Also available from the Hound

VideoHound's® Golden Movie Retriever

VideoHound's Vampires on Video

VideoHound's Sci-Fi Experience:
Your Quantum Guide to the Video Universe

VideoHound's Complete Guide to Cult Flicks and Trash Pics

VideoHound's Video Premieres:
The Only Guide to Video Originals and Limited Releases

VideoHound's Independent Film Guide

VideoHound's Family Video Guide, 2nd Edition

VideoHound's Soundtracks:
Music from the Movies, Broadway, and Television

MusicHound® Rock:
The Essential Album Guide, 2nd Edition

MusicHound Country:
The Essential Album Guide

MusicHound Blues:
The Essential Album Guide

MusicHound R&B:
The Essential Album Guide

MusicHound Jazz:
The Essential Album Guide

MusicHound Folk:
The Essential Album Guide

MusicHound Lounge:
The Essential Album Guide to Martini Music and Easy Listening

YOU DESERVE THE FINER THINGS IN LIFE!

These guides will point you in the right direction

MUSICHOUND® CLASSICAL

The Essential Album Guide

Do you think classical music is just a bunch of squeaky violins … or can you name all of the characters in *Don Giovanni*? Whether you're a rank amateur or a seasoned collector, you'll love *MusicHound Classical*. From Mozart to McCartney, this guide includes profiles of more than 300 composers and gives you quick advice on what to buy and what to avoid. You'll enjoy reviews and recommendations on orchestral works, chamber music, solo instrumentalists, opera, and sacred and choral vocals. Also included is "Classical's Greatest Hits," which explains how well-known works are used in popular culture (television, movies, radio themes, cartoons, commercials, etc.). Check out *MusicHound Classical* today and build a collection that would make your childhood piano teacher proud.

David Wagner • 1999 • Paperback • 700 pages
ISBN 1-57859-034-5

"A series that does the job well in terms of both scope and accuracy ... a lot of data that's a lot more reliable than some other volumes can claim."
— Bruce Sylvester, DJ at WMBR Radio, Cambridge, MA

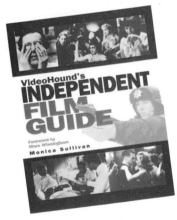

VIDEOHOUND'S® INDEPENDENT FILM GUIDE

Audacious. Risk-taking. Spirited. Original. These are some of the qualities that separate independent films from the mainstream studio concoctions. And recently, the indies have evolved from critics' choice to commercial powerhouses, influencing studio releases and dominating the Oscars. *Pulp Fiction*, with earnings of $210 million on an $8 million investment, is an outstanding example of such success. In this guide, you'll find insight and recommendations on more than 1,000 of the best and the most innovative works in the independent film industry. If you love indies – or think you might – *VideoHound's Independent Film Guide* is an indispensable companion.

Monica Sullivan • 1998 • Paperback • 558 pages
ISBN 1-57859-018-3

"Filled with stinging views, fascinating historical tidbits, cogent tributes and thoughtful critical appraisals."
– San Francisco Chronicle

VISIBLE
INK
PRESS

VideoHound's

WORLD
CINEMA

VideoHound's
WORLD CINEMA

The Adventurer's Guide to Movie Watching

Elliot Wilhelm

Detroit London

VideoHound's®
WORLD CINEMA

Copyright © 1999 by Visible Ink Press

Published by Visible Ink Press®, a division of Gale Research,
27500 Drake Rd., Farmington Hills, MI 48331-3535.

Visible Ink Press, *VideoHound*, the *VideoHound* logo, and A Cunning Canine Production are trademarks of Gale Research.

Most Visible Ink Press books are available at special quantity discounts when purchased in bulk by corporations, organizations, or groups. Customized printing, special imprints, messages, and excerpts can be produced to meet your needs. For more information, contact Special Markets Manager, Gale Research, 27500 Drake Rd., Farmington Hills, MI 48331-3535.

Art Director: Eric Johnson

Photos: The Kobal Collection

Library of Congress Cataloging-in-Publication Data

Wilhelm, Elliot.
VideoHound's world cinema: the adventurer's guide to movie watching / Elliot Wilhelm.
     p. cm.
     Includes indexes.
     ISBN 1-57859-059-0 (softcover)
       1. Foreign films--Catalogs. 2. Video recordings--Catalogs.
I. Title.
PN1995.9.F67W56 1999
016.79143'75--dc21
                                                 98-36337
                                               CIP

ISBN 1-57859-059-0 Printed in the United States of America
All Rights Reserved
10 9 8 7 6 5 4 3 2 1

A Cunning Canine Production™

For Dorothy and Seymour

CONTENTS

THE REVIEWS: A TO Z

SIDEBARS

ABOUT THE AUTHOR

Elliot Wilhelm has been director of the Detroit Film Theatre series at the Detroit Institute of Arts since 1973, and Curator of Film at the DIA since 1984. More than 100,000 people attend the 1,200-seat theatre each year. According to Larry Kardish, Curator of Film Exhibitions at the Museum of Modern Art in New York, the Detroit Film Theatre is "a pilgrimage cathedral for those who love cinema in its appropriate and proper surroundings," he says, showcasing foreign and independent cinema that otherwise would not be seen. In his capacity as director, Wilhelm has given hundreds of prominent films their area debut, including *Ran*, *Jean de Florette* and *Manon of the Spring*, *Taxi Driver*, *My Left Foot*, and *Breaking the Waves* (not to mention, *sex, lies and videotape*). For his indefatigable work in presenting leading-edge cinema for area film enthusiasts, he was awarded a "Michiganian of the Year" honor by *The Detroit News* in 1984.

A lifelong resident of the Detroit area, Wilhelm hosts a weekly film series on the local PBS station, and has served as film critic at numerous Detroit area radio and television stations.

INTRODUCTION

On a Friday evening in the fall of 1978, I was pacing anxiously in the lobby of the Detroit Institute of Arts Auditorium while the film being shown to the 900 or so people inside was drawing to a close. The newspaper reviews had been good, but as programmer of the series—which featured a new first-run film every weekend and had been running since 1974—I was anxious to hear the crowd's comments as they departed for home, restaurants, bars, and cafes. I heard the music come up and the theatre doors bang open and suddenly I was surrounded by hundreds of people. While I stood still trying to pick up snatches of conversation, a familiar looking gentleman—a "regular"—walked up to me, looked me straight in the eye, and proclaimed: "That was the worst picture I've ever seen. I'll see you next week."

He *did* see me next week, though I can't for the life of me remember what film he saw then or what his reaction was. Yet I'll never forget the startling, matter-of-fact juxtaposition of his two-sentence comment that first evening, not only because his remark was not nearly as symptomatic of aesthetic masochism as it at first sounded, but in fact amounted to an elegantly terse encapsulation of the simple philosophy that had always unconsciously directed my own moviegoing, eventually leading to the creation of the book that you're holding.

The customer at the movies that night was less concerned with the pleasure or displeasure he felt during a single 90-minute moviegoing experience than he was in the value of the sum total of *all* of his moviegoing experiences. This doesn't mean he was incapable of passing judgment, but he was far less troubled by the idea of having sat through something he thought was lousy than he was by the notion of possibly missing something great.

I identified with him. I still do. It's why I get my hopes up *every time I go to the movies.*

Movies are little glimpses of the world—visions of life—as seen through the eyes of people we would otherwise never meet. Perceived that way, they can be as mysterious, precious, and intense as the personal relationships we have with other people, for when we're involved with the images on the screen, we *are* involved with other people—writers, directors, actors, technicians, characters. More than that, though, their work combines to form a sensory experience unique in all the arts—a communal dream that we can share together when the lights dim in a theatre or in our living room. Whether the experience is as endearingly silly as *Plan 9 From Outer Space* or as breathtakingly transporting as *Vertigo*, it's rare that a movie doesn't leave some part of itself—and its creators—with us, even long after we swear we've forgotten it.

In Ray Bradbury's now-classic fable "A Sound of Thunder," a man goes back in time and steps on a butterfly, only to discover upon his return to the present that everything has changed. The influence of that seemingly insignificant act on the course of history is something that the story's time traveler could never in a million years have anticipated or predicted. And while it's not likely that missing just one of the 800 or so movies in this book would have caused me to take my life in a substantially different direction, how can I be sure? How many of us can claim that we remember each of the little revelatory moments in childhood, the fantasies of our private nighttime dreams or the euphoria and pain of pleasures and disappointments that—taken together—influenced our lives without our knowing it, in ways that continue to affect every aspect of our daily decision making?

The answer, of course, is that we can *never* be sure just which of our millions of experiences come together to give us our perspective and judgment. (Remember Mr. Bernstein's story about his memories of the woman with a parasol in *Citizen Kane*?) Bad movies, however, would have us see such complexities much more simply; when Michelangelo (Charlton Heston) is lacking inspiration for the Sistine Chapel ceiling in *The Agony and the Ecstasy*, he looks up at a laughably phony cloud formation, hears a blast of heavenly stereophonic music, and before him is The Answer. (It's like the young disciple's admiring remark about a fascistic political candidate in Hal Hartley's extraordinary *Henry Fool*: "He has a way of taking extremely complex ideas and making them…simple.") Yet if I hadn't seen *The Agony and the Ecstasy* as a kid, I might be less aware of how movies—like other parts of life—can seductively con us as if we were potential real estate suckers in a David Mamet play. *The Agony and the Ecstasy* is a bad movie, but it's bad in such an outrageously fraudulent way that it became a significant part of my film—and therefore my life—experience. For that reason alone, I wouldn't have missed it. (Nor, had I missed it, would I have been able to appreciate, say, Maurice Pialat's remarkable *Van Gogh*, which celebrates its protagonist's genius as gloriously unfathomable rather than as a sentence to be dutifully diagrammed.)

All those images, moments and memories from good and bad movies do, ultimately, add up to something, and that something, to paraphrase Pogo, is us. The most alarming concept in the hit science fiction movie *Men in Black* isn't a giant cockroach from another planet, but the idea of the little flashing light that can wipe out selected portions of our memories. Given the chance, would we really choose to forget *anything*? The death of a loved one? An obsessive, disastrous love affair? *Moon in the Gutter*? *Armageddon*? In the end, aren't we shaped as much by the unpleasant—even grueling—experiences of our lives as by the seemingly joyous ones? Despite the vast number of truly terrible movies that I've sat through, I can't imagine actually wanting to remove the memory of any of them (though I've come close, as you'll discover thumbing through this guide). They're all experiences I've had, and I'm not giving up any of them.

Though it's a cliche, it's nevertheless a safe bet that few people on their deathbeds have ever said "I should have spent more time at the office." Yet I must confess that I've been more than a little lucky to have had the experience of seeing movies—and then presenting them to others—as a way of making a living. While I don't exactly think I'm guilty of confusing movies with "real life," I do regard the experiences I've had at the movies—my intimate, personal, lifelong, emotional involvement with them—to be every bit as valid, powerful, and resonant as other forms of contact with humanity, be that contact in the form of literature, painting, conversation, food, friendship, work, or love.

Time to confess. I really don't like cilantro. But I'm sure as hell glad I know what it tastes like, just in case anybody offers me any, or in case I ever want to describe something as *cilantro-*

like. Likewise, there are some films in this book that I feel no emotional bond with, I respect mightily and admire enormously. Conversely, and perhaps more frequently, I can find myself moved beyond reason by a movie that by every traditional standard doesn't seem to deserve such a profound response. Does such a reaction make the viewer *wrong*? Hardly. Love is vastly more than the sum of its parts, which, appropriately enough, is true of art in all its forms and that includes the film medium itself.

The great Soviet director Sergei Eisenstein often wrote about the miracle of film editing—of how the juxtaposition of two seemingly unrelated images could result in the creation of an emotional response of undreamed richness. The same principle extends to the response movies generate in us when seen at different times in our lives. The movies we loved as kids may look silly to us now, while the movies that seemed cold and distant to us when we were in high school may seem almost embarrassingly intimate—as if the director followed us around with a camera—when we see them again as more experienced adults.

This volume, then, is designed as both guidebook and notebook—a record of experiences commonly called movies, some of which I've loved, some of which I haven't, but all of which are a part of one individual's lifetime at the movies.

What's different about *VideoHound's World Cinema* from most other film and video guides is that this cinematic journey is primarily international in scope, taking a look at some of the most extraordinary, often acclaimed, occasionally undiscovered visions of filmmakers from beyond America's borders.

Finding many of these films in your local video outlet may not always be an easy task; those two or three sparsely populated shelves marked "foreign" are often stocked only with the same battered, sticky copies of *Rashomon* or *La Dolce Vita* year after year, while neglecting most of the dazzling new films from abroad that are released in the U.S. each year. (Those shelves might more accurately be labeled "foreign language," since British, Australian and most Canadian films are usually not segregated from the "regular" movies.) To help you along your way you'll find a guide here to some of the more enterprising and helpful video retailers, who can help you track down the films that sound intriguing to you. Just because university and museum film societies—not to mention small, independently programmed and managed film theatres—are an endangered species, there's no reason in this video age that you can't program your own film festival based on some of the links between themes, countries, directors, and genres that you'll run across as you peruse this book.

And just what exactly is a "foreign film" anyway? In an era when what we once thought of as Japanese cars are built in Kentucky and Ohio, and a goodly sized portion of the American population thinks that espresso was invented in Seattle, it's not always so easy—nor should it be, perhaps—to tell. My memories of actual travels abroad are vivid, but no more vivid than my first glimpses of Rome or Dakar or Madrid as seen in the movies. Whether it's Belmondo being gunned down in the streets of Paris or a little girl looking for her lost money in the streets of Teheran, the journeys taken to other places via the cinema can be *true* journeys—of the mind, the eye, and the heart. Who has experienced Rome more fully—someone who's walked around the Coliseum with a guidebook, or someone who's never set foot in Italy but has seen *The Bicycle Thief*?

Videohound's World Cinema isn't meant to be a definitive list of foreign titles, but the movies described here are a good place to jump in if you're new to international cinema. If you make your way through all of them, many more await your discovery in future editions.

The medium of film has only been around for 100 years or so, yet a veritable universe of inspired, visionary work has yet to be discovered by much of the moviegoing world. If the films described in this volume help you to begin exploring that universe, I'll have done my job.

It's time to look beyond your own backyard. Some priceless journeys await.

ACKNOWLEDGMENTS

Thanks are due to many people for helping me to embark upon and ultimately complete this adventure, especially Hannah Klein, Joseph Miner, Barbara and Raymond Sneider, Andrea Sneider, Michael, Elizabeth, and Isabel Dorothy Sneider, Robert Nirkind, and Meryl Greenblatt.

My editors at Visible Ink Press have been so delightful and encouraging to work with that they've probably given me a completely false impression of the publishing world. My thanks to Marty Connors for suggesting the book in the first place, and to Beth Fhaner, Carol Schwartz, and Julia Furtaw for everything. Also thanks to Jay Nelson at Channel 56 for suggesting the initial get-together.

A lifetime achievement award goes to editor Devra Sladics, who not only worked hard to make me look good, but ought to get a bonus for not buckling under the onslaught of my whining and deadline-stretching.

Thanks to Tracey Rowens for designing the cover, Eric Johnson for the page design, and Linda Mahoney for the typesetting job.

Finally, my deepest gratitude goes to my friends and colleagues in the Department of Film and Video at the Detroit Institute of Arts, whose graciousness and generosity allowed me to take the time to tackle this project: Associate Curator Lawrence Baranski (a prince), Departmental Coordinator Matthew Breneau and Curatorial Assistant Deborah Haddrill.

Special thanks also to the DIA's Interim Director Maurice Parrish, whose encouragement, assistance and enthusiasm made the book's completion possible.

VIDEO SOURCES

Some of the movies in this book are not available on video, and some may be difficult to find using conventional sources such as the neighborhood video rental chain. Many independent and mail-order video outlets specialize in rare or hard-to-find movies. We have included a small list of such outlets to assist you in your search.

Thomas Video
122 S. Main St.
Clawson, MI 48017
248-280-2833
fax: 248-280-4463

Video Vision
Attn: Chris Hendlin
4603 Bloomington Ave.
Minneapolis, MN 55407
612-728-0000

Video Oyster
145 W. 12th St.
New York, NY 10011
fax: 212-989-3533

Facets Video
1517 W. Fullerton Ave.
Chicago, IL 60614
800-331-6197

**A Million and One
    World-Wide Videos**
PO Box 349
Orchard Hill, GA 30266
770-227-7309
800-849-7309
fax: 770-227-0873
fax: 800-849-0873

Movies Unlimted
3015 Darnell Rd.
Philadelphia, PA 19154
800-4-MOVIES

Home Film Festival
PO Box 2032
Scranton, PA 18501
800-258-3456

ALPHABETIZATION

Titles are arranged on a word-by-word basis, including articles and prepositions. Leading articles (A, An, The) are ignored in English-language titles; the equivalent foreign articles are not ignored (because so many people—not you, of course—don't recognize them as articles); thus, *The Brothers McMullen* appears in the Bs, but *La Femme Nikita* appears in the Ls. Acronyms appear alphabetically as if regular words; for example, *D.O.A.* is alphabetized as "DOA." Common abbreviations in titles file as if they were spelled out, so *The Cabinet of Dr. Caligari* will be alphabetized as "Cabinet of Doctor Caligari" and *Mr. Arakin* as "Mister Arakin." Movie titles with numbers, such as *8 1/2* are alphabetized as if the number was spelled out—so this title would appear in the Es as if it were "Eight and a Half."

SAMPLE REVIEW

Each review contains up to 17 tidbits of information, as enumerated below. Please realize that we faked a bit of info in this review for demonstration purposes.

BREATHLESS

A Bout de Souffle

French hoodlum and petty thug Michel (Jean-Paul Belmondo) is on the run from the law after shooting a cop and stealing a car. He hooks up with Patricia, a beautiful American girl (Jean Seberg) who hawks papers ("New York Herald *Tribune!*") on the Champs Élysées. They make love, they make faces, they kill some time, she turns him in. They're going nowhere, of course, but that's not the point; what excites them is that they're doing it fast. The pacing of [*Breathless*] ([*À Bout de Souffle*] originally, which is more like "out of breath") is key because these amoral characters—who do what they want when they want to, whether it's killing, stealing, making love or turning the other in—never stop for a second to contemplate cause and effect or their place in the world, unless it's to immediately satisfy themselves. Belmondo and Seberg looked great and had fun on the streets of Paris; the city was filmed with an electric immediacy and a restless camera by Raoul Coutard, and much of the editing is violently blunt.

NEXT STOP. . . *8 1/2, Marcello Mastroianni: I Remember, Star 80*

1959 **(R)** **90m** **B** *FR* Jean-Paul Belmondo, Jean Seberg, Daniel Boulanger, Jean-Pierre Melville, Liliane Robin; **D:** Jean-Luc Godard; **W:** Jean-Luc Godard. **C:** Jean-Luc Godard **M:** Jean-Luc Godard Berlin International Film Festival '60: Best Director (Godard). **VHS, Beta** NOS, MRV, CVC

1. Title (see also the Alternative title below, and the "Alternative Titles Index")
2. Alternative title
3. Description/review
4. Suggested viewings
5. Year released
6. MPAA rating
7. Length in minutes
8. Black and white (B) or Color (C)
9. Foreign film code (if produced outside the U.S.); see next page
10. Cast, including cameos and voiceovers (V)
11. Director(s)
12. Writer(s)
13. Cinematographer(s)
14. Music composer(s)/lyricist(s)
15. Awards, including nominations
16. Format(s), including VHS, Laservideo/disk (LV), letterbox, and others
17. Distributor code(s), if available on video (see also "Distributor List" and "Distributor Guide")

A NOS AMOURS
To Our Loves

Despite nearly continuous international critical accolades and a parade of film festival awards, Maurice Pialat's low-concept, intimate slice-of life dramas have never really caught on with the American art-house crowd. A good example of his work is this startlingly intimate domestic nightmare about a teenage girl (the amazing, 17-year-old Sandrine Bonnaire's screen debut) whose bed-hopping seems excessive until it's seen against the backdrop of her utterly dysfunctional, violent, and incestuous family life. Pialat's specialty is the detailed portrayal of such hothouse family dynamics; but it's his steadfast refusal to draw neat, simplistic conclusions about his characters that is the primary reason for his unjustly remaining one of the least-known of France's contemporary masters. Not surprisingly, *A Nos Amours* received little exposure in the U.S. outside of film festival showings, yet it was awarded France's César—the equivalent of the Oscar—as Best Picture of 1984. One year later, Bonnaire herself would capture the Best Actress César for her equally intense incarnation of disaffected youth in Agnes Varda's *Vagabond.*

NEXT STOP . . . *Vagabond, Loulou, Monsieur Hire*

1984 (R) 99m/C *FR* Sandrine Bonnaire, Dominique Besnehard, Maurice Pialat, Evelyne Ker; *D:* Maurice Pialat; *W:* Arlette Langmann, Maurice Pialat; *C:* Jacques Loiseleux; *M:* Henry Purcell. **VHS, LV** *COL*

A NOUS LA LIBERTÉ
Freedom for Us

Having established a reputation as a brilliant satirist during the silent era with films like 1924's *Paris Qui Dort,* in which an experimental ray gun causes Parisians to reveal their own hypocrisy, René Clair worried—as did so many other directors of comic films at the time—about the prospect of sound intruding on their fantastic and surrealistic silent world. While Chaplin actually managed to dodge the auditory bullet until the final minutes of *Modern Times* in 1936, Clair's 1931 *A Nous la Liberté* tackled the possibilities of sound head on, with the not inconsiderable help of composer Georges Auric. This is a tale of a prison escapee (Raymond Cordy) who makes his way to freedom and becomes rich by opening a highly regimented, prison-like factory manufacturing phonograph records. (An image undoubtedly meant to symbolize Hollywood's new obsession with early talkies: prefabricated, stiff entertainments that only had to make noise to become hits.) The ironies compound as Clair adds a another former prisoner to the mix, a free-spirited and gentle soul (Henri Marchand) who seems fully modeled on Chaplin's ragingly popular "little tramp." Apparently Chaplin himself was more flattered than offended by Clair's "homage," so he felt free to do a little borrowing himself five years later. The assembly line scenes of *Modern Times,* which bear more than a passing resemblance to Clair's, so blatantly outraged Clair that he sued Chaplin over it, apparently forgetting that the inspiration for *A Nous la Liberté*'s "gentle soul" was clearly none other than Chaplin himself. The suit was eventually dropped as Clair admitted that Chaplin was a spiritual father to all screen comedy, and history has rightly made a place for both films as the original and visionary works that they are. Both, of course, have always remained influential, and for a witty reference to the scene in *A Nous la Liberté* in which well-dressed dandies scramble over each other

1

for ill-gotten cash, take a look at the 1956 Peter Sellers classic *I'm All Right, Jack,* perhaps the one film in movie history that makes a believable case for labor and management having but a single, common purpose—greed.

NEXT STOP . . . *Le Million, Modern Times, I'm All Right, Jack*

1931 87m/B *FR* Henri Marchand, Raymond Cordy, Rolla France, Paul Olivier, Jacques Shelly, Andre Michaud; *D:* Rene Clair; *W:* Rene Clair; *C:* Georges Perinal; *M:* Georges Auric. Nominations: Academy Awards '32: Best Interior Decoration. **VHS, 8mm** *NOS, MRV, VYY*

THE ACCOMPANIST
L'Accompagnatrice

Richard Bohringer, one of the fixtures of contemporary French cinema in films such as *The Last Metro, Diva,* and *Le Grand Chemin,* may be best remembered by future generations not as a fine actor but as a great actress's father; Romane Bohringer has been appearing in small roles for years, but in Claude Miller's 1992 *The Accompanist* she pulled off something surprising and spectacular. In this quietly eloquent drama set during the German occupation of Paris, Bohringer plays the 20-year-old Sophie Vasseur, an aspiring pianist who lands a job as accompanist to a highly regarded singer, Irene Brice (Elena Safonova). Irene and her husband Charles (played by Bohringer's father Richard) are fond enough of their luxurious lifestyle that the viewer becomes suspicious, unsure at first whether the Brice household maintains its privilege through collaboration with the Nazis. Yet *The Accompanist* turns out to be a far smarter film than such a potential revelation might suggest; before long it's up to Sophie to decide just how far she's willing to go in a deception of her own, when Irene's affair with a member of the resistance becomes apparent to all but her husband. Like all of the films of the exceptionally gifted but unjustly unknown writer-director Claude Miller, *The Accompanist* is driven more by character than plot, and more by actor than action. As the wide-eyed young woman looking upon a corrupt world with all possibilities before her, Bohringer's performance is both a revelation and the spine of the film. She's called upon to straddle that border between success and selling one's soul, but with none of the clear-cut, rear-view-mirror certainties of a position-paper exercise like István Szabó's *Mephisto* (1981). From moment to moment, her Sophie seems absolutely real: open, unformed, malleable, and vulnerable. She makes *The Accompanist* as engrossing and suspenseful as it is disquieting.

NEXT STOP . . . *The Sorrow and the Pity, Europa, Europa, A Self-Made Hero*

1993 (PG) 111m/C *FR* Elena Safonova, Romane Bohringer, Richard Bohringer, Samuel Labarthe, Nelly Borgeaud, Julien Rassam; *D:* Claude Miller; *W:* Claude Miller, Luc Beraud, Claude Rich; *C:* Yves Angelo; *M:* Alain Jomy. **VHS** *COL*

THE ADJUSTER

Canadian wunderkind Atom Egoyan's films can be as tantalizing as they are frustratingly distant (including his breakthrough hit, *The Sweet Hereafter*), and his 1991 *The Adjuster* is one of the films that demonstrates his strengths and weaknesses most clearly. It's the story of an insurance adjuster named Noah (Elias Koteas) whose clients have had catastrophic accidents, forcing them to become utterly dependent on this seemingly benevolent man. But Noah is something of a voyeur, as is his wife, Hera, a film censor who secretly videotapes the pornography she sits through and passes judgment on day after day. Noah, however, carries his little fetish a bit further, placing his clients in "temporary" motel housing where he can keep a close eye on them, manipulating them, deciding their futures, rewriting their lives. Together, this quietly ghoulish couple spend their days in a creepy suburban dream home, which happens to be the only completed house in an unfinished subdivision. *The Adjuster* raises its extraordinary central conceit about the delicate lines separating curiosity, voyeurism, and sadism, and then unceremoniously drops the ball, introducing still another couple who are even more insistently manipulative than Noah and Hera, but in far less surprising or darkly funny ways. *The Adjuster* is one of those memorable failures that you root for during most of its running time, even when it's limping to a halt. A key, though incomplete, piece of the mystery of Atom Egoyan, *The Adjuster* irritates more than it should, perhaps because its first hour so intoxicatingly raises such great expectations.

NEXT STOP . . . *Calendar, Exotica, The Stepfather*

1991 (R) 102m/C *CA* Elias Koteas, Arsinee Khanjian, Maury Chaykin, Gabrielle Rose, David Hemblen, Jennifer Dale, Don McKellar, Raoul Trujillo; *D:* Atom Egoyan; *W:* Atom Egoyan; *C:* Paul Sarossy; *M:* Mychael Danna. Toronto-City Award '91: Best Canadian Feature Film. **VHS** *ORI*

AFTER THE REHEARSAL
Efter Repetitionen

If you've seen *Deconstructing Harry* and you're more than a bit curious as to why Woody Allen has always been so fascinated with Ingmar Bergman, the modestly mounted but deeply moving *After the Rehearsal* is as good a place as any to start. As an aging and legendary director named Henrik Vogler (Erland Josephson) prepares work on a new production of August Strindberg's *A Dream Play*, a young actress (Lena Olin) enters the theatre, joins him on the ghostly, not-quite-bare stage, and engages him in a conversation that will prove revelatory to them both. Will this exquisite young woman be another in the director's parade of sexual conquests? Or is it possible that she is, in fact, the child of an affair he had with her mother? As Vogler (the name so often given to the protagonists of Bergman's most outwardly autobiographical films) ruminates about his compulsive couplings and the theatrical creations that have in every sense constituted his work and his life, he ultimately arrives at that point at which he faces the big questions about the convergence of art and life. Is being a great creator justification for leading a dishonest and often sordid life of one's own? As in most of his films, Bergman doesn't claim to have the answer.

But who else could so bluntly and chillingly pose the question?

NEXT STOP . . . *The Magician, Persona, Face to Face*

1984 (R) 72m/C *SW* Erland Josephson, Ingrid Thulin, Lena Olin; *D:* Ingmar Bergman; *W:* Ingmar Bergman; *C:* Sven Nykvist. **VHS** *COL*

AGUIRRE, THE WRATH OF GOD
Aguirre, der Zorn Gottes

In one of the 16th century's more spectacular follies, would-be conqueror Gonzalez Pizarro mounted an expedition through the jungles of Peru to seek El Dorado—the shining, legendary city of gold. One of the many unlucky and unprepared men to accompany him was one Gaspar de Carvajal, who kept a journal of the nightmarish adventure which would eventually find its way into the hands of Germany's Werner Herzog, who fashioned Gaspar's account of the bizarre quest into his own demented and irresistible masterpiece. Don Lope de Aguirre (Klaus Kinski) is sent ahead with a group of soldiers by an exhausted Pizarro, and as the small army makes its way through the Peruvian jungles, their physical and emotional ties to civilization become increasingly tenuous. Rarely in screen history has an actor embodied madness and megalomania with the authority and hypnotic power of Klaus Kinski in *Aguirre*. His face seems to change shape (which it literally would years later when he starred in Herzog's *Nosferatu*) as he becomes more and more convinced that "the earth trembles with his steps." I don't mean to dismiss the power of Popol Vuh's musical score, but Kinski and Herzog have created a film that works on such powerful visual terms that if you watch it without sound, you may not notice that anything's missing. Herzog presents Aguirre's dementia not as a descent into madness, but as an *ascent*. He achieves a kind of holy state as he lords over a wooden raft teeming with wild monkeys, for it's apparent that this conqueror has indeed found his El Dorado, and it would be almost rude to inform him otherwise. That task was left to Francis Coppola,

TOSHIRO MIFUNE

The world's most famous Japanese screen actor was born in China—on April 1, 1920 to be exact. An aerial photographer with the Imperial Army during World War II, Toshiro Mifune first set foot in Japan at the age of 25, immediately following the Japanese surrender. He was comfortable with—and skilled at—photography, so it seemed like a logical move to apply for a job in the photographic department at Toho, a major Japanese film studio.

Mifune never got the job, and accounts differ as to what happened next. Accepted movie folklore says that his application was sent to the wrong department, and he was mistakenly auditioned as an aspiring actor. Another version is that Mifune's background was politically unacceptable to the cinematographers' union, so he tried to break into acting out of simple expediency.

Legend has it that Mifune blew up and lost his cool at Toho's 1946 "Wanted: New Faces" audition, throwing a physically spectacular fit that made him immediately stand out among hundreds of other, more seasoned applicants. One of those present that day, a 37-year-old director named Akira Kurosawa, described it a bit differently in his book, *Something Like an Autobiography*: "I opened the door and stopped dead in amazement. A young man was reeling around the room in a violent frenzy…It turned out that this young man was not really in a rage, but had drawn 'anger' as the emotion he had to express in his screen test. He was acting."

Indeed.

By 1948, he would be acting for Kurosawa, playing a tough gangster in the director's *Drunken Angel*. Over the next 16 years, Mifune and Kurosawa would work together almost constantly, creating some of the most extraordinary and memorable works of art in the history of cinema: *Rashomon*, *Seven Samurai*, *Throne of Blood*, *Yojimbo*.

Every Mifune character in a Kurosawa film is absolutely indelible and distinct—the panic-stricken, morally confused businessman in *High and Low*; the comically cynical, surprisingly principled general in *The Hidden Fortress*; the demanding and deeply humane physician in *Red Beard*.

It was after the 1964 *Red Beard* that a personal rift developed between the two men; they were never to work together after that. Mifune tried his hand at Hollywood with varying degrees of success in *Hell in the Pacific*, *Grand Prix*, *1941* and the hit TV miniseries "Shogun." He always had work, and remained one of the cinema's most recognized and respected actors until his death in 1997.

Yet it's impossible to hear Toshiro Mifune's name without specific images coming to mind, and those images always seem to be from his films with Kurosawa. Whether it's the weather-beaten, scheming, out-of-work samurai scratching himself on a dusty road in *Yojimbo*, or a defeated warlord clinging furiously to life while pierced with countless arrows in *Throne of Blood*, Mifune's characters for Kurosawa are among the cinema's greatest glories.

whose *Apocalypse Now* was almost certainly influenced to some degree by Herzog's visionary epic, when "civilization" would finally put Kurtz/Aguirre out of his misery. Oddly enough, *Aguirre, the Wrath of God* was originally filmed in English (read the actors' lips as you watch the film), but the expressionist visuals combined disastrously with American accents, and Aguirre was released successfully in America with a German soundtrack.

NEXT STOP . . . *Fitzcarraldo, Burden of Dreams, Apocalypse Now*

1972 94m/C *GE* Klaus Kinski, Ruy Guerra, Del Negro, Helena Rojo, Cecilia Rivera, Peter Berling, Danny Ades, Alejandro Repulles; *D:* Werner Herzog; *W:* Werner Herzog; *C:* Thomas Mauch; *M:* Popul Vuh. National Society of Film Critics Awards '77: Best Cinematography. **VHS** *NYF*

AKIRA

A recent news story out of Japan reported that hundreds, if not thousands, of Japanese children suffered seizures after watching an episode of an animated TV series that used a particularly mesmerizing stroboscopic visual effect. *Akira,* Katsuhiro Otomo's 1988 pioneering example of the particular Japanese animation form known as anime, is not known to have produced such an effect on anyone, but it did elevate this science-fiction/fantasy form to worldwide cult status and ultimately to a popularity of such magnitude that Japan's government is currently examining legislation to try to control its impact and influence. Based on Otomo's own graphic novel (a.k.a. comic book), which could serve as the very definition of "cyberpunk," *Akira* is a post-apocalyptic tale a la *Mad Max* set in the year 2019 about a society of teenage gangs slugging it out in a stunningly designed Neo-Tokyo. As the government conspires to harness human mental capacity into a palpable physical weapon, layer after layer of teenage angst and anxiety are peeled away, making *Akira* a nightmarishly oppressive though always eye-popping experience. Otomo insisted on shooting Akira in a 70mm format, making sure that the images, though animated, would be no less

impressive than similar live-action special effects extravaganzas. Despite its extraordinary visual sophistication, however, *Akira* is a claustrophobic and largely joyless affair—a kind of *Speed Racer Goes to Nuke 'Em High*—providing plenty of pow but surprisingly little exhilaration.

NEXT STOP . . . *Tetsuo: The Iron Man, The Road Warrior, Ghost in the Shell*

1989 124m/C *JP D:* Katsuhiro Otomo, Sheldon Renan; *W:* Katsuhiro Otomo, Izo Hashimoto; *C:* Katsuji Misawa; *M:* Shoji Yamashiro. **VHS, LV** *STP, CRC*

AKIRA KUROSAWA'S DREAMS
Dreams
Yume
I Saw a Dream Like This
Konna Yume Wo Mita

I compare the critics who've labeled *Akira Kurosawa's Dreams* "uneven" to therapists who've listened attentively to a brilliant patient as he confides his innermost secrets, only to tell him when his hour is up that two or three of his private fantasies went on a little too long. If ever a director has earned the right to be self-indulgent, then surely it is this unparalleled visionary storyteller who may well be the most influential filmmaker of the century's second half. The eight short films that Kurosawa conjures here—they can't all properly be called "stories"—show the imagination and visual energy of the then-80-year-old artist in full flower and splendid color. The film leaps gracefully from the tale of a child who casually observes gods who sprang from a living orchard, to an eloquent and strangely reassuring brush with Vincent Van Gogh (played, in an inspired bit of casting, by Martin Scorsese), and inevitably to a horrifying vision of the nuclear devastation of Japan—an image that can never, it seems, be extracted from Japan's collective consciousness. If *Akira Kurosawa's Dreams* seems less of a coherent vision than some of his more formally perfect masterworks, it is because he wanted us to see his frailties and his fears. By sharing them with us, the world's

5

VideoHound's
WORLD CINEMA

greatest living filmmaker has given us an invaluable—and frequently thrilling—glimpse into the mind of a genius.

NEXT STOP . . . *Amarcord, Kwaidan, The Phantom of Liberty*

1990 (PG) 120m/C *JP* Akira Terao, Mitsuko Baisho, Meiko Harada, Chishu Ryu, Hisashi Igawa, Mitsunori Isaki, Toshihiko Nakano, Yoshitaka Zushi, Toshie Negishi, Martin Scorsese; *D:* Akira Kurosawa; *W:* Akira Kurosawa; *C:* Kazutami Hara, Takao Saito, Masaharu Ueda; *M:* Shinichiro Ikebe. **VHS, LV, Letterbox** *WAR, FCT*

ALEXANDER NEVSKY

Few movies have been subjected to as much revisionist criticism as has Sergei Eisenstein's staggering action epic about the legendary Russian prince who defeated the savage Teutonic hordes on a vast frozen lake in 1242. Commissioned by Stalin to whip the Russian masses into an anti-Nazi frenzy, Eisenstein understood that there should be no reason why propaganda couldn't be rip-snorting fun as well as effective. Nevsky is portrayed by Nikolai Cherkassov (who later would play Ivan the Terrible in the film that drove Stalin to turn in his Eisenstein fan club membership card) and his deep voice and impressively sculpted features made him an extraordinarily popular screen hero—the 13th-century Indiana Jones. The Teutonic knights, a band of blonde religious fanatics who burn alive the Russian babies of each town they conquer, appear to be unstoppable until Prince Nevsky makes his nation's population—no matter how old or how young—realize the true magnitude of the German threat. In structure, *Alexander Nevsky* resembles a classic western, though the cattle rustlers are replaced here by religious tyranny and fascism. Eisenstein's first sound film features a fabulous score by Sergei Prokofiev that has since been turned into a cantata and is still performed regularly by symphony orchestras worldwide. The most celebrated sequence in the film is the famous "battle on ice" that finally deals a death blow to the Germans on the frozen lake Peipus. The battle concludes as the ice cracks, sending the heavy, armor-laden knights to the bottom in an image of—ironically—biblical-style justice that recalls the Red Sea closing over the armies of Egypt. *Alexander Nevsky* was made in 1938, but Eisenstein's film did encounter a rocky road to release. It seems that just as it was ready to hit every screen in Russia, the Nazi-Soviet pact was signed and the film was sent to the showers. But the phony peace didn't hold, and soon the images of German invaders became all-too-real, and *Alexander Nevsky* became the hit the Eisenstein needed to resuscitate his career. Incidentally, for parents who think that movie tie-in merchandise is a recent phenomenon, Moscow stores couldn't keep the official *Alexander Nevsky* swords and helmets in stock after the picture's release.

NEXT STOP . . . *Ivan the Terrible Parts 1 & 2, Henry V (1945), Chimes at Midnight*

1938 110m/B *RU* Nikolai Cherkassov, Nikolai P. Okholopkov, Andrei Abrikosov; *D:* Sergei Eisenstein; *W:* Sergei Eisenstein, Pyotr Pavlenko; *C:* Eduard Tisse; *M:* Sergei Prokofiev. **VHS, LV** *BMG, MRV, NOS*

ALFREDO, ALFREDO

Dustin Hoffman plays a shy, nervous, continuously sweating bank clerk who manages to marry the ravishingly pretty Stefania Sandrelli, discovering too late that what should have been his dream come true—his beautiful bride's unquenchable sexual appetite—has become his worst nightmare. Pietro Germi specialized in a highly popular subcategory of domestic Italian comedy, the zenith of which he probably reached a decade earlier with the vulgar but irresistibly funny *Divorce—Italian Style* (which starred Marcello Mastroianni and featured Sandrelli). *Alfredo, Alfredo* is considerably less inventive and outrageous, and though then-35-year-old Hoffman made a surprisingly convincing Italian nebbish, he was no Mastroianni. Pauline Kael wrote upon the film's release that she found the dubbed voice of Hoffman (that's right, his subtitled dialogue was dubbed by an Italian actor) gave the picture "an extra dimension." Be that as it may, it's nearly as disconcerting as hearing a strange actor's voice come out of Mel Gibson's mouth in the American version of *Mad Max*.

NEXT STOP... *Divorce—Italian Style, Seduced and Abandoned, The Pizza Triangle (A Drama of Jealousy)*

1972 (R) 97m/C *IT* Dustin Hoffman, Stefania Sandrelli, Carla Gravina, Clara Colosimo, Daniela Patella, Dulio Del Prete; **D:** Pietro Germi; **W:** Pietro Germi, Leo Benvenuti; **C:** Aiace Parolini; **M:** Carlo Rustichelli. **VHS, Closed Caption** *PAR*

ALI: FEAR EATS THE SOUL
Fear Eats the Soul
Angst Essen Selle auf

Rainer Werner Fassbinder was a man in a hurry to make the films he wanted to make, having created some 40-odd pictures by the time he died at age 36, reportedly found face down at his editing table and filled with your run-of-the-mill combo of cocaine, vodka, and Valium. An admirer of the tragic American melodramas of Douglas Sirk (*Written on the Wind, Imitation of Life*), it was logical that Fassbinder would be drawn to a tale of star-crossed, interracial romance, and here he's created a love story set in Munich between two holy innocents—a German scrub woman and a Moroccan mechanic. Indeed, as if to prove that he was in a hurry to out-Sirk Sirk, as well as to up the ante and prove that true love knows no boundaries, Fassbinder has made the mechanic a tall, handsome man in his thirties and the floor-washer a short, squat woman in her sixties. Fortunately, this unlikely duo is played by the extraordinary Brigitte Mira and Fassbinder "protégé" El Hedi Ben Salem, who, though he may have gotten the part by other than traditional means (who doesn't?), is nevertheless a spellbinding screen presence; Fassbinder himself is also fascinating in one of the many small but significant roles in which he frequently cast himself. We know from square one that this physically mismatched couple is going to be in for a rough ride from "society," but then the movie surprises us, taking their marriage to an unexpected conclusion. Fassbinder's deadpan directorial style and smooth, elegant visuals are justly celebrated, but his ability to make material like *Ali* work ultimately depended on his cast. That so many of his films, *Ali* included, cast such a powerful spell with such baroque material suggests that it may be as a director of actors that Rainer Werner Fassbinder will ultimately be best remembered.

NEXT STOP... *Mother Küsters Goes to Heaven, The Merchant of Four Seasons, All That Heaven Allows* (1959)

1974 68m/C *GE* Brigitte Mira, El Hedi Ben Salem, Irm Hermann; **D:** Rainer Werner Fassbinder; **W:** Rainer Werner Fassbinder; **C:** Jurgen Jurges. **VHS** *NYF, FCT*

ALLEGRO NON TROPPO

In the 1960s baby-boomers discovered Walt Disney's part-grand and part-bizarre *Fantasia* (1940) and promptly proclaimed it an early head film. For some of their parents, *Fantasia* had served as an early and important introduction to classical music. This newly rediscovered classic proved to be a revelation worldwide. In Italy it captured the heart of one of the most celebrated creators of short, comic animation, Bruno Bozzetto, who made the rather courageous decision to do ... well ... sort of a remake. Or would it be a tribute? Perhaps a parody. Then again ... an homage? A deconstruction? Whatever it was to be, it turned out to be *Allegro Non Troppo*, featuring a few wonderfully imaginative segments (the best, involving a discarded Coke bottle, is set to Ravel's *Bolero*) which were unfortunately juxtaposed with enough flat moments to make you wish you were watching the real *Fantasia*. The film's orchestra conductor, Leopold Stowkowski in the Disney original, was here played by the wacky Italian comic Maurizio Nichetti (*The Icicle Thief*), who also contributed to the script. This time out, Dvořák, Ravel, Sibelius, and Stravinsky were among those to have cartoons drawn to their music, but none was alive to complain. One of those composers, however, *did* live to see the premiere of the original *Fantasia*, of which his music was an important part. Igor Stravinsky, having been invited by Walt Disney in 1940 to an advance

A

Seaside villagers gather to talk in Federico Fellini's *Amarcord*.

preview screening of *Fantasia*, was startled to see Walt's animated dinosaurs roaming the earth to the accompaniment of an unexpectedly "abridged" version of his masterpiece, *The Rite of Spring*. The great composer was, according to legend, so outraged by what he saw and heard that he stormed furiously out of the screening room just minutes after the segment began, swearing loudly. When reporters who hadn't been able to catch up with the fast-moving maestro asked the Disney people for Stravinsky's response to the film, they were given one of the smoothest answers in the history of public relations. "Mr. Stravinsky," the press people announced, "was visibly moved."

NEXT STOP . . . *Fantasia, Volere Volare, The Icicle Thief*

1976 (PG) 75m/C *IT* Maurizio Nichetti; *D:* Bruno Bozzetto; *W:* Bruno Bozzetto, Guido Manuli; *C:* Mario Masini. **VHS, LV** *BMG, IME, BTV*

ALLONSANFAN

An aging anarchist (Marcello Mastroianni) wants to give up the fight for a comfy rocking chair, but is goaded into action once more by colleagues who fear that fatigue—both individual and collective—is the greatest enemy of revolution. *Allonsanfan* (sing the title and you've got the opening words of France's national anthem, "allons enfants," or "goodbye children") is blessed with three distinguishing characteristics: the writing-directing team of Paolo and Vittorio Taviani, and the incomparable Mastroianni. *Allonsanfan* is one of the Tavianis's least flashy vehicles, and one must assume that the style is designed around their star. Mastroianni embodies the old revolutionary fully and convincingly, and by eschewing much of their usual stylized imagery, the Tavianis have made us a gift of his performance. Indeed, it's unusual to think back on films like

Padre Padrone or The Night of the Shooting Stars without the Tavianis's dazzling imagery coming to mind; remembering Allonsanfan, it's Marcello's grizzled, still-innocent face that pops into our minds first, transforming a pretty good picture into a memorable one.

NEXT STOP... *Padre Padrone, Fiorile, A Special Day*

1973 115m/C *IT* Marcello Mastroianni, Laura Betti, Renato de Carmine, Lea Massari, Mimsy Farmer, Claudio Cassinelli, Bruno Cirino, Michael Berger; *D:* Paolo Taviani, Vittorio Taviani; *W:* Paolo Taviani, Vittorio Taviani; *C:* Giuseppe Ruzzolini; *M:* Ennio Morricone. **VHS** *FCT, WBF*

ALPHAVILLE
Alphaville, a Strange Case of Lemmy Caution
Alphaville, une Etrange Aventure de Lemmy Caution

In the history of motion pictures there have been innumerable ways of imagining the future. Yet even when examining the medium's entire first 100 years, it is entirely possible that there has never been a vision as bleak or as radically beautiful as that which was conjured by Jean-Luc Godard in his 1965 pulp fiction opus about a future controlled by a giant, all-encompassing, emotionless computer. Godard was able to realize his vision using "found materials"—that is, the city of Paris at night, automobiles as spacecraft, neon-lit office corridors as futuristic bastions of power. Trench coated detective Lemmy Caution (American actor Eddie Constantine) had been the hero of other French crime films, and Godard hit upon the concept of taking this well-known and well-worn character—known not as a genius but a man of action—and placing him matter-of-factly in the fantastic setting of Alphaville. Lemmy's mission is to get to the bottom of the disappearance of the agent who preceded him and to bring back, dead or alive, one mysterious Professor Von Braun. When Lemmy meets the professor's beautiful daughter (Anna Karina), all bets are off as Lemmy's Raymond Chandler-style, pistol-packing code of behavior runs smack into the nightmarish emotional controls imposed by Alphaville's gigantic controlling computer, Alpha 60. *Alphaville*

was photographed in glistening black and white by the great cinematographer Raoul Coutard, and it is a visionary work of such startling visual density that certain images, ones that may only make sense on a subliminal level, will nevertheless remain with the viewer for years. In a single astonishing leap, Godard not only anticipated the science-fiction mania that would engulf the cinema a decade later, but surpassed most of it on both an intellectual and a visual level without ever even imagining what a computer-generated special effect was. I'm still not certain what *Alphaville* adds up to (Lemmy wasn't either), but I've never experienced a rain-soaked night in a big city without recalling it. Godard understood that the future is now.

NEXT STOP... *Weekend, Le Samourai, Blade Runner*

1965 100m/B *FR* Eddie Constantine, Anna Karina, Akim Tamiroff, Howard Vernon, Laszlo Szabo, Michel Delahaye, Jean-Pierre Leaud; *D:* Jean-Luc Godard; *W:* Jean-Luc Godard; *C:* Raoul Coutard; *M:* Paul Misraki. Berlin International Film Festival '65: Golden Berlin Bear. **VHS** *HMV, SNC, MRV*

AMARCORD
I Remember

For those who would separate the films of Federico Fellini into the films made before *La Dolce Vita* (1960) and those that came after, *Amarcord* is often cited as the summation of the director's later work. This haunting and self-consciously dreamlike movie, featuring a lilting yet vaguely frightening score by Nino Rota, is a loosely autobiographical kaleidoscope of moments in the life of a young boy growing up in a small, Italian seaside town in the 1930s. Also known as *I Remember, Amarcord* is a film that viewers tend to recall in fragments, which is probably exactly what its creator intended. In attempting to find a cinematic equivalent for the selective memory that we all use when remembering the pleasures and pains of childhood, Fellini forces us to take the bitter with the sweet—most literally exemplified by the nightmarish sequence in which the young protagonist's father, suspected of disloyalty, is forced by the town's new fascist regime to drink castor oil until he collapses. Yet as hard as Fellini tries to

bring the harsh lights of reality and cruelty to his remembered universe, it is the small joyous moments that always triumph. An uncle whose liltingly musical farting becomes as reassuring as a town crier; a gloriously lit ocean liner, stylized and mysterious, suggesting unimagined destinies to come; and, perhaps the simplest and most stunning of all, a peacock displaying its feathers during an unexpected, silent snowfall. These images—photographed by the great Giuseppe Rotunno—which might simply form a few privileged moments by an ordinary director, are at the heart of Fellini's art.

NEXT STOP . . . *The White Sheik, Fellini's Roma, Akira Kurosawa's Dreams*

1974 (R) 124m/C *IT* Magali Noel, Bruno Zanin, Pupella Maggio, Armando Brancia; ***D:*** Federico Fellini; ***W:*** Federico Fellini, Tonino Guerra; ***C:*** Giuseppe Rotunno; ***M:*** Nino Rota. Academy Awards '74: Best Foreign Film; New York Film Critics Awards '74: Best Director (Fellini), Best Film; Nominations: Academy Awards '75: Best Director (Fellini), Best Original Screenplay. **VHS, DVD** *HMV*

THE AMERICAN FRIEND
Der Amerikanische Freund

Bruno Ganz is Jonathan, a mild-mannered picture framer, originally Swiss but living in Germany, who discovers that his rare blood disease will result in a death sentence. At the same time, a mysterious American art dealer and all-around shady profiteer named Ripley (Dennis Hopper) has a friend who wants a hit performed on a gangster, pointing out to Jonathan what an ideal assassin a doomed man such as he would make. That's just the premise around which Wim Wenders constructs this elegant but sometimes impenetrable puzzle of a film, based on the novel *Ripley's Game* by *Strangers on a Train* author Patricia Highsmith. Cinematographer Robby Müller's deeply saturated color images give *The American Friend* an ominousness and appropriate sense of dread even when the plot is opaque. But the cameo appearances by a host a directors that Wenders admires—Nicholas Ray, Samuel Fuller, Jean Eustache, Daniel Schmid—seem gratuitous at best; at

worst they are premature and self-congratulatory comparisons. What carries the picture, as is so often the case in anything in which he appears, is the quiet and utterly assured intelligence of Bruno Ganz's performance. Note: the character of Tom Ripley—this time played by Alain Delon—made an appearance in a remarkable French film that was recently restored and reissued: René Clement's 1960 *Purple Noon.*

NEXT STOP . . . *The Goalie's Anxiety at the Penalty Kick, Kings of the Road, Strangers on a Train*

1977 127m/C *FR GE* Bruno Ganz, Dennis Hopper, Elisabeth Kreuzer, Gerard Blain, Jean Eustache, Samuel Fuller, Nicholas Ray, Daniel Schmid, Wim Wenders; ***D:*** Wim Wenders; ***W:*** Wim Wenders; ***C:*** Robby Muller; ***M:*** Jurgen Knieper. **VHS, LV** *FCT, GLV, TPV*

THE AMERICAN SOLDIER
Der Amerikanische Soldat

If pictures like *The American Soldier* hadn't been followed by the flood of far more sophisticated films that he churned out throughout the remainder of the 1970s, Rainer Werner Fassbinder might have been relegated to a minor footnote in the history of modern European cinema. This shaky tribute to American noir reveals a director whose love of directors like Samuel Fuller, Nicholas Ray, and Douglas Sirk hadn't yet found its own means of expression, and therefore comes off as limp parody. It's the story of an American hit man who completes his assignments without emotion or regret, but who radiates not the existential mystery of Alain Delon in Jean-Pierre Melville's *Le Samourai,* but rather the self-satisfied American imperialism so prevalent in films of the Vietnam era. As social criticism, *The American Soldier* is sophomoric; as Fuller-esque melodrama, it's a flabby and as-yet unformed harbinger of the inspired works that would follow.

NEXT STOP . . . *The Bitter Tears of Petra von Kant, In a Year of 13 Moons, Pierrot le Fou*

1970 80m/C *GE* Rainer Werner Fassbinder, Karl Scheydt, Elga Sorbas, Jan George, Ingrid Caven, Ulli Lommel, Kurt Raab; ***D:*** Rainer Werner Fassbinder; ***W:***

Rainer Werner Fassbinder; *C:* Dietrich Lohmann; *M:* Peer Raben. **VHS** *NYF*

AND GOD CREATED WOMAN
And Woman…Was Created
Et Dieu Crea la Femme

If it's possible for a movie to change the history of the medium as well as to more generally alter popular culture—all without being a particularly good picture—then *And God Created Woman* will serve nicely as an example of how it can be done. This overheated, widescreen, brightly colored roundelay of sexual longing, lusting, and coupling was neatly packaged by 28-year-old writer-director Roger Vadim into a modern moralistic fable that managed to tsk-tsk what it presented on the screen while making sure that it was all presented as explicitly as possible. Though both Brigitte Bardot and the village of Saint Tropez existed prior to *And God Created Woman,* the picture's astonishing worldwide success—most notably in America—put both of these incomparable sights on the radar screens of the rich and famous. Bardot's lovemaking scenes were filmed in multiple versions for the anticipated objections—and desires—of various worldwide markets. American "adult" magazines ran still photos of the notorious European "uncut" version, meaning you could get a glimpse of BB's breasts at your local barber shop, but just the knowledge of what we were NOT seeing in the U.S. was enough to pack audiences in to see the picture anyway, and provided the added titillation of imagining that the French were seeing explicit scenes well beyond anything Vadim and his wife Bardot had actually put on film. Curt Jurgens, Jean-Louis Trintignant, and Christian Marquand are the men whom Bardot dazzles in this pioneering triumph of packaging and marketing—a picture that would forever put a slightly perverse, leering, sexual spin on that tired and uniquely condescending term, the "art" film. Bardot's future, of course, was assured. As for the mania for Saint-Tropez that the film ignited, BB herself gave this quote to the International Herald Tribune when she finally left her home there in 1989: "I am leaving the town to the invaders: increasingly numerous, mediocre, dirty, badly behaved, shameless tourists." C'mon, BB. Remember who brought them there.

NEXT STOP . . . *Contempt, Breathless, La Dolce Vita*

1957 (PG) 93m/C *FR* Brigitte Bardot, Curt Jurgens, Jean-Louis Trintignant, Christian Marquand; *D:* Roger Vadim; *W:* Roger Vadim, Raoul Levy; *C:* Armand Thirard; *M:* Paul Misraki. **VHS** *NO*

AND THE SHIP SAILS ON
El la Nave Va

One of the most unjustly neglected of Fellini's later films (along with *Ginger & Fred*), *And the Ship Sails On* is a nearly plotless epic about the various passengers who've gathered on a fabulous ocean liner in the early 1900s to be on the final journey with a legendary opera star. If the jaw-droppingly realistic, digitally enhanced recreations of James Cameron's *Titanic* inspire a very specific kind of awe in moviegoers, then Fellini's defiantly unreal ship of dreams is both its antithesis and its equal. From the painted, two-dimensional backdrops assembled at impossible scale and angles, to the gently undulating ripples of plastic sheeting that stand in quite elegantly—and dryly—for waves, this is a fantastic frigate. It's like German expressionism with a sense of humor, a child's Colorforms construction come to life. The passengers are no less stylized, and the reporter who speaks directly to the audience throughout is played by British actor Freddie Jones, whose larger-than-life features earned him prime spots in David Lynch's *The Elephant Man* and *Dune.* At well over two hours, *And the Ship Sails On* takes its time. But since it really has no particular place to go, the journey is all the fun. It's best enjoyed as a vacation as vacations ought to be—all anticipation, all what if, a dream of genuine, otherworldly escape that somehow never seems as exquisite as the travel folders promise but that we know exists somewhere. Reality, like beauty, can often be in the

Mother and daughter lead a procession of male friends in *Antonia's Line*.

eye of the beholder—and what a beholder Federico Fellini was.

NEXT STOP . . . *Amarcord, 8 1/2, Stagecoach* (1939)

1983 (PG) 130m/C *IT* Freddie Jones, Barbara Jefford, Janet Suzman, Peter Cellier, Philip Locke; *D:* Federico Fellini; *W:* Federico Fellini, Tonino Guerra; *C:* Giuseppe Rotunno; *M:* Gianfranco Plenizio. **VHS, LV** *COL*

ANDREI RUBLEV

Among the many glories that I had the privilege of discovering at the 1973 New York Film Festival was a two-and-a-half-hour version—a big fragment, really, some 30 minutes shorter than the original—of Andrei Tarkovsky's already-legendary *Andrei Rublev*. Tarkovsky's second feature, a sprawling, three-hour mosaic of imagined moments in the life of the 15th-century icon painter, was in trouble with Soviet authorities from the moment of its completion some seven years earlier, and had been screened only sporadically, usually clandestinely, and even then in versions of varying length. Since not much was ever known about the real Rublev, the authorities were hard-pressed to claim distortion of the facts, but Tarkovsky's emphasis on the importance of art and the artist, particularly in a time of savagery, tyranny, and general barbarism, clearly made *Andrei Rublev* a hotter potato than Mosfilm Studios had bargained for. (As if to twist the knife of censorship still further, *Andrei Rublev*'s American distributor, which picked up the film in time for the New York Film Festival press screening, decided to cut the already shortened version by another 20 minutes, most likely to get in one extra show each day!) It wasn't until the 1980s that the efforts of those such as New York—based distributor Corinth Films resulted in the availability of the full version of *Andrei Rublev*. It was immediately apparent that Tarkovsky's film was indeed the masterpiece that its shorter versions hinted at; this is a stunning, visionary, hallucinatory portrait not only of an artist but of the times that create one. Far from a standard "biopic," *Andrei Rublev* is at times only obliquely about the painter himself; its eight distinct sections—not episodes exactly—suggest living frescoes that collectively provide a feeling for an era in which art was not a luxury, it was almost literally the only means by which the human soul might survive, and even then by the slenderest of threads. The film is photographed in a spellbindingly beautiful black and white, and Tarkovsky generously presents us with Rublev's actual surviving creations, in widescreen and full color, at the conclusion. It is the ultimate tribute to the filmmaker that, while it's a joy to be able to see the real icons, they ironically have less impact than the dark and unforgettable work of art that Tarkovsky himself has created. The script, incidentally, was co-authored by Andrei Mikhalkov-Konchalovsky, brother of *Burnt by the Sun* director Nikita Mikhalkov, and later a transplant to Hollywood, where he ended up directing Sylvester Stallone in *Tango & Cash*. Go figure.

NEXT STOP . . . *Ivan the Terrible Parts 1 & 2, The Wild Bunch, Mother and Son*

1966 185m/C *RU* Anatoli Solonitzin, Ivan Lapikov, Nikolai Grinko, Nikolai Sergueiev; *D:* Andrei Tarkovsky; *W:* Andrei Tarkovsky, Andrei Konchalovsky; *C:* Vadim Yusov; *M:* Vyacheslav Ovchinnikov. **VHS, LV** *FXL, NOS, FCT*

ANGI VERA

In 1948 Hungary, during the early and increasingly dehumanizing days of socialism, a young woman who is deeply committed to the cause finds herself falling in love with the charming—and married—group leader of her Party "re-education" school. Veronika Papp's Angi is one of the most memorable and convincing characters to come out of the great wave of Eastern European cinema of the 1970s. Her dilemma is hardly unique to her time or place, yet her solution to that dilemma—revealed in an unexpected climax that still packs a wallop—represents a quietly revolutionary but genuinely revelatory intersecting of sex and politics. Director Pál Gábor's film is a graceful, entertaining and haunting love story that received great critical acclaim when it appeared on the international film festival circuit, yet received such limited release here that it failed to reach the crossover audience that it deserved. A glittering, beguiling, and ultimately devastating little gem, *Angi Vera* is ripe for rediscovery.

NEXT STOP . . . *Tito and Me, When Father Was Away on Business, My Twentieth Century*

1978 96m/C *HU* Veronika Papp, Erszi Pasztor, Eva Szabo, Tamas Dunai, Laszlo Horvath; *D:* Pal Gabor; *W:* Pal Gabor; *C:* Lajos Koltai; *M:* Gyorgy Selmeczi. **VHS** *NO*

ANNA
Anna: From Six Till Eighteen
Anna: Ot Shesti do Vosemnadtsati

Filmed over a period of thirteen years beginning in 1980, this extraordinary work by Russia's justly celebrated Nikita Mikhalkov (*A Slave of Love, Burnt by the Sun*) is both a documentary portrait of the collapse of the Soviet Union and, simultaneously, a tender, fascinating, epic home movie chronicling the maturing of the director's daughter Anna, from ages six through 18. Each year, Mikhalkov asks Anna the same five questions, and her changing answers reflect not only the ordinary and universal evolution of concerns that a young person faces, but also unexpectedly parallel the dramatic changes that the Soviet Union itself went through, from hard-line party rule to Perestroika to the brink of capitalism itself. Anna is that rare political documentary that manages to reveal a huge, changing landscape through the eyes of one individual. As always, the fate of millions is vastly more difficult to relate to than the emotions and choices of a single human being. Knowing this, Mikhalkov has fashioned a human-scaled vision of recent history that is accessible, moving, and honest. *Anna* is a modest undertaking, but a stirring achievement.

NEXT STOP . . . *A Slave of Love, Oblomov, 28 Up*

A

13

SATYAJIT RAY

Ray is India's most internationally acclaimed filmmaker. Born in Calcutta in 1921, he was encouraged to appreciate the arts, and while studying at the University of Calcutta he was already viewing Western films and writing his own film scenarios. In the early 1940s he began working as a layout artist for an English advertising agency. He continued to enjoy films, and he eventually corresponded with film critics in England. In 1949, after being transferred to England, Ray realized the opportunity of seeing many more films. He was especially drawn to *Bicycle Thief*, Vittorio De Sica's neorealist masterpiece in which a worker determines to retrieve his stolen bicycle.

Around this time, Ray drew an assignment to illustrate an edition of Bannerjee's popular novel "Pather Panchali." He felt that the story would lend itself to a neo-realist rendering, and upon returning to India he determined to make such a film. Despite meager funds and amateur technicians, Ray—with personal encouragement from such directors as Jean Renoir and John Huston—persevered over a three-year period. The result of his considerable efforts was a film that ultimately won praise as a realistic, humanistic drama about a boy, Apu, and his long journey with his mother.

Even as *Pather Panchali* reaped acclaim, Ray finished a sequel, *Aparajito*, which concerns Apu's adolesence and his family hardships in Benares. Like *Pather Panchali*, *Aparajito* shows Ray to be a master of evocative imagery ranging from landscapes to facial expressions, and it too proved a success outside India. Ray followed *Aparajito* with *Jalsaghar*, the story of a foolhardy nobleman's tragic faith in tradition, and then he concluded the Apu saga with *Apur Sansar*, an account of Apu's marriage and his early years as a writer.

Throughout the 1960s Ray wrote and directed some of his greatest films. In 1960 he completed *Devi*, in which a household is undone after a father comes to suspect his daughter of being a reincarnated goddess, and in 1962 he produced *Kanchenjungha*, wherein a domineering father attempts to engineer his daughter's marriage to an arrogant suitor even as she finds love with a less promising fellow. *Charulata*, arguably Ray's masterpiece, premiered in 1964. In this understated film, which won Ray comparisons with Russian master Anton Chekhov, a love triangle threatens to undo a marriage in Victorian India.

In 1974 Ray brought a more broadly humanistic approach to *Asani Sanket*, which details life in a small village during the widespread famine that ravaged India in 1943. He then returned to the cynical world of capitalism with the satiric *Jana Aranya*, wherein a struggling businessman finally finds work in a less-than appealing profession.

Among Ray's final films, *Shatranj Ke Khilari*, is noteworthy for its English and Hindi—as opposed to Bengali—dialogue. This film, in which Ray again indulges in satire, concerns two nobleman who revel in chess even as their independent state is about to fall under British rule. Another notable film, *Ghare Bahire*, recalls *Charulata* in relating a destructive human triangle. Ray completed still another domestic tale, *Agantuk*, in 1991. He died the next year in Calcutta.

1993 99m/C Nikita Mikhalkov, Nadia Mikhalkov, Anna Mikhalkov; **D:** Nikita Mikhalkov; **W:** Nikita Mikhalkov; **C:** Pavel Lebeshev, Vadim Yusov; **M:** Eduard Artemyev. *NYR*

✓ ANTONIA'S LINE

Marleen Gorris's exquisite recounting of the loves and trials of several generations of women in a rural village in the Netherlands has been nearly as popular with audiences as it has been with critics. *Antonia's Line* unfolds in a series of flashbacks that gently cascade through the memory of the now-90-year-old Antonia (the wonderful Willeke van Ammelrooy) who tells us in her narration that this is the day on which she will die. Though the film has been misread in some quarters as an idealized vision of a world of women in which men are unnecessary, *Antonia's Line* is in fact far from that simplistic. It presents a universe in which men and women have made a kind of uneasy peace with each other, and the film goes so far as to imagine a community in which sexuality in all its incarnations is a genuinely liberating force rather than a guilt-inducing need for which a steep price must be paid. Simply but elegantly photographed and directed, with a particularly evocative score by Ilona Sekacz, *Antonia's Line* is one of those small surprises that is often referred to—justifiably in this case—as a gem. It won the 1995 Academy Award for Best Foreign Language Film.

NEXT STOP . . . *Career Girls, Fire, The Women*

1995 (R) 102m/C NL Willeke Van Ammelrooy, Els Dottermans, Veerle Van Overloop, Thyrza Ravesteijn, Jan Decleir, Mil Seghers, Jan Steen, Marina De Graaf; **D:** Marleen Gorris; **W:** Marleen Gorris; **C:** Willy Stassen; **M:** Ilona Seckaz. Academy Awards '95: Best Foreign Film; Nominations: British Academy Awards '96: Best Foreign Film. **VHS** *BMG*

ANTONIO DAS MORTES
O Dragao da Maldade contra o Santo Guerreiro

The most outspoken and brilliantly talented member of the Cinema Novo movement in Brazil, Glauber Rocha came to the film world's attention with his 1964 *Black God, White Devil.* In this sequel, made five years later, the bounty hunter from the earlier film comes to realize that his true enemies are not the revolutionaries he's being paid to kill, but rather the land barons and government functionaries who are using him so cynically. Rocha's first film in color is a rich, imagist epic that immediately established him as one of the world's most important new cinematic voices. *Antonio Das Mortes* brought Rocha a shared Best Director prize at Cannes, and became the most widely distributed of the Cinema Novo films in the west, even receiving a moderately successful art house release in the U.S. Yet despite the worldwide critical acclaim that the film garnered—or perhaps because of it—Rocha was hounded mercilessly by the Brazilian establishment and was ultimately forced to flee to Europe, where he would continue to work as both a filmmaker and critic until just prior to his untimely death at age 43. When he discovered that a lung infection was going to kill him, Rocha flew back to his beloved Brazil to die, a gesture reminiscent of the sweeping romanticism of this film, his masterpiece.

NEXT STOP . . . *Black God, White Devil, Quilombo, Bye Bye Brazil*

1968 100m/C BR Mauricio Do Valle, Odete Lara, Jofre Soares, Lorival Pariz; **D:** Glauce Rocha; **W:** Glauce Rocha; **C:** Alfonso Beato. **VHS** *FCT*

APARAJITO
The Unvanquished

The centerpiece of Satyajit Ray's renowned *Apu Trilogy,* which traces the life of a poor Bengali boy from childhood through fatherhood, is an act of both grace and quiet revolution. It begins where its predecessor, *Pather Panchali,* left off, as the Bengali family arrives in the holy city of Benares in 1920. Apu's father becomes ill in his new home, and though the father believes that his immersion in the Ganges has purified him, it merely hastens his death. Apu, now on the brink of adulthood, discovers that he has been awarded a scholarship to the University of Calcutta. In order to make use of it, however,

he must wrestle with his mother's pleas to stay with her and train for the priesthood, which is the family's tradition. What elevates *Aparajito*—and all of Ray's work—far above any suggestion of soap opera is the purity of his near-documentary approach, which is so unfussy and natural in its observation of human behavior that his films simply enter our bloodstream and become experience. His generally non-professional casts are so without affectation that his performers seem to hone in on the essence of each scene, each moment of small revelation, with the accuracy of a laser. It's the compounding of these moments that result in films that are remembered as more real than real life, and though *Aparajito* necessarily serves a somewhat mechanical function in getting Apu from the opening film to the trilogy's transcendental conclusion, it remains an essential and unforgettable link in a great master's triptych.

NEXT STOP... *Pather Panchali, The World of Apu, I Vitelloni*

1958 108m/B *IN* Pinaki Sen Gupta, Karuna Banerjee, Kanu Banerjee, Ramani Sen Gupta; **D:** Satyajit Ray; **W:** Satyajit Ray; **C:** Subrata Mitra; **M:** Ravi Shankar. Venice Film Festival '57: Best Film. **VHS** *FCT, MRV, TIM*

ARABIAN NIGHTS
Il Fiore delle Mille e Una Notte
Flower of the Arabian Nights
A Thousand and One Nights

In the last years of his career and his life, Pier Paolo Pasolini turned to an unexpected source for inspiration: cinematic interpretations of literary classics, including *Medea* (1970), *The Decameron* (1971), *The Canterbury Tales* (1972), and this colorful but oddly disjointed 1974 telling of the *Arabian Nights*. Some of the narrative lapses may be due to cuts that the film suffered at the hands of censors who dogged Pasolini through his entire career. Still, much of the insistent eroticism that permeated his versions of *Oedipus Rex* (1967) and *The Decameron* had become largely an uninspired, rote exercise by the time of this film, Pasolini's second-to-last prior to his scandalous *Salo, or the 120 Days of Sodom* and his subsequent murder. Be that as it may, the film's relaxed mood, open structure, and occasional flashes of deep humor, most of which relate to sexual stereotyping and the nature of truth, now seem precious and fragile reminders of the gifted and often humane director who would present us next with his horrifying parting shot, *Salo*—perhaps the most utterly bleak and despairing vision of the human condition that the cinema has yet given us.

NEXT STOP... *The Decameron, Fellini Satyricon, The Milky Way*

1974 130m/C *IT* Ninetto Davoli, Franco Merli, Ines Pellegrini, Luigina Rocchi, Franco Citti; **D:** Pier Paolo Pasolini; **W:** Pier Paolo Pasolini; **C:** Giuseppe Ruzzolini; **M:** Ennio Morricone. **VHS, LV, Letterbox** *WBF*

ARIEL

When his mining job falls prey to Finnish downsizing, Taisto (Turo Pajala) hops into the new Cadillac his father has given him and sets off for the wide open spaces of Finland to find a brand-new future, and, perhaps, romance. This dark 1988 comedy from Finland's Aki Kaurismäki is an early and superb example of the way Kaurismäki spins his shaggy-dog tales with a uniquely dry, minimalist wit. Kaurismäki's movies have been compared to those of Jim Jarmusch (*Stranger than Paradise*), yet there is something uniquely Scandinavian in this movie's humor, despite the pervasive influence of American pop culture throughout. (That influence would continue the next year not with Kaurismäki going Hollywood exactly, but in his startlingly effective, feature-length sketch on popular culture-clash, *Leningrad Cowboys Go America*.) The joy of *Ariel* is in truly not knowing where this road trip is headed, yet being so confident in the director's vision that we go along for the ride happily, and with no questions asked.

NEXT STOP... *Drifting Clouds, La Vie de Bohème, Stroszek*

1989 74m/C *FI* Susanna Haavisto, Turo Pajala, Matti Pellonpaa; **D:** Aki Kaurismaki; **W:** Aki Kaurismaki; **C:** Timo Salminen; **M:** Dimitri Shostakovich. National Society of Film Critics Awards '90: Best Foreign Film. **VHS** *KIV, FCT*

ARSENAL

At the end of the silent era, Russian filmmakers created masterworks of power and lyricism that frequently transcended their propagandistic purposes. Alexander Dovzhenko, a cinematic poet and brilliant theorist, created in his *Arsenal* a sweeping chronicle of the war of 1914 and the conflict between nationalists and revolutionaries. Startling images—a group of well-heeled bourgeois listening in silence in their homes for the sound of revolution, a crushed accordion that suggests the revolution's dashed hopes—are so potent in their evocative power that it would be a disservice to Dovzhenko's art to label them mere symbolism. Although *Arsenal,* as well as his *Zvenigora* (1928) and *Earth* (1930), is a superb representative of the Soviet cinema's golden era, the mutilated versions of it that have been circulated in the west for years have caused many viewers and a few critics to find the picture nearly incomprehensible. Try to find a complete version; seen in its original form, *Arsenal* is a model of storytelling and pacing that is the equal of the greatest work of Griffith and Eisenstein.

NEXT STOP . . . *Earth, Chapayev, Strike*

1929 70m/B *RU* Semyon Svashenko, Luciano Albertini; **D:** Alexander Dovzhenko; **W:** Alexander Dovzhenko; **C:** Daniil Demutsky. **VHS** *NOS, MRV, IHF*

THE ASCENT
Voskhozhdeniye

At the 1976 Telluride Film Festival, audiences were justifiably blown away by this daring and dynamic tale of World War II, in which the Nazis were not the only enemy of the beleaguered Russian people. Even hinting at the possibility of Russian collaboration with Germany during the war was almost unheard of in Soviet cinema, yet *The Ascent* focuses on it so unblinkingly that it seemed to take glasnost out to an almost undreamed of—and perhaps dangerous—precipice. Even viewed as just a "war movie," *The Ascent* shows the sure hand of its remarkably skilled director every inch of the way. The picture, memorably photographed in a crisp black and white, is

set in the cold, snowy expanses of Belarus, and it focuses on a captured partisan whose physical battles are nothing compared to the psychological war he faces against his Russian collaborationist interrogator. *The Ascent's* enormously talented, then-38-year-old director, Larissa Shepitko, answered questions with as much candor as she could after the Telluride screening, charming the audience and receiving great admiration for her courage and skill. Three years later she was dead, reportedly the victim of a traffic accident on a road as snowy as those depicted in her film. Whether it was life (or death) imitating art, a simple traffic accident, or causes unknown, the cinema world was robbed of an accomplished and hugely promising talent. Ultimately receiving a very limited release in the United States, *The Ascent* is ripe for rediscovery on video, and will, one hopes, spark interest in the life and work of its creator.

NEXT STOP . . . *Prisoner of the Mountains, The Confession, Grand Illusion*

1976 105m/B *RU* Boris Plotnikov, Vladimir Gostyukhin; **D:** Larisa Shepitko; **W:** Larisa Shepitko, Yuri Klepikov; **C:** Pavel Lebeshev, Vladimir Chukhnov; **M:** Alfred Schnittke. **VHS** *IFC*

ASHES AND DIAMONDS
Popiol i Diament

Long before the collapse of the Soviet Union and the ensuing chaos, confusion, and factionalizing, Polish director Andrej Wajda created this complex and insightful work about the new and unexpected perils that arise when a hated regime is toppled. Taking place in a small Polish town in 1945, on the day that Germany surrendered, *Ashes and Diamonds* is the story of Maciek (Zbigniew Cybulski in a brooding and memorable performance), an underground freedom fighter whose superiors have now instructed him to assassinate a local communist party official before he can place the town under the control of a Russian-backed government. By focusing the film on Maciek's dilemma, Wajda is able to show us a world in which the enemies are no longer so clear-cut. Those who fought side-

by-side against the common Nazi enemy suddenly find themselves violently divided as to what direction to take next, and this would-be assassin is forced to contemplate what, if anything, military victory has meant, as long as the enemy remains hidden within us all. Based on a 1948 novel by Jerzy Andrzejewski, *Ashes and Diamonds* is the third part of Wajda's "War Trilogy," which includes *A Generation* (1954) and *Kanal* (1957). A piercing story of love, politics, and revolution, and the surprising yet recurring ways in which they intersect, *Ashes and Diamonds* is marred only by a modest amount of overly insistent symbolism—a minor flaw in an otherwise powerful and still-relevant work.

NEXT STOP . . . *A Generation, Kanal, Man of Marble*

1958 105m/B PL Zbigniew Cybulski, Eva Krzyzewska, Adam Pawlikowski, Bogumil Kobiela, Waclaw Zastrzezynski; **D:** Andrzej Wajda; **W:** Andrzej Wajda; **C:** Jerzy Wojcik; **M:** Jan Krenz, Filip Nowak. **VHS, LV** ING, MRV, NLC

ASHIK KERIB
The Lovelorn Minstrel
The Hoary Legends of the Caucasus

In a weirdly mythical age that seems to exist only in the stunningly fertile imagination of the director, a musician who has fallen in love with a rich man's daughter is punished by being made to spend his years wandering the countryside. The visions and adventures that he encounters are what interests the director, Sergei Parajanov, whose 1964 *Shadows of Forgotten Ancestors* remains one of the great visionary masterpieces of the 1960s. *Ashik Karib* has a narrative, all right, but it takes a bit of digging to sort it out. Parajanov's storytelling is subordinated to poetic evocation—an attempt to use the medium of film to animate impossible and magnificent dreams, the kind of thing that becomes literalized and flattened in the hands of lesser directors. Featuring a soundtrack as shockingly beautiful as its images, *Ashik Karib* can clearly be seen as a major influence on recent films such as Iran's *Gabbeh,* in which surrealistic tableaux transport us to a world of the subconscious, far beyond that which is merely mystical or symbolic. Not a film that will likely be optioned for a remake by Touchstone, *Ashik Karib* is a complete original, as rewarding as it is demanding.

NEXT STOP . . . *The Color of Pomegranates, Mother and Son, Gabbeh*

1988 75m/C *RU* Yiur Mgoyan, Veronkia Metonidze, Levan Natroshvili, Sofiko Chiaureli; *D:* Dodo Abashidze, Sergei Paradjanov; *W:* Giya Badridze; *M:* Djavashir Kuliev. **VHS** *KIV, FCT*

AU REVOIR LES ENFANTS
Goodbye, Children

Louis Malle was a filmmaker so interested in telling different kinds of stories that the questions of what he would do next and *how* he would do it were always gloriously unpredictable—all that remained constant was the generosity and humanity he brought to each of his films, regardless of subject. Here, that subject is autobiographical. In 1944, during the German occupation of France, three Jewish students were hidden in the Catholic boarding school that Malle attended. What ultimately happened to those children should not be surprising to any citizen of this century, yet the story that Malle has decided to share with us is not nearly as simple as good versus evil. Near its conclusion, this suspenseful, devastating, and ultimately ennobling memoir about guilt, honor, and responsibility, about bravery that—tragically and ironically—fell short of its goal *because* of the compassion that inspired it, distills a lifetime of trying to make sense of human nature into a few perfectly edited frames of film in which a child's eyes shift their gaze from one part of a schoolroom to another. Malle's simple, profoundly eloquent film is an uncluttered yet stunningly complex account of a moment that would change the story's teller forever. As all of his best films do, *Au*

Revoir les Enfants adds to our knowledge of the human condition.

NEXT STOP . . . *Lacombe, Lucien, The Sorrow and the Pity, The Designated Mourner*

1987 (PG) 104m/C *FR* Gaspard Manesse, Raphael Fejto, Francine Racette, Stanislas Carre de Malberg, Philippe Morier-Genoud, Francois Berland, Peter Fitz, Francois Negret, Irene Jacob; *D:* Louis Malle; *W:* Louis Malle; *C:* Renato Berta; *M:* Franz Schubert, Camille Saint-Saens. British Academy Awards '88: Best Director (Malle); Cesar Awards '88: Best Art Direction/Set Decoration, Best Cinematography, Best Director (Malle), Best Film, Best Sound, Best Writing; Los Angeles Film Critics Association Awards '87: Best Foreign Film; Venice Film Festival '87: Best Film; Nominations: Academy Awards '87: Best Foreign-Language Film, Best Original Screenplay. **VHS, LV** *ORI, FCT, HMV*

AUGUSTIN

Anne Fontaine's hour-long film is precisely the kind of picture that could have been made in the U.S. only as a film school project, unlikely to ever be seen by paying audiences. In France, however, this remarkable little comedy was actually a success, thanks mainly to the unprepossessing charm of the film's lead, the gangly and rubber-faced Jean-Chretien Sibertin-Blanc (a name that wouldn't even fit on a multiplex marquee). Sibertin-Blanc, real life brother of writer/director Fontaine, portrays Augustin, a geeky but oddly ingratiating insurance clerk who processes death claims for a living, but dreams of fame as an actor. As *Augustin* ambles amiably along, Sibertin-Blanc uses his natural ease in front of the camera to pull off a neat trick, namely suggesting his character's *unease* whenever *he's* in front of a camera. This is a shaggy-dog, star-is-born story with a kicker at the close, suggesting at the fade-out that Augustin's spaced-out qualities may be symptoms of a slightly more serious disorder than we had imagined. And keep your eye on Augustin when he's doing research as a hotel room-service waiter; Sibertin-Blanc would reprise the part nearly identically later the same year in director Benoit Jacquot's *A Single Girl.*

NEXT STOP . . . *Son of Gascogne, When the Cat's Away, Irma Vep*

1995 61m/C *FR* Jean-Chretien Sibertin-Blanc, Thierry Lhermitte, Stephanie Zhang, Nora Habib, Guy

"Mom, I want a child. But no husband to go with it."

—Danielle (Els Dottermans) to Antonia (Willeke van Ammelrooy) in *Antonia's Line.*

Casabonne; **D:** Anne Fontaine; **W:** Anne Fontaine; **C:** Jean-Marie Dreujou. **VHS** *KIV*

AN AUTUMN AFTERNOON
Sanma No Aji

The final film by the great Yasujiro Ozu is a story about a widowed father who must come to terms with having to give up his only daughter to marriage. As in Ozu's *Late Spring* (1949), the father needs to convince the daughter that it's a part of life for her to get married and to leave her father to fend for himself. She's reluctant to do so, he's reluctant to lose her, and yet it's the duty of both of them to accept the flow of traditional life despite the accompanying sadness. It's a story Ozu had told many times before, but rarely with more power or grace than in this nearly sublime summation of the knowledge and insight of a career that spanned 53 features in 60 years. There's a unique joy in turning yourself over to Ozu; it's like having an eternally wise (and eternally living) father on call for the kind of therapy that is, in the end, simply the shared wisdom of a great soul, dispensed with patience, wit, compassion, and artistry. As usual, the amazing Chishu Ryu played the role of the father whose understanding usually advanced while downing a few sakés or Johnny Walkers (Red). It wasn't that different for Ozu himself, whose scripts were often completed in all-night writing marathons—aided by a few cocktails—together with his writing collaborator, Kogo Noda. The colors of the film are muted, and, as in all Ozu films, the camera remains still and most images are photographed from the vantage point of someone seated cross-legged on a *tatami* mat, eyes approximately three feet off the ground. If *An Autumn Afternoon* isn't, in the end, Ozu's masterpiece, it's only because of the existence of his *Tokyo Story*. Nevertheless, it's a great experience.

NEXT STOP . . . *Late Spring, Tokyo Story, Babette's Feast*

1962 112m/C *JP* Chishu Ryu, Shima Iwashita, Shin-Ichiro Mikami, Mariko Okada, Keiji Sada; **D:** Yasujiro Ozu; **W:** Yasujiro Ozu; **C:** Yushun Atsuta; **M:** Kojun Saito. **VHS** *NYF*

AUTUMN SONATA
Hostsonaten

Autumn Sonata marked the only time that the cinema's two most treasured Bergmans —Ingrid and Ingmar—worked together. When two legends get together the results are often less than the sum of the two brilliant parts, possibly because the very pairing can be intimidating to all. Happily, *Autumn Sonata* is an exception. The story is of a mother (Bergman) who spends a long and painfully revealing evening as she attempts to rekindle a relationship with her oldest child (Liv Ullmann). The friction comes from the fact that the Bergman character deserted her family years before in order to pursue her career as a concert pianist. Ingmar Bergman's career has been marked by films that are, to varying degrees, autobiographical. But the boldness of Ingrid Bergman portraying a character who deserted her family for a greater passion has an unmistakable parallel to the real-life "scandal" in which she left her family and career in the United States for the love of director Roberto Rossellini. All of this would seem to be the kind of baggage that even the most insightful of artists would have trouble handling, but both Bergmans pull off near-miracles here. Photographed with a characteristic lack of fussiness by Bergman collaborator Sven Nykvist, *Autumn Sonata* is a superbly orchestrated and surprisingly moving demonstration that in families—no matter how severe the damage or how bitter the resentments—it's never too late to discard what's unimportant and to try just one more time to learn the meaning of forgiveness.

NEXT STOP . . . *Fanny and Alexander, Tokyo Story, Terms of Endearment*

1978 97m/C *SW* Ingrid Bergman, Liv Ullmann, Halvar Bjork, Lena Nyman, Gunnar Bjornstrand, Erland Josephson; **D:** Ingmar Bergman; **W:** Ingmar Bergman; **C:** Sven Nykvist. Golden Globe Awards '79: Best Foreign Film; National Board of Review Awards '78: Best Actress (Bergman), Best Director (Bergman); New York Film Critics Awards '78: Best Actress (Bergman); National Society of Film Critics Awards '78: Best Actress (Bergman); Nominations: Academy Awards '78: Best Actress (Bergman), Best Original Screenplay. **VHS, LV** *FOX*

BABETTE'S FEAST
Babettes Gaestebud

On the Danish seacoast in the late 19th century, two elderly sisters living in a village of modest, abstinent puritans take in a housekeeper and preparer of modest meals named Babette (Stéphane Audran), a mysterious Frenchwoman who does what the women ask, yet asks little in return for herself. Fourteen years later, she makes them dinner *her* way. Actually, the meal that Babette prepares is served to a somewhat larger party than just the sisters, but the resulting feast provides lasting and magical nourishment—not only for the characters, but for everyone who has ever had the good fortune to encounter this miraculous little film. Based on an Isak Dinesen short story and directed with exemplary restraint by Gabriel Axel, *Babette's Feast* is a multi-layered mystery that dares to provide a lot of answers, including more than a vague hint at the meaning of life itself. But who is this strange woman and what is she doing in this incredibly out-of-the-way landscape? Will Babette's true talents ever be appreciated by people who, by their very strict beliefs, seem opposed to everything her life stands for? Will they be able to understand the real meaning of her gift to them, or must the joys of this world always be rejected by them as dangerous hedonism? In the crowning, sybaritic dinner sequence of *Babette's Feast,* all is revealed; by the film's starry fadeout, we've been taken to a transcendental moment, and been rewarded with the answer to a question we may never have even dared to ask. (When *Babette's Feast* was released in the U.S., restaurants in some cities recreated, at a hefty price, the spectacular dinner that Babette makes on screen. Without Babette's generosity, however, the dinner was only dinner—the vain and hollow temptation the sisters feared it was. Moral: rent the film, but don't try this at home. Just order a pizza—but do get a good one.)

NEXT STOP . . . *Tampopo, Late Spring, Ikiru*

1987 102m/C *DK FR* Stephane Audran, Bibi Andersson, Bodil Kjer, Birgitte Federspiel, Jean-Philippe LaFont, Ebbe Rode, Jarl Kulle; *D:* Gabriel Axel; *W:* Gabriel Axel; *C:* Henning Kristiansen; *M:* Per Norgard. Academy Awards '87: Best Foreign Film; British Academy Awards '88: Best Foreign Film. **VHS, LV** *ORI, FCT, AUD*

THE BAD SLEEP WELL
The Worse You Are, the Better You Sleep
Waru Yatsu Hodo Yoku Nemuru

Filmed during the break between two of Kurosawa's greatest action epics, *The Hidden Fortress* and *Yojimbo, The Bad Sleep Well* is a well-crafted but ultimately unfocused thriller about high-level government corruption. Toshiro Mifune—secretary to a corrupt corporate bigshot—marries his boss's daughter during the film's stunning opening sequence. The marriage ceremony concludes with the arrival of a wedding cake in the shape of an office building, and placed in one "window" of the building is a single rose—it's the window from which a former employee plunged to his death years before. The man who died—unbeknownst to his new father-in-law—was Mifune's father, and Mifune has sworn to find out the true circumstances of his mysterious death, officially labeled a suicide by the company. Ultimately Mifune gets to the bottom of things, but by then *The Bad Sleep Well* reveals such a bleak and corrupt landscape that the film can only end one way, and does. One of the few Kurosawa pictures that gets less interesting as it goes along, *The Bad Sleep Well* nevertheless contains a number of memorable moments, including that truly unforgettable wedding sequence.

NEXT STOP . . . *Stray Dog, Z, JFK*

1960 135m/B *JP* Toshiro Mifune, Masayuki Kato, Masayuki Mori, Takashi Shimura, Akira Nishimura; *D:* Akira Kurosawa; *W:* Akira Kurosawa, Shinobu Hashimoto, Riyuzo Kikushima, Hideo Oguni; *C:* Yuzuru Aizawa; *M:* Masaru Sato. **VHS** *HMV, COL*

THE BAKER'S WIFE
La Femme du Boulanger

In a small French village, the new baker's arrival is greeted with great anticipation by

the locals, since the previous baker's suicide has left the population breadless. The baker (Raimu) turns out to be quite talented, but his lovely wife (Ginette Leclerc) decides that not everything about him is completely satisfying, and she promptly runs off with her new lover, a local shepherd. Despondent, the baker turns to drink and, worst of all for the villagers, loses interest in his craft. It is up to the townspeople, therefore, to reunite the pair if they ever expect to get a decent loaf of bread again. *The Baker's Wife* has charmed audiences worldwide for 60 years; not only was it a rare foreign language hit in American theatres, but luminaries such as Marlene Dietrich, Orson Welles, and Albert Einstein extolled its virtues in the most grandiose of terms. *The Baker's Wife is* pretty irresistible, yet the film's strength derives not from the grandiosity of either theme or style, but from the very simplicity of its conception. Pagnol's ability to let us comfortably soak up his little village's atmosphere, allowing us to virtually move in for a couple of hours, is part of the secret; but it's the central performance of Raimu as the baker that is the real yeast in this recipe. Raimu may not actually have been, as Welles claimed, "the greatest screen actor of all time," but while watching him balance comedy and pathos in the perpetually enchanting performance he gives here, you just might be inclined to agree.

NEXT STOP . . . *The Fanny Trilogy, The Well-Digger's Daughter, Harvest*

1933 101m/B *FR* Raimu, Ginette LeClerc, Charles Moulton, Charpin, Robert Vattier; *D:* Marcel Pagnol; *W:* Marcel Pagnol; *C:* Georges Benoit; *M:* Vincent Scotto. New York Film Critics Awards '40: Best Foreign Film. **VHS** *INT, MRV, DVT*

BALLAD OF A SOLDIER
Ballada o Soldate

Winner of the *Palme d'Or* at the 1960 Cannes Film Festival and an Academy Award nominee for best original screenplay, *Ballad of a Soldier* was the breakthrough film for the Soviet film industry following World War II. It tells the story of a young Russian soldier named Alësha who's given a few days' leave as a reward for taking out a couple of German tanks, and on his journey home meets a number of people who have been affected by the war in various and sometimes surprising ways. A young legless veteran is afraid to go home to his wife, and Alësha arranges their reunion; when Alësha visits the wife of a fellow soldier to bring her a gift from her husband, he's shocked and embarrassed to find her with another man; without warning, Alësha meets a young girl with whom he shares a few hours, only to be parted from her quickly, and forever. Finally, the moments he actually gets to spend with his mother are far too short, but all the more precious as a result of the experiences of his brief but eventful journey. *Ballad of a Soldier,* while certainly a tender, intelligent, and affecting film, may have been overpraised a bit on its initial release, partly because its appearance in the USSR in 1960 was so unexpected, and partly because its anti-war message was— and still is—hungered for so universally.

NEXT STOP . . . *Commissar, The Ascent, Paisan*

1960 88m/B *RU* Vladimir Ivashov, Shanna Prokhorenko, Antonina Maximova, Nikolai Kryuchkov; *D:* Grigori Chukrai; *W:* Grigori Chukrai, Valentin Yezhov; *C:* Sergei Mukhin; *M:* Mikhail Ziv. British Academy Awards '61: Best Film; Nominations: Academy Awards '61: Best Story & Screenplay. **VHS** *NYF, HHT, IHF*

THE BALLAD OF NARAYAMA
Narayama-Bushi-Ko

Even in an era in which debates about assisted suicide have become standard TV news sound bites, Imamura's magnificent *The Ballad of Narayama*—the tale of a 70-year-old woman who, by village custom, has reached the age when she must be taken to a mountaintop to die—retains all of its shocking, spellbinding power. Imamura intercuts the woman's struggle to tie up the loose ends of her life—most of which have to do with orchestrating her sons' sex lives— with startling close-ups of insects, animals, and other natural wonders as they complete their sometimes beautiful, sometimes horri-

An elderly woman accepts help in *The Ballad of Narayama*.

fying natural processes. In his portrait of humanity as simply another facet of the natural world, Imamura doesn't denigrate or belittle human beings; on the contrary, the vision of a universe filled with necessary cruelties leading logically to the acceptance of the ultimate sadness of existence (a particularly Japanese concept known as *mono no aware*) is, in the end, strangely reassuring. It's a unique, unforgettable picture.

NEXT STOP . . . *In the Realm of the Senses, The Human Condition, Near Death*

1983 129m/C *JP* Ken Ogata, Sumiko Sakamota, Takejo Aki, Tonpei Hidari, Shoichi Ozawa; *D:* Shohei Imamura; *W:* Shohei Imamura; *C:* Maseo Tochizawa; *M:* Shinichiro Ikebe. Cannes Film Festival '83: Best Film. **VHS** *HMV, FCT, KIV*

BAND OF OUTSIDERS
Bande à Part
The Outsiders

Though they have a reputation for despising things American, the French have always been the first to recognize the beauty and daring in so many of the American movies that we considered to be disposable. Jean-Luc Godard dedicated his pioneering *Breathless* to "poverty row" studio Monogram Pictures, and in his *Band of Outsiders* he dared to throw away the nuts and bolts of traditional American crime movies, and kept only the passion, the sentiment, and the joy of movement he felt emanating from them. Would-be tough guys Sami Frey and Claude Brasseur plan and execute a robbery with their new-found girlfriend/gun moll Anna Karina, but this is hardly a traditional suspense film. The spontaneity and capriciousness of what they're doing—despite, or perhaps because of, its movie-like implausibility—is what the picture's about, and the effect of seeing these three enacting scenes from other movies and other lives while creating a screen legend of their own is like looking into one of those double sets of mirrors that reflects a reflection of a reflection, ad infinitum. This is, of course, what Godard himself has always been doing with

his art—using his reverence for the cinema to spin riffs on genre films that both break them down into their basic elements while reverentially defending them against anyone who would deny their status as art. "To me style is just the outside of content," Godard was quoted as saying, "and content the inside of style, like the outside and the inside of the human body—both go together; they can't be separated." It's a film—and a philosophy—that was adopted by another immense talent who refuses to dis the genre film, Quentin Tarantino, whose own production company, A Band Apart, is a playful variation on *Bande à part,* the French title of *Band of Outsiders.* The movie's based on *Fool's Gold* by American author Dolores Hitchens, and it was photographed by the great Raoul Coutard.

NEXT STOP . . . *Pierrot le Fou, Going Places, Reservoir Dogs*

1964 97m/B *FR* Sami Frey, Anna Karina, Claude Brasseur, Louisa Colpeyn; *D:* Jean-Luc Godard; *W:* Jean-Luc Godard; *C:* Raoul Coutard; *M:* Michel Legrand. **VHS** *HTV, NOS, MRV*

BANDIT QUEEN

The true story of Phoolan Devi, a relentlessly abused woman from a low caste who almost single-handedly staged a bloody revolt against the male-dominated, oppressive system that tried to beat her into submission. That revolt—which turned the real Phoolan into the legendary folk hero of the title—is not simply implied or referred to offscreen; it's shown in the same graphic detail as the abuse and rapes that Phoolan and so many other women were subjected to. The violence in *Bandit Queen* is loud, bloody, and relentless. Though it's shocking at first, the non-stop parade of battles, massacres, and wholesale slaughter ultimately produces something approaching an anesthetizing effect; we find ourselves almost less interested in seeing justice done than in seeing the butchery simply end. Nevertheless, this nightmarish vision of the fruits generated by the now-illegal but deeply entrenched roots of the caste system has a primal power that steamrollers over a lot of reservations one might have about *Bandit Queen* as a film. It's a tough movie to watch, but a far tougher one to forget.

NEXT STOP . . . *Bhaji onhe Beach, Fire, Switchblade Sisters*

1994 119m/C *GB IN* Seema Biswas, Nirmal Pandey, Manoj Bajpai, Raghubir Yadav, Rajesh Vivek, Govind Namdeo; **D:** Shekhar Kapur; **W:** Mala Sen; **C:** Ashok Mehta; **M:** Nusrat Fateh Ali Khan, Roger White. **VHS, LV** *HMK*

BANDITS OF ORGOSOLO
Banditi a Orgosolo

A Sardinian shepherd named Michele, falsely accused of both murder and sheep rustling (perhaps the greater crime in his community), is forced to "take it on the lam" (sorry) with his brother when the villagers come after him. Most of his flock does not survive the journey, and Michele is forced into crime in order to survive. Performed primarily by a non-professional cast and photographed with the purity and unobtrusiveness of a great documentary, *Bandits of Orgosolo* feels like equal parts *Man of Aran* and *The Bicycle Thief,* with a bit of *I Am a Fugitive from a Chain Gang.* The overall effect is of life observed, and the director-writer-cinematographer Vittorio de Seta (not to be confused with *The Bicycle Thief's* Vittorio de Sica), has built on the principles of post-World War II neo-realism, but has taken that style to an even more uncluttered, unsentimental level. *Bandits of Orgosolo* had a wider influence than its relative obscurity would suggest, and it likely had an impact on another Italian director, Pier Paolo Pasolini, whose similarly stripped-down 1964 *The Gospel According to St. Matthew* would itself forever revolutionize the historical and religious cinema.

NEXT STOP . . . *The Miracle (1948), Accatone!, Louisiana Story*

1961 98m/B *IT* Michele Cossu, Peppeddu Cuccu; **D:** Vittorio de Seta; **W:** Vittorio de Seta, Vera Gherarducci; **C:** Vittorio de Seta, Luciano Tovoli; **M:** Valentino Bucchi. **VHS** *NOS, FCT, VYY*

BASILEUS QUARTET
Il Quartetto Basileus

A well-regarded string quartet that has played, recorded, and toured together for decades is stunned by the sudden death of one of the four. His replacement turns out to be a fine musician but a much younger and livelier man, whose womanizing and drinking and occasional marijuana use appear outrageous and disruptive to the other three; but what really dogs this older trio— who have until now lived modestly and only for their music—is that the "wild" lifestyle of the new man doesn't seem to be taking its toll on his musicianship. As the quartet members, Omero Antonutti, Hector Alterio, Michel Vitold (the older, nearly monk-like musicians), and Pierre Malet (the new young whippersnapper) all give superbly, uh, orchestrated performances. *The Basileus Quartet* is an original and nicely executed piece, with a surprisingly potent aftertaste. Watch for American cult actress Mimsy Farmer (*Hot Rods to Hell*) in a cameo.

NEXT STOP . . . *Un Coeur en Hiver, Vanya on 42nd Street, The Gig*

1982 118m/C *FR IT* Pierre Malet, Hector Alterio, Omero Antonutti, Michel Vitold, Alain Cuny, Gabriele Ferzetti, Elisabeth Kreuzer; **D:** Fabio Carpi; **W:** Fabio Carpi; **C:** Dante Spinotti; **M:** Claude Debussy. **VHS, LV** *TPV*

THE BATTLE OF ALGIERS
La Bataille d'Alger
La Battaglia di Algeri

Gillo Pontecorvo's powerful and remarkably balanced depiction of the Algerian rebellion against the French in the 1950s has one especially surprising effect when seen again today, nearly 30 years after its initial release. The massive demonstration scenes and breathtakingly realistic glimpses of urban guerrilla warfare remind us not so much of a film that we may have seen decades ago, but rather of a real moment in history. Just as that actual footage of a lone man standing in front of a tank in Tienanmen Square *became*

B

25

VideoHound's
WORLD CINEMA

JEAN-LUC GODARD

Godard is among the greatest pioneers of post-World War II cinema. He was born in Paris in 1930. Having developed into an avid film enthusiast, especially with regard to Hollywood productions, Godard began his own filmmaking career in the mid-1950s even as he established himself as a provocative film critic for the French publication "Cahiers du Cinema." He scored his first triumph in 1959 with *A Bout de Souffle*, at once an homage and a reshaping of the conventional crime drama. In this film, which follows the banal activities of an endearing hoodlum being tracked by police, style is paramount. Indeed, the cinematography, notably the use of handheld camera, and the editing, particularly the employment of jump cutting, readily established Godard as a filmmaker for whom the medium is the message.

Godard followed *A Bout de Souffle* with *Une Femme est une Femme*, a relatively frenetic comedy about a woman's flirtations with her husband's best friend, and the more impressive *Vivre sa Vie*, which traces a housewife's degeneration into prostitution. Both films marked a radical departure from *A Bout de Souffle*, yet both films are equally notable for their stylistic attributes. *Vivre sa Vie*, as Godard conceded, constitutes a fairly formal film, despite the spontaneity with which he filmed. It also serves as a valentine, of sorts, to actress Anna Karina, whom Godard married and continued to cast in his ensuing films.

Godard turned to political themes for *Le Petite Soldat*, in which a young soldier refuses to sympathize his country's cause, and *Les Caribiniers*, wherein two soldiers uncover the illogical consequences of warfare. During this period, the early 1960s, Godard also made a slight concession to commercial filmmaking with *Les Mepris*, a compelling drama derived from a novel by Alberto Moravia. In making this film, Godard ran afoul of his producers, who had perceived it as a vehicle for sexy actress Brigitte Bardot, and he eventually yielded to their demands for footage of Bardot nude. Despite this compromise, *Les Mepris* remains among Godard's most accomplished, and accessible, efforts.

Throughout the 1960s Godard continued to make characteristically self-conscious and therefore, unique films, including *Bande a Part*, an endearing, deliberately accessible film about young criminals; *La Femme Mariee*, a freewheeling account—replete with ethnological asides—of a woman with marital problems; *Alphaville*, which merges the crime and science-fiction genres; *Pierrot le Fou*, a notably wide-ranging work that addresses alienation and artistic expression; and *Weekend*, which concerns the grotesque nature of capitalism. By the early 1970s Godard was devoting himself to films espousing, in his own maddeningly inaccessible way, to radical politics. These films, including the relatively commercial *Tout va Bien*, which featured Yves Montand and Jane Fonda, failed to realize the recognition accorded Godard's earlier works.

Godard continued to make obscure political films until 1980, when he completed *Sauve qui peut*, a somewhat approachable work—about various individuals in various stage of romance—that he described as his second first film. But much of his ensuing work, while shedding the strident politicism of his '70s efforts, remains frustratingly obscure. Exceptions include *Prenom: Carmen*, a compelling, if typically offbeat, reworking of the "Carmen" story; and *Je Vous salue, Marie*, a moving modernization of Christ's immaculate conception.

that entire uprising in the eyes much of the world, Pontecorvo's recreated revolution in *The Battle of Algiers* has *become* the event to us—it's what most of us flash on when the Algerian anti-colonial uprising is mentioned. Told in flashback as the rebellion's leaders are about to be flushed out, *The Battle of Algiers* intercuts personal stories (including that of the surprisingly complex French colonel at the film's core) with the terrorist bombings and retaliatory violence that grows and spirals logically, inexorably, and terrifyingly, ultimately ripping apart the lives of characters we've come to know. A landmark work of power and passion, the picture generates much of its power from a lack of stereotyping that leads to the tragic inevitability of what we see; each side is seen as having its reasons, its prejudices, and its blindness. Supercharged by an Ennio Morricone score, *The Battle of Algiers* was designed to be—and remains—a wake-up call every bit as powerful as any of the explosions depicted in the film.

NEXT STOP . . . *The Battleship Potemkin, I Am Cuba, Burn!*

1966 123m/B *AL IT* Yacef Saadi, Jean Martin, Brahim Haggiag, Tommaso Neri, Samia Kerbash, Fawzia el Kader, Michele Kerbash, Mohamed Ben Kassen; *D:* Gillo Pontecorvo; *W:* Gillo Pontecorvo, Franco Solinas; *C:* Marcello Gatti; *M:* Gillo Pontecorvo, Ennio Morricone. Venice Film Festival '66: Best Film; Nominations: Academy Awards '66: Best Foreign-Language Film; Best Story & Screenplay. **VHS, LV** *IHF, TPV*

THE BATTLESHIP POTEMKIN
Potemkin
Bronenosets Potemkin

Sergei Eisenstein's depiction of the 1905 navy mutiny that ultimately led to the Russian Revolution is considered a classic and deserves to be. With *Potemkin*, Eisenstein took the lessons of D.W. Griffith ever further in the use of quick editing and the subtle, psychological expansion of screen time to create overwhelming emotional responses in the viewer. Early scenes of maggot-ridden meat that the Potemkin's sailors are expected to eat

become an intricately threaded visual metaphor that will ultimately lead to a kind of "gag reflex" or revolt in the body of each sailor as well as the body of the masses. The film's rhythm is astounding: musical, pulsating, increasingly intense. Ultimately, the long sequence in which Cossacks massacre civilians on the Odessa steps—including a woman precariously holding on to a baby carriage—is so brilliantly orchestrated and edited that it has justifiably become one of the most often-cited bits of film in history. Aside from its general impact on movie history and editing theory, the Odessa steps sequence itself, complete with baby carriage, has been referred to and recreated in part by filmmakers such as Woody Allen (in *Bananas*) and Brian de Palma (*The Untouchables*). In his books *Film Form* and *The Film Sense*, Eisenstein writes fascinatingly about his theories of film editing, or "montage"; but instead of reading them you may just want to run *The Battleship Potemkin* for yourself a few dozen times; before long, the infinite possibilities of putting two pieces of film together to create an entirely new emotion will become apparent, as will the infinite, potential power of the medium. Note: the film is now in the public domain and has been released in many versions, some cut, some "time expanded" or "step printed" which can make the action look like its underwater, and many with different musical scores. None of the scores is necessary, and most are intrusive and counterproductive. Watch it silently, and discover the movies all over again.

NEXT STOP . . . *Strike, Ten Days That Shook the World, The Battle of Algiers*

1925 71m/B *RU* Alexander Antonov, Vladimir Barsky, Grigori Alexandrov, Mikhail Gomorov, Sergei Eisenstein; *D:* Sergei Eisenstein; *W:* Sergei Eisenstein; *C:* Eduard Tisse. **VHS, LV** *REP, MRV, NOS*

BAXTER

Baxter is a movie about a dog, but it will never play on a double bill with *Beethoven*. (Still, it would be fun to hear Charles Grodin ranting, outraged, about the decadent "values" of *Baxter* on his cable show.) Not for the kiddies, this dog is pure bad news. His

thoughts—heard in deep, carefully pronounced French—are generally evil, least dangerous when they're simply voyeuristic observations, downright scary when they're more "pro-actively" homicidal. Baxter is jealous of human affection that may be diverted from him to other humans, but his response is less like a dissed Lassie than the Siamese cats who'd like to off the new baby in *Lady and the Tramp.* Baxter is obsessed with sex—human sex—and likes to look toward the window of a young couple, listening to their sounds through the fluttering curtains, speculating in his malevolently silky thought-voice about what they might be doing, and whether or not he approves. Generally, the human cast members of this shocking and original horror film are much better off when Baxter approves. We've seen the world from the point-of-view of animals before—it's a staple in kids' movies like *The Adventures of Milo and Otis* and even in more celebrated pictures like Jean-Jacques Annaud's *The Bear*—and we've seen stories about killer bees, ants, gorillas, and dogs before as well. But no one has thought of melding the two genres until this unnerving little picture by Jerome Boivin, and the effect is not unlike *The Incredible Journey* meets *Henry: Portrait of a Serial Killer*—subversive, nasty fun.

NEXT STOP . . . *Psycho, Monsieur Hire, Christine*

1989 82m/C *FR* Lisa Delamare, Jean Mercure, Jacques Spiesser, Catherine Ferran, Jean-Paul Roussillon, Sabrina Leurquin; *D:* Jerome Boivin; *W:* Jerome Boivin, Jacques Audiard; *C:* Yves Angelo; *M:* Marc Hillman, Patrick Roffe. **VHS, LV** *FXL, PMS*

BÉATRICE
La Passion Béatrice

In the Middle Ages, young Béatrice (Julie Delpy) has been pining for the return of her father (Bernard-Pierre Donnadieu) who was taken prisoner by the English while fighting the Crusades. When dad returns, however, he instigates a reign of domestic terror with a puzzled and shattered Béatrice as his primary target. This elaborate and effectively claustrophobic period drama from Bertrand Tavernier is like a variation on *The Stepfather*

as directed by Cecil B. DeMille. The reasons for the father's cruelty—including his wife's infidelity while he was away fighting the good fight—are alluded to throughout, yet there is still an undeniably creepy core of almost instinctive familial abuse running through the film. One of the least-known and least characteristic of the many superb movies by Tavernier, *Béatrice* (a.k.a. *La Passion Béatrice*) features a really scary performance by Donnadieu as the dad from hell, and a remarkably nuanced one from the very young Julie Delpy. A one-of-a-kind, unclassifiable historical epic, *Béatrice* will get under your skin and stay there.

NEXT STOP . . . *Life and Nothing But, The Judge and the Assassin, Lancelot of the Lake*

1988 (R) 132m/C *FR* Julie Delpy, Barnard Pierre Donnadieu, Nils Tavernier; *D:* Bertrand Tavernier; *W:* Colo Tavernier O'Hagan; *C:* Bruno de Keyzer; *M:* Lili Boulanger. Cesar Awards '88: Best Costume Design. **VHS, LV** *NO*

BEAU PÈRE
The Stepfather

When the wife of 30-year-old pianist Remy (Patrick Dewaere) dies in a traffic accident, he and his 14-year-old stepdaughter, Marion (Ariel Besse), are left alone to make the best of it. Soon, however, her biological father comes to take her away, but her concern for and adoration of Remy leads her back to his door, and ultimately to his bed. As always, writer/director Bertrand Blier (*Get Out Your Handkerchiefs*) stands convention on its head. He films a sexually unconventional subject, one that sounds like pure exploitation, but confounds our expectations by creating a funny, touching, and, in the case of *Beau Père,* deeply insightful look at the undeniable bonds between sexuality, security, and family values. Especially noteworthy in *Beau Père* is the tender and extremely sweet performance of Blier veteran Patrick Dewaere, who made his first screen appearance in Blier's subversive 1974 debut film, *Going Places.* A suicide at the height of his career, just one year after the release of *Beau Père,* Dewaere may well be best remembered for this courageous and delicately shaded portrayal of a fully grown man whose confusion and loneliness and ultimate contentment are nearly palpable.

NEXT STOP . . . *Mon Homme, Get Out Your Handkerchiefs, The Sweet Hereafter*

1981 125m/C *FR* Patrick Dewaere, Nathalie Baye, Ariel Besse, Maurice Ronet; *D:* Bertrand Blier; *W:* Bertrand Blier; *C:* Sacha Vierny; *M:* Philippe Sarde. **VHS**

BEAUTIFUL THING

We're used to seeing fairy-tale romances set in unlikely surroundings, but Hettie MacDonald's *Beautiful Thing*—the story of two teenagers in a London housing project who gradually discover their love for each other—is nevertheless a disarming and welcome surprise. For one thing, the kids who discover their mutual affection are both boys; for another, the picture ends with acceptance, understanding, and happiness all around. Knowing the outcome in no way diminishes the fun of *Beautiful Thing,* for it's the feast of performances (though many of the decidedly non-royal accents may at first be impenetrable to Americans) together with the picture's well-drawn working-class milieu that make so much of this fable of well-placed faith a pleasure to watch. Glenn Berry and Scott Neal are quite fine as the two boys—initially aware to very different degrees of their feelings for each other—but Linda Henry as the outspoken mother of one of the boys, and Tameka Empson the girl next door who has a Mama Cass fixation, steal the film by sheer force of personality. *Beautiful Thing* falls apart the instant you place its vision of universal acceptance and its wouldn't-it-be-great finale in the real world, but director MacDonald has been wise enough to keep reality at considerably more than arm's length. Adapted by Jonathan Harvey from his play, and featuring a good-time soundtrack stuffed to the brim with faves from the Mamas and the Papas.

NEXT STOP . . . *Ma Vie en Rose, Different for Girls, Fire*

1995 (R) 89m/C *GB* Glen Berry, Scott Neal, Linda Henry, Tameka Empson, Ben Daniels; *D:* Hettie Macdonald; *W:* Jonathan Harvey; *C:* Chris Seager. **VHS, Closed Caption** *COL*

BEAUTY AND THE BEAST
La Belle et la Bete

In an era in which special-effects companies like Industrial Light & Magic and Digital Domain can convince us of the absolute reality of anything we see on the screen, from a T-Rex to the Titanic, a danger exists that lazy filmmakers who rely solely on this realism of the impossible to astonish us may inadvertently neglect the one element of the fantastic that realism has nothing to do with: a sense of wonder. (The new Godzilla looks real, but the flat concept of the movie he stars in makes him a big green bore.) When Jean Cocteau conceived his thrilling *Beauty and the Beast,* he was well aware that we would know "how they did it." The secret here has nothing to do with technique. Rather, it's the imagination of the poet who can conceive of such images, who has the genius to place them on the screen so straightforwardly and with such shimmering elegance that we delight as a child does, looking at the simplest and most perfect of toys, charmed to have it in our possession to curl up with as we prepare to dream. We know that those candelabra-bearing arms and eyeball-rolling faces protruding from the walls of the beast's castle are attached to actors on the other side of the wall; it doesn't diminish the boldness of Cocteau's vision, but enhances it. Would *Beauty and the Beast* been more "special-effects savvy," more digitally seamless if Cocteau were making it today? In our time, I suppose, the question has no meaning. Yet a viewing of the enormously popular Disney animated version shows much of the Cocteau film's influence, and surprisingly few big show-stopping fx. It's more than conceivable that they learned something by watching this example of real screen magic, but even Disney artists couldn't figure out how to match the sympathy or frighteningly seductive power of Jean Marais's beast. If *Beauty and the Beast* isn't the greatest filmed fairy tale in cinema history, then I indeed have riches beyond my wildest dreams to anticipate.

THE HOUND SALUTES:
CATHERINE DENEUVE
Beautiful French Legend

Ethereal, elegant, enigmatic Catherine Deneuve has made scores of films since becoming a star in 1964 with her role in *The Umbrellas of Cherbourg*. But she is more well-known in America for her Chanel commercials than for her movies. More the pity. Few actresses can match Deneuve for range, beauty and intelligence—qualities which haven't dimmed over the years.

"I've always been more choosy for directors than parts," Deneuve says. She's worked with legends like Francois Truffaut (*The Last Metro*), Luis Bunuel (*Belle de Jour* and *Tristana*), Roman Polanski (*Repulsion*), and Andre Techine (*Thieves* and *My Favorite Season*). Belatedly honored by Hollywood, she was nominated for an Oscar for her role in 1992's *Indochine*. Most recently, she was awarded the Golden Bear for lifetime achievement at the 48th Berlin Film Festival in 1998.

Born on October 22, 1943 in Paris, she is the daughter of two actors, Maurice Dorleac and Renee Deneuve. Her older sister, actress Francoise Dorleac, was killed in a car accident. Catherine made her screen debut at 13, taking her mother's name, and soon became a protege and lover of director Roger Vadim.

Umbrellas, Polanski's *Repulsion,* and Bunuel's *Belle de Jour,* in which she coolly plays a bored housewife who turns to prostitution by day, established Deneuve as a sexy star. Her willingness to take risks is underlined by 1983's *The Hunger,* in which she plays a vampiress who feasts on Susan Sarandon.

Deneuve has produced two actor children: Chiara Mastroianni, with Marcello Mastroianni; and Christian Vadim, with Vadim. She was married once, for five years, to British photographer David Bailey, but later declared: "Marriage is obsolete and a trap."

NEXT STOP . . . *Orpheus, Donkey Skin, Pinocchio*

1946 90m/B *FR* Jean Marais, Josette Day, Marcel Andre, Mila Parely, Nane Germon, Michel Auclair; *D:* Jean Cocteau; *W:* Jean Cocteau; *C:* Henri Alekan; *M:* Georges Auric. **VHS, LV, DVD** *HMV, MLB, CRC*

BED AND BOARD
Domicile Conjugal

The fourth film (the third feature) in François Truffaut's semi-autobiographical Antoine Doinel cycle finds Antoine (Jean-Pierre Léaud) right on schedule; he's a bourgeois husband and new father who's feeling trapped and having an affair that he doesn't even seem to really want. Though Antoine seems on first glance to be light years from the grim, juvenile delinquent driven to the brink of catastrophe in *The 400 Blows,* he endearingly reveals himself to be exactly the same kid in a slightly bigger body; still juvenile, still delinquent, and still flirting with disaster—though in grown-up-speak it's called a mid-life crisis. Christine (Claude Jade, still as enchanting as she was as Antoine's fiancee in

Stolen Kisses) is now Antoine's wife and still adores him, though he does his best to test her with his continual, self-centered whining. Hiroko Berghauer is the object of Antoine's stab at manly freedom, and she's both lovely enough to attract Antoine and smart enough to keep it simple. *Bed and Board* is often cited as the weakest of the major Antoine Doinel films (*Love on the Run* being a kind of *Reader's Digest* condensed Antoine Doinel). It may be that art house audiences find Antoine's dilemmas here less "exotic" than they'd prefer; his travails may also strike a bit too close to home for many of the ego-maniacal male critics who tend to dismiss the film even while they squirm uncomfortably. *Bed and Board* was photographed with characteristic aplomb by Nestor Almendros.

NEXT STOP . . . *The 400 Blows, Love at Twenty, Stolen Kisses, Love on the Run*

1970 100m/C Jean-Pierre Leaud, Claude Jade, Barbara Laage, Daniel Ceccaldi, Daniel Boulanger, Pierre Maguelon, Jacques Jouanneau, Jacques Rispal, Jacques Robiolles, Pierre Fabre, Billy Kearns, Hiroko Berghauer, Daniele Girard, Claire Duhamel, Sylvana Blasi, Claude Vega, Christian de Tiliere, Annick Asty, Marianne Piketi, Guy Pierauld, Marie Dedieu, Marie Irakane, Yvon Lec, Ernest Menzer, Christophe Vesque; **D:** Francois Truffaut; **W:** Francois Truffaut, Bernard Revon, Claude de Givray; **C:** Nestor Almendros; **M:** Antoine Duhamel. *NYR*

BEFORE THE RAIN
Po Dezju
Pred dozhdot

The failure of this extraordinary picture to reach a wide American art house audience—despite nearly unanimous rave reviews—is part of a sad, consistent chain of evidence that most Americans will do anything to avoid the subject of the Bosnian/Serbian/Croatian conflicts, perhaps out of fear that they won't understand the complexities and ancient animosities that seem to thrive in any nation referred to as "the former" anything. In the case of *Before the Rain*, the focus of which is the Republic of Macedonia (which was, yes, part of the former Yugoslavia, as was Bosnia), those animosities are laid out in the form of a trilogy of inter-linked stories. The film begins and ends in Macedonia, detouring for an electrifying centerpiece in London. The tales are told simply but grippingly, and take on considerable additional power when the movie's ingeniously conceived but non-gimmicky circular structure becomes clear at the fade-out. The director, Milcho Manchevski, a Macedonian native who has chosen to live and work in America, has a command of the wide screen and a cinema sense that is immediately striking, and ultimately overwhelming. His portrait of a violent conflict that seems to involuntarily perpetuate itself would be an important statement about the human condition even if it weren't so specific in its time and place. Its authenticity, however, makes it all the more valuable, and all the more heartbreaking.

NEXT STOP . . . *All Quiet on the Western Front (1930), Prisoner of the Mountains, Underground*

1994 120m/C *GB FR MA* Rade Serbedzija, Katrin Cartlidge, Gregoire Colin, Labina Mitevska, Phyllida Law; **D:** Milcho Manchevski; **W:** Milcho Manchevski; **C:** Manuel Teran; **M:** Anastasia. Independent Spirit Awards '96: Best Foreign Film; Venice Film Festival '94: Golden Lion; Nominations: Academy Awards '94: Best Foreign-Language Film. **VHS** *PGV*

BEFORE THE REVOLUTION
Prima della Rivoluzione

Those of us who either toyed with or obsessed on the idea of revolution in the 1960s, only to retreat home each evening to the safety of spouse, bed, and television, will respond as powerfully as ever to the second film by Bernardo Bertolucci, made when he was only 24. Based loosely on Stendahl's *The Charterhouse of Parma*, *Before the Revolution* is the story of a young man (Francisco Barilli) who takes up Marxism as if it were a hobby, but finds himself thinking ahead too quickly; imagining the privileges and bourgeois pleasures (including, perhaps, his newly kindled affair with his lovely young aunt) that will be lost to him should his newfound "idealism" actually succeed. An early example of the grand, operatic style that Bertolucci

B

Four beautiful sisters surround their mother in Fernando Trueba's romantic comedy *Belle Epoque.*

would take still further with *The Conformist, 1900,* and *Luna* (his most underrated film), *Before the Revolution* also represents his first commercial breakthrough, possibly because the movie's theme of romanticism and pleasure versus idealism and pain is the kind of dilemma that patrons of "art" movies are well aware of. (Despite the fact that the festival prize-winner we may be sitting through is probably good for us, who among us doesn't also crave an occasional, "decadent," mayhem-heavy Hollywood entertainment?) Bertolucci's emotional honesty here is both admirable and moving; his directorial assurance is quietly staggering.

NEXT STOP . . . *The Conformist, La Chinoise, The Garden of the Finzi-Continis*

1965 115m/C *IT* Francesco Barilli, Adrianna Asti, Alain Midgette, Morando Morandini, Domenico Alpi; *D:* Bernardo Bertolucci; *W:* Bernardo Bertolucci; *C:* Aldo Scavarda; *M:* Ennio Morricone, Gino Paoli. **VHS** *NYF*

BELLE DE JOUR

In a British edition of the published screenplay of *Belle de Jour,* Luis Buñuel reveals not only that his most popular masterpiece—a film in which each image seems painstakingly planned and executed—was completely edited in twelve hours, but also decides one very big, previously controversial issue for us all: "You know of course," Buñuel remarks, "that it's a pornographic film?" He qualifies this statement by describing his movie as containing "chaste eroticism," but then adds the ringer: "I never try to scandalize people," the director says, "but they sometimes scandalize themselves." Amen. And when we do, we usually find that Luis Buñuel has already made a movie about us. Take this one. The impossibly beautiful Catherine Deneuve, at her chilliest and most impenetrable, is Séverine, the seemingly contented bourgeois wife of an affluent, handsome physician. Yet if Séverine is so contented, why is she daydreaming of being tied to a tree at the command of her husband in preparation for being whipped and ravished by a vile, foul coachman? It would seem that Séverine's sexual fantasies are struggling to find expression, but there is clearly no place for them in the spotless, neat apartment in which the couple live. Nor is there any room for them in Séverine's ordered life. So, in the only way she knows how, Séverine creates a neat, orderly place in which to put them. The house of prostitution where she allows herself to be pleasurably abused on weekday afternoons becomes another part of Séverine's ordered routine—until her other, "normal" world collides with it in an unexpected way, causing Séverine's repressed sexual world to explode in a kind of bourgeois critical mass. Buñuel, irrepressible anarchist that he was (as well as the cinema's only true surrealist) has made something far more exciting than a pornographic movie. The deep humor inherent in poor Séverine's quiet, unacknowledged sexual frenzy, rendered poignant by her cluelessness and comic by her beauty, receives such a delicate, multi-layered presentation from Buñuel that it only seems appropriate to refer to him as a master. As long as sexual feelings—at least some of them—are "inappropriate" (or now, perhaps, un-PC) in bourgeois life, Séverine's story will remain touching, powerful, and deeply, darkly funny. Hail to the master.

NEXT STOP . . . *Tristana, La Cérémonie, The Piano*

1967 (R) 100m/C *FR* Catherine Deneuve, Jean Sorel, Genevieve Page, Michel Piccoli, Francesco Rabal, Pierre Clementi, Georges Marchal, Francoise Fabian; *D:* Luis Bunuel; *W:* Luis Bunuel, Jean-Claude Carriere; *C:* Sacha Vierny. **VHS, LV** *TOU*

BELLE EPOQUE ✓
The Age of Beauty

In the relatively untroubled Spain of 1931, prior to the rise of fascism, a young army deserter is given food and shelter by a charming old anarchist. The young man is grateful and prepares to leave, but discovers

that the old man also happens to be father to four enchanting, beautiful, and sensuous daughters. Not so much a male fantasy as a kind of national longing for a more innocent, predictable era in which the possibilities of life were ripening right in front of you, *Belle Epoque* is an erotic fairy tale about a more guileless, less cynical age—a time when spontaneity suggested fulfillment rather than retaliation. A lush, smart, glossy entertainment, *Belle Epoque* was something of a worldwide phenomenon at the boxoffice. A financial success in Spain and the winner of the Academy Award for Best Foreign Film, *Belle Epoque*'s idyllic eroticism seemed to offer a welcome respite for a world that had learned not just about the responsibilities but also the dangers that come with casual, unbridled sexual desire. *Belle Epoque* indeed.

NEXT STOP . . . *Like Water for Chocolate, Jamón, Jamón, La Ronde*

1992 (R) 108m/C *SP* Jorge Sanz, Fernando Gomez, Ariadna Gil, Maribel Verdu, Penelope Cruz, Miriam Diaz-Aroca, Mary Carmen Ramirez, Michel Galabru, Gabino Diego; *D:* Fernando Trueba; *W:* Rafael Azcona; *C:* Jose Luis Alcaine; *M:* Antoine Duhamel. Academy Awards '93: Best Foreign Film. **VHS, LV** *COL*

THE BELLY OF AN ARCHITECT

An American architect named Stourley Kracklite (Brian Dennehy) arrives in Rome to act as curator of an exhibition in tribute to a legendary 18th-century architect. Strange events and goings-on abound, including Kracklite's suspicions that his expectant wife Louisa (Chloe Webb) is having an affair—possibly with an unctuous professional rival (Lambert Wilson). This is a moderately interesting addition to the Greenaway canon, filmed between his clever *A Zed and Two Noughts* and the far more tantalizing *Drowning by Numbers, Belly of an Architect,* but its rigidity finally becomes deadly. Brian Dennehy's plugged-in, fully awake screen presence periodically sparks the proceedings to life, but even he can't survive the director's strict and stifling structural mold. Even if you can't make heads or tails of this movie (or

stop caring to), take heart; at the very least there's always something fabulous to look at—Rome itself has rarely appeared more mysterious or seductive on-screen. Greenaway's eye never fails him, even when his storyline does.

NEXT STOP . . . *The Draughtsman's Contract, The Pillow Book, The Fountainhead*

1991 (R) 119m/C *GB IT* Brian Dennehy, Chloe Webb, Lambert Wilson, Sergio Fantoni, Geoffrey Copleston, Marino Mase; **D:** Peter Greenaway; **W:** Peter Greenaway; **C:** Sacha Vierny; **M:** Glenn Branca, Wim Mertens. **VHS, LV** *NO*

BERLIN ALEXANDERPLATZ

The generally derogatory expression "made for television" is pretty much without meaning in the case of Rainer Werner Fassbinder's adaptation of psychiatrist Alfred Döblin's epic 1929 novel of Germany in the late 1920s. Without the backing of television, how else could Fassbinder have created a 15-and-a-half hour movie, including a two-hour epilogue in which the director recapitulates the preceding 13-and-a-half hours as an hallucinatory dream? The question, I suppose, is how did Fassbinder do it even with the backing of television? Whatever the answer, Fassbinder's creation, despite its occasional niggling flaws as drama and its surprisingly rare repetitiveness, is a genuinely great achievement. The intimate and richly detailed chronicle of Franz Biberkopf's journey from prison to an underworld of intrigue, love, and crime that would eventually overwhelm him proves overwhelming to the viewer as well. The sheer magnitude of *Berlin Alexanderplatz* is no small element of its power to seduce. In the not inconsiderable pleasure of simply being immersed in a story this size, with such a huge number of sub-plots and characters, the film reminds us of reading Dickens—arguably the last author most of us would mention when speaking of Fassbinder. Gunter Lamprecht as Franz gives a truly memorable performance that holds everything together, and he's ably supported by Fassbinder regulars

Hanna Schygulla, Barbara Sukowa, Gottfried John, Brigitte Mira, and Margit Castensen. Peer Rabin's score is insistent but never unwelcome, adding to the operatic, larger than life feel of the whole enterprise. (Those who have seen this film tend to carry it around with them. Shortly after *Berlin Alexanderplatz* played to sold-out houses at the Detroit Institute of Arts in 1981, an anonymous gentleman, who paid to have one of the theatre's seats refurbished, simply requested that his seat's commemorative plaque read: "In Memory of Fifteen-and-a-Half Hours with Franz Biberkopf.")

NEXT STOP . . . *The Godfather Parts I & II, Little Dorrit, The Kingdom, Parts I & II*

1980 930m/C *GE* Gunter Lamprecht, Hanna Schygulla, Barbara Sukowa, Gottfried John, Elisabeth Trissenaar, Brigitte Mira, Karin Baal, Ivan Desny, Margit Castensen; **D:** Rainer Werner Fassbinder; **W:** Rainer Werner Fassbinder; **C:** Xaver Schwarzenberger; **M:** Peer Raben. **VHS FCT, MGM**

THE BEST INTENTIONS

In 1991, Ingmar Bergman completed a screenplay based on the courtship and marriage of his parents, but rather than direct this extremely personal material himself, he entrusted it to friend and colleague Bille August. August's *Pelle the Conqueror* had just found worldwide success, and Bergman's intimate drama of marital tension and class/culture-clash appealed enormously to August, as did the fact that Bergman would entrust such a responsibility to him. August had a full, six-hour canvas on which to tell the story, thanks to Swedish television's interest, but the theatrical version that played around the world ended up as a condensed, three-hour film—hardly rushed, but severely abridged nevertheless. This does seem to create gaps in the tale of Anna Akerblom (played superbly by the director's wife, Pernilla August), the strong-willed daughter of a proudly bourgeois family, and her involvement and ultimate marriage to the poor, working-class theology student named Henrik Bergman (Samuel Froler). *The Best*

Intentions is a physically splendid epic about the small tensions and incidental moments in a relationship that evolve into the big issues that, ultimately, will affect the lives of everyone in the family, including those yet unborn. Set between 1909 and 1918, the film can be seen as a kind of "prequel" to Bergman's own 1973 *Scenes from a Marriage* (itself originally a serial for Swedish TV, and also edited down to three hours for theatrical release). While the movie is filled with insights into the issue of class difference—perhaps the most skimmed over but explosive of all marital differences—we keep unconsciously looking for clues about the background of the child we know is coming: little Ingmar. He's on the screen only *in utero* but his presence is felt throughout; toward the end, the suspense of his impending birth tends to feel a bit too much like an expected holy event that would be unseemly to actually depict on screen. (What infant actor could carry the weight of portraying Ingmar Bergman, and how could even Bille August deal with the implications of showing Ingmar Bergman's umbilical cord being cut?) *The Best Intentions,* as fine as it is, cries out to be seen in its full version, simply to see the full shape of Bergman's conception, as well as to discover what he and August found acceptable to leave out.

NEXT STOP . . . *Sunday's Children, Jerusalem, Pelle the Conqueror*

1992 182m/C *SW* Samuel Froler, Pernilla August, Max von Sydow, Ghita Norby, Mona Malm, Lena Endre, Bjorn Kjellman; *D:* Bille August; *W:* Ingmar Bergman; *C:* Jorgen Persson; *M:* Stefan Nilsson. Cannes Film Festival '92: Best Actress (August), Best Film. **VHS** *FCT*

THE BEST WAY
The Best Way to Walk
La Meilleure Façon de Marcher

A longtime assistant to such directors as Robert Bresson, Jean-Luc Godard and François Truffaut, Claude Miller made his feature-directing debut with this wise and witty dramatic comedy set in the early 1960s. Patrick Dewaere plays Marc, a rugged and proudly masculine counselor at a boys' summer camp, who is startled (to say the least) when he stumbles unannounced into the cabin of fellow counselor Philippe (Patrick Bouchitey), only to find him attired in a dress and full makeup. *The Best Way,* originally titled *The Best Way to Walk,* is the story of Marc's method of dealing with this information, which begins with his steady taunting of Philippe (who also happens to be the son of the camp's director) and quickly escalates to full psychological torture. Miller's carefully shaded script also shows us how—despite his revulsion—Marc is fascinated by the spectacle he happened on, and how that fascination ultimately evolves into an unexpected and surprisingly moving bond of understanding between the two men. Unsentimental yet genuinely touching, *The Best Way* marks the debut of an important and gifted director, whose subsequent films would include such major works as *The Little Thief* (1989) and *The Accompanist* (1993).

NEXT STOP . . . *Beautiful Thing, Different for Girls, Ma Vie en Rose*

1976 85m/C *FR* Patrick Dewaere, Patrick Bouchitey, Christine Pascal, Claude Pieplu; *D:* Claude Miller; *W:* Luc Beraud, Claude Miller; *C:* Bruno Nuytten; *M:* Alain Jomy. **VHS** *FCT*

A BETTER TOMORROW
Ying Huang Boon Sik
Gangland Boss

Two brothers—one a mobster who longs to again be a decent citizen, the other a cop who's convinced that their father's death is his brother's fault—live to see their combined rivalry and affection explode against a backdrop of Hong Kong mob violence. If it sounds like you've been there and done that, you're not taking the most important element into consideration; *A Better Tomorrow* was directed by John Woo, who may be the most brilliantly gifted director of genre action films of his generation. *A Better Tomorrow* marked the first appearance in a Woo film of Chow Yun-fat, the sullen, handsome, stoic actor who would instantly become director Woo's alter ego. With a gun in each hand and

Betty (Beatrice Dalle) takes a moment to read a good book in *Betty Blue.*

an forbidding, Elvis-like sneer, Chow makes a socko impression here as a syndicate enforcer who may break the laws of the state, but whose sense of outrage and personal honor will never let him knuckle under to real scum. Woo and Chow were an unbeatable boxoffice combination, and *A Better Tomorrow* quickly spawned two sequels, as well as such now-classic Woo/Chow action films as *The Killer* and *Hard-Boiled.* Both men eventually made the trip to Hollywood, with Woo achieving spectacular commercial and artistic success with *Face/Off,* and Chow making his first major U.S. appearance opposite Mira Sorvino in the stylish, Woo-produced *The Replacement Killers.*

NEXT STOP . . . *The Killer, Hard-Boiled, The Public Enemy*

1986 95m/C *CH* Chow Yun-Fat, Leslie Cheung, Ti Lung; *D:* John Woo; *W:* John Woo; *C:* Wing-hang Wong; *M:* Ka-Fai Koo. **VHS** *REP, FCT*

BETTY BLUE
37.2 le Matin
37.2 Degrees in the Morning

There's a lot to hoot at in the third feature film by *Diva* creator Jean-Jacques Beineix, but watching an obviously gifted director's talent dribble away bit by bit is hardly a pleasurable experience. The expectations raised by *Diva,* Beineix's surprise 1982 hit (which took off in France only after American critics and audiences championed it), were unceremoniously dashed by his second picture, the ill-conceived style-*über-alles* marathon of would-be visual poetry, *Moon in the Gutter.* One can only assume that his third film, the sexually explicit *Betty Blue,* was conceived as a fallback, sure-fire career resuscitator that would at least demonstrate Beineix's ability to make both news and noise at the worldwide boxoffice. But what Beineix may have overlooked was the fact that movie sex was not exactly impossible to come by in the U.S. in 1986, and Americans no longer had to look overseas to see previously forbidden nudity or simulated orgasm. You get them both in *Betty Blue,* and as these things go, you get your money's worth. (Ironically, it was the French who packed theatres for this picture; it barely made a ripple over here.) Beatrice Dalle is Betty, the apparently unstable but remarkably energetic lover of Zorg (not an alien), played by Jean-Hughes Anglade. Zorg, who has found time somehow to write a manuscript that impresses Betty, agrees to go to Paris with her and ultimately to the south of France, where things take an ugly but not entirely unexpected turn. For a movie that makes very little sense, Betty Blue goes down pretty easily and you can have a good time with it. Mistaking Beineix for a great, unappreciated talent, however, would be less than wise. (If two hours of *Betty Blue* aren't satisfying, the inevitable three-hour "director's cut" has been recently made available. I haven't seen it, so I can't report if it contains any more "good parts.")

NEXT STOP . . . *I Am Curious (Yellow), Birds in Peru, Moon in the Gutter*

1986 (R) 121m/C *FR* Beatrice Dalle, Jean-Hughes Anglade, Gerard Darmon, Consuelo de Haviland, Clementine Celarie, Jacques Mathou, Vincent Lindon; *D:* Jean-Jacques Beineix; *W:* Jean-Jacques Beineix; *C:* Jean-Francois Robin; *M:* Gabriel Yared. Nominations: Academy Awards '86: Best Foreign-Language Film; Cesar Awards '86: Best Actor (Anglade). **VHS, LV, Closed Caption** *FOX*

BEWARE OF A HOLY WHORE
Warnung Vor Einer Helligen Nutte

The holy whore of the title refers to the combined villain, hero, and seductress of the story: the cinema itself. Made as a response to a particularly difficult film shoot that Fassbinder experienced (the picture was called *Whity*), *Beware of a Holy Whore* finds cast and crew at a seaside resort, simmering with anger, sexual anxiety, and seething with repressed resentment—though it doesn't stay repressed for long. A tough, leather-jacketed Lou Castel stands in for Fassbinder, though Fassbinder himself, a remarkably magnetic though generally creepy presence, performs in the film as well. The sullen star of the picture within the picture is none other than European cult figure and American expatriate Eddie Constantine, whose square-jawed, pockmarked presence is always in itself a commentary on Europe's eternal love/hate relationship with the American cinema. Regulars Hanna Schygulla and Ulli Lommel are here as well, completing what is probably best described as *Day for Night* without the day.

NEXT STOP . . . *The Bitter Tears of Petra von Kant, Passion* (1982), *Two Weeks in Another Town*

1970 103m/C *GE* Lou Castel, Eddie Constantine, Hanna Schygulla, Marquard Bohm, Ulli Lommel, Margarethe von Trotta, Kurt Raab, Ingrid Caven, Werner Schroeter, Rainer Werner Fassbinder; *D:* Rainer Werner Fassbinder; *W:* Rainer Werner Fassbinder; *C:* Michael Ballhaus; *M:* Peer Raben. **VHS** *ORI*

BHAJI ON THE BEACH

This gentle and pleasingly shaped picture is part of a new subcategory in British cinema that deals with the specific problems encountered by many of the nation's Indian immigrants—in this case, women. *Bhaji* is the story of a group of women linked by family and friendship who decide to travel by bus from their Birmingham homes to spend a day together in pure sisterhood at the seaside resort of Blackpool. They're determined to have what they demand on the bus: "a female good time." Their men, however, will not be denied, and as they've got various axes to grind, vendettas to visit, and posturing male face to save, they're determined to manipulate this "girls' day out" for their own controlling purposes. (It's true that the men are all stereotypes, but who cares? The movie's not about them.) *Bhaji on the Beach* is perhaps a bit too neatly worked out and states its political position a tad too clearly, yet the movie is for the most part a joy because of the unforced and thoroughly

fresh performances of its female cast members, notably Shaheen Khan, Lalita Ahmed, and Zohra Segal. A promising and generally charming debut film from director Gurinder Chadha.

NEXT STOP . . . *Fire, Bandit Queen, Antonia's Line*

1994 (R) 100m/C *GB* Kim Vithana, Jimmi Harkishin, Sarita Khajuria, Mo Sesay, Lalita Ahmed, Shaheen Khan, Zohra Segal; *D:* Gurinder Chadha; *W:* Meera Syal, Gurinder Chadha; *C:* John Kenway; *M:* John Altman, Craig Preuss. **VHS, Closed Caption** *COL*

✓

THE BICYCLE THIEF
Ladri di Biciclette

Boris Karloff, Bela Lugosi, Marilyn Monroe, and Elvis can be found on America's postage stamps, but in Italy, for 650 lira, you can mail a letter featuring the trusting, confused, heartbreakingly eloquent face of little

Bruno (Enzo Staiola), son of the desperate and shattered character whose story is at the heart of Vittorio de Sica's masterpiece, *The Bicycle Thief.* I mention this only because in an age of instantly proclaimed greatness and ever-escalating critical hyperbole, it's reassuring to know that this 1948 triumph of Italy's neo-realist cinema movement is indeed regarded as a national treasure. It is. Bruno's father is a decent man who, like so many after the war, is in need of a job. He's finally hired as a poster-hanger, but when the bicycle that he needs for the job is stolen, he and his son commence a hopeless search through the streets, alleys, and black markets of Rome to retrieve the thread that is tenuously holding the family's lives together. The image on that stamp is of Bruno's face at the end, after the inevitable yet still shocking climax of the film, which gives a full and deep resonance to the movie's title (which is in the more accurate plural form, *Ladri di Biciclette,* in its original Italian title). Cesare Zavattini's screenplay was actually nominated for a 1949 Academy Award for Best Screenplay, and the film itself received an Oscar for Best Foreign Film. Though the film seems to go in and out of fashion over the years, appearing near the top of critics' ten-best-of-all-time lists and then disappearing from the lists completely, this trendiness is meaningless. *The Bicycle Thief* is a great, timeless cry of despair that many of us like to put away during good times, especially good economic times. Yet just like an undeniable conscience, *The Bicycle Thief*—a truly inspired masterwork and one of the most indelible of all cinematic visions of the human condition—returns to us whenever its needed.

NEXT STOP . . . *Shoeshine, Forbidden Games, Los Olvidados*

1948 90m/B *IT* Lamberto Maggiorani, Lianella Carell, Enzo Staiola, Elena Altieri, Vittorio Antonucci, Gino Saltamerenda, Fausto Guerzoni; *D:* Vittorio De Sica; *W:* Vittorio De Sica, Cesare Zavattini; *C:* Carlo Montuori; *M:* Alessandro Cicognini. Academy Awards '49: Best Foreign Film; British Academy Awards '49: Best Film; Golden Globe Awards '50: Best Foreign Film; National Board of Review Awards '49: Best Director (De Sica); New York Film Critics Awards '49: Best Foreign Film; Nominations: Academy Awards '49: Best Screenplay. **VHS, LV** *NOS, MRV, FCT*

THE BIG CITY
Mahanagar

In the mid 1950s, a young Calcutta housewife—whose marriage is suffering from the same financial anxieties as much of the rest of the lower-middle-class—decides out of necessity to break with tradition and enter the work force. Her experience turns out to be liberating, but not in the manner she expected. Her crash course in office politics, racism, classism, sexism, and, ultimately, unemployment, marks a subtle shift in director Satyajit Ray's generally poetic tone from quiet observation toward social criticism sprinkled with a deeply knowing sense of humor. Ray was always a keen and sympathetic chronicler of women's issues in India, and *The Big City* remains one of his most heartfelt and persuasive depictions of a society in which women's progress has been slow in coming; the ironic result is that with a degree of equality comes a woman's hard-earned right to be just as out of work as her husband.

NEXT STOP . . . *Two Daughters, Charulata, The Middleman*

1963 131m/B *IN* Anil Chatterjee, Majhabi Mukherjee, Vicky Redwood, Haren Chatterjee; *D:* Satyajit Ray; *W:* Satyajit Ray; *C:* Subrata Mitra; *M:* Satyajit Ray. **VHS** *COL*

BIG DEAL ON MADONNA STREET
The Usual Unidentified Thieves
I Soliti Ignoti
Persons Unknown

The poverty depicted in neo-realist classics like *Shoeshine* and *The Bicycle Thief* may not seem like the stuff of comedy, but Mario Monicelli's *Big Deal on Madonna Street* proves that humor is in the eye of the beholder; this simple, brilliant farce is indeed something to behold. Five down-on-their-luck characters decide to pull off a heist as their only possible ticket out of the day-to-day misery of their lives in the back alleys of Rome. Giving us sharp, terse comic vignettes illustrating the desperation of each of the major characters, Monicelli—a former film critic whose understanding of the crime genre is dazzling—efficiently proceeds to the brilliantly bungled robbery itself, designed as a mirror image send-up of such classic movie heists as those in Jules Dassin's *Rififi*, John Huston's *The Asphalt Jungle,* and Stanley Kubrick's *The Killing.* A surprisingly big hit in the U.S., where the picture crossed over from art houses to many mainstream theatres in major cities, *Big Deal on Madonna Street* was itself an inspiration for later films like Peter Yates's *The Hot Rock,* Louis Malle's *Crackers* (a direct remake of *Big Deal*), and even—in spirit at least—Mel Brooks's *The Producers.* The dream cast includes Marcello Mastroianni, Vittorio Gassman, Renato Salvatori, and Claudia Cardinale.

NEXT STOP . . . *The Lavender Hill Mob, Topkapi, The Pink Panther*

1958 90m/B *IT* Marcello Mastroianni, Vittorio Gassman, Claudia Cardinale, Renato Salvatori, Memmo Carotenuto, Toto, Rosanna Rory; *D:* Mario Monicelli; *W:* Mario Monicelli, Furio Scarpelli, Suso Cecchi D'Amico; *C:* Gianni Di Venanzo; *M:* Pierro Umiliani. Nominations: Academy Awards '58: Best Foreign-Language Film. **VHS** *CVC, MRV, DVT*

A BIGGER SPLASH

Jack Hazan's dramatized portrait of the life of, friends of, and work of painter David Hockney is one of the more bizarre and curious cultural artifacts of the 1970s. A semi-improvised and hugely self-aggrandizing examination of how the split between Hockney (playing himself) and his lover influenced, inspired, and generally affected his work. This kind of biopic about artists usually doesn't get made until the subject has passed on, and even then the direct connections often made between actual events and the art they inspire come off as hooey—like Charlton Heston gazing at a cloud formation and suddenly realizing what's missing from the Sistine Chapel. Here Hockney prattles on about his work, (which, of course, is rather wonderful and not to be confused with this film) and writer/director/cinematographer Hazan records it all in arresting images that are slavishly "suggested" by Hockney's paint-

ings (as was the movie's title). If Vanity Press had a film distribution arm, *A Bigger Splash* would be available in coffee-table sized cassette packaging, personally autographed in limited, numbered, mass-produced quantities complete with a certificate of inauthenticity. "Art has to move you and design does not," Hockney told the *Guardian* in 1988, "unless it's a good design for a bus." This film, as carefully designed as it is, will get you nowhere.

NEXT STOP . . . *Lust for Life, I Shot Andy Warhol, Basquiat*

1974 105m/C *GB* **D:** Jack Hazan; **W:** Jack Hazan, David Mingay; **M:** Patrick Gowers. **VHS**

THE BIRD WITH THE CRYSTAL PLUMAGE

L'Ucello dalle Plume di Cristallo
The Phantom of Terror
The Bird with the Glass Feathers
The Gallery Murders

After collaborating on the original story of Sergio Leone's great *Once Upon a Time in the West* with Leone and Bernardo Bertolucci, Dario Argento plunged head first into the horror genre with his first directorial effort, the now tamely gory *The Bird with the Crystal Plumage*. It's the story of an American writer (Tony Musante) who witnesses an attempted murder (the scene toys playfully with *Rear Window* and was itself later saluted by Brian de Palma in his *Dressed to Kill*) and quickly becomes obsessed with capturing the likely serial killer. The real subject of the film is Argento's simple and unrepentant love of going to the movies to be scared, and the creation of widescreen images that are both horrifying and beautiful at the same time. In the latter Argento has been blessed with the talent of the gifted Vittorio Storaro, whose first feature film (photographed when he was 29) this is. Soon Storaro would achieve fame working for Argento's former co-author Bertolucci, photographing his visual feasts *The Spider's Stratagem, The Conformist*, and *1900*, ultimately receiving Oscars for Bertolucci's *The Last Emperor*, Fran-

cis Coppola's *Apocalypse Now,* and Warren Beatty's *Reds.*

NEXT STOP . . . *Suspiria, Four Flies on Gray Velvet, The Beyond*

1970 (PG) 98m/C *IT* Tony Musante, Suzy Kendall, Eva Renzi, Enrico Maria Salerno, Mario Adorf; **D:** Dario Argento; **W:** Dario Argento; **C:** Vittorio Storaro; **M:** Ennio Morricone. **VHS, LV** *VCI, MRV*

BIRTHPLACE

Henryk Greenberg, a Polish-born American who lost much of his family in the Holocaust, is the subject of Pavel Lozinski's mind-blowing, 47-minute, 1992 documentary chronicling Greenberg's return to the village of his childhood. Certain of the location where his father and younger brother were murdered, Greenberg returns to find most of his former neighbors predictably claiming foggy memories at first; but soon their recollections come more easily. Even Greenberg, however, isn't fully prepared for the evidence that is uncovered before the camera in *Birthplace*—evidence that is presented to the audience so straightforwardly and simply that the sudden invention of a time machine couldn't make the past come more vividly, horribly alive. Though it runs just three-quarters of an hour, *Birthplace* is as full, as complete, and as powerful a work of art as any feature film on this subject that I've ever seen. To call it unforgettable is an understatement. For any citizen of this century, to miss it is unforgivable.

NEXT STOP . . . *Night and Fog, Shoah, Hotel Terminus: The Life and Times of Klaus Barbie*

1992 47m/C D: Pavel Lozinski. *NYR*

BITTER RICE
Riso Amaro

After collaborating with Luchino Visconti on the 1942 *Ossessione*, Visconti's bleakly overwhelming—not to mention scandalous, suppressed, and unauthorized—version of James M. Cain's *The Postman Always Rings Twice,* Giuseppe De Santis set out to create a major neo-realist work of his own with his

1948 *Bitter Rice*. Conceived and promoted as a heavy-hitting expose of worker exploitation in Italy's impoverished, agriculture-dependent Po Valley, the story is a slightly sordid, sexual pulp thriller in neo-realist clothing. This hardly renders *Bitter Rice* insignificant, and it should be noted that the same label was slapped on *Ossessione*—though considerably less justifiably. In *Bitter Rice,* the poor, trusting, bovine rice-field worker Silvana (Silvana Mangano) falls for a slick thief and confidence man (Vittorio Gassman) who talks her into helping him steal the area's precious rice harvest. But when the overripe Silvana discovers she's been taken for a fool, events turn bitter indeed. Though it was clearly Silvana Mangano's unbridled sexual presence that helped sell tickets around the world (in the U.S., the famous image of Mangano knee-deep in a rice field with her skirt hiked up was featured in "men's" magazines for years as typical of European "art" films), *Bitter Rice,* which nevertheless *did* expose truly horrendous working conditions, may still be unfairly maligned for simply not being *The Bicycle Thief.* It's no masterpiece, but Mangano's undisguiseable lushness shouldn't be used to dismiss this engaging postwar *noir.*

NEXT STOP . . . *Ossessione, Open City, Double Indemnity*

1949 96m/C *IT* Silvana Mangano, Vittorio Gassman, Raf Vallone, Doris Dowling; *D:* Guiseppe de Santis; *W:* Guiseppe de Santis, Carlo Lizzani, Giani Puccini; *C:* Otello Martelli; *M:* Goffredo Petrassi. Nominations: Academy Awards '50: Best Story. **VHS** *FCT*

THE BITTER TEARS OF PETRA VON KANT
Die Bitteren Traenen der Petra von Kant

Writing about Rainer Werner Fassbinder in *The Village Voice* when *The Bitter Tears of Petra von Kant* debuted at the 1973 New York Film Festival, Molly Haskell should have received the Accuracy in Media terseness prize for describing the film as "a tragicomic love story disguised as a lesbian slumber party in high-camp drag." And they said Fassbinder wasn't high-concept. *Bitter Tears* was the picture that won me over to Fassbinder, and despite Haskell's on-target summary, there's really no description of any of his melodramatic plots that could begin to suggest the nearly maniacal, single-minded sincerity with which he filmed his tales of doomed love, hopeless lust, and unrelenting, comically overwhelming *angst.* The word "stylized" seems inadequate to suggest the colors and shifting images of this three-character chamber-piece, the story of celebrated fashion designer Petra von Kant (Margit Carstensen), her fawning secretary/sex slave Marlene (Irm Hermann), and the exquisite, unattainable Karen (Hanna Schygulla), the young, bisexual model who Petra dreams of being enslaved by. With music by Giuseppe Verdi, the Walker Brothers, and the Platters, and glistening images by Michael Ballhaus (later of *Goodfellas, The Last Temptation of Christ,* and *Air Force One*), this remains one of Fassbinder's most absurd, sinewy, irresistible spectacles.

NEXT STOP . . . *The Merchant of Four Seasons, Fox and His Friends, There's Always Tomorrow*

1972 124m/C *GE* Margit Carstensen, Hanna Schygulla, Irm Hermann, Eva Mattes; *D:* Rainer Werner Fassbinder; *W:* Rainer Werner Fassbinder; *C:* Michael Ballhaus. **VHS** *NYF, FCT*

BLACK GIRL
Une Noire de...
La Noire de...

The first feature-length film by Senegal's Ousmane Sembène tells the tragic, inevitable story of a young Senegalese maid's forced exile when her white employers want to use her as a servant at their home in the south of France. The film that is most often cited as marking the birth of the African cinema, *Black Girl* (the original French title of which was the far more telling *Une Noire de ...*) remains one of the most powerfully disturbing depictions of the dehumanizing power of racism in the history of cinema. Sembène has said that his early interest in the power of film was sparked by the overt racism of Leni Riefenstahl's *Olympia,* in

which the 1936 Olympic Games were portrayed as a paean to white—particularly German—"superiority." (Even Riefenstahl, however, couldn't figure out a way to remove Jesse Owens from the final cut.) Sembène knew that if this great medium could be used to promote racism, it could be used even more effectively to expose and denounce it. His heartbreakingly spare and unflinching debut feature proved that he was right, and it remains a chilling and unforgettable experience.

"You'll like her. She's a real aristocrat."

—Madame Anais
(Genevieve Page)
to a customer
about Severine
(Catherine Deneuve)
in *Belle de Jour.*

NEXT STOP . . . *Mandabi, Ceddo, Guelwaar*

1966 65m/B Robert Fontaine, Anne-Marie Jelinek, Therese N'Bissine Diop, Momar Nar Sene; **D:** Ousmane Sembene; **W:** Ousmane Sembene; **C:** Christian Lacoste. *NYR*

BLACK GOD, WHITE DEVIL
Deus e o Diabo na Terra do Sol

Manuel and Rosa, an impoverished couple trying to survive in the drought-ridden Brazilian countryside of 1940, desperately grasp at various systems of belief, hoping to make sense of their chaotic world. Religious cults and gangs of self-proclaimed revolutionaries both turn out to be dead ends for the couple, but ultimately they come to the realization that servitude and slavery come in many forms—sometimes disguised as the church, sometimes disguised as the liberator—and that true awareness must first come from an *internal* revolution, in which colonialist frames of reference can only be replaced with an untainted perception of the reality of the Third World. The fourth film by Cinema Novo founder Glauber Rocha contains the seeds of what would be developed in his masterful *Antonio Das Mortes,* but *Black God, White Devil* is itself a formidable achievement. Filmed in an explosively stark black and white and edited with a driving, inevitable rhythm, this is a poetic vision of not only a specific time and place, but of human awakening from a complacency that is often so deep-rooted that it is no longer perceptible. Reminding us of that complacency was Rocha's calling, and he rose to it with artistry.

NEXT STOP . . . *Antonio das Mortes, Ganga Zumba, Quilombo*

1964 102m/C BR Yona Magalhaes, Geraldo Del Rey, Othon Bastos, Mauricio De Valle, Lidio Silva; **D:** Glauce Rocha; **W:** Glauce Rocha; **C:** Waldemar Lima. **VHS** *FCT*

BLACK MOON

Okay, go on, call me a shameless apologist, rationalizer, toady or sycophant. The fact remains that the late and dearly missed Louis Malle made so many magnificent films during his all-too-brief but indispensable career that he was thoroughly entitled to an occasional, ill-conceived howler on the order of *Black Moon.* That being said, I'm reminded of Joseph Cotten as Jed Leland ambling into Charles Foster Kane's office in the early days of *The Inquirer,* holding up a rather pathetic drawing and saying "I'm no good as a cartoonist." Louis Malle, gifted and brilliant in so many ways, was no good as a surrealist. We've got the proof, and it's in the form of this ghastly *Alice in Wonderland*—inspired vision of a futuristic land in which men and women are officially in a state of war. (So what else is new?) *Black Moon* is set in a mysterious country house where an old woman (Theresa Giehse), a twin sister and brother (Alexandra Stewart and the comatose Andy Warhol/Paul Morrisey discovery Joe Dallesandro), and a young girl (Cathryn Harrison) engage in mind games of a puzzling, dreamlike, and intensely uninteresting nature. These are the only four cast members, unless you count the talking unicorn and the armadillo that gets squashed in the movie's opening shot. The movie's surrealist pedigree—it must have been hoped—was provided by co-writer Joyce Buñuel (daughter of Luis). She didn't help. Nor did the cinematography of Bergman collaborator Sven Nykvist. Nothing helped. Nevertheless, it must be remembered that *Black Moon* followed Malle's *Lacombe, Lucien. Lacombe, Lucien* is a masterpiece. *Black Moon* is just a very bad movie. Louis Malle, a great filmmaker who made his bones many times over, was entitled.

NEXT STOP . . . *Dreamchild, Diva, The Milky Way*

1975 100m/C FR Cathryn Harrison, Joe Dallesandro, Alexandra Stewart, Therese Giehse; **D:** Louis Malle; **W:**

Louis Malle, Joyce Bunuel, Ghislain Uhry; *C:* Sven Nykvist; *M:* Diego Masson. **VHS** *NYR*

BLACK NARCISSUS

Having established a school, hospital, and religious outpost high in the Himalayas, a group of nuns finds that the tensions of daily life—physical, emotional, sexual—become magnified in their claustrophobic world in ways both deadly and revelatory. Deborah Kerr is the nun who remembers, in flashback, the pleasures of her former, worldly life—feelings that resurface in the presence of a handsome, local British official (David Farrar). His presence causes other problems, however, and soon *Black Narcissus* turns into a veritable pressure cooker of repressed sexuality; the tension comes from guessing how—and where—it will surface. That at least one of the film's most memorable images recalls another masterwork of a decade later—Alfred Hitchcock's *Vertigo*—seems only natural. *Black Narcissus,* stunningly designed and photographed entirely in Britain's Pinewood Studios, where light and color was tightly controlled for maximum psychological impact, remains a brilliant example of how to treat remarkably controversial subject matter in a commercially acceptable manner. If co-producers/directors/writers Michael Powell and Emeric Pressburger had an impact on Hitchcock, and vice-versa, who can blame these great artists for respecting and for absorbing—on some level—each others' inspired, potent images? A revelation also is Deborah Kerr, whose fully human Sister Clodagh is quietly unforgettable, as is the amazing Kathleen Byron (unforgettable, but not quietly) as Sister Ruth, the most tortured and repressed of the nuns. With Sabu, Flora Robson, and Jean Simmons in her first major screen role. Oscars went to Jack Cardiff for his color cinematography and Alfred Junge for the bold and intensely Freudian set design.

NEXT STOP . . . *A Matter of Life and Death, The Red Shoes, Vertigo*

1947 101m/C *GB* Deborah Kerr, David Farrar, Sabu, Jean Simmons, Kathleen Byron, Flora Robson, Esmond Knight, Jenny Laird, Judith Furse, May Hallitt, Nancy Roberts; *D:* Michael Powell, Emeric Pressburger; *W:* Michael Powell, Emeric Pressburger; *C:* Jack Cardiff; *M:* Brian Easdale. Academy Awards '47: Best Art Direction/Set Decoration (Color), Best Color Cinematography; New York Film Critics Awards '47: Best Actress (Kerr). **VHS, LV** *MLB*

BLACK ORPHEUS
Orfeu Negro

A retelling of the Greek legend of Orpheus and Eurydice set in modern day Rio, *Black Orpheus* took home the Palme d'Or at the 1959 Cannes Film Festival and remained one of the darlings of art houses and repertory film theatres throughout the 1960s. While the immensely influential musical score of Antonio Carlos Jobim and Luis Bonfa still has the power to intoxicate (despite becoming familiar to elevator passengers and K-Mart shoppers as well), the film itself has not aged as gracefully as we might wish. Orpheus (soccer star Breno Mello), a streetcar conductor who enchants the denizens of his slum with his singing, falls hard for Eurydice (Pittsburgh dancer Marpessa Dawn), a fresh-faced young girl who's making her first visit to the big city in time for Rio's famous carnival. They sing, they dance, they fall in love in the most colorful and tuneful setting imaginable, and they are, of course, pursued by death. Even if one doesn't find a certain inherent condescension in the way Marcel Camus conceived of and handles this material, there's still a hefty dollop of thick, unearned sentimentality that has to be waded through before the final samba fades into memory. Perhaps a bit too genuinely poignant to actually be called the art house *Flashdance, Black Orpheus* may nevertheless be best remembered as a smashing soundtrack album, with lots of "exotic," brightly colored pictures to illustrate the tunes.

NEXT STOP . . . *Quilombo, Bye Bye Brazil, Umbrellas of Cherbourg*

1958 103m/C *BR FR PT* Breno Mello, Marpessa Dawn, Lea Garcia, Fausto Guerzoni, Lourdes De Oliveira; *D:* Marcel Camus; *W:* Vinitius De Moraes, Jacques Viot; *C:* Jean Bourgoin; *M:* Antonio Carlos Jobim, Luis Bonfa. Academy Awards '59: Best Foreign Film; Cannes Film Festival '59: Best Film; Golden Globe Awards '60: Best Foreign Film. **VHS, LV** *CVC, FOX, FCT*

BLACK RAIN
Kuroi Ame

Japan's Shohei Imamura, whose career included serving as assistant director on Ozu's 1953 *Tokyo Story* and who wrote and directed the extraordinary *The Ballad of Narayama* in 1983, turned his attention in 1989 to the inevitable subject that Japan can never fully turn away from. Many films have dealt with the bombing of Hiroshima, yet the direct, indelible, and uncompromisingly horrifying vision that Imamura brings to the screen in *Black Rain* is both new and necessary. The black rain of the title is, of course, radiation; the film's subject is not the blast itself (though the bombing is not shied away from and is graphically depicted) but rather the after-effects of the explosion. The black-and-white images of *Black Rain* were filmed in such high contrast that they appear to have been burned into the film itself—like the shadows that still exist on walls found near the bomb's ground zero. We've seen documentaries that chronicle the effects of radiation poisoning on the bodies of survivors and their offspring, but in telling the story of a young girl who survived the bombing with no apparent visible effect, Imamura forces us to examine psychological issues that survivors of other holocausts must also confront. The young protagonist, Yasuko, lives with the knowledge of her "contamination." But how and when will it manifest itself? What kind of life can she plan, and—most importantly in both the movie and the book on which it was based—what does she do with the shame she feels for being so different from others, the undeserved guilt of being "contaminated"? This mournful, sobering picture attained an extra degree of resonance being released in the wake of the AIDS epidemic. (The film's American release may well have been hurt by that same year's release of another *Black Rain*—also set in Japan—but that one a mediocre Ridley Scott thriller starring Michael Douglas.)

NEXT STOP . . . *The Ballad of Narayama, Fires on the Plain, Rhapsody in August*

1988 123m/B *JP* Kazuo Kitamura, Yoshiko Tanaka, Etsuko Ichihara, Shoichi Ozawa, Norihei Miki, Keisuke Ishida; *D:* Shohei Imamura; *W:* Shohei Imamura, Toshiro Ishido; *C:* Takashi Kawamata; *M:* Toru Takemitsu. **VHS** *FXL, FCT*

BLACK SUNDAY
La Maschera del Demonio
The Demon's Mask
House of Fright
Revenge of the Vampire

This *Brigadoon* of terror, in which the devil walks the earth for one horrifying day each century, marks the fully credited debut feature of Italy's Mario Bava. His full-bodied, all-stops-out, Gothic Grand Guignol style produces some memorable images (Bava was also co-cinematographer), most of them built around the striking, sculpted face of Barbara Steele in a dual role as a beautiful princess and a centuries-old evil witch. It's her witch we remember, of course, and that single close-up of her eyes popping open (you'll know it when you see it) may put much of the rest of this ridiculous yet genuinely unsettling horror movie in the background. It's understandable that a Bava cult grew out of *Black Sunday,* yet few if any of his later films, including the gory *Hatchet for the Honeymoon* and the wonderfully titled *Twitch of the Death Nerve,* made the stylish impact of his first. *Black Sunday* was released in the U.S. in a dubbed version, and the army of kids who saw it nationwide in 1961 at Saturday kiddie matinees were effectively freaked for weeks, if not (in my case, at least) permanently.

NEXT STOP . . . *Suspiria, The Bird with the Crystal Plumage, Night of the Living Dead* (1968)

1960 83m/B *IT* Barbara Steele, John Richardson, Ivo Garrani, Andrea Checchi, Arturo Dominici, Antonio Pierfederici, Tino Bianchi, Clara Bindi, Enrico Oliveri, Germana Dominici; *D:* Mario Bava; *W:* Mario Bava, Ennio de Concini, Mario Serandrei; *C:* Mario Bava, Ubaldo Terzano; *M:* Les Baxter. **VHS** *SMW, SNC, MRV*

BLEAK MOMENTS
Loving Moments

The word "bleak" in a movie's description can be counted on to sell almost as many tickets

as such ever-popular adjectives as "boring," "political," or "demanding." When the offending word is actually in the title, however, there's a good chance the film will go totally unnoticed. Happily, this was not the case with *Bleak Moments*, the poignant and bracingly intelligent 1972 debut film by the then-29-year-old Mike Leigh. A tale of two sisters who have a lot to tell each other but don't know how, *Bleak Moments* envisions—in miniature—a world of wounded and hurt human beings, all desperate to communicate their longings but lacking the tools to do so. The product of numerous improvisational workshops involving Leigh and his cast, the finished product—as with all of Leigh's films including *Naked, Secrets and Lies,* and *Career Girls*—is meticulously and tightly constructed by the director. The wise and deeply grim humor, naturalistic performances, and non-schematic structure of *Bleak Moments*—together with its central dilemma surrounding human communication and the lack thereof—would become the hallmarks of Mike Leigh's later films, beginning with his breakthrough second feature (which didn't arrive until 17 years after *Bleak Moments*), the brilliant 1988 *High Hopes*.

NEXT STOP . . . *Life Is Sweet, Career Girls, Riff Raff*

1971 110m/C *GB* Anne Raitt, Eric Allen, Mike Bradwell, Joolia Cappleman; *D:* Mike Leigh; *W:* Mike Leigh; *C:* Bahram Manocheri; *M:* Mike Bradwell. **VHS** *WBF*

THE BLOOD OF A POET
Le Sang d'un Poete

There was a time when the greatest and most innovative of our artists and writers wanted to work in the cinema. It couldn't have been for the money; films like the 1928 Buñuel/Dali *Un Chien Andalou* and Jean Cocteau's 1930 *The Blood of a Poet* were not, I feel certain, designed to keep Chaplin or Griffith awake at night worrying about competition at the boxoffice. These were visionaries who understood the potentially revolutionary power of this relatively new art form, and who were anxious to subvert the expectations of an already complacent viewing pub-

lic by turning the cinema's established storytelling conventions on their head. "I applied myself only to the relief and to the details of the images that came forth from the great darkness of the human body," Cocteau wrote of the creation of this, his first film, "I adopted them then and there as the documentary scenes of another kingdom." Indeed, the overwhelming power of *The Blood of a Poet* stems from that matter-of-fact way in which the impossible is visualized. A series of four episodes that all happen in the fraction of a second that it takes for a chimney to collapse, *The Blood of a Poet* shows us internal emotional states—not vaguely symbolized, but as if filmed during sleep by a camera focused on our dreams. An artist draws a mouth and tries to erase it—whereupon it comes to life in his hand. His inability to flee from his own creation leads to his confinement in the "Hotel of Dramatic Follies," where he clambers along the walls of a gravity-defying, dreamlike corridor, peeking into keyholes through which he is forced to witness unspoken human desires. There is much more, and it's all powerful, primal, funny, and frightening—even today. *The Blood of a Poet* also features the brilliant first film score by the legendary Georges Auric.

NEXT STOP . . . *L'Age d'Or, Beauty and the Beast, Orpheus*

1930 55m/B Enrique Rivero, Feral Benga, Jean Desbordes; *D:* Jean Cocteau; *W:* Jean Cocteau; *C:* Georges Perinal; *M:* Georges Auric. **VHS** *VYY, MRV, HHT*

BLOOD WEDDING
Bodas de Sangre

The first in an acclaimed trilogy of dance films by Spain's Carlos Saura, *Blood Wedding* achieves its power through the purity and simplicity of its concept and execution. Star and choreographer Antonio Gades drives his dancers through a rehearsal of his ballet adaptation of Garcia Lorca's story of thwarted passion and bloody revenge, and for once a filmed ballet generates real heat from the screen. Saura's not afraid to use facial close-ups to accentuate the story's power, but he never fails to keep his focus on his dancers' bodies in their entirety. Chopping bodies into

THE HOUND SALUTES:

MICHELANGELO ANTONIONI
Italian Avant-Garde Director

The tennis players feint and thrust. They grunt and sweat. But there is no ball.

The famous scene from *Blow-Up* is one of the defining moments of avant-garde 1960s cinema. Italian director Michelangelo Antonioni is a master at depicting alienation. His challenging films strive for a new cinematic language, abandoning conventional narrative and plot and using striking visuals and jarring techniques to evoke the psychic horrors of modern life.

"Some people believe I make films with my head, a few others think they come from the heart," Antonioni once said. "For my part, I feel as though I make them with my stomach."

Born to a middle-class family in Ferrara, Italy on September 29, 1912, Antonioni was a student of economics, college tennis champion, painter, film critic, and anti-Fascist activist who cut his teeth on short documentaries in the 1950s. He burst to international fame with *L'avventura* in 1961, a film that remains on many critics' all-time top ten list. His innovative 1964 film *The Red Desert* used colors to illustrate its fragile heroine's changing moods. *Blow-up,* about a British fashion photographer who becomes a murder witness, was released in 1966. Some critics consider his 1975 thriller, *The Passenger,* which starred Jack Nicholson, the director's best and most accessible work. Unfortunately, in 1985 Antonioni suffered a stroke and now works with a co-director on his films, including Wim Wenders for 1995's *Beyond the Clouds.*

Antonioni, divorced from his first wife Letizia Balboni, lives in Rome with Enrica Fico, whom he married in 1986. In 1995, he was honored with a lifetime achievement Academy Award.

a series of over-edited close-ups in an attempt to make dance on film more "cinematic" is one of the usual failings of this kind of thing, yet Saura has far too much feeling for the rhythm of this piece—and for the talents of Gades and co-star Cristina Hoyos—to fall into that trap. A model of its genre, *Blood Wedding* was followed by *Carmen* (1983) and *El Amor Brujo* (1986), both created with the full collaboration of Gades.

NEXT STOP . . . *Carmen, Flamenco, Tango* (1998)

1981 71m/C *SP* Antonio Gades, Christina Hoyos, Marisol, Carmen Villena; **D:** Carlos Saura; **W:** Carlos Saura, Antonio Gades; **C:** Teo Escamilla; **M:** Emillo De Diego. **VHS** *XVC, CTH*

BLOW-UP

The story appears to be simple; a photographer thinks he may have accidentally taken pictures of a murder. He "blows up" the photos, and reaches a surprising conclusion. Although his 1960 *L'Avventura* changed the language of movies, it was Michelangelo Antonioni's widely seen, 1966 *Blow-Up* that ultimately changed the expectations of moviegoers, exposing a new generation of young people to the tantalizing possibility that the cinema could offer the viewer considerably more than meets the eye. (Part of its theme, ironically, is that reality may consist of considerably *less* than we imagine.) Some of us were enticed into attending *Blow-Up* with the promise of a glimpse of the "happening" world of Carnaby Street in the 1960s, not to mention all that London-style free love with those half-naked birds—would-be cover girls—frolicking on purple paper with hopes that photographer David Hemmings would make them famous for fifteen minutes. And while we laughed knowingly and shifted in our seats as Hemmings seduced the gangly Verushka with his long lens, we baby boomers who packed into *Blow-Up* felt proud that we were fully understanding and keeping up with the plot of this famous foreign director's "art" movie. Even the mysterious body in the park, which showed up in Hemmings's pictures, was one part of a fascinating but very real puzzle that we were keeping up with. Then, the lights came up—and we questioned everything. Everything about the dead body, everything about that airplane propeller, everything about the Yardbirds' anger at the nightclub, not to mention the purple paper, Vanessa Redgrave's manic nervousness, the existence of the photographs themselves and, lest we forget, the meaning of the final shot. And there were those *mimes*…. In retrospect, the whole mod "swinging London" aspect of *Blow-Up* may still get in the way of its appreciation as a modern classic, which is unjust. In asking a generation to consider how we make sense of the images we see, and how we construct—out of need and loneliness—a reality that suits our purposes, Antonioni worked a miracle. Also starring Sarah Miles, with Jane Birkin and Gillian Hills as the purple paper girls. The legendary score is by Herbie Hancock, and the Antonioni/Tonino Guerra/ Edward Bond screenplay (Oscar nominated) is based on a story by Julio Cortázar.

NEXT STOP . . . *The Passenger, Living in Oblivion, The Crying Game*

1966 111m/C *GB IT* David Hemmings, Vanessa Redgrave, Sarah Miles, Jane Birkin, Veruschka; **D:** Michelangelo Antonioni; **W:** Tonino Guerra, Michelangelo Antonioni; **C:** Carlo Di Palma; **M:** Herbie Hancock. Cannes Film Festival '67: Best Film; National Society of Film Critics Awards '66: Best Director (Antonioni), Best Film; Nominations: Academy Awards '66: Best Director (Antonioni), Best Story & Screenplay. **VHS, LV, Letterbox** *MGM, FCT*

BLUE

"I'm not afraid of death but I am afraid of dying," wrote filmmaker Derek Jarman in 1992. "Pain can be alleviated by morphine but the pain of social ostracism cannot be taken away." In 1993, only months before his death from AIDS, Jarman completed his final film, a contemplation of his life and impending death featuring a dense, carefully orchestrated soundtrack of voices, sound effects, and music, but containing only a single visual image. Yet such a description is misleading, for the lone image—a deep, unchanging, solid blue light projected onto the screen of the darkened theatre—is the canvas on which we see the pictures that Jarman forces us to conjure. Since *we* do the conjuring, the images we see—and we do see them—are private visual communications between Jarman and the viewer, allowing us the freedom to visualize our own lives, our own decay and our own deaths with an hallucinatory intensity that is at once shocking, surprising, and liberating. This is a great film as well as a brilliant stunt, perhaps the only successful example in movie history of a filmmaker preparing a last will and testament for himself that inspires awe, tears, and joy in people who never knew him. *Blue* takes us directly to the specifics of the disease's effects on Jarman's body, and then, in what seems like an instant, stares intense suffering in the eye and molds it—as if pain were being used as a material for *origami*—into a creative grace that shames each of us into an overwhelming gratitude for being able to feel at all. With a score by Simon Fisher Turner, and a cast that includes Jarman, John Quentin, Nigel Terry, and Tilda Swinton.

NEXT STOP . . . *Ikiru, Parting Glances, Near Death*

1993 (R) 76m/C *GB* **D:** Derek Jarman; **W:** Derek Jarman; **M:** Simon Fisher Turner. **VHS** *KIV*

THE BLUE ANGEL
Der Blaue Engel

Near the end of *The Blue Angel*, disgraced professor Immanuel Rath (Emil Jannings) is reduced to the lowest point of his life:

"Perhaps we can find out what this word love entails."

—Anna (Pernilla August) to Henrik (Samuel Froler) in *Best Intentions.*

Young Tietou (Lu Liping) hangs on to his cherished toy in *The Blue Kite*.

dressed as a clown and forced to crow like a rooster on the stage of a seedy Berlin nightclub—the Blue Angel—as an audience of former students hoots and taunts him. Rath, the strict disciplinarian who was feared by his students, had first come to the Blue Angel to see if his young charges were patronizing this sinful place, wasting time that should have been devoted to study. But when he got a load of singer Lola Lola (Marlene Dietrich) in her lewd costume, her stockinged legs wrapped intoxicatingly around her chair as she sang "Falling in love again ... never wanted to ...," Rath helplessly turned control of all discipline in his life over to her. Far more graphically explicit—even hardcore—movies about erotic enslavement will come and go, but there will never be as fully realized a depiction on screen of utter sexual humiliation as the moment of Rath's crowing (during which Lola toys with her lover in the wings).

The character had still more depths to plumb (as did the actor who played him), but screen history had already been made; *The Blue Angel,* the first collaboration between Josef von Sternberg and Dietrich and the director's only collaboration with Jannings, was—and still is—an electrifying melodrama that only gains in power over the years. Von Sternberg (who had been in Hollywood for 15 years already) filmed the project in Germany at the desperate request of Jannings, whose great career in German silent film had crashed with the onset of sound. Incredibly, Marlene Dietrich wasn't von Sternberg's first choice for Lola. (He wanted Brigitte Helm, the blonde who played Maria and her evil robot twin in Fritz Lang's 1925 *Metropolis;* but the author of the book on which it was based said *nein.*) This was to be Emil Jannings's last great performance. Following it, he elected to stay in Germany and work for the Nazis, suffering an ignominious death in 1950 not unlike Rath's in the film. After the shoot, von Sternberg hightailed it back to the U.S. with Dietrich in tow, where they later collaborated on stylish melodramas like *Morocco* and *Shanghai Express. The Blue Angel* was shot in both German and English versions, but Rath's maniacal obsession with order, discipline, and ritual—finally subjugated by his passion—makes full emotional sense only when heard in the original German.

NEXT STOP . . . *Pandora's Box, The Marriage of Maria Braun, The Last Seduction*

1930 90m/B *GE* Marlene Dietrich, Emil Jannings, Kurt Gerron, Rosa Valetti, Hans Albers; *D:* Josef von Sternberg; *W:* Karl Vollmoller, Robert Liebmann, Carl Zuckmayer; *C:* Gunther Rittau; *M:* Friedrich Hollander. **VHS, 8mm** *NOS, FCT, BAR*

THE BLUE KITE
Lan Feng Zheng

Many of history's most significant epochs—those that cause upheaval in the lives of millions—tend to be treated on screen in ways that try to demonstrate the "big picture" results of this change, but at a cost of de-emphasizing the day-to-day human experience of living through such an era. Chinese director Tian Zhuangzhuang's *The Blue Kite* achieves its considerable power by taking exactly the opposite road—by giving us one family's daily struggles in Beijing between the years 1953 and 1967. In film after film set during the Cultural Revolution, we've seen individuals accused of crimes and reaction told to "go home and engage in some constructive self-criticism." In *The Blue Kite,* the protagonist is a child whose father is taken away for "reeducation," and whose world and family structure will never be the same after. This child—played by three different actors during the film's 14 year span—attempts to come to terms with the changes taking place both inside his home and in the streets of China, but he's able in the end to draw no easy conclusions about the course that his family's lives have taken. As with a great many recent Chinese films, *The Blue Kite* is exquisitely designed and structured. It also, like so many other superb Chinese

films, has been banned and suppressed at home. Perhaps it's time for the regime that bans such eloquent, humane and—dare I say it?—"non-reactionary" works of art as *The Blue Kite,* Zhang Yimou's *To Live,* and Chen Kaige's *Farewell My Concubine* to engage in just a bit of constructive self-criticism itself.

NEXT STOP . . . *To Live, Farewell My Concubine, The Gate of Heavenly Peace*

1993 138m/C *CH* Lu Liping, Zhang Wenyao, Pu Quanxin; *D:* Tian Zhuangzhuang; *W:* Xiao Mao; *C:* Yong Hou; *M:* Yoshihide Otomo. Nominations: Independent Spirit Awards '95: Best Foreign Film. **VHS** *KIV*

THE BLUE LIGHT
Das Blaue Licht

Mount Cristallo emanates a mysterious light that mesmerizes climbers from the nearby village, who ultimately fall to their deaths trying to reach it. But Junta, a beautiful girl who is pure at heart, innocent, and virtuous (Leni Riefenstahl), conquers the precipice—only to be persecuted by other villagers who assume that her survival must mean that she's a witch. Her ultimate destruction comes as a result of the greed of her would-be lover (an artist), who, when he discovers that the mysterious blue light is emanating from precious crystals, has them removed, causing Junta to lose her footing in the darkness when she climbs Cristallo again. Leni Riefenstahl's first directorial effort is a cannily designed, thoroughly demented extension of the peculiar German genre of "mountain films" that had been popularized by directors Arnold Fanck and Luis Trenker, but which in Riefenstahl's hands takes on unmistakably ominous overtones of a struggle between "natural German purity" and "cosmopolitan" moneygrubbing. With her enormous talent as a director already evident, and her themes of imperiled purity firmly in place, Riefenstahl was soon enthusiastically working directly for Hitler (a fan of *The Blue Light* and of Riefenstahl herself), filming the meticulously choreographed 1934 Nazi Party Rally with an army of photographers at her command, later editing the miles of footage into

Compulsive gambler Bob (Roger Duchesne) is caught up in another game in *Bob le Flambeur*.

her numbing, supremely insidious Nazi recruiting poster *Triumph of the Will*.

NEXT STOP . . . *Triumph of the Will, Olympia, The Wonderful, Horrible Life of Leni Riefenstahl*

1932 77m/B *GE* Leni Riefenstahl, Matthias Wieman, Max Holsboer; ***D:*** Leni Riefenstahl; ***W:*** Bela Belazs, Leni Riefenstahl; ***C:*** Hans Schneeberger; ***M:*** Giuseppe Becce. **VHS** *VYY, MRV, FCT*

THE BOAT IS FULL
Das Boot Ist Voll

One of the least known (in the U.S.) films on the subject of the Holocaust is also one of the finest. *The Boat Is Full* is Swiss director Markus Imhoof's moving and detailed depiction of a group of German Jewish refugees who pose as a family in order to reach asylum in Switzerland, only to find that strictly maintained quotas are causing many to be turned back from this supposed haven of neutrality, resulting in certain death. "The boat is full" was, in fact, the Swiss Parliament's unofficial term for having accepted all the Jews they were going to take, and in this they joined many other nations of the world (including the U.S.) in officially denouncing the German policy of extermination, then looking the other way when refugees pounded on the door. Imhoof, who was born at about the time this story takes place, has said that he always wondered about Swiss policy on this subject, especially since his uncle—living in America during the war—had financed the smuggling of some Jews from Switzerland to the U.S. This austere and appropriately claustrophobic work—featuring not a note of music—was rather surprisingly financed as a Swiss/Austrian/West German co-production; it won prizes for Best Direction and Best Screenplay at the Berlin Film Festival.

NEXT STOP . . . *The Sorrow and the Pity, Hotel Terminus: The Life and Times of Klaus Barbie, Shoah*

1981 104m/C *SI* Tina Engel, Curt Bois, Renate Steiger, Mathias Gnaedinger, Hans Diehl, Martin Walz, Gerd David; *D:* Markus Imhoof; *W:* Markus Imhoof; *C:* Hans Liechti. Berlin International Film Festival '81: Best Director (Imhoof); Nominations: Academy Awards '81: Best Foreign Film. **VHS** *FRF, GLV, SWC*

BOB LE FLAMBEUR
Bob the Gambler

There's a brief, throwaway moment in Stanley Donen's comedy *Bedazzled* in which the devil (Peter Cook) is seen casually ripping the last page out of Agatha Christie thrillers before shipping them off to book stores. If he'd *really* wanted to be devilish, he would have snipped the priceless, soul-satisfying final line of dialogue out of all prints of Jean-Pierre Melville's wonderful 1955 *film noir* about an aging, gentleman gambler out to make one last big score. Bob Montagne (Roger Duchesne)—the "Bob the Gambler" of the title—has been compulsively placing bets all his life, but now he needs to call in his chips and settle the bets of a lifetime. Bob's scheme involves putting together a team to knock over a posh Deauville casino, but as the clock ticks down, all odds seem to be stacked against him. *Bob le Flambeur* is often cited as a seminal work of the French cinema's New Wave movement, in large part because of the freewheeling nighttime and location cinematography of legendary cinematographer Henri Decaë. Discovered by American critics at the 1982 New York Film Festival and later released commercially in the U.S. for the first time, *Bob le Flambeur*'s success helped to raise awareness of Melville in this country, a process which continued with the recent release of the restored version of his 1967 masterpiece, *Le Samourai*.

NEXT STOP . . . *Touchez pas au Grisbi, Le Samourai, The Killing*

1955 97m/B *FR* Roger Duchesne, Isabel Corey, Daniel Cauchy, Howard Vernon, Gerard Buhr, Guy Decomble; *D:* Jean-Pierre Melville; *W:* Jean-Pierre Melville, Auguste Le Breton; *C:* Henri Decae; *M:* Jean Boyer, Eddie Barclay. **VHS, LV** *COL, CVC, ING*

BOCCACCIO '70

An army of screenwriters—and three of Italy's most celebrated directors—collaborated with decidedly mixed results on this three-part updating of *The Decameron*. Federico Fellini opens the show with *The Temptation of Dr. Antonio*, in which a Milquetoast is outraged by a milk poster—a billboard actually—on which Anita Ekberg's mammaries push the dairy's bovine advertising thrust about as far as it can go. Luchino Visconti is next up with a segment featuring Romy Schneider as the stunning wife of a wealthy man who's excited by the idea of taking a mistress—so Schneider convinces him to keep the home fires burning by paying *her* to play the part. Sophia Loren steals the show in the final episode, *The Raffle*, directed by Vittorio De Sica. The prize attraction of a small, traveling carnival, Loren takes the concept of the "kissing booth" to a whole new dimension for the lucky raffle winner in each small town on the tour. One of the many multi-part films to come out of Italy in the 1960s, *Boccaccio '70* is by its very nature an uneven affair; it's diverting enough, though, with memorable little glories sprinkled generously throughout.

NEXT STOP . . . *Yesterday, Today and Tomorrow, Spirits of the Dead, Love at Twenty*

1962 145m/C *IT* Anita Ekberg, Romy Schneider, Tomas Milian, Sophia Loren, Peppino de Filippo, Luigi Gilliani; *D:* Vittorio De Sica, Luchino Visconti, Federico Fellini; *W:* Luchino Visconti, Federico Fellini, Tullio Pinelli, Ennio Flaiano, Cesare Zavattini; *C:* Otello Martelli, Giuseppe Rotunno; *M:* Nino Rota, Armando Trovajoli. **VHS** *NO*

BOROM SARRET

A celebrated writer and social critic in the 1950s, Senegal's Ousmane Sembène traveled to Moscow in 1961 to study filmmaking, believing that the cinema was the most effective way for his voice to reach the largest possible audience. Upon his return, Sembène directed this riveting 20-minute film that packs the power of a full-length feature. *Borom Sarret* chronicles—in the uninsistent, straightforward manner that would

become the hallmark of Sembène's style—one day in the life of a cart-driver in the bustling city of Dakar. As the small details and cumulative indignities of his life compound, the film achieves a haunting and precise sense of outrage that grows organically out of the near-documentary images. Though *Borom Sarret* doesn't aspire to the same richness and complexity that some of Sembène's later features like *Black Girl, Emitai,* and *Ceddo* reached, it remains not only a pioneering work of African cinema, but an early example of the cinematic skills of a master.

NEXT STOP . . . *Black Girl, Mandabi, Ceddo*

1966 20m/B D: Ousmane Sembene. *NYR*

BORSALINO

You could say that *Borsalino* is an example of style over substance—if there were any substance. Come to think of it, the picture doesn't have much style, either. Fortunately, Jean-Paul Belmondo and Alain Delon are asked to provide just about everything that this buddy-buddy comic gangster picture has to offer, and that turns out to be enough to have even spawned a sequel (*Borsalino and Co.*). Belmondo and Delon portray rival mobsters in 1930s Marseilles, and they dress better than their Chicago counterparts. The gunplay and mob violence is all of the wink-wink variety, the vintage cars are colorful and shiny, and the catchy, bouncy, incessant score is used to fill in any holes in the plot or gaps between wardrobe changes. All in all, *Borsalino* is harmless—though I can't quite bring myself to call it fun—but Belmondo and Delon, sartorially splendid, obviously fond of each other, and in their prime, are something to see.

NEXT STOP . . . *Bob le Flambeur, Bugsy Malone, My New Partner*

1970 (R) 124m/C *FR* Jean-Paul Belmondo, Alain Delon, Michel Bouquet, Catherine Rouvel, Francoise Christophe, Corinne Marchand; **D:** Jacques Deray; **W:** Jacques Deray, Jean Cau, Claude Sautet, Jean-Claude Carriere; **C:** Jean-Jacques Tarbes; **M:** Claude Bolling. **VHS** *PAR*

BOUDU SAVED FROM DROWNING
Boudu Sauve des Eaux

If it's true that no good deed goes unpunished, perhaps there's a good reason. When the tramp called Boudu (Michel Simon) jumps into the Seine at the beginning of Jean Renoir's great *Boudu Saved from Drowning,* the bookseller who rescues him is sure that he's doing the right and decent thing. He takes Boudu home with him, proud to offer this pathetic outcast of society the comfort and privilege of his middle-class home, but the man he has rescued stubbornly refuses to be grateful. Moreover, he not only seduces the bookseller's wife but his maid, too (what nerve—the bookseller was trying to get to her himself). Renoir's classic comic fable about bourgeois expectations and, yes, liberal pieties, is still a great, rude, welcome blast of fresh air. Once seen, it's impossible to ever again be seriously surprised about a favor not returned or a dinner invitation not reciprocated. Michel Simon is so perfect as the gloriously independent Boudu that the full achievement of Renoir's casual-seeming cheer for anarchy may go almost unnoticed: it shouldn't. *Boudu Saved from Drowning* is a classic and timeless moral fable—a perfect illustration of Renoir's oft-quoted observation that "the terrible thing about this world is that everybody has his reasons." (Modern American version: "You want gratitude? Get a puppy.") *Boudu* was indeed the basis for Paul Mazursky's *Down and Out in Beverly Hills.* I like Paul Mazursky, but *Boudu* is incomparable.

NEXT STOP . . . *La Chienne, Rules of the Game, Toni*

1932 87m/B *FR* Michel Simon, Charles Granval, Jean Daste, Marcelle Hainia, Severine Lerczinska, Jacques Becker; **D:** Jean Renoir; **W:** Jean Renoir; **C:** Marcel Lucien. **VHS** *INT, MRV, DVT*

BOY
Shonen

One of the most overtly confrontational of the new generation of Japanese filmmakers,

Nagisa Oshima is best known in the U.S. for *In the Realm of the Senses,* his scandalous, widely banned marathon of copulation, strangulation, and castration that was based on an actual 1936 incident. Also drawn from a real event was this 1969 Oshima film about a nearly impoverished family whose only income came from shoving their 10-year-old son in front of unsuspecting motorists' cars. The boy would feign injury, and the terrified, guilt-ridden drivers were virtually blackmailed into paying for the child's "medical bills." Oshima uses this nightmarish scenario to create a portrait of the modern Japanese family *in extremis;* as terrified and confused as the boy is by this strange set of family values, it is, nevertheless, a system. As the boy questions that system, his grasp of the world around him—what is real and what is not; what other aspects of his life involve performance, ritual, and lying—becomes increasingly uncertain. Though in the end it's a bit too analytical for its own good, *Boy* is a disturbing look at the nuclear family reaching critical mass.

NEXT STOP . . . *Diary of a Shijuku Thief, Night of the Hunter, The Family Game*

1969 97m/C Tetsuo Abe, Tsuyoshi Kinoshita, Akiko Koyama, Fumio Watanabe; *D:* Nagisa Oshima; *W:* Nagisa Oshima; *C:* Seizo Sengen, Yasuhiro Yoshioka; *M:* Hikaru Hayashi. *NYR*

BOY MEETS GIRL

Two lonely young people wander the dark streets, cafés, and clubs of a strange, otherworldly Paris. In the strangest of ways, they meet. That would be all, folks, except for the fact that this 1984 feature by France's Léos Carax is so visually suggestive and transporting that the black-and-white images take on a chilling, edgy life of their own. Paris has been imagined in countless ways on screen, but perhaps not since Jean-Luc Godard's *Alphaville* has there been such an original and poetic vision of a city at night—and we're not talking digitally enhanced Gotham City stuff, either. Carax's camera can creep over a pinball machine as a desolate young man whaps robotically at the flippers and the image seems to have an electrically charged life of its own—it's completely familiar yet it's all strange, new, and eerie. The same can be said of the talent of this remarkable, yet-to-be-discovered-in-the-U.S. director, whose equally astounding, big-budget *Les Amants du Pont-Neuf* has been seen here only at film festivals, but not (as of this writing) in theatres. Watch out for Léos Carax.

NEXT STOP . . . *Les Amants du Pont-Neuf, Diva, The Devil, Probably*

1984 100m/B *FR* Denis Lavant, Mireille Perrier, Carroll Brooks, Anna Baldaccini; *D:* Leos Carax; *W:* Leos Carax; *C:* Jean-Yves Escoffier; *M:* Jacques Pinault. **VHS** *FCT, MGM*

BOYFRIENDS & GIRLFRIENDS
My Girlfriend's Boyfriend
L'Ami de Mon Ami

Eric Rohmer's films seem to acquire almost as many titles as his characters do paramours. This sixth in his series of "Comedies and Proverbs," for example, was known in England as *My Girlfriend's Boyfriend,* which is considerably closer to the original title of *L'Ami de Mon Ami* than is the vastly less specific American title *Boyfriends and Girlfriends.* (Still, it's less bizarre than *The Green Ray*'s American title of *Summer,* which will now likely be confused with Rohmer's recent *A Summer's Tale.*) Whatever you call it, it's an absolutely delightful romantic comedy about a young woman living in a disorientingly neat and clean looking Parisian suburb, who indeed finds herself increasingly attracted to the boyfriend of her girlfriend. On the other hand, is she as attracted to him as she is attracted to the idea of being able to snare him? And what's her girlfriend up to in the meantime? Rohmer's films are a kind of reverse *Seinfeld:* they can appear to be about nothing, but in fact are almost always profoundly stirring and emotionally resonant in ways that may make you smile contentedly to yourself, hours, days, or weeks afterward.

NEXT STOP . . . *Claire's Knee, Summer, Rules of the Game*

ERIC ROHMER

French New Wave Director

Born Jean-Marie Maurice Scherer on April 4, 1920 in Nancy, France, Eric Rohmer is one of the legendary figures of modern cinema. His classic films include *My Night at Maud's* (1969), *Claire's Knee* (1970), and *The Marquise of O* (1976). A critic and television director as well, he is considered part of the French "New Wave" of cinema directors, who took an all encompassing view of themselves as the authors ("auteurs") of their films. Their attitude inspired a whole generation of American film critics to revise their notions of Hollywood films by taking directors more seriously and lending less weight to the influence of the Hollywood studio system. He was the editor-in-chief of the influential New Wave journal "Cahiers Du Cinema" from 1957–1963.

Rohmer concentrates on character studies and on sly and subtle satires of the European middle class. Often there is not much action in a Rohmer film. Instead the camera is used as a psychological probe revealing the characters' self-deceptions. Or as one critic puts it, Rohmer is concerned with the "confrontation between word and image." He endows images with an "introspective aura" and words with vivid imagery. Consequently, his films often have an architectural feel that has been compared to the elaborate tableaux of French 18th-century paintings.

In a 1988 interview Rohmer referred to himself as a director-architect who is creating a stage for events and characters who are already latent in the world. In other words, he sees the world as incipiently aesthetic, as having a beautiful potentiality his films fulfill. Thus dialogue in a Rohmer film becomes a way of illustrating the landscape, and the characters become, so to speak, part of the scenery. If this sometimes makes for slow-moving cinema, it also conveys a depth of vision that lingers long after the film's plot fades from memory. He works in "film cycles," including six moral tales, the four seasons, and six films in the comedies and proverbs series. His latest film is 1998's *Conte d'Automne*.

1988 (PG) 102m/C *FR* Emmanuelle Chaulet, Sophie Renoir, Eric Viellard, Francois-Eric Gendron, Anne-Laure Meury; *D:* Eric Rohmer; *W:* Eric Rohmer; *C:* Bernard Lutic; *M:* Jean-Louis Valero. **VHS, LV** *ORI*

THE BOYS OF ST. VINCENT

A two-part, three-and-a-half hour film originally made for Canadian television, *The Boys of St. Vincent* is based on an actual case in which scores of children were abused for years in a Catholic orphanage. Legal proceedings started by those accused in the actual case were successful in delaying its broadcast, but the complete film surfaced at the 1993 Telluride Film Festival, where critics and festivalgoers were overpowered by the electrifying performance of Henry Czerny as the monstrous Brother Peter Lavin. Molesting little boys like clockwork and then terrorizing all the children into keeping quiet when police finally investigate, Lavin is portrayed not as the usual, pathetic, multi-sided, tortured soul who wants someone to stop him, but as a consummately evil, arrogant monster, believing himself to be fully above the laws of god and man. It's a great performance, and Czerny never lets it get away from him. As the swaggering, arrogant tyrant who enjoyed lording over his little boys in a Newfoundland orphanage in 1975, he's right up there with the great movie monsters, but vastly more alarming. He's equally impressive in the more demanding second half, set 15 years after the molestations, when Lavin—now married with sons of his own—is finally going to be tried for his crimes and is furious to find himself backed into a corner and running out of lies. The cumulative impact of this picture gets to you, and it feels—appropriately—like an ordeal. Never released to commercial theatres in the U.S. (only non-profit theatres were licensed to exhibit it), it did play in a cut version on cable, and was eventually aired in its entirety by the CBC.

NEXT STOP . . . *The 400 Blows, The Mystery of Kaspar Hauser, M*

1993 186m/C *CA* Henry Czerny, Johnny Morina, Sebastian Spence, Brian Dodd, David Hewlett, Jonathan Lewis, Jeremy Keefe, Phillip Dinn, Brian Dooley, Greg Thomey, Michael Wade, Lise Roy, Timothy Webber, Kristine Demers, Ashley Billard, Sam Grana; *D:* John N. Smith; *W:* Sam Grana, John N. Smith, Des Walsh; *C:* Pierre Letarte; *M:* Neil Smolar. Nominations: Independent Spirit Awards '95: Best Foreign Film. **VHS** *NYF*

THE BRAINIAC
El Baron del Terror
Baron of Terror

Abel Salazar produced a series of horror films in Mexico in the late 1950s and 1960s, and while it would be fair to categorize most of them as truly terrible, some of them—such as *Curse of the Doll People* and *The Brainiac*—have a nightmarish quality that's not easy to dismiss. This one has a plot about a centuries-old sorcerer who continues to survive by devouring the brains of the descendants of his executioners. Sometimes he uses a long, forked tongue to ingest his cranial nourishment, and sometimes he simply eats them out of a dish with a spoon—at least as

I remember it. I get the feeling that these pictures (dubbed) were heavily edited for American release, making the silly stories even more incoherent. Yet a nightmare with imagery this ... well, disgusting, can sometimes be even more effective when the plot makes no sense at all. *The Brainiac* (*El Baron del Terror*) is outrageous enough to be my personal favorite of the series, but do take my rating as a warning to those who think that foreign cinema should be—pardon the expression—more *cerebral*.

NEXT STOP . . . *The Conqueror Worm, Black Sunday, Suspiria*

1961 75m/B *MX* Abel Salazar, Ariadne Welter, Mauricio Garces, Rosa Maria Gallardo, Ruben Rojo, German Robles; *D:* Chano Urueto; *W:* Frederick Curiel, Alfredo Torres Portillo; *C:* Jose Ortiz Ramos; *M:* Gustavo Cesar Carrion. **VHS** *SNC, MRV, HHT*

BREAKING THE WAVES

Fritz Lang is reputed to have said that the widescreen CinemaScope process was only fit for photographing snakes and funerals. If he had lived long enough, he would have included a happier image in that brief list: the face of Emily Watson. As Bess, the holy innocent and devoted wife in Lars von Trier's exhilarating and gloriously wacky *Breaking the Waves,* Watson is a woman whose love for her disabled husband, Jan (Stellan Skarsgärd) is so pure and all-encompassing that she's willing to do anything he wants to try to preserve their shattered intimacy. The fact that this includes sexual encounters with other men may disturb the residents of the small Scottish village where Jan and Bess were wed, but Bess's burning passion for her husband is of such magnitude that even her humiliation becomes something she's proud to bear, all the way to its logical end. How we know all this about Bess, and the reason that *Breaking the Waves* doesn't simply collapse under the weight of all that male-fantasy-disguised-as-religious-experience baggage, can be explained in those same two words: Emily Watson. Every time this risky, sexually frank fairy tale threatens to simply turn into a

Michel (Jean-Paul Belmondo) walks a Paris street with girlfriend Patricia (Jean Seberg) in *Breathless*.

long, silly parable about inner purity versus public hypocrisy, von Trier reminds us whose show this is. The supremely expressive face of this small woman is filmed in huge close-ups by von Trier, with a camera that is always in motion, suggesting the ocean of feeling that moves continually within her. You can't take your eyes off her, and Jan's obsession with her needs no explanation whatsoever; he knows he was the luckiest man in the world before the accident that left him paralyzed, and his fury and his passion collide in ways that make emotional sense. *Breaking the Waves* shouldn't work, but it does. It does despite an ending that seems out of character with the rest of the picture not because of the leap of faith that it requires, but because Emily Watson's face isn't on the screen. Jan misses her, but not as much as we do.

NEXT STOP . . . *Wings of Desire, Beauty and the Beast* (1946), *The Kingdom, Parts I & II*

1995 (R) 152m/C *DK FR* Emily Watson, Stellan Skarsgard, Katrin Cartlidge, Adrian Rawlins, Jean-Marc Barr, Sandra Voe, Udo Kier, Mikkel Gaup; *D:* Lars von Trier; *W:* Lars von Trier; *C:* Robby Muller; *M:* Joachim Holbek. Cannes Film Festival '96: Grand Jury Prize; Cesar Awards '97: Best Foreign Film; New York Film Critics Awards '96: Best Actress (Watson), Best Cinematography, Best Director (von Trier); National Society of Film Critics Awards '96: Best Actress (Watson), Best Cinematography, Best Director (von Trier), Best Film; Nominations: Academy Awards '96: Best Actress (Watson); British Academy Awards '96: Best Actress (Watson); Golden Globe Awards '97: Best Actress—Drama (Watson), Best Film—Drama; Independent Spirit Awards '97: Best Foreign Film. **VHS, Letterbox, Closed Caption** *EVE*

ᐯ BREATHLESS
A Bout de Souffle

French hoodlum and petty thug Michel (Jean-Paul Belmondo) is on the run from the law after shooting a cop and stealing a car. He hooks up with Patricia, a beautiful American girl (Jean Seberg) who hawks papers ("New York Herald *Tribune!*") on the Champs Élysées. They make love, they make faces, they kill some time, she turns him in. They're going nowhere, of course, but that's not the point; what excites them is that they're doing it fast. The pacing of *Breathless* (*Bout de Souffle* originally, which is more like "out of breath") is key because these amoral characters—who do what they want when they want to, whether it's killing, stealing, making love, or turning the other in—never stop for a second to contemplate cause and effect or their place in the world, unless it's to immediately satisfy themselves. Belmondo and Seberg looked great and had fun on the streets of Paris; the city was filmed with an electric immediacy and a restless camera by Raoul Coutard, and much of the editing is violently blunt. In his first feature, Godard dared to glamorize this beautiful, deadly couple without moralizing, and the effect was galvanizing. *Breathless* is generally regarded as the seminal film of the French New Wave, and it still feels revolutionary—and seductively dangerous—today. (It makes sense that Godard was Warren Beatty's original choice to direct his 1967 *Bonnie and Clyde*.) *Breathless* is famously dedicated to the American "poverty row" studio Monogram Pictures, and features cameos by directors Philippe de Broca, Jean-Pierre Melville, and Godard himself (as a stool pigeon). The true story on which it was based was brought to Godard's attention by François Truffaut, who is credited with the story idea. (American director Jim McBride's 1983 remake starring Richard Gere wasn't exactly awful, but it was pointless.)

NEXT STOP . . . *Pierrot le Fou, Bonnie and Clyde, Gun Crazy* (1949)

1959 90m/B *FR* Jean-Paul Belmondo, Jean Seberg, Daniel Boulanger, Jean-Pierre Melville, Liliane Robin; *D:* Jean-Luc Godard; *W:* Jean-Luc Godard; *C:* Raoul Coutard; *M:* Martial Solal. Berlin International Film Festival '60: Best Director (Godard). **VHS** *NOS, MRV, CVC*

THE BRIDE WORE BLACK
La Mariee Etait en Noir

François Truffaut's obsession with the films of Alfred Hitchcock influenced his films in two separate and distinct ways. Many of Truffaut's most personal and inspired works—*The Soft Skin, The Wild Child, The Story of Adele H., The Woman Next Door*—possess the frighteningly intense, clear-eyed obsessiveness of Hitchcock at his peak. Others, like *Mississippi Mermaid, Fahrenheit 451,* and *The Bride Wore Black,* are more Hitchcockian in superficial ways—homages to the master, if you will; variously charming and touching as tokens of Truffaut's esteem, but in a manner more concerned with style than substance. Truffaut's 1968 *The Bride Wore Black,* based on a book by *Rear Window* author Cornell Woolrich (as was *Mississippi Mermaid*), is the story of a woman whose husband is killed on their wedding day, and whose life is transformed into an obsessive crusade to track down and dispatch those responsible. *The Bride Wore Black* is so filled with direct references to Hitchcock pictures—including a pulsating score by Bernard Herrmann—that it sometimes feels like *High Anxiety.* But Truffaut's genuine adoration of Hitchcock makes this tribute a heartfelt one, and Jeanne Moreau, who's quite wonderful here, smooths over any of our niggling misgivings with her usual, glorious panache.

NEXT STOP . . . *Rear Window, Jules and Jim, The Man Who Loved Women*

1968 107m/C *FR* Jeanne Moreau, Claude Rich, Jean-Claude Brialy, Michel Bouquet, Michael Lonsdale, Charles Denner, Daniel Boulanger; *D:* Francois Truffaut; *W:* Francois Truffaut, Jean-Louis Richard; *C:* Raoul Coutard; *M:* Bernard Herrmann. **VHS, LV** *MGM, MLB, FCT*

BRIEF ENCOUNTER
✓

Noel Coward's one-act play *Still Life* was the basis for David Lean's classy tearjerker about two strangers—both married—who meet by chance and gradually come to the realization that they've fallen in love. Celia Johnson and Trevor Howard broke moviegoers' hearts and made grown men—and women—sniffle in theatres the world over when they decided to do the right thing, to go home to their spouses and to never see each other again. (It's been described as the story of upper lips so stiff they're afraid to touch.) A good part of *Brief Encounter*'s continuing appeal is the audience's ability to vicariously share in the "nobility" of the lovers' decision, which constitutes a nearly foolproof gimmick. After all, if you're carrying on an affair yourself, you get to imagine for a moment what it must be like to be brave, courageous, and honorable; if you're not involved with someone else (and perhaps regretting it), you get to pride yourself on never having succumbed. Johnson and Howard's restrained performances help enormously, but it's Lean's elegant craftsmanship that ultimately saves the day, preventing Coward's supremely British domestic fairy tale from being an insufferably maudlin wallow, and turning it instead into a canny, satisfyingly guilty pleasure. If only Lean had lost the Rachmaninoff. (For a darker twist on a similar marital sacrifice, see Douglas Sirk's claustrophobic 1956 gem *There's Always Tomorrow,* with Fred MacMurray and Barbara Stanwyck.)

NEXT STOP . . . *Strangers on a Train, There's Always Tomorrow, Le Bonheur*

1946 86m/B *GB* Celia Johnson, Trevor Howard, Stanley Holloway, Cyril Raymond, Joyce Carey, Everley Gregg, Margaret Barton, Dennis Harkin, Valentine Dyall, Mar-

B

"Have a female fun time!"

—Tour organizer Simi (Shaheen Khan) in *Bhaji on the Beach.*

Young Nadia (Nadia Mikhalkov) enjoys life in the country in *Burnt by the Sun*.

jorie Mars, Irene Handl; *D:* David Lean; *W:* Noel Coward, David Lean, Ronald Neame, Anthony Havelock-Allan; *C:* Robert Krasker. New York Film Critics Awards '46: Best Actress (Johnson); Nominations: Academy Awards '46: Best Actress (Johnson), Best Director (Lean), Best Screenplay. **VHS** *PAR, HMV*

THE BURMESE HARP

Harp of Burma
Birumano Tategoto

Director Kon Ichikawa's exquisite, heartfelt 1956 film—set in Burma at the close of World War II—is the story of a Japanese private who finds himself emotionally unprepared for Japan's defeat, as well as for the unimaginable death and destruction around him. Almost instinctively, he undergoes a religious experience that causes him to refuse to return to his defeated homeland, choosing instead to remain behind and face the massive task of burying the dead. The private's obsession at first seems a kind of national penance, in which an individual suddenly awakens to the results of a collective madness; as it continues, however, *The Burmese Harp* becomes a universal act of grieving for the human and emotional toll taken by all wars, on all sides. In addition to the private's obsession, Ichikawa himself was reportedly obsessed with committing Michio Takeyama's novel to film, and despite the praise and near-classic status with which it was greeted, the director chose to make the picture yet again in 1985.

NEXT STOP . . . *Enjo, Fires on the Plain, Rhapsody in August*

1956 115m/B *JP* Shoji Yasui, Rentaro Mikuni, Tatsuya Mihashi, Tanie Kitabayashi, Yunosuke Ito; *D:* Kon Ichikawa; *W:* Natto Wada; *C:* Minoru Yokoyama; *M:* Akira Ifukube. Nominations: Academy Awards '56: Best Foreign-Language Film. **VHS, LV** *CVC, TPV*

BURN!
Quemimada!

"Very often, between one historical period and another, ten years suddenly might be enough to reveal the contradictions of a whole century. And so often we have to realize that our judgments, and our interpretations—and even our hopes—may have been wrong." So says Sir William Walker (Marlon Brando), the British agent who's sent to a Portugese-controlled Caribbean island in 1845 to help ensure the success of a slave revolt, by any means necessary. After doing so, the island's residents continue to suffer for ten more years, this time under the yoke of their British "liberators." Gillo Pontecorvo (*The Battle of Algiers*) directed this extraordinarily intelligent action epic about the deadly cycle of colonialism, which was released during the height of the Vietnam war. Dumped unceremoniously into the American marketplace by its distributor, *Burn!* nevertheless quickly found a cult following and remains an amazingly potent piece of work. Brando is extraordinary as the imperious Walker (in 1969 he was still years away from his official "comeback" in *The Godfather*), but just as impressive is non-professional actor Evaristo Marquez as the slave who Brando hand-picks to lead his anti-Portugese revolt, but who years later finds himself fighting against his former "teacher." Marcello Gatti's color cinematography is lush and intoxicating, and Ennio Morricone's score is one of his most memorable. An overlooked classic.

NEXT STOP . . . *The Battle of Algiers, I Am Cuba, The Dogs of War*

1970 (PG) 112m/C *IT* Marlon Brando, Evarist Marquez, Renato Salvatori; *D:* Gillo Pontecorvo; *C:* Marcello Gatti; *M:* Ennio Morricone. **VHS, LV, Letterbox** *MGM, CRC, FCT*

BURNT BY THE SUN
Outomlionnye Solntsem

Nikita Mikhalkov's seductive film takes place at a lively, warm, well-lived-in Russian country estate in 1936. It's a year in which many of the old veterans of the Revolution (one of whom is the head of this household, played by Mikhalkov himself) are taking the nation's direction for granted and are letting their guard down, not yet fully aware of the nightmare that Stalin was about to create. It's in this Chekhovian setting that Mikhalkov and his wife and daughter are visited by a mysterious stranger, as well as by an even more mysterious plague of fireballs, which race through the sky, zip in and out of windows, and just do not look like good omens at all. *Burnt by the Sun* is an easy-to-take cautionary tale about resting on one's laurels and the dangers of ceasing to be vigilant, and on that level it's a sobering experience. As drama, however, it tends to cross the border at some point from being leisurely to flaccid, and at two-and-a-half hours the picture seems like a long slog. The part of Mikhalkov's daughter is played by the enchanting young Nadia Mikhalkov, real-life daughter of the director; she neatly steals every scene that she's in. (When *Burnt by the Sun* won the Oscar for Best Foreign Language Film, it was Nadia who charmed the L.A. crowd when she and her dad made their acceptance speech together.)

NEXT STOP . . . *A Slave of Love, Oblomov, Close to Eden*

1994 (R) 134m/C *RU FR* Nikita Mikhalkov, Ingeborga Dapkounaite, Oleg Menshikov, Nadia Mikhalkov, Andre Oumansky, Viatcheslav Tikhonov, Svetlana Krioutchkova, Vladimir Ilyine; *D:* Nikita Mikhalkov; *W:* Nikita Mikhalkov, Rustam Ibragimbekov; *C:* Vilen Kalyuta; *M:* Eduard Artemyev. Academy Awards '94: Best Foreign Film; Cannes Film Festival '94: Grand Jury Prize; Nominations: Australian Film Institute '96: Best Foreign Film; British Academy Awards '95: Best Foreign Film. **VHS, LV** *COL*

BUTTERFLY KISS

I've been waiting in vain for Michael Winterbottom to make another film as original and subversive as *Butterfly Kiss,* but then again, with material this strong, maybe once is enough. Amanda Plummer is Eunice, a woman who roams the English countryside murdering women after asking them if their name is Judith. Eunice is a mess; she wears chains under her clothing and is pierced in places that must hurt. She is, in fact, obsessed with punishment—both inflicting it on others and on herself. Eventually, *Butterfly Kiss* turns into a strange love story between Eunice and a woman named Miriam (Saskia Reeves), whom Eunice has elected not to kill. Some of this film will be hard to watch—simply on a graphic level—for many viewers. But if you're able to mesh with this director's sensibilities, the surprisingly human—and often appallingly funny—undercurrent of *Butterfly Kiss* might surprise you. Plummer is electrifying, engaging, and terrifying throughout, and she (fortunately) never has to do a scene in which she explains or justifies her disorder or her behavior. There she is, and that's that. That was enough for me, but one viewing will do it, thank you very much.

NEXT STOP . . . *Henry: Portrait of a Serial Killer, Badlands, The Vanishing*

1994 90m/C *GB* Amanda Plummer, Saskia Reeves, Paul Brown, Des McAleer, Ricky Tomlinson; *D:* Michael Winterbottom; *W:* Frank Cottrell Boyce; *C:* Seamus McGarvey; *M:* John Harle. **VHS** *FRF*

BYE BYE BRAZIL

A traveling company of entertainers—whose ragged costumes and refusal to throw in the towel can be seen as the very definition of trouper—make their way over the paved and dirt roads of tiny Brazilian towns and villages, putting on shows, collecting what money they can, picking up an occasional hitchhiker, and moving on. The shows themselves aren't much, even for these small-town, generally impoverished audiences who haven't been to Vegas lately, yet the troupe is able to create a genuine, unique magic out of the sheer fabric of their show-business spirits. Creating a neat bit of magic himself, director Carlos Diegues uses his troupe as a kind of metaphor for the way the soul of his country is responding to external change and Americanization, but he pulls it all off so sweetly that *Bye Bye Brazil* rarely seems rueful or angry. Even a moment in which an entire town is too preoccupied to come to the traveling carnival because they're all entranced by the town's single TV set is more than offset by a more theatrical but less technological wonder: an indoor

dusting of fake snowflakes, falling to the accompaniment of *der Bingle* crooning "White Christmas." If Americanization is inevitable, Diegues seems to suggest, there's no reason to not get there in style.

NEXT STOP . . . *Quilombo, The Traveling Players, Kings of the Road*

1979 115m/C *BR* Jose Wilker, Betty Faria, Fabio Junior, Zaira Zambello; *D:* Carlos Diegues; *W:* Carlos Diegues; *M:* Chico Buarque. **VHS, LV** *FXL, TPV*

THE CABINET OF DR. CALIGARI
Das Cabinet des Dr. Caligari

In the early 19th century, Dr. Caligari (Werner Krauss) exhibits a sleepwalker, Cesare (Conrad Veidt), at a carnival. Soon after, a murder takes place and it is Caligari, the "master" of Cesare, who is the chief suspect. Before long, however, it's discovered that Caligari is actually the director of a nearby insane asylum, but is himself quite insane. But wait! As those who have seen *The Cabinet of Dr. Caligari* will remember, everything we have seen up until that point of revelation turned out to be the fantasy of a *real* inmate in that same asylum, who has imagined that the hospital's director (Krauss) is the dreaded "Dr. Caligari." It's all simpler than it sounds, but the plot is not what makes Robert Wiene's film a landmark (admittedly, some aspects of the plot, such as those that touch on blind obedience to authority, are ripe for study when examining German film history). The expressionist style of the film was the brainchild not of Wiene but of the film's producer Erich Pommer, who wanted to bring to the cinema an example of the expressionist movement taking hold in the art world at the time. The result was the movie's extraordinary visual representation of madness through the use of distorted and twisted streets, doorways, windows, and rooms, as well as makeup that provided a ghostly and terrifying approximation of a nightmare. Though it was made on a low budget and directed by Wiene in generally pedestrian fashion, it is the ingenious and daring visual design of *The Cabinet of Dr. Caligari* that makes it the head-turning shot from a starter pistol that began the race toward a new era of cinematic expression. A pointless Hollywood remake was done in 1962.

NEXT STOP... *The Last Laugh, A Page of Madness, Invaders from Mars* (1953)

1919 92m/B *GE* Conrad Veidt, Werner Krauss, Lil Dagover, Friedrich Feher, Hans von Twardowski, Rudolf Klein-Rogge, Rudolf Lettinger; **D:** Robert Wiene; **W:** Carl Mayer, Hans Janowitz; **C:** Willy Hameister. **VHS, LV** *KIV, REP, MRV*

CACTUS

Australia's Paul Cox created one of his most elliptical and mysterious films in *Cactus,* the story of a woman who has to decide whether or not to have one of her eyes removed so as to possibly preserve the remaining vision in the other. Isabelle Huppert plays the woman, whose dilemma is caused by an accident while she's on vacation in Australia. Things become even more complicated when Huppert falls in love with a man who's blind (Robert Menzies). For Cox, her choice is a jumping off point for larger questions of love and commitment, as well as a contemplation of the subject with which so many filmmakers are obsessed: the way in which we see the world, and how we interpret what we see. Though one of his less well-focused efforts (no pun intended—really), *Cactus* is still a deeply thought-provoking work from one Australia's least-known but most gifted directors. With Norman Kaye and Sheila Florance (*A Woman's Tale*).

NEXT STOP... *My First Wife, Man of Flowers, A Woman's Tale*

1986 95m/C *AU* Isabelle Huppert, Robert Menzies, Monica Maughan, Sheila Florance, Norman Kaye, Banduk Marika; **D:** Paul Cox; **W:** Norman Kaye, Paul Cox, Bob Ellis; **C:** Yuri Sokol; **M:** Giovanni Pergolese, Yannis Markopolous, Elsa Davis. **VHS** *ORI*

CAFÉ AU LAIT
Metisse

Lola (Julie Mauduech) is an 18-year-old West Indian woman living in Paris, who happily discovers that she's pregnant. Not quite as happy, however, are Julie's two boyfriends, Jamal (Hubert Kounde) and Felix (Mathieu Kassovitz, the versatile star of *A Self-Made Hero*), who are as miserable in each other's company as they are wondering which of them is the father. In the interest of fairness, the two men—one black and the son of diplomats, one Jewish and without a cent—finally decide to put their petty squabbles aside and move in with Lola, to help share in their parental responsibilities. *Café au Lait* was written and directed by Kassovitz (his directorial debut) in a breezy, colorful, romantic fashion that feels like a calculated nose-thumbing at societal conventions. Such formulas can sometimes be miscalculated, however, and while the relatively harmless *Café au Lait*'s heart is most assuredly in the right place, the picture pulls off the unusual feat of being both preachy *and* uncomfortably stereotypical in its characterizations and conclusions. A new wave *Brigitte Loves Bernie/Abie's Irish Rose* with a healthy dose of *Jules and Jim* tossed in, *Café au Lait* is intended to be both liberated and liberating, but it feels mighty familiar. (Kassovitz seems to have anticipated *She's Gotta Have It* popping into the viewer's mind by having Lola accuse Felix of thinking he's in a Spike Lee picture.)

NEXT STOP... *Jules and Jim, She's Gotta Have It, La Haine (Hate)*

1994 94m/C *FR* Mathieu Kassovitz, Julie Mauduech, Hubert Kounde, Vincent Cassel, Tadek Lokcinski, Jany Holt; **D:** Mathieu Kassovitz; **W:** Mathieu Kassovitz; **C:** Pierre Aim; **M:** Marie Daulne, Jean-Louis Daulne. **VHS** *NYF*

CAMILLE CLAUDEL

In the late 19th century, the gifted sculptress Camille Claudel (Isabelle Adjani), desperate for artistic success and obsessively involved with the womanizing sculptor Auguste Rodin (Gérard Depardieu), descends further and further into emotional instability, ultimately ending her life in an asylum. Though it's ostensibly the brutally insensitive treatment she receives at the hands of her ego-

maniacal lover Rodin that causes Camille's mental breakdown, she's depicted as wacko from the movie's opening frames. On her hands and knees in a pit of mud, digging for the best clay for sculpting, we understand that Camille's frantic flailing and her huffing and puffing is supposed to symbolize the essence of a dedicated, possessed artist searching for the truth in the dirt—but Adjani's bug-eyed, operatic frenzy torpedoes any possibility of multiple meanings. She just looks nuts. With the lead character opening the film at this kind of fever pitch, there's no way for the first-time director, cinematographer Bruno Nuytten, to modulate her escalating madness. We spend much of the film's two-and-a-half hours (cut down from nearly three) watching her slapping and pounding mud, as if the intensity of her blows were indicative of the power of the genius within (the Academy must have believed it—she got an Oscar nomination for Best Actress).

Depardieu provides a bit of a respite, though it's embarrassing to identify with him when you know he'd like to see the lead character carted off. Adjani may have felt that this project—and the character she plays—had much in common with her Adele Hugo in Truffaut's *The Story of Adele H*. But where that film took the viewer every step of the way along a remarkable internal journey, *Camille Claudel* is as stiff as one of the real Camille's sculptures—and far less expressive.

NEXT STOP . . . *Isadora (The Loves of Isadora), Savage Messiah, Edvard Munch, Artemisia*

1989 (R) 149m/C FR Isabelle Adjani, Gerard Depardieu, Laurent Grevill, Alain Cuny, Madeleine Robinson, Katrine Boorman; **D:** Bruno Nuytten; **W:** Bruno Nuytten, Marilyn Goldin; **C:** Pierre Lhomme; **M:** Gabriel Yared. Cesar Awards '89: Best Actress (Adjani), Best Art Direction/Set Decoration, Best Cinematography, Best Costume Design, Best Film; Nominations: Academy Awards '89: Best Actress (Adjani), Best Foreign-Language Film. **VHS, LV** *ORI, IME*

CAMP DE THIAROYE
The Camp at Thiaroye

As World War II was coming to an end, black Senegalese troops who had been fighting in the French Army were brought back to Senegal by the French and confined in "transit camps" for what stretched into an interminable and inexcusable period of time. Many of these men—those fortunate enough to have survived the war—had not only been fighting heroically for the French, but had been captured and placed in Nazi prison camps during their service. Now that their usefulness to the French cause was over, however, the system of "transit camps" that the French created soon revealed itself as simply a thinly veiled way of reestablishing the old colonialist formula of white domination. Ousmane Sembène's majestic and moving 1987 epic about a bloody rebellion at one such camp is one of the least-seen but most important of the great Senegalese director's works, and it chronicles a singular event in modern African history about which far too little is written. Co-directed with Thierno Faty Sow.

NEXT STOP . . . *Black Girl, Emitai, Ceddo*

1987 147m/C Sijiri Bakaba, Dansogho Camara, Pierre Orma, Ibrahim Sane, Jean-Daniel Simon; *D:* Ousmane Sembene, Thierno Faty Sow; *W:* Ousmane Sembene, Thierno Faty Sow; *C:* Ismail Lakhdar Hamina; *M:* Ismaila Lo. *NYR*

THE CANTERBURY TALES

The second of Pier Paolo Pasolini's Medieval Trilogy is the one best forgotten. It consists of four Chaucerian episodes, which, rather amazingly, all manage to miss the mark. The movie has a mean-spiritedness and graphically unpleasant tone, which feels more like a dare than a daring reinterpretation. In a modest and self-effacing bit of casting, Pasolini himself plays Chaucer; others in the largely wasted cast include Hugh Griffith, Laura Betti, and Jenny Runacre. *Arabian Nights* and *The Decameron* are more fun, more substantial, and less gratuitously vicious.

NEXT STOP . . . *Arabian Nights, Mamma Roma, Fellini Satyricon*

1971 109m/C *IT* Laura Betti, Ninetto Davoli, Pier Paolo Pasolini, Hugh Griffith, Josephine Chaplin, Michael Balfour, Jenny Runacre; *D:* Pier Paolo Pasolini. Berlin International Film Festival '72: Golden Berlin Bear. **VHS** *WBF*

CAPTAIN CONAN
Capitaine Conan

In 1918, as World War I nears its end, a band of French soldiers—fierce, despondent, dazed, disease-ridden, and lusting for revenge—refuses to stop fighting. Slogging through the mud in Bulgaria, this small regiment doesn't find out about the end of the war until months after the armistice, which only increases their frustration and rage. Based on a true and long-forgotten chapter of French history as chronicled in a 1934 autobiographical novel by Roger Vercel, this is a compassionate and gripping portrait of the tragic choices even honorable men can make when existing under savage conditions. *Capitaine Conan* is like a large-scale epic as seen through a microscope—while spectacle and horror are a major part of the landscape, the actual focus is on those private, instantaneous moments of judgment that we make, for better or worse, in the midst of chaos. *Capitaine Conan*'s director, Bertrand Tavernier, is one of France's most humane and generous-spirited national treasures. On this occasion at least, the French film industry recognized that fact by awarding the film the César (France's Oscar) for Best Picture of the Year.

NEXT STOP . . . *Life and Nothing But, Béatrice, Paths of Glory*

1996 129m/C *FR* Philippe Torreton, Samuel Lebihan, Bernard Le Coq, Pierre Val, Francois Berleand, Claude Rich, Catherine Rich; *D:* Bertrand Tavernier; *W:* Bertrand Tavernier, Jean Cosmos; *C:* Alain Choquart; *M:* Oswald D'Andrea. Cesar Awards '97: Best Actor (Torreton), Best Director (Tavernier), Best Film. **VHS, Letterbox** *KIV*

HENRI LANGLOIS

Though I was only 15, I had already been a film enthusiast for some time when my parents took my sister and me on our first European vacation in the fall of 1965. We were scheduled to spend just two days in Paris, so on arrival I immediately cajoled my father into accompanying me to the legendary Cinémathèque Française located in the Pallais de Chaillot, not far from the Eiffel Tower.

After a search through what seemed like an awful lot of vegetation, we spotted a small flight of stairs leading down to a set of open doors. Inside we saw no crowds—only a rotund, imposingly large man in casual, rumpled clothing whose longish, stringy hair flopped back and forth as he energetically pushed a broom over the floor. This man, who was obviously a janitor, looked up and began speaking in—of all things—*French*. He then put down his broom and said something in broken English about an Eisenstein exhibit, gestured around the room, and said that there were no films showing, but we could look around. Afterward, he *smiled* and told us to return sometime.

Three years later, when I read about the French government's unsuccessful efforts at ousting Langlois from his position as head of the Cinémathèque, American papers ran his photo. It was the "janitor," of course, and even without knowing all the facts of the *affaire Langlois* I immediately understood why the French film world came to a screeching halt to ensure that this great and triumphantly non-bureaucratic rescuer of endangered films would continue in his post.

Born in 1914, little Henri's early fascination with moving pictures led him to begin collecting discarded films and storing them in his family's apartment, until—as legend has it—films cans in the bathtub were interfering with his family's hygiene. They got a bigger place. He saved every reel of film he could get his hands on, knowing instinctively that it was *all* to be saved, and that debates on quality and artistic importance could only take place if the films existed to be argued about.

In 1936 he and Georges Franju founded the Cinémathèque Française, which would eventually consist of thousands of films acquired in almost as many ways as there were titles. Langlois wasn't satisfied to simply collect; he *showed* the films in the Cinémathèque's collection, and his brilliantly eclectic programming influenced a generation of French filmmakers who were, in effect, the children of the Cinémathèque—Jean-Luc Godard, François Truffaut, Claude Chabrol, Jacques Demy, Eric Rohmer, Jacques Rivette and so many others. His love for American films, and his championing of so many great artists who had been underappreciated at home changed the face of film criticism and scholarship, and influenced every aspect of the so-called "film generation."

Langlois died in 1977. During much of his career, his unusual and eccentric managerial and curatorial methods came under much criticism, but if a man is to judged by the results of his labors, then Langlois—who by saving *everything* he possibly could helped to preserve much of the cinema's history for future generations—was a complete and shining success. His work didn't go unappreciated in his lifetime; in 1974 he received a special, honorary Academy Award for his achievements, and was described at the ceremony by Jack Valenti as "the conscience of the cinema."

CAPTAIN'S PARADISE

Alec Guinness redefines compartmentalizing in this charming, lightweight British farce from 1953. He's the sailor with a girl in every port, but there are only two ports, and the two girls are both his wives. *Brief Encounter's* Celia Johnson is the respectable, traditional British wife who keeps their neat, genteel home in Gibraltar, and Yvonne De Carlo provides a considerably more spicy brand of domesticity whenever Guinness docks in Morocco. The implication of course is that the two women are symbolic of that eternal dual-circuit impulse every man is reputed to have about what he wants in a woman—and what he wants in a wife. The captain's blissful bigamy is the not-so-simple answer to having it all. *Captain's Paradise* eventually wears a little thin, particularly when old boy's two worlds threaten to collide, but the performers provide enormously compensating fun along the way. (The theme of one man obsessed with two very different women must have been dear to the heart of *Captain's Paradise* author Alec Coppel, for five years later he would co-author the great screenplay of *Vertigo* for Alfred Hitchcock. Of the two, it was *Captain's Paradise* for which Coppel received an Oscar nomination.)

NEXT STOP . . . *Monsieur Verdoux, Kind Hearts and Coronets, The Lavender Hill Mob*

1953 89m/B *GB* Alec Guinness, Yvonne De Carlo, Celia Johnson, Miles Malleson, Nicholas Phipps, Ferdinand "Ferdy" Mayne, Sebastian Cabot; **D:** Anthony Kimmins; **W:** Alec Coppel, Nicholas Phipps; **C:** Edward Scaife; **M:** Malcolm Arnold. Nominations: Academy Awards '53: Best Story. **VHS** *FCT*

CARAVAGGIO

By combining the familiar shape and structure of Hollywood biography with a vividly bold, colorful, avant-garde visual design, Derek Jarman won over many of his detractors with this elegant, entertaining, and engagingly witty dissection of the life, art, and passion of Caravaggio. The film opens in 1610 when, near death, Caravaggio reflects back on scenes from a life in which many of the same issues that have affected young artists throughout the centuries—money, commitment, independence, sexuality—parade through his memory in a series of revealing, Caravaggio-influenced *chiaroscuro* tableaux. Nigel Terry makes a riveting and full-bodied Caravaggio, Sean Bean plays Ranuccio, the model Caravaggio adored both on and off the canvas, and Tilda Swinton (*Orlando, Female Perversions*) is Lena, Ranuccio's lover and the model for Caravaggio's Magdalene. Neatly packaging a great deal of information—and perhaps a few too many assumptions—into its 93 minutes, this is one of the few biographical films about an artist that offers more than a simple by-the-numbers tour, leaving the viewer tantalized rather than saturated.

NEXT STOP . . . *Edward II, Wittgenstein, Blue (Jarman)*

1986 97m/C *GB* Nigel Terry, Sean Bean, Tilda Swinton; **D:** Derek Jarman; **W:** Derek Jarman; **C:** Gabriel Beristain; **M:** Simon Fisher. **VHS, LV** *TPV, FCT, CCN*

CAREFUL

In a mythical Alpine valley, ominously surrounded by steep, ice-covered mountains, lives a population of bizarrely dysfunctional, pathologically repressed villagers who speak only in hushed of tones due to their constant fear of causing a catastrophic avalanche. With this mass anxiety at the core of their daily existence, the villagers logically but disastrously evolve into a society that exists for the sole purpose of taking no risks. It's a funny idea, but avant-garde Winnipeg director Guy Maddin does a great deal more with it than simply going for cheap laughs. *Careful* is an ingenious, absurd, visionary work of filmmaking that will enthrall as many people as it will exasperate. Maddin's hallucinatory/stoned/expressionist style is inspired by lots of sources: the German "mountain" films of the early 1930s, Fritz Lang, Georges Melies, Ed Wood. Yet these influences don't begin to suggest the essence of Maddin's true originality; he's come as close as any other filmmaker to putting dreams on screen, and those—when seen while awake—can be alternately hilarious, breathtaking, silly and terrifying. Maddin's refusal to conform to filmmaking norms or audience expectations seems all the more startling in the context of the movie's theme—*Careful* is anything but. It could be the nightmare of someone who ate too much bratwurst and beer during some grotesque, unending *Oktoberfest,* and who then fell asleep on the couch while watching television public service announcements for safe sex. The visual artificiality, the scratchy, flat soundtrack, the wildly exaggerated acting all breeze past any hint of "camp" in the first few minutes, and then drop us squarely into an unexplored, satirical, dangerous realm of the cinematic unconscious.

NEXT STOP . . . *Tales from the Gimli Hospital, Archangel, The Tenant*

1994 100m/C Kyle McCulloch, Gosia Dobrowolska, Jackie Burroughs, Sarah Neville, Brent Neale, Paul Cox, Victor Cowie, Michael O'Sullivan, Vince Rimmer, Katya Gardner; *D:* Guy Maddin; *W:* Guy Maddin, George Toles; *C:* Guy Maddin; *M:* John McCulloch. **VHS** *KIV*

CAREFUL, HE MIGHT HEAR YOU

Careful, He Might Hear You is based on an autobiographical novel by Sumner Locke Elliot, who during the 1930s as a six-year old boy was the object of a custody fight between two of his aunts, both of whom had very different reasons for wanting the youngster. When director Carl Schultz was preparing the project, he knew that he wanted the disorientation and emotional vulnerability of the boy to be the movie's focus, so he made the crucial decision to design the entire film from the child's point-of-view. It's a risky move, of course, and the kind of thing that can become cutesy and precious when handled badly, but *Careful, He Might Hear You* manages to avoid the most obvious trap of over-romanticizing a child's universe. The other-worldly quality that seems totally at home in many of the films from Australia and New Zealand is nicely suited to this story of a child (Nicolas Gled-

hill) growing up with a strange, distant, and very beautiful new aunt (Wendy Hughes). Yet even though the images have a way of creeping into your memory and staying put, the film as a whole has a naggingly schematic feel, and never really connects emotionally. One more note of caution: much of the dreamy lyricism of *Careful, He Might Hear You* can be attributed to its exquisite widescreen images. Many of these will lose their impact on video.

NEXT STOP . . . *My Brilliant Career, An Angel at My Table, Two Friends*

1984 (PG) 113m/C *AU* Nicholas Gledhill, Wendy Hughes, Robyn Nevin, John Hargreaves; *D:* Carl Schultz; *W:* Michael Jenkins; *C:* John Seale; *M:* Ray Cook. Australian Film Institute '83: Best Actress (Hughes), Best Film. **VHS, Closed Caption** *FOX*

CARMEN

The centerpiece of Spanish director Carlos Saura's trilogy of dance films—which included *Blood Wedding* and *El Amor Brujo*—was the most popular of the three, and with good reason. Cross-cutting between rehearsal and performance of the flamenco version of Bizet's opera, revealing the parallel stories of passion that exist on and off the stage, Saura reinforces the story of Carmen as an eternal, ever-contemporary legend of eroticism and tragedy. Saura and his choreographer/star Antonio Gades (playing a choreographer/star named Antonio) have enriched and stretched the borders of the musical film, even while conceiving it as a widely accessible entertainment. The stunning Laura Del Sol is the "ultimate" Carmen whom Gades becomes hopelessly enslaved by, and watching her dance we don't feel that his reaction is particularly extreme. *Carmen* is one of the rare movies in which filmed dance has the excitement and immediacy of live performance, and Saura knows instinctively how to edit with the intelligence and restraint required to keep from mangling the rhythm of the dances. This is terrific filmmaking.

NEXT STOP . . . Blood Wedding, El Amor Brujo, Flamenco

1983 (R) 99m/C *SP* Antonio Gades, Laura Del Sol, Paco DeLucia, Christina Hoyos; *D:* Carlos Saura; *W:* Antonio Gades, Carlos Saura; *C:* Teodoro Escamilla. British Academy Awards '84: Best Foreign Film; Nominations: Academy Awards '83: Best Foreign-Language Film. **VHS** *CTH*

CARNIVAL IN FLANDERS
La Kermesse Heroique

When the Spanish army invades Flanders in the early 17th century, the men of one small town act on their cowardly impulses by hiding; the women, however, prepare a feast—and themselves—to appease the invaders in high style. An amazingly frank sexual comedy that still startles today, *Carnival in Flanders* was directed in 1935 by Jacques Feyder, who later wasted no time in departing France ahead of the German invasion. Feyder was well aware that this subversive comic scenario for "collaboration" with—and distraction of—an occupying army would not have gone down well with the Nazi's propaganda machine. (It was in fact banned by Goebbels in 1939.) The production itself—wittily designed in the style of Breughel paintings like "The Wedding Dance"—was supervised by Marcel Carné (*Children of Paradise*) and photographed by Harry Stradling, who would go on the become one of Hollywood's most legendary cinematographers.

 **NEXT STOP . . .** *Children of Paradise, Rembrandt, Tous les Matins du Monde*

1935 90m/B *FR* Francoise Rosay, Louis Jouvet, Jean Murat, Andre Aleme, Micheline Cheirel; *D:* Jacques Feyder; *C:* Harry Stradling; *M:* Louis Beydts. New York Film Critics Awards '36: Best Foreign Film; Venice Film Festival '36: Best Director (Feyder). **VHS** *HTV, MRV, HHT*

CARO DIARIO
Dear Diary

Some movies—like certain wines—need to be consumed in their country of origin for their full flavor to be revealed. Put another way, some pictures just don't travel well, and that would seem to be the case with the gentle comic essays of Italy's acclaimed and popular (at home) Nanni Moretti, who is still largely unknown in the U.S. Despite its limited American release, Moretti's *Caro Diario* (*Dear Diary*) may be his best known film here, having been picked up for distribution after winning a Best Director Prize at Cannes. Though its pace proved too leisurely for American art house audiences, *Caro Diario* is an intriguing little three-part cinematic sketch pad of observations, confessions, and complaints. In the first section, Moretti (as Moretti) zips around Rome on his little motor scooter, at one point encountering Jennifer Beals on the street, and later visiting the spot where writer/director Pier Paolo Pasolini was murdered. Moretti travels south in the clever part two, to spend time with a friend whose aversion to television soon becomes an addiction. The final section reveals that Moretti has been battling skin cancer, but deals with the fact in the same dryly witty manner as the rest of the film's observations, refusing to milk it for sympathy. (Nevertheless, I remember mentally kicking myself at that point in the film for being impatient with the first section, and that subtle "guilt" factor may one reason that the film was distributed more widely than Moretti's other, equally good work). One inspired highlight in this generally sweet and insightful picture: Moretti reads a rave review of *Henry: Portrait of a Serial Killer*, buys a ticket, hates the picture, and then tracks down the critic, forcing him to listen to his own pretentious review. How could any reviewer of *Caro Diario* be unkind to such a humbling, cautionary tale?

 **NEXT STOP . . .** *Palombella Rossa, Fellini's Roma, Sherman's March*

1993 100m/C *IT* Nanni Moretti, Renato Carpentieri; *D:* Nanni Moretti; *W:* Nanni Moretti; *C:* Giuseppe Lanci; *M:* Nicola Piovani. Cannes Film Festival '94: Best Director (Moretti). **VHS, LV** *NLC*

CASANOVA '70

Marcello Mastroianni is an Italian NATO official who finds no challenge in seducing modern, emancipated women. Without external threats he is unable to achieve arousal, which leads him into a series of "dangerous" encounters, such as a female lion

tamer (*in* the cage, *with* her lions), a married woman (at her home, at the moment her husband is expected), and a peasant girl (he poses as a doctor to examine the girl, so that her family may be reassured that she's "pure"). Mario Monicelli's film was hardly inspired comedy to begin with, and it seems painfully dated today. Marcello's lively dedication keeps us watching, though, and it's fun to be reminded of just how stunning Virna Lisi was in her heyday. Look for director Marco Ferreri (*The Grande Bouffe*) in the role of Count Ferreri. Academy Award Nominee, Best Original Screenplay.

NEXT STOP . . . *Il Bell'Antonio, Yesterday, Today and Tomorrow, Alfredo, Alfredo*

1965 113m/C *IT* Marcello Mastroianni, Virna Lisi, Michele Mercier, Guido Alberti, Margaret Lee, Bernard Blier, Liana Orfei; **D:** Mario Monicelli; **W:** Tonino Guerra. Nominations: Academy Awards '65: Best Story & Screenplay. **VHS** *FOX*

THE CASE OF THE MUKKINESE BATTLE HORN

Thief uses brick to smash glass case containing priceless Mukkinese Battle Horn. Thief reaches into smashed case, picks up brick, and runs away. Thief's footsteps fade into the distance, stop, then return. Thief puts back brick, takes Mukkinese Battle Horn, runs away again. If you don't find this bit amusing, take a pass. If, on the other hand, this is just the sort of groan-inspiring that tickles you (I'm admittedly in that camp), then *The Case of the Mukkinese Battle Horn* will be a tasty and refreshing little reminder of the golden age of one school of very British comedy. The popular and gloriously demented *The Goon Show* was at its peak in Britain in the mid-'50s, and Peter Sellers and Spike Milligan collaborated on this short subject featuring the talents of much of the regular cast. It's awfully silly, and awfully funny. And what the hell—it's only 27 minutes.

NEXT STOP . . . *The Ladykillers, I'm All Right, Jack, And Now for Something Completely Different*

1956 27m/C *GB* Peter Sellers, Spike Milligan, Dick Emery; **M:** Edwin Astley. **VHS, 8mm** *VYY*

CASQUE D'OR
Golden Marie
Golden Helmet

Based on an actual murder case that took place in Paris in 1898, Jacques Becker's *Casque d'Or* (Golden Helmet) is both gangster film and period melodrama, as well as one of the great romantic epics of all time. The 31-year-old Simone Signoret is Marie, the woman known by her "golden helmet" of hair in the dance hall where she spends her evenings. It's in that small riverside establishment where she first meets her lover, Manda (Serge Reggiani); it's also where the unsavory leader of a gang known as *apaches*—who's in love with Marie himself—first marks Manda as his target. Becker's straightforward storytelling plunges us into the seamy and forbidding underworld of a Paris of the imagination; it's an assured and intoxicating work, though oddly enough it was in England where *Casque d'Or* first gained its deserved reputation as a masterpiece—the French were late to discover its timeless pull. Reggiani and Claude Dauphin are perfectly cast as the two men obsessed with Marie, but it's Simone Signoret who elevates *Casque d'Or* to a celestial plane—this is the performance of her life. (Another of Becker's masterworks has *still* not received the acclaim it deserves; his 1959 prison drama *Le Trou (The Hole)*—Becker's final film—is rarely screened today, and has yet to be released in the U.S.)

NEXT STOP . . . *Touchez Pas au Grisbi, Le Trou (The Hole), Room at the Top*

1952 96m/B *FR* Serge Reggiani, Simone Signoret, Claude Dauphin, Raymond Bussieres, Gaston Modot; **D:** Jacques Becker; **W:** Jacques Becker, Jacques Companeez; **C:** Robert Le Febvre; **M:** Georges Van Parys. **VHS** *FCT*

CAT AND MOUSE
Le Chat et la Souris

When a woman's rich, unfaithful husband turns up dead, the hard-boiled and exceedingly unorthodox Inspector Lechat (get it?) is determined to track down his prey. Claude Lelouch's lighthearted, picturesque *policier* is more enjoyable than it has a right to be, but just give in and enjoy the vivid Parisian scenery, not to mention the all-in-fun scenery-chewing from veterans Serge Reggiani, Jean-Pierre Aumont, Michèle Morgan, and Philippe Léotard. *Cat and Mouse* was a hit in France in 1975, but it only found release in the U.S. three years later thanks to the unexpected stateside success of Lelouch's 1978 comedy *Robert et Robert*. For those of us who tended to dismiss Lelouch in the 1970s for seeming out of touch with serious themes and the world's social turmoil, it just might be time to reassess some of his breezy and energetic genre entertainments such as the painlessly pleasurable *Cat and Mouse*.

NEXT STOP . . . *A Man and a Woman, The Crook, And Now My Love*

1978 (PG) 107m/C *FR* Michele Morgan, Serge Reggiani, Jean-Pierre Aumont, Philippe Labro, Philippe Leotard, Valerie Lagrange, Michel Perelon, Christine Laurent; **D:** Claude Lelouch; **W:** Claude Lelouch; **C:** Andre Perlstein; **M:** Francis Lai. **VHS** *COL*

CEDDO

Ceddo (translated loosely as "the feudal class") is unquestionably one of the most important films yet produced in Africa—an engrossing and magnificent national epic that defines its culture at a particular moment in history. On the surface, *Ceddo* is a riveting and thoroughly entertaining political thriller; set in the 19th century, it concerns the kidnapping of a beautiful princess, whose status as hostage becomes a symbol in the standoff between opposing cultures in the face of religious expansion. On a deeper and more subtle level, though, Sembène's masterwork is a meditation on philosophy, fantasy, and militant politics, and its boldly imaginative structure includes at least two startling and boldly conceived leaps

"I don't know if I'm unhappy because I'm not free or not free because I'm unhappy."

—Patricia (Jean Seberg) to journalist in *Breathless*.

**Yves Montand and
Romy Schneider
star in Claude
Sautet's** *Cesar &
Rosalie.*

across the centuries. If there can be such a thing as a single modern film that resonates with nearly every aspect of the African experience, it is Sembène's *Ceddo.*

NEXT STOP . . . *Mandabi, Emitai, Xala*

1978 120m/C Matoura Dia, Ismaila Diagne, Tabata Ndiaye, Moustapha Yade; *D:* Ousmane Sembene; *W:* Ousmane Sembene; *C:* Georges Caristan; *M:* Manu Dibango. *NYR*

CÉLESTE

Percy Adlon's *Céleste* is based on the published memoirs of one Céleste Alberet, the woman who served as housekeeper to the reclusive, chronically ill Marcel Proust for the eight years leading up to his death in 1922. Wisely avoiding the temptation to resemble a miniature *Remembrance of Things Past,* or even to suggest a full portrait of the great writer's last years, *Céleste* instead is an impressionistic but unromanticized recreation of what one curious and intelligent woman observed in the everyday occurrences of Proust's life. If there are *madeleine*-style bites of information here that can lead to nuggets of literary revelation, they are hardly forced down our throats. In place of the standard creative artist biopic's insistence on linking specific events with artistic achievements, *Céleste* offers the pleasures of a keen observer's fascination with a flesh-and-blood man—albeit a mighty talented one. Adlon's film is refreshingly restrained in every way, as are the performances of Fassbinder discovery Eva Mattes as Céleste and Jürgen Arndt as Proust.

NEXT STOP . . . *The Bitter Tears of Petra von Kant, Stroszek, Swann in Love, Sugarbaby*

1981 107m/C *GE* Eva Mattes, Jurgen Arndt, Norbert Wartha, Wolf Euba; *D:* Percy Adlon; *W:* Percy Adlon; *C:* Jurgen Martin; *M:* Cesar Franck. **VHS** *NYF, FCT*

CELESTIAL CLOCKWORK
Mecaniques Celestes

A highly favorable but curiously defensive review of *Celestial Clockwork*—written by an otherwise invaluable and brilliantly perceptive critic—maintains that the film was approached with "suspicion" in cinema circles here because it was made by an unknown director. Had it been made by Almodóvar, the critic believes, the picture would have been widely acclaimed. Oh come on. Critics and public embraced *Cinema Paradiso* without ever having heard of Giuseppe Tornatore, and I doubt that *Il Postino* was so widely accepted because the public had been salivating for the new Michael Radford film. I doubt that most people (and probably a few critics) even *remember* the name of *Il Postino*'s director. The fact is that I found myself quite captivated during the first ten minutes or so of Fina Torres's colorful *Celestial Clockwork*—a modern-day remake of *Cinderella*—but soon I found that the movie's exhausting, frantic pace wasn't able to distract me from the one-note, plodding, episodic plot developments. Ariadna Gil is the woman who abandons her fiancee at the altar, jets off to Paris with hopes of becoming the next Maria Callas. There she encounters the rest of the fairy-tale cast, including an evil and jealous rival (the stunning Arielle Dombasle of *Pauline at the Beach*), a gay waiter, a lesbian psychiatrist, a witch doctor, and other assorted wacky characters who work so hard at being free spirits that they're just the opposite—and are trapped by the cliches of their conception. The title is a warning: this piece of aggressively feel-good, mechanical, by-the-numbers whimsy is indeed possessed of all the soul and spontaneity of clockwork.

NEXT STOP . . . *Orpheus, Donkey Skin, Cinderfella*

1994 85m/C *FR* Ariadna Gil, Arielle Dombasle, Evelyne Didi, Frederic Longbois, Lluis Homar, Michel Debrane; **D:** Fina Torres; **W:** Fina Torres; **C:** Ricardo Aronovich; **M:** Michel Musseau, Francois Farrugia. **VHS** *EVE*

CÉSAR

See *Fanny* (1932).

1936 117m/B *FR* Raimu, Pierre Fresnay, Orane Demazis, Charpin, Andre Fouche, Alida Rauffe; **D:** Marcel Pagnol; **W:** Marcel Pagnol; **M:** Vincent Scotto. **VHS, LV** *NOS, MRV, INT*

CÉSAR & ROSALIE

Claude Sautet is an anomaly as well as a magician. Here, as in so many of the delicately drawn love stories he's directed since 1970, there's no real "hook" to suggest that the familiar plotline—in this case a couple wrestling with the emotional turmoil of an old lover suddenly reappearing—is going to result in anything special. And yet Sautet knows that behind every cliche there's an interesting story. The challenge he's created for himself, and successfully met, is to show us the minute-to-minute motivations of his characters, making them comfortably and sympathetically human. The action in Sautet's films is the stuff that happens *between* scenes in most other movies; the tension comes not from whether successful industrialist César (Yves Montand) is going to stay with Rosalie (Romy Schneider), or whether she's going to run off with her old flame David (Sami Frey). *César & Rosalie* is about the ways in which love legitimizes decisions that make no sense on paper, and it's a tribute to the knowing, gentle hand of Claude Sautet that he's able to carry us along with these very human beings, never condescending to them even when an easy laugh is there for the taking. As in most of his work, this is a film without villains; what's more, Sautet has the wisdom to make such everyday emotions as love and regret seem positively heroic.

NEXT STOP . . . *Vincent, François, Paul and the Others, Un Coeur en Hiver, Nelly and Monsieur Arnaud*

1972 (PG) 110m/C *FR* Romy Schneider, Yves Montand, Sami Frey, Umberto Orsini; **D:** Claude Sautet; **W:** Jean-Loup Dabadie, Claude Neron, Claude Sautet; **C:** Jean Boffety; **M:** Philippe Sarde. **VHS, LV** *TPV*

THE CHANT OF JIMMIE BLACKSMITH

Set against the magnificent landscapes of New South Wales at the exact turn of the century, *The Chant of Jimmie Blacksmith* tells the story of a half-caste aborigine who's determined—through hard work and enormous resilience, even in the face of obscenely entrenched racism—to work within the limitations of his society in order to better his life. Jimmie is not by any means *accepting* of racism—nor is his good-natured half-brother, Mort—but he's got a grip on reality, and he understands where he is. He does the odd jobs and fence-building that he's hired to do, aware that he is paid less than white men but that he has no alternative. Insults, poverty, and general degradation are a way of life for him, and Jimmie's disgust at this inequity is obvious. Nevertheless, he continues out of necessity to play by rules he didn't make, withstanding treatment designed to grind his will into dust. One day, in an unplanned split-second, that changes. In the theatre where this film played in Detroit, that moment of reckoning provoked one viewer to hobble slowly to the lobby, where he fainted. His response was understandable. Jimmie's pent-up fury—the long-festering, undeniable fruit of racism—has to manifest itself somehow, and when it finally appears it takes the form of an unexpectedly shocking physical and emotional explosion. Based on a novel by *Schindler's List* author Thomas Keneally, *The Chant of Jimmie Blacksmith* was written for the screen and directed by Australia's Fred Schepisi, who has made a film so good, so instructive, and so necessary that it evokes astonishment. This is uncompromising, fabulously intelligent filmmaking that—once seen—will never be forgotten. (If at all possible, see the film in a letterboxed format; its majestic images and soundtrack contribute mightily to its epic impact.)

NEXT STOP . . . *The Devil's Playground, A Cry in the Dark, Do the Right Thing*

1978 (R) 120m/C *AU* Tommy Lewis, Bryan Brown, Ray Barrett, Elizabeth Alexander, Jack Thompson, Peter Car-roll, Liddy Clark, Ruth Cracknell, Arthur Dignam, Ian Gilmour, John Jarratt, Ray Meagher, Kevin Miles, Robyn Nevin, Angela Punch McGregor, Peter Sumner; *D:* Fred Schepisi; *W:* Fred Schepisi; *C:* Ian Baker; *M:* Bruce Smeaton. *NYR*

CHAPAYEV

A down-to-earth, iconoclastic, peasant-born Red Army commander takes on the White Russians in the bloody Civil War of 1919. Based on a biography of Chapayev written by one of his military associates, this enormously popular epic film was directed in a grandly pictorial, sweepingly energetic style, rousing yet not bombastic. Its creators, Sergei and Georgy Vassiliev, worked under the collective name of "The Brothers Vassiliev" but were in fact not brothers. (Go know.) Boris Babochkin makes a dashing and heroic Chapayev, though the pleasant surprise is that he's portrayed throughout as both a military hero *and* an ordinary human being—albeit one who rises to the occasion when circumstances demand. *Chapayev* contains a rather amazing and terrifying battle sequence in which the White Army forms what amounts to a parade of the dead; the instant that any one of their neatly uniformed soldiers is felled by gunfire, the dead man is instantly replaced by an identically uniformed man; the unit marches forward without the slightest disruption of its formation. The actual incident was designed to scare the hell out of the Red Army, of course, but its eerie recreation does a number on the viewer as well. (As a gentle reminder of how political climates can be even more unpredictable than El Niño, America's National Board of Review—originally founded in 1909 as the National Board of Censorship—gave *Chapayev* its Best Foreign Film of the Year Award in 1935.)

NEXT STOP . . . *Strike, Ten Days That Shook the World, The End of St. Petersburg*

1934 101m/B *RU* Boris Chirkov, Varvara Myasnikova, Illarian Pevzov, Boris Babochkin, Leonid Kmit; *D:* Sergei Vassiliev, Georgy Vassiliev; *W:* Sergei Vassiliev, Georgy Vassiliev; *C:* Aleksander Sigayev, Alexander Xenofontov; *M:* Gavriil Popov. **VHS** *VYY, AUD, IHF*

CHARULATA
The Lonely Wife

In 19th-century Bengal, Charulata (Madhabi Mukherjee) is bored and frustrated by her wealthy, pretentious, and self-aggrandizing husband, Bhupati, who has no time for her. When the naive but insensitive Bhupati suggests that his cousin Amal might make an innocently diverting companion for his wife, he has no way of knowing that Charulata's friendship with Amal will quickly turn sexual. Satyajit Ray's astounding and revolutionary *Charulata,* based on a story by Rabindranath Tagore, is the story of a woman awakening not only to discover her own repressed sexuality, but discovering that the restraints and oppression of her male-dominated society are becoming intolerable. Pleasing her husband is impossible, as is pleasing her lover, who gets out of the kitchen as soon as the pilot light is lit. Forbidden to express herself through writing, her idleness enforced as a status symbol of her class, Charulata's self-awareness dawns on her gradually, but then pours into her like an emotional flood, which Ray has held back until the end. Ruthlessly honest, bracingly satirical, and deeply moving, *Charulata*—which was Ray's favorite of his own films—is a masterpiece.

NEXT STOP . . . *The Music Room, Mahanagar, The Silences of the Palace*

1964 117m/B *IN* Shailan Mukherjee, Shyamal Ghoshal, Gitali Roy, Bholanath Koyal, Suku Mukherjee, Dilip Bose, Joydeb, Bankim Ghosh, Subrata Sensharma, Majhabi Mukherjee, Soumitra Chatterjee; *D:* Satyajit Ray; *W:* Satyajit Ray; *C:* Subrata Mitra; *M:* Satyajit Ray, Rabindranath Tagore. **VHS** *COL*

A CHEF IN LOVE
Les Mille et une Recettes
du Cuisinier Amoureux
The Cook in Love

Told primarily in flashback, Georgian director Nana Djordjadze's romantic epic is the story of a French chef named Pascal (Pierre Richard of *The Tall Blond Man with One Black Shoe*) whose love affair with the beautiful Cecilia (Nino Kirtadze) is rivaled in intensity only by the flavors and textures of the culinary creations he so lovingly fashions. Pascal had come to Tbilisi in the 1920s in search of recipes, but his love for Cecilia led him to stay and open a restaurant that quickly became legendary—a holy site for gastronomes the world over. Suddenly, with the communist revolution invading Pascal's idyllic setting, the great chef's traditions are forced to meet an explosive new world order—the flavors of food, love, and politics will be altered forever. *A Chef in Love* is a pleasant and lushly filmed romantic fantasy that gains its real appeal from neither sex nor politics, but from food. Part of a recent (and welcome) tradition of "food films" that include *Tampopo, Babette's Feast,* and *Big Night, A Chef in Love*'s old world portrait of gastronomy as civilization has a primal appeal; the luscious, sybaritic food scenes are like a spoonful of sugar, making us willingly, and even eagerly, swallow the picture's occasionally labored lyricism.

NEXT STOP . . . *Babette's Feast, Like Water for Chocolate, Tampopo*

1996 (PG-13) 95m/C *FR* Pierre Richard, Nino Kirtadze, Temur Kahmhadze, Jean-Yves Gautier, Vladimir Ilyine, Danielle Darrieux, Micheline Presle; *D:* Nana Dzhordzadze; *W:* Irakli Kvirikadze; *C:* Georgi Beridze; *M:* Goran Bregovic. Nominations: Academy Awards '96: Best Foreign Film. **VHS** *COL*

CHILDREN OF PARADISE
Les Enfants du Paradis

If you're ever asked to provide proof that movies can indeed weave a spell unlike any other medium—unlike literature, unlike painting, unlike music, and yet containing elements of all of them—then consider a single screening of Marcel Carné's incomparable cinematic dream, *Children of Paradise (Les Enfants du Paradis).* A complex but crisply told love story set in the romantic back streets of Paris in the early 19th century, *Children of Paradise* is the ultimate answer to those who would insist that art is irrelevant to daily life; it's a film in which

JEANNE MOREAU
Legendary French Actress

The legendary French actress Jeanne Moreau continues to augment her legend. Now in her late sixties, she keeps up an active schedule of movie making. Born on January 23, 1928 in Paris to an English music hall performer and a French father, Moreau began acting at age 19. After ten years of working in film and on stage, she finally came into her own in two films directed by Louis Malle, *L'ascenseau pour l'echafaud (Elevator to the Gallows)* (1957) and *Les Amants (The Lovers)* (1958). In these movies Moreau established an iconoclastic image for herself—that of the sensual independent woman—that she would play to perfection in other films like *Moderato Cantabile* (1960). Perhaps her most memorable personification of this image was as the femme fatale in Francois Truffaut's *Jules and Jim* (1961).

One key to Moreau's longevity surely has been her ability to hang on to this image throughout the years. Even as recently as *The Summer House,* released in 1994, she played a seductive senior. Although she began writing an autobiography around that time, she also continued to act in films such as Ismail Merchant's *The Proprietor* (1996) and to direct, working most recently on a film version of the Joyce Carol Oates novel "Solstice." She actually made her directing debut in 1976's *Lumiere* and also directed *L'adolescente.* And she continues to be the embodiment of the free woman—free of false vanity, free of guilt, and full of zest for life. As she says, "[I]f you want to live, and live your life through to the end, you have to live dangerously. And one thing you have to give up is attaching importance to what people see in you."

Moreau is divorced from French director Jean-Louis Richard by whom she had a son, Jerome, and American director Willaim Friedkin.

---

art—performance, commitment, *theatricality*—are inseparable from our minute-by-minute interactions with each other. During the movie's three hours, the huge cast of characters—actors, criminals, and lovers—mesh with their surroundings in such a thrillingly detailed way that their world seems absolutely real; the film is perhaps better described as a work of faith than as a work of fiction. Filmed during the Nazi occupation of France, much of *Children of Paradise* was filmed clandestinely, with the threat of arrest by secret police constantly in the minds of cast and crew, many of whom were Resistance members. And what a cast and crew; Jean-Louis Barrault, Arletty, Pierre Brasseur, Maria Casarés, and Marcel Herrand are among the stars, and the physically astounding production was designed by Alexander Trauner, Lucien Barsacq, and Raymond Gabutti. Jacques Prévert's screenplay was nominated for an Oscar in 1946.

NEXT STOP . . . *Les Visiteurs du Soir, Le Jour Se Lève, Carnival in Flanders*

1944 188m/B *FR* Jean-Louis Barrault, Arletty, Pierre Brasseur, Maria Casares, Albert Remy, Leon Larive, Marcel Herrand, Pierre Renoir, Jeanne Marken, Gaston Modot; ***D:*** Marcel Carne; ***W:*** Jacques Prevert; ***C:*** Roger Hubert; ***M:*** Maurice Thiriet, Joseph Kosma. Nominations: Academy Awards '46: Best Original Screenplay. **VHS, LV** *HMV, CRC, FCT*

CHIMES AT MIDNIGHT
Falstaff
Campanadas a Medianoche

When considering the work of the late Orson Welles, pundits still tend to drone on about the lost opportunities, the unfinished projects, the technical sloppiness. It's the schoolboy's nightmare of being reminded that he's "not living up to his potential"; and if Welles is looking down on us now, he knows he's destined to hear it for all eternity. There are still a few of us, though, who take much more pleasure in sifting through the astonishing riches he left us, not the least of which is his brilliant, 1966 *Chimes at Midnight* (also known as *Falstaff*), the storyline of which is a surprisingly deft juggling of plots and characters from at least five of Shakespeare's plays. Yes, the post-synchronized sound is a mess, and the images often don't match what the characters are saying—many are given voices by Welles himself for reasons we can only imagine—but in the final analysis it doesn't matter; indeed, one can even see its technical shortcomings as obstacles that make the film's triumph all the more moving. Welles's performance as Falstaff reminds us of what is often forgotten in the age of the *auteur,* and that is how a great actor can make familiar material appear to have been just invented—even improvised. Keith Baxter and Margaret Rutherford give no hint of the chaos that must have surrounded the production, and when he's front and center as Henry IV, the great and irreplaceable John Gielgud makes us grieve at the prospect of a cinema that will lack his incomparable presence. *Chimes at Midnight,* one of the greatest of all screen adaptations of the work of William Shakespeare, is rumored to be under "renovation"—due for a "clean-up" of both its image and soundtrack. If it's a true restoration of Welles's original accomplishment, three cheers. If, however, it's fiddled with and "repaired" in an effort to "smooth over" the passionate and crazy risks that made Welles the great director that he was—to make his *Chimes at Midnight* acceptable to an audience for whom stereo and seamless technology are all—it will be a far greater tragedy than the never-ending myth of this magnificent genius's "unrealized potential."

NEXT STOP... *Othello (1952), Henry V, Throne of Blood, Touch of Evil*

1967 115m/B *SP SI* Orson Welles, Jeanne Moreau, Margaret Rutherford, John Gielgud, Marina Vlady, Keith Baxter, Fernando Rey, Norman Rodway; **D:** Orson Welles; **W:** Orson Welles; **C:** Edmond Richard; **M:** Angelo Francesco Lavagnino. **VHS** *FCT*

CHLOE IN THE AFTERNOON
L'Amour l'Après-Midi

The final installment in Eric Rohmer's series of "Six Moral Tales" finds the director contemplating a familiar but ever-tantalizing situation; a married man's contemplation of a no-strings-attached dalliance with a beautiful and intriguing "other" woman. Frederic (Bernard Verley) is afflicted with the usual Rohmer curse; he examines his dilemma from so many angles that the pluses and minuses of expressed physical passion with Chloe (Zouzou) add up to a more daunting choice than selecting a mutual fund—and a somewhat less erotic choice to boot. Less well-known than some of Rohmer's other major works, his 1972 *Chloe in the Afternoon* (*L'Amour l'après-midi*) is nevertheless a thoroughly engaging, refreshingly cerebral examination of guilt, lust, and indecision—a fitting conclusion to the director's priceless "Moral Tales" cycle. (Keep a sharp eye out for one of the film's treats—cameo appearances by characters from earlier films in the cycle, such as *Claire's Knee, My Night at Maud's,* and *La Collectionneuse.*) Photographed in dark, saturated colors by the great Nestor Almendros.

NEXT STOP... *La Collectionneuse, My Night at Maud's, Claire's Knee, Summer*

1972 (R) 97m/C *FR* Bernard Verley, Zouzou, Francoise Verley, Daniel Ceccaldi, Malvina Penne, Babette Ferrier, Suze Randall, Marie-Christine Barrault; **D:** Eric Rohmer; **W:** Eric Rohmer; **C:** Nestor Almendros; **M:** Arie Dzierlatka. **VHS** *FCT*

CHRIST STOPPED AT EBOLI

Eboli

Cristo si e fermato a Eboli

In 1935, at the start of the Abyssinian War, Italian artist, writer, and physician Carlo Levi was banished to a small village in southern Italy due to his unwavering opposition to fascism. It was an extraordinary and life-changing year that Levi spent in exile, though he would only write about the experience years later—while living in Florence during World War II—in what would become his acclaimed 1943 memoir, *Christ Stopped at Eboli.* In 1979, filmmaker Francesco Rosi completed a two-and-a-half hour film adaptation of Levi's book, with Gian Maria Volonté in the role of the author. Astoundingly, and against the odds for successful non-fawning screen biographies of this sort, Rosi's *Christ Stopped at Eboli* is an epic in every sense; an enriching, un-sentimentalized journey of fear, hope, and self-discovery that never loses its human-scaled focus despite its grand scale. The gradual and novelistic way in which Rosi immerses the audience in Levi's story was apparently lost on the film's American distributor, which released it here with more than half-an-hour removed, changing the title simply to *Eboli,* lest the public think they were seeing a religious picture. (The title is a reference to Levi's description of the impoverished village of Basilicata: "Christ never came this far, nor did time, nor the individual soul, nor hope, nor the relation of cause to effect, nor reason nor history.") Fortunately, the full version of *Christ Stopped at Eboli* was eventually made available here, allowing one of Rosi's masterworks—as well as Volonté's most exquisitely etched performance—to be seen in its full splendor. With Lea Massari and Irene Papas.

1979 118m/C *IT FR* Gian Marie Volonte, Irene Papas, Paolo Bonacelli, Francois Simon, Alain Cuny, Lea Massari; *D:* Francesco Rosi; *W:* Francesco Rosi; *C:* Pasquale De Santis. British Academy Awards '82: Best Foreign Film. **VHS** *COL*

CHUNGKING EXPRESS
Hong Kong Express
Chongqing Senlin

Hong Kong's *Breathless.* The two most memorable stars of Wong Kar-Wai's snappy and intoxicating *Chungking Express* are not the two actors who play the two cops at the center of the movie's two plots; the real stars are Hong Kong itself and the man whose electric images seem to reinvent the city from minute to minute, cinematographer Christopher Doyle. Faye Wang is the lovestruck waitress who makes salads while dancing to the Mamas and the Papas whenever she's not obsessively but sweetly stalking cynical cop Tony Leung. A veteran of John Woo's *Bullet in the Head* and *Hard-Boiled,* Leung may unfortunately be best known in the west for his conventionally "exotic" role in Jean-Jacques Annaud's glossy, would-be-erotic epic *The Lover.* Director Wong Kar-Wai (*Happy Together*) paints an exhilarating portrait of unrequited love and desperate loneliness amid the youthful energy and perpetual motion of Hong Kong's glittering, pop-culture labyrinth of malls, fast food, and crime; it's that energy that makes the movie flow, and it's what we take home with us when the lights come up. You may not remember what happens to these characters a day after seeing *Chungking Express,* but it's likely that the sound and sights of the city that surrounds them will create in most viewers an unconscious, palpable dream of Hong Kong to be recalled with joy in sudden, Proust-style flashbacks at unexpected moments years from now.

NEXT STOP . . . *Breathless, The Killer, Happy Together*

1995 (PG-13) 102m/C *HK* Bridget Lin, Takeshi Kaneshiro, Tony Leung, Faye Wang, Valerie Chow, Piggy Chan; *D:* Wong Kar-Wai; *W:* Wong Kar-Wai; *C:* Christopher Doyle, Lau Wai-Keung; *M:* Frankie Chan, Roel A. Garcia. Nominations: Independent Spirit Awards '97: Best Foreign Film. **VHS, LV, Closed Caption** *MAX*

CINEMA PARADISO
Nuovo Cinema Paradiso

When Salvatore, a movie director, learns of the death of the projectionist at the cinema in the small Sicilian town of his youth, he returns home—both physically and by way of flashback sequences—to relive and rediscover the primal childhood joy that he discovered at the movies so many years before. Giuseppe Tornatore's 1988 *Cinema Paradiso* has an enchanting premise, but somewhere into the second hour the seemingly endless reaction shots of the dazzled young hero and his fellow villagers begin to wear thin, and we realize that *Cinema Paradiso* might have made a wonderful, brief subplot in one of Fellini's memory films, but is far too cloying, relentlessly sentimental, and monotonous to pad out an entire feature. (And the American release was about half-an-hour shorter than the original.) One gimmick is memorable, though; in the flashbacks, the local priest demands that the projectionist (the usually wonderful Philippe Noiret in his aggressively sweet, full teddy bear mode) remove all offending kissing scenes from the movies he shows. As a child, Salvatore saved all of those "naughty" pieces of film, and that leads to *Cinema Paradiso*'s payoff—which possesses the genuine charm that most of the rest of the movie lacks—by letting us and the adult Salvatore watch happily and gratefully as all of those sweet, romantic, censored moments unspool end to end. It's a touching sequence, but not quite worth the wait.

NEXT STOP . . . *Amarcord, The Clowns, Sherlock Jr.*

1988 123m/C *IT* Philippe Noiret, Jacques Perrin, Salvatore Cascio, Marco Leonardi, Agnes Nano, Leopoldo Trieste; *D:* Giuseppe Tornatore; *W:* Giuseppe Tornatore; *C:* Basco Giurato; *M:* Ennio Morricone. Academy Awards '89: Best Foreign Film; British Academy Awards '90: Best Actor (Noiret), Best Foreign Film, Best Original Screenplay, Best Supporting Actor (Cascio); Cannes Film Festival '89: Grand Jury Prize; Golden Globe Awards '90: Best Foreign Film. **VHS, LV, 8mm** *HBO*

C

THE CITY OF LOST CHILDREN
La Cite des Enfants Perdus

In one of the coolest high-concept plots in the history of fantasy films, a fiendish scientist named Krank—who lacks the ability to dream—kidnaps innocent children to steal their nocturnal imaginings. France's Marc Caro and Jean-Pierre Jeunet (*Delicatessen, The Fifth Element*) have dreamed up a darkly dazzling visual wonderland that suggests some of the more terrifying sequences of Disney's animated classics come to life. Ron Perlman plays the strongman/hero who sets out to destroy this evil conspiracy when his younger brother becomes one of Krank's victims. While the movie's narrative thrust never achieves the power of its visual scheme, there are enough memorable sights—such as the opening sequence of a parade of evil Santa Clauses (cloned henchmen of Krank's) coming down the chimney to whisk away an unsuspecting child—to make the picture reverberate long afterward.

NEXT STOP . . . *Delicatessen, Pinocchio, The 5,000 Fingers of Dr. T*

1995 (R) 114m/C *FR* Ron Perlman, Daniel Emilfork, Joseph Lucien, Judith Vittet, Dominique Pinon, Jean Claude Dreyfus, Odile Mallet, Genevieve Brunet, Mireille Mosse; **D:** Jean-Pierre Jeunet, Marc Caro; **W:** Jean-Pierre Jeunet, Marc Caro, Gilles Adrien; **C:** Darius Khondji; **M:** Angelo Badalamenti; **V:** Jean-Louis Trintignant. Cesar Awards '96: Best Art Direction/Set Decoration; Nominations: Cesar Awards '96: Best Cinematography, Best Costume Design, Best Score; Independent Spirit Awards '96: Best Foreign Film. **VHS, LV, Closed Caption** COL

CITY OF WOMEN
La Citte delle Donne

This big, colorful Fellini circus is a gloriously un-PC extension and expansion (not necessarily deepening) of the sexual fantasies in which he gloried in *8 1/2* and *Juliet of the Spirits,* and then embalmed in the self-flagellating, interminable *Casanova.* Maybe it's a guy thing, but I found *City of Women* a sweet, poignant, and—dare I say it?—*honest* carnival of sexual anxiety, regret, and celebration.

Since it's true that this garishly spectacular, stylized parade of fetishes, pneumatically adjusted bodies, and lascivious lip-licking probably wouldn't be watchable without Marcello Mastroianni in the lead, one thing ought to be pointed out: Marcello Mastroianni is in the lead. We've been through a lot with this great actor, and over the decades he has become—through the screen persona he and Fellini fashioned—a very close friend indeed. As Guido (a.k.a. Snaporaz), the hero of *City of Women*, Mastroianni plays that friend of ours whose midlife crisis has reached critical mass; we don't need to endorse or disavow his individual fantasies to be touched by this extraordinary yet common man who is still puzzled and eternally enslaved by the very idea of woman. In this hallucinatory, sexual rendition of *A Christmas Carol,* Marcello/Guido/Snaporaz, in visiting the women he's loved, the women he's feared, and the women he's invented, finally comes to realize that in the truest sense, he's invented them all.

NEXT STOP . . . *8 1/2, Marcello Mastroianni: I Remember, Star 80*

1981 (R) 140m/C *IT* Marcello Mastroianni, Ettore Manni, Anna Prucnall, Bernice Stegers; **D:** Federico Fellini; **W:** Federico Fellini; **C:** Giuseppe Rotunno; **M:** Luis Bacalov. **VHS** NYF, FCT

CLAIRE'S KNEE
Le Genou de Claire

Jerome (Jean-Claude Brialy), a young man who's engaged to be married, decides he needs a bit of a breather beforehand in order to rest and contemplate the step he's about to take; you could say Jerome needs to get himself together. The spot he chooses for his R and R is a kind of beautiful no man's land, a lake that exists just between France and Switzerland. While in this idyllic setting, Jerome runs into an old flame, Aurora (Aurora Cornu). As if this weren't enough of a distraction, it seems that Aurora is vacationing with another family in which there are two daughters: Laura (Béatrice Romand in a film-stealing performance), a wise-beyond-her-years and somewhat gawky teenager, and Claire (Laurence de Monaghan), Laura's not-so-brilliant older sister, who happens to be a knockout. Laura's completely infatuated with Jerome, but their relationship remains non-physical. Jerome's problem is Claire—her knee, to be more specific. His physical obsession with the young woman (who has a sharply observed, self-absorbed boyfriend) is focused on this single body part in a way that is both absurd and honest, and Jerome spends a lot of time analyzing his fascination before deciding that action must be taken. How writer/director Eric Rohmer fashions all of this into a supremely witty *suspense* film about eroticism, fetishism, and self-delusion is one of the cinema's modern miracles, and one of its glories. This fifth of Rohmer's "Six Moral Tales" is a brilliantly structured, hugely enjoyable sex comedy disguised as a series of casual, individually inconsequential encounters. Rohmer's talent is truly magical, because he never allows us to see how he does it.

NEXT STOP . . . *Pauline at the Beach, My Night at Maud's, Vertigo*

1971 105m/C *FR* Jean-Claude Brialy, Aurora Cornu, Beatrice Romand, Laurence De Monaghan, Gerard Falconetti; *D:* Eric Rohmer; *W:* Eric Rohmer; *C:* Nestor Almendros. National Society of Film Critics Awards '71: Best Film. **VHS, LV** *FCT*

THE CLOWNS

Federico Fellini's seductive personal memoir about the joys and terrors of childhood, and how they can often be the same thing, is not a documentary in the traditional sense— thank goodness. With his simple admission that circus clowns both fascinated and frightened him as a boy, Fellini sells us a ticket to a young person's view of theatricality; a spectacle that we can't look away from, partly to make sure it's not getting any closer. The images of little Federico sneaking into a newly erected circus tent alone, under a sky full of impossibly bright stars, is indelible and dreamlike. Yet *The Clowns* is not all nostalgia. The film is brave enough to take us on the mature Fellini's search for a rare bit of film footage of the man who is reputedly the greatest clown of all time. Fellini finds the footage in his film-within-a-film, and he

allows us to see it. It's a sad affair; some guy getting up and down off of a chair holding an umbrella, as I remember it, and the director's disappointment as he watches it with us is palpable. It's all a staged put-on, of course, but the impact and the message are loud and clear—perhaps the legends we cling to and the fantasies that reassure us should remain just that, safely tucked away in our imaginations. If it's the harsh and unforgiving light of "reality" we seek, then it's best to avoid the circus—and essential to avoid the movies.

NEXT STOP . . . *8 1/2, Bye Bye Brazil, Bronco Billy*

1971 (G) 90m/C *IT D:* Federico Fellini; *W:* Federico Fellini, Barnardino Zapponi; *C:* Dario Di Palma; *M:* Nino Rota. **VHS** *HTV, NOS, MRV*

COMFORT AND JOY

It could be that there's a logical explanation for what makes Scottish director Bill Forsyth's comedies so exceptionally engaging and strangely moving, but I prefer to think that his talent is as magical as the stories he tells. In his 1984 *Comfort and Joy,* Forsyth tells the tale of a Glasgow disk jockey whose personal life is falling apart—and whose job hardly provides the needed solace—until he finds himself in the unexpected position of mediator in a war between rival ice cream vendors named Mr. McCool and Mr. Bunny. How Forsyth manages to keep such a plot from veering off into either pointlessness or gooey sentimentality is a part of his mystery and appeal, but after 20 minutes or so we simply accept, gratefully, our presence in the writer/director's magical, miniature world. Bill Patterson plays the bleary-eyed, dawn-patrol DJ Alan "Dickie" Bird with a resigned, cynical hopelessness that feels completely honest; when his ice cream adventure begins, his willingness to get involved seems logical and right—like David Hemmings's need to solve a mystery in *Blow-Up.* Forsyth makes his films from the plot elements that other directors might throw away, and, as in kinds of "found art," he sees beauty in much of the human folly that could be considered ridiculous in the hands of less observant directors. When Forsyth's cooking, as he is in *Local Hero, Housekeeping,* and *Comfort and Joy,* you nod with the recognition that these decent and wounded characters are all on the right track, even though the track itself may be far from the beaten path of traditional, plot-driven movies.

NEXT STOP . . . *Local Hero, Breaking In, Big Night*

1984 (PG) 93m/C *GB* Bill Paterson, Eleanor David, Clare P. Grogan, Alex Norton, Patrick Malahide, Rikki Fulton, Roberto Berrardi; *D:* Bill Forsyth; *W:* Bill Forsyth; *C:* Chris Menges; *M:* Mark Knopfler. National Society of Film Critics Awards '84: Best Cinematography. **VHS** *USH*

COMMISSAR
Komissar

Filmed in 1967 but suppressed until 1988, Soviet director Alexander Askoldov's film is an unexpected thunderbolt. Set during the 1922 civil war, *Commissar* is the story of a Red Army officer whose pregnancy forces her to go into hiding with a Jewish family until the birth of her child. Coming to acknowledge the family as human despite the virulent anti-Semitism that is the norm is but one side of what the film shows us; at the same time, her disguising as part of the family forces her to understand what being the object of racial hatred feels like. Photographed in a series of powerful, widescreen images that are at once epic and claustrophobic, *Commissar*'s narrative flow moves in fits and starts, and at times declares its humanist intentions a bit too overtly; nevertheless, a film this potent on this subject from a Soviet director in 1967 is in and of itself a true rarity. Apparently the authorities wanted to keep it that way; in addition to keeping *Commissar* under wraps for more than two decades, director Askoldov was stopped after this promising and brave piece of work.

NEXT STOP . . . *Bitter Harvest, The Boat Is Full, The Ascent*

1968 105m/B *RU* Nonna Mordyukova, Rolan Bykov, Raisa Nedashkovskaya, Vasily Shukshin, Pavlik Levin, Ludmilla Volinskaya; *D:* Alexander Askoldov; *W:* Alexander Askoldov; *C:* Valery Ginsberg; *M:* Alfred Schnittke. **VHS** *KIV*

THE CONFESSION
L'Aveu

It's amazing how rarely this film—one of the finest works by Costa-Gavras (*Z, State of Siege, The Music Box*)—shows up in repertory film programs or even on lists of important films of the 1970s. It may be that audiences that embraced Costa-Gavras's thunderously powerful *Z* were so caught up in the unraveling of the fascist conspiracy depicted in that film that they felt betrayed by *The Confession,* an even more detailed and brilliant depiction of the inherent dangers of a police state. The problem may be that *this* police state—the Czechoslovakia of 1951—called itself Communist when it arrested Under-Secretary of Foreign Affairs Artur London (fictionalized as "Gerard" in the film and played by Yves Montand) and 13 others for the crimes of spying for the U.S. and being "Zionists" (they were all Jews). The Stalinist show trial that ensued resulted in the execution of 11 of the men, though London himself was eventually tortured into signing a "confession" of his non-existent "crimes." It wasn't long after *The Confession*'s release that Montand himself became disillusioned with his own socialist leanings, and former friends found the film's uncompromising refusal to romanticize the movement both impossible to swallow yet impossible to refute. The result was that *The Confession*—perhaps the most gruelingly detailed portrait of psychological, political terrorism ever seen in a narrative film—was received politely and then politely ignored. Montand and real-life wife Simone Signoret are both wrenching and poignant in this resonant and memorable film: an intelligent, resolute, and unflinching portrait of the evil inherent in unchecked, absolute power, regardless of the label it slaps on itself.

NEXT STOP . . . *State of Siege, Missing, The Thin Blue Line*

1970 160m/C *FR* Yves Montand, Simone Signoret, Gabriele Ferzetti, Michel Vitold, Jean Bouise; *D:* Constantin Costa-Gavras; *W:* Jorge Semprun; *C:* Raoul Coutard. *NYR*

CONFIDENTIALLY YOURS

Vivement Dimanche!
Finally, Sunday

François Truffaut's final film—a larky pastiche of gumshoe noir and Hitchcock homage about a trench-coated secretary determined to clear her boss of suspicion by tracking down a murderer—hardly feels like a summing up of the great director's career. *Confidentially Yours* (*Vivement Dimanche*) feels tired and rote, and neither the crisp black-and-white images of Nestor Almendros nor the lilting melodies of Georges Delerue can keep us from drifting off to reflect back on other, deeper pleasures that Truffaut has given us. Yet if *Confidentially Yours* leaves us with a surprising number of aftershocks, it surely is due to the presence of its star, Fanny Ardant. Truffaut's love for so many of his leading ladies was legendary, and there's something reassuringly moving in his last film being so obviously a love letter to its star. The director Truffaut "played" in *Day for Night* assures Jean-Pierre Léaud in that film that the cinema is what is important to the two of them—that they are not like other people. But in so many of his films, from the *Antoine and Colette* episode of *Love at Twenty* (Marie-France Pisier) through *Jules and Jim* (Jeanne Moreau), *Mississippi Mermaid* (Catherine Deneuve), *The Story of Adele H.* (Isabelle Adjani), and *The Woman Next Door* (Fanny Ardant), women are the irresistible, inexplicable force that generate the gravitational pull of his storytelling. (His *The Man Who Loved Women* is only one more example, despite the fact that the miracle of the director's attraction to *all* women was the film's very subject.) Some have expressed disappointment that Truffaut didn't give us something more overtly "profound" as his last statement; but what could be purer, more consistent, and more honestly profound than his last gaze being fixed on a woman he loved, showing her off to us proudly, asking us with his last breath: "Isn't she something?" Confidentially, Mr. Truffaut, you were something too.

NEXT STOP... *Stolen Kisses, The Bride Wore Black, Gumshoe*

1983 (PG) 110m/B *FR* Fanny Ardant, Jean-Louis Trintignant, Philippe Morier-Genoud, Philippe Laudenbach, Caroline Sihol; **D:** Francois Truffaut; **W:** Francois Truffaut, Suzanne Schiffman, Jean Aurel; **C:** Nestor Almendros; **M:** Georges Delerue. **VHS, LV** *FOX, HMV*

THE CONFORMIST

Il Conformista

Marcello Clerici (Jean-Louis Trintignant) wants so much to blend in with those around him that he's willing to suppress, sacrifice, and sublimate his own instincts and desires in order to be "normal." Seeking this "normality" in Mussolini's Italy of the 1930s, Clerici marries a pretty, empty-headed girl (Stefania Sandrelli) to cover up any suspicion of his own homosexual impulses. Becoming an assassin for the Fascists, he promptly snares the assignment of murdering his liberal former professor. Though Clerici could be the evil twin brother of Woody Allen's "chameleon man," Leonard Zelig, Bernardo Bertolucci's *The Conformist,* based on the novel by Alberto Moravia, is more precisely concerned with the connection between sexual repression and political oppression (whereas Zelig just wanted to be liked). What's great about *The Conformist,* however, isn't the tired old saw about repressed homosexuals making the best Fascists; what makes it memorable is the glistening richness of its surface, which is so visually intoxicating that it's easy to overlook the less-than-profound thesis lurking underneath. Photographed by Vittorio Storaro (*Apocalypse Now*) in deeply saturated colors and gliding camera movements, the film is constructed in a series of memorable visual tableaux, its operatic feel underscored by Georges Delerue's haunting musical score. One of the weirdest and most beautifully choreographed episodes is a party at which the Fascist guests—all but Clerici—are blind. The scene was cut from American prints after the New York engagement, and when this fan of the film wrote to the American distributor inquiring about the cut, the studio's then-VP of Distribution (now a *very* prominent show business journalist) fired back a vitriolic, enraged response, decrying "kids like you who know nothing" and assuring me that the cut was Bertolucci's idea. Nevertheless, the same studio in 1996 issued a restored "director's cut" of *The Conformist* with much fanfare; the "party of the blind" is in it, and I've heard of no complaints from the director. The film also stars Dominique Sanda and Pierre Clementi, and it was nominated in 1971 for the Best Adapted Screenplay Academy Award.

NEXT STOP . . . *Before the Revolution, Lacombe, Lucien, Zelig*

1971 (R) 108m/C *IT FR GE* Jean-Louis Trintignant, Stefania Sandrelli, Dominique Sanda, Pierre Clementi, Gastone Moschin, Pasquale Fortunato; **D:** Bernardo Bertolucci; **W:** Bernardo Bertolucci; **C:** Vittorio Storaro; **M:** Georges Delerue. National Society of Film Critics Awards '71: Best Cinematography (Storaro), Best Director (Bertolucci); Nominations: Academy Awards '71: Best Adapted Screenplay. **VHS, LV** *PAR*

CONTEMPT
Le Mepris
Il Disprezzo

Jean-Luc Godard's adaptation of Alberto Moravia's *A Ghost at Noon* stars Brigitte Bardot as the disgusted wife of a talented and formerly principled writer (Michel Piccoli) who signs to do a rewrite of *The Odyssey* for a vulgar American producer (Jack Palance). The fact that *The Odyssey*'s director is to be Fritz Lang, and is actually played by Fritz Lang, adds far more than simply a knowing, inside wink to this legendary and recently restored dream of a film—it brings the fantasy-making apparatus full circle, forcing us to see that the creative process of making connections between art and life doesn't end at the edge of the screen. *Contempt* is so rich, so stuffed with ideas that Godard couldn't bear to toss out (unlike Palance, the predatory film-within-a-film's producer) that it becomes a veritable treasure trove of playful and disturbingly on-target observations about art, commerce, sex, and disillusionment; the long, brilliant sequence in which Piccoli and Bardot bicker and dig into each other's motives and "deconstruct" their rela-

tionship is painful, great, and like nothing you've ever seen on screen before. Photographed in deeply saturated, widescreen colors by Raoul Coutard and graced by a stunningly evocative score from Georges Delerue (partially borrowed with intelligence and wit by Martin Scorsese in his *Casino*), *Contempt* is a knockout—as much a hate letter to Hollywood as it is a love letter to all of cinema. Whether it is, as *Sight & Sound*'s Colin McCabe claims, "the greatest work of art produced in post-war Europe" is questionable; that it is indeed a great work of art is not.

NEXT STOP . . . *Pierrot le Fou, The Player, Irma Vep*

1964 102m/C *IT FR* Brigitte Bardot, Jack Palance, Fritz Lang, Georgia Moll, Michel Piccoli; **D:** Jean-Luc Godard; **W:** Jean-Luc Godard; **C:** Raoul Coutard; **M:** Georges Delerue. **VHS, LV** *COL*

CONTRACT

When a bride abandons her groom at the altar, the assembled wedding guests decide that they can't let a little problem like that interrupt the festivities. The resulting two-day wedding party encompasses every imaginable kind of comedy, scandal, insult, and humiliation as the throng turns into a mob and from there takes on an uncontrollable, intimidating life of its own. In this and other films by Poland's enormously talented Krzysztof Zanussi, a nation's precarious and tumultuous political realities are illustrated in startlingly imaginative metaphorical situations that have the grace and verve of modern, cinematic Aesop's fables. As with so many film artists who've had to produce their work under the oppressive eye of the political censor—before, during, and after production—Zanussi has wittily made the most of his situation by scoring his points in what appears at first glance to be a decidedly non-political story. The films that directors like Zanussi, Andrej Wajda, Jerzy Skolimowski, and Krzysztof Kieslowski created in the Poland of the 1970s and 1980s were certainly influential cinematically, yet their political impact was such that they were an integral part of the sweeping changes that reshaped the world in the 1990s. If that weren't enough, it should also be noted that *Contract* is a very funny picture. With Leslie Caron and the extraordinary Maja Komorowska.

NEXT STOP . . . *The Constant Factor, A Wedding, The Exterminating Angel*

1980 111m/C *PL* Maja Komorowska, Tadeusz Lomnicki, Magda Jaroszowna, Leslie Caron, Ignacy Machowski; *D:* Krzysztof Zanussi; *W:* Krzysztof Zanussi; *C:* Slawomir Idziak; *M:* Wojciech Kilar. **VHS** *FCT*

CONVERSATION PIECE
Violence et Passion
Gruppo di Famiglia in un Interno

Mark Twain once wryly commented that "Wagner's music is actually better than it sounds." The same comment—in spirit— might be adapted to many of the more "operatic" films of Luchino Visconti, and the unfairly maligned *Conversation Piece* is most certainly one of them. It's a gentle, introspective chamber piece done on a visually sumptuous, grand scale, about a former professor (Burt Lancaster) who's introduced to a countess's lover (Helmut Berger) and soon becomes obsessed with him. There's always been something silly about Helmut Berger, and in *Conversation Piece* this quality makes sense for his character, and provides much of the reason for the stodgy professor's fascination with him; yet the outraged, mocking audience response to *Conversation Piece* when it opened the 1977 New York Film Festival may well have ended Berger's ability to be taken seriously by American art house audiences. It also ended the movie's commercial possibilities, period. Sitting in that audience was like being a new chapter of Charles MacKay's indispensable book *Extraordinary Popular Delusions and the Madness of Crowds*—the audience had become a mob, and each line of the film set off new waves of derisive laughter. (Intentional laughs were, at a certain point, no longer distinguishable from unintentional.) The film's brave distributor later scrapped the English-language version that produced this horrifying response, replacing it with the dubbed

Italian (English subtitled) version in the futile hope that a successful release could be salvaged. Alas, it went virtually unseen here, and too bad—it's better than it sounds. With Silvana Mangano and Claudia Cardinale.

NEXT STOP . . . *The Damned, Death in Venice, The Leopard*

1975 (R) 112m/C *IT FR* Burt Lancaster, Silvana Mangano, Helmut Berger, Claudia Cardinale, Claudia Marsani; *D:* Luchino Visconti; *W:* Luchino Visconti, Suso Cecchi D'Amico, Enrico Medioli; *C:* Pasquale De Santis; *M:* Franco Mannino. **VHS** *NO*

THE COOK, THE THIEF, HIS WIFE & HER LOVER

Every night, an expansive—and expanding—gangster (Michael Gambon) holds court in the posh London restaurant he owns. As he wolfs down plate after plate of food prepared by the expensive French chef (Richard Bohringer) whom he constantly belittles, he holds court to a slew of sycophants and low-lifes who guffaw at his crude humor and never dis his gluttony. Among those at the table is his elegant and attractive wife (Helen Mirren), whose response to the gazes of a distinguished-looking diner at a nearby table leads to an affair that kicks off with their flamboyant copulation in one of the ladies' room's stalls. Sex, food, and excrement find their common bond in gluttony in Peter Greenaway's *The Cook, the Thief, His Wife & Her Lover,* a visionary epic of theoretical eroticism that inspires as much critical admiration as it does contempt—which appears to be exactly what its creator intended. Though visually astonishing, the picture might be insufferable had Greenaway not cast Gambon and Mirren; Gambon is terrifying and exhausting as the maniacal mobster, and Mirren is the very model of a woman whose repression of both hatred and desire finally force the two emotions to become indistinguishable. At the end of Greenaway's earlier *The Draughtsman's Contract*, a statue that comes to life turns his head toward us and spits in our (the audience's) face. *The Cook, the Thief, His Wife & Her*

PETER GREENAWAY
Art House Director

When film director Peter Greenaway burst onto the international scene in 1983 with *The Draughtsman's Contract*, he was hailed by critics for his painterly eye. Small wonder—Greenaway, born in 1942 in Newport, Wales, trained as a painter in London and worked for a few years as a starving artist. The realization that he was destined to be an artist came when he was 12 years old, but just four years later another, equally compelling calling in cinema began to assert itself. And indeed, just one year after graduating from art school, Greenaway took a low level position at the British Film Institute in order to find his way into the world of motion pictures.

During the 11 years he spent directing and editing films for the British government, Greenaway also began to release a series of highly experimental short films of his own, and in 1978 he released his first feature, the surrealist *A Walk through H*. The obsession with symbolism and order Greenaway evinced there reappeared in the films that followed—perhaps most conspicuously in *Drowning by Numbers* (1988). In the U.S., Greenaway's films drew mostly art house crowds, until the release in 1989 of *The Cook, the Thief, His Wife & Her Lover*, a comic—some said pornographic—parable about greed and the consumer society. As with his past films, critics were sharply divided over the merits of *The Cook, the Thief...*, but the X-rating bestowed by the Motion Picture Association of America seemed only to increase the film's box office receipts.

In recent years, although Greenaway has continued to make movies, his attention has shifted to other venues, and he has devoted more and more time to creating CDROMs, Imax films, live operas, and art installations. One of his latest efforts was a project called "The Stairs: Location," which took over the entire city of Geneva with its one hundred pieces installed throughout the city streets. His most recent film is *The Pillow Book*. He is married with two daughters, both who are studying art.

Lover is an infernal and occasionally inspired two-hour version of that gesture—carefully structured, of course, as political metaphor—yet you can't take your eyes off it (except for the occasional glance at one's watch). As this monstrous circus of gluttony enters its second hour, we fear that the only sin we haven't seen—literal cannibalism—has to show up here someplace, and in this Greenaway doesn't (or perhaps does) disappoint.

NEXT STOP . . . La Grande Bouffe, The Pillow Book, The Long Good Friday, 301, 302

1990 (R) 123m/C *GB* Richard Bohringer, Michael Gambon, Helen Mirren, Alan Howard, Tim Roth; *D:* Peter Greenaway; *W:* Peter Greenaway; *C:* Sacha Vierny; *M:* Michael Nyman. **VHS, Letterbox, Closed Caption** *THV*

CRASH

After a sex scene in one of his movies, Woody Allen remarked "that was the most fun I ever had without laughing." The characters of *Crash* might say that their sex is the most fun they've ever had without dying. It's dying—not what the French call "the little death" but what Canadian director David Cronenberg would call "the big one"—that these characters want to snuggle up to before leaving in the morning. In Cronenberg's visionary, ice-cold adaptation of J.G. Ballard's novel, the damaged victims/lovers/survivors of a head-on collision (James Spader and Holly Hunter) inhabit not just another state of mind; they seem to be living on another planet as well. It's a plane of existence well beyond "eroto-mania" or simple fetishism, induced by the near-death experience of a high-speed car crash that has almost literally "knocked the stuffing" out of the survivors. That stuffing was the filler of their lives; anything that gets in the way of reliving that moment of impact followed by the realization of survival—the greatest orgasmic intensity imaginable. Considering what a struggle it was to get the picture released, *Crash* hasn't provoked the outrage that its subject might suggest. The mechanical, repetitive quality of the sex scenes—mirroring the characters' helpless surrender to their poignantly obsessive, fetishistic impulses—is either alarmingly arousing to audiences or utterly absurd; either way couples find it safer to laugh the whole thing off as silly on the ride home, and quickly flip on Letterman when they climb into bed and crash for the night. A darkly funny vision of erotic obsession that has a lot more in common with *Vertigo* than it does with *Grand Prix* may, ironically, be one of the least pornographic movies ever made. "Those people are all so *sad*," a disappointed, sensitive-sounding man complained after the lights went up, "isn't sex more *fun* than that?" His girlfriend flashed a look at him as if she wanted to say something, but she thought better of it and off they went to have *fun*. I think that Mr. Cronenberg—an extraordinary and witty artist—would have been pleased.

NEXT STOP . . . *Dead Ringers, Last Tango in Paris, Damage*

1995 (NC-17) 98m/C *CA* James Spader, Holly Hunter, Elias Koteas, Deborah Kara Unger, Rosanna Arquette, Peter MacNeill; *D:* David Cronenberg; *W:* David Cronenberg; *C:* Peter Suschitzsky; *M:* Howard Shore. Cannes Film Festival '96: Special Jury Prize; Genie Awards '96: Best Adapted Screenplay, Best Cinematography, Best Director (Cronenberg), Best Film Editing; Nominations: Genie Awards '96: Best Film, Best Sound. **VHS, LV, Closed Caption** *NLC, CRC*

CRIA
Cria Cuervos
Raise Ravens
Rear Ravens

When a young girl's father dies, the child mistakenly believes that the "poison" she has been playing with is responsible for his death. Carlos Saura's exquisite memory film is set primarily in the waning days of Spanish Fascism, touching delicately but not insistently on the themes of misplaced guilt and collective responsibility. Geraldine Chaplin has the showiest part in *Cria* (originally *Cria Cuervos,* or *Rear Ravens*), playing multiple roles in her own story as she reconstructs the mysterious memories of her childhood. But it's the amazing Ana Torrent as the 9-year-old Ana who does more than steal the show—she *is* the show. Torrent is the actress who first made a splash in Victor Erice's 1973 *Spirit of the Bee-hive,* and here, three years later, those huge eyes still have the ability to transform this simple tale of a child's discovery of her own power into something haunting and genuinely magical. If Chaplin's presence is perhaps less impressive than Saura (her real-life companion) intended, young Torrent more than makes up for it. The kid is something to see.

NEXT STOP . . . *Dreamchild, Spirit of the Beehive, The Nest*

1976 (PG) 115m/C *SP* Geraldine Chaplin, Ana Torrent, Conchita Perez, Maite Sanchez; *D:* Carlos Saura; *W:* Carlos Saura; *C:* Teo Escamilla; *M:* Federico Mompoll. Cannes Film Festival '76: Grand Jury Prize. **VHS, LV, Letterbox** *INT, TPV*

CRIES AND WHISPERS
Viskingar Och Rop

At the turn of the century, a dying woman and her servant are visited by the woman's two sisters. Though we do learn a bit about all the sisters' lives—and their relationships with each other—through flashbacks, it is

"Two women, each with half of the things a man wants."

—Bigamist Captain St. James (Alec Guinness) in *The Captain's Paradise.*

their increasingly revelatory conversations that gradually probe the depths of their fears, exploring ever more honestly the love, sexuality, hatred, and dread that have formed them, driven them together, and torn them apart. The amazing cast is headed by Ingrid Thulin, Liv Ullmann, and Harriet Andersson, and the movie's look—filmed by Sven Nykvist in a darkly claustrophobic, red-saturated color scheme—allows the country house itself to become a principal, emotionally charged character in the story. Though *Cries and Whispers* is clearly a masterwork, it seemed to me on first viewing that its many wrenching and painful moments would have limited its audience to the traditional art house crowd—those already familiar with Ingmar Bergman's themes and obsessions. Not so. *Cries and Whispers* received an ingenious and intelligent promotional push from distributor Roger Corman (yes, *that* Roger Corman, director of *Little Shop of Horrors* and *Attack of the Crab Monsters*), who vowed that it would be the first Bergman film to saturate the American marketplace and even play drive-ins. The campaign worked, and word-of-mouth did the rest. A bona fide hit in the U.S., receiving five Oscar nominations including Best Picture and Best Director (though cinematographer Nykvist was the only winner), *Cries and Whispers* allowed Bergman to reach a vastly wider American audience than he ever had before, paving the way for his future breakthroughs, *Scenes from a Marriage* and *Fanny and Alexander*.

NEXT STOP . . . *Persona, The Passion of Anna, Mother and Son*

1972 (R) 91m/C *SW* Harriet Andersson, Ingrid Thulin, Liv Ullmann, Kary Sylway, Erland Josephson, Henning Moritzen; *D:* Ingmar Bergman; *W:* Ingmar Bergman; *C:* Sven Nykvist. Academy Awards '73: Best Cinematography; National Board of Review Awards '73: Best Director (Bergman); New York Film Critics Awards '72: Best Actress (Ullmann), Best Director (Bergman), Best Film, Best Screenplay; National Society of Film Critics Awards '72: Best Cinematography, Best Screenplay; Nominations: Academy Awards '73: Best Costume Design, Best Director (Bergman), Best Picture, Best Story & Screenplay. **VHS, LV** *HMV, WAR, BTV*

THE CRIME OF MONSIEUR LANGE
Le Crime de Monsieur Lange

One of the earliest screenplays on which surrealist Jacques Prévert collaborated was this charmingly witty and easily digested bit of anti-capitalist entertainment from Jean Renoir. A deeply pleasurable fantasy of what socialism might be if it could ever actually be made to work, *The Crime of Monsieur Lange* is set at a publishing house run by the slimy and oppressive profiteer, Batala (Jules Berry). Monsieur Lange (René Lefèvre) is a humble employee who loves good literature as well as pulp fiction, and in his spare time is writing a rip-roaring western adventure with the wonderful title (especially when pronounced in French) of *Arizona Jim*. When Batala appropriates the book as a picture-book for quick cash, he also fills it with gratuitous commercial mentions of a patent medicine—perhaps one of the cinema's first references to the still-obnoxious practice of product placement. This isn't enough to take care of the unscrupulous boss's debts, however, and when he takes it on the lam, his employees band together to create a harmonious collective where there was once a grim sweatshop. Batala's eventual return drives Lange to the satisfying crime of the title, which is recounted in relaxed and richly textured flashback form by the incomparable Renoir. Created in the wake of the formation of France's left-wing Popular Front, *Monsieur Lange* served as a rallying point for audiences who wanted this publishing collective to be more than just a fantasy. Despite the Popular Front's victories later that year (1936), their dreamed-of goals quickly proved elusive. Renoir's elegant and enchanting film, however, has yet to lose any of its luster.

NEXT STOP . . . *Boudu Saved from Drowning, La Chinoise, Our Daily Bread*

1936 90m/B *FR* Rene Lefevre, Jules Berry, Florelle, Sylvia Bataille, Jean Daste, Nadia Sibirskaia, Henri Guisol; *D:* Jean Renoir; *W:* Jean Renoir, Jacques Prevert; *C:* Jean Bachelet; *M:* Jean Wiener, Joseph Kosma. **VHS** *FCT, INT*

THE CRIMINAL LIFE OF ARCHIBALDO DE LA CRUZ

Ensayo de un Crimen
Rehearsal for a Crime

While it's generally acknowledged that this 1955 Mexican film by Luis Buñuel never fully measures up to its underlying premise, that premise itself may be as hilariously, perversely "Buñuelian" as anything the great surrealist ever conjured (and may be *so* ingenious as to have been impossible to live up to). A young boy is intruded upon by his governess at the very moment he happens to be trying on his mother's clothes. His embarrassment at her scolding is short-lived, because in addition to the (revolutionary?) act of cross-dressing, another, bloodier revolution is taking place in the streets outside his home. That revolt converges with little Archibaldo's, producing a stray—or divinely aimed—shot that shuts the governess up by killing her, instantly transforming little Archibaldo's guilt and shame into gratified and enormously relieved sexual pleasure. Alas, the powerful and thoroughly ingrained fetish that has been created in Archibaldo at that moment proves a difficult and unwieldy one for him to recreate later in life—though not for lack of trying. This theme of the unendingly frustrated quest for genuine sexual fulfillment would go on to become the spine of many of Buñuel's later masterworks, including *Tristana, Belle de Jour,* and *The Discreet Charm of the Bourgeoisie.*

NEXT STOP . . . *The Exterminating Angel, Viridiana, That Obscure Object of Desire*

1955 95m/B *MX SP* Ernesto Alonso, Ariadne Welter, Rita Macedo, Rodolfo Landa, Andrea Palma, Miroslava Stern; **D:** Luis Bunuel; **W:** Luis Bunuel; **C:** Augustin Jimenez; **M:** Jorge Perez. **VHS** *FCT, WBF*

A CRY IN THE DARK
Evil Angels

During a recent, high-profile murder investigation near my hometown of Detroit, the guilt of the victim's spouse was virtually assumed by many in the community, not because of any facts, but because of the extremely polished, calm, and emotionless manner in which the spouse answered reporters' questions on television. As it turned out, the eventual solution to the case proved the spouse's complete innocence. This kind of public lynching by mannerism is nothing new; it is, in fact, the subject of one of the most powerfully unsettling (and unjustly neglected) films of the 1980s, Australian director Fred Schepisi's *A Cry in the Dark.* It's based on the true story of an Australian woman named Lindy Chamberlain, who was found guilty of murdering her baby despite her claims that the infant was carried off from the family's campsite by a wild dingo. Chamberlain was found guilty by the public long before the jury chimed in, and the "incriminating evidence" all centered around her cool, unemotional attitude in TV interviews as well as on the witness stand. If you've ever thought that Meryl Streep's talent has been over-hyped, one look at her riveting performance here as Lindy Chamberlain will cure you of that notion. She didn't win the Oscar the year she was nominated for *A Cry in the Dark,* but that may simply be because not enough tickets were sold to the movie—and *that* may be because people don't *like* Lindy Chamberlain, which of course is what got her convicted in the first place. Issues of popularity aside, this is an extraordinary picture.

NEXT STOP . . . *The Chant of Jimmie Blacksmith, Six Degrees of Separation, The Thin Blue Line*

1988 (PG-13) 120m/C *AU* Meryl Streep, Sam Neill, Bruce Myles, Charles Tingwell, Nick Tate, Neil Fitzpatrick, Maurice Fields, Lewis Fitz-gerald; **D:** Fred Schepisi; **W:** Fred Schepisi, Robert Caswell; **C:** Ian Baker; **M:** Bruce Smeaton. Australian Film Institute '89: Best Actor (Neill), Best Actress (Streep), Best Film; Cannes Film Festival '89: Best Actress (Streep); New York Film Critics Awards '88: Best Actress (Streep); Nominations: Academy Awards '88: Best Actress (Streep). **VHS, LV, 8mm, Closed Caption** *WAR, FCT*

CURSE OF THE DEMON
Night of the Demon
The Haunted

Montague James's story "Casting the Runes" was the basis for this satisfyingly creepy hor-

ror film, made in 1958 by the legendary director Jacques Tourneur (*Out of the Past, Cat People*). While visiting London, psychologist and believer in all things rational John Holden (Dana Andrews) has an unpleasant encounter with one Dr. Karswell (Niall MacGinnis in an exhilaratingly villainous performance). Karswell, it seems, has been toying with the occult and rather successfully conjuring demons. His method: a slip of paper on which Karswell has transcribed ancient runes must be passed to another person—when that person accepts the paper, even unwittingly, a demon will, at the appointed hour, materialize and carry the hapless victim to hell. By the time Holden becomes a believer and realizes what the paper he's carrying in his pocket means, only minutes remain for him to alter his horrible fate. *Curse of the Demon* builds from a carefully shaded series of scenes that suggest the evil at work here without rubbing our

faces in it. Against Tourneur's wishes, the picture's American distributor insisted that a real monster be shown at least once, so a demon was built for the film's final sequence (it even made the cover of *Famous Monsters of Filmland*). All purists are supposed to hate this big rubber demon, but I've always liked him. Blame it on my less refined side. With or without him though, this is a genuinely unnerving and richly atmospheric horror film—one of the very best of the 1950s. Recently restored to its original British running time, but not to its British title, which is *Night of the Demon.*

NEXT STOP . . . *Cat People (1942), I Walked with a Zombie, Carnival of Souls*

1957 81m/B *GB* Dana Andrews, Peggy Cummins, Niall MacGinnis, Maurice Denham, Athene Seyler, Liam Redmond, Reginald Beckwith, Ewan Roberts, Peter Elliott, Brian Wilde; *D:* Jacques Tourneur; *W:* Charles Bennett, Hal E. Chester; *C:* Edward Scaife. **VHS, LV** *GKK, MLB*

DAY FOR NIGHT
La Nuit Americaine

At the American premiere of François Truffaut's *Day for Night* at the 1973 New York Film Festival, I overheard a critic in the lobby loudly pronouncing that Truffaut had finally revealed himself as a phony; he had made a movie about moviemaking that was devoid of passion and suffering. The critic (a reactionary jerk then and now) was wrong on both counts, for one of the glories of Truffaut's art lay in his ability to blind us with images of sunlight sparkling on a calm sea, forgetting for just a moment about the coming storm. The "characters" of *Day for Night*— actors, crew, their lovers, a narrator/director (played by Truffaut)—are as much children as the kids of Truffaut's later *Small Change*. As the director of what's apparently going to be a mediocre film (at best), Truffaut tells us—as if he were talking about a homework assignment late Sunday night—that at first he hoped to make a great film, then a good one, but now he hopes simply to finish it. He tells his sullen star (Jean-Pierre Léaud) to stop whining, that for them there is only the cinema—they aren't like normal people. *This* is the real world to them. And at that moment when the sun does come out and everything works—and the simple crane shot that the director wants to shoot is perfect—Georges Delerue's triumphant music rolls and the director confirms to us that "cinema is king." At a moment of supreme nakedness, Truffaut's character listens to a playback of Delerue's music over the phone while he opens a parcel. It contains books—a copy of Robin Wood's *Hitchcock's Films,* a copy of Dreyer's unfilmed screenplay for "Jesus," and more. This remarkable, talented man was always in thrall to his own gods, for whom his passion was boundless. That critic was wrong—Truffaut *was* possessed of passion. But since the director's departure, it is the cinema that suffers.

NEXT STOP . . . *8 1/2, Alex in Wonderland, The Player*

1973 (PG) 116m/C *FR* Francois Truffaut, Jean-Pierre Leaud, Jacqueline Bisset, Jean-Pierre Aumont, Valentina Cortese, Alexandra Stewart, Dani, Nathalie Baye; *D:* Francois Truffaut; *W:* Suzanne Schiffman, Jean- Louis Richard, Francois Truffaut; *C:* Pierre William Glenn; *M:* Georges Delerue. Academy Awards '73: Best Foreign Film; British Academy Awards '73: Best Director (Truffaut), Best Film, Best Supporting Actress (Cortese); New York Film Critics Awards '73: Best Director (Truffaut), Best Film, Best Supporting Actress (Cortese); National Society of Film Critics Awards '73: Best Director (Truffaut), Best Film, Best Supporting Actress (Cortese); Nominations: Academy Awards '74: Best Director (Truffaut), Best Original Screenplay, Best Supporting Actress (Cortese). **VHS** *WAR*

DAY OF WRATH
Vredens Dag

Of the 14 films that Denmark's Carl Dreyer completed during his 60-year career, few received significant distribution here, and even fewer are seen much today. His 1928 *The Passion of Joan of Arc* and his 1932 *Vampyr* are probably his best known in the U.S.; less seen is Dreyer's great 1943 *Day of Wrath,* the story of a young 17th-century woman who falls in love with her stepson, and is tried and burned as a witch after her husband—a pastor—dies. This is a majestic and uncompromising movie, inexorably moving us toward that point at which a victim is so thoroughly overwhelmed by her accusers that she no longer has the luxury of recognizing reality; she becomes, in a sense, the otherworldly creature she is accused of being. That the viewer can understand her final inner state is proof of Dreyer's genius. His stark images and dreamlike pacing have the searing inevitability of being conveyed into a psychological crematorium—which will soon become real—as inch by inch we're encompassed by her nightmare until at some final instant of higher awareness, it all makes a kind of mad, simple sense. Dreyer's honesty and aversion to cheap or easy manipulation of emotion has traditionally led the attention-span-challenged to dismiss him as tedious or boring (*The New York Times*'s Bosley Crowther called *Day of Wrath*'s "slow and ponderous tempo...a presumptuous imposition"), but others, such as screenwriters James Agee (*Night of the Hunter*) and Paul Schrader (*Taxi Driver*), have written eloquently about Dreyer's style and his ability to express the seemingly inexpressible on screen.

NEXT STOP . . . *The Passion of Joan of Arc, The Confession, The Last Temptation of Christ*

1943 110m/B *DK* Thorkild Roose, Sigrid Neiiendam, Lisbeth Movin, Preben Lerdorff, Anna Svierker; *D:* Carl Theodor Dreyer; *W:* Carl Theodor Dreyer; *C:* Karl Andersson; *M:* Poul Schierbeck. **VHS** *HTV, NOS, SNC*

THE DAY THE SUN TURNED COLD
Tianguo Niezi

Director Yim Ho's quietly jolting, Hong Kong *noir* is the story of a young man who goes to the police with his suspicion that his father's death a decade earlier wasn't an accident. The killer, he's convinced, is his own mother. Selective memory (seen in flashback) gradually becomes "repressed memory" in *The Day the Sun Turned Cold,* a taut little thriller that can be read on many levels and never loses sight of its crime-drama origins. The young man's near-pathological attachment to mom ultimately reaches critical mass when circumstantial evidence—real and remembered—can no longer be denied. Though the solution to the crime is presented without ambiguity, the age-old mystery of how we manage to see only those "truths" that we want to see remains as puzzling and disturbing as ever.

NEXT STOP . . . *The Postman Always Rings Twice (1946), Rashomon, The Conversation*

1994 99m/C *HK* Siqin Gowa, Tuo Zhong Hua, Wai Zhi, Ma Jingwu, Li Hu; *D:* Yim Ho; *W:* Yim Ho; *C:* Hou Yong; *M:* Yoshihide Otomo. **VHS** *KIV*

DAYS AND NIGHTS IN THE FOREST
Aranyer Din Ratri

Four thirty-something middle-class Bengali men take a road trip into the countryside where they promptly get lost, rhapsodize about the forgotten ideals of their youth, and decide that they will stop shaving and become "all hippies." It may have sounded like a romantic notion in 1970, but the supremely wise Satyajit Ray was hip to the true bourgeois aspirations of these self-centered men; in the end, they reveal themselves to be "all yuppies." Along the way, the four—quietly smug friends who appear to have remarkably different personalities, at least on the surface—discover considerably more about themselves than they wanted to. The gentle but stinging social and political satire of *Days and Nights in the Forest*—a film that was largely overlooked in America due to its initial, bungled distribution—might be described as *Deliverance* as directed by Jean Renoir. Perhaps the most insightful and relaxed of Ray's contemporary social comedies, it's a deeply compassionate, amusingly critical, refreshingly unforced glimpse at a hypocritical society about to devour itself as casually as a picnic lunch on a warm summer day.

NEXT STOP . . . *The Middleman, Smiles of a Summer Night, Vanya on 42nd Street*

1970 120m/C *IN* Soumitra Chatterjee, Sharmila Tagore, Shubhendu Chatterjee, Samit Bhanja; *D:* Satyajit Ray; *W:* Satyajit Ray; *C:* Soumendu Roy; *M:* Satyajit Ray. **VHS** *FCT*

DEAD OF NIGHT

When a nervous architect arrives at a British country estate, he and the others present begin describing their recent nightmares, with shocking results. Four directors collaborated to create this five-part 1945 British horror classic, which unfolds seamlessly enough to be the work of a single, impressively twisted mind. *Dead of Night* is the granddaddy of all multi-part horror films, though many who've seen it remember only the sequence starring Michael Redgrave as the frantic, paranoid ventriloquist who's certain that his dummy, Hugo, is out to kill him. There are two reasons our memories are fuzzy on the rest of the picture: one is that two stories were cut from the original American release prints (to pick up the picture's pace and to get one extra showing per day in at theatres). The second and most important reason is that the Redgrave sequence is quite simply one of the most perfectly terrifying and genuinely nightmarish little horror films ever made. I first encountered it on TV when

I was five (don't ask why my parents allowed it) and when I next saw it—more than two decades later—it was *exactly* as I had remembered it, and just as scary. I had forgotten the other stories completely, but now that *Dead of Night* has been restored to its original, five-story 102 minutes, it's somehow even scarier; you can see the circular logic that has the true flavor of an inescapable night terror. And oh, that Hugo. The directors are Alberto Cavalcanti, Basil Dearden, Robert Hamer, and Charles Crichton (*The Lavender Hill Mob*). The screenplay is by John Baines, Angus MacPhail, and T.E.B. Clarke, with an ominous, dissonant score by Jean Cocteau's favorite composer, Georges Auric (*Orpheus*).

NEXT STOP . . . *The Night My Number Came Up, The Great Gabbo, Devil Doll* (1964), *The Glass Eye* (TV episode of *Alfred Hitchcock Presents*)

1945 102m/B *GB* Michael Redgrave, Mervyn Johns, Sally Ann Howes, Basil Radford, Naunton Wayne, Roland Culver, Googie Withers, Frederick Valk, Antony Baird, Judy Kelly, Miles Malleson, Ralph Michael, Mary Merrall, Renee Gadd, Michael Allan, Robert Wyndham, Esme Percy, Hartley Power, Elizabeth Welch, Magda Kun, Carry Marsh; **D:** Alberto Cavalcanti, Charles Crichton, Basil Dearden, Robert Hamer; **W:** T.E.B. Clarke, John Baines, Angus MacPhail; **C:** Stanley Pavey, Douglas Slocombe; **M:** Georges Auric. **VHS** *NO*

DEAD RINGERS

When you read the advance description of a forthcoming David Cronenberg movie—whether it's *Crash,* his remake of *The Fly,* or *Dead Ringers*—it's only natural to assume that either he's lost his mind or that he's simply trying to be outrageous for the hell of it. Then you see the film, and it's immediately apparent that Cronenberg is far more than a great showman—he's one of the boldest and most eloquent poets to work in the medium of cinematic fantasy since Jean Cocteau. The description that preceded *Dead Ringers*'s release was that it was based on the true story of twin gynecologists who shared a lover. Well, sure, but... how interesting can that be? As star Jeremy Irons commented in another film: "You have no idea." *Dead Ringers* (which was originally set to be released as *Twins,* but had to scuttle the name because of the then-forthcoming

Danny De Vito—Arnold Schwarzenegger fiasco) is, as are all of Cronenberg's best films, an exploration of the twin mysteries of desire and revulsion that Cronenberg likes to explore by "externalizing internal states." As Hitchcock did with Norman Bates and his mother, Cronenberg is able to use the love/hate relationship between twin doctors Beverly and Elliot Mantle to look at the thin borders separating love from manipulation, genius from paranoia, pride from megalomania. I don't know what it is to be a twin, but I do know what it is to look in the mirror and wonder just exactly who it is I'm looking at. The performance that Jeremy Irons gives in *Dead Ringers* is just as personal and embarrassingly private, and despite the movie's ostensibly outrageous (and gruesome) premise, it's equally unshakable.

NEXT STOP . . . *The Fly* (1986), *Naked Lunch, Psycho*

1988 (R) 117m/C *CA* Jeremy Irons, Genevieve Bujold, Heidi von Palleske, Barbara Gordon, Shirley Douglas, Stephen Lack, Nick Nichols; **D:** David Cronenberg; **W:** David Cronenberg, Norman Snider; **C:** Peter Suschitzky; **M:** Howard Shore. Genie Awards '89: Best Actor (Irons), Best Director (Cronenberg), Best Film; Los Angeles Film Critics Association Awards '88: Best Director (Cronenberg), Best Supporting Actress (Bujold); New York Film Critics Awards '88: Best Actor (Irons). **VHS, LV** *VTR, CRC*

DEATH OF A BUREAUCRAT
La Muerte de un Burocrata

This early work from Cuba's foremost filmmaker, Tomás Gutiérrez Alea, is the witty and sharply funny story of a man whose efforts to dig up and rebury the corpse of his uncle lead to a bureaucratic nightmare of epic—and comic—proportions. Alea was to use a similar comic metaphor (trying to move a corpse) as the basis of his final film, the 1996 *Guantanamera!,* but with a gentler, more resigned, more melancholy tone than he uses here. *Death of a Bureaucrat* is more of a flat-out slapstick farce with political underpinnings, which pokes fun at red tape, regulations, and "official policy" that flies in the face of common sense; it's an eternally frustrating aspect of modern society that is hardly unique to

D

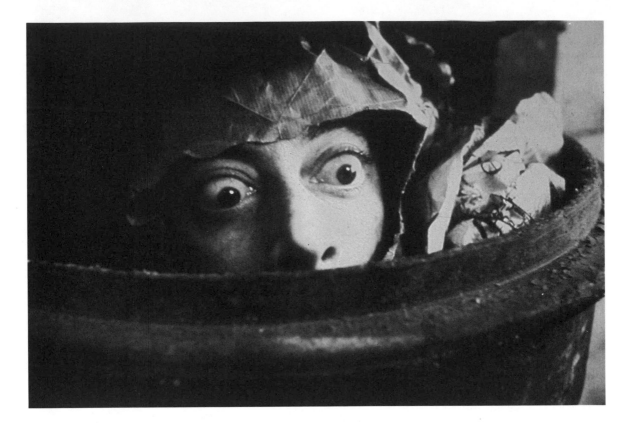

socialism. To paraphrase the classic Levy's Rye Bread ad, you don't have to be communist to enjoy *Death of a Bureaucrat*.

NEXT STOP . . . *Memories of Underdevelopment, Guantanamera!, The Trouble with Harry*

1966 87m/B *CU* Salvador Wood, Silvia Planas, Manuel Estanillo, Gaspar de Santelices, Carlos Ruiz de la Tejera, Omar Alfonso, Ricardo Suarez, Luis Romay, Elsa Montero; *D:* Tomas Gutierrez Alea; *W:* Tomas Gutierrez Alea, Ramon Suarez; *C:* Ramon Suarez; *M:* Leo Brower. **VHS** *NYF, FCT*

THE DECAMERON
Il Decameron

Probably the most spirited, faithful, and purely entertaining of the many screen adaptations of Boccaccio's writings, Pier Paolo Pasolini's 1970 rendering of eight bawdy and charming stories from *The Decameron* was

hot stuff when originally released; few theatres would play it thanks to a then-deadly "X" rating, and many of the customers who showed up at those few theatres may have been expecting something considerably more graphic—perhaps *porno*graphic. This squeamishness on the part of censors was partly due to some nudity in the films, but also due to the film establishment's fear and loathing of Pasolini's outspoken political positions and his "unsavory" private life. The perception of Pasolini himself as taboo, if not the personification of evil, was a major "spin" problem that would continue to hamper the director's marketability, right through the limited release of the two other films of his self-described "Trilogy of Life": *The Canterbury Tales* (1971) and *The Arabian Nights* (1974). By 1975, frustrated with compromise, Pasolini erupted with the cinematic equivalent of Ivan the Terrible's angry declaration: "From this day forward I will be what you call me."

He finally lived up to the reputation that had been imposed on him, by following his gentle *The Arabian Nights* with what was to be not only his last film, but one of the most horrifying non-documentary visions in all cinema—perhaps the only movie in history to really *deserve* an "X"—*Salo, or the 120 Days of Sodom*. But I do digress. *The Decameron* is a charmer. (Look for Pasolini in the role of the painter Giotto.)

NEXT STOP . . . *The Gospel According to St. Matthew, Mamma Roma, The Arabian Nights*

1970 (R) 111m/C *FR IT GE* Franco Citti, Ninetto Davoli, Angela Luce, Patrizia Capparelli, Jovan Jovanovich, Silvana Mangano, Pier Paolo Pasolini; *D:* Pier Paolo Pasolini; *C:* Tonino Delli Colli; *M:* Ennio Morricone. Berlin International Film Festival '71: Silver Prize. **VHS, LV, Letterbox** *WBF*

DEEP END
Na Samyn Dnie

There was a comic strip from the early years of *Peanuts* in which a kid (I don't remember whether it was Charlie Brown or Linus) was asked how his first conversation with the little girl he had a crush on went. "I didn't know what to do," he replied, "so I hit her." It's immediately apparent that that strip was *not* published in the PC nineties, yet I remember it coming to mind in 1970 when I was watching director Jerzy Skolimowski's subversive and devilishly engrossing *Deep End*. John Moulder-Brown plays the 15-year-old Michael, whose job in a seedy London public bath surrounds him with all manner of grotesque characters, but more importantly introduces him to his pretty co-worker, Susan (Jane Asher), who instantly becomes the physical embodiment of every romantic and erotic fantasy rattling around in Michael's adolescent head. A German/American co-production with a British cast and a Polish director, *Deep End* nevertheless has a coherence and a singular comic tone that seems the product of one highly individual vision. You may know where it's going, but you'll be pleasantly on edge until you get there.

NEXT STOP . . . *Knife in the Water, Moonlighting, The Tenant*

1970 88m/C *GB GE* Jane Asher, John Moulder-Brown, Diana Dors, Karl Michael Vogler, Christopher Sandord; *D:* Jerzy Skolimowski; *W:* Jerzy Skolimowski, Jerry Gruza, Bloeslav Sulik; *C:* Charly Steinberger; *M:* Cat Stevens. **VHS** *NO*

DELICATESSEN

In a post-nuclear future, the tenants of a dilapidated rooming house—including a group of militant vegetarians—do their best to keep from becoming dinner for the building's aggressively carnivorous landlord. A large-scale visionary fable distinguished by a polished and genuinely original visual style, this energetic tale of love and cannibalism from French directors Marc Caro and Jean-Pierre Jeunet (*The City of Lost Children, The Fifth Element*) sometimes achieves a spectacular comic grace. A sequence in which Jeunet and Caro weave together the various sounds that tenants are making behind the closed doors of their rooms into a hilarious but grisly cinematic symphony is of near-classic stature, but the whole film works best (as much of the best grim screen humor does) when seen with an audience that's plugged in to the directors' temperament. While watching *Delicatessen* you may be reminded of some of director Terry Gilliam's elaborate fantasy films, like *Brazil* and *The Adventures of Baron Munchausen;* apparently Gilliam himself was reminded of them, as he's listed in the film's credits as *Delicatessen*'s "presenter."

NEXT STOP . . . *The City of Lost Children, Brazil, A Boy and His Dog*

1992 (R) 95m/C *FR* Marie-Laure Dougnac, Dominique Pinon, Karin Viard, Jean Claude Dreyfus, Ticky Holgado, Anne Marie Pisani, Edith Ker, Patrick Paroux, Jean-Luc Caron; *D:* Jean-Pierre Jeunet, Marc Caro; *W:* Gilles Adrien, Jean-Pierre Jeunet, Marc Caro; *C:* Darius Khondji; *M:* Carlos D'Alessi. Cesar Awards '92: Best Art Direction/Set Decoration, Best Writing. **VHS, LV, Closed Caption** *PAR, BTV*

DERSU UZALA

As a result of the critical and popular failure (unjustified, I think) of his 1970 fairy-tale-like portrait of slum residents, *Dodes 'ka-den*, the

A Russian soldier (Yuri Solomine) befriends a Mongolian trapper (Maxim Munzuk) in the Siberian wilderness in *Dersu Uzala*.

despondent Akira Kurosawa attempted suicide. The work he plunged himself into—partly as comeback, partly as therapy—was this simple tale set early in this century of a Russian explorer who encounters a wise, aging hunter along the border between Russia and Manchuria. Dersu the hunter (played with considerable charm by Maxim Munzuk) becomes a great and unexpected friend to the explorer, saving his life during a fearsome blizzard, which is just one of many memorable images in the film. Featuring a flashback structure not unlike that which John Ford used in *The Man Who Shot Liberty Valance,* Kurosawa's film is, also like Ford's, a tale of unlikely heroism and secret honor in the face of a galvanic clash between nature and "civilization." A Japanese and Soviet co-production, *Dersu Uzala* tries to achieve its impact through both length (nearly two-and-a-half hours) and sheer size. Though photographed in a 70mm multi-track stereo

format, it was seen that way in the U.S. only at a few festival showings; its general release here was in standard 35mm. The grainy, brownish color (a sad hallmark of much Russian cinema) in the release prints certainly didn't help, but even in its original 70mm version *Dersu Uzala* never gels into the visionary epic of friendship and adventure that it clearly wants to be. It's a sluggish, schematic, and only fitfully moving pageant. But if it indeed provided the therapy that Kurosawa needed (it snared an Academy Award as Best Foreign Language Film), then *Dersu Uzala*—which was followed by the stunning *Kagemusha* and the brilliant *Ran*—may well be one of the most important (if not best) films in Kurosawa's life.

NEXT STOP . . . *Red Beard, The Man Who Shot Liberty Valance, Close to Eden*

1975 124m/C *JP RU* Yuri Solomin, Maxim Munzuk; **D:** Akira Kurosawa; **W:** Akira Kurosawa, Yuri Nagibin; **C:**

Asakazu Nakai, Yuri Gantman, Fyodor Dobronravov; **M:** Isaak Shvartz. Academy Awards '75: Best Foreign Film. **VHS** *KIV*

THE DESIGNATED MOURNER

In an unnamed country in the not-too-distant future, a bourgeois couple (Mike Nichols and Miranda Richardson) find the tensions of their marriage strained to the breaking point when a brutal, fascist regime tightens its grip on their privileged, intellectual world. A straightforward record of the 1995 London stage production of a play by Wallace Shawn (better known as an actor in films like *My Dinner with André* and *Clueless*), *The Designated Mourner* was directed by another playwright, David Hare, with the goal of recreating the power and claustrophobia of the original theatrical experience. He achieved that goal, and then some. The three person cast, which includes David de Keyser in addition to Nichols and Richardson, is seated on a stage, directly facing the camera as they speak. They talk of the day-to-day experience of having their rights and dignity stripped away, and soon Nichols's character becomes the center of attention. He draws us in with his easy and confessional manner, but gradually we're chilled as we understand how an intelligent, seemingly decent human being can rationalize his own monstrous behavior until he sees it as not only *not* monstrous, but as a welcome relief from the hypocrisy of caring about others. Shawn and Nichols provide us with a window onto one of the greatest mysteries, how portions of some of civilization's most "enlightened" populations—such as Germany's during World War II—were and are able to rationalize behavior that seems to us unimaginable. Nichols's character isn't a monster; he's a charming and witty man whose monstrous behavior is a part of human nature, and that's what makes him more terrifying than any tentacled, digitized special effect. All the performances are fine, but Mike Nichols's is beyond that. He's a superb director, but judging from this performance—his screen debut—we've been missing out on his *real* talent all these years.

NEXT STOP . . . *Shame* (Bergman), *Fires on the Plain*, *The Sorrow and the Pity*

1997 (R) 94m/C *GB* Mike Nichols, Miranda Richardson, David de Keyser; **D:** David Hare; **W:** Wallace Shawn; **C:** Oliver Stapleton; **M:** Richard Hartley. **VHS** *NYR*

DEVI
The Goddess

In 19th-century Bengal, a well-to-do man (Chhabi Biswas) dreams that his 17-year-old daughter-in-law (Sharmila Tagore) is the reincarnation of the goddess Kali. Believing his dream to be a holy message, the father publicly proclaims this "miracle" and promptly ensconces the startled girl on an altar at his home; soon, the area's peasants—and the girl herself—become convinced of her divinity. Satyajit Ray's bold, perceptive, and extraordinarily haunting drama touches on issues of faith, fanaticism, class, and, as in so many of his films, the subjugation of women. *Devi*'s themes caused the film to be the subject of protest by fundamentalist Hindus in 1960, but after a brief ban, the government approved it for both domestic and international distribution.

NEXT STOP . . . *The Music Room*, *Charulata*, *Days and Nights in the Forest*

1960 93m/B *IN* Chhabi Biswas, Sharmila Tagore, Soumitra Chatterjee; **D:** Satyajit Ray; **W:** Satyajit Ray; **C:** Subrata Mitra; **M:** Ali Akbar Khan. **VHS** *COL, WFV, DVT*

DEVIL IN THE FLESH
Le Diable au Corps

An autobiographical novel by Raymond Radiguet, who died at age 20, is the basis for this poetic, powerfully bitter love story between adolescent French schoolboy François (Gérard Philipe) and unhappy soldier's wife Marthe (Micheline Presle) during World War I. Though the movie is by every standard an elegantly modulated and exceptionally sensitive love story, it is the mesmerizing performance of the 24-year-old Gérard Philipe that elevates the picture to classic status. Rocketing past major stardom and heading straight to idol status

"No! No Italians allowed. Music is a serious business."

—Music teacher Grigorief (Michel Debrane) tells Ana (Ariadna Gil) she can't sing Rossini in *Celestial Clockwork*.

THE HOUND SALUTES:

IRENE JACOB
Inspiring French-born Actress

In the 1991 global hit film, *The Double Life of Veronique*, dark-eyed French-born actress Irene Jacob sparkled in a difficult dual role, playing two identical young women in Paris and Krakow. The performance for revered Polish director Krzystof Kieslowski garnered Jacob a best actress award at Cannes at the age of 25 in her first starring role. More European art films followed before Jacob was reunited with Kieslowski in *Red*, the final installment in a well-received trilogy. Jacob was linked romantically to Kieslowski, and she functioned for him much as Catherine Deneuve did for Luis Bunuel: She was the magnetic and romantic center of both films.

Born July 15, 1966 in Paris, Jacob attended the Dramatic School in London and the Geneva Conservatory of Music. She debuted in a small role in Louis Malle's 1987 film *Au Revoir les Enfants*. Kieslowski, seeing her in the film, auditioned her for *Veronique*. One critic said she was "unquestionably a great and beguiling presence" in the mysterious film. In *Red*, where she plays a model who stumbles upon an old judge who spies on his neighbors, she was both radiant and harried in a performance one critic called "wonderfully exhausting." Recently, she played Desdemona in the 1995 British/U.S. film *Othello* and played Wesley Snipes's girlfriend in 1998's *U.S. Marshal*.

---

thanks to his internationally acclaimed portrayal of François, Philipe would remain a popular actor until his untimely death in 1959. A decade after the successful release of *Devil in the Flesh (Le Diable au Corps)*, the film's director, Claude Autant-Lara, was one of those cited by the young François Truffaut and other founders of the *Cahiers du Cinéma*/New Wave movement as being representative of the staid and formal quality of French cinema—a cinema that this new group of critics/filmmakers would soon alter forever. (Italy's Marco Bellocchio directed an updated remake in 1986.)

 **NEXT STOP** . . . *La Traversée de Paris (Four Bags Full), Sylvia and the Phantom, Devil in the Flesh* (1986)

1946 112m/B *FR* Gerard Philipe, Micheline Presle, Denise Grey; *D:* Claude Autant-Lara; *W:* Jean Aurenche, Pierre Bost; *C:* Michel Kelber; *M:* Rene Cloerec. **VHS** *NOS, FCT*

DEVIL IN THE FLESH
Il Diavolo in Corpo

This unnecessary remake of the 1946 Claude Autant-Lara classic *Devil in the Flesh (Le Diable au Corps)* is a modern-day updating of the original story, about a schoolboy who becomes sexually involved with a soldier's wife in World War I. Director Marco Bellocchio has changed the war to the one which modern terrorists are waging in Italy; Giulia (Maruschka Detmers) is engaged to Giacomo (Riccardo De Torrebruna), an imprisoned terrorist who's on trial for killing her father, and who claims he's seen the light and given up his violent ways. As the trial continues, Giulia makes the acquaintance (through *very* odd circumstances) of a handsome young student named Andrea (Federico Pitzalis). Before long they're lovers, and they move with all deliberate speed from a discussion of urban guerrilla warfare to the long and explicit fellatio sequence that made this version of *Devil in the Flesh* a hot topic on the art house circuit (though more people expressed opinions about it than could have possibly seen it in its limited American run). Except for "the big scene," which was certainly a first for a studio release (it went out with an "X" rating), *Devil in the Flesh* isn't much of a picture, lacking the genuine eroticism of the original as well as political bite. You almost get the feeling that Bellocchio gave Giulia a touch of insanity as an excuse for the movie's flabby, motivationless screenplay. Detmers is one of the most heart-stoppingly exquisite actresses in movies, but she was far better served by Godard in 1983 in his witty and intelligent *First Name: Carmen*. As for *Devil in the Flesh*, there's a well-worn slang term for the movie's famous sex act that could be used to describe the whole picture.

NEXT STOP . . . *Fists in the Pocket, First Name: Carmen, Patty Hearst*

1987 (R) 110m/C *IT* Riccardo De Torrebruna, Maruschka Detmers, Federico Pitzalis; *D:* Marco Bellocchio; *W:* Ennio de Concini, Enrico Palandri, Marco Bellocchio; *C:* Giuseppe Lanci; *M:* Carlo Crivelli. **VHS, LV** *ORI*

THE DEVILS
The Devils of Loudun

Oy. For those too young to remember, there was, once upon a time, an outlandish movie director named Ken Russell. It's been a decade or so since he's caused anything resembling a stir, but for the nearly 20 years beginning with 1969, the unveiling of a new Ken Russell movie was awaited with anticipation, fear, and a fistful of Dramamine. His historical epics in particular took more than a few liberties with traditional textbook versions of the facts, and students who wrote book reports based on movies like *The Devils* discovered that they should have stuck with Cliff's Notes. Aldous Huxley's *The Devils of Loudun* is the ostensible source material for Russell's brightly colored, unapologetically vulgar portrait of the 17th-century French

town that was purported to be stuffed to the rafters with sexually degenerate nuns, tortured priests, demonic pacts, and countless varieties of murder. The only thing they *didn't* do in 1634 was photograph all of these lewd and disgusting goings-on in leering, widescreen Technicolor close-ups, but Russell has thoughtfully served history by doing that job himself. *The Devils* would be genuinely offensive if it weren't so patently stupid, but it's so hilariously overwrought that you just can't bring yourself to despise it; it's a movie Ed Wood might have made if his goal in life was to be a big-budget pornographer. Vanessa Redgrave and Oliver Reed both survived Russell's onslaught (though Reed claims that Russell wanted to actually pierce his tongue in one close-up, but Reed dodged that indignity by convincing Russell that as an actor, his tongue would come in handy in the future). The film's one genuinely striking element is the production design, which marked the first screen credit of director Derek Jarman.

NEXT STOP . . . *The Music Lovers, Savage Messiah, Lisztomania*

1971 (R) 109m/C *GB* Vanessa Redgrave, Oliver Reed, Dudley Sutton, Max Adrian, Gemma Jones, Murray Melvin, Michael Gothard, Georgina Hale, Christopher Logue, Andrew Faulds; *D:* Ken Russell; *W:* Ken Russell; *C:* David Watkin; *M:* Peter Maxwell Davies. National Board of Review Awards '71: Best Director (Russell). **VHS** *WAR*

THE DEVIL'S EYE
Djavulens Oga

"A woman's chastity is a sty in the devil's eye," or so goes a legend as related in an old Danish radio play called *Don Juan Returns*. In 1960, fresh from the worldwide acclaim he received for *The Virgin Spring*, Sweden's Ingmar Bergman decided on an adaptation of the play for his next project. *The Devil's Eye* was conceived as a grand comedy about bourgeois hypocrisy in which the Devil (Stig Järrel) tries to cure his ocular irritation by sending Don Juan (Jarl Kulle) back to Earth from Hell in order to take care of business with a pastor's chaste daughter (Bibi Andersson). Despite what must have sounded like

Simone Signoret and Vera Clouzot are partners in crime in *Diabolique*.

prime material for an elegant, archly theatrical comedy on the order of his *Smiles of a Summer Night, The Devil's Eye* turned out to be not so much theatrical as merely stagy. There's a tired and uninspired feel to the sexual satire as well as to most of the performances, betraying, perhaps, some of the tensions that existed between the director and his cast. By one report, Bergman was calling *The Devil's Eye* "a bad film" while he was shooting it, and the all-around anxiety level on the set wasn't helped by a reporter/photographer team from *Life* magazine hanging around and eavesdropping on all the squabbles. Hardly a disgrace, but by no means one of Bergman's best.

NEXT STOP . . . *Smiles of a Summer Night, The Magic Flute, Sunday's Children*

1960 90m/B *SW* Stig Jarrel, Bibi Andersson, Jarl Kulle; *D:* Ingmar Bergman; *W:* Ingmar Bergman; *C:* Gunnar Fischer; *M:* Erik Nordgren, Domenico Scarletti. **VHS** *NLC*

THE DEVIL'S PLAYGROUND

At a Catholic boarding school, adolescent boys are discovering their own sexuality; their confusion and anxiety is matched only by that of their instructors. Fred Schepisi's superb 1976 debut film is—to whip out the old cliche—"controversial," as films on this subject always are by their very nature. What sets *The Devil's Playground* apart is the compassion and humor with which Schepisi treats his subjects, not to mention his elegant storytelling abilities. This is the first film by this extraordinary Australian director, but its lack of flashy, show-offiness makes it feel like the creation of someone who's blessedly without the need to call attention to his own style, focusing it instead on his characters. It's a rich and powerful debut. (Look for *Schindler's List* author Thomas Keneally in the small role of Father Marshall; Keneally went on to write Schepisi's next film, the brilliant *The Chant of Jimmie Blacksmith*.)

NEXT STOP . . . *The Chant of Jimmie Blacksmith, The Boys of St. Vincent, Zero for Conduct*

1976 107m/C *AU* Arthur Dignam, Nick Tate, Simon Burke, Charles Frawley, Jonathon Hardy, Gerry Dugan, Thomas Keneally; *D:* Fred Schepisi; *W:* Fred Schepisi; *C:* Ian Baker; *M:* Bruce Smeaton. Australian Film Institute '76: Best Actor (Tate), Best Actor (Burke), Best Film.

DIABOLIQUE
Les Diabolique

It's as great as it's cracked up to be, but perhaps for different reasons than you've heard. Henri-Georges Clouzot's 1955 thriller is the story of a monstrous, philandering schoolteacher (Paul Meurisse) whose wife (Vera Clouzot) and lover (Simone Signoret) get together to do him in. *Diabolique* was originally promoted and described as a shocker, and though there are certainly a few pleasurable jolts left in the gas tank, today's Freddy Krueger—raised audiences are a bit harder to stun with unexpected twists. Fortunately for Clouzot—and us—this darkly funny and sexually suggestive fun house offers considerably more than a stunner of an ending (though it *does* happen to have one). The bickering, jealousy, and fear that bonds weak, victimized wife Clouzot to tough-as-nails mistress/murderess Signoret boils over when their victim's body vanishes; they seem to suspect each other and are driven nearly to the breaking point by the casual but insistent questioning of the wiser-than-he-seems, raincoated Inspector Fichet (Charles Vanel). The audience isn't sure what—or who—to believe, but since all of those involved in the crime are such monsters, the whole picture has a misanthropic, deeply perverse atmosphere unlike any other thriller I know. It's fun, all right, but you might want to go to confession afterward. (Remade clumsily and pointlessly in 1996; the casting of Isabelle Adjani and Sharon Stone was clever but to no avail.) From a novel by Pierre Boileau and Thomas Narcejac, who went on to write the story that would form the basis of Hitchcock's *Vertigo*.

NEXT STOP . . . *The Wages of Fear, Vertigo, Psycho*

1955 107m/B *FR* Simone Signoret, Vera Clouzot, Paul Meurisse, Charles Vanel, Michel Serrault; *D:* Henri-Georges Clouzot; *W:* Frederic Grendel, Jerome Geronimi, Rene Masson; *C:* Armand Thirard; *M:* Georges Van Parys. New York Film Critics Awards '55: Best Foreign Film. **VHS, LV, 8mm** *VYY, NOS, SNC*

DIARY OF A CHAMBERMAID
Le Journal d'une Femme de Chambre
Il Diario di una Cameriera

Octave Mirbeau's novel about bourgeois decadence in the face of budding fascism was originally filmed in Hollywood in 1946 by Jean Renoir, but it was an unhappy clash of cultures that resulted in an amiable but negligible mess of a film. This savagely witty remake, made in France in 1964 by Luis Buñuel, sets the story in 1928. Célestine (Jeanne Moreau at her best) is the scheming, irresistible housekeeper who climbs up the social ladder by using the political and sexual fantasies of everyone in her well-to-do employer's household as the rungs on which she steps. Both deeply funny and genuinely appalling, Buñuel's *Diary of a Chambermaid* is a sobering and boldly witty vision of a self-deluded, refined society hungrily feeding on itself. With Georges Geret, Michel Piccoli, and longtime Buñuel writing collaborator Jean-Claude Carrière.

NEXT STOP . . . *Diary of a Chambermaid* (1946), *L'Age d'Or, Viridiana*

1964 97m/C *FR* Jeanne Moreau, Michel Piccoli, Georges Geret, Francoise Lugagne, Daniel Ivernel; *D:* Luis Bunuel; *W:* Luis Bunuel, Jean-Claude Carriere; *C:* Roger Fellous. **VHS, LV** *IME, XVC*

DIARY OF A COUNTRY PRIEST
Le Journal d'un Cure de Campagne

Just see it. Describing director Robert Bresson's masterpiece is inevitably to trivialize it; it's an experience that was conceived for and can only be experienced as cinema.

The story is simple. A priest, dying of cancer, is in a state of despair because he believes that he has failed in his life's task of raising the moral level of his parish. As he examines his life mercilessly, the priest ultimately is able to contemplate the possibility and meaning of redemption, and this is conveyed by the director with such subtle and eloquent imagery that the film itself becomes a kind of answer to the largest of all questions. *Diary of a Country Priest* is an example not only of the cinema's great, largely untapped powers, but also an irrefutable answer to those who question the relevance of art to everyday life. One of the greatest films of all time.

NEXT STOP . . . *A Condemned Man Has Escaped, Mouchette, Pickpocket*

1950 120m/B *FR* Nicole Maurey, Antonine Balpetre, Claude Layou, Jean Riveyre, Nicole Ladmiral; *D:* Robert Bresson; *W:* Robert Bresson; *C:* L.H. Burel; *M:* Jean Jacques Grunenwald. **VHS** *DVT, IGP, FCT*

DIARY OF A LOST GIRL
Das Tagebuch Einer Verlorenen

The plot is part Dickens, part Jerry Springer; a wealthy pharmacist's daughter has a child by her father's assistant, then lands in a reform school commanded by a sadistic matron, moves on to a brothel, and ultimately becomes the wife of a wealthy count whose sexual secrets lead to his suicide. The last silent film by director Georg Wilhelm Pabst was based on a best-selling novel by Margaret Böhme, and was a perfect vehicle for the beautiful Kansas-born showgirl Louise Brooks to use as a follow-up to her enormously successful 1928 collaboration with Pabst, *Pandora's Box*. *Diary of a Lost Girl* ran into censorship troubles immediately, in practically every country where it was permitted to be shown at all. In the U.S. it was simply unavailable in anything resembling its complete form for many decades, until a restored and relatively full version was released in 1984. A director whose interest leaned toward the realities of street life, Pabst treaded into a bold new cinematic frankness with his 1925 *The Joyless Street* starring Greta Garbo, and took no prisoners with the legendary Louise Brooks's character Lulu in *Pandora's Box*. While not quite on that film's dramatically intoxicating level, *Diary of a Lost Girl* is nevertheless an enjoyably scandalous concoction.

NEXT STOP . . . *The Joyless Street, Pandora's Box, The Threepenny Opera* (1931)

1929 99m/B *GE* Louise Brooks, Fritz Rasp, Josef Rovensky, Sybille Schmitz; *D:* G.W. Pabst; *W:* Rudolf Leonhard; *C:* Sepp Allgeier, Fritz Arno Wagner; *M:* Timothy Brock. **VHS, LV** *GPV, MRV, VDM*

DIARY OF A SEDUCER
Le Journal du Seducteur
The Seducer's Diary

When a mysterious Parisian student loans Claire (Chiara Mastroianni, daughter of Marcello and Catherine Deneuve) a rare copy of a novel called *Diary of a Seducer,* she falls hopelessly in love with him. Her realization that the book possesses the uncanny power of an aphrodisiac leads to a bizarre and rather unexpected web of desire, as the book is passed from one reader to another. Director Daniele Dubroux came from a background in film criticism, and if her generally engrossing tale of obsession and sexual manipulation has a flaw, it may be that she's been a bit too dryly analytical in structuring the action. Still, this is a clever, gloomy little dark comedy about the male capacity for compartmentalizing passion. It has an appropriately bitter aftertaste, and a wonderfully understated performance from Chiara Mastroianni.

NEXT STOP . . . *La Discrete, Rendezvous in Paris, Captain's Paradise*

1995 98m/C *FR* Danielle Dubroux, Chiara Mastroianni, Melvil Poupaud, Mathieu Amalric, Micheline Presle, Hubert Saint Macary, Jean-Pierre Leaud; *D:* Danielle Dubroux; *W:* Danielle Dubroux; *C:* Laurent Machuel; *M:* Jean-Marie Senia. **VHS, Letterbox** *FXL, FCT*

DIE LIEBE DER JEANNE NEY
The Loves of Jeanne Ney
Lusts of the Flesh

G.W. Pabst's adaptation of Ilya Ehrenburg's novel is the story of the love between a young French girl (Edith Jehanne) and a young Russian communist (Uno Henning), and the manipulating adventurer (Fritz Rasp) who comes between them. This beautifully photographed and richly detailed drama is famous for Pabst's experiments in making the film's editing "invisible." He discussed his method in an interview at the time of its production: "Every shot is made on some movement. At the end of one cut somebody is moving, at the beginning of the next, the movement is continued. The eye is thus so occupied in following these movements that it misses the cuts." What he couldn't have known was that the technique he was describing, "cutting on movement," would become standard practice years later, and that *The Loves of Jeanne Ney* would become the textbook for the future of film editing.

NEXT STOP . . . *The Joyless Street, Pandora's Box, Kameradschaft*

1927 102m/B *GE* Brigitte Helm, Eugen Jenson, Edith Jehanne, Uno Henning, Fritz Rasp, Vladimir Sokoloff; *D:* G.W. Pabst; *W:* Ladislao Vajda, Ilya Ehrenburg, Rudolf Leonhard; *C:* Walter Robert Lach, Fritz Arno Wagner. **VHS** *FCT, GLV*

DIE NIBELUNGEN
Siegfried and Kriemhild's Revenge
Die Nibelungen: Siegfried und Kriemhilds Rache

As hard as it may be to imagine *Die Nibelungen* as anything other than Wagnerian, Fritz Lang's great silent epic about the death of Siegfried and the revenge of his wife Kriemhild was based not on Wagner's operatic interpretation of the story but on the original legend, which Lang envisioned as a hot-blooded, spectacular epic fantasy. Filmed and released in two separate parts—one year after the other—*Siegfried* and *Kriemhild's*

Revenge are adventure films on a scale that James Cameron can only dream of. Film historian Lotte Eisner has written definitively about the massive and monumental architectural design of Lang's epic, but the still images reproduced in her books can give only a hint of the overwhelming scale and the physical and dramatic symmetry of the most astounding interpretation of a mythological legend in all cinema. In part one, Siegfried attains invulnerability in battle by bathing in the blood of a slain dragon, only to later die at the behest of a wronged and enraged Queen Brunhild. In part two, Siegfried's wife, Kriemhild, who has sworn to avenge her husband's death, marries Attila the Hun and arranges for the massacre of all those who had a hand the death of her beloved Siegfried. (Attila is played to the hilt by Rudolf Klein-Rogge, best-remembered as Rotwang the inventor in Lang's *Metropolis*.) For a modern audience, it's impossible not to think, at least for an instant, of Kriemhild's enemies as "the heads of the five families," but that's a tribute to the lasting power of Lang's vision, the influence of which can be seen in every subsequent epic film to touch on the themes of loyalty, betrayal, and revenge. (In 1933, nine years after *Die Nibelungen*'s release and the year that Lang fled Germany for America, Hitler arranged for a re-release of *Siegfried*, yet found *Kriemhild's Revenge* a bit too rousing for the public, banning it until his death.)

NEXT STOP . . . *Dr. Mabuse: Der Spieler, Metropolis, M*

1923 280m/B *GE* Paul Richter, Margareta Schoen, Rudolf Klein-Rogge, Georg August Koch; *D:* Fritz Lang; *C:* Carl Hoffmann, Gunther Rittau; *M:* Gottfried Huppertz. **VHS, LV** *CVC, GLV*

THE DISCREET CHARM OF THE BOURGEOISIE
Le Charme Discret de la Bourgeoisie

I've never really been sure whether the "Buñuelian" moments that have happened to me since 1972—the year in which *The Discreet Charm of the Bourgeoisie* was released—were a result of seeing the film, or

The Ambassador
(Fernando Rey)
takes aim as his
friends watch in
amazement in *The
Discreet Charm of
the Bourgeoisie.*

if I simply *noticed* them because of the film. It doesn't matter, I suppose, yet even as recently as last week, when I was presented at a McDonald's with the unlikely and down-right alarming story that they were "out of french fries," I felt the smiling presence of Luis Buñuel and his strangely comforting chronicle of a group of self-centered, middle-class adults who have the damnedest time getting something to eat. *The Discreet Charm of the Bourgeoisie* can certainly be inter-preted in a number of ways, but on its sim-plest and most accessible level, it's a com-edy—one which takes place as a series of dreams within dreams—about the eternal quest for human satisfaction, whether it be carnal or culinary. This quest, of course, can never be fully satisfied, nor is it ever over (God forbid we no longer long for anything), yet when Buñuel makes us look at it in such a literal manner—as a meal that is set out before us but which we can never quite get

into our mouths—he makes us appreciate the bitter and inspired comedy behind the Creator's little jokes. Buñuel has said that given the choice, people will always select slavery over freedom; his genius lies in his ability to not only show us the evidence, but to amuse us with the notion of such a fate. His six characters trudging bravely down the road at the end of *The Discreet Charm* is as close to Buñuel's version of solidarity as we'll ever get; we're all in this together, and we might as well have a few laughs. A fabulous movie. With Stéphane Audran, Delphine Seyrig, Bulle Ogier, Michel Piccoli, Milena Vukotic, Jean-Pierre Cassel, and the great Fer-nando Rey. Academy Award for Best Foreign Film, Nominee for Best Original Screenplay.

NEXT STOP . . . *Viridiana, Simon of the Desert, The Phan-tom of Liberty*

1972 (R) 100m/C *FR* Milena Vukotic, Fernando Rey, Delphine Seyrig, Jean-Pierre Cassel, Bulle Ogier, Michel

Piccoli, Stephane Audran, Luis Bunuel; **D:** Luis Bunuel; **W:** Luis Bunuel, Jean-Claude Carriere; **C:** Edmond Richard. Academy Awards '72: Best Foreign Film; British Academy Awards '73: Best Actress (Seyrig), Best Screenplay; National Society of Film Critics Awards '72: Best Director (Bunuel), Best Film; Nominations: Academy Awards '72: Best Story & Screenplay. **VHS, LV**

DISTANT THUNDER
Ashani Sanket

In a remote Bengali village, Gangacharan (Soumitra Chatterjee) is a well-respected Brahmin who serves many functions: priest, physician, schoolteacher, and general spiritual leader. But it is 1942, and World War II will soon affect even the most remote reaches of the globe, causing panic, profiteering, and inflation, and this will cause even the carefully structured, privileged world of Ganga to face the realities of hatred, division, and famine. One of the least-seen of Ray's major films, *Distant Thunder* is a quietly devastating portrait of a society being tested by the most horrifying of human tragedies. Photographed in rich, dark colors that bring the landscapes to life with an almost shocking vividness, *Distant Thunder*'s physical beauty serves as a staggeringly beautiful but mocking counterpoint to its portrait of large-scale human tragedy.

NEXT STOP . . . *The Music Room, Mahanagar, Days and Nights in the Forest*

1973 92m/C IN Soumitra Chatterjee, Sandhya Roy, Babita, Gobinda Chakravarty, Romesh Mukerji; **D:** Satyajit Ray; **W:** Satyajit Ray; **C:** Soumendu Roy; **M:** Satyajit Ray. Berlin International Film Festival '73: Golden Berlin Bear. **VHS** *FCT*

DISTANT VOICES, STILL LIVES

This autobiographical work from England's Terence Davies is constructed as a series of living tableaux ripped freshly bleeding yet ominously tranquil from the memory of a child growing up in a working class family in the 1940s and 1950s. The brutality of Davies's father (Pete Postlethwaite) is presented without anesthesia, though the antidotes

seen in the film range from the family's regular attendance at the pub— with songs of the era making a stinging yet poignant counterpoint to the father's savagery—to the young protagonist's desperate escape to the dream families of Hollywood at the local movie house. Some of this film's set pieces—the mother's bruises unblinkingly photographed by a gliding, tracking camera to the tune of "Taking a Chance on Love"—are unforgettably moving and almost shockingly brave. In one's heart of hearts it must be admitted that this is indeed a musical, the likes of which has never been seen before. Bravo. (A sequel, *The Long Day Closes,* was finished six years later, in 1993.)

NEXT STOP . . . *The Long Day Closes, The Neon Bible*

1988 87m/C *GB* Freda Dowie, Pete Postlethwaite, Angela Walsh, Dean Williams, Lorraine Ashbourne; **D:** Terence Davies; **W:** Terence Davies; **C:** Patrick Duval. Los Angeles Film Critics Association Awards '89: Best Foreign Film. **VHS, LV** *ART*

DIVA

This plush and sparkling romantic thriller—the debut feature of director Jean-Jacques Bieneix—is the story of Jules (Frédéric Andrei), a young messenger who becomes obsessed with the operatic voice and person of American opera star Cynthia Hawkins (Wilhelminia Wiggins Fernandez). Jules has made a secret, bootleg recording of Cynthia's performance of *La Wally,* and when his tape becomes mixed up with a recording sought by drug dealers, *Diva* splinters into a crystalline kaleidoscope of chases, hideouts, and unexpectedly romantic moments, all set in a glistening, neon-lit Paris. Whenever *Diva* appears to be veering toward the utterly shallow, an inspired bit of decor or music or motion lifts it out of the merely fashionable and into that privileged realm of dazzling movies that exist merely for the love of movies. It's true that some films that toss in a little bit of everything in their search for hipness end up being mere uncommitted pastiches, but *Diva* has style and personality to burn. A lot of films since—including some by Bieneix himself—have clearly been *Diva* wannabees, but this film's pungent formula

comic timing in Pietro Germi's brutally funny 1962 black comedy. The title refers to the quickest and cleanest method of separating from one's spouse in Italy, which isn't divorce, exactly; it's murder. (Crimes of passion are permitted; divorce is not.) Marcello's demanding wife (Daniela Rocca) has driven him to the breaking point, and the beautiful young girl—his cousin—he'd like to replace her with (Stefania Sandrelli) won't wait forever. Taking matters into his own hands proves tricky, however, and director Germi provides suspense and comedy in equal, generous measure. Mastroianni received the first of his three Academy Award nominations for his performance here as the frustrated, hilariously desperate Ferdinando; it came as a double honor since comic performances—not to mention foreign language performances—are notoriously snubbed by the Oscars. Germi was nominated for Best Director as well, and his ingenious screenplay, written in collaboration with Ennio de Concini and Alfredo Gianetti, won the 1962 Oscar for Best Original Screenplay.

NEXT STOP... *Seduced and Abandoned, Alfredo, Alfredo, Marcello Mastroianni: I Remember*

1962 104m/B *IT* Marcello Mastroianni, Daniela Rocca, Leopoldo Trieste, Stefania Sandrelli; *D:* Pietro Germi; *W:* Pietro Germi, Ennio de Concini, Alfredo Giannetti; *C:* Leonida Barboni; *M:* Carlo Rustichelli. Academy Awards '62: Best Story & Screenplay; British Academy Awards '63: Best Actor (Mastroianni); Golden Globe Awards '63: Best Actor—Musical/Comedy (Mastroianni), Best Foreign Film; Nominations: Academy Awards '62: Best Actor (Mastroianni), Best Director (Germi). **VHS** *HTV*

Scheming married Ferdinando (Marcello Mastroianni) contemplates *Divorce—Italian Style.*

is more than simply original; it's got legs. Unfortunately, the same wasn't true of Bieneix's career, which sank like a rock with the subsequent *Moon in the Gutter,* and has yet to recover.

NEXT STOP... *Moon in the Gutter, Betty Blue*

1982 (R) 123m/C *FR* Frederic Andrei, Roland Bertin, Richard Bohringer, Gerard Darmon, Jacques Fabbri, Wilhelmenia Wiggins Fernandez, Dominique Pinon; *D:* Jean-Jacques Beineix; *W:* Jean-Jacques Beineix; *C:* Philippe Rousselot; *M:* Vladimir Cosma. Cesar Awards '82: Best Cinematography, Best Sound, Best Score; National Society of Film Critics Awards '82: Best Cinematography. **VHS, LV** *MGM*

DIVORCE— ITALIAN STYLE
Divorzio All'Italiana

Marcello Mastroianni dazzled audiences worldwide with his impeccable, deadpan

DR. MABUSE, PARTS 1 & 2
Doktor Mabuse der Spieler

Fritz Lang's two-part film is a massive fresco of depravity and violence—a portrait of a society so close to the brink of self-destruction that a single madman can come close to pushing it over. Dr. Mabuse (Rudolf Klein-Rogge) is a brilliant criminal mastermind whose designs are nothing less than to profit from—as well as accelerate—the wholesale decadence that already exists in the Berlin of

1922. Mabuse's powers of persuasion are incomparable, as is his ability to disguise himself in countless insidious but familiar forms. Part one—originally subtitled *An Image of Our Times*—shows Mabuse unable to control himself when losing at the gambling tables, but equally unable to handle winning. His thirst for power—in the form of money—struck a chord with German audiences of the day, who were used to the staggering inflation and wild revelry that made the stylized nightclubs and pumped-up passions of Lang's film seem like a tame documentary. A decade later, in 1933, when the nation had indeed found one man to be in charge of its national criminal empire, Lang produced a sequel—*The Testament of Dr. Mabuse*—following which he fled the country for Hollywood. More than simply a prescient warning, however, *Dr. Mabuse: Der Spieler* remains a fascinating, sprawling spectacle, and one of the most powerful visions of evil ever committed to film.

NEXT STOP . . . *Spies, The Testament of Dr. Mabuse, M*

1922 242m/B *GE* Rudolf Klein-Rogge, Aud Egede Nissen, Alfred Abel, Gertrude Welcker, Lil Dagover, Paul Richter; **D:** Fritz Lang; **W:** Thea von Harbou, Fritz Lang; **C:** Carl Hoffmann. **VHS** *SNC, MRV, NOS*

DR. PETIOT
Le Docteur Petiot

Docteur Petiot is the true story of a physician in occupied Paris who assured Jews that he could transport them safely out of the country for a price; after taking their possessions, however, he turned them over to the Nazis to be murdered. Considering the intrinsic fascination of this real-life horror story, and in spite of the casting of the reliable Michel Serrault as Petiot, director Christian de Chalonge has achieved the nearly impossible; he's made a dull, flatly uninteresting film that strains credulity despite its factual basis. The problem is the director's basic approach to the character. He portrays Petiot almost literally as a movie monster; with his wild eyes, pale makeup, and swirling, joyous dance steps, we expect this Petiot to get into his coffin at sunrise, or to need some sort of liquid

concoction to keep him so animated. It's not even vaguely shocking to see a vampire murder without conscience, but to see an actual human being—which, despite their inhuman behavior, is what the Nazis and their collaborators were, after all—rationalize sending friends and strangers to their deaths is what would have made *Docteur Petiot* both valuable and truly horrifying. This Petiot isn't human on any level; despite Serrault's dazzling theatrics, the character as conceived here could have been played just as convincingly by Bela Lugosi or Robert Englund.

NEXT STOP . . . *The Sorrow and the Pity, Hotel Terminus: The Life and Times of Klaus Barbie, Point of Order*

1990 102m/C *FR* Michel Serrault, Berangere Bonvoisin, Aurore Prieto, Nita Klein, Dominique Marcas, Andre Lacombe, Pierre Romans, Zbigniew Horoks, Claude Degliame, Martine Montgermont, Nini Crepon, Andre Julien, Andre Chaumeau, Axel Bogousslavsky, Maxime Collion, Nadege Boscher, Jean Dautremay, Michel Hart; **D:** Christian de Chalonge; **W:** Christian de Chalonge, Dominique Garnier; **C:** Patrick Blossier; **M:** MIchel Portal. **VHS** *WAC, FCT*

DODES 'KA-DEN
Clickety Clack

After a five year hiatus following the release of his magnificent *Red Beard* (a period that also included his brief, disastrous participation in the production of *Tora! Tora! Tora!*), Akira Kurosawa returned to the screen with this gentle, humane fantasy about the daily lives of the residents of a slum. Based on a previously published collection of short stories, the film's title comes from the sound that one of the residents makes when he imagines himself a uniformed streetcar driver. He repeats the word over and over (not unlike Walter Mitty's "pocketa pocketa") until it becomes a kind of metaphorical refrain for the courage each of these people demonstrates in simply getting through one more seemingly hopeless day. This was Kurosawa's first film in color, and he uses his bright, fantastic palette to suggest a different emotional tone for each of the stories he tells. Though *Dodes 'ka-den* is minor Kurosawa, its downright hostile reception by film critics was almost inexplicable (unless a modest

THE HOUND SALUTES:
KRZYSZTOF KIESLOWSKI
Trilogy Director

Krzysztof Kieslowski, the Polish born director who died in 1996, has been called the greatest film maker of his generation. Born in Warsaw in 1941, in his youth Kieslowski knew illness and poverty. Because his father, a civil engineer, suffered from tuberculosis, the family had to subsist on the meager salary his mother made as an office clerk. And Kieslowski himself was a sickly child who was frequently admitted to sanatoriums.

Kieslowski declined to apply to college, but he was admitted to a school for theater technicians, where he initially conceived the idea of becoming a director. Kieslowski's goal at the time was to become a stage director, but he decided to pursue it by studying to be a film director. After several tries, he was finally admitted to the prestigious School of Cinema and Theatre in Lodz, Poland, and after graduating he spent more than a decade making documentary films about the lives of ordinary Poles under communism. In 1981, realizing that his films might be used to incriminate some of the people who appeared in them, he turned his attention full-time to feature films.

After the Polish government imposed martial law in 1981, Kieslowski, a member of the Solidarity trade union, made one more politically oriented film, *Bez Konca* (*No End,* 1984) before tackling a series of ten one-hour segments for Polish television. Released together as *Decalogue: The Ten Commandments* (1988), this film about ethics in everyday life finally brought Kieslowski international attention. His next film, *The Double Life of Veronique* (1991), a joint Polish-French production, was also well-received abroad. His next project, the *Three Colors* trilogy, was based on the symbolic meaning of the three colors in the French flag, and proved to be a triumph. For the third installment, *Red* (1994), Kieslowski was nominated for a best director Oscar. Afterward, the director announced his retirement from filmmaking. However, he apparently changed his mind and began working with screenwriter Krzysztof Piesiewicz on a new script thought to be the first in a new trilogy of films, *Heaven, Hell, and Purgatory.* He died from a heart attack on March 13, 1996 in Warsaw.

---

picture following a lifetime of masterworks must be judged a catastrophe by comparison). Its reception proved a disaster for its creator as well; less than a year after its release, Kurosawa attempted suicide.

NEXT STOP... *The Lower Depths (1957), Red Beard, Kagemusha*

1970 140m/C *JP* Yoshitaka Zushi, Junzaburo Ban, Kiyoko Tange; **D:** Akira Kurosawa; **W:** Shinobu Hashimoto, Hideo Oguni, Akira Kurosawa; **C:** Takao Saito, Yasumichi Fukuzawa; **M:** Toru Takemitsu. Nomi-nations: Academy Awards '71: Best Foreign-Language Film. **VHS** *NO*

DON QUIXOTE
Don Kikhot

This is an intelligent and generally enchanting Soviet adaptation of Cervantes, directed with flair and color (and a big budget) by Grigori Kozintsev. The picture's comedy rarely gets in the way of its gracious poignancy, and Kozintsev deserves credit for maintaining a high-wire act that never collapses into the maudlin. But what's really priceless about this version is the elegant, transfixing performance of Nikolai Cherkassov as the would-be gallant knight. Best remembered as the title characters in Sergei Eisenstein's historical epics *Alexander Nevsky* and *Ivan the Terrible,* Cherkassov here reveals a sweet vulnerability under his proud hero's surface; his deep, amazingly versatile voice provides Quixote with a real but very human elegance. Filmed in the Crimea, the picture is as physically exquisite as it is sincere. A gem.

NEXT STOP . . . *Alexander Nevsky, Ivan the Terrible, Peter the First*

1957 110m/B *SP RU* Nikolai Cherkassov, Yuri Tobubeyev; *D:* Grigori Kozintsev; *W:* Yevgeni Schwarz; *C:* Appolinari Dudko, Andrei Moskvin; *M:* Kara Karayev. **VHS** *FCT*

DONA FLOR AND HER TWO HUSBANDS
Dona Flor e Seus Dois Maridos

Dona Flor (Brazilian natural resource Sonia Braga) becomes a widow when her husband's womanizing and drinking and other bad habits finally causes the simultaneous expiration of most all of his organs. She's glad to get rid of the bum, and remarries—this time to a respectable, tasteful man who's moderate in all things. It doesn't take long before Dona Flor wishes for the return of husband number one, and in director Bruno Barreto's lively, brainless fantasy, she gets her wish. A novel by Jorge Amado was the basis for this hugely successful film, which outgrossed *Ghostbusters* in Brazil. It was a hit in the U.S. too, at least on the art house circuit, and one might conceivably attribute this to Sonia Braga's numerous, highly energetic sex scenes. The movie's pretty bad, but the American remake, *Kiss Me Goodbye,* starring Sally Field (yes, in the Sonia Braga part), was worse. It was *so* serious and self-important (and sexless) that it made me long—just like

Dona Flor did—for the dirtier, raunchier, less responsible fun of the first one.

NEXT STOP . . . *Gabriela, Belle Epoque, Lovers*

1978 106m/C *BR* Sonia Braga, Jose Wilker, Mauro Mendonca; *D:* Bruno Barreto; *W:* Bruno Barreto; *M:* Chico Buarque. **VHS, LV** *FXL, IME, TPV*

DONKEY SKIN
Peau d'Ane

As if to imagine a Hollywood musical as filmed by Jean Cocteau (years before Disney's *Beauty and the Beast,* mind you), Jacques Demy and musical collaborator Michel Legrand continued the partnership that began with their *The Umbrellas of Cherbourg* with this bizarrely straightforward yet surprisingly engaging fairy tale. Jean Marais (Cocteau's Beast in his *Beauty and the Beast*) is the widower king who refuses to marry a woman less beautiful than his dead queen, so he settles on his daughter. Since she's played by Catherine Deneuve, we can't exactly blame him, but it is a little tough to explain to kids why the king's plan is undesirable. All ends well, the scenery and costumes are clever and colorful, and the Legrand songs are never worse than harmless (some are better than that). Delphine Seyrig makes a knockout fairy godmother, but it's Marais's resonant presence that provides *Donkey Skin* with its emotional center.

NEXT STOP . . . *Lola, The Umbrellas of Cherbourg, Jacquot de Nantes.*

1970 89m/C *FR* Catherine Deneuve, Jean Marais, Delphine Seyrig, Jacques Perrin; *D:* Jacques Demy; *C:* Ghislan Cloquet; *M:* Michel Legrand. **VHS** *NO*

THE DOUBLE LIFE OF VERONIQUE
La Double Vie de Veronique

The late Krzysztof Kieslowski's 1991 film picks up in a sense where Ingmar Bergman's *Persona* left off. In Bergman's 1966 film, the personalities of what may be two separate women (Liv Ullmann and Bibi Andersson) seem to combine and blend into each other.

In Kieslowski's film, two identical women—one living in Poland and one in France—have an enormous number of similarities, or does it only seem that way because of their physical appearance? This mysterious puzzle of a movie—exactly the kind of picture so many timid filmgoers fear they're going to encounter when they hear the term "art film"—suggests many tantalizing possibilities but insists on leaving any conclusions about the inevitability of human behavior or predestination solely on the audience's shoulders. That, of course, is where it belongs, and thanks to the mesmerizing dual performance of Irène Jacob, the fascinating questions that Kieslowski poses become immediate and somewhat scary. This is a journey that will take you to a new destination with each viewing.

NEXT STOP . . . *Blue* (Kieslowski), *White*, *Red*

1991 (R) 96m/C *FR PL* Irene Jacob, Phillipe Volter, Sandrine Dumas, Aleksander Bardini, Louis Ducreux, Claude Duneton, Halina Gryglaszewska, Kalina Jedrusik; **D:** Krzysztof Kieslowski; **W:** Krzysztof Kieslowski, Krzysztof Piesiewicz; **C:** Slawomir Idziak; **M:** Zbigniew Preisner. Cannes Film Festival '91: Best Actress (Jacob); National Society of Film Critics Awards '91: Best Foreign Film. **VHS, LV, Closed Caption** *PAR*

DOWN & DIRTY
Brutti, Sporchi, e Cattivi
Ugly, Dirty and Bad

The title was whittled down by the American distributor from *Ugly, Dirty and Bad*, but *Down & Dirty* is still a perfectly apt title for Ettore Scola's hilarious, raw portrait of a riotously degenerate extended family living outside of Rome. Nino Manfredi plays the head of this clan, who's so mean that when his family spikes his mostaccioli with what seems like a pound of rat poison, it barely slows him down—though it does make him meaner.

(He's a wealthy miser, having gotten a big insurance payout for losing an eye. It was an accident that left this mean, dirty man—to paraphrase Henny Youngman's famous second opinion joke—ugly, too.) *Down & Dirty* features the kind of broad, fork-waving, violent physical humor that's simply a matter of taste, and there are certainly those who'll find this whole sordid group of characters utterly without redeeming features. That, of course, is exactly what I love about it.

NEXT STOP . . . *The Pizza Triangle, We All Loved Each Other So Much, Passione d'Amoré*

1976 115m/C *IT* Nino Manfredi, Francesco Anniballi, Maria Bosco; *D:* Ettore Scola; *W:* Ruggero Maccari, Ettore Scola; *C:* Dario Di Palma; *M:* Armando Trovajoli. Cannes Film Festival '76: Best Director (Scola). **VHS, Closed Caption**

THE DRAUGHTSMAN'S CONTRACT

At a lavish English country estate in 1694, a young painter (Anthony Higgins) makes a deal with the estate's owner (Janet Suzman) to complete a dozen renderings of the place, but the terms of his employment are unusual indeed. Strange goings-on are replaced by even stranger goings-on, and just what exactly the draughtsman is up to is revealed slowly, in the form of the drawings he produces. Stepping back a level, the film's director, Peter Greenaway, is performing precisely the same function as the draughtsman, allowing the meanings of his film to develop slowly, in the details, though when it's over you may well wonder if anything at all has been revealed other than Greenaway's extraordinary capacity for producing striking *mise en scène*. It's a film that seems the product of a brilliant smart-ass; when it's over you may want to congratulate Greenaway on his vision and originality, and then punch him in the mouth.

NEXT STOP . . . *The Falls, Drowning by Numbers, The Pillow Book*

1982 (R) 103m/C *GB* Anthony Higgins, Janet Suzman, Anne Louise Lambert, Hugh Fraser; *D:* Peter Green-

away; *W:* Peter Greenaway; *C:* Sacha Vierny; *M:* Michael Nyman. **VHS** *MGM, FCT*

DREAMCHILD

An unexpected delight. *Dreamchild,* written by Dennis Potter (*The Singing Detective*) and directed by Gavin Millar, is a fantasy about a real person whose fame stemmed from being someone else's fantasy. The central portion of the story is set in New York in the 1930s, when 80-year-old Mrs. Alice Hargreaves (Coral Browne) arrives from England to celebrate the centennial of the birth of the Rev. Charles Dodgson (Ian Holm), known to the world as Lewis Carroll. As a child, we learn, Mrs. Hargreaves was Dodgson's model for the Alice of *Alice in Wonderland*. The trip jogs Mrs. Hargreaves's memory, and we get to spend—through flashback—time with little Alice and Hargreaves at the time of his inspired creation. But all her memories are not happy, and though the film could hardly be classified as an expose, it deals frankly and compassionately with Dodgson's strong feelings for the child. Coral Browne is quite wonderful as the grown Alice, and her scenes of interaction with characters from *Alice's Adventures in Wonderland*—designed and performed by Jim Henson's Creature Shop—are surprisingly touching. Ian Holm is riveting as Dodgson, and Amelia Shankley is more than adequate portraying Alice as a child. *Dreamchild* sneaks up on you, and will stay with you a long time.

NEXT STOP . . . *Pennies from Heaven, The Singing Detective*

1985 (PG) 94m/C *GB* Coral Browne, Ian Holm, Peter Gallagher, Jane Asher, Nicola Cowper, Amelia Shankley, Caris Corfman, Shane Rimmer, James Wilby; *D:* Gavin Millar; *W:* Dennis Potter; *C:* Billy Williams; *M:* Max Harris, Stanley Myers. **VHS** *MGM*

DREAMS
Kvinn Odrom
Journey into Autumn

Two women—one who owns a fashion photography studio (Eva Dahlbeck) and one who's a friend and model (Harriet Andersson)—make a trip to Göteborg to visit the studio-owner's former, now-married lover (Ulf Palme). The model, who herself is recovering from a broken engagement, unexpectedly finds herself wooed on the journey by a leering, huffing-and-puffing old consul (Gunnar Björnstrand). While the men in *Dreams* (also known as *Journey into Autumn*) all turn out to be jerks, Bergman seems uninterested as to why, and consequently the film has little impact or staying power beyond its considerable physical beauty. In fact, in a 1968 interview Bergman himself stated:"I don't remember much about *Journey into Autumn*."To tell you the truth, neither do I.

NEXT STOP . . . *Sawdust and Tinsel, The Seventh Seal, Wild Strawberries*

1955 86m/B *SW* Harriet Andersson, Gunnar Bjornstrand, Eva Dahlbeck, Ulf Palme; *D:* Ingmar Bergman; *W:* Ingmar Bergman; *C:* Hilding Bladh; *M:* Stuart Gorling. **VHS, LV** *HMV, NLC*

DROWNING BY NUMBERS

A coroner named Henry Madgett (Bernard Hill) is startled to discover that three male drowning victims were all married to three generations of women who are all named Cissie Colpitts (Joan Plowright, Juliet Stevenson, and Joely Richardson). The coroner—who has a dead-bug and dead-animal collecting son named Smut—agrees to keep quiet in exchange for an "arrangement" with the ladies. While all of this is taking place within the confines of writer/director Peter Greenaway's ostensible plot, another story is being told within the images themselves; the numbers 1 through 100 appear on screen—sequentially—during the course of *Drowning by Numbers,* and sometimes they show up in the *strangest* places. You'll see them on key chains, trees, clocks, and cows, but what they add up to is anybody's guess. As is always the case with Greenaway's films, the cinematography is both lushly beautiful and stubbornly enigmatic, but then again so are the movies themselves. I rather like *Drowning by Numbers;* as much of a puzzle as it is, it's somehow one of Greenaway's most pleasantly annoying achievements.

NEXT STOP . . . *The Falls, The Draughtsman's Contract, The Cook, the Thief, His Wife & Her Lover*

1987 (R) 121m/C *GB* Bernard Hill, Joan Plowright, Juliet Stevenson, Joely Richardson; *D:* Peter Greenaway; *W:* Peter Greenaway; *C:* Sacha Vierny; *M:* Michael Nyman. **VHS, LV** *ART*

✓ DRUNKEN ANGEL
Yoidore Tenshi

This superb 1948 Kurosawa picture was seen by much of the world only after *Rashomon* took the cinema world by storm two years later. It's the story of a swaggering gangster (played wonderfully by the 28-year-old Toshiro Mifune) who visits a doctor (*Ikiru*'s Takashi Shimura) to have a bullet removed, only to be informed that he has tuberculosis. Uninterested in this news, the gangster not only refuses treatment from the alcoholic doctor, he also slaps him around a bit in the bargain. Outraged by the gangster's refusal to deal with any of the sad truths of his life, yet well aware that he is not without flaws himself, the doctor engages the gangster in a duel of wills that results in a surprising—though violent—resolution. This story of a wounded man and his would-be healer was also seen by many in post-war Japan as an allegory of a wounded nation; it won Japan's highest film prize, the Kinema Jumpo ("Best One") Award, Japan's equivalent of the Oscar. Though it wasn't his first film as a director, many feel that *Drunken Angel* is the first major work of Kurosawa's career. Just as importantly, it marks the first collaboration between Kurosawa and Toshiro Mifune—a partnership that would change the face of world cinema for all time.

NEXT STOP . . . *Stray Dog, Ikiru, Red Beard*

1948 108m/B *JP* Toshiro Mifune, Takashi Shimura, Choko Iida; *D:* Akira Kurosawa; *W:* Keinosuke Uegusa; *C:* Takeo Ito; *M:* Fumio Hayasaka. **VHS** *DVT, MRV*

DRUNKEN MASTER
Drunken Monkey in a Tiger's Eye

Depending on exactly how you count, *Drunken Master* was Jackie Chan's third movie, and it's one of his best. Jackie Chan (called Jacky in the credits of this movie) is listed everywhere you look as a martial arts star, but—while not wishing to denigrate martial arts stardom—he is considerably more than that. He's often compared to Buster Keaton in his ability to set up and execute elaborate visual gags, and when he's really sailing, as he is here, the comparison is apt. The plot here has something to do with Naughty Panther (Chan) studying under a geezer-ish, liquor-saturated martial arts master (Siu Tien Yuen) who hardly seems equipped to teach him what it takes to tackle the ubiquitous "big boss." And that's the secret of Jackie's appeal; he's funny, but incredibly skilled. The combination works wonderfully, and some of the ballet-like stunts and fight sequences in *Drunken Master* are as good as anything in his more elaborate *Police Story* or *Project A*. The dubbing in *Drunken Master* is terrible enough to add yet another level of comedy, and you can't exactly become exorcized over any damage it does to the dramatic "subtleties" of the characterizations. Just enjoy. (There's also the added bonus of the wonderful Michelle Yeoh; she plays Jackie's aunt, and if she looks familiar, you may have caught her big-budget debut in the James Bond picture *Tomorrow Never Dies*.)

NEXT STOP . . . *Police Story, Supercop (Police Story III), Sherlock Jr.* (1924)

1978 90m/C *CH* Jackie Chan, Siu Tien Yuen, Michelle Yeoh; *D:* Woo-Ping Yuen. **VHS** *FCT*

THE DYBBUK
Der Dibuk

Recently revived in a restored version that features exquisitely expressionistic images and a clear, rich, Yiddish-language soundtrack, this 1937 Polish film by director Michael Waszynski is a stately and elegantly mounted adaptation of Sh. Ansky's legendary stage play. *The Dybbuk* is the story of Khonen (Leon Liebgold) and Leah (Lili Liliana), a couple who cannot be married because Leah's father has decided on a more well-to-do son-in-law. Angered, frustrated, and with no alternative, Khonen attempts to use powers of the occult

to stop the wedding, resulting first in his death and then in the transfer of his spirit—a dybbuk—into Leah at the moment of her wedding. The tragedy builds further from that point, and it's told in an exceptionally graceful, darkly unsettling labyrinth of deep-shadowed, Gothic images. A major success in its initial 1937 engagement in Warsaw, *The Dybbuk,* according to film historian J. Hoberman in his invaluable book on Yiddish film, *Shadows of Light,* attracted Gentile audiences as well as the traditional Jewish audience that attended Yiddish films. Still mesmerizing as drama and now profoundly moving as an artifact of a world that would soon cease to exist, the restored version successfully toured a number of American cities in the 1980s.

NEXT STOP . . . *Green Fields, The Light Ahead (Fishke der Krumer), Tevye the Milkman*

1937 123m/B *PL* Abraham Morewski, Isaac Samberg, Moshe Lipman, Lili Liliana, Dina Halpern, Leon Liebgold; *D:* Michal Waszynski; *W:* S.A. Kacyzna, Marek Arenstein; *C:* Albert Wywerka; *M:* Krzysztof Komeda. **VHS** *IHF, FCT, NCJ*

THE EARRINGS OF MADAME DE...
Diamond Earrings
Madame de...

Narcissistic and spoiled, Madame de ... (Danielle Darrieux) lives in ostentatious comfort with her military husband (Charles Boyer); she's so accepting of their unemotional marital arrangement—and their separate bedrooms—that she's unashamed to pawn for a little extra cash the earrings her husband gave her. But when the same earrings find their way back to her by way of her new lover, the dashing Baron Donati (Vittorio De Sica), her desire now to keep them as precious symbols of his love drives this dizzyingly romantic, heartbreaking masterpiece to its inevitable, tragic conclusion. The physical perfection and ingeniously symmetrical structure of Max Ophuls's *The Earrings of Madame de...* is easy to see; its surface glitters with the opulent palaces and opera houses of a long-ago Paris, and the ceaseless, fluid camera movement plunges the viewer headlong into

1954 105m/C *FR* Charles Boyer, Danielle Darrieux, Vittorio De Sica, Lea di Lea, Jean Debucourt; **D:** Max Ophuls; **W:** Max Ophuls, Marcel Archand, Annette Wademant; **C:** Christian Matras; **M:** Oscar Straus, Georges Van Parys. Nominations: Academy Awards '54: Best Costume Design (B & W). **VHS** *FCT, MRV, CVC*

EARTH
Zemlya
Soul

"I wanted to show the state of a Ukrainian village in 1929," wrote director Alexander Dovzhenko in 1930 of his masterpiece, *Earth,* "that is to say, at the time it was going through an economic transformation and a mental change in the masses." The change that the great director portrays is the struggle to establish a collective farm program in the face of the murderous old-line landowners, the kulaks. But though this struggle forms the spine of *Earth's* plot at its most conventional level, Dovzhenko's film is far more than a sophisticated piece of advocacy drama. *Earth* bites off a great deal; it attempts to be nothing less than a poetic cinematic tribute to the cyclical glory of nature, as seen through the eyes of those who tend to and love the land. The complete, stunning success of Dovzhenko's film is all the more staggering when you consider the immensity of its goal. It is capable, even 70 years after its creation, of making one marvel anew at the majesty and logic of the natural world, as well as producing the sheer elation that comes with rediscovering—with all the force of a tidal wave—the primal, incomparable power of cinema. Correctly voted one of the ten greatest films of all time by more than one international panel of film critics.

NEXT STOP . . . *Arsenal, Shchors, Nanook of the North*

1930 57m/B *RU* Semyon Svashenko, Mikola Nademsy, Stephan Shkurat, Yelena Maximova; **D:** Alexander Dovzhenko; **W:** Alexander Dovzhenko; **C:** Daniil Demutsky. **VHS** *VYY, CCB, IHF*

THE ECLIPSE
L'Eclisse

Deciding that they have nothing more to say to each other, lovers Vittoria (Monica Vitti)

her vertiginous romantic plunge. Yet that surface is only an elegant means of transportation into the romantic world that Ophuls ruled; his famous tracking shots and swirling images were like the mirrors in a Cocteau film, on the other side of which existed a world of dreams vastly more real and affecting than our own. The power of *Madame de...* is achieved by Ophuls's alchemy—a confluence of form and truth that is, to say the least, vastly more wrenching than the sum of its parts. There are a dozen or so films—not exactly twelve, perhaps, but hardly a huge number by any measure—that I consistently believe to be *the* best movie I've ever seen, every time I see it. That *Madame de...* is among that number each time I see it remains rapturous proof to me that despite frequent suspicions to the contrary, my lifetime in the dark has not been entirely misspent.

NEXT STOP . . . *La Ronde, Letter from an Unknown Woman, Lola Montès*

and Riccardo (Francisco Rabal) break off their affair; before long, Vittoria becomes involved with a swaggering young stockbroker named Piero (Alain Delon) who is working for her mother. The final chapter of the Michelangelo Antonioni trilogy that began with *L'Avventura* and continued with *La Notte* carries the director's concerns about the individual's sense of alienation in modern society to their logical extremes. The famous final sequence of the film doesn't even show us any human beings at all—just the location where we expect them to be and the space that surrounds them. Where such images in an Ozu film would indicate a world in balance with the characters about to enter the frame, the same images in *The Eclipse* imply a world in which human actions are no longer effectual—the landscape is the same, with or without people. It's a view of man's fate that's as bleak as they come, but expressed by an artist of extraordinary talent. If you've seen the first two films in this cycle, you may feel you've gone down this road far enough. Depending on your appetite for the director's world view, *The Eclipse* will either be the most uncompromising—or the most superfluous—of Antonioni's major works.

NEXT STOP . . . *L'Avventura, La Notte, Zabriskie Point*

1966 123m/B *IT* Monica Vitti, Alain Delon, Francesco Rabal, Louis Seigner; **D:** Michelangelo Antonioni; **W:** Tonino Guerra, Elio Bartolini, Ottiero Ottieri, Michelangelo Antonioni; **C:** Gianni Di Venanzo; **M:** Giovanni Fusco. **VHS** *TPV, MRV, FCT*

EDITH & MARCEL

Too reverential, too dull, and too long. Claude Lelouch must have embarked on this project as if it were some kind of historical biopic about founding fathers who were never actually alive—just mythological. Chanteuse Edith Piaf and boxer Marcel Cerdan were both French national treasures, of course, but just because they got together, do they have to be turned into waxworks—*Raging Stiffs*? And *why* did they get together? We don't have a clue, but Francis Lai's sticky musical score insistently tries—and fails—to fill in the Grand Canyon—like storytelling gaps. Eve-lyne Bouix lip-synchs to Piaf recordings of *Ma Vie en Rose,* while Cerdan's kid, Marcel Jr. (who unfortunately got talked into playing his old man in this dog) jumps rope and punches his punching bag, waiting for his title shot. In the French version, it takes two-and-a-half hours until the tragic finish. The best thing about the American prints is that they're almost an hour shorter. Nice costumes.

NEXT STOP . . . *A Man and a Woman, Happy New Year, Sweet Dreams*

1983 104m/C *FR* Evelyne Bouix, Marcel Cerdan Jr., Charles Aznavour, Jacques Villeret; **D:** Claude Lelouch. **VHS**

EDVARD MUNCH

I've never been completely sure why this extraordinary film casts the spell that it does, yet its eerie, documentary-like quality does seem to constantly be on the brink of capturing some cataclysmic, violent eruption, which, of course, perfectly mirrors the temperament of the tortured artist who is its subject. British director Peter Watkins made a number of acclaimed films prior to *Edvard Munch.* The best of them—*Culloden* and *The War Game*—were portraits of wars past and future and were filmed in the style of documentaries (his style was so convincing that *The War Game,* his fictional, 47-minute what-if portrait of nuclear disaster in a British town, won the 1966 Oscar for Best Documentary Feature). His nearly three-hour, Norwegian production *Edvard Munch* sticks pretty much to the early years of the life of this seminal, 19th-century giant of the Expressionist movement. It does what biographies of this sort should never do—analyze the works in relation to specific portions of the artist's life—yet Watkins's film is so assured and convincing that it packs an irresistible psychological punch. This is an eye-opening, groundbreaking biography, and an entertaining one to boot.

NEXT STOP . . . *The War Game, Van Gogh, La Belle Noiseuse*

1974 167m/C *NO* Geir Westby, Gro Fraas, Eli Ryg; **D:** Peter Watkins; **W:** Peter Watkins; **C:** Odd Geir Saether. **VHS** *FCT, NYF*

"Every time I hear the word culture, I bring out my checkbook."

—Prokosch (Jack Palance) in *Contempt.*

EFFI BRIEST
Fontane Effi Briest

In 19th-century Germany, a teenage girl (Hanna Schygulla in an exceptionally fine performance) is pressed into marriage with a much older Prussian diplomat (Wolfgang Schenck). Years later, in the far away Baltic port in which they live, Effi enters into a brief affair with a soldier (Ulli Lommel), the long term unexpected effects of which will alter the course of her future. Theodor Fontaine's acclaimed 1895 novel is the basis of this quietly devastating film from Germany's Rainer Werner Fassbinder; it paints a portrait of a woman's fate completely linked to an unbending and utterly unforgiving code of societal behavior. This is an uncharacteristically stately epic from Fassbinder, and its classical, visually resplendent images reinforce the rigidity of the world in which Effi lives. Yet the film's formal design, while chilling, in no way diminishes the heartfelt cry of despair at the movie's core.

NEXT STOP . . . *The Merchant of Four Seasons, The Marriage of Maria Braun, Veronika Voss*

1974 135m/B *GE* Hanna Schygulla, Wolfgang Schenck, Lilo Pempeit, Ulli Lommel; **D:** Rainer Werner Fassbinder; **W:** Rainer Werner Fassbinder; **C:** Jurgen Jurges, Dietrich Lohmann; **M:** Camille Saint-Saens. **VHS** *NYF, PMS*

EGG
Ei

The problem with movies that run less than an hour is that it's very difficult for them to get adequate distribution. The public tends to feel they're being ripped off if they see something as short as *Egg* (58 minutes) and so the movie has to be paired with a short. The short may be good, but it's perceived as filler—the audience resents this and is in a foul mood by the time the feature comes on. All of this is assuming the picture lands in a theatre at all, which is iffy at best. In the case of *Egg,* that's tragic, because this is delicate and elegant little gem of a movie that deserves a wide audience. Directed and written by Danniel Danniel for Dutch television, it's the story of a quiet, emotionally vulnerable middle-aged baker (Johan Leyson) who responds to a lonelyhearts ad in the personals column. The ad was placed by a teacher (Marijke Veugelers), and she's intrigued enough by the response to continue the correspondence. As the day for her visit to the baker's little village grows near, the tension and anticipation become remarkably strong, and we feel there's a lot at stake here. Miracles happen, but not always. *Egg* is perfect at its 58-minute length. It needs no chaser—just an audience.

NEXT STOP . . . *Combination Platter, Dragon Chow, Sugarbaby*

1988 58m/C *NL* Johan Leysen, Marijke Veugelers; **D:** Danniel Danniel; **W:** Danniel Danniel. **VHS, LV** *KIV, LUM*

8 1/2
Otto e Mezzo
Federico Fellini's 8 1/2

In that fickle and specialized world of the "art film," Federico Fellini had indeed been crowned "King of the World" (sorry, Mr. Cameron) following the worldwide reception that greeted his 1960 *La Dolce Vita.* Though he subsequently worked on a minor, short film for the omnibus feature *Boccaccio '70,* the search for ideas for his next major feature resulted in something unexpected, but ridiculously logical: a film about a successful filmmaker with a big hit on his hands who wasn't sure what to do as his next feature. It's hard to imagine anything riskier, and even harder to imagine a payoff as successful as Fellini's *8 1/2,* a brilliant, irritating, immovable object of a movie that has become one of the basic building blocks of the language of modern cinema. Guido (Marcello Mastroianni) is the director in Fellini's vision, whose expenditures on sets for his next, only-vaguely-conceived movie are large enough to cause Guido distracting anxiety, as well as "director's block." At the spa where Guido goes to take stock, the characters of his life—his wife, his mistress, his childhood memories, and his movies' characters—all come to visit him, either in the flesh or in the form of palpable fantasies. Many individual sequences in *8 1/2*—Guido keeping all the women of his life at bay with a whip—are well known and well-remembered, but it's as a cohesive whole and through the power of its enormously influential, redemptive ending that Fellini achieves a sometimes messy but unmistakable greatness. There have been—and will be—lots of other fine movies about the making of movies. But from the opening shot of a terrified Guido trapped in his car to the final seconds of him in the center of the celebratory circus ring that is his life, *8 1/2* remains an incomparable experience. (The title is derived from the fact that Fellini had previously directed six features, plus portions of longer films that added up to a movie and a half—this, therefore, was film number 8 1/2. Years later, a Broadway musical based on the film would be—bizarrely enough—titled *9*.)

NEXT STOP . . . *La Dolce Vita, Ginger & Fred, Alex in Wonderland*

1963 135m/B *IT* Marcello Mastroianni, Claudia Cardinale, Anouk Aimee, Sandra Milo, Barbara Steele, Rossella Falk, Eddra Gale, Mark Herron, Madeleine LeBeau, Caterina Boratto; **D:** Federico Fellini; **W:** Tullio Pinelli, Ennio Flaiano, Brunello Rondi, Federico Fellini; **C:** Gianni Di Venanzo; **M:** Nino Rota. Academy Awards '63: Best Costume Design (B & W), Best Foreign Film; New York Film Critics Awards '63: Best Foreign Film; Nominations: Academy Awards '63: Best Art Direction/Set Decoration (B & W), Best Director (Fellini), Best Story & Screenplay. **VHS, LV, Letterbox** *VES, MRV, MPI*

ÉL
This Strange Passion

One of a series of films Luis Buñuel made in Mexico while in exile from Spain, *Él* (a Spanish pronoun for he) was released in the United States as *This Strange Passion,* which is not an entirely terrible title. *Él* is the story of Francisco (Arturo de Cordova), a wealthy, 40-year old Catholic virgin who persuades the beautiful Gloria (Delia Garcés) to marry him. But all is not well with Francisco, whose commitment to Gloria begins to merge the forces of his repressed paranoia, sexual anxiety, and religious mania. As one would expect—and secretly hope—in Buñuel, these impulses lead Francisco not to a 12-step group but to his sleeping wife's bedside

as he clutches a needle, thread, and anesthetic. *Él* is an unblinking look at one man's rapid descent into madness, but what makes the film so riveting and entertaining is the straightforward matter-of-factness with which Francisco's deterioration is depicted, as well as the irrefutable logic of his response to the conflicting religious and sexual impulses within him. (A subtitle for the film might be *Well, What Did You Expect?*) This is a truly subversive and wonderful movie, a picture that, had it been made today—and it couldn't be—would be referred to as "a low-budget independent triumph." More important than its budget, however, is the fact that it's a major, overlooked chapter in the cinematic career of a genius.

NEXT STOP . . . *Wuthering Heights (Buñuel, 1954), The Criminal Life of Archibaldo de la Cruz, The Milky Way*

1952 88m/B *MX* Arturo de Cordova, Delia Garces, Luis Beristain, Aurora Walker; **D:** Luis Bunuel; **W:** Luis Bunuel, Luis Alcoriza; **C:** Gabriel Figueroa; **M:** Luis Hernandez Breton. **VHS** *HTV*

EL TOPO
The Gopher
The Mole

It's sometimes tempting—especially when sitting through one of the glut of mediocre, machine-tooled Gen-X entertainments that often pass for "cutting edge" visions in today's art houses—to think back to the "good old days" of the late 1960s and early 1970s, when it seemed that a committed, new generation of filmmakers truly was reinventing the cinema. But then you remember *El Topo,* and you snap right out of it. Alexandro Jodorowsky's surrealistic, self-aggrandizing fantasy was not just the first official "cult film" of the 1970s, but seemed conceived and born as a fully formed religious cult in and of itself. Divided into sections with names like "Genesis," "Psalms" and "Apocalypse" (mustn't leave *that* one out—it was 1970), *El Topo* is the story of a mysterious character (played by Jodorowsky) and his seven-year-old son, who first appear on horseback in a mysterious desert landscape. After telling the boy to bury his first toy and a picture of his dead mother, El Topo (the mole)

LUIS BUÑUEL

Buñuel is the greatest surrealist of the cinema. He was born in Spain in 1900 and studied entomology in Madrid, where he befriended artists such as playwright Federico Garcia Lorca and surrealist painter Salvador Dali. Buñuel and Dali shared an affinity for the cinema, and they soon became close friends. During a brief stint in Paris, where he attended the Academie du Cinema and apprenticed under director Jean Epstein, Buñuel met more artists, including painters Pablo Picasso and Max Ernst, with whom he shared a disdain for social convention and the bourgeoisie. Buñuel eventually called Dali to Paris and collaborated with him on *Un Chien Andalou*, a silent, 25-minute film replete with outrageous imagery.

Un Chien Andalou had been designed as an offense to bourgeois sensibilities, and when the film actually met with praise, Buñuel and Dali endured abuse from their fellow surrealists. Still determined to outrage the public, Buñuel, after breaking with Dali, concocted *L'Age d'Or*, a truly subversive film. Here, coupling lovers disrupt a public address, a father shoots his adorable son, and Christ conducts orgiastic revelers from the Marquis de Sade's palace. Although *L'Age d'Or* premiered without incident, a second screening succeeded in violently offending viewers, who responded with epithets and the destruction of surrealist paintings shown in the theatre lobby. For Buñuel, *L'Age d'Or* thus constituted a great success.

While Paris buzzed with controversy, Buñuel toured Hollywood under the assumption that he would find work there as a film director. When no offers came, he returned to his native Spain in 1932 and filmed *Las Hurdes*, a documentary set in a poor Spanish village. *Las Hurdes* would be Buñuel's final film before a 15-year period in which he worked occasionally at Warner Brothers, where he supervised dubbing, and at the Museum of Modern Art, where he tried, without success, to re-edit German filmmaker Leni Riefenstahl's films to undermine their effectiveness as propaganda. After World War II Buñuel moved to Mexico and resumed his career with *Los Olvidados*, a grim drama about slum life.

In 1962 Buñuel returned to Spain and directed *Viridiana*, in which a devout woman is defiled by a relative and exploited by beggars and cripples. With *Viridiana*, Buñuel once again managed to disturb viewers, and in the ensuing decades, if he failed to match the sheer outrageousness of his earliest efforts, he nonetheless managed to produced suitably idiosyncratic works. Among the finest of these films is *Belle du jour*, starring Catherine Deneuve as a devout Catholic who longs for degradation; *Tristana*, with Deneuve as a young woman undermined by the sexual double-standard of her guardian; and *That Obscure Object of Desire*, in which a French businessman blindly engages in sexual pursuit even as terrorist activity rages around him.

That *Obscure Object of Desire*, released in 1977, proved to be Buñuel's final film. In his final years, as his hearing failed, Buñuel—who had long indulged an appetite for self-concocted martinis, called Buñuelionis, and maintained an appreciation for insects—produced an autobiography, "My Last Sigh," which abounds in personal insights and typically surreal recollections. He died in Mexico City in 1983, having earlier threatened—in a final act of gleeful surrealism—to leave his belongings to the already rich.

and his son ride off to embark on numerous symbolic adventures involving disemboweled animals, turtle eggs, fat decadent generals, master gunfighters, and a dwarf. After two hours of this El Topo immolates himself (you may be tempted as well), but his son rides off into the sunset, ready for further self-discovery. *El Topo* is less interesting for what it is (its director/star/writer unintentionally summed it up when he said "*El Topo* is endless") than for what it began in the world of movie exhibition. Run only at midnights, seven nights a week at New York's now-vanished, then-seedy Elgin Theatre, *El Topo* attracted SRO audiences comprised of reverential repeat business, would-be hipsters, and the merely curious, mostly via word-of-mouth (there was almost no advertising). The "midnight movie" as we know it today was officially born, and the way was paved for *Pink Flamingos, Eraserhead,* and *The Rocky Horror Picture Show* to add a new, "private club" dimension to the moviegoing experience for a generation.

NEXT STOP . . . *The Holy Mountain, Billy Jack, The Last Movie*

1971 123m/C *MX* Brontis Jodorowsky, Alfonso Arau, Alejandro Jodorowsky; *D:* Alejandro Jodorowsky; *W:* Alejandro Jodorowsky; *C:* Rafael Corkidi; *M:* Nacho Mendez, Alejandro Jodorowsky. **VHS** *NYR*

ELÉNA AND HER MEN
Paris Does Strange Things
Eléna et les Hommes

This lushly designed comedy of manners, set in Paris in the 1880s, tells of the Polish Princess Eléna (Ingrid Bergman) who decides to abandon her true love, Henri de Chevincourt (Mel Ferrer), so that she can instead attain political power by way of a liaison with the Minister of War, General Rollan (Jean Marais). Originally, Renoir wanted this to be a serious portrait of the real General Boulanger's reach for dictatorial power in the same period, but the involvement of Bergman led him to take what he described as "a more lighthearted approach." The last in a trilogy of lush period films that Renoir directed in the 1950s—the earlier films

being *The Golden Coach* and *French Can-Can*—*Eléna et les Hommes* was cut and dubbed in its original 1956 American release, and released under the title *Paris Does Strange Things*. (So do film distributors.) A few years ago, new, fully restored color prints were made available of *Eléna,* but, alas, this was one restoration that did not reveal an undiscovered masterpiece. Curiously distant, the restored *Eléna* is no *Lola Montès;* it's not even *French Can-Can.* It *is* a Renoir film, however, and therefore not without its glories. Chief among the glories in *Eléna et les Hommes* is one of the greatest glories in all of cinema—the staggering, heartbreaking beauty of Ingrid Bergman. No film that features such a sight could ever be dismissed as a failure.

NEXT STOP . . . *La Chienne, Rules of the Game, The Golden Coach*

1956 98m/C *FR* Ingrid Bergman, Jean Marais, Mel Ferrer, Jean Richard, Magali Noel, Pierre Bertin, Juliette Greco; *D:* Jean Renoir; *C:* Claude Renoir. **VHS, LV** *INT, FCT, TPV*

ELVIRA MADIGAN

Not as bad as you may remember, but you may still want to turn off the sound. The late Bo Widerberg's film about a young, married soldier (Thommy Berggren) and a circus tightrope artist (Pia Degermark) who run off together in Sweden in the late 1800s was based on the true story of a couple who chose death over living apart. The picture might have gained a little much-needed friction had the two principals not both been so beautiful; Pia Degermark has a face that simply astonishes, and Widerberg makes the most of it. The lush, almost oppressively lyrical photography and the soundtrack's ceaseless repetition of Mozart's Piano Concerto No. 21 (commonly referred to now on those middle-of-the-night, "Greatest Classical Hits" TV commercials as the "Elvira Madigan Theme") can distract the viewer from the movie's political subtext, yet Widerberg was making a clear and specific statement about a society that would impose such a rigid morality that these two harmless individuals would find no recourse other than suicide.

E

Widerberg's next films, *dalen '31* and *Joe Hill,* were concerned with directly political subject matter; it was only then that he was thought of here as something more formidable than the guy who made that gauzy love story with all the Mozart. (*Elvira Madigan* was a surprise hit in the U.S., thanks largely to a brilliant marketing campaign orchestrated by the New York based independent distributor/exhibitor Donald Rugoff.)

NEXT STOP . . . *dalen '31, The Man on the Roof, Jerusalem*

1967 (PG) 90m/C *SW* Pia Degermark, Thommy Berggren, Lennart Malmer, Nina Widerberg, Cleo Jensen; *D:* Bo Widerberg; *W:* Johan Lindstroem Saxon, Bo Widerberg; *C:* Jorgen Persson; *M:* Ulf Bjorlin. Cannes Film Festival '67: Best Actress (Degermark). **VHS, LV** *WAC, FCT, TPV*

THE EMIGRANTS
Utvandrarna

In the middle of the 19th century, horrendously impoverished living conditions couple with severe religious and moral intolerance led more than a quarter of Sweden's population to leave their country, and a vast proportion of those came to America. Swedish director Jan Troell set out in the early 1970s to create a gigantic epic in two parts that would tell of this extraordinary moment in his nation's history; it would also, of course, be the story of an equally significant moment in *this* country's history. Released in 1971, the first of these films, *The Emigrants,* portrays the day-to-day struggle for existence of the Nilssons: Karl Oskar (Max von Sydow), his wife Kristina (Liv Ullmann), and Karl Oskar's young brother Robert (Eddie Axberg). The Nilsson farm is a physically magnificent setting, and Troell never pretends this isn't so. Even when a hungry child dies of eating raw grain, Troell refuses to make the physical setting anything less than majestic; Troell wants to be sure that when it is time for the family to finally pull up stakes and begin the long, dangerous voyage to America, we understand that they are not simply leaving behind poverty. They are leaving their home because they are suffering, but they also suffer in leaving it behind. The ocean voyage itself is a harrowing nightmare, and their early American experience doesn't bring them the paradise they've imagined; how could it? Nevertheless, they move on, and their journey will come to a profoundly moving conclusion in the second half of this magnificent epic, which is titled *The New Land.* (European prints of *The Emigrants* run over three hours, but the director shortened the film for America to just under two-and-a-half hours. Whatever you do, steer clear of the English-dubbed version.) Oscar nominations for Best Picture, Director, Actress, Adapted Screenplay (it was based on Vilhelm Moberg's novels), and Foreign Language Film.

NEXT STOP . . . *The New Land, The Ox, The Godfather, The Godfather, Part II*

1972 (PG) 151m/C *SW* Max von Sydow, Liv Ullmann, Allan Edwall, Eddie Axberg, Svenolof Bern, Aina Alfredsson, Monica Zetterlund, Pierre Lindstedt; *D:* Jan Troell; *W:* Jan Troell, Bengt Forslund; *C:* Jan Troell; *M:* Erik Nordgren. New York Film Critics Awards '72: Best Actress (Ullmann); Nominations: Academy Awards '72: Best Actress (Ullmann), Best Adapted Screenplay, Best Director (Troell), Best Picture. **VHS** *WAR, MOV*

EMITAI
Dieu de Tonnerre
God of the Sun

On a weekday afternoon in New York in the early 1970s, I wandered into the now-defunct Fifth Avenue Cinema where I watched—along with three other patrons who were scattered through the tiny theatre—this Senegalese film about an African tribe's encounter with French colonialists near the end of World War II. As the French exploit and systematically destroy the tribe—the Diolas—by turning them against each other, the elder members of the tribe engage in a dialogue with the gods, lashing out at them for their impotence as protectors. The gods—actors in costume—are defensive and bullying, but no match for the furious elders who clearly expect more from their deities. The scene is simply but elegantly staged, bold, daring, and devastatingly satirical—as is the rest of *Emitai* (*God of the Sun*), the third feature film by Senegal's Ousmane Sembène but the first that I encountered. In the lobby after the film, the four patrons (including me) became acquainted quickly, sharing that pleasurable jolt of unexpected discovery and the knowledge that we had experienced something truly revelatory, albeit in a nearly empty theatre. Looking back, however, it's probably remarkable that the film played in a commercial theatre in this country at all. Would it now? One worries about the chances of Third World cinema finding any American theatrical venues in the crowded, youth-obsessed marketplace of the 1990s. Yet thanks to video, this extraordinary picture continues to live and breathe. It remains one of Sembène's key works, a strongly worded warning of the evils of colonialism, and one of the seminal moments in the history of African cinema.

NEXT STOP . . . *Mandabi, Ceddo, Guelwaar*

1971 103m/C Pierre Blanchard, Robert Fontaine, Michel Remaudeau; *D:* Ousmane Sembene; *W:* Ousmane Sembene; *C:* Michel Remaudeau. *NYR*

ENJO
Conflagration
The Flame of Torment

A young priest (Raizo Ichikawa) develops an obsession with what he perceives as the perfection of a beloved temple; rather than see it corrupted or commercialized in any way, he vows to destroy it. Adapted from the story *The Temple of the Golden Pavilion* by novelist and militarist/cult figure Yukio Mishima, Kon Ichikawa's *Enjo* (also known as *Conflagration*) may be the most delicately perceptive and engaging film to come from any of the writer's works. Though filmed in widescreen, Ichikawa's film has an intimacy and intensity that is in no way diffused by the size of the image, nor is the director attempting to graft any external, "cinematic" notions of beauty on the young man's obsessive vision. That vision—and its accompanying obsession—remain his, and remain appropriately mysterious. His passion, on the other hand, together with the decision he must make as a result of it, are presented logically and without judgment. The true story that forms the basis of *Enjo* was also depicted as one section of Paul Schrader's unjustly overlooked 1985 biographical film, *Mishima*.

NEXT STOP . . . *The Burmese Harp, Odd Obsession, Mishima*

1958 98m/B *JP* Raizo Ichikawa, Ganjiro Nakamura, Tatsuya Nakadai; *D:* Kon Ichikawa; *W:* Natto Wada, Keiji Hasebe, Toshiro Mayazumi; *C:* Kazuo Miyagawa. **VHS** *NYF*

ENTRE-NOUS
Between Us
Coup de Foudre
At First Sight

In the 1950s, Madeleine and Lena (Miou-Miou and Isabelle Huppert), two married women, meet and learn about each other; only then do they come to realize how disillusioned and dissatisfied each of them is with her marriage and her life. Diane Kurys's glossy 1983 film (released in France as *Coup de Foudre*) was widely championed on the film festival circuit as a pioneering feminist film, but its status as a pioneering work—as well as its feminist credentials—may be open to some question. The husbands of Madeleine and Lena (Guy Marchand and Jean-Pierre Bacri) are jerks, and while it's difficult for their wives to readily dismiss them as such, it's easy for the audience. The multi-year friendship that bonds the two women is pleasant enough to be around while the picture's on, but it feels insubstantial; an hour later you'll be hungry again. As with all of Kurys's work, *Entre-Nous* is splendidly crafted and beautiful to look at. I only wish it were more engaging.

NEXT STOP . . . *Peppermint Soda, Cocktail Molotov, C'est la Vie*

1983 (PG) 112m/C *FR* Jean-Pierre Bacri, Patrick Bauchau, Jacqueline Doyen, Isabelle Huppert, Miou-Miou, Guy Marchand; *D:* Diane Kurys; *W:* Alain Henry, Diane Kurys; *C:* Bernard Lutic; *M:* Luis Bacalov. Nominations: Academy Awards '83: Best Foreign-Language Film. **VHS** *MGM*

ERENDIRA

When her house burns down as the result of a mysterious fire, an old woman (Irene Papas) decides that the otherworldly vision reported by her exquisite granddaughter,

E

Erendira (Claudia Ohana), is the cause. Immediately and unforgivingly holding the teenager responsible, the old woman decides that the only way for the girl to pay for the damage she has caused is through prostitution. Director Ruy Guerra sends the pair off into a mystical, surreal, richly colored desert setting, where their adventures take the strange and haunting twists and turns one would expect from the movie's screenwriter, Gabriel García Márquez. *Erendira* rambles along entertainingly enough, though it always feels a bit schematic and rarely attains the startling narrative magic that this kind of fantasy calls for. The picture looks great, though, and Irene Papas is formidable, frightening, and altogether irresistible.

NEXT STOP . . . *Quilombo, The Gods and the Dead, The Milky Way*

1983 103m/C *FR MX GE* Sergio Calderon, Blanca Guerra, Ernesto Cruz, Michel Lonsdale, Pierre Vaneck, Irene Papas, Claudia Ohana, Michael Lonsdale, Rufus, Jorge Fegan; **D:** Ruy Guerra; **W:** Gabriel Garcia Marquez; **C:** Denys Clerval; **M:** Maurice Lecouer. **VHS** *XVC*

ERMO

An enchanting surprise. Ermo (Ailiya) is a noodle maker who lives in a rural Chinese area. She works like a dog to support her son and her lazy, goldbricking husband, but despite her scrimping and saving, she can't get over the fact that her neighbor—known as "fat woman" (Zhang Haiyan)—has the biggest color TV set that Ermo has ever seen. Desperate to outdo "the Jonses," Ermo sets out on a new mission in life: to work so hard that she'll be able to afford a bigger TV than her neighbor. In this madly direct and poignantly hilarious microcosm of the new found spirit of capitalism colliding head-on with basic human nature, obsession blossoms like a rose. Ermo can't stay out of the store where the TV of her dreams awaits the swelling of her purse; she asks the store owner to turn it on so that she can see it, but then orders him to shut it off so as to not wear it out before she can afford it. Director Zhou Xiaowen makes sure that Ermo herself remains gloriously human throughout and refuses to reduce her to a cartoon for extra laughs; her three-dimensional vulnerability is why the film's final irony packs such a powerfully poignant punch, and why *Ermo* is such a find.

NEXT STOP . . . *The Story of Qiu Ju, Woman from the Lake of Scented Souls, To Live*

1994 93m/C *CH* Alia, Liu Peiqi, Ge Zhijun, Zhang Haiyan; **D:** Zhou Xiaowen; **W:** Lang Yun; **C:** Lu Gengxin; **M:** Zhou Xiaowen. **VHS** *EVE*

ETERNAL RETURN
L'Eternel Retour
Love Eternal

Director Jean Delannoy's updating of the Tristan and Isolde legend was a big hit in France, where it was filmed during the German Occupation. Jean Marais and Madeleine Sologne are Patrice and Nathalie, modern lovers who are repeating the age old tragic love story. Jean Cocteau's screenplay would most likely have been better served by Jean Cocteau the director; many of the "poetic" touches of director Delannoy are laid on with a trowel. Despite the presence of Marais and a score by Cocteau's composer Georges Auric, the film never radiates the grace or simple startling inventiveness of the films of Cocteau. On the other hand, it's not exactly the collaborationist debacle some have claimed, the blond protagonists notwithstanding.

NEXT STOP . . . *Beauty and the Beast, Les Enfants Terribles, Orpheus*

1943 111m/B *FR* Jane Marken, Alexandre Rignault, Roland Toutain, Yvonne de Bray, Jean Marais, Madeleine Sologne, Jean Murat; **D:** Jean Delannoy; **W:** Jean Cocteau; **C:** Roger Hubert; **M:** Georges Auric. **VHS** *WBF, NLC, FCT*

EUROPA, EUROPA
Hitlerjunge Salomon

I attended an early screening of Agnieszka Holland's *Europa, Europa* with the same skepticism and, yes, dread that I generally carry with me to new films about the Holocaust. It's not that I don't want to see new takes on the subject, but rather that movies have so rarely dealt with it effectively or honestly—for a host of reasons—that I often find such films more disappointing than eye-opening. This film, however, which is based on the remarkable, true-life, World War II odyssey of a teenager named Solomon Perel, is a quietly staggering piece of work. Perel's saga of survival would be laughed out of a Hollywood story conference if it were fiction. Escaping to Russia from Nazi-occupied Poland, the Jewish Perel survives by impersonating a German when the Nazis enter Russia. Having no choice but to continue his charade, Perel becomes a member of the Hitler Youth, where he's held up as an example of a model Aryan. When he becomes romantically involved with a German girl while impersonating everything he hates and fears, the delicate juggling act that Perel must perform to survive causes him to question the very nature of what we all comfortably consider our "identity." *Europa, Europa* is on one level an exciting and profoundly moving adventure about the resilience, ingenuity, and courage of one human being; it is also a simple but brilliantly told lesson about the fascinating, often terrifying, and occasionally inspiring ways in which ordinary people adapt when the universe around them turns mad.

NEXT STOP . . . *Olivier, Olivier, The Boat Is Full, Shoah*

1991 (R) 115m/C *GE* Marco Hofschneider, Klaus Abramowsky, Michele Gleizer, Rene Hofschneider, Nathalie Schmidt, Delphine Forest, Julie Delpy; **D:** Agnieszka Holland; **W:** Agnieszka Holland; **C:** Jacek Petrycki, Jacek Zaleski; **M:** Zbigniew Preisner. Golden Globe Awards '92: Best Foreign Film; National Board of Review Awards '91: Best Foreign Film; New York Film Critics Awards '91: Best Foreign Film; Nominations: Academy Awards '91: Best Adapted Screenplay. **VHS** *ORI, BTV*

EVERY MAN
FOR HIMSELF
Slow Motion
Sauve Qui Peut
Sauve Qui Peut la Vie

In 1967, Jean-Luc Godard told a film critic:"To me, style is just the outside of content, and content the inside of style, like the outside and the inside of the human body—both go together, they can't be separated."Then why must so many of Godard's critics try to do precisely that? By the time *Every Man for Himself*—his 1980 portrait of modern sexuality in an emotionally frozen world—was released, much of the critical world had already given up on Godard as a once-great pioneer who had in recent years gone off the deep end with political diatribes like *Wind from the East, Tout va Bien,* and *Letter to Jane.* Yet with *Every Man for Himself,* a beautiful and eloquent film that focuses—however despairingly—on a marketable topic ("Topic A," as Preston Sturges referred to it), the critics were jockeying to be first in line to declare that "Godard is back." America may not have wanted to see Godard's takes on Vietnam as the war continued to drag on, but sex was another matter and *Every Man for Himself,* which is just as elliptical and elusive in structure as some of his earlier films, became a major art house event, complete with "Francis Ford Coppola Presents" featured over the title in the film's American advertising. Don't get me wrong, however—I'm hardly complaining about its PR (though I wish that more of his films had received the same treatment), for this *is* one of the funniest, most beautiful, and most deeply disturbing films of Godard's career. Set in the cold, symbolic neutrality of Switzerland, the three loosely intertwined plot threads tell of lovers who manipulate and control each other with varying degrees of passion and disgust, and for very different reasons. (A businessman's precisely choreographed "scene" with a prostitute is one of the more appalling and brilliant depictions of joyless, power-centered sexuality in cinema history.) Often hard to follow and maddeningly fragmented, it is also so rich that you leave the theatre with

your priorities realigned. For better or worse, the work of a genius. With Isabelle Huppert, Nathalie Baye, and Jacques Dutronc.

NEXT STOP . . . *Contempt, Passion, First Name: Carmen*

1979 87m/C Roland Amstutz, Nathalie Baye, Jacques Dutronc, Isabelle Huppert, Anna Baldaccini, Monique Barscha, Michel Cassagna, Nicole Jacquet, Paule Muret, Fred Personne, Cecile Tanner; **D:** Jean-Luc Godard; **W:** Jean-Luc Godard, Jean-Claude Carriere, Anne-Marie Mieville; **C:** Renato Berta, William Lubtchansky, Barnard Menoud; **M:** Gabriel Yared. *NYR*

EVERY MAN FOR
HIMSELF & GOD
AGAINST ALL
The Mystery of Kaspar Hauser
Jeder fur Sich und Gott Gegen Alle
The Enigma of Kaspar Hauser

In Nuremberg in the 1820s, a mysterious man was discovered standing in the town square bearing a letter. Having been locked in a cellar and abused by his... master?... father?...until he was grown, and never having met another human being until the day that he appeared in town, Kaspar is in essence a newborn in the utterly confused body of an adult. And what a body. The origins of the actor who plays Kaspar—whose name is only given as Bruno S.—are nearly as mysterious as those of the actual Kaspar, though the public relations value of the carefully concealed mystery of Bruno S. himself can't be discounted. (While undeniably an artist, director Werner Herzog is also a consummate showman; Bruno S.—though possessed of an electrifying screen presence—is in real life no holy innocent, though Herzog has brilliantly transformed Bruno's orchestrated enigma into the art house equivalent of one of schlockmeister William Castle's horror movie gimmicks.) Though there is still contention and controversy over the origins and history of the actual Kaspar Hauser, the version of events depicted by Herzog in this enormously popular 1975 film, originally titled *Every Man for Himself & God Against All,* is the kind of fable that we accept as truth because we *want* it to be.

That being said, *The Mystery of Kaspar Hauser* is nevertheless a visually staggering and seductively told legend that manages—in images such as a baby's tiny hand clutching at one of Kaspar's thick, rough fingers—to transcend most of its easy heart-tugging. Its last moments—in which a grotesque, Teutonic bureaucrat arrogantly declares the discovery of a physical explanation for the metaphysical mystery at the movie's center—have a surprising resonance, and are likely to stay with you permanently.

NEXT STOP . . . *Stroszek, Woyzeck, The Wild Child*

1975 110m/C *GE* Bruno S, Brigitte Mira, Walter Laderigast, Hans Musaus, Willy Semmelrogge, Michael Kroecher, Henry van Lyck; ***D:*** Werner Herzog; ***W:*** Werner Herzog; ***C:*** Jorge Schmidt-Reitwein; ***M:*** Albinoni Pachelbel, Orlando Di Lasso. **VHS** *NYF, GLV, COL*

EXOTICA

At a strange, somewhat dreamlike strip club in Toronto, a regular named Francis (Bruce Greenwood) spends hours, and many dollars, in the company of the beautiful Christina. Francis's obsession—and Christina's response—form the core of director Atom Egoyan's remarkably engaging wisp of a film, but there are enough subplots and peripheral characters with hidden agendas to make Robert Altman salivate. Egoyan—to his credit—refuses to tie all of these loose ends into a neat, boy scout's knot. We're never quite sure of the motives behind a lot of what happens in and around club Exotica, but we stay riveted because from scene to scene, these people are all beautifully delineated and consistent in their impulses and behavior. *Exotica* is a puzzle that we hope we won't discover *the* answer to, because we instinctively suspect that simple explanations aren't going to account for the deep, reassuring mystery of eroticism that permeates every moment of the film. *Exotica*—winner of Canada's Best Picture of the Year Award—features a feast of intriguing performances from a largely unknown cast, but it's Mia Kirshner's maddeningly mysterious Christina who serves as the movie's centerpiece, and our tour guide into a seedy but irresistible heart of darkness.

NEXT STOP . . . *The Adjuster, Calendar, The Sweet Hereafter*

1994 (R) 104m/C *CA* Mia Kirshner, Elias Koteas, Bruce Greenwood, Don McKellar, Victor Garber, Arsinee Khanjian, Sarah Polley, Calvin Green, David Hemblen; ***D:*** Atom Egoyan; ***W:*** Atom Egoyan; ***C:*** Paul Sarossy; ***M:*** Mychael Danna. Genie Awards '94: Best Art Direction/Set Decoration, Best Cinematography, Best Costume Design, Best Director (Egoyan), Best Film, Best Original Screenplay, Best Supporting Actor (McKellar), Best Score; Toronto-City Award '94: Best Canadian Feature Film; Nominations: Genie Awards '94: Best Actor (Greenwood), Best Actor (Koteas); Independent Spirit Awards '96: Best Foreign Film. **VHS, LV, Closed Caption** *MAX*

THE EXTERMINATING ANGEL
El Angel Exterminador

"Basically," wrote Luis Buñuel in his autobiography, "I simply see a group of people who couldn't do what they wanted to—leave a room." He was describing the basis of this hilarious and terrifying 1962 masterwork, filmed in Mexico on a modest budget. Nobile (Enrique Rambal) has invited guests to his splendid home for dinner, and though the cooks have managed to flee, the guests just can't seem to tear themselves away after dinner. It's not that they don't want to, mind you, they just … can't. They stay. The days go on and on, accompanied by madness, suicide, disease, hunger, an attempted military rescue, and an invasion of sheep. The situation is ultimately resolved, though it's inevitably replaced by one even more ominous. While Buñuel has said of *The Exterminating Angel* that "there is no explanation," the great surrealist has also said more: "it is a deeply felt, disturbing reflection of the life of modern man," he has written, but his latter statement in no way conflicts with his former. No one in his right mind would attempt to literally interpret each image and dilemma in *The Exterminating Angel*, but we understand after watching it—and examining where we are in our own lives in relation to our desires—that it all makes perfect sense. Even the sheep.

E

ATOM EGOYAN
Canadian Indie Director

Since independent Canadian director Atom Egoyan is himself a striptease artist, expert at hiding and revealing key parts of his tantalizing films, it is fitting that his sixth feature, *Exotica*, has finally brought him wider audiences. Set in a Toronto strip joint but not at all about sex, *Exotica* is, like all of Egoyan's films, an intricate puzzle that exploits the gap between what people appear to be doing and their real purposes.

Egoyan's films often feature characters with seemingly mundane jobs—an insurance adjuster in *The Adjuster*, a hotel laundry room worker in *Speaking Parts*, a tax auditor in *Exotica*. The characters usually are engaged in seemingly innocuous rituals which serve deeper needs.

"Finding a system or ritual to safeguard yourself from pain actually makes you more vulnerable," Egoyan believes. That's true with the man in *Exotica* whose attentions to a stripper are attempts to undo his daughter's murder. "I want to make people feel emotional against all possible odds, by things they don't immediately understand or that they have to work hard for," Egoyan explains. His sly, wry, delicately crafted, and technically innovative films do just that.

His award-winning 1997 film *The Sweet Hereafter* was the first film Egoyan adapted. The film is based on the novel by Russell Banks and was nominated for best director and best adapted screenplay Oscars. It won the 1997 Grand Jury Prize at Cannes and was nominated for 16 Canadian Genie awards. It won eight, including best picture and best director. His latest work has been with the opera, including directing "Doctor Ox's Experiment" for the English National Opera in June 1998 in London.

Egoyan was born to Armenian immigrants in Cairo July 19, 1960, and named after Egypt's first nuclear reactor. His parents, who ran furniture stores, moved to Victoria, British Columbia, when he was three. Egoyan started writing plays at 13 and continues to write his own scripts. To relax, he plays classical guitar. He and his wife, Arsinee Khanjian, who appears in all his films, have a son, Arshile.

NEXT STOP . . . *Simon of the Desert, The Discreet Charm of the Bourgeoisie, Woman in the Dunes*

1962 95m/B *MX SP* Claudio Brook, Cesar del Campo, Lucy Gallardo, Enrique Garcia Alvarez, Tito Junco, Ofelia Montesco, Bertha Moss, Pancho Cordova, Silvia Pinal, Enrique Rambal, Jacqueline Andere, Jose Baviera, Augusto Benedico, Luis Beristain; *D:* Luis Bunuel; *W:* Luis Alcoriza, Luis Bunuel; *C:* Gabriel Figueroa; *M:* Raul Lavista, Domenico Scarletti. **VHS** HTV, FCT

EYES WITHOUT A FACE
The Horror Chamber of Dr. Faustus
Les Yeux sans Visage
Occhi Senza Volto

It sounds like a horror movie plot you've watched a thousand times: a deranged plastic surgeon is obsessed with restoring his disfigured daughter's face to its original beauty. But this time, the atmosphere of dread and spiritual devastation that France's Georges Franju has brought to this nightmarish fable has elevated it to the truly magical—and thoroughly disturbing. Pierre Brasseur is the surgeon whose careless driving has mangled the delicate features of daughter Edith Scob, and his solution is to roam through the dark streets of Paris with his sinister, leather-clad assistant (Alida Valli), looking for young women to capture so that he might graft their faces onto his daughter's. Jean Cocteau wrote that "Franju takes us implacably to the end of what our nerves can bear," and there are moments in *Eyes without a Face* when we think we can't look at what we're about to be shown. Of course we can, and we do. (The film's original American release was in a dubbed version sent to drive-ins called *The Horror Chamber of Dr. Faustus,* which also cut short one of the film's most perversely graphic scenes of facial surgery. Despair not, however: the voices of the original French soundtrack—as well as every evil stroke of the surgeon's scalpel—have been fully and lovingly restored.)

NEXT STOP . . . *Beauty and the Beast, The Wasp Woman, Face/Off*

1959 84m/B *FR* Alida Valli, Pierre Brasseur, Edith Scob, Francois Guerin; *D:* Georges Franju; *W:* Jean Redon; *C:* Eugene (Eugen Shufftan) Shuftan; *M:* Maurice Jarre. **VHS, LV** *INT, TPV*

FABULOUS ADVENTURES OF BARON MUNCHAUSEN
Baron Munchausen
The Fabulous Baron Munchausen
The Original Fabulous Adventures of Baron Munchausen
Baron Prasil

This eye-popping follow-up to Czech animator Karel Zeman's *The Fabulous World of Jules Verne* (*Vynález zkázy*) was conceived on a larger scale than the earlier film, and was

filmed in color. Nevertheless, it's just not as much fun, and that's probably a result of the plodding, episodic, "tall tale" nature of the Baron Munchausen legend; the story's clunky structure has been a drag on every one of the many filmed versions of the story, from the 1943 German version through Terry Gilliam's in 1989 (there were silent versions as well, but they were shorter). What this version of the legend does have, however, is the enchanting, refined, and elegant imagery that was the hallmark of all of Zeman's productions. Like miniature Gustave Dore engravings come to life, each of the Baron's adventures—whether in a whale's belly, riding a cannonball, or walking on the moon—is designed with a graceful understatement that makes you rethink your definition of "special effects." Original title: *Baron Prásil.*

NEXT STOP . . . *The Fabulous World of Jules Verne, Baron Müenchhausen (1943), The Adventures of Baron Munchausen* (1989)

1961 84m/C *GE* Milos Kopecky, Jana Brejchova, Rudolph Jelinek, Jan Werich; *D:* Karel Zeman; *W:* Karel Zeman; *C:* Jiri Tarantik; *M:* Zdenek Liska. **VHS** *ART, VES, TPV*

THE FABULOUS WORLD OF JULES VERNE
Vynález zkázy
Invention of Destruction

Czech artist and animator Karel Zeman adapted this extraordinary fantasy film—originally titled *Vynález zkázy* and released in much of the world as *The Deadly Invention*—from a number of Jules Verne stories, primarily "For the Flag." It's a successful attempt at recreating the look of engraved, highly detailed 19th-century illustrations that might have accompanied such fantastic stories when originally published. Zeman has animated the images, and added live actors to the mix. How he brought it all about is anybody's guess, and to tell you the truth, I don't want to know. The illusion is so ingenious and utterly charming that it leaves the category of special effects and belongs more

"You haven't had any experience till I have it, too."

—Elliot (Jeremy Irons) to identical twin Beverly in *Dead Ringers.*

to the province of the magician. You feel the same electric jolt that audiences attending the earliest traveling shadow shows must have felt; you know it's a trick, but it's such an elegant one that you're not just willing to suspend disbelief—you're eager to. This is a movie that modern special effects wizards ought to take a look at, just to be reminded that the technologically perfect creation of an impossible reality—as in a *Jurassic Park*—should never be mistaken for the one thing that can truly inspire awe: the unleashed imagination. Filmed in 1958, the picture was reworked for its brief American release by Joseph E. Levine and Warner Bros. and ultimately released in 1961 with a weird, tacked-on introduction by Hugh Downs.

NEXT STOP . . . *Fabulous Adventures of Baron Munchausen* (1961), *Alice* (Svankmajer, 1988), *The Adventures of Baron Munchausen* (1989)

1958 83m/B *CZ* Lubor Tolos, Arnost Navratil, Miroslav Holub, Zatloukalova; *D:* Karel Zeman; *W:* Frantisek Hrubin, Karel Zeman; *C:* Antonin Horak, Bronislau Pikhart, Jiri Tarantik; *M:* Zdenek Liska. **VHS**

THE FACE OF ANOTHER
Tanin No Kao
I Have a Stranger's Face
Stranger's Face

A scientist named Okuyama (Tatsuya Nakadai) severely burns his face in an accident. He seeks the assistance of a brilliant plastic surgeon, who fashions a lifelike mask for him. The mask gives him a normal appearance, though a decidedly different one than before. His life becomes further complicated when his wife (Machiko Kyo) furiously seduces him even before he tells her who he is, causing him to accuse her of adultery. It's only then that he begins to absorb the subtle, existential changes that are taking place as a result of his new appearance—changes that are not only altering his view of himself, but of his place in the world. This tantalizing and physically stunning 1966 film from Japan's Hiroshi Teshigahara was the follow up to his acclaimed 1964 *Woman in the Dunes*. Like the earlier film, *The Face of Another* was based on a novel by Kobo Abe,

who again collaborated with Teshigahara on the screenplay. But unlike *Woman in the Dunes,* this decidedly disturbing, Kafkaesque examination of the nature of identity—and of the masks we all design for ourselves—was not well received in the U.S., and got very limited release. It's a shame, for this is a striking and fascinating work.

NEXT STOP . . . *Woman in the Dunes, Eyes without a Face, Seconds, Face/Off*

1966 124m/B *JP* Minoru Chiaki, Robert Dunham, Kyoko Kishida, Beverly Maeda, Eiji Okada, Koreya Senda, Tatsuya Nakadai, Machiko Kyo; *D:* Hiroshi Teshigahara; *W:* Kobe Abe; *C:* Hiroshi Segawa; *M:* Toru Takemitsu. **VHS** *NO*

FACE TO FACE
Ansikte mot Ansikte

Successful psychiatrist Dr. Jenny Isaksson (Liv Ullmann) makes a trip to her family home, and soon thereafter finds herself in the grip of a full-blown mental collapse. Neither her husband, also a psychiatrist, nor her lover is able to help her; but after a long tortuous journey (which includes a suicide attempt) and the help of another doctor who cares enormously about her (Erland Josephson), Jenny is ready to look her crippling anxieties in the eye. With the doctor's help, many of the mysteries of her past are revealed, but overcoming the emotional paralysis they've left her with will be a lifetime struggle. *Face to Face* is not an easy ride, even in the abridged 136 minute American version, which was trimmed by the director from the original four-hour Swedish TV presentation. If you have misgivings about Bergman in the first place, *Face to Face* will only reinforce them. Yet despite patches of dialogue that read like self-parody (would you like to hear *yourself* in therapy?), there's a bracing power in seeing Jenny through to her tenuous victory over demons. It may not be everyone's first choice for an evening's light entertainment, but there may be a day—you'll know it when you get there—when it will be just the ticket. Oscar nominations for Best Director and Best Actress.

NEXT STOP . . . *Cries and Whispers, Scenes from a Marriage, Autumn Sonata*

Oskar Werner and Julie Christie in François Truffaut's chilling film, *Fahrenheit 451.*

Fanny (Pernilla Allwin) and her brother Alexander (Bertil Guve) survey the situation in *Fanny and Alexander.*

1976 136m/C *SW* Liv Ullmann, Erland Josephson, Gunnar Bjornstrand, Aino Taube-Henrikson, Sven Lindberg, Kary Sylway, Sif Ruud; *D:* Ingmar Bergman; *W:* Ingmar Bergman; *C:* Sven Nykvist. Golden Globe Awards '77: Best Foreign Film; Los Angeles Film Critics Association Awards '76: Best Actress (Ullmann), Best Foreign Film; National Board of Review Awards '76: Best Actress (Ullmann); New York Film Critics Awards '76: Best Actress (Ullmann); Nominations: Academy Awards '76: Best Actress (Ullmann), Best Director (Bergman). **VHS** *PAR*

FAHRENHEIT 451

It's easy to see what's wrong with François Truffaut's risky and foolhardy adaptation of Ray Bradbury's seminal science-fiction novel, *Fahrenheit 451*. The English-language dialogue is stilted and awkward; Oskar Werner appears to be struggling to stay awake; the special effects and process photography are ludicrously bad. Yet if so much of *Fahrenheit 451* is all wrong, why is it so moving? The answer, I think, has to do not with the awkwardness of many of the film's individual pieces, but with the passion and sincerity that surges quite powerfully through its entire conception. *Fahrenheit 451* is a cautionary tale about a future society in which the printed word—and therefore the controversies and conflicting ideas that books bring—is banned. With all new houses fireproof, the job of firemen in Bradbury's future will be to *start* fires—to burn books whenever a neighbor or a jealous lover decides to turn someone possessing a private library over to the guardians of the police state. Truffaut's affection for books comes through far more strongly than does the new-found passion of his lawbreaking protagonist, Montag the fireman (Werner), and it's the director's obvious love for his subject—expressed in eloquent sequences like the snow-covered camp of "book people" at the film's end—that gives the picture a startling emotional immediacy in spite of all its conventional "flaws." Composer Bernard Herrmann's heartbreaking score doesn't hurt either, and Truffaut knew it. In a journal the director kept for *Cahiers du Cinema* on the making of the film, he stated "if one is bored by the film at least it will be boredom set to music, and when it's Bernard Herrmann's music no one will be tired by two or three minute sections like those in *Vertigo* or *Psycho*." But the director needn't have worried. Truffaut's spirit lives in this film, just like the authors whose words are remembered by the book people in its transcendent ending. With Julie Christie and Cyril Cusack. Cinematography by Nicolas Roeg.

NEXT STOP . . . *Mississippi Mermaid, Two English Girls, Testament*

1966 112m/C *FR* Oskar Werner, Julie Christie, Cyril Cusack, Anton Diffring; *D:* Francois Truffaut; *W:* Ray Bradbury, Jean-Louis Richard, Francois Truffaut; *C:* Nicolas Roeg; *M:* Bernard Herrmann. **VHS, LV** *USH, MLB*

THE FAMILY GAME
Kazoku Gaimu
Kazoku Game

The director of this bitter 1983 Japanese satire, Yoshimitsu Morita, is probably not a psychic, but he could certainly pass for one based on this cautionary tale about a manic, over-achieving *Japan, Inc.* on the verge of collapsing under its own unbearable weight. The parents portrayed in *The Family Game* are frantic about the upcoming exams that will decide the academic fate of their younger son, Shigeyuki (Ichirota Miyagawa). With dad (played by Juzo Itami, the late director of *Tampopo*) constantly at work and mom (Saori Yuki) continually cleaning, a tutor named Yoshimoto (Yusaku Matsuda) is brought into the family's tiny home to assure that Shigeyuki will be admitted to the most prestigious high school possible. The tutor, however, is a little wackier than the family bargained for, and his impact on Shigeyuki and the entire family structure is like a delicate pinprick on the surface of a huge, vastly over-inflated, thin-skinned balloon. *The Family Game* looks like an episode of *Leave it to Beaver* that was directed by Luis Buñuel; it's subversive, funny, and always on the verge of shocking. In the end, the *The Family Game*'s bleak, unblinking honesty—despite all its comic, surrealist flourishes—becomes downright sobering.

NEXT STOP . . . *The Crazy Family, Léolo, Welcome to the Dollhouse*

1983 107m/C *JP* Junichi Tsujita, Yusaku Matsuda, Juzo Itami, Saori Yuki, Ichirota Miyagawa; *D:* Yoshimitsu Morita; *W:* Yoshimitsu Morita; *C:* Yonezo Maeda. **VHS** *FCT*

FANNY

César (Raimu) is a cafe owner in Marseilles whose son, Marius (Pierre Fresnay) is in love with Fanny (Orane Demazis). Fanny is terrified that Marius will abandon her because of his love for the sea, and soon her fears are realized. Soon after, when Fanny realizes that she's pregnant by Marius, she agrees to marry an understanding and loving friend who's willing to give the child his name. Two decades later, it is that now-grown child who sets in motion the enormously satisfying conclusion to this remarkable trilogy of films, each written and produced by the great Marcel Pagnol. Though each part was fashioned by a different director—*Marius* was directed

by Alexander Korda in 1931, *Fanny* by Marc Allegret in 1932, and *César* by Pagnol himself in 1933—the films as a whole all have the same full-bodied, richly lived-in quality that makes immersion into the trilogy an unforgettable emotional journey. Pagnol insisted on bringing his cameras from the film studios of Paris to Provence, and thanks to his use of natural sounds and settings, the brilliant performers seem to blend into their environment with a natural, vividly real quality that gives life and breath to each moment of the trilogy's seven hours. The subject of assorted remakes over the years—including Joshua Logan's limp, 1960 *Fanny* with Leslie Caron and Maurice Chevalier—Pagnol's monumental trilogy has stood the test of time not only dramatically, but as a reminder of the unparalleled power with which the cinematic image can transport us to another time and another place, and make it live again.

NEXT STOP . . . *Harvest, The Baker's Wife, Letters from My Windmill*

1932 128m/B *FR* Raimu, Charpin, Orane Demazis, Pierre Fresnay, Alida Rauffe; *D:* Marc Allegret; *W:* Marcel Pagnol; *M:* Vincent Scotto. **VHS, LV** *INT, MRV, HHT*

FANNY AND ALEXANDER
Fanny och Alexander

For those who've never had the opportunity or the interest—for whatever reason—to experience one of the films of the great Swedish director Ingmar Bergman, there is probably no better place to jump in than with his 1983 *Fanny and Alexander*. As with so many great films, this one has a simple story; ten-year-old Alexander and his eight-year-old sister Fanny, growing up in a glowingly happy home in a turn-of-the-century Swedish town, find their life turned horrifyingly upside-down following the unexpected death of their father. Their mother remarries—this time to a pathologically strict clergyman—and the privileged, comfortable life that the children used to know is suddenly replaced by punishment, deprivation, and cruelty. All of this is seen through the eyes of a child, as is the film's miraculous,

CHEN KAIGE
Epic Director

Director Chen Kaige is a Mandarin, born to privilege in Bejing August 12, 1952. His father, a well-known film director, was frequently away on location, and Chen was raised by his actress mother and a Manchu nanny. Then, with the advent of the Cultural Revolution, Chen's life changed dramatically, as the Red Guards ransacked his home and forced him to publically denounce his own father.

Chen tells his story in a 1989 memoir titled "The Young Kaige," but autobiographical aspects also show up—albeit in disguise—in his films. After performing military service in the 1970s, Chen entered the Beijing Film Academy, to emerge in the 1980s as one of the "Fifth Generation" of directors, freed by the passing of Mao to explore Chinese culture and history. Initially, Chen was considered the natural leader of this group, but soon his reputation was eclipsed by the achievements of one of his classmates, Zhang Yimou.

Chen had hired Zhang, a cinematography major, as his director of photography for his first major project, *Yellow Earth* (1984), hailed as an instant classic. Chen's subsequent films, however, proved less successful, and while he became known as a "philosophical" director, Zhang went on to achieve international renown with films like *Ju Dou*. It was therefore especially sweet for Chen when his epic film *Farewell My Concubine* won the Palme d'Or at the Cannes Film Festival in 1994, as well as box office success in the United States. His latest effort, *Temptress Moon*, starring Zhang's former lover, the actress Gong Li, was released in 1996. His next film, also with Gong Li, is called *The Assassin*.

redemptive ending. It's an ending that the children deserve, of course, and one that Bergman has wisely and rather generously chosen to not deny to either himself or his audience. In a sense, seeing this tormented filmmaker allow himself a note of grace after so many films drenched in self-doubt, fear, and despair makes an already marvelous experience into a celebration. The movie makes us happy, and it makes us happy for its creator as well. But even if those other films aren't present in your mind at the end of *Fanny and Alexander*—it may actually *be* your first Bergman, after all—you'll probably be enchanted enough to begin exploring others. By the way, you should know that *Fanny and Alexander* runs three hours and seventeen minutes, but you should also know that it doesn't run a second too long.

Academy awards for Best Cinematography, Art Direction, Costume Design, and Foreign Language Film; nominations for Best Director and Best Original Screenplay.

NEXT STOP . . . *The Seventh Seal, The Magician, Night of the Hunter*

1983 (R) 197m/C *SW* Pernilla Allwin, Bertil Guve, Gunn Walgren, Allan Edwall, Ewa Froling, Erland Josephson, Harriet Andersson, Jarl Kulle, Jan Malmsjo; *D:* Ingmar Bergman; *W:* Ingmar Bergman; *C:* Sven Nykvist; *M:* Daniel Bell. Academy Awards '83: Best Art Direction/Set Decoration, Best Cinematography, Best Costume Design, Best Foreign Film; Cesar Awards '84: Best Foreign Film; Golden Globe Awards '84: Best Foreign Film; Los Angeles Film Critics Association Awards '83: Best Cinematography, Best Foreign Film; New York Film Critics Awards '83: Best Director (Bergman), Best Foreign Film; Nominations: Academy Awards '83: Best Director (Bergman), Best Original Screenplay. **VHS, LV, Closed Caption** *COL, NLC*

FANTASTIC PLANET

La Planete Sauvage
Planet of Incredible Creatures
The Savage Planet

Czech graphic artist Roland Topor and French animator René Laloux adapted Stefan Wul's cautionary novel about interplanetary class struggles, *Oms en Serie,* into one of the most visually innovative animated features of the 1970s. The civilized Oms are living under the heel—literally—of their giant, 40-foot-tall masters, the Draags, and they have no other way to restore the dignity of their traditions but to rebel. *Fantastic Planet* (*La Planète sauvage*) runs just 72 minutes but feels padded; the graphic designs are quite wonderful, but the animation itself is limited and rigid. The flat English-language dubbing doesn't help, but the alternative of subtitling is something that distributors of animated films tend to be understandably leery of. It's an interesting attempt at a grown-up, progressive animated film, but dramatically it's as flat as the paper it was drawn on. (For an example of animation on a similar theme that *is* compelling, try to find Jacques Cardon's 7-minute, 1975 French short, *Imprint.*)

NEXT STOP . . . *Twilight of the Cockroaches, Laputa: Castle in the SkyMy Neighbor Totoro*

1973 (PG) 68m/C *FR D:* Roland Topor, Rene Laloux; *W:* Roland Topor, Steve Hayes, Rene Laloux; *C:* Boris Baromykin, Lubomir Rejthar; *M:* Alain Goraguer; *V:* Barry Bostwick. **VHS** *VYY, MRV, SNC*

FARAWAY, SO CLOSE!

In Weiter Ferne, So Nah!

He just couldn't leave well enough alone. The "well enough" I refer to is Wim Wenders's delicate and miraculously successful 1988 *Wings of Desire,* the story of an angel (Bruno Ganz) who chooses to fall to earth in a divided Berlin in order to experience—even if for a relatively short time—the sensory and emotional pleasure and pain that we all tend to take for granted. *Faraway, So Close!* is *Wings II,* in which Ganz's angelic buddy from the first

film, Cassiel (Otto Sander), decides to take the fall himself. It's now a very different Berlin, of course, and though the fetid and spiritually bereft underside of this new city is probably the very thing that caused Wenders to revisit the story in the first place, it's also what makes *Faraway, So Close!* such a downer. Things don't work out neatly for Cassiel, and if there's a symbol of moral bankruptcy that he doesn't run into—be it pornographers, gangsters, or black market weapons—I'll be darned if I can remember it. Bruno Ganz is back from the first film, as are Solveig Dommartin and Peter Falk. Lou Reed shows up—why not? Mikhail Gorbachev drops in as well. (You don't want to know.) *Faraway, So Close!* isn't truly awful, but it is truly unnecessary. It's a tribute to the originality and strength of *Wings of Desire* that the memory of that film is in no way diminished by this one—nor by the cloying American remake *City of Angels.* (*Faraway, So Close!* originally clocked in at 164 minutes. It's had 24 minutes trimmed since then, yet is virtually indistinguishable from the long version. This should tell you something.)

NEXT STOP . . . *Wings of Desire, The Man Who Fell to Earth, Carousel*

1993 (PG-13) 146m/C *GE* Otto Sander, Peter Falk, Horst Buchholz, Nastassia Kinski, Heinz Ruhmann, Bruno Ganz, Solveig Dommartin, Ruediger Vogler, Willem Dafoe, Lou Reed; *D:* Wim Wenders; *W:* Ulrich Zieger, Richard Reitinger, Wim Wenders; *C:* Jurgen Jurges; *M:* David Darling, Laurent Petitgrand. Cannes Film Festival '93: Grand Jury Prize; Nominations: Golden Globe Awards '94: Best Song ("Stay"). **VHS, LV, Closed Caption** *COL*

FAREWELL MY CONCUBINE

Bawang Bie Ji

Chen Kaige is one of many directors who've attempted to portray the human price of the massive cultural upheavals that have taken place within China. What sets his *Farewell My Concubine* apart is the sweeping, universally accessible structure that he's chosen for his story, as well as the humanity with which he portrays his flawed, damaged, yet heroic characters. It's the story of two men who've been trained since childhood for a life in the

revered Peking Opera. As children, the pair had no say over what their roles were going to be in this enormously popular, traditional art form; Douzi (played by Leslie Cheung as an adult) was deemed the one to portray the female role of a concubine, while Shitou (Zhang Fengyi) was groomed to play the king. (Their early scenes as children at the Opera's school are grueling enough to make you feel you're watching a kids' version of the gladiatorial training in *Spartacus*.) Their experience in the Opera is, of course, far more than a job, and their stage personas mirror their actions in the "real" world; Douzi is gay, and his unreciprocated affection for Shitou—in the face of Shitou's affair with and eventual marriage to prostitute Juxian (Gong Li)—is a lifelong source of anguish for him. The picture's half-century time span—taking in World War II *and* the Cultural Revolution—puts the characters through enormous changes, but Kaige ingeniously uses the Peking Opera as a constant factor around which the country's upheavals swirl. It's a bold and brilliant concept, and Kaige pulls it off. The most powerful screen epics have always worked by keeping a tight focus on the well-drawn characters at their center, and *Farewell My Concubine* is no exception. Yes, it's a physically magnificent movie—but while that may be what got it into the world's theatres, it's the moving, eloquent portrait of history's indelible impact on individual human beings that makes it a classic.

NEXT STOP . . . *Life on a String, The Blue Kite, To Live*

1993 (R) 157m/C *HK* Leslie Cheung, Zhang Fengyi, Gong Li, Lu Qi, Ying Da, Ge You; **D:** Chen Kaige; **W:** Lilian Lee, Lu Wei; **C:** Gu Changwei; **M:** Zhao Jiping. British Academy Awards '93: Best Foreign Film; Cannes Film Festival '93: Best Film; Golden Globe Awards '94: Best Foreign Film; Los Angeles Film Critics Association Awards '93: Best Foreign Film; National Board of Review Awards '93: Best Foreign Film; New York Film Critics Awards '93: Best Foreign Film, Best Supporting Actress (Li); Nominations: Academy Awards '93: Best Cinematography, Best Foreign-Language Film. **VHS, LV** *TOU*

FARINELLI
Farinelli the Castrato
Farinelli il Castrato

Carlo Broschi, whose stage name was "Farinelli," was the most famous of the 18th-century music world's many *castrati*—male singers whose high, heavenly voices were preserved for a lifetime by a flick of the knife in their youth. Broschi was the Sinatra of his day—in terms of popularity, that is—and he reportedly drove his cult-like following of young women into adoring frenzies at his performances. Director Gérard Corbiau has focused his film on the intense sexual and professional rivalries between Broschi (Stefano Dionisi), his brother Riccardo (Enrico Lo Verso), and composer George Frederick Handel (Jeroen Krabbé), and dressed up the whole, rather campy enterprise with all-stops-out costumes and sets. Unfortunately, Corbiau forgot to bother with anything like a compelling script, so once the gimmick of hearing Farinelli's digitally synthesized, Dolby surround-o-fied voice has grown tiresome, the whole picture grows tiresome with it. Carlo and Riccardo do have a pretty amusing routine for seducing women, but it's not *that* amusing, and once would have been enough. Not an embarrassment, but a bungle. If you want to hear the tunes, get the CD.

NEXT STOP . . . *Amadeus, The Music Teacher, Tous les Matins du Monde*

1994 (R) 110m/C *FR IT BE* Stefano Dionisi, Enrico Lo Verso, Jeroen Krabbe, Elsa Zylberstein, Caroline Cellier, Omero Antonutti, Jacques Boudet; **D:** Gerard Corbiau; **W:** Gerard Corbiau, Andree Corbiau, Marcel Beaulieu; **C:** Walther Vanden Ende; **M:** Christopher Rousset. Cesar Awards '95: Best Art Direction/Set Decoration, Best Sound; Golden Globe Awards '95: Best Foreign Film; Nominations: Academy Awards '94: Best Foreign-Language Film. **VHS, LV** *COL*

FAUST
Faust-Eine deutsche Volkssage

This visually brilliant expressionist fantasy by Germany's F.W. Murnau is based on Goethe's version of the story of a man who exchanges his soul for worldly pleasures. It is also, as is widely acknowledged, flawed by the meandering and melodramatic love scenes that take up a good portion of the film's center section. That said, don't miss it for anything. The opening sequence alone—in which Mephisto (Emil Jannings) makes his deal with Faust (Gösta Ekman) and then sweeps

him away on his satanic coattails—are enough to provide nightmares for a month. Murnau was one of the greatest visual stylists in the history of cinema, and his masterpieces—*Nosferatu, The Last Laugh, Sunrise*—were all characterized by a perfectly worked-out visual scheme that was continually at the service of the material. The inconsistent visual audacity of *Faust*, which has phenomenal power in its opening sequences and its final third, but an unremarkable center, is what prevents it from achieving greatness. Nevertheless, if all flawed films were this amazing, then flawed films would be all I'd care to see. Note: there are lots of "public domain" prints and tapes of *Faust* in circulation, which generally indicates poor visual quality. Since the images are the whole reason for *Faust*'s classic status, do everything you can to find the best quality copy—laser *or* video—or better yet, wait for a museum retrospective.

NEXT STOP . . . *Nosferatu* (1922), *The Last Laugh, Mephisto* (1981)

1926 117m/B *GE* Emil Jannings, Warner Fuetterer, Gosta Ekman, Camilla Horn; *D:* F.W. Murnau; *W:* Hans Kyser, Christopher Marlowe, Carl Hoffmann; *M:* Timothy Brock, Werner R. Heymann. **VHS** *GPV, MRV, NOS*

THE FEARLESS VAMPIRE KILLERS
Pardon Me, Your Teeth Are in My Neck
Dance of the Vampires

Professor Abronsius (Jack McGowran) and his bumbling assistant Alfred (Roman Polanski) bring along a sack full of wooden stakes when they visit the desolate, Transylvanian castle where they hope to destroy an ancient family of vampires. For years I've read heavily qualified, polite reviews of Roman Polanski's 1967 *The Fearless Vampire Killers*. Most of the reviews talk about how the film was butchered by its American distributor (it was indeed). They talk about how infuriated Polanski was by this, and how he tried to have his name removed from the credits (he did try, unsuccessfully). They talk about the poignancy of seeing Sharon Tate in the film, with fangs for teeth and blood dripping from

the corners of her mouth (it *is* tough to look at that scene, even today). What few of the reviews point out, however, is that *The Fearless Vampire Killers* (which has been restored) is a knockout. That a comedy can be this saturated not just with blood but with *dread* and still be deeply, darkly hilarious is quite a feat. There are fabulous set pieces in the picture—the ball of the vampires, the prowl along the roof of the castle—but it's the consistency of Polanski's comic tone that's so remarkable. This is a simple but subversive little story about how, despite our best intentions, evil occasionally triumphs. *The Fearless Vampire Killers* is a comedy, but one without comic relief; there are no concessions to the audience's equilibrium and no escape, not even in the unhappy ending. But it's a visionary work, and a visually thrilling one as well (do your best to see it letterboxed, or better yet, on the big screen). Polanski once accurately reminded an interviewer: "What is horrible to you is not necessarily horrible to me." Though his art has always reminded us of that which makes us "uncomfortable," perhaps it's time—in this sanitized cinematic era—to be grateful for that. Perhaps it's time for this extraordinary artist to receive a little *unqualified* praise.

NEXT STOP . . . *Repulsion, Rosemary's Baby, The Tenant*

1967 98m/C *GB* Jack MacGowran, Roman Polanski, Alfie Bass, Jessie Robbins, Sharon Tate, Ferdinand "Ferdy" Mayne, Iain Quarrier, Terry Downes, Fiona Lewis, Ronald Lacey; *D:* Roman Polanski; *W:* Gerard Brach, Roman Polanski; *C:* Douglas Slocombe. **VHS, LV, Letterbox** *MGM*

FELLINI SATYRICON
Satyricon

Using the *Satyricon* of Petronius as a jumping off-point, Federico Fellini created the first historical head film, and right on time; the picture became a cult item in American art houses less than a year after the release of *2001: A Space Odyssey*. But issues of timing aside, it's difficult to argue with assessments like the one by Pauline Kael, who found *Fellini Satyricon* to be "full of cautionary images of depravity that seem to have come out of the imagination of a Catholic school-

boy." For this viewer, however, those images can't be dismissed simply because the primal fears they sprang out of aren't sophisticated—the artist who put them on the screen sure is. I recently watched an *A & E Biography* program on Caligula, and it contained every bit as much of the detailed "depravity" that you'll find in *Fellini Satyricon*, but none of the beauty. And that, of course, is what you remember from Fellini's thrillingly imaginative film—the darkly shimmering, labyrinthine, widescreen images; the sexual pleasures of a world that hasn't yet passed judgment on sexual pleasures (even if the director has); the fragmented, splintered, fantastic universe that is far closer to science-fiction than it is to historical epic. (Looking at the film today, one almost expects it to open with the words: "A Long Time Ago in a Galaxy Far, Far Away.") There's no such thing as a movie that's beyond criticism, but there is such a thing as a movie I choose to accept—even embrace—in the same way I accept an obsessive trait in a trusted friend. That person's fantasy may not be one I would have conjured myself, but that's the whole point of going to the movies. I'm a sucker for hearing about a really good dream.

NEXT STOP . . . *Juliet of the Spirits, Fellini's Roma, Fellini's Casanova*

1969 (R) 129m/C *IT* Martin Potter, Capucine, Hiram Keller, Salvo Randone, Max Born; *D:* Federico Fellini; *W:* Federico Fellini; *C:* Giuseppe Rotunno; *M:* Nino Rota. Nominations: Academy Awards '70: Best Director (Fellini). **VHS, LV, Letterbox** *MGM, FCT, TVC*

FELLINI'S ROMA
Roma

Fellini's Roma, a heartfelt series of vignettes about the city the maestro loves, was promoted in 1972 as Fellini's "documentary" about the city, but with a few fantasy sequences thrown into the mix. I've always had trouble defining the term "documentary" anyway, but to assume that Federico Fellini was going to present us with *cinema vérité*—whatever the hell that really means—is a howler. If Fellini points a camera at Gore Vidal when he's blathering on at his most obnoxious and unctuous, does that

mean we're no longer watching a film by Fellini? No siree, but as *Fellini's Roma* goes on, you get the feeling that the director himself wanted to make sure we knew it was his show. Hence the joyously subversive ecclesiastical fashion show that Fellini stages here, which detractors and fans alike still can't stop talking about. *Fellini's Roma* is as wildly uneven as anyone's imagination is likely to be in different settings and at different times of the day. You feel guilt for going out to the lobby during an irritating moment, because a second later you'll want to rush back for fear of missing something. The something that you'll be missing is the companionship of this dear, irreplaceable genius as he asks us to look at pictures of his trip. They're some pictures, and it was some trip, but the film nevertheless has the same modest, strangely endearing combination of warmth and tediousness as does sitting in a living room at a friend's house seeing narrated slides of a vacation—some will be excruciatingly, picture-post-card boring, some will be spontaneous, unexpected, and surprisingly touching. All things considered, you feel privileged to have been invited. Cameos, in addition to Mr. Vidal, include Anna Magnani and Marcello Mastroianni.

NEXT STOP . . . *Love in the City, Nights of Cabiria, La Dolce Vita, Marcello Mastroianni: I Remember*

1972 (R) 128m/C *FR IT* Peter Gonzales, Britta Barnes, Pia de Doses, Fiona Florence, Marne Maitland, Renato Giovannoli; *Cameos:* Gore Vidal, Anna Magnani, Marcello Mastroianni; *D:* Federico Fellini; *W:* Federico Fellini; *C:* Giuseppe Rotunno; *M:* Nino Rota; *V:* Federico Fellini. **VHS, LV, Letterbox** *MGM, FCT*

FIORILE
Wild Flower

Two children—descendants of a Tuscan family that has a long, unusual history—are being driven by their father to meet their grandfather for the first time. Before they arrive, the father decides to arm the children with the truth about the family's past—200-year-old curse and all. This exquisitely delicate memory film from directors Paolo and Vittorio Taviani (*The Night of the Shooting Stars*) proceeds to tell us in flashback—using

F

"I would have given anything this morning for one human word of compassion—or tenderness."

—Priest (Claude Laydu) in *Diary of a Country Priest*.

135

Chiara Caselli in a pensive moment in the Taviani brothers' *Fiorile*.

a graceful, sophisticated, yet uncluttered visual style that suggests a fable told to children—about the centuries-old, star-crossed love story at the heart of one family's protracted, multi-generational misery. We hear all of it, as do the children, and when they finally arrive for their visit, they look at their old grandfather—perhaps the last living figure in the curse's path—as if he were the central figure in the scariest ghost story they've ever heard. And when he serves them mushrooms, just like the mushrooms in the story they've been listening to in terror…no, you're going to have to squirm through that electric final sequence without any guide other than the Tavianis. They're among the most fabulous storytellers in all cinema, and though *Fiorile* may not quite be up there with Taviani triumphs like *Padre Padrone* and *Kaos*, it's nevertheless one of the most haunting campfire stories you'll ever hear.

NEXT STOP . . . *Padre Padrone, The Night of the Shooting Stars, Kaos*

1993 (PG-13) 118m/C *IT* Michael Vartan, Galatea Ranzi, Claudio Bigagli, Lino Capolicchio, Constanze Engelbrecht, Athina Cenci, Giovanni Guidelli, Chiara Caselli; *D:* Paolo Taviani, Vittorio Taviani; *W:* Paolo Taviani, Vittorio Taviani, Sandro Petraglia; *C:* Giuseppe Lanci; *M:* Nicola Piovani. **VHS, LV** *NLC*

THE FIRE WITHIN
Le Feu Follet
Fuoco Fatuo

Louis Malle's great 1964 film (his fourth feature) is a compassionate but scrupulously unsentimental account of the final 48 hours in the life of a man determined to commit suicide. Though contemporary in setting, *The Fire Within* is based on a 1931 novel called *Le Feu follet* (the film's French title) by Pierre Drieu Le Rochelle, who himself committed suicide in 1945 after being accused of collaboration with the Nazis. Malle's film version is the story of a wealthy and emotionally exhausted man, Alain (Maurice Ronet), whose lifestyle might have at one time caused him to be called a playboy. Alain is also an alcoholic, and upon being released from a clinic where he is being treated, he visits a number of old friends and acquain-

tances, hoping to find a single reason to continue his increasingly difficult struggle to keep living. He cannot find one. Alain's story is told in myriad small details that add up over the course of the movie's two hours to a remarkably intimate portrait of someone who—in the traditional sense—we don't really know at all. Malle was apparently going through a personal crisis of his own during the preparation and filming of *The Fire Within,* and if the film was an act of therapy, so be it. It is also an extraordinary achievement in its own right, a clear-eyed, unblinking look at an intelligent, tormented individual who is tired of wrestling with the demons within him, and who simply decides to declare that the match is over. With Jeanne Moreau and Alexandra Stewart.

NEXT STOP . . . *Mouchette, Drunks, Affliction*

1964 104m/B *FR* Bernard Noel, Jeanne Moreau, Alexandra Stewart, Henri Serre, Maurice Ronet, Lena Skerla, Yvonne Clech, Hubert Deschamps, Jean-Paul Moulinot; *D:* Louis Malle; *W:* Louis Malle; *C:* Ghislan Cloquet; *M:* Erik Satie. **VHS** *NYF, PMS*

THE FIREMEN'S BALL
Hori, Ma Panenko

Milos Forman's third feature film—set in a small Czech town not long before Soviet tanks invaded the country—is a poignant, brilliantly inventive comedy in which the smallest moments converge to form an enormous impression. At this year's edition of the annual celebration held by the town's volunteer fire brigade, the main order of business is to stage a beauty pageant to produce one lucky girl whose privilege it will be to present a gift to the 86-year-old, terminally ill, retiring commander. Things begin to go wrong— such as the head cheese being stolen—but soon the smaller catastrophes spiral into a hopelessly funny series of unexpected but all-too-human failings, ultimately resulting in the one disaster that the brigade exists to prevent. A wry, metaphorical microcosm of an old and traditional society on the brink of collapse, *The Firemen's Ball* remains one of the key works of the glorious Czech film renaissance of the 1960s, and a bitter reminder of its brutal and violent demise. In 1968, following the Soviet takeover, Forman emigrated to Hollywood, where an enormously successful career awaited him (his credits here include *One Flew over the Cuckoo's Nest, Amadeus,* and *The People vs. Larry Flynt*). (American prints of *The Firemen's Ball* begin with Forman himself placing the film in context; if you can read between the lines, you'll find his comments a sly and priceless commentary.)

NEXT STOP . . . *Loves of a Blonde, The Deserter and the Nomads, Taking Off*

1968 73m/C *CZ* Vaclav Stockel, Josef Svet; *D:* Milos Forman; *W:* Ivan Passer, Jaroslav Papousek, Vaclav Sasek, Milos Forman; *M:* Karel Mares. Nominations: Academy Awards '68: Best Foreign-Language Film. **VHS** *HMV, COL, BTV*

FIRES ON THE PLAIN
Nobi

It's often the case that great novels make mediocre movies; it may be that filmmakers are too fearful of rejection by critics and audiences to impose a personal vision on already venerated material. I haven't read the novel that was the basis for Kon Ichikawa's 1959 story of World War II, *Fires on the Plain,* but if it's half as powerful, original, and shocking as the film, I'd be too frightened to open it. Set on an island in the Philippines as the war is drawing to an end, this is a portrait of the end of civilization in miniature. Japanese soldiers have been fighting for months; exhausted, without supplies, and insane with hunger, they begin eating one another. At first devouring corpses killed in battle, they soon begin doing their own killing, describing their prey to each other—and to themselves—as "monkey meat." The story's protagonist, Tamura (Eiji Funakoshi) is known to have tuberculosis, and he's therefore the last person on the island in danger of becoming dinner. Yet his affliction also gives him another kind of distance from the horror around him—he's not desperate to live another day because he knows that it's pointless for him, so he remains a dignified, horrified observer: the only sober man at a nightmarish bacchanal. The widescreen black-and-white images and stark makeup

effects help to fill out this film's infernal vision; the sights resemble what we might imagine as the landscape of another planet, yet we're constantly reminded by this true story that the world we're seeing is not another, but our very own.

NEXT STOP . . . *The Burmese Harp, Forbidden Games, Europa, Europa*

1959 105m/B *JP* Eiji Funakoshi, Osamu Takizawa, Mickey Custis, Asao Suno; *D:* Kon Ichikawa; *W:* Natto Wada; *C:* Setsuo Kobayashi; *M:* Yashushi Akutagawa. **VHS** *MRV, HHT, NLC*

A FISTFUL OF DOLLARS

An open letter to Clint Eastwood. Dear Mr. Eastwood: In 1971, you came to Detroit on a publicity tour for your first directorial effort, *Play Misty for Me.* At a crowded press lunch (You had a steak sandwich and a Heineken. You could have had anything you wanted.) I asked you in my geekiest "film generation" college-paper film-critic style about the genesis of a movie of yours I liked a lot, Sergio Leone's *A Fistful of Dollars.* You looked right at me, narrowed those eyes, leaned forward, and quietly said:"We all *know* it was based on *Yojimbo,* son." I didn't mess with you anymore, but in case you ever read this, Mr. Eastwood, I was *sure* you knew it—I was just rather awkwardly trying to talk to you about Sergio Leone. I guess since you came to town for *Misty,* I should have stuck to that, but I just couldn't resist. You see, as much as I love *Yojimbo,* I've always been astonished at how you and Leone rethought Mifune and Kurosawa into something that was absolutely all your own, but was nevertheless a clear spiritual descendant of Kurosawa's movie. Nope. Never thought you were trying to put one over on anybody—I just thought *A Fistful of Dollars* was ingenious and terrific. Thought you were terrific too. Still do. C'mon back to Detroit sometime. The steak's on me.

NEXT STOP . . . *Yojimbo, The Good, the Bad, and the Ugly, Unforgiven*

1964 (R) 101m/C *IT* Clint Eastwood, Gian Marie Volonte, Marianne Koch; *D:* Sergio Leone; *C:* Massimo

PEDRO ALMODÓVAR
Spain's Unconventional Filmmaker

"Society is preoccupied with controlling passion because it's a disequilibrium, but for the individual it is undeniably the only motor that gives sense to life," director Pedro Almodóvar wrote in his press notes for *Tie Me Up! Tie Me Down!*

Passion is everything for Spain's leading pop icon. Almodóvar's kinky, wacky, irreverent fantasies deflate pretension. His aim, he admits, is to destroy the repressive legacy of Spanish dictator Francisco Franco. He does so with films that are blackly comic, blasphemous, violent, and erotic.

Almodóvar, a control freak, writes, casts, directs, produces, designs, and promotes his own films, buying knickknacks on his travels to use in sets. He is openly gay. His films mock machismo while featuring large roles for powerful, brazen women.

Born on September 24, 1951 in a poor village in southwestern Spain, Almodóvar was raised, with three siblings, mostly by his mother, who has cameos in many of his films. His father was a bookkeeper and gas station attendant. Almodóvar survived sexual abuse by local priests, rejected Catholicism, and fled to Madrid at age 17. In his twenties, he worked for a telephone company while earning a cult following in the underground film, theater, and music scene. He dressed as a transvestite while fronting a punk rock band.

Almodóvar made his first feature in 1980. His 1988 *Women on the Verge of a Nervous Breakdown*, nominated for an Oscar, earned him a large cult following in the United States. *Tie Me Up! Tie Me Down!* earned a disastrous X rating, but Almodóvar refused to cut it. He remains Spain's top celebrity and a prolific, uncompromising filmmaker who concocts amazing movies from his fertile imagination. His other films include *High Heels* (1991), *Kika* (1993), *Flower of My Secret* (1995), and *Live Flesh* (1997).

Dallamano, Federico G. Larraya; *M:* Ennio Morricone. **VHS, LV, Letterbox, Closed Caption** *MGM, FCT, TLF*

FITZCARRALDO

Werner Herzog's *Fitzcarraldo* is the story of an obsessive, perhaps maniacal, self-styled entrepreneur (Klaus Kinski at his most possessed) whose dream it is to build a full-scale opera house in one of the deepest jungles of the Amazon's rain forest. Since the story is set at the end of the last century, it's only logical that Fitzcarraldo's dream will be complete only if Caruso sings there. (As someone who's worked in a museum most of his life, seeing this movie cured me of ever again carping about "community outreach" programs.) To get the money to build the opera house, Fitzcarraldo believes that he must find a way to get a huge steamship into an uncharted and inaccessible river in order to open up new trade routes. The only way to do it—and the reason for the movie's existence—is for Fitzcarraldo to drag the massive ship over the top of a huge mountain and gently lower it into the waiting river on the other side. His life boils down to this single feat, and so does

Herzog's film. The startling sight of Fitzcarraldo in his white suit and tie, supervising this clearly impossible task for the sake of importing "culture" to the Peruvian jungles is an obvious but undeniably compelling sysiphian metaphor for much about western society, and much about many of our lives. As a cohesive film, however, *Fitzcarraldo's* got a bit of a limp; much of it feels sluggish and padded, as if there were too much plot concocted to justify Fitzcarraldo's stunt. Yet every time that we want to tell Herzog to cut to the chase, an unexpectedly lyrical image or note of music delights and astonishes us, and we settle back into the spectacle. The making of this movie was as difficult as the task that Fitzcarraldo sets for himself; the nightmare of filming it was captured in a superb documentary called *Burden of Dreams* by Herzog's friend Les Blank. One tip: see *Fitzcarraldo before* seeing *Burden of Dreams,* otherwise the more astounding journey won't be saved for last.

NEXT STOP . . . *Burden of Dreams, Aguirre, the Wrath of God, Apocalypse Now*

1982 (PG) 157m/C *GE* Klaus Kinski, Claudia Cardinale, Jose Lewgoy, Miguel Angel Fuentes, Paul Hittscher; *D:* Werner Herzog; *W:* Werner Herzog; *C:* Thomas Mauch; *M:* Popul Vuh. Cannes Film Festival '82: Best Director (Herzog). **VHS** *WAR*

THE FLOWER OF MY SECRET
La Flor de My Secreto

An unexpected and refreshingly welcome surprise, particularly after the (unintentionally, I hope) misogynistic misfire of *Kika,* Pedro Almodóvar's *The Flower of My Secret* is a sparklingly witty, genuinely moving portrait of a middle-aged writer (Marisa Paredes in a fabulous performance) who tries desperately to find a meaningful shred of *something* to hang on to when every aspect of her life comes apart at the seams. Leo (Paredes) is a fabulously successful author of pulp romances, which she churns out under a nom de plume. Yet when it comes to her disastrous, real-life marriage, she exists in an even sadder state of denial and self-delusion than

her fictional heroines. Just as Leo keeps her other literary identity a secret from the world, she also keeps her own sexual identity compartmentalized and hidden from herself. Yet when her carefully arranged double life reaches critical mass, thanks to an explosive and unexpected series of mishaps, Leo must redefine herself, deciding, perhaps for the first time, which of her identities is the "real" one. Though it's dramatically different in tone from the manic farce of his equally wonderful *Women on the Verge of a Nervous Breakdown, Flower* demonstrates—as did *Women*—the heights that Almodóvar can reach when his comic talents and his love for his female characters are kept in balance. It's a gem.

NEXT STOP . . . *What Have I Done to Deserve This?, Women on the Verge of a Nervous Breakdown, A Self-Made Hero*

1995 (R) 107m/C *SP FR* Marisa Paredes, Juan Echanove, Imanol Arias, Carmen Elias, Rossy de Palma, Chus Lampreave, Joaquin Cortes, Manuela Vargas; *D:* Pedro Almodovar; *W:* Pedro Almodovar; *C:* Alfonso Beato; *M:* Alberto Iglesias. **VHS, LV, Closed Caption** *COL*

THE FLOWERS OF ST. FRANCIS
Francesco, Giullare di Dio
Francis, God's Jester

I saw Roberto Rossellini's 1950 *The Flowers of St. Francis* just once, at a screening at London's National Film Theatre more than 30 years ago. I remember it as being a charmingly relaxed, documentary-style series of episodes in the life of St. Francis and his disciples—a film so uninsistent in tone that it struck me as being unlike any film on a religious subject that I had ever seen. Rossellini created a number of such uncluttered, neo-realist films on religious and historical figures such as Socrates, Augustine of Hippo, Descartes, and Jesus. His extraordinary 1966 film *The Rise of Louis XIV* was originally made for French television, but was screened theatrically in the U.S. Like *The Flowers of St. Francis,* the Louis XIV film consists of a series of terse episodes photographed flatly and without sentimentality, giving the viewer the vicarious experience of looking at history

Michel. She understands the need for survival, though she's confused by her new rural lifestyle, and she's utterly uncomprehending of the meaning of this thing called death that has come to her parents. Together, the two children try to grasp what death is about; ultimately, Paulette's eyes are opened in a final scene that is one of the most emotionally harrowing sequences in all cinema. *Forbidden Games,* one of the greatest and most heartbreaking films ever made, is the work of France's René Clément, who, though he's unquestionably done other fine work (notable is the 1960 *Purple Noon,* starring Alain Delon), never again approached the power or majesty of this haunting, obviously heartfelt fable. All of the acting is exemplary, but the performance of little Brigitte Fossey is astounding. (She's so powerful in the role that you'll want to look her up in one of the films she made as an adult—like *The Man Who Loved Women*—just to assure yourself that she's really OK.) The legendary score is by Narciso Yepes. Academy Award, Best Foreign Language Film.

NEXT STOP . . . *Grand Illusion, Shame (Bergman, 1968), Au Revoir les Enfants*

1952 90m/B *FR* Brigitte Fossey, Georges Poujouly, Amedee, Louis Herbert, Suzanne Courtal, Jacques Marin, Laurence Badie, Andre Wasley, Louis Sainteve; *D:* Rene Clement; *W:* Rene Clement, Jean Aurenche, Pierre Bost, Francois Boyer; *C:* Robert Juillard; *M:* Narciso Yepes. Academy Awards '52: Best Foreign Film; British Academy Awards '53: Best Film; New York Film Critics Awards '52: Best Foreign Film; Venice Film Festival '52: Best Film; Nominations: Academy Awards '54: Best Story. **VHS, LV** *NOS, NLC*

THE FORBIDDEN QUEST

Dutch filmmaker Peter Delpeut has fashioned something of a cottage industry out of turning archival documentary footage into a spine on which to hang newly spun yarns. In his *The Forbidden Quest,* Delpeut begins with spectacular images of polar expeditions—probably shot between 1905 and 1925—and adds a soundtrack, actors, and newly staged scenes to create a hybrid, fake "documentary" in which the old gen-

Brigitte Fossey is orphaned by war in Rene Clement's *Forbidden Games.*

photographed *by* the camera, rather than recreated *for* the camera.

NEXT STOP . . . *The Gospel According to St. Matthew, The Rise of Louis XIV, The Last Temptation of Christ*

1950 75m/B *IT* Aldo Fabrizi, Brother Nazario Gerardi, Arabella Lemaitre; *D:* Roberto Rossellini; *W:* Father Antonio Lisandrini, Father Felix Morion, Federico Fellini, Roberto Rossellini; *C:* Otello Martelli; *M:* Enrico Buondonno, Renzo Rossellini. **VHS** *FCT*

FORBIDDEN GAMES
Les Jeux Interdits

Paulette (Brigitte Fossey), a five-year-old girl whose parents are killed as the family flees Nazi occupied Paris, is taken in by a peasant family that includes 11-year-old Michel (Georges Poujouly). Paulette adapts as best she can thanks to the help of the adoring

uine footage becomes part of the new, fictitious tale. Sounds crazy, but it works. Delpeut has an extraordinary flair for capturing the feel of isolation and dread that can be found only the most wide-open of spaces, and the incredibly beautiful, color-tinted archival footage is incorporated into his story in a genuinely chilling manner; it gives his whole absurd tale—about an underground passage to Antarctica—the flavor of a classic ghost story. Delpeut's films (he also made the extraordinary *Lyrical Nitrate*) aren't for everyone, but for those who can be awestruck by rare old film footage of places that we normally visit only in dreams, there's nothing like them.

NEXT STOP . . . *Lyrical Nitrate, The Saltmen of Tibet, Nanook of the North*

1993 75m/C *NL* Joseph O'Conor, Roy Ward; *D:* Peter Delpeut; *W:* Peter Delpeut. **VHS** *KIV*

47 RONIN, PART 1
The Loyal 47 Ronin
47 Samurai

The tale has been filmed many times, but Kenji Mizoguchi's 1942 two-part epic of Seika Mayama's story is the best remembered and the most gripping. Part one chronicles how the early 18th-century samurai warriors of Lord Asano set out to avenge their leader, who was forced by an enemy to commit seppuku (harakiri, to use the more vulgar term). In part two, vengeance is theirs. This wartime production—known in Japan as *The Loyal 47 Ronin*—was designed as a total sensory experience for Japanese audiences, and was filmed on a scale that was new to Mizoguchi and to the Japanese film industry in general. The detail within each sequence, whether it be a huge vista or an intimate interior, is what sets Mizoguchi's direction apart here, and that passion for historical, physical, and emotional accuracy would be seen in his subsequent, superior masterworks, such as Life of Oharu and Ugetsu.

NEXT STOP . . . *Sansho the Bailiff, Ugetsu, Seven Samurai*

1942 111m/C *JP D:* Kenji Mizoguchi. **VHS** *FCT*

47 RONIN, PART 2

See *The 47 Ronin, Part 1.*

1942 108m/C *JP D:* Kenji Mizoguchi. **VHS** *FCT*

THE 400 BLOWS ✓
Les Quatre Cents Coups

The debate over just *how* autobiographical François Truffaut's first feature film really is has faded somewhat over the years, while its stature as one of the most influential of all films about childhood has continued to rise. The troubled, 13-year-old Antoine Doinel, played by an extraordinary young actor named Jean-Pierre Léaud, lives in a tiny Parisian apartment with his bickering, miserably unhappy parents. Antoine escapes through reading and through movies, but his need for attention leads him down a road of truancy, deceit, and petty crime that finally corners him—in one of the most powerful images in modern cinema—with literally no place to run. This heartbreaking final image of the film is typical of Henri Decae's cinematography; the camera freely but glamourlessly roams the streets of Paris, yet pulls off the rare feat of reinforcing the lead character's claustrophobia, even though the images are in a widescreen format. The impact of *The 400 Blows* in 1959 was enormous; Truffaut took the Best Director Award at Cannes and the his script even received an Oscar nomination—a rare occurrence for any foreign language film in the 1950s. More than the awards, however, the film's naturalistic and accessible qualities endeared it to American audiences, and Truffaut became—along with Fellini, Bergman, and perhaps Kurosawa—one of a handful of foreign directors whose names became familiar to American audiences beyond the strict boundaries of the art house. Forty years later, the film itself remains quite magnificent—a marvel of complexity disguised as the simplest and most straightforward of stories. (It was followed years later

F

Julien (Maurice
Ronet) leans on
lover Florence
(Jeanne Moreau)
in *Frantic*.

by a number of sequels, in which Léaud
starred as the same character.)

NEXT STOP . . . *Love at Twenty, Stolen Kisses, Bed and Board, Love on the Run*

1959 97m/B *FR* Francois Truffaut, Jean-Pierre Leaud,
Claire Maurier, Albert Remy, Guy Decomble, Georges
Flament, Patrick Auffay, Jeanne Moreau, Jean-Claude
Brialy, Jacques Demy, Robert Beauvais; *D:* Francois Truf-
faut; *W:* Francois Truffaut, Marcel Moussey; *C:* Henri
Decae; *M:* Jean Constantin. Cannes Film Festival '59:
Best Director (Truffaut); New York Film Critics Awards
'59: Best Foreign Film; Nominations: Academy Awards
'59: Best Story & Screenplay. **VHS, LV, Letterbox, DVD**
HMV, MRV, FOX

THE 4TH MAN
Die Verde Man

Later in his career, the Dutch director Paul
Verhoeven would again attempt to meld a
murder mystery with comically intense eroticism, but the result then—the Sharon
Stone/Michael Douglas *Basic Instinct*—
would be less inventive, less witty, less interesting, and just less fun than his diabolically
clever 1979 thriller *The 4th Man*. Gerard
(Jeroen Krabbé) is a writer who wants to get
to the bottom of the mystery surrounding
hairdresser Christine Halsslag (Renee Soutendijk)—that is, the mystery of her three
dead husbands. In order to find out if she's a
murderer, he needs to get closer to her. She's
a stunningly attractive woman, but as Gerard
is gay, he finds himself far more attracted to
Christine's latest boyfriend. Filled with outrageous fantasy sequences and a satisfyingly
shocking ending, *The 4th Man* is good, dirty
fun. *The 4th Man* has nudity to spare, but
refuses to spare any. It went out in the U.S.
without a rating, rather than submit to what
would have been an inevitable "X." (The
inventive cinematography is by Jan De Bont,
whose Hollywood directorial career included
Speed and *Twister*.)

NEXT STOP... *Soldier of Orange, Diabolique (1955), House of Games*

1979 104m/C NL Jeroen Krabbe, Renee Soutendijk, Thom Hoffman, Jon DeVries, Geert De Jong; **D:** Paul Verhoeven; **C:** Jan De Bont; **M:** Loek Dikker. Los Angeles Film Critics Association Awards '84: Best Foreign Film. **VHS, LV** *XVC*

FRANTIC
Elevator to the Gallows
Ascenseur pour L'Echafaud

Louis Malle was 25 when he made his directorial feature debut with this 1957 thriller about an ex-paratrooper named Julien (Maurice Ronet) in love with his boss's wife (Jeanne Moreau). Julien knows what has to be done, and the perfect murder he has planned will leave nothing to chance—nothing, that is, except the elevator he becomes stuck in after the murder, leading to his false implication in a different killing. Though *Frantic* (*Elevator to the Gallows* in France) is a nifty little suspense film, it's difficult to detect the presence of the extraordinarily gifted director who would burst on the film scene a year later with *The Lovers.* Incidentally, *Frantic* was released in America only after the successful release of *The Lovers;* audiences here must have been a bit puzzled as to why Malle would chose this as his "followup." (Malle is one of many famous directors whose early career included a suspense thriller; as with Kubrick's *The Killing* and Spielberg's *Duel,* it would seem to be a straightforward and often profitable way to develop the basics of film technique.)

NEXT STOP... *The Lovers, The Postman Always Rings Twice (1946), Double Indemnity*

1958 92m/B FR Maurice Ronet, Jeanne Moreau, Georges Poujouly; **D:** Louis Malle; **C:** Henri Decae; **M:** Miles Davis. **VHS, 8mm** *SNC, NOS, VYY*

FREEZE-DIE-COME TO LIFE
Zamri Oumi Voskresni

Near the end of World War II, two children (Pavel Nazarov and Dinara Drukarova) living in poverty in the remote mining village of Suchan, have only their wits and their precious sense of humor to guide them though the bleakness of their situation. This humane, sensitive, and inventively photographed Russian film marks the directorial debut of Vitaly Kanevski, who himself spent eight years in a Soviet labor camp prior to commencing production. Kanevski was given a green light on the production, but then was told that the finished product was unacceptable in the version in which he delivered it. Editing was done and redone in a race to make the film ready for competition at Cannes, while still appeasing official party censors. Ultimately, *Freeze-Die-Come to Life* did make it to Cannes, where it won the coveted *Camera d'Or* award for Best First Feature. As a result, this poetic and stirring little film did receive American distribution, though it was sadly limited.

NEXT STOP... *Repentance, Commissar, Cardiogram*

1990 105m/B RU Pavel Nazarov, Dinara Drukarova; **D:** Vitaly Kanevski; **W:** Vitaly Kanevski; **C:** Vladimir Brylyakov; **M:** Sergei Banevich. **VHS** *FXL, BST, ING*

FRENCH CAN-CAN
Only the French Can!

In the Paris of 1888, a nightclub owner named Danglard (Jean Gabin) has fallen on hard times; he decides that the only way to restore himself to financial health is to revive the Can Can. To do it properly, he'll need to present it in a dazzling, spectacular cabaret, but since nothing already in existence is good enough, Danglard sets out to build the nightclub of his dreams—he will call it the Moulin Rouge. Of the trilogy of lushly colorful period films that Jean Renoir directed in the 1950s (*The Golden Coach* and *Eléna et les Hommes* were the others), *French Can-Can* may be the most purely and gloriously entertaining. What seems at first to be a subplot—Danglard's love affair with the dancer he wants to make into a star—culminates in the revelation of Danglard's true passion: his art. The sacrifice he is willing to make for that passion makes the opening night sequence at the Moulin Rouge into a powerful and surprisingly moving climax; we feel Renoir and Gabin speaking to us directly, and what had threatened to

Loli (Victoria Abril) tries to separate her lover (Josiane Balasko) from her husband (Alain Chabat) in *French Twist*.

be just a glossy, polished entertainment is suddenly, magically transformed into a profoundly touching tribute to all artists, and all dreamers. Happily, *French Can-Can* was restored in 1985 to its full, colorful glory.

NEXT STOP . . . *The Golden Coach, Children of Paradise, Singin' in the Rain*

1955 93m/C *FR* Jean Gabin, Francoise Arnoul, Maria Felix, Jean-Roger Caussimon, Edith Piaf, Patachou; **D:** Jean Renoir. **VHS, LV** *INT*

FRENCH PROVINCIAL
Souvenirs d'en France

Former film critic André Téchiné was yet another of the gifted *Cahiers du Cinéma* set who decided to put his money where his mouth is, and the result was this striking if maddeningly disjointed portrait of a seamstress (Jeanne Moreau) who marries into a bourgeois family and works her way to the top. The movie's conceived as a kind of supersoaper—an ungainly blend of *Rules of the Game* and *Dallas,* with a dash of Pagnol thrown in—but it's Téchiné's audacious, lilting sense of style that rides to the rescue. There are lovely passages of such visual ingenuity that the already convoluted narrative takes a backseat, and we can simply luxuriate in the rich, fluid images of Bruno Nuytten (who later would photograph the Pagnol-inspired *Jean de Florette* and *Manon of the Spring,* and, less successfully, would direct *Camille Claudel*). With Marie-France Pisier and Orane Demazis (of Pagnol's *Harvest* and *The Fanny Trilogy*).

NEXT STOP . . . *Wild Reeds, Ma Saison Préférée, The Marriage of Maria Braun*

1975 95m/C *FR* Jeanne Moreau, Michel Auclair, Marie-France Pisier, Orane Demazis, Claude Mann, Julien

Guiomar, Michele Moretti, Aram Stephane; **D:** Andre Techine; **W:** Andre Techine, Marilyn Goldin; **C:** Bruno Nuytten; **M:** Philippe Sarde. *NYR*

FRENCH TWIST

Bushwhacked
Gazon Maudit

All praise to Victoria Abril for her stalwart efforts at trying to keep this helpless, sinking ship of a sex comedy afloat; it goes down to the bottom anyway, and it seems to take longer to do it than the entire running time of *Titanic*. Josiane Balasko (who played the other woman in Bertrand Blier's *Too Beautiful for You*) was the perp of this high-concept gender-bender about a philandering husband (Alain Chabat) whose lonely wife (Abril) begins an affair with a husky, sensitively masculine woman (Balasko). Hubby isn't happy about this, but reluctantly agrees to an "arrangement," whereby Abril spends a few nights with her husband followed by a few with her new lover. They'll just all have to get along (but of course that doesn't mean *we* have to stay). The biggest problem with *French Twist* isn't necessarily the moronic premise; I've seen great filmmakers do remarkable things with mighty thin material. But Josiane Balasko, who wrote *French Twist* in addition to directing it, is not even a passable filmmaker. This thing is all situation and no comedy; you want to elbow Balasko in the ribs and tell her "I get the premise. Now *do* something with it." Alas, the premise, such as it is, is all. Balasko deserts her cast, and her audience, to do a slow *French Twist* in the wind.

NEXT STOP . . . Anything else.

1995 (R) 100m/C *FR* Victoria Abril, Alain Chabat, Josiane Balasko, Ticky Holgado; **D:** Josiane Balasko; **W:** Josiane Balasko, Telsche Boorman; **C:** Gerard de Battista; **M:** Manuel Malou. Cesar Awards '96: Best Writing; Nominations: Cesar Awards '96: Best Actor (Chabat), Best Director (Balasko), Best Film, Best Supporting Actor (Holgado); Golden Globe Awards '96: Best Foreign Film. **VHS, LV, Closed Caption** *TOU*

FULL MOON IN PARIS

Les Nuits de la Pleine

Louise (Pascale Ogier) is feeling suffocated in her relationship with her architect boyfriend. Explaining to the befuddled guy that she needs her own space, Louise takes a small apartment in Paris where she can be on her own. But space, it seems, it not what Louise really gravitates toward, and before long she's being pushed and pulled into relationships without even realizing it. Eric Rohmer's charming comedy features a truly enchanting performance from Ogier, whose confusion, misunderstandings, and disappointments become palpably poignant. Rohmer's comedy isn't so much about situations as it is about the human response to them. We feel for his characters because no matter how absurd the situations they get into, their indecisiveness and simple human weaknesses are reassuring, refreshing, and familiar. Those are real people up there on the screen, and they're terrific company.

NEXT STOP . . . *Summer, Boyfriends & Girlfriends, Rendezvous in Paris*

1984 (R) 101m/C *FR* Pascale Ogier, Tcheky Karyo, Fabrice Luchini; **D:** Eric Rohmer; **W:** Eric Rohmer; **C:** Renato Berta. Venice Film Festival '84: Best Actress (Ogier). **VHS** *XVC*

THE FUNERAL

Funeral Rites
Ososhiki

The TV careers of a married couple are interrupted by the sudden death of the wife's father. The couple gets considerably more than they bargained for, however, when the carefully laid plans for what was to be a traditional, three-day Buddhist funeral service begin to unravel into a series of out-of-control misadventures. Juzo Itami's 1985 debut film has fewer big laughs than his subsequent hits, *Tampopo* and *A Taxing Woman*, but it's every bit as dryly and bitterly satiri-

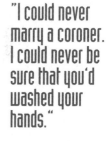

"I could never marry a coroner. I could never be sure that you'd washed your hands."

—Cissie 2 (Juliet Stevenson) to Madgett (Bernard Hill) in *Drowning By Numbers.*

145

Frank (Mel Gibson) and Archy (Mark Lee) are Aussie soldiers in WWI in *Gallipoli*.

cal. A scathing portrait of a Japan in which ceremony and appearance are vastly more important than simple human feeling, *The Funeral* is a bleak vision of the last manic days of Japan, Inc. just prior to the nation's economic reckoning, which is eerily—if only metaphorically—foreshadowed here. In sequences such as the inappropriate arrival of the husband's mistress, a mix-up by the sushi delivery man, and the couple's careful study of what may be the ultimate self-help video, "The ABC's of Funerals," the sure, sharp eye of Itami is at its most wicked and brutally funny.

NEXT STOP . . . *Tampopo, A Taxing Woman, The Loved One*

1984 112m/C *JP* Tsutomu Yamazaki, Nobuko Miyamoto, Kin Sugai, Ichiro Zaitsu, Nekohachi Edoya, Shoji Otake; *D:* Juzo Itami; *W:* Juzo Itami; *C:* Yonezo Maeda; *M:* Joji Yuasa. **VHS** *REP, FCT*

GABBEH

At the center of Iranian filmmaker Mohsen Makhmalbaf's exquisitely told tale of unrequited love is a nomadic world in which an ancient form of rug-weaving results in the precious gabbeh—a carpet in which is woven the images of timeless tales and legends. Makhmalbaf has extended the folk art tradition that produced the gabbeh itself to the filmmaking process, fashioning a kaleidoscopic love story out of brightly colored images of varying textures and tones. With a visual boldness that recalls the works of Sergei Parajanov and Andrei Tarkovsky, Makhmalbaf presents us with startling, enchanting moments; a teacher points to the sky to indicate the color of sunlight, and when his hand next appears it is golden. The sound of cascading water seems to spring from the deep blues of the gabbeh, as the two lonely characters woven into it speak of a heartache that seems as timeless as the weaver's art. Haunting and unforgettable as it shifts between legend, dream, and reality, *Gabbeh* is one of the many extraordinarily delicate and poetic works of art to emerge from the new, rich cinematic tradition of Iran.

NEXT STOP... *Shadows of Forgotten Ancestors, Andrei Rublev, The White Balloon*

1996 75m/C Shaghayeh Djodat, Hossein Moharami, Rogheih Moharami, Abbas Sayah; **D:** Mohsen Makhmalbaf; **W:** Mohsen Makhmalbaf; **C:** Mahmoud Kalari; **M:** Hossein Alizadeh. *NYR*

GALLIPOLI

Frank (Mel Gibson) and Archy (Bill Kerr) are friends who enlist in the Australian military in World War I. After a period of training together in Egypt, the two men become fodder in the battle between Australia and the German-allied Turks. This large scale recreation of the catastrophic battle of Gallipoli was staged by Australia's Peter Weir (*Picnic at Hanging Rock, The Truman Show*) and is clearly intended as a powerful anti-war statement. Those sentiments certainly get through, but much of the film is nevertheless filler, demonstrating in unconvincing detail the friendship of these two athletes in order that we may be all the more devastated by the final outcome. Trouble is, their friendship is unspontaneous and stereotypical, as is the long Egyptian training sequence at the film's center. The final battle scenes are magnificently designed and staged with stunning, widescreen images, but as impressive as *Gallipoli* is both visually and as a concept, its ultimate impact is disappointingly muted. The film's superb score is by Brian May.

NEXT STOP... *Paths of Glory, Full Metal Jacket, The Year of Living Dangerously*

1981 (PG) 111m/C *AU* Mel Gibson, Mark Lee, Bill Kerr, David Argue, Tim McKenzie, Robert Grubb; **D:** Peter Weir; **W:** David Williamson, Peter Weir; **C:** Russell Boyd; **M:** Brian May. Australian Film Institute '81: Best Actor (Gibson), Best Film. **VHS, LV** *PAR*

THE GARDEN OF DELIGHTS

When a millionaire industrialist (J.L. López Vásquez) is wheelchair-bound and afflicted with amnesia after an auto accident, his greedy family turns all of their attention to him, hoping to find a way to get him to reveal the number of his Swiss bank account. They're not exactly gentle in their methods; at one point they put him in a room with a large pig, and tell him he's about to be eaten. In another, they make him relive his first communion, which turned out to be nightmarishly traumatic. Carlos Saura's pitch-black comedy is cynical but surprisingly touching. It can be seen as a multi-leveled commentary on fascism, greed, and overall family values, and it ultimately succeeds by never losing sight of the protagonist's humanity. It's often overlooked, possibly because of similarly toned films by Luis Buñuel, but it's a fine, haunting piece of work.

NEXT STOP... *Tristana, Simon of the Desert, Cria*

1970 95m/C *SP* Jose Luis Lopez Vasquez, Lina Canelajas, Luchy Soto, Francisco Pierra, Charo Soriano; **D:** Carlos Saura. **VHS** *HMV, CVC, FCT*

THE GARDEN OF THE FINZI-CONTINIS
Il Giardino del Finzi-Contini

Vittorio de Sica's extraordinary, unexpected (at least by me) late-career masterwork is the story of a wealthy Jewish-Italian family living in luxurious, sheltered elegance—and in denial. It is World War II, and the Finzi-Continis are living in Ferrara. They will not believe that their way of life is endangered, let alone about to end catastrophically. The family's garden is a magnificent and tranquil setting, but it is walled. Each of the family members feels secure inside, but as the reality of their situation begins, bit by bit, to sink in, they feel secure *only* inside. In flashback we learn about the childhood of Micol (Dominique Sanda), the daughter whose romantic and

G

sexual confusion is at the heart of the film. Through her character, De Sica gives us a portrait of people who create their own realities, their own carefully crafted universe, until, disastrously, the illusion is violently shattered. Simple, eloquent, and finally devastating, *The Garden of the Finzi-Continis* is a breathtaking classic from of one of the cinema's genuine masters. Academy Award for Best Foreign Language Film, nomination for Best Adapted Screenplay.

NEXT STOP . . .   *The Bicycle Thief, Miracle in Milan, The Boat Is Full*

1971 (R) 94m/C *IT* Dominique Sanda, Helmut Berger, Lino Capolicchio, Fabio Testi, Romolo Valli; **D:** Vittorio De Sica; **W:** Cesare Zavattini; **C:** Ennio Guarnieri; **M:** Bill Conti, Manuel De Sica. Academy Awards '71: Best Foreign Film; Berlin International Film Festival '71: Golden Berlin Bear; Nominations: Academy Awards '71: Best Adapted Screenplay. **VHS, LV** *COL, IME, WAR*

GATE OF HELL
Jigokumen

One of the seminal moments of my moviegoing life occurred in 1965, when a local art house ran a new-to-me triple bill of Japanese films: Hiroshi Teshigahara's *Woman in the Dunes,* Kenji Mizoguchi's *Ugetsu,* and Teinosuke Kinugasa's 1954 *Gate of Hell.* Calling the evening sensory overload would be an understatement. Set in the 12th century, *Gate of Hell* is the story of a victorious warrior whose grateful lord rewards his loyalty by offering to give him anything he wants. When the warrior asks for the hand of a beautiful noblewoman (*Rashomon's* Machiko Kyo) who happens to already be married, a riveting contest of wills ensues, resulting in tragedy. It's a majestic and powerful drama on every level, but it derives a huge amount of its impact from the truly astounding color cinematography. More than 30 years later, *Woman in the Dunes* and *Ugetsu* remain widely acknowledged classics, seen and written about on a regular basis, yet *Gate of Hell*—which I still recall as the real jaw-dropper of that evening—is rarely screened. The reason for its scarcity has nothing to do with the quality of the film, and everything to do with the quality of film *stock*. *Gate of Hell* was photographed with Eastmancolor film, and its color palette—so immediate and vivid that it felt like 3-D—retained its majesty in prints that were circulated for many years. Inevitably, however, those prints faded into a pale, ghostly magenta, leaving not even a hint of the film's original beauty. Finding a decent print today is impossible. Current video versions have partially resuscitated the color, but a full-scale restoration is needed to rescue this amazing experience for a new generation. *Gate of Hell* won the Academy Award for Color Costume Design, as well as a Special Award for Best Foreign Film (two years before that Oscar was given annually.)

NEXT STOP . . . *A Page of Madness, Ugetsu, Chikamatsu Monogatari*

1954 89m/C *JP* Kazuo Hasegawa, Machiko Kyo, Isao Yamagata, Koreya Senda; *D:* Teinosuke Kinugasa; *W:* Teinosuke Kinugasa; *C:* Kohei Sugiyama; *M:* Yashushi Akutagawa. Academy Awards '54: Best Costume Design (Color), Best Foreign Film; Cannes Film Festival '54: Best Film. **VHS, 8mm** *VYY, DVT, VDM*

GENERAL IDI AMIN DADA

"Do you see?," points out General Idi Amin to director Barbet Schroeder as they take a boat ride together through a Ugandan jungle, "the elephants on the shore are saluting me." If Werner Herzog can be called a risk-taker to film a documentary on the edge of the *La Soufrière* volcano at the moment it was predicted it would erupt, what would you call Schroeder for putting himself in a small boat, deep in the Ugandan countryside, with only a cinematographer (Nestor Almendros) and Idi Amin for company? It would not be inappropriate to sit through the entire 90 minutes of Schroeder's documentary *General Idi*

Amin Dada in disbelief, but it would also not be odd to wonder at its conclusion just what exactly you've been looking at. Amin clearly enjoys playing to the camera, and the focus of the film quickly boils down not to whether Almendros and Schroeder will come to harm (Hollywood success followed for both), but rather the old con artist's "who'll blink-first-since-I-know-that-you-know-that-I-know" routine; Amin orchestrates it with the skill of Joe Mantegna in Mamet's *House of Games*. In the end, the film doesn't provide a whole lot of information that wasn't already known in 1974; as an exercise in macho bravado, however, it does give Schroeder boasting rights. (Herzog's volcano didn't erupt either, at least not until he left the mountain.)

NEXT STOP . . . *The Wonderful, Horrible Life of Leni Riefenstahl, God's Angry Man* and *La Soufrière* (two short films by Werner Herzog)

1975 113m/C D: Barbet Schroeder; **W:** Barbet Schroeder; **C:** Nestor Almendros. **VHS** *WAR, BTV, FCT*

GENERALE DELLA ROVERE
Il Generale Della-Rovere

Many of us will always think of *Generale Della Rovere,* though it was directed by Roberto Rossellini, as a Vittorio De Sica picture. Not because he had a hand in the direction—he didn't—but because as the star of the film he turns in one of the most memorably magnificent portrayals in film history. *Generale Della Rovere* takes place during World War II, as the Italian resistance movement is taking a strong stand against the Nazi presence. When a resistance leader is shot, the Germans decide that no one has to know about it: By sending someone who can impersonate the dead man to a prison where other resistance members are being held, the fascists can get valuable information. The spy they settle on is Vittorio Emanuele Bardone, a thief and black marketeer played by De Sica. What the Nazis don't count on, of course, is that once he's surrounded by real heroes, all of whom believe that *he's* a hero, Vittorio will persuade himself to rise to the occasion and do the right thing. De Sica's

G

transformation from lowlife to freedom fighter is brilliantly delineated—he'd given fine performances before, as in *The Earrings of Madame de ...*, but his Vittorio is a spectacular, heartbreaking creation. If the film as a whole has occasional moments that are a bit heavy-handed, the same can't be said for De Sica's performance. He leads this *Generale* to a triumphant victory.

NEXT STOP . . . *Open City, To Be or Not to Be* (1942), *Kagemusha*

1960 139m/B *IT* Vittorio De Sica, Otto Messmer, Sandra Milo; *D:* Roberto Rossellini; *W:* Diego Fabbri, Indro Montanelli, Roberto Rossellini; *C:* Carlo Carlini; *M:* Renzo Rossellini. **VHS** *NOS, CVC, HHT*

A GENERATION
Pokolenie

Polish director Andrzej Wajda made his directorial debut with this stark and absorbing tale about a young man named Stach (Tadeusz Lomnicki) whom we first meet searching for work in Nazi occupied Poland. Stach gets a job in a woodworking shop, where he meets Dorota (Urszula Modrzynska), a woman who introduces him to the resistance movement, and with whom he falls in love. Stach may be less drawn into the resistance at first for political reasons than for the companionship of Dorota, but when she dies attempting to help prisoners of the ghetto escape, Stach's grief will be channeled into continuing the movement, and to teaching a new, younger generation about the fascist menace. *A Generation* is clearly the work of a major new film artist, though he would surpass this achievement quickly. It was the first film in what was to be known as Wajda's "war trilogy"; the films that followed were *Kanal* in 1956, and the widely acclaimed *Ashes and Diamonds* in 1958, the later making a major star of Zbigniew Cybulski. (Look for Cybulski in the small role of Kostek in *A Generation*. And look for Roman Polanski here as well, in the role of Mundek.)

NEXT STOP . . . *Kanal, Ashes and Diamonds, Man of Marble*

1954 90m/B *PL* Tadeusz Lomnicki, Urszula Modrzynska, Zbigniew Cybulski, Roman Polanski; *D:* Andrzej Wajda; *W:* Bohdan Czeszko; *M:* Andrzej Markowski. **VHS** *FCT, HMV, ING*

A GENTLE WOMAN
A Gentle Creature
Une Femme Douce

In 1969, France's celebrated director Robert Bresson made *Une Femme Douce* (*A Gentle Woman*), his first color film, which begins with the suicide of the title character (Dominique Sanda). Attempting to make sense of what—at least at first—does not make sense, the woman's husband looks back on their brief time together, remembering moments, gestures, pleasures, and heartaches, all leading to a single, mysterious instant at which her life became unbearable. Using Dostoevsky's *A Gentle Creature* as his source material, Bresson has fashioned a kaleidoscopic, minimalist *Scenes from a Marriage* that never attempts to justify or blame; it possesses, as does all of his work, a spiritual intensity that depends solely on the purity of his images, and demands the absolute attention of the viewer. (This was Dominique Sanda's film debut; she quickly moved on to Bertolucci's *The Conformist* and De Sica's *The Garden of the Finzi-Continis*, eventually appearing in a few Hollywood productions.)

NEXT STOP . . . *Diary of a Country Priest, Pickpocket, L'Argent*

1969 89m/C *FR* Dominique Sanda, Guy Frangin, Jane Lobre; *D:* Robert Bresson; *W:* Robert Bresson; *C:* Ghislan Cloquet; *M:* Jean Wiener. **VHS** *NYF, FCT*

GERMINAL

Emile Zola's 1884 novel about the appalling working conditions of French coal miners was the basis for what was widely touted as the most expensive film in the history of the French film industry. Claude Berri (who's made such genuinely engaging movies as *Jean de Florette*) produced and directed this sprawling, nearly three-hour-long production that tells the story of the members of the Maheu family, who, each in his or her own way, are both in thrall to and repelled by the mines that control every aspect of their lives. Into this inferno comes an outsider, who stirs up the dormant resentment of the indigenous families and introduces the idea of an organized work force. It's hard to know exactly where *Germinal* goes wrong, but go wrong it does, and quickly; despite the widescreen, graphic scenes of horror, passion, and outrage, Berri achieves the nearly impossible—he makes this shameful, true chapter in the history of modern human cruelty not merely unaffecting, but *irritatingly* unaffecting. This is by-the-numbers epic filmmaking, in which the structure alone is supposed to be enough to engage us and the enraged townspeople shouting and shaking their fists in well-choreographed, eye-popping groupings are supposed to make us grasp their plight—yet it all comes off as dry, schematic, and bloated. Despite the energetic and valiant presence of Gérard Depardieu, Jean Carmet, Judith Henry, pop star Renaud, and the always captivating, ever-reliable Miou-Miou, *Germinal* just sits there. It's France's answer to John Wayne's *The Alamo;* lots of money, lots of detail, lots of talent—everything but inspiration.

NEXT STOP . . . *Kameradschaft, Jean de Florette, Manon of the Spring*

1993 (R) 158m/C *FR* Gerard Depardieu, Miou-Miou, Bernard Fresson, Jean Carmet, Laurent Terzieff, Anny Duperey, Renaud, Jacques Dacqmine, Judith Henry; **D:** Claude Berri; **W:** Claude Berri, Arlette Langmann; **C:** Yves Angelo; **M:** Jean-Louis Roques. Cesar Awards '94: Best Cinematography, Best Costume Design. **VHS, LV** *COL*

GERTRUD

In the early 1970s I managed to get on the wrong side of my college film studies instructor by suggesting that the newly released *Claire's Knee* was a wonderful piece of cinematic storytelling. "Rohmer's movies aren't even *cinematic*," the young scholar informed me sternly. "His camera hardly ever *moves*." It's a lucky thing, I suppose, that my chosen example wasn't Carl Theodor Dreyer's *Gertrud,* or I might have been tossed out of the third story window bodily. The "instructor" wasn't—and isn't—alone in his thinking, of course; there are legions of moviegoers, and movie critics, who equate the notion of "cinematic" with constant motion, or at least with an egomaniacal camera calling attention to itself, as in, say, *Arabesque.* But by the end of his career, Denmark's great Carl Dreyer didn't just want to simplify his technique; he wanted to purify it by making all mechanical barriers between the audience and his actors vanish. *Gertrud,* set in 1910, is the story of a woman who is unhappily married, who examines the possibilities of seeking passion elsewhere, and who ultimately chooses to live alone. The actors deliver their lines directly to us, and Dreyer photographs them in long, fluid takes that surround them with space and force us to focus our attention on what they are saying, judging it for ourselves rather than being bludgeoned into accepting what to think or what to feel by the filmmaker's traditional editorializing methods of punctuation-style close-ups or "cue card" reaction shots. It's a demanding, sophisticated, daring technique, which, like any tool, can prove disastrous when placed in the wrong hands. These aren't the wrong hands. Thanks to Dreyer's rigorous, uncompromising, visionary brilliance, *Gertrud* (with all due respect to my former "instructor") is as "cinematic" an experience as any I've ever had.

NEXT STOP . . . *The Passion of Joan of Arc, Day of Wrath, Pickpocket*

1964 116m/B *DK* Nina Pens Rode, Bendt Rothe, Ebbe Rode; **D:** Carl Theodor Dreyer; **W:** Carl Theodor Dreyer; **C:** Arne Abrahamsen, Henning Bendtsen; **M:** Jorgen Jersild. **VHS** *FCT, DVT, HEG*

GET OUT YOUR HANDKERCHIEFS
Preparez Vous Mouchoirs

While he isn't a surrealist in the same league as Luis Buñuel, Bertrand Blier took upon himself in the 1970s the task of shaking much of the movie world—particularly the French movie world—out of its perceived stagnation. His 1974 debut, *Going Places,* was a violent, funny, and highly controversial vision that caused a sensation in France but left

Carol Laure is the bored wife caught between lover and husband (Patrick Dewaere, Gerard Depardieu) in *Get Out Your Handkerchiefs.*

American viewers colder than the movie's thug protagonists. But his 1978 *Get Out Your Handkerchiefs*—the story of a beautiful, listless woman whose husband procures lovers for her to cheer her up—was not only a smash on the American art house circuit, it won an Academy Award as the Best Foreign Language Film of that year. Dan Quayle wasn't yet in a position to deliver a nationally televised tirade against the highly unconventional family structure that *Get Out Your Handkerchiefs* fades out on, but if he went to French movies in 1978 (care to bet?) he would not have been pleased. Gérard Depardieu is at his most goofily endearing as the husband who only wants to be a good provider, and Patrick Dewaere is characteristically superb as the first lover Depardieu selects for his down-in-the-mouth wife. Carol Laure has the toughest job, having to retain our interest while impersonating a zombie-like knitting machine for most of the picture, but she's so intoxicatingly beautiful that Blier

is able to get away with keeping her on screen as much as he does. *Get Out Your Handkerchiefs,* like all of Blier's best work, is designed to provoke, infuriate, and dare us not to laugh. The most delicate of terrorists, Blier turns the safety of our prejudices upside down and then dares to ask: what's wrong with this picture?

NEXT STOP . . . *Going Places, Beau Père, Too Beautiful for You*

1978 (R) 109m/C *FR* Gerard Depardieu, Patrick Dewaere, Carole Laure; **D:** Bertrand Blier; **W:** Bertrand Blier; **C:** Jean Penzer; **M:** Georges Delerue. Academy Awards '78: Best Foreign Film; Cesar Awards '79: Best Score; National Society of Film Critics Awards '78: Best Film. **VHS, LV** *WAR, INT*

GINGER & FRED

Ginger & Fred has been dismissed in some circles as being "an old man's movie." Fine. If all old men can make movies like this, you can check me into a nursing home so that I can be around more of them. Federico Fellini's 1986 valentine of a movie is the story of a pair of aging, retired dancers named Amelia and Pippo (Giulietta Masina and Marcello Mastroianni), who worked during their vaudeville years under the stage names Ginger and Fred. Summoned to Rome for a nostalgic television reunion, Amelia and Pippo are uneasy and awkward reliving their former celebrity (which was originally based on their imitation of celebrities Rogers and Astaire). The unhappy realities of their lives since the old days are revealed (these are the film's most banal, occasionally maudlin scenes) as they prepare for their appearance on what promises to be a vulgar and insensitive broadcast. The show looks to be a washout, but at the last moment, the unexpected happens. Amelia and Pippo, as Ginger and Fred, begin to dance, and everything that was once magical about their momentary stardom comes flooding back; for a few, glorious minutes, the joy of simply performing together returns to them, and they—and Fellini—share it with us. Much of *Ginger & Fred*'s unexpected poignancy comes from Masina's elegant performance, and it suddenly dawns on you that it's been over two decades since she acted in one of her husband's films—reunions within reunions, and we're privileged to be present.

NEXT STOP . . . *Variety Lights, Nights of Cabiria, The Sunshine Boys*

1986 (PG-13) 126m/C *IT* Marcello Mastroianni, Giulietta Masina, Franco Fabrizi, Frederick Von Ledenberg, Martin Blau, Toto Mignone; *D:* Federico Fellini; *W:* Federico Fellini, Tonino Guerra, Tullio Pinelli; *C:* Tonino Delli Colli; *M:* Nicola Piovani. **VHS** *MGM, FCT*

THE GO-BETWEEN

In the early 1900s, Leo (Dominic Guard), a young boy spending the summer with an aristocratic family on their British estate, becomes involved in an affair between a beautiful young member of the household (Julie Christie) and her lower-class, secret lover (Alan Bates). Leo is persuaded to carry notes between the two lovers—there is a price to pay, however, for what at first seems to the boy simply a game. Caught up in the secrecy of his mission, and eager to be a slave to the exquisite, enchanting Christie, Leo pursues his mission with zeal, unaware of how seriously the society around him regards class differences—and unaware of what a dangerous game he is really playing. L.P. Hartley's novel was adapted by Harold Pinter (who can't seem to resist tossing in his patented technique of tinkering with chronology, recently parodied on *Seinfeld*) and directed with restraint and admirable clarity by Joseph Losey. Bates and Christie are remarkable (it could be your only chance to hear Bates sing Gilbert and Sullivan), as is young Dominic Guard. But the show belongs to Margaret Leighton as Christie's quietly terrifying mother, waging war to protect the privileges of her class at all costs. The film is beautifully photographed by Gerry Fisher, and Michel Legrand's score is, unfortunately, overbearing.

NEXT STOP . . . *Betrayal, Butley, Howards End*

1971 (PG) 116m/C *GB* Julie Christie, Alan Bates, Dominic Guard, Margaret Leighton, Michael Redgrave, Michael Gough, Edward Fox; *D:* Joseph Losey; *W:* Harold Pinter; *C:* Gerry Fisher; *M:* Michel Legrand. British Academy Awards '71: Best Screenplay, Best Supporting Actor (Fox), Best Supporting Actress (Leighton); Cannes Film Festival '71: Best Film; Nominations: Academy Awards '71: Best Supporting Actress (Leighton). **VHS** *COL*

THE GOALIE'S ANXIETY AT THE PENALTY KICK
Die Angst Tormannes beim Elfmeter

In his program notes for the Telluride Film Festival screening of *Henry: Portrait of a Serial Killer*, admirer Errol Morris wrote: "*Henry* provides the perfect answer to the Hollywood executive's favorite question: 'what makes these characters sympathetic?' The answer in *Henry*: absolutely nothing!" Wim Wenders's 1971 *The Goalie's Anxiety at the Penalty Kick* will never be mistaken for *Henry*, but what it shares with that film—in addition to seemingly random murder—is a steadfast refusal to explain the protagonist's actions in conventional terms. While playing a match in Vienna, Joseph Bloch (Arthur Brauss) suddenly decides to simply walk out of the soccer game in which he's tending goal. The journey he begins at that point includes a murder and the search for an old girlfriend, both undertaken with the same matter-of-fact, uninsistent quality that makes Bloch—and the film—quietly unnerving. What prevents the movie from alienating us into the same numb listlessness as its protagonist is that very refusal to explain what makes Bloch "tick." It's a new and disturbing kind of suspense film, in which what we fear most—our inability to make an irrational universe fit into our Day Runners—comes to pass. Screenplay by Wenders and Peter Handke, from Handke's novel.

NEXT STOP . . . *Kings of the Road, In the White City, Jeanne Dielman*

1971 101m/C *GE* Arthur Brauss, Erika Pluhar, Kai Fischer; **D:** Wim Wenders; **W:** Peter Handke, Wim Wenders; **C:** Robby Muller; **M:** Jurgen Knieper. **VHS** *FCT, GLV*

GODZILLA, KING OF THE MONSTERS
Gojira

About 20 years ago, New York's Japan House cleared the calendar of its normally high-toned film series—works of directors like Ozu, Mizoguchi, and Naruse were the typical fare—for a special event: a retrospective of Toho Studios' most popular monster films, titled "Thank You, Godzilla." There was a lot to be thankful for, as by some measures the infusion of cash that Godzilla, Mothra, and Rodan pumped into the financially troubled Japanese film industry in the 1950s may have saved it from an extinction similar to that which Tokyo suffered in so many of those films. Godzilla made a big impression in more ways than monetary, as evidenced by his enduring international popularity and his recent big-budget Hollywood resurrection. In director Inoshiro Honda's *Godzilla, King of the Monsters,* the old boy (whose Japanese name, Gojira, is a combination of gorilla and kujira, or whale) was not the hero and protector of children (or proud daddy of little Minya) that he became in later years. Godzilla was the terrible manifestation of Japan's nuclear legacy, a submerged but undead beast that was the living, fire-breathing proof that the nuclear holocaust suffered by the Japanese was neither gone nor forgotten, and was ready to wreak further destruction anytime atomic weapons were again unleashed. King of the Monsters, indeed. The original film, in stark black and white, includes something few of the others in the series would ever show again—human carnage, including bandaged, bleeding children who are suffering as a result of what these terrible weapons have unleashed. Though the audience isn't beaten over the head with this symbolism, *Godzilla's* release during the height of the Cold War may have been a more effective, subliminal anti-nuke message than many of us assume. If so, then we *all* owe you a note of thanks, Godzilla. With Takashi Shimura, Momoko Kochi, and Raymond Burr as correspondent Steve Martin. (Burr's sequences for the American version were directed by Terry Morse.)

NEXT STOP . . . *Rodan, Mothra, Black Rain* (1989, Imamura)

1956 80m/B *JP* Momoko Kochi, Raymond Burr, Takashi Shimura; **D:** Inoshiro Honda, Terry Morse; **W:** Takeo Murata; **C:** Masao Tamai; **M:** Akira Ifukube. **VHS, LV** *PAR, VES*

GOING PLACES
Les Valseuses
Making It

Bertrand Blier's portrait of a pair of petty, sadistic thugs remains a source of controversy a quarter-century after its release. Blier adapted his own novel for the screen, and gave the leads to virtual unknowns Gérard Depardieu and Patrick Dewaere—one wonders what might have happened to Blier's career without that inspired bit of casting. *Going Places* was something of a hipness/litmus test when it was released; if you found these bullying rapists and thieves sympathetic and funny, you were in the vanguard. Not to do so made you something of a cinematic reactionary, or worse yet, someone who "didn't get it." It's a male fantasy, right? So it's OK. In fact, it's more than OK. It's art! I maintain, however, that it *is* possible to both "get it" and "not like it." Just because *Going Places* is calculated to provoke bourgeois outrage doesn't mean that you're necessarily an imperialist running dog if you don't think Jeanne Moreau shooting herself in the vagina is a riot. (Or as Orson Welles's Hank Quinlan put it in *Touch of Evil:* "Just because he talks a little guilty don't make him innocent.") Anyway, the cast is wonderful; in addition to Depardieu, Dewaere, and Moreau, it includes Miou-Miou, Isabelle Huppert, and, as the woman who provides the milk of human kindness, Brigitte Fossey, who played the five-year-old Paulette in *Forbidden Games.* Blier went on to better films, as did everybody else.

NEXT STOP . . . *Get Out Your Handkerchiefs, Mon Homme, A Clockwork Orange*

1974 (R) 122m/C *FR* Gerard Depardieu, Patrick Dewaere, Miou-Miou, Isabelle Huppert, Jeanne Moreau, Brigitte Fossey; *D:* Bertrand Blier; *W:* Bertrand Blier; *C:* Bruno Nuytten; *M:* Stephane Grappelli. **VHS, LV, Letterbox** *COL, INT*

THE GOLDEN COACH
Le Carrosse d'Or

Jean Renoir was fascinated by the way that our lives mirror, and are mirrored by, the theatrical experience. The stories of love and passion that recur again and again through the ages, in many guises, articulated in different ways, are what Renoir sees as a kind of continuing, generation-to-generation grand performance. It's there in the many little re-creations of theatre that he includes in *Grand Illusion, Rules of the Game,* and *The Little Theatre of Jean Renoir,* as well as in his two great films *about* theatre, *French Can-Can* and *The Golden Coach.* The first in a trilogy of colorful period films in which the theatre plays a central role (the others being *French Can-Can* and *Eléna et les Hommes*), *The Golden Coach* is

blessed by a magnificent, incomparable force of nature named Anna Magnani. The plot—a *very* distant cousin to *Fitzcarraldo*—tells of a troupe of Italian *commedia dell'arte* players who are bringing their art to 18th-century Peru. Pursued by at least three suitors, Magnani struggles to remain true to her heart, and, most importantly, true to her art. At a certain point—and we can't be absolutely sure where that is—her theatrical life and her "real" romantic life become one. The heartbreakingly funny and touching performance she gives *onstage* is also—quite literally—the performance of her life. Magnani is astounding and unforgettable, and Renoir is a match for her. *The Golden Coach* is a priceless moment in movie history in which theatre, love, and cinema converge, becoming—ever so briefly—inseparable.

NEXT STOP . . . *French Can-Can, Eléna et les Hommes, Boudu Saved from Drowning*

1952 101m/C *FR* Anna Magnani, Odoardo Spadaro, Nada Fiorelli, Dante Rino, Duncan Lamont; *D:* Jean Renoir; *W:* Ginette Doynel, Jack Kirkland, Giulio Macchi, Jean Renoir; *C:* Claude Renoir, Ronald Hill; *M:* Antonio Vivaldi. **VHS, LV** *FCT, CRC, INT*

THE GOLEM
Der Golem, wie er in die Welt kam

The legend of the Golem—a humanoid clay figure brought to life by Rabbi Loew in 16th-century Prague in order to defend the Jews against pogroms—has been the basis of a number of films from 1914 through the 1950s. The best of them, this 1920 silent German film directed by Paul Wegener, is a starkly stylized film filled with ominous shadows and disturbing, Gothic settings; much of the visual scheme is directly influenced by the theatrical work of Max Reinhardt. *The Golem* turns into a strange and nightmarish love story when the creature falls in love with the rabbi's daughter (Lyda Salmonova); but he later meets his end by the hand of an unwitting child. The figure of the Golem itself is an imposing visual design featuring huge eyes and a mammoth, bulky body, which in some scenes is made of stone and in others is played by Wegener. A clear precursor to James Whale's 1931 *Frankenstein, The Golem* was stunningly photographed by the legendary Karl Freund, who, in addition to shooting Fritz Lang's *Metropolis* in 1926, would, in his later Hollywood years, become director of photography for *I Love Lucy*.

NEXT STOP . . . *The Cabinet of Dr. Caligari, Nosferatu* (1922), *Frankenstein*

1920 80m/B *GE* Paul Wegener, Albert Steinruck, Ernst Deutsch, Lyda Salmonava, Otto Gebuehr, Max Kronert, Loni Nest, Greta Schroder, Hans Sturm; *D:* Carl Boese, Paul Wegener; *W:* Henrik Galeen, Paul Wegener; *C:* Karl Freund; *M:* Hans Landberger. **VHS** *VYY, SNC, MRV*

THE GOOD, THE BAD, AND THE UGLY

With the final chapter in Sergio Leone's epic trilogy, which began with *A Fistful of Dollars* and continued with *For a Few Dollars More*, highbrow critics began to notice that there was something going on here, and they'd better reckon with it. Some took the easy way out, switching their writing on these films from "reviewing" to "criticism" by fishing out that holy grail, symbolism. "The Man with No Name" (Clint Eastwood) was a Christ figure, the films are about the individual's rebellion against imperialism, yadda yadda yadda. I won't quarrel with that (because it's true), but what some savvy folks also happened to notice is that Sergio Leone had made a bold, visionary Western epic that seemed to cross all national—and interplanetary—boundary lines. This was a West that existed in our collective memories—through photographs, stories, legends, but above all, through movies. Leone—like Renoir before him—understood the theatrical, near-operatic quality of some of the oldest, most often repeated stories. Further, he had the daring to take that most universally beloved and widely understood of all theatrical conventions—the American Western—and portray it with the panache and romantic stylization of Giuseppe Verdi. And if that weren't brilliant enough, he topped himself by putting Clint Eastwood at the center of it. *The Good, the Bad, and the Ugly* is hilarious, moving, and fantastically complex, but on the surface it's just a simple tale, set in the Civil War years, of three guys looking for a buried treasure. The real treasure is the pleasure of a narrative texture this thick and luxurious, acted by faces that seem to have been carved by tumbleweeds—Eastwood, Lee Van Cleef, and Eli Wallach. Tonino Delli Colli photographed it spectacularly on locations in the south of Spain, and the great Ennio Morricone provided the score that is its pulsing lifeblood.

NEXT STOP . . . *Stagecoach, The Wild Bunch, Once Upon a Time in the West*

1967 161m/C *IT* Clint Eastwood, Eli Wallach, Lee Van Cleef, Chelo Alonso, Luigi Pistilli; *D:* Sergio Leone; *W:* Sergio Leone; *C:* Tonino Delli Colli; *M:* Ennio Morricone. **VHS, LV, Letterbox** *FOX, MGM, FCT*

THE GOSPEL ACCORDING TO ST. MATTHEW
Il Vangelo Secondo Matteo
L'Evangile Selon Saint-Matthieu

This extraordinary picture is one of the most eloquent ever made about a religious figure. The antithesis of every bloated Hollywood religious epic, *The Gospel According to St. Matthew* was filmed in a modest black-and-white format without the usual vulgar trickery or, in fact, special effects of any kind. Most of the dialogue is lifted directly from Gospel, and the episodes that are presented are filmed without excessive flourish or ornamentation. This is not to say that the director, Pier Paolo Pasolini, has made a film without personality. Quite the contrary. Pasolini sees the story as one of a fighter against injustice of all kinds, and he emphasizes the meanings of scenes not through theatrical grandiosity (the cast is comprised of all non-professional actors) but through the delicacy of his staging, and, especially, through his use of music. Using everything from Prokofiev's score for Eisenstein's *Alexander Nevsky,* to Mozart and Bach, and, most effectively, to Odetta's stirring rendition of "Sometimes I Feel Like a Motherless Child," Pasolini brings a contemporary relevance and immediacy to the drama while never disturbing the purity of the images. This is a model of how such material can be brought to the screen without trashing it. Photographed by Tonino Delli Colli. Oscar nominations for Best Art Direction, Costume Design, and Adapted Score.

NEXT STOP... *Open City, Bandits of Orgosolo, The Last Temptation of Christ*

1964 142m/B *IT* Enrique Irazoqui, Susanna Pasolini, Margherita Caruso, Marcello Morante, Mario Socrate; *D:* Pier Paolo Pasolini; *W:* Pier Paolo Pasolini; *C:* Tonino Delli Colli; *M:* Luis Bacalov. Nominations: Academy Awards '66: Best Adapted Score, Best Art Direction/Set Decoration (B & W), Best Costume Design (B & W). **VHS, LV, 8mm, Letterbox** *NOS, MRV, WBF*

GRAND ILLUSION
La Grande Illusion

A portrait of war, friendship, gallantry, and respect in a world that has now—in every sense—vanished. Jean Renoir's great *Grand Illusion* is the story of all of this, as well as a suspenseful and gripping tale of French soldiers determined to escape their German captors during World War I. Pierre Fresnay and Erich von Stroheim are, respectively, the French and German officers of "the old school," who are adversaries on the field of battle but who are at heart both citizens of the same, vanishing civilization—one where the formal, chivalrous rules of combat are paramount, and where honor is more highly prized than victory. Jean Gabin and Marcel Dalio co-star as prisoners whose eyes are focused on escaping, but the show belongs to Fresnay as the refined and brave Captain de Boeldieu, and, most indelibly, von Stroheim, in whose hands the noble and elegant German air ace von Rauffenstein becomes one of the unlikeliest romantic figures in movie history. *Grand Illusion* deserves all the praise it's ever received; it's one of the great film experiences. (That greatness wasn't achieved easily; early in the shoot, Renoir, in tears, told the egomaniacal von Stroheim that he would shut down the film if von Stroheim didn't stop trying to direct. The tears worked, and von Stroheim was docile for the remainder of the production.) *Grand Illusion*'s humanitarian vision didn't sit well with

the Nazis; Goebbels tried to destroy every European print in existence, calling it "cinematic enemy number one." He failed. It seems that after the war, one was found—in Germany. Von Rauffenstein would have loved it.

NEXT STOP... *Kameradschaft, Rules of the Game, Paths of Glory*

1937 111m/B *FR* Jean Gabin, Erich von Stroheim, Pierre Fresnay, Marcel Dalio, Julien Carette, Gaston Modot, Jean Daste, Dita Parlo; *D:* Jean Renoir; *W:* Charles Spaak, Jean Renoir; *C:* Christian Matras; *M:* Joseph Kosma. New York Film Critics Awards '38: Best Foreign Film; Nominations: Academy Awards '38: Best Picture. **VHS, LV, DVD** *VYY, MRV, FOX*

THE GREEN ROOM
La Chambre Verte

For hard-core fans of the films of the late François Truffaut, *The Green Room* can be an extraordinarily moving and powerful experience. But even some Truffaut fanatics may have their patience tested by this adaptation of Henry James's *The Altar of the Dead,* the story of a man whose obsession with death became his life. Beginning with *Two English Girls* in 1972, many of Truffaut's films embraced a new intensity and darkness that took him into unexplored emotional territory. He went very far in this regard in his 1975 masterpiece *The Story of Adele H.,* but goes all the way with it—uncompromisingly—in *The Green Room.* In the film, Truffaut himself takes the role of a French journalist who, following the First World War, writes obituaries for a newspaper. But writing about the dead isn't enough for him, and the physical altar that he builds as a monument to the dead—his late wife as well as others—becomes all that he lives for. The woman who falls in love with him (Nathalie Baye) is unable to get through to him, precisely because she is so very much alive. (It's a bit reminiscent of one of Truffaut's favorite movies, *Vertigo,* in that the Jimmy Stewart character there was obsessed with the image of a "dead" woman, later rejecting the actual woman when he found she was

François Truffaut stars with Nathalie Baye in a film about obsession in *The Green Room.*

alive.) Fact and fiction are blended here, in that the altar itself contains photos of people who were important to Truffaut the director, rather than Truffaut the character; one of them, composer Maurice Jaubert, was "resurrected" by Truffaut when he used the late composer's compositions in *The Story of Adele H.*, as well as in *The Green Room.* These elements all run together, and now, with Truffaut's own death at 53, the film becomes both a touchstone and the most difficult to watch of his films. (It may be doubly difficult to watch because the picture is so dark physically—images that were barely visible on screen may not be visible at all on video.)

NEXT STOP . . . *The Story of Adele H., Forbidden Games, Vertigo*

1978 (PG) 95m/C *FR* Antoine Vitez, Jane Lobre, Marcel Berbert, Francois Truffaut, Nathalie Baye, Jean Daste; **D:** Francois Truffaut; **W:** Jean Gruault; **C:** Nestor Almendros; **M:** Maurice Jaubert. **VHS** *MGM*

THE GREEN SLIME

Gamma Sango Uchu Daisakusen
Battle Beyond the Stars
Death and the Green Slime

Whatever happened to those innocent days when you could release a picture like *The Green Slime* that was made for ten bucks and looked it, featured a bunch of one-eyed octopi with rubber tentacles that were being waved by stagehands, and boasted an "international cast" of low-rent performers like Robert (*Wagon Train*) Horton and Luciana (*99 Women*) Paluzzi? I suppose we should be glad they're gone, but I'm stubbornly resisting the New World Order as it applies to this kind of trash. For the record, *The Green Slime* is a Japanese/American co-production about a space station overrun by ... green slime. The slime turns into the rubber octopi, and therein lies a tale. An advantage of such films was that you could go on opening night and not worry about advance ticket purchase (as with, say, the new, unimproved *Godzilla*). And you got more bang for your buck—MGM released *The Green Slime* on a double bill with Roman Polanski's *The Fearless Vampire Killers,* thus bridging the class gap between the art house and what was then the meat-and-potatoes of the 42nd St. grind house. It was a more democratic world. The American version of *The Green Slime* features a peppy theme song sung by Richard Delvy ("You'll believe it when you're DEAD," instructively warn the lyrics), and was directed by Kinji Fukasaku, who a decade later would make the energetic *Star Wars* ripoff *Message from Space,* in which Vic Morrow finds an extraterrestrial walnut in his scotch. Go ahead—tell me movies are better now. I dare you.

NEXT STOP . . . *It! The Terror from Beyond Space, Alien, Invasion of the Neptune Men*

1968 (G) 90m/C *JP* Robert Horton, Richard Jaeckel, Luciana Paluzzi, Bud Widom, Ted Gunther, Robert Dunham; *D:* Kinji Fukasaku; *W:* Ivan Reiner, Charles Sinclair, Bill Finger; *C:* Yoshikazu Yamasawa; *M:* Charles Fox, Toshiaki Tsushima. **VHS** *MGM*

GUELWAAR

The most recent masterwork from Senegal's great Ousmane Sembène is a stinging, potent comedy focusing on the unexplained circumstances surrounding the death of a local political dealmaker, a man who was also an unapologetic philanderer, the self-proclaimed moral anchor of the community, and was so widely admired that he was referred to respectfully as "Guelwaar," or "Noble One." The mysterious goings-on don't end with Guelwaar's death; his body vanishes as well, but that little detail is soon explained. It seems that Guelwaar, a Christian, has been buried in a Muslim cemetery by mistake. Almost instantaneously a bureaucratic nightmare kicks into high gear, resulting in an anxious and near-surrealistic standoff at the unintended grave site. Still, that's just the beginning of an extraordinarily witty fable about corruption and colonialist politics,

related by master storyteller Sembène with his characteristic blend of comedy, political allegory, social satire, insight, and deeply compassionate humanity.

NEXT STOP . . . *Emitai, Xala, Ceddo*

1994 115m/C *D:* Ousmane Sembene; *M:* Baaba Maal. **VHS** *NYR*

GUMSHOE

A nice surprise. Albert Finney is Eddie Ginley, a working-class dreamer whose drab, Liverpool existence is relieved only by the daydreams in which he cracks murder cases with the style and aplomb of Bogart's Philip Marlowe. Soon, Eddie gets the chance to live out his fantasies when he's plunged headlong into a real—and dangerous—murder case. Avoiding all of the "cutes" that spread out like a minefield in this sort of thing, director Stephen Frears (*My Beautiful Laundrette, The Grifters*) has made a captivating and beguilingly understated debut film, held in place by the amazing Finney. Billie Whitelaw, Janice Rule, and Frank Finlay co-star in this sweet, rarely seen winner. Cinematographer Chris Menges (*Local Hero*) provides the just-right, warmly romantic images; even Andrew Lloyd Webber's bombastic score can't trip up *Gumshoe.*

NEXT STOP . . . *The Hit, Don Quixote* (1957), *Shoot the Moon*

1972 (G) 85m/C *GB* Albert Finney, Billie Whitelaw, Frank Finlay, Janice Rule, Carolyn Seymour; *D:* Stephen Frears; *C:* Chris Menges; *M:* Andrew Lloyd Webber. **VHS** *NO*

THE HAIRDRESSER'S HUSBAND
Le Mari de la Coiffeuse

The director of the transfixing *Monsieur Hire* is back with another tale of obsession and fetishism, but this time far less successfully. *The Hairdresser's Husband* is about a man (the sweetly droopy-faced Jean Rochefort) who—as a boy—developed an erotic association with the act of having his hair cut. We see these childhood scenes in flashback, as

H

"Life is color! Love is color!"

—Teacher (Abbas Sayahi) in *Gabbah.*

STEPHEN FREARS

British Filmmaker Invades Hollywood

Filmmaker Stephen Frears is part of Hollywood's British Invasion. The stiff-upper-Brit has directed mostly for television in Great Britain for two decades until he established a beach-head in the United States in 1986 with the release of the quirky comedy *My Beautiful Laundrette* which deals with immigrants dazed and confused by Merry-Old-England. He clinched his international rep with his first foray into big-budget filmmaking *Dangerous Liaisons*(1988), that baroque boudoir schemer that copped an Oscar nod for best picture of the year. He followed up with the dog-eat-dog world of *The Grifters* (for which he was nominated for a Best Director Oscar) which made him a frequent flyer to the Hollywood sound stages of L.A. *The Snapper*, on the other hand, was shot on the Emerald Isle. His most recent films include *Mary Reilly* (1996), *The Van* (1996), and *Hi-Lo Country*.

Stephen Arthur Frears was born on June 20, 1941 in Leicester to a physician and social worker. He recieved a law degree in 1963 at Cambridge University but left his heart at the student theatre stage door. Among his group were David Frost, Monty Python madcaps like John Cleese, and people who now run the BBC. Frears says he "eventually became a very well-trained person and therefore of value."

He shares his Victorian digs with painter Ann Rothenstein and their son in London's Notting Hill section. His favorite pastimes are reading and walking in the fells.

Antoine remembers his first, pubescent sexual arousal at the hands of a stimulating and gently encouraging female barber. As an adult, it just takes one shampoo for him to fall head and shoulders for Mathilde (the dreamily beautiful Anna Galiena), whose subsequent marriage to Antoine leads to the movie's bittersweet but painfully contrived outcome. Maybe it's just that some fetishes are more suited to the movies than others, but it seems unlikely that there'll be a run on Flow-Bees anytime soon. The lilting score is by Michael Nyman (*The Piano*).

NEXT STOP . . . *Monsieur Hire, Vertigo, Shampoo*

1992 (R) 84m/C *FR* Jean Rochefort, Anna Galiena, Roland Bertin, Maurice Chevit, Philippe Clevenot, Jacques Mathou, Claude Aufaure; **D:** Patrice Leconte; **W:** Claude Klotz, Patrice Leconte; **C:** Eduardo Serra; **M:** Michael Nyman. **VHS, LV, Closed Caption** *PAR, BTV*

HALF OF HEAVEN
La Mitad del Cielo

Rosa (Angela Molina) is a young peasant woman who has inherited strange but not-always-wonderful telepathic powers from her grandmother (Margarita Lozano). Grandma uses her occult abilities to warn Rosa away from unsuitable suitors, and if she doesn't listen, the men meet singularly unpleasant fates. *Half of Heaven* is a pleasant, handsomely photographed fable about heredity, desire, and the twin family curses of poverty and success. The director, Manuel Gutiérrez Aragon, doesn't quite have the flair for surrealism that the material requires, but the spirited performances, particularly from Molina (*That Obscure Object of Desire*) help considerably.

NEXT STOP . . . *The Garden of Delights, Tristana, Like Water for Chocolate*

1986 95m/C *SP* Angela Molina, Margarita Lozano; *D:* Manuel Gutierrez Aragon. VHS *PBS, FCT, AUD*

HAMLET

You wonder sometimes why anyone ever bothers to do movie versions of Shakespeare when there are so many purists, scholars, and fans waiting in the wings to tell the filmmaker just exactly why he's gotten it all wrong. (Kenneth Branagh tried to head critics off by making a four-hour *Hamlet* that included every last line, but some of us found things to complain about anyway, like the fact that it ran four hours, or Jack Lemmon.) When Laurence Olivier set out to film his version of *Hamlet* in 1948, he had already fallen in love with the possibilities of Shakespeare on film via his stunning 1945 *Henry V.* His two-and-a-half hour *Hamlet* is streamlined, reworked, and chock full of compromises, altered lines and missing characters. And it's great. Olivier seemed less interested in a definitive, time-capsule *Hamlet* than one that would be seen, felt, and considered, perhaps by a whole new audience that was never tempted to even be exposed before. We're fortunate that so many extraordinary Olivier performances have been captured on film; more fortunate still that some of the finest of them have been in films he directed: *Hamlet, Henry V, Richard III.* With Jean Simmons, Eileen Herlie, Basil Sydney, Norman Wooland, Felix Aylmer, Stanley Holloway, Anthony Quayle, and John Gielgud, offscreen, as the voice of the ghost. Oscars for Best Picture, Actor, Art Direction, and Costume Design, nominations for Director, Supporting Actress (Simmons), and Score (Sir William Walton).

NEXT STOP . . . *Henry V, Chimes at Midnight, Othello* (1965)

1948 153m/B *GB* Laurence Olivier, Basil Sydney, Felix Aylmer, Jean Simmons, Stanley Holloway, Peter Cushing, Christopher Lee, Eileen Herlie, John Laurie, Esmond Knight, Anthony Quayle; *D:* Laurence Olivier; *W:* Alan Dent; *C:* Desmond Dickinson; *M:* William Walton; *V:* John Gielgud. Academy Awards '48: Best Actor (Olivier), Best Art Direction/Set Decoration (B & W), Best Costume Design (B & W), Best Picture; British Academy Awards '48: Best Film; Golden Globe Awards '49: Best Actor—Drama (Olivier); New York Film Critics Awards '48: Best Actor (Olivier); Nominations: Academy Awards '48: Best Director (Olivier), Best Supporting Actress (Simmons), Best Original Dramatic/Comedy Score. VHS *PAR, BTV, HMV*

HANUSSEN

After his dazzling breakthrough performance in István Szabó's Faustian parable *Mephisto,* Klaus Maria Brandauer looked like the next big thing. He was to work in two other films of Szabó's over the subsequent six years—*Colonel Redl* and *Hanussen*—which completed Szabó's historical trilogy on the themes of collaboration and denial. Based on a factual case, *Hanussen* tells the story of Klaus Schneider, an Austrian soldier who suffered a head wound in World War I, following which he cashed in on his purported newfound ability to foresee future events. Schneider decides to resurrect a mind-reading act he staged before the war (using the stage name Hanussen), but this time, he claims, the act is for real. As in *Mephisto,* Brandauer's character is—despite his exploitation of those around him—strangely compelling. His manipulation of those around him can be seen as a foreshadowing of the Nazi regime waiting in the wings, and of course there's the uncomfortable question of how we would behave in similar circumstances. Brandauer played a number of character roles since working in the Szabó films—even stopping to play a fiend in the James Bond picture *Never Say Never Again*—but he's had no roles as commanding as *Hanussen* since completing it a decade ago.

NEXT STOP . . . *Mephisto, Colonel Redl, Nightmare Alley*

1988 (R) 110m/C *GE HU* Klaus Maria Brandauer, Erland Josephson, Walter Schmidinger; *D:* Istvan Szabo; *W:* Peter Dobai, Istvan Szabo; *C:* Lajos Koltai; *M:* Gyorgy Vukan. Nominations: Academy Awards '88: Best Foreign-Language Film. VHS, LV *COL*

HAPPY TOGETHER
Cheun Gwong Tsa Sit

From Hong Kong cult fave Wong Kar-Wai comes a neon-lit love story about a pair of

pher Doyle; **M:** Danny Chung. Cannes Film Festival '97: Best Director (Kar-Wai); Nominations: Independent Spirit Awards '98: Best Foreign Film. **VHS** *KIV*

HARAKIRI
Seppuku

In 17th-century Japan, following the downfall of a number of powerful clans, the samurai who once held allegiance to these families were now unemployed and without masters. These masterless samurai, or *ronin*, had no means by which to support themselves but were nevertheless expected to live by the same code of honor they were bound by previously. Masaki Kobayashi's wrenching, thoroughly gripping *Harakiri* is the story of one aspect of the hypocrisy of such codes, which—as many periods throughout history have demonstrated— tend to be applied disproportionately to the detriment of the weak and the powerless. Though *Harakiri* is presented in the guise of the traditional—albeit exceptionally elegant—sword picture, it is a piece of social criticism as bitter and stinging as they come. Tatsuya Nakadai (*Yojimbo, Fires on the Plain*) is galvanizing as the ronin who explains his tragic family saga—in a series flashbacks— to the increasingly anxious, sadistic old warlords who are his intended victims. (The term *harakiri,* or "stomach-cut," is actually a vulgarized term for the traditional Japanese suicide ritual of *seppuku*. You'll know all about it by the end of this film.) The score is by the brilliant Toru Takemitsu; the gleaming, widescreen black-and-white cinematography by Yoshio Miyajima is best seen in a letterboxed format.

NEXT STOP . . . *Rebellion (a.k.a. Samurai Rebellion), Yojimbo, The Human Condition*

1962 135m/B Hisashi Igawa, Yoshio Inaba, Akira Ishihama, Shima Iwashita, Rentaro Mikuni, Masao Mishima, Tatsuya Nakadai, Tetsuro Tamba, Shichisaburo Amatsu, Yoshio Aoki, Jo Azumi, Akiji Kobayashi, Ichiro Nakaya, Kei Sato, Ryo Takeuchi; **D:** Masaki Kobayashi; **W:** Shinobu Hashimoto, Yasuhiko Takiguchi; **C:** Yoshio Miyajima; **M:** Toru Takemitsu. *NYR*

Chow Yun-Fat stars as a cop seeking revenge in John Woo's *Hard-Boiled.*

gay lovers (Leslie Cheung and Tony Leung) who travel from Hong Kong to Buenos Aires in hopes of resurrecting their stormy relationship. *Happy Together* is a sometimes lyrical/sometimes disjointed series of moments from a love affair, filtered through the stylized, constantly moving images of Christopher Doyle's dazzling camerawork. It's more of a beautiful object than it is an engaging film, however, and though individual scenes—a mountain of cigarettes collected by one man to eliminate the other's excuse for going out—jump out at you as little nuggets of ingenuity, the total effect is of a fleeting, incomplete creation that never fully anchors itself in our imaginations. Best Director Award, 1997 Cannes Film Festival.

NEXT STOP . . . *Chungking Express, Fallen Angels, Days of Being Wild*

1996 93m/C *HK* Leslie Cheung, Tony Leung, Chang Chen; **D:** Wong Kar-Wai; **W:** Wong Kar-Wai; **C:** Christo-

HARD-BOILED
Lashou Shentan

You can say that again. Hong Kong action ace John Woo has designed a complex conspiracy of illegal arms traffic and international corruption just so that a pair of renegade cops (Tony Leung and sullen, legendary action star Chow Yun-Fat) can team to wipe them off the map—in style. The action sequences in Woo's films are not gratuitous—they're the reason that his movies exist. There's a joy in the balletic choreography and two-gun orgasmic score-settling that Woo stages in his films, and he's brilliant at straddling the line between violent excess and the beloved conventions of the genre. The big, final shoot-out in *Hard-Boiled* revels in the unthinkable—the whole sequence is staged in a hospital ward packed with crying newborns, all endangered by the thousand of flying bullets. Since everything we know about Chow Yun-Fat's character (and Woo's) tells us that he'll never let a single baby come to harm, we can relax and enjoy the spectacle for its sheer exhilarating audacity. If you're going to see a movie—*any* movie—in which the ostensible subject is male bonding, then it might as well be one that's as excitingly, hilariously enjoyable as *Hard-Boiled*.

NEXT STOP . . . *A Better Tomorrow, The Killer, Face/Off*

1992 126m/C *HK* Chow Yun-Fat, Tony Leung, Philip Chan, Anthony Wong, Teresa Mo; *D:* John Woo; *W:* John Woo, Barry Wong; *C:* Wing-Heng Wang; *M:* Michael Gibbs. **VHS** *ORI, FCT*

HARVEST
Regain
La Femme du Boulanger

Itinerant scissors-grinder Gedemus (Fernandel), and his lover Arsule (Orane Demazis) come upon a rural French town that seems almost deserted—except for a single, lonely hunter named Panturle (Gabriel Gabrio). It is Panturle's belief that as long as a single person remains in this place, it is a town. Otherwise, the town—his home—will cease to exist. When Arsule goes to live with the hunter—thanks to the "generosity" of Gedemus—the cycle of life begins anew. Soon the land will be enriched with a new, self-replenishing harvest of life in every one of its many forms. Marcel Pagnol's *Harvest* (the French title is *La Femme du Boulanger*), adapted from the novel by Jean Giono, is a unique masterpiece of the French cinema; a radical yet simple bit of storytelling/mythmaking that startles audiences of every generation with its elegant, visionary power. *Harvest* is neither religious epic nor humanist manifesto; it is, rather, a primal and enormously moving tale of the eternal, cyclical regeneration of life and spirit that goes by many names, but never ceases. Magnificent.

NEXT STOP . . . *The Fanny Trilogy, The Baker's Wife, Jean de Florette and Manon of the Spring*

1937 128m/B *FR* Fernandel, Gabriel Gabrio, Orane Demazis, Edouard Delmont, Henri Poupon; *D:* Marcel Pagnol; *W:* Marcel Pagnol; *C:* Willy; *M:* Arthur Honegger. New York Film Critics Awards '39: Best Foreign Film. **VHS** *INT, MRV, FCT*

HATE
La Haine
Hatred

Matthieu Kassovitz (*Café au Lait*) snared the Best Director prize at the 1995 Cannes Film Festival for his grim, bleak portrait of disaffected, gun-toting Parisian youth. You can't deny his talent, but you can remain unaffected by it. *Hate* (*La Haine*) caused a sensation in France, where the urgency of the film's message was not lost on the audience; the problems of teenage crime there are an epidemic that isn't always discussed in polite company, and Kassovitz's film simply kicked the door in. *Hate,* while an obviously accomplished piece of filmmaking, has a journalistic relevance that doesn't travel well. There's no way for this film to be seen here in the same, revelatory way it was at home; consequently, it feels busy but routine—like a pumped-up, obscenity-laden, skillfully photographed *Dead End,* complete with its own Huntz Hall (Vincent Cassel as Vinz). With Hubert Kounde and Saïd Taghmaoui.

NEXT STOP . . . *Zero for Conduct, A Clockwork Orange, Kids*

plot, but the movie's genuine power comes from its stylized, operatic imagery, which Herzog has said was designed to convey an atmosphere of "hallucination and collective madness." To ensure this effect, as well as to provide a high-toned gimmick for getting the film noticed on the festival circuit, Herzog claimed that the entire cast of the film was hypnotized during production, so that any critic who described *Heart of Glass* as "hypnotic" wouldn't just be whistling Dixie. To reinforce his goal of depicting collective madness, Herzog tried—at the Telluride Film Festival screening I attended—to hypnotize the entire audience prior to the screening. Though he was restrained from doing so by Festival officials, I suppose there's nothing to stop you from hypnotizing yourself prior to watching it on tape. But since *Heart of Glass* actually is mesmerizing enough all by itself, my advice remains the same: *kids, don't try this at home.*

NEXT STOP . . . *Fata Morgana, Aguirre, the Wrath of God, Vernon, Florida*

1974 93m/C *GE* Josef Bierbichler, Stefan Guttler, Clemens Scheitz, Volker Prechtel, Sonia Skiba; *D:* Werner Herzog; *W:* Werner Herzog, Herbert Achternbusch; *C:* Jorge Schmidt-Reitwein; *M:* Popul Vuh. **VHS** *NYF, FCT*

Melanie Lynsky and Kate Winslet occupy their own secret world in *Heavenly Creatures.*

1995 95m/B *FR* Vincent Cassel, Hubert Kounde, Said Taghmaoui, Francois Levantal; *D:* Mathieu Kassovitz; *W:* Mathieu Kassovitz; *C:* Pierre Aim, Georges Diane. Cannes Film Festival '95: Best Director (Kassovitz); Cesar Awards '96: Best Film, Best Film Editing; Nominations: Cesar Awards '96: Best Actor (Cassel), Best Cinematography, Best Director (Kassovitz), Best Sound, Best Writing. **VHS** *PGV*

HEART OF GLASS
Herz aus Glas

One of the pictures that best typifies the characteristically outrageous showmanship of Werner Herzog's early career is his bizarrely compelling, quite demented portrait of a small German town that—at some undetermined point in the "pre-industrialized past"—loses the secret for making a unique form of glass. That's pretty much the

HEAVENLY CREATURES

The old "senseless crime" myth is hung out to dry again, this time with freshness and energy by Peter Jackson. *Heavenly Creatures* is the real-life story of two teenage girls—Juliet Hulme and Pauline Parker—who, in 1952, rocked New Zealand by brutally murdering one of their mothers. The killing and the events that led up to it—as well as the sensational trial and its aftermath—are the subjects of this swirling and vertiginous portrait of paranoia, friendship, and romantic/sexual obsession. Jackson takes his theory of the girls' mindset at the moment of the killings and has constructed, from that point backward, a foundation on which their actions—while never seeming "justified"—are comprehensible. Melanie Lynskey and

Titanic's Kate Winslet are remarkable as the girls, but more remarkable still is what happened in the aftermath of the film's release. The real Hulme came forward after years of self-imposed secrecy to reveal that she has been living and working under the name of Anne Perry, and is today a successful writer of ... crime fiction. As stylized and fanciful as much of *Heavenly Creatures* is, it never—even in its wildest moments—could have predicted a zinger like *that*.

NEXT STOP . . . *An Angel at My Table, The Piano, Rope*

1994 (R) 110m/C *NZ* Melanie Lynskey, Kate Winslet, Sarah Pierse, Diana Kent, Clive Merrison, Simon O'Connor; **D:** Peter Jackson; **W:** Peter Jackson, Frances Walsh; **C:** Alun Bollinger, **M:** Peter Dasent. Nominations: Academy Awards '94: Best Original Screenplay; Australian Film Institute '95: Best Foreign Film; Writers Guild of America '94: Best Original Screenplay. **VHS, LV, Closed Caption** *TOU*

HEAVENS ABOVE!

Probably the weakest of the Boulting brothers' comedies of the 1960s, this is the story of a prison chaplain (Peter Sellers) who's transferred by clerical error to an upscale parish. The movie's tongue-in-cheek satirical digs at the hypocrisies of the church and its flock are like an undistinguished slice of cheese: too mild, too many holes, not particularly sharp, but harmless. Sellers is a joy, however, in one of his less-flamboyant performances of the period. Immediately after *Heavens Above!*, Sellers would make *Dr. Strangelove* for Stanley Kubrick, and his career would enter hyperdrive. If *Heavens Above!* is significant in any way, it's that it provides one last look at the great comic actor prior to the long, fruitful Hollywood period that would follow. (The pre-Clouseau Sellers has a certain shining purity, not unlike the pre-Army Elvis.) With Cecil Parker, Isabel Jeans, Ian Carmichael, Brock Peters and Roy Kinnear.

NEXT STOP . . . *I'm All Right, Jack, The Wrong Arm of the Law, Lolita*

1963 113m/B *GB* Peter Sellers, Cecil Parker, Isabel Jeans, Eric Sykes, Ian Carmichael; **D:** John Boulting, Roy Boulting; **M:** Richard Rodney Bennett. **VHS** *FCT*

HEIMAT 1
Heimat-Eine Deutsche Chronik

Sixteen hours, with barely a single memorable moment. Director Edgar Reitz's multigenerational family soap is intended as nothing less than the history of modern Germany, seen through the eyes of its central character/cipher, Maria (Marita Breuer), who had the symmetrically good fortune to be born in 1900. From the vantage point of Maria's little village, childhood blooms into young womanhood while romance, family obligations, and all those pesky wars keep everybody hopping. About six hours into *Heimat* (the high-steroid word for "homeland") you realize that it's going to be all buildup and no payoff; when the Nazis finally pass through as just one more speed bump on the road to the '80s, you simply sit back and stare at this thing with the same interest you'd feel for a local access/cable TV city council meeting. (The switching back and forth between black-and-white and color seemed arbitrary to me at first, until I realized it was probably tossed in just to add *some* mystery to the interminably dull goings-on.) The musical crescendos cue you in to the importance of certain scenes, particularly the ones that are not important. Originally filmed in eleven parts for German television.

NEXT STOP . . . *Berlin Alexanderplatz, The Godfather and The Godfather Part II, 1900*

1984 924m/C *GE* Marita Breuer; **D:** Edgar Reitz; **W:** Edgar Reitz, Peter F. Steinbach; **C:** Gernot Roll; **M:** Nikos Mamangakis. **VHS** *FCT*

HENRY V

If greater joys await, this will do nicely until they come along. Conceived with the goal of building morale among a beleaguered, Nazi-bombarded British public, Laurence Olivier also knew that the mounting of this film was a rare opportunity to bring Shakespeare to the screen with an audacity and freshness that could make it accessible to millions. Olivier sought other directors before accepting the task himself, but the final, glorious result looks like anything *but* the work of a

H

director selected by default. The ingenuity of every aspect of this chronicle of the events leading up to the (stunningly recreated) Battle of Agincourt in 1415 is still astounding, particularly the ingeniously fashioned screenplay. The film opens by placing the viewer in London's Globe Theatre at a 16th-century performance of Henry V; we get a feel for the original conception of the play's staging, followed by Olivier's fantastically exciting "full-dress" interpretation. Everything works, and, blessedly, the color film materials used in *Henry V* have been restored and preserved for future generations. That it will ever lose its captivating power, or will ever become "dated," is unimaginable. If nothing else, its restoration will prove that. With Renée Asherson as Princess Katherine (Olivier wanted Vivien Leigh, but couldn't get her out of her Selznick contract), Robert Newton, Leslie Banks, Leo Genn, and Felix Aylmer. Robert Krasker filmed the magnificent color images, and William Walton composed the rousing score. Olivier received a special Oscar in 1946 for outstanding achievement for creating *Henry V.*

NEXT STOP . . . *Henry V* (1989), *Richard III, Ran*

1945 136m/C *GB* Laurence Olivier, Robert Newton, Leslie Banks, Esmond Knight, Renee Asherson, Leo Genn, George Robey, Ernest Thesiger, Felix Aylmer, Ralph Truman; *D:* Laurence Olivier; *W:* Laurence Olivier, Alan Dent; *C:* Robert Krasker; *M:* William Walton. National Board of Review Awards '46: Best Actor (Olivier); New York Film Critics Awards '46: Best Actor (Olivier); Nominations: Academy Awards '46: Best Actor (Olivier), Best Interior Decoration, Best Picture, Best Original Dramatic/Comedy Score. **VHS** *PAR, HMV*

HENRY V

Kenneth Branagh's visually handsome, full-bodied film of Shakespeare's *Henry V* was generally received well by critics, yet it likely would have received an even more rousing reception had it not been for the obvious need to compare it with Laurence Olivier's 1945 masterpiece. Was that fair? Probably not. But it was inevitable. And part of the pleasure in Branagh's brash achievement is that he, probably more than anyone, was aware that such comparisons were being readied, like the arrows in the tightly drawn bows at Agincourt, for firing directly into his pugnacious little heart. For Branagh, choosing *Henry V* for his directorial debut was like deciding to take on Joe Louis for his first professional fight; he had to perform better than adequately just to keep from being knocked out. And he did; Branagh's *Henry V* is rich and vibrant and filled with wonderful performances, not the least of which is his own (Derek Jacobi and Ian Holm are also standouts among the well-chosen cast). Yet I have the feeling that even if I were able to remove Olivier's film from my memory for the duration of Branagh's (I can't), I would still find it less fully, triumphantly exhilarating than Olivier's, as well as dotted with nagging little weaknesses such as a calculatedly "cute" ending that Olivier had the wits to toss off far more quickly. A nice job, nevertheless, and you *do* have to admire his chutzpah. Oscar nominations for Best Director and Actor, winner for Costume Design.

NEXT STOP . . . *Henry V* (1945), *A Midwinter's Tale, Hamlet* (1996)

1989 138m/C *GB* Kenneth Branagh, Derek Jacobi, Brian Blessed, Alec McCowen, Ian Holm, Richard Briers, Robert Stephens, Robbie Coltrane, Christian Bale, Judi Dench, Paul Scofield, Michael Maloney, Emma Thompson; *D:* Kenneth Branagh; *W:* Kenneth Branagh; *C:* Kenneth Macmillan; *M:* Patrick Doyle. Academy Awards '89: Best Costume Design; British Academy Awards '89: Best Director (Branagh); National Board of Review Awards '89: Best Director (Branagh); Nominations: Academy Awards '89: Best Actor (Branagh), Best Director (Branagh). **VHS, LV, Letterbox, Closed Caption** *FOX, SIG, TVC*

HEY, BABU RIBA

Four middle-aged men gather in Belgrade in the 1980s for the funeral of a girl they all loved as youngsters. In flashback, we get glimpses of the fun they had in the 1950s, saturated with American rock and roll, American movies, and American cigarettes. Far from American, however, was their local Communist Youth Group leader, who's the villain of the piece on both a personal and political level. The four boys comprised a rowing team, with the girl their coxswain, and the metaphorical implications of that image—with the foursome gliding through history to the rhythm of their now-

Henry (Laurence Olivier) sits regally on the English throne in *Henry V* (1944).

dead muse—can be seen as typical of the film. It's not a subtle movie, nor is it a bad one, yet the specificity of time and place that it describes make it a film that doesn't travel all that well. You had to be there.

NEXT STOP . . . *Twist & Shout, Time Stands Still, American Graffiti*

1988 **(R)** 109m/C *YU* Gala Videnovic, Nebojsa Bakocevic, Dragan Bjelogric, Marko Todorovic, Goran Radakovic, Relja Basic, Milos Zutic; **D:** Jovan Acin; **W:** Jovan Acin. **VHS, LV** *ORI*

THE HIDDEN FORTRESS

Kakushi Toride No San Akunin
Three Rascals in the Hidden Fortress
Three Bad Men in the Hidden Fortress

During the civil wars of Japan's 16th century, a princess bearing an important and priceless treasure is being chased by a ruthless enemy bent on her destruction. If you change the era and geography (or galaxy) you'll immediately see why George Lucas has cited Kurosawa's 1958 *The Hidden Fortress* as one of the sources of inspiration for his *Star Wars*. So much of that film's basic structure is here, right down to the bickering, comic farmers who tag along on the princess's journey (and would evolve into R2D2 and C3PO), as well as the stirring sword play, which would remain the same conceptually while evolving from steel to lasers. That being said, it would be a shame to designate Kurosawa's magnificent and rousingly dynamic adventure epic as simply the early version of something else. *The Hidden Fortress* is a true original; funny, action-packed, and spectacular, and one of the most deeply satisfying and elegantly structured films of Kurosawa's career. Clearly and inventively conceived as a live-action fairy-tale, *The Hidden Fortress* is further energized by Toshiro Mifune as the princess's protector, and by the boldly designed, widescreen black-and-white images. (If at all possible, see *The Hidden Fortress* in a letter-boxed version.)

NEXT STOP . . . *Yojimbo, The Good, the Bad and the Ugly, Star Wars*

1958 139m/B *JP* Toshiro Mifune, Misa Vehara, Minoru Chiaki; **D:** Akira Kurosawa; **W:** Akira Kurosawa, Shinobu Hashimoto, Riyuzo Kikushima, Hideo Oguni; **C:** Kazuo Yamazaki; **M:** Masaru Sato. Berlin International Film Festival '59: Best Director (Kurosawa). **VHS, LV, Letterbox** *HMV, FCT, CRC*

HIGH & LOW
Tengoku To Jigoku

Akira Kurosawa's dense, crackling thriller is based on *King's Ransom,* an *87th Precinct* novel by Ed McBain (Evan Hunter). In Kurosawa's version, a high-powered shoe tycoon (Toshiro Mifune) is interrupted during a business meeting with the news that his son has been kidnapped. After agreeing in front of associates that he will pay the enormous ransom demanded (money he recently raised for a pending business deal by mortgaging everything he owns), the boy walks in the house. It seems that the kidnappers have taken the son of Mifune's chauffeur by mistake, and now the ruthless businessman must decide if he's willing to risk everything to save a child who is not his own. *High & Low* is neatly divided into two sections; the first half (entirely set in the tycoon's luxurious, high-rise home overlooking Tokyo) deals with the difficult decision that Mifune has to make, while the second half (set in the "lower" depths of the city's dark, labyrinthine streets) deals with the pursuit of the kidnapper and the aftermath of his arrest. *High & Low* provides the physical tension and gut-level excitement one expects from a detective thriller, but also provides what one has come to expect from Kurosawa: a story that resonates in surprising and universal ways for all of us who would separate actions from consequences. A visual knockout, but be sure you look at a letterboxed copy. (And you're not going crazy—there is *one* color image in this otherwise black-and-white film.)

NEXT STOP . . . *Stray Dog, The Bad Sleep Well, Face/Off*

1962 **(R)** 143m/B *JP* Toshiro Mifune, Tatsuya Mihashi, Tatsuya Nakadai; **D:** Akira Kurosawa; **W:** Evan Hunter, Riyuzo Kikushima, Hideo Oguni, Akira Kurosawa; **C:** Asakazu Nakai, Takao Saito; **M:** Masaru Sato. **VHS, LV, Letterbox** *IME, TPV*

HIGH HOPES

The seven principal characters in Mike Leigh's ironically titled *High Hopes* are sharply drawn and indelible, and though they all represent different dead ends of Margaret Thatcher's England, they don't symbolize political positions to the point of simply being labels. One aging mother and three couples—one poor but sane, one maniacally desperate to climb socially, one yuppified beyond human recognition—interact over the course of a few days in a series of plot twists that is both excruciatingly witty and inevitable. We learn an enormous amount about these people as individuals, and we also come away with a surprisingly solid take on the society that created them and then dropped them right in their little traps. It's a poignant and profound little film about class distinctions, yes, but it's also a brilliant, devastatingly funny comedy about human ambition and a society that creates enemies naturally, simply as a cruel but everyday by-product of what it deems to be "progress." Philip Davis, Ruth Sheen, Philip Jackson, and Heather Tobias are marvelous, while Lesley Manville and Edna Doré are better than that. Leigh (*Secrets and Lies, Naked*) employs an innovative method of preparation that involves cast members working out their own characters prior to the final script stage. It has never served him better. A classic.

NEXT STOP . . . *Life Is Sweet, Career Girls, A Sense of History* (a short film available in a package called *Two Mikes Don't Make a Wright*)

1988 110m/C *GB* Philip Davis, Ruth Sheen, Edna Dore, Philip Jackson, Heather Tobias, Leslie Manville, David Bamber; *D:* Mike Leigh; *W:* Mike Leigh; *C:* Roger Pratt; *M:* Rachel Portman, Andrew Dixon. **VHS**

HIMATSURI
Fire Festival

Mitsuo Yanagimachi's *Himatsuri* (*Fire Festival*) is a powerful, poetic, visionary work about one individual's increasing disillusionment with the world of man, and his growing, obsessive, and ultimately religious relationship with nature. The hero is a lumberjack in a small, magnificently scenic Japanese vil-

lage, where the stately trees that the lumberjack veritably worships seem to take on a phallic suggestiveness without the director forcing the issue. If this all sounds hopelessly symbolic and pretentious on paper, I'd have to agree. Yanagimachi's art is in his ability to wrap this skeleton of an idea in a visual cloak that is so awe-inspiring that the underlying silliness of the film's conceit is replaced by an electrifying foreboding. The explosive climax that *Himatsuri* seems to be building toward is very real, and doesn't disappoint; the stormy, wind-whipped sound effects and towering, living, ominous living landscapes that suggest what is to come are evidence of an artist who is in total control of his medium. (Note: *Himatsuri* is a film that will particularly benefit from being seen on laserdisc or DVD, if available. To put it in sixties speak, it will blow your mind.)

NEXT STOP . . . *The Ballad of Narayama, Nanook of the North, 2001: A Space Odyssey*

1985 120m/C *JP* Kinya Kitaoji, Kwako Taichi, Ryota Nakamoto, Norihei Miki; *D:* Mitsuo Yanagimachi; *W:* Kenji Nakagami; *C:* Masaki Tamura; *M:* Toru Takemitsu. **VHS** *ORI, WAR, AUD*

HIROSHIMA MON AMOUR

Alain Resnais had made a number of acclaimed documentaries (one of them—*Night and Fog*—was already considered a masterpiece) when he directed his first feature film, *Hiroshima Mon Amour*. The two stars are simply called he and she (Eiji Okada and Emmanuelle Riva); they are both married to others, and meet in modern Hiroshima. They become lovers, and during the night the woman, who is from Nevers, describes her past, which involved a now-dead German soldier she once loved. She tells the man, whose home is Hiroshima, that her heartbreak allows her to know everything about his city, but he tells her she knows nothing. Even a far more detailed plot description would not suffice, since the power of *Hiroshima Mon Amour* comes from Resnais's juxtaposition of images from past and present—including documentary footage—as a counterpoint to the feel-

JOHN WOO
Action Film Director

Director John Woo achieved cult status with his work on the stylishly violent films, *The Killer* and *Hard Boiled*. His 1996 release, *Broken Arrow*, made number one at the box office, and now he finds himself on the A-list of action directors. He followed up the success of *Broken Arrow* with equally successful *Face/Off* (1997). Still he finds it difficult to think of himself as a success. Perhaps he is still recovering from the disappointing reception of *Hard Target*, a Jean-Claude Van Damme movie he directed.

Terrence Rafferty, "The New Yorker" film reviewer, lauds Woo's non-stop momentum, which often overrides considerations of plot and verisimiltude. For Woo making movies is not about violence: "Actually, I hate violence, I hate it."

Woo was born May 1, 1946 in Guangzhou, Canton, China. Woo grew up in Hong Kong's slums among gang crime, drugs, and prostitutes. His family experienced homelessness. People turned up dead in front of the shacks he found for shelter. Woo, approaching 50, calls that time "a living hell." He consoled himself with fantasies, of just flying away to another world. His mother took him to movie musicals, and he loved watching Gene Kelly and Fred Astaire dance.

A Christian family from the United States sponsored Woo and paid for his early education. By the late 1960s, Woo was experimenting with films in Super-8 and 16-millimeter, avidly reading books about film theory, and studying films by Federico Fellini, Francois Truffaut, Arthur Penn, and Elia Kazan. It is that attention to style and construction, perhaps, that once made a reviewer call Woo "the Mozart of mayhem."

---

ings the couple express. Eventually, the film—which was written by Marguerite Duras—evokes the notion of the senselessness of war as well as the futility of love in a world of such transience, misery, and devastation. For better or worse, *Hiroshima Mon Amour* was one of the films that sprang to a generation's mind when the term "art film" came up. It obviously *is* a work of art, and indeed has moments of quiet passion and extreme beauty; it also, I'm afraid, has a preciousness and self-consciousness that seen today nudges it just a bit closer than ever to self-parody.

NEXT STOP . . . *Night and Fog, Providence, Mon Oncle d'Amerique*

1959 88m/B *JP FR* Emmanuelle Riva, Eiji Okada, Bernard Fresson, Stella Dassas, Pierre Barbaud; *D:* Alain Resnais; *W:* Marguerite Duras; *C:* Sacha Vierny; *M:* Georges Delerue, Giovanni Fusco. New York Film Critics Awards '60: Best Foreign Film; Nominations: Academy Awards '60: Best Story & Screenplay. **VHS** *HMV, MRV, HHT*

THE HIT

Terence Stamp turns in a knockout performance in this witty, off-kilter little picture about a mob informer (Stamp) who's managed to escape the long arm of the "family" for a decade. As *The Hit* begins, his luck runs out. Killing him right away would mean no movie, however, so world-weary, zombie-like hit man John Hurt and his moronic, weasely gunsel Tim Roth (making a terrific impression in his film debut) are charged with transporting him to the ordained place and time of his execution. Stamp confounds the two men by accepting his fate like a gentleman; he's so suave and cool that they're both incredulous (with good reason, it turns out). *The Hit* was directed by Stephen Frears (*The Grifters, The Snapper*) as a darkly comic shaggy-dog story about courage and machismo not always being what they seem. He's got a point. Highly recommended. With Laura Del Sol (*Carmen*), Bill Hunter (*Muriel's Wedding*), and Fernando Rey (*The Discreet Charm of the Bourgeoisie*).

NEXT STOP . . . *Goodfellas, The Adventures of Priscilla, Queen of the Desert, Reservoir Dogs*

1985 (R) 105m/C *GB* Terence Stamp, John Hurt, Laura Del Sol, Tim Roth, Fernando Rey, Bill Hunter; *D:* Stephen Frears; *W:* Peter Prince; *C:* John A. Alonzo; *M:* Eric Clapton. **VHS, LV** *NLC*

HOLLOW REED
Believe Me

When the nine-year-old son of a divorced couple begins to show signs of physical abuse, the boy's physician father (Martin Donovan)—now openly gay—finds himself unable to prove his suspicion that his ex-wife's new lover is the cause. *Hollow Reed* looks for all the world like a made-for-cable movie during its first ten minutes or so, but soon its texture begins to appear, and the plot takes you in directions you don't see coming. Martin Donovan, who for years was the effectively blank protagonist of Hal Hartley's existential downtown comedies, displays a range I was both surprised and impressed by. It's an issue picture about battered children, yes, but it's more than that; it's also about how well-meaning, intelligent people manage to sheath themselves with denial despite—perhaps because of—unbearably ugly realities that they know to be true. Most importantly, *Hollow Reed* is engaging enough to make us *care* about the issues at its center.

NEXT STOP . . . *Amateur, Flirt, Patty Hearst*

1995 105m/C *GB* Martin Donovan, Joely Richardson, Ian Hart, Jason Flemyng, Sam Bould; *D:* Angela Pope; *W:* Paula Milne; *C:* Remi Adefarasin; *M:* Anne Dudley. **VHS, Closed Caption** *COL*

THE HORSE THIEF
Daoma Zei

Tian Zhuangzhuang's *The Horse Thief* is an epic Chinese film of startling visual and emotional richness, set against the fantastic landscape of Tibet. It's the story of a horse thief named Norbu, who is banished from his tribe in order to keep it cleansed of evil. Refusing to renounce his Buddhist faith, Norbu and his wife attend temples as often as possible. But the odd jobs Norbu has to take and the nomadic existence the family is forced to adopt takes its toll on their young son, and eventually these believers reach a powerfully moving breaking point. *The Horse Thief* has the simple, elegant plot structure of a folk tale (large portions are without dialogue) but ultimately becomes such a remarkably rich portrait of a culture and its way of life that it bursts the boundaries of its storyline. It's like a glimpse into a world we've always suspected existed, but never had the means to look at until now.

NEXT STOP . . . *Red Sorghum, The Wooden Man's Bride, Close to Eden*

1987 88m/C *CH* Daiba, Jiji Dan, Drashi, Gaoba, Jamco Jayang, Rigzin Tseshang; *D:* Tian Zhuangzhuang; *W:* Rui Zhang; *C:* Fei Zhao, Hou Yong; *M:* Xiao-Song Qu. **VHS** *KIV, FCT*

THE HOUR OF THE WOLF
Vargtimmen

Artist goes nuts; audience pays price. That's the cinematic version of frontier justice, perhaps. Still, Ingmar Bergman's 1968 *The Hour of the Wolf*—the story of a painter who vanishes, leaving behind only the diary in which he describes his descent into mad-

"No Turk in his right mind is going to waste a bullet on you."

—Archy (Mark Lee) to Frank (Mel Gibson) in *Gallipoli*.

ness—is the closest the great Swedish director has ever come to making a psycho-analytical slasher film; a Jungian *Halloween*. Max von Sydow is the tortured, imploding Johan Borg, whose wife Alma (Liv Ullmann) conveys the story of his breakdown to us in an increasingly grotesque series of Gothic-style flashbacks. Some of these are power-fully suggestive images; Johan's terrified nights of insomnia, during which he tries to convince his wife of his terror by demon-strating to her—and us—how long one minute can be during the deepest period of the night, or "hour of the wolf"; a centuries-old woman who peels off her face; a dead body that suddenly springs to life. They're amazing and chilling sights, photographed with impeccable artistry by Sven Nykvist. But do we really want to see the hallucina-tions of a psychotic artist presented in such a straightforward, literal-minded manner? Somewhere in here are hints of the conver-gence of fantasy and reality, and the diffi-culty the artist has in distinguishing between the two at certain, critical junc-tures in his life. All well and good, but *The Hour of the Wolf* is such a non-stop flow of nightmares that the whole picture is like Ray Milland's one-minute "DTs" sequence in *The Lost Weekend*. One minute can be a long time, as Johan correctly points out, and *The Hour of the Wolf* has 88 of them. Sometimes, less is more.

NEXT STOP . . . *The Magician, The Cabinet of Dr. Caligari, A Page of Madness*

1968 89m/B *SW* Max von Sydow, Liv Ullmann, Ingrid Thulin, Erland Josephson, Gertrud Fridh, Gudrun Brost, Georg Rydeberg, Naima Wifstrand, Bertil Anderberg, Ulf Johansson; *D:* Ingmar Bergman; *W:* Ingmar Bergman; *C:* Sven Nykvist; *M:* Lars Johan Werle. National Board of Review Awards '68: Best Actress (Ull-mann); National Society of Film Critics Awards '68: Best Director (Bergman). **VHS** *MGM, FCT, BTV*

HOW I WON THE WAR

I went to see Richard Lester's rabidly anti-war comedy the night it opened, at a small "art" theatre just north of Detroit in 1967. The place was packed with teenagers (I shouldn't complain, since I was one, too) who had gotten word that John Lennon was making his first non-Beatle film appearance. The audience talked through the entire film, more loudly when Lennon showed up on screen, and I could barely understand a word any of the actors said. A few days later, I went back on a weekday afternoon and saw the film in a nearly empty theatre. I *still* couldn't understand a word, but I got the drift. Like most of the anti-war films made during the Vietnam years, *How I Won the War* is set in another place and time—in this case it's a British regiment deployed in Africa during World War II. (In the 1960s, Vietnam existed only on television, and there only on the news. It was banned from movie screens—except by allusion—as if by court order.) Lester and his screenwriter Charles Wood (who morphed Vietnam into the Crimean War the next year in Tony Richardson's *The Charge of the Light Brigade*) created a knockabout farce about frivolous, dim-witted officers putting the lives of their hapless infantry at risk. It's packed with bitter, sarcastic one-liners that you strain to hear through the muffled, rapid-fire Cockney accents, but the ones you do hear turn out to be leaden and obvious. You wait for the most innocent and sweet of the wits and pranksters to come to bloody, tragic ends, and they do. The frantic, kaleidoscopic editing doesn't help, but with a script like this it doesn't hurt, either. With the young, pre-Vegas Michael Crawford, Roy Kinnear, and Michael Hordern.

NEXT STOP . . . *M*A*S*H, The Charge of the Light Brigade* (1968), *Oh! What a Lovely War*

1967 (PG) 111m/C *GB* Roy Kinnear, John Lennon, Michael Crawford, Michael Hordern; **D:** Richard Lester; **W:** Charles Wood; **C:** David Watkin; **M:** Ken Thorne. **VHS, LV** *MGM*

THE HUMAN CONDITION: A SOLDIER'S PRAYER

One of the most extraordinary achievements of the post-war Japanese cinema is director Masaki Kobayashi's epic trilogy of films, each more than three hours in length, based on the acclaimed novel by Jumpei Gomikawa. Together, the three films—*No Greater Love, The Road to Eternity,* and *A Soldier's Prayer* (*The Human Condition* is the name of the trilogy)—tell the story of Kaji (Tatsuya Nakadai), a pacifist who attempts to avoid military service in 1943, but is drafted when a catastrophe ensues at his draft-exempt job. As Kaji endures a mind-numbing military ordeal that eventually leads to imprisonment in Manchuria following the Russian invasion, his last shreds of idealism are stripped away as he discovers that the brutality under which he served in the Imperial Japanese Army was not unique; the horrors do not vanish because one's captors wear different uniforms—it is, he tragically discovers, the human condition. Kobayashi's own military experience led to his fight to make this masterwork, the first large-scale Japanese production to be openly critical of Japan's military policies. Kobayashi's own military experience was not unlike that of his hero—"I am Kaji," he has written. Putting that story in the form of this sweeping, nine-hour, widescreen saga was a four-year struggle for the director; *The Human Condition*'s success in Japan—as well as its prizes at the Venice Film Festival—gave him the power to follow it with a series of superb, socially critical period dramas that would secure his reputation both at home and abroad.

NEXT STOP . . . *Harakiri, Kwaidan, Rebellion* (a.k.a. *Samurai Rebellion*)

1961 190m/B *JP* Tatsuya Nakadai, Michiyo Aratama, Yusuke Kawazu, Tamao Nakamura, Chishu Ryu, Taketoshi Naito, Reiko Hitomi, Kyoko Kishida, Keijiro Morozumi, Koji Kiyomura, Nobuo Kaneko, Fujio Suga; **D:** Masaki Kobayashi. **VHS** *NO*

H

THE HUMAN CONDITION: NO GREATER LOVE

See *The Human Condition: A Soldier's Prayer.*

1958 200m/B *JP* Tatsuya Nakadai, Michiyo Aratama, So Yamamura, Eitaro Ozawa, Akira Ishihama, Chikage Awashima, Ineko Arima, Keiji Sada, Shinji Nambara, Seiji Miyaguchi, Toru Abe, Masao Mishima, Eijiro Tono, Yasushi Nagata, Yoshio Kosugi; *D:* Masaki Kobayashi. **VHS** *NO*

THE HUMAN CONDITION: ROAD TO ETERNITY

No Greater Love
Ningen No Joken

See *The Human Condition: A Soldier's Prayer.*

1959 180m/B *JP* Tatsuya Nakadai, Michiyo Aratama, Kokinji Katsura, Jun Tatara, Michio Minami, Keiji Sada, Minoru Chiaki, Ryohei Uchida, Kan Yanagidani, Kenjiro Uemura, Yusuke Kawazu, Susumu Fujita; *D:* Masaki Kobayashi; *W:* Zenzo Matsuyama; *C:* Yoshio Miyajima; *M:* Chuji Kinoshita. **VHS** *NO*

I AM CUBA

Soy Cuba
Ja Cuba

In 1964, Soviet director Mikhail Kalatozov (*The Cranes Are Flying*) collaborated with poet Yevgeny Yevtushenko and writer Enrique Pineda Barnet to create a propagandistic portrait of an oppressed Cuba—one that was ripe for a rebellion against decadent, imperialist enslavement of the Cuban people's bodies and minds. The film consists of four "chapters" that show us different aspects of the same problem—the human misery caused by colonialist influences, primarily American. *I Am Cuba* has the broad caricatures you'd expect—noble but degraded peasants, contaminated by American corruption; sexually decadent American businessmen, their women, and their armed forces; valiant, committed, revolutionary youth. But simply calling *I Am Cuba* advocacy filmmaking is like calling *The Godfather* a movie about rival mobsters—it is, but that's not the half of it. The creators of this film set out to make an epic, visionary fantasy about liberation, and they succeeded to a staggering degree. When I tell you that I've never seen anything like the images in *I Am Cuba*, it's not just hyperbole. This is a movie so visually inventive and audacious that about halfway through the picture I actually realized that my mouth was open out of a combination of astonishment and disbelief—astonishment at the inventiveness of the visual scheme, disbelief because I couldn't figure out how it was achieved. There are acrobatic camera movements in this movie far too complex and sinewy to describe, but which sound unbelievable anyway—until you see them. And when you do see them, they're *still* unbelievable. A unique, insane, exhilarating spectacle. Kudos to Francis Ford Coppola and Martin Scorsese for helping to make the American release of the restored version possible.

NEXT STOP . . . *Memories of Underdevelopment, Improper Conduct, The Battleship Potemkin*

1964 141m/B *CU RU* Luz Maria Collazo, Jose Gallardo, Sergio Corrieri, Jean Bouise, Raul Garcia, Celia Rodriguez; *D:* Mikhail Kalatozov; *W:* Yevgeny Yevtushenko, Enrique Pineda Barnet; *C:* Sergei Urusevsky; *M:* Carlos Farinas. Nominations: Independent Spirit Awards '96: Best Foreign Film. **VHS** *MIL, FCT*

I AM CURIOUS (YELLOW)

Jag Ar Nyfiken—Gul
Jag Ar Nyfiken—En Film i Gult

There *is* a plot; Swedish filmmaker Vilgot Sjöman, playing Swedish filmmaker Vilgot Sjöman, decides to make a film starring actress Lena Nyman. Her character, Lena, is curious about Vietnam, the Swedish class system, and civil rights. She is also curious about sex, and has it many times during the film, usually with her boyfriend Börje (played by her boyfriend Börje), but also with Swedish filmmaker Vilgot Sjöman. Swedish and Danish "art" movies about sex were legion in the 1960s, and *I Am Curious (Yellow)* is the most pretentiously highfalutin' of the bunch. It was distributed by Grove Press Films, a division of the pioneering publishing house that printed *Naked Lunch* and *Tropic of Cancer* when others would not. Grove Press agreed to send *I Am Curious* out with an "X" rating, despite the fact that many theatres wouldn't touch an "X" rated movie lest the theatre be labeled a porno house. (It shouldn't go unmentioned that the sex scenes were simulated.) One of those in attendance at the packed, opening-day matinee at the art house that ran it in suburban Detroit was that suburb's mayor; when local news stations stuck cameras in his face after the premiere, he flatly and authoritatively pronounced that "the film is definitely obscene in three places." I would have said four, myself, but that's neither here nor there. It ran unfettered for months to a audience of half suits and half raincoats. Within two years, the theatre—which had premiered *Blow-Up* the year prior to *I Am Curious*—was running hard-core sex films. It's now a church. If there's a moral here, I do not know what it is. Nor, for that matter, do I know the whereabouts of Swedish filmmaker Vilgot Sjöman.

NEXT STOP . . . *I Am Curious (Blue), I, a Woman, I, a Woman Part II*

1967 95m/B *SW* Lena Nyman, Peter Lindgren; *D:* Vilgot Sjoman. **VHS** *HTV*

I CAN'T SLEEP
J'Ai Pas Sommeil

In the back alleys of Paris, a number of seemingly disparate story fragments simultaneously spin into motion during the course of a summer. An actress arrives from Lithuania, looking for a job; a series of murders is taking place in which the victims are all elderly women; a West Indian musician is imploring his wife to move back to Martinique with him. Not all of the loose ends of Claire Denis's *I Can't Sleep* are neatly tied up by the film's end (you may not even be sure what some of the ends are), but her film is less a whodunit than a gently poetic mood piece about uncertainty and *angst* at a particular moment in contemporary European history. There's a dreamlike mood about the whole enterprise that is effectively unnerving,

though you're never sure exactly where it comes from. You may tell yourself afterwards that nothing much really happened in this film, yet you can't easily shake off its dank mood or its creeping sense of dread. If that's what Denis was after, she hit the bull's eye. (The killings alluded to in *I Can't Sleep* are drawn from an actual case of a decade ago.)

NEXT STOP . . . *Chocolat, Nenette et Boni, A Single Girl*

1993 110m/C *FR* Richard Courcet, Vincent Dupont, Katerina Golubeva, Alex Descas, Beatrice Dalle, Laurent Grevill; *D:* Claire Denis; *W:* Claire Denis, Jean-Pol Fargeau; *C:* Agnes Godard; *M:* Jean Murat. **VHS** *NYF*

I DON'T WANT TO TALK ABOUT IT
De Eso No Se Habla

The widowed Dona Leonor (Luisina Brando), who lives in a small Argentine town in the 1930s, is determined to see that her daughter, Charlotte (Alejandra Podesta), achieves as much happiness in life as possible. She refuses, though, to as much as acknowledge the fact that her daughter is extremely short, and will not allow any mention of the girl's size in her presence (the word these days is *denial*). Leonor's zealous overprotectiveness (she torches copies of *Snow White and the Seven Dwarfs*) is challenged when a worldly newcomer (a genteel Marcello Mastroianni) finds himself completely enchanted by Charlotte. Maria Luisa Bemberg's film remains sensitive throughout, never going after easy laughs or condescending to her characters. That's about all she does, however, and the net emotional effect of *I Don't Want to Talk about It* is one of vague relief at all the mines the director avoids stepping on. The picture might have had considerably more punch if she'd been a little less obsessed with taste, and a little more dedicated to dramatic friction.

NEXT STOP . . . *Camila* (1984), *Bye Bye Brazil, The Incredible Shrinking Man*

1994 102m/C *AR* Marcello Mastroianni, Luisina Brando, Alejandra Podesta; *D:* Maria-Luisa Bemberg; *W:* Maria-Luisa Bemberg, Jorge Goldenberg. **VHS, LV** *COL*

I KNOW WHERE I'M GOING

Joan Webster (Wendy Hiller), a smart and determined young working woman whose journey through life has been planned for years, is committed to marrying a wealthy and socially well-positioned Scottish fuddy-duddy. But while on her way to marry him, Joan becomes stranded by a storm in a small coastal town where she meets the handsome young Naval officer Torquil MacNeil (Roger Livesey); for the first time in her life, Joan considers a change of plan. Michael Powell and Emeric Pressburger wrote, produced, and directed this completely enchanting, supremely atmospheric romantic comedy, which has rightfully achieved cult status in recent years. (Powell and Pressburger were known collectively as the Archers—they provided British cinema with some of its most memorable and beloved triumphs, including *A Matter of Life and Death, Black Narcissus,* and *The Red Shoes.*) *I Know Where I'm Going*'s plot is as simple and uncomplicated as the town in which it's set, but the small and unexpectedly rich details—not to mention the town itself— provide this film with its unique and lilting personality. This is a film that, like a beguiling new acquaintance who later becomes a best friend, you'll want to visit again and again until you can't remember a time before you met.

NEXT STOP . . . *The Life and Death of Colonel Blimp, L'Atalante, Local Hero*

1945 91m/B *GB* Roger Livesey, Wendy Hiller, Finlay Currie, Pamela Brown, George Carney, Walter Hudd; **D:** Michael Powell, Emeric Pressburger; **W:** Michael Powell, Emeric Pressburger; **C:** Erwin Hillier; **M:** Allan Gray. **VHS, LV** *HMV, BFA*

I LIVE IN FEAR
Record of a Living Being
Kimono No Kiroku

As daring as Stanley Kubrick's 1964 *Dr. Strangelove* may be, you might be surprised to know that Japan's Akira Kurosawa conceived of a satirical film on the subject of the bomb as early as 1955. Though he finally realized that a darkly comic essay on the subject of nuclear war would be far too contro-versial—this was, after all, just ten years after the bombings of Hiroshima and Nagasaki— Kurosawa did create a film that dealt with one man's fear of nuclear holocaust, and he gave the movie a core of deep and bitter irony rather than flat-out humor. *I Live in Fear* is the story of a wealthy industrialist (Toshiro Mifune) whose fear of the escalating 1950s nuclear arms race between the U.S. and the Soviet Union is driving him past the point of simple anxiety. Mifune has fixated on the idea that Brazil will be the one safe place on Earth in the event of atomic war, so he begins to make preparations to move there, along with his wife, his family, and his mistresses. They resist, and Mifune's steep descent into paranoia and madness finally leads to his complete hallucinatory break with reality in the film's *Twilight Zone*-ish final moments. Kurosawa was making a sophisticated statement for such an early period in the Cold War; he wasn't asking whether or not the world was going to blow itself up, but rather was questioning how mankind was going to live with the knowledge that it *might.* Though *I Live in Fear* is a bit more static and talky than much of Kurosawa's other work of the period, the film gets under your skin in ways that "issue" films rarely do. It's like that classic description of a paranoiac; psychiatrist to patient: "What can I—or anyone you can think of—do, say, or show you to prove that your fear of X is unfounded?" Patient to psychiatrist: "Nothing." While it's hardly irrational to fear nuclear war, the genius of Kurosawa lies in his knowing that the fear can be far more deadly than the bomb.

NEXT STOP . . . *Rashomon, The Atomic Cafe, Dr. Strangelove*

1955 105m/C *JP* Toshiro Mifune, Takashi Shimura, Eiko Miyoshi, Haruko Togo; **D:** Akira Kurosawa; **W:** Akira Kurosawa, Shinobu Hashimoto, Hideo Oguni; **C:** Asakazu Nakai; **M:** Fumio Hayasaka. **VHS** *FCT*

I VITELLONI
The Young and the Passionate
Vitelloni
Spivs

Fellini's third feature—his second solo directing effort—is a spellbinding portrait of aimless, post-World War II youth adrift in a small Italian town. It is also, quite possibly, his finest film. Designed neither as an exploitative exposé nor as a fully sympathetic portrait of "misunderstood" youth, *I Vitelloni* ("the fatted calves") is a clear-eyed and brilliantly conceived portrait of a group of clueless, self-centered young men whose inevitable "come-uppance" is presented touchingly but without sentimentality. Fellini does an extraordinary job of balancing comedy, drama, and tragedy, without ever making his well-differentiated protagonists seem in the least bit inconsistent. Featuring exceptionally rich performances and lyrical, naturalistic, unforced direction, *I Vitelloni* feels closer to the neo-realist tradition of directors like De Sica and Rossellini than do any of Fellini's subsequent films; the powerful ray of hope at the movie's conclusion, however, is pure Fellini. (And the heartbreaking score is pure Nino Rota.) With Franco Interlenghi, Alberto Sordi, Leopoldo Trieste, and Riccardo Fellini. Academy Award Nominee, Best Original Screenplay.

NEXT STOP . . . *La Dolce Vita, American Graffiti, Diner*

1953 104m/B *IT* Alberto Sordi, Franco Interlenghi, Franco Fabrizi, Leopoldo Trieste, Riccardo Fellini; *D:* Federico Fellini; *W:* Federico Fellini, Ennio Flaiano; *C:* Carlo Carlini, Otello Martelli; *M:* Nino Rota. Nominations: Academy Awards '57: Best Story & Screenplay. **VHS, LV** *MOV*

THE ICICLE THIEF
Ladri di Saponette

A movie director (Maurizio Nichetti) is invited to host an Italian TV station's screening of one of his classic, neo-realist films: *The Icicle Thief* (*Ladri di saponette*). The black-and-white movie about an impoverished family (a movie-within-a-movie parody of De Sica's *The Bicycle Thief*) is constantly being interrupted by commercials—all in color—but the worst is yet to come; a power glitch at the studio causes characters from the commercials to appear in the film, and vice-versa. Nichetti wrote, directed, and starred in what is essentially a clever and imaginative idea for a short

subject; the problem is that it's 90 minutes long. *The Icicle Thief* goes down relatively easily for a gag that's so over-extended, but you get impatient once you see where Nichetti's headed. It's a harmless diversion. (The visual effects look a bit clunky now, but may seem a little less crude on the more forgiving small screen. Nichetti's subsequent *Volere Volare* is less successful still, and features a similar plot gimmick involving a sound-effects man who becomes a cartoon character.)

NEXT STOP . . . *Volere Volare, Who Framed Roger Rabbit, Sherlock Jr.*

1989 93m/C *IT* Maurizio Nichetti, Cateria Sylos Labini, Claudio G. Fava, Renato Scarpa, Heidi Komarek; *D:* Maurizio Nichetti; *W:* Maurizio Nichetti; *C:* Mario Battistoni; *M:* Manuel De Sica. **VHS** *FXL, FCT*

IF...

Director Lindsay Anderson created enormous controversy in a year in which controversy was the norm with his 1968 epic about tradition, cruelty, and, finally, machine-gun-totin' rebellion at a British boys' school. Malcolm McDowell plays Mick Travis, the angry young man whose anti-establishment leanings contrast with the embalmed tradition of the British public education system portrayed here, and who eventually leads an armed assault on the school. Writer David Sherwin began working on the concept a decade earlier, after he saw *Rebel without a Cause*—this script was titled *The Crusaders* in its embryonic stage—but *If...*'s eventual release in 1968 couldn't have been timed better. With French students taking to the streets in Paris and American students being beaten by police at Chicago's Democratic National Convention, critics were able to write Sunday newspaper "think" pieces about whether *If...* was inspired by, or was inspiring, real-life events. The narrative—a series of progressively surrealistic "chapters" building up to the bloody climax—flows entertainingly and often ingeniously, demonstrating at every turn the school's brutal, often sadistic traditions until the students' assault on the school at the film's finish seems eminently sensible. But as there are almost no sympathetic characters in *If...*

MARCELLO MASTROIANNI
Legend of Italian Film

Italian actor Marcello Mastroianni was born on September 28, 1924 in Fontana Liri, a small town midway between Naples and Rome. He began acting as a child in the little theater in his church's basement in Rome. At university he studied architecture, but after graduating, he kept his hand in the theater, acting with an amateur group. By chance, they were joined for one production by Federico Fellini's wife, Giulietta Massina, who was already a famous actress. Her presence generated attention, including that of the manager of Italy's largest theater company, then directed by Luchino Visconti. Mastroianni was asked to join Visconti's company, where he spent the next ten years.

Mastroianni began his film career appearing in a series of romantic comedies with Sophia Loren, and with Visconti's *White Nights,* he became a star. He has appeared in films, such as Michelangelo Antonioni's *La Notte,* directed by other important figures in world cinema, and for *Divorce: Italian Style* he was nominated for a British Film Academy award. But Mastroianni will forever be remembered for his partnership with Fellini. He began playing Fellini's alter ego in 1960, when he starred in *La Dolce Vita,* and made the role more explicit in *8 1/2,* in which the actor appeared as a beleaguered director. He literally revisited the latter role in 1987 in Fellini's autobiographical *Intervista,* in which Mastroianni played himself. Mastroianni died December 19, 1996, but not before completing over 120 films. He worked well into his seventies. Director Anna Maria Tato filmed a series of interviews with Mastroianni that was released in 1997 as *Marcello Mastroianni, I Remember.*

Mastroianni was married for more than forty years to the former actress Flora Carabella, with whom he has a daughter. Famed for his appreciation of women, he has been romantically linked with many of his leading ladies, including Faye Dunaway, said to be the love of his life, and Catherine Deneuve, with whom he had a ten-year affair as well as a daughter, actress Chiara.

(McDowell is likable by default), you just can't get worked up by it like you can with agit-prop classics like *The Battleship Potemkin* or even *Easy Rider.* That's probably why *If...* was never a smash in the States, though the initial "X" rating didn't help (there may also have been just too many scenes set in *school* for student audiences to comfortably plunk their money down). Critics debated the significance of *If...*'s switching back and forth between black-and-white and color, but years later Anderson said he simply ran out of money one day and had to shoot whatever was left in less expensive black-and-white. Palme d'Or, Cannes Film Festival.

NEXT STOP . . . *Zero for Conduct, O Lucky Man!, Britannia Hospital*

1969 (R) 111m/C *GB* Malcolm McDowell, David Wood, Christine Noonan, Richard Warwick, Robert Swann, Arthur Lowe, Mona Washbourne, Graham Crowden, Hugh Thomas, Guy Rose, Peter Jeffrey, Geoffrey Chater, Mary MacLeod, Anthony Nicholls, Ben Aris, Charles Lloyd Pack, Rupert Webster, Brian Pettifer, Sean Bury, Michael Cadman; *D:* Lindsay Anderson; *W:* David Sherwin; *C:* Miroslav Ondricek; *M:* Marc Wilkinson. Cannes Film Festival '69: Best Film. **VHS, LV** *PAR*

IKIRU
To Live
Doomed
Living

Describing *Ikiru* to friends who haven't seen it often provokes a polite but unenthusiastic response. When they learn that it's about a aging bureaucrat who's been diagnosed with terminal cancer, they may understandably think that, well, it may indeed be a classic and sure, it might actually be good ... but why should they put themselves through it? All I can say to that is that there probably hasn't been a day of my life since seeing *Ikiru* (nearly 30 years ago) that I haven't been reminded of how it has become a companion to me—an indispensable part of my experience. Mr. Watanabe (Takashi Shimura), the everyman who is the hero of *Ikiru* (*To Live*), sits behind his stack of ever-growing papers at his desk in a city office, as he has each workday for a quarter-century, waiting out his time. His wife died years ago and his child is no longer close to him—he has only his meaningless, ineffectual job, and perhaps six more months in which to contemplate what his life has been and now has become. In the hands of Akira Kurosawa, this seeming recipe for a maudlin movie-of-the-week is transformed into a thrilling adventure—an interior journey by an ordinary man that is free of unearned sentiment or false gloss. Kurosawa's unflinching vision of a man with no excuses left, searching for a way to make a mark on his bleak universe—to find *some* meaning to his life before he vanishes without a trace—is one of the cinema's noblest, most humane pinnacles. With one wrenching but deeply reassuring image of an old man on a swing, quietly pulling something from deep within him for the first and last time, Kurosawa—while refusing to tie all the senseless strands of our lives into a neat bow—has advanced humankind's knowledge of itself, and justified one of its arts.

NEXT STOP . . . *The Magnificent Ambersons, Rashomon, A Matter of Life and Death (Stairway to Heaven)*

1952 134m/B *JP* Takashi Shimura, Nobuo Kaneko, Kyoko Seki, Miki Odagari, Yunosuke Ito; *D:* Akira Kurosawa; *W:* Akira Kurosawa, Shinobu Hashimoto, Hideo Oguni; *C:* Asakazu Nakai; *M:* Fumio Hayasaka. **VHS, LV** *HMV, CRC, FCT*

IL BELL'ANTONIO
Handsome Antonio

One of the high points in the great career of the irreplaceable Marcello Mastroianni was his immensely poignant portrayal of Antonio Magnano, a man who decides to stop bedding down all the "easy" women of the lower classes who have taken up so much of his life and, instead, finally embraces the sanctity of the Catholic church's teachings by marrying a well-bred, "pure," religious girl (Claudia Cardinale). With her, and for the first time in his life, Antonio is impotent. This is not, however, another of the many broad social comedies (many of them wonderful) that Italy produced in the 1960s; *Il Bell'Antonio* is instead a delicate and razor-sharp illustration of one man's inability to reconcile that age-old dichotomy—the good, publicly proclaimed, sacred love that the church teaches, versus the secret, "profane" love that only "bad" girls enjoy. It's like the response of Woody Allen when he was asked if sex was dirty. "Yes, if you're doing it right," he replied. (To bastardize Groucho Marx, while Antonio is willing to be a member of the holy matrimony club, his member isn't.) The screenplay by Pier Paolo Pasolini and Gino Vissentini refuses to ridicule Antonio. His anguish is treated with respect and intelligence, for it is the very real hypocrisy and cultural/religious need to compartmentalize that is under the microscope here. But thanks to Mastroianni, the issues always assume human proportions. In the recent, authorized, enormously engaging screen biography of Mastroianni titled *I Remember,* the actor speaks with fondness and pride of his heartbreaking and revelatory performance in this film. He was justified in that pride. Marcello will be missed.

NEXT STOP . . . *Big Deal on Madonna Street, Divorce—Italian Style, Marcello Mastroianni: I Remember*

1960 115m/C *IT* Marcello Mastroianni, Claudia Cardinale, Pierre Brasseur, Tomas Milian, Rina Morelli; *D:* Mauro Bolognini; *W:* Pier Paolo Pasolini, Gino Vissentini; *C:* Armando Nannuzzi; *M:* Piero Piccioni. **VHS** *KIV, FCT*

ILLUMINATION
Illuminacja

Krzysztof Zanussi was one of the most interesting directors of the Polish film renaissance of the 1960s and 1970s. Many of his films centered around earnest, well-meaning intellectuals who were attempting to use their science or their art to clarify some of the emotional mysteries of their lives. *Illumination*, Zanussi's fourth film, deals with the intellectual dilemmas of a young physicist (Stanislaw Latallo) in his 20s, spanning the period until he turns 30. The mysteries of love and death, sex and money, fatherhood and freedom—all of these are enormously confusing and demanding of his time and attention. Can't mathematics and physics provide the answers to some of the seemingly random patterns of life? And what of religion, which never held much sway over his life? So many of his friends are experimenting with mind-altering drugs; can they be the source of the enlightenment—or illumination—he's looking for? As Zanussi's quietly adventurous hero explores the limits of the answers science can provide, his curiosity reminds us of questions we may simply have stopped asking long ago. This is a stimulating, witty, and thought-provoking work.

NEXT STOP . . . *Contract, The Constant Factor, Camouflage*

1973 91m/C *PL* Stanislaw Latallo, Monika Denisiewicz-Olbrzychska, Malgorzata Pritulak, Edward Zebrowski; *D:* Krzysztof Zanussi; *W:* Krzysztof Zanussi; *C:* Edward Klosinski; *M:* Wojciech Kilar. **VHS** *FCT*

I'M ALL RIGHT, JACK

During the 1950s, Peter Sellers appeared in a number of modestly budgeted British comedies of varying quality and staying power.

The one constant in all of the films was Sellers, who didn't simply seem to be a different *character* each time, he seemed to be a different *actor*. In John and Roy Boulting's gloriously funny 1959 *I'm All Right, Jack*, Sellers plays the Hitler-mustached factory union leader Mr. Kite, whose self-serving blather about his union "brothers" fails to conceal the bullying, greedy little tyrant lurking underneath his brush cut. Management comes off no better, of course, and the final moments of the movie—in which both labor and management appear on a TV show to discuss their differences and end up trampling each other to snatch up a pile of loose pound notes—perfectly sums up the movie's utterly refreshing cynicism. Sellers is miraculous in this movie—he's always able to show us Kite's thoughts as if they were written on his forehead, yet never for a second gives up his comic timing to do it. It's a smart, bitter, hilarious little classic. With Terry-Thomas, Ian Carmichael, Richard Attenborough, and Margaret Rutherford. Based on Alan Hackney's novel *Private Life*. (Film editor Anthony Harvey went on to fame as a director, with credits including *The Lion in Winter*.)

NEXT STOP . . . *The Ladykillers, The Wrong Arm of the Law, Lolita*

1959 101m/B Peter Sellers, Ian Carmichael, Terry-Thomas, Victor Maddern; *D:* John Boulting. British Academy Awards '59: Best Actor (Sellers), Best Screenplay. **VHS** *FCT*

IN A YEAR OF 13 MOONS
In a Year with 13 Moons
In einem Jahr mit 13 Monden

If you've ever felt rejected, victimized, or just plain misunderstood, take a look at Rainer Werner Fassbinder's *In a Year of 13 Moons* and you'll probably decide you're not so bad off after all. Volker Spengler gives a legendary performance as Elvira Weishapt, who started life as Erwin but remedied all that with a sex-change operation. Problem is, the guy Erwin became Elvira for no longer loves him (or her), and now Erwin's stuck as Elvira and regrets it. Constantly teetering on the edge of self-parody, this is a tragedy so funny you can't cry, and a comedy so surprisingly touching you find yourself unable to shrug it off with a laugh. *The New York Times'* Vincent Canby wrote that "the film's redeeming feature is genius," which may well be true, but Volker Spengler's awesomely theatrical, operatic performance is hardly chopped liver. This is one Fassbinder that you simply can't take your eyes off of, even when you *really* want to.

NEXT STOP . . . *The Bitter Tears of Petra von Kant, Fox and His Friends, Ali: Fear Eats the Soul*

1978 119m/C *GE* Volker Spengler, Ingrid Caven, Gottfried John, Elisabeth Trissenaar, Eva Mattes, Gunther Kaufman; *D:* Rainer Werner Fassbinder; *W:* Rainer Werner Fassbinder; *C:* Rainer Werner Fassbinder; *M:* Peer Raben. **VHS** *NYF*

IN FOR TREATMENT

It's tempting to blame the obscurity of this superb little picture on insensitive movie distributors or unadventurous audiences, but really, the movie did play theatres and it did get seen by a few people. The fact is that it's a Dutch movie with an unknown cast about a man (Helmert Woudenberg) who checks into a hospital for tests and discovers he's dying of cancer. A miracle cure does not happen. Nor does the hospital do right by him; his care is inefficient and lackadaisical, particularly after his unfavorable diagnosis is revealed. Where on Earth will this movie pack them in? *In for Treatment* is a movie about loneliness, about rising to the occasion, about the priceless value of simple, unexpected kindnesses. And it is about dying. It is also wonderful. Should the opportunity ever arise, don't avoid seeing this film by using the "I'm sure it's good but I just don't need to see that kind of thing right now" excuse. If you don't need to see it now, can you name a better time? Produced and performed by the Werkteater Collective.

NEXT STOP . . . *Near Death* (1988), Frederick Wiseman), *On the Bridge* (1992, Frank Perry)

1982 92m/C *NL* Helmut Woudenberg, Frank Groothof, Hans Man Int Veld; *D:* Eric Van Zuylen, Marja Kok. **VHS** *NO*

IN THE REALM OF THE SENSES
Ai No Corrida

Japan's Nagisa Oshima based his 1976 film on an actual murder case that took place in Japan in 1936. A woman had strangled her lover to death during intercourse, after which she cut off his penis and carried it around with her until the police arrested her. (It *had* to be love; after all, Lorena Bobbitt simply tossed her husband John's freshly severed penis out of the car window.) The actual case was a sensation, and Oshima's film version was as well. The graphic sexuality depicted in the film, and the dangerous practice of heightening excitement through asphyxiation, were absolutely essential elements in demonstrating how and why the murder happened; still, Oshima had such a controversial movie on his hands that the previously obscure filmmaker—whose serious, fascinating works such as *Boy* and *Death by Hanging* had been shown primarily only at film festivals outside of Japan—suddenly found himself at the center of a publicity-generating censorship battle. *In the Realm of the Senses* isn't terrible by any stretch, but its high-toned, painterly, coffee-table-book style does suggest art house porn gussied up just enough to be called "erotica." The couple's desperate, nearly non-stop couplings begin to provoke titters after a while, although Oshima understands that there's a vein of humor inherent in the material, and he lets it break through on occasion. (In the realm of special effects, however, it must be noted that the man's post-surgical member still seems semi-erect; a neat trick considering it was still decades before Viagra.) The film was widely suppressed, and in fact U.S. Customs prevented its public showing at the 1976 New York Film Festival (the press screening went on as scheduled, I'm happy to report). There were still censorship problems, even after it won American distribution. In Detroit, for example, those waiting in line to see it on its scheduled opening day found it was replaced by *Rocky*. Not such a strange substitute, since Rocky was another guy who went the distance.

Plantation owner Elaine (Catherine Denevue) discusses political matters in *Indochine*.

NEXT STOP . . . *Last Tango in Paris, Damage, The Woman Next Door*

1976 (NC-17) 105m/C *JP FR* Tatsuya Fuji, Eiko Matsuda, Aio Nakajima, Meika Seri; *D:* Nagisa Oshima; *W:* Nagisa Oshima; *C:* Hideo Ito; *M:* Minoru Miki. **VHS** *FXL, CVC*

IN THE WHITE CITY
Dans la Ville Blanche

Swiss director Alain Tanner directed this absorbing and visually intoxicating dream of a movie about a sailor (Bruno Ganz of *Wings of Desire*) who jumps ship in Lisbon, where he blends into the hallucinatory landscapes and alleyways of the hauntingly beautiful "white city." Ganz becomes sexually involved with a waitress, loses most of his money, and takes 8mm home movies of his new surroundings to send home to his wife (those movies taken by Ganz—which we see—are contrasted eerily with the "real" images that constitute the film itself). What's remarkable here is the tight grip that Tanner maintains on his simple story, an oft-told tale that's tough to do on film because most of the "action" is happening in the protagonist's head. Nevertheless, the film has the structure and feel of an adventure story, and you can't really take your eyes off it. Much of the film's success is due to the beguiling, intuitive performance of Bruno Ganz; but Tanner also pulls off something else exciting: He and his cinematographer have found a languid cinematic equivalent for the feeling of actually *being* a stranger in a strange land—a cosmic tourist, in a sense—and the textures, the heat, and the labyrinthine streets of Lisbon seem to surround us in a way that's eerily transporting, as well as liberating.

NEXT STOP . . . *Messidor, The Sheltering Sky, Kings of the Road*

1983 108m/C *PT SI* Bruno Ganz, Teresa Madruga, Julia Vonderlinn, Jose Carvalho; *D:* Alain Tanner; *W:* Alain Tanner; *C:* Acacio De Almeida; *M:* Jean-Luc Barbier. **VHS** *NYΓ*

Awards '93: Best Foreign Film; National Board of Review Awards '92: Best Foreign Film; Nominations: Academy Awards '92: Best Actress (Deneuve); British Academy Awards '93: Best Foreign Film. **VHS, LV, 8mm, Letterbox, Closed Caption** *COL, FCT, BTV*

INDOCHINE ✓

Vietnam lite. The proud and beautiful Eliane (Catherine Deneuve) is the owner of a rubber plantation in French Indochina in the 1930s. She lives there with her father (symbol of the old world) and her adopted Indochinese daughter Camille (symbol of the new world). After mom has a brief fling with the handsome young French naval officer Jean-Baptiste (Vincent Perez), he and Camille realize that they're in love, and spend the next few hours trying to reunite after he's stationed on a faraway island. The evil of colonialist rule eventually becomes apparent to Jean-Baptiste, and his resistance of the oppressive system results in his death. Not long after, Camille becomes a dedicated Communist freedom fighter, giving the child she had with Jean-Baptiste to her still-proud, still-beautiful mother, who will raise the boy (symbol of the future world) in France. There was probably a way to make a low, juicy entertainment out of this kind of soap opera, but director Régis Wargnier insists on presenting it with a completely straight face as highbrow art, it as if it were a grand, operatic statement about the birth of a revolutionary movement. (It almost looks as if musical numbers had been removed at the last minute.) Deneuve's great to look at, and so is the cinematography, but the whole thing would have seemed more at home—and probably more affecting—as a Lifetime Channel made-for-TV two-parter starring Lisa Hartman.

NEXT STOP . . . *The Scent of Green Papaya, Ramparts of Clay, Ceddo*

1992 (PG-13) 155m/C *FR* Catherine Deneuve, Linh Dan Pham, Vincent Perez, Jean Yanne, Dominique Blanc, Henri Marteau, Carlo Brandt, Gerard Lartigau; *D:* Regis Wargnier; *W:* Erik Orsenna, Louis Gardel, Catherine Cohen, Regis Wargnier; *C:* Francois Catonne; *M:* Patrick Doyle. Academy Awards '92: Best Foreign Film; Cesar Awards '93: Best Actress (Deneuve), Best Art Direction/Set Decoration, Best Cinematography, Best Sound, Best Supporting Actress (Blanc); Golden Globe

THE INNOCENT
L'Innocente
The Intruder

Director Luchino Visconti's final film is a satisfyingly rich, 19th-century drama about a spoiled, hypocritical aristocrat (Giancarlo Giannini) who's sexually bored by his seemingly meek wife (Laura Antonelli). He takes up with a beautiful countess (Jennifer O'Neill) who becomes a pleasant enough distraction for him, until he learns that his "timid" wife is having a furiously passionate affair with another man. Giannini's refusal to acknowledge his double standard, together with his sudden "feelings of love," for his wife, discovered only when she's no longer his alone, provides a foundation of deeply ironic comedy for this stately and elegantly designed and paced melodrama. Antonelli had been appearing at the time in a series of slightly risqué sex comedies that were popular in the U.S., and the strength of her performance here may well have surprised some critics who hadn't taken her seriously until then. Giannini is superb as well, giving a finely graded performance that is the precise opposite of his manic flailing and mugging when acting under the direction of Lina Wertmüller. *The Innocent* is photographed in widescreen format with deeply saturated colors by Ruggero Mastroianni; try to find a letterboxed version.

NEXT STOP . . . *Senso, The Leopard, The Age of Innocence*

1976 (R) 125m/C *IT* Laura Antonelli, Jennifer O'Neill, Giancarlo Giannini, Didier Haudepin, Marc Porel; *D:* Luchino Visconti; *W:* Luchino Visconti, Suso Cecchi D'Amico; *C:* Pasquale De Santis. **VHS** *CVC, FCT, VES*

INSIGNIFICANCE

Better than it sounds. Terry Johnson's screenplay (based on his play) is a kind of compressed *Ragtime,* in which a number of his-

> "Turns out that normal people are all the same."
>
> —Lai (Tony Leung) in *Happy Together.*

laugh from the audience. Curtis plays McCarthy as if he'd been cross-bred with Roy Cohn; it's a neat bit of shorthand, and it works fine. Emil is a gentle wonder; you fully understand his attraction to Marilyn, and you hope down in your heart of hearts that the real Einstein was *exactly* like him.

NEXT STOP . . . *Don't Look Now, The Man Who Fell to Earth, Time After Time* (1979)

1985 110m/C *GB* Gary Busey, Tony Curtis, Theresa Russell, Michael Emil, Will Sampson; *D:* Nicolas Roeg; *W:* Terry Johnson; *C:* Peter Hannan; *M:* Hans Zimmer. **VHS, LV** *ORI, WAR*

INSOMNIA

A Swedish homicide cop (Stellan Skårsgard of *Breaking the Waves* and *Good Will Hunting*) is sent to Norway to investigate what appears to be the sexually motivated murder of a teenage girl. But the 24-hour daylight makes sleep impossible for the detective, and soon a disturbing, ominous and previously repressed side of the already tense and anxiety-plagued investigator begins to surface. *Insomnia* is an unnerving and creepy detective thriller that is that rare thing in the genre: original. Director Erik Skjoldbjaerg looks to be a serious student of Hitchcock's, and it's the psychology of the Master's films that interests him most, not merely "technique." This clever little picture will stay with you, and might even keep you awake.

NEXT STOP . . . *The Vanishing* (1988), *Angel Heart, Out of the Past*

1997 97m/C Stellan Skarsgard, Sverre Anker Ousdal, Maria Bonnevie, Bjorn Floberg, Gisken Armand, Kristian Figenschow, Thor Michael Aamodt, Bjorn Moan, Marianne O. Ulrichsen, Frode Rasmussen, Maria Mathiesen, Guri Johnson; *D:* Erik Skjoldbjaerg; *W:* Nikolaj Frobenius; *C:* Erling Thurmann-Andersen; *M:* Geir Jenssen. *NYR*

INTERVISTA
Federico Fellini's Intervista

There's no point in briefly criticizing or, God forbid, analyzing Federico Fellini's *Intervista,* because that's something each of us

Orson Welles looks appropriately grim in Rene Clement's WWII drama *Is Paris Burning?*

torical figures cross paths—and more—on one 1954 summer night. Marilyn Monroe (Theresa Russell) is the warm and life-giving sun around whom Joe DiMaggio (Gary Busey), Joe McCarthy (Tony Curtis), and Albert Einstein (Michael Emil) find themselves in orbit, all within the universe of a single New York hotel room (the celebs are clearly the aforementioned persons, though the film never uses their names). What could easily have been a slamming door, French style farce instead turns into a gently charming, tantalizing game of what if, with insights and agendas blending into satisfying, civilized, and ultimately liberating collision of ideas. The too-often underrated Theresa Russell does a glorious job with Marilyn; a lesser director than Nicolas Roeg might have urged Russell to camp her up mercilessly, but instead Marilyn's intuitive wit and intelligence aren't shown to be incongruous characteristics in order to get a startled, easy

will do on a very personal level, based on our own feelings about this legendary artist. The maestro's second-from-final film (his *Voices of the Moon* has yet to receive American release) is designed as a "mockumentary" made by a Japanese TV crew about the life of filmmaker Federico Fellini. In *Intervista,* the character of Fellini (he plays himself) is supposed to be preparing an adaptation of Kafka, which makes perfect sense amid the strange goings-on. Set at Rome's Cinecittà Studios, where Fellini shot many of his greatest works, the studio's hallways become corridors of memory for both the director and the viewer, as familiar figures like Anita Ekberg and Marcello Mastroianni drop in for brief appearances, watching along with us some indelible, wrenchingly moving film clips from the past—they're snippets from the dreams that Fellini shared not only with his actors, but with the entire world. *Intervista* isn't much of a movie in the conventional sense, but as a glimpse of a great artist free-associating messily but sincerely through the passions of a lifetime, it's an offer few film lovers will be able to refuse.

NEXT STOP . . . *La Dolce Vita, 8 1/2, Ginger & Fred*

1987 108m/C *IT* Marcello Mastroianni, Anita Ekberg, Sergio Rubini, Lara Wendell, Antonio Cantafora, Antonella Ponziani, Maurizio Mein, Paola Liguori, Nadia Ottaviani, Federico Fellini; **D:** Federico Fellini; **W:** Federico Fellini, Gianfranco Angelucci; **C:** Tonino Delli Colli; **M:** Nicola Piovani. **VHS** *TRI*

IS PARIS BURNING?
Paris Brule-t-il?

What a mess. This international super-production was designed to dramatize the liberation of Paris from the Nazis, and to detail the events that halted the German plan to burn the city to the ground before the Allies reached it. In the "style" of *The Longest Day,* an international cast of stars was assembled to impersonate actual historical figures as well as fictional composites. No characters are developed; instead, the filmmakers simply drop Orson Welles or Glen Ford or Jean-Paul Belmondo or Kirk Douglas into a scene, and then these actors proceed to speak their colorless, purely informational dialogue haltingly—an attempt, I suppose, to infuse their lines with some significance, or at least a little tension. It doesn't work. Amazingly, this script was written by Francis Ford Coppola and Gore Vidal, but I have a feeling that more than a little of it mutated in the transition from page to premiere. The director, René Clément, had years before made one of the greatest of all films on the subject of war, *Forbidden Games.* But here he's directing traffic, and it's torturously slow, bumper-to-bumper Parisian traffic at that. This movie isn't just a dinosaur stylistically; it was also one of the last films to assume that the vast majority of the French population was in the Resistance; four years later, Marcel Ophuls's *The Sorrow and the Pity* would shatter that illusion forever. *Is Paris Burning?*'s catchy score is by Maurice Jarre; we get to hear way too much of it.

NEXT STOP . . . *The Sorrow and the Pity, Lacombe Lucien, The Accompanist*

1966 173m/C *FR* Jean-Paul Belmondo, Charles Boyer, Leslie Caron, Jean-Pierre Cassel, George Chakiris, Claude Dauphin, Alain Delon, Kirk Douglas, Glenn Ford, Gert Frobe, Daniel Gelin, E.G. Marshall, Yves Montand, Anthony Perkins, Claude Rich, Simone Signoret, Robert Stack, Jean-Louis Trintignant, Pierre Vaneck, Orson Welles, Bruno Cremer, Suzy Delair, Michael Lonsdale; **D:** Rene Clement; **W:** Gore Vidal, Francis Ford Coppola; **C:** Marcel Grignon; **M:** Maurice Jarre. Nominations: Academy Awards '66: Best Art Direction/Set Decoration (B & W), Best Black and White Cinematography. **VHS, Closed Caption** *PAR, FCT*

IVAN THE TERRIBLE, PART 1
Ivan Groznyi

Soviet filmmaker Sergei Eisenstein's brilliant, two-part historical epic *Ivan the Terrible* was filmed between 1944 and 1946. Though it was conceived of and written as a two-part film, what now exists as *Ivan the Terrible, Part 2* is really just the first portion of Eisenstein's envisioned second half of the story; as the production grew in scope, he intended to turn the remainder of the script into a third and final film. He never got the chance. Production was halted by authorities after their horrified reaction to the completed portion of *Part 2,* which was promptly banned and went unseen for over 13 years. This was a blow that was especially puzzling to the great director, since *Part 1* of *Ivan*—which had already been released separately—was not only a success, it won Eisenstein the coveted Order of Lenin. Then again, *Part 1* didn't give us an ostensibly heroic *tsar* who was beginning to show distinctly paranoid and homicidal tendencies; *Part 2* did. *Ivan the Terrible* is not what one would call a "personality driven" epic; it paints monumental historical events on a monumental canvas, and its considerable emotional power results from something akin to the wonder of geometry. Eisenstein wrote: "With Ivan we wished to convey a sense of majesty, and this led us to adopt majestic forms." The Ivan portrayed here had a majestic goal as well; he wanted to prevent the dissolution of Russia into smaller sovereign states run by profiteers. He gets the mandate to do just that at the end of *Part 1,* and by the end of *Part 2* Ivan and his secret police are knocking off whoever they have to accomplish his goal. Stalin wasn't pleased, and the fact that Eisenstein didn't anticipate that fact is a clear indicator of just how totally—and perhaps naively—he immersed himself in his art. It's also easy to see why this is a favorite film of *The Godfather* director Francis Ford Coppola, whose epic portrait of the corruption of Michael Corleone may have had its stylistic genesis here. (*Ivan's* influence reaches into surprising places; Peter Weller said that his movements as *RoboCop* were fully based on Nikolai Cherkassov's elegantly stylized performance as Ivan.) Music by Sergei Prokofiev. Portions of *Part 2* are in color.

NEXT STOP . . . *Alexander Nevsky, Lawrence of Arabia, The Godfather Parts I & II*

1944 96m/B *RU* Nikolai Cherkassov, Ludmila Tselikovskaya, Serafina Birman, Piotr Kadochnikev; **D:** Sergei Eisenstein; **W:** Sergei Eisenstein; **C:** Eduard Tisse; **M:** Sergei Prokofiev. **VHS, 8mm, Letterbox** *NOS, MRV, WST*

IVAN THE TERRIBLE, PART 2
Ivan the Terrible, Part 2:
The Boyars' Plot
Ivan Grozny 2

See *Ivan the Terrible, Part I.*

1946 84m/B *RU* Nikolai Cherkassov, Ludmila Tselikovskaya, Serafina Birman, Piotr Kadochnikev; **D:** Sergei Eisenstein; **W:** Sergei Eisenstein; **C:** Eduard Tisse, Andrei Moskvin; **M:** Sergei Prokofiev. **VHS, 8mm, Letterbox** *NOS, MRV, WST*

JACQUOT
Jacquot de Nantes

Filmmakers Jacques Demy and Agnès Varda had been married for nearly 30 years when Demy was diagnosed with an inoperable brain tumor. Their life together had been based on their mutual passion for the cinema, and it was only natural that Demy's last project should be a cinematic portrait of how the love for movies developed in him as a child growing up in Nantes. It wasn't, however, to be his project alone. Varda scripted and directed, based on the stories he told her of his childhood, and together—through his failing health—they shaped this eloquent and heartfelt love letter to a life in the movies, which would be simply titled *Jacquot de Nantes.* Reenactments of Demy's childhood—which included the Nazi occupation—take us up to the period of his young adulthood and his realization that movies are his destiny. Clips from some of Demy's most well-remembered films, including *The Umbrellas of Cherbourg, Lola,* and *Donkey Skin,* are used to enrich and widen the meaning of these childhood anecdotes, as are interview segments with the aging and ill director. Demy never lived to see the finished film, but he must have sensed what a personal and almost private memoir Varda was creating. A showman as well as an artist, however, Demy would have been proud that his wife invited all the moviegoers of the world to celebrate his life with her. (The title was shortened simply to *Jacquot* for American release.)

1991 (PG) 118m/C *FR* Philippe Maron, Edouard Joubeaud, Laurent Monnier, Brigitte de Villepoix, Daniel Dublet; **D:** Agnes Varda; **W:** Agnes Varda; **C:** Patrick Blossier; **M:** Joanne Bruzdowicz. **VHS** *COL*

JALSAGHAR
The Music Room

Biswambhar Roy (Chhabi Biswas) is a still-arrogant member of the declining aristocracy of Bengal in the 1920s. The proud patriarch of a once-wealthy family, Roy has spent the family fortune on self-indulgent, ruinously expensive concerts at his home; these expenses have fed his ego and sense of cultural refinement, but have also, through a terrible twist of fate, cost the lives of his wife and son. Roy's pride is such, however, that nothing can make him understand the mad consequences of his obsession with his own superiority. Nearly impoverished, sitting in his decaying mansion's music room, Roy spends his final days trying to show that he has more refined musical tastes than, and is culturally superior to, his wealthy, *nouveau riche* neighbor—he'll spend his last coins and his last breath to prove it. It's one thing to simply say "pride goes before a fall"; this is what it means. Satyajit Ray's *The Music Room* (*Jalsaghar*) springs to life fully formed as a great, cautionary fable illustrating the logical consequences of utterly unbridled pride. It's a chilling, brilliantly simple, darkly funny vision, and a masterpiece.

NEXT STOP . . . *Pather Panchali, Aparajito, The World of Apu*

1958 100m/B *IN* Chhabi Biswas, Padma Devi, Tulsi Lahnin, Pinaki Sen Gupta, Kali Sarkar; **D:** Satyajit Ray; **W:** Satyajit Ray; **C:** Subrata Mitra; **M:** Satyajit Ray. **VHS** *COL*

JAMÓN, JAMÓN
Ham Ham

Stop the presses! It's a movie about sex and food! OK, so it's not the first time. But writer/director Bigas Luna's 1992 Spanish comedy is so gleefully, joyously vulgar that it is a breakthrough of sorts; it allows a generation of refined art house attendees to guiltlessly let their hair down a bit even while learning about the class structure of modern Spain. Stefania Sandrelli is Conchita, a harridan of a mother who's dead set against her son José's possible marriage to Silvia, daughter of the town prostitute, Carmen. Conchita's solution is to find a hunk to take Silvia's mind—and body—off of her son. This she does, but Conchita finds him irresistible as well. And so it goes, with the pairings becoming ever more inclusive, and the sex becoming ever more energetic. The universe of *Jamón, Jamón* (literally "ham, ham," a tasty title that fully bridges the gap between food and sex when explained in the film), where it seems completely natural that the family business is manufacturing underwear, is such a surrealistic, self-contained, isolated rural universe that it's like being in a soft-core Dogpatch. Luna goes well past being offensive early on, never looks back, and wisely and successfully occupies himself with the serious business of being funny. With Anna Galiena, Jordi Molla, Javier Bardem, and the spectacular Penelope Cruz as Silvia. Silver Lion, Venice Film Festival.

NEXT STOP . . . *Like Water for Chocolate, The Story of Boys and Girls, Tampopo*

1993 95m/C *SP* Penelope Cruz, Anna Galiena, Javier Bardem, Stefania Sandrelli, Juan Diego, Jordi Molla; **D:** Bigas Luna; **W:** Bigas Luna, Cuca Canals; **C:** Jose Luis Alcaine; **M:** Nicola Piovani. **VHS, LV**

JAN SVANKMEJER'S FAUST
Faust

Admirers of Jan Svankmajer's short animated films should be aware that much of his modern adaptation of the Faust legend is actually live action, complete with real, photographed human beings. But don't be put off by that; *Faust* is as strange and disturbing a film as Svankmajer has ever made, and one of the most nightmarish movies to come out of Europe in years. There's a decidedly Kafka-like flavor here, as well as a touch of Lewis Carroll; the man who will be Faust (the late Petr

Cepek) exits a subway in Prague, and is handed a map that directs him to a bizarre theatrical setting. Needless to say, he goes. Once there he encounters a puppet/marionette gallery that begins to come to ominous life after he starts thumbing through a thoughtfully placed copy of Goethe's *Faust*. The puppets—acting out portions of the Faust story, and repeating the creepiest scenes over and over—are operated by hand, by string, and by animation, and all with the shocking and unexpected logic of a dream. The puppets and marionettes were carved by Svankmajer, and are as integral to his vision as the filmmaking process itself. If *Faust* isn't completely satisfying, it's difficult to imagine how anything this personal could be; after all, nightmares are not written by committee (at least not yet), and do tend toward asymmetry.

NEXT STOP . . . *Faust* (1926), *Alice* (Svankmajer, 1988), *Conspirators of Pleasure*

1994 87m/C *CZ GB* **D:** Jan Svankmajer, Ernst Gossner; **W:** Jan Svankmajer; **C:** Svatopluk Maly. **VHS** *KIV*

JEAN DE FLORETTE

French author and filmmaker Marcel Pagnol made the first version of *Manon des Sources* (*Manon of the Spring*) in 1952, following which he expanded the same story into a two-part novel called *The Water of the Hills*. This was the source that director Claude Berri and co-screenwriter Gérard Brach drew from when conceiving their 1986 epic two-part screen version of Pagnol's tale, ultimately released as *Jean de Florette* and *Manon of the Spring*. This first part of the story, set in the 1920s, is a stately, novelistic portrait of human greed and suffering. Gérard Depardieu is Jean de Florette, the hunchbacked farmer who, together with his wife and small child, Manon, are trying to make a go of it on their newly inherited farmland despite the ravages of drought. What Jean doesn't know is that his land sits on a natural spring that would give him all the irrigation he needs, if only his viciously greedy old neighbor hadn't plugged up the spring in hopes of driving Jean away and getting the farm for himself. That neighbor and his dim nephew (Yves Montand and Daniel Auteuil) are the villains of this piece; they're as despicable as movie villains get, and we sit in our seats hoping quietly and ever more despairingly that their avarice and inhumanity will be punished somehow. But for now, it's not to be. This absorbing and physically magnificent production was a worldwide hit; the story's second part, *Manon of the Spring*, was released a few months later. Cinematographer Bruno Nuytten's exquisite widescreen images justify seeking out a letterboxed version of *Jean de Florette*.

NEXT STOP . . . *Manon of the Spring, The Fanny Trilogy, Harvest*

1987 (PG) 122m/C *FR* Gerard Depardieu, Yves Montand, Daniel Auteuil, Elisabeth Depardieu, Ernestine Mazurowna, Margarita Lozano, Armand Meffre; **D:** Claude Berri; **W:** Claude Berri, Gerard Brach; **C:** Bruno Nuytten; **M:** Jean-Claude Petit. British Academy Awards '87: Best Adapted Screenplay, Best Film, Best Supporting Actor (Auteuil); Cesar Awards '87: Best Actor (Auteuil), Best Supporting Actress (Beart). **VHS, LV** *ORI, IME, FCT*

JERUSALEM

Sweden's Bille August, director of the Cannes prize-winner *Pelle the Conqueror*, used a celebrated, fact-based novel by Nobel Prize-winning Swedish author Selma Lagerlof as the basis for this extraordinary story of hardship and disillusionment. Set in an impoverished rural Sweden at the turn of the century, *Jerusalem* is a portrait of a small community torn apart not just by hunger, but by a mysterious and compelling outsider who claims to have the answer to the community's prayers. This fire-and-brimstone fundamentalist preacher (Sven-Bertil Taube) assures all in the community that God has proclaimed an end to the world in the very near future. Their only hope, he tells them, is to leave behind all their

worldly possessions and accompany him on a pilgrimage to Jerusalem, where a Christian community organized by a mysterious woman from Chicago (Olympia Dukakis) will help them to build the New Jerusalem. Families, friends, and lovers are bitterly divided over what to do, and August follows the stories of both those who make the pilgrimage and those who stay behind. A rich, engrossing, thickly textured film about the nature of faith and about living with the choices that faith entails, *Jerusalem* is haunting and surprising; it's a large-scale movie with an extremely intimate focus, never forgetting the individual stories that comprise its epic design.

NEXT STOP . . . *Pelle the Conqueror, The Emigrants, The New Land*

1996 (PG-13) 166m/C *SW* Maria Bonnevie, Ulf Friberg, Lena Endre, Pernilla August, Olympia Dukakis, Max von Sydow, Sven-Bertil Taube; **D:** Bille August; **W:** Bille August; **C:** Jorgen Persson; **M:** Stefan Nilsson. **VHS** *FXL*

JESUS OF MONTREAL
Jesus de Montreal

A Montreal church has decided that its annual Passion Play is becoming overly rigid in its staging, and perhaps is becoming less relevant to its parishioners as a result. The church decides to appoint a young, talented actor named Daniel (Lothaire Bluteau) to rework and revamp the Passion Play, but the church gets more than it bargained for. Daniel casts himself as Jesus and puts a number of non-professionals from the fringes of society into pivotal roles; when his innovative staging becomes the subject of the church's wrath—and the media's latest feeding frenzy—Daniel is compelled to live the play offstage as well, taking a lonely but righteous stand for the principles in which he believes. Canadian director Denys Arcand has fashioned an intriguing spiritual parable about truth, hypocrisy, and faith in the modern age, as well as a wry look at the eternal dilemma of artists whose means of expression are influenced by the constraints of their society. The recent furor over a New York theatre's cancel-

ing—and then reinstating—the premiere of Terrence McNally's play *Corpus Christi* over advance reports that it contained a gay Jesus-like figure might well spark revived interest in Arcand's thoughtful, absorbing, and relevant film. If it doesn't, it should; forcing the audience to see a two-thousand-year-old story as relevant to their lives was the whole idea in the first place. Academy Award Nominee, Best Foreign Language Film.

NEXT STOP . . . *The Gospel According to St. Matthew, The Last Temptation of Christ, The Golden Coach*

1989 (R) 119m/C *FR CA* Gilles Pelletier, Lothaire Bluteau, Catherine Wilkening, Robert Lepage, Johanne-Marie Tremblay, Remy Girard, Marie-Christine Barrault; *D:* Denys Arcand; *W:* Denys Arcand; *C:* Guy Dufaux; *M:* Jean-Marie Benoit, Francois Dompierre, Yves Laferriere. Cannes Film Festival '89: Special Jury Prize; Genie Awards '90: Best Actor (Girard), Best Director (Arcand), Best Film, Best Supporting Actor (Girard); Nominations: Academy Awards '89: Best Foreign-Language Film. **VHS, LV** *ORI, FCT*

JOHNNY STECCHINO

I admit it; I'm a Benigni fan. There are a lot of us around, yet until now, the movies of Italy's premier cinematic comic, Roberto Benigni, have simply not caught on in the United States. There are lots of reasons; some of his comedy, as in every country, is based on a national sense of humor and simply doesn't travel well—inadequate subtitling doesn't help. Some members of the audience, as with a Jerry Lewis or a Jim Carrey, just won't find him funny. But I suspect that the biggest reason for Benigni's relatively unknown status in the U.S. is simply the huge core audience that never would dream of going to a foreign language movie at all. And Roberto Benigni not only speaks a "foreign" language, he seems to inhabit another planet. (His luck may change when America gets a look at his *Life Is Beautiful,* which snatched one of the top awards at the 1998 Cannes Film Festival and is poised to put Benigni in a different league.) *Johnny Stecchino* is a typical Benigni vehicle (though less inspired than *The Monster*), in which the skinny nebbish plays a sweet school bus driver who's mistaken for a ruthless mob boss. (Benigni, of course, plays both the bus driver and the gangster.) That's about it plotwise, but if you find yourself watching *Johnny Stecchino* (*Johnny Toothpick*), think of yourself as being in quicksand; you're going to come out way ahead if you don't struggle. Maybe you don't like big, noisy pratfalls, confused identities, or slamming doors, but if you let your guard down for 100 minutes or so, you just might find that your natural defenses are worn down enough so that you laugh in spite of yourself. When that happens—and there's a good chance that it will—Benigni's benign invasion of America will, with a little luck, be one step closer to reality.

NEXT STOP . . . *The Monster, Down by Law, The Nutty Professor* (1963)

1992 (R) 100m/C *IT* Roberto Benigni, Nicoletta Braschi, Paolo Bonacelli, Ignazio Pappalardo, Franco Volpi; *D:* Roberto Benigni; *W:* Roberto Benigni, Vincenzo Cerami; *C:* Giuseppe Lanci; *M:* Evan Lurie. **VHS, LV** *NLC, IME, FCT*

JONAH WHO WILL BE 25 IN THE YEAR 2000
Jonas—Qui Aura 25 Ans en l'An 2000

Movie directors are usually not great at summarizing their own films; that's why they make movies. But I have to hand it to Swiss director Alain Tanner, who once described his dazzlingly beguiling *Jonah Who Will Be 25 in the Year 2000* as "a dramatic tragicomedy as political science fiction." *Jonah* is set eight years after that pivotal and convulsive year for the world's young people, 1968. It's a series of stories—fragments of stories, really—concerning eight survivors of that traumatic time, all of whom now face the responsibilities of adulthood, and all of

whom have been altered to varying degrees by the 1960s. These characters are seen in splintered, kaleidoscopic terms, but Tanner manages to keep them distinctive, consistent, and memorable by use of ingenious cinematic shorthand that includes both fantasy sequences and densely distilled snippets of the characters' everyday lives. A schoolteacher (Jacques Denis) demonstrates the relationship between time and history by use of a giant sausage; a man (Jean-Luc Bideau) complains about the cost of cigarettes while chain smoking; a supermarket cashier (Miou-Miou) continues her '60s dream of revolutionary liberation by undercharging customers she deems worthy—often those she deems worthy are simply those she likes. Whether they're misguided, hypocritical, or simply clueless, their ideas and their passion become infectious, and their refusal to stop searching for answers becomes thrillingly reassuring. Tanner loves these characters and wishes them well as they lurch forward through their lives, and through ours. There was an era, not long ago, when filmmakers of Tanner's intelligence and curiosity were not uncommon. With luck, we'll have a new and restless crop of such filmmakers well before the year 2000.

NEXT STOP . . . *No Man's Land , Return of the Secaucus Seven, The Big Chill*

1976 110m/C *SI* Jean-Luc Bideau, Myriam Meziere, Miou-Miou, Jacques Denis, Rufus, Dominique Labourier, Roger Jendly, Miriam Boyer, Raymond Bussieres, Jonah; *D:* Alain Tanner; *W:* Alain Tanner; *C:* Renato Berta; *M:* Jean-Marie Senia. National Society of Film Critics Awards '76: Best Screenplay. **VHS** *NYF*

JOUR DE FETE
The Big Day
Holiday

In *The Silent Clowns,* his indispensable book about the golden era of silent comedy, Walter Kerr examines the phenomenal success of a few of the most famous figures from 1920s, including Buster Keaton, Charlie Chaplin, and Harry Langdon. But in examining their staying power, Kerr notes that

Langdon, major star that he was, was a phenomenon of his time. While films of Keaton and Chaplin can get the same laughs now as they did 70 years ago, Langdon's comedy was more contemporary than classic—the cultural context of his gags existed in a limited time span, and the window has closed. France's Jacques Tati, whose work was strongly influenced by those comics, may have quietly succumbed in the last couple of decades to a fate similar to Langdon's. His first feature, the 1949 *Jour de Fete,* develops a character Tati created earlier in a short film: François the Postman. A bicycle-riding civil servant in a small French village, François (Tati) sees a documentary film at a local carnival on the high-speed, automated wizardry of the United States Postal Service. The light flashes on in François's head, and he sets about designing increasingly bizarre, charmingly Rube Goldberg—esque ways to bring the little town's mail delivery into the modern age. The result is chaos, built on a series of intricate, interlocking visual gags that place the earnest but bumbling François at the mercy of his own, unnecessarily complex solutions to a problem that never existed; no one in town is in a hurry to get mail. (One wonders what Tati's reaction would have been—had he not died in 1982—to the now nearly common phenomenon we Americans call "going postal.") As in Tati's subsequent theatrical features (there were to be only four more), the world he envisions is an expansion of Chaplin's *Modern Times.* Tati warns us—through a strategy of slow, gradually escalating physical comedy—that the fast pace of modern life is a threat to humanity's more delicate sensibilities; furthermore, it's rude. The relative rarity of Tati retrospectives, and their sparse attendance when they do happen, may be bittersweet proof that his fears were well-founded. (Most video versions now contain the hand-colored sequences that Tati added in 1964.)

NEXT STOP . . . *Modern Times, Mon Oncle, Playtime*

1948 79m/B *FR* Jacques Tati, Guy Decomble, Paul Fankeur, Santa Relli; *D:* Jacques Tati; *W:* Henri Marquet, Jacques Tati; *C:* Jacques Mercanton; *M:* Jean Yatove. **VHS, LV** *VDM, CRC, NLC*

THE JOYLESS STREET
Street of Sorrow
Die Freudlosse Gasse

German director G.W. Pabst's famous silent film *The Joyless Street* created a sensation in 1925 because of its dramatized, vivid portrayal of Vienna's post—World War I economic collapse. The film tells multiple stories of the residents of a single despair-ridden street: a professor's daughter (Greta Garbo) does her best to get food for her starving family, nearly falling into the clutches of a procuress (Valeska Gert); another woman (Asta Nielsen) nearly descends to prostitution, but is rescued by a valiant American (Einar Hanson). *The Joyless Street* is relatively clumsy as drama; today it seems almost hopelessly cliched, though Garbo (her third film) and Nielsen manage extraordinary performances with their cardboard roles. What the film is really remarkable for is its deign, decor, and cinematography, which brought a haunting, expressionistic touch to the nightmarish reality of Vienna's ever-spiraling poverty and inflation.

NEXT STOP . . . *Pandora's Box, The Last Laugh, Dr. Mabuse*

1925 96m/B *GE* Greta Garbo, Werner Krauss, Asta Nielson, Jaro Furth, Loni Nest, Max Kohlhase, Silva Torf, Karl Ettlinger, Ilka Gruning, Agnes Esterhazy, Alexander Musky, Valeska Gert; *D:* G.W. Pabst; *W:* Willi Haas; *C:* Guido Seeber, Curt Oertel, Walter Robert Lach. **VHS, LV** *VYY, MRV, FST*

JU DOU

In 1920s China, the elderly owner of a textile factory buys a young, beautiful bride for himself, though he proves to be both impotent and abusive. In despair, she takes the young man who is the factory's only employee as her lover, and together they have the son the old man could not give her. The unforeseen yet inevitably violent twists and turns that follow are more reminiscent of James M. Cain than of any other Chinese films of its day, and this fact—together with *Ju Dou*'s steamy sex scenes—did not go unnoticed by government censors. Banned domestically but widely seen internationally, it became the breakthrough film for the great Chinese director Zhang Yimou, whose previous and equally extraordinary *Red Sorghum* had not been seen very widely in America (primarily at film festivals). *Ju Dou* was another matter, and after its successful New York Film Festival showings, it went on to play at art houses in every major American city, ultimately receiving (over Chinese authorities' objections) an Oscar nomination as Best Foreign Language Film of 1989. This was the second of the six remarkable films that Zhang would make with actress Gong Li; their partnership—both personally and professionally—was dissolved after the 1995 *Shanghai Triad*. (If you're looking at it on video, try to see *Ju Dou*—which features exceptional color cinematography—on a carefully adjusted, high-resolution TV, ideally on laserdisc or DVD.)

NEXT STOP . . . *Red Sorghum, Raise the Red Lantern, The Postman Always Rings Twice* (1946)

1990 (PG-13) 98m/C *CH* Gong Li, Li Bao-Tian, Li Wei, Zhang Yi, Zheng Jian; *D:* Zhang Yimou; *W:* Liu Heng; *C:* Gu Changwei, Yang Lun; *M:* Xia Ru-jin, Jiping Zhao. Nominations: Academy Awards '90: Best Foreign-Language Film. **VHS, LV** *ART, BTV*

THE JUDGE AND THE ASSASSIN
Le Juge et l'Assassin

In late 19th-century France, a sergeant (Michel Galabru) is discharged from the army as a result of his raging, violent episodes, which seem to alternate between anger and religious outbursts. After attempting to kill his wife, the sergeant is sent to an asylum, does a little time, is sent home over his own objections, and then commits a series of rapes and murders. From this point on, the sergeant falls under the care of a provincial judge (Philippe Noiret), whose interest in the killer and his crimes begins to border on the obsessive, and whose own precarious state of "normalcy" becomes more and more open to question. One of our most humane and probing directors, Bertrand Tavernier (*A Sunday in the Country, 'Round Midnight*) has fash-

ioned another of his fascinatingly open-ended portraits of the human condition, unflinchingly posing questions about the validity of our definitions of both justice and insanity. It's also a riveting, beautifully acted drama. With Isabelle Huppert, Jean-Claude Brialy, and Yves Robert.

NEXT STOP . . . *The Clockmaker, L.627, The Silence of the Lambs*

1975 130m/C *FR* Philippe Noiret, Michel Galabru, Isabelle Huppert, Jean-Claude Brialy, Yves Robert, Rene Faure; *D:* Bertrand Tavernier; *W:* Bertrand Tavernier, Jean Aurenche, Pierre Bost; *C:* Pierre William Glenn; *M:* Philippe Sarde. Cesar Awards '77: Best Writing, Best Score. **VHS, LV, Letterbox** *CVC, IME, TPV*

JUGGERNAUT

It sounds like something you'd want to avoid at all costs; a psycho has planted a number of bombs on a luxury ocean liner, and the legendary demolition expert sent to the scene sweats heavily while deciding whether to cut the blue wire or the red wire. As it happens, director Richard Lester's 1974 *Juggernaut* is probably one of the most enjoyable and breezy thrillers of this type ever made; when it took a dive at the boxoffice, it was probably because its distributor sold it as a disaster movie in the *Poseidon Adventure* mold. (Those who couldn't stomach another disaster movie stayed away, and those who *wanted* to see a disaster movie were disappointed. Now *that's* marketing.) Richard Harris plays the poor guy who has to figure out how to keep the 1,200 passengers from being blown to bits, while the portly, wonderfully spry Roy Kinnear is in charge of keeping the paying customers cheered up. *Juggernaut* followed a four-year hiatus for Lester, which he took after a series of ambitious movies that disappointed either commercially (*Petulia*), artistically (*How I Won the War*), or both (*The Bed-Sitting Room*). *Juggernaut* may have simply been conceived as an exercise to see what kind of condition his moviemaking muscles were in, but his energy and imagination and crackling juxtaposition of comedy and suspense make it one of Lester's most exhilarating rides. With

J

Anthony Hopkins, Omar Sharif, Ian Holm, Shirley Knight, and David Hemmings.

NEXT STOP . . . *Help!, Petulia, Cuba*

1974 (PG-13) 109m/C *GB* Richard Harris, Omar Sharif, David Hemmings, Anthony Hopkins, Shirley Knight, Ian Holm, Roy Kinnear, Freddie Jones; ***D:*** Richard Lester; ***W:*** Richard DeKoker; ***C:*** Gerry Fisher; ***M:*** Ken Thorne. **VHS** *MGM, FOX*

JULES AND JIM
Jules et Jim

For his third feature, François Truffaut selected an autobiographical novel by Henri-Pierre Roché about the complicated relationship between two men and the woman they both love. *Jules and Jim* opens just prior to the outbreak of World War I, presenting us with the friendship between the reserved German, Jules (Oskar Werner), and the extroverted Frenchman, Jim (Henri Serre). When they meet the blazing, irresistible Catherine (Jeanne Moreau), their lives become more complex yet remain joyous; following the two men's service—on different sides—in the war, their lives all take a decidedly darker, far more melancholy path. *Jules and Jim*, a movie that's absolutely alive, minute to minute, is a triumph of intuitive filmmaking by a director who proudly and wisely refuses to rationalize his characters' every move. The passion of these three is understood by the viewer; when that passion spawns painful consequences, and leads to comings and goings that might seem gratuitously capricious in a less accomplished movie, we stay with them because the movie's director has formed them *fully*. It's a breathtaking feeling to realize, at some early point into a movie, that you've placed your absolute trust in the director; you don't know where the adventure will lead, yet you go along, and without reservation. It's no different than what Jules, Jim, and Catherine experience in the film; their instincts and desires carry them along, so when we see that passion so diminished and deflated in the scenes following World War I (which include the rise of fascism), we not only mourn for them, but for ourselves. Each time *Jules and Jim* begins, we marvel again at its ability to carry us off into memories of our own youthful, enthusiastic passions. Each time we see it end, we grieve; not just for the friends lost on screen or for the lost joys of their youth, but for our own knowledge that all joys—whether friendship, love, cinema, or life—are bound to end.

NEXT STOP . . . *Shoot the Piano Player, The Soft Skin, Two English Girls*

1962 104m/B *FR* Jeanne Moreau, Oskar Werner, Henri Serre, Marie DuBois, Vanna Urbino; *D:* Francois Truffaut; *W:* Jean Gruault, Francois Truffaut; *C:* Raoul Coutard; *M:* Georges Delerue. **VHS, LV, Letterbox** *HMV, FOX*

JULIET OF THE SPIRITS

Giulietta Degli Spiriti

Fellini seemed to be so concerned with the fantastic images in his first color feature that he allowed most of his ideas to escape through the back door. *Juliet of the Spirits* is the story of a woman (Giulietta Masina) whose life is a disappointment on just about every level; her husband has forgotten their anniversary, and his philandering is a considerably larger problem. Her sex-obsessed, orgy-throwing neighbor (Sylva Koscina) can only offer diversions in which Juliet has no interest. Her response is to retreat into her daydreams, but the brightly colored, romantic, asexual fantasies that Fellini provides her with are long on design but short on longing. We want her to come to terms with her own identity, and for a good portion of the film it appears that she's headed in that direction; but as the set pieces and machinery of her elaborate unconscious stagings grow, her image of herself becomes even more diffuse. *Juliet of the Spirits* followed the director's brilliant *8 1/2*, in which he pre-

sented a famous director who was at a complete loss for ideas about his next project; all he had were grand sets, and didn't know what to do with them. Whether *8 1/2* became self-fulfilling prophecy, or was simply Fellini's way of breaking the news about his next movie to us gently, *Juliet of the Spirits* remains a richly colored, gift-wrapped package containing not much more than additional richly colored gift-wrapping.

NEXT STOP . . . *The White Sheik, Nights of Cabiria, Ginger & Fred*

1965 142m/C *IT* Giulietta Masina, Valentina Cortese, Sylva Koscina, Mario Pisu, Sandra Milo, Caterina Boratto, Valeska Gert; *D:* Federico Fellini; *W:* Federico Fellini, Tullio Pinelli, Ennio Flaiano, Brunello Rondi; *C:* Gianni Di Venanzo; *M:* Nino Rota. New York Film Critics Awards '65: Best Foreign Film; Nominations: Academy Awards '66: Best Art Direction/Set Decoration (Color), Best Costume Design (Color). **VHS, LV** *VYY, VDM, MRV*

KAGEMUSHA

The Shadow Warrior
The Double

When a 16th-century warlord is killed during a period of civil wars, the warlord's clan settles on the idea of replacing him with a double in order to prevent chaos and ruin. A petty thief is found who bears an astounding resemblance to the fallen leader, and he is groomed for the difficult job of fooling both the enemy and the warlord's own family. Akira Kurosawa's magnificent *Kagemusha* (*The Shadow Warrior*) marked a welcome return to form for the great director, who had completed only two relatively minor works in the previous decade. *Kagemusha* features spectacular battle sequences and the epic visual power that had been lacking in his films for so long; it's also an intensely engaging film on a human level. The thief at first envisions his situation as the opportunity to perform a huge con and live in luxury; later, as he becomes accustomed to his role and position, he assumes not only the trappings of a leader but the soul as well. The thief becomes the warrior, and is no longer playing a part; it is, in a sense, what great acting is about. It is also a brilliantly telescoped parable of what the responsibility of leadership

"You bring it on yourself, Ollie, you really do."

—Frank (Jason Flemyng) to Ollie (Sam Bould) about hitting him in *Hollow Reed*.

can bring out even in the most seemingly irresponsible, as Prince Hal pointed out to the devastated Falstaff. This Shakespearean dimension is not accidental; Kurosawa's next film would be a masterpiece based on Shakespeare's *King Lear: Ran*. *Kagemusha* features a stunning performance by Tatsuya Nakadai in the dual roles of the thief and the warlord. If the film has a major failing, it is the overbearing, sentimental musical score by Shinichiro Ikebe, who replaced the brilliant composer Masaru Sato after Sato crossed paths with the intractable director. Produced by Francis Ford Coppola and George Lucas.

NEXT STOP . . . *Generale Della Rovere, To Be or Not to Be* (1942), *Ran*

1980 (PG) 160m/C *JP* Tatsuya Nakadai, Tsutomu Yamazaki, Kenichi Hagiwara, Hideji Otaki; *D:* Akira Kurosawa; *W:* Akira Kurosawa, Masato Ide; *C:* Kazuo Miyagawa, Masaharu Ueda; *M:* Shinichiro Ikebe. British Academy Awards '80: Best Director (Kurosawa); Cannes Film Festival '80: Best Film; Cesar Awards '81: Best Foreign Film; Nominations: Academy Awards '80: Best Art Direction/Set Decoration, Best Foreign-Language Film. **VHS, LV, Letterbox** *FOX*

KAMERADSCHAFT
La Tragedie de la Mine
Comradeship

Based on an actual 1906 mine disaster, G.W. Pabst's noble *Kameradschaft* (*Comradeship*) is set on the German-French border shortly after World War I. An explosion traps French miners, and German workers come to their aid in an emotional demonstration of human kindness, brotherhood, and solidarity. *Kameradschaft* is a moving and affecting plea for peace, and a call for the healing of old wounds that the war had only deepened. The suspenseful and sometimes nerve-shattering dramatic structure is concealed just below the movie's surface, which has the immediacy and visual punch of a documentary. Pabst spices that surface up with startling images, such as the sight of a German rescuer in a gas mask causing an oxygen-starved French miner to flash back to the war; in an instant the Frenchman loses his grasp on reality, attacking his would-be savior. The film features no scored music (though an orchestra is heard within the film); the primary sounds are those of frightened men, rumbling machinery, and creaking support beams, threatening to collapse still further. *Kameradschaft* resonates in another way, of course, when we think of the nightmare in Europe that would follow the film's 1931 release. That doesn't diminish Pabst's achievement, and in fact it makes *Kameradschaft*'s poignant if unsuccessful plea for peace seem all the more noble in retrospect. (Hindsight, however, also brings out an irony that's worth mentioning here. Unlike other European artists and filmmakers who expatriated themselves at the time—Fritz Lang is perhaps the most notable example—Pabst, who had traveled and worked around Europe and the United States before the war, returned to Austria in 1940–41, for reasons of health he claimed, and continued his career under the Nazis.)

NEXT STOP . . . *Metropolis, All Quiet on the Western Front* (1930), *Ace in the Hole (The Big Carnival)*

1931 80m/B *GE* Ernst Busch, Alexander Granach, Fritz Kampers, Gustav Puttjer, Daniel Mendaille, Elizabeth Wenst; *D:* G.W. Pabst; *W:* Laszlo Wajda, Karl Otten, Peter Martin Lampel; *C:* Fritz Arno Wagner, Robert Barberske. **VHS** *MRV, IHF, NLC*

KANAL
They Loved Life

In September of 1944, while Nazis are advancing through Warsaw, a group of Polish partisans must retreat to the city's center by way of the sewers ("kanal"). During their ordeal, the characters' individual stories come into focus, giving a personal, human face to the horrors of war. *Kanal*'s subterranean, claustrophobic visual scheme is an ingenious metaphorical image for the impact of occupation, it's in this deep, pressurized desperate world that the protagonists' suppressed secrets, fears, and breaking points are revealed. This second film in Polish director Andrej Wajda's celebrated war trilogy followed his *A Generation,* and it would soon be followed by his widely acclaimed *Ashes and Diamonds*. Special Jury Prize, Cannes Film Festival.

NEXT STOP... *A Generation, Ashes and Diamonds, Underground*

1956 96m/B *PL* Teresa Izewska, Tadeusz Janczar, Vladek Sheybal, Emil Kariewicz, Wienczylaw Glinski; *D:* Andrzej Wajda; *W:* Jerzy Stefan Stawinski; *C:* Jerzy Lipman; *M:* Jan Krenz. Cannes Film Festival '57: Grand Jury Prize. **VHS** *ING, NLC, HMV*

KAOS
Chaos

The Taviani brothers—Paolo and Vittorio—created this vast mosaic consisting of four stories framed by a prologue and epilogue. The picture isn't well known here, probably because its length was daunting, and because movies comprised of short stories are rarely big at the boxoffice. The stories that the Tavianis tell here are all based on Pirandello tales, and are all set in Sicily. I've read review after respectful review of *Kaos*, most of which feel obliged to point out that the short stories are "uneven" in quality, and that some are better yarns than others. So what? *Kaos* is a transporting, magical recreation of folk legends as seen through the eyes of master storytellers, and if you should find one or two of these enchanting tales to be not quite as celestial, funny, or scary as the others, it still leaves you with an evening of entertainment difficult to match elsewhere. Many of us regret one aspect of adulthood above all others; the loss of that electric sensation of hearing a disturbing fairy tale for the first time, and not knowing how to react, other than with a mixture of fascination and fear. This is what the Tavianis have often brought to the movies, and in this film, in particular, their stories are best experienced just before being tucked in. (It's true that even the Tavianis thought that one of the stories should be removed from the American release version of *Kaos*, but the distributor didn't agree and left in all four. For my money, I wish there was a fifth.) This great looking movie was photographed by Giuseppe Lanci and features a sweeping, magical score by Nicola Piovani.

NEXT STOP... *Padre Padrone, The Night of the Shooting Stars, Fiorile*

1985 (R) 188m/C *IT* Margarita Lozano, Claudio Bigagli, Massimo Bonetti, Omero Antonutti, Enrica Maria Modugno, Ciccio Ingrassia, Franco Franchi, Biagio Barone, Salvatore Rossi, Franco Scaldati, Pasquale Spadola, Regina Bianchi; *D:* Paolo Taviani, Vittorio Taviani; *W:* Paolo Taviani, Vittorio Taviani; *C:* Giuseppe Lanci; *M:* Nicola Piovani. **VHS** *MGM, BTV*

KASPAR HAUSER

The circumstances behind the real Kaspar Hauser—a man who mysteriously appeared in a Nuremberg town square in 1828 without the ability to talk—have been the subject of speculation for more than a century. At the conclusion of Werner Herzog's *Every Man for Himself & God Against All*, also known as *The Mystery of Kaspar Hauser*, a functionary at Kaspar's autopsy notes something strange about the shape of one of Kaspar's organs. "At last we have an explanation for this strange man," he pronounces, and wanders off into the distance as the film fades out. Herzog's movie gave us a Kaspar who was a holy innocent, and as his ironic ending shows us, Herzog was less interested in the hard, scientific realities of Kaspar Hauser than in the spiritual substance of his legend. And now we have another Kaspar Hauser film, this one by German director Peter Sehr, and wouldn't you know it—it could have been made by that little man who triumphantly reaches his conclusions at the end of Herzog's film. This *Kaspar Hauser* is based on speculation as to who Kaspar may have actually been, and how his society might have used him for nefarious political purposes. Sehr concocts as good an explanation as any, but it's fiction, and it's hard to care if it's true or not (not that we'll ever know). Herzog's movie, as naive and soft-hearted as much of it is, is based on a far more universal truth—an emotional one—and it leaves this vast, handsomely photographed conspiracy theory in the dust.

NEXT STOP... *Every Man for Himself & God Against All, The Wild Child, E.T.: The Extra-Terrestrial*

1993 137m/C *GE* Andre Eisermann, Jeremy Clyde, Katharina Thalbach, Udo Samel, Uwe Ochsenknecht; *D:* Peter Sehr; *W:* Peter Sehr; *C:* Gernot Roll; *M:* Nikos Mamangakis. **VHS** *KIV*

Juana (Rossy de Palma) in a beauty moment in *Kika.*

KIKA

The problem with being a director who traffics in risky material is that when you fail, your failure will be that much more noticeable. This is the case with Pedro Almodóvar's 1993 *Kika,* a fog bound "satire" that sinks beneath the waves early on—and takes quite a while to actually hit bottom. The Kika of the title is a wacky makeup artist (Veronica Forque) who falls for the stepson of an up-to-no-good American writer (Peter Coyote). Into the mix comes Andrea Scarface (Victoria Abril), the host of a notorious tabloid TV show who wears S/M outfits and is never without her video camera. We know from all the signs that she's supposed to be a riot, but the comedy's stalled. With the next subplot, it stops dead. The retarded brother of Kika's maid Juana (the equine visaged Rossy de Palma of *Women on the Verge of a Nervous Breakdown*) knocks Juana out and proceeds

to rape the sleeping Kika. This is intended as the movie's big comic centerpiece; Kika thoroughly enjoys what's happening to her, and as the scene goes on and on, we can see that this mutually pleasurable rape is supposed to be disarming us and winning us over. The scene is extremely long because Almodóvar's trying to build an elaborate gag—making us laugh in a liberated way at what is the ultimate non-PC comic situation. The problem is, the scene *isn't* funny, it *isn't* liberating, and it *is* endless. It's a big, fat, miscalculation, and it stops cold what wasn't a funny film to begin with. The scene seems to have been filmed by Almodóvar's critics, as if to publicly reveal a deep misogynistic streak in the director. Yet Almodóvar's best movies show that his gay sensibility and an empathy with women are not mutually exclusive; on the contrary, *Women on the Verge, The Flower of My Secret,* and the recent *Live Flesh* feature some of the richest female characters in years. It's tempting but pointless to speculate on how that awful rape scene would—or wouldn't—play had *Kika* been a rousing comedy to that point. Better to move on to the director's more successful works and chalk this one up to the ever-lurking downside that comes with risk.

NEXT STOP . . . *What Have I Done to Deserve This?, Matador, The Flower of My Secret*

1994 115m/C *SP* Veronica Forque, Peter Coyote, Victoria Abril, Alex Casanovas, Rossy de Palma; *D:* Pedro Almodovar; *W:* Pedro Almodovar; *C:* Alfredo Mayo; *M:* Enrique Granados. **VHS** *THV*

THE KILLER
Die Xue Shuang Xiong

The ads read: "Guaranteed: Ten Thousand Bullets." And Hong Kong director John Woo is as good as his word. Hit man Jeffrey Chow (Chow Yun-Fat), better known on the streets as Mickey Mouse, feels responsible for accidentally blinding night club singer Jenny (Sally Yeh) while pulling a job. The demoralized Jeffrey decides to take on one last assignment to pay for surgery to restore Jenny's eyesight; the dedicated Detective Lee (Danny Lee), better known as Dumbo, develops a strange respect for the driven, secretive hit man, though he's bound by law to bring him to justice. "You're an unusual cop," says Mickey Mouse to Dumbo. "Well, you're an unusual killer," is his reply. If the plot sounds like a bonkers blend of *City Lights, La Bohème,* and *The Wild Bunch,* you're not far off. Yet the utter originality and stylistic power of John Woo's *The Killer* makes real comparisons of any kind impossible. It's a violent movie, all right, but Woo's violence is an expressionistic form of pure, unashamed melodrama, rooted in new urban mythology. (If *West Side Story* had been made by John Woo, my childhood would have been a lot more fun.) Chow's nobility is visible through his sneer. He's a great action star; sullen, deeply sentimental, unhesitatingly violent. He shoots with a gun in each hand, as do so many characters in Woo's movies—it's almost a symbol of his commitment. Mickey

Mouse and Dumbo are an endangered movie species; gallant, world-weary men of action who are capable of respecting each other, regardless of their being on opposite sides of the law. If you thought such sentiments went out with *Grand Illusion,* take a look at *The Killer.* Describing it as "gratuitously" violent seems itself gratuitous; violence—what it can do, what it can't do, its natural expressive power in the cinema—is the subject of the film. Funny, shocking, outrageous, and sweet, this is Woo's demented, glorious masterpiece.

NEXT STOP . . . *A Better Tomorrow, Hard-Boiled, Face/Off*

1990 (R) 110m/C *HK* Chow Yun-Fat, Sally Yeh, Danny Lee, Kenneth Tsang, Chu Kong; *D:* John Woo; *W:* John Woo; *C:* Wing-hang Wong, Peter Pau; *M:* Lowell Lo. **VHS, Letterbox** *FXL, BTV, FCT*

KIND HEARTS AND CORONETS

At the turn of the century, young Louis Mazzini (Dennis Price) is appalled at the injustice of his being *ninth* in line to inherit the dukedom that he believes should be rightfully his. Though there are complicated reasons for Louis's dilemma, he hits upon a simple solution; murder the eight who are in the line of inheritance before him. An even simpler—and more brilliant—solution was the one hit upon by the film's producer, Michael Balcon; casting Alec Guinness as all eight of the intended victims. Balcon and director Robert Hamer fashioned a darkly satirical assault on traditional British values, and British, American, and worldwide audiences ate it up. The biting, acidic wit is served up in a quick-witted and completely unsentimental screenplay that had considerable shock value in 1949, and it still packs a kick a half-century later. But it's the genius of Guinness's performance(s) in *Kind Hearts and Coronets* that elevates it to classic status. And for a generation that knows Guinness only as Obi-Wan Kenobi in *Star Wars,* his work here will be more than a delight—it will be a revelation. Based on Roy Horniman's 1907 novel *Israel Rank, Kind Hearts and Coronets* was one of the best of the many extraordinary British comedies produced under Michael Balcon's supervision at Ealing Studios. With Joan Greenwood, Valerie Hobson, and Hugh Griffith.

NEXT STOP . . . *The Lavender Hill Mob, The Ladykillers, A Sense of History* (1992, Mike Leigh, available in the anthology *Two Mikes Don't Make a Wright*)

1949 104m/B *GB* Alec Guinness, Dennis Price, Valerie Hobson, Joan Greenwood, Audrey Fildes, Miles Malleson, Clive Morton, Cecil Ramage, John Penrose, Hugh Griffith, John Salew, Eric Messiter, Anne Valery, Arthur Lowe, Jeremy Spenser; *D:* Robert Hamer; *W:* Robert Hamer, John Dighton; *C:* Douglas Slocombe; *M:* Ernest Irving. **VHS, LV** *REP, FCT, HMV*

A KIND OF LOVING

British director John Schlesinger's directorial debut is one of the best of the ubiquitous "kitchen-sink," working-class British melodramas of the 1950s and early 1960s. Alan Bates is Vic, the the kind of young, blustery bloke who likes to boast at the pub over a pint or two about the "birds" he's known and those he plans to know. But Vic's fling with attractive young Ingrid (June Ritchie) has left her in the family way, and has left the couple with no alternative but marriage. There's nothing show-offy or pretentious about *A Kind of Loving;* it's a memorable, poignant, and well-detailed little drama, modest in scope and performed by a first-rate cast. This was one of Bates's early films, and his command of the screen is impressive and strong. Equally as fine, however, is June Ritchie, whose disappearance from British screens soon after *A Kind of Loving* is regrettable; she remains an under-appreciated, powerfully sympathetic performer, best remembered for her performance here.

NEXT STOP . . . *Billy Liar, The Entertainer, Saturday Night and Sunday Morning*

1962 107m/B *GB* Alan Bates, Thora Hird, June Ritchie, Pat Keen, James Bolam; *D:* John Schlesinger; *W:* Willis Hall, Keith Waterhouse; *C:* Denys Coop; *M:* Ron Grainer. **VHS** *NO*

KING KONG VS. GODZILLA
King Kong Tai Godzilla

The erroneous but widespread belief that Bogart said "Play it again, Sam" in *Casablanca* is nothing compared to the ultimate false movie myth: that different endings were filmed for Japan and the United States for *King Kong vs. Godzilla.* We Americans can chill; on no screens in the world are audiences seeing Kong get his ass kicked. It *is* true that Kong has an extra off-screen roar at the end of the American prints, but that's it; in both versions he leaves for home in one piece. One *big* piece. The major differences between the Japanese and American versions are the usual thing—an American actor (Michael Keith) who plays a reporter is inserted intrusively throughout the film, and an English-language narration is added (the always-reliable Les Tremayne has the honors). Much of the film's original score is replaced by stock library music in American prints, but nothing changes the big picture; both monsters survive in *King Kong vs. Godzilla,* regardless of your country of origin. Now, don't you feel better?

NEXT STOP . . . *Godzilla vs. Megalon, Frankenstein Meets the Wolf Man, Wrestling Women vs. the Aztec Mummy*

1963 105m/C *JP* Inoshiro Honda, Michael Keith, Tadao Takashima; *D:* Thomas Montgomery. **VHS** *GKK*

THE KINGDOM
Riget

There are some mighty strange things happening at the mammoth Copenhagen hospital known as "The Kingdom." Spirits seem to be roaming the corridors, while sexual shenanigans, bizarre ritualistic ceremonies, and administrators' meetings that threaten to erupt in violence at any moment are all in a days' work. From Denmark's Lars von Trier, director of *Breaking the Waves,* comes this soap opera to end all soap operas, originally made for Danish television but released theatrically in the U.S. *The Kingdom* has been compared to *Twin Peaks,* but that's unfair to von Trier's film, which has the dangerously demented, absurdly comic bursts of pent-up rage that David Lynch was looking for but never got hold of. *The Kingdom* doesn't rip you off on a narrative level, either; each of its plot threads is followed through, and all is explained, to a point. With some of these characters, like the psychotic, fiercely chauvinistic, Denmark-hating Swedish consultant, you become almost obsessively involved in watching their blossoming insanity. You want to see him get his, and he does—better than you imagined. *The Kingdom*'s first part is four-and-a-half hours long—consisting of four episodes—and the whole thing ends with a "to be continued" title at a crucial moment. Von Trier has now completed the next four episodes—another four-and-a-half hours—and it's been released in the U.S. as *The Kingdom, Part II.* But be prepared—it too is "to be continued," and based on where the story leaves off at the end of *Part II,* the third segment will be something to see. (*The Kingdom*'s strange, brownish visual quality was achieved by doing a lot of juggling in the lab between video and film. Throw in von Trier's constant, gently rocking camera movements, and you just might—literally—feel at sea.)

NEXT STOP . . . *Zentropa, Berlin Alexanderplatz, The Hospital*

1995 279m/C *DK* Kirsten Rolffes, Ghita Norby, Udo Kier, Ernst Hugo Jarogard, Soren Pilmark, Holger Juul Hansen, Baard Owe, Birgitte Raabjerg, Peter Mygind; **D:** Lars von Trier; **W:** Lars von Trier, Tomas Gislason; **C:** Eric Kress; **M:** Joachim Holbek. **VHS** *HMK*

KINGS OF THE ROAD—IN THE COURSE OF TIME
Im Lauf der Zeit

Bruno (Rüdiger Vogler) is a traveling, freelance movie-projector repairman, whose route takes him along the borderline separating what had been East and West Germany. While parked in his van one day, a VW comes whizzing by and crashes into a nearby river. Out of the river comes Robert (Hanns Zischler), a man who has just fled his family.

Bruno takes him along. The original title of Wim Wenders's hypnotic *Kings of the Road* was *In the Course of Time;* that title is far more accurate about where we're headed, for toward the end of this deceptively rambling series of modest adventures set in towns with old, decaying movie theatres, an epiphany is reached. Bruno flashes on the trip they've made, on the pieces of film that run through projectors, on the cinematic histories of nations that can—as was the case with Germany after the war—suddenly and abruptly stop. He sees his own life as both a piece of time and a history, and realizes that the years—the course of time—in which his life has unspooled has become his history. Wenders places this thought at the heart of a long, epic movie that takes us from one point in a divided, dispirited land to another in a way that lets us *feel* that forward motion and the time the journey takes. We're reminded by Bruno's revelation that the film we're watching—and the people in it whom we've come to consider friends—are slipping away from us as the frames of the film we're looking at race through the projector. Bruno tries to keep those machines in good working order, but eventually they give out too. It's Wenders's inspiration to be able to make us remember that cinema is life, and that our life—our lives—are history that we make in the finite period of time given to us. A gentle, poetic, physically stunning film, *Kings of the Road* acquires new power and richer meaning with each viewing.

NEXT STOP . . . *Alice in the Cities, The State of Things, Wings of Desire*

1976 176m/B *GE* Ruediger Vogler, Hanns Zischler, Elisabeth Kreuzer; **D:** Wim Wenders; **W:** Wim Wenders; **C:** Robby Muller, Martin Schafer; **M:** Axel Linstadt. **VHS** *FCT, GLV, TPV*

KNIFE IN THE WATER
Noz w Wodzie

An affluent couple are driving off to spend a weekend on their yacht when they pick up a young hitchhiker. He accepts their invitation to accompany them on their vacation, but

Sportswriter Leon Niemczyk is jealous of young drifter Zygmunt Malanowicz, who likes to play with his knife in *Knife in the Water*.

once on the water their vicious interpersonal tensions begin to escalate into a day-long series of confrontations that will change all of their lives forever. Roman Polanski's compact, ingenious first feature looks much simpler than it is; the young director's probing, hovering camera sees the ugly behavior of this isolated little family and stares at it with the detached fascination of a scientist watching mutating germs in a petri dish. Envy, sex, greed, and anger are the fuels that power this little vacation, and they take the viewer along as well for 94 nerve-wracking but wryly funny minutes. Polanski's debut feature was based on a three-page story he developed while in film school in Poland. The project, originally turned down in 1960 by his country's film production board, was finally approved two years later. (Though *Knife in the Water* has the shape and economy of scale of a film-school exercise, that's only apparent in retrospect; while you're

watching the movie, it captivates thoroughly.) It went before the cameras with a script by Polanski, Jakub Goldberg, and Jerzy Skolimowski (who went on to direct his own features including *Deep End* and *Moonlighting*), and went on to become an international sensation, despite being attacked at home by Poland's communist press. *Knife in the Water* snared the International Film Critics' Award at the Venice Film Festival, an Oscar Nomination for Best Foreign Film, and even made the cover of *Time*. It also marked the beginning of Polanski's successful multi-feature collaboration with the late, gifted composer Krzysztof Komeda.

NEXT STOP . . . *Repulsion, Cul-de-Sac, Rosemary's Baby*

1962 94m/B *PL* Leon Niemczyk, Jolanta Umecka, Zygmunt Malandowicz; *D:* Roman Polanski; *W:* Jakub Goldberg, Jerzy Skolimowski, Roman Polanski; *C:* Jerzy Lipman; *M:* Krzysztof Komeda. Nominations: Academy Awards '63: Best Foreign-Language Film. **VHS, LV** *HMV, FOX, BTV*

KOLYA

Set in Czechoslovakia in 1988—the final days of its Communist regime—*Kolya* alarmingly begins like yet another version of *Green Card,* with middle-aged violinist and confirmed bachelor Frantisek (Zdenek Sverak) agreeing to a sham marriage with a Russian woman. Instead of falling for her, though, he falls for the woman's 10-year-old son, Kolya (Andrej Chalimon), who Frantisek believes he's been stuck with in perpetuity when the woman disappears. For this grumpy and randy musician (for whom a Viagra prescription would be carrying coals to Newcastle) having a kid around is the last thing he needs, but soon the inevitable bonding takes place, as does the even more inevitable resurfacing of Kolya's mother. The remarkable thing about *Kolya* is that despite its loaded premise and its unavoidable tearjerker finale, the picture goes down easier than one might expect. Some of this has to do with the easygoing and generally non-manipulative direction of Jan Sverak, who refuses to bludgeon us with the political implications of his story of painful change. Credit must also be given to Sverak and young Chalimon for keeping the mugging in check and bringing out the humanity in characters who could have easily degenerated into insufferable stereotypes. *Kolya* offers proof that even "high concept" pictures can be affecting when their creators make an effort to respect their audience.

NEXT STOP . . . *The Two of Us, Spirit of the Beehive, Tito and Me*

1996 (PG-13) 105m/C *CZ* Zdenek Sverak, Andrej Chalimon, Libuse Safrankova; **D:** Jan Sverak; **W:** Zdenek Sverak; **C:** Vladimir Smutny; **M:** Ondrej Soukup. Academy Awards '96: Best Foreign Film; Golden Globe Awards '97: Best Foreign Film; Nominations: British Academy Awards '96: Best Foreign Film. **VHS, LV, Closed Caption** *TOU*

KWAIDAN

This visually masterful rendering of four ghostly stories by Lafcadio Hearn remains one of the most beautiful and gently disquieting visions of the supernatural ever committed to film. Japan's Masaki Kobayashi mounted these four stories in a majestic, widescreen, richly colored style, each with a distinctive look. "Black Hair" is the story of a man who returns to his wife after leaving her for a younger woman, only to make a terrifying discovery. "Woman of the Snow" tells of an exhausted, nearly frozen woodcutter whose life is spared by a ghostly spirit, after which he tries to live by the spirit's one condition: to never reveal to *anyone* what he has seen this night. The intriguingly titled "Hoichi the Earless" is the tale of a blind musician who entertains an audience of ghosts each evening; when a priest tells Hoichi that the ghosts will tear him apart if he keeps singing, Hoichi allows his entire body to be covered with holy verses to protect himself. There are two parts of his body, however, that the priest neglects to protect. The final episode, "In a Cup of Tea," is the story of a warrior who first sees his enemy reflected in a teacup. Unfortunately, the image proves startlingly elusive when the time for combat arrives. *Kwaidan* achieves its exhilaratingly other-worldly feel through highly stylized settings, such as the magnificent design for the "Woman of the Snow" sequence, which features huge painted eyes hovering in the sky at strategic moments. The film was shot entirely in a studio with lighting and color tightly controlled, and the effect is of a living, moving Japanese scroll that illustrates the fantastic with boldly imaginative designs. The film's deliberate pacing was too much for its original American distributor, though, and that "Woman of the Snow" sequence was excised from *Kwaidan*'s original American release. It's been restored in the letterboxed video and laserdisc versions of this lush, haunting, elegantly scary film. Portions of Toru Takemitsu's chilling score can be heard on a recent CD compilation of his film music. Special Jury Prize, Cannes Film Festival.

NEXT STOP . . . *Ugetsu, Onibaba, Dead of Night*

1964 164m/C *JP* Michiyo Aratama, Rentaro Mikuni, Katsuo Nakamura, Keiko Kishi, Tatsuya Nakadai, Takashi Shimura; **D:** Masaki Kobayashi; **W:** Yoko Mizuki; **C:** Yoshio Miyajima; **M:** Toru Takemitsu. Cannes Film Festival '65: Grand Jury Prize; Nominations: Academy

"The earth is the only country I belong to. When I die, that's the end of it. I live now."

—Tullio (Giancarlo Giannini) in *The Innocent.*

Five-year-old Kolya (Andrej Chalimon) is befriended by the cynical Louka (Zdenek Sverak) in *Kolya*.

Awards '65: Best Foreign-Language Film. **VHS, LV, Letterbox** *VYY, NOS, SNC*

L.627

Director Bertrand Tavernier (*Capitain Conan, Life and Nothing But*) created a sensation at the French boxoffice with this hard-hitting and uncompromising policier about a side of Paris that never appears in travel brochures. Written in collaboration with Parisian police inspector Michel Alexandre, *L.627* chronicles the day-to-day frustrations—and occasional victories—of an undercover narcotics cop named Lulu (Didier Bezace). Lulu's personal relationships with hookers, dealers, and informers make the lines between criminal, associates, and friends ever more obscure; the concern Lulu feels when an HIV-infected prostitute and informer named Cecile (Lara Guirao) suddenly disappears is typical not only of Lulu's blurring identities, but also his humanity. American audiences will probably find much of the action in the streets to be old hat; our police procedurals have for years shown the difficulties cops have in making home life and street life co-exist, and their frustration with legal technicalities and bureaucracy. In terms of action, most half-hour episodes of *Cops* contain more shocks and genuine horror. Nevertheless, Tavernier's particularly humanistic slant is a refreshing take on this largely familiar material; at the very least, he gives us electric, pulsating images of a Paris never seen.

NEXT STOP . . . *The Clockmaker, The Judge and the Assassin, Serpico*

1992 145m/C *FR* Didier Bezace, Jean-Paul Comart, Cecile Garcia-Fogel, Lara Guirao, Charlotte Kady, Jean-Roger Milo, Philippe Torreton, Nils Tavernier; **D:** Bertrand Tavernier; **W:** Bertrand Tavernier, Michel Alexandre; **C:** Alain Choquart; **M:** Philippe Sarde. **VHS** *KIV*

LA BELLE NOISEUSE
Divertimento
The Beautiful Troublemaker

An aging, retired painter, whose marriage has become more of a deep friendship than a love affair, is introduced to an exquisite young woman and decides that he must paint her. He does. Four hours of screen time later, the painter has completed his work, the three principal characters have undergone unexpected changes, and the audience has been moved in ways that movies rarely lead us to expect. When I saw *La Belle Noiseuse* on screen for the first and only time, I became so involved with it, so excited by the supremely risky way in which the director, the then 63-year-old Jacques Rivette, told a story that in retrospect seems entirely unsuited to movies, that it seemed less like a screening than a real experience. Having emerged satisfied and with rich memories of the four hours I had just spent, I decided I would never mess with perfection by ever watching it in its entirety again. (It was Gene Siskel, I think, who once noted that you can only see a movie for the first time once.) That my reaction parallels an important moment in the film is an irony that only struck me later, yet because I never have experienced this astonishing movie again, I have no idea how it works on video. My only caution to you is this: don't break *La Belle Noiseuse* into shorter viewing sessions, don't pause it, fast-forward it, back it up, or mess with it in any way. Just watch it. Rivette's miraculous ability to capture the process of creating a drawing, then a painting, all influenced by the emotional drama taking place between model and artist, is something I've never seen on film before. Michel Piccoli, Emmanuelle Béart, and Jane Birkin are ideal as the artist, model, and wife, and cinematographer William Lubtchansky's images are breathtaking. But it's Rivette's uncanny feel for an artist's creative rhythms—the rhythms of life and its creation—that makes it all work.

NEXT STOP . . . *Divertimento, Edvard Munch, Dream of Light*

1990 240m/C *FR* Michel Piccoli, Emmanuelle Beart, Jane Birkin, David Bursztein, Marianne Denlcourt; **D:** Jacques Rivette; **W:** Jacques Rivette, Christine Laurent, Pascal Bonitzer; **C:** William Lubtchansky; **M:** Igor Stravinsky. Cannes Film Festival '91: Grand Jury Prize; Los Angeles Film Critics Association Awards '91: Best Foreign Film. **VHS** *NYF, FCT, ING*

LA BETE HUMAINE
The Human Beast

Jean Renoir's *La Bete Humaine* (*The Human Beast*) stars Jean Gabin as railroad engineer Jacques Lantier, a man whose deep-seated hatred of women—and unresolved resentment over inheriting his parents' alcoholism—produces in him a periodic, uncontrollable compulsion to kill. His bitter life takes a new turn when he falls in love with a railroad executive's wife (Simone Simon); but frustrated over her marital status, he makes plans to murder her husband. *La Bete Humaine* is based on Emile Zola's novel, and it remains one of the bleakest and most despairing visions Renoir has given us. Visually, the movie is a triumph of powerful, realistic imagery; Renoir's experiments with deep-focus cinematography bring a startling immediacy to the drama (it's a technique that would be further experimented with three years later by Orson Welles and cinematographer Gregg Toland in *Citizen Kane*). These deep-focus images allow the viewer to more freely select what or who he's going to look at within a frame, imparting a more open and naturalistic quality to the action. Much of *La Bete Humaine* is set on trains, and Renoir's evocative location photography—particularly in the celebrated opening sequence of the train's Paris to Le Harve run—remains indelible in the memories of those who've seen it. As usual, Gabin is a wonder, as is Simon as the seductive wife. (Look for Renoir himself playing a poacher.)

NEXT STOP . . . *La Chienne, The Crime of Monsieur Lange, The Lower Depths* (1936)

1938 90m/B *FR* Jean Gabin, Simone Simon, Julien Carette, Fernand Ledoux; **D:** Jean Renoir; **W:** Jean Renoir; **C:** Curt Courant; **M:** Joseph Cosma. **VHS, 8mm** *NOS, HHT, CAB*

his engagement—not to just *any* girl, but to the daughter of the secretary-general of the "Union of Moral Order." The upshot: Renato has to pretend to be heterosexual when the prospective in-laws visit, and Albin ends up posing as the mother, which becomes a big problem when the boy's *real* mother shows up. Predictably well-orchestrated chaos ensues. *La Cage aux Folles* became a word-of-mouth hit in its initial New York engagement, and settled in to run—seemingly—forever. It may not have been *quite* as big in some of the smaller markets of the heartland, but *La Cage aux Folles'* structure is so sure-fire and sentimental that it's perceived as non-threatening by all but the most resistant audiences. Tognazzi and Serrault make an inspired couple, and with the exception of a few lumpy expository sections, the whole, big, whirling machine zips harmlessly along, creaking loudly on occasion, but never quite breaking down. Édouard Molinaro directed from a screenplay he co-authored with Francis Veber, Marcello Danon, and Jean Poiret, who wrote the play on which it was based. It spawned a sequel (*La Cage aux Folles II*), a Broadway musical (*La Cage aux Folles*), and an American remake (*The Birdcage*) directed by Mike Nichols and starring Robin Williams and Nathan Lane.

Albin (Michel Serrault) disguises Monsieur Charrier (Michel Galabru) as a woman in *La Cage aux Folles.*

LA CAGE AUX FOLLES
Birds of a Feather

When it began life 20 years ago it was called daring; now it feels indestructible enough to call it an old war horse. A comedy about the intrinsic humor of gender and role-playing in society, as well as the true meaning of "family values," *La Cage aux Folles* is also a sure-fire, old-fashioned French farce of mixed-up identities and slamming doors, freshly fitted out in drag. In case you don't know, Renato (Ugo Tognazzi) is the gay owner of a notorious cross-dressers' nightclub in the south of France. One of the club's veteran performers, the flamboyantly effeminate Albin (Michel Serrault), has been Renato's lover for decades. A married couple for all intents and purposes, they even have a son (Renato's from an earlier fling), but the plot's ringer is that the son has announced

NEXT STOP . . . *La Cage aux Folles II, To Be or Not to Be* (1942), *Pain in the A***

1978 (R) 91m/C *FR* Ugo Tognazzi, Michel Serrault, Michel Galabru, Claire Maurier, Remy Laurent, Benny Luke; *D:* Edouard Molinaro; *W:* Edouard Molinaro, Francis Veber, Jean Poiret; *C:* Armando Nannuzzi; *M:* Ennio Morricone. Cesar Awards '79: Best Actor (Serrault); Golden Globe Awards '80: Best Foreign Film; Nominations: Academy Awards '79: Best Adapted Screenplay, Best Costume Design, Best Director (Molinaro). **VHS, LV** *MGM, FOX, CRC*

LA CÉRÉMONIE
A Judgment in Stone

Isabelle Huppert took home France's highest film honor, the César, for her performance as a deranged post office worker (another American trait the French have picked up?) who befriends a shy, illiterate, live-in housekeeper (Sandrine Bonnaire, who shared the Venice Festival's Best Actress Prize with Huppert) in Claude Chabrol's tense, satisfying, darkly funny thriller about class, sex, and rage. The pair team up to chip away at the smug and hypocritical bourgeois family Bonnaire works for, played with creepy efficiency by Jacqueline Bisset and Jean-Pierre Cassel as the couple, Valentin Merlet as the young son, and Virginie Ledoyen (*A Single Girl*) as the exquisite, harmlessly vacuous, 19-year-old daughter. It doesn't take long to see where the picture's going, but that doesn't keep it from being deliciously voyeuristic, nasty fun. The violence in *La Cérémonie* isn't overly graphic, but middle-class audiences get so spooked imagining themselves as the decadent, class-proud homeowners that when the moment of reckoning arrives, they tend to take it personally—and jump out of their seats. The film won the National Society of Film Critics and Los Angeles Film Critics Awards for Best Foreign Language Film.

NEXT STOP . . . *Repulsion, The Chant of Jimmie Blacksmith, Badlands*

1995 111m/C *FR* Sandrine Bonnaire, Isabelle Huppert, Jacqueline Bisset, Jean-Pierre Cassel, Virginie Ledoyen; *D:* Claude Chabrol; *W:* Claude Chabrol, Caroline Eliacheff; *C:* Bernard Zitzermann; *M:* Matthieu Chabrol. Cesar Awards '96: Best Actress (Huppert); Los Angeles Film Critics Association Awards '96: Best Foreign Film; National Society of Film Critics Awards '96: Best Foreign Film; Nominations: Cesar Awards '96: Best Actress (Bonnaire), Best Director (Chabrol), Best Film, Best Supporting Actor (Cassel), Best Supporting Actress (Bisset), Best Writing. **VHS** *NYF*

LA CHIENNE
Isn't Life a Bitch?
The Bitch

Jean Renoir's first sound film is the tale of Maurice Legrand, an unhappily married bank teller (Michel Simon) who finds a bit of refuge from his harridan of a wife (Madeleine Bérubet) in the arms of an attractive street prostitute named Lulu (Janie Marèze). When Maurice discovers that Lulu and her lover/pimp, Dédé (Georges Flammand) have been setting him up, he kills her and lets Dédé take the rap. *La Chi-* enne (*The Bitch*), which is a masterful and deeply satisfying movie, has had a long and difficult time getting seen by the public. Though it was initially unsuccessful in its French release, due reputedly to the public's disappointment in discovering that Simon's role was not a comic one, Renoir wrote in his memoirs about a resourceful film distributor who saved the day. Instead of running ads featuring quotes from the best reviews, the distributor placed notices in papers advising that *La Chienne* was so horrifying that "families should stay away—it's not fit for sensitive viewers." The film sold out that very night, and went on to great success, according to the director. One of *La Chienne*'s most intriguing aspects is its exquisitely photographed portrait of life in the Montmartre section of Paris. We also *hear* the area's sounds, since Renoir insisted on natural sound recording techniques rather than post-synchronized dubbing, a process the director disdainfully called "equivalent to a belief in the duality of the soul." It didn't get seen in America until the 1950s, and then it was with incomplete subtitles and a refusal to translate the title. *La Chienne*'s basic story elements have been part of many movies since, but a faithful remake— *Scarlet Street*—was filmed in Hollywood in 1945 by Fritz Lang.

NEXT STOP . . . *La Bete Humaine, The Crime of Monsieur Lange, The Woman in the Window*

1931 93m/B *FR* Michel Simon, Janie Mareze, Georges Flament, Madeleine Berubet; *D:* Jean Renoir; *W:* Andre Girard, Jean Renoir. **VHS, LV** *INT, TPV*

LA COLLECTIONNEUSE
The Gentleman Tramp

Is it the third or the fourth of Eric Rohmer's "six moral tales" cycle? Both, actually; it was the third to be filmed, but the fourth to be released, seeing the light of day only after the success of *My Night at Maud's*. *La Collectionneuse* is the story of Adrien (Patrick Bauchau), an antiques dealer who spends his vacation at a villa near Saint-Tropez; while there he meets Haydee (Haydee

"I'm afraid she will never be happy on this earth. She is a vision for all men, not for one."

—Jim (Henri Serre) about Catherine (Jeanne Moreau) in *Jules and Jim.*

Politoff), a woman he nicknames "la collectionneuse" because of what appears to be her m.o. of "collecting" men. Adrien is appalled by Haydee's promiscuous behavior, but it isn't too long before he feels an attraction and has to make a decision on whether or not to act on it. Though he ultimately is able to make that choice, it turns out to be the result of an unforeseeable but most fortunate confluence of events—a situation that is pure Rohmer. Seeing *La Collectionneuse* after *My Night at Maud's* may be a bit of a letdown, since in retrospect this film feels like a less fully formed version of the other. It's nevertheless filled with Rohmer's characteristic sparkling wit and deeply felt sympathy for the circumstances of *all* of his characters. And the Mediterranean never looked better than when photographed by Nestor Almendros.

NEXT STOP . . . *My Night at Maud's, Claire's Knee, Chloe in the Afternoon*

1967 88m/C *FR* Patrick Bauchau, Daniel Pommereulle, Haydee Politoff, Alain Jouffroy; *D:* Eric Rohmer; *W:* Eric Rohmer; *C:* Nestor Almendros. **VHS** *FXL*

LA DISCRETE
The Discreet

Antoine (Fabrice Luchini) is an arrogant writer who is clearly not the lothario he imagines himself to be. Outraged and wounded by his latest girlfriend dumping him, he huddles with his publisher to plan a revenge that will kill two birds with one stone. He will advertise for a young female typist whom he will seduce and abandon—all the while keeping a diary of the experience for publication. All bets are off when the ad is answered by the lovely and irresistibly intriguing Catherine (Judith Henry), who messes with Antoine's mind in ways even he never dreamed of. *La Discrete* looks at first like it's going to be a simple-minded tale of a male chauvinist's come-uppance, but writer/director Christian Vincent is interested in much more. Both of these people pay a price for their manipulation, and the viewer is drawn into a relationship that's far more touching and complex than we bargained for. This picture never made much of a splash on the American art house circuit, possibly because of its refusal to draw easy conclusions. Had it caught on, it might have made Judith Henry the star she deserves to be; watching her Catherine try to calm down the steaming Antoine by repeating his name—beckoning him to bed—is one of the most seductive and charming scenes in any French film of the '90s. It's a notable directorial debut.

NEXT STOP . . . *Diary of a Seducer, Rendezvous in Paris, The Disenchanted*

1990 95m/C *FR* Fabrice Luchini, Judith Henry, Maurice Garrel, Marie Bunel, Francois Toumarkine; *D:* Christian Vincent; *W:* Jean-Pierre Ronssin, Christian Vincent; *M:* Jay Gottlieb. Cesar Awards '91: Best Writing. **VHS** *NYF, FCT*

LA DOLCE VITA
The Sweet Life

Upon returning to my hotel after a late movie during the 1997 Telluride Film Festival, the TV informed me that a car accident had taken the life of Princess Diana. The CNN newscaster reported that the crash scene had been besieged by *paparazzi*. For an instant I wondered if the image that next popped into my head was only there because I was at a film festival, but I don't think so. The sudden flashback to the flashbulbs, snapping shutters, and pushing and shoving of the viciously aggressive photographers in Federico Fellini's *La Dolce Vita* would have entered my head anywhere I heard the news. It's not only that the term *paparazzo* was coined in reference to the movie's Signor Paparazzo; the film itself has become a nearly universal, communal vision of modern society's fascination with celebrity, glamour, scandal, and decadence, trapped forever in amber by *The Maestro*. For the three hours of *La Dolce Vita* (*The Sweet Life*), the bored tabloid reporter Marcello (Marcello Mastroianni) complains, suf-

fers, and vents his frustration over not being a journalist of a higher caliber. But Marcello knows who he is, and he is in thrall to the decadent and hedonistic pleasures that surround him. (And if Fellini has given us a single bit of visual shorthand for that hedonism, it's Marcello and movie starlet Sylvia (Anita Ekberg) frolicking at night in the Trevi Fountain.) Eventually, after a friend commits a horribly violent act, and after reporting on a faked religious miracle that has shattered the faith of hundreds, Marcello throws in the towel. He can no longer—literally—hear the words of the one "good" woman he's encountered, and he wanders off to lose himself completely in a world of shallowness. A vast morality play disguised as a mesmerizing peep show, *La Dolce Vita* is, on the one hand, tempting to dismiss as Fellini's knee-jerk, overreaction to a generation's vanishing sense of purpose—the kind of movie Dan Quayle might make if he could spell *paparazzi*. Still, one can't deny that *La Dolce Vita*'s mythological cultural landscape has both staying power *and* artistic power. It's a part of us, ready to spring back to buoyant life whenever events warrant—just like tabloid journalism, and just like our own nagging regrets about the high road not taken. Oscar nominations for Director, Screenplay, and Art Direction; Oscar Winner for Costume Design.

NEXT STOP . . . *I Vitelloni, Fellini Satyricon, Ikiru*

1960 174m/B *IT* Marcello Mastroianni, Anita Ekberg, Anouk Aimee, Alain Cuny, Lex Barker, Yvonne Furneaux, Barbara Steele, Nadia Gray, Magali Noel, Walter Santesso, Jacques Sernas, Annibale Ninchi; *D:* Federico Fellini; *W:* Tullio Pinelli, Ennio Flaiano, Brunello Rondi, Federico Fellini; *M:* Nino Rota. Academy Awards '61: Best Costume Design (B & W); Cannes Film Festival '60: Best Film; New York Film Critics Awards '61: Best Foreign Film; Nominations: Academy Awards '61: Best Art Direction/Set Decoration (B & W), Best Director (Fellini), Best Story & Screenplay. **VHS, LV, Letterbox** *REP*

LA FEMME INFIDÈLE
The Unfaithful Wife

Charles (Michel Bouquet) and Helene (Stéphane Audran) are a civilized, cultured, well-heeled bourgeois couple whose mar-

riage has become passionless. Helene's response to this missing part of her life has been to take a lover (Maurice Ronet); Charles' rejoinder is to kill him. *La Femme Infidèle* is one of Claude Chabrol's most celebrated films, and with good reason. It's an elegantly designed black comedy about the sometimes-paradoxical nature of sexual passion—a kind of refined, more overtly intellectual version of *Straw Dogs*—that also functions quite efficiently as a conventional thriller. As usual, Chabrol gets superb performances from his stock company; Audran is just right as the adulterous wife whose passion for her husband begins to swell again after he acts decisively, and Ronet is appropriately slick and elegantly sleazy as the other man. But the movie belongs to Michel Bouquet, as is always the case when he works with Chabrol. Bouquet's Charles is a quietly ticking time bomb whose ultimate, explosive attainment of self-esteem leads ironically and touchingly to both his downfall and his recaptured virility. This picture is a model of its genre, and one of the most pleasurable movies of Chabrol's career.

NEXT STOP . . . *Just Before Nightfall, Le Boucher, This Man Must Die*

1969 98m/C Stephane Audran, Michel Bouquet, Michael Duchaussoy, Henri Marteau, Maurice Ronet, Dominique Zardi; **D:** Claude Chabrol; **W:** Claude Chabrol; **C:** Jean Rabier; **M:** Pierre Jansen. *NYR*

LA FEMME NIKITA

A young French woman (Anne Parillaud) is reprieved from her death sentence (she's been bad) and taught to be a much neater, better-looking killer. After years of training and New Wave charm school (yes, it's *Pygmalion* again), she starts her new job as assassin for a super-secret government agency. The irony is that once she's taught style, grace, manners, and class, she no longer *wants* to kill—but she has no choice. *La Femme Nikita* was a worldwide hit, and I'll confess that I predicted otherwise when I first saw a preview screening. My assumption was that this was an American movie at heart, and that audiences for French cinema—including the French—would reject it for the real thing.

Oops. The movie didn't just catapult Luc Besson into the big time—it changed the direction of French cinema. Depending on your point of view, the movie can be considered a much-needed economic savior for a national film industry that was struggling—or, it can be seen as a death-knell for the kind of small, delicate drama that the French cinema is known for, and which is increasingly difficult to finance, distribute, and market worldwide. Is the movie good at what it does? Not bad. It looks great, and so does Anne Parillaud, but to put it politely, it's a waste of time. *La Femme Nikita*'s violence is never stirring or even very exciting. The movie is all about style, and style is all that it's about. We're not talking about a lyrical, expressively violent style, like, say, Peckinpah or John Woo; it's just *stylish,* like a huge, bloody Gap ad. The emptiness turned out to be prophetic, for Besson (whose Bruce Willis vehicle, *The Fifth Element,* is one of the most successful French productions in history) is regarded—as Truffaut and Godard once were—as the French cinema's savior. Now *that's* scary. (The original French title is just plain *Nikita,* but the American distributor thought it might be considered a documentary on Khrushchev.) It became the basis for an American TV series as well as a flat-out remake called *Point of No Return,* starring Bridget Fonda.

NEXT STOP . . . *Le Dernier Combat, Diva, Face/Off*

1991 (R) 117m/C *FR* Anne Parillaud, Jean-Hugues Anglade, Tcheky Karyo, Jeanne Moreau, Jean Reno, Jean Bouise; **D:** Luc Besson; **W:** Luc Besson; **C:** Thierry Arbogast; **M:** Eric Serra. Cesar Awards '91: Best Actress (Parillaud). **VHS** *THV, FCT, BTV*

LA GRANDE BOUFFE
The Blow-Out

There are food movies and there is *La Grande Bouffe.* Director Marco Ferreri's spectacularly unnecessary movie about four affluent, middle-aged men who decide to commit suicide by gorging can't exactly be called a cautionary fable; we see what the physical effects of non-stop eating are, but they're nothing we didn't suspect. Stomach pains, diarrhea, endless, high-decibel farting, chest pains, incontinence, death. The plush chateau where Mar-

Starlet Sylvia (Anita Ekberg) poses in a Roman fountain in *La Dolce Vita.*

cello Mastroianni, Ugo Tognazzi, Michel Piccoli, and Philippe Noiret do themselves in is also equipped with a plump, sexually starved schoolteacher (Andrea Ferreol), with whom the men attain other forms of pleasure (she gets to share the men's food, too). I can't deny that there's a certain fascination for the audience in all this—kind of like stopping by the pie-eating contest at the state fair to see how many of ma's peach pies little Timmy can wolf down before he throws up. But at the state fair you can at least move on to the swine exhibit; here you're trapped in the theatre for over two hours, with no place to hide while that ominous dark puddle begins to gently fan out under Michel Piccoli's pants. *La Grande Bouffe* provides shocks, all right, but since the movie's not really about anything, the shocks have no power. Each man's death is like a new dish-spinning act on Ed Sullivan; you may be impressed, but you won't exactly go away with food for thought. I'm sure there's a pointed metaphor in the movie somewhere about gluttony, fascism, and the bourgeois-capitalist value system. I tell you what—*you* find it, and get back to me. I'm going to see *Tampopo.*

NEXT STOP . . . *Salo, or the 120 Days of Sodom, The Last Woman, Tales of Ordinary Madness*

1973 125m/C *FR* Marcello Mastroianni, Philippe Noiret, Michel Piccoli, Ugo Tognazzi, Andrea Ferreol; *D:* Marco Ferreri; *W:* Marco Ferreri, Rafael Azcona; *C:* Mario Vulpiani; *M:* Philippe Sarde. **VHS** *WBF*

LA JETÉE
The Pier

In 1962, French film poet Chris Marker's 29-minute *La Jetée* was *de rigueur* at university film societies and experimental film co-ops, but only with the release of the overwritten, overheated, Terry Gilliam/Bruce Willis remake, *12 Monkeys,* did the original begin to receive exposure on a few "independent" cable networks. More than 35 years have passed since the first showings of this tale of a post-apocalyptic time-traveler's journey back to an earlier age, but as the subject of *La Jetée* is itself the passage of time and the impact of memory, the years have only added

a haunting resonance to what may well be the greatest—and scariest—science-fiction film ever made. Comprised of an assemblage of still images (with one very moving exception) and a French-language narration, *La Jetée* unquestionably owes much to the cinematic time-traveling pioneered by Alain Resnais, yet has its own, highly distinctive atmosphere that recreates with uncanny skill the feeling and circular structure of a deeply private night dream. It's a deeply disturbing, supremely beautiful creation. (Though the original narration is in French, an English-dubbed version was circulated in the 1960s, and, surprisingly, it's superb. More than simply the fact that there's no lip synchronization problem to worry about, the English track version is as beautifully performed and affecting as the original.)

NEXT STOP . . . *Hiroshima Mon Amour, Last Year at Marienbad, The Koumiko Mystery*

1962 28m/B *FR* **D:** Chris Marker; **W:** Chris Marker; **C:** Chris Marker; **M:** Trevor Duncan. **VHS** *FCT*

LA LECTRICE
The Reader

A Raymond Jean novel titled *La Lectrice*—the story of a woman whose seductive powers blossom when she reads aloud—is taken to heart by Constance (Miou-Miou), who's inspired enough by the book to try reading to her boyfriend in bed. Constance is quite smitten with the novel's premise, and imagines herself as its heroine, offering her services as a professional reader, and serves a varied clientele in a series of surreal, teasing episodes that appear to be part real and part fantasy In the course of the film, Constance reads to a young paraplegic, to a judge whose tastes run to pornography, and to a radical, socialist widow. Director Michel Deville was on to something here—the idea of a woman taking such pleasure in the written word that she gets sexual pleasure from sharing it with others is novel but not absurd, and filled with possibilities. So where are they? *La Lectrice* entices at first with the idea that it might turn into a literary *Klute,* but the individual encounters never generate much interest, sympathy, or heat. The comic possibilities are certainly there, as well—the idea isn't all that different from Woody Allen's brilliant comic essay *The Whore of Mensa*—but Deville avoids flat-out laughs as if they were beneath him. Instead, the movie's just a tease—soft-core intellectual porn, for librarians in raincoats.

NEXT STOP . . . *Diary of a Seducer, Fahrenheit 451, Belle de Jour*

1988 (R) 98m/C *FR* Miou-Miou, Christian Ruche, Sylvie Laporte, Michael Raskine, Brigitte Catillon, Regis Royer, Maria Casares, Pierre Dux, Patrick Chesnais; *D:* Michel DeVille; *W:* Rosalinde DeVille, Michel DeVille. Cesar Awards '89: Best Supporting Actor (Chesnais); Montreal World Film Festival '88: Best Film. **VHS, LV** *ORI*

LA MARSEILLAISE

In 1938, Jean Renoir accepted the task of producing a film designed primarily to kindle strong feelings of patriotism and anti-fascism. He chose the most natural subject of all: the march on Paris of the Marseilles volunteers, and the capture of the Tuilleries in 1793, ending the Revolution and overthrowing the monarchy. The story is told in a series of vignettes, presented in rapid succession, with two young volunteers as the focal point. Renoir shows us the decadent court of Louis XVI, and juxtaposes scenes of the oppressed peasantry. He moves on to the storming of the Bastille, the Marseilles rebellion and so on, until the triumphant finish accompanied by the song that was ultimately known as "La Marseillaise." The film is simple, sweeping, and occasionally thrilling. Though one can hardly call it the most multi-leveled and complex of epics, there are reassuring human touches throughout—small details that humanize the characters beyond the mere types they threaten to become. Ironically, the show is almost stolen by the performance of Renoir's brother, Pierre, as Louis XVI. He's always hungry, always eating, always worried about his image—and always, as we well know, missing the point. It's a generous, sympathetic performance in a film teeming with them.

NEXT STOP . . . *Napoleon, Orphans of the Storm, Danton*

1937 130m/B *FR* Pierre Renoir, Lisa Delamare, Louis Jouvet, Alme Clarimond, Andrex Andrisson, Paul Dullac; *D:* Jean Renoir; *W:* Jean Renoir; *C:* Jean Bourgoin. **VHS** *NOS, INT, HHT*

LA NOTTE
The Night
La Nuit

In Milan, a middle-class writer (Marcello Mastroianni) and his wife (Jeanne Moreau) appear to have come to the end of their road together; without passion or a conviction that they need to stay together, they spend one long and lonely night observing the shapes and sounds of the city around them, trying to make sense of what appears to be a chaotic and uncaring world. Without specific references to the post-war/cold war angst that saturates the 1961 of *La Notte,* Michelangelo Antonioni nevertheless evokes that world with the vividness that only a true poet can. By dawn, the couple have indeed come to an understanding, but it's not the simple Hollywood solution of simply staying or leaving. Antonioni's concern is with the daunting prospect of coping with the modern world while not living in denial; in *La Notte* the terrors of the night may not lead to reborn, romantic dawn, but they also don't lead to utter despair. We mustn't be afraid to dig down into ourselves, he seems to tell us, for even though self-knowledge may not lead to happiness, the alternative leads only to oblivion. *La Notte* won the Grand Prize (Golden Bear) at the Berlin Film Festival.

NEXT STOP . . . *L'Avventura, Red Desert, The Magician*

1960 122m/B *IT* Jeanne Moreau, Marcello Mastroianni, Monica Vitti, Bernhard Wicki, Maria Pia Luzi, Rosy Mazzacurati, Grigor Taylor; *D:* Michelangelo Antonioni; *W:* Michelangelo Antonioni, Ennio Flaiano, Tonino Guerra; *C:* Gianni Di Venanzo; *M:* Girogio Gaslini. *NYR*

LA NUIT DE VARENNES

This historical dramatic comedy is based on a celebrated chapter in French history, when Louis XVI (Michel Piccoli) and Marie

Antoinette (Eleonore Hirt) fled from a Paris in the throes of revolution to Varennes in 1791. On their journey, they meet an unlikely and altogether remarkable group of characters, including Casanova (Marcello Mastroianni), Thomas Paine (Harvey Keitel), and the popular writer Restif de la Bretonne (Jean-Louis Barrault). All the elements are in place for a completely fascinating take on politics, revolution, sex, and power, but the film—despite some engaging and wonderfully witty passages—just never takes off. This is the kind of conceit that needs the goosing of a genuinely inspired script, not merely an adequate one, but writer/director Ettore Scola and his co-author Sergio Amidei seem to feel that the setup is enough to carry the picture. The movie reminded me a bit of the old Steve Allen TV series *Meeting of Minds,* in which historical figures who couldn't have sat down together sat down together. (*Meeting of Minds* was more intriguing.) The performances are delightful, particularly those of Mastroianni and the great Barrault (Baptiste in *Children of Paradise*). The film is cut by about 20 minutes from its original running time, although prints of various lengths have circulated in the U.S.

NEXT STOP . . . *Passione d'Amoré, Danton, Stagecoach* (1939)

1982 (R) 133m/C *FR IT* Marcello Mastroianni, Harvey Keitel, Jean-Louis Barrault, Hanna Schygulla, Jean-Claude Brialy, Michel Piccoli, Jean-Louis Trintignant; *D:* Ettore Scola; *W:* Ettore Scola. **VHS, LV** *COL, IME*

LA PROMESSE
The Promise

Just outside of Antwerp, Roger, a man running an illegal immigration mill, allows a critically injured immigrant laborer to die, and then covers up the crime by burying him in cement. Roger's 15-year-old son, Igor, has long assisted his father in running what is essentially a slave market, and he's forced to help bury the laborer and then lie to the dead man's frantic wife about her husband's whereabouts. Wracked with guilt and humiliated by his father's treatment not only of the man's wife but of him, Igor is forced to make an agonizing decision about the direction of his own life. Belgian directors Jean-Pierre and Luc Dardenne have created one of the most complex and devastating moral tales in modern film; the lives of the characters in *La Promesse* are never going to made whole, and no matter what road Igor takes he's going to leave at least some part of his world in ruin. Living with the pain of moral choices—even those that appear at first glance to be clear-cut—is at the heart of this riveting and powerful movie, which never pretends that doing the right thing will provide the rewards of riches, satisfaction, or even simple gratitude. Films this multi-layered, richly textured, and uncondescending are a rarity now, and that's one of the many reasons that audiences tend to file out speechless after screenings of *La Promesse*. It is, in just about every sense, a knockout.

NEXT STOP . . . *Lacombe, Lucien, The Butcher Boy, Affliction*

1996 93m/C *FR BE* Jeremie Renier, Olivier Gourmet, Assita Ouedraogo, Rasmane Ouedraogo; *D:* Jean-Pierre Dardenne, Luc Dardenne; *W:* Jean-Pierre Dardenne, Luc Dardenne; *C:* Alain Marcoen; *M:* Jean-Marie Billy. Los Angeles Film Critics Association Awards '97: Best Foreign Film; National Society of Film Critics Awards '97: Best Foreign Film. **VHS** *NYR*

LA RONDE

Arthur Schnitzler's play was the basis for this lyrical and bittersweet series of linked episodes depicting love in all its tragic, comic, and unexpected manifestations. Linked by the image of love as a merry-go-round, the master of ceremonies (Anton Walbrook at his most suavely elegant) narrates and explains what we see as the carousel of love comes full circle. It begins with prostitute Simone Signoret and soldier Serge Reggiani; he takes up with chambermaid Simone Simon. She introduces young Daniel Gélin to love; with his new confidence, he seduces the married Danielle Darrieux. Darrieux's husband, Fernand Gravet, is maintaining mistress Odette Joyeux. But she's in love with poet Jean-Louis Barrault, which will come to naught because he loves actress Isa Miranda. She, however, prefers a Count,

Gérard Philipe, who has occasion to visit prostitute Simone Signoret. And there—where it began—the carousel stops. Filled with witty and charming performances, and directed with the sweeping fluidity of movement that was Ophüls's signature, *La Ronde* is an exceptionally satisfying romantic fable. It was a major success for Ophüls upon its release in France, but censors prevented its American debut until 1954. The censors may have been alarmed by the casual sex, but they may well have missed the other aspect of Schnitzler's clever structural metaphor, which illuminates not only the path of love, but the path of those pesky little microbes that have been known to accompany it on its rounds. Best Screenplay Award, Venice Film Festival; Oscar Nominations for Screenplay and Art Direction.

NEXT STOP . . . *The Earrings of Madame de …, Caught, Lola Montès*

1951 97m/B *FR* Simone Signoret, Anton Walbrook, Simone Simon, Serge Reggiani, Daniel Gelin, Danielle Darrieux, Jean-Louis Barrault, Fernand Gravet, Odette Joyeux, Isa Miranda, Gerard Philipe; *D:* Max Ophuls. British Academy Awards '51: Best Film; Nominations: Academy Awards '51: Best Art Direction/Set Decoration (B & W), Best Screenplay. **VHS** *NLC, HMV*

LA RUPTURE
The Breakup

One of Claude Chabrol's more lurid and intense thrillers, *La Rupture* (*The Break-Up*) wastes no time plunging you into its alarming premise. Charles, the husband of Helene, is in a rage. Before the movie's credits he picks up their young son and throws him, injuring him severely enough to be hospitalized. After the credits, Charles has run off to his rich parents' house, where they shelter him and baby him, and—in true enablers' fashion—blame Helene for making their darling boy into a violent psychopath. But it's not enough that Charles's parents manage to keep him out of jail—they want to ruin Helene lest she get the judge's sympathy in the upcoming custody battle over the recuperating child. Charles's parents hire a ruthless and perverse private detective to nail Helene, and at this point *La Rupture* goes

steadily and pleasurably off the deep end. Chabrol, one of the earliest of the French film critics to take Alfred Hitchcock seriously as both an entertainer and an artist, is aware that an apparently conventional thriller can also be a superb vehicle for affecting audiences on a much deeper level. *La Rupture* does just that, presenting us with a disquietingly grotesque parody of the family dynamic at its most savagely self-destructive. As usual, Stéphane Audran (Helene) provides the center around which Chabrol's anxious universe revolves.

NEXT STOP . . . *This Man Must Die, Le Boucher, Psycho*

1970 124m/C *FR* Stephane Audran, Jean-Claude Drouot, Michel Bouquet, Jean-Pierre Cassel, Catherine Rouvel, Jean Carmet, Annie Cordy; *D:* Claude Chabrol; *W:* Claude Chabrol; *M:* Pierre Jansen. **VHS** *CVC, FCT*

LA SALAMANDRE
The Salamander

The debut of Swiss director Alain Tanner is a funny and assured little comedy with a sharp, stinging aftertaste. When a journalist (Jean-Luc Bideau) notices an item in the paper about a young woman who's been accused by her uncle of attempting to kill him, he decides that the incident would make a swell made-for-TV movie. He contacts a novelist friend of his (Jacques Denis)—a *real* writer—to see if he can help him whip it into something marketable. With the novelist searching for an "emotional truth," and the journalist looking for what actually happened, we're left with the alleged perpetrator herself—an angry, defiant handful of a woman (Bulle Ogier) who's completely fed up with all of it. If we don't ever learn the absolute truth about why a gun went off the day her uncle was wounded, we sure do learn about the explosive, unpredictable, and erotically rebellious young woman who claims that it was all a misunderstanding. *La Salamandre* is the film that put both Tanner and Swiss cinema on the map; it is, ironically enough, a dark and lively comedy about the explosive consequences of trying to remain neutral—particularly when you're crazy.

THE HOUND SALUTES:

ENNIO MORRICONE
Composer of the "Spaghetti Westerns"

As one of the most eclectic and prolific composers of the 20th century, Ennio Morricone has created soundtracks for over 350 films and television productions released in English, Italian, and French. Although he established his "name" by composing scores for Italian westerns (often called "spaghetti westerns"), Morricone has composed for mystery thrillers, romantic dramas, comedies, and epics, including *The Untouchables, City of Joy, In the Line of Fire, Wolf,* and *Disclosure.*

Morricone's work with director Sergio Leone on the classic 1960s "man with no name" trilogy vaulted both Morricone and actor Clint Eastwood to instant cult stardom. In scores for *A Fistful of Dollars, For a Few Dollars More,* and *The Good, the Bad, and the Ugly,* Morricone mirrored the violence, irony, and campy humor pervading the classic Eastwood western. Besides his work with Leone, Morricone has worked with major directors such as Franco Zefferelli, Federico Fellini, Roman Polanski, and Roland Joffe.

Born in Rome, Italy, in 1928, Morricone started writing music at the age of six. He holds diplomas in composition, trombone, and orchestra direction from the Santa Cecilia Conservatory in Rome, and he still plays trombone with a local music group called Nuova Consonaza. Along with his classical compositions, he has composed a ballet (Requiem for Destiny) but little other non-film music.

Nominated for five Academy Awards for best score, Morricone is perhaps best known for his work on the 1968 film *Once Upon a Time in the West.*

NEXT STOP . . . The Middle of the World, Jonah Who Will Be 25 in the Year 2000, Maîtresse

1971 119m/B *SI* Bulle Ogier, Jean-Luc Bideau, Jacques Denis; *D:* Alain Tanner; *W:* Alain Tanner, John Berger; *M:* Patrick Moraz. **VHS** *NYF*

LA SCORTA
The Bodyguards
The Escorts

This is a taut and intelligent fact-based thriller about four carabinieri who struggle to maintain some semblance of their normal lives after being assigned to protect a judge (Carlo Cecchi) who's volunteered to investigate political corruption and murder in a crime-ridden Sicilian town. The previous judge, and his escort, were assassinated while on the same case, and the tension of waiting for another explosion of violence soon reaches the breaking point. Many of these men are at cross-purposes, suspecting and double-crossing each other as the investigation tightens its noose, and director Riccardo (Ricky) Tognazzi sometimes drops the ball when it comes to keeping clean track of who's spying on whom. It's still a tight, high-energy police story, centering on the sometimes-precarious balance of power between the mob and the state, with a few dedicated individuals struggling to deliver some kind of justice between two corrupt extremes. *La Scorta (The Escort)* is helped enormously by the pulse-pounding music of Ennio Morricone; it's an effective, energizing variation on his classic score for Elio Petri's 1970 police corruption thriller, *Investigation of a Citizen Above Suspicion*. With Enrico Lo Verso (*The Stolen Children, Lamerica*).

NEXT STOP . . . *Z, Who Killed Pasolini?, Serpico*

1994 92m/C *IT* Claudio Amendola, Enrico Lo Verso, Tony Sperandeo, Ricky Memphis, Carlo Cecchi, Leo Gullotta; *D:* Ricardo Tognazzi; *W:* Graziano Diana, Simona Izzo; *M:* Ennio Morricone. **VHS** *NYF*

LA SIGNORA DI TUTTI

Unavailable for many years in a subtitled print, this enchanting early work by Max Ophüls stars Isa Miranda as Gaby Doirot, "Everybody's Sweetheart," a movie star whose professional success did not bring her happiness. Her story is told in flashback while she's hospitalized after an attempted suicide, and this structure lends a bittersweet tone to all of the events we see. This was the only film Ophüls was to make in Italy; he was forced by politics to work outside of his native Germany, a situation which would last until after World War II. In tone and visual style (lyrical and elegant camera movement throughout, always at the service of the story), *La Signora di Tutti* is clearly the work of a master; the themes and structure of this little jewel box of a film would be most closely echoed by his heartfelt final work, *Lola Montès*.

NEXT STOP . . . *Liebelei, The Earrings of Madame de…, Lola Montes*

1934 92m/B *IT* Isa Miranda; *D:* Max Ophuls. **VHS** *CVC, FCT*

LA STRADA
The Road

At the price of a dish of pasta, a dim-witted peasant girl named Gelsomina (Giulietta Masina) is literally sold to a traveling performer named Zampano (Anthony Quinn), who will use her in his strong-man act, and will use her sexually as well. During their travels around the country, Zampano's brutality to Gelsomina is unrelenting—yet she stays with him for many reasons. Even Gelsomina has a breaking point, however, and its arrival is perhaps the most wrenching moment in any of the films of Federico Fellini. *La Strada*, a heartbreaking and powerful fable about shattered faith, loneliness, and the possibility of redemption, was a worldwide sensation, catapulting Fellini to international fame. Giulietta Masina's tender, waif-like performance—which owes quite a bit to the work of great silent performers like Chaplin—proved not only a revelation, but was accessible to audiences everywhere; even people who had never considered attending a foreign-language film found themselves touched and haunted by the memory of her victimized, loyal Gelsomina. It is here in which the real power of *La Strada* can be found; though Gelsomina's treatment by Zampano almost literally as baggage is an exaggerated theatrical image, the dynamics of the relationship are not nearly so exaggerated—or rare—as they might look. If women respond to *La Strada* with recognition, and men with guilt, it may be time to see it as considerably more than a simple fable about the bleak fates awaiting one strongman and his victim. With Richard Basehart as the gentle high-wire walker Il Matto. Nino Rota's brilliant score, with its haunting, circus-like themes, is one of the most important contributions to *La Strada*'s success. Academy Award Winner, Best Foreign Language Film; Nominee for Best Original Screenplay.

NEXT STOP . . . *I Vitelloni, Nights of Cabiria, 8 1/2*

1954 107m/B *IT* Giulietta Masina, Anthony Quinn, Richard Basehart, Aldo Silvani; *D:* Federico Fellini; *W:* Ennio Flaiano, Brunello Rondi, Tullio Pinelli, Federico Fellini; *M:* Nino Rota. Academy Awards '56: Best Foreign Film; New York Film Critics Awards '56: Best Foreign Film; Nominations: Academy Awards '56: Best Original Screenplay. **VHS, LV** *IME, HMV*

LA TERRA TREMA
Episoda Del Mare
The Earth Will Tremble

Luchino Visconti's portrait of an impoverished family in a Sicilian fishing village is a

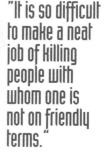

"It is so difficult to make a neat job of killing people with whom one is not on friendly terms."

—Louis (Dennis Price) in *Kind Hearts and Coronets*.

stately and magnificent achievement. As was the case in other Italian works of the neo-realist period, Visconti used a non-professional cast. Yet the film's visual style is a long way from the off-the-cuff look of the Rossellini and De Sica films; Visconti's operatic visual scheme consists of long takes and slow, sweeping, hypnotic camera movements intended to draw the viewer into what is essentially an alien landscape. Visconti went all the way with his realistic approach by having his actors speak in a Sicilian dialect that was unintelligible throughout much of Italy, resulting in the movie being later dubbed into Italian. Further, a narration was added and the movie was extensively cut, effectively demolishing its entire structure. Not surprisingly, the movie was a boxoffice disaster, and wasn't commercially released in the U.S. until more than 20 years after its completion. The director was discouraged enough to abandon movies for a time, but eventually, he was vindicated; the restored, original *La Terra Trema* can at last be rediscovered as the masterwork it is. (It was conceived as part of a trilogy of films: one on the sea, one on the mines, and one on the countryside. As a result of *La Terra Trema*'s commercial failure, only this first part, the subtitle of which is *Episode of the Sea,* was filmed.)

NEXT STOP . . . *Ossessione, Rocco and His Brothers, Christ Stopped at Eboli*

1948 161m/B *IT* Antonio Pietrangeli; *D:* Luchino Visconti. **VHS** *FCT*

THE LACEMAKER
La Dentielliere

A shy young assistant at a beauty shop (Isabelle Huppert) and the student she falls in love with (Yves Beneyton) seem perfectly matched at the deserted Normandy resort where they meet. Upon their return to Paris, however, the myriad differences between them begin to reveal themselves one by one, creating, like the delicate lace the girl makes, a thinly transparent but very real barrier between them. *The Lacemaker*'s conclusion, inevitable perhaps, but shocking neverthe-

less, completes a briefly blazing arc for the troubled woman at the film's center; her character's gradual descent into an intolerable emotional whirlpool is richly and indelibly drawn by Huppert and Swiss director Claude Goretta, even while they use the most delicate of brushstrokes. This 1977 movie was Huppert's breakthrough film; it became a major hit on the international film festival circuit, and created brief but widespread fame for its director.

NEXT STOP . . . *The Wonderful Crook, Violette, Une Femme Douce*

1977 107m/C *FR SI GE* Isabelle Huppert, Yves Beneyton, Florence Giorgetti, Anna Marie Duringer; *D:* Claude Goretta. **LV, Letterbox** *HMV, CRC*

LACOMBE, LUCIEN

Louis Malle's memories of a childhood incident in which classmates were sent to their deaths during the German Occupation of France wouldn't actually be recreated in one of his films until *Au Revoir les Enfants* in 1987. But years earlier, in 1974, the incident was the inspiration for Malle's *Lacombe, Lucien,* a completely gripping and brilliant movie about a young man who becomes one of the hunters, rather than one of the victims. Lucien Lacombe (first-time actor Pierre Blaise) is a teenager in rural France in 1944; his mother is living with another man while his father is in a POW camp. Lucien's education is limited, and he seems not the brightest or most sophisticated of 17-year-olds, so when he approaches the local cell of the resistance movement, his expressed desire to join is rejected. Angered at being turned away, Lucien joins up with the German occupiers instead. This is the true, revelatory shocker in Malle's masterwork. Lucien isn't looking to further the cause of humanity, but as he initially tried to side with the Resistance, he wasn't trying to destroy it, either. How then, could he switch sides "just like that?" That, of course, is our problem to sort out. Malle poses the question of what a moral choice is, how one is made, and just what is the precise point at which one crosses from self-interest to evil? Later in the film, Lucien becomes involved with a Jewish tailor and his daughter who are in hiding—or at least doing their best to not be obvious—and the pair are forced to engage in a subtle attempt to keep Lucien placated so they will not be turned in. In one of Malle's stunning set pieces, the tailor—unable to stand a moment more of hiding—goes out to a plush restaurant even though Gestapo officers are plentiful. He needs this moment of simple, civilized dignity just as he needs air and water, and Malle makes the moment funny, terrifying, and poignant. The tailor has his reasons, as does Lucien. The complexity of those reasons is typical of the entire film, which poses huge moral questions through its matter-of-fact, tight dramatic structure. This is a great movie about how evil happens, and about the overwhelming task of trying to pinpoint that exact moment at which the innocent become guilty. With Holger Lowenadler as the tailor Albert Horn, and Aurore Clément as his daughter, France. Academy Award Nominee, Best Foreign Language Film.

NEXT STOP . . . *The Sorrow and the Pity, Au Revoir les Enfants, The Story of Women*

1974 130m/C *FR* Pierre Blaise, Aurore Clement, Holger Lowenadler, Therese Giehse; *D:* Louis Malle; *W:* Louis Malle, Patrick Modiano; *C:* Tonino Delli Colli; *M:* Django Reinhardt, Andre Claveau. Nominations: Academy Awards '74: Best Original Screenplay. *NYR*

THE LADY WITH THE DOG

Chekhov's *The Lady with the Little Dog* was the basis for this little-seen, completely wonderful Soviet film by director Josef Heifitz. In Yalta at the turn of the century, a vacationing married man named Dmitri (Alexei Batalov) meets a lovely young married woman, Anna (Iya Savvina), when he notices her on her daily walks with her little dog. They begin an affair, but can't bring themselves to end their marriages. Instead, they continue to meet through the years, briefly and in hiding. Their heartbreaking dilemma remains unresolved as the film closes. *The Lady with the Dog* is one of the rare films in which indecisiveness

isn't presented tediously. The movie is gracefully conceived and beautifully performed; many of the images, such as Anna seated at the pier, her little dog by her side as she waits for Dimitri to appear, are quite unforgettable. It's a nearly perfect love story, and has a considerable cult following (Ingmar Bergman is a fan). It was photographed by Andrei Moskvin, one of the two cinematographers of Eisenstein's *Ivan the Terrible*. Special Prize, 1960 Cannes Film Festival.

NEXT STOP . . . *Oblomov, The Overcoat (1959), Brief Encounter*

1959 86m/B *RU* Iya Savvina, Alexei Batalov, Ala Chostakova, N. Alisova; *D:* Yosif Heifitz. **VHS** *WST, FCT, TPV*

L'AGE D'OR
The Age of Gold
The Golden Age

Explicitness and outrageousness should never be confused; it's because of the difference between them that even though highly graphic depictions of human sexuality are not unusual in the cinema of the 1990s, the release in today's cultural climate of a film as proudly subversive as Luis Buñuel's revolutionary 1930 *L'Age d'Or* would be impossible. Written together with Salvador Dali as a calculated affront to even the most liberal bourgeois values, *L'Age d'Or* does contain the bones of a conventional story, but the flesh that Buñuel heaps on them is sensuous, suggestive, and deeply disturbing. A man and a woman (those are their only names) are so anxious to make love that it's difficult for him to fit all of her fingers into his mouth, even though doing so causes his eyes to roll back into his head alarmingly far. Distractions are everywhere—including the now-legendary cow on the bed—and the church's antipathy toward the couple's physical desires may be the most daunting of all to overcome. Pauline Kael has described *L'Age d'Or* as "the most anti-religious, anti-bourgeois of all of Luis Buñuel's films," which is saying something. (In Detroit, an observant Catholic attacked a projector that was unspooling Buñuel's *The Milky Way* as recently as 1980, and the story made page one of the *Detroit News*.) *L'Age d'Or* was indeed widely banned following the riots and demonstrations that greeted its initial release, and until 1984 it was still rarely screened in the U.S. Perhaps less shocking now but every bit as brilliantly, hilariously honest, *L'Age d'Or* retains the power to do that single thing that Jean Cocteau always put highest on his list: "Astonish me."

NEXT STOP . . . *Un Chien Andalou, The Milky Way, The Blood of a Poet*

1930 62m/B *FR* Gaston Modot, Lya Lys, Max Ernst, Pierre Prevert, Marie Berthe Ernst, Paul Eluard; **D:** Luis Bunuel; **W:** Salvador Dali, Luis Bunuel; **C:** Albert Duverger; **M:** Claude Debussy. **VHS, LV** *FCT, IME, GVV*

LAMERICA

Two Italian carpetbaggers (Enrico Lo Verso and Michele Placido) head for poverty-stricken Albania in 1991, the first year after the collapse of the communist dictatorship. Hoping to bleed money out of the instability and general chaos that the country has fallen into, the men attempt to set up a phony corporation with the goal of scamming government grant money, but they need an Albanian national as a figurehead and puppet to pose as chief of their "corporation." They settle on a simple-minded old man (Carmelo Di Mazzarelli) who's spent much of his life in prison camps, and they place him in yet another prison—this time an orphanage—for safekeeping. When the old man escapes, one of the con artists (Lo Verso) goes looking for him, and his search turns into a voyage of discovery that becomes unexpectedly personal, political, and, ultimately, philosophical. This extraordinary and heartbreaking film from director Gianni Amelio is a large-scale, spectacular portrait of humanity in upheaval, yet within it beats the heart of an intimate, tightly focused, neo-realist master-work on the order of *The Bicycle Thief* or *Open City*. Amelio has long been carrying on the tradition of neo-realism in films like *Open Doors* and *The Stolen Children,* but with *Lamerica* (the title's full meaning and impact is best discovered while watching the film) his directorial powers have clearly reached the level of a master. Amelio has taken a complex situation—both politically and emotionally—and has clarified it, rather than simplified it, allowing us to see our own lives within this magnificent, sweeping portrait of the human condition. One of the great films of the 1990s. (See it letterboxed to appreciate its remarkable visual power.)

NEXT STOP . . . *The Stolen Children, The Tree of Wooden Clogs, Paisan*

1995 116m/C *IT* Enrico Lo Verso, Michele Placido, Carmelo Di Mazzarelli, Piro Milkani; **D:** Gianni Amelio; **W:** Gianni Amelio, Andrea Porporati, Alessandro Sermoneta; **C:** Luca Bigazzi; **M:** Franco Piersanti. Nominations: Independent Spirit Awards '97: Best Foreign Film. **VHS, Letterbox** *NYF*

LANCELOT OF THE LAKE
Lancelot du Lac
The Grail
Le Graal

A masterpiece. France's Robert Bresson dreamed of making a film about the King Arthur legend for more than 20 years. By the time he was able to film his *Lancelot of the Lake* (*Lancelot du Lac*) in 1974, Bresson's style had been honed to the point where he was able to tell his story with images that are reduced to their absolute bare essentials. Each moment in the film is an evocation rather than a recreation, and the result is a dreamlike vision that embeds itself in the mind with a force most conventional movies never approach. We sometimes see only portions of a particular action, accompanied by off-screen sounds (as in the astounding jousting tournament), but each moment seems to capture the essence of Bresson's evocation of the failure of Arthur's mission, and the subsequent death of the age of chivalry. *Lancelot of the Lake* is so stylized and distilled that it can draw hoots of derision from audiences unwilling to go along with its uncompromising, minimalist vision. For the adventurous, there's absolutely nothing else like it; *Lancelot of the Lake* becomes the legend in our memories. (Accurate reproduction of the film's color cinematography and dark imagery is essential for the film to work; with luck, new DVD or laserdisc transfers from original print materials will become available.)

NEXT STOP . . . *Diary of a Country Priest, Pickpocket, Day of Wrath*

1974 85m/C *FR* Luc Simon, Laura Duke Condominas, Vladimir Antolek-Oresek, Humbert Balsan, Patrick Bernard, Arthur De Montalembert; *D:* Robert Bresson; *W:* Robert Bresson; *C:* Pasquale De Santis; *M:* Philippe Sarde. **VHS** *NYF*

LAND AND FREEDOM

In her great 1989 documentary *American Dream,* Barbara Kopple chronicled a grueling strike at a Minnesota meat-packing plant and showed how the strikers were constantly in danger of losing their war because they fought so many small skirmishes among themselves. It's not a new syndrome, and it crops up as the central issue in Ken Loach's *Land and Freedom,* his riveting portrait of division among the left during the Spanish Civil War. Loach's film has much of the immediacy of a documentary, but it's a well-crafted narrative about a young British man (Ian Hart) who volunteers to fight Franco for a host of romantic and idealistic reasons. As he gets further into complexities of what he originally perceived to be a simple case of good versus evil, he comes to see that division within his ranks may well be the most formidable impediment to victory. A long sequence in which the fighters debate seemingly minor political points demonstrates—rather agonizingly—that with so many agendas active and so many individual and incompatible goals at play, the identity of the "enemy" became maddeningly unclear. Some of the film's melodramatic sections—such as a predictable romantic subplot—feel like forced, obvious padding to create a more "human" story. But overall, *Land and Freedom* is a valuable and fascinating look at why even the best-intentioned political movements seem to often do their damndest to try and snatch defeat from the jaws of victory.

NEXT STOP . . . *The Good Fight, American Dream, Raining Stones*

1995 109m/C *GB SP GE* Ian Hart, Rosana Pastor, Iciar Bollain, Tom Gilroy, Frederic Pierrot, Marc Martinez; *D:* Ken Loach; *W:* Jim Allen; *C:* Barry Ackroyd; *M:* George Fenton. Cesar Awards '96: Best Foreign Film; Nominations: British Academy Awards '95: Best Film. **VHS** *PGV*

LANDSCAPE IN THE MIST
Topio Stin Omichli

As parents have been known to do when there's a family secret they want to hide from the children, the mother of young Voula and Alexander concocts an elaborate myth to explain an unpleasant truth. The 14-year-old girl and her younger brother have never met their father, and when the kids continue to press for answers to his whereabouts, their mother tries to protect them from learning that they were born out-of-wedlock by telling them that dad is "in Germany." Believing their mother and desperate to find their father, the children take to the road and embark on what will become an epic, life-changing journey. This extraordinary film by Greece's Theo Angelopoulos has the episodic structure and grand design of Greek mythology. Long, wordless passages accompanied by only natural sounds (sequences stunningly photographed by Giorgos Arvanitis) evoke visions of a strange landscape as seen though the eyes of hopeful children: visions that are soon dramatically challenged by a universe teeming with chance and danger. Be aware that *Landscape in the Mist* will prove insufferable to those whose attention-span-o-meters are set to "get to the point already," or "just tell me what happens to the kids." For everyone else (count me among them), Angelopoulos's intoxicating, masterful, magnificent real-life fairy-tale possesses the rare, precious power to transport attentive and willing viewers to a new and unforgettable world.

NEXT STOP . . . *Ulysses' Gaze, The Stolen Children, Forbidden Games*

1988 126m/C *GR FR IT* Tania Palaiologou, Michalis Zeke, Stratos Tzortzoglou, Eva Kotamanidou, Alika

Theatre director
Marion (Catherine
Denevue) with the
company's lead
actor, Bernard
(Gerard Depardieu)
in *The Last Metro.*

Georgouli; ***D:*** Theo Angelopoulos; ***W:*** Thanassis Valti̧-
nos, Tonino Guerra, Theo Angelopoulos; ***C:*** Yorgos
Arvanitis; ***M:*** Eleni Karaindrou. **VHS** *NYF, FCT, BTV*

L'ARGENT
Money

In 1983, at the age of 76, France's Robert Bresson returned to the screen with an unexpected and undeniable masterpiece. A coun-
terfeit 500 franc note is given to a delivery
man by a store clerk. The man uses the bill, is
arrested, and sees everything in his universe
devastatingly altered as a result. Bresson's
L'Argent ("Money") is a portrait of how corruption taints not only the innocent but all
who come in contact with the carrier; the
inevitable downward spiral of so many lives
as a result of one seemingly simple act is a
precise and terrifyingly beautiful visualiza-
tion of the progressively larger, rippling

waves that are generated by casual, thought-
less sin. Watching *L'Argent* you're reminded
of the Ray Bradbury story in which a man
travels back in time and is warned against
touching anything; he accidentally steps on
a single butterfly, and when he returns to the
present, the world has changed completely.
Performed—as are all of Bresson's films—by
a non-professional cast, and photographed
in a stripped-down, uncluttered series of perfectly evocative images, *L'Argent* poses more
questions that it can conceivably answer. The
clear-eyed but open-ended vision of a master, *L'Argent,* based loosely on Tolstoy's *The
False Note,* is a mesmerizing portrait of a universe the delicate balance of which can be
tipped at any instant—with disastrous and
unplanned results.

NEXT STOP . . . *Pickpocket, The Earrings of Madame
de…, Tales of Manhattan*

1983 82m/C *FR* Christian Patey, Sylvie van den Elsen,

Michel Briguet, Caroline Lang; **D:** Robert Bresson; **W:** Robert Bresson; **C:** Pasquale De Santis. Cannes Film Festival '83: Best Director (Bresson); National Society of Film Critics Awards '84: Best Director (Bresson). **VHS** *NYF, FCT*

THE LAST LAUGH
Der Letzte Mann

The great moment of German silent star Emil Jannings's career was his performance as the proud hotel doorman who is demoted to washroom attendant in F.W. Murnau's brilliant expressionist fable *The Last Laugh*. The doorman, whose age prevents him from lifting the guests' overstuffed baggage as easily as he used to, is so humiliated by the demotion that he hides the fact from his wife and neighbors. He stashes his doorman's uniform in a closet, putting it on just before returning to his apartment's courtyard. Though he is degraded at having to descend (literally, as if going down to Hell) to the bustling Berlin hotel's basement washroom as his new station in life, it's the loss of his elaborate, gold-buttoned doorman's uniform that seems to be the real source of his shame. (There's something peculiarly Teutonic about this obsession with uniform and rank, and when students look at *The Last Laugh* in film history classes they sometimes just can't connect with the whole uniform thing; they figure if his pay's the same, what's the difference?) Murnau's camera reveals the doorman's internal states through dizzying motion, distorted, rotating lenses, lighting, and set design—the entire film, including the street scenes, were photographed under strictly controlled conditions within the huge UFA film studios. Murnau was forced by the studio to tack on a happy ending to what was obviously intended to be an operatic-style tragedy, but he made the most of it; it's impossible to leave *The Last Laugh* unmoved or unimpressed.

NEXT STOP . . . *The Joyless Street, Sunrise, The Crowd*

1924 77m/B *GE* Emil Jannings, Maly Delshaft, Max Hiller; **D:** F.W. Murnau. **VHS** *NOS, FCT, IHF*

THE LAST METRO
Le Dernier Metro

In Nazi-occupied Paris, an acclaimed theatre director (Heinz Bennent) hides in the basement of his theatre, knowing that his German-Jewish heritage will cost him his life if he's discovered. Above ground, his beautiful wife (Catherine Deneuve) keeps productions running while dealing both personally and professionally with the theatre's daily trials, which include the company's intriguing new leading man (Gérard Depardieu). The movie is a romantic fantasy about theatrical troupers—a group of show-business professionals from different economic, social, and cultural backgrounds who share the common passion of their trade/art—and how they stick together under extreme circumstances. What hurts the effectiveness of the film's melodramatic plot is that those extreme circumstances just happen to be the Occupation. The lyrically romantic tone that Truffaut is after here is sabotaged by our own knowledge of the period; it's not what he leaves out—it's what we automatically bring in. Knowing how enthusiastically so many French citizens turned in other French citizens, we naturally fear the worst. When that doesn't happen we don't feel the elation we're supposed to experience—we may instead feel we've fallen prey to a well-meaning but unconvincing sleight-of-hand routine. You wonder during the movie's happy ending if others seeing the film are going to naively think that every sophisticated Parisian was hiding a Jew in his basement. (It doesn't help that *The Sorrow and the Pity* had already enlightened us about French complicity in the war years.) For me such unavoidable thoughts dampened—but didn't completely sink—*The Last Metro*'s many real pleasures. We bring a lot with us to movies—even when they're fairy tales—but sometimes too much carry-on baggage is enough to prevent a light vehicle from ever taking off. Academy Award Nominee, Best Foreign Language Film.

NEXT STOP . . . *Europa, Europa, Commissar, Au Revoir les Enfants*

American Marlon Brando with his young French lover Maria Schneider in *Last Tango in Paris.*

1980 135m/C *FR* Catherine Deneuve, Gerard Depardieu, Heinz Bennent, Jean-Louis Richard, Jean Poiret, Andrea Ferreol, Paulette Dubost, Sabine Haudepin; *D:* Francois Truffaut; *W:* Suzanne Schiffman; *C:* Nestor Almendros; *M:* Georges Delerue. Cesar Awards '81: Best Actor (Depardieu), Best Actress (Deneuve), Best Art Direction/Set Decoration, Best Cinematography, Best Director (Truffaut), Best Film, Best Sound, Best Writing, Best Score; Nominations: Academy Awards '80: Best Foreign-Language Film. **VHS, LV** *HMV, FOX, SWC*

THE LAST SUPPER

An ostensibly repentant, pious Cuban slave owner in the 18th century decides to simultaneously cleanse his soul and convert his slaves to Christianity by having a dozen of them reenact the Last Supper. Based on a true incident, this bitterly satirical swipe at the ties between colonialism, religious repression, and racism is one of the angriest films by Cuba's Tomás Gutiérrez Alea. The picture exists for the purpose of its long, blas-

phemous final sequence, which is an amazing bit of theatrical construction and performance. Overall, though, the movie's politics are really hammered home past the point of overkill—as such it's an anomaly in the generally subtle and generous-spirited works of this extraordinary director.

NEXT STOP . . . *Memories of Underdevelopment, Guantanamera!, I Am Cuba*

1976 110m/C *CU* Nelson Villagra, Silvano Rey, Lamberto Garcia, Jose Antonio Rodriguez, Samuel Claxton, Mario Balmasada; *D:* Tomas Gutierrez Alea. **VHS** *NYF, FCT*

LAST TANGO IN PARIS

Marlon Brando, an expatriate American in Paris in an emotional daze after the suicide of his wife, meets a young girl (Maria Schneider) who's about to get married and is looking for an apartment. They spontaneously begin an affair while at the same time attempting to remain anonymous—meeting in the apartment for uninhibited sexual encounters while pretending to not reveal anything about themselves. Bernardo Bertolucci's extraordinary and stunningly beautiful landmark film is like an Aesop's Fable with orgasms; we discover, as we already may have suspected, that our struggle to see sex as something "other," something separate and distinct from our "real" lives, is both ludicrous and futile. To dramatize this visually, Bertolucci includes scenes of both that sun-drenched "real" world, which exists under an open sky, and the hidden, secret world, where this couple desperately tries to maintain a private universe. The apartment that Brando and Schneider meet in is dark and bare-walled and closed-off; it works visually in the way that the dark, enclosed rooms in *The Godfather* did, suggesting the private recesses of the imagination. This image is also like a child's clubhouse, in which a kid can make up his own rules and fantasize the day away, but at a certain point he's got to leave, as do Brando and Schneider, each by a different route. Brando's performance is legendary, and deservedly so. It's an amazing, visionary work. Co-starring Jean-Pierre Léaud, with cinematography by the brilliant Vittorio Storaro. Oscar Nominations for Best Actor and Director.

NEXT STOP . . . *The Spider's Stratagem, Every Man for Himself* (1980, Jean-Luc Godard), *The Story of Adele H.*

1973 (R) 126m/C *IT FR* Marlon Brando, Maria Schneider, Jean-Pierre Leaud; *D:* Bernardo Bertolucci; *W:* Bernardo Bertolucci; *C:* Vittorio Storaro; *M:* Gato Barbieri. New York Film Critics Awards '73: Best Actor (Brando); National Society of Film Critics Awards '73: Best Actor (Brando); Nominations: Academy Awards '73: Best Actor (Brando), Best Director (Bertolucci). **VHS, LV, Letterbox** *MGM, FOX*

LAST YEAR AT MARIENBAD
L'Anee Derniere a Marienbad

In a huge chateau, "X" (Giorgio Albertazzi) tries to convince "A" (Delphine Seyrig) that they've met before. "M" (Sacha Pitoeff) may

be "A"'s husband or may not be. That's about it. What writer Alain Robbe-Grillet and director Alain Resnais do with these plot elements is to rearrange and reconstruct them, trying to illustrate the flow of memory and time as something malleable or amorphous. It could be likened to the "time warp" concept so popular in science-fiction, but the best science-fiction does its best to keep you awake. Alain Resnais has done great work using the manipulation of time and viewpoint as his principal storytelling tool; *Night and Fog, Providence,* and *Mon Oncle d'Amerique* are extraordinary films in which the shifting of time and remembrance are central to the films' resonant power. But *Last Year at Marienbad* is so theoretical as to be of almost solely academic interest; it's a standard item in film studies classes, and that's where it's perhaps best left. It was a much talked-about movie when released in the U.S., confirming "lowbrow" moviegoers' worst fears about "highbrow" cinema—but everybody liked the clothes. Speaking of clothes—the emperor's new ones—this largely indecipherable movie received, in one of film history's most amusing ironies, a nomination for Best Original Screenplay at the 1962 Academy Awards.

NEXT STOP . . . *Hiroshima Mon Amour, The Truck (Le Camion), La Guerre Est Finie*

1961 93m/B *FR IT* Delphine Seyrig, Giorgia Albertazzi, Sacha Pitoeff, Luce Garcia-Ville; *D:* Alain Resnais; *C:* Sacha Vierny. Nominations: Academy Awards '62: Best Story & Screenplay. **VHS, 8mm** *FXL, MRV, NOS*

L'ATALANTE
Le Chaland Qui Passe

Juliette (Dita Parlo) is a newly married bride whose husband Jean (Jean Dasté) is a mate aboard the barge named l'Atalante. Unhappy with her unglamorous life aboard ship, and frustrated by tales of the outside world's wonders—spun magically by the cantankerous old first mate Père Jules (Michel Simon)—Juliette makes a break for it when the barge docks in Paris. Alone in separate beds, his on the barge and hers in a cheap Parisian hotel, Jean and Juliette toss and turn, utterly confused by the turn their

"Everything in this world is good for something."

—Il Matto (Richard Basehart) to Gelsomina (Giulietta Masina) in *La Strada.*

lives have taken while longing restlessly for each other's familiar bodies. That the satisfying conclusion that *L'Atalante* soon reaches is, perhaps, predictable, is the least important element of the film. In fact, nothing about this simple tale is, on the surface, all that exceptional; as the outline of a film script it reads like a sketchy treatment that needs fleshing out. That might have been the case with the finished product, if it hadn't been directed by a genius. Jean Vigo was 29 when he directed what may be the most purely poetic and eloquently primal love story ever put on film. The power of *L'Atalante* is cumulative, as a series of what appear to be offhanded and quirky moments, both melodramatic and comic, culminate in a simple but shockingly moving moment of rescue—from pride, from danger, from one's self—that is as sure to provoke tears on each viewing as is the single, transcendent sentence that John Wayne speaks to Natalie Wood at the end of *The Searchers.* Photographed by the legendary Boris Kaufman (brother of Soviet director Dziga Vertov) and scored with an easy majesty by Charles Goldblatt and Maurice Jaubert (whose music would be reprised for some of the later films of François Truffaut), *L'Atalante* would be the last film by Jean Vigo, who died before the film's final editing. The studio found *L'Atalante* self-indulgent (nothing ever changes in the movie business), retitled it *Le Chaland qui Passe,* and opened and closed it quickly. The full *L'Atalante* was only released in 1945, and in the 1990s, a restored version was circulated in American art houses to the rapturous reviews and public acceptance it has always deserved.

NEXT STOP . . . *Zero for Conduct, A Propos de Nice, Harvest*

1934 82m/B *FR* Dita Parlo, Jean Daste, Michel Simon; *D:* Jean Vigo; *W:* Jean Vigo, Jean Guinee, Albert Riera; *C:* Boris Kaufman, Louis Berger; *M:* Maurice Jaubert. **VHS** *NOS, HHT, PMS*

LATE SPRING

This masterpiece by Japan's Yasujiro Ozu tells a story that Ozu has related, with variations, many times: A widower (Chishu Ryu) living with his unmarried daughter is torn between the joy of her companionship and care, and the knowledge that she needs to create a life of her own apart from him. He knows that her devotion to him will prevent her from seeking a husband, so he tells her that he's going to remarry, knowing that she'll have no choice but to go out on her own and begin the independent life that is the natural state of things. Alone in his home at the end of the film, his plan successfully accomplished, the old man sits silently and peels a piece of fruit, growing completely still momentarily as he contemplates his future and the inexorable pattern of life. It may be the most powerful and characteristic single image in all of Ozu's films, perfectly summing up his philosophy of *mono no aware,* or the serene acceptance of the inevitable sadness of life. For many years, Ozu's films were thought to be "too Japanese" for export—that western audiences in particular would find them less appealing than some of the action-packed samurai films they were used to. In fact, Ozu's films, like some of Chaplin's masterworks, are as universal as the cinema—or any art form—can be. Films like *Late Spring, Tokyo Story,* and *An Autumn Afternoon* are brilliant distillations of our great human dilemma; how can we experience joy when we know that suffering inevitably awaits? Neither depressing nor maudlin, Ozu's view is both reassuring and bracing, and one of the highest, noblest peaks of the cinema's first century.

NEXT STOP . . . *Floating Weeds, Late Autumn, Tokyo Story*

1949 107m/B *JP* Setsuko Hara, Chishu Ryu, Jun Usami, Haruko Sugimura; *D:* Yasujiro Ozu. **VHS** *NYF, FCT*

L'AVVENTURA
The Adventure

Is it possible to refer to 1960 as *just one of those years*? It's not every year that sees the release of landmarks like *La Dolce Vita, Hiroshima Mon Amour,* or *Rocco and His Brothers.* It was even a great year for popular entertainments like *The Apartment, Spartacus, The Entertainer,* and even—on a different plane, perhaps—*Little Shop of Horrors.* All well and good, yet how often in modern times have *two* films been released in a single year that have altered forever not only the language of cinema itself, but have also influenced for all time the way in which a society views itself? One of these movies, Alfred Hitchcock's *Psycho,* introduced Americans to what was to be one of the most turbulent decades in its recent history by unexpectedly replacing the point-of-view of a victim with that of her killer. The other, Michelangelo Antonioni's *L'Avventura,* didn't play the commercial movie houses that Hitchcock's film did, yet its influence on popular culture and the intelligentsia was such that it had a trickle down impact that is still with us. A young woman (Lea Massari) on a yachting trip disappears from an island near the Sicilian coast. Her lover Sandro (Gabriele Ferzetti) and her best friend Claudia (Monica Vitti) go searching for her, and they begin an affair—almost wordlessly—in the emptiness of her absence. The tensions created by Antonioni's stark, barren compositions are, in a sense, the framework of the story he's telling. He depicts a world as vacuum, a world in which sex is the instinctual human response to what we were always told about nature—that it abhors a vacuum. *L'Avventura* isn't just a picture about the decadent idle rich—it's a vision of a universe without direction, in which the inhabitants who have been unable or unwilling to find a meaning to their existence are drawn into the far easier escape of purely physical coupling. It's a world in which Eros, as the director himself has put it, "is sick." *L'Avventura* showed us that the cinema was capable of reinventing itself when necessary in order to express that which can only told through the images and rhythm of film. This script wouldn't have survived a modern story conference, if for no other reason than the "mystery" that Sandro and Claudia initially set out to solve is not only left a mystery at the end, it's *forgotten* about. *L'Avventura,* a Rosetta stone for the post-1960 cinema and one of the greatest films of all time, is available in well-mastered letterbox laserdiscs and cassettes.

NEXT STOP . . . *The Eclipse, Red Desert, Landscape in the Mist*

1960 145m/C *IT* Monica Vitti, Gabriele Ferzetti, Lea Massari, Dominique Blanchar, James Addams; *D:* Michelangelo Antonioni; *W:* Tonino Guerra, Michelangelo Antonioni; *C:* Aldo Scavarda; *M:* Giovanni Fusco. Cannes Film Festival '60: Special Jury Prize. **VHS, LV, Letterbox** *CVC, VDM, HMV*

LE BEAU MARIAGE
A Good Marriage
The Well-Made Marriage

More than a decade before Eric Rohmer made *Le Beau Mariage,* he cast the very young Béatrice Romand in his great *Claire's Knee* as Laura, a brilliant, precocious child almost frighteningly wise in the ways of romance. But while the earlier film was a tale of erotic obsession fulfilled, *Le Beau Mariage* finds Romand as Sabine, a 20-something yuppie driven by a decidedly non-erotic agenda: the nailing down of a reasonably adequate male specimen—the first one she can find—to assume the role of immediate husband and future father. Sabine settles on a lawyer and zeros in for the kill, and watching her at work on the guy is both fascinating and depressing. You keep hoping for both of their sakes that she won't succeed, yet one's sense of traditional movie suspense makes you root unconsciously for this misdirected powerhouse to get what she wants. It's a little like the mixed feelings you have seeing the evil Robert Walker's fingers almost touching the incriminating lighter through the grating in Hitchcock's *Strangers on a Train*—you don't want an innocent man convicted of a crime, yet something in you roots for him to reach down just a *little* bit further to grab his undeserved prize.

NEXT STOP . . . *The Aviator's Wife, Boyfriends & Girlfriends, Claire's Knee*

1982 (R) 97m/C *FR* Beatrice Romand, Arielle Dombasle, Andre Dussollier, Feodor Atkine, Pascal Greggory, Sophie Renoir; *D:* Eric Rohmer; *W:* Eric Rohmer; *C:* Bernard Lutic; *M:* Ronan Girre, Simon des Innocents. Venice Film Festival '82: Best Actress (Romand). **VHS** *NO*

LE BONHEUR
Happiness

In a picturesque French suburb, a young carpenter named François shares an idyllic exis-

227

tence with his wife, Thérèse, and their two children. When I say idyllic, I mean it; when the family isn't on picnics in the sun-dappled woods near their home, François and Thérèse are making love, usually with Mozart on the soundtrack. My early memories of Agnes Varda's 1965 *Le Bonheur* ("Happiness") are centered on this gauzy, dreamy depiction of marriage, which I found intolerably corny in my teen years during the Vietnam era. The fact that François later began an affair with Emilie, a post office clerk, with whom he and the children live happily ever after following the death of his wife, only made the picture seem sillier to me at the time. Fast forward. In 1997, some 30 years after I first saw it, a friend invited me to a screening of a restored color print of *Le Bonheur* at New York's Museum of Modern Art. My, my. What a difference living a life makes. Not only is this film *not* the candy-colored, sentimental pabulum that I had remembered, it's the opposite: complex, wise,

and darkly, almost breathtakingly subversive. What escaped me as a teen? Everything. For starters, the open, sunny honesty of the married couple's relationship leads to François telling Thérèse of his feelings for Emilie. She tells him that she loves him so much that his happiness is what counts. Right after telling him that, she drowns. (While her death is presented ambiguously, I'm convinced she did herself in.) After what seems like a few minutes of mourning, François does indeed find himself as happy as can be with Emilie, and they go off picnicking, guilt-free and grief-free, with the same Mozart riffs on the soundtrack that we heard at the beginning. The bone-chilling irony of *Le Bonheur*'s ending outdoes the moment in Woody Allen's *Crimes and Misdemeanors* in which Martin Landau describes waking up one day—after he sanctions his lover's murder—and feels no guilt whatsoever. That Varda's film is so damned honest only makes it more hair-raising. It's a fairy tale for grown-ups who harbor no illusions whatsoever. As much as any film from its time, *Le Bonheur* is ripe for fresh look.

NEXT STOP . . . *The Umbrellas of Cherbourg, Jacquot, The Soft Skin*

1965 87m/C *FR* Jean-Claude Drouot, Claire Drouot, Marie-France Boyer; *D:* Agnes Varda; *W:* Agnes Varda; *C:* Jean Rabier, Claude Beausoleil. **VHS** *HMV, FCT*

LE BOUCHER
The Butcher

In a small French village, a serial killer is spreading deep shadows of fear through the normally quiet, sheltered streets. A schoolteacher (Stéphane Audran) suspects the town's butcher (Jean Yanne) of the crimes, yet she doesn't want to believe that it's so. The clues that lead her to suspect him are also clues to the man's tortured, traumatic military past, and the more she understands about him, the more sympathetic—and emotionally close—she feels. There's more than a touch of Alfred Hitchcock's *Shadow of a Doubt* in Claude Chabrol's brooding and surprisingly poignant *Le Boucher* (*The Butcher*). Like Hitchcock's film, which portrayed a serial killer hiding in a small California town, Chabrol is concerned not only with the lasting impact of evil on the innocent, but with the more subversive notion that good and evil share common emotional ground. In *Shadow* it was the widow-murdering Uncle Charlie (Joseph Cotten) who shared a psychic bond with his namesake, his trusting niece Charlie (Teresa Wright). Here, Audran also knows what she must do to eliminate the evil in front of her, yet she's aware that she'll be changed forever by the experience. The true horror, in both this film and in Hitchcock's movie, is that the evil cannot be objectified; what gives us—and the protagonists/survivors—nightmares is knowing that the enemy's thoughts, feelings, and unquenchable drives are far from incomprehensible.

NEXT STOP . . . *M, Shadow of a Doubt, Just Before Nightfall*

1969 94m/C *FR* Stephane Audran, Jean Yanne, Antonio Passallia; *D:* Claude Chabrol; *W:* Claude Chabrol. **VHS, LV** *CVC*

LE DERNIER COMBAT
The Last Battle

Luc Besson was 24 when he directed this visually striking, post-nuke survival pic about a group of youthful survivors who quickly remember what it means to be territorial. The widescreen black-and-white compositions are gorgeous; they have to be, because there's no dialogue in the movie—just grunts and heavy breathing. That heavy breathing you hear on the couch next to you may be your significant other snoring. The French film industry didn't sleep through *Le Dernier Combat,* however. They took note of this young upstart, who eventually became the most powerful force in France's film universe, thanks to his splashy worldwide hits *La Femme Nikita* and *The Fifth Element.*

NEXT STOP . . . *Subway, The Road Warrior, Hell in the Pacific*

1984 (R) 93m/B *FR* Pierre Jolivet, Fritz Wepper, Jean Reno, Jean Bouise, Christiane Kruger; *D:* Luc Besson; *W:* Luc Besson. **VHS** *COL, OM*

LE DOULOS
Doulos—The Finger Man

Jean-Paul Belmondo is a shady hoodlum who's suspected of being a police informer (a stool-pigeon/finger-man, or *doulos*) by the criminals who number themselves among his associates. As the film unfolds, we're let in on the secrets of this underworld bit by bit, tantalizingly, as the suspense mounts and the shocks and unexpected twists both surprise and delight us. The biggest surprise is saved for the end, however; as the late, wonderfully gifted film critic (and friend) Kathy Huffhines put it: "a simple phone call is the world's suavest good-bye...you discover that the director himself has been a stoolie and that life itself is the real double-crosser." With the recent restoration and rediscovery of Melville's great *Le Samourai*, it's time for a similar rehabilitation for the spectacularly atmospheric, gloriously corrupt *Le Doulos.*

"No, no, I don't —I don't want to know your name. You don't have a name, and I don't have a name either. No names here. Not one name."

—Paul (Marlon Brando) to Jeanne (Maria Schneider) in *Last Tango in Paris.*

NEXT STOP . . . *Bob le Flambeur, Le Samourai, Chinatown*

1961 108m/B *FR* Serge Reggiani, Jean-Paul Belmondo, Michel Piccoli; *D:* Jean-Pierre Melville. **VHS** *INT, TPV*

LE JOLI MAI

Chris Marker is an extraordinary artist; his films are varied, bold, and utterly fresh in their concept and concerns. His *Le Joli Mai* was conceived as a two-part examination of Paris in May of 1962, the month that the war in Algeria came to an end. Since this was, in effect, the first time France had been fully at peace since 1939, Marker wanted to document the city at this important moment in history. Part one of the film, titled *A Prayer From the Eiffel Tower,* is an overview of ordinary life in the city—salesmen, lovers, poets and children go about their daily business. Part two, *The Return of Fantomas,* is a more overtly political analysis of Paris, in which street demonstrators and students explain their positions, their anger, their fear and their heartbreak. In the film's stirring epilogue, which focuses on a prison, Marker draws a parallel; he suggests that unburdened by France's colonialist adventures, its citizens may now look upon their city as if they themselves had been released from jail, and are breathing the air of freedom for the first time in decades. Beautifully photographed, poetic and elliptical, *Le Joli Mai* remains an audacious encapsulation of a significant moment in modern history. Narrated by Yves Montand and Simone Signoret in both the French and English versions.

NEXT STOP . . . *La Jetée, The Koumiko Mystery, The Battle of Chile*

1962 180m/B *FR D:* Chris Marker. **VHS** *FCT*

LE JOUR SE LÈVE
Daybreak

A lone man (Jean Gabin) sits locked behind the door of a rooming-house apartment as police downstairs discover the body of the man he has just murdered. As the police attempt to arrest him, Gabin remembers in flashback the lifelong series of events that inexorably led to this most desperate of moments. A brilliantly structured and stunningly designed example of "poetic realism," *Le Jour Se Lève* (*Daybreak*) is the product of an inspired collaboration between director Marcel Carné and screenwriter Jacques Prévert, who years later would be the principal forces behind the great *Children of Paradise. Le Jour Se Lève* is a riveting and emotionally complex piece of storytelling that expands as we watch it into a fully formed vision of humanity at the mercy of forces beyond its control. The look of the film is both dreamlike and gritty; Alexander Trauner's set designs and Curt Courant's cinematography are completely at one with the movie's haunting, disturbingly claustrophobic tone. Arletty, Jacqueline Laurent, and Jules Berry co-star with Gabin. The magnificent score is by Maurice Jaubert (*L'Atalante*), who died in World War II combat the following year. (In 1975, 35 years after Jaubert's death, François Truffaut revived interest in the composer by brilliantly using older Jaubert works to score *The Story of Adele H..*)

NEXT STOP . . . *The Crime of Monsieur Lange, Children of Paradise, Crimes and Misdemeanors*

1939 89m/B *FR* Jean Gabin, Jules Berry, Arletty, Jacqueline Laurent; *D:* Marcel Carne. **VHS** *HMV, GVV, HHT*

LE MILLION

Starving artist Michel (René Lefèvre) is thrilled to discover that he's the owner of a winning lottery ticket, but his joy turns to panic when he realizes that the ticket was in the pocket of a coat he sold at a secondhand store. In a splendid touch of irony, the artist's coat is purchased by an operatic tenor, who finds it authentically tattered enough to use as part of his costume for a production of *La Bohème.* Director René Clair's inspired comic musical is the story of Michel's desperate pursuit of that lottery ticket—which eventually leads him to a chaotic and hilarious night at the opera—and is also the tale of the frantic parade of creditors, cops, thieves, and hangers-on who are pursuing Michel. *Le Million* is weird, funny, and ingenious; surrealistic comic *schtick* erupts unexpectedly, and much of that well-orchestrated anarchy was to be influential for years to come. The Marx Brothers had already established a beachhead on screen, but *The Cocoanuts* was a filmed play, and *Monkey Business*—released the same year as *Le Million*—still felt stagebound. Clair's ideas, which rethought the concept of musical comedy in cinematically innovative and visually inventive ways, inspired much of the subsequent liberating Marx madness of *Horse Feathers* and *Duck Soup,* and, more specifically, the hilariously mangled *Il Trovatore* of *A Night at the Opera.* Still, there's nothing quite like *Le Million*, which looks as hip and startling today as it must have when first released. It's *almost* as much fun as winning the lottery.

NEXT STOP . . . *A Nous la Liberté, Modern Times, Duck Soup*

1931 89m/B *FR* Annabella, Rene Lefevre, Paul Olivier, Louis Allibert; *D:* Rene Clair. **VHS** *VYY, NOS, DVT*

LE PLAISIR
House of Pleasure

The three stories of which Max Ophüls's exhilarating *Le Plaisir* is comprised are based on tales by Guy de Maupassant. A woman explains to a doctor that her husband is phobic about becoming wrinkled. A *madame* agrees to shut down her business temporarily, so that she and her employees can attend her niece's first communion. Finally, a painter and his model have an affair, which has tragic, and then marvelous, consequences. Made immediately after his triumphant *La Ronde,* the whirling, lyrical, deeply romantic *Le Plaisir* displays in every frame Ophüls's joy at returning to the romantic Europe that the Nazis forced him to leave behind. Narrated by Peter Ustinov, who would appear as the ringmaster in Ophüls's final masterpiece, *Lola Montès.*

NEXT STOP . . . *La Signora di Tutti, La Ronde, The Earrings of Madame de. . .*

1952 97m/B *FR* Claude Dauphin, Simone Simon, Jean Gabin, Danielle Darrieux, Madeleine Renaud, Gaby Morlay; *D:* Max Ophuls. Nominations: Academy Awards '54: Best Art Direction/Set Decoration (B & W). **VHS** *NOS, DVT, GVV*

LE SAMOURAI
The Samurai

The steely eyed 32-year-old Alain Delon is Jef Costello, an ice-cold, contract killer who lives—and is prepared to die—by a personal code of honor, in a world where betrayal is the norm on *both* sides of the law. Jef's latest job, which requires him to murder a nightclub owner, has plunged him into a whirlpool of intrigue, treachery, and revenge that the trenchcoated hit man will either extricate himself from via his own rules, or die trying. French director Jean-Pierre Melville's justly legendary *Le Samourai* is a thrillingly stylized, mythic epic of revenge set in the dark and seedy back alleys of a Paris that seems to have been dreamed rather than filmed. What little talk there is is tougher than a two-dollar steak, yet buried deep in the unforgiving universe of *Le Samourai* is a breathtakingly romantic heart, grieving for the loss of an era when there was honor among thieves. The bitter realization that such a time never existed is what ultimately destroys Jef, and it makes *Le Samourai* the *noir* of *noirs.* Though it was made in 1967, *Le Samourai* wasn't seen in the U.S. until the early 1970s—and then only in a cut, dubbed version that was ludicrously but opportunistically titled *The Godson.* The original finally reached American screens in 1997, and it was greeted by a well-deserved, too-long-delayed outpouring of critical raves. Add mine. With François Perier as the police inspector determined to nail Jef, Nathalie Delon as Jef's longtime lover, and Caty Rosier as the nightclub singer who could finger Jef as the killer, but doesn't. The hallucinatory, barely colored images are by the brilliant cinematographer Henri Decaë.

NEXT STOP . . . *Le Doulos, Bob le Flambeur, The Killer*

1967 95m/C *FR* Alain Delon, Francois Perier, Cathy Rosier, Nathalie Delon, Jacques Leroy, Jean-Pierre Posier; *D:* Jean-Pierre Melville; *W:* Jean-Pierre Melville; *C:* Henri Decae; *M:* Francois de Roubaix. **VHS** *NYF*

Group shot of
the outlandish
Finnish band in
*Leningrad Cowboys
Go America.*

LE TROU
The Hole
The Night Watch
Il Buco

Based on the true story of five prisoners who attempted a seemingly impossible escape from a notorious French prison in 1947, French director Jacques Becker's *Le Trou* (*The Hole*) has never received theatrical distribution in the United States. The distributors who turned it down should be sent to the slammer themselves, because *Le Trou* is one of the great prison films—nearly on a level with Bresson's *A Condemned Man Has Escaped*—and a textbook example of how to generate true suspense on screen. There have been a lot of movies about digging tunnels out of prisons, but after experiencing *Le Trou* and feeling the steady, rhythmic clanging of tools pounding at cement hour after hour, day after day, this claustrophobic,

uncompromising stunner is the one you'll remember. Without wanting to reveal the ending, it's safe to tell you that one of the five men whose true story is told in the film—Jose Giovanni—was still very much alive as of this writing and was the author of the autobiographical novel on which Becker based this film. In a rather amazing example of art becoming indistinguishable from life, Giovanni not only collaborated on the screenplay of *Le Trou,* but also went on to write scripts for other French filmmakers before trying his own hand at directing.

NEXT STOP . . . *A Condemned Man Has Escaped, Grand Illusion, Casque d'Or*

1959 118m/B Phillippe LeRoy, Marc Michel, Catherine Spaak, Andre Bervil, Michel Constantin, Jean-Paul Coquelin, Jean Keraudy, Raymond Meunier, Eddy Rasimi, Dominique Zardi; **D:** Jacques Becker; **W:** Jacques Becker, Jose Giovanni, Jean Aurel; **C:** Ghislan Cloquet. *NYR*

LENINGRAD COWBOYS GO AMERICA

Finnish wunderkind Aki Kaurismäki has built an international reputation with ironic, dead-pan comedies like *Ariel, The Match Factory Girl,* and *Drifting Clouds.* His 1989 *Leningrad Cowboys Go America* was Kaurismäki's version of a "breakout" film, designed with enough physical comedy and bizarre sight gags to get wider play in the U.S. than his usual art house engagements. But Kaurismäki seems to be both too cynical and too gifted to be a successful panderer, and his hysterical *Leningrad Cowboys* played to nearly empty theatres here, despite his best efforts at selling out. It's the story of a Finnish rock band called Leningrad Cowboys, who sport hep gray suits, lethally pointy shiny leather boots, and outrageous, mile-high pompadours. Their music is as terrible as their look, so they decide their best chance at stardom is to go to America, where "they'll listen to anything." *Leningrad Cowboys* is the story of their American "tour"; it's a less raucous, hallucinatory *This Is Spinal Tap,* in which most of the laughs are muted, and stem not from a Finnish-American culture clash, but from the Cowboys' cultural clash with the rest of the human race. If you either don't get it or *do* get it and *wish* you didn't, this could be the longest 79 minutes of your life. On the other hand, if you find the movie funny, as I do, you'll want to watch it repeatedly, as I do. It features the late Matti Pellonpää and Kaurismäki's American counterpart, Jim Jarmusch. You'll also want to catch the Leningrad Cowboys' astonishing, already legendary 1994 hour-long concert film, *The Total Balalaika Show,* in which good-time standards like "The Volga Boatman," "Knockin' on Heaven's Door," and "Happy Together" are hilariously demolished for all eternity.

NEXT STOP . . . *The Total Balalaika Show, Stroszek, Mystery Train*

1989 (PG-13) 78m/C *FI* Jim Jarmusch, Matti Pellonpaa, Kari Vaananen, Nicky Tesco; **D:** Aki Kaurismaki; **W:** Aki Kaurismaki. **VHS, LV, Letterbox** *ORI, FCT*

LÉOLO

French-Canadian director Jean-Claude Lauzon's 1992 *Léolo* is a powerful, frightening, sometimes magical movie that suggests the work of a true visionary. This is a portrait of a child growing up in a mad Montreal household, and it's told—both in its narration and its expressionist images—from that child's point of view. Young Leo has renamed himself Léolo for what he believes to be a very good reason; he's convinced that his heritage is at least partly Italian, due to the fact that his mother was directly impregnated by a sperm-laden Italian tomato—a Sicilian tomato, to be precise. Therefore the sperm that sired him was presumably provided by a Sicilian as well, relieving Léolo of the burden of being the offspring of his ghoulish father, and distancing him from his equally creepy siblings. Léolo spends more time in the bathroom than the adolescent Alex Portnoy, but bowel movements—and proof thereof—are his family's *raison d'etre.* The hours there provide him with the opportunity to fantasize both sexually and homicidally, devising a fantastic, Rube Goldberg—style demise for his vile grandfather. *Léolo* does what a lot of more conventional "family" films do, and that is to show us the world through an imaginative child's eyes. But *Léolo* is no ordinary child, and his fantasies reflect the grim, ugly realities of his life. One of the rare intelligent films about children that is not *for* children, this is obscenely witty yet genuinely shocking moviemaking; as befits a perceptive and uncompromising film about an abusive upbringing, *Léolo* is a nightmare.

NEXT STOP . . . *The Blood of a Poet, Heavenly Creatures, Cria*

1992 107m/C *CA* Maxime Collin, Julien Guiomar, Ginette Reno, Pierre Bourgault, Yves Montmarquette, Roland Blouin, Giuditta del Vecchio; **D:** Jean-Claude Lauzon; **W:** Jean-Claude Lauzon. Genie Awards '92: Best Costume Design, Best Film Editing, Best Original Screenplay. **VHS, LV** *NLC, ING*

LES BICHES
The Heterosexuals

A rich, amoral, sexually hungry socialite named Frédérique (Stéphane Audran) picks

"I never lose, not ever."

—Costello (Alain Delon), playing cards in *Le Samourai.*

up a young artist named Why (Jacqueline Sassard) drawing on the streets of Paris, seduces her, and takes her to St. Tropez. Things heat up considerably when an architect (Jean-Louis Trintignant) appears on the scene, threatening the lovers' stability by tempting the sexually ambiguous artist. Claude Chabrol's *Les Biches* was mighty hot stuff when first released, but it's no less silly today than it was in 1968. It's the perfect thing when you're in the mood for a nice, healthy wallow in European decadence (Audran is a veritable poster child for slinky, self-satisfied degeneracy), but it's not necessarily the best introduction to the work of the enormously gifted Claude Chabrol.

NEXT STOP... *Wedding in Blood, Just Before Nightfall, Violette*

1968 (R) 95m/C *FR* Stephane Audran, Jean-Louis Trintignant, Jacqueline Sassard; **D:** Claude Chabrol; **W:** Claude Chabrol. **VHS, LV** *CVC, LUM*

LES BONS DEBARRAS

Michelle (Marie Tifo) is the unmarried mother of the 13-year-old Manon (Charlotte Laurier), who live in near poverty outside of Montreal. Almost obsessively in love with her mother, Manon becomes enraged and desperately jealous when she learns that her mother has become pregnant by a local cop (German Houde). Directed by Francis Mankiewicz, this is an intense and weird little psychodrama that never exactly takes off, yet its portrait of the lives and environment of the protagonists is so indelibly sketched that you almost don't mind. Tifo and Laurier are lively and often startling in their roles, and cinematographer Michel Brault (*Mon Oncle Antoine*) has provided a rich but desolate look. Winner of Canada's Genie Awards for Best Picture, Director, Actress (Tifo), and Supporting Actor (Houde).

NEXT STOP... *Mon Oncle Antoine, Proof, La Cérémonie*

1981 114m/C *CA* Marie Tifo, Charlotte Laurier, German Houde; **D:** Francis Mankiewicz. Genie Awards '81: Best Actress (Tifo), Best Director (Mankiewicz), Best Film, Best Supporting Actor (Houde). **VHS** *NO*

LES CARABINIERS
The Soldiers

Two young jerks decide that it makes sense to enlist in the army and fight for their king, thanks to the irresistible lure of looting, rape, torture and killing without justification. Calling Jean-Luc Godard's *Les Carabiniers* controversial would be an understatement. It appeared in 1963 as France was getting over its Indochinese "adventure" and America's was just beginning. The film's purposely "tasteless" frontal assault on knee-jerk patriotism rewarded those who sat through it (there weren't a lot), with a final sequence that makes you rethink everything that's gone before. What doesn't work dramatically does work allegorically, and vice versa. Only Godard would have dared to make this picture, which was generally reviled yet remains an indispensable, fascinating artifact of its era. (Kenneth Tynan wrote upon seeing it: "If this is not a masterpiece, it will do until one comes along.") Suppressed and difficult to see for years, *Les Carabiniers* finally surfaced in the U.S. at the 1967 New York Film Festival, and went into limited commercial release the following year. Screenplay by Godard, Jean Grualt, and Roberto Rossellini.

NEXT STOP... *La Chinoise, Weekend, Grand Illusion*

1963 80m/B *GB IT FR* Anna Karina, Genevieva Galea, Marino Mase; **D:** Jean-Luc Godard. **VHS** *FCT*

LES COMPÈRES

In yet another Francis Veber sitcom starring Pierre Richard and Gérard Depardieu, a woman (Anny Duperey) suckers two former lovers into finding her wayward son (Stephane Bierry) by secretly telling each that he is the kid's father. That's all there is to the high-concept setup, so it's up to Richard (as a grotesquely hypochondriacal nervous wreck) and Depardieu (a tough-talking reporter) to make the picture watchable through comic chemistry. They succeed fitfully, but eventually you're run over by this thing and find that it's easier to lie down and surrender to it than to resist. Actually, this is one of the easiest to take (and, not coincidentally, the shortest) of Veber's ubiquitous buddy movies.

NEXT STOP . . . *Le Chèvre, The Tall Blond Man with One Black Shoe, Pain in the A***

1983 92m/C *FR* Pierre Richard, Gerard Depardieu, Anny Duperey, Michel Aumont; *D:* Francis Veber; *W:* Francis Veber; *M:* Vladimir Cosma. **VHS, LV** *FCT*

LES ENFANTS TERRIBLES
The Strange Ones

"I like it in the middle of the night when I am writing," director Jean-Pierre Melville said in an interview 30 years ago, "working completely alone in my room at three in the morning. This I enjoy." Melville's version of Jean Cocteau's *Les Enfants Terribles,* which he co-authored for the screen with Cocteau, feels like it was also *filmed* at three in the morning, in a deep and hallucinatory dream state. This is the story of Elisabeth and Paul, a brother and sister whose fascination for each other leads them to shut themselves off from the rest of the world, creating a private, self-imposed prison where society's taboos are irrelevant. It's crude and perhaps misleading to use the word "incest" in the poetic context of *Les Enfants Terribles,* yet such a word evokes more than a sexual encounter between siblings; there is also the emotional and romantic fact of the deep-seated, obsessive, pathological narcissism at its core, and this is what Cocteau and Melville have tapped. They couldn't have done it without the astounding and ethereal performance of Nicole Stéphane as Elisabeth—what she does with the role is deservedly legendary. Édouard Dermithe is Paul, and Cocteau's own voice hovers over these elegant proceedings as the narrator. The cinematography is by Henri Decaë, and the costumes are by Christian Dior. Suppressed in America for decades after its initial appearance, *Les Enfants Terribles* (also known as *The Strange Ones*) was re-released here in a restored version in 1975.

NEXT STOP . . . *Blood of a Poet, Orpheus, Heavenly Creatures*

1950 105m/B *FR* Edouard Dermithe, Nicole Stephane; *D:* Jean-Pierre Melville; *W:* Jean Cocteau, Jean-Pierre Melville. **VHS** *FCT, WBF*

LES MISTONS
The Mischief-Makers

François Truffaut's first feature was his 1959 *The 400 Blows;* his first film was *Les Mistons* (known in the U.S. as *The Mischief-Makers*). It's a half-hour portrait of a group of small boys who are both fascinated and repelled by a pair of lovers (Bernadette Lafont and Gérard Blain). The kids spy on them, laugh at them, follow them everywhere on their bicycles. Though the situation and concerns are different than those that little Antoine Doinel would encounter in the abusive, darker world of *The 400 Blows,* the characterizations here are distinguished by Truffaut's consistent sensitivity and his remarkable emotional honesty in portraying the motives and needs of children. *Les Mistons* looks and feels a bit like an audition film—as if Truffaut were testing his wings and trying to discover if he had the ability to make a movie at all. He needn't have worried; he aced this test.

NEXT STOP . . . *The 400 Blows, The Wild Child, Small Change*

1957 18m/C *FR D:* Francois Truffaut. **VHS** *HMV*

LES VISITEURS DU SOIR
The Devil's Envoys

Marcel Carné's elegantly conceived fairy tale is the story of how the devil's henchmen try to wreak havoc on the love between ordinary mortals in 15th-century France. The devil himself ultimately discovers he is powerless in the face of deeply committed, true love. *Les Visiteurs du Soir* was—like Carné's great *Children of Paradise*—filmed during the Occupation. On one level the film offered escape and fantasy to audiences starved for it, but at the same time the movie was seen as a thinly disguised allegory about the need for the French people to remain true to their ideals at a difficult moment in history. Writ-

ten by Jacques Prévert and brilliantly photographed by Roger Hubert (both were Carné's collaborators on *Children of Paradise*), the picture was a success at home and abroad. As a coherent work of art, *Les Visiteurs du Soir* can't hold a candle to *Le Jour se Lève* or *Children of Paradise*; nevertheless, it remains a diverting and often enchanting entertainment.

NEXT STOP . . . *Le Jour Se Lève, Children of Paradise, The Devil's Eye*

1942 120m/B *FR* Arletty, Jules Berry, Marie Dea, Alain Cuny, Fernand Ledoux, Marcel Herrand; **D:** Marcel Carne; **W:** Jacques Prevert, Pierre Laroche. **VHS** *HMV, FCT, TPV*

LES VOLEURS
Thieves

You keep hoping that this plot-heavy, complicated new film from the gifted André Téchiné is going to reward you mightily for the effort of adding it all up as it races along, jumping back-and-forth through time and defining the relationships between characters in tiny increments. It turns out to be a perfectly OK little thriller, but you can't dismiss that nagging voice in your ear at the end, asking "is that all there is?" Daniel Auteuil is a cop whose brother is murdered at the film's opening, and Catherine Deneuve is a troubled professor of philosophy whose connection with the dead man—and with a young thief—is established gradually as Auteuil's investigation proceeds. Téchiné gives us characters who are battered by life and circumstance, and who are considerably more than simple cliches; yet the fragmented shape he imposes on the movie gets in the characters' way, and it keeps us from becoming deeply involved with their uniformly grim situations. At a certain point we lower our expectations for the movie and simply want to find out what happened, and we are left to wonder if the kaleidoscopic editing isn't simply a fancy wrapping for a tale not particularly worth telling. (To see Téchiné, Auteuil, and Deneuve working together at peak form, take a look at their extraordinary 1993 *Ma Saison Préférée*.)

NEXT STOP . . . *Wild Reeds, Ma Saison Préférée, L.627*

1996 (R) 116m/C *FR* Catherine Deneuve, Daniel Auteuil, Laurence Cote, Benoit Magimel, Didier Bezace, Fabienne Babe, Ivan Desny, Julien Riviere; **D:** Andre Techine; **W:** Andre Techine, Gilles Taurand; **C:** Jeanne Lapoirie; **M:** Philippe Sarde. Nominations: Cesar Awards '97: Best Actress (Deneuve), Best Director (Techine), Best Film. **VHS, LV** *COL*

LIEBELEI

This lovely and characteristically elegant turn-of-the-century love story was the last film Max Ophüls made in Germany; upon its completion, the rising Nazi tide forced his emigration to France, and, later, to America. *Liebelei* is based—as was Ophüls's later, 1950 *La Ronde*—on an Arthur Schnitzler play. This time, it's the story of a young Viennese woman who falls in love with a handsome lieutenant; their idyllic romance leads to a tragic confrontation when the lieutenant's previous indiscretion with a baroness is discovered by her husband, the baron. *Liebelei* is an exquisitely conceived jewel-box of a creation, featuring enchanting performances from Wolfgang Liebeneiner as the lieutenant, and especially from Magda Schneider (Romy's mother) as the tragic heroine. The celebrated sleigh ride sequence in which the two young lovers reveal their feelings to each other on a ride through snowy woods is typical of the expressive cinematography of Franz Planer, who would also soon depart Germany for America, eventually working on such famous Hollywood hits as *20,000 Leagues under the Sea, Breakfast at Tiffany's*, and *The Nun's Story*. Though *Liebelei* was released in Germany after Ophüls's departure, his name and that of Arthur Schnitzler were removed from the credits of all prints. The film was unavailable in America for almost 40 years following its initial release, finally surfacing to charm a new generation at the 1974 New York Film Festival.

NEXT STOP . . . *La Ronde, The Earrings of Madame de ..., The Umbrellas of Cherbourg*

1932 82m/B *GE* Magda Schneider, Wolfgang Liebeneiner, Gustav Grundgens; **D:** Max Ophuls. **VHS** *KIV*

THE LIFE AND DEATH OF COLONEL BLIMP
Colonel Blimp

Roger Livesey delivers a legendary performance as major General Clive Candy, a British officer whose confusion over the loss of honorable behavior by the military during World War II causes him to reflect back over his long and extraordinary career. This first production by the Archers—the British film company that consisted of Michael Powell and Emeric Pressburger as co-producers, co-authors, and co-directors—was a rich, complex, and satisfying film (based on a popular comic strip of the day) that became immediately controversial upon its release in 1943, the height of World War II. It didn't please Winston Churchill that this film's hero makes a lifelong friend of a German officer (Anton Walbrook) prior to World War I, or that at the end of his life Candy is so appalled by the loss of honorable behavior in a now-savage world that he claims he'd rather lose the war than sink to the Nazis' level of fighting. Livesey and Walbrook are superb, as is Deborah Kerr, who portrays all three of the women in Candy's life. *Colonel Blimp* is above all a magnificently drawn character study, brilliantly photographed in Technicolor by Jack Cardiff and Georges Périnal. Yet Churchill saw the picture simply as dangerous, anti-British propaganda, all the more outrageous in his eyes because of its British pedigree. His ire had an immediate impact, and he kept the film from being exported. When it finally did get seen abroad, it had been cut into various butchered versions; the American prints, for example, had 80 minutes removed and were released in black and white. The film has finally been restored to its full, 163-minute version thanks in no small measure to the support of admirer Martin Scorsese. (The wonderful Criterion laserdisc version features Scorsese and the late Powell on an alternate soundtrack, discussing the film's production.)

NEXT STOP . . . *Grand Illusion, A Matter of Life and Death (Stairway to Heaven), The Red Shoes*

1943 115m/C *GB* Roger Livesey, Deborah Kerr, Anton Walbrook, Ursula Jeans, Albert Lieven; *D:* Michael Powell, Emeric Pressburger; *C:* Georges Perinal. **VHS, LV** *NO*

LIFE AND NOTHING BUT
La Vie et Rien d'Autre

Two women—one aristocratic (Sabine Azéma), one a provincial schoolteacher (Pascale Vignal)—search for their missing men on a bloody French battlefield following World War I. They are helped in this seemingly impossible task by a Major Dellaplanne (Philippe Noiret), whose commitment to accounting for the hundreds of thousands of men missing in action is tempered by his deep cynicism. By the time the film is over, he has reached a very particular kind of peace with his grim, seemingly endless task. Bertrand Tavernier's *Life and Nothing But* is a large-scale film with an extremely intimate focus; this is necessary to convey the enormity of the task Dellaplanne has before him, as well as to contrast the scale of the war's carnage against the individual faces that it affects. One of those faces belongs to actress Sabine Azéma, who here is a match for the great Noiret. Azéma appeared in a great many films that were not thundering hits in the U.S., but she ought to be more well known. She has an extraordinarily delicate and expressive presence, and this is one of her most extraordinary performances. As for Noiret, one might call Dellaplanne's exhausted nobility the role he was born to play, except that *whatever* Noiret does seems the role he was born to play. He's extraordinary here. Do what you can to see *Life and Nothing But* in a well-mastered letterboxed version; Bruno De Keyser's widescreen images are quite stunning. César Award to Philippe Noiret as Best Actor of 1990.

NEXT STOP . . . *The Judge and the Assassin, Coup de Torchon, Paths of Glory*

1989 (PG) 135m/C *FR* Philippe Noiret, Sabine Azema, Francoise Perrot; *D:* Bertrand Tavernier; *W:* Bertrand Tavernier; *C:* Bruno de Keyzer. British Academy Awards '89: Best Foreign Film; Cesar Awards '90: Best Actor (Noiret), Best Score; Los Angeles Film Critics Association Awards '90: Best Foreign Film. **VHS** *ORI, FCT*

L

MIKE LEIGH
Provacative English Director

Mike Leigh has directed three of the most provocative and realistic films of the nineties—from *Life is Sweet*, to *Naked* to the 1996 *Secrets and Lies*. He has done extensive work for television and theater as well, beginning in the 1960s.

Leigh, in his mid-fifties, is known for working with his actors closely, developing stories out of lower class life and out of the personalities of his actors and their improvisations. His 30-year career has been marked by his devotion to what has been called "social-realist comedies." Critic Vincent Canby has called him the most innovative of contemporary British filmmakers and also the most subversive. Leigh's characters are desperate and terribly funny. They can be extraordinarily articulate about their condition. Their self-criticism blocks any sentimental view of them.

Leigh was born February 20, 1943 in Salford, England, the son of a doctor. Both parents, he has said, were leftwingers but unaligned, which perhaps accounts for his own striking independence and freedom from leftist cliches about working people.

Beginning in his teens Leigh knew he wanted to make films. He trained as an actor at the Royal Academy of Dramatic Art in London. After various jobs in theater and in television, he made one film in 1971. But the pressures of film production and commercialization seemed to stand in the way of his iconoclastic work, which often began with no script and no pitch for film backers and producers to invest in. So he returned to the freedom of the stage.

Everything began to change for Leigh in the late 1980s, when he cobbled together enough support to make *High Hopes*, which attracted an American audience and great reviews. Making films is still a struggle for Leigh, but he has the reputation now that demonstrates he can bring projects to fruition. *Secrets and Lies* was nominated for five 1996 Academy Awards, including best picture and best director. After *Secrets*, he directed *Career Girls* (1997).

He is divorced from actress Alison Steadman, who worked in his earlier films.

LIFE AND NOTHING MORE …
And Life Goes On…
Zendegi Va Digar Hich…

Following a catastrophic earthquake in northern Iran, a filmmaker who recently worked in the stricken area returns with his son to discover the fates of those he knew. Iran's master filmmaker Abbas Kiarostami examines the impact of a disaster on a human population by showing it through the eyes of a storyteller—a man who is used to supplying a neat and organized structure for his portraits of the human condition. This is one of Kiarostami's most beautiful and eloquent films, a profound and uninsistent look at a shattered population attempting to restore the structure of real life, which, it turns out, must be as carefully and diligently ordered as any work of art. One of the most talked-about films at the 1992 Cannes and New York Film Festivals, *And Life Goes On* was a breakthrough film for Kiarostami, and an important moment in the history of Iranian cinema.

NEXT STOP . . . *Where Is My Friend's House?, Through the Olive Trees, The White Balloon*

1992 91m/C Farhad Kheradmand, Pooya Payvar; **D:** Abbas Kiarostami; **W:** Abbas Kiarostami; **C:** Homayun Payvar. **VHS** *FCT*

LIFE IS SWEET

You can read about his unique, inclusive methods for preparing a film, and then you can watch the resulting picture over and over until you're blue in the face, but when a movie by Mike Leigh succeeds on the scale of *Life Is Sweet,* there's simply no way to figure out how he does it. This time, his plot centers on parents Andy and Wendy (Jim Broadbent and Allison Steadman) who have twin daughters (Jane Horrocks and Claire Skinner) who are as different from each other as they are from dad and mum. The sisters are the spine of *Life Is Sweet,* but the totality of their relationship—and their complex problems—reveal themselves when least expected, as in life. Andy is one of this movie's two chefs; he decides that the key to his family's future security is a rolling food-cart, which is as liberating an image to him as Albert Brooks's Winnebago in *Lost in America.* Aubrey (Timothy Spall of Leigh's *Secrets and Lies*) is a friend who aims higher, opening a hopelessly pretentious pseudo-French restaurant and persuading Wendy to fill in as a waitress. The sequence contains some of the biggest laughs in any of Leigh's films, but as always in Leigh the comedy is used as a brace for the film's delicate and genuinely insightful examination of human frailty, loneliness, and need. In achieving this balance with such a miraculous combination of honesty, wit, and insight, *Life Is Sweet* may be Leigh's masterpiece—his most deeply affecting, magically conjured film, and the one that seems continually richer after repeated viewings.

NEXT STOP . . . *High Hopes, Naked, Secrets and Lies*

1990 (R) 103m/C *GB* Alison Steadman, Jane Horrocks, Jim Broadbent, Claire Skinner, Timothy Spall, Stephen Rea, David Thewlis; **D:** Mike Leigh; **W:** Mike Leigh. Los Angeles Film Critics Association Awards '91: Best Supporting Actress (Horrocks); National Society of Film Critics Awards '91: Best Actress (Steadman), Best Film, Best Supporting Actress (Horrocks). **VHS, LV, Closed Caption** *REP, BTV*

LIFE OF OHARU
Diary of Oharu
Saikaku Ichidai Onna

In 17th-century Japan, a prostitute (Kinuyo Tanaka) describes via flashbacks the long and terrible journey that has taken her from being the young, beautiful, sought-after daughter of a samurai, to the bottom rung of society on which she now exists. Kenji Mizoguchi's magnificent *Life of Oharu* was based on a novel by Ibara Saikaku that the director waited for many years to film, so that—by his own account—he could grow emotionally closer to the material through careful reflection. Oharu's downfall is the result of a social system that extracts a terrible and irreparable price for indiscretions that are the result of normal human emotions; that price is, as Mizoguchi demonstrated in so many of his films, considerably higher for that society's women. Each step in her descent is seen as both tragic and inevitable, and is depicted with the stately grace and sheer narrative skill of a master storyteller. Mizoguchi's restless camera travels with Oharu on her journey, and the film's elegant forward motion suggests the passage of a single human life through the course of history. Whether or not it is, as some critics have stated, one of the cinema's few great feminist works, *Life of Oharu* is unquestionably one of the most powerful screen portraits of a woman objectified—treated as a thing, with a physical value that declines with her social position. Mizoguchi's masterwork is an unforgettable portrait of one woman's quest to at least find redemption in a world that systematically denies her justice. The large cast includes Toshiro Mifune. Silver Lion, 1952 Venice Film Festival. (Cut by 30 minutes for export, the complete, 146-minute version has recently been beautifully restored for American release.)

L

NEXT STOP . . . *Sansho the Bailiff, Harakiri, When a Woman Ascends the Stairs*

1952 136m/B *JP* Kinuyo Tanaka, Toshiro Mifune; *D:* Kenji Mizoguchi. **VHS** *HMV, TPV*

LIFE ON A STRING

Though director Chen Kaige's tale of an aged musician and his young apprentice may seem just a bit too leisurely from time to time, the film's enchantingly spiritual story and poetic imagery more than compensate. The old musician has been blind since childhood, but he is not without hope; the teacher who taught him to master his stringed instrument, the sanxian, has assured him that when a lifetime of perfecting his music causes him to break his one-thousandth string, his sight will be restored. Whether this is meant to be a literal restoration of sight or a symbolic path to understanding through art is open to debate, and the old man and his young assistant do precisely that. As they travel through the magnificent landscapes that one of them can see with his eyes and one of them can feel with his heart, *Life on a String* becomes a consciousness-expanding journey of faith, spirituality and knowledge—a memorable and powerfully felt modern fable. Though *Life on a String* received only limited release in the U.S., Chen's next film, *Farewell My Concubine,* would bring him international recognition as well as two Academy Award nominations.

NEXT STOP . . . *Farewell My Concubine, The Horse Thief, Kundun*

1990 110m/C *CH D:* Chen Kaige; *C:* Gu Changwei. **VHS** *FCT, KIV*

LIKE WATER FOR CHOCOLATE
Como Agua para Chocolate

In the early part of the century, an old widow (Regina Torne) raises three daughters, the youngest of whom, Tita (Lumi Cavazos), knows her way around the kitchen. She knows her way around Pedro (Marco Leonardi) as well, and the two are anxious to marry. Family obligations are in the way, however; it seems that Tita's older sister Rosaura (Yareli Arizmendi) must marry first, and Tita must stay home and care for her manipulative and tyrannical mother. Rosaura does marry, but Tita is shocked when she discovers that it is Pedro who has become her husband. Not to worry, he tells Tita, they won't be parted so easily. Tita believes him, and begins to prepare a little food to celebrate. Soon, her skills in the kitchen will become the unexpected secret ingredient to change lives, light fires of desire, and open a world of magical, sensory delight to all who taste her cuisine. Before there was Viagra, there was food. *Like Water for Chocolate* is a celebration of that eternal joy, and it's presented as a magical, fabulist fable—a fairy tale of arousal. Enjoyable enough entertainment (though far from the masterwork some have claimed), *Like Water for Chocolate*'s bountiful food scenes developed strong word-of-mouth; the resulting repeat business made it one of the most successful foreign-language releases in American history. The film was adapted by Laura Esquivel from her novel, and was directed by her husband, Alfonso Arau. (You may remember him as the toothy bandit in Sam Peckinpah's *The Wild Bunch,* pleading with William Holden to "*Please* cut the fuse!") The American release prints run 105 minutes, about half an hour shorter than the original.

NEXT STOP . . . *The Story of Boys and Girls, Babette's Feast, Big Night*

1993 (R) 105m/C *MX* Lumi Cavazos, Marco Leonardi, Regina Torne, Mario Ivan Martinez, Ada Carrasco, Yareli Arizmendi, Caludette Maille, Pilar Aranda; *D:* Alfonso Arau; *W:* Laura Esquivel; *C:* Steven Bernstein; *M:* Leo Brower. Nominations: British Academy Awards '93: Best Foreign Film; Independent Spirit Awards '94: Best Foreign Film. **VHS, LV** *TOU*

LITTLE DORRIT, FILM 1: NOBODY'S FAULT

Little Dorrit is an adaptation of Charles Dickens's novel. It runs six hours, in two big chunks, and it's all plot. All you need to know of that plot here is that it's about a father and

Marco Leonardi worships Lumi Cavazos in *Like Water for Chocolate*.

daughter trapped in debtor's prison, and that a great many things happen to them to change the course of their lives. Is it as good as being immersed in the novel? No, but it's hypnotic and beautifully done. The director, Christine Edzard, has created what is clearly a labor of love, if not maniacal dedication, and though she may not have reproduced absolutely every sentence in the novel, you'd never know it. There are said to be more than two hundred speaking parts in the two films—titled *Nobody's Fault* and *Little Dorrit's Story*—which form one big overlapping narrative, with the story told from different points of view. Edzard didn't have a huge budget for this project, but she's produced some memorable scenes using dark, close-up images that produce an appropriately claustrophobic effect. The sheer bulk and size of the narrative is capable of producing great pleasure if you try to allow yourself to be taken over by it, but Edzard's skill has limits. There's never a moment of lyrical, crazy joy in *Little Dorrit* that makes the film turn into more than the sum of its parts; everyone seems to be so busy keeping the story going that there's no room for such "privileged moments." That dogged faithfulness is why the movie remains an impressive, highly enjoyable stunt, but may also be why it will never be thought of as a classic.

NEXT STOP . . . *Great Expectations* (1946), *Oliver Twist* (1948), *David Copperfield* (1935)

1988 369m/C *GB* Alec Guinness, Derek Jacobi, Cyril Cusack, Sarah Pickering, Joan Greenwood, Max Wall, Amelda Brown, Daniel Chatto, Miriam Margolyes, Bill Fraser, Roshan Seth, Michael Elphick, Eleanor Bron, Patricia Hayes, Robert Morley, Sophie Ward; *D:* Christine Edzard; *W:* Christine Edzard; *C:* Bruno de Keyzer; *M:* Giuseppe Verdi. Los Angeles Film Critics Association Awards '88: Best Film, Best Supporting Actor (Guinness); Nominations: Academy Awards '88: Best Adapted Screenplay, Best Supporting Actor (Guinness). **VHS, LV, Closed Caption** *WAR, SIG, TVC*

LITTLE DORRIT, FILM 2: LITTLE DORRIT'S STORY

See *Little Dorrit, Film 1.*

1988 369m/C *GB* Alec Guinness, Derek Jacobi, Cyril Cusack, Sarah Pickering, Joan Greenwood, Max Wall, Amelda Brown, Daniel Chatto, Miriam Margolyes, Bill Fraser, Roshan Seth, Michael Elphick, Patricia Hayes, Robert Morley, Sophie Ward, Eleanor Bron; *D:* Christine Edzard; *W:* Christine Edzard; *C:* Bruno de Keyzer; *M:* Giuseppe Verdi. Los Angeles Film Critics Association Awards '88: Best Film, Best Supporting Actor (Guinness). **VHS, LV, Closed Caption** *WAR, SIG, TVC*

THE LITTLE THIEF

The Little Thief was based on a story by François Truffaut, which Truffaut was reportedly preparing to film not long before his death. It's a delicately conceived story about an adolescent girl (Charlotte Gainsbourg) who reacts to her loveless environment by engaging in a series of petty crimes. *The Little Thief* was filmed in 1989 by Truffaut's long-time assistant Claude Miller, who later became a major director on his own (*The Best Way, The Accompanist*). Unfortunately, *The Little Thief* seems to suffer from a case of over-reverence; the material has been treated as if everyone involved was afraid to touch it for fear of infusing it with a personality or style that might depart from Truffaut's original concept. The result is a curiously lifeless picture with no strong point of view, built around the otherwise mesmerizing performance of Charlotte Gainsbourg as the young girl.

NEXT STOP . . . *Small Change, Rebel without a Cause, Vagabond*

1989 (PG-13) 108m/C *FR* Charlotte Gainsbourg, Simon de la Brosse, Didier Bezace, Raoul Billerey, Nathalie Cardone; *D:* Claude Miller; *W:* Annie Miller, Claude Miller; *C:* Dominique Chapuis; *M:* Alain Jomy. **VHS, LV** *HBO*

LITTLE VERA

Malenkaya Vera

Natalya Negoda stars in this punkish blast of western-style rebellion, a 1988 harbinger of the soon-to-follow Soviet upheaval. Negoda (a lively, pretty actress) plays a young working-class woman in Ukraine who smokes, drinks, has sex with her boyfriend, wears leather, loves rock and roll, lives with her parents, and ridicules the system. Just as in American youth-rebel movies, the older generation points an accusatory finger at Vera's wicked ways, but she comes right back at em by zeroing in on their HYPOCRISY, pointing out that all they do is sit around watching TV in their liquor-stained underwear. And they say there's a *new* world order. *Little Vera* isn't much of a movie, but it's comforting social history. (It also proves that we live in One World when it comes to movie *marketing,* too; as part of her dedicated belief in glasnost, Negoda posed nude for *Playboy* to boost *Little Vera*'s American ticket sales.)

NEXT STOP . . . *Rebel without a Cause, Look Back in Anger, Taxi Blues*

1988 130m/C *RU* Natalia Negoda, Andrei Sokolov, Yuri Nazarov, Ludmila Zaisova, Alexander Niegreva; *D:* Vassili Pitchul. **VHS, LV** *FCT, LUM, WBF*

LOCAL HERO

Mac (Peter Riegert) is an up-and-coming Texas oil company executive whose boss (Burt Lancaster) sends him to Scotland to acquire a prize piece of coastal property—which includes an entire town—as an oil drilling site. As Mac settles in and meets the locals, making them cash offers they're hard-pressed to refuse, he finds himself attached to the place in ways that he never expected—and some of the townspeople begin to feel the same way about him. As charming as *Local Hero*'s plot turns out to be, it's only half the story; the beauty of Bill Forsyth's film is that Mac's strange new love of the place and his intoxicating, first-time sensation of *belonging* somewhere are depicted by the director without ever resorting to obvious or cheap sentimentality. Mac's enchantment with his new-found world is fully felt and so delicately delineated that months after seeing the movie you don't just remember it fondly, you feel *nostalgic* for it—as if the film itself were a place you've visited and dream of getting back to (this mirrors the final moments of the movie). Wondrous little moments remain in your head—a visiting Russian sings a sweet, unexpected song at a local dance; Mac discovers the pleasures

of *really good* Scotch; an injured rabbit's shocking fate is suddenly discovered; a phone booth takes on spiritual importance. Forsyth constructs a classic fable out of such small details, and it's presented in such an unforced, gently persuasive fashion that you can't see how he does it. As in any great act of magic, that's part of the appeal. Photographed by Chris Menges, and featuring a perfectly elegant score by Mark Knopfler.

NEXT STOP . . . *Comfort and Joy, Housekeeping, I Know Where I'm Going*

1983 (PG) 112m/C *GB* Peter Riegert, Denis Lawson, Burt Lancaster, Fulton Mackay, Jenny Seagrove, Peter Capaldi, Norman Chancer; *D:* Bill Forsyth; *W:* Bill Forsyth; *C:* Chris Menges; *M:* Mark Knopfler. British Academy Awards '83: Best Director (Forsyth); New York Film Critics Awards '83: Best Screenplay; National Society of Film Critics Awards '83: Best Screenplay. **VHS, LV, Closed Caption** *WAR*

LOLA

Jacques Demy's audacious first feature—a pioneering work of the French New Wave—is every bit as startling and fresh as it was when it captivated worldwide audiences in 1961. *Lola* is a romantic fable with music and dancing but it is in no way the conventional movie musical we've come to know. Lola (Anouk Aimée) is the dancer who was left with a baby in her home in Nantes seven years before; she always believes the baby's father will come back to her—and will, of course, be wealthy. The romantic encounters that happen in *Lola* are a part of life's own erotic choreography; it's no coincidence that the film is dedicated to Max Ophüls, whose *La Ronde* gave us a carousel of love that eventually took us back to where we began, as does Demy's whirling, magical *Lola*. Aimée is enchanting as the unashamedly trusting dancer whose faith carries her along to the conclusion she knew would come. Demy's first choice was to film *Lola* in color, but he didn't have the budget; that turned out to be a turn of events as miraculous as those in his film. Raoul Coutard's glistening black-and-white widescreen images allow Demy's sweetly imagined fantasy to remain delicately alive; the burden of realistic color

L

could have crushed it. The Michel Legrand score includes Bach and Mozart as well.

NEXT STOP . . . *On the Town, The Umbrellas of Cherbourg, Jaquot*

1961 90m/B *FR* Anouk Aimee, Marc Michel, Elina Labourdette, Jacques Harden; *D:* Jacques Demy. **VHS** *INT, TPV*

LOLA MONTÈS

The final film by the great Max Ophüls is a whirling and sensuous portrait of the famous 19th-century courtesan Lola Montès, who was mistress to Franz Liszt and King Ludwig of Bavaria, but who ended up as a circus attraction, recounting tales from her past in exchange for coins from the audience. Ophüls conceived the film as the culmination of his life's work; used to working on limited budgets and with technical limitations, he had created masterpiece after masterpiece (*The Earrings of Madame de …* and *La Ronde* are but two) out of the most meager of means. Now he had the backing to make one of his jewel-like romances on a large scale, and for a much wider audience. Martine Carol was signed to play Lola, and Anton Walbrook, Ivan Desny, and Oskar Werner joined Peter Ustinov, who had the central role of the circus ringmaster who narrates Lola's history to the circus patrons—and to us. The film was shot in color and in the widescreen CinemaScope process, which Ophüls uses to breathtaking effect, particularly in the brilliantly choreographed and heartbreaking circus sequences which "bracket" the flashbacks of Lola's life. (The film's closing sequence, in which customers line up to pay a dollar to kiss Lola's hand, is one of the most emotionally complex and heartbreaking passages in all of Ophüls's work.) *Lola Montès* was unveiled in France in 1955 with great fanfare, but its premiere was a disaster with both the public and the newspaper critics. The producers, desperate for a return on their investment, began cutting away at the 140-minute film until they had hacked away almost an hour, rearranging the film's chronology in the process. This 92-minute version was dubbed and sent to America as *The Sins of Lola Montès,* where it sank to the depths of late-night local TV broadcasts. Ophüls never survived the indignity, and died in 1957 as the truncated *Lola Montès* was being shipped off to the few theatres that played it. In 1969, when a partially restored, 110-minute version was assembled from the surviving print materials and was reissued in the U.S., film critic and historian Andrew Sarris pronounced it the greatest film of all time. Agreeing or disagreeing is beside the point; the very fact that the broken pieces of Ophüls's beloved creation could, in true labyrinthine Ophülsian fashion, wend their way across the sea to touch hearts in the way he intended is a triumphant coda to the great director's brilliant career. (The 110-minute version has been lovingly transferred to letterboxed laserdiscs and videocassettes.)

NEXT STOP . . . *Liebelei, The Earrings of Madame de …, Le Plaisir*

1955 140m/C *FR* Martine Carol, Peter Ustinov, Anton Walbrook, Ivan Desny, Oskar Werner; *D:* Max Ophuls; *W:* Max Ophuls; *M:* Georges Auric. **LV, Letterbox** *CRC, NLC*

THE LONG DAY CLOSES

A companion/sequel to his brilliant *Distant Voices, Still Lives,* Terence Davies's poetic and hauntingly lyrical *The Long Day Closes* is an autobiographical portrait set in the 1950s of an impressionable 11-year-old, whose obsession with movies is a way of escaping from the still-painful wounds of an abusive childhood. The palatial Liverpool movie house where Bud spends as much of his time as possible is lovingly and eloquently filmed by Davies as a cathedral of dreams, hopes, and possibilities, and the choir we hear on the soundtrack overflows with melodies from Nat King Cole's "Stardust" to "The Carousel Waltz" to—as the accompaniment to a breathtakingly moving montage of gently gliding, overhead images—Debbie Reynolds's "Tammy." There's a narrative structure within *The Long Day Closes,* but the movie's power is a result of Davies's freedom to create a true work of cinematic poetry that seems to spring directly from his unconscious. (It's the perfect antidote to the saccharine tidiness of *Cinema Paradiso*.) Considerably less bitter than *Distant Voices* but no less potent, this is a unique work of art that richly rewards the adventurous filmgoer. It can stand on its own, but is an especially powerful experience after viewing *Distant Voices, Still Lives*. The stunning color cinematography is by Michael Coulter (*Four Weddings and a Funeral*.)

NEXT STOP . . . *Distant Voices, Still Lives, Dreamchild, Léolo*

1992 (PG) 84m/C *GB* Leigh McCormack, Marjorie Yates, Anthony Watson, Ayse Owens; *D:* Terence Davies; *W:* Terence Davies; *C:* Michael Coulter. **VHS, Closed Caption** *COL*

THE LONG GOOD FRIDAY

Harold Shand (Bob Hoskins) is a self-important, self-made London mob boss on the brink of his greatest achievement; he's about to greet a delegation of American gangsters who just might pony up millions to invest in his bold, hands-across-the-sea casino/real estate venture. But on the eve of his biggest triumph, somebody's knocking off members of Harold's gang, one by one. What's worse, they're blowing up his businesses in broad daylight, humiliating him in front of the Americans and his own wife (Helen Mirren). If Harold can't get to the bottom of the mayhem and convince the American "delegate" (Eddie Constantine) that the deal isn't risky, he's going to lose his dream. Frantic, furious, and enraged, Harold does get to the bottom of it, but the would-be little Caesar is almost pitifully incapable of comprehending the magnitude of the danger he uncovers. Gripping, hilarious, and enormously pleasurable, *The Long Good Friday* is one of the few genuinely original crime movies in decades. Hoskins is almost frighteningly perfect as the sawed-off, stocky, bullying Harold. You can't help feeling sorry for him, just as his wife

does. Helen Mirren is remarkable; sympathetic but angry, needing Harold's protection, yet aware at all times of her superior intelligence (and aware of the danger of flaunting the fact). Barrie Keefe's script is clever enough to keep the audience guessing, and wise enough to never let them fall behind. It was the first time Americans had seen Hoskins in a leading role, and it remains his best. This is a rare example of how genre filmmaking does not have to leave wit, passion, or originality behind. Directed by John Mackenzie.

NEXT STOP . . . *Mona Lisa, The Crying Game, Alphaville*

1980 109m/C *GB* Bob Hoskins, Helen Mirren, Dave King, Bryan Marshall, George Coulouris, Pierce Brosnan, Derek Thompson, Eddie Constantine, Brian Hall, Stephen Davies, P. H. Moriarty, Paul Freeman, Charles Cork, Paul Barber, Patti Love, Ruby Head, Dexter Fletcher, Roy Alon; *D:* John MacKenzie; *W:* Barrie Keefe; *C:* Phil Meheux; *M:* Francis Monkman. **VHS** *VTR*

LOOK BACK IN ANGER

When we speak of the "angry young man" period of British films in the 1950s and 1960s, we can include any number of movies, but we *always* include this one. John Osborne's searing play is the story of a grown man (Richard Burton) who's still a rebel without a cause, and who takes it out on his wife (Mary Ure), his mistress (Claire Bloom), and his friend (Gary Raymond). Burton is astounding as Jimmy Porter; the rage is as terrifying to us as it is to those around him, and we may be frightened while watching him because his fury seems both real and, in a way, justified. This may be one of those movies you've heard about so often or seen so many references to that you feel you don't actually need to see it. You'd be wrong. This was Tony Richardson's first film, and it's a powerhouse of a debut.

NEXT STOP . . . *The Entertainer, Saturday Night and Sunday Morning, Room at the Top*

1958 99m/B *GB* Richard Burton, Claire Bloom, Mary Ure, Edith Evans, Gary Raymond; *D:* Tony Richardson; *W:* John Osborne; *C:* Oswald Morris; *M:* John Addison. **VHS, LV**

LOS OLVIDADOS
The Young and the Damned

After an eighteen-year hiatus from filmmaking—for political reasons that had the surreal, nightmarish logic of one of his films—the surrealist master Luis Buñuel returned to the screen triumphantly with this brilliantly lucid and utterly haunting portrait of gang youths in the slums of Mexico. Buñuel's vision is disturbing because these aren't kids who steal a loaf of bread to feed their poor mothers, or to buy clothes for school. These are children who kill each other; who throw a legless man in the street to see him in pain; who stone a blind man trying to earn money as a street musician. Buñuel claimed that the genesis of *Los Olvidados* (released in the U.S. as *The Young and the Damned*) was in the impoverished children of Vittorio De Sica's *Shoeshine;* yet this unsparing portrait of a sociopathic generation seems light years away from De Sica's tender neo-realist work. The images here are unforgettable and searing, but their clarity and honesty negate any hint of exploitation. It's as passionate and fully felt as any "coming-of-age" film ever made, but without the reassuring balm of condescending sentimentality. The reaction was hostile at the film's initial screenings in Mexico. Buñuel wrote later that Diego Rivera's wife wouldn't speak to him after the movie, and that the Mexican ambassador to France claimed that the film dishonored his country. Yet when Buñuel was awarded the Best Director Prize for *Los Olvidados* at the Cannes Film Festival, the movie became an international hit, and even played to full houses in Mexico. For a number of years Buñuel continued to work in Mexico, returning to his native Spain in 1961 to begin the great final portion of his career with his brilliant—and shocking—*Viridiana*.

NEXT STOP . . . *Nazarin, The Exterminating Angel, Pixote*

1950 88m/B *MX* Alfonso Mejias, Roberto Cobo; *D:* Luis Bunuel. Cannes Film Festival '51: Best Director (Bunuel), Best Film. **VHS** *HHT, DVT, NOS*

THE LOST HONOR OF KATHARINA BLUM
Die Verlorene Ehre der Katharina Blum

When a woman (Angela Winkler in a strong, memorable performance) spends the night with a young man about whom she knows virtually nothing, she discovers to her horror that her brief "association" with this man—who is suspected of being a terrorist—will change her life forever in ways she could never have imagined. With tabloid and television microphones shoved mercilessly and recklessly in her face, Katharina finds that without so much as a day in court, her honor and reputation have become nothing but memories, and her guilt is all but established by viciously judgmental press and affirmed by a scandal-hungry, gullible public. Based on a novel by Heinrich Böll, *The Lost Honor of Katharina Blum* feels contemporary despite the quarter-century that's passed since its release; its portrait of a news-addicted society eager to eat itself alive for ratings and circulation is uncomfortably familiar. The film has the feel of a classic fable for our time, and was adapted for the screen and directed with restraint and intelligence by the husband and wife team of Volker Schlöndorff and Margarethe von Trotta. Remade a decade later for American television as *The Lost Honor of Kathryn Beck,* starring Marlo Thomas and Kris Kristofferson.

NEXT STOP . . . *The Tin Drum, A Free Woman, Life of Oharu*

1975 (R) 97m/C *GE* Angela Winkler, Mario Adorf, Dieter Laser, Juergen Prochnow; *D:* Volker Schlondorff, Margarethe von Trotta. **VHS** *GLV*

LOULOU

In the 1950s, Louis Malle's *The Lovers* struck a cultural nerve with its portrait of a bourgeois woman (Jeanne Moreau) who—refusing to deny her repressed sexuality any longer—bolts her suffocating marriage for the passion of a younger lover. In the 1980s, it was

Nelly (Isabelle Huppert), wife of a middle-class, modestly successful executive, whose chance disco encounter with the leather-clad, brutish sexual athlete Loulou (Gérard Depardieu) diverts her well-planned life off onto a high-speed but dangerously unpaved road. Nelly's guilt-free honesty is apparent when her jilted husband demands to know what Loulou's got that he hasn't got. "He never stops," she replies. Neither does the film, which is a headlong dive into a pool of unbridled passion, directed with wit, intelligence, and matter-of-fact directness by the gifted Maurice Pialat. Depardieu was born to play this role; his performance feels lived-in and completely fleshed out. Likewise, Huppert as a performer seems liberated by Nelly's lack of pretense, and her cool, controlled exterior creates an extraordinarily sensual chemistry with her big, impatient, explosively narcissistic co-star. One of the most underrated French films of the 1980s.

 NEXT STOP . . . *Police, A Nos Amours, Breathless*

1980 (R) 110m/C *FR* Isabelle Huppert, Gerard Depardieu, Guy Marchand; *D:* Maurice Pialat. **VHS** *NYF*

LOVE
Szerelem

When a man is arrested by Stalin's secret police, his wife (Mari Töröcsik) is alarmed at the prospect of telling his aged mother (Lili Darvas) the truth about his arrest and probable fate. Instead, she takes matters into her own hands by telling the ailing old woman—who she lives with in a cramped apartment—what she wants to hear: fabricated stories of her son's success as a movie director in America. Károly Makk's bittersweet, wonderfully intelligent comic drama, appropriately titled *Love,* is a small, gentle masterwork, powered to near-greatness by Darvas's memorable and ingenious performance. This is no "cute old lady" movie, but rather a simple, convincing, unadorned portrait of the decency that can be found in even the darkest corners of human experience. This was Darvas's final film, and she's extraordinary. Based on novellas by Tibor Déry. Special Jury Prize, Cannes Film Festival.

NEXT STOP . . . *When Father Was Away on Business, Tito and Me, Underground*

1971 92m/B *HU* Lili Darvas, Mari Torocsik, Ivan Darvas; *D:* Karoly Makk. **VHS, LV** *CVC, IME, HMV*

LOVE AND ANARCHY
Film d'Amore et d'Anarchia

In 1932, a peasant (Giancarlo Giannini), who's reached the end of his rope after a friend is murdered, decides that he will be the one to assassinate Mussolini. The center of his assassination attempt is to be a bustling brothel, but as soon as he settles in, he falls in love with one of the help (Lina Polito), and suddenly his mission seems considerably less urgent. Lina Wertmüller's *Love and Anarchy* is big, boisterous, and noisy, but it also gets more interesting and engaging as it goes along. Giannini does most of the hamming in the big, dreamy close-ups his director gives him, but it's Mariangela Melato as his political contact and the brothel's resident madam who's really the star; she takes over the movie whenever that worried but determined face of hers is onscreen. Melato and Giannini were paired again in Wertmüller's big hit *Swept Away…,* but this is their best work together, and it's probably Wertmüller's most accomplished and least offensive movie as well. Nino Rota wrote the score, and the exceptionally handsome cinematography is by Giuseppe Rotunno.

NEXT STOP . . . *Swept Away…, Seven Beauties, Land and Freedom*

1973 108m/C *IT* Giancarlo Giannini, Mariangela Melato; *D:* Lina Wertmuller; *W:* Lina Wertmuller; *M:* Nino Rota. Cannes Film Festival '73: Best Actor (Giannini). **VHS** *COL*

LOVE IN THE CITY
Amore in Citta

Not everything that came out of Italy's postwar, neo-realist period was a masterpiece, and here's the proof. The five-episode film

NINO ROTA

Composer of Italian Epics

Italian composer Nino Rota, best known for his prolific composition of film scores, was also an esteemed music teacher and classical composer who worked on operas, ballets, masses, and orchestral and chamber pieces. Although he worked with several directors, he attained prominence by providing the musical scores for the most memorable films of Federico Fellini and Francis Ford Coppola.

Rota's distinctive soundtracks set the dramatic tone of more than 40 films, starting with *His Young Wife* in 1945. In the United States, the films that brought Rota the most exposure were Coppola's *Godfather* and *The Godfather, Part II*. However, Fellini film enthusiasts throughout the world lauded the composer's scores for 1954's *La Strada,* 1960's *La Dolce Vita,* 1965's *Juliet of the Spirits,* and 1974's *Amarcord*.

Rota was born and raised in Milan, Italy, and was the grandson of pianist/composer Giovanni Rinaldi. At the age of eight, he began studying the piano and composing. When he was 12, he entered the Milan Conservatory and studied under Italy's most distinguished musical teachers, including Casella and Pizzetti. He later attended the Curtis Institute in Philadelphia on a special musical scholarship and studied composition with Rosario Scalero while in the United States. Upon returning to Italy, Rota resumed his studies and received an arts degree in literature from Milan University.

In 1974, Rota shared a best original dramatic score Oscar for his work with Carmine Coppola on the music to *The Godfather, Part II*. He continued composing soundtracks until shortly before is death in 1979.

about the different kind of love that can be found on the streets of Rome at any given moment was the work of six directors: Michelangelo Antonioni, Federico Fellini, Dino Risi, Alberto Lattuada, Francesco Maselli and Cesare Zavattini. The film was conceived by Zavattini, who based the picture on actual incidents and used—as was often the case in the neo-realist films of the era—a completely non-professional cast. Fellini's episode, about a matrimonial agency, is a comic romp in the style of his *The White Sheik,* while Antonioni's, not surprisingly, is about three failed suicide attempts. The strength of the Fellini episode works to the detriment of the far more modest success of the others (though Lattuada's "girl-watchers" sequence isn't successful on *any* level), and the ultimate effect is distractingly uneven. A sixth episode, directed by Carlo Lizzani, was removed by the film's American distributor prior to release in the U.S. (The Fellini sequence is one of the short films that he used in calculating his numerical resume, totaling it up to get the title of his *8 1/2*.)

NEXT STOP . . . *Paisan, Open City, Yesterday, Today and Tomorrow*

1953 90m/B *IT* Ugo Tognazzi, Maresa Gallo, Caterina Rigoglioso, Silvia Lillo; *D:* Michelangelo Antonioni, Federico Fellini, Dino Risi, Carlo Lizzani, Alberto Lattuada, Francesco Maselli, Cesare Zavattini; *W:* Aldo Buzzi, Luigi Malerba, Luigi Chiarini, Tullio Pinelli, Vittorio Vettreni; *C:* Gianni Di Venanzo; *M:* Mario Nascimbene. **VHS** *NOS, FCT, AUD*

LOVE ON THE RUN
L'Amour en Fuite

François Truffaut's fifth and final film about his cinematic alter ego, Antoine Doinel (Jean-Pierre Léaud), finds Antoine divorced from Christine (Claude Jade) and coping with the death of his mother. *In Love of the Run,* Antoine, now in his thirties, is looking back over his life and loves, which necessarily entails the inclusion of film clips from the previous films in the cycle—*The 400 Blows,* the *Antoine and Colette* sequence from *Love at Twenty, Stolen Kisses,* and *Bed and Board.* This is both a *Reader's Digest*—style "condensed Antoine Doinel" as well as a sobering and melancholy moment of reflection for Antoine, who never stopped moving forward and taking risks as he searched continuously for the love he was denied in childhood. Antoine's tragic legacy was his deep-seated belief that he was not deserving of love, but his nobler instincts always propelled him toward it; at the end of *Love on the Run*—which might have been called "The Man Who Loved Women" had Truffaut not already used the title—Antoine seems to understand this, but whether or not that is sufficient to bring him happiness is a question that Truffaut and his great star Léaud left us to decide for ourselves. It's a strangely sad but appropriately unfinished final chapter in Truffaut's remarkably personal and pioneering series about the emotional adventure that we call youth. Marie-France Pisier, who made her debut opposite Léaud in *Antoine and Colette,* is credited as one of four co-authors of *Love on the Run*'s screenplay. (Composer Georges Delerue's wistful theme song, sung by Alain Souchon on the soundtrack, was released on a French CD of music from Truffaut's films.)

NEXT STOP . . . *The 400 Blows, Love at Twenty, Stolen Kisses, Bed and Board*

1978 95m/C *FR* Jean-Pierre Leaud, Marie-France Pisier, Claude Jade; *D:* Francols Truffaut; *C:* Nestor Almendros; *M:* Georges Delerue. Cesar Awards '80: Best Score. **VHS** *HMV, WAR*

LOVE SERENADE

Into the strange and barren little town of Sunray, Australia ambles D.J. and self-appointed king of cool Ken Sherry (George Shevtsov)—fresh from Brisbane—to take over the town's airwaves (such as they are) and position himself as a heartthrob/dreamboat fantasy to the town's female population. Two of those females are sisters Vicki-Ann (Rebecca Frith) and Dimity (Miranda Otto), whose manipulation by—and, eventually, of—the sleazy, disingenuous and philandering lord of radio provides the driving force behind this demented and surrealistically hilarious debut film from writer-director Shirley Barret. *Love Serenade*'s amiably slow, seemingly casual rhythm gradually draws us in to a wonderfully detailed, pitch-black comedy that—despite its small-town setting—feels epic in its perversely cynical kick. If the "surprise" ending is vaguely disappointing in its predictability—the only element in the picture that really feels like a gratuitous afterthought—it's only because what's gone before has been so starkly and refreshingly original. If Jim Jarmusch and Luis Buñuel had ever had a few drinks together and decided to make a movie in Australia, it might well have turned out something like the bizarre, suspenseful, quietly witty *Love Serenade.* Mandy Walker's widescreen, wide-open-spaces cinematography should be seen letterboxed for the maximum comic effect. And get your Barry White albums together—you'll be looking for them afterward.

NEXT STOP . . . *Sweetie, Comfort and Joy, Muriel's Wedding*

1996 (R) 101m/C *AU* Miranda Otto, Rebecca Frith, George Shevtsov, John Alansu, Jessica Napier; *D:* Shirley Barrett; *W:* Shirley Barrett; *C:* Mandy Walker. **VHS, LV, Closed Caption** *TOU*

"Sometimes I talk to myself—it's less exhausting than talking to someone else."

—Berthe (Marthe Villalonga) in *Ma Saison Preferee.*

THE LOVERS

The film that secured an international reputation for Louis Malle was his second feature,
a portrait of a rich, unsatisfied, provincial wife
(Jeanne Moreau) and her two adulterous
affairs. *The Lovers* was controversial for a few
reasons, and the biggest one was the fact
that Moreau drives off at the end of the film
with the second—and younger—of her
lovers (Jean-Marc Bory), both he and she free
of guilt; they don't even go over a cliff in a
traffic accident. The film scored in American
art houses for its then-candid love scenes,
which look modest by today's standards yet
still reveal an erotic abandon in the narrative
that was unusual in its day. *The Lovers* is the
movie that made Moreau a recognized
screen presence, and established the restless
sexuality that she would continue to be associated with. Henri Decaë provided the
dreamy black-and-white images that always
stop short of hazy, calendar-art eroticism.
The Brahms on the soundtrack is the perfect,
witty accompaniment to this pleasurable,
high-toned, high-fashion snapshot of low-
down longings among the bourgeoisie.

NEXT STOP . . . *The Fire Within, La Dolce Vita, Damage*

1959 90m/B *FR* Jeanne Moreau, Alain Cuny, Jose-Luis
De Villalonga, Jean-Mark Bory; **D:** Louis Malle; **W:** Louis
Malle. Venice Film Festival '59: Special Jury Prize. **VHS**
NYF, FCT, ING

LOVERS: A TRUE STORY
Amantes

Paco (Jorge Sanz), a young man recently discharged from the army, searches for a job and
an apartment so that he can begin to earn
enough money to make an honest woman of
his sweet and trusting fiancée, Trini (Maribel

Verdu). But Paco doesn't realize that the apartment building he chooses comes complete with a scheming, sexually insatiable (and inventive) landlady, Luisa (Victoria Abril). Soon poor Trini is willing to sacrifice her virginity just to regain Paco from the landlady's clutches, but Luisa isn't about to give up so easily. Set in Franco's Spain of the 1950s, *Lovers* could have been a grindingly predictable melodrama were it not for the wry and resourceful direction of Vincente Aranda, who balances the story between Buñuelian irony and James M. Cain—style intensity. The sex scenes in *Lovers* between Paco and Luisa are something to see, and they're persuasive enough to make Paco's confusion and malleability perfectly understandable. Victoria Abril took the Best Actress Prize at the Berlin Film Festival for her performance here, and you'll get no argument from me. As evil as Luisa may be, Abril manages to make her sexual frenzy so needy and intense that she becomes a surprisingly sympathetic figure, even while luring an innocent young couple to their doom and edging the picture tantalizingly close to soft porn (I give this movie's scarf scene the edge over *Last Tango in Paris*'s famous butter sequence, if for nothing else than sheer surprise). Abril is a versatile and stunning actress who's appeared in some of Pedro Almodóvar's films, yet never had the breakthrough role that would give her name recognition with a wider American audience. When you see *Lovers,* however, you will remember her.

NEXT STOP . . . *The Postman Always Rings Twice (1946), Ossessione, Tristana.*

1990 (R) 105m/C *SP* Victoria Abril, Jorge Sanz, Maribel Verdu; *D:* Vicente Aranda; *W:* Vicente Aranda, Alvaro del Amo; *C:* Jose Luis Alcaine; *M:* Jose Nieto. Berlin International Film Festival '91: Best Actress (Abril). **VHS** *REP*

LOVES OF A BLONDE
A Blonde in Love
Lasky Jedne Plavovlasky

Andula (Hana Brejchova) is a shy teenage factory worker who falls in love with Milda (Vladimir Pucholt), a compulsively womaniz-

ing musician, after spending a night with him. She's convinced that the pianist is truly in love with her, and she decides the next weekend to visit his parents, arriving unannounced at their home. Andula's heartbreak at what she learns there is matched only by her deep-seated need to perpetuate her romantic illusions. The film that established Milos Forman as the foremost Czech filmmaker of his generation displays his early mastery of understatement and the poignant, emotionally devastating subtlety that would become his trademark. Forman allows us to observe the naturalness of his characters' behavior—as in the simply staged but emotionally complex sequence in Milda's home—and lets the truth of a scene emerge before us through their actions rather than through their declarations. As with subsequent American films of Forman's, such as *Taking Off, One Flew over the Cuckoo's Nest,* and *The People vs. Larry Flynt,* the marvelous comic sequences in *Loves of a Blonde* are the director's way of easing us into what is essentially an unhappy story; it's a seductive storytelling method, and it ultimately allows the film's underlying tragic dimension to stand out in powerful relief. Brejchova and Pucholt are natural and convincing, and the images of cinematographer Miroslav Ondricek (who would accompany Forman to America) provide an extra level of intimacy. Academy Award Nominee, Best Foreign Language Film.

NEXT STOP . . . *The Fireman's Ball, Heartburn, Nights of Cabiria*

1965 88m/B *CZ* Jana Brejchova, Josef Sebanek, Vladimir Pucholt; *D:* Milos Forman. Nominations: Academy Awards '66: Best Foreign-Language Film. **VHS** *HMV, COL*

THE LOWER DEPTHS
Les Bas Fonds
Underground

Renoir's adaptation of Maxim Gorky's play is set in no specific land, and yet it's a universal location; this is the bottom rung of the human ladder, a cramped world of derelicts,

thieves, and gamblers, scrambling over each other for the meager crumbs they find. Renoir assembled a fine cast, including Jean Gabin as the thief and Louis Jouvet as the baron whose gambling has brought him low, but though the film is beautifully acted, it never finds an adequate rhythm to hold our attention throughout. Wonderful in spots and certainly containing Renoir's spirit of humane generosity, *The Lower Depths* is nevertheless one of the great director's rare missteps. (Gorky's story had an appeal that the world's best directors found irresistible—*The Lower Depths* would be filmed again 20 years later, this time by Akira Kurosawa.)

NEXT STOP . . . *The Lower Depths* (1957), *Dodes 'ka-den, The Iceman Cometh*

1936 92m/B *FR* Jean Gabin, Louis Jouvet, Vladimir Sokoloff, Robert Le Vigan, Suzy Prim; *D:* Jean Renoir; *W:* Jean Renoir, Charles Spaak; *C:* Jean Bachelet; *M:* Jean Wiener. **VHS** *FCT, DVT, GVV*

THE LOWER DEPTHS
Donzoko

Akira Kurosawa has transported the characters of Maxim Gorky's 1902 classic to an old Edo tenement at the beginning of the 19th century. In an ancient lodging house, a number of derelicts are assembled, including a kabuki actor, a sick old woman, a prostitute, a shamed, former samurai, and a thief (Toshiro Mifune). Lording over them are a corrupt, greedy landlord and his sexually insatiable wife (Isuzu Yamada). In this oppressive, nightmarish milieu, the characters on the bottom rung of society's ladder have only their fantasies to comfort them, and fantasize they do, with humor and fury. Kurosawa has made one of the most intentionally claustrophobic films of his career in *The Lower Depths;* we leave the theatre having felt trapped in this world he's shown us with such vividness, and the experience can be disconcerting. There's a lot of conversation in *The Lower Depths,* which can be trying simply from the standpoint of reading almost constant subtitles for a straight two hours plus. Nevertheless, this is a fascinating and near-experimental piece of work (the abrupt ending *is* experi-

mental, and it outraged Japanese film critics when they first got a load of it). Previously filmed by Jean Renoir in 1936.

NEXT STOP . . . *The Lower Depths* (1936), *Dodes'ka-den, The Iceman Cometh*

1957 125m/B *JP* Toshiro Mifune, Isuzu Yamada, Ganjiro Nakamura, Kyoko Kagawa, Bokuzen Hidari; *D:* Akira Kurosawa; *W:* Akira Kurosawa, Hideo Oguni; *C:* Kazuo Yamazaki; *M:* Masaru Sato. **VHS** *HMV, FCT, COL*

M

If you make even a modest survey of the trauma that the coming of sound in 1927 inflicted on the art of motion pictures, you'll encounter legions of actors, directors, writers, and cinematographers who, having mastered that pinnacle of 20th-century artistic expression known as the silent film, were suddenly told to invent a whole new way of telling stories. Many celebrated directors of the silent era, such as D.W. Griffith, were never able to adapt to this new world, and simply vanished. One who didn't vanish was Germany's Fritz Lang, whose silent expressionist classics *Metropolis, Die Nibelungen,* and *Dr. Mabuse* were known the world over. Yet even though Lang understood that the move to sound was inevitable, even he might not have guessed that his first attempt at a talking picture would produce not simply a success, but the single greatest achievement of his entire career. Based on an actual case, Fritz Lang's *M* is the story of a serial child molester/murderer (Peter Lorre) whose impact on every aspect of life in Berlin was so profound that the police place the city under what amounts to a state of siege. When the cops fail to catch him, the city's criminal underworld—paralyzed in their livelihood because of increased police crackdowns—vows to catch the killer by banding together to form a dragnet of their own. In its use of natural sounds coupled with dark, shadowy imagery suggesting the danger and decadence of city life, director Lang creates a spellbinding thriller with something extra: Peter Lorre. In his first major screen role, Lorre pulls off the unthinkable; he makes this killer monstrous, all right, but at the same time he makes him a human being—not exactly sympathetic, but a living, suffering human being nevertheless.

Though Lorre doesn't have a huge amount of screen time his scenes are all indelible, and his climactic plea for mercy from the "court" of criminals remains one of the most riveting moments in screen history. (Lang's original choice for a title was "Murderers Among Us," but it was nixed—not surprisingly—by the up-and-coming Nazis.)

 **NEXT STOP** . . . *Dr. Mabuse, The Big Heat, Short Eyes*

1931 111m/B *GE* Peter Lorre, Ellen Widmann, Inge Landgut, Gustav Grundgens, Otto Wernicke, Ernest Stahl-Nachbaur, Franz Stein, Theodore Loos, Fritz Gnass, Fritz Odemar, Paul Kemp, Theo Lingen, Georg John, Karl Platen, Rosa Valetti, Hertha von Walther, Rudolf Blumner; *D:* Fritz Lang; *W:* Fritz Lang, Thea von Harbou; *C:* Fritz Arno Wagner, Gustav Rathje; *M:* Edvard Grieg. **VHS** *HMV, NOS, HHT*

MA SAISON PRÉFÉRÉE
My Favorite Season

Emilie (Catherine Deneuve) is a lawyer whose reserved and "civilized" persona is being challenged daily by the swelling tensions and increasingly unavoidable dissatisfactions of her marriage. Her brother Antoine (Daniel Auteuil), a doctor and confirmed bachelor who refuses to conceal his disgust for family life and bourgeois hypocrisy, is Emilie's polar opposite. Though these estranged siblings have had contact with each other only rarely in their adult years, that situation changes radically when their aging mother begins to show unmistakable signs of being unable to care for herself any longer. Even if *Ma Saison Préférée* had merely been an adequate domestic melodrama, director André Téchiné would have probably struck a receptive nerve among baby boomer audiences simply because so many of them are now caring for newly dependent parents. But far from being merely adequate, *Ma Saison Préférée* is one of the subtlest, most insightful, most delicately nuanced portraits of repressed family tensions ever made. Blessedly unpreachy, unmanipulative, and unpredictable, this is 124 minutes of powerful and affecting family therapy wrapped in the glittering and brilliantly honest performances of Catherine Deneuve and Daniel Auteuil. It's one of the finest films in the career of Téchiné, a director whose extraordinary output has remained largely unseen in the United States.

NEXT STOP . . . *Scene of the Crime, Wild Reeds, Thieves (Les Voleurs)*

1993 124m/C *FR* Daniel Auteuil, Catherine Deneuve, Marthe Villalonga, Jean-Pierre Bouvier, Chiara Mastroianni, Anthony Prada, Carmen Chaplin; *D:* Andre Techine; *W:* Andre Techine; *C:* Thierry Arbogast; *M:* Philippe Sarde. **VHS, Letterbox** *FXL*

MADAME ROSA
La Vie Devant Soi

Intolerable. This maudlin, sentiment-sodden tearjerker is so intensely and single-mindedly determined to rip at your heartstrings that you should only see it with a cardiologist. Simone Signoret plays the world-weary Madame Rosa, an aging prostitute and holocaust survivor who stays young at heart by taking in street kids as if they were kittens. (Will Mia Farrow star in the Disney remake?) But wait, there's more. Our worst fears become reality when Madame Rosa takes in a little Arab boy, and our noses are rubbed in the Big Question: if these misfits can live together in peace and harmony, why can't we? Can't we all get along? Chances are *you'll* want to get along, long before *Madame Rosa*'s interminable 105 minutes are over.

NEXT STOP . . . *Madame Sousatzka, Madame X* (1966), *Madam Satan* (1930)

1977 (PG) 105m/C *FR IS* Simone Signoret, Claude Dauphin, Samy Ben Youb, Michal Bat-Adam; *D:* Moshe Mizrahi; *W:* Moshe Mizrahi; *C:* Nestor Almendros; *M:* Philippe Sarde. Academy Awards '77: Best Foreign Film; Cesar Awards '78: Best Actress (Signoret); Los Angeles Film Critics Association Awards '78: Best Foreign Film. **VHS** *HTV, VES*

MÄEDCHEN IN UNIFORM
Girls in Uniform

When a young girl (Herta Thiele) arrives at an upper-crust girls' boarding school, she nearly collapses under the weight of the school's

Prussian, regulation-crazed authoritarianism. Her only ray of hope comes in the form of one sympathetic, patient, and understanding female teacher (Dorothea Wieck), with whom the girl falls completely in love—with disastrous consequences. The 1931 German film *Mädchen in Uniform* was directed by Leontine Sagan and based on the play *Gestern und Heute* by Christa Winsloe. It's an unusual and remarkable film in a number of respects, not the least of which is the fact that it was directed by a woman from a play by a woman. Far from simply an "issue" picture, this is a sleek, elegantly told, poignant fable about individuality and special needs being crushed mercilessly by authoritarianism, which comes in many forms. The film's sexual subtext seems merely an eloquent means of expressing this larger idea about the dehumanizing qualities of power, and in fact the overt lesbian theme is perhaps less startling in retrospect than its more subver-

sive (for Germany) anti-militarist thrust. With Hitler's rise to power shortly after the release of *Mädchen in Uniform*, Sagan and most of the cast were—not surprisingly—forced to leave the country. Banned briefly in the U.S., the film was finally restored to its original, uncut version in the 1960s. (An undistinguished German remake was filmed starring Romy Schneider and Lili Palmer in 1958.)

NEXT STOP . . . *The Blue Angel, M, All Quiet on the Western Front* (1930)

1931 90m/B *GE* Dorothea Wieck, Ellen Schwannecke, Hertha Thiele; *D:* Leontine Sagan. **VHS** *MRV, NLC*

THE MAGIC FLUTE

Ingmar Bergman was commissioned in 1975 to create a special television presentation of

Mozart's *The Magic Flute,* a broadcast which would commemorate the fiftieth anniversary of Swedish radio. As a concept it made sense, of course, since there's always been a streak of Mozart's elegant romanticism in Bergman films like *Smiles of a Summer Night* (*The Magic Flute* is even referenced directly in *The Hour of the Wolf*). Still, it seems almost miraculous that Bergman's delicately theatrical staging of the opera works as well as it does on film. Far from attempting to disguise the opera's stagebound qualities, Bergman revels in them; the movie is actually *about* the experience of seeing a theatrical performance, and of surrendering oneself to it. The young girl's face that we see during the overture (Bergman's daughter) is settled in and anticipating, open to the experience that is about to begin, and we jump right in with her. It's a variation on Olivier's device of taking us to the Globe for a performance of *Henry V,* the difference being that Bergman keeps us in the theatre as the opera progresses, making the charming artificiality of sets and scenery such as a fire-breathing dragon and a passenger balloon an integral part of the performance. Photographed in color with characteristic ingenuity by Sven Nykvist, *The Magic Flute* remains the most successful and rapturously rewarding of filmed operas. Bergman's own pleasure in Mozart's artistry seems to have brought out a welcome warmth in the great director; it is—for composer, director, and audience—a marriage made in heaven.

NEXT STOP . . . *Smiles of a Summer Night, Fanny and Alexander, Babette's Feast*

1973 (G) 134m/C *SW* Josef Kostlinger, Irma Urrila, Hakan Hagegard, Elisabeth Erikson; *D:* Ingmar Bergman. Nominations: Academy Awards '75: Best Costume Design. **VHS, LV** *HMV, PAR, MVD*

THE MAGICIAN

Before David Mamet carved a niche for himself as America's most perceptive and provocative chronicler of modern man as con artist (that's con as in confidence), Sweden's Ingmar Bergman created this dark, scary, and brutally funny portrait of a 19th-century hypnotist/artist/con-man who must wrestle with private demons—as well as the supernatural—in order to regain confidence in himself. Max von Sydow is Vogler, a traveling magician and mesmerist who tours with his grandmother (Naima Wifstrand) and his wife (Ingrid Thulin), who, in one of the film's many examples of things not being as they appear, dresses as his male assistant. Upon the troupe's arrival in Stockholm, a committee of "rational" thinkers sets out to expose Vogler as a fraud. But after witnessing Vogler being killed by a servant (who's been too quickly awakened from a trance), the committee's medical officer (Gunnar Björnstrand) performs an autopsy on Vogler; the "rational" physician can't believe his eyes—or the intensity of his terror—when the magician's corpse comes back to life and pursues him though the house. In the end, the mechanics of Vogler's illusion are revealed to all, and, as with any artist stripped of his ability to astonish, he's ready to throw in the towel. That isn't to be, however, for at his lowest point, the magician is pulled back from the brink by the summons to a royal, command performance. The bleak, unforgiving face of reality can once again be hidden behind the glorious mask of theatricality, at least for one more day. According to Bergman, *The Magician* (originally titled *The Face*) was inspired by a similar moment in his own creative career, when his own self-loathing and anxiety over critical rebukes were instantly overcome by the announcement that he had received a grant from Sweden's King's Fund. Anyone who's experienced that common syndrome of feeling fraudulent—that critical, crippling moment of self-doubt—will be mesmerized by Bergman's chilling, ironic, and elegantly witty Gothic fable about the importance of remembering that to create any illusion, you must fool *yourself* first.

NEXT STOP . . . *The Seventh Seal, Wild Strawberries, The Miracle (1948)*

1958 101m/B *SW* Max von Sydow, Ingrid Thulin, Gunnar Bjornstrand, Bibi Andersson, Naima Wifstrand; *D:* Ingmar Bergman; *W:* Ingmar Bergman. Venice Film Festival '59: Special Jury Prize. **VHS, LV** *HMV, MRV, HHT*

M

"I usually start the month with a postman."

—Serial killer Poelvoorde (Benoit Poelvoorde) in *Man Bites Dog.*

THE MAKIOKA SISTERS

Kon Ichikawa's leisurely but always engaging film—set in 1938 Osaka—is a portrait of four lovely Japanese sisters who are heiresses to a dwindling but still considerable family fortune. The movie is about the traditional system that dictates how the two youngest sisters are to be matched with proper husbands, and how the desires or stubbornness of any one of the sisters can set machinery in motion that will impact all of them. The older sisters may be frustrated by what they perceive to be the rebelliousness and irresponsibility of the younger, but they're also aware that the family's entire way of life is being altered by the realities of a rapidly changing world. The picture is based on a celebrated novel by Junichiro Tanizaki called *A Light Snowfall,* which was filmed two times prior to this splendid and moving 1983 version. Ichikawa (*Fires on the Plain*) plunges us into the sisters' world immediately and without traditional road maps; it takes a while to catch up to the details of the sisters' lives and their specific situations, but it's such a joy to be with them that the time it takes to get our bearings is like a gift. As each woman's personality and longing becomes clear, we feel as if our understanding of her is something we gleaned a little at a time—as we do with people in real life—rather than as neat, pre-ordained plot developments. The film is alive, and its effect on attentive audiences can be magical. Happily, *The Makioka Sisters* wasn't cut down by a plot-mad American film distributor for its release here; the full 140-minute version is available theatrically, as well as on videocassette. Keiko Kishi, Yoshiko Sakuma, Yuko Kotegawa, and Sayuri Yoshinaga are the sisters, and director Juzo Itami (*Tampopo*) is a suitor. They—and the film—are wonderful.

NEXT STOP . . . *Early Spring, Tokyo Story, The Heiress*

1983 140m/C *JP* Keiko Kishi, Yoshiko Sakuma, Sayuri Yoshinaga; *D:* Kon Ichikawa. **VHS, LV** *FCT, TPV*

MAMMA ROMA

The great Anna Magnani is Mamma Roma, the Roman prostitute who hopes to turn her life around and win respectability for the sake of her 16-year-old son. In his second feature film, director Pier Paolo Pasolini clearly implies that Magnani's feeling for her son goes somewhat beyond the traditional mother-son bond, but that doesn't diminish the purity or sincerity of Magnani's mission to provide him with a better life than she has given him until now. Tragic complications get in Magnani's way—as we might predict from the tense and raucous wedding reception for her pimp that opens the film—and her son finds it all but impossible to avoid the pitfalls and temptations of the city's mean streets. Beautifully written and directed, and featuring one of Magnani's most electrifying screen performances, *Mamma Roma* was nevertheless the target of heated criticism when it was first presented; denounced as immoral and scandalous when it premiered at the 1962 Venice Film Festival, the movie's overtones of incest and its raw, overheated melding of Catholicism, eroticism, and crime kept it out of most theatres. Despite five minutes' worth of cuts the producers thought would make it more palatable, *Mamma Roma* went unreleased in the United States for 33 years. It was 1994 when Martin Scorsese and the invaluable Milestone Films arranged for the restored *Mamma Roma*'s American premiere. This is the video version now available, and it's a must—a major, no-longer-missing link between the neo-realist tradition and the incendiary street dramas of Scorsese himself.

NEXT STOP . . . *Accatone!, The Gospel According to St. Matthew, Mean Streets*

1962 110m/B *IT* Anna Magnani, Ettore Garofolo, Franco Citti, Silvana Corsini, Luisa Loiano; *D:* Pier Paolo Pasolini; *W:* Pier Paolo Pasolini; *C:* Tonino Delli Colli. **VHS** *CVC*

A MAN AND A WOMAN
Un Homme et une Femme

A man and a woman (Jean-Louis Trintignant and Anouk Aimée), both widowed, meet and become interested in one another, but find that it's not easy committing their past lives to the past. Claude Lelouch's swirling, insistently lyrical love story was one of the most popular foreign films of the 1960s. It's become a part of many people's lives, as when they hear "their song" suddenly pop up on the radio; for them, criticism of *A Man and a Woman* is both impossible and pointless. For the rest of us, however, this is simply a not-quite-as-terrible-as-you-remembered little romance that leaned a bit too heavily on the sunsets and la-la-la Francis Lai soundtrack. Aimée and Trintignant have never gotten the credit they deserve for bringing off their non-characters with such aplomb, particularly in light of the fact that Lelouch (who also photographed) did everything he could to call attention to himself, except, perhaps, give himself a cameo singing *Nessun Dorma*.

NEXT STOP . . . *Another Man, Another Chance, Happy New Year, A Man and a Woman: 20 Years Later*

1966 102m/C *FR* Anouk Aimee, Jean-Louis Trintignant, Pierre Barouh, Valerie Lagrange; *D:* Claude Lelouch; *W:* Claude Lelouch, Pierre Uytterhoeven; *C:* Claude Lelouch; *M:* Francis Lai. Academy Awards '66: Best Foreign Film, Best Story & Screenplay; British Academy Awards '67: Best Actress (Aimee); Cannes Film Festival '66: Best Film; Golden Globe Awards '67: Best Actress—Drama (Aimee), Best Foreign Film; Nominations: Academy Awards '66: Best Actress (Aimee), Best Director (Lelouch). **VHS, Closed Caption** *WAR, HMV*

MAN BITES DOG
C'est Arrive Pres de Chez Vous

Ben (Benoît Poelvoorde) is a serial killer being followed by a two-man camera/sound crew (which he's hired). They record his casual carnage without lifting a finger to stop him, and they have a good reason; the robberies he commits while on his murderous rampage are paying for the film being shot, and therefore providing a living for his chroniclers/co-conspirators. There's no such thing as journalistic objectivity. Get it? Think carefully, now. It's a deep message, so concentrate. The above plot description might be enough to let you get the point—the ostensible point, at least—of this intention-

ally scandal-provoking 1992 Belgian film by cast members Rémy Belvaux, André Bonzel, and Benoît Poelvoorde. The *real* point, however, is for the audience to laugh with hip delight at the rape and baby-slaughtering sequences, which, we are assured, are enacted in near-pornographic detail so that the satire might be hammered home that much more forcefully. You may prefer to hammer yourself home instead, and bolt this obnoxious, self-important exploitation film long before half-time. International Critics' Prize, 1992 Cannes Film Festival.

NEXT STOP . . . *Hate (La Haine), Wrong Is Right (1982), Medium Cool*

1991 (NC-17) 95m/B *BE* Benoit Poelvoorde, Remy Belvaux, Andre Bonzel; *D:* Benoit Poelvoorde, Remy Belvaux, Andre Bonzel; *W:* Benoit Poelvoorde, Remy Belvaux, Andre Bonzel, Vincent Tavier; *C:* Andre Bonzel; *M:* Jean-Marc Chenut, Laurence Dufrene. **VHS** *FXL, FCT*

A MAN ESCAPED
Un Condamne a Mort s'Est Echappe, Ou le Vent Souffle ou Il Vent
A Man Escaped, or the Wind Bloweth Where It Listeth
A Condemned Man Has Escaped

Describing director Robert Bresson's art by any method other than showing it is a tantalizing but futile task. "I have been influenced by no one," Bresson said in a 1966 interview, "I am a painter as well as a director, which perhaps explains why I feel the meaning must reside in the image alone." Based on the true story of a Frenchman imprisoned by the Gestapo for his affiliation with the Resistance, this film about the experience of imprisonment builds to a transforming, perhaps transcendental, moment for both the prisoner and the viewer. Since the title lets us know the outcome of the story, the almost unbearable suspense the film generates has to do with the moment-by-moment details of survival and awareness that lead ultimately to the hero's experiencing what can only be described as a miracle. Using natural sounds, objects, and shadows, as well as a non-professional actor at the film's center, Bresson has fashioned a work of supernat-

M

ural mystery and spiritual purity. For those of us who tend to regard the cinema with a reverence that borders on the religious, the existence of this film—and indeed all of the work of Robert Bresson—stands as one small bit of justification for the reverence that we feel.

NEXT STOP . . . *Le Trou, Pickpocket, Escape from Alcatraz*

1957 102m/B Francois Leterrier, Charles Le Clainche, Roland Monot, Maurice Beerblock, Jacques Ertand; *D:* Robert Bresson; *W:* Robert Bresson; *C:* L.H. Burel. Cannes Film Festival '57: Best Director (Bresson). **VHS** *NYF*

THE MAN IN THE WHITE SUIT

A humble laboratory assistant (Alec Guinness) in a textile mill invents a white cloth that won't stain, tear, or wear out, and it can't be dyed. The panicked garment industry sets out to destroy him and the fabric, resulting in sublimely comic passages. Guinness achieves (once again) perfection, this time as the prototypical, eccentric, absent-minded professor, Sydney Stratton. Daphne Bimley (Joan Greenwood) is not only enchanted by Sydney, but is also the one person who doesn't think he's bonkers. In addition to being already engaged to a stiff (Michael Gough, Alfred the butler of Tim Burton's *Batman*), Daphne's life is further complicated by being the daughter of a textile mogul for whom Sydney's discovery is his worst nightmare. The social criticism at the heart of director Alexander Mackendrick's *The Man in the White Suit* never undercuts its potent comic poignancy; like the fabric Guinness dreams of, this movie continues to look as good as new with each passing year. (A similar plot hook—this time about a gasoline substitute—was used witlessly in Steve Shagan's awful, reactionary 1980 *The Formula*.)

NEXT STOP . . . *Tight Little Island (Whiskey Galore), The Ladykillers, Kind Hearts and Coronets*

1951 82m/B *GB* Alec Guinness, Joan Greenwood; *D:* Alexander MacKendrick. Nominations: Academy Awards '52: Best Screenplay. **VHS** *REP, HMV*

MAN IS NOT A BIRD
Covek Nije Tica

A factory engineer and a hairdresser meet and fall in love in a small Yugoslavian town. The first feature film from the gifted Dusan Makavejev is a disarming and truly bizarre comedy/drama mixing sex, politics, and hypnotism, for reasons that happily defy conventional analysis. This is a freewheeling film that was influenced by the early 1960s films of Jean-Luc Godard, but has a sweet and inventive tone that is fresh and new. Makavejev will frequently stop the movie's conventional storyline to deliver weird asides on various topics, and while these scenes are not always completely relevant, they're always fun and weird. Makavejev would move into the international spotlight in a bigger way with his *WR: Mysteries of the Organism, Montenegro* and *The Coca-Cola Kid,* but *Man Is Not a Bird* remains his most proudly demented and purely enjoyable achievement. Note: the subtitles on the original American prints of *Man Is Not a Bird* were not only inadequate as translations, they actually *slid out of the frame* while they were on screen. They weren't supposed to, but they were applied to the prints so cheaply that no one seemed to have the money to fix them.

NEXT STOP . . . *Love Affair, or The Case of the Missing Switchboard Operator, Innocence Unprotected, Manifesto*

1965 80m/B *YU* Eva Ras, Milena Dravic, Janez Urhovec; *D:* Dusan Makavejev; *W:* Dusan Makavejev; *C:* Aleksandar Petkovic; *M:* Petar Bergamo. **VHS** *FCT*

MAN OF FLOWERS

Because of his strict, religious upbringing, Charles (Norman Kaye), a reclusive art collector has great and embarrassing difficulty coping with his sexual impulses. His (partial) solution is to pay a beautiful young woman—an artist's model—to disrobe in front of him once a week, though she's instructed to stop short of reaching compete nudity. As they begin learning a bit more about each other's troubled private lives, it becomes clear that they are going to mean a great deal more to each other than a simple, secretive business transaction. This remarkable and quietly startling film from Australia's Paul Cox seems to have slipped between the cracks as far as American distribution is concerned; it did play in a few theatres nationally, but it's never achieved the critical reputation that it deserves. This could be because the tone of *Man of Flowers* is so dark and elusive, and because the thread of voyeuristic humor contrasts so sharply with the deeply personal psychological pain experienced by the repressed man at the movie's center. Whatever the cause, *Man of Flowers* is ripe for rediscovery. The vulnerably dignified Norman Kaye is extraordinary as Charles, and there are disturbing flashback cameos by Werner Herzog as Charles's monstrous father.

NEXT STOP... *My First Wife, A Woman's Tale, Monsieur Hire*

1984 91m/C *AU* Norman Kaye, Alyson Best, Chris Haywood, Sarah Walker, Julia Blake, Bob Ellis, Werner Herzog; ***D:*** Paul Cox; ***W:*** Bob Ellis, Paul Cox; ***C:*** Yuri Sokol; ***M:*** Gaetano Donizetti. Australian Film Institute '83: Best Actor (Kaye). **VHS, LV** *ART, VES*

MAN OF IRON
Czlowiek z Zelaza

Andrzej Wajda's sequel to his 1976 *Man of Marble* focuses on a reporter who's been sent as a government shill to cover the Gdansk shipyards' strike. He's been instructed to do a smear of one of the most outspoken of the strikers, Tomczyk (Jerzy Radziwilowicz), the son of the central figure in *Man of Marble,* now married to the reporter (Krystyna Janda) who in the earlier film uncovered the truth about Tomczyk's father. As the reporter becomes caught up in the passion and intensity of the history-changing events that he's been assigned to derail, even the copious amounts of vodka that he consumes can't stop the truth from flooding into his conscience. Wajda's film, made as the Gdansk upheaval was actually taking place, combines documentary footage and narrative fiction in a seamless, often brilliant fashion. Real figures (Lech Walesa among them) take their place within the same frame as fictional ones, and the distinction begins to matter

less and less. *Man of Iron* is a less dramatically satisfying film than its predecessor, but it's an undeniably astounding cultural artifact.

NEXT STOP... *Man of Marble, Medium Cool, Danton*

1981 (PG) 116m/C *PL* Jerzy Radziwilowicz, Marian Opania, Krystyna Janda; ***D:*** Andrzej Wajda; ***W:*** Aleksander Scibor-Rylski; ***C:*** Edward Klosinski; ***M:*** Andrzej Korzynski. Cannes Film Festival '81: Best Film; Nominations: Academy Awards '81: Best Foreign-Language Film. **VHS** *MGM*

MAN OF MARBLE
Czlowiek z Marmur

In Poland in the mid-1970s, a young filmmaker (Krystyna Janda) sets out to make a documentary about a bricklayer (Jerzy Radziwilowicz) who, because of his exceptional skill, once gained popularity with other workers. The bricklayer became a champion for workers' rights and was the subject of many newsreels and much media attention. The filmmaker—who has chosen this worker's history as the subject of her graduate project for film school—uncovers his story in reels of locked-away and suppressed film, which show the bricklayer's rise to hero's status being officially sanctioned by the government, followed by the same bricklayer's descent into "non-personhood" when that same government found him getting a bit too influential. Andrej Wajda's gripping and bitterly satirical *Man of Marble* is structured like an epic and paced like a thriller; the ugly truth about state-sanctioned heroes unravels interview by interview, reel by reel, and culminates in a powerful indictment of Poland's communist regime as a police state. Needless to say, *Man of Marble* was not seen in Poland in its complete form (the ending was considerably more upbeat) but it sank in nonetheless. Just five years later, Wajda would more specifically chronicle the rise of the Solidarity movement in his sequel, *Man of Iron*. Lech Walesa, Solidarity's own real-life hero, appeared in that film as himself.

NEXT STOP... *Man of Iron, Tito and Me, Z*

1976 160m/C *PL* Krystyna Janda, Jerzy Radziwilowicz, Tadeusz Lomnicki, Jacek Lomnicki, Krystyna Zachwatowicz; ***D:*** Andrzej Wajda; ***W:*** Aleksander Scibor-Rylski; ***M:*** Andrzej Korzynski. **VHS** *NYF, FCT*

THE MAN ON THE ROOF
Manen Pa Taket

The director of *Elvira Madigan* shifts gears dramatically in this tense and effective little thriller, which begins with a policeman being gruesomely murdered in his hospital bed. Soon, the investigating team suspects police corruption may be at the heart of the case, and it all leads to a rooftop sniper endangering a densely populated section of busting Stockholm. *The Man on the Roof* divides its time equally between the domestic lives of the cops on the case and the red tape and bureaucracy they need to go through to nail their suspect. The picture never really catches fire, but the slick, location camerawork and tough-talking script (from a Martin Beck novel by Maj Sjowall and Per Wahloo) makes for a taut and moderately diverting couple of hours.

NEXT STOP . . . *High & Low, Dirty Harry, Garde a Vue*

1976 110m/C *SW* Carl Gustav Lindstedt, Ingvar Hirdwall, Sven Wollter, Thomas Heelberg; ***D:*** Bo Widerberg; ***W:*** Bo Widerberg; ***C:*** Odd Geir Saether, Per Kallberg. **VHS** *NYF*

THE MAN WHO ✓ LOVED WOMEN
L'Homme Qui Aimait les Femmes

A charming, intelligent, and thoroughly obsessed bachelor writes his memoirs and remembers the many women he's loved, which is pretty much the same number of women he's known. François Truffaut's movie is heartfelt, risky, sophisticated, and—for the most part—joyous, though after the hero's accidental death some larger questions about the meaning and purpose of desire are raised. Charles Denner's Bertrand radiates just the right combination of frantic intensity, religious adoration, and total confusion as he struggles and flails about, desperately trying to hold on to the memory of all the couplings of his life. He never really looks like he's having fun, and I think that's intentional on the director's part; his drive is so absolute and all-encompassing that it can never be satisfied or stilled—perhaps not even by death, Truffaut suggests. The last moments of the film are a privileged dream sequence for both Bertrand and Truffaut, as a vision of tout les femmes features virtually every woman in the world in a skirt and high heels, perfect legs crossed, smiling, ready to be adored, fantasized over, fetishized, obsessed on. Dismissing this as a male fantasy isn't exactly fair; it proudly proclaims that that's *exactly* what it is, and that despite the inherent sadness and disappointment that accompanies Bertrand's compulsion, he knew exactly what he wanted, and died with his passion still proudly burning. By all accounts, so did the film's gifted creator. (In Blake Edwards's dour 1983 remake of the same title, Burt Reynolds isn't fun *or* passionate; that version's just a slightly titillating sensitivity training session, with only the saving grace of Kim Basinger to redeem it.)

NEXT STOP . . . *The Story of Adele H., The Soft Skin, City of Women*

1977 119m/C *FR* Charles Denner, Brigitte Fossey, Leslie Caron, Nelly Borgeaud, Genevieve Fontanel, Nathalie Baye, Sabine Glaser; ***D:*** Francois Truffaut; ***W:*** Francois Truffaut, Suzanne Schiffman, Michel Fermaud; ***C:*** Nestor Almendros; ***M:*** Maurice Jaubert. **VHS, LV, Closed Caption** *MGM, BTV*

THE MAN WITH A MOVIE CAMERA
Chelovek s Kinoapparatom

Soviet filmmaker and theorist Dziga Vertov set out to create a new way of looking at the world through the use of experimental editing and innovative special effects. In his near-cubist 1929 film, *The Man with a Movie Camera*—a pulsating and rousing portrait of one day in the life of the Soviet Union—Vertov stretched the envelope to the near-breaking point. The man of the movie's title shows up in the darndest places, pointing his lens at myriad people and places that simultaneously recreate the life of a nation each day. The rhythm of the picture is critically important, so to reinforce the concept of his nation as a living thing with lifeblood pulsing to its corners, Vertov made extensive notes as to what kind of music and sound effects should accompany his silent film. (These even included the astoundingly avant-garde notion of having live radio broadcasts of big city noises piped into theatres at critical moments in the film.) In 1995, the brilliantly talented Alloy Orchestra of Cambridge, Massachusetts, created a complete score—city noises included—based on Vertov's original notes. The score is a part of a recent reissue of the film on video and laserdisc, which was mastered from a beautiful print preserved by the George Eastman House. Live concert performances of this event are must-sees, but the video version is the next best thing. It's staggering.

NEXT STOP . . . *Earth, Berlin, Symphony of a Great City, Koyaaniqatsi*

1929 69m/B *RU* **D:** Dziga Vertov; **W:** Dziga Vertov; **C:** Mikhail Kaufman; **M:** Pierre Henry. **VHS** *IHF, MRV, DVT*

MANDABI
The Money Order
Le Mandat

Unlocking—perhaps for the first time on screen—the complex daily world of modern Africa, Senegalese filmmaker Ousmane Sembène's second feature was a bright burst of lightning on the world cinema scene. *Mandabi* (*The Money Order*) is a deceptively simple story of a man who receives a money order and runs straight into a barrage of bureaucracy—Third World bureaucracy, but bureaucracy nevertheless—when he attempts to cash it. Gradually but unmistakably gaining deeper and more far-reaching meaning as it progresses, Sembène's moving, witty, altogether masterful piece of storytelling is also a sharply etched portrait of a civilization in the throes of change. Thirty years after its initial release, Sembène's pioneering *Mandabi* remains fresh, exciting, warm, subtle, and heartbreaking—a seminal moment in the history of African cinema.

NEXT STOP . . . *Black Girl, Emitai, Guelwaar*

1968 90m/C Christoph Colomb, Makhouredia Gueye, Isseu Niang, Mustapha Ture; **D:** Ousmane Sembene. *NYR*

MANON OF THE SPRING
Manon des Sources
Jean de Florette 2

The conclusion of Claude Berri's two-part epic that began with *Jean de Florette* finds that Jean's young child, Manon, has grown into a stunningly beautiful woman (Emmanuelle Béart). Manon inadvertently discovers a horrible secret; that her father's death and her own childhood misery were needless, because an underground spring on what was her family's property was blocked on purpose, preventing precious water from touching the family's crops. It is Manon's purpose from that moment on to extract revenge from César and Ugolin (Yves Montand and Daniel Auteuil), the greedy and heartless neighbors who were the cause of her family's ruin. The brilliance of *Manon of the Spring*'s plotting isn't found in Manon's ingenuity in achieving her goal, but in the "come-uppance" that really does César in. His greed causes him to bring the worst imaginable fate upon himself; the scene in which discovers it is worth sitting through every moment of this epic's four hours. It's Montand's scene, and it's a piece of screen acting—performed almost silently—that will leave you shaken. Béart and Auteuil are superb as well. Whatever one's reservations about Berri's epic—and my own are too minor to carp about—it represents a grand, sumptuous form of storytelling that is near extinction at the movies, and we are all the poorer for it. As with *Jean de Florette,* do what you can to see the sequel in a letterboxed format. And though it may be tempting to watch them in a four-hour marathon, give yourself the luxury of least one day between them, just to let the first part of the story settle comfortably into your bones.

NEXT STOP . . . *Jean de Florette, The Fanny Trilogy, Harvest*

1987 (PG) 113m/C *FR* Yves Montand, Daniel Auteuil, Emmanuelle Beart, Hippolyte Girardot, Margarita Lozano, Elisabeth Depardieu, Yvonne Gamy, Armand Meffre, Gabriel Bacquier; **D:** Claude Berri; **W:** Claude Berri, Gerard Brach; **C:** Bruno Nuytten; **M:** Jean-Claude Petit, Roger Legrand. **VHS, LV** *ORI, HMV*

EMMANUELLE BEART
The New French Phenom

Emmanuelle Beart costars with Tom Cruise in the blockbuster hit, *Mission Impossible* (1996), but her first film released in this country was *Manon of the Spring* (1986). However, her first Hollywood picture was the 1987 disaster *Date With an Angel*. She has been compared to the great women of French cinema such as Catherine Deneuve, Isabelle Huppert, and Isabelle Adjani. She has also been called the French Michele Pfeiffer.

Beart's mystique has been enhanced by roles in two films directed by Claude Sautet, *Un Coer en Hiver* (1992) and *Nelly et Monsieur Arnaud* (1996). In both, she plays reserved, almost silent characters. Beart says that she welcomed these roles as a contrast to the passionate, outgoing parts she had played before. The role of observer who says little actually suits her personality, Beart suggests.

Compared to the slow, sometimes agonizing process of filmmaking in France, work on *Mission Impossible* seemed fun to Beart. She could not believe the film's huge budget, which would cover the cost of 20 films in France. She was impressed with Tom Cruise, pointing out that it takes as much mental and physical preparation for an action movie as it does for an intimate French one.

Beart was born August 14, 1965 in Saint Tropez, France, but her father, singer/poet Guy Beart, raised his children on a farm in Gassin. After three years in Montreal, she went to Paris and took drama classes and made her debut on French television in 1984. Shortly after she met husband Daniel Auteuil while making the 1985 film *L'Amour en Douce* and they also worked together in *Manon of the Spring*. Her most recent films include *Stolen Life* and *Don Juan*, both 1998.

THE MANSTER
The Manster—Half Man, Half Monster
The Split

This cheapo 1959 exploitation picture—a Japanese/American co-production—is truly awful. Yet the picture sticks with you because there's a weird kind of sincerity in its ineptitude, and it approaches being truly grotesque as opposed to merely gross. An extremely American reporter (Peter Dyneley in a bizarrely stilted "performance") on assignment in Japan has a run-in with a mad scientist, Dr. Suzuki, whose inhuman experiments on humans never fail to go wrong. Suzuki injects the reporter with his latest experimental serum, and soon the poor Yankee lug becomes a sex-crazed, bad-tempered drunk. Worse, he discovers that he has a new eyeball, and it's growing out of his shoulder. Soon he's sprouting a whole new head, and then a second body, which he ends up wrestling with in the film's big finish. (Did Bergman see this before writing *Persona*? You be the judge!) At first you may think of Raymond Burr's sequences as American reporter Steve Martin in the original *Godzilla, King of the Monsters*, but here it's the reporter who's the monster—er, manster; it's as if

Burr's Steve Martin dropped some bad acid, though *we* get the hallucinations. *The Manster* may remind you of grade Z American 1950s schlock filler like *The Black Sleep*, but there's nothing else exactly like it. (Count your blessings.) Recommended for aficionados of this stuff—or fanatical chroniclers of "duality of the soul" movies—only.

NEXT STOP . . . *The Thing with Two Heads, Shadow of a Doubt, Persona*

1959 72m/B *JP* Peter Dyneley, Jane Hylton, Satoshi Nakamura, Terri Zimmern; *D:* Kenneth Crane, George Breakston. **VHS** *SNC, MRV*

MARGARET'S MUSEUM

In a small New Brunswick town in the 1940s, Margaret (Helena Bonham Carter) neglects her mother's stern and hard-earned advice by falling in love with a man who works in the area's dangerous mines. Though he tries to stay away, the disastrous economy leaves him no alternative. Yes, there's an inevitability and even a predictability about the direction in which events will unfold in director Mort Ransen's *Margaret's Museum,* but the wonder is how fresh and alive so much of the movie is. Both Carter and Kate Nelligan, who plays Margaret's emotionally devastated mother, are extraordinary, and Clive Russell takes Margaret's headstrong lover Neil in unexpected, quirky directions. This is a handsome romantic tragedy suffused with both feeling and social conscience, but blessedly little easy sentimentality. Winner of a number of Canada's Genie Awards, including Best Actress, Supporting Actress, Screenplay, and Score.

NEXT STOP . . . *Germinal, Kameradschaft, dalen '31*

1995 (R) 114m/C *CA GB* Helena Bonham Carter, Clive Russell, Kate Nelligan, Kenneth Welsh, Craig Olejnik; *D:* Mort Ransen; *W:* Mort Ransen, Gerald Wexler; *C:* Vic Sarin; *M:* Milan Kymlicka. Genie Awards '95: Best Actress (Bonham Carter), Best Adapted Screenplay, Best Costume Design, Best Supporting Actor (Welsh), Best Supporting Actress (Nelligan), Best Score. **VHS** *CAF*

MARIANNE AND JULIANE
The German Sisters
Die Bleierne Zeit

Personal and historical politics combine in Margarethe von Trotta's portrait of two German sisters in the 1970s. Juliane (Jutta Lampe) is the editor of a left-wing feminist journal, while Marianne (Barbara Sukowa) is active in a notorious, well-organized gang of deadly terrorists. Juliane's natural tendency toward compassion leads her to want to prevent her sister's apparently inevitable, headlong leap into oblivion; her obsessive attachment to Marianne leads her to do everything she can think of to bring her out of her murderous and suicidal rage. Based on an actual case, Von Trotta's *Marianne and Juliane* has a fascinating theme, but her connect-the-dots structure drains the juice out of it. The performances, however, are so good as to almost compensate.

NEXT STOP . . . *Sisters, or the Balance of Happiness, A Free Woman, Patty Hearst*

1982 106m/C *GE* Jutta Lampe, Barbara Sukowa, Ruediger Vogler, Doris Schade, Franz Rudnick; *D:* Margarethe von Trotta; *W:* Margarethe von Trotta; *C:* Franz Rath; *M:* Nicolas Economou. **VHS** *NYF*

MARIUS

See *Fanny* (1932).

1931 125m/B *FR* Raimu, Pierre Fresnay, Charpin, Orane Demazis; *D:* Alexander Korda; *W:* Marcel Pagnol; *M:* Francis Gromon. **VHS, LV** *NOS, MRV, INT*

THE MARQUISE OF O

During the Franco-Prussian War, a lovely young Italian widow (Edith Clever) is saved by a gallant Russian soldier (Bruno Ganz) from an impending rape. Yet months later, she is alarmed—and utterly puzzled—to find herself pregnant. Eric Rohmer's elegantly reserved and wonderfully witty adaptation of an 18th-century novella by Heinrich von Kleist has the narrative quality of a classic fable and the charming visual style (thanks to

THE MARRIAGE OF MARIA BRAUN
Die Ehe der Maria Braun

Hanna Schygulla, Rainer Werner Fassbinder's discovery, is given the full-blown movie star treatment in Fassbinder's 1978 breakthrough film. She stars as a woman who refuses to accept the loss of her husband—a soldier in World War II—as a personal defeat, using every tool at her disposal (including those Dietrich-like legs of hers that appear on the film's celebrated poster) to reinvent herself following the Hitler years. Clearly designed to be a major statement about the sacrifices, rewards, and lessons that sprang from Germany's defeat and subsequent recovery, *The Marriage of Maria Braun* is, perhaps, more successful as a lush, juicy soap opera than as an instructive metaphor. As dynamic, funny, erotically charged, and symmetrically structured as it is, *The Marriage of Maria Braun*—perhaps the single best-known example of the New German Cinema—nevertheless feels less personal and passionate than Fassbinder's fifteen-and-a-half-hour *Berlin Alexanderplatz* or even his dark, doom-ridden, visionary *Veronika Voss*. As a display of Schygulla's talents, however, it remains a worthy and beautifully crafted showcase for one of the most talented performers in modern cinema.

NEXT STOP . . . *Lili Marleen, Veronika Voss, Mommie Dearest*

1979 (R) 120m/C *GE* Hanna Schygulla, Klaus Lowitsch, Ivan Desny, Gottfried John, Gisela Uhlen; *D:* Rainer Werner Fassbinder; *W:* Rainer Werner Fassbinder, Peter Marthesheimer, Pea Frolich; *C:* Michael Ballhaus; *M:* Peer Raben. Berlin International Film Festival '79: Best Actress (Schygulla). **VHS** *NYF, COL, GLV*

A MARRIED WOMAN
La Femme Mariee

A young married woman (Macha Méril) tries to make up her mind whether to leave her husband or her lover. The urgency of her crisis is prompted by her pregnancy, though she's not sure which of the two men is the baby's

Bruno Ganz stars as a dissolute count in Eric Rohmer's *The Marquise of O.*

cinematographer Nestor Almendros) of a series of living, period tableaux. Created by Rohmer after completing *Chloe in the Afternoon,* the final film in his *Six Moral Tales* cycle, *The Marquise of O* looks at first glance like a major departure from the contemporary romantic comedies he had become famous for. But though the century, clothes, and customs are different (as is the language—these characters speak German), Rohmer's wonderfully confused, deeply romantic characters are not all that different on the inside from those we'd meet in one of his films set in a Paris suburb or a resort in the south of France. (With luck, video versions will capture Almendros's dark and velvety color scheme, which is one of the film's great pleasures.)

NEXT STOP . . . *Claire's Knee, The Aviator's Wife, The Magic Flute*

1976 102m/C *FR GE* Edith Clever, Bruno Ganz, Peter Luhr, Edda Seipel, Otto Sander, Ruth Drexel; *D:* Eric Rohmer; *W:* Eric Rohmer; *C:* Nestor Almendros. *NYR*

co-founder. Jean-Luc Godard's film looks and feels like it could have been made by a wicked student of his trying to imitate—or poke fun at—the master. Many of Godard's visual and storytelling innovations are here, such as quick jump cuts, interpretive titles, dry, ironic narration (by Godard) and bold fantasy sequences, but the subject matter is trifling and the method isn't exciting enough to make us not care about the flimsiness. He made *Band of Outsiders* the same year; *that's* the one to rent. (The French distributor forced Godard to change the movie's title from *The Married Woman*—suggesting they're all like this—to the more character-specific *A Married Woman*. This French sensibility toward the institution of marriage may be the most interesting nugget to emerge from the film.)

NEXT STOP . . . *My Life to Live, Two or Three Things I Know About Her, Contempt*

1965 94m/B *FR* Macha Meril, Phillippe LeRoy, Bernard Noel; *D:* Jean-Luc Godard; *W:* Jean-Luc Godard; *C:* Raoul Coutard. **VHS, 8mm** *VYY, MRV, DVT*

MASCULINE FEMININE
Masculin Feminin

In the Paris of 1965, a young interviewer who questions authority (Jean-Pierre Léaud) meets a young would-be pop star (Chantal Goya); they're the pair that the film's brilliant, pioneering director, Jean-Luc Godard, has dubbed "the children of Marx and Coca-Cola." Their affair progresses through a series of 15 loose and wildly inventive sketches/encounters that encompass parody, interviews, satire, movies, TV, violence, sex, and politics. Godard is at his most playful and insightful in these seemingly offhanded slices of gentle, intellectual street theatre, showing us a generation raised on pop culture and advertising struggling with questions of whether war and revolution can be packaged and marketed just like everything else. Though *Masculin Feminin* is a traditional love story at heart, Léaud and Goya are clearly representative of the generation of young people who, just three years after *Masculin Feminin*'s release, would take to the streets of Paris

in the traumatic days of May, 1968.

NEXT STOP . . . *Band of Outsiders, La Chinoise, Weekend*

1966 103m/B *FR* Jean-Pierre Leaud, Chantal Goya, Marlene Jobert; *D:* Jean-Luc Godard. Berlin International Film Festival '66: Best Actor (Leaud). **VHS** *NYF, DVT, VDM*

THE MASK
Eyes of Hell
The Spooky Movie Show

This wacky Canadian horror movie from 1961 tried—as happens every few years—to resuscitate the brief 3-D craze of the 1950s. It's the story of a psychiatrist (Paul Stevens) who comes into the possession of an ancient Aztec mask, and sees the physical manifestations of his unconscious sexual desires whenever he puts it on. We get to see his fantasies, too—and in 3-D—because every time he puts the mask on in the movie, the narrator instructs us to put on the cardboard mask (with red and blue cellophane eyes) that we were given when we bought our tickets (or bought the tape). It's kind of a cool, Freudian gimmick, but the director, Julian Roffman, dropped the ball by making the film unnecessarily dull, and the fantasy scenes laughably cheesy. The gimmick itself is really not very different from the premise of the 1994 Jim Carrey movie, except that Carrey simply lives out his fantasies. (Carrey also has the ability to pop through any movie screen *without* the need for special glasses.) Also known as *Eyes of Hell*.

NEXT STOP . . . *X—The Man with the X-Ray Eyes, Tightrope, The Dead Zone*

1961 85m/B *CA* Paul Stevens, Claudette Nevins, Bill Walker, Anne Collings, Martin Lavut, Leo Leyden, Bill Bryden, Eleanor Beecroft, Steven Appleby; *D:* Julian Roffman; *W:* Slavko Vorkapich, Franklin Delessert, Sandy Haver, Frank Taubes; *C:* Herbert S. Alpert; *M:* Louis Applebaum. **VHS, LV** *RHI, MLB*

MATADOR

Pedro Almodóvar's inventive, erotically charged, non-PC black comedy stars Nacho Martinez as a retired matador who satiates his deeply rooted desire to kill by guest-

M

"I know I'm not normal, but I can change."

—Muriel (Toni Colette) in *Muriel's Wedding*.

VICTORIA ABRIL
Star of Sexy Cinema

Spanish sexpot Victoria Abril knows how to get attention. To prove to director Jean-Jacques Beineix she could do nude scenes, she jumped naked into a pool minutes after meeting him. On screen, she sheds inhibitions just as freely. In *Tie Me Up! Tie Me Down!*, she portrayed a heroin-addicted ex-porn star. In *On the Line*, she played a prostitute who caresses a client's ears with her boots while wearing nothing else. In *Kika*, she was a cruel reality-show TV hostess clad in a black-rubber dominatrix outfit with a camera on her head and spotlights mounted on her breasts. In *Robin and Marian*, clad only in an animal skin, she invited the King of England to make love to her. She was 15 at the time and had already perfected the Glance. "When Victoria looks at you, she blows you away," says director Pedro Almodóvar. "Victoria is a predatory actress whose mere presence manages to attract everyone's attention."

Born July 4, 1957, Victoria was a skinny tomboy at 15, when she turned from dancing to film. "Compared to dancing, films seemed to me to be the work of lazy bums," she says. "There was no physical pain…It was very easy for me." So easy that Abril has vamped through 70 films and countless nude scenes. "There's nothing more human than two people making love," she says.

In 1994, Abril finally landed an English-speaking part as the hairdresser girlfriend of Joe Pesci in *Jimmy Hollywood*. Then she was cast in *Disclosure* as Michael Douglas's lawyer. "My only plan is not to play the same character twice," she says. In 1995, she played a married woman who takes a lesbian lover in *French Twist*, and she won a best actress Goya Award for *Nobody Will Speak of Us When We're Dead*. Her most recent film is 1997's *La Femme du Cosmonaute*.

To escape her family, Abril married impulsively at age 16; it ended in divorce. French cinematographer Gerard de Battista is the father of her two sons. Bringing hope to her typical male fan, she swears: "I like men with some belly who are a little over the hill."

starring in snuff films. He meets his match in the equally deadly Assumpta Serna, and the two are drawn together by a young bullfighting student who confesses to a series of murders. This early work of Almodóvar's shows him at his daring and outrageous best, walking a very fine line between comedy and horror. Though it's not for the squeamish or timid, *Matador* is one of the director's boldest and most visually arresting achievements. Still, those who only know Almodóvar by his high-gloss *Women on the Verge of a Nervous Breakdown* may be horrified by the links between violence and sexuality.

NEXT STOP . . . *Law of Desire, Live Flesh, The Criminal Life of Archibaldo de la Cruz*

1986 90m/C *SP* Assumpta Serna, Antonio Banderas, Nacho Martinez, Eva Cobo, Carmen Maura, Julieta Serrano, Chus Lampreave, Eusebio Poncela; **D:** Pedro Almodovar; **W:** Pedro Almodovar, Jesus Ferrere; **M:** Bernardo Bonazzi. **VHS, LV, Letterbox** *CCN, TPV*

THE MATCH FACTORY GIRL
Tulitkkutehtaan Tytto

Iris (the wonderfully deadpan Kati Outinen) is a plain, shy outsider who shares a drab dwelling with her one-dimensional mother and stepfather, works in a match factory, and hopes desperately for romantic love. Her world is transformed when the extraordinary occurs—she spots a brightly colored party dress in a shop window, buys it, wears it to a bar, and meets the creep who will soon get her pregnant and dump her. When she seeks revenge, Iris is ironically transformed into the most passionate of human beings. Finland's Aki Kaurismäki—who produced, wrote, directed, and edited *The Match Factory Girl*—has created a perfectly bleak, horrifyingly funny fable about love, loneliness, and betrayal; this surprisingly touching modern horror story is a sick but perfectly polished little jewel, and may well be the director's masterpiece. Truly, truly scary.

NEXT STOP . . . *Ariel, I Hired a Contract Killer, La Vie de Bohème*

1990 70m/C *SW FI* Kati Outinen, Elina Salo, Esko Nikkari, Vesa Vierikko; *D:* Aki Kaurismaki; *W:* Aki Kaurismaki. **VHS** *KIV, BTV, FCT*

MAX, MON AMOUR
Max, My Love

Peter (Anthony Higgins), a refined British diplomat living in Paris, has become suspicious of the occasional disappearances of his wife, Margaret (Charlotte Rampling). He follows her, and discovers that she's in love with a chimpanzee named Max. Ever the British gentleman, Peter suggests that everything would be neater if Max simply moved in with them, and soon their double bed has a freshly prepared cage nearby. *Max, Mon Amour* was written by longtime Buñuel collaborator Jean-Claude Carrière, and one can see how Buñuel might have been amused enough by the concept to perhaps include it as a short dream sequence in a film like *The Phantom of Liberty*. But it makes for an awfully thin feature, particularly in the leaden hands of Nagisa Oshima, who directs without a feel for surrealism, comedy or irony. What you see is what you get, and what you get is Charlotte Rampling in love with a chimp. Next!

NEXT STOP . . . *In the Realm of the Senses, In the Realm of Passion, Everything You Wanted Always to Know About Sex…But Were Afraid to Ask*

1986 97m/C *FR* Anthony Higgins, Charlotte Rampling, Victoria Abril, Christopher Hovik, Anne-Marie Besse, Pierre Etaix; *D:* Nagisa Oshima; *W:* Jean-Claude Carriere, Nagisa Oshima; *C:* Raoul Coutard; *M:* Michel Portal. **VHS** *CVC, ING*

MAY FOOLS
Milou en Mai
Milou in May

A bourgeois family gathers at a country estate for the funeral of the clan's matriarch, while the student riots of May 1968 unfold far from the peaceful sanctuary. The political effects are felt even here, however, for the national strikes which have seized the country are making it impossible to bury the woman on schedule. As the family members wait, the squabbles—some petty, some long-festering—begin to blossom. Few among the family members mourn the old woman's death, with the exception of her grown son, Milou (Michel Piccoli), who leads a pastoral existence tending grapes on the estate. Milou's daughter (Miou-Miou) also fails to reflect a note of sadness over the loss of continuity; she suggests, to her father's dismay, that the estate be divided in three. Louis Malle's *May Fools*, a portrait of individuals collectively experiencing personal upheaval against the backdrop of social upheaval, is a warm and delicately sketched pastorale made between the far more intense *Au Revoir les Enfants* and *Damage*. The most self-consciously Renoir-ish of Malle's films, it may also be one of the most underrated, precisely because of that unavoidable comparison. Chances are you'll enjoy it if you refuse to compare it to anything, and instead take in the setting, the food, the wine, and the relaxed performances of Michel Piccoli, Miou-

Theatre life takes its toll in Istvan Szabo's *Mephisto,* an adaptation of the novel by Klaus Mann.

Miou, and Harriet Walter. The original title is *Milou in May.*

NEXT STOP . . . *My Dinner with André, Vanya on 42nd Street, Picnic on the Grass*

1990 (R) 105m/C *FR* Michel Piccoli, Miou-Miou, Michael Duchaussoy, Dominique Blanc, Harriet Walter, Francois Berleand, Paulette Dubost, Bruno Carette, Martine Gautier; *D:* Louis Malle; *W:* Jean-Claude Carriere, Louis Malle; *C:* Renato Berta; *M:* Stephane Grappelli. Cesar Awards '91: Best Supporting Actress (Blanc). **VHS, LV** *ORI, FXL, FCT*

MEMORIES OF UNDER-DEVELOPMENT
Memorias del Subdesarrollo

Tomás Gutiérrez Alea's remarkable 1968 film—the first feature produced in Castro's Cuba to receive American release—is the story of a thoughtful and sympathetic man caught between two worlds. He believes—in theory, at least—in the revolution, but he's far too attached to the comforts and privileges he enjoyed before the revolution to become fully committed to the cause. With an intelligence, insight, and sensitivity similar to that which Bernardo Bertolucci displayed in his *Before the Revolution, Memories of Underdevelopment* took the film festival circuit by storm in 1968 and rightly signaled the arrival of a major new filmmaker. Until his death in 1997, Tomás Alea would make the films that the hero of this film might have made: probing, romantic, humane, and idealistic, yet always nostalgically aware of the value of what he must leave behind. His films would forever redefine our often simplistic notion of the parameters of Third World Cinema.

NEXT STOP . . . *Death of a Bureaucrat, Strawberry and Chocolate, Guantanamera!*

1968 97m/B *CU* Sergio Corrieri, Daisy Granados, Eslinda Nunez, Beatriz Ponchora; *D:* Tomas Gutierrez Alea; *W:* Tomas Gutierrez Alea, Edmundo Desnoes; *C:* Ramon Suarez; *M:* Leo Bower. **VHS** *NYF, FCT*

THE MEN WHO TREAD ON THE TIGER'S TAIL

Tora No O Wo Fumu Otokotachi
They Who Step on the Tiger's Tail
Walkers on the Tiger's Tail

The wartime Japanese government commissioned Akira Kurosawa to film the most popular of kabuki dramas, the story of a 12th-century lord forced to escape with only six retainers to guard him. The expectation was that Kurosawa would produce a rousing, patriotic movie that would sing the praises of obedience and feudal values. Instead, he turned out this satire of not only the original kabuki piece, but of militarism as well. The picture was promptly banned and remained banned until the end of the war, when it was unexpectedly—and ironically—banned again, this time for allegedly being in favor of feudalism. Though it's not typical Kurosawa fare, the compact, hour-long *Those Who Tread on the Tiger's Tail* is enormously enjoyable, highly theatrical fun—low comedy of a high order.

NEXT STOP . . . *The Hidden Fortress, Yojimbo, At War with the Army*

1945 60m/B *JP* Denjiro Okochi, Susumu Fujita, Masayuki Mori, Takashi Shimura, Yoshio Kosugi; *D:* Akira Kurosawa; *W:* Akira Kurosawa; *C:* Takeo Ito; *M:* Tadashi Hattori. **VHS** *IHF*

MEPHISTO

An egomaniacal, ambitious German actor (Klaus Maria Brandauer) sides with the Nazis to further his career. Hungary's István Szabó directed a trilogy of films starring the gifted Brandauer, all of which explored different aspects of selling one's soul for personal gain throughout German history. Szabó makes no bones about this story being a modern reworking of the Faust legend, and though he's unambiguous about his protagonist's guilt, the film remains fascinating throughout as a well-sculpted portrait of the cost of rationalization when carried to its logical end. Brandauer is a wonder; his energy level is staggering, but he never lets his sheer whirlwind force substitute for expressiveness. Academy Award Winner, Best Foreign Language Film.

NEXT STOP . . . *Colonel Redl, Hanussen, Faust (1926)*

1981 144m/C *HU* Klaus Maria Brandauer, Krystyna Janda, Ildiko Bansagi, Karin Boyd, Rolf Hoppe, Christine Harbort, Gyorgy Cserhalmi, Christiane Graskoff, Peter Andorai, Ildiko Kishonti; *D:* Istvan Szabo; *C:* Lajos Koltai. Academy Awards '81: Best Foreign Film. **VHS** *REP, SWC, GLV*

MESSIDOR

An acutely bored university student (Clementine Amoroux) meets a shop assistant (Catherine Retore) while hitchhiking. They decide to travel together across a desolate, faceless, modern Europe, stealing what they need when they run out of money. This poetic, elegant, and disturbing parable about a generation blessed with everything but purpose is one of Swiss director Alain Tanner's most experimental works. It may add up to less than the sum of its beautiful parts, but many of the images and incidents—visually stunning and paced with the slow inevitability of a dream—will stay with you long afterward.

NEXT STOP . . . *La Salamandre, Jonah Who Will Be 25 in the Year 2000, Butterfly Kiss*

1977 118m/C *SI* Clementine Amouroux, Catherine Retore, Franziskus Abgottspon, Gerald Battiaz, Hansjorg Bedschard; *D:* Alain Tanner; *W:* Alain Tanner; *C:* Renato Berta; *M:* Arie Dzierlatka. **VHS** *NYF, FCT*

METROPOLIS

Fritz Lang's astounding 1925 science-fiction epic is a classic of the German cinema's golden age. It's the story of a future in which society is neatly divided into haves and have-nots; the "masters" run the city from their palatial above-ground digs, while the

M

workers are squeezed into underground tenements and work like slaves. (Did I say science fiction?) The plot includes a great mad scientist named Rotwang (Rudolph Klein-Rogge, who was also Lang's *Dr. Mabuse*), who invents a robot who—disguised as a trusted female worker—incites the unsuspecting workers to riot and destroy their own homes. The film's message is for understanding between workers and management, but what the movie's really about is its incredible expressionist design. A restored version—including tinted sequences and some heretofore missing footage—was issued in 1984, and included a truly horrendous soundtrack by Giorgio Moroder featuring Loverboy, Pat Benatar, and Queen. Just turn off the sound, or better yet, try to catch a performance of *Metropolis* when the Alloy Orchestra accompanies the film on tour. Their score for the film is rousing, witty, and respectful—everything Moroder's is not.

NEXT STOP . . . *Woman in the Moon, Dr. Mabuse, Die Nibelungen*

1926 115m/B *GE* Brigitte Helm, Alfred Abel, Gustav Froehlich, Rudolf Klein-Rogge, Fritz Rasp, Heinrich George, Theodore Loos, Erwin Biswanger, Olaf Storm, Hans Leo Reich, Heinrich Gotho; **D:** Fritz Lang; **W:** Fritz Lang, Thea von Harbou; **C:** Karl Freund, Gunther Rittau, Eugene Schufftan; **M:** Gottfried Huppertz. **VHS, LV** *SNC, NOS, MRV*

THE MIDDLEMAN
Jana Aranya

Even among diehard devotees of foreign film, the late Satyajit Ray remains one of the directors whose work is more frequently discussed or alluded to than actually experienced. A case in point is this 1975 tale of a university graduate applying for a job in Calcutta. Carefully and thoughtfully, the young man puts the finishing touches on his job application, seals the envelope and drops it in the mail. The next image Ray gives us is of an undulating wave, a mountain of mail—what appear to be thousands, if not tens of thousands, of applications literally pouring in to a single office, all representing graduates seeking the same position. With this quick and simple juxtaposition of hope versus reality, Ray begins his tale of this young man's journey toward ultimate self-reliance by way of disillusionment. Yet Ray's concern isn't unemployment as such but rather the human spirit and the various and surprising ways it so often survives, particularly in the face of seemingly insurmountable odds. This is, he suggests, the story of his country, retold time and again in epics like *The Middleman*, in which humanity is forced to reach a truce with poverty, overpopulation, and loneliness. The very specificity of *The Middleman*'s Indian setting makes it obvious why Ray refused to make films outside of India. Tempted as he was, time and again, by offers to direct stories in other places (Hollywood included), he remained instead his nation's cinematic voice, proud to spin his miraculously eloquent stories without compromise or awkwardness.

NEXT STOP . . . *Days and Nights in the Forest, Mahanagar, Taxi Driver*

1976 131m/B *IN* Pradip Mukherjee; **D:** Satyajit Ray; **W:** Satyajit Ray; **C:** Soumendu Roy. **VHS** *COL.*

THE MILKY WAY

Two tramps on a religious pilgrimage encounter all manner of startlingly surrealistic sights, incidents, and adventures. As they wander through this series of dreamlike, often hilarious sketches, they discuss and debate Catholic religious doctrine even while the shape of the film itself suggests a somewhat unconventional reinterpretation of the Trinity. (Having an intimate knowledge of that doctrine is necessary to fully understand the film; but, ironically, those who have that knowledge are the ones most likely to be offended.) *The Milky Way* remains one of the most controversial movies by the great Spanish surrealist Luis Buñuel. While some regard it as a reverential film in the guise of a satire, others do not agree. Its power to disturb and enrage those with relatively inflexible religious beliefs should not be taken lightly; at a museum screening in Detroit in the late 1970s, an offended viewer attacked the movie projector as the film was in progress, shouting about blasphemy and demanding to be arrested. As quite a few in the audience later noted, *The Milky Way*'s provoking that manner of response was a sight that Buñuel himself—an old, irascible anarchist—might well have enjoyed.

NEXT STOP . . . *Nazarin, Viridiana, Simon of the Desert*

1968 102m/C *FR* Laurent Terzieff, Paul Frankeur, Delphine Seyrig, Alain Cuny, Bernard Verley, Michel Piccoli, Edith Scob; **D:** Luis Bunuel; **W:** Jean-Claude Carriere. **VHS, LV** *XVC, FCT, IME*

MINA TANNENBAUM

Mina (Romane Bohringer) and Ethel (Elsa Zylberstein) meet at the age of seven, and together they experience childhood and teenage traumas, including the desperate pangs of first love. As adults, Mina is consumed by her passionate commitment to her painting, while Ethel, a journalist, remains passionate only about her incorrigible flirtatiousness, as well as her friendship and lifelong rivalry with Mina. Martine Dugawson's *Mina Tannenbaum* is conceived as an epic portrait of the changes that friends create in each other over a quarter-century, but while the movie certainly feels long, it rarely wields the resonance or narrative power required of a genuine epic. It contains wonderful sequences, but they never flow into the sweeping story that you hope for. The performances by Bohringer and Zylberstein are, considering the fractured storytelling, captivating.

NEXT STOP . . . *Old Acquaintance, Rich and Famous, Antonia's Line*

1993 128m/C *FR* Romane Bohringer, Elsa Zylberstein, Nils Tavernier, Florence Thomassin, Jean-Philippe Ecoffey, Stephane Slima; **D:** Martine Dugowson; **W:** Martine Dugowson; **C:** Dominique Chapuis; **M:** Peter Chase. **VHS** *NYF*

MINBO—OR THE GENTLE ART OF JAPANESE EXTORTION
Minbo No Onna
The Gangster's Moll
The Anti-Extortion Woman

The Japanese mobsters known as *yakuza* are known for shakedowns and general intimidation of businesses. In Juzo Itami's 1992 *Minbo—or the Gentle Art of Japanese Extortion,* a group of obnoxious, ill-mannered *yakuza* enjoy congregating at a plush hotel, much to the detriment of business and much to the consternation of the management. Finally, the hotel bosses decide to hire a specialist they've heard of—a tough, hardball-playing female lawyer (Nobuko Miyamoto) who's become an expert at the new cottage industry of driving out *yakuza*. Miyamoto (Mrs. Itami) is completely captivating as the industrious *yakuza*-chaser; her schemes are often hilarious, and though it's clear from the start that the criminals have met their match, they won't go easily. Miyamoto became a specialist of sorts herself, playing a similar role here to that of the irrepressible tax collector in Itami's *A Taxing Woman.* Japan loves her too, and they made *Minbo* a smash hit at home. The *yakuza* weren't as pleased, however—they didn't like being made fun of, and consequently attacked Itami after the film's release, sending him to the hospital with multiple stab wounds. He recovered, but tragically fell victim to suicide in 1997.

NEXT STOP . . . *A Taxing Woman, A Taxing Woman's Return, Tampopo*

1992 123m/C *JP* Nobuko Miyamoto, Akira Takarada, Takehiro Murata, Yasuo Daichi, Hideji Otaki; **D:** Juzo Itami; **W:** Juzo Itami; **C:** Yonezo Maeda; **M:** Toshiyuki Honda. **VHS** *HMV*

THE MIRACLE
Ways of Love

The great Anna Magnani is the peasant woman who believes that her pregnancy by

M

a shepherd will produce a holy offspring. That the shepherd is played by Federico Fellini (who wrote the story on which the film is based) is but one of the many extraordinary aspects of Roberto Rossellini's stunning, 43-minute parable; *The Miracle* may have generated more controversy per minute of running time than any motion picture ever made. It was the subject of major censorship battles in many countries, including the U.S., where the Supreme Court finally upheld the public's right to see the film. What was lost in some of the controversy is what an exquisite and delicate piece of filmmaking it is, and how, in its unconventional way, the film is an enormously sensitive and highly reverent piece of work. (Echoes of the film can be found in the "miracle" sequence in Fellini's later *La Dolce Vita*.)

NEXT STOP . . . *Open City, The Flowers of St. Francis, La Dolce Vita*

1948 43m/B *IT* Anna Magnani, Federico Fellini; *D:* Roberto Rossellini; *W:* Federico Fellini. VHS *NOS, FCT, HEG*

MIRACLE IN MILAN
Miracolo a Milano

Vittorio De Sica's incomparable fantasy is an immensely satisfying neo-realist fable about heavenly intervention in the form of the miracle-working Toto the Hero (Francesco Golisano), whose missions include driving capitalists out of a Milanese ghetto while showering undreamed of blessings on the city's impoverished. De Sica managed to address the very real and dispiriting problem of Europe's displaced newly poor after World War II, and the fantasy form he uses for his moral tale is itself miraculously poetic, extraordinarily touching, and thoroughly uncondescending. An exquisite work of fantasy, adapted from Cesare Zavattini's story *Toto the Good.*

NEXT STOP . . . *Shoeshine, The Bicycle Thief, Umberto D*

1951 95m/B *IT* Francesco Golisano, Brunella Bova, Emma Gramatica, Paolo Stoppa; *D:* Vittorio De Sica; *W:*

Cesare Zavattini. Cannes Film Festival '51: Best Film; New York Film Critics Awards '51: Best Foreign Film. VHS, LV *HMV, FCT*

THE MIRROR
Zerkalo
A White White Boy

Andrei Tarkovsky's *The Mirror* is a stunning, imagist memoir of a child's life in Russia during World War II, but that's only on the surface. Beneath that exquisite surface is an emotional history of his nation, told through flashbacks to key moments in Russian history which are then juxtaposed with the "modern" story, blending past and present in a way that infuses the film with truths well beyond the specific. This is an historical film about feeling, which seems, in the end, as valid a method of documenting the march of time as any—perhaps more so. It's a one-of-a-kind, masterful work of art.

NEXT STOP . . . *My Name Is Ivan, Andrei Rublev, The Sacrifice*

1975 106m/C *RU* Margarita Terekhova, Philip Yankovsky, Ignat Daniltsev, Oleg Yankovsky; *D:* Andrei Tarkovsky; *W:* Andrei Tarkovsky; *C:* Georgy Rerberg; *M:* Eduard Artemyev. VHS *TPV, KIV*

MISS JULIE
Froken Julie

Miss Julie (Anita Björk), a wealthy but confused noblewoman, is irritated and angered by—as well as attracted to—the masculine butler who works for her and her father. It is Midsummer's Eve and a celebration is planned, but Miss Julie is heartbroken over the breaking off of her engagement. To console herself, she carefully plans the seduction of her butler (Ulf Palme), assuring him afterward that she will run away with him. In a series of flashbacks following the seduction, we learn of her background, her mother's attitude toward men, and the incidents in her past that have brought her to this moment. We also discover that Miss Julie finds it impossible to live with the shame of what she's done. This is a lean, strong, and generally superb film, with marvelous performances from Anita Björk and Ulf Palme. Director Alf Sjöberg has captured a nearly unbearable sexual tension while remaining completely faithful to Strindberg's play. Grand Prize, Cannes Film Festival (shared with *Miracle in Milan*).

NEXT STOP... *Torment, Sawdust and Tinsel, After the Rehearsal*

1950 90m/B *SW* Anita Bjork, Ulf Palme, Anders Henrikson, Max von Sydow; *D:* Alf Sjoberg; *W:* Alf Sjoberg; *C:* Goran Strindberg; *M:* Dag Wiren. Cannes Film Festival '51: Best Film. **VHS** *HMV, COL*

MISSISSIPPI MERMAID
Le Sirene du Mississippi

François Truffaut's dark romance about a plantation owner (Jean-Paul Belmondo) who sends for a mail-order bride and ends up with the very special delivery of Catherine Deneuve was indifferently received by critics and largely ignored by audiences (the dubbed version shown in many American cities was no help). The film's neglect is tragic, however, because *Mississippi Mermaid*—based on a novel by *Rear Window* author Cornell Woolrich—is one of the most delicately shaded, moving, and personal films of Truffaut's career. Belmondo's love for the duplicitous, ice-cold woman who cleans him out of everything except his passion for her is an early version of what would ultimately become the obsessive mania depicted in Truffaut's masterpiece, *The Story of Adele H. Mississippi Mermaid* is the converse of David Mamet's *House of Games,* in which broken trust instantly reshapes love into hate. Here, it's just another obstacle that makes an inevitable journey toward a common destiny take a little longer; it's foreplay, like the brief moment in the film in which Belmondo's arrival home prompts Deneuve to quickly put *on* her stockings before lying down on his bed, just to give him the pleasure of taking them off of her. If the sadomasochistic bond at the center of this heartbreaking and complex movie seems inexplicable, consider the film's dedication, which is to Jean Renoir. It was Renoir who wrote that "the terrible thing about this world is that everybody has his reasons."

NEXT STOP... *La Chienne, The Soft Skin, The Woman Next Door*

1969 (PG) 110m/C *FR IT* Jean-Paul Belmondo, Catherine Deneuve, Michel Bouquet, Nelly Borgeaud, Marcel Berbert, Martine Ferriere; *D:* Francois Truffaut; *W:* Francois Truffaut; *C:* Denys Clerval; *M:* Antoine Duhamel. **VHS, LV, Letterbox** *MGM, FCT*

MR. ARKADIN
Confidential Report

As in *Citizen Kane,* Orson Welles here looks at and stars in the story of another ruthless millionaire, but Gregory Arkadin (Welles) isn't anxious to admit the unsavory source of his wealth. Also as in *Kane,* an outsider (Robert Arden) is our investigator/guide into the man's mysterious world, examining the trail of his life through strange—and strangely photographed—witnesses such as Mischa Auer playing the owner of a seedy little flea circus. By any conventional standards, *Mr. Arkadin* (also known as *Confidential Report*) is a mess. Conventional standards, however, make little sense when looking at much of Welles's post-Kane work, particularly a film that took two years to shoot and seven years to edit (it finally saw the light of day in 1962). During that editing process, it became impossible to round up all the actors for post-synchronization of the soundtrack; Welles's solution was to rival the vocal productivity of Mel Blanc by dubbing 18 of the soundtrack's voices himself. *Mr. Arkadin* remains a nightmarish, highly personal, bizarrely fascinating failure. With Michael Redgrave, Akim Tamiroff, and Katina Paxinou. (A reworked reissue a la *Touch of Evil* is reputed to be in the works.)

NEXT STOP... *Citizen Kane, The Lady from Shanghai, The Immortal Story*

1955 99m/B *GB* Orson Welles, Akim Tamiroff, Michael Redgrave, Patricia Medina, Mischa Auer; *D:* Orson Welles; *C:* Jean Bourgoin. **VHS, LV** *HMV, HTV, HEG*

M

MON ONCLE
My Uncle
My Uncle, Mr. Hulot

Jacques Tati's justly celebrated comedy contrasts the simple life of his Monsieur Hulot with the technologically complicated life of his family when he aids his nephew in war against his parents' ultramodern, pushbutton home. Tati's first film in color is an often inspired work in which an impersonal, mechanized future clashes with Hulot's quirky individualism in a series of ingeniously choreographed comic vignettes. *Mon Oncle* is a reaction to modernization of all sorts, and a visually concise argument against France being overtaken by what was seen as a sterile invasion of glass-and-steel modernism creeping in from America. Tati's obvious genius, however, may strike one as being a bit impersonal itself; his carefully designed gags make their points, but rarely emit the spontaneity of a Buster Keaton or (pardon me) Jerry Lewis. Despite such reservations, *Mon Oncle*—a sequel to Tati's *Mr. Hulot's Holiday*—is a formidable achievement, and an undeniable comic landmark.

NEXT STOP . . . *Mr. Hulot's Holiday, Playtime, The General*

1958 110m/C *FR* Jacques Tati, Jean-Pierre Zola, Adrienne Serrantie, Alain Bacourt; **D:** Jacques Tati; **C:** Jean Bourgoin. Academy Awards '58: Best Foreign Film; Cannes Film Festival '58: Grand Jury Prize; New York Film Critics Awards '58: Best Foreign Film. **VHS, LV, 8mm** *HMV, MRV, HHT*

MON ONCLE ANTOINE

This portrait of a young boy's Christmas in a small Quebec mining town in the 1940s is no saccharine, rose-colored remembrance; Canada's gifted Claude Jutra has blended the natural beauty of the surroundings with the community's grim economic realities to create a bittersweet, heartbreakingly beautiful masterwork. The small joys and humiliations that the boy, his working-class family, and his wonderful, generous-spirited uncle experience daily seem unfocused at first, as if we were seeing random incidents; before long, however, *Mon Oncle Antoine* becomes a fully formed portrait of a way of life that takes on a surprising emotional power. You may find yourself overwhelmed by moments that you don't fully absorb until the film's over, and there are images (and an extraordinarily haunting musical score) that you will always remember. Quiet, devastating, brilliant.

NEXT STOP . . .   *Act of the Heart, King of the Hill, Sugar Cane Alley*

1971 104m/C *CA* Jean Duceppe, Olivette Thibault; *D:* Claude Jutra. **VHS** *HMV, HMV, AUD*

MON ONCLE D'AMERIQUE
Les Somnambules

Director Alain Resnais tracks three characters as they encounter success of various kinds in modern Paris. Their adventures are interspersed with ironic, enlightening, and hilariously relevant lectures from Professor Henri Laborit, about the biology that impels and influences human behavior. (When these lectures are particularly impersonal or scientific in nature, we will see the actors appear with the heads of huge laboratory rats protruding from their clothing. Yes, it's a gimmick—but it's a riot, and it works brilliantly.) As each of the characters experiences inevitable setbacks in love or career, they dream of their proverbial—and generic—American uncle, who someday will grant all their wishes and make their dreams come true. Resnais's witty and bracingly intelligent *Mon Oncle d'Amerique* suggests *Death of a Salesman* as reworked by benevolent space aliens; it provides the

experience of seeing our lives under the microscope, yet refuses to find anything depressing about our remarkably predictable behavior. One of the best and most shamefully neglected French films of the 1980s. With Gérard Depardieu, Nicole Garcia, and Roger Pierre. Jean Grualt's deft screenplay, based on the works of the real Henri Laborit, received an Oscar nomination.

NEXT STOP . . .   *Providence, A Clockwork Orange, The Young Poisoner's Handbook*

1980 (PG) 123m/C *FR* Gerard Depardieu, Nicole Garcia, Roger-Pierre, Marie DuBois; *D:* Alain Resnais; *W:* Jean Gruault; *C:* Sacha Vierny. Cannes Film Festival '80: Grand Jury Prize; New York Film Critics Awards '80: Best Foreign Film; Nominations: Academy Awards '80: Best Original Screenplay. **VHS** *NYF, BTV*

MONDO CANE
A Dog's Life
A Dog's World

It's hard to remember, but there was a time when the Italian word "mondo" was *not* an official part of the English language. That was the day before the release of *Mondo Cane* (*A Dog's World*), a 1963 exploitation film about bizarre human behavior around the world, directed by Gualitero Jacopetti and produced by Franco Prosperi. *Mondo Cane* billed itself as a documentary, though everything seen in the movie—the "cargo cult," body painting, ritzy New Yorkers eating insects, etc.—was staged in such a bald-faced, phony-baloney way that even the makers of Sunn Classics' pictures like *Beyond and Back* and *In Search of Noah's Ark* would have blushed with embarrassment. *Mondo Cane* came complete with a "love theme"—"More," which was nominated for an Oscar—and played its initial engagements in art houses, billed as a foreign oddity. (I tried to get in at an art house in Detroit, but they said thirteen was too young to be exposed to the "mature" subject matter of *Mondo Cane*. Actually, being *over* thirteen should have disqualified you.) The picture developed a buzz and moved on to more mainstream theatres, which is when distrib-

"You have to compare so you can keep perspective. It helps to keep a little distance."

—Ingemar (Anton Glanzelius) in *My Life as a Dog*.

utors and exhibitors became aware of the huge crossover potential of the geek audience. They wasted no time. *Mondo Cane* was followed by *Mondo Pazzo, Mondo Balardo* and *Mondo Trasho* (OK, OK, that's John Waters), and later its spiritual heirs—the pseudo-snuff *Faces of Death* series—would show up just in time for the video era, so that viewers would be able to watch the "good" parts over and over, day in and day out. What a wacky mondo we live in.

NEXT STOP . . . The Blood of the Beasts, Koyaanisqatsi, Powaqqatsi

1963 (R) 105m/C *IT* **D:** Gualtiero Jacopetti; **W:** Gualtiero Jacopetti; **C:** Antonio Climati, Benito Frattari; **M:** Riz Ortolani, Nino Oliviero. Nominations: Academy Awards '63: Best Song ("More"). **VHS** *SNC, VDC, VDM*

A MONGOLIAN TALE
Hei Ma

A young boy is sent to live with an orphan girl and a foster grandmother in the Mongolian grasslands. The boy and girl become extremely close, and when she's grown and becomes pregnant by a lover, the brother runs off out of anger and jealousy. Twelve years later he comes back; he's a celebrated musician now, but his "sister" and his entire remembered world have changed in ways he couldn't have imagined. Xie Fei's film reaches for epic sweep and comes very close, though the director has insisted on just a bit too much plot in slightly too short a time. Nevertheless, this is a physically magnificent film with many exquisite and haunting sequences, and its portrait of the inevitability of change rings universally true. Tengger, an allegedly popular Chinese rock star, is the lead actor in *A Mongolian Tale,* and also provided the inventive musical score.

NEXT STOP . . . Girl from Hunan, Close to Eden, The Searchers

1994 105m/C *CH HK* Narenhua, Tengger; **D:** Xie Fei; **W:** Zhang Chengzhi; **C:** Jing Sheng Fu; **M:** Tengger. Montreal World Film Festival '95: Best Director (Fei). **VHS** *NYF*

MONIKA
Summer with Monika

Teenagers Harry and Monika (Lars Ekborg and Harriet Andersson), one an errand boy and the other a beautiful shopgirl, run away together for the summer and find that the winter brings more responsibility than they can handle when Monika becomes pregnant and gives birth. That changes the family dynamic, so to speak, because before long Monika decides that she's just not cut out for motherhood. This OK early Ingmar Bergman film achieved a reputation beyond its quality, primarily because of Harriet Andersson's nude scenes. *Monika* was imported to America in a dubbed version that played both art theatres and commercial houses, with ad campaigns to match. (For the dubbed runs here, Erik Nordgren's original score was stripped off and replaced by some supposedly hot 'n' sassy licks laid down by Les Brown and his Band of Renown.) *Monika* (also known as *Summer with Monika*) wasn't considered a lascivious item in the U.S. alone; in Truffaut's *The 400 Blows,* little Antoine (Jean-Pierre Léaud) can be seen swiping stills from the film from the front of a Parisian movie house.

NEXT STOP . . . Illicit Interlude, Through a Glass Darkly, Sawdust and Tinsel

1952 96m/B *SW* Harriet Andersson, Lars Ekborg, John Harryson, Georg Skarstedt, Dagmar Ebbesen, Ake Gronberg; **D:** Ingmar Bergman; **W:** Ingmar Bergman; **M:** Les Baxter. **VHS** *HMV, CVC, TPV*

MONSIEUR HIRE
M. Hire

As Monsieur Hire spends his time trying to peer through his window at his beautiful young neighbor (Sandrine Bonnaire), he is transfixed—and appalled—by her romantic encounters. But, as Hitchcock showed us in *Rear Window,* voyeurs pay a price for their obsession, and rarely remain passive observers no matter how desperately they try. Patrice Leconte's brilliant and hypnotic thriller *Monsieur Hire,* based on the Georges Simenon novel *Les Fiançailles de Monsieur Hire,* is both the story of Hire's repressed desires and a murder mystery involving unrestrained passions. We watch breathlessly as these events unfold, knowing that we're in the hands of a master filmmaker. Leconte's storytelling is subtle and absolutely lucid at the same time; he adds layer upon layer of meaning and possibility while building tension visually, using dialogue only in the rare instances when an image won't do. Michel Blanc seems to have a direct pipeline into his role, and Sandrine Bonnaire is tantalizingly mysterious as the object of his nearly desperate obsession. Denis Lenoir's widescreen cinematography and Michael Nyman's sad, mocking score are absolutely right. Just 81 minutes long, *Monsieur Hire* is a perfect, darkly glistening gem. (If you're seeing it on video, be sure it's a letterboxed version.)

NEXT STOP . . . The Tenant, The Hairdresser's Husband, Ridicule

1989 (PG-13) 81m/C *FR* Michel Blanc, Sandrine Bonnaire, Luc Thuillier, Eric Berenger, Andre Wilms; ***D:*** Patrice Leconte; ***W:*** Patrice Leconte. Cesar Awards '90: Best Sound. **VHS, LV** *FXL, FCT, IME*

MONSIEUR VINCENT

Monsieur Vincent is the true story of the 17th-century priest who became St. Vincent de Paul. Monsieur Vincent forsakes his worldly possessions and convinces members of the aristocracy to finance charities for the less fortunate. Pierre Fresnay gives a legendary performance in a film that managed to rise to the occasion in every sense. Jean Anouilh wrote the simple and elegant screenplay, and Claude Renoir provided the glowing cinematography. Director Maurice Cloche backed Fresnay with an extraordinary supporting cast, all of them members of the Comédie Française. *Monsieur Vincent* received a dozen international prizes including a special Academy Award for Best Foreign Language Film. (Critics everywhere seemed happily startled that the film wasn't just about a good person, but was actually a good *film.*)

NEXT STOP . . . Thérèse, The Flowers of St. Francis, The Gospel According to St. Matthew

1947 112m/B *FR* Pierre Fresnay, Lisa Delamare, Aime Clarimond, Jean Debucourt, Pierre Dux, Gabrielle Dorziat, Jean Carmet, Michel Bouquet; ***D:*** Maurice Cloche; ***W:*** Jean Anouilh, Jean-Bernard Luc; ***C:*** Claude Renoir; ***M:*** Jean Jacques Grunenwald. Academy Awards '48: Best Foreign Film. **VHS** *INT*

THE MONSTER
Il Mostre

In *The Monster,* the Italian comic actor and director Roberto Benigni plays an ordinary, lovesick nebbish who's mistaken for a serial killer. Benigni finds endless possibilities for mistaken identity gags, double takes, pratfalls and slamming doors in this admittedly obvious farce, but while it's obvious, it's also hilarious. Benigni takes running gags further than you think he's going to, and his frenzied repetition, electric-socket hair and manic energy can wear down your defenses no matter how hard you resist. Watching a Benigni film is like being a guest on the TV show *Make Me Laugh;* you see where things are headed, you know what's coming, but when you try to keep from laughing—*that's* when you explode. Benigni's films have been massive hits in Italy, but he's yet to make a significant dent in the American box office. That's likely to change with the release of his 1998 Cannes Jury Prize winner *Life is Beautiful,* which had even stone-faced, diehard cinéastes on their feet applauding in the most prestigious movie theatre in the world. In the meantime, rent *The Monster* and invite a couple of friends over. And don't be surprised at who laughs first.

NEXT STOP . . . Johnny Stecchino, Night on Earth, Down by Law

1996 (R) 110m/C *IT* Roberto Benigni, Nicoletta Braschi, Michel Blanc, Dominque Lavanant, Jean-Claude Brialy, Ivano Marescotti, Laurent Spielvogel, Massimo Girotti, Franco Mescolini; ***D:*** Roberto Benigni; ***W:*** Roberto Benigni, Vincenzo Cerami; ***C:*** Carlo Di Palma; ***M:*** Evan Lurie. **VHS** *COL*

ROBERTO BENIGNI
Italy's Answer to Woody Allen

The man called "Italy's Woody Allen" sounds like the neurotic American when he notes: "Comedy works best when he is surrounded by misery." But Roberto Benigni is more aptly compared to Charlie Chaplin or Buster Keaton. He is an adept physical comic with a perpetual mask of mystified innocence.

"His true gift is improvisation…and disruption," said director Jim Jarmusch, who cast Benigni in his first American film, *Down by Law*, as a tourist/murderer who carries a notebook of fractured English phrases.

Benigni had been a national antihero in Italy for a decade but was virtually unknown elsewhere until Blake Edwards cast him as a new Inspector Clouseau in the 1993 film, *Son of the Pink Panther*. Benigni, who was born October 27, 1952 in a poor village in Tuscany and cut his teeth on avant-garde theater in Rome in the 1970s, hosted a wildly popular TV show where he played a befuddled film critic. He has written, directed, and acted in several smash films. His *Little Devils*, with Walter Matthau, set new Italian box-office records. His next film, *Johnny Stecchino*, in which Benigni plays a bus driver mistaken for a Mafia boss, doubled the gross of *Devils* and got limited release across the Atlantic.

Benigni combines his trademark impassive face with a shy, sweet demeanor, outrageous slapstick stunts and wicked, often anti-religious, satire. His wife, actress/comedian Nicoletta Braschi, often appears in his films. They met on the set of *Tu Mi Turbi*, where he cast her as the Virgin Mary. In his next film, she played the devil. They also worked together in 1994's *The Monster*.

He won the Grand Jury Prize at Cannes for the Holocaust comedy/drama *Life is Beautiful*, which he directed, co-wrote, and starred in. (His wife Braschi played his wife in the film.)

A MONTH IN THE COUNTRY

This is a gentle, eloquently told story of two British World War I veterans, one an archaeologist (Kenneth Branagh) and the other an expert in the conservation and restoration of paintings (Colin Firth), who come together when working in a small Yorkshire town. Firth's character suffered great emotional damage during the war, and as he removes layers of grime from a medieval church painting, gradually revealing the glorious work of art underneath, the simple but not overstated metaphor for the healing of his own damaged psyche comes into focus. Branagh, Firth, and Miranda Richardson are superb in this rarely seen, small jewel of a film. J.R. Carr's novel was adapted by playwright Simon Gray (*Butley*) and was directed by Pat O'Connor.

NEXT STOP . . . *Life and Nothing But, Mrs. Dalloway, La Belle Noiseuse*

1987 92m/C *GB* Colin Firth, Natasha Richardson, Kenneth Branagh, Patrick Malahide, Tony Haygarth, Jim

Carter; **D:** Pat O'Connor; **W:** Simon Gray; **C:** Kenneth Macmillan; **M:** Howard Blake. **VHS, LV** *ORI, WAR*

MONTY PYTHON'S THE MEANING OF LIFE

The last of the Monty Python feature films is a strong contender for their best—most of it is truly inspired stuff. Notable among the linked sketches are a live sex enactment performed before bored schoolboys, a student-faculty rugby game that turns quite violent, and an encounter between a physician and a reluctant organ donor. The amazing—and amazingly funny—sequence in which a glutton (played by the film's director, Terry Jones) eats just one bite too many in a posh restaurant deserves its legendary status, and it's a perfect illustration of how the Pythons were able to walk that razor-thin line between silly grossness and comic brilliance. Hilarious, smart, and surprisingly touching. Special Jury Prize, Cannes Film Festival (no kidding).

NEXT STOP . . . *And Now for Something Completely Different, Monty Python's Life of Brian, The Seventh Seal*

1983 (R) 107m/C *GB* Graham Chapman, John Cleese, Terry Gilliam, Eric Idle, Terry Jones, Michael Palin, Carol Cleveland, Matt Frewer; **D:** Terry Jones; **W:** Graham Chapman, John Cleese, Terry Gilliam, Eric Idle, Terry Jones, Michael Palin; **M:** John Du Prez. Cannes Film Festival '83: Grand Jury Prize. **VHS, LV, Letterbox, DVD** *USH, CCB, SIG*

MOON IN THE GUTTER
La Lune dans le Caniveau

In a ramshackle harbor town, a stevedore (Gérard Depardieu) searches the docks for the person who killed his sister many years before. Supposedly the screenplay for *Moon in the Gutter* was based on a novel by American crime writer David Goodis; if that's true, how did Goodis make a living? Not having read the novel on which the film is based, something tells me that it was messed with more than a little by director Jean-Jacques Beineix, whose *Diva* was a smash hit in the

U.S. *Moon in the Gutter* makes little—if any—literal sense. You can't follow it, and when you can, you don't want to. This isn't really a movie—it's a wallow. A wallow in "style," in trendiness, in pretentious lighting and cinematographic effects. It's everything but characters, a story, and a movie—the things we came to see. It's appallingly awful.

NEXT STOP . . . *Diva, The Long Voyage Home, Shoot the Piano Player*

1983 (R) 109m/C *IT FR* Gerard Depardieu, Nastassia Kinski, Victoria Abril, Vittorio Mezzogiorno, Dominique Pinon; **D:** Jean-Jacques Beineix; **W:** Jean-Jacques Beineix; **C:** Philippe Rousselot; **M:** Gabriel Yared. Cesar Awards '84: Best Art Direction/Set Decoration. **VHS** *COL*

MOONLIGHTING

A group of Polish workers is illegally brought into London to renovate a house. But when martial law is declared back in Poland, the group's foreman (Jeremy Irons) makes the god-like decision to keep the men in the dark so as to get the project completed on time and on budget. Jerzy Skolimowski's simple but brilliantly worked out fable about manipulation and power is a political parable told on such convincingly human terms that its significance as metaphor may not bowl you over until the very end—which is as it ought to be. Irons is an inspired choice as the tyrannical, sociopathic foreman who plays with his charges' lives and feels no anxiety doing so—until, of course, he considers the consequences of being caught. *Moonlighting* is one of the most elegant and convincing—and bitterly funny—movies ever made about the eternal lure of fascism and the universal specter of the bully. Best Screenplay Award to Skolimowski, Cannes Film Festival.

NEXT STOP . . . *Deep End, Man of Marble, Death and the Maiden*

1982 (PG) 97m/C *PL GB* Jeremy Irons, Eugene Lipinski, Jiri Stanislay, Eugeniusz Haczkiewicz; **D:** Jerzy Skolimowski; **C:** Tony Pierce-Roberts; **M:** Hans Zimmer. **VHS, LV** *USH*

MOSCOW DOES NOT BELIEVE IN TEARS

Moscow Distrusts Tears

Moskwa Sljesam Nje Jerit

Three man-hungry girls arrive in Moscow in the 1950s, hoping to find love and happiness. Over the course of the next 20 years, we discover their successes, their compromises, and share in what they've learned about love and life. If you change the setting to New York or Los Angeles, you'll be reminded of glossy 1950s Hollywood movies that aren't all that different except for the factories and the decor. Nevertheless, the dull *Moscow Does Not Believe in Tears* got a lot of playdates in U.S. theatres, not because the film is particularly radical or exhilarating (it isn't either), but because everyone remembered the name from the 1980 Academy Awards show. There were a few titters in the audience when the nominees were announced (it was the title that got laughs), but there was a general gasp when this film was announced as the winner. It hadn't been released here yet, so no one knew what to make of it, but there was a kind of "with-a-name-like-Smuckers-it's-got-to-be-good" buzz surrounding the movie's surprise victory. When it was released, critics seemed to be getting in line to proclaim its virtues, though its scanty charms did manage to elude American audiences in general. (It was a smash in the USSR.) The video release is a full half-hour shorter than the original cut, yet is no less enervating.

NEXT STOP . . . *Little Vera, Repentance, How to Marry a Millionaire*

1980 115m/C *RU* Vera Alentova, Irina Muravyova, Raisa Ryazanova, Natalie Vavilova, Alexei Batalov; *D:* Vladimir Menshov; *W:* Valentin Chernykh; *C:* Igor Slabnevich; *M:* Sergei Nikitin. Academy Awards '80: Best Foreign Film. **VHS, LV** *COL, IME, KIV*

THE MOTHER AND THE WHORE

La Maman et la Putain

Arriving on the international film scene in 1973 amid a glut of self-indulgent films about student unrest, Jean Eustache's epic was mistaken in some quarters as just one more of those, especially since the young man at its center—played by Jean-Pierre Léaud in his prime—is perhaps the screen's ultimate self-indulgent student. Comfortably ensconced in a womb-like, self-contained Paris, completely obsessed with himself and his own (as he sees it) intelligence, Léaud lords over his little domain by practicing the sexual freedom he espouses while at the same time demanding fidelity from the woman he lives with (Bernadette Lafont). Toss in the film's three-hour-and-forty-minute running time, which is almost entirely taken up by alternately passionate and disingenuous conversation between the three principals (the third being Françoise Lebrun, the new woman Léaud brings home, whose astonishing, furious tirade takes up the last half-hour of the picture), and *The Mother and the Whore* became an easy target for those anxious to shoot down subtitled toy ducks. But look out, because *The Mother and the Whore* is so utterly engaging, so blazingly honest and indelible, that it in no way appears to be a period piece a quarter-century after its release. Recent, real-life political events are simply additional proof that sexual politics in a male-dominated society rarely budge an inch from where they started, regardless of the amount of passionate lip service (pardon the expression) that men in positions of power care to pay. Recently remastered from the film's original negative and fitted with much-needed new subtitles (the original prints kept huge chunks of conversation a secret from non-French-speaking audiences, giving us subtitles that periodically read "untranslatable French pun"!), *The Mother and the Whore* is fresher than ever—one of the most essential films to emerge from the French New Wave.

NEXT STOP . . . *Rules of the Game, La Belle Noiseuse, Masculine Feminine*

1973 210m/B Bernadette LaFont, Jean-Pierre Leaud, Isabelle Weingarten, Francoise Lebrun, Jean-Noel Picq, Jessa Darrieux, Genevieve Mnich, Marinka Matuszewski; *D:* Jean Eustache; *W:* Jean Eustache; *C:* Pierre Lhomme. *NYR*

A young country girl comes to Moscow in *Moscow Does Not Believe in Tears.*

TONI COLLETTE
Actress Who Took a Chance

Most actresses that Australian director Paul Hogan called wanted no part of playing weird, fat, uncool Muriel Heslop, central character of *Muriel's Wedding*. But Toni Collette loved the script about the ugly ducking's search for Prince Charming. And she wanted to protect the character from being mangled. "Muriel could easily be made fun of. I didn't want to trust anyone else with her," she said. "I just knew I was Muriel."

Physically, she wasn't. Collette is lithe and striking. To play Muriel, Collette wolfed down doughnuts and gained 42 pounds, changed her sleek hairdo into a stringy mess and listened constantly to Abba, the Swedish pop group that Muriel worships. She became a gawky, provincial dumpling with freckles and a toothsome grin.

The unglamorous part that nobody wanted propelled Collette into sudden stardom. She even won the Australian Film Institute Best Actress Award for the role. Critic Andrew Sarris called Muriel "a spectacular, subversive heroine." Collette's unmocking portrayal of a modern Everygirl connected with audiences worldwide.

Born November 1, 1972, Collette grew up a tomboy in the Sydney suburb of Blacktown and quit high school at 14 to pursue a stage career. In her first film, she played a factory worker in Mark Joffe's little-known 1992 comedy *The Efficiency Expert*. After *Muriel*, she thinned down and again became a chic diva. For her next project, she teamed again with Joffe and *Muriel* co-star Rachel Griffiths on another quirky film, *Cosi* (1996). Her latest film is the 1998 Australian movie *The Boys* and her other films include *The Pallbearer* (1996), *Emma* (1996), *The James Gang* (1997), *Clockwatchers* (1997), and *Velvet Goldmine* (1998).

MOTHER KÜSTERS GOES TO HEAVEN
Mutter Kusters Fahrt Zum Himmel

Mrs. Küsters's husband is a frustrated factory worker who flips out and kills the factory owner's son and himself. Left alone, Mrs. Küsters (Brigitte Mira) discovers that everyone is using her husband's death to further their own needs, including her daughter, who uses the publicity to enhance her singing career. Savagely criticizing a modern media-mad world in which politics, journalism, and personal agendas all intersect at the point of personal gain, Rainer Werner Fassbinder's darkly funny and searingly angry film is, at heart, the story of Mrs. Küsters's heroic efforts to rise above the muck. Its politics earned the film expulsion from the Berlin Film Festival, which alone makes the picture worth a look. Brigitte Mira, gloomy veteran of Fassbinder films such as *Ali: Fear Eats the Soul* is splendid. (The film's original title, *Mutter Küsters Fahrt zum Himmel*, has also been translated as *Mother Küster's Trip to Heaven*.)

NEXT STOP . . . *The Merchant of Four Seasons, Ali: Fear Eats the Soul, Patty Hearst*

1976 108m/C *GE* Brigitte Mira, Ingrid Caven, Armin Meier, Irm Hermann, Gottfried John, Margit Carstensen, Karl-Heinz Boehm; *D:* Rainer Werner Fassbinder; *W:* Rainer Werner Fassbinder; *C:* Michael Ballhaus. **VHS** *NYF*

MOTHRA

Mosura

Daikaiju Masura

Most fans of Japanese monster movies have their favorites, though sometimes this is a tough fact to drag out of adults in public. All the monsters have their charms. Godzilla is the king—this of course is undeniable—and his little smoke-ring-blowing son, Minya, is heir apparent. Rodan has that great wing span, and can knock over buildings (the same three buildings, actually, over and over) just by doing a fly-by. Gamera has to apologize to no one—he's the world's only jet-propelled, prehistoric flying turtle. Yet there's something about Mothra, and we all know what it is. It's the little twin princesses—the Alilenas—who sing their hearts out, pining to be reunited with the big moth who really belongs with them. They're great, and they're played by Emi and Yumi Itoh, who deserve some sort of lifetime achievement award. Where is justice? *Mothra* was one of the films that started to turn the tide in these movies, shifting certain monsters from destructors to good guys so that kids could root for them. They eventually all moved to Monster Island, a kind of Sun City for Japanese monsters.

NEXT STOP . . . *Godzilla vs. Mothra, Destroy All Monsters, Godzilla on Monster Island*

1962 101m/C *JP* Yumi Ito, Frankie Sakai, Lee Kresel, Emi Ito; *D:* Inoshiro Honda; *W:* Shinichi Sekizawa; *C:* Hajime Koizumi; *M:* Yuji Koseki. **VHS** *GKK*

MOUCHETTE

A lonely 14-year-old French girl (Nadine Nortier), daughter of an alcoholic father and a terminally ill mother, exhausts her capacity to live with her spiritual and emotional pain. Based on the novel *La Nouvelle Histoire de Mouchette* by Georges Bernanos, Bresson's film is a structurally simple yet emotionally complex portrait of a tortured soul achieving redemption and release though the only means she believes to be available. In an interview, director Robert Bresson described the title character's larger significance: "Mouchette offers evidence of misery and

cruelty. She is found everywhere: wars, concentration camps, tortures, assassinations." This is a film about suffering, and though it's a magnificent, overpowering experience—perhaps even a transcendental one—it requires as much dedication on the part of the viewer as Bresson summoned in creating it.

NEXT STOP . . . *Diary of a Country Priest, Une Femme Douce, Day of Wrath*

1967 80m/B *FR* Nadine Nortier, Maria Cardinal, Paul Hebert; *D:* Robert Bresson; *C:* Ghislan Cloquet. **VHS** *FCT, TPV, HTV*

MURIEL

Muriel, Ou le Temps d'un Retour

The Time of Return

Muriel, Or the Time of Return

Alain Resnais's 1963 *Muriel* is the story of Hélène (Delphine Seyrig), a middle-aged widow living in Boulogne with her stepson, Bernard (Jean-Baptiste Thierée). Recently returned from the war in Algeria, Bernard is something of a mess. He's obsessed with memories of an incident that took place in Algeria—the torture and murder of a girl named Muriel—in which Bernard apparently participated. Concurrently, Hélène's lover of 20 years earlier (Jean-Pierre Kerien) shows up for a visit, with his new young mistress (Nita Klein) in tow. These characters—and others—interact in the film, reflecting on their unresolved, haunting memories of days past. As in *Last Year at Marienbad* and *Hiroshima Mon Amour*, it is the relationship of those memories to the present that most intrigues the director, yet the structure of *Muriel* is so fragmented and splintered that the film—while beautiful and disturbing—is nearly abstract. It's almost as if a Dadaist had picked up the various pieces of film shot for the movie, tossed them in the air, and assembled them just as they came down. Interpretations of *Muriel* tend to speculate not only on the film's meaning, but on its plot—you can't be sure of what's going on here, but in Resnais's scheme, emotional reality seems to be more important than linear continuity. That's not necessarily all bad, but it's instructive to know before seeing it that even for

M

It's the big moment for Muriel (Toni Collette) and her family in *Muriel's Wedding*.

Resnais, *Muriel* is an experimental film in the extreme, and will be a completely different experience for each viewer.

NEXT STOP . . . *Last Year at Marienbad, Mrs. Dalloway, Providence*

1963 115m/C *FR IT* Delphine Seyrig, Jean-Pierre Kerien, Nita Klein, Jean-Baptiste Thierree; **D:** Alain Resnais; **W:** Jean Cayrol; **C:** Sacha Vierny; **M:** Georges Delerue. Venice Film Festival '63: Best Actress (Seyrig). **VHS** *HTV, FCT*

MURIEL'S WEDDING

The overweight, dowdy, achingly lonely Muriel (Toni Collette) dreams of a fairy-tale wedding to a vague, fantasized Mr. Right, yet has a classic case of low self-esteem, thanks to her unsupportive family (dad Bill Hunter gives a terrifically flamboyant performance)

and creepy, bitchy, back-stabbing "girl-friends." How Muriel fulfills her obsessive wedding fantasies—and then sails elegantly beyond them—is the basis for this hilariously sweet, surprisingly poignant ugly-duckling tale from Australia's P.J. Hogan. Collette (who gained 40 pounds for the part á la Robert De Niro) is enchanting as the utterly sympathetic Muriel, who spends much of her time grooving to 70s Europop superstars ABBA. The tunes both punch up the film and make sense for Muriel's character—in essence they're effective, plot-advancing musical numbers. *Muriel's Wedding* has a not-unpleasant, slightly bitter aftertaste that gives the picture a satisfying punch. It's better than you think it's going to be, and you won't be ashamed of yourself in the morning. Australian Film Institute Awards for Best Picture and Actress.

NEXT STOP . . . *Georgy Girl, Love Serenade, Two Friends*

1994 (R) 105m/C *AU* Toni Collette, Bill Hunter, Rachel Griffiths, Jeanie Drynan, Gennie Nevinson Brice, Matt Day, Daniel Lapaine, Sophie Lee, Rosalind Hammond, Belinda Jarrett; **D:** P.J. Hogan; **W:** P.J. Hogan; **C:** Martin McGrath; **M:** Peter Best. Australian Film Institute '94: Best Actress (Collette), Best Film, Best Sound, Best Supporting Actress (Griffiths); Nominations: Australian Film Institute '94: Best Director (Hogan), Best Original Screenplay, Best Supporting Actor (Hunter), Best Supporting Actress (Drynan); British Academy Awards '95: Best Original Screenplay; Golden Globe Awards '96: Best Actress—Musical/Comedy (Collette); Writers Guild of America '95: Best Original Screenplay. **VHS, LV, Closed Caption** *MAX*

MURMUR OF THE HEART
Dearest Love
La Souffle au Coeur

Louis Malle's smashing 1971 *Murmur of the Heart,* a brilliantly comic and delicately persuasive portrait of a smart, sensitive, confused 14-year-old French boy and his smart, sensitive, confused Italian mom, remains one of the most audacious and exhilarating movies of Malle's career. Young Laurent Chevalier (Benoit Ferreux) and his brothers are the sons of a physician, living a privileged life in Dijon in the early 1950s. The boys and their mother (Lea Massari) take their status and pleasures for granted, and guess what? They don't pay with their lives! They don't pay with their souls! They don't even fall into poverty. Laurent, however, is found to have a heart murmur which leads to his mother taking him on a recuperative holiday away from family and friends. For everyone involved, it turns out to be a vacation to remember. The close relationship between the mutually adoring mother and her son is presented with a natural, spontaneous, totally convincing consistency of character. As you've probably heard, there *is* a taboo-shattering moment of mother-son incest near the end of the film; though startling, it's neither shocking nor gratuitous. The transportingly sweet, laughter-filled moments which follow the scene *do* seem revolutionary, however, and appropriately so. Malle's characters find their salvation in the unconditional, gloriously unrepentant bond of love between a woman and her sons, rather than in the far more easy (and traditional) slathering on of guilt as the solution to everything—as a way to punish the characters, and to punish us for liking them. (Whether it was an unconscious stunt or simply an accident—not that Freud would believe in such a thing—I first saw *Murmur of the Heart* with my mother. Well, I *was* 21. She loved the picture, though I recall that she did slide all the way over to the other side of the taxi afterward.)

NEXT STOP . . . *Zazie dans le Metro, My Life As a Dog, Luna*

1971 (R) 118m/C *FR* Benoit Ferreux, Daniel Gelin, Lea Massari, Corinne Kersten, Jacqueline Chauveau, Marc Wincourt, Michael Lonsdale; **D:** Louis Malle; **W:** Louis Malle; **C:** Ricardo Aronovich; **M:** Charlie Parker. Nominations: Academy Awards '72: Best Story & Screenplay. **VHS, LV** *ORI*

THE MUSIC LOVERS

Ken Russell hit the skids relatively early in his career with a film that made his *The Devils* (also made in 1971) look like a 1950s educational filmstrip. *The Music Lovers* purports to contrast Tchaikovsky's musical achievements with his tormented private life—but do *we* have to be tormented too? The gay Tchaikovsky marries out of convenience, only to discover to his horror that his blushing bride (Glenda Jackson) is a nymphomaniac. The film includes a metaphorical fellatio scene involving Tchaikovsky, his boyfriend, and a peach, and Mrs. Tchaikovsky ends up in an asylum, sitting on an open grating with men reaching up underneath it to touch her while she moans her approval. (There's a great symmetry in this shot: Jackson the actress reaches bottom while her character's bottom is being reached. Thanks, Ken.) *The Music Lovers* is the worst musical biography ever made—even worse than Russell's own *Lisztomania*. It's the film that Ed Wood would have killed to make, if only he'd had the budget, the clout and even less talent. (Melvyn Bragg—who hosts the splendid *South Bank Show* on the BBC and Bravo—was the screenwriter.)

NEXT STOP . . . *Lisztomania, Mahler, The Gene Krupa Story*

"Could your puritanical rigor in fact border on intolerance?"

—Nelly (Emmanuelle Beart) to Monsieur Arnaud (Michel Serrault) in *Nelly and Monsieur Arnaud.*

Christy Brown
(Daniel Day-Lewis)
with his teacher
(Fiona Shaw) in *My
Left Foot.*

1971 (R) 122m/C *GB* Richard Chamberlain, Glenda Jackson, Max Adrian, Christopher Gable, Kenneth Colley, Izabella Telezynska, Maureen Pryor; *D:* Ken Russell; *W:* Melvin Bragg; *C:* Douglas Slocombe; *M:* Andre Previn. **VHS, LV, Letterbox** *MGM, MLB, FCT*

MY BRILLIANT CAREER

A headstrong young woman (Judy Davis) spurns the social expectations of turn-of-the-century Australia and pursues opportunities to broaden her intellect and preserve her independence. Davis is a knockout—wonderfully intriguing and completely surprising at every turn—as the energetic and charismatic community trendsetter, and Sam Neill makes a strong impression as the rich bachelor who falls for her (it's the role that first got him worldwide recognition). Miles Franklin's autobiographical novel—

written when she was 16—was the basis for this widely admired debut feature by director Gillian Armstrong, the international success of which helped to put Australian cinema on the map. The rich, widescreen color cinematography is by Don McAlpine.

NEXT STOP . . . *Starstruck, Little Women, An Angel at My Table*

1979 (G) 101m/C *AU* Judy Davis, Sam Neill, Wendy Hughes; *D:* Gillian Armstrong. Australian Film Institute '79: Best Film; British Academy Awards '80: Best Actress (Davis); Nominations: Academy Awards '80: Best Costume Design. **VHS** *VES*

MY LEFT FOOT

This miraculously unsentimental and profoundly moving drama is based on the life and autobiography of writer, artist, and cerebral palsy victim Christy Brown. Considered an imbecile by everyone but his mother (Brenda Fricker) until he teaches himself to write, Brown survives his impoverished Irish roots to become a painter and writer using his left foot, the only appendage over which he has control. The elements were all in place for a maudlin, by-the-numbers, triumph over adversity pic, but this is one case where everyone involved more than rose to the occasion. Daniel Day-Lewis's staggering performance was immediately the stuff of legend; he took home an Oscar for his performance, as did Fricker as his adoring mother. Smaller roles are handled with equal skill, particularly Ray McAnally as Brown's hard-drinking da, and Hugh O'Conor (*The Young Poisoner's Handbook*) as the young Christy in the film's flashback sequences. Jim Sheridan directed from a script he and Shane Connaughton adapted from Brown's book. This is a stunning achievement, all the more so because of the many cliches it so deftly avoids. Bravo.

NEXT STOP . . . *In the Name of the Father, The 400 Blows, A Brief History of Time*

1989 (R) 103m/C *IR* Daniel Day-Lewis, Brenda Fricker, Ray McAnally, Cyril Cusack, Fiona Shaw, Hugh O'Conor, Adrian Dunbar, Ruth McCabe, Alison Whelan; *D:* Jim Sheridan; *W:* Shane Connaughton, Jim Sheridan; *M:* Elmer Bernstein. Academy Awards '89: Best Actor (Day-Lewis), Best Supporting Actress (Fricker); British Academy Awards '89: Best Actor (Day-Lewis), Best Supporting Actor (McAnally); Independent Spirit Awards '90: Best Foreign Film; Los Angeles Film Critics Association Awards '89: Best Actor (Day-Lewis), Best Supporting Actress (Fricker); Montreal World Film Festival '89: Best Actor (Day-Lewis); New York Film Critics Awards '89: Best Actor (Day-Lewis), Best Film; National Society of Film Critics Awards '89: Best Actor (Day-Lewis); Nominations: Academy Awards '89: Best Adapted Screenplay, Best Director (Sheridan), Best Picture. **VHS, LV, Closed Caption** *HBO, BTV, HMV*

MY LIFE AS A DOG
Mitt Liv Som Hund

12-year-old Ingemar Johansson (Anton Glanzelius in a charmingly intelligent, unsentimental performance) is separated from his brother and sent to live with relatives in the country when his brother is taken ill. Unhappy, confused, and going through the normal nightmare of puberty, little Ingemar is struggling to understand sexuality and love while trying to find security and acceptance (not to mention having to live up to the name he shares with the boxing champion). Based on an autobiographical novel by Reidar Jonsson, Swedish director Lasse Hallström's film quickly became one of the cinema's most beloved tales of the joys and trials of growing up, and was one of Sweden's biggest international hits of all time. (It has also been released in an inferior dubbed version, which should be avoided.) Academy Award Nominations, Best Director and Best Adapted Screenplay.

NEXT STOP . . . *The 400 Blows, The Slingshot, Fanny and Alexander*

1985 101m/C *SW* Anton Glanzelius, Tomas Van Bromssen, Anki Liden, Melinda Kinnaman, Kicki Rundgren, Ing-mari Carlsson; *D:* Lasse Hallstrom. Golden Globe Awards '88: Best Foreign Film; Independent Spirit Awards '88: Best Foreign Film; New York Film Critics Awards '87: Best Foreign Film; Nominations: Academy Awards '87: Best Adapted Screenplay, Best Director (Hallstrom). **VHS, LV** *PAR, HMV*

MY LIFE TO LIVE
Vivre Sa Vie
It's My Life

A woman (Anna Karina) struggling to pay her bills is evicted from her apartment and turns to prostitution. Jean-Luc Godard's probing and eloquent examination of sexual and social relations in the early 1960s is structured as 12 episodes in the woman's life, and it is directed and edited with a tender directness that is both complex and extremely lucid. The film is part documentary, part gangster melodrama, and Godard's attempts at distancing the audience from the action (with what Bertolt Brecht called "alienation effects") don't succeed, because we're more absorbed by Karina's story than he may realize. There's no doubt that Godard is utterly fixated by the face of his star (to whom he was married at the time), but that obsession seems justified when absorbing the poetic street tragedy that unfolds around the char-

M

287

acter's abused and delicate heart. A beautiful, haunting, maddening film, brilliantly photographed by Raoul Coutard. Score by Michel Legrand (*The Umbrellas of Cherbourg*). Special Jury Prize, Venice Film Festival.

NEXT STOP . . . *Pierrot le Fou, Band of Outsiders, Contempt*

1962 85m/B *FR* Anna Karina, Sady Rebbot, Andre S. Labarthe, Guylaine Schlumberger; *D:* Jean-Luc Godard; *W:* Jean-Luc Godard; *M:* Michel Legrand. Venice Film Festival '62: Special Jury Prize. **VHS** *FXL, NYF, DVT*

MY NEW PARTNER
Les Ripoux

The French need their popcorn movies too, and sometimes they recruit great actors to star in them. *My New Partner* (*Les Ripoux*) is a pleasant but undistinguished police buddy movie featuring amiable performances from Philippe Noiret as a cynical, been-around-the-block detective, and heartthrob Thierry Lhermitte as his by-the-book, young rookie partner. There's nothing really wrong with *My New Partner,* and I'm sure it made a perfectly adequate Saturday evening choice after dinner on the Champs-Elysées, but you'll be hard-pressed to figure out why it took home César awards for Best Picture and Best Director (Claude Zidi). (Then again, I'm sure the French do a lot of tsk-tsking at *our* Oscars, too.)

NEXT STOP . . . *My New Partner II, Cat and Mouse, L.627*

1984 (R) 106m/C *FR* Philippe Noiret, Thierry Lhermitte, Regine, Grace de Capitani, Claude Brosset, Julien Guiomar; *D:* Claude Zidi; *W:* Claude Zidi; *C:* Jean-Jacques Tarbes; *M:* Francis Lai. **VHS, LV** *IME*

✓ MY NIGHT AT MAUD'S
My Night with Maud
Ma Nuit Chez Maud

Jean-Louis (Jean-Louis Trintignant) is an engineer who is also a practicing Catholic; he's designed his life as if it were one of his engineering projects, but a moral crisis

ensues when he's forced to spend a snow-bound night at the home of the beautiful—and atheistic—Maud (Françoise Fabian). Not long after, Jean-Louis meets the girl of his dreams—or at least the girl of his plans—in the person of the pretty, blonde, and Catholic Françoise (Marie-Christine Barrault). One of the most celebrated of director Eric Rohmer's *Six Moral Tales* cycle, *My Night at Maud's* is a smart and engaging series of conversations, confrontations, and dilemmas of conscience. A witty dissection of human frailties, feelings, desires, and guilt, Rohmer's razor-sharp interplay of character and situation may look "talky," but is in fact one of the most intellectually dynamic films of the modern era. The crystalline black-and-white images are courtesy of the great Nestor Almendros. Academy Award Nominee, Best Foreign Language Film, Best Original Screenplay.

NEXT STOP . . . *Claire's Knee, Summer, Rendezvous in Paris*

1969 111m/B *FR* Jean-Louis Trintignant, Francoise Fabian, Marie-Christine Barrault, Antoine Vitez; *D:* Eric Rohmer; *W:* Eric Rohmer; *C:* Nestor Almendros. New York Film Critics Awards '70: Best Screenplay; National Society of Film Critics Awards '70: Best Cinematography, Best Screenplay; Nominations: Academy Awards '70: Best Foreign-Language Film.; Best Story & Screenplay. **VHS, LV**

MY SWEET LITTLE VILLAGE
Vesnicko Ma Strediskova

This wistful, charming film from Czech director Jiri Menzel (*Loves of a Blonde*) is a seemingly simple portrait of everyday events in a small rural community—a teenager develops a crush on a schoolteacher, a woman cheats on her husband, a doctor keeps getting into accidents. Yet as the film progresses, you can see a pattern in the "simplicity;" despite the trials and tribulations of daily life, there's a spirit in this little town that's going to remain civilized despite any unwelcome intrusions. It's a barely visible political metaphor, but a powerful one. It gives the film a tartness and poignancy that seems all the more rich more a decade after its original release. This is a picture that got largely lost in the American distribution shuffle, but it's well worth a look.

NEXT STOP . . . *The Fireman's Ball, Loves of a Blonde, Kolya*

1986 100m/C CZ Rudolf Hrusinsky, Janos Ban, Marian Labuda, Milena Dvorska, Ladislav Zupanic, Petr Cepek; *D:* Jiri Menzel; *W:* Zdenek Sverak; *C:* Jaromir Sofr; *M:* Jiri Sust. Nominations: Academy Awards '86: Best Foreign-Language Film. **VHS** HTV

MY TWENTIETH CENTURY
Az en XX. Szazadom

This bracingly intelligent and often overlooked gem is a charming and perceptive journey through the early 1900s. Twins Dora and Lili are separated in early childhood. They reunite as grown (very different) women traveling on the Orient Express after they both (unknowingly) have sex with the same man. Dora is coquettish and seductive; Lili is a radical, toting her own bombs (those little round ones that movie and cartoon anarchists always carry). When the two sisters come together, they lose their respective dependence on men and politics, and grasp at true independence. Ildiko Enyedi's funny and poignant look at human progress—or lack thereof—as opposed to scientific advancements is an original and bewitching Hungarian *Ragtime*, jump-started by Dorotha Segda's triple role as Dora, Lili, and their mother. The black-and-white cinematography is a gracious and witty enhancement to the fairy-tale atmosphere.

NEXT STOP . . . *The Fireman's Ball, My Sweet Little Village, Underground*

1990 104m/B HU CA Dortha Segda, Oleg Jankowsky, Peter Andorai, Gabor Mate, Paulus Manker, Laszlo Vidovszky; *D:* Ildiko Enyedi; *W:* Ildiko Enyedi. **VHS** FXL

THE MYSTERY OF RAMPO

Legendary mystery writer Hirai Taro, whose pen name was Edogawa Rampo, was consid-ered Japan's Edgar Allan Poe (pronounce Rampo's entire name slowly and phoneti-cally—get it?); he's propelled into his own stories in this lush, slightly mad, visually stunning fantasy. Set in the period just prior to World War II. Rampo (Naoto Takenaka) is despondent when his story about a woman suffocating her husband in a trunk is censored by the government, and then he is stunned when a newspaper reports an almost identical murder. When he investigates on his own, Rampo discovers that the widow is a dead ringer for his fictional character—at least the way he imagined her. Soon fact and fantasy collide in increasingly disturbing—and erotically obsessive—ways, culminating in a truly mind-blowing finale steeped in apocalyptic special effects. (The telling of Rampo's original murder story at the film's opening is done in a hauntingly animated—or *anime*—sequence.) The film's original director was hauled off the project and replaced by producer Kazuyoshi Okuyama, but the final result is a seamless, visionary whole. (The widescreen images deserve to be seen in a letterboxed version.) Akira Senju's lush, dreamy score was performed by the Czech Philharmonic, and it is available on a beautifully engineered CD.

NEXT STOP . . . *Odd Obsession, Kwaidan, Vertigo*

1994 (R) 96m/C JP Naoto Takenaka, Michiko Hada, Masahiro Motoki, Teruyuki Kagawa, Mikijiro Hira; *D:* Kazuyoshi Okuyama; *W:* Kazuyoshi Okuyama, Yuhei Enoki; *C:* Yasushi Sasakibara; *M:* Akira Senju. **VHS** HMK

NAPOLEON

Abel Gance's *Napoleon*, completed in 1927 and restored by historian Kevin Brownlow in 1980, remains one of the world's great film experiences. The picture follows the conqueror's life from childhood through his Italian Campaign, and in its execution the film is an astonishingly successful blend of traditional and experimental storytelling techniques; with its sweeping camera movements, rapid editing, tinting, grand special effects, and a final three-panel sequence that encompasses all of these techniques and combines them into more than the sum of

N

their parts, *Napoleon* seemed in many ways to suggest the future of the cinema. Alas, following its original premiere, the film was carved into many different, shortened versions for export and conventional theatrical projection (the final sequence of the film, photographed in what Gance dubbed "Polyvision," originally required three projectors in synchronization). Much of the original footage was reputed to be lost over the subsequent years, but Brownlow's dedication led to a premiere of a thrillingly restored four-hour version at the 1980 Telluride Film Festival, with the 91-year-old Gance triumphantly in attendance. (I was one of those lucky enough to be shivering up in the Colorado mountains at 3 a.m. when *Napoleon* ended, but it was hard to distinguish whether the goosebumps were from the cold or from the astonishment of seeing the restored final sequence, and then looking behind me and seeing Gance alone in a window, watching his recovered masterpiece with the rest of us.) Though Gance died the following year, *Napoleon* toured the U.S. under the sponsorship of Francis Ford Coppola, whose father, Carmine, composed and conducted a live orchestral score. Brownlow has returned a precious and irreplaceable treasure to all of us, and deserves our gratitude. (Gance reworked portions of *Napoleon* cleverly in his 1971 *Bonaparte and the Revolution*.)

NEXT STOP . . . *Intolerance, Orphans of the Storm, Chimes at Midnight*

1927 235m/B *FR* Albert Dieudonne, Antonin Artaud, Pierre Batcheff, Gina Manes, Armand Bernard, Harry Krimer, Albert Bras, Abel Gance, Georges Cahuzac; **D:** Abel Gance; **M:** Carmine Coppola. **VHS, LV** *USH*

NELLY ET MONSIEUR ARNAUD
Nelly and Mr. Arnaud

Films like Claude Sautet's thoroughly wonderful *Nelly and Monsieur Arnaud* are what many of us immediately flash on when we dream the dream of French cinema: a complex tapestry of relationships, revelations, and longing in which the romantic dilemmas and real-life despair of wounded human beings can be dealt with over coffee and croissants, rather than AK-47s and Uzis. There's something immensely satisfying—and subtly voyeuristic—in settling back and immersing one's self in the story of Nelly (Emmanuelle Béart), an exquisite young woman who finds little satisfaction in either her marriage or her job and decides to do something about it. Nelly is introduced to a much older man, Monsieur Arnaud (Michel Serrault), a judge who offers her a job typing his dictated memoirs. As she begins to find power in how attracted he is to her, the two engage in a delicate erotic duel in which each is intrigued what the other is hiding; Arnaud wants the truth of Nelly's body, while Nelly wants to be the one who can make the judge reveal his real secrets instead of the heroic cliches he dictates. Without revealing the outcome, I can tell you that a single, memorable image of Nelly's back as she sleeps becomes one of the most evocative and erotic images you'll ever see in a film. Perhaps it's simply an adult movie fantasy, but Sautet's film rekindles our hopes that somewhere, adults really do speak to each other, interact with each other, and behave with gallantry, sensitivity, thoughtfulness, and restraint. And if they don't—well, I suppose that's what movies are for.

NEXT STOP . . . *Vincent, François, Paul and the Others, Un Coeur en Hiver, La Belle Noiseuse*

1995 105m/C *IT GE FR* Emmanuelle Beart, Michel Serrault, Jean-Hugues Anglade, Francoise Brion, Claire Nadeau, Michael Lonsdale, Charles Berling, Michele Laroque; **D:** Claude Sautet; **W:** Jacques Fieschi, Claude Sautet; **C:** Jean-Francois Robin; **M:** Philippe Sarde. Cesar Awards '96: Best Actor (Serrault), Best Director (Sautet); Nominations: British Academy Awards '96: Best Foreign Film; Cesar Awards '96: Best Actress (Beart), Best Film, Best Film Editing, Best Sound, Best Supporting Actor (Anglade, Lonsdale), Best Supporting Actress (Nadeau), Best Writing, Best Score. **VHS, Letterbox** *NYF*

THE NEST
El Nido

The extraordinary Ana Torrent, who was the wide-eyed young star of *Cria* and *Spirit of the Beehive*, is a 13-year-old schoolgirl who's the target of the unhealthy, obsessive interest of an aging, wealthy don (Hector Alterio). *The Nest* looks at first to be a teasing exploitation film disguised as art, but then something unexpected happens; it *does* become art. *The Nest* gets better as it goes along, evolving into a dark and witty examination of the dynamics of desire, repression and guilt. While it never reaches Buñuelian heights, it's a smart, compassionate and highly engaging surprise, featuring yet another remarkable performance from Torrent.

NEXT STOP . . . *Spirit of the Beehive, Lolita (1962), Viridiana*

1980 109m/C *SP* Ana Torrent, Hector Alterio, Patricia Adriani, Luis Politti, Augustin Gonzalez; *D:* Jaime de Arminan; *W:* Jaime de Arminan; *C:* Teo Escamilla. Nominations: Academy Awards '80: Best Foreign-Language Film. **VHS**

THE NEW LAND
Nybyggarna

In the second half of director Jan Troell's epic about an impoverished Swedish family's mid-19th-century emigration to America (the first half of the story was told in *The Emigrants*), the family settles in their new home in Minnesota, where a different but equally difficult struggle lies ahead. As you settle into the opening scenes of this film, even if it's a year after seeing *The Emigrants* (as it was for me) you feel an immediate and surprisingly powerful wave of emotion. You *know* these people, and it's a joy to be with them again. Part of the joy of experiencing *The New Land* also comes from the sheer pleasure of a big but controlled narrative, in which a huge and deeply significant story is being told, but not in platitudes. This is an epic that reveals itself gradually, scene by scene, always remaining on an intimate, focused, human level, so that when the movie's inevitable last revelation comes—and it's one that will hit home with any American who's descended from ancestors who spoke a language other than our own—it's only then that we fully grasp the magnitude of the story that we've seen. Though they're one gigantic story, *The Emigrants* and *The New Land* were designed to be seen separately, with, perhaps, a bit of

time between them. Like most great art they will stay with you permanently, providing a kind of equilibrium and perspective that will not fade, regardless of where you or your family came from, and regardless of where you're headed. A masterpiece.

NEXT STOP . . . *The Emigrants, The Godfather, The Godfather, Part II*

1973 (PG) 161m/C *SW* Max von Sydow, Liv Ullmann, Allan Edwall, Eddie Axberg, Hans Alfredson, Halvar Bjork, Peter Lindgren, Monica Zetterlund, Pierre Lindstedt, Per Oscarsson; *D:* Jan Troell; *W:* Jan Troell, Bengt Forslund; *C:* Jan Troell; *M:* Bengt Ernryd, George Oddner. National Board of Review Awards '73: Best Actress (Ullmann); National Society of Film Critics Awards '73: Best Actress (Ullmann). **VHS** *WAR, MOV*

NIGHT AND FOG
Nuit et Brouillard

In the case of Alain Resnais's *Night and Fog*—the existence of which constitutes proof for all time that the motion picture is a great and unique art form—the comparatively brief running time (30 minutes) must never be used to relegate the film to some arbitrary category of lesser importance than what we normally consider the "feature-length film" or "major motion picture." They don't come any more major than *Night and Fog*. Created ten years after the liberation of Auschwitz, *Night and Fog* juxtaposes black-and-white archival footage of the camp—including scenes still rarely shown because of the staggering horror of the images—with fluid, full-color glimpses of Auschwitz ten years later: green and partially lush fields that each year grow to cover up a bit more of the history that lies there. Described by its director as a "warning siren" to the world, *Night and Fog* includes poetic and heartbreaking narration written by Jean Cayrol, who described it as "not only a film of memory, but also a film of great uneasiness." Resnais would revisit this relationship between past and present in many of his greatest feature films, including *Hiroshima Mon Amour, Last Year at Marienbad,* and *Providence,* but the power and beauty of *Night and Fog*—which François Truffaut called the greatest film of all time—would remain unparalleled.

N

THE HOUND SALUTES

JEAN-JACQUES ANNAUD

A Groundbreaking Director

Who else but Jean-Jacques Annaud would attempt the first commercial 3-D Imax feature film, 1995's *Wings of Courage*? Annaud always likes to break new ground and invent new perspectives, even new languages, in his films.

Annaud's global blockbuster hit, *The Bear,* is a graceful nature story told from the perspective of the animals. His erotic film, *The Lover,* is told from the perspective of a young woman. In *Quest for Fire,* Annuad had his collaborators invent a new language for his Stone Age protagonists.

Born in Draveil, France, on October 1, 1943, Annaud trained at the Sorbonne in Paris. He launched his directorial career with the Oscar-winning *Black and White in Color* in 1976, a story of colonialists in French West Africa in 1915. *Quest for Fire* was a serious attempt to recreate prehistory; it got mixed reviews. In 1986, Annaud scored with Unberto Eco's bizarre story about monks and the Inquisition, *In the Name of the Rose,* starring Sean Connery. *The Bear,* released in 1988, grossed over $100 million before it was released in the United States. Like all Annaud's films, his 1991 *The Lover* was controversial, getting an NC-17 rating in America but a G in France. His most recent film, *Seven Years in Tibet* (1997), also controversial, has caused such a fuss that he has been banned from entering China.

Annaud married Monique Rossignol in 1970; they had a daughter, Mathilde, and divorced in 1980. He then married Laurence Duval; they have a daughter, Louise.

NEXT STOP . . .   *Birthplace, Shoah, Hiroshima Mon Amour, The Sorrow and the Pity*

1955 30m/B *FR* **D:** Alain Resnais; **W:** Jean Cayrol; **C:** Ghislan Cloquet, Sacha Vierny; **M:** Hanns Eisler. **VHS** *HMV, IHF, HMV*

THE NIGHT OF COUNTING THE YEARS

al-Mummia

This extraordinary modern classic of Egyptian cinema is based on a true event: the discovery of ancient treasures near Thebes in 1881. Perhaps the most suspenseful and disturbing of all cinematic attempts to equate the plundering of a nation's treasures with the violation of its soul, *The Night of Counting the Years* centers on the inevitable conflicts that arise when a mountain tribe is caught in a mysterious and unholy struggle between archeologists, antique dealers, and the ever-present voices of the distant past. Egyptian director Shadi Abdelsalam's fantastic, spellbinding imagery seduces us with what appear at first to be mirages—a ship sailing through the desert, human figures that emerge from stone—but soon we realize that the only illusions are those we have created to rationalize the gutting of a nation's center. This is strong, unforgettable stuff, more haunting than all the *Mummy* films wrapped together.

NEXT STOP . . . *Navigators of the Desert, Cairo Station, Landscape in the Mist*

1969 102m/C Zouzou El Hakim, Ahmad Hegazi, Nadia Loutfy, Ahmed Marei; **D:** Chadi Abdel Salam; **W:** Chadi Abdel Salam, Mario Nascimbene; **C:** Abdel Aziz Fahmy. NYR

THE NIGHT OF THE SHOOTING STARS
The Night of San Lorenzo
La Notte di San Lorenzo

In a small Tuscan village during the closing days of World War II, the Nazi occupiers and their fascist collaborators react to the knowledge that the Allied forces are only days away. This remarkable film by Italy's Paolo and Vittorio Taviani is quite unlike any other historical film ever made; it's told through the eyes of a woman who was just six at the time, and now, as an adult, is telling the story of what happened in the little village of San Lorenzo to her own young daughter. What we see is filtered not only through years of memory, but is also told to us as a bedtime story. The Tavianis have found a cinematic equivalent for the fairy tale embellishment that the mother soothes her child with, and the stylized images and rich soundtrack are as intoxicating and fresh to adults as the story she's telling must be to the child. It's a staggeringly imaginative work, and the kind of picture that makes you remember all over again that the possibilities of the cinema are all still before us. The ingeniously stylized cinematography is by Franco Di Giacomo, and the lyrical score is by Ennio Morricone. Grand Jury Prize, Cannes Film Festival; Best Picture and Best Director, National Society of Film Critics.

NEXT STOP . . . *Padre Pardone, Kaos, Grand Illusion*

1982 (R) 106m/C *IT* Omero Antonutti, Margarita Lozano, Claudio Bigagli, Massimo Bonetti, Norma Martel; **D:** Paolo Taviani, Vittorio Taviani; **W:** Tonino Guerra, Giuliani G. De Negri, Paolo Taviani, Vittorio Taviani; **C:** Franco Di Giacomo; **M:** Nicola Piovani. Cannes Film Festival '82: Grand Jury Prize; National Society of Film Critics Awards '83: Best Director (Taviani), Best Director (Taviani), Best Film. **VHS** MGM, AUD

THE NIGHT PORTER
Il Portiere de Notte

This pathetic trash was considered hot, chic stuff when it was unveiled in art theatres in 1974 (there were lines down the block in New York). It's a soft-core continuation/exploitation of the associations Visconti made between degenerate sexuality and fascism in his 1969 *The Damned*. Charlotte Rampling is the woman who was sexually abused as a girl when she was imprisoned in a concentration camp; Dirk Bogarde is the Nazi who abused her. Years after the war they meet in Vienna, and they can't wait to get it on. They take turns wearing his old uniform, and at first the only real problem in their relationship is deciding who gets to use the riding crop on any given night. Things get a bit stickier later on, but you'll probably be gone by then. That *The Night Porter* is offensive and insulting goes without saying, but it's so jaw-droppingly inept that it almost fails to achieve even that.

NEXT STOP . . . *The Damned, Seven Beauties, Ilsa: She Wolf of the SS*

1974 (R) 115m/C *IT* Dirk Bogarde, Charlotte Rampling, Phillippe LeRoy, Gabriele Ferzetti, Isa Miranda; **D:** Liliana Cavani; **W:** Liliana Cavani; **C:** Alfio Contino; **M:** Daniele Paris. **VHS, LV** HMV, GLV, NLC

NIGHTS OF CABIRIA
Le Notti de Cabiria
Cabiria

In one of the most heartbreakingly poignant performances in screen history, Giulietta Masina plays Cabiria, the Roman street prostitute whose grasp on the value of continuing to live is tested to the breaking point. Fellini described the character of Cabiria as "fragile, tender, and unfortunate; after all that has happened to her, and after the collapse of her naive dream of love, she still carries in her heart a touch of grace." *Nights of Cabiria* has long been recognized as a masterpiece, but happily, in 1997, film archivists carefully and lovingly returned it to its original visual

delicacy, and in addition restored seven minutes of critically important footage, never before seen in America. The result is a fuller and more complete narrative, making *Cabiria*'s great final sequence more powerfully moving than ever. (*Nights of Cabiria* was later used as the basis for Bob Fosse's stage and screen musical, *Sweet Charity*.) Academy Award, Best Foreign Language Film; Best Actress Award, Cannes Film Festival.

NEXT STOP . . . *I Vitelloni, La Strada, Mamma Roma*

1957 111m/B *IT* Giulietta Masina, Amedeo Nazzari; **D:** Federico Fellini; **W:** Federico Fellini, Tullio Pinelli, Ennio Flaiano; **M:** Nino Rota. Academy Awards '57: Best Foreign Film; Cannes Film Festival '57: Best Actress (Masina). **VHS** *NOS, VYY, TPV*

1900
Novecento

Bernardo Bertolucci's impassioned, sprawling, operatic epic about two Italian families, one aristocratic, the other peasant. With enormous ambition, Bertolucci's attempts to portray nothing less than the changes brought about by the history of the 20th century, beginning with the trauma of World War I and culminating with the arrival of socialism and the corresponding death throes of fascism. Robert De Niro and Gérard Depardieu are the lifelong friends—born on the same day in 1901—who turn against each other as adults as a result of the class structure that controls their lives. The political and symbolic baggage that the film's cast must haul around eventually drains the picture of human drama, and we stare at the screen not really out of interest in the characters but amazed by the sheer bulk and physical spectacle that parades before us. Not the disaster some would claim, but exasperating nonetheless, mainly because one feels so many elements of greatness are here for the plucking—and yet, as Martin Balsam said in *Psycho*, "If it doesn't jell, it's not aspic. And this ain't jelling." With Dominique Sanda, Burt Lancaster, Sterling Hayden, Alida Valli, and, as the fiendish, sadistic cat-murdering fascist Attila, Donald Sutherland. Despite the stellar cast, the real stars of *1900*—the artists who try to supply the feeling that the script does not—are cinematographer Vittorio Storaro and composer Ennio Morricone. (Originally shown at Cannes in a five-hour version, it was shortened by an hour for American release and dubbed into English. The missing hour was put back for a 1991 reissue.)

NEXT STOP . . . *The Leopard, Before the Rain, Underground*

1976 (R) 255m/C *FR IT GE* Robert De Niro, Gerard Depardieu, Burt Lancaster, Donald Sutherland, Dominique Sanda, Sterling Hayden, Laura Betti, Francesca Bertini, Werner Bruhns, Stefania Sandrelli, Anna Henkel, Alida Valli; **D:** Bernardo Bertolucci; **W:** Giuseppe Bertolucci, Bernardo Bertolucci; **C:** Vittorio Storaro. **VHS, LV** *PAR*

NOSFERATU
Nosferatu, Eine Symphonie des Grauens
Nosferatu, A Symphony of Terror
Nosferatu, A Symphony of Horror
Nosferatu, the Vampire
Terror of Dracula
Die Zwolfte Stunde

F.W. Murnau's silent 1922 adaptation of Bram Stoker's *Dracula* remains one of the creepiest and most eerily atmospheric horror films ever made. The film follows Stoker's plot relatively closely, though the characters' names had to be changed to avoid copyright infringement problems (there's nothing new under the sun, if the Count will pardon the expression). Max Schreck plays Count Orlok, who sleeps in his unadorned wooden coffin by day, and seeks fresh blood by night. Schreck seems to be the cinema's first expressionist human being; his makeup and movements suggest a huge, scrawny rodent—giant, pointed ears, protruding teeth, sunken eyes, and massive, talon-like hands. He's envisioned as a nightmare personification of corruption, and the brilliant conception and execution of his character carries *Nosferatu* through the few patches that might otherwise seem uninspired. *Nosferatu* also contains the most startling—and practical—image in any vampire film ever: Count Orlok carrying his own coffin over his shoulder as he prepares to move in to his new home in Bremen. The word "atmosphere" gets tossed around a lot, sometimes when discussing movies that are simply well-designed; *Nosferatu* has *real* atmosphere—its powerful, primal aura of dread is unique in movie history. (Werner Herzog directed a remake/homage in 1979, which starred Klaus Kinski as Nosferatu.)

NEXT STOP. . . *Vampyr, Dracula (1931), Nosferatu the Vampyre* (1979)

1922 63m/B *GE* Max Schreck, Alexander Granach, Gustav von Wagenheim, Greta Schroeder, John Gottowt, Ruth Landshoff, G.H. Schnell; **D:** F.W. Murnau; **W:** Henrik Galeen; **C:** Fritz Arno Wagner. **VHS, LV** *KIV, MRV, NOS*

NOSFERATU THE VAMPYRE

Werner Herzog's 1979 reworking of F.W. Murnau's 1922 silent classic is often dissed or dismissed for largely being a shot-by-shot remake of the original. There's no denying that many images are based on Murnau's, but Herzog has also infused the Dracula legend with unnervingly nightmarish qualities that seem entirely Herzog's. Klaus Kinski's performance is a brilliant updating of Max Schreck's original rodent-like vampire, and Herzog goes all the way with that theme—rats carry the plague to a doomed population here, and as the dying dance madly in the streets, the rats scurry about at the command of their evil, disease-carrying master to infect still more. The picture is stylized in the expressionist manner of Murnau's original, but reconfigured for consumption by modern audiences (i.e. it's in color and has sound). Herzog and Kinski reportedly had a difficult relationship while shooting this movie (a year after its release I overheard Kinski complaining loudly to a stranger about "those f*****g teeth Herzog made me wear," but you'd never know it from the elegant finished product. Kinski's makeup—bald head, pointed ears, and yes, those great rodent teeth—would be useless without his deliberate, theatrical movements. He's great, and the picture's a creepy joy. With Bruno Ganz, Isabelle Adjani, and Roland Topor (*Fantastic Planet*) as the bug-hungry Renfield. (Beware at all costs the English-language version. This kind of stylization seems natural in German, but impossibly silly in English.)

NEXT STOP. . . *Nosferatu, A Symphony of Horror, Dracula (1931), The Fearless Vampire Killers*

1979 107m/C *FR GE* Klaus Kinski, Isabelle Adjani, Bruno Ganz, Roland Topor, Walter Ladengast; **D:** Werner Herzog; **W:** Werner Herzog; **C:** Jorge Schmidt-Reitwein. **VHS** *VTR*

OBLOMOV
A Few Days in the Life of I.I. Oblomov
Neskolko Dnel iz Zhizni I.I. Oblomov

This is a wonderful film version of the classic 19th-century Ivan Goncharov novel about a symbolically inert Russian aristocrat whose childhood friend helps him find a reason to get up out of the house and back into life. This is a stately, deliberate, funny, and eloquent picture that in some ways represents a triumph of cinematic resourcefulness on the part of director Nikita Mikhalkov (*Burnt by the Sun*); he manages to show a man doing almost literally nothing for the better part of two hours, and keeps it not only interesting but lively and suspenseful. Goncharov's Oblomov (played engagingly here by Oleg Tabakov) is a character whose name has entered the language as shorthand for any person who's existing in this kind of disinterested, sedentary state.

NEXT STOP. . . *A Slave of Love, Burnt by the Sun, The Designated Mourner*

1981 145m/C *RU* Oleg Tabakov, Elena Solovei; **D:** Nikita Mikhalkov. **VHS** *TPV, KIV, AUD*

ODD OBSESSION
The Key

Kon Ichikawa's dark comedy is the story of an elderly Japanese gentleman (Ganjiro Nakamura) whose sexual impotence leads to a bizarre series of events. His idea for producing his desired erection through an elaborate scheme does indeed work, but it also generates considerably more excitement

THE HOUND SALUTES:

AGNIESZKA HOLLAND
Challenging Polish Filmmaker

Uncompromising Polish-born filmmaker Agnieszka Holland sees psychological violence and moral ambiguity everywhere. Her sharp dramatic films prick consciences and deflate political and religious orthodoxy. Even her version of the children's story *The Secret Garden* was dark, claustrophobic, and sinister, albeit with an uncustomary happy ending.

Born on November 28, 1948 in Warsaw, Holland had journalist parents who divorced when she was 11. Her mother, a Catholic, was a Polish resistance fighter during World War II. Her father, a Jew, fled Hitler, fought in the Red Army and became a prominent Polish Communist Party figure killed in an anti-Semitic purge. Holland's background leads her to work which mixes religious and political traditions and firmly avoids political correctness of any kind.

Holland studied filmmaking in Prague, Czechoslovakia. As a young filmmaker, Holland struggled against Communist disapproval of her work. Her scripts constantly were rejected. She was exiled to France when martial law was imposed in 1981 and doggedly continued her career. Her 1991 *Europa, Europa* became the second-highest-grossing foreign film in U.S. history but was attacked in France as anti-Semitic. However, the film was nominated for a Best Adapted Screenplay Oscar. It's the remarkable story of a young German Jew who survives the Holocaust by pretending to be a Nazi.

A woman without a country, Holland shuttles between America and France and rarely returns to Warsaw, where her estranged husband, Slovak director Laco Adamik, lives. Their daughter Katarzuna often travels with Holland. Her other films include *Olivier, Oliver* (1991), *Total Eclipse* (1995), *Washington Square* (1997), and *Angry Harvest* (1985), which was nominated for the Best Foreign Language Film Oscar and which she both wrote and directed.

---

than he bargained for. *Odd Obsession* suffers somewhat from a necessary obfuscation of some of the plot's specifics—it's unlikely that the film could have been fully realized in 1959 and legally projected anywhere, so compromises had to be made (including the unsatisfying ending.) Overall, however, it's a vicious, cynical, and highly entertaining examination of fetishism, desperation, and denial. With Machiko Kyo and Tatsuya Nakadai. It's a widescreen film—look for a letterboxed copy.

NEXT STOP . . . *In the Realm of the Senses, The Face of Another, Rear Window*

1960 96m/C *JP* Machiko Kyo, Ganjiro Nakamura; **D:** Kon Ichikawa. Golden Globe Awards '60: Best Foreign Film. **VHS** *HMV, COL*

OKOGE
Fag Hag

Syoko (Misa Shimizu) is a single young working woman living in an apartment that's small even by Tokyo standards. Syoko meets a gay man and his older, married, closeted lover and when they become friendly she lets them use the apartment as their love nest. Complications ensue, but not before we get a peek into the motives and personal rewards of Syoko's preference for hanging out with gay men. It's a phenomenon that's not unique to Japan, but the film nevertheless was the source of controversy when released domestically. Such women are so ubiquitous in Japan that a phrase has entered the language to refer to them, and it was used as the title of this interesting, low-key but thin comedy, which fits more comfortably into the category of "issue" picture.

NEXT STOP . . . *The Celluloid Closet, Crush, Menage*

1993 120m/C *JP* Misa Shimizu, Takehiro Murata, Takeo Nakahara, Masayuki Shionoya, Noriko Songoku, Kyozo Nagatsuka, Toshie Nogishi; **D:** Takehiro Nakajima; **W:** Takehiro Nakajima; **C:** Yoshimasa Hakata; **M:** Hiroshi Ariyoshi. **VHS** *FCT, CCN*

OLIVIER, OLIVIER

Agnieszka Holland's wrenching film is based on a 1984 French newspaper story that evoked themes explored in *The Return of Martin Guerre*. An adored 9-year-old boy disappears from his home in a small French town and his family comes completely unstrung. The mother (Brigitte Rouan) obsesses on Olivier's disappearance and lapses into trances; the father (François Cluzet) escapes to North Africa; and the boy's sister (Marina Golovine) copes by developing telekinetic powers (which the film portrays as quite real). Six years later a detective brings an amnesiac teenager (Gregoire Colin), found hustling on the streets of Paris, to the boy's family. At that point, everyone involved must balance their natural curiosity and need for facts with their near-desperate desire to believe what they *want* to believe. This is an extraordinary, very disturbing, highly intelligent piece of filmmaking, but viewers should also know that it's an experience not easily shaken.

NEXT STOP . . . *Europa, Europa, The Return of Martin Guerre, Sommersby*

1992 (R) 110m/C *FR* Francois Cluzet, Brigitte Rouan, Gregoire Colin, Marina Golovine, Jean-Francois Stevenin, Emmanuel Morozof, Faye Gatteau, Frederic Quiring; **D:** Agnieszka Holland; **W:** Agnieszka Holland. Los Angeles Film Critics Association Awards '93: Best Score. **VHS, LV** *COL*

ONCE UPON A TIME IN THE WEST

Incredible, incomparable, great. Sergio Leone's amazing *Once Upon a Time in the West* is, on one level, an ingeniously scripted western in which a number of characters slowly reveal their purposes to each other and the audience, culminating in a grandly designed finale. But what director Sergio Leone and his co-writers Segio Donati, Dario Argento, and Bernardo Bertolucci have achieved is something considerably more; they've bred the traditional structure of the western with the sweeping, operatic expansiveness of Giuseppe Verdi, producing a visionary, thrilling dream of what the western form means to us on a subliminal level. Though the film's setting is specific, it could be taking place on another planet; this film achieves what *Star Wars* may have been after—to root the mythic shape of the western in our minds as a universal and timeless idea. It's a masterpiece. With Charles Bronson, Jason Robards, Claudia Cardinale, Woody Strode, Lionel Stander, Keenan Wynn, Gabriele Ferzetti, Jack Elam, and Henry Fonda as Frank, the coldest damned villain you've ever seen. In its original American release the film was brutally butchered, removing 25 crucial minutes of plot. With the help and support of Martin Scorsese, the complete version was presented in the U.S. for the first time in 1980, and is now available on video. (You *must* see cinematographer Tonino Delli Colli's images in their widescreen, letterboxed version.) The incomparable score, which fully complements Leone's operatic vision, is by Ennio Morricone.

NEXT STOP . . . *The Good, the Bad, and the Ugly, Once Upon a Time in America, Johnny Guitar, Seven Samurai*

1968 (PG) 165m/C *IT* Henry Fonda, Jason Robards Jr., Charles Bronson, Claudia Cardinale, Keenan Wynn, Lionel Stander, Woody Strode, Jack Elam; **D:** Sergio Leone; **W:** Sergio Leone, Bernardo Bertolucci, Dario Argento; **C:** Tonino Delli Colli; **M:** Ennio Morricone. **VHS, LV** *PAR*

ONCE WERE WARRIORS

This is the violent and deeply poignant story of a struggling Maori family, the Hekes, who have left their rural New Zealand roots to live in the city. Feisty mother Beth (Rena Owen) is struggling with five children and her abusive, volatile husband Jake (Temuera Morrison) who's always out of work, always drunk, always brawling, and always blaming everybody but himself for his sorry state. *Once Were Warriors* is a horrifying picture, but never gratuitously so. Jake could be a poster child for uncontrolled, alcoholic, addictive behavior as he brings his battling "mates" home to destroy what little domestic life he and his family have left. Ultimately, his wife understands what she has to do. Owen's remarkable portrayal won her the Best Actress Prize at the Montreal World Film Festival, but all the performances are superb. This was director

Lee Tamahori's first film; his recent Alec Baldwin/Anthony Hopkins survivalist bear hunt picture, *The Edge,* marked a step up in pay and a step down in importance.

NEXT STOP . . . *Broken English, Ladybird, Ladybird, Distant Voices, Still Lives*

1994 (R) 102m/C *NZ* Rena Owen, Temuera Morrison, Mamaengaroa Kerr-Bell, Julian (Sonny) Arahanga, Taungaroa Emile, Rachael Morris, Joseph Kairau, Pete Smith; **D:** Lee Tamahori; **W:** Riwia Brown; **C:** Stuart Dryburgh; **M:** Murray Grindlay, Murray McNabb. Australian Film Institute '95: Best Foreign Film; Montreal World Film Festival '94: Best Actress (Owen), Best Film. **VHS, LV, Closed Caption** *NLC*

ONE SINGS, THE OTHER DOESN'T

L'Une Chante, L'Autre Pas

Two very different women who met and became friends in the 1960s share personal and political experiences as they journey together into the 1970s. Valérie Mairesse and Thérèse Leotard star as Pomme, a radical feminist and singer, and Suzanne, a don't-rock-the-boat conservative and wife, in Agnes Varda's schematic, dramatically inert and instantly dated snapshot of the state of the women's movement 20 years ago. *One Sings, the Other Doesn't,* which was the opening night presentation of the 1977 New York Film Festival, is a legendary film for having pleased almost no one, and for different reasons. Much of the feminist press gagged on the movie's olive branches to the bourgeoisie, while the bourgeois press thought that Varda's personal hearth-and-home sentiments were being hidden behind half-hearted, pseudo-radical blather. Then there were those of us who felt the movie had no characters at all—just some actors with signs around their neck identifying what they stood for. On a more serious note, there's just too much street-singing in *One Sings, the Other Doesn't,* which is a punishable offense where I come from. I think there's a mime in the film as well, though my memory is failing me. I thought I should warn you anyway, just in case.

NEXT STOP . . . *Zabriskie Point, Baby Boom, Marianne and Juliane*

1977 105m/C *FR BE* Valerie Mairesse, Therese Liotard, Robert Dadies, Ali Affi, Jean-Pierre Pellegrin; *D:* Agnes Varda; *W:* Agnes Varda; *C:* Charlie Van Damme; *M:* Francois Wertheimer. **VHS** *COL*

ONIBABA
The Demon
The Devil Woman

A brutal parable about a mother and her daughter-in-law in war-ravaged medieval Japan who subsist by murdering stray soldiers and selling their armor. One soldier beds the daughter, setting the mother-in-law on a vengeful tirade. She dons a grisly looking samurai mask in order to scare the girl away from the soldier, but discovers to her horror that she is unable to remove it. Director Kaneto Shindo's *Onibaba* has a considerable cult following, and with good reason. It's a

truly disturbing blend of feudal brutality and supernatural horror, photographed and directed with spellbinding intensity. The picture is really an extended ghost story but has the authentically unpleasant texture of a nightmare—Shindo is able to make the swaying of a patch of reeds seem like a harbinger of the end of the world. (Shindo's less-well-known 1968 *Kuroneko* is a horror film that's every bit as creepy as *Onibaba,* but even more erotic and perverse.) *Onibaba's* widescreen black-and-white images are best seen in a letterboxed version.

NEXT STOP . . . *Kuroneko, Kwaidan, Carnival of Souls*

1964 103m/B *JP* Nobuko Otowa, Yitsuko Yoshimura, Kei Sato; *D:* Kaneto Shindo. **VHS** *HMV, CVC, TPV*

OPEN CITY
Roma, Citta Aperta
Rome, Open City

A leader in the Italian underground resists Nazi control of the city. Roberto Rossellini's landmark work was filmed in actual locations within months of the Allied liberation of Italy. The film changed virtually everything about the possibilities of moviemaking, since it once and for all discarded all the old certainties about what constituted "documentary" and what was clearly narrative fiction. *Open City* looked like it was being photographed as events were really happening, and the impact on the movie world was nothing short of revolutionary. The movie paved the way for much of the "New Wave" filmmaking revolution that would follow a decade later, as higher speed film would soon allow shooting on city streets in all sorts of lighting and weather conditions. Rossellini also successfully perpetuated the illusion of real life by blending non-professional cast members with seasoned actors like Anna Magnani, further reducing the visibility of the cinema's already fine border between art and life. A humane, powerful, pioneering work. The screenplay by Rossellini, Sergio Amidei, and Federico Fellini was nominated for an Academy Award.

NEXT STOP . . . *Paisan, The Bicycle Thief, I Vitelloni*

Orlando (Tilda Swinton) with lover Shelmerdine (Billy Zane) in *Orlando*.

1945 103m/B *IT* Anna Magnani, Aldo Fabrizi, Marcel Pagliero, Maria Michi, Vito Annicchiarico, Nando Bruno, Harry Feist; **D:** Roberto Rossellini; **W:** Federico Fellini, Sergio Amidei. New York Film Critics Awards '46: Best Foreign Film; Nominations: Academy Awards '46: Best Screenplay. **VHS** *VYY, NOS, DVT*

ORCHESTRA REHEARSAL
Prova d'Orchestra

Federico Fellini's clever and entertaining *Orchestra Rehearsal* is the result of a commission Fellini received from Italian television for the production of a short film about—an orchestra rehearsal. The resulting political satire is not exactly what was expected, and the 72-minute film set off a firestorm of controversy when it was first screened (the Prime Minister was among the most vocal critics). The Aldo Moro kidnapping, rampant terrorism and high-and-low-level corruption were what was on Fellini's mind when he created this portrait of well-orchestrated governmental madness thinly disguised as elegantly conducted chaos. It's a one-joke satire, but the brief length, colorful cinematography and Nino Rota score conspire to make that single joke a potent and memorable one.

NEXT STOP . . . *Variety Lights, Basileus Quartet, Un Coeur en Hiver*

1978 72m/C *IT* Balduin Baas, Clara Colosimo, Elisabeth Labi, Ronaldo Bonacchi, Ferdinando Villella, Giovanni Javarone, David Mauhsell, Francesco Aluigi; **D:** Federico Fellini; **W:** Federico Fellini, Brunello Rondi; **C:** Giuseppe Rotunno; **M:** Nino Rota. **VHS** *FXL, FCT*

ORDET
The Word

A man who believes he is Christ (Preben Lerdorff-Rye) is ridiculed until be begins performing miracles—including a resurrection—that result in the healing of a broken family. Danish director Carl Dreyer's statement on the continuing struggle between religious dogma and personal faith is a profoundly demanding work of art from the deeply religious Dreyer. *Ordet* (*The Word*) was based on the play by Kaj Munk, a Danish pastor who was murdered by the Nazis in 1944. A rigorous intellectual exercise, the film is itself an act of faith in the power of cinema to transform human thought and beliefs. As derided as it is praised, *Ordet* is the spellbinding, utterly sincere, and overwhelmingly beautiful work of a great artist.

NEXT STOP . . . *The Passion of Joan of Arc, Diary of a Country Priest, Simon of the Desert*

1955 126m/B *DK* Henrik Malberg; **D:** Carl Theodor Dreyer. Golden Globe Awards '56: Best Foreign Film; Venice Film Festival '55: Best Film. **VHS** *NOS, WFV, HEG*

ORLANDO

Sally Potter's stylistically inventive, witty adaptation of Virginia Woolf's 1928 novel—covering 400 years in the life of an English nobleman whose defiance of death is small potatoes next to his evolution from a man into a woman—is as elegant visually as it is conceptually. Orlando (played charmingly throughout by the coolly androgynous Tilda Swinton) is first glimpsed as a young man in the court of Queen Elizabeth I, whose deadpan portrayal by Quentin Crisp sets both the movie's playful tone as well as its sexual agenda. In bed, the grateful queen beseeches Orlando to "not fade, wither or grow old," and he complies, becoming a she after a fade out/fade in that slips us quickly past the next 40 years. By the end of the movie's swift 92 minutes, Orlando (now a single mother) has arrived in the 20th century with all of its accompanying modern problems, yet her resourcefulness, intelligence and adaptability reassure us that despite appearances, there's nothing new—at least not alarmingly so—under the sun. Highly theatrical and proudly stylized, *Orlando* became a surprise hit at film festivals worldwide, and continues to enjoy a sizable cult following. *Orlando* looks and feels like a major statement on sexuality and the role of gender in society, yet—happily— it's more of a joyous lark than a serious position paper, which may well be the reason for its heartening commercial success. With Billy Zane and John Wood.

NEXT STOP . . . *The Tango Lesson, Female Perversions, Career Girls*

1992 (PG-13) 93m/C *GB* Tilda Swinton, Charlotte Valandrey, Billy Zane, Lothaire Bluteau, John Wood, Quentin Crisp, Heathcote Williams, Dudley Sutton, Thom Hoffman, Peter Eyre, Jimmy Somerville; **D:** Sally Potter; **W:** Sally Potter; **C:** Alexei Rodionov; **M:** Bob Last. Nominations: Academy Awards '93: Best Art Direction/Set Decoration, Best Costume Design; Independent Spirit Awards '94: Best Foreign Film. **VHS, LV, Letterbox, Closed Caption** *COL*

ORPHEUS
Orphee

The legend of Orpheus, the poet whose fascination with death takes him on a search that leads from this world to the next, is updated to a modern Parisian setting by perhaps the only other poet up to the job: Jean Cocteau. Cocteau's Orpheus (Jean Marais) is a brooding, masculine, dissatisfied dreamer whose earthly wife, Eurydice (Marie Déa), is disposed of by the jealous Princess of Death (Maria Casarés) when the Princess's obsession with Orpheus begins to equal his fascination with her. We've seen lots of figures of death in the movies, from Bengt Ekerot in Bergman's *The Seventh Seal* to Royal Dano in *The Right Stuff,* but only Casarés—cloaked in black, irresistibly sensuous, as comfortable on an earthbound motorcycle as she is floating through the next world—has made us feel death's darkly glamorous appeal. A miracle of elegance and ingenuity on just about every level, Cocteau's *Orpheus* allows his poet/hero to receive messages from beyond on his car radio and to plunge through mirrors as the gateway to Death's underworld kingdom; these are notions far more thrilling than mere "special effects," for they allow a poet's vision to transform the world we live in into a magical land-

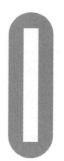

scape fraught with possibilities, wonders, and mystery. With this audacious and moving fairy tale for grown-ups, Cocteau has visualized our eternal struggle with sensuality and death by conjuring the power of a child's view of the world, making us see the simplest and most basic things around us as if for the first time.

NEXT STOP . . . *The Blood of a Poet, Beauty and the Beast* (1946), *The Testament of Orpheus, The Seventh Seal*

1949 95m/B Jean Marais, Francois Perier, Maria Casares, Marie Dea, Edouard Dermithe, Juliette Greco; *D:* Jean Cocteau; *W:* Jean Cocteau; *C:* Nicolas Hayer; *M:* Georges Auric. **VHS, 8mm** *SNC, NOS, VYY*

OSSESSIONE

Luchino Visconti's legendary first feature was an adaptation of James M. Cain's *The Postman Always Rings Twice,* transferred to fascist Italy. The classic story of a drifter who conspires with a innkeeper's wife to murder her husband, *Ossessione* is widely considered to be the first example of what would later be classified by film historians as cinematic "neo-realism." The picture was shot in natural settings, forsaking the usual studio setups, and startled Italian moviegoers with realistic glimpses of rural life. This visual forthrightness was so new that the fascist censors of 1942 were at first confused as to whether the picture was or wasn't subversive. Mussolini thought it was swell, however, and gave it the green light for release. Since Visconti's use of the Cain novel had been unauthorized, the film wasn't legally shown in America until 1975. Though today the movie feels a bit sluggish, it's indisputably an impressive achievement, infused throughout with Visconti's characteristically operatic style. (In 1988, the Italian government issued a series of stamps in commemoration of neo-realism; *Ossessione* was on the 500 lira.)

NEXT STOP . . . *The Postman Always Rings Twice* (1946), *Double Indemnity, Rocco and His Brothers*

1942 135m/B *IT* Massimo Girotti, Clara Calamai, Juan deLanda, Elio Marcuzzo; *D:* Luchino Visconti. **VHS** *FCT, TPV*

OUTBACK
Wake in Fright

A horror movie about beer: that's something you don't see everyday, and neither is a film that manages to be this unnerving while containing this much sunlight. *Outback* is the story of an Australian schoolteacher (Gary Bond) on summer vacation, who gets off his train at a stop just to stretch his legs, promptly gambles away his money, and finds himself stranded among beer-swilling, kangaroo-hunting dimwits. One of the swillers is a vaguely depraved, alcoholic ex-doctor (Donald Pleasance) who meets the teacher in a bar and insists he order the house special: a steak with a fried egg on it for only one dollar. After his dinner arrives, the teacher stares down at the fatty gray mass queasily. "You gonna eat that?" queries Pleasance, who then spears the fried egg with his fork and stuffs it in his mouth. "Best dollar *you'll* ever spend," Pleasance mumbles, washing it all down noisily with warm beer. You keep hoping that someone from American Express will show up with Bond's travelers' checks, but instead, blokes keep buying him more beer. At first the teacher tries to drink and hunt with "the boys" because he's afraid they'll pummel him if he doesn't; soon, though, his civilized veneer begins to crack, and his newly conjured macho brutality starts getting good to him. *Outback* marks a considerable change of pace from the better known Australian films that American art house audiences are accustomed to, perhaps because the director, Ted Kotcheff (*The Apprenticeship of Duddy Kravitz*), is really Canadian. The slightly longer, original cut, released under the title *Wake in Fright,* was rediscovered a few years back by the Telluride Film Festival.

NEXT STOP . . . *The Chant of Jimmie Blacksmith, A Cry in the Dark, Night of the Living Dead* (1968)

1971 109m/C *AU* Gary Bond, Donald Pleasence, John Armstrong, Charles Hughes, John Meillon, Chips Rafferty, Al Thomas, Jack Thompson, John Dalleen, Slim De Gray, Maggie Dence, Norman Erskine, Buster Fiddess, Tex Foote, Mark "Jacko" Jackson, Sylvia Kay; *D:* Ted Kotcheff; *W:* Evan Jones; *C:* Brian West; *M:* John Scott. *NYR*

THE OVERCOAT
The Cloak
Shinel

A meek little clerk named Akaky Akakyevich (Roland Bykov), who is the tiniest of cogs in the huge wheel of a Dickensian 19th-century St. Petersburg, believes there will be a change in the heartless world in which he lives once he finally attains the magnificent new overcoat of which he has long dreamed. Bykov's performance as the pathetic little man tossed about in a sea of bureaucratic heartlessness is quite amazing; for years after seeing this nearly perfect, 73-minute adaptation of Gogol's story, Bykov's rubbery, brilliantly expressive face will be clearly visible whenever the story is referred to or remembered. This haunting, quietly disturbing little movie was directed by the gifted and versatile Alexei Batalov, who himself starred that same year in another extraordinary Soviet adaptation of a literary classic, director Josef Heifitz' film of Chekhov's *The Lady with the Dog*. *The Overcoat* was filmed many times before, including a silent version in 1926 by Grigori Kozintsev and a 1951 short starring Marcel Marceau, but Batalov's 1959 film remains the most moving and vivid of them all.

NEXT STOP... *The Lady with the Dog, The Cranes Are Flying, Oliver Twist* (1948)

1959 93m/B *RU* Rolan Bykov, Yuri Tolubeyev; **D:** Alexei Batalov; **W:** L. Solovyov; **C:** Heinrich Marandzhjan; **M:** N. Sidelnikov. **VHS** *HTV*

PAISAN

Roberto Rossellini followed the international triumph of his *Open City* with this six-part look at Italy during World War II. Each of the film's sequences tells a different aspect of the Allies' arrival. One sequence is the story of a man from New Jersey who tries to develop a relationship with a young woman without knowing a word of Italian. Another focuses on a young street robber who is confronted by one of his victims. The final episode involves a battle between German and British forces. Much of the film has an open, improvisational feel, and the dramatic changes in tone that take place with each new episode tend to reinforce the feeling of spontaneity. As in *Open City*, nonprofessionals blend with seasoned actors seamlessly. It was clear after the success of both *Open City* and *Paisan* that Rossellini had paved new roads with his "caught-on-the-run" neo-realist filmmaking techniques; his influence on the cinema world would be profound and permanent. The screenplay, which Federico Fellini collaborated on, was nominated for an Oscar.

NEXT STOP... *Open City, Generale Della Rovere, Shoeshine*

1946 115m/B *IT* Maria Michi, Carmela Sazio, Gar Moore, William Tubbs, Harriet White, Robert Van Loon, Dale Edmonds, Carla Pisacane, Dots Johnson; **D:** Roberto Rossellini; **W:** Federico Fellini, Roberto Rossellini. National Board of Review Awards '48: Best Director (Fellini); New York Film Critics Awards '48: Best Foreign Film; Nominations: Academy Awards '49: Best Story & Screenplay. **VHS** *HTV, HHT, CAB*

PANDORA'S BOX
Die Buechse der Pandora

The era of German expressionism was drawing to a close by the time of G.W. Pabst's silent classic *Pandora's Box*, which established Louise Brooks as one of most electrifying, erotically charged screen personalities in movie history. Brooks plays Lulu, a tempestuous, irresistible knockout who seduces or murders (or both) just about everyone she comes in contact with, eventually descending into the depths of prostitution and a fateful encounter with Jack the Ripper. Brooks was a struggling Hollywood actress under contract to Paramount when Pabst—who had been searching for the right actress to play Lulu—tried to arrange for her to be loaned out to shoot *Pandora's Box* in Germany. Legend has it that Paramount never even informed her of Pabst's offer until she threatened to quit the studio anyway over money. Ultimately, the deal was made, and Brooks became an instantaneous international sensation (still not in America, however). What wowed audiences wasn't just Brooks's beauty and natural screen presence, but her powerfully erotic, remarkably natural performance. The movie was censored and

P

suppressed in many countries, and in France it was reedited almost beyond recognition and fitted out with a completely new storyline. (According to Sadoul's *Dictionary of Films,* the Jack the Ripper climax was eliminated in French prints, and an ending was substituted in which Lulu joined the Salvation Army.) There are still lots of different unauthorized versions of *Pandora's Box* floating around, but the superb near-definitive 1983 restoration is available from Home Vision Cinema. The film that Pabst and Brooks followed up with, *Diary of a Lost Girl,* is available as well. (A fan organization, the Louise Brooks Society, maintains an elegant and well-stocked web site at www.pandoras box.com.)

NEXT STOP . . . *Canary Murder Case, Diary of a Lost Girl, Prix de Beaut… (Miss Europe)*

1928 110m/B *GE* Louise Brooks, Fritz Kortner, Francis Lederer, Carl Goetz, Alice Roberts, Gustav Diesl; *D:* G.W. Pabst; *W:* G.W. Pabst. **VHS** *GPV, MRV, VDM*

THE PASSION OF ANNA
A Passion

Ingmar Bergman's film is a complex psychological drama about four people alone on an isolated island. Max von Sydow is an ex-convict living a hermit's existence when he becomes involved with a widow (Liv Ullmann) and her friends (Erland Josephson and wife Bibi Andersson), all of whom have secrets in their past that they would prefer to conceal. Exquisitely photographed in color by Sven Nykvist, *The Passion of Anna* (its somewhat exploitative and misleading American title; the original was *A Passion*) is another of Bergman's examinations of human isolation and loneliness, photographed on Bergman's secluded and symbolically rich island home, Fårö. (The following year, Bergman would make a documentary about the island.) Though the specific characters change from film to film in Bergman's work from the mid 1950s onward, they will often share names with earlier characters; in this film, an opening narration informs us that "This time, his name

(literally, von Sydow's, but more to the point, the director's alter ego) was Winkelman." The couple played by Andersson and Josephson have the name Vergerus, which was the name of the skeptical medical officer who performed an autopsy on a body he thought was von Sydow's in Bergman's *The Magician.* This is one of Bergman's most emotionally violent yet accessible films of the period—it followed his extraordinary examination of human behavior in wartime, *Shame,* also filmed on Fårö.

NEXT STOP . . . *Through a Glass Darkly, Winter Light, The Silence*

1970 (R) 101m/C *SW* Max von Sydow, Liv Ullmann, Bibi Andersson, Erland Josephson, Erik Hell; *D:* Ingmar Bergman; *W:* Ingmar Bergman; *C:* Sven Nykvist. National Society of Film Critics Awards '70: Best Director (Bergman). **VHS** *MGM, BTV*

THE PASSION OF JOAN OF ARC

Renée Maria Falconetti appeared in one film in her lifetime, Carl Theodor Dreyer's 1928 *The Passion of Joan of Arc.* To call her performance legendary would be a gross understatement; to call the film a masterpiece is not enough. The film is based on historical records of Joan's trial, which took place when she was 19. The film is extremely straightforward, and it is unrelenting in its cumulative emotional power. Much has been written about Dreyer's dramatic use of close-ups, which are generally presented from a very strong, subjective viewpoint, making the viewer a participant in the horrifying spectacle that's unfolding (it's a technique that Hitchcock would master as well, using it to prevent audiences from being able to experience disturbing material from a "safe" distance.) The power of Falconetti's performance is astounding and exhausting. Rudolph Maté's photography is at every turn an active participant with the performers, and has to be considered one of the greatest achievements of not just the silent cinema, but of cinema. Dreyer's refusal to compromise is evident in every aspect of the film. The actors wore no makeup, which gave

Dreyer much greater freedom when photographing in close-up the expressiveness of faces. The choice of Falconetti was also controversial, since she was only a modestly successful stage actress who had had no experience in film. The set itself was by all reports boiling over with passion, as performers stayed in character after the cameras stopped rolling, profoundly stirred by the scenes they had just played. The effect of the finished film may have been best summed up by Jean Cocteau, who wrote that "it seems like an historical document from an era in which the cinema didn't exist." Censored by the Catholic Church in France, banned in England for years after its completion, *Joan* has survived it all, and is one of the most frequently revived films of the silent era. Live orchestras frequently provide musical accompaniment to the film, but it isn't necessary; the music of *The Passion of Joan of Arc* is generated within us, by the succession of magnificent images on the screen.

NEXT STOP . . . *The Battleship Potemkin, Day of Wrath, The Trial of Joan of Arc* (1962)

1928 114m/B *FR* Renee Maria Falconetti, Eugena Sylvaw, Maurice Schultz, Antonin Artaud; *D:* Carl Theodor Dreyer. **VHS** *VYY, MRV, NOS*

PATHER PANCHALI
The Song of the Road
The Saga of the Road
The Lament of the Path

Apu, a young Bengali boy, is growing up in rural India with his parents, his sister Durga, and his aged, beloved Auntie, who is somewhat disabled and more than a little cranky. While Apu's father goes off to the city on one of his many attempts to find work, his mother becomes overwhelmed by the difficulty of keeping her family together and healthy in such impoverished conditions. The first feature film by India's Satyajit Ray became part one of an epic, but intimate, trilogy chronicling the coming-of-age and young adulthood of Apu. Together, the three films— which include *Aparajito* and *The World of Apu,* and which have come to be known collectively as "The Apu Trilogy"—constitute one of the richest, most eloquent, most deeply moving of all cinematic portraits of the human condition. *Pather Panchali* is one of the most heartbreaking of the trilogy, for it includes the death from fever of Apu's sister, as well as Auntie's death after she's driven out into the forest by Apu's overwrought mother. But this is hardly a maudlin tearjerker. Ray achieves the miraculous from the opening moments of his masterwork. Every step along the way we share in the emotional and intellectual development of this curious, sweet, knowledge-hungry little boy, and we see him wrestle with countless obstacles that his poverty places before him and his family. In its intimacy and specificity, "The Apu Trilogy" becomes utterly universal. The quiet delicacy of Ray's assured vision is finally staggering in its larger implications, and the series of small incidents we've lived through become emotionally overwhelming. *Pather Panchali* was dismissed as primitive when it was first screened at the Cannes Film Festival, but the great French critic André Bazin championed it behind the scenes and the Cannes jury gave it a special award. (In 1991, after a lifetime of brilliant achievements, Ray received a special Academy Award; he was forced to accept it from the hospital bed in which he would die just weeks later.) "The Apu Trilogy" was unavailable in the U.S. for more than a decade when Merchant-Ivory productions assisted in the restoration of new prints of many of Ray's major films, including those in "The Apu Trilogy." It's available at last in a beautifully remastered video edition. Score by Ravi Shankar.

NEXT STOP . . . *Aparajito, The World of Apu, Forbidden Games*

1954 112m/B *IN* Kanu Banerjee, Karuna Banerjee, Uma Das Gupta, Subir Banerji, Runki Banerji, Chunibala Devi; *D:* Satyajit Ray; *W:* Satyajit Ray; *M:* Ravi Shankar. **VHS** *NOS, FCT, MRV*

PAULINE AT THE BEACH
Pauline á la Plage

15-year old Pauline (Amanda Longlet) accompanies her beautiful, considerably

more experienced older cousin Marion (Arielle Dombasle) to the French coast, vaguely considering the possibility of romance. As is typical in the comedies of Eric Rohmer, a great deal of conversation takes place on the subjects of fidelity, love, sex, and trust. And as is inevitable in Rohmer, a series of gently amusing but thoroughly unpredictable events produce some startling coincidences and some surprising romantic couplings (and uncouplings). *Pauline at the Beach* is part of Rohmer's "Comedies and Proverbs" cycle; it might be crudely summarized as a sexual cross between "The Tortoise and the Hare" and that old saw about "those who can, do; those who cannot, teach." But if *Pauline at the Beach* feels just a tad less substantial than some of Rohmer's other films, there are compensating factors. Nestor Almendros's high-calorie color cinematography makes the film seem like ... well, a day at the beach. And the young cast, as always in

Rohmer's films, is remarkable. But it's Arielle Dombasle who provides much of *Pauline*'s comic sparkle and visual appeal—when she's on screen, she's the film. (She was extensively featured in the advertising for *Pauline at the Beach,* and—wonder of wonders—the film became Rohmer's biggest American hit.) A pleasure.

NEXT STOP . . . *Claire's Knee, Summer, Rendezvous in Paris*

1983 (R) 95m/C *FR* Amanda Langlet, Arielle Dombasle, Pascal Greggory, Rosette; ***D:*** Eric Rohmer; ***W:*** Eric Rohmer; ***C:*** Nestor Almendros. **VHS, LV** *XVC*

PELLE THE CONQUEROR

This is an overpowering tale of a Swedish boy (Pelle Hvenegaard) and his widower father (Max von Sydow) who serve landowners in late 19th-century Denmark. Director Bille August's compassionate saga of the human spirit contains many wonderfully conceived, aria-like sequences of hardship, tragedy, and intrigue, all of them anchored on the stunning performances of young Hvenegaard and, in particular, von Sydow. The demands of this film seemed to bring out something new in von Sydow, though he's long been one of our great screen actors. Here, his exceptional power and sympathy as Papa Lasse suggest the unintended summation of a career, and if this should be the film he's ultimately remembered by (which would be a trick, considering his long partnership with Ingmar Bergman), he can be extremely proud. It's a magnificent, wonderfully conceived performance. Unfortunately, *Pelle the Conqueror* was trimmed for U.S. release by more than 20 minutes following its capture of the Grand Prize at the Cannes Film Festival. The New York Film Festival ran the full version as well, but it was cut immediately afterwards for theatrical release. Some films can weather such cuts well (some even improve by them, though you didn't read that here) but *Pelle's* rhythm and cumulative narrative force were unnecessarily wounded by the inflicted cuts; it's worth searching for a complete, 160-minute version on video. Based on Martin Anderson Nexo's celebrated four-volume novel. Academy Award Winner, Best Foreign Language Film; Nomination to von Sydow for Best Actor.

NEXT STOP . . . *The Emigrants, The New Land, Jerusalem*

1988 160m/C *SW DK* Max von Sydow, Pelle Hvenegaard, Erik Paaske, Bjorn Granath, Axel Strobye, Astrid Villaume, Troels Asmussen, John Wittig, Anne Lise Hirsch Bjerrum, Kristina Tornqvist, Morten Jorgensen; **D:** Bille August; **W:** Bille August. Academy Awards '88: Best Foreign Film; Cannes Film Festival '88: Best Film; Golden Globe Awards '89: Best Foreign Film; Nominations: Academy Awards '88: Best Actor (von Sydow). **VHS, LV** *HBO*

PÉPÉ LE MOKO

Julien Duvivier's incomparable *Pépé le Moko* is the story of a gang leader (Jean Gabin), living in the Casbah of Algiers, who survives by successfully playing an intricate game of cat-and-mouse with the police. Pépé's charmed life changes dramatically when he falls under the spell of a stunning Parisian woman (Mireille Balin), whose sophistication and elegance make Pépé long—with tragic consequences—for the glorious but risky world of his beloved Paris. The brilliantly atmospheric gangster film is often cited as the picture that gave birth to the expression "film noir." True or not, the movie was enormously influential in France and later in the U.S. (where it was remade two years later as *Algiers,* starring Charles Boyer). Its stirring portrait of a Frenchman's homesickness for Paris got the picture banned in France during the Nazi Occupation, but it became wildly popular immediately after the war. Simply on the level of a gangster film, *Pépé le Moko* may be the greatest romantic genre movie of its kind prior to *The Godfather,* which unquestionably displays its influence. Though the film is based on a French story by Henri La Barthe (which, like Puzo's *The Godfather,* achieved its full dramatic potential only on screen), it was, ironically, Duvivier's goal to make a gangster picture in the style of an American movie. Though he succeeded, *Pépé le Moko* may nevertheless be the most *spiritually* French movie ever made.

NEXT STOP . . . *Le Jour Se Lève, Port of Shadows, Bob le Flambeur*

1937 87m/B *FR* Jean Gabin, Mireille Balin, Gabriel Gabrio, Lucas Gridoux; **D:** Julien Duvivier; **W:** Julien Duvivier, Henri Jeanson; **C:** Jules Kruger; **M:** Vincent Scotto. **VHS, 8mm** *VYY, NOS, HHT*

PERSONA

A famous actress (Liv Ullmann) decides that she will stop speaking, and is treated by a lively, talkative, forthcoming nurse (Bibi Andersson) at a secluded cottage. As they learn more about each other and their relationship turns increasingly tense, the women's personalities begin to merge and they become psychologically—and perhaps physically—indistinguishable. Much of Ingmar Bergman's *Persona* has the form of an experimental film. The opening sequence shows a movie projector's light flickering to life, and begins the story proper only after we've seen a young boy looking through the screen at us, while a slightly hazy image of ourselves as the audience is visibly reflected in front of him. Like the rest of the film, it's suggestive of the sensation of stepping outside one's self and observing the world through a proscenium—or screen—while we remain detached and disconnected; the elements of a mental breakdown. Bergman touched a great but maddeningly elusive pinnacle of his art with *Persona,* a brilliant, 88-minute Rorschach test that moves. It's about the importance of language—whether that language be vocal or cinematic—and about the inherent limitations of ever being truly intimate with either a mate or an audience. Beyond that, as in a true Rorschach, it's about whatever you see in its suggestive, galvanizing images, and whatever you hear in these conversations about the need for silence to ward off both war and the risk of sexual abandon. It's great, and it's too much. Bergman knew it, and brought persona to a close with the image of film slipping out of its sprockets and spilling out of the projector, followed by silence and darkness. For him, as for his voluntarily mute protagonist, there is a moment at which feeling is so strong that communication—like a circuit breaker—shuts down. Like any truly inspired artwork, *Persona* will spark new interpretations and vigorous arguments for years to come. Named one of the ten greatest films of all time in a *Sight & Sound* international critics' poll.

NEXT STOP . . .   *The Silence, The Passion of Anna, L'Avventura*

1966 100m/C *SW* Bibi Andersson, Liv Ullmann, Gunnar Bjornstrand, Margareta Krook; *D:* Ingmar Bergman; *W:* Ingmar Bergman; *C:* Sven Nykvist. National Society of Film Critics Awards '67: Best Actress (Andersson), Best Director (Bergman), Best Film. **VHS, 8mm** *MGM, VYY, VDM*

PHANTOM INDIA
L'Inde Fantome

In 1967, after a disappointing critical reception for his still-underrated *The Thief of Paris,* Louis Malle took a cinematographer and a sound recorder and flew to India. Malle wanted to recharge his creative batteries and to get away from the rat-race of the commercial film business by making a documentary on Calcutta. The resulting 90-minute film, *Calcutta,* is remarkable, but Malle achieved still more on his journey. Continuing to film as he toured the rest of the country, he accumulated hundreds of hours of footage, which he sorted and edited over the following year into a seven-part, 6 1/2 hour documentary diary titled *Phantom India.* The experience of *Phantom India* is unique; not because of the movie's length (there are longer) or because of its subject (India has been the focus of countless documentaries), but because of the probing, brilliant, generous-spirited man who accompanies us. And the word "accompanies" is the key, because Malle doesn't condescend to us as a guide to any predigested sights or sounds. *Phantom India* is thrilling because we're on this journey with him—discovering, marveling, hearing him ask the questions that have just popped into our heads at the moment he voices them. The seven parts of the movie examine different aspects of the country, but they all affect each other; the multitude of religions, the concept of the sacred, the arts, poverty, literacy, hunger, and the caste system are all examined, but the closer Malle looks, the more he and we realize that definitive conclusions are impossible. *Phantom India* is perhaps better described as a cycle of films rather than a series, since in the end we're led back to the questions that brought us there in the first place; we may well be left with the feeling that we're less certain about *everything* than we were when we came in. The experience of *Phantom India* is awesome, moving, and humbling, as much for what we see as for the artistry by which we see it. Narrated in English by Malle.

NEXT STOP . . .   *Pather Panchali, Aparajito, The World of Apu*

1969 378m/C *D:* Louis Malle; *C:* Etienne Becker. *NYR*

THE PHANTOM OF LIBERTY

Le Fantome de la Liberte
The Specter of Freedom

Master surrealist Luis Buñuel's immensely enjoyable, episodic funhouse glides from character to character and bizarre event to bizarre event with the sure logic of a dream. A man rearranging the objects on his mantel disgustedly proclaims, "I'm fed up with symmetry." A child comes home with a set of pornographic postcards that depict only historical French landmarks. Her parents are outraged. A group of well-dressed, sophisticated friends sitting around a table appear to be gathered for dinner, but are in fact sitting on toilets. (They quietly ask the hostess for directions to the individual cubicles—down the hall and to the left, she tells them—where they can eat in locked privacy.) A missing girl stands before her parents even as they futilely attempt to determine her whereabouts. Buñuel himself is among the firing squad victims in the film's opening recreation of Goya's *May 3, 1808*. This time, however, the victims shout "Down with liberty!" just before their deaths. That's the crux of Buñuel's thesis, and why his films—despite their surface outrageousness—never seem absurd. Given the choice, Buñuel convincingly and hilariously informs us, we will always choose slavery over freedom. We can reject that discomforting truth if we prefer, but the shot of an ostrich that closes the film seems placed to gently remind us of what denial looks like. This was Buñuel's second-to-last film, made between *The Discreet Charm of the Bourgeoisie* and his 1977 *That Obscure Object of Desire*.

NEXT STOP . . . *L'Age d'Or, The Exterminating Angel, The Milky Way*

1974 104m/C *FR* Adrianna Asti, Jean-Claude Brialy, Michel Piccoli, Adolfo Celi, Monica Vitti, Milena Vukotic, Michel Lonsdale, Claude Pieplu, Julien Bertheau, Paul Frankeur, Paul Leperson, Bernard Verley; **D:** Luis Bunuel; **W:** Luis Bunuel, Jean-Claude Carriere; **C:** Edmond Richard. **VHS, LV** *XVC*

THE PIANO

Ada (Holly Hunter), a mute Scottish widow with a young daughter (Anna Paquin), agrees to an arranged marriage with Stewart (Sam Neill), a colonial landowner in 19th-century New Zealand. Absent speech, Ada expresses her feelings by playing her cherished piano, left behind on the beach by her new husband. Another settler, George (Harvey Keitel), buys the piano, arranges for lessons with Ada, and soon the duo begin a grand passion leading to Stewart's coldly calculated revenge. Jane Campion's Cannes Grand Prize Winner (shared with *Farewell My Concubine*) is a strikingly conceived fable about sexuality, sublimation, and emotional liberation, packed with symbolism and dream imagery that works well set amid the dense vegetation of New Zealand's jungles. In both a literal and figurative sense, it's the story of a woman who finds her voice, and is thus open to an infinite number of highly individual interpretations by its audience. Hunter is extraordinary—she's a knockout, to be more precise—and she took home nearly every known film acting award to prove it. Paquin, Neill, and Keitel bring exactly the right tension and friction to their roles, and Stuart Dryburgh and Michael Nyman respectively provided the all-important cinematography and lush musical score that provide *The Piano* with its other-worldly, fairy-tale feel. *The Piano* is a classic of sorts, and watching it has become akin to a religious experience to some of its fans. On the other hand, those unwilling or unable to go along with Campion's romantic and operatic leap-of-faith storytelling may simply sit through it with a case of the giggles. However one responds, there's no denying that this is a brave and formidable piece of moviemaking. Academy Awards for Best Actress, Best Supporting Actress (Paquin), and Best Original Screenplay. Nominated for Best Picture, Cinematography, Costumes, and Editing.

NEXT STOP . . . *Sweetie, An Angel at My Table, My Brilliant Career*

1993 (R) 120m/C *AU* Holly Hunter, Harvey Keitel, Sam Neill, Anna Paquin, Kerry Walker, Genevieve Lemon; **D:** Jane Campion; **W:** Jane Campion; **C:** Stuart Dryburgh;

P

THE HOUND SALUTES:

JACKIE CHAN

Action Star Extraordinaire

Jackie Chan left Hong Kong for this country 15 years ago, a young kung fu star aiming to succeed in the American market. Four movie flops later, he returned home. But in 1995's *Rumble in the Bronx* he seems to have finally triumphed in the one part of the world that had thwarted him. His recent U.S. releases include *First Strike* (1996), *Mr. Nice Guy* (1997), and *Rush Hour* (1998).

Chan does more than stunts. He is great at physical comedy, and at 41 has come to terms with himself in a way that makes his screen persona more appealing. He relies on charm and cleverness, not merely physical strength. He does all of his own stunts and includes outtakes during his films' closing credits of failed stunts and other mishaps.

Chan got his training at the Chinese Opera Research School. Beginning at age seven, he spent a decade studying acting, singing, dance, mime, acrobatics, and martial arts. His career developed slowly, for he had to spend most of the 1970s coping with the enormous appeal of Bruce Lee. To make himself stand out, Chan turned to comedy, inspired by Charlie Chaplin, Buster Keaton, and the graceful movement of Fred Astaire and Gene Kelly.

In Asia and Europe, Chan's unique blend of action and comedy made him a huge star, but he could not seem to find the right vehicle in the U.S.—even in the highly successful *Cannonball Run* films. Chan admits his lackluster performances were humbling. Now he just wants people to come see his work. "It's like art. If you just put it in a trunk, it hurts me." Having won the MTV Life Achievement Award in 1995, it looks as though Chan will find the recognition and the audience he craves.

M: Michael Nyman. Academy Awards '93: Best Actress (Hunter), Best Original Screenplay, Best Supporting Actress (Paquin); Australian Film Institute '93: Best Actor (Keitel), Best Actress (Hunter), Best Cinematography, Best Costume Design, Best Director (Campion), Best Film, Best Film Editing, Best Screenplay, Best Sound, Best Score; British Academy Awards '93: Best Actress (Hunter); Cannes Film Festival '93: Best Actress (Hunter), Best Film; Golden Globe Awards '94: Best Actress—Drama (Hunter); Independent Spirit Awards '94: Best Foreign Film; Los Angeles Film Critics Association Awards '93: Best Actress (Hunter), Best Cinematography, Best Director (Campion), Best Screenplay, Best Supporting Actress (Paquin); National Board of Review Awards '93: Best Actress (Hunter); New York Film Critics Awards '93: Best Actress (Hunter), Best Director (Campion), Best Screenplay; National Society of Film Critics Awards '93: Best Actress (Hunter), Best Screenplay; Writers Guild of America '93: Best Original Screenplay; Nominations: Academy Awards '93: Best Cinematography, Best Costume Design, Best Director (Campion), Best Film Editing, Best Picture; British Academy Awards '94: Best Director (Campion), Best Film, Best Original Screenplay, Best Score; Directors Guild of America Awards '93: Best Director (Campion); Golden Globe Awards '94: Best Director (Campion), Best Film—Drama, Best Screenplay, Best Supporting Actress (Paquin), Best Score. **VHS, LV, Closed Caption, DVD** *ART*

PICKPOCKET

Though Robert Bresson's great *Pickpocket* is a scripted film, meticulously photographed, edited, and performed, it leaves you with the feeling that you have seen something more authentic, naked, and *true* than any work of so-called *cinéma vérité*. The movie's protagonist (played by a non-professional actor, as are most of the parts in Bresson's films) is obsessed with the exhilaration he experiences while stealing, and he practices his craft with an intensity and concentration that borders on the holy. The details of his acts of theft are depicted by Bresson with this same kind of near-religious respect; watching him and other thieves at work in a crowded train station is such a pure, focused, and exacting piece of cinema that it becomes, as writer/director Paul Schrader (*Taxi Driver, Patty Hearst*) has written, a "transcendental" experience. The thief attempts at one point—following an arrest—to give those who care for him a higher priority by abandoning his trade, but its pull proves irresistible. Even so, the possibility of redemption lurks everywhere in *Pickpocket,* and when that moment finally arrives it is simpler and vastly more affecting than we could have anticipated. Incidentally, the same Paul Schrader who wrote of *Pickpocket*'s brilliance so convincingly wasn't above adapting virtually the same climactic moment of redemption to end—considerably less effectively than Bresson—his otherwise witty and entertaining *American Gigolo*.

NEXT STOP . . . *A Condemned Man Has Escaped, L'Argent, The Thief of Paris, American Gigolo*

1959 75m/B *FR* Martin LaSalle, Marika Green, Pierre Leymarie, Pierre Etaix, Jean Pelegri, Dolly Scal; *D:* Robert Bresson; *W:* Robert Bresson; *C:* L.H. Burel. **VHS** *NYF, FCT, TPV*

PICNIC AT HANGING ROCK

A school outing in 1900 to a mountainous outback region of Australia ends tragically when a schoolteacher and three young girls vanish without a trace. The eerie, early film by director Peter Weir (*Witness, The Truman Show*) is haunting, intriguing, and memorably unnerving—an achievement that is all the more formidable because so much of the film takes place in daylight-saturated, wide open spaces. Anne Lambert (Louise) is extremely photogenic—and suitably subdued—as one of the girls to disappear, but the entire cast is suitably stylized and appears vaguely possessed by unseen forces. *Picnic at Hanging Rock* was originally released in a form that Weir disapproved of, and in fact one entire sequence the director considered "unconvincing" was included anyway, causing the picture to, as Weir put it, "come to a dead stop." Consequently, Weir reedited *Picnic at Hanging Rock* in 1998, creating new widescreen prints and remixing the soundtrack, the result being a nearly anomalous quirk in this era of reworked "director's cuts": a film seven minutes *shorter* than the original. (It's slated for video release in early 1999). Russell Boyd's widescreen cinematography deserves to be seen in the letterboxed format. From the novel by Joan Lindsay.

NEXT STOP . . . *The Last Wave, The Year of Living Dangerously, Outback*

1975 (PG) 110m/C *AU* Margaret Nelson, Rachel Roberts, Dominic Guard, Helen Morse, Jacki Weaver, Vivean Gray, Anne Lambert; *D:* Peter Weir; *C:* Russell Boyd; *M:* Bruce Smeaton. **VHS** *FCT*

PIERROT LE FOU

A woman (Anna Karina) fleeing gangsters joins a man (Jean-Paul Belmondo) fleeing his wife and together they race across the South of France in their shiny, 1962 Ford Galaxie. This exhilarating and unclassifiable work from New Wave pioneer Jean-Luc Godard is a brilliantly colored, romantic, melodramatic, funny, and shocking tale of a political and cinematic world in transition. References to classic Hollywood storytelling abound (at a cocktail party early in the film, hard-boiled American director Samuel Fuller utters the now-legendary words: "The cinema is a battleground. Love, hate, violence, action, death. In one word, emotion."). Yet under *Pierrot le Fou*'s glossy and glamorous surface beats the heart of a gleefully revolutionary filmmaker, one whose storytelling methods are anything but conventional. "A film should have a beginning, middle, and end," Godard has said, "but not necessarily in that order." *Pierrot le Fou*'s storytelling indeed comes to a dynamite-laden big finish when the movie's

THE PILLOW BOOK

A young Japanese girl, whose calligrapher father celebrates her birthdays by lovingly painting a ritualized message on her face, grows into a woman (Vivian Wu) who's driven inexorably into an obsessive, all-encompassing quest for erotic perfection. *The Pillow Book* is one of director Peter Greenaway's most accessible and visually intoxicating works, exploring themes of the parent-child bond, eroticism, fetishism, feminism, and intellectual freedom, all within the context of one woman's search for the perfect male body on which to practice her family's treasured art of calligraphy. (And therein lies *The Pillow Book*'s first major power shift—she began her quest for erotic enlightenment by looking for a man to write on *her*.) Greenaway seems to have found a near-perfect subject with which to exercise his visual technique. The electronic, computer-enhanced, video/film fusions that he's been experimenting with since his 1991 *Prospero's Books* seemed like a style in search of some substance, but now, happily, that particular yin and yang have settled cozily into Greenaway's unique and delicately satisfying *The Pillow Book*. (Cinematographer Sacha Vierny's images are dense, busy, and complex. To make sense of them on video try to use the largest, highest-definition TV or monitor you can find, and look at a laserdisc version of the film if at all possible.)

NEXT STOP . . . *Drowning by Numbers, The Draughtsman's Contract, In the Realm of the Senses*

1995 (NC-17) 126m/C *NL FR GB* Vivian Wu, Ewan McGregor, Yoshi Oida, Ken Ogata, Hideko Yoshida, Judy Ongg, Ken Mitsuishi, Yutaka Honda, Ronald Guttman; **D:** Peter Greenaway; **W:** Peter Greenaway; **C:** Sacha Vierny. **VHS** *COL*

PIXOTE

Director Hector Babenco's wrenching portrait of an orphaned boy's nightmarish existence on the crime-ridden streets of Sao Paolo, Brazil, is one of the most grueling, powerful, and disturbing films of the last quarter-century. *Pixote* has justly been compared to Luis Buñuel's great *Los Olvidados*,

Jean-Paul Belmondo, seaside, in Jean-Luc Godard's *Pierrot le Fou.*

ideas simply become too numerous for the narrative to hold; but before that Godard takes us on an erotically charged and breathless tour of a society attempting to force a neat commercialized structure on even the most violent acts of political, individual, and economic terrorism. That the movies have always been a part of this isn't lost on Godard, and in *Pierrot le Fou* he's looking for ways in which the cinema—the most dynamic and immediate of the arts—can destroy and reinvent itself, just like Belmondo's character. The incomparable widescreen color cinematography is by Raoul Coutard. Based (loosely) on the novel *Obsession* by Lionel White.

NEXT STOP . . . *Breathless, Contempt, My Life to Live*

1965 110m/C *FR IT* Samuel Fuller, Jean-Pierre Leaud, Jean-Paul Belmondo, Anna Karina, Dirk Sanders; **D:** Jean-Luc Godard; **M:** Antoine Duhamel. **VHS, LV, Letterbox** *FXL, FCT, IME*

yet there has perhaps never been a vision of childhood on screen as thoroughly horrifying as Babenco's. This 10-year-old's descent into the lowest level of hell is presented in a series of what seem like inevitable moments, all leading with inexorable and terrifying logic to the creation of a little murderer. *Pixote* isn't the kind of "social problem" movie we're used to, in which a cliche of a caseworker will manage to turn around one child and show everybody what's wrong with the state's methods for dealing with juvenile crime; in these teeming slums of Sao Paolo, to paraphrase Martin Sheen in *Apocalypse Now,* there are no methods at all. At the time the film was made, more than half the city's population was under 18. Fernando Ramos da Silva, a non-professional actor and a young orphan himself, gives an amazing, chilling performance as Pixote. But perhaps calling it a performance isn't fully accurate: a few years after *Pixote*'s release, young da Silva died in those same streets, during a shootout with police. The film is genuinely great, but the experience of watching it is so devastating that one recommends it to others with caution. From the novel *Infancia dos Mortos* by Jose Louzeiro.

NEXT STOP . . . *Los Olvidados, The Bicycle Thief, River's Edge* (1986)

1981 127m/C *BR* Fernando Ramos Da Silva, Marilia Pera, Jorge Juliao, Gilberto Moura, Jose Nilson dos Santos, Edilson Lino; *D:* Hector Babenco; *W:* Hector Babenco; *M:* John Neschling. Los Angeles Film Critics Association Awards '81: Best Foreign Film; New York Film Critics Awards '81: Best Foreign Film; National Society of Film Critics Awards '81: Best Actress (Pera). **VHS** *FCT, COL*

PLAYTIME

Monsieur Hulot (Jacques Tati) tries in vain—but with remarkable tenacity—to keep an appointment in a forbidding modern landscape of glass and steel. The third film in Jacques Tati's trilogy about Hulot's struggle with modernization (after *Mr. Hulot's Holiday* and *Mon Oncle*) was an extraordinarily ambitious and costly production, featuring huge and elaborate sets. Many of the film's most intricate sight gags depended on the sheer scale of the settings, such as an overhead shot of a linked maze of glass-enclosed office cubicles, or a gigantic nightclub set. Tati's concept was for a movie as massive as its gags, and so it was prepared as a 70mm, five-track stereo super-production with a three-hour running time. In many of the film's most audacious sequences, comic bits are happening simultaneously in different parts of the frame; in order to even see them clearly, let alone respond to their comic rhythm, the screen image needs to be very large and razor sharp—hence the wide film gauge Tati selected. Alas, *Playtime* was not only cut by more than an hour by the time it reached the U.S. (six years after its completion), but it was never available here in its 70mm version. The fuzzier and smaller 35mm prints circulated here were vastly less detailed than Tati's original film, rendering much of *Playtime*'s most brilliantly choreographed comedy nearly unintelligible. Even seen under ideal conditions, *Playtime* showcased a Hulot whom the world had little time or sympathy for in the late 1960s and early 1970s. Ironically, Hulot was essentially an "anti-establishment" character, and while his message of the dangers of depersonalization may have been timely, his age and his gentle comic methods were out of step with moviegoers of the era. Placing his trust in the audience, Tati refused to force his gags—instead letting us freely and democratically select what we wanted to see from within his vast, enveloping, generous images. The failure of that trust broke his heart and his pocketbook, and sent Tati into bankruptcy.

NEXT STOP . . . *Jour de Fete, Mon Oncle, Our Hospitality*

1967 108m/C *FR* Jacques Tati, Barbara Dennek, Jacqueline Lecomte, Jack Gautier; *D:* Jacques Tati. **VHS** *HMV, NLC*

POLICE STORY
Jackie Chan's Police Force
Police Force
Jackie Chan's Police Story
Ging Chaat Goo Si

As of this writing, Jackie Chan was still making movies, still doing his own stunts, and still

ambulatory (on most days). Diehard fans of the great Hong Kong action star like to debate which of his films is the best, which has the best stunts, and which has the best outtakes—a signature of Jackie Chan films in which during the closing credits we're shown the stunts that may not have worked out so well, often including an upbeat Jackie being carted away on a stretcher. If I have a particularly soft spot for Chan's 1985 *Police Story*, that's because it's the first of his films that I got to experience on the big screen, complete with an appreciative audience. Whether he's hanging out the top window of a careening double decker bus as it takes a sharp corner, or crashing through sheet after sheet of glass while slugging it out with mobsters on a tall department store escalator, Chan is likely to provoke the same giddy wonder as Buster Keaton does when being tossed around by a cyclone in *Steamboat Bill, Jr.* You see it, you have no choice but to believe it, and then you laugh, gasp, and applaud all at once. For the record, Chan here plays a cop assigned to protect a witness. But in a Jackie Chan movie, *everything* other than Jackie Chan is the MacGuffin. With Maggie Cheung (*Irma Vep*).

NEXT STOP . . . *Project A, Project A, Part II, Seven Chances (1925, Buster Keaton)*

1985 (PG-13) 92m/C *HK* Jackie Chan, Bridget Lin, Maggie Cheung, Cho Yuen, Bill Tung, Kenneth Tong; *D:* Jackie Chan; *C:* Yiu-tsou Cheung. **VHS** *NLC, TAI*

PONETTE

Four-year-old Ponette (Victorie Thivisol), whose mother has died in a car accident, progresses through stages of grieving, ultimately emerging—together with the audience—at a glorious and completely new awareness of what it means to be alive. Ponette wants to know what death is—what it means—and the more questions she asks grown-ups, the more we realize they haven't a clue. She must answer the question for herself, as we all must sooner or later. This searingly emotional new film from the gifted Jacques Doillon is one of the most powerful and affecting works ever made about childhood, and about the different ways we leave it. It is a daring film on a number of levels, not the least of which was Doillon's simple commercial gamble that anyone would voluntarily sit down in a theatre for an hour and a half to see a child go through this kind of emotional wringer. But as in any great film on a difficult, or "non-commercial" subject, *Ponette*'s unblinking honesty and its refusal to sentimentalize allows us the privilege of reaping the exhilarating rewards that accompany emergence from the other side of a black hole. One might conceivably question whether a four-year-old's performance can truly be called "acting," but the Venice Film Festival jury sure thought so—they gave little Victorie Thivisol the Festival's Best Actress Prize. As Ponette, she gives—and there is simply no other word—a miraculous performance. She's an equal partner with Doillon in allowing us to understand the emotional growth and thought processes of a child, thereby letting us all understand our adult selves that much better.

NEXT STOP . . . *Forbidden Games, The 400 Blows, Pather Panchali*

1995 107m/C *FR* Victorie Thivisol, Marie Trintignant, Claire Nebout, Xavier Beauvois; *W:* Jacques Doillon; *D:* Jacques Doillon. New York Film Critics Awards '97: Best Foreign Film; Venice Film Festival '96: Best Actress (Thivisol). **VHS** *NYR*

THE POSTMAN
Il Postino

A bittersweet, charming film about Mario (Massimo Troisi), a shy postman who winds up the personal postman of poet Pablo Neruda (Philippe Noiret), who is exiled from his beloved Chile in 1952, granted asylum by the Italian government, and who finds himself living in the tiny Italian community of Isla Negra. The tongue-tied Mario has fallen in love with barmaid Beatrice (Maria Grazia Cucinotta) and asks the poet's help in wooing the dark-eyed beauty, striking up an unlikely friendship with the worldly Neruda. (It's Neruda's seeming ease with women that the shy postman seems most impressed by.) The picture's ever-so-slightly-over-the-top sentimentality—which finally surfaces by having what seems like one too many drawn-out endings, jeopardizing the delicacy of what

P

Jackie tries to reassure a screaming woman that everything will be okay in *Police Story*.

has gone before—can't exactly be called a bad decision, at least on the basis of the movie's popularity. *The Postman (Il Postino)* is one of the most popular foreign-language films ever released in America, and while a brilliant ad campaign helped to get it jump-started, it was word-of-mouth that made it a long-running hit, even in smaller cities. (It also started a run on Neruda's poetry.) Since *The Postman* is in many ways what one might conjure when imagining a prototypical "small" Italian art house film, it's more than a little surprising that it's actually the product of British director Michael Radford (*1984*, *White Mischief*). *The Postman*'s considerable pleasures are provided in large part by the gentle and rich performances of Philipe Noiret and Massimo Troisi. Troisi, a beloved comic actor in Italy, was gravely ill during the picture's production, and died less than one day after its completion. He was posthumously nominated for an Academy Award as Best Actor for his performance. *The Postman* also received nominations for Best Picture, Director, and Adapted Screenplay; Luis Bacalov's lilting score did take home an Oscar.

NEXT STOP . . . *Christ Stopped at Eboli, Cinema Paradiso, Cyrano de Bergerac* (1990)

1994 (PG) 115m/C *IT* Massimo Troisi, Philippe Noiret, Maria Grazia Cucinotta, Linda Moretti, Renato Scarpa, Anna Buonaiuto, Mariana Rigillo; *D:* Michael Radford; *W:* Massimo Troisi, Michael Radford, Furio Scarpelli, Anna Pavignano, Giacomo Scarpelli; *C:* Franco Di Giacomo; *M:* Luis Bacalov. Academy Awards '95: Best Original Dramatic/Comedy Score; British Academy Awards '95: Best Director (Radford), Best Foreign Film, Best Score; Broadcast Film Critics Association Awards '95: Best Foreign Film; Nominations: Academy Awards '95: Best Actor (Troisi), Best Adapted Screenplay, Best Director (Radford), Best Picture; British Academy Awards '95: Best Actor (Troisi), Best Adapted Screenplay; Cesar Awards '97: Best Foreign Film; Directors Guild of America Awards '95: Best Director (Radford); Screen Actors Guild Award '95: Best Actor (Troisi). **VHS** *TOU*

PRINCESS YANG KWEI FEI
Yokihi
The Empress Yang Kwei Fei

Set in 8th-century China, Kenji Mizoguchi's elegant film is based on the life of the last T'ang emperor and the beautiful servant girl he loves and makes his bride. She falls victim to court jealousies and he to his greedy family, though even death cannot end their love (which we see in a staggering final sequence that rivals anything in Mizoguchi). *Princess Yang Kwei Fei* is a mystical and miraculous combination of fairy tale and ghost story, saturated throughout with a graceful supernatural aura. Mizoguchi's gently moving camera and richly evocative color scheme combine to make this one of the most memorably touching and delicately haunting of the great director's masterworks. With Machiko Kyo and Masayuki Mori, both of whom were in Kurosawa's *Rashomon* as well as Mizoguchi's great erotic ghost story, *Ugetsu*.

NEXT STOP . . . *Life of Oharu, Sansho the Bailiff, Ugetsu*

1955 91m/C *JP* Machiko Kyo, Masayuki Mori, Sakae Ozawa, So Yamamura; *D:* Kenji Mizoguchi. **VHS** *NYF*

PRISONER OF THE MOUNTAINS
Kavkazsky Plennik
Prisoner of the Caucasus

Two Russian soldiers whose small unit has been ambushed are taken prisoner by Chechen rebels who hope to swap them for hostages held in a Russian jail. The mother of one of the soldiers (who's played by director Sergei Bodrov's son)—angered by the conflict and determined to get her boy back—sets off on foot to do what she can to deal directly with his captors and arrange for his release. Unexpected events, old antagonisms and sheer chance conspire to produce an unforeseen yet somehow inevitable conclusion for the hostages, yet nothing in the film happens exactly as we suspect it will. Though the recent conflict in Chechnya is the specific focal point, the story on which the movie is based is actually Tolstoy's 150-year-old *Prisoner of the Caucasus;* its updating here doesn't seem in the least a stretch. The universality of Bodrov's devastating *Prisoner of the Mountains* is such that the sudden appearance on the soundtrack at a crucial moment of Louis Armstrong's "What a Wonderful World" seems novel only in retrospect—the film's emo-

Mario (Massimo Troisi) asks for advice from poet Pablo (Philippe Noiret) in *The Postman*.

tional power throughout is very real, deeply felt, and anything but a gimmick.

NEXT STOP . . . *The Bridge, Kanal, Before the Rain*

1996 (R) 98m/C *RU* Sergei Bodrov Jr., Oleg Menshikov, Djemal Sikharulidze, Susanna Mekhralieva, Alexander Burejev; *D:* Sergei Bodrov; *W:* Sergei Bodrov, Arif Aliev, Boris Giller; *C:* Pavel Lebeshev; *M:* Leonid Desyatnikov. Nominations: Academy Awards '96: Best Foreign Film; Golden Globe Awards '97: Best Foreign-Language Film. **VHS, LV** *ORI, MET*

PROJECT GRIZZLY

At the moment I sat down to watch director Peter Lynch's National Film Board of Canada production *Project Grizzly* last year I considered myself a relatively sophisticated moviegoer, able to separate—to a reasonable degree, anyway—complete fabrications from photographed reality. That's why when the lights went up after the screening was over I was able to assure myself that the utterly hilarious 72 minutes I had just laughed all the way through was in fact a terrifically entertaining and imaginative example of a "mockumentary"—a work of fiction in the *style* of a documentary, á la *This Is Spinal Tap* or *Forgotten Silver*. My pride in my own sophistication turned out to be premature, however, for the movie's biggest joke was on me. *Project Grizzly*—the mind-blowing chronicle of a colorful North Bay, Ontario adventurer and zealot named Troy Hurtubise who is determined to create the world's first grizzly bear-proof suit—is a *real* documentary. Apparently Hurtubise is something of a folk hero back home, and the film was created to chronicle his field testing of his latest model, a seven-foot-tall, 147-pound, two-piece suit made of titanium, chain mail and plastic, designed to take the ultimate licking while permitting its wearer's pulse to keep on ticking. A planned but unsuccessful confrontation with a free-roaming grizzly is the movie's denouement, but before that's attempted we get to see the fast-talking, utterly obsessed, feverishly enthusiastic, suited-up Hurtubise knocked on his ass by a 300-pound log, only to assure us after his reinforced helmet is removed that "I feel great, eh?" Take my word for it, you will too. Unbelievable.

NEXT STOP . . . *Gates of Heaven, Fast, Cheap and Out of Control, General Idi Amin Dada*

1996 72m/C Troy Hurtubise; *D:* Peter Lynch; *C:* Tony Wannamker; *M:* Anne Bourne, Ken Myhr. *NYR*

PROOF

Jocelyn Moorehouse's directorial debut is a quietly engaging tale of manipulation, friendship, and erotic obsession between a young blind man named Martin (Hugo Weaving), his housekeeper (Genevieve Picot), and the young man he befriends (Russell Crowe). Martin, mistrustful since his youth of those around him, takes photographs of his environment (labelled in braille) as an attempt to prove that others are being honest with him. A chance meeting with Andy provides Martin with descriptive "eyes," offering the opportunity to expand his world and his sensual connection with it—something his housekeeper, Celia, would be only too happy to help him with. This satisfyingly perverse, darkly witty, nasty little movie proceeds further than you think it will, ultimately inspiring the three corners of the story's erotically charged triangle to reevaluate their lives, behavior, and motives. This is a crisp and assured examination of the borders between curiosity and voyeurism, loneliness and desperation, proof and paranoia. A sophisticated, pleasingly creepy, overlooked gem.

NEXT STOP . . . *Rear Window, Love Serenade, House of Games*

1991 (R) 90m/C *AU* Hugo Weaving, Genevieve Picot, Russell Crowe, Heather Mitchell, Jeffrey Walker, Frank Gallacher; *D:* Jocelyn Moorhouse; *W:* Jocelyn Moorhouse. Australian Film Institute '91: Best Actor (Weaving), Best Director (Moorhouse), Best Film, Best Film Editing, Best Screenplay, Best Supporting Actor (Crowe). **VHS, LV, Closed Caption** *NLC, COL*

A PROPOS DE NICE
Nizza

Jean Vigo was 24 when he bought a camera to make his first, short film, *A Propos de Nice*. The cinema club he had started in Nice wasn't enough for him, and though he devoured the films of others, he felt the need to create

"Poetry doesn't belong to those who write it; it belongs to those who need it."

—Mario (Massimo Troisi) in *The Postman (Il Postino).*

Raw Russian Army recruit Vania (Sergei Bodrov Jr.) is a *Prisoner of the Mountains.*

his own. Reminiscent of the "Kino Eye" films of the brilliant Soviet theorist and filmmaker Dziga Vertov, *A Propos de Nice* is social criticism of a high order, a documentary portrait of a beautiful seaside town as well as a biting, satirical indictment of much of the society that makes Nice what it is. That Vigo himself was the offspring of two dedicated anarchists is apparent throughout *A Propos de Nice.* But two things were undoubtedly not obvious at the film's 1929 premiere. One was that Jean Vigo would go on from this brave, amusing, and ingeniously experimental little film to create two of the greatest and most studied films in cinema history, *Zero for Conduct* (1933) and *L'Atalante* (1934). The other was that Vigo would die of tuberculosis barely five years later at the age of 29, having completed only two short films and two features, the latter two now universally recognized as seminal masterworks. Representing, therefore, a quarter of Vigo's life's work and an early clue to the vision of a master, *A Propos de Nice* is both a charming social document and an invaluable cinematic artifact.

NEXT STOP . . . *L'Atalante, Zero for Conduct, The Man with the Movie Camera*

1929 25m/B *FR* **D:** Jean Vigo; **W:** Jean Vigo; **C:** Boris Kaufman. **VHS** *FST, MRV, GVV*

PROVIDENCE

A dying writer (John Gielgud) spends a sleepless night in nearly intolerable pain, which he tries to fight off with bottle after bottle of cold white wine. As the night wears on, his imagination weaves his terror, his memories, and his desires into a fantastic, hallucinatory novel in which the members of his family act out a mysterious melodrama—though his story's progress occasionally halts for unwanted intrusions such as a recurring vision of his own impending autopsy. An English-language film written by playwright David Mercer and directed by France's Alain Resnais (*Hiroshima Mon Amour, Last Year at Marienbad*), *Providence*'s cast includes—in addition to Gielgud—Ellen Burstyn, Dirk Bogarde, David Warner, and Elaine Stritch. Their performances all seem disconcertingly stiff and bizarrely theatrical at first, but soon it's clear that the decidedly "unrealistic" manner of speech and the correspondingly expressionistic sets are exactly right for the unfinished, continually revised rough draft that Gielgud desperately rattles off as both dawn and the final deadline for making sense of his life close in. To say that everything comes together in the end would be quite an understatement—*Providence* has the kind of knockout finish that can make you see the world differently when you leave the theatre—yet the film is still seen and discussed only rarely. (The lilting themes of Miklos Rozsa's spellbinding score may actually be better known than the film itself.) Ten years after its quiet American release, *Providence* was screened as a sidebar event at the Telluride Film Festival; in a passionate and memorable 20-minute introduction to that screening, Norman Mailer called it simply the greatest film ever made about the creative process. On this single occasion at least, Mr. Mailer's opinion may very well be unassailable.

NEXT STOP . . . *32 Short Films about Glenn Gould, Last Year at Marienbad, Rashomon*

1977 (R) 104m/C *GB* John Gielgud, Dirk Bogarde, Ellen Burstyn, David Warner, Elaine Stritch; **D:** Alain Resnais; **W:** David Mercer; **C:** Ricardo Aronovich; **M:** Miklos Rozsa. Cesar Awards '78: Best Art Direction/Set Decoration, Best Director (Resnais), Best Film, Best Sound, Best Writing, Best Score; New York Film Critics Awards '77: Best Actor (Gielgud). **VHS** *COL*

PURPLE NOON
Plein Soleil
Lust for Evil

An amoral, social-climbing, money-hungry American named Ripley (Alain Delon) is hired by a wealthy businessman to go to Europe to bring back the man's wealthy playboy son, Philippe (Maurice Ronet). It soon dawns on Ripley that there might be considerably more money and power (i.e. women) in it for him if he were to find a way to impersonate Philippe rather than return him. That, however, would mean that the spoiled, irresponsible Philippe would have to disappear—permanently. Based on the novel *The*

Talented Mr. Ripley by Strangers on a Train author Patricia Highsmith, René Clément's decadent and enormously pleasurable suspense thriller features one of Delon's best and most chilling performances (and a knockout surprise ending). With the exception of his great Forbidden Games, this is the film for which director Clément is most famous. Purple Noon was unavailable in America for over 25 years, but was recently returned to circulation thanks to the efforts of Martin Scorsese, who rightly called it "a forgotten classic." Purple Noon's slightly faded colors are still not everything they should be—there's a certain vibrancy missing—but Henri Decaë's tension-packed images are still effective. My favorite shot in the movie involves a roast chicken. I'll say no more. (Anthony Minghella, fresh from the success of his The English Patient, has announced that the same Highsmith novel on which Purple Noon was based will be the basis for his next film.)

NEXT STOP . . . *The American Friend, Strangers on a Train, Rope*

1960 (PG-13) 118m/C *FR* Alain Delon, Maurice Ronet, Marie Laforet, Erno Crisa, Billy Kearns; *D:* Rene Clement; *W:* Rene Clement, Paul Gegauff; *C:* Henri Decae; *M:* Nino Rota. **VHS, LV** *TOU*

QUE VIVA MEXICO
Da Zdravstvuyet Meksika

In 1930, the great Soviet director Sergei Eisenstein was getting ready to end his visit to California, having been told by Paramount Pictures that they weren't interested in his proposed adaptation of Theodore Dreiser's *An American Tragedy.* (Paramount and George Stevens *would* make that film 21 years later, as *A Place in the Sun.*) The studio handed Eisenstein a ticket back to the U.S.S.R. (by way of Japan), but before using it the director decided he would go south to explore the possibility of fulfilling his longtime dream of making a film on the history of Mexico and its peoples. Eisenstein was able to secure financing for the project, and soon he and his brilliant cinematographer Eduard

Tisse were shooting hours and hours of stunning, spectacular footage of every imaginable aspect of Mexican society. The shoot went on through 1931, but only after the miles of film were in the can did it become apparent that Eisenstein's deal for the film did not include his right to final approval of its editing—the single aspect of filmmaking that Eisenstein believed to be the most critical. Disagreements with his collaborators and rumors about his behavior and affiliations that were circulating back home contributed to what was to become a legendary catastrophe—a potentially great film that would remain eternally unfinished. Footage from the project was assembled into many different forms during the years—including a study for the completed project called *Time in the Sun*—but it wasn't until 1979 that Eisenstein's original collaborator, Grigori Alexandrov, released an 85-minute *Que Viva Mexico* that was said to approximate Eisenstein's intentions. The shape may indeed be similar to what was envisioned by Eisenstein, yet the footage—while visually overwhelming—remains only footage. Whatever *Que Viva Mexico* might have become under Eisenstein's control remains a subject for speculation, but this "reconstruction," which is comprised of film by Sergei Eisenstein, should never be mistaken for *a* film by Sergei Eisenstein.

NEXT STOP . . . *It's All True, The Epic That Never Was, Queen Kelly*

1932 85m/B *RU D:* Sergei Eisenstein; *W:* Sergei Eisenstein, Grigori Alexandrov; *C:* Eduard Tisse. **VHS** *KIV*

QUILOMBO

The title refers to a legendary settlement of runaway slaves in 17th-century Brazil; this epic chronicles its fortunes as leadership passes from a wise and beloved ruler named Ganga Zumba (the subject of an earlier film by director Carlos Diegues) to a more sternly militant one named Zumbi, who fears that Ganga Zumba's old ways smack of appeasement and who insists on mounting a full-scale war against the oppressive government. Carlos Diegues's groundbreaking

Quilombo tells this richly complex saga to the accompaniment of a powerfully evocative musical score by Gilberto Gil; it's one of the few fact-based historical spectaculars from which you emerge humming the tunes. Revolutionary in form, *Quilombo* is nevertheless a colorful, compelling, and ultimately heartbreaking work. Though self-contained, *Quilombo* is one of a series of films by Diegues chronicling different aspects of the Brazilian people's centuries-old struggles to free themselves from the curses of colonialism and slavery.

NEXT STOP . . . *Ganga Zumba, Xica, Bye Bye Brazil*

1984 114m/C *BR* Vera Fischer, Antonio Pompeo, Zeze Motta, Toni Tornado; **D:** Carlos Diegues; **W:** Carlos Diegues. **VHS** *NYF, FCT*

RAISE THE RED LANTERN

In the 1920s in China, Songlian (Gong Li), an educated 19-year-old beauty, is forced into marriage as the fourth wife of a wealthy and powerful old man. She soon discovers that each wife has her own separate quarters and servants, and spends most of her time battling to attract her husband's attention. (A red lantern is placed outside the door of the wife the old man chooses to spend the night with.) Over the course of her first year in this luxurious servitude, Songlian's humiliation, resentment, and fury swell until rebellion, as self-defeating as it may be, is her only impulse. Zhang Yimou's thrilling *Raise the Red Lantern* is an extraordinary work of art, as visually dazzling as it is deeply heartbreaking. Gong Li's third film collaboration with Zhang produced what may be her most delicately nuanced and memorable performance, as a woman struggling to accept a life formed by circumstance and tradition, but ultimately—and nobly—unable to bury her dignity beneath a silken mountain of "privilege." From the novel *Wives and Concubines* by Su Tong. Academy Award Nominee, Best Foreign Language Film.

NEXT STOP . . . *Red Sorghum, The Story of Qiu Ju, Life of Oharu*

1991 (PG) 125m/C *CH* Gong Li, Ma Jingwu, He Caifei, Cao Cuifeng, Jin Shuyuan, Kong Lin, Ding Weimin; **D:** Zhang Yimou. British Academy Awards '92: Best Foreign Film; Los Angeles Film Critics Association Awards '92: Best Cinematography; New York Film Critics Awards '92: Best Foreign Film; National Society of Film Critics Awards '92: Best Cinematography, Best Foreign Film; Nominations: Academy Awards '91: Best Foreign-Language Film. **VHS, LV, Closed Caption** *ORI, BTV*

RAMPARTS OF CLAY

In contemporary Tunisia, a young woman (Leila Schenna) attempts to reconcile her village's traditional way of life with what she learns of the outside world following a strike by the villagers against a powerful corporation. A tale of the enormous psychological and economic consequences of independence from colonialism, Jean-Louis Bertucelli's *Ramparts of Clay* is a magnificent visual experience. Through extremely expressive camera movements and design, Bertucelli replicates the sensation of one individual's discovery of a universe beyond her immediate borders. This is a thrilling, poignant, and wholly unforgettable work of art. Though small in scale, I hesitate to refer to it as "a small classic"; it's a classic, all right, yet its impact and power are anything but small.

NEXT STOP . . . *The Silences of the Palace, Emitai, Al Leja (The Land of Leja)*

1971 (PG) 87m/C *FR* Leila Schenna **D:** Jean-Louis Bertucelli. **VHS** *COL*

RAN

Medieval warlord Hidetora Ichimonji (Tatsuya Nakadai) cedes power over his empire to the oldest of his three sons, setting off a chain of tragic events fueled by greed, ambition, anger, and betrayal. With the 1985 release of his epic adaptation of Shakespeare's *King Lear,* Akira Kurosawa achieved considerably more than a mere resuscitation of his career. *Ran* is an emotionally wrenching, awe-inspiring spectacle that takes its place alongside the few great cinematic interpretations of Shakespeare—a handful of films that includes Olivier's *Henry V,* Welles's *Chimes at Midnight,* and Kurosawa's own *Throne of Blood*. Kurosawa boldly took liberties with *Lear* (Lear's daughters are now sons, for starters) and he added—as Welles did with *Chimes at Midnight*, the main sources of which are the two parts of *Henry IV*—elements from other Shakespeare plays. In *Ran*, a Lady Macbeth—inspired character named Lady Kaede (brilliantly played by Mieko Harada) would have easily walked off with the picture, were the picture as a whole not so astonishing. Much has been written about *Ran*'s visual qualities, and understandably so, yet it's the film's narrative flow and emotional fullness that give those images their overwhelming resonance, making them far more than pretty pictures. Even in such passages as the deceptively calm opening sequence, in which the savagely ruthless but now old Hidetora, peacefully seated on a sun-drenched mountainside, explains his catastrophically ill-conceived plans for his impending "retirement," Kurosawa maintains absolute control over the tone of his material. It's in *Ran*'s battle sequences that that control is most apparent, and those scenes are among the greatest depictions of combat in cinema history. Horrifying, staggeringly beautiful, yet as carefully delineated on an emotional level as any of the film's more intimate moments, *Ran*'s battle scenes evoke the full power of Shakespeare's tragedy. Kurosawa and his production team (a major contributor being composer Toru Takemitsu) have placed all of their technological power at the service of their story, and the performers—particularly Tatsuya Nakadai in the demanding role of Hidetora—live up to the challenge as well. Kurosawa is one of the very few filmmakers who created several masterpieces in his career. *Ran*—Kurosawa's 27th film, made when he was 75 years old—is one of them.

NEXT STOP . . . *Seven Samurai, Throne of Blood, Alexander Nevsky*

1985 (R) 160m/C *JP FR* Tatsuya Nakadai, Akira Terao, Jinpachi Nesu, Daisuke Ryu, Meiko Harada, Hisashi Igawa, Peter; *D:* Akira Kurosawa; *W:* Akira Kurosawa, Hideo Oguni, Masato Ide; *M:* Toru Takemitsu. Academy Awards '85: Best Costume Design; British Academy Awards '86: Best Foreign Film; Los Angeles Film Critics Association Awards '85: Best Foreign Film; National Board of Review Awards '85: Best Director (Kurosawa); New York Film Critics Awards '85: Best Foreign Film; National Society of Film Critics Awards '85: Best Cinematography, Best Film; Nominations: Academy Awards '85: Best Art Direction/Set Decoration, Best Cinematography, Best Director (Kurosawa). **VHS, LV, Letterbox, Closed Caption** *FXL, HMV*

RASHOMON ✓
In the Woods

It's happened to you. You've gone to a movie with someone, either loved or hated what you saw on the screen, and as you leave the theatre together, you realize that you've each had the exact *opposite* response. Then one of you pops the inevitable, rhetorical question: "Did we see the same movie?" The answer, of course, is no. You both *looked* at the same movie, but what you *saw* is another story. In describing what we see to each other—and not just our *response* to what we see—we possess the power to distort and rework some very simple truths to suit our own purposes. That uncomfortable fact is the subject of Akira Kurosawa's 1950 masterpiece, which not only introduced the Japanese cinema to much of the world, it also introduced a new expression into the language. The film's title actually refers to the huge stone gate under which three men take refuge from a rainstorm in 11th-century Japan, and whose talk soon turns to a notorious crime—a rape and murder—and the resulting trial that took place. Since all the varying versions of the crime that the men describe and that we see enacted in the film (a fourth is related by a spirit) conflict with each other, the unfolding labyrinthine mystery soon encompasses not just the crime itself, but the motives of those describing it. Toshiro Mifune and Machiko Kyo are remarkable as the criminal and his prey in this ingeniously assembled and endlessly fascinating portrait of human greed and fallibility. *Rashomon* took the film world by storm on its release in 1950, winning the Grand Prize at the Venice Film Festival and the Academy Award for Best Foreign Language Film.

NEXT STOP . . . *Ikiru, Citizen Kane, The Conversation*

R

DANIEL TALBOT

At a morning press screening at the 1997 New York Film Festival, Daniel Talbot plopped down next to me and said: "So what is this rumor about you retiring?" I was celebrating my 25th year of exhibiting films at the Detroit Institute of Arts, and a sarcastic remark I had made about being ready for a gold watch had apparently made it around the room and into one or both of Talbot's ears. Before I could swallow the coffee in my mouth and assure him that it was only a rumor, he added with the terseness that is his trademark: "You can't do that. The films have to be shown, and you need to stay there and show them." Then he turned to greet someone else, and that was that.

I could have pointed out to him that there are plenty of other people capable of doing my job, but I was hardly about to argue with a man who has been a hero of mine since I was ten years old, and who was telling me that my job—exhibiting motion pictures at a museum—might actually be valuable work. When the lights dimmed for the film we had all come to see, I began to fantasize that I *had* been planning retirement, just so that I that I could later claim I'd been talked out of it by one of the pioneers in bringing great international cinema to America.

Daniel Talbot's fondly remembered New Yorker Theatre was located at Broadway near 88th Street in New York City, and for decades was regarded as an American Cinematheque long before such a concept became formalized. In the 1960s, The New Yorker ran a different double feature of classic films every day of the year, usually in the best 35mm prints available. Before VCRs were even an idea, Daniel Talbot was providing New Yorkers with a daily opportunity to explore the history of the cinema. The theatre's programming could be eclectic (the cover of 1970's Film Culture Reader features a famous photograph of a New Yorker marquee announcing a double bill of Jack Kerouac's *Pull My Daisy* and Orson Welles's *The Magnificent Ambersons*) as well as down-home comforting (my first double bill there—on my first day ever in New York—was a packed Saturday night showing of *North by Northwest* and *Shane*). The place had a lived-in feel and a wealth of personality; the inner lobby doors were graced by cartoon figures painted by regular patron Jules Feiffer, and Dan's mother-in-law often worked the concession stand. The New Yorker is the theatre in which Woody Allen suddenly produces Marshall McLuhan to an obnoxious patron who's ahead of him in line in order to prove a point in *Annie Hall*.

1951 83m/B *JP* Machiko Kyo, Toshiro Mifune, Masayuki Mori, Takashi Shimura, Minoru Chiaki, Kichijiro Ueda, Daisuke Kato; *D:* Akira Kurosawa; *W:* Akira Kurosawa, Shinobu Hashimoto; *C:* Kazuo Miyagawa; *M:* Fumio Hayasaka. Academy Awards '51: Best Foreign Film; National Board of Review Awards '51: Best Director (Kurosawa); Venice Film Festival '51: Best Film; Nominations: Academy Awards '52: Best Art Direction/Set Decoration (B & W). **VHS, LV** *CRC, NLC*

THE RED BALLOON

Little Pascal (Pascal Lamorisse) is a lonely French boy who befriends a wondrous red balloon that follows him everywhere. When catastrophe in the form of bullying, jealous children causes the balloon's demise, every other balloon in Paris comes flying to the aid

Yes, I said "in" line, not "on" line, which means I'm not a New Yorker. Growing up as a movie lover in Detroit in the 1950s and 1960s, I longed to see many of the foreign classics I had only read about—films like *The Bicycle Thief, Metropolis, Grand Illusion, Battleship Potemkin* and *Seven Samurai*—which, thanks to my family's subscription to the Sunday New York Times, I often saw listed as playing that very day at the New Yorker Theatre, causing me to wonder why inhabitants of Manhattan would ever do anything else on a Sunday afternoon.

As many films as he presented, however, Talbot, who is a scholar of the cinema and the editor of a classic 1959 book of essays titled *Film: An Anthology*, found that there were movies he wanted to present at the theatre which were not available through traditional distribution sources. His response was to become a film distributor himself and import those films; today the hundreds of titles he distributes on both film and video constitute one of the most important single sources of world cinema anywhere. Talbot's New Yorker Films gave American moviegoers—and not *just* New Yorkers—their first opportunity to see Yasujiro Ozu's *Tokyo Story* and *Late Spring*, Bernardo Bertolucci's *Before the Revolution* and *The Spider's Stratagem*, Louis Malle's *The Fire Within* and *My Dinner with André*, Ousmane Sembène's *Emitai* and *Ceddo*, Rainer Werner Fassbinder's *The Merchant of Four Seasons* and *The Marriage of Maria Braun*, Robert Bresson's *Pickpocket*, Juzo Itami's *Tampopo*, Werner Herzog's *Aguirre, the Wrath of God*, Ermanno Olmi's *The Tree of Wooden Clogs*, Zhang Yimou's *Red Sorghum*, Theo Angelopoulos's *Landscape in the Mist* and Claude Lanzmann's *Shoah*.

Dan Talbot once autographed a copy of his book for me with the words "better to see movies than read about them." Because of his groundbreaking and ongoing efforts in exhibition (he still owns theatres in New York) and distribution (New Yorker Films is more active than ever), he has helped to make it possible for those intrigued by the movies described in this book to do more than simply read about them. Without businessmen of Talbot's generosity, taste, and bravery, many of the artists who've committed their visions to film might never have been able to bring those visions to an American audience.

Dan Talbot loves movies, and he loves to share his joy in them by making it possible for others to see them; that's why he's appalled at the mere *rumor* of a lone Midwesterner defecting from the ranks of this religion. It's also why, in 1979, the George Eastman House presented New Yorker Films with a special award which read in part: "No distribution company has performed a greater service to serious moviegoers in this country than has New Yorker Films." I couldn't have said it better—or more tersely—myself.

and comfort of the devastated Pascal. Directed by the resourceful and inventive Albert Lamorisse (Pascal's father), *The Red Balloon* is a charmingly imaginative, elegantly conceived, marvelously done 34-minute fable about friendship, loyalty, and love. *The Red Balloon* was one of the few short films to achieve a significant following on its initial release, partly due to its immense appeal to children, as well as the fact that the story is told with music and images, but without any need for dialogue (it is the *least* foreign of foreign films, regardless of what country you live in). *The Red Balloon's* simple photographic effects work even on today's allegedly sophisticated, special-

Ballet dancer Moira Shearer is eyed by impresario Anton Walbrook in *The Red Shoes*.

effects-savvy kids, because the story it tells is primal and universal; by the big finish, everybody's too moved to care "how it was done." And like all great children's films, it's even more affecting for adults. Academy Award Nominee, Best Original Screenplay.

NEXT STOP . . . *Stowaway in the Sky, The Black Stallion, E.T.: The Extra-Terrestrial*

1956 34m/C *FR* Pascal Lamorisse; *D:* Albert Lamorisse. Academy Awards '56: Best Original Screenplay. **VHS, LV, 8mm** *HMV, HHT, DVT*

RED BEARD
Akahige

Akira Kurosawa's engrossing epic is the story of a tough but compassionate physician (Toshiro Mifune) in 19th-century Japan who does his best to treat patients from every walk of life, while simultaneously training a young intern. *Red Beard* was mistakenly dismissed by some upon its release as a soap opera in disguise. While it may share some of the plot elements of an episode *Dr. Kildare* or *ER,* it's also a powerful and sweeping portrait of the human spirit in the grand Kurosawa style. It was the last film that Kurosawa and Toshiro Mifune would make together, and as the grizzled physician with the hard exterior and compassionate heart (who knows the martial arts as well), Mifune gives one of his most memorable and touching performances. This is a stately, visually grand three-hour film that remains one of Kurosawa's most unjustly overlooked masterworks. With Takashi Shimura (*Ikiru*) and Chishu Ryu (*Tokyo Story*). The stunning widescreen compositions deserve to be seen in the letter-boxed video format.

NEXT STOP . . . *Seven Samurai, Dodes 'ka-den, Ikiru*

1965 185m/B *JP* Toshiro Mifune, Yuzo Kayama, Yoshio Tsuchiya, Reiko Dan; *D:* Akira Kurosawa. **VHS, LV, Letterbox** *CRC, FCT*

THE RED DESERT
Il Deserto Rosso

Michelangelo Antonioni went for broke in designing the images of his first color film, the story of an alienated woman (Monica Vitti) who searches for meaning and purpose in the industrial, lunar-like landscape of northern Italy. Antonioni uses settings and carefully controlled colors to represent Vitti's deteriorating, increasingly fractured mental state. His plan, which is often remarkably successful, is to show us a world that is both recognizable and realistic but also obviously "heightened," the subjective "reality" of someone whose understanding of her world is splintering into something resembling primary colors and basic shapes, with very little middle ground. *Red Desert* is a fascinating, if less than utterly gripping, experiment by a master filmmaker. But beware; it makes no sense whatsoever if seen in a faded or poorly processed copy. Be sure that you see it in a recently restored and letterboxed videocassette, DVD (if available) or laserdisc version.

NEXT STOP . . . *L'Avventura, The Passenger, The Cabinet of Dr. Caligari*

1964 120m/C *IT* Monica Vitti, Richard Harris, Carlos Chionetti; *D:* Michelangelo Antonioni; *W:* Michelangelo Antonioni, Tonino Guerra; *C:* Carlo Di Palma; *M:* Giovanni Fusco. Venice Film Festival '64: Best Film. **VHS** *FCT, CVC, TPV*

THE RED SHOES

A masterpiece. Though it was inspired by a Hans Christian Andersen fairy tale, *The Red Shoes* is an absolute original, and the quintessential film from writers/producers/directors Michael Powell and Emeric Pressburger, known together as the Archers. It's the story of a talented young ballerina named Victoria Page, (Moira Shearer) who studies under the unforgiving, tyrannical impresario Boris Lermontov (Anton Walbrook). As she trains to perform in a ballet of *The Red Shoes,* the story

of an enchanted pair of ballet slippers that cause their wearer to dance herself to death, it becomes apparent to Shearer that her life and her art have come together with overwhelming intensity. If *Citizen Kane* is the movie that started the most number of filmmakers on their careers, then surely *The Red Shoes* did the same for dancers. It's a perfectly realized, thrillingly conceived adult fairy tale, every bit as powerful (and disturbing) today as it was 50 years ago. (It's still popular, as well. Perhaps *too* popular; a few years ago at a museum showing in Detroit, the audience and staff made the unpleasant discovery that a still-unknown "collector" who had temporary possession of the commercially distributed print previously had removed the entire, 14-minute ballet sequence that is pivotal to the film.) Seeing *The Red Shoes* in a good quality, color-restored videocassette or laserdisc is essential to appreciating and enjoying it; seeing a restored 35mm print projected in a theatre is ideal.

NEXT STOP . . . *Black Narcissus, A Matter of Life and Death, Carmen*

1948 136m/C *GB* Anton Walbrook, Moira Shearer, Marius Goring, Leonide Massine, Robert Helpmann, Albert Basserman, Ludmila Tcherina, Esmond Knight; *D:* Emeric Pressburger, Michael Powell; *W:* Emeric Pressburger, Michael Powell; *C:* Jack Cardiff. Academy Awards '48: Best Art Direction/Set Decoration (Color), Best Original Dramatic/Comedy Score; Golden Globe Awards '49: Best Score; Nominations: Academy Awards '48: Best Film Editing, Best Picture, Best Story. **VHS, LV, Closed Caption** *PAR, HMV*

RED SORGHUM

A stunning visual and narrative achievement, this extraordinary film from China—the directorial debut of the gifted Zhang Yimou—succeeds on every level. Set in rural China in the 1920s, the sweeping plot—comprised of equal parts romance, comedy, drama, and horror—is the story of a beautiful young woman (Gong Li) who arrives at a provincial winery betrothed to one man but in love with another. The widescreen color images of Zhang's epic conjure the punch and resonance of stories told by John Ford, Sergio Leone, Sam Peckinpah, and Akira

Kurosawa, but with a uniquely eloquent emotional control. Despite the relatively modern setting of the story, the significance of the year in which it is set only begins to sink in during the harrowing last third of the film, when the brutal Japanese invasion suddenly takes place. *Red Sorghum* is a knockout—one the most auspicious debut films in cinema history. Grand Prize, Berlin Film Festival.

NEXT STOP . . . *Ju Dou, Once Upon a Time in the West, Ride the High Country*

1987 91m/C *CH* Gong Li, Jiang Wen, Ji Cun Hua; *D:* Zhang Yimou; *C:* Gu Changwei. **VHS** *NYF*

RENDEZVOUS IN PARIS
Les Rendez-vous de Paris

The three tales of young love that comprise Eric Rohmer's twentieth feature are engaging, wise, revealing, and deeply funny, demonstrating anew that at age 75, Rohmer may well be the most perceptive chronicler of young people in all cinema. The first story tells of a trusting woman whose refusal to believe the rumors about her boyfriend's alleged infidelities leads to a series of coincidental encounters, culminating in a surprising discovery. The picturesque centerpiece tells of a deceptively free-spirited young woman whose erotic fascination with her lover is based on an unusual formula of risk and reward. As enchanting as these two stories are, however, they're no match for the film's finale, a tiny, jewel-like classic about a self-absorbed artist who meets his match when he picks up a beautiful woman at the Picasso Museum. This sequence shifts mood almost continuously, evolving from low comedy to improbable, impeccably timed farce, and finally becoming a startlingly clear-eyed—and ruthlessly honest—psychological profile of a serial womanizer. *Rendezvous in Paris*

proves that Eric Rohmer—who still makes eloquence look easy— remains one of the cinema's great masters of romantic comedy.

NEXT STOP . . . *Summer, Claire's Knee, Boyfriends & Girlfriends*

1995 100m/C *FR* Clara Bellar, Antoine Basler, Mathias Megard, Judith Chancel, Aurore Rauscher, Serge Renko, Michael Kraft, Benedicte Loyen, Veronika Johansson; *D:* Eric Rohmer; *W:* Eric Rohmer; *C:* Diane Baratier; *M:* Sebastien Erms. **VHS** *NYF*

REPULSION

Above all, there's the rabbit. Movie history is littered with symbols of characters' madness and gradual descent into insanity, but the dish containing the unrefrigerated, rotting rabbit in Roman Polanski's great thriller *Repulsion* will have to be given a place of honor at the entrance to the Psycho Killer Hall of Fame. Catherine Deneuve is the manicurist whose unresolved sexual anxieties turn deadly when she spends a fateful few days alone in a London apartment. Though the film features some graphic violence that had audiences jumping out of their seats in 1965, the movie's real power to disturb comes from Polanski's uncanny ability to present Deneuve's deteriorating grip on reality in visual terms. Sexually suggestive images such as sudden cracks in a ceiling and grasping arms protruding from walls are seen from Deneuve's point-of-view, though her vicious killings are not sanitized. All the while that rabbit slowly decays, and it's both a reassuring, darkly comic image for the audience to grab on to as well as an indelible reminder of the face of death, contrasting starkly with the young, pristine beauty of the young Catherine Deneuve. Though they both had previous cinematic successes, *Repulsion* is the film that propelled the careers of both Polanski and Deneuve into the stratosphere.

NEXT STOP . . . *The Tenant, Rosemary's Baby, Psycho*

1965 105m/B *GB* Catherine Deneuve, Yvonne Furneaux, Ian Hendry, John Fraser, Patrick Wymark, James Villiers, Renee Houston, Helen Fraser, Mike Pratt, Valerie Taylor; *D:* Roman Polanski; *W:* Roman Polanski, Gerard Brach, David Stone; *C:* Gilbert Taylor. **VHS, LV** *COL*

THE RETURN OF MARTIN GUERRE
Le Retour de Martin Guerre

In this intriguing, well-written fable set in 16th-century France, a dissolute village husband disappears soon after his marriage. Years later, someone who appears to be Martin Guerre returns (Gérard Depardieu), allegedly from war, and appears kinder, more educated, and far more sympathetic than the man that most of the village (including his wife) remembers. In this popular and quietly suspenseful love story about second chances and the power of hope to alter the way we see, Gérard Depardieu gives one of his most memorable and finely layered performances. Daniel Vigne's film was based on an actual incident, and it became a surprise art house hit in the U.S. upon its 1983 release. National Society of Film Critics' Award to Depardieu as Best Actor. The better-than-average 1993 Hollywood remake, *Sommersby*, was set after the American Civil War, and starred Richard Gere and Jodie Foster (in a superb performance).

NEXT STOP . . . *Béatrice, Persona, Olivier, Olivier*

1983 111m/C *FR* Gerard Depardieu, Roger Planchon, Maurice Jacquemont, Barnard Pierre Donnadieu, Nathalie Baye; *D:* Daniel Vigne; *W:* Daniel Vigne, Jean-Claude Carriere. Cesar Awards '83: Best Writing, Best Score; National Society of Film Critics Awards '83: Best Actor (Depardieu); Nominations: Academy Awards '83: Best Costume Design. **VHS, Letterbox** *FXL, HMV*

RHAPSODY IN AUGUST
Hachigatsu no Kyoshikyoku

This 1992 Kurosawa film was regarded as minor and uncharacteristic by some, yet I find it to be one of the most moving and heartfelt pictures of his career. The basic story is contemporary; a group of teenagers take a trip to Nagasaki to see their aging grandmother, whose husband died in the atomic bombing of the city. As her story is gradually and tenderly revealed, Kurosawa shows us and the children many remaining

"What kind of game is this?"

—Margo (Marge Dval) to Philippe (Maurice Ronet) and Tom (Alain Delon) in *Purple Noon*.

physical manifestations of the bombing, including the melted, twisted bars of what was once a children's jungle gym, and which now serves as a formal memorial—a stark, powerful reminder of what was lost in an instant. The superb cast includes Richard Gere in a small but pivotal role, but the most important and memorable "performers" in *Rhapsody in August* may be the colony of ants that climb silently up the stem of a rose in a sequence near the film's conclusion; it's a moment so inspired and so breathtakingly expressive that it reminds us in the same instant of both man's power to destroy, as well as the artist's power to fashion hope from the ashes.

NEXT STOP . . . *I Live in Fear, Black Rain (Imamura), Ikiru*

1991 (PG) 98m/C JP Sachiko Murase, Narumi Kayashima, Hisashi Igawa, Richard Gere; **D:** Akira Kurosawa; **W:** Akira Kurosawa; **C:** Takao Saito, Masaharu Ueda; **M:** Shinichiro Ikebe. **VHS, LV** *ORI*

RIDICULE

In 1783, a young French engineer (Charles Berling) is determined to drain the dangerous, disease-infested swamps he lives near, and which are causing illness and death among the area's children. He finds, however, that to have his case even heard at the Versailles court of Louis XVI requires the manipulative skills of a politician, the clarity of thought of a philosopher and the wit and humor of a stand-up comic, yet the urgency and goodness of his cause is barely a part of the formula. Patrice Leconte's *Ridicule* is a remarkably entertaining and intelligent piece of storytelling about the human costs of a society based on arrogance, ego, and social stratification. The esteem that "wit" is held in in this society is eclipsed only by the price paid by those who don't have it. The prized bits of verbal repartee which can scoot one up the ladder of aristocratic acceptance are depicted with the graphic coldness of sex without emotion (the difference being that this aristocratically mandated "cleverness" without conscience is *truly* pornographic). A costume epic with a brain is rare enough, but Leconte (*Monsieur Hire, The Hairdresser's Husband*) has gone one better. His indictment of wit without soul is itself a marvelously witty creation; *Ridicule* demonstrates what perspective coupled with mental dexterity can achieve when used in the service of humanity, rather than at its expense. César awards for Best French Film, Best Director, Best Costumes and Production Design. With Jean Rochefort, Fanny Ardant, and Judith Godrèche (The Disenchanted).

NEXT STOP . . . *Monsieur Hire, La Nuit de Varennes, La Marseillaise*

1996 (R) 102m/C FR Charles Berling, Jean Rochefort, Fanny Ardant, Bernard Giraudeau, Judith Godreche, Bernard Dheran, Carlo Brandt, Jacques Mathou; **D:** Patrice Leconte; **W:** Remi Waterhouse, Michel Fessler, Eric Vicaut; **C:** Thierry Arbogast; **M:** Antoine Duhamel. Academy Awards '96: Best Foreign Film; Cesar Awards '97: Best Director (Leconte), Best Film; Broadcast Film Critics Association Awards '96: Best Foreign Film; Nominations: Academy Awards '96: Best Foreign Film; Cesar Awards '97: Best Actor (Berling); Golden Globe Awards '97: Best Foreign Film. **VHS, LV, Closed Caption** *TOU*

THE RISE OF LOUIS XIV
La Prise de Pouvoir par Louis XIV

Roberto Rossellini's masterful and remarkably intimate "docudrama" details the life and court intrigues of the 17th century's Sun King. The best and most frequently screened of a series of historical portraits Rossellini created for French television, *The Rise of Louis XIV* is disorienting at first because of its straightforward, workmanlike style, which includes TV-style zoom shots that seem utterly incongruous in a lush, historical epic. But it's precisely that method of recording the "action" that makes watching the film feel so much like being present as events took place. Carrying on the tradition of his "caught-on-the-run" style used so brilliantly in his *Open City* and *Paisan*, Rossellini here has added a new tranquility and almost voyeuristic observational technique, creating the impression that this was somehow a film made during Louis's reign, and only now has been discovered to give us a view of history never before available. It's a remarkable, ingenious illusion, unlike almost every other period film ever made.

NEXT STOP . . . *The Private Life of Henry VIII, The Gospel According to St. Matthew, Blaise Pascal*

1966 100m/C *FR* Jean-Marie Patte, Raymond Jourdan, Dominique Vincent, Silvagni, Pierre Barrat; *D:* Roberto Rossellini. **VHS** *HTV, FCT*

ROCCO AND HIS BROTHERS
Rocco et Ses Freres
Rocco e I Suoi Fratelli

A classic film from Italy's Luchino Visconti, about the impact on the lives of four brothers when they move with their widowed mother (Katina Paxinou) from the Italian countryside to a very different lifestyle in Milan. The fate of each of the sons is chronicled in marvelous detail over the course of the film's three hours, and the cumulative effect is extraordinary. Visconti gives us a portrait of the impact of environment and cor-

ruption on family bonds, love, and loyalties in a way that would be taken further—and in a different direction—years later by Francis Coppola and Mario Puzo in *The Godfather*. The assured narrative flow and extraordinary performances (in particular those of Alain Delon, Renato Salvatori, Annie Girardot, and Claudia Cardinale) require a longer attention span than some of today's audiences are used to, but the rewards of Rocco are mighty. Seen originally in the U.S. in a butchered and pointless 90-minute version, *Rocco and His Brothers* has at last been restored to its original length and visual quality. The evocative black-and-white images, most shot on location, were photographed by Giuseppe Rotunno (*The Leopard, Fellini Satyricon, Popeye*); the haunting score is by Nino Rota (*La Dolce Vita, The Godfather*).

NEXT STOP . . . *Ossessione, I Vitelloni, Mean Streets*

1960 175m/B *IT* Alain Delon, Renato Salvatori, Annie Girardot, Katina Paxinou, Claudia Cardinale, Roger Hanin; *D:* Luchino Visconti; *M:* Nino Rota. **VHS, LV, Letterbox** *VDM, CVC, TPV*

THE ROUND-UP
Szegenylegenyek Nehezeletuck
The Hopeless Ones
The Poor Outlaws

In a 19th-century prison camp, Hungarian peasants and herdsman are rounded up, terrorized, and brutally tortured by the Austrian Army following their suspected participation in a popular uprising. Miklós Jancsó's grim and incendiary historical epic was made in 1965, and was clearly intended—despite the period setting—as an outraged cry against the brutalities and injustices of a far more contemporary regime. Jancsó's visual style is elegant, carefully choreographed, and highly stylized, providing a powerful contrast to the savagery depicted on screen. *The Round-Up* created a sensation when screened at the Cannes Festival and later at the New York Film Festival, launching its director into the international spotlight.

NEXT STOP . . . *The Red and the White, Andrei Rublev, Red Sorghum*

1966 90m/B *HU* Janos Gorbe, Tibor Molnar, Andras Kozak; *D:* Miklos Jancso; *W:* Gyula Hernadi. **VHS** *FST, HTV*

THE SACRIFICE

Soviet filmmaker Andrei Tarkovsky's enigmatic, mesmerizing final film was released following his death in 1986. *The Sacrifice* is the story of a retired intellectual (Erland Josephson) living in a magnificent country estate, who learns that the world is about to be destroyed in an inevitable nuclear holocaust. Unable to bear the idea of the loss of his family, he digs deep within himself, past the faith that he lost over the years, and offers himself as a sacrifice to his creator if only his family and their world can be spared. Tarkovsky was aware that he was dying during the preparation and production of this film. Its stylized formalism is so utterly demanding and uncompromising that one can construe that Tarkovsky was not interested in his film's commercial possibilities, but rather wanted to create a last will and testament on film. In this light *The Sacrifice* is a magnificent achievement, though a highly personal one. (If you're unfamiliar with Tarkovsky's work, it might be useful to know, and be forewarned, that he remarked at a film festival in the 1980s that no film that's any good should actually be "enjoyable.") In what seems a nod to the influence of Ingmar Bergman's films on Tarkovsky's career, *The Sacrifice*, in addition to starring Bergman veteran Josephson, is a Swedish language production, and features astonishing color cinematography by Sven Nykvist (*Cries and Whispers, Fanny and Alexander*).

NEXT STOP . . . *Stalker, Solaris, Shame*

1986 (PG) 145m/C *FR SW* Erland Josephson, Susan Fleetwood, Valerie Mairesse, Allan Edwall, Gudrun Gisladottir, Sven Wollter, Filippa Franzen; *D:* Andrei Tarkovsky; *C:* Sven Nykvist. British Academy Awards '87: Best Foreign Film. **VHS, LV, Letterbox** *KIV, TPV*

SALAAM BOMBAY!

This gritty and engaging directorial debut by Mira Nair is a lively, poignant, ultimately heartbreaking portrait of a child who begs in the streets of contemporary Bombay in order to raise enough money to return to his mother's house in the country. Using a largely non-professional cast—selected from the streets and trained in special, improvisational workshops—Nair's simple tale takes on added tragic dimension with each new obstacle and blind alley that the boy runs into. It's soon apparent that *Salaam Bombay!*—one of the most talked-about films at Cannes in 1988—is more than just the compassionate and moving story of one desperate child; the tightly focused microcosm of this boy's world is representative of a larger tragedy that continues to enfold impoverished young people and their families the world over. Academy Award Nominee, Best Foreign Language Film.

NEXT STOP . . . *Mississippi Masala, Phantom India, Aparajito*

1988 114m/C *IN GB* Shafiq Syed, Hansa Vithal, Chanda Sharma, Nana Patekar, Aneeta Kanwar, Sarfuddin Quarassi, Raju Barnad, Raghubir Yadav; *D:* Mira Nair; *W:* Sooni Taraporevala; *C:* Sandi Sissel; *M:* L. Subramaniam. Nominations: Academy Awards '88: Best Foreign-Language Film. **VHS, LV** *NO*

SALO, OR THE 120 DAYS OF SODOM

Sixteen children—eight boys and eight girls—are kidnapped by Fascists in World War II Italy. After arriving at a secluded, palatial villa, the children are bound, stripped, trained like dogs to follow strict orders, and then are systematically subjected to sexual humiliation, sadomasochistic torture, rape, indescribable violence, and finally savage, unbearable mutilation. Based on a novel by the Marquis de Sade (you didn't guess?) and adapted by the director Pier Paolo Pasolini, *Salo* is one of the most genuinely horrifying, deeply disturbing experiences in cinema history. Far from an exploitation film, however, this final film of Pasolini's is, in this viewer's opinion, at least, a deeply felt depiction of what Pasolini believed to be the essence—and the logical, final destination of—the mentality that embraces fascism, that mindset's depraved descent into absolute, unchecked, limitless power. Pasolini cuts right to the chase; first the trains are made to run on time, and then, he convincingly argues, comes *this*. Simultaneously great and unwatchable, *Salo* is a work of art that needs to exist and continue to be available as a part of this century's legacy, but it's also an experience that I could never recommend to another human being. I can acknowledge its importance and perhaps even its brilliance, but to this day it remains the only film in my experience that I genuinely wish I had never seen.

NEXT STOP . . . *Night and Fog, Hotel Terminus: The Life and Times of Klaus Barbie, Shoah*

1975 117m/C *IT* Giorgio Cataldi, Umberto P. Quinavalle, Paolo Bonacelli; *D:* Pier Paolo Pasolini; *C:* Tonino Delli Colli; *M:* Ennio Morricone. **VHS, LV** *FCT, HHE, WBF*

SAMBIZANGA

The groundbreaking first feature by Angolan director Sarah Maldoror is the story of a black resistance leader arrested in 1961 by Portuguese colonialists, at the height of one of the early anti-Portuguese uprisings. Unaware that her husband has been locked up in a brutal and infamous political prison, she embarks on a search that takes her from village to village; her journey illustrates both poignantly and powerfully the effect that the oppressive regime has had on Angolan society, and how the impact of colonialism seeps into the very fabric of a culture, draining it of strength, identity, and purpose. One of the most important and influential African films of the 1970s, *Sambizanga* was co-scripted by Maldoror's husband, who himself was an important force in the Angolan resistance.

NEXT STOP . . . *Xala, Camp de Thiaroye, Burn!*

1972 ?m/C *D:* Sarah Maldoror. *NYR*

SAMURAI REBELLION
Rebellion

In this powerful and hugely entertaining blend of social commentary and rip-roaring swordplay, Toshiro Mifune plays a father liv-

ing under the feudal rules of Japan in the 18th century. But when a neighboring warlord claims that Mifune's daughter-in-law and new grandchild are the warlord's property and demands they be turned over to him, Mifune and his family have no choice but to take a stand against the warlord, the entire feudal system, and hundreds of well-trained samurai. *Rebellion* (originally released in the U.S. as *Samurai Rebellion*) is one of director Masaki Kobayashi's most visually splendid and stirring films. In tone, attitude, and plot, it's a first cousin to the same director's earlier (and equally stunning) *Harakiri,* but it goes further in both its social criticism and in its splendidly choreographed violence. *Rebellion*'s score is by Toru Takemitsu, whose music for Harakiri is part of an excellent, recently issued compilation CD that includes portions of his scores for *Woman in the Dunes, The Face of Another,* and *Dodes 'ka-den.*

NEXT STOP . . . *Yojimbo, If..., The Chant of Jimmie Blacksmith*

1967 121m/B *JP* Toshiro Mifune, Tatsuya Nakadai; *D:* Masaki Kobayashi; *W:* Shinobu Hashimoto. **VHS** *HMV*

SANJURO
Tsubaki Sanjuro

In Akira Kurosawa's witty, jaunty, satiric sequel to his samurai classic *Yojimbo,* a talented but lazy samurai (Toshiro Mifune) comes to the aid of a well-meaning group of naive, bumbling young would-be warriors. Much more of a lark than the director's previous, darkly cynical samurai epics (particularly the pitch-black, hilariously bitter *Yojimbo*), *Sanjuro* nevertheless packs its share of surprises, most notably an unexpected, perfectly timed, outrageously exaggerated gusher of blood signaling the spectacular demise of a key villain. The image is a signature Kurosawa moment—a warning against becoming too complacent or letting our guard down too completely, even in a comic adventure as light as this one. As with the dog carrying the severed hand in *Yojimbo, Sanjuro*'s climactic red gusher ups the ante of movie violence, and would not go

unnoticed by such upcoming filmmakers as Sam Peckinpah, Arthur Penn, Robert Altman, and Brian de Palma. With Takashi Shimura and Tatsuya Nakadai, and a score by *Yojimbo*'s Masaru Sato.

NEXT STOP . . . *The Hidden Fortress, The Good, the Bad, and the Ugly, Little Big Man*

1962 96m/B *JP* Toshiro Mifune, Tatsuya Nakadai; **D:** Akira Kurosawa. **VHS, LV** *NOS, HHT, HEG*

SANSHIRO SUGATA

Akira Kurosawa's assured and entertaining 1943 debut film as a director—based on a popular story about the rivalry between judo and jujitsu—chronicles an eager young student's education and training at the hands of a martial arts master. Kurosawa was 33 when he made *Sanshiro Sugata,* and since it was made during World War II, he wasn't allowed to tackle any story that contained big, possibly controversial moral issues (which would be the only type of film he *would* make after the war). Nevertheless, the action sequences that Kurosawa has staged here are stunningly controlled, and the very human, personal relationship between the young student Sugata and his *sensei* is both charming and affecting. A simultaneously funny and poignant sequence in which Sugata clings tenuously to a post protruding from a pond while all the teachings of his *sensei* come together in his head is one the most memorable and moving scenes in all of Kurosawa's films. (The picture was such a hit that Kurosawa was talked into doing a sequel the following year, but *Sanshiro Sugata Part Two* was a disaster for a number of reasons, and has been happily forgotten.)

NEXT STOP . . . *Stray Dog, Sanjuro, A Touch of Zen*

1943 82m/B *JP* Denjiro Okochi, Yukiko Todoroki, Ranko Hanai, Ryonosuke Tsukigata, Sugisaku Aoyama, Kokuten Kodo, Susumo Fusuita, Takashi Shimura; **D:** Akira Kurosawa. **VHS** *HMV, FCT, COL*

SANSHO THE BAILIFF
The Bailiff
Sansho Dayu

In 11th-century Japan, a woman (Kinuyo Tanaka) decides to go searching for her husband, a former official who was banished from his province years ago. She takes her two children with her on her quest, but soon the family is broken up and sold—the mother into prostitution, the children into slavery in the service of the cruel and ruthless Sansho (Eitaro Shindo). As a decade passes, the mother and her children maintain their hope of being united, despite the cruelty and violence of the system under which they live. Kenji Mizoguchi's adaptation of Ogai Mori's popular novel could have been—in lesser hands—a protracted soap opera. It is, instead, among the most moving and poetic portraits of human courage and suffering the cinema has yet given us. In its narrative structure, visual magnificence, and overwhelmingly poignant cumulative power, Mizoguchi's *Sansho the Bailiff* is one of the world's great cinematic folk legends, and an achievement of absolutely timeless beauty. (Though the film had its American premiere at the First New York Film Festival in 1963, its commercial debut in the U.S. wasn't until 1969, which is when I saw it—if I'm not mistaken—on a staggering double feature with the restored *Lola Montès* at Manhattan's now long-defunct Bleecker Street Cinema.)

NEXT STOP . . . *Life of Oharu, Ugetsu, Princess Yang Kwei Fei*

1954 132m/B *JP* Kinuyo Tanaka, Yoshiaki Hanayagi, Kyoko Kagawa, Eitaro Shindo, Ichiro Sugai; **D:** Kenji Mizoguchi; **W:** Yoshikata Yoda; **M:** Fumio Hayasaka. **VHS, LV** *HMV*

THE SARAGOSSA MANUSCRIPT
Rekopis Znaleziony W Saragossie

This highly ambitious epic yarn is perhaps the best-known of the many rarely screened works of Polish director Wojciech Has. A movie that's become as legendary as the Jan

Potocki novel on which it's based, *The Saragossa Manuscript* is the long and winding tale of a Belgian military officer (Zbigniew Cybulski) who encounters two beautiful princesses while on his travels during the Napoleonic era. Demanding to know if the officer is worthy of their affections, they send him on a fantastic and surrealistic series of adventures during which he is expected to prove that he is up to their challenge. *The Saragossa Manuscript* is three hours long, and since it's something of a shaggy-dog, Baron Munchausen-ish legend at heart, film distributors apparently felt free over the years to chop the picture down into smaller versions. Riding to the restoration rescue came—and even Criswell couldn't have predicted this one—the late Jerry Garcia, whose *favorite* movie this was. Though the Martin Scorsese—assisted full restoration happened too late for Jerry to see, the full-length version of *The Saragossa Manuscript* was screened to a sold-out house at the 1997 New York Film Festival. After two attempted viewings, I have to confess that I've never been able to get into this movie's rhythm for more than an hour or two, but that's just my stodgy temperament, I suppose. It's obviously an original, truly weird creation, and what the hell—it was good enough for Jerry. (Be sure to see it in a letterboxed version, or you'll miss the splendid widescreen compositions.)

NEXT STOP . . . *Orpheus, The Fabulous World of Jules Verne, Kaos*

1965 174m/B *PL* Zbigniew Cybulski, Iga Cembrzynska, Joanna Jedryka, Slawomir Linder; *D:* Wojciech Has; *W:* Tadeusz Kwiatkowski; *M:* Krzysztof Penderecki. **VHS** *FCT*

SATURDAY NIGHT AND SUNDAY MORNING

One of a flood of movies from that period about the bleak lives of the British working class, director Karel Reisz's *Saturday Night and Sunday Morning* is possibly the simplest most affecting of the bunch. The story—about a young machine operator (Albert Finney) who's so stifled by his family, his job,

and his small town that he lives for the night life, booze, and affairs he can work in between punches of the time clock—may well be the inspiration for another disaffected youth movie that was to come along 17 years later, the similarly themed—and titled—*Saturday Night Fever*. And though it doesn't have the Bee Gees, it does have the mesmerizing, raw rhythm of the 23-year-old Albert Finney's performance, a major debut that seems all the more satisfying now, because we know the astonishingly rich career that followed. Finney's performance here made him, according to legend, David Lean's first choice to play the lead in his upcoming *Lawrence of Arabia*. The desert didn't agree with Finney, however, and Peter O'Toole took over, while Finney bit heartily into Tony Richardson's *Tom Jones*. They all lived—and worked—happily ever after.

NEXT STOP . . . *The Entertainer, Two for the Road, Gumshoe*

1960 98m/B *GB* Albert Finney, Rachel Roberts, Shirley Anne Field, Bryan Pringle, Norman Rossington, Hylda Baker, Robert Cowdra, Elsie Wagstaff, Frank Pettitt; *D:* Karel Reisz; *W:* Alan Sillitoe; *C:* Freddie Francis; *M:* John Dankworth. British Academy Awards '60: Best Actress (Roberts), Best Film; National Board of Review Awards '61: Best Actor (Finney). **VHS** *HMK*

SAWDUST AND TINSEL
The Naked Night
Sunset of a Clown
Gycklarnas Afton

This somber 1953 Ingmar Bergman film details the grisly and humiliating experiences of a second-rate traveling circus as it rolls across a barren, desolate Swedish countryside. One of Bergman's darkest and most pessimistic films is built around the central story of the circus's owner (Ake Grönberg) and his relationship with his mistress Anne (Harriet Andersson), whom he tries to dump in order to return to the wife he originally abandoned for a life with the circus. The images in *Sawdust and Tinsel* (also known in the U.S. as *The Naked Night*) are haunting, disturbing, and nightmarish; clowns and a

tawdry theatrical milieu have rarely been depicted with such leering dread. The movie's distinctive look was the result of the first of many collaborations between Bergman and Sven Nykvist, who was called in to work on the picture when Bergman's regular cinematographer was unavailable.

NEXT STOP... *Torment, Through a Glass Darkly, The Silence*

1953 87m/B *SW* Harriet Andersson, Ake Gronberg; *D:* Ingmar Bergman; *W:* Ingmar Bergman. **VHS, LV** *HMV, NLC, FCT*

SCENE OF THE CRIME

A beautiful single mother (Catherine Deneuve), stifled and unfulfilled in her small French town, is sexually reawakened by an escaped convict (Wadeck Stanczak) who's hiding out near her home. Things become considerably more sticky when the convict resorts to physical violence to protect Deneuve's young son, who's already suffering the emotional effects of the nastiness of his parents' divorce. André Téchiné has conceived this psychological thriller with the same multi-layered complexity that has graced his best movies (*Wild Reeds, Ma Saison Préférée*), but here the pieces never quite come together in a meaningful way. *Scene of the Crime* has some of the elements and tone of Hitchcock, but without the clarity of narrative or emotional resonance. The picture is lyrical and lush, but seems to evaporate even while it's being projected.

NEXT STOP... *Le Boucher, Gun Crazy, Mississippi Mermaid*

1987 90m/C *FR* Catherine Deneuve, Danielle Darrieux, Wadeck Stanczak, Victor Lanoux, Nicolas Giraudi, Jean Bousquet, Claire Nebout; *D:* Andre Techine; *W:* Olivier Assayas. **VHS** *KIV, FCT*

SCENES FROM A MARRIAGE

The husband and wife are Marianne (Liv Ullmann) and Johan (Erland Josephson), and their marriage is in trouble long before she finds out about his affair with a younger woman (Bibi Andersson). Word has it that all of Sweden tuned in for director Ingmar Bergman's six-part television series chronicling the disintegration of Marianne and Johan's unhappy household; America got a version of about half that length, which was edited into a single feature film and successfully released to theatres. Even in its shortened form, *Scenes from a Marriage* is realistic and volcanic enough to be alarming, frightening, and familiar. (I have a feeling some couples watched it with hands over their faces, as if it were a slasher film.) As you would expect, the performances are superb and the individual confrontations—which occur with the regularity of rounds in a prizefight—are timed and tweaked to the same nerve-wracking perfection as the couple's Volvo. After its theatrical run, PBS broadcast the complete version in its original six episodes, but regardless of which version you see, it's still a galvanizing, devastating experience. National Society of Film Critics' awards for Best Picture, Screenplay, Actress, and Supporting Actress.

NEXT STOP . . . *Face to Face, The Passion of Anna, Shoot the Moon*

1973 (PG) 168m/C *SW* Liv Ullmann, Erland Josephson, Bibi Andersson, Jan Malmsjo, Anita Wall; **D:** Ingmar Bergman; **W:** Ingmar Bergman; **C:** Sven Nykvist. Golden Globe Awards '75: Best Foreign Film; New York Film Critics Awards '74: Best Actress (Ullmann), Best Screenplay; National Society of Film Critics Awards '74: Best Actress (Ullmann), Best Film, Best Screenplay, Best Supporting Actress (Andersson). **VHS** *HMV*

THE SCENE OF ✓ GREEN PAPAYA
Mui du du Xanh

The debut feature from director Tran Anh Hung is so assured and quietly intoxicating that—despite its deceptively languid pace—it may be nearly over before you realize that more than 90 minutes have passed. Set in Saigon in the 1950s and 1960s, this is the story of a young peasant girl who arrives from the countryside to take a job as servant to a bourgeois family. The day-to-day and minute-by-minute details of her routine are documented with a fluid, poetic intensity that creates a palpable tension seemingly out of thin air. As the child grows into a woman and the dynamics of the film's power structure begin to shift (she finds herself working for a seductive composer in the story's second half), *The Scent of Green Papaya* gradually takes on an inevitable political dimension that is wondrously devoid of stridency. Filmed in rich, dreamlike colors that make you think you've seen a 3-D movie, the film also features one of the most delicately powerful soundtracks in recent memory. (These carefully designed and richly lit images of the Vietnam of the director's memory were—rather astoundingly—filmed on a sound stage in France.) Tran's stunning and auspicious first feature was followed by the equally impressive but very different *Cyclo*.

NEXT STOP . . . *Cyclo, Chocolat, Ramparts of Clay*

1993 104m/C *VT* Tran Nu Yen-Khe, Lu Man San, Truong Thi Loc, Vuong Hoa Hoi; **D:** Tran Anh Hung; **W:** Tran Anh Hung, Patricia Petit; **C:** Benoit Delhomme; **M:** Ton That Tiet. Nominations: Academy Awards '93: Best Foreign-Language Film. **VHS, LV** *COL*

SECRETS AND LIES

Hortense (Marianne Jean-Baptiste) is an optometrist who decides to seek information about her birth mother when her beloved adoptive mother dies. She discovers that she was born to Cynthia (Brenda Blethyn), an anxious and unhappy middle-aged single mother who is different from Hortense in many ways, perhaps the least of which is the color of her skin. Director Mike Leigh's splendid, involving, and generous-spirited *Secrets and Lies* was the deserving Grand Prize Winner at the 1996 Cannes Film Festival, and Brenda Blethyn was the just-as-deserving winner of the Festival's Best Actress Award. Her towering performance is but one element in Leigh's brilliantly cast and eloquently written intimate epic about repressed jeal-

ousies and family secrets, which features sterling work from Phyllis Logan, Claire Rushbrook, and in particular, Leigh veteran Timothy Spall (*Life Is Sweet*). If there's a flaw, it can be found in a too-pat speech near the end that plays more like a defense attorney's summation than the spontaneous outburst it purports to be (though Spall almost brings it off entirely). And while the picture's overall shape seems a bit neater than some of Leigh's earlier work, these are minor quibbles over an overall achievement of enormous power, grace, and intelligence.

NEXT STOP . . . *High Hopes, Life Is Sweet, Career Girls*

1995 (R) 142m/C *GB* Brenda Blethyn, Marianne Jean-Baptiste, Timothy Spall, Claire Rushbrook, Phyllis Logan, Lee Ross, Ron Cook, Leslie Manville, Irene Handl; *Cameos:* Alison Steadman; *D:* Mike Leigh; *W:* Mike Leigh; *C:* Dick Pope; *M:* Andrew Dickson. Australian Film Institute '97: Best Foreign Film; British Academy Awards '96: Best Actress (Blethyn), Best Original Screenplay; Cannes Film Festival '96: Best Actress (Blethyn), Best Film; Golden Globe Awards '97: Best Actress—Drama (Blethyn); Los Angeles Film Critics Association Awards '96: Best Actress (Blethyn), Best Director (Leigh), Best Film; Nominations: Academy Awards '96: Best Actress (Blethyn), Best Director (Leigh), Best Original Screenplay, Best Picture, Best Supporting Actress (Jean-Baptiste); British Academy Awards '96: Best Actor (Spall), Best Director (Leigh), Best Film, Best Supporting Actress (Jean-Baptiste); Cesar Awards '97: Best Foreign Film; Directors Guild of America Awards '96: Best Director (Leigh); Golden Globe Awards '97: Best Film—Drama, Best Supporting Actress (Jean-Baptiste); Independent Spirit Awards '97: Best Foreign Film; Screen Actors Guild Award '96: Best Actress (Blethyn); Writers Guild of America '96: Best Original Screenplay. **VHS** *FXV*

A SELF-MADE HERO
Un Heros Tres Discret
A Very Discreet Hero

When a young Frenchman (Mathieu Kassovitz) misses his chance to become an actual hero in World War II, he ingeniously fabricates an intricate and detailed scenario for himself in which he becomes widely known as a hero of the Resistance. Until the film's surprising ending, he is the only one who's aware that he is a hero who never was. On one level, Jacques Audiard's terrific film is a wry and convincing portrait of a man who's so superb at fashioning a fully formed character out of himself that his life becomes a movie in which he plays a part. By the end, however, *A Self-Made Hero* assumes much larger proportions, as Audiard's tale becomes a vision of a France which has, with the passage of time, convinced itself through a revisionist, collective imagination that its entire population was in the Resistance—even the collaborators. Kassovitz (the director of *Café au Lait* and *Hate*) turns in a smooth, charming and chillingly convincing performance in this clever, clear-eyed, and chillingly honest dark comedy.

NEXT STOP . . . *The Sorrow and the Pity, Lacombe, Lucien, Sunday*

1995 105m/C *FR* Mathieu Kassovitz, Anouk Grinberg, Albert Dupontel, Sandrine Kimberlain, Jean-Louis Trintignant, Nadia Barentin; **D:** Jacques Audiard; **W:** Jacques Audiard, Alain Le Henry; **C:** Jean-Marc Fabre; **M:** Alexandre Desplat. **VHS, Letterbox** *NYF*

✓ SENSO
The Wanton Contessa

In Venice in 1866, as loyal patriots join forces against the occupying Austrian military, an Italian noblewoman (Alida Valli) very nearly betrays her country as a result of her desperate, obsessive love for a cynical, handsome, greedy young Austrian officer (Farley Granger). Luchino Visconti's visually stunning, richly colored spectacle was conceived as a cinematic grand opera complete with huge, sweeping dramatic arcs and sequences of such visual grandeur that they become the equivalent of arias. The film's richly detailed, visually seductive settings draw you in to another world, but Visconti is clear about his purpose—the lust, sloth, and treachery that results from the aristocrats' way of life is a high price to pay for the luxury. *Senso* was an over-the-top experience for

audiences prepared for another neo-realist work like *Ossessione* or *La Terra Trema* from Visconti, and some felt that his new reliance on visual lushness was in itself a form of decadence. The shortened English-language version—released as *The Wanton Countess*—didn't help matters, nor did the florid dialogue supplied for it by Tennessee Williams and Paul Bowles. An even bigger problem now is finding a print (or videocassette) with the fully restored color scheme that Visconti envisioned. But if you can, or if you have the opportunity to see a well-preserved archival copy, *Senso* remains an extraordinarily beautiful and startlingly subversive work of art.

NEXT STOP . . . *Rocco and His Brothers, The Leopard, The Innocent*

1954 125m/C *IT* Alida Valli, Massimo Girotti, Heinz Moog, Farley Granger; **D:** Luchino Visconti; **C:** Robert Krasker. **VHS** *VCD*

✓ SEVEN BEAUTIES
Pasqualino Settebellezze
Pasqualino: Seven Beauties

During World War II, Pasqualino (Giancarlo Giannini), a small-time, low-level Italian *mafioso* with seven ugly sisters (the "seven beauties") to support, finds himself in a German prison camp under the tyrannical control of a grotesquely fat guard (Shirley Stoler). Using his sleazy but highly practical con-man's gifts, Pasqualino does whatever he must to survive his ordeal. *Seven Beauties* was *the* art house phenomenon of 1976, with nationally renowned critics almost literally tripping over each other to be quoted in the *New York Times* ads. One compared *Seven Beauties* to *Citizen Kane,* another to *Tokyo Story.* The latter claimed that the film propelled its director, Lina Wertmüller, into the "highest regions of cinematic art." In fairness, that critic wrote the most intelligently reasoned defense of the film, but I like his review a lot more than the picture. It's been about twenty years since I've seen it, but I recall *Seven Beauties* to be an obnoxious, misogynistic freak show bursting at the seams with self-aggrandizing rationalizations designed to let its viewers off the hook for whatever

"...be witty, sharp and malicious and you'll succeed."

—Bellegarde's (Jean Rochefort) advice to Malavoy (Charles Berling) in *Ridicule.*

they may be feeling guilty over. If that guilt happened to be over using concentration camps for attention-getting slapstick, as Wertmüller has done, well, I'm still not in the mood to let her—or her Pasqualino—off the hook. The film turned out to be Wertmüller's last gasp, however; though she's made films since, none has been "bold" enough to be declared the new *Kane,* or even the new *Seven Beauties.* As for Shirley Stoler, I found her earlier work in *The Honeymoon Killers* and her subsequent stint on *Pee-Wee's Playhouse* more gratifying. Considering the smug obscenity at the core of *Seven Beauties,* it's ironic that Pee-Wee Herman was the one who was fired on a morals charge.

NEXT STOP . . . *Love and Anarchy, Swept Away…, The Honeymoon Killers*

1976 116m/C *IT* Giancarlo Giannini, Fernando Rey, Shirley Stoler, Elena Fiore, Enzo Vitale; *D:* Lina Wertmuller; *W:* Lina Wertmuller; *C:* Tonino Delli Colli. Nominations: Academy Awards '76: Best Actor (Giannini), Best Director (Wertmuller), Best Original Screenplay, Best Foreign-Language Film. **VHS, LV** COL

SEVEN SAMURAI
Shichinin No Samurai
The Magnificent Seven

In 16th-century Japan, a small village is plundered annually by bandits who steal not only the food supply, but some of the farmers' lives and all of their self-respect. After the intimidating raid that opens the film, the farmers reach a breaking point; they're divided, however, between whether to simply hand over the grain and beg for mercy or to make a stand and fight, which will at least lead to a death that will finally put them out of their misery. Yet there is a third way. The farmers recall hearing about a village that was protected by hiring freelance samurai— but since all these poor farmers can offer as pay is a roof and meals, the village elder offers some pointed and practical advice: "Find *hungry* samurai." They do, and much of the greatness of Akira Kurosawa's masterpiece has to do with the not-so-simple reasons for each man's decision to become a part of this makeshift army. With each viewing, this nearly four-hour film seems richer

and more exciting; the personal dramas that drive each of the seven toward the film's final battle are etched with crystalline precision, and the battle scenes themselves are miracles of choreography, design, and power. Much has been written about the film's visual style—the use of telephoto lenses to bring the action shockingly close and the relentless motion that propels everything forward—yet *Seven Samurai* is, above all, a great story: a timeless fable told with an electrifying yet eloquent grace. Toshiro Mifune's Kikuchiyo—buffoonish at first but ultimately tragic—makes the biggest splash among the players; yet the quiet, thoughtful power of Takashi Shimura as Kambei, the first samurai to sign on, provides the film's memorable moral anchor. Remade in the U.S. as *The Magnificent Seven* (which itself spawned a number of sequels), *Seven Samurai*'s debt to the American western is clear. Yet what Kurosawa has fashioned is a wholly original vision of modest men standing against a chaotic universe. It's one of the greatest films ever made. (Cut to various lengths over the years by American distributors, it's now available in the definitive 208 minute version.)

NEXT STOP . . . *The Hidden Fortress, Yojimbo, Harakiri, The Wild Bunch*

1954 204m/B *JP* Toshiro Mifune, Takashi Shimura, Yoshio Inaba, Kuninori Kodo, Ko Kimura, Seiji Miyaguchi, Minoru Chiaki, Daisuke Kato, Bokuzen Hidari; *D:* Akira Kurosawa; *W:* Akira Kurosawa, Shinobu Hashimoto, Hideo Oguni; *C:* Asakazu Nakai; *M:* Fumio Hayasaka. Venice Film Festival '54: Silver Prize; Nominations: Academy Awards '56: Best Art Direction/Set Decoration (B & W), Best Costume Design (B & W). **VHS, LV, DVD** HMV, HHT, CAB

SHADOWS OF FORGOTTEN ANCESTORS
Tini Zabutykh Predkiv
Shadows of Our Ancestors
Shadows of Our Forgotten Ancestors
Wild Horses of Fire

Sergei Parajanov's luminous, electrifying folk tale is set in the Carpathians in the 19th century; it's the story of a peasant who enters into a loveless marriage as a result of a bitter, murderous feud involving his own family and that of the woman he truly loved. This breathtaking Soviet landmark—a one-of-a-kind masterpiece—is one of the most richly poetic and powerful cinematic fables of the last half-century. The picture got Parajanov in trouble with Soviet authorities because of its visually astounding, highly expressionistic avant-garde surface, as well as its deeply rooted lesson about the dangers inherent in mindless obedience to tradition. An international prize-winner, *Shadows of Forgotten Ancestors* was cut by nineteen minutes in its initial American release, and the title was changed to *Wild Horses of Fire,* a reference to one of the most striking images in the film. Though the title was subsequently changed to the almost original *Shadows of Our Forgotten Ancestors,* the nineteen minutes weren't restored until the 1980s, when Parajanov's other suppressed films were rediscovered in the West. (If the amazing score for the film is available on CD, *somebody* please let me know.)

NEXT STOP . . . *The Color of Pomegranates, Emitai, Gabbeh*

1964 99m/C *RU* Ivan Micholaichuk, Larisa Kadochnikova; *D:* Sergei Paradjanov. **VHS** *CVC, AUD, HMV*

SHALL WE DANCE?
Shall We Dansu?

A sense of *deja vu* isn't uncommon at the movies, but there was something weirdly familiar about the Japanese sleeper hit *Shall We Dance?* that kept tugging at my sleeve as it rolled innocuously on. The obvious suspects popped into my head: *Strictly Ballroom*? Yes, but that's obvious. *Saturday Night Fever*? Well, sure—*Sensei Night Fever,* perhaps—though the hero, Mr. Sugiyama (Koji Yakusho), never becomes a master a la John Travolta. No, there was something *else* about this story of an overachieving businessman whose original goal in signing up for dance lessons was to inflate his own ego by getting next to an attractive dancing teacher (Tamiyo Kusakari), but who ends up going beyond such selfish concerns and learns the joy of this new sport and the value of teamwork by working together with a bunch of lovable misfits and...of course! I knew where I'd seen this before! It was *The Mighty Ducks*! And *D2: The Mighty Ducks II* and *D3: The Mighty Ducks* and *The Big Green* and *Little Giants* and every other kids' sports movie about lovable, goofy misfits who come from behind and give up their individual hot-dogging to connect spiritually with team values, thanks to the patience of a well-meaning though personally troubled coach (or sensei) who ends up learning just as much as the kids. More! There's always one goofball class clown who ends up a hero (Naoto Takenaka), one fat kid who everyone roots for in gratuitous reaction shots during the triumphant finish (Hiromasa Taguchi), and an older, wiser teacher (Reiko Kasamura) whose pure joy in the sport is eventually grasped by the younger, life's-dealt-me-unfair-blows coach (Kusakari). And, of course, the hero, who learns that with teamwork—coupled with the art of being a strong leader—comes true victory. *Shall We Dance?* comes complete with several rousing "training" montages set to peppy pop songs—a staple of kids' sports movies—to get everyone ready for the big competition. The football, baseball, soccer, and hockey versions of this come-from-behind fable seem to be enjoyed over and over again by kids, and more power to them. Once I realized what I was seeing, it was just a matter of waiting—and waiting—for the inevitable lesson to be learned, though you might find the going more pleasurable than I did. The performances are this movie's saving grace, and they're wonderful (Kusakari is completely charming). To give the picture its due, when was the last time you saw a movie that featured both Rodgers and Hammerstein *and* The Drifters? If you *have* to have musical montages, at least that's going in style.

NEXT STOP . . . *Strictly Ballroom, Footloose, Cold Fever*

1997 118m/C *JP* Koji Yakusho, Tamiyo Kusakari, Naoto Takenaka, Akira Emoto, Eriko Watanabe, Yu Tokui, Hiromasa Taguchi; *D:* Masayuki Suo; *W:* Masayuki Suo; *C:* Naoke Kayano; *M:* Yoshikazu Suo. National Board of Review Awards '97: Best Foreign Film; Broadcast Film Critics Association Awards '97: Best Foreign Film. **VHS, LV, Closed Caption** *TOU*

S

THE HOUND SALUTES:

GONG LI
China's Shining Star

China's leading young actress, Gong Li has starred in most of the recent Chinese films to become U.S. hits. For Western audiences, she has become something of a guide to the cruelties of Chinese life in this century. She immolates herself in *Ju Dou,* is betrayed by her husband in *Farewell My Concubine* and is driven mad by a husband in *Raise the Red Lantern.* In *To Live,* she ages over 30 years as the matriarch of a family torn apart by political turmoil.

Born December 31, 1965 in Shenyang, China, Gong Li's parents were university professors and therefore targets of the Cultural Revolution, which scattered her family. She still is battling repression. Many of her films were held up by Chinese censors and *To Live* remains unreleased in China.

Gong rose quickly from a shy provincial actress to a voluptuous, radiant international star. Her face has been called "a map of cool insurrection." She has had a professional and romantic partnership with *To Live* director Zhang Yimou since he cast her in the lead in his acclaimed debut, *Red Sorghum,* in 1988. Zhang left his wife and child to be with her. The relationship ended, however, in 1995 after filming *Shanghai Triad.* She married Ooi Hoe-Seong, a businessman, in 1997 and lives in Hong Kong. Spurning most offers from Hollywood, Gong Li continues to be a beacon of hope in her own country. Her latest film is 1997's *Chinese Box,* by director Wayne Wang.

SHAME

Married concert musicians Jan (Max von Sydow) and Eva (Liv Ullmann) flee a violent and terrible civil war by seeking refuge on a small island near their unnamed country's coast. Inevitably, they discover that even on their island the war's impact is felt, and before long their lives become a struggle not only for mere survival, but to maintain a measure of dignity and civilized behavior in an increasingly chaotic, anarchic universe. Along with *Persona* and *Through a Glass Darkly,* *Shame* is one of the great Bergman films of the 1960s, as well as one of the most affecting and terrifying films ever made about the delicate, easily shattered surface of the civilization we take for granted. Though the film was released during the height of the Vietnam War, it's rarely included when anti-war films of the period are cited; perhaps it didn't seem specific enough at the time, or it may simply be too universally unnerving. Whatever the reason, *Shame* remains, twenty years later, a brilliant, unsettling, great work of art. National Society of Film Critics' Awards for Best Picture, Director, and Actress.

NEXT STOP . . . *Grand Illusion, Forbidden Games, Fires on the Plain*

1968 (R) 103m/C *SW* Max von Sydow, Liv Ullmann, Gunnar Bjornstrand, Sigge Furst, Birgitta Valberg, Hans Alfredson, Ingvar Kjellson; *D:* Ingmar Bergman; *W:* Ingmar Bergman; *C:* Sven Nykvist. National Society of Film Critics Awards '68: Best Actress (Ullmann), Best Director (Bergman), Best Film. **VHS** *MGM, BTV*

SHANGHAI TRIAD
Yao a Yao Yao Dao Waipo Qiao

In the corrupt, gangster-run Shanghai of the 1930s, a young rural boy named Shuisheng is brought to town by a gang boss to become the personal servant of the boss's mistress, Bijou (Gong Li). Told primarily though the progressively less innocent eyes of Shuisheng, *Shanghai Triad* begins as an explosion of color, music, and sensual decadence that dramatically presents the Chicago-style mob violence that permeates Bijou's world. An escalating gang war sends Shuisheng and his employers to a remote island hideout, where Shuisheng sees another side of the beautiful and mysterious Bijou, and where he also begins to understand the inevitable consequences awaiting those who either wield or live under absolute power. Though suppressed by Chinese authorities (natch), the haunting and emotionally complex *Shanghai Triad* is clearly director Zhang Yimou's effort at "breaking out" into a wider international market. As mistress and nightclub singer Bijou, Gong Li gets to do some flashy production numbers complete with singing, dancing, and Vegas-style costumes, yet *Shanghai Triad* is no mindless entertainment; it is, in fact, the relentlessly bleak, no-nonsense denouement that both assured the film's status as a highly personal vision and, ironically, may have sabotaged its boxoffice potential. Widely underrated, *Shanghai Triad* is a rich and universally relevant fable about the price of corruption. This was Gong's sixth and final film collaboration with Zhang—their personal and professional relationship concluded during its production.

NEXT STOP . . . *Ju Dou, Raise the Red Lantern, The Godfather*

1995 (R) 108m/C *FR CH* Gong Li, Li Bao-Tian, Li Xuejian, Shun Chun Shusheng, Wang Xiaoxiao Cuihua, Jiang Baoying; **D:** Zhang Yimou; **W:** Bi Feiyu; **C:** Lu Yue; **M:** Zhang Guangtain. Nominations: Academy Awards '95: Best Cinematography; Golden Globe Awards '96: Best Foreign Film. **VHS, LV** *COL*

SHOESHINE

Two young shoeshine boys, struggling to survive in a wartime Rome occupied by American GIs ("shoeshine" is what the street kids of Rome shouted at GIs to make money during the war), become involved in the black mar-

ket and are jailed. Once in prison, their sense of abandonment and hopelessness becomes overwhelming, and even their friendship ultimately falls victim to the ever-widening tragedy that envelops them. In a 1957 interview, director Vittorio de Sica said: "What hit Zavattini (his co-screenwriter) and me at the end of the war was human solitude. The real sense of my films is the search for the human solidarity, the fight against egoism and indifference; in *Shoeshine,* the theme was treated in tragedy...." Indeed. De Sica's heartbreaking 1946 classic is one of the great achievements of neo-realist cinema, though not always ranked quite as highly by critics as the same director's *The Bicycle Thief* or Rossellini's *Open City* and *Paisan*. This may simply be because portions of *Shoeshine* were photographed in studios, rendering the film less "purely" neo-realist than the Rossellini films (I disagree strongly with such simplistic categorizing); or it may simply be because *Shoeshine* has a more conventional overall structure than *The Bicycle Thief.* Where *Shoeshine* is ranked on some abstract, numerical scale, however, ultimately matters a lot less than the fact that it's a great, unforgettable experience—one of the most searingly powerful films ever made about the loss of innocence.

NEXT STOP . . . *The Bicycle Thief, Forbidden Games, Pixote*

1947 90m/B *IT* Franco Interlenghi, Rinaldo Smordoni, Anniello Mele, Bruno Ortensi, Pacifico Astrologo; **D:** Vittorio De Sica; **W:** Cesare Zavattini, Sergio Amidei, Adolfo Franci, C.G. Viola. Nominations: Academy Awards '47: Best Original Screenplay. **VHS** *FCT*

SHOOT THE PIANO PLAYER
Tirez sur le Pianiste
Shoot the Pianist

Former concert pianist Edouard Saroyan (Charles Aznavour), disillusioned, unlucky in love, and world-weary, has changed his name to Charlie Kohler and now plays a very different kind of tune at the piano of an undistinguished Parisian bar. Yet even here he's unable to avoid commitments, and the underworld types he falls in with lead him down an unpredictable and poignantly

tragic path. Based on the novel *Down There* by American crime writer David Goodis, François Truffaut's second feature film marked a total change of pace from his stunning portrait of a shattered childhood, *The 400 Blows*, yet it's every bit as successful. *Shoot the Piano Player* is a risky and audacious blend of genres, in which slapstick asides are successfully juxtaposed with romantic wistfulness, all in the middle of a chase scene. The film may be an affectionate tribute to Hollywood "B" pictures, but Truffaut and his enormously gifted star never lose sight of the pianist's human dimension, and they refuse to allow the inventive cinematic techniques to run away with the movie's heart. A classic of the French New Wave period, it remains one of Truffaut's most exuberant and touching films. (It also marked the beginning of Truffaut's long, fruitful collaboration with composer Georges Delerue.) Be sure to see a letterboxed version.

NEXT STOP . . . *Breathless, Gun Crazy, Mississippi Mermaid*

1962 92m/B *FR* Charles Aznavour, Marie DuBois, Nicole Berger, Michele Mercier, Albert Remy; *D:* Francois Truffaut; *W:* Marcel Moussey, Francois Truffaut; *M:* Georges Delerue. **VHS, LV, Letterbox** *HMV, HHT, WFV*

THE SILENCE
Tystnaden

The third in Ingmar Bergman's so-called "crisis-of-faith" trilogy, *The Silence* is at once the most enigmatic and the most disturbing of the three (the earlier films were *Through a Glass Darkly* and *Winter Light*). The two women in the film, Ester (Ingrid Thulin) and Anna (Gunnel Lindblom) have checked into a large, somewhat decayed hotel in an unnamed city that appears to be at war. The women, who may or may not be sisters, clearly have a sexual relationship. Anna has a young son who curiously wanders the halls of the hotel, but all three of them are voyeurs—Anna's strong, nearly desperate erotic impulses are tied to her desire to see others having sex, and in a famous, frequently censored sequence set in a theatre, she does. Ester is gravely ill, and she quenches her fears and anxieties with alcohol, cigarettes, and masturbation. The two women have filled their lives with activity and are still spiritually impoverished, but by the end of the film, Anna and her son have taken action, which may signal enlightenment and hope. *The Silence* is a dark and rather terrifying portrait of a universe without faith, and its dreamlike structure is both logical and undefined. The picture contains very little dialogue, but it's specific enough to suggest that these women may represent two halves of one soul—and only one of them leaves the hotel at the conclusion. It's a structure that would be echoed in the director's great *Persona* just three years later, and though the issues of communication and faith are raised in that film as well, Bergman's conclusion would be no more certain.

NEXT STOP . . . *Through a Glass Darkly, The Passion of Anna, Shame*

1963 95m/B *SW* Ingrid Thulin, Gunnel Lindstrom, Birger Malmsten; *D:* Ingmar Bergman; *W:* Ingmar Bergman; *C:* Sven Nykvist. **VHS, LV** *HMV, NLC*

THE SILENCES OF THE PALACE
Les Silences du Palais

This elegant and quietly powerful debut film from Tunisian director Moufida Tlatli is the story of Alia (Ghalia Lacroix), whose mother is a servant in the palace of the Bey. Her mother's lifelong role has been to serve food and make her body available for the amusement of Tunisia's royal princes. Alia is now an admired and talented singer in a modern but not altogether different Tunisia; as she reflects on her 1960s childhood years spent observing her mother's humiliation, she must come to terms with the tragic, quiet suffering that marked her mother's life and the tradition of bondage that has not yet vanished from her culture. Winner of a special mention at the 1994 Cannes Film Festival, *The Silences of the Palace* is a sensitive, moving, tough-minded film that's a potent piece of social criticism. Woven into the fabric of the tale are a number of exquisite songs, though at least one musical sequence was removed by the film's American distributor before it played in theatres. The original version's running time is 127 minutes.

NEXT STOP . . . *Ramparts of Clay, The Band and the Bracelet, Mahanagar*

1994 116m/C *FR* Ghalia Lacroix, Amel Hedhili, Kamel Fazaa, Hend Sabri, Najia Overghi; *D:* Moufida Tlatli; *W:* Moufida Tlatli, Nouri Bouzid; *C:* Youssef Ben Youssef. **VHS** *CTL*

SIMON OF THE DESERT
Simon del Desierto

Based loosely on the life of the 15th-century saint Simeon Stylites, Buñuel's dark, 43-minute comedy is the story of Simon (Claudio Brook), who dwells in self-imposed solitude at the top of a 30-foot pillar in the middle of a barren desert in order to devote himself to repentance and contemplation. But Simon discovers that solitude doesn't come easily; below him passes a parade of strange characters, all of whom either want something from him or simply want to toss in their two cents worth. He blesses many and performs miracles for others, including restoring hands to a man who is without them (the man's first use for his miraculous new gift is to slap his kid). In addition, the devil (*Viridiana*'s Silvia Pinal) pops up in a variety of alternately tempting and horrifying forms, all designed to test Simon's resolve, and leading to a witty and surprisingly contemporary apocalyptic conclusion. This is a compact, wickedly funny, thoroughly blasphemous satire that packs an astounding amount of cynicism about the human condition into a remarkably short amount of screen time. This is a striking and hilarious little surrealist classic.

NEXT STOP . . . *Viridiana, Nazarin, The Milky Way*

1966 46m/B Claudio Brook, Silvia Pinal, Enrique Alvarez Felix; *D:* Luis Bunuel; *W:* Luis Bunuel; *C:* Gabriel Figueroa; *M:* Raul Lavista. **VHS** *HTV, HHT, DVT*

A SINGLE GIRL
La Fille Seule

At an early morning meeting over coffee, a young woman tells her boyfriend that she's pregnant and that she's not sure what she's going to do about it. After a bit of tense discussion, she leaves abruptly and walks the short distance to a small Parisian hotel, where she begins her first day on the job as a room service waitress. For the next hour or so, we follow the woman in real time as she brings breakfast to guests' rooms, intruding on couples as they fight or make love, conversing briefly with men on their way to business meetings, arguing with co-workers. The star of *A Single Girl* (*La Fille Seule*), Virginie Ledoyen, is on screen for virtually the entire running time of the movie, and her face is expressive enough to let us in on her reactions to the sights and sounds she encounters, but it's also mysterious enough to keep us from feeling like voyeurs. Indeed, we feel not only privileged to accompany her, but invited, too. Benoit Jacquot's film is every bit as fresh and surprising as his star; he transforms the physically tedious repetition of her delivering orange juice, croissants, and coffee into a surprising voyage of spiritual self-discovery, without letting us see how he pulls it off. *A Single Girl* is a magical balancing act that probably shouldn't work but does; it carries us along with Ledoyen on her rounds, and behind each door she opens is a clue—for both her and us—to the innumerable possibilities of life, and the responsibility we all have in deciding our own fates. It's never strident or preachy, and its simplicity is almost purifying. This is a director—and a star—to keep your eyes on.

NEXT STOP . . . *The Ceremony, The Lacemaker, La Désenchantée*

1996 90m/C *FR* Virginie Ledoyen, Benoit Magimel, Vera Briole, Dominique Valadie; *D:* Benoit Jacquot; *W:* Benoit Jacquot, Jerome Beaujour; *C:* Caroline Champetier; *M:* Kvarteto Mesta Prahi. **VHS** *FXL*

A SLAVE OF LOVE

The enchanting directorial debut from Soviet director Nikita Mikhalkov (*Oblomov, Dark*

1978 94m/C *RU* Elena Solovei, Rodion Nakhapetov, Alexander Kalyagin; *D:* Nikita Mikhalkov; *M:* Eduard Artemyev. **VHS** *COL, AUD*

SMALL CHANGE
L'Agent de Poche

Truffaut followed his dark *The Story of Adele H.* with this deceptively sunny look at the world of children—some who thrive and some who barely survive. *Small Change* was lambasted in many quarters for what was considered sentimentality, yet Truffaut's treatment of children—a subject he began with in *The 400 Blows* and returned to regularly—was based on his belief in their original innocence. The kids in *Small Change,* like Antoine Doinel in *The 400 Blows* and Victor, the boy raised by wolves in *The Wild Child,* are reacting to their environment in the most sensible way possible. These films are about kids as survivors—physically and emotionally. The corruption of some of them is on the horizon, but that wasn't Truffaut's interest. When we discover that one of the quiet "loners" of *Small Change* is being nightmarishly abused in the shack to which he must return every night, Truffaut is less interested in this kid passing abuse on to others than he is in marveling at his capacity for getting himself to school every day in the face of his private holocaust. A child falls from a high apartment window only to get up and giggle, while his mother passes out. "There's no time in life in which people are more resilient than in childhood," notes an observer. Truffaut's own childhood is an example, but *Small Change* is not meant to be a balanced portrait of good and "bad" kids, nor does it need to kill any off to show us that they don't always make it. It's simply a portrait of small, vulnerable human beings doing their best to cope with unfathomable rules and injustice—a liberating, unapologetic celebration of the human capacity for survival.

NEXT STOP . . . *The 400 Blows, The Wild Child, Forbidden Games, Night of the Hunter*

1976 (PG) 104m/C *FR* Geory Desmouceaux, Philippe Goldman, Jean-Francois Stevenin, Chantal Mercier, Claudio Deluca, Frank Deluca, Richard Golfier, Laurent Devlaeminck, Francis Devlaeminck, Sylvie Grezel, Pascale Bruchon, Nicole Felix; *D:* Francois Truffaut; *W:* Fran-

Gunnar Bjornstrand and Ulla Jacobsson play romantic games in Ingmar Bergman's comedy *Smiles of a Summer Night.*

Eyes) is the story of a film crew trying to complete a project they're shooting in the Crimea in 1917, even as the revolution erupts all around them. *A Slave of Love* is a romantic and poignant love story on a number of levels, including the director's nostalgic longing for a time long past. The female star of the film-within-a-film (Elena Solovei) learns all-too-well the reason for the revolution (which she at first finds merely an annoyance), and her heartbreak at the loss of what seems a simpler, gentler era is finally tempered by a stiff dose of reality and replaced by her optimism for a better world in the future. One of the most sophisticated Soviet films of the 1970s, it marked the beginning of Mikhalkov's intriguing career—one which would be marked by both disillusionment and a vastly refined point of view by the era of the 1990s.

NEXT STOP . . . *Burnt by the Sun, Before the Revolution, Anna*

cois Truffaut, Suzanne Schiffman; *C:* Pierre William Glenn; *M:* Maurice Jaubert. **VHS, LV** *MGM, FCT, WAR*

SMILES OF A SUMMER NIGHT
Sommarnattens Leende

Eight Swedish aristocrats become romantically and comically intertwined over a single weekend in Ingmar Bergman's charming, witty, and exceptionally graceful comedy of manners, sex, and blank cartridges. Bergman's elegantly worked-out screenplay keeps all of the simultaneous intrigues and bedroom farces spinning zestily, and keeps the overall effect uplifting, sweet, and sly. It's a razor-sharp, lyrical piece of filmmaking, which seems every bit as knowing and sophisticated today as it did when it was first released. Stephen Sondheim must have thought so too; he used *Smiles of a Summer Night* as the basis for his successful and widely admired Broadway musical *A Little Night Music*. Winner of a special Grand Prize for Comedy at the 1955 Cannes Film Festival.

NEXT STOP . . . *Rules of the Game, Boudu Saved from Drowning, The Magic Flute*

1955 110m/B *SW* Gunnar Bjornstrand, Harriet Andersson, Ulla Jacobsson, Eva Dahlbeck, Jarl Kulle, Margit Carlquist; *D:* Ingmar Bergman; *W:* Ingmar Bergman. **VHS, LV** *HMV, DVT, CRC*

THE SOFT SKIN
Le Peau Douce
Silken Skin

Truffaut's first feature following the worldwide triumph of his *Jules and Jim* was a decided flop in the United States. It may have been that, following *Jules and Jim*'s perceived assault on bourgeois values (represented by that film's central *ménage-à-trois*), this seemingly conventional tale of a married man's affair with an airline stewardess came across as routine. Whatever the reason, it's unfair. *The Soft Skin* remains the most shamefully and unjustly neglected of Truffaut's early features—it's a darkly funny, powerfully unnerving story of how repressed passion can sud-

denly surface in exactly the wrong time and place, with disastrous results. Though it begins as a seductive, erotic male fantasy, *The Soft Skin* gradually and inexorably evolves into the ultimate nightmare of anyone who's ever had or contemplated an affair—it's a logical response to anyone who's ever acted on impulse while rhetorically asking: "What's the worst that can happen?" Jean Desailly is the clueless, middleaged husband whose rediscovered passion sets the plot in motion; and Nelly Benedetti is his less-than-sympathetic wife. The late Françoise Dorleac plays the object of Desailly's obsession; the combination of her casual compliance and her chilly, unattainable beauty prove irresistibly erotic to the bourgeois, intellectual husband. (The immensely talented Dorleac, who died in an accident four years later, was the sister of Catherine Deneuve. Without meaning to slight one of the most beautiful women alive, one can get an idea of Dorleac's beauty by the fact that some who knew both sisters referred to Françoise as "the pretty one.")

NEXT STOP . . . *The Blue Angel, Mississippi Mermaid, Fatal Attraction, Damage*

1964 120m/B *FR* Jean Desailly, Nelly Benedetti, Francoise Dorleac, Daniel Ceccaldi; *D:* Francois Truffaut; *W:* Francois Truffaut, Jean-Louis Richard; *C:* Raoul Coutard; *M:* Georges Delerue. **VHS, LV** *HMV, FOX*

SOLARIS

Near the planet Solaris, a space station orbits as the cosmonauts inside try to understand why they've been having emotionally overwhelming visions of their earlier lives on Earth. They discover that the ocean of Solaris is actually a vast, intelligent entity that is affecting their memories and thought processes in life-changing ways. The brilliant Soviet filmmaker Andrei Tarkovsky tried to borrow chapters from Stanley Kubrick and Jean-Luc Godard in this adaptation of Stanislaw Lem's novel, but the result is hampered by the movie's dirge-like pacing and its generally shoddy technical effects. (The plot isn't all that fresh, either; just as *Alien* was a high-tech version of the 1956 *It! The Terror from Beyond Space, Solaris* seems an intellectual-

"The best lives are invented, someone said that. I think it was me."

—Albert (Mathieu Kassovitz) in *A Self-Made Hero.*

ized, art house retread of Sid Pink's 1961 cheese fest *Journey to the Seventh Planet.*) There are exquisite sequences and unforgettable images in *Solaris,* but it never achieves the cumulative power of such extraordinary—and thematically similar—Tarkovsky works as *Stalker, Nostalghia,* or *The Sacrifice.* Brutally cut by almost an hour when first released in the U.S., *Solaris* has been restored to its original, nearly three-hour length and released on video in a widescreen, letterbox format. Grand Jury Prize, Cannes Film Festival.

NEXT STOP . . . *2001: A Space Odyssey, Stalker, Mother and Son*

1972 167m/C *RU* Donatas Banionis, Natalya Bondarchuk; **D:** Andrei Tarkovsky; **M:** Eduard Artemyev. Cannes Film Festival '72: Grand Jury Prize. **VHS, LV, Letterbox** *FXL, FCT*

THE SORROW AND THE PITY

Marcel Ophüls's great 1971 *The Sorrow and the Pity* is the result of the questioning of a widely held belief—that every man, woman, and child who lived in Nazi-occupied France either joined the Resistance or helped it. Ophüls turned his attention to a single French town—Clermont-Ferrand—and interviewed those residents who remembered and would speak, as well as government officials, writers, artists, and a stray German veteran or two. What Ophüls found has rewritten modern history, and changed forever the way we think of and understand the issues of collaboration and resistance, specifically as they apply to one particular nation at one particular moment in time. *The Sorrow and the Pity* is four-and-a-half hours long, and unfolds at the breathless pace of a great thriller. In fact, it *is* a great thriller. We learn bits and pieces about the way people behaved and how they rationalized their behavior; and our assimilation of these facts, each and cumulatively, results in a staggeringly clear and powerful portrait of how real human beings behaved in the most demanding of circumstances. Needless to say, not everyone was a hero. But Ophüls's intelligence and craft invites us to continually try to place ourselves in the positions of these witnesses; the more we hear the more we try to imagine how *we* would have behaved—what *we* would have done under the same circumstances. *The Sorrow and the Pity* opens our eyes and our minds in ways that predigested, pat documentaries cannot. It leaves us with more questions than we had when we went in, but feeling more wide awake—and more aware of the power and responsibility we each possess—than we have ever been. Exhilarating in its impact even though so much of what it shows us is appalling, *The Sorrow and the Pity* takes its place among the most valuable achievements in the histories of cinema and journalism. (As a gauge of the "infallibility" of the Academy Awards, you might want to know that *The Sorrow and the Pity* lost the Best Documentary award to *The Hellstrom Chronicle,* a science-fiction movie about bugs that was completely scripted and staged—a "mockumentary." Bet you haven't heard of it lately.)

NEXT STOP . . . *The Memory of Justice, Hotel Terminus: The Life and Times of Klaus Barbie, The Troubles We've Seen*

1971 265m/B *FR* **D:** Marcel Ophuls. **VHS** *COL, OM*

A SPECIAL DAY
Una Giornata Speciale
The Great Day

The day of a huge rally celebrating Hitler's visit to Rome in 1939 serves as the backdrop for an affair between a weary housewife (Sophia Loren) and a lonely, gay radio announcer (Marcello Mastroianni). Marcello and Sophia give it their all, but Ettore Scola's film never ignites. There's a predetermined, schematic feel to the proceedings, which is all the more disappointing—and surprising—considering the many exceptional, spontaneous, lively films Scola has fashioned out of material less compelling than the maudlin *A Special Day.* Sitting through this movie is like being forced to eat your vegetables; you know that it's good for you—like one of Stanley Kramer's plodding, well-meaning, "liberal" fifties pictures—but it's hard to get it all down without occasionally gagging.

NEXT STOP . . . *We All Loved Each Other So Much, Passione d'Amoré, The Object of My Affection*

1977 105m/C *IT* Sophia Loren, Marcello Mastroianni, John Vernon, Francoise Berd; *D:* Ettore Scola; *W:* Ettore Scola, Ruggero Maccari, Maurizio Costanzo; *C:* Pasquale De Santis; *M:* Armando Travaioli. Golden Globe Awards '78: Best Foreign Film; Nominations: Academy Awards '77: Best Actor (Mastroianni), Best Foreign-Language Film. **VHS, LV, Letterbox** *COL*

THE SPIDER'S ✓ STRATAGEM

Thirty years after his father's murder by fascists, a young man (Giulio Brogi) returns to that small Italian town to learn why the killing took place. When the townspeople resist his inquiry, he becomes trapped in a mysterious and ever-widening web where history and its convenient revision exert a stranglehold on the truth. (That truth, by the way, turns out to be stranger than you will guess.) Based on the short story "The Theme of the Traitor and the Hero" by Jorge Luis Borges, Bernardo Bertolucci's *The Spider's Stratagem* is an ingeniously worked-out mystery/thriller laced with darkly comic psychological and political undertones. It's one of Bertolucci's most visually stunning achievements as well, featuring intoxicatingly lush color cinematography by the legendary Vittorio Storaro (*Last Tango in Paris*, *Apocalypse Now*). A find.

NEXT STOP . . . *Luna, Ulysses' Gaze, Birthplace*

1970 97m/C *IT* Giulio Brogi, Alida Valli; *D:* Bernardo Bertolucci; *W:* Bernardo Bertolucci. **VHS** *NYF, FCT, AUD*

SPIES
Spione

A master criminal (Rudolph Klein-Rogge) poses as a reputable, well-recognized financier in order to gain access to secret government plans and instigate worldwide economic chaos. Fritz Lang's lively, highly enjoyable 1928 thriller gives Klein-Rogge—the mad scientist of *Metropolis* and the fiendish mastermind of *Dr. Mabuse*—another opportunity to place all of civilization in peril.

Rolling all the thrills, chases, and stunts of a 13-episode serial into one sleek, compact, 90-minute entertainment, Lang's breathless adventure is packed with seductive female spies, ingenious traps, and breathtaking, expressionist sets and scenery. *Spies* remains one of the most suspenseful, inventive, and purely enjoyable thrillers of the silent era.

NEXT STOP . . . *Dr. Mabuse, M, The 39 Steps*

1928 88m/B *GE* Rudolf Klein-Rogge, Lupu Pick, Fritz Rasp, Gerda Maurus, Willy Fritsch; *D:* Fritz Lang. **VHS, LV** *GPV, NOS, VYY*

SPIRIT OF THE BEEHIVE
El Espiritu de la Colmena

A lonely young Spanish girl named Ana (Ana Torrent of *Cria*) becomes enthralled and eventually obsessed by a Saturday matinee screening of the 1931 Boris Karloff version of *Frankenstein*. Encouraged by her older sister Isabel (Isabel Telería), intrigued by the creature's emotional vulnerability, and completely convinced by the illusion of cinema, Ana embarks on a quest to locate the monster somewhere in the Spanish countryside. The acclaimed 1973 debut feature from Spain's Victor Erice is both an insightful political allegory and a haunting parable about the loneliness and longings of childhood. Torrent, an extraordinary young actress with huge, expressive eyes, is perfectly cast as the child searching for her place in the world.

NEXT STOP . . . *Cria, The White Balloon, Welcome to the Dollhouse*

1973 95m/C *SP* Fernando Gomez, Teresa Gimpera, Ana Torrent, Isabel Telleria, Laly Soldevilla; *D:* Victor Erice; *W:* Victor Erice; *C:* Luis Cuadrado; *M:* Luis De Pablo. **VHS, LV** *HMV, CVC, TPV*

STALKER

A meteorite crashing to Earth has created a desolate wasteland area known as the Zone. The Zone is forbidden to anyone except special guides known as Stalkers. Soviet director Andrei Tarkovsky's epic metaphysical fantasy focuses on three Stalkers who enter the Zone, searching for "the room," a spot at the Zone's center that supposedly has the power to reveal and materialize the deepest of human fantasies. Working with themes similar to his science-fiction epic *Solaris,* Tarkovsky here creates a disorienting and powerfully hypnotic visual experience that makes great demands on the patience of viewers, but provides sights and sounds vastly different from virtually any film you've ever seen. What it all adds up to is up to you; in a sense, the film itself provides the same opportunity for the projection of our own fantasies as does "the room" at the Zone's center.

NEXT STOP . . . *Solaris, Nostalghia, La Jetée*

1979 160m/C *RU* Alexander Kaidanovsky, Nikolai Grinko, Anatoli Solonitzin, Alice Freindlikh; *D:* Andrei Tarkovsky; *M:* Eduard Artemyev. **VHS** *FXL, FCT*

STATE OF SIEGE
Etat de Siege

Costa-Gavras—arguably the original Oliver Stone—directed this rip-snorting, fact-based conspiracy thriller about the events surrounding the death of U.S. Agency for International Development employee Daniel Mitrone (here called Philip Michael Santore and played by Yves Montand), suspected to be involved in the torture and murder of Uruguayan dissidents in the 1960s. This is one of the director's more complex and multi-leveled political powerhouses, but unless you know the players, you may find it difficult to keep score. (Names have been changed, characters have been invented and the country is unnamed.) Nevertheless, *State of Siege* is a skillfully constructed and persuasive combination of reporting and propaganda, even when its bombast overpowers its intended thoughtfulness. Much of the skilled production team and cast of *Z* were united here, including producer/performer Jacques Perrin, editor Françoise Bonnot, and composer Mikis Theodorakis.

NEXT STOP . . . *Z, Missing, The Battle of Chile*

1973 119m/C *FR* Yves Montand, Renato Salvatori, O.E. Hasse, Jacques Perrin; *D:* Constantin Costa-Gavras. **VHS, LV** *COL*

THE STATIONMASTER'S WIFE

In Weimar Germany, a provincial stationmaster's wife (Elisabeth Trissenaar) expresses her boredom with her ineffectual, servile husband (Kurt Raab) by entering into a series of shallow sexual affairs. Both a stylized portrait of dead-end marital despair and a thinly veiled political parable about a Germany too hedonistically self-absorbed to grasp the dangers fast approaching, Rainer Werner Fassbinder's *The Stationmaster's Wife* was originally filmed as a three-and-a-half hour miniseries for German television (the original title was *Bolweiser,* the stationmaster's name), and was edited into its current 111-minute length for international theatrical release. Though overall it's one of Fassbinder's less compelling chamber-pieces, Trissenaar's full-bodied, sensation-hungry Hanni and Raab's frustrated, sexually subservient husband are indisputably potent characterizations, and the cinematography by Michael Ballhaus (*Goodfellas, The Fabulous Baker Boys*) is magical.

NEXT STOP . . . *The Bitter Tears of Petra von Kant, Berlin Alexanderplatz, The Blue Angel*

1977 111m/C *GE* Elisabeth Trissenaar, Kurt Raab, Gustal Bayrhammer, Bernard Helfrich, Udo Kier, Volker Spengler; *D:* Rainer Werner Fassbinder; *W:* Rainer Werner Fassbinder; *C:* Michael Ballhaus; *M:* Peer Raben. **VHS** *NYF, FCT*

THE STOLEN CHILDREN
Il Ladro di Bambini

Every so often a picture just seems to loom up out of nowhere and—totally and unexpectedly—overwhelms you. In 1992, that film, for me at least, was Gianni Amelio's *The Stolen Children* (*Il Ladro di Bambini*), the saga of a shy and sensitive *carabiniere* (Enrico Lo Verso) and the two children he's been assigned to escort from Milan to a Sicilian orphanage. The children—an emotionally battered 11-year old girl who was forced into prostitution by her now-imprisoned mother, and the girl's 9-year-old brother—become more attached to the gentle *carabiniere* each day, and more confused about the nightmare of their past. Amelio's delicate, graceful handling of this heartbreaking material seems a direct descendent of the great neo-realist classics such as de Sica's *The Bicycle Thief,* but with a haunting and ethereal quality all its own. The same issues of guilt, innocence, and human responsibility are present here as they were in Italy's post-war films, and much of *The Stolen Children*'s staggering power comes from the fact that despite the passage of years, surprisingly little about the human condition has changed for the better. This is a great, unforgettable experience. Grand Jury Prize, Cannes Film Festival.

NEXT STOP . . . *The Bicycle Thief, Shoeshine, Open Doors*

1992 108m/C *IT* Enrico Lo Verso, Valentina Scalici, Giuseppe Ieracitano, Florence Darel, Marina Golovine, Fabio Alessandrini; *D:* Gianni Amelio; *W:* Gianni Amelio, Sandro Petraglia, Stefano Rulli; *M:* Franco Piersanti. Cannes Film Festival '92: Grand Jury Prize. **VHS** *NYR*

STOLEN KISSES
Baisers Voles

Antoine Doinel, the troubled 13-year-old of François Truffaut's *The 400 Blows,* had already made a second screen appearance when this full-fledged sequel—the third Doinel film—was released. (He appeared as a love-struck teenager in the *Antoine and Colette* segment of the 1962 omnibus film *Love at Twenty.*) *Stolen Kisses* begins with Antoine's discharge from the army under questionable circumstances (mirroring Truffaut's own military experience) and follows his exploits as a rookie private detective. Infatuated as he is with his girlfriend (Claude Jade), Antoine is nevertheless not immune to the charms of an attractive older woman (Delphine Seyrig) who happens to be married to the store owner who's hired Antoine to do some undercover work. A genuinely sweet film that is especially reassuring in light of the many possibilities that awaited Antoine at the end of *The 400 Blows, Stolen Kisses* nevertheless is marked by a melancholy, resigned

tone that is underscored by the wistful Charles Trenet tune that closes the film. That vaguely unsettled quality is no accident: 1968 was a tumultuous year in France—as in much of the rest of the world, of course—and the furor over the French Ministry of Culture's short-lived removal of Henri Langlois, the beloved head of the Cinémathèque Française, from his post was a galvanizing event for French filmmakers and critics. This crisis took place during the filming of *Stolen Kisses,* which is why Truffaut dedicated it to the Cinémathèque, complete with an image of its then-padlocked gates.

NEXT STOP . . . *The 400 Blows, Love at Twenty, Bed and Board, Love on the Run*

1968 90m/C *FR* Jean-Pierre Leaud, Delphine Seyrig, Michel Lonsdale, Claude Jade; *D:* Francois Truffaut; *W:* Francois Truffaut, Claude de Givray; *C:* Denys Clerval; *M:* Antoine Duhamel. National Society of Film Critics Awards '69: Best Director (Truffaut); Nominations: Academy Awards '68: Best Foreign-Language Film. **VHS** *COL*

STORM OVER ASIA
The Heir to Genghis Khan

In Central Asia in 1920, a wounded Mongolian trapper is discovered to be a descendent of Genghis Khan, and he is placed in the position of puppet emperor of a British-controlled Mongolian province. As he regains his health, the evil designs of the oppressive, would-be colonialist rulers—in league with treacherous White troops—becomes clear to him, and he turns his anger and his soldiers against them in a great "storm" of Mongolian military might. Soviet filmmaking pioneer Vsevolod Pudovkin created an overwhelming, exhilarating visual spectacle in his 1928 silent masterpiece *Storm over Asia.* Using actual locations and stunning, documentary-like photography, Pudovkin assembled the film using the sophisticated, multiple-story, cross-cutting techniques that seem bold and breathtaking even today.

NEXT STOP . . . *Mother (1926), Strike, Kagemusha*

1928 70m/B *RU* I. Inkizhinov, Valeri Inkizinov, A. Christiakov, A. Dedinstev, V. Tzoppi, Paulina Belinskaya; *D:* Vsevolod Pudovkin. **VHS** *IHF, FST, VYY*

S

THE HOUND SALUTES:

ISABELLE ADJANI
Controversial Leading Lady of French Film

Tempestuous Isabelle Adjani loves to smash expectations. "I am not here to walk in the average footsteps of an average sensibility," she said once. "I am here to disturb, to destabilize, to disarm the invincibles, the living dead, so that they can let themselves be swept away by the best and most lyrical parts of themselves."

On and offscreen, Adjani has been disturbing and disarming. While still a teenager, she swept away audiences as the romantically obsessed heroine of François Truffaut's *The Story of Adele H.* Critic Pauline Kael observed: "She hardly seems to be doing anything, yet you can't take your eyes off her."

Adjani spurned marketable roles, preferring bizarre or artsy parts for maverick directors such as Roman Polanski (*The Tenant*), Werner Herzog (*Nosferatu the Vampyre*), Walter Hill (*The Driver*), and Andrzej Zulawsky (*Possession,* in which she played a housewife who mates with her demon child.) To film the life of tortured sculptress Camille Claudel, she started her own production company, picked Bruno Nuytten as director and Gérard Depardieu as co-star, co-wrote the screenplay, and played the title role.

Her career started and has stayed controversial. To film *Adele H,* Adjani broke a contract with the prestigious Comedie-Francaise, enraging theater patrons. She stormed off the set of Jean-Luc Godard's *Carmen,* blasting the revered director. She shocked French fans by revealing her father was Algerian, not Turkish. Accepting a César (the French equivalent of Oscar) for *Camille Claudel,* she read a passage from Salman Rushdie's banned Satanic Verses. But her career has also been successful. She has been nominated for two Best Actress Oscars, one for *Camille Claudel* and one for *The Story of Adele H.* She also won a Cesar in 1995 for Best Actress in *Queen Margot.*

Her personal life has been stormy too. In 1979, she had a child, Barnabe Said, with Nuytten. Later, she had an affair with Warren Beatty. Her recent beau has been Daniel Day-Lewis; they had a son, Gabriel-Kane in 1995.

THE STORY OF ✓ ADELE H.
L'Histoire d'Adele H.

François Truffaut called his 1975 film *The Story of Adele H.* "a musical composition for a solo instrument," though it's impossible to discern whether that instrument is the character (Victor Hugo's daughter Adele) or the actress who plays her (Isabelle Adjani). In the final analysis it doesn't matter, because the seamless perfection of Truffaut's masterpiece extends to every aspect of this transporting film, from the dark, terrifyingly beautiful images of cinematographer Nestor Almendros to the tight, brilliant screenplay (surprisingly, the result of a collaboration by four writers), to the overwhelmingly potent score by Maurice Jaubert, whose death 35 years earlier didn't stop Truffaut from reworking his music so triumphantly. (Jaubert wrote the score for Jean Vigo's supremely romantic *L'Atalante*.) The story, which begins in Halifax in 1863, is simple enough on the surface: Adele Hugo has fallen in love with a young lieutenant (Bruce Robinson) and decides to recapture his love *by whatever means necessary*. She keeps a journal (as she did in life—it's the basis for the screenplay) and as her obsession deepens into a bottomless madness, the burning passion that pours out of Adele is eventually not even directed at the lieutenant—who becomes a kind of erotic "McGuffin"—but becomes an overwhelming and all-encompassing end in itself. At least one critic has called Adele's final delusional moments "triumphant," and she's right. I would extend that word to describe every aspect of *The Story of Adele H.*, and at the same time I hope that in the near future a restored version—approximating Almendros's original color scheme—will replace the visually muddy, unsatisfactory video version currently in release.

NEXT STOP . . . *Vertigo, The Searchers, The Green Room, Breaking the Waves*

1975 (PG) 97m/C *FR* Isabelle Adjani, Bruce Robinson, Sylvia Marriott; *D:* Francois Truffaut; *W:* Suzanne Schiffman, Jean Gruault; *C:* Nestor Almendros; *M:* Maurice Jaubert. National Board of Review Awards '75: Best Actress (Adjani); New York Film Critics Awards '75: Best Actress (Adjani), Best Screenplay; National Society of Film Critics Awards '75: Best Actress (Adjani); Nominations: Academy Awards '75: Best Actress (Adjani). **VHS, LV** *MGM, FCT*

THE STORY OF QIU JU
Qiu Ju Da Guansi
Qiu Ju Goes to Court

The pregnant Qiu Ju's husband is assaulted and injured by the head of their rural Chinese village. Outraged and angered at the lack of any justice or compensation for the injury, the determined, quietly obsessive Qiu Ju (a nearly unrecognizable Gong Li) slowly climbs up the labyrinthine Chinese administrative ladder from official to higher official as she insistently seeks redress. A novel called *The Wan Family's Lawsuit* was the basis for the film, but China's great Zhang Yimou has created a work that has the unmistakable imprint of his own humanity, humor, and eloquence. The stunning Gong's peasant outfit and her labored, waddling gait mark a new kind of character for her, and she brings the sweet, sympathetic performance off with total control. The movie marks a new look for Zhang as well; the formal, richly stylized images we're used to in films like *Raise the Red Lantern* are here replaced by a near-documentary, hand-held visual design that is absolutely right for this small story, which by its conclusion has assumed the much larger proportions of a classic fable. Venice Film Festival Award for Best Actress.

NEXT STOP . . . *The Horse Thief, Red Sorghum, Ermo*

1991 (PG) 100m/C *CH* Gong Li, Lei Lao Sheng, Liu Pei Qu, Ge Zhi Jun, Ye Jun, Yang Liu Xia, Zhu Qanging, Cui Luowen, Yank Huiquin, Wang Jianfa, Lin Zi; *D:* Zhang Yimou; *W:* Liu Heng; *C:* Chi Xiaonin, Yu Xaioqun; *M:* Zhao Jiping. National Society of Film Critics Awards '93: Best Foreign Film; Venice Film Festival '92: Best Actress (Li), Best Film; Nominations: Independent Spirit Awards '94: Best Foreign Film. **VHS, LV** *COL*

THE STORY OF WOMEN
Une Affaire de Femmes

One of the last women to be guillotined in France was Marie Latour, whose hand-to-mouth existence was supplemented with a little extra cash when she began performing illegal abortions in occupied France during World War II. Her story is the centerpiece of Claude Chabrol's dark and disturbing *The Story of Women*, which gives us a Marie (Isabelle Huppert) who is neither hero nor villain, but does what she does out of her will to survive. She goes about her work with the same grim, matter-of-factness that characterizes the sex she shares with her lover (she can no longer muster any interest in making love to her husband), and it's only a matter of time before the French police—puppets of the Gestapo—arrest, "try," and execute her with that same emotionless determination; everyone here is simply a worker doing a job.

S

With his gray, bleak, cold-as-ice vision of a world that has learned to function without the concept of moral responsibility, Chabrol asks not only if we are any more entitled to pass judgment on this woman than the Nazis were, but begs a larger question; at what point do survival and collaboration become indistinguishable? This rich, multi-leveled portrait of infectious, festering hypocrisy wouldn't have nearly the same impact without the calm, rigorous, terrifyingly glacial performance of the remarkable Isabelle Huppert.

NEXT STOP . . . *Violette, Le Boucher, The Sorrow and the Pity, Shadow of a Doubt*

1988 110m/C *FR* Isabelle Huppert, Francois Cluzet, Marie Trintignant, Nils Tavernier, Louis Ducreux; *D:* Claude Chabrol; *W:* Claude Chabrol, Colo Tavernier O'Hagan; *C:* Jean Rabier; *M:* Matthieu Chabrol. Los Angeles Film Critics Association Awards '89: Best Foreign Film; New York Film Critics Awards '89: Best For-

eign Film; Venice Film Festival '88: Best Actress (Huppert). **VHS** *NYF*

STRAWBERRY AND CHOCOLATE
Fresa y Chocolate

Sex, politics, and friendship set in 1979 Havana. University student David (Vladimir Cruz) is slouching morosely in a cafe eating chocolate ice cream when he's eyed by the older, educated, gay, strawberry-eating Diego (Jorge Perugorria), who persuades David to visit him at his apartment. Resolutely heterosexual (and just as committedly communist), David is appalled both by David's sexuality and his "subversive" politics. Gradually, David is seduced by both friendship and ideas into questioning the harsh policies of the existing regime, including its homophobia. Based on the short story "The Wolf, the Forest, and the

New Man" by co-screenwriter Senel Paz, Tomás Gutiérrez Alea's *Strawberry and Chocolate* is a witty, often hilarious, profoundly humane entertainment, which serves as both a political parable and a deeply touching story of friendship in the face of differences. Alea's illness forced him to complete the film with the aid of an associate, but it's every inch the work of the brilliant and probing creator of *Memories of Underdevelopment* and *Death of a Bureaucrat.*

NEXT STOP . . . *Memories of Underdevelopment, Guantanamera!, Kiss of the Spider Woman*

1993 (R) 110m/C *CU* Jorge Perugorria, Vladimir Cruz, Mirta Ibarra, Francisco Gattorno, Jorge Angelino, Marilyn Solaya; *D:* Tomas Gutierrez Alea, Juan Carlos Tabio; *W:* Tomas Gutierrez Alea, Senel Paz; *C:* Mario Garcia Joya; *M:* Jose Maria Vitier. Nominations: Academy Awards '94: Best Foreign-Language Film. **VHS** *TOU*

STRAY DOG

This tense, smart, assured early feature from Akira Kurosawa is the story of a rookie police detective (Toshiro Mifune) whose service revolver is plucked from his pocket while he's riding on a bus. Soon after its theft, he comes to the horrifying realization that his gun being used to commit a series of murders. Together with his seasoned, cynical older partner (Takashi Shimura), Mifune methodically and obsessively hunts down the "stray dog" who's stolen the deadly weapon; in the process, he learns more than he bargained for about guilt, responsibility, and justice. A powerful, tough, gripping detective picture that's also a fascinating portrait of postwar Japan, the 1949 *Stray Dog* was the last film Kurosawa made prior to achieving worldwide fame the following year with his brilliant *Rashomon.*

NEXT STOP . . . *Drunken Angel, High & Low, Blue Steel*

1949 122m/B *JP* Toshiro Mifune, Takashi Shimura, Isao Kimura; *D:* Akira Kurosawa. **VHS** *HMV, COL*

STRIKE

Sergei M. Eisenstein's 1924 debut film is an audacious and astonishing depiction of a pre-revolutionary (1912) factory strike and the resulting violent clash between strikers and the Czar's brutal military forces. *Strike* is an electrifying film in which Eisenstein first demonstrated the power of his theories of film editing, which he characterized as "montage." Perhaps more than any other filmmaker of the silent era, Eisenstein grasped the rhythmic power that could be unleashed in the editing process, and in *Strike* he masterfully displays his ability to seemingly expand time, creating entire dramatic structures within actions that would normally take only seconds of screen time. He orchestrates the violence like a conductor after suspensefully building up to it, and he provides full, operatic design within confrontations that would otherwise seem mere chaos. His ability to create silent "music" with these dynamic, juxtaposed images would fully flower in his next film, the 1925 *The Battleship Potemkin.* But *Strike,* which resulted from Eisenstein's frustrations with the limitations of the stage, is still a breathtaking eruption of artistry and inspiration that seems to leap to the screen directly from the mind of its brilliant creator. (A superbly mastered version of *Strike* is contained on a multi-film laserdisc of Soviet classics; the set also includes Dziga Vertov's *The Man with the Movie Camera,* accompanied by the Alloy Orchestra's stunning original score.)

NEXT STOP . . . *The Battleship Potemkin, Ten Days That Shook the World, Intolerance*

1924 78m/B *RU D:* Sergei Eisenstein. **VHS** *NOS, KIV, IHF*

STROSZEK

Three unlikely friends, all misfits to varying degrees and all fed up with the brutal and uncaring Berlin neighborhood they live in, decide to chuck it all for a shot at the American Dream in rural Wisconsin. Eva Mattes (*Céleste*) stars with Clemens Scheitz and the enigmatic Bruno S. (*The Mystery of Kaspar Hauser*) in Werner Herzog's bizarre, hilarious, and tragic portrait of a culture clash so extreme that it seems positively interplanetary. For every easy laugh and cheap shot in *Stroszek*—and there are more than a few— there is an equally strange and wonderful

S

"Bad luck isn't brought by broken mirrors, but by broken minds."

—Dr. Mandel (Udo Kier) in *Suspiria.*

SOPHIE MARCEAU

Award-Winning Beauty

Sophie Marceau got into the entertainment business so that she could avoid unloading one more truck for her parents' cafe in the Paris suburbs. Born November 17, 1966 in Paris as Sophie Maupu, Marceau at 13 answered an advertisement placed by a modeling agency, and within six months she was chosen to play the part of a plucky teenager in the successful 1980 film, *La Boum*. She was nominated for a French Oscar, the César, for her performance, and won the award after she appeared in a sequel, *La Boum II*, three years later.

Marceau put up with her schoolgirl image for only a few years, and when, at the age of sixteen, she was offered the role of a prostitute in *L'Amour Braque* (1984), she jumped at the chance to play a different sort of role. Needless to say, her performance, which included a nude scene, proved to be highly controversial among her French fans. What troubled them was not just her new image, but the fact that she had been transformed by the Polish director Andrzej Zulawski who, besides being 24 years her senior, also became her lover. And Zulawski had a reputation as a demanding, even humiliating taskmaster—the public began to wonder if he was acting as Marceau's Svengali.

Today, Marceau laughs at the notion that Zulawski has manipulated her. The couple is still together after a decade, and they have a son, Vincent, born in 1995. And her film career has taken a new direction. With her appearance as Princess Isabelle in Mel Gibson's Oscar-winning *Braveheart*, Marceau hopes that she will gain an American audience and access to bigger and better acting parts. She has since starred in the title roles of 1997's *Anna Karenina* and *Marquise*. She has a role in the latest all-star version of *A Midsummers Night's Dream* due in 1999.

---

moment of sheer, inspired visionary power. These can show up in the form of everything from a frozen turkey to a dancing chicken, and somehow they all add up to a remarkably coherent, melancholy road movie—a visionary glimpse of a universe spinning hopelessly out of control. *Stroszek*'s assistant director was Errol Morris (whose great *Gates of Heaven* would debut the following year) and the soundtrack features remarkably appropriate music by Chet Atkins and Sonny Terry.

NEXT STOP . . . *The Mystery of Kaspar Hauser, Gates of Heaven, Stranger than Paradise*

1977 108m/C *GE* Eva Mattes, Bruno S, Clemens Scheitz; *D:* Werner Herzog; *W:* Werner Herzog; *C:* Thomas Mauch; *M:* Chet Atkins, Tom Paxton. **VHS** *NYF, FCT*

SUBWAY

France's Luc Besson first drew attention with his stylized, post-apocalyptic, New New Wavish *Le Dernier Combat*; his 1985 *Subway* was a more direct bid for the francs of disenfranchised, movie-loving French punks. It's the story of a spike-haired renegade (Christopher Lambert) on the lam from the law, the mob, and a rich man's beautiful wife (Isabelle

Adjani). When he chooses the Parisian subway system as his hideout, he discovers a complete—and completely bizarre—subculture of youthful rebels living beneath the city streets. As is the case with all of Besson's work (including *La Femme Nikita* and *The Fifth Element*), *Subway* looks great. As is also the case with most of Besson's work, that's about *all* there is to say for it. This particular package of eye candy is packed with nothing but empty calories, though the set designs by the legendary Alexander Trauner (*The Man Who Would Be King*, *Land of the Pharaohs*) are cool. And no film with Isabelle Adjani can ever be *completely* worthless.

NEXT STOP . . . *Le Dernier Combat, Diva, THX 1138*

1985 (R) 103m/C *FR* Christopher Lambert, Isabelle Adjani, Jean-Hugues Anglade, Jean Reno; *D:* Luc Besson; *W:* Luc Besson. Cesar Awards '86: Best Actor (Lambert), Best Art Direction/Set Decoration, Best Sound; Nominations: Cesar Awards '86: Best Supporting Actor (Anglade). **VHS, LV, Closed Caption** *FOX*

SUGAR CANE ALLEY
Rue Cases Negres

An utter, unexpected delight. Euzhan Palcy's glowing coming-of-age story is set in Martinique in 1931, when much of the population toiled in the sugar cane fields under French colonial rule. Jose (Garry Cadenat) is an 11-year-old who lives with his wise and spirited grandmother (Darling Legitimus, the eccentric concierge in Bertolucci's *Last Tango in Paris*); the movie's gentle portrait of their love for each other gradually moves toward that moment at which she knows what she must do to assure the boy's future. With Ozu-like humanity and a sharp eye for the spiritual and physical beauty that exists even amid the poverty, Ms. Palcy's debut film was made for less than a million dollars, but it in no way looks like a shoestring production; even the French film industry recognized this, by awarding *Sugar Cane Alley* the 1984 César for Best First Film. This eloquent, truly moving film—remembered fondly by nearly everyone who sees it—is one of the loveliest and most affecting of all films about childhood.

NEXT STOP . . . *The 400 Blows, Small Change, Sounder*

1983 (PG) 106m/C *FR* Garry Cadenat, Darling Legitimus, Douta Seck; *D:* Euzhan Palcy; *W:* Euzhan Palcy; *C:* Dominique Chapuis. **VHS, LV** *NYF, FCT*

SUGARBABY
Zuckerbaby

Marianne (Marianne Sägebrect) is a hefty, lonely mortuary attendant living in Munich who falls for a young, handsome subway conductor (Eisi Gulp). When she's not dolling herself up, Marianne spends her time tracking down the man of her dreams, stalking and staking out trains and stations to discover who he is, where he lives, and how she can make him fall in love with her. The candy-colored, neon-lit stylization of Johanna Heer's cinematography is amusing but distracting; the real attraction in director Percy Adlon's fable is Sägebrect's sweet, poignant performance, and all the unnecessary expressionist trappings—which suggest the director's lack of confidence in his material—just keep getting in the way. The director and star would team up again for *Bagdad Cafe* and *Rosalie Goes Shopping*.

NEXT STOP . . . *Céleste, Ali: Fear Eats the Soul, Too Beautiful for You*

1985 (R) 103m/C *GE* Marianne Saegebrecht, Eisi Gulp, Toni Berger, Will Spendler, Manuela Denz; *D:* Percy Adlon; *W:* Percy Adlon. **VHS** *ORI, GLV, KIV*

SUMMER INTERLUDE
Illicit Interlude
Summerplay
Sommarlek

Just before an opening night performance, a prima ballerina, Marie (Maj-Britt Nilson), receives the diary of a boy she had an affair with ten years ago, when they were both students. The boy has since died, and the diary stirs memories in the dancer that will alter the course of her life, and will clear her mind and heart in ways she could never have imagined. Ingmar Bergman's 1950 *Summer Interlude* remains one the director's favorite films, and with good reason. This is a genuinely touching and heartfelt testament to the power of memory, and it's a bracing reminder of our too-often untapped capacity for self-healing and for spiritual regeneration. Intelligent, sensitive, and profound, Bergman's delicate movie is also—indirectly—about the cinema, the medium's ability to transport its audience through eloquent epiphanies like the joy regained by Marie in *Summer Interlude*.

NEXT STOP . . . *Smiles of a Summer Night, Fanny and Alexander, Babette's Feast*

1950 95m/B *SW* Maj-Britt Nilsson, Birger Malmsten, Alf Kjellin; *D:* Ingmar Bergman; *W:* Ingmar Bergman. **VHS** *HMV, NLC*

SUNDAYS & CYBELE
Les Dimanches de Ville d'Arvay
Cybele

A traumatized war veteran (Hardy Kruger) suffering from amnesia *and* vertigo develops a strong emotional bond with a young orphaned girl (Patricia Gozzi). When the innocent relationship between the two is misunderstood and greeted with hostility by the local townspeople, an inevitable but tragic series of events converge to destroy their happiness. A well-meaning but overly "artistic" work of carefully calculated poignancy, *Sundays & Cybele* feels forced and overbearing just when it needs to back off and simply let its story happen. Spontaneity is replaced by swanky widescreen compositions that call attention to the director rather than the protagonists' pain, but at least all that art did get noticed; this won the Academy Award for Best Foreign Language Film in 1962. The overly noticeable cinematography is by Henri Decaë (who can be far less showy), and the I-get-it-already score is by Maurice Jarre.

NEXT STOP . . . *The Lacemaker, Manny & Lo, Mrs. Dalloway*

1962 110m/B *FR* Hardy Kruger, Nicole Courcel; *D:* Serge Bourguignon; *M:* Maurice Jarre. Academy Awards '62: Best Foreign Film; Nominations: Academy Awards '63: Best Adapted Score, Best Adapted Screenplay. **VHS** *NYF, DVT, VYY*

SUNDAY'S CHILDREN

This lyrical and lovely exploration of childhood continues the complex Bergman family saga that began with the autobiographical *Fanny and Alexander* and left off just prior to the birth of little Ingmar in *The Best Intentions. Sunday's Children* takes up the story eight years after the director's birth (though it never turns into the story of little Ingmar's fascination with the movies). Many of the same issues and family conflicts carry over from the previous film (both were scripted by Bergman, though *The Best Intentions* was directed by Bille August), but the story soon narrows to the relationship between young Ingmar (Henrik Linnros) and his stern, minister father, Henrik (Thommy Berggren of *Elvira Madigan*). This collection of memories generates a strong emotional pull; being familiar with the extraordinarily expressive art that this little boy up on the screen would someday produce, we stretch and crane our necks in hopes of catching a glance of that spark of genius being born. That's impossible, of course, just as it's impossible for the adult Ingmar Bergman to understand the coldness and apparent unhappiness of his father, whom he shows in this film as being a mystery to him still. But in reaching out to him, as his script does here—a script which has been directed with sweetness and sensitivity by Bergman's own son Daniel—Ingmar Bergman the father and Ingmar Bergman the son offer a welcome ray of light, closing this unique series of films on a generous note of grace.

NEXT STOP . . . *Fanny and Alexander, The Best Intentions, Pelle the Conqueror*

1994 118m/C *SW* Thommy Berggren, Lena Endre, Henrik Linnros, Jacob Leygraf, Maria Bolme, Bjorje Ahistedt, Per Myrberg; *D:* Daniel Bergman; *W:* Ingmar Bergman. **VHS** *FRF*

SUSPIRIA

An American dancer (the petite, frail-looking Jessica Harper) arrives at a strange European ballet school and finds she has to do some fancy pirouetting to get out of the way of all the bodies, blood, and mayhem. Italian fearmaster Dario Argento directed this certifiably weird cult item in 1977, and its American release was spotty. Some cities saw the film in a pruned, less gory version, while others claimed to be running the original cut, complete with a then-avant-garde multi-channel stereo soundtrack. The full, widescreen version of *Suspiria* has shown up recently on premium cable channels, but however you see it, see it. Argento's horror films are unique in their ability to recreate the mood and look of a bad dream, yet they also capture the undeniable visual majesty of an unleashed, fullthrottle psychotic episode. His careful attention to the psychological impact of color, shadow, and sound effects is akin to a great illusionist's ability to create an elephant out of thin air; it provides his moldy, *Tales from the Crypt*—style plots with a lot more staying power than they deserve. *Suspiria* is easy to laugh off, but images and unexpected shocks will return to you later at remarkably inappropriate moments. For a maker of horror films, that's the ultimate compliment. With Joan Bennett, Alida Valli, and (horrors) Udo Kier. Music by Goblin.

NEXT STOP . . . *Four Flies on Gray Velvet, Creepers, Dawn of the Dead*

1977 (R) 92m/C *IT* Jessica Harper, Joan Bennett, Alida Valli, Udo Kier, Stefania Casini, Flavio Bucci, Barbara Magnolfi, Rudolf Schuendler; *D:* Dario Argento; *W:* Dario Argento, Daria Nicolodi; *C:* Luciano Tovoli. **VHS, LV, Letterbox, Closed Caption** *FXL*

THE SWEET HEREAFTER

In the aftermath of a tragic, small-town accident in British Columbia that takes the lives of 14 schoolchildren, a sophisticated big-city lawyer (Ian Holm) arrives on the scene to convince parents of the need to assign blame—and to collect a settlement. Atom Egoyan's thoughtful and skillfully performed adaptation of Russell Banks's story is a carefully layered piece of storytelling that touches on many issues. *The Sweet Hereafter*

begins as a simple search for the truth; it gradually evolves into a far more complex exploration of the not-so-easily solved mysteries of guilt, collective responsibility, and victimization, within both society and the family. Much of *The Sweet Hereafter*'s power emerges in small, seemingly throwaway moments such as Holm's irritation with an airplane meal; in such sequences Egoyan suggests motivations and character history with a breathtaking economy of means. He couldn't do it without his exceptional cast, of course; young Sarah Polley is a real discovery, and Ian Holm is just plain brilliant, as usual. Egoyan seems to have faltered in his faith in his audience, however, by including a naggingly insistent rereading of the story of the Pied Piper of Hamelin—it's a bit much the first time we hear it, and more than a bit much every time thereafter. Special Jury Prize, Cannes Film Festival.

NEXT STOP . . . *The Adjuster, Exotica, Affliction*

1996 (R) 110m/C *CA* Ian Holm, Sarah Polley, Bruce Greenwood, Tom McCamus, Arsinee Khanjian, Alberta Watson, Gabrielle Rose, Maury Chaykin, David Hemblen, Earl Pastko, Peter Donaldson, Caerthan Banks; *D:* Atom Egoyan; *W:* Atom Egoyan; *C:* Paul Sarossy; *M:* Mychael Danna. Cannes Film Festival '97: Grand Jury Prize; Genie Awards '97: Best Actor (Holm), Best Cinematography, Best Director (Egoyan), Best Film, Best Film Editing, Best Sound, Best Score; Independent Spirit Awards '98: Best Foreign Film; Toronto-City Award '97: Best Canadian Feature Film; Nominations: Academy Awards '97: Best Adapted Screenplay, Best Director (Egoyan); Genie Awards '97: Best Actor (Greenwood), Best Actress (Polley, Rose), Best Screenplay. **VHS, LV, Closed Caption, DVD** *NLC*

SWEETIE

Jane Campion's stylized and striking tragicomedy is the story of two sisters—Kay, a withdrawn, nearly paranoid Plain Jane (Karen Colston), and Dawn (Genevieve Lemon in a brave and amazingly effective performance), a manic, corpulent, wildly extroverted misfit who reenters her family's life with a vengeance and turns it upside down. Dawn, who was, and still is, called Sweetie by her family, is both victim and victimizer. She's your worst nightmare of what

will become of a "spoiled child," and she's a monstrously effective but tragically self-destructive manipulator—a certifiable Georgie Minafer without any constraints whatsoever. By the time Sweetie ends up naked in a tree, with her father quietly pleading "Come down from the tree, Sweetie," the picture has gone through all of its many stages of comedy, melodrama, heartbreak, and simple weirdness, and it achieves at last the dimension of a classic, tragic, emotionally overwhelming fable for our times. Campion, a New Zealand native, has set *Sweetie* in Australia, and there's something so otherworldly about the country that I doubt that her story—or her comic-book-like, strongly graphic visual style, photographed by Sally Bongers—would make sense in any other location. This is a very upsetting movie, and a fine one.

NEXT STOP . . . *Two Friends, An Angel at My Table, The Magnificent Ambersons*

1989 (R) 97m/C *AU* Genevieve Lemon, Karen Colston, Tom Lycos, Jon Darling, Dorothy Barry, Michael Lake, Andre Pataczek; *D:* Jane Campion; *W:* Gerard Lee, Jane Campion; *M:* Martin Armiger. Nominations: Academy Awards '91: Best Foreign-Language Film. **VHS, LV** *ART*

SWEPT AWAY...
Swept Away...By an Unusual Destiny in the Blue Sea of August

A rich, beautiful, arrogant Milanese woman (Mariangela Melato) is shipwrecked on a desert island with the masculine deckhand (Giancarlo Giannini) she used to treat like a slave. Lina Wertmüller's sexual fable takes on a not-so-subtle political dimension when material girl Melato becomes the eager, adoring sexual slave of the fiercely communist Giannini. She's dependent in other ways, too, since Giannini is the only one skilled enough to catch a fish and start a fire, but whatever lessons Melato learns melt away when their rescue portends a return to their traditional roles. The full title of the film was too long to fit on the marquee of the small Manhattan theatre—conveniently opposite Bloomingdale's—where *Swept Away...* opened, but the lines that stretched a full city block let the trendsetters know where it was playing. *Swept Away...* was the subject of lots of allegedly serious discussions about sexual roles, stereotypes, and politics, but more than anything else it became a high-toned make-out movie for upper east-siders and aspiring yuppies everywhere. It was the movie that started the blessedly brief American art house craze for the heavy-handed Wertmüller, which reached its frenzied height with the director's near-deification following the release of her *Seven Beauties* the following year.

NEXT STOP . . . *Love and Anarchy, Sotto, Sotto, Tristana*

1975 (R) 116m/C *IT* Giancarlo Giannini, Mariangela Melato; **D:** Lina Wertmuller; **W:** Lina Wertmuller; **C:** Julio Battiferri; **M:** Piero Piccioni. **VHS, Letterbox** *FXL*

SYMPATHY FOR THE DEVIL
One Plus One

Jean-Luc Godard's legendary experiment tells two simultaneous stories; one is of the death of a young revolutionary, while the other is of the creation of a song by the Rolling Stones. One works, the other doesn't. Yet the sequences chronicling the Stones' assembly of "Sympathy for the Devil," lick by lick and track by track, while the camera glides gracefully through their recording studio in a kind of visual counterpoint to the music, are exciting enough to make you wish Godard had made the song's creation his only subject. The film was originally to be called *One Plus One,* and the metaphor for revolution that the director was looking to capture depended on the Stones coming right up to the brink of giving birth to their creation, but never actually completing it.

Hence, Godard's *One Plus One* never features the complete, "final" version of the song "Sympathy for the Devil." One of the film's producers, however, thought that he had a better chance of recouping his costs from what looked to him like a disaster by running the finished song over the film's end credits, and by changing the movie's title to that of the song. Godard politely disagreed with the decision, allegedly jumping the producer as the reworked version of the film unspooled at the London Film Festival.

NEXT STOP . . . *Wind from the East, Gimme Shelter, The Rolling Stones Rock and Roll Circus*

1970 110m/C *FR* Mick Jagger, Rolling Stones; **D:** Jean-Luc Godard. **VHS** *FOX, OM*

A TALE OF SPRINGTIME

First up in the recent "Tales of the Four Seasons" cycle by France's Eric Rohmer is the story of Natasha (Florence Darel), a romantically minded, meddling young high-school student who hopes her father (Hugues Quester) will dump the woman he's been dating in order to take up with Natasha's smart and charming philosophy teacher (Anne Teyssedre). From plot elements that sound like a typical episode of *Bachelor Father* (I guess that dates *me*), Rohmer has built a suspenseful, wise, and witty entertainment that's every bit as welcome as the season it's named after. This is a simple but tart story of that well-worn point in the heart where the hopes of youth and the memories of middle-age converge, and it's blended with Rohmer's typical good humor and generosity. Rohmer's previous film cycles included his "Comedies and Proverbs" and "Six Moral Tales."

NEXT STOP . . . *A Tale of Winter, A Summer's Tale, Summer*

1992 (PG) 107m/C *FR* Anne Teyssedre, Hugues Quester, Florence Darel, Eloise Bennett, Sophie Robin; **D:** Eric Rohmer; **W:** Eric Rohmer. **VHS, Closed Caption** *ORI*

S

The master
(Ryutaro Otomo)
gives his opinion on
the noodles in Juzo
Itami's *Tampopo*.

A TALE
OF WINTER
Conte d'Hiver

The second chapter in Eric Rohmer's "Tales of the Four Seasons" cycle tells of the romantic trials of Félicie (Charlotte Véry), a young woman who simply cannot choose between her two smitten lovers and the man she truly longs for (and the father of her child), Charles (Frédéric Van Den Driessche). It seems that five years earlier, when Félicie and Charles parted after the summer holiday that produced their baby, Félicie mistakenly provided Charles with the wrong address. Having fruitlessly searched for him all this time, Félicie refuses to give up; though her current lovers keep her hopping, she refuses to give up hoping. That is, until a moment of revelation during a performance of Shakespeare's *The Winter's Tale* snaps her into a new awareness, which propels her dilemma forward into a *very* unexpected resolution, and the most graceful surprise ending of any of Rohmer's romantic comedies. Though it's less screened than many of Rohmer's more conventional romances, *A Tale of Winter* is one of his wittiest, most moving, most effortlessly elegant films.

NEXT STOP . . . *A Tale of Springtime, A Summer's Tale, Summer*

1992 114m/C *FR* Charlotte Very, Frederic Van Dren Driessche, Michel Voletti, Herve Furic, Ava Loraschi, Jean-Luc Revol, Haydee Caillot, Jean-Claude Biette, Rosette, Marie Riviere; *D:* Eric Rohmer; *W:* Eric Rohmer; *C:* Luc Pages; *M:* Sebastien Erms. **VHS** *NYF*

TAMPOPO
Dandelion

When it premiered here in 1986, this second film from the late Juzo Itami (his debut, *The Funeral,* caused something of a modest scandal in Japan) seemed all the sweeter for being so thoroughly unexpected. Yet recent, repeated viewings—minus the element of surprise—reveal *Tampopo* to be a marvel of comic structure so inventive, knowing, sweet, and tart that this trailblazer of the recent flood of "food" movies feels more like a classic than ever. The movie's heroine is Tampopo (Dandelion), a woman whose noodle shop is failing because she's a terrible cook. To the rescue comes Goro, a swaggering, macho truck driver with cattle horns on the cab of his truck, who makes Tampopo's cause his own. Swearing to make her noodles the best in the east, Goro and Tampopo embark on a fantastic gastronomical odyssey of epicurean research that keeps spinning the picture's plot off into darkly hilarious shaggy-food stories. *Tampopo* is a celebration of movies, food, and sex, and Itami's whirling vision of a ravenous, unrepentantly insatiable world is never interested in separating the three. *Tampopo* is played by the wonderful Nobuko Miyamoto (Mrs. Itami), who would later go on to become the closest thing to a Japanese superwoman as a corruption-buster in Itami's subsequent, controversial comic exposés *A Taxing Woman, A Taxing Woman's Return,* and *Minbo.*

NEXT STOP . . . *The Funeral, A Taxing Woman, Babette's Feast*

1986 114m/C *JP* Ken Watanabe, Tsutomu Yamazaki, Nobuko Miyamoto, Koji Yakusho, Rikiya Yasuoka, Kinzo Sakura, Shoji Otake; *D:* Juzo Itami; *W:* Juzo Itami; *C:* Masaki Tamura; *M:* Kunihiko Murai. **VHS, LV, Letterbox** *REP*

THE TANGO LESSON

A talented filmmaker named Sally (Sally Potter) who has a single hit movie behind her (not unlike, perhaps, Potter's own successful *Orlando*) becomes distracted from her new film project when she finds herself immersed in the sensuous world of the tango. Her passion for the dance—and for other things—deepens when she meets and takes lessons from a handsome and legendary Argentinean dancer named Pablo (Pablo Veron). With their outsized egos a match for each other, Pablo and Sally practice the tango on and off the stage, literally and metaphorically, against the backdrop of a glittering, intensely romantic Paris. Granted—there's an unapologetic, Vanity Press tone to Potter's placement of herself at the center of all this romantic and artistic sensuality, but in a sense that's just the idea; *The Tango Lesson* is a celebration of the personal liberation that the unconditional love of one's self can bring about, including receptivity to the love of others. Potter's brave and intentionally provocative casting of herself in this movie's central role was the justification for many of the critical pot-shots that have been taken at *The Tango Lesson,* but if critics can accept movies like *The Wild Bunch, 8 1/2, Wings of Desire* and *Naked* for what they are—fine films and male fantasies—then why not female fantasies as well? Robby Müller's stunning black-and-white cinematography ought to be seen in a letterboxed video version. The musical score features Carlos Gardel, Yo-Yo Ma and the Klezmatics, and is available on a beautifully produced, cleverly packaged soundtrack CD.

NEXT STOP . . . *Orlando, Carmen, Danzón*

1997 (PG) 101m/B *GB* Sally Potter, Pablo Veron, Gustavo Naveira, Fabian Salas, David Toole, Carolina Iotti, Carlos Copello, Peter Eyre, Heathcote Williams; *D:* Sally Potter; *W:* Sally Potter; *C:* Robby Muller; *M:* Sally Potter, Fred Frith. Nominations: British Academy Awards '97: Best Foreign Film. **VHS** *COL*

TASTE OF CHERRY
Ta'm e Guilass
Taste of Cherries

A man drives around the outskirts of Teheran on a bright, airy day, stopping people at random and engaging them in small talk, looking for someone who has the time and the willingness to help him with a project—his own suicide. Well, perhaps his own suicide. If he changes his mind—which he's not ruling out—he'll need that same person to pull him out of the dark hole he's planning to jump into, just in case it doesn't become his grave. In this masterwork from Iranian filmmaker

Gong Li and Leslie
Cheung are
unhappy lovers in
1920s Shanghai in
Temptress Moon.

Abbas Kiarostami, the specific reason for the man's despair never becomes clear, nor is it particularly important. What does become clear in *Taste of Cherry* is how unimaginably important simple human interaction can be, and how the continual, relentless march toward death that we're all engaged in has to—at some point—be reckoned with and made sense of. A metaphysical mystery that goes down easily thanks to its slyly seductive, voyeuristic structure, *Taste of Cherry* is no simple-minded, feel-good, "choose life" message picture. I have a feeling that *Taste of Cherry*—a work of art as complex and multi-leveled as Kurosawa's *Ikiru*—will appear to be a very different film at different times in one's life (my guess is that some of the critics who have dissed it are precisely the ones who are going to think of it when they least expect to), and I look forward with great anticipation to finding new riches in it in future years. It won the Palme d'Or at the Cannes Film Festival.

NEXT STOP . . . *And Life Goes On, Under the Olive Trees, The Fire Within*

1996 95m/C Homayon Ershadi, Abdolrahma Bagheri; *D:* Abbas Kiarostami; *W:* Abbas Kiarostami; *C:* Homayun Payvar. Cannes Film Festival '97: Best Film. **VHS** *NYR*

A TAXING WOMAN
Marusa No Onna

On the heels of the popular domestic success of Japanese director Juzo Itami's first two films, *The Funeral* and *Tampopo,* Itami turned his attention to the very real and very hot topic of tax evasion in Japan. In his smartly comic "issue film," *A Taxing Woman,* the crooked boss of a chain of quick-turnover "love hotels" is successfully escaping the tentacles of the government's tax laws until he meets the tax bureau's secret weapon: an ingenious and infinitely resourceful female tax collector named Ryoko (Nobuko Miyamoto, the star of *Tampopo*). Half James Bond and half super—girl scout, Ryoko goes about her job with the hilariously single-minded, unstoppable determination of "the Terminator." Itami uses the classic gambit of mutual respect between a thief and his pursuer, as in pictures like *The Fugitive* and *Heat;* Ryoko's methods draw admiration from the gangster even while his elaborate money-laundering schemes force Ryoko to think like a thief. Some American critics dissed *A Taxing Woman* for being a bit flabbier in the middle than Itami's tight earlier films (it *is* looser, though no less focused), yet I found the sheer audacity of the tax-shunning schemes (based on reality, we're told), together with the sweetly militaristic, crackerjack comic performance from Miyamoto (Mrs. Itami) to be enormous, richly rewarding fun.

NEXT STOP . . . *A Taxing Woman's Return, Tampopo, Minbo*

1987 127m/C JP Nobuko Miyamoto, Tsutomu Yamazaki, Hideo Murota, Shuji Otaki; *D:* Juzo Itami; *W:* Juzo Itami; *C:* Yonezo Maeda; *M:* Toshiyuki Honda. **VHS, LV** *FXL, LUM, FCT*

TEMPTRESS MOON
Feng Yue

Conceived as a sweeping romantic drama depicting years of tumultuous change in China, Chen Kaige's *Temptress Moon* features the stars of Chen's *Farewell My Concubine,* Leslie Cheung and Gong Li, as childhood friends who grow up to be adversaries in a complex test of wills involving rival gangs and rival families. Complex is the key word, since I must confess that I lost track of the plot about halfway through the film each of the two times I viewed it. Everyone agrees that *Temptress Moon*—photographed by Wong Kar-Wai associate Christopher Doyle—is visually lush and stunning to look at; if it weren't, I doubt that the picture ever would have made it into American theatres

at all. Word has it that *Temptress Moon* was cut a bit for American release, but since reviews from international film festivals also allude to continuity problems, I have a feeling that any changes that may have been made here were not the primary source of audience confusion. *Temptress Moon* reminds you of those incomplete Michelangelo sculptures in which the carved figures are only partially freed from their marble blocks, and we are only allowed to see tantalizing portions of what might have been. Likewise, there's a beautiful epic living somewhere inside *Temptress Moon,* but Chen and his editor—for whatever reason—never finished freeing it from its prison.

NEXT STOP . . . *Farewell My Concubine, Shanghai Triad, McCabe & Mrs. Miller*

1996 (R) 113m/C *HK* Gong Li, Leslie Cheung, Kevin Lin, Xie Tian, Zhou Jie, He Saifei; *D:* Chen Kaige; *W:* Shu Kei; *C:* Christopher Doyle; *M:* Zhao Jiping. **VHS, LV, Closed Caption** *TOU*

TEN DAYS THAT SHOOK THE WORLD
October

The book of the same name by American reporter John Reed (who in turn was the subject of Warren Beatty's *Reds*) was the basis for Sergei Eisenstein's incredibly ambitious, government-commissioned, 10th-anniversary commemoration of the 1917 Bolshevik Revolution. Eisenstein turned what had been recent history into a sweeping, spectacular epic of mythological proportions, complete with an evil villain (the Czar), a traitorous, self-aggrandizing, false hero (Kerensky, head of the first provisional government), and a shining knight (Lenin). In sheer technique, and in his bold experimentation with the possibilities of film editing, Eisenstein's achievement here is frequently astonishing. To show us the imperial designs fulminating in Kerensky's head, Eisenstein cuts between his face and mechanical peacocks, yet the cuts in sequences like this are so swift as to be nearly subliminal (if you look at a copy of

ROMAN POLANSKI
Controversial Director

Roman Polanski's life has been as dramatic and tragic as any of his movies: his rise to great success in his native Poland, directing one of the landmark post-World War II films, *Knife in the Water,* his triumphant transition to Hollywood, directing *Rosemary's Baby* and *Chinatown* (in which he also played a vicious thug who slits Jack Nicholson's nose), and then the murder of his pregnant wife, Sharon Tate by followers of Charles Manson, and his arrest for seducing a 14-year-old girl. As one profile of the actor-director puts it, there is no escaping his history.

Yet this is precisely what Polanski claims he has done—vehemently claiming that his films should not be taken as disguised autobiography. He has a point. His sardonic and Gothic view of life was formed long before events in his life caught up with his vision. He was born August 18, 1933 in Paris, France. His parents were native Poles and returned to Poland in the late 1930s. He was a child of World War II and the Holocaust, a Polish Jew who managed to survive by pretending to be Catholic, hiding with various families in the countryside. However, his parents were taken to a concentration camp, where his mother died. He wasn't reunited with his father until 1945.

Polanski's choices as a film director have been eclectic, unified only by his sensibility. Externally, there is no obvious connection between films like *Tess of the D'Urbervilles, Bitter Moon,* and *Death and the Maiden.* But what such films seem to have in common are characters who share Polanski's plight—in the sense that they are cut off from their fellows and have to confront the issue of survival, not always successfully.

Polanski lives in Paris and continues to make films. Although he has reached a settlement with the young woman who said he seduced her, he cannot return to the United States without facing charges. He would like to resolve the matter, but he says there have been no negotiations with American authorities. He's been married to French actress Emmanuelle Seigner since 1989, whom he directed in *Frantic* and *Bitter Moon.* As for his career, he concludes: "I don't think I've yet made a movie that completely satisfies me. I hope that one day I may make it."

the film that's projected at too high a speed such images may not even register). The big action sequences, like a massacre in a public square and the storming of the Winter Palace, are masterful and frighteningly realistic. (The director might have been dispirited, however, if he knew that modern audiences react more vocally to the smashing of the Czar's wine cellar than to the slaughtering of civilians.) After the film's completion, Eisenstein was informed that Leon Trotsky had just been declared an enemy of the people. He had no choice but to remove every one of the heroic images of Trotsky scattered throughout the finished film, as if he were plucking raisins out a huge, perfectly baked muffin without disturbing its shape.

NEXT STOP . . . Strike, The Battleship Potemkin, The Battle of Algiers

1927 104m/B *RU* Nikandrov, N. Popov, Boris Livanov; **D:** Grigori Alexandrov, Sergei Eisenstein; **M:** Dimitri Shostakovich. **VHS, LV** *VYY, IHF, WFV*

THE TENANT
Le Locataire

Roman Polanski's supremely creepy *The Tenant* is a Kafkaesque story about a meek, hapless office worker (Polanski) who moves into a big, decaying, spooky Parisian apartment building (*How* spooky? The concierge is Shelley Winters, *that's* how spooky.) Once ensconced in his new digs, Polanski spends much of his time obsessing on the previous tenant, who committed suicide by defenestrating herself. The discovery of her clothes prompts Polanski to dress in them, but when the neighbor below him tells him to make less noise, Polanski sits down without moving, terrified of being chastised, and of wrinkling his (her) dress. He spends so much time imagining how his neighbors would like to force him to jump out of that same window that he has no time for his sexually aggressive co-worker (Isabelle Adjani). Though it suffers a bit from the disembodied, post-synchronized English-language soundtrack, *The Tenant* may be Polanski's most unjustly neglected film. This portrait of a quick and inevitable descent into madness is bitterly funny and outrageous—you get the feeling that Polanski was trying out ideas that he had had for a long time, but didn't know where to use them. An example is the priceless scene in a bar in which a cowering man proclaims that everyone's against him; Polanski's character tries to comfort the man and assure him that he's being silly—not *everyone* could be against him. Suddenly a stranger bellows "drinks for everyone!," after which he slowly approaches the cowering man, points directly at him and says "Except *him*." With *The Tenant*, Polanski has created the *Lawrence of Arabia* of paranoia.

NEXT STOP . . . Repulsion, Rosemary's Baby, Dead of Night

1976 (R) 126m/C *FR* Roman Polanski, Isabelle Adjani, Melvyn Douglas, Jo Van Fleet, Bernard Fresson, Shelley Winters; **D:** Roman Polanski; **W:** Gerard Brach, Roman Polanski; **C:** Sven Nykvist. **VHS** *NO*

THE TESTAMENT OF DR. CORDELIER
Testament in Evil
Le Testament du Docteur Cordelier

Jean Renoir's strange and disturbing experimental fantasy, freely adapted from Robert Louis Stevenson's *Dr. Jekyll and Mr. Hyde,* is the tale of a physician (played brilliantly by the great Jean-Louis Barrault of *Children of Paradise*) who, transformed by his own hand into a murderous lunatic, stalks the streets and dark alleys of an unsuspecting Paris. Originally conceived as a television play, Renoir combined his own bold concepts of mise-en-scène with standard TV production techniques, using multiple cameras to record action in a scene from different angles simultaneously. The result is a strangely poetic—and intimate—horror film, which suggests a kind of demented variation on the themes of the director's *Boudu Saved from Drowning*. This time, however, the unanticipated interloper's anarchic impulses result in behavior considerably more antisocial than seducing the maid. It's a weird and claustrophobic little film, a vessel that can barely contain the startlingly awesome gracefulness of Barrault's electrifying, deeply scary performance.

NEXT STOP . . . Dr. Jekyll and Mr. Hyde (1932), Boudu Saved from Drowning, The Nutty Professor (1963)

1959 95m/C *FR* Jean-Louis Barrault, Michel Vitold, Teddy Billis, Jean Topart, Micheline Gary; **D:** Jean Renoir; **W:** Jean Renoir; **C:** Georges Leclerc; **M:** Joseph Kosma. **VHS** *FCT*

THE TESTAMENT OF ORPHEUS
Le Testament d'Orphee

Cocteau's final film is usually compared unfavorably to his masterworks like *Beauty and the Beast* and *Orpheus,* but this kind of com-

help him to bid an elegant, amusing, and characteristically esoteric farewell to the screen, to life, and to us. Though he may indeed have been misunderstood by the men of his time, Jean Cocteau's extraordinary films will continue to live so that they may once again work their unique magic on generations yet to come.

NEXT STOP . . . *The Blood of a Poet, Orpheus, Les Enfants Terribles*

1959 80m/B *FR* Jean Cocteau, Edouard Dermithe, Maria Casares, Francois Perier, Yul Brynner, Jean-Pierre Leaud, Daniel Gelin, Jean Marais, Pablo Picasso, Charles Aznavour; *D:* Jean Cocteau; *W:* Jean Cocteau; *C:* Roland Pointoizeau; *M:* Georges Auric. **VHS** *HMV, FCT, HEG*

TETSUO: THE IRON MAN
The Ironman

Well, *here's* something you don't see every day (though the film is so successful at what it does that I feared we might). Thematically, *Tetsuo* is a movie that seems a natural progression of all fears modern: man's gradual loss of his humanity, his enslavement to technology, his fears of disease, plus the particularly Japanese obsession and dread surrounding the subject of mutation. On a visual level, however, *Tetsuo* is—quite literally—something else. Shinya Tsukamoto's instant cult classic is the story of a white-collar worker (Tomoroh Taguchi) who discovers that he's being transformed bit by bit into a walking collection of metallic cables, drills, wires, and gears. In an homage to Fernando Rey's remark to Catherine Deneuve that "some men would find you even more attractive now" as he strokes her newly attached artificial leg in Buñuel's *Tristana,* the newly formed metal man finds himself confronted by a bizarre metals fetishist (played by the director in what I'd have to call an homage to himself). *Tetsuo* is amusing, disgusting, and beautifully crafted, but so unengaging on a narrative level that even at 67 minutes, it feels like an ordeal. (The sequel, *Tetsuo II: Body Hammer,* must have been what Tsukamoto was after the first time. The sequel is visually spectacular—this time in color—and it's

Fernando Rey with his beautiful young girlfriend Angela Molina in *That Obscure Object of Desire.*

parison is both unfair and absurd. *The Testament of Orpheus* is designed as a personal and highly poetic home movie (pointedly subtitled "Don't Ask Me Why"), in which Cocteau, at age 70, looks back at his career and his life, wanders through time, and playfully addresses the crucial importance of art in a chaotic world. The director described the film as "my farewell to the screen.... The events are linked as in a dream, with no logical sequence. My great desire is to live a reality which is truly mine and which is beyond time. *Testament* is my legacy to the youth of today—the youth in the shadows who helps the poet to bear being misunderstood by the men of his time." Consider it, then, a kind of artist's sketchpad constructed as a last will and testament, in which Cocteau and his fellow artists and friends (Maria Casarés, Jean-Pierre Léaud, Jean Marais, Charles Aznavour, Yul Brynner, and Pablo Picasso among them) pay him tribute as a poet of the cinema, and

hung on a stronger narrative core. It's still mighty grotesque stuff, but it's also a one-of-a-kind, visionary work.)

NEXT STOP . . . *Tetsuo II: Body Hammer, Videodrome, The Fly* (1986)

1992 67m/B *JP* Tomoroh Taguchi, Kei Fujiwara, Shinya Tsukamoto; **D:** Shinya Tsukamoto; **W:** Shinya Tsukamoto; **C:** Shinya Tsukamoto; **M:** Chu Ishikawa. **VHS** *FXL*

THAT OBSCURE ✓ OBJECT OF DESIRE
Cet Obscur Objet du Desir

A wealthy, widowed Spanish aristocrat (Fernando Rey) becomes erotically obsessed with his beautiful, seductive new maid, but she refuses to give in to his pleadings. In the hands of master director Luis Buñuel, Pierre Louÿs's often-filmed novel *La Femme et le Pantin,* becomes a savagely funny portrait of a man endlessly stimulated by his own frustration, like a dog chasing another dog's tail. Fernando Rey gives his usual deadly serious—and therefore hilariously vulnerable—performance, but the real show-stopper of *That Obscure Object of Desire* is his casting of two different women, Angela Molina and Carole Bouquet, in the single role of the maid, Conchita. It's the closest Buñuel has ever come to using a "gimmick" in one of his films, and you study the movie intensely hoping to see different specific qualities in Conchita when played by one actress as opposed to the other. But Buñuel, the old anarchist, refuses to let us off with an explanation so logical or obvious. Conchita simply is played by a two different actresses, sometimes within the same sequence, and that's that. In the spirit of his prank, Buñuel has given different explanations at different times, telling one interviewer that the talent of Maria Schneider—the *Last Tango in Paris* star who was originally cast in the part—was such that when she departed he needed two women to replace her. He told others that he simply couldn't bring himself to choose. Regardless, Buñuel's last film is as mischievous, wise, and subversive as his first (*Un Chien Andalou*); it's reassuring to know that the same questions and paradoxes that delighted him all his life were still nipping at his heels at the end, resulting in one of his most pleasurable entertainments.

NEXT STOP . . . *The Exterminating Angel, The Discreet Charm of the Bourgeoisie, Baby Doll*

1977 (R) 100m/C *SP* Fernando Rey, Carole Bouquet, Angela Molina, Julien Bertheau; **D:** Luis Bunuel; **W:** Luis Bunuel, Jean-Claude Carriere; **C:** Edmond Richard. Los Angeles Film Critics Association Awards '77: Best Foreign Film; National Board of Review Awards '77: Best Director (Bunuel); National Society of Film Critics Awards '77: Best Director (Bunuel); Nominations: Academy Awards '77: Best Adapted Screenplay, Best Foreign-Language Film. **VHS, LV, Letterbox** *COL*

THÉRÈSE

Thérèse is based on the true story of the 15-year-old Thérèse Martin (Catherine Mouchet) whose desire to become a Carmelite nun—and whose love for Jesus—bursts through the boundaries of exhilaration and religious exaltation, becoming romantic, obsessive, and, at least in its intensity, implicitly sexual. Thérèse was granted the permission she sought to join the Carmelite order, but she died of tuberculosis at the age of just 24. Later canonized, Thérèse became St. Theresa of Lisieux. Alain Cavalier's remarkable movie achieves an amazing purity of its own; he strips away all unnecessary trappings from the images we see, and uses dramatic and boldly lit chiaroscuro compositions to keep us focused on Thérèse's inner journey. Cavalier is wise enough to not try to *explain* Thérèse's faith or her rapturous joy in serving her Christ; her commitment speaks for itself. The simplicity and intensity of these stark and beautiful tableaux from Thérèse's short life (including, as I recall, an inexplicably wonderful scene involving a lobster) constitute mysterious and memorable flashes of a human being burning with passion and spiritually insatiable. *Thérèse* received the Special Jury Prize at the Cannes Film Festival, and César awards for Best Picture, Screenplay, Direction, and Cinematography.

NEXT STOP . . . *The Passion of Joan of Arc, Diary of a Country Priest, The Gospel According to St. Matthew*

1986 90m/C *FR* Catherine Mouchet, Aurore Prieto, Sylvie Habault, Ghislaine Mona; *D:* Alain Cavalier; *W:* Alain Cavalier; *C:* Isabelle Dedieu. Cannes Film Festival '86: Special Jury Prize; Cesar Awards '87: Best Cinematography, Best Director (Cavalier), Best Film, Best Writing. **VHS** *TPV*

THEY CAME FROM WITHIN

Shivers
The Parasite Murders
Frissons

The parasites on the rampage in a neat and tidy Canadian apartment building seem like a blessing in disguise at first. They stimulate intense sexual desire among the tenants with more high-powered effectiveness than a pound of Viagra dumped into the water supply. But, alas, they entail far more gruesome side effects than just "blue vision." David Cronenberg's first theatrical feature, the 1975 *They Came from Within,* is a gruesome, hilarious, splashy orgy of sex, gore, and dread that features just about all the themes that the gifted director would later explore in far more elegant but no less insistent films. The movie's title is suggestive enough to be that of Cronenberg's autobiography (a superb book about his work *is* titled *The Shape of Rage*), for the director's greatest talent throughout his career has been to dig deeply into the cinema's unique capacity for giving a physical shape to feelings—for externalizing internal states. His fascination with sexual appetite as a means of delaying the inevitable decay of the flesh has been the subtext, if not the direct subject, of most of his best-known, most powerfully operatic works, such as *Dead Ringers, The Fly,* and *Naked Lunch,* as well as his two most unjustly neglected masterworks, *The Dead Zone* and *Crash.* This is where it started, but even if you're not a general fan of this great, subversive, Canadian visionary, *They Came from Within* still packs a good scare. It's known alternately as *The Parasite Murders* and *Shivers* (*Frissons* in Quebec), and—heads up,

Jesse Helms!—it was partially funded by the Canadian government.

NEXT STOP . . . *The Brood, Scanners, Eraserhead*

1975 (R) 87m/C *CA* Paul Hampton, Joe Silver, Lynn Lowry, Barbara Steele, Susan Petrie, Allan Magicovsky; *D:* David Cronenberg; *W:* David Cronenberg; *C:* Robert Saad. **VHS** *ART, VES*

THE THIEF
Vor

In 1952, Katya (Ekaterina Rednirkova) and her six-year-old son Sanya (Misha Philipchuk) are traveling across Russia by train, struggling for food and shelter in the difficult post-World War II era. On board, Katya meets a handsome young officer named Tolyan (Vladimir Mashkov) and is immediately entranced, but soon learns that far from being a military hero, Tolyan is merely a thief—a common criminal. Finding that she doesn't have the strength—or the will—to leave him, she drinks to dull her sense of guilt as she gradually evolves into his accomplice, while at the same time naively hoping to protect her son from the long-term, corrupting effects of his influence. The specific metaphorical aspects of writer/director Pavel Chukhrai's portrait of the relationship between a dishonest tyrant and his helpless subjects (little Sanya is both frightened and impressed when Vladimir, who wears a tattoo of Stalin, claims to be the dictator's son) is the least subtle aspect of this otherwise tightly structured, gripping drama about the natural human tendency toward psychological dependence. Visually dynamic and featuring superb performances, *The Thief,* which was a 1998 Academy Award nominee for Best Foreign Language Film, is a potent and memorable cautionary fable about the dangers inherent in placing blind faith in *any* form of authority.

NEXT STOP . . . *Prisoner of the Mountains, A Friend of the Deceased, The Mirror*

1997 (R) 110m/C *RU* Vladimir Mashkov, Ekaterina Rednikova, Misha Philipchuk; *D:* Pavel Chukhrai; *W:* Pavel

Chukhrai. Nominations: Academy Awards '97: Best Foreign Film; Golden Globe Awards '98: Best Foreign Film. **VHS** *NYR*

THE THIEF OF PARIS

Le Voleur

This gentle study of a 19th-century burglar, Georges (Jean-Paul Belmondo), who enters his profession out of necessity but stays because of obsession, is one of the most unjustly overlooked films of Louis Malle's career. *The Thief of Paris* has many light moments, but at heart it's a gloomy and melancholy tale of a man lost in the details of his job—his work means everything to him, and he's willing to give everything up for it. Georges's obsession could have been based on that of an artist—a filmmaker such as Orson Welles, perhaps— but Georges has much more in common with the protagonist of Robert Bresson's 1959 masterpiece, *Pickpocket*. Bresson's thief was past mere obsession; his thefts took on a religious, transcendental intensity that went well beyond pride of craft, and I think that's what Malle is getting at here, but expressed in a lighter way, designed to be accessible to wider audiences. Still, the downbeat tone of *The Thief of Paris* (simply *Le Voleur* in France) didn't go over in the U.S.; it seemed to get lost in the much noisier, more violent world of 1967 cinema, and that's rather a shame. It's a delicate and surprisingly affecting work. It's visually beautiful too, yet when the movie was reissued in the late 1970s, the colors looked muddy and faded. It could use a genuine restoration.

NEXT STOP . . . *Pickpocket, Breathless, To Catch a Thief*

1967 120m/C Jean-Paul Belmondo, Genevieve Bujold, Marie DuBois, Julien Guiomar, Francoise Fabian, Marlene Jobert, Bernadette LaFont, Martine Sarcey, Roger Crouzet, Charles Denner, Paul Le Person, Christian Lude; *D:* Louis Malle; *W:* Louis Malle, Jean-Claude Carriere, Georges Darien; *C:* Henri Decae. *NYR*

32 SHORT FILMS ABOUT GLENN GOULD

Using an approach as unconventional as his subject, Canadian director François Girard has illuminated the life of the enigmatic pianist Glenn Gould with ingenuity, intelligence, and frequent flashes of brilliance. Gould's genius came complete with a thick layer of eccentricity and controversial decisions, not the least of which was his sudden retirement from live performance in order to dedicate himself exclusively to recording. Gould, who died in 1982 at the age of 50, is played here—"channeled" might be a better word—by the mesmerizing Colm Feore in a demanding and elegantly modulated performance, all the more impressive due to the intentionally fragmented nature of the movie's structure. The 32 short films of the title are all incidents or moments in Gould's life that may be representative of him (and may or may not be literally true), but are never meant to be seen as the definitive solution to the puzzle of his life. This is that rare "biopic" that doesn't try to explain the unexplainable, but instead celebrates it. In one particularly haunting, stunning sequence called "Truck Stop," Gould sits in a roadside restaurant and listens selectively to the conversations and sounds around him. Just as Robert Altman has done with the sound mix of so many of his films, Gould tunes in and out of the noises and voices he hears (as do we via the soundtrack) and we can see on his face that he is pulling rhythms—music—out of the everyday cacophony all around him. It's a small, thrilling moment in a film that provides many. *32 Short Films about Glenn Gould* marvels at the unfathomable mystery of human creativity, yet is itself creative enough to make us feel we've witnessed it.

NEXT STOP . . . *Tous les Matins du Monde, Nashville, Providence, Shine*

1993 94m/C *CA* Colm Feore, Gale Garnett, David Hughes, Katya Ladan, Gerry Quigley, Carlo Rota, Peter Millard, Yehudi Menuhin, Bruno Monsaingeon; *D:* Francois Girard; *W:* Don McKellar, Francois Girard; *C:* Alan Dostie. Genie Awards '93: Best Cinematography, Best Director (Girard), Best Film, Best Film Editing; Nominations: Independent Spirit Awards '95: Best Foreign Film. **VHS, LV** *COL*

T

Pianist Glenn Gould (Colm Feore) listens to a playback of his work in the recording studio in *32 Short Films about Glenn Gould.*

THIS MAN MUST DIE

Que la Bete Meure
Uccidero Un Uomo
Killer!

When a young boy is killed by a hit-and-run driver, the boy's father (Michel Duchaussoy) swears revenge. But after successfully locating his child's killer, the man decides that to simply dispatch the monster isn't enough; it's at this point that the complex and brilliantly insightful *real* plot of Claude Chabrol's thriller kicks in, as the father, the killer, and the audience all get far more in the way of suspense and surprises than they bargained for. Featuring exceptional performances all around, particularly from Duchaussoy and from Jean Yanne as the despised object of the father's search, this is one of the finest of Claude Chabrol's tantalizingly ambiguous

thrillers, in which guilt, justice, and retribution are always far less simple than they seem. Based on Nicholas Blake's novel *The Beast Must Die,* with cinematography by Jean Rabier. (Look for director Maurice Pialat in the role of a cop.)

NEXT STOP . . . *Le Boucher, Violette, The Sweet Hereafter*

1970 (PG) 112m/C *FR* Michael Duchaussoy, Caroline Cellier, Jean Yanne, Anouk Ferjac, Maurice Pialat; *D:* Claude Chabrol; *W:* Paul Gegauff; *C:* Jean Rabier. **VHS** *FOX*

THIS SPORTING LIFE

One of the best and most-discussed of the British working-class "angry young man" films of the 1960s was this gritty and despairing portrait of Frank (Richard Harris), a former

coal miner who breaks into the violent world of professional rugby. Handling social differences off the field becomes as difficult and confrontational as his sport, and when Frank begins an affair with his landlady (Rachel Roberts), he finds himself unable to move their relationship past the physical. The highly acclaimed *This Sporting Life* marked the directorial feature debut of Lindsay Anderson, a former film critic and documentary filmmaker who would roar back into the public eye five years later with his startling, controversial portrait of revolution at a boy's school, *If....* Harris won the Best Actor Prize at the Cannes Film Festival for *This Sporting Life,* and the film's success made him an international star. Adapted by David Storey from his novel.

NEXT STOP . . . *Look Back in Anger, A Kind of Loving, In Celebration*

1963 134m/B *GB* Richard Harris, Rachel Roberts, Alan Badel, William Hartnell, Colin Blakely, Vanda Godsell, Arthur Lowe; *D:* Lindsay Anderson; *W:* David Storey; *C:* Denys Coop; *M:* Roberto Gerhard. British Academy Awards '63: Best Actress (Roberts); Cannes Film Festival '63: Best Actor (Harris); Nominations: Academy Awards '63: Best Actor (Harris), Best Actress (Roberts). **VHS** *PAR*

THREE BROTHERS
Tre Fratelli

Three adult brothers—one a judge (Philippe Noiret), one a teacher (Vittorio Mezzogiorno), and one a mechanic (Michele Placido)—whose lives, concerns, and politics have become very different, are summoned to their small Italian village on the occasion of their mother's death. Over the course of the next few days these men will not only mourn their shared pain over the loss of their mother, but they will also grieve over the social, political, and economic differences that have separated them, and that may now be a bridge to bring them back together. Francesco Rosi's *Three Brothers* is a cumulatively powerful, eloquent portrait of the kinds of differences and jealousies that can fracture families everywhere, but beyond that it's a fascinating look at the very specific differences that exist between regions in Italy, and how those differences can bring about the fateful, gradual decisions that send once-close siblings into so many conflicting directions. *Three Brothers* isn't designed to race by; so, just relax, listen, and look—the experience is profound, and it will stay with you. Rosi's screenplay was adapted from Platonov's story *The Third Son.*

NEXT STOP . . . *Christ Stopped at Eboli, The Moment of Truth, Lamerica*

1980 (PG) 113m/C *IT* Philippe Noiret, Charles Vanel, Michele Placido, Vittorio Mezzogiorno, Andrea Ferreol; *D:* Francesco Rosi; *W:* Francesco Rosi; *C:* Pasquale De Santis; *M:* Piero Piccioni. Nominations: Academy Awards '81: Best Foreign-Language Film. **VHS**

301, 302

In a modern high-rise in Seoul, two women living across the hall from each other—each identified only by her apartment number—discover that they have something in common: a fascination with food. Fascination is not a one-size-fits-all word, however, especially in this case of the obsessive, endlessly cooking, slightly deranged gourmet chef in 301 (Eun-Jin Pang) who doesn't understand why all the food she makes for the woman in 302 (Sin-Hye Hwang) vanishes so quickly, or why her reclusive neighbor is so thin. By the time she finds out, *301, 302* has turned its attention to sexual sublimation, eating disorders, and cannibalism, with all the energy and—ahem—relish of an episode of *Essence of Emeril* as directed by Freddy Krueger. Director Chul-Soo Park's urban horror fable is pretty gruesome and sometimes pretty funny, but while it seems to be getting at real issues about hunger, lust, revulsion, and guilt, you may be heading for the bathroom long before you find out what they are. Eat first.

NEXT STOP . . . *Repulsion, They Came from Within, The Grande Bouffe*

1994 99m/C Eun-Jin Bang, Sin-Hye Hwang, Chu-Ryun Kim; *D:* Chul-Soo Park; *W:* Suh-Goon Lee. **VHS** *EVE*

THE THREEPENNY OPERA

Die Dreigroschenoper
L'Opera de Quat'Sous
Beggars' Opera

Set in the Soho section of London in the late 19th century, G.W. Pabst's 1931 screen adaptation of Bertolt Brecht and Kurt Weill's brilliant reworking of John Gay's *The Beggar's Opera* is a near-perfect melding of director and subject. The creator of a number of classic German "street" films such as *The Joyless Street* and *Diary of a Lost Girl,* Pabst had a relationship with the underside of Berlin in the 1920s that was similar to that which Martin Scorsese would have with New York's Little Italy in the 1970s. The *Threepenny Opera*'s cast of thieves, beggars, and prostitutes may be walking the streets of Victorian London, but for Germany in 1931 the mood of cynicism, despair, and tragedy couldn't be closer to home. *The Threepenny Opera* has been cut, censored, condensed, and reworked over the years, but most of the versions circulating in the last decade have been fully restored (the sound quality remains poor, however, but doesn't seriously diminish the picture's still-remarkable impact). With Rudolph Forster as Mack the Knife, Carola Neher as Polly Peachum, Ernst Busch as the Street Singer, and the legendary Lotte Lenya as Jenny, the part she would own for the rest of her life.

NEXT STOP . . . *The Joyless Street, Pandora's Box, The Beggar's Opera*

1931 107m/B Rudolph Forster, Lotte Lenya, Carola Neher, Reinhold Schunzel, Fritz Rasp, Valeska Gert, Ernst Busch; **D:** G.W. Pabst; **W:** Ladislao Vajda, Bela Balazs, Leo Lania; **C:** Fritz Arno Wagner; **M:** Kurt Weill. **VHS** *VDM, AUD, HEG*

THRONE OF BLOOD

Kumonosujo, Kumonosu-djo
Cobweb Castle
The Castle of the Spider's Web

After seeing Akira Kurosawa's ingenious screen adaptation of *Macbeth,* which sets the timeless story of greed, ambition, and murder in 16th-century Japan, it's tempting to think that this is how Shakespeare should have done it in the first place. Isuzu Yamada is absolutely mesmerizing as the Lady Macbeth figure—her name here is Asaji—who goads her warrior husband Washizu (Toshiro Mifune) into murdering his warlord and seizing the throne for himself. As the lies and deceit pile up as high as the corpses, the prophecy of a ghostly figure that Washizu encountered early in the film comes to pass, and the movie's action shifts into high gear; Washizu meets his end in a violent, outrageous, stunningly designed climax which has been burned into the memory of anyone who's seen the film. *Throne of Blood* lays its tale out with the same swift, muscular narrative thrust found in any of John Ford's greatest films, but without the cloying scenes of comic relief. Still, there's humor here too, but of a much darker variety; it's found in the deep ironies of the nightmarish "comeuppance" that Washizu suffers when the forest "moves" toward his castle, and in the legendary "pincushion" finale, which is both a nod to the American western and as stylized as kabuki. Mifune is a wonder. This is a picture that requires his quiet, pensive moments to have the same impact as his big, spectacular death scene—and he brings it off with grace and power. *Throne of Blood* is a perfect example of not only Shakespeare's universality, but also of how a classic can be reinterpreted in another medium without forsaking its soul.

NEXT STOP . . . *Macbeth* (1948), *Macbeth* (1971), *Forbidden Planet, Ran*

1957 105m/B *JP* Toshiro Mifune, Isuzu Yamada, Takashi Shimura, Minoru Chiaki, Akira Kubo; **D:** Akira Kurosawa; **W:** Hideo Oguni, Shinobu Hashimoto, Riyuzo Kikushima, Akira Kurosawa; **C:** Asakazu Nakai; **M:** Masaru Sato. **VHS, LV** *HMV, CRC, IHF*

THROUGH A GLASS DARKLY

Sasom I En Spegel

The first in a series of Ingmar Bergman films known as his religious or "crisis of faith" trilogy, *Through a Glass Darkly* is the story of Karin (Harriet Andersson), a young woman who has read in her psychologist father's journal his diagnosis of her incurable schizophrenia. Karin's husband (Max von Sydow) is unable to help her as her hallucinations accelerate, but the consolation Karin finds in her closeness to her young brother becomes incestuous, sending her over the precipice of sanity and into a terrifying vision of a monstrous God. That vision is all the more horrifying because we experience it only in Karin's description and in the look on her face, allowing us to later recall having seen a specific image, but it's one that *we* supply. One of the most painful and unsparing visions of madness ever put on film, Bergman's film is nevertheless one of his most beautiful and insightful. The cast is extraordinary, particularly Andersson as Karin, Lars Passgard as her confused brother, and the young Max von Sydow as Karin's tortured, helpless husband. Academy Award, Best Foreign Language Film.

NEXT STOP . . . *Winter Light, The Silence, The Rapture*

1961 91m/B *SW* Harriet Andersson, Max von Sydow, Gunnar Bjornstrand, Lars Passgard; **D:** Ingmar Bergman; **W:** Ingmar Bergman; **C:** Sven Nykvist. Academy Awards '61: Best Foreign Film; Nominations: Academy Awards '62: Best Story & Screenplay. **VHS** *NOS, NLC*

THROUGH THE OLIVE TREES

Under the Olive Trees
Zire Darakhtan Zeyton

This third in a trilogy of films about village life by Iranian director Abbas Kiarostami concerns the production of a film about the making of the trilogy's second film, *And Life Goes On.* The director of the film-within-the-film is a thinly veiled portrayal of Kiarostami, and he's portrayed by the actor Mohamad Ali Keshavarz. (Take it from me—it all makes

T

"You want to give up the taste of cherries?"

—Bagheri (Abdolrahman Bagheri) to suicidal Badiei (Homayon Ershadi) in *The Taste of Cherry.*

sense on the screen.) The director of the film-within-the-film, filming in an earthquake-ravaged village, discovers that the young bricklayer playing the bridegroom in his film is actually in love with the local woman who's playing the bride. However, she's turned down his real-life marriage proposal, feeling that the uneducated man is not of her social class. As is evident here and in the final sequence of his great *Taste of Cherry,* Kiarostami is fascinated by the convergence of cinema and real life, and in *Through the Olive Trees* he dares us to clearly identify the dividing line between them. The more we try, the more we realize how fully our lives have melded with the movies that we live and breathe. Kiarostami's films are not for the attention-span challenged, but their rewards are considerable; this is a memorable, quietly profound human comedy about the universal longings for acceptance, love, and creativity.

NEXT STOP... *Where Is My Friend's House?, And Life Goes On, Day for Night*

1994 (G) 104m/C Hossein Rezai, Mohamad Ali Keshavarz, Taherek Ladania, Zarifeh Shivah; **D:** Abbas Kiarostami; **W:** Abbas Kiarostami; **C:** Hossein Jafarian, Farhad Saba. Nominations: Independent Spirit Awards '96: Best Foreign Film. **VHS** *NYR*

TICKET TO HEAVEN

Canada's Ralph L. Thomas directed this bombastic but engrossing and often nastily funny portrait of a troubled young man (Nick Mancuso) whose unhappiness over a romantic breakup leads him straight into the waiting arms of a religious cult. *Ticket to Heaven* compresses his entire cycle—despair, vulnerability, indoctrination, kidnapping by family, deprogramming—into a whiz-bang, highly one-sided 109 minutes. Many of the performers in *Ticket to Heaven,* including Saul Rubinek, Kim Cattrall, Meg Foster, and Mancuso, went on to Hollywood success, but the movie's most riveting performance is given by the legendary Canadian stage actor R.H. Thomson, playing the "tough love"-style deprogrammer. Thomson reportedly avoids

the limelight and most offers of higher-profile roles; his hypnotic performance here of a man who's as obsessed and perhaps as unbalanced as his prey offers a rare chance to see him wail. From the novel *Moonwebs* by Josh Freed. Winner of Canada's Genie Awards for Best Film, Actor (Mancuso), and Supporting Actor (Rubinek).

NEXT STOP... *Scanners, Videodrome, Exotica*

1981 (PG) 109m/C *CA* Nick Mancuso, Meg Foster, Kim Cattrall, Saul Rubinek, R.H. Thomson, Jennifer Dale, Guy Boyd, Paul Soles; **D:** Ralph L. Thomas; **W:** Anne Cameron; **C:** Richard Leiterman; **M:** Micky Erbe. Genie Awards '82: Best Actor (Mancuso), Best Film, Best Supporting Actor (Rubinek). **VHS** *MGM*

TIE ME UP! TIE ME DOWN!
Atame

Psychiatric patient Antonio Banderas kidnaps a former porno actress and prostitute (Victoria Abril) he's long had a crush on and holds her captive, convinced that he can make her fall in love with him. Pedro Almodóvar's comedy is neither as witty or subversive as its champions would suggest nor as vile as its detractors would have you believe. Banderas and Abril attack their respective psycho-who-just-needs-love and junkie-hooker-with-a-heart-of-gold roles with cartoonish gusto, which perfectly fits Almodóvar's directorial style, visual scheme, and over-the-top screenplay. Never patently offensive, *Tie Me Up! Tie Me Down!* just seems too carefully calculated to outrage us, which consequently drains the movie of much-needed spontaneity, despite all the frantic and frenzied bondage and sexuality. The flap over the movie being released without a rating, together with a talked-about scene in a bathtub involving a toy submarine (you got it) brought people into theatres to see it, but only for a couple of weeks.

NEXT STOP... *Matador, What Have I Done to Deserve This?, The Collector*

1990 (NC-17) 105m/C *SP* Victoria Abril, Antonio Banderas, Loles Leon, Francesco Rabal, Julieta Serrano, Maria Barranco, Rossy de Palma; **D:** Pedro Almodovar;

T

Victoria Abril falls in love with her kidnapper (Antonio Banderas) in *Tie Me Up! Tie Me Down!*

W: Pedro Almodovar; C: Jose Luis Alcaine; M: Ennio Morricone. **VHS, LV, Letterbox** COL

TILAÏ
The Law

Though the setting is African, the opening scene suggests *The Ox-Bow Incident;* a rider (on donkey, not horseback) is returning home to his village after a long journey, and immediately stops to ask about his fiancée. It's bad enough that he learns she's gotten married while he was away, but it's quite another matter when he finds out that the other man is his own father. Not letting a little thing like that get in his way, he begins an illicit affair with the woman who is now his stepmother, and soon finds himself in an even tougher spot—the affair is considered incest in the tribe's *tilaï* (the law), and the punishment it carries is death. With a plot that recalls James M. Cain and imagery that conjures John Ford, this remarkable, engaging, and richly moving drama from Burkina Faso's Idrissa Ouedraogo was the deserving winner of the Special Jury Prize at the 1990 Cannes Film Festival. *Tilaï* confirms Ouedraogo's status as one of the most important cinematic talents to emerge from the new African cinema.

NEXT STOP . . . *Yaaba, Emitai, Ceddo*

1990 81m/C Rasmane Ouedraogo, Ina Cisse, Roukietou Barry; **D:** Idrissa Ouedraogo; **W:** Idrissa Ouedraogo; **C:** Pierre-Laurent Chenieux, Jean Monsigny; **M:** Abdullah Ibrahim. Cannes Film Festival '90: Grand Jury Prize. **VHS** NYF

TIME STANDS STILL
Megall Az Ido

In Budapest in the 1960s, two schoolboys are dogged by their classmates because a decade earlier the boys' father fled Hungary for the promise of America. Branded "an enemy of the people," the father unwittingly bequeathed a legacy to his children that turns out to be a social and political nightmare given the realities of Hungary's oppressive socialist regime. Péter Gothár's *Time Stands Still* shows us how living in a police state can pervert the simplest of relationships and the ordinary, day-to-day trials of school life. With its ironic, American pop soundtrack and stylized look, *Time Stands Still* is an expressionistic, Kafkaesque, out-of-time-and-space glimpse at some of the forgotten victims of political tyranny.

NEXT STOP . . . *Tito and Me, Angi Vera, Institute Benjamenta*

1982 99m/C HU Istvan Znamenak, Henrik Pauer, Aniko Ivan, Sander Soth, Peter Galfy; **D:** Peter Gothar; **W:** Peter Gothar; **C:** Lajos Koltai; **M:** Gyorgy Selmeczi. New York Film Critics Awards '82: Best Foreign Film. **VHS** COL

THE TIN DRUM
Die Blechtrommel

Oskar (David Bennent), a horrified German child of the 1920s, wills himself to stop growing in response to the ballooning Nazi presence in his country. As his chosen means of expression, the boy communicates his anger, fear, and outrage by pounding on a tin drum. Loudly. Director Volker Schlöndorff's widely praised adaptation of Günter Grass's novel goes for strong, often grotesque, nearly expressionistic imagery in its portrait of a shocked innocent who would rather distort himself than blend unobtrusively into a distorted world. The problem for me was that all that distorting—which the director and his cinematographer participate in as well—ends up being far too showy for the film's own good. The filmmaking style is Schlöndorff's cinematic equivalent of pounding on that drum, and as a result you may end up emerging from *The Tin Drum* feeling more pummeled than enlightened. The film is constructed out of schematic, hard-hitting symbolism, and what power it achieves comes from striking, individual images and set pieces, such as Oskar's ability to shatter windows with his scream (it was a big year for explosive bellowing at the movies—Jerzy Skolimowski's *The Shout* had been released just months earlier). Videocassettes of *The Tin Drum* have idiotically been banned from some American communities because of explicit content. That, of course, is an outrage that should not be tolerated, but being

"My mother was my first teacher and I've never doubted her methods. After all, she introduced me to Bach."

—Glenn Gould (Colm Feore) in *32 Short Films about Glenn Gould.*

banned doesn't make the film a classic. Have students read the book instead (if they haven't banned *that* yet). With Angela Winkler, Daniel Olbrychski, Mario Adorf, Charles Aznavour, and Heinz Bennent. Co-winner of the Grand Prize (with *Apocalypse Now*) at the 1979 Cannes Film Festival; Academy Award, Best Foreign Language Film.

NEXT STOP . . . *Forbidden Games, Au Revoir les Enfants, The Quiet Room*

1979 (R) 141m/C *GE* David Bennent, Mario Adorf, Angela Winkler, Daniel Olbrychski, Katharina Thalbach, Heinz Bennent, Andrea Ferreol, Charles Aznavour; *D:* Volker Schlondorff; *W:* Jean-Claude Carriere, Volker Schlondorff; *C:* Igor Luther; *M:* Maurice Jarre. Academy Awards '79: Best Foreign Film; Cannes Film Festival '79: Best Film; Los Angeles Film Critics Association Awards '80: Best Foreign Film. **VHS** *KIV, GLV, AUD*

TITO AND ME
Tito i Ja
Tito and I

If you've ever looked at old newsreels in which the schoolchildren living under repressive regimes line up to adoringly smile and wave to their fascist leader, you might have wondered what was actually going through their little heads at that very moment. This remarkable but sadly neglected picture by Goran Markovic—which holds the distinction of being the very last film to claim Yugoslavia as its country of origin—is set in the Belgrade of 1954. A captivating, chubby, perpetually hungry 10-year-old named Zoran has a crush on 12-year-old Jasna, but he can't get next to her because Jasna's too busy being obsessed with her leader, her idol and her hero, Comrade Tito. Zoran hopes she'll notice him if he sings the praises of their fearless leader loudly enough, so he writes an essay for school on "Why I Love Tito." Not only does his essay win a prize, it assures him a place in the upcoming "Children's Walk through Comrade Tito's Country," during which his hope of being noticed by Jasna leads to a series of mishaps that will change the little boy's life—and beliefs—forever. Dimitrie Vojnov gives an extraordinary performance as young Zoran in one of the most effortlessly

profound, wise, and witty political comedies of the decade.

NEXT STOP . . . *When Father Was Away on Business, Hey, Babu Riba, Underground*

1992 104m/C *YU* Dimitrie Vojnov, Lazar Ristovski, Anica Dobra, Predrag Manojlovic, Olivera Markovic; *D:* Goran Markovic; *W:* Goran Markovic; *C:* Radoslav Vladic; *M:* Zoran Simjanovic. **VHS** *FXL, FCT*

TO LIVE
Huozhe

The fifth feature film from China's Zhang Yimou follows the lives and fortunes of one family—the weak but adaptable Fugui (Ge You), his strong-willed wife Jiazhen (Gong Li), and their young daughter and son—from pre-revolutionary China in the 1940s through the Cultural revolution of the 1960s. Fugui's loss of the family fortune to gambling becomes a life-saving blessing when the communists assume power, though the family must struggle to survive the increasingly violent and unpredictable winds of change brought about by the "Great Leap Forward." Zhang's *To Live* is a sweeping epic about an ordinary family's struggle in extraordinary times. Intimate in focus but awesome in its breadth, the film's day-to-day events—humorous and tragic—compound into a saga of the human spirit that sneaks up on you gently, and becomes overwhelmingly moving in its final scenes. Zhang has become a master not only of story structure and visual nuance, but of coaxing natural and startlingly spontaneous performances from his casts. (A hospital sequence involving arrogant bureaucrats, an old, starving doctor, and steamed buns is a brilliantly orchestrated example of comedy horribly but inevitably evolving into tragedy—the scene's complex perfection is typical of Zhang.) *To Live* is additional proof (if any is needed) that Zhang Yimou is one of the world's greatest living filmmakers. Grand Jury Prize and Award for Best Actor (Ge You), Cannes Film Festival.

NEXT STOP . . . *The Story of Qiu Ju, Farewell My Concubine, The Blue Kite*

1994 130m/C *CH* Ge You, Gong Li, Niu Ben, Guo Tao, Jiang Wu; **D:** Zhang Yimou; **W:** Lu Wei, Yu Hua; **C:** Lu Yue; **M:** Zhao Jiping. British Academy Awards '94: Best Foreign Film; Cannes Film Festival '94: Best Actor (You), Grand Jury Prize; Nominations: Golden Globe Awards '95: Best Foreign Film. **VHS, LV** *HMK, IME*

TOKYO OLYMPIAD

Of the many big-screen documentaries that have tried to convey a sense of the excitement, drama, and physical splendor of the Olympic Games, Kon Ichikawa's spectacular 1966 *Tokyo Olympiad* may be the most elegant, the least agenda-laden, and—sadly—the least-well-known, at least in the United States. Ichikawa (*Fires on the Plain, The Makioka Sisters*) had the usual army of photographers at his disposal to record the 1964 Tokyo Olympics (not to mention two years of continuous editing), but he wasn't interested in just a mind-numbing chronicling of statistics. Instead, Ichikawa created a poetic and visually astonishing tribute to the endurance and capabilities of the human spirit—a three-hour epic that builds in power and possibilities until the athletes and the team of filmmakers who are recording them truly do seem to merge into a single force. All of that was thrown away when *Tokyo Olympiad* was cut *in half* when released in the U.S. in 1966; and as if to try to make up for the butchery, the American distributor added an insufferable, pedestrian narration, sprinkling unnecessary sentimentality on what was now a cold corpse of a film. (Leni Riefenstahl's Nazi-glorifying *Olympia* was shown in America without cuts, but with an English-language soundtrack.) Fortunately, *Tokyo Olympiad* has been restored to its original glory and is available in its original, full-length, widescreen version, complete with freshened color. The sad irony is that in this age of lightweight video cameras and full TV coverage of the Olympics, few moviegoers took the time to see the rejuvenated *Tokyo Olympiad* when it was reissued to theatres a few years back. Its video and laserdisc release should finally give this enduring, long-distance runner the second wind it deserves.

NEXT STOP . . . *Olympia, Visions of Eight*

1966 170m/C *JP* **D:** Kon Ichikawa; **W:** Kon Ichikawa; **C:** Kazuo Miyagawa. **VHS, LV, Letterbox** *TPV, WFV, CRC*

TOKYO STORY
Tokyo Monogatari
Their First Trip to Tokyo

An aging couple (Chieko Higashiyama and Chishu Ryu) decides to make the trip from their small town to Tokyo to visit their busy children, but the trip is strenuous and—in many ways—disappointing. On their journey home one of the parents becomes ill and dies, and the children and surviving parent must come to terms with the experience. Yasujiro Ozu had made over 40 movies by the time he filmed *Tokyo Story* (a.k.a. *Their First Trip to Tokyo*) in 1953. Though a few Ozu films were seen in the United States in the 1950s and 1960s, *Tokyo Story* never actually received American release until 1972, when it showed up at Daniel Talbot's invaluable New Yorker Theatre. The impact for those of us who discovered the picture then was immeasurable; it was as if film history—as some of us had come to understand it—had to be rewritten. Ozu had refined a kind of storytelling that was similar from film to film. These "home dramas," as they have been called, reflect a simple but shockingly profound philosophy, which—if it could be boiled down to "high concept"—might be described as a character's acceptance of the ultimate sadness of life. In Ozu, this is the opposite of defeat. In fact, the moment of epiphany in *Tokyo Story,* in which a loving daughter-in-law (the sublime Setsuko Hara) is asked tearfully if life is disappointing and states her certain answer with a magnificent smile, is as surprisingly reassuring a vision as any work of 20th-century art has offered us. *Tokyo Story* is one of the greatest films of all time. Seeing it once a year is reason enough to own a VCR.

NEXT STOP . . . *Late Spring, Floating Weeds, An Autumn Afternoon*

1953 134m/B *JP* Chishu Ryu, Chieko Higashiyama, So Yamamura, Haruko Sugimura, Setsuko Hara; **D:** Yasujiro Ozu; **W:** Yasujiro Ozu; **C:** Yushun Atsuta; **M:** Kojun Saito. **VHS** *NYF, FCT*

TONI

Toni (Charles Blavette) is an Italian farm worker who comes to Provence in the 1930s looking for work. He falls in love, but the woman he adores (Jenny Hélia) marries Toni's new boss (Max Dalban), a brute whose subsequent death leads to Toni being accused of a murder he didn't commit. Though made in 1934, Jean Renoir's film—shot in natural locations with a high degree of realism—foreshadowed the Italian neo-realist cinema that would emerge after World War II. Despite the soap opera—ish aspects of the plot, the movie's visual power and breathtaking sincerity seem revolutionary today, particularly when compared to other sound films of the period. Renoir succeeded in his aims, which he stated in an introduction to the film's 1956 reissue: "No stone was left unturned to make our work as close as possible to a documentary. Our ambition was that the public would be able to imagine that an invisible camera had filmed the phases of a conflict without the characters unconsciously swept along by their being aware of its presence." The simple, affecting cinematography is by Claude Renoir, the director's nephew. So influential was this film that Truffaut, Godard, Melville, Resnais, and many of France's other New Wave pioneers frequently described themselves as "the children of *Toni*."

NEXT STOP . . . *Rules of the Game, Harvest, Greed*

1934 90m/B *FR* Charles Blavette, Jenny Helia, Edouard Delmont, Celia Montalvan; *D:* Jean Renoir; *W:* Jean Renoir; *C:* Claude Renoir; *M:* Paul Bozzi. **VHS** *DVT*

TOO BEAUTIFUL FOR YOU
Trop Belle pour Toi

Successful car salesman Gérard Depardieu, married for years to the extraordinarily beautiful Carole Bouquet, discovers to his surprise that he is irresistibly drawn to his overweight, physically unexceptional secretary (Josiane Balasko). Bertrand Blier's screenplay contains the seeds of a rich, complex dramatic comedy that touches on a number of subjects—masculine insecurity, women's fear of objectification, the nature of romantic love, etc. The problem is, all Blier does *is* touch on them, and what we're left with is a thin, protracted, gimmicky trifle that feels like a skillfully filmed first draft, never finding a way to develop the core situation far beyond its superficial shock value. As a result, the movie's talented cast is left to flounder; still, if you're determined to hire a floundering cast, you could do a lot worse than to hire these three. They not only make *Too Beautiful for You* watchable, they also suggest the unexplored possibilities in this material, thereby inviting us—to Blier's detriment, unfortunately—to imagine the movie that might have been.

NEXT STOP . . . *Get Out Your Handkerchiefs, Mon Homme, Passione d'Amoré*

1988 (R) 91m/C *FR* Gerard Depardieu, Josiane Balasko, Carole Bouquet, Roland Blanche, Francois Cluzet; *D:* Bertrand Blier; *W:* Bertrand Blier; *C:* Philippe Rousselot. Cannes Film Festival '89: Grand Jury Prize; Cesar Awards '90: Best Actress (Bouquet), Best Director (Blier), Best Film, Best Writing. **VHS** *ORI, FXL, FCT*

TORMENT
Hets
Frenzy

The 25-year-old Ingmar Bergman wrote the screenplay for this gripping 1944 tragedy—rarely seen now—that was directed by Alf Sjöberg. It's the story of Jan-Erik (Alf Kjelin), a student who becomes romantically involved with Bertha (Mai Zetterling), a troubled girl who lives nearby. Eventually it's revealed that Bertha has become the unwilling sexual slave of an older man, and Jan-Erik soon learns that the man is none other than his sadistic, tyrannical, feared teacher, Caligula (Stig Jarrel). *Torment* is a stark and crisply directed parable of the dynamics of fascism and sexual terrorism, as well as a snapshot *in extremis* of the looming post-war generation gap. If it weren't for the monstrous teacher's unnecessarily obvious moniker, this disturbing little movie would be just about perfect.

NEXT STOP . . . *Monika, Sawdust and Tinsel, The Blue Angel (1930)*

JOSIANE BALASKO
Bold French Actress/Director

French actress/director Josiane Balasko's *French Twist* (*Gazon Maudit*) was one of the most daring comedy hits of the 1996 film season. Both adultery and lesbianism figure in the plot.

With her orange hair and outspoken manner, Balasko has been called "an unreconstructed Roseanne." Balasko says she wanted to make a light comedy with a lesbian instead of the usually serious films that deal with same-sex relationships. To complicate the farce, she introduced a suburban housewife played by Victoria Abril, tired of her philandering husband. She is attracted to a female truck driver, played by Balasko. "I wrote the part for myself," she confesses, "because I always wanted to play a butchy woman like that."

In her mid-forties, Balasko first got attention for her part as the heavy set secretary who seduces Gérard Depardieu in *Too Beautiful for You*. In France, she has a significant reputation as both a screenwriter and director, and has been acting since 1975, having got her start in the cafe theaters, where she honed her comic skills and observations of ordinary people. She acted and directed in the 1997 film *Un Grand Cri d'Amour*. She is also the happily married mother of two children. Indeed, she is proud that two years ago she was chosen by the children of France as the perfect mother and was asked to lead the gay pride parade.

Balasko realizes her film may offend some American audiences. In France, it was considered mainstream—similar to *Three Men and a Baby*. She hopes that people see that the film is about "not taking ourselves and our sexual roles so seriously. After all, it has a happy ending, you know? I like it when everything turns out happy."

1944 90m/B *SW* Alf Kjellin, Mai Zetterling, Stig Jarrel, Olof Winnerstrand, Gunnar Bjornstrand; *D:* Alf Sjoberg; *W:* Ingmar Bergman; *C:* Martin Bodin; *M:* Hilding Rosenberg. **VHS** *HMV, NLC*

TOTO LE HEROS
Toto the Hero

As a child, Thomas always believed that he'd grow up to do fabulous things—in particular, he saw himself becoming the super secret agent "Toto the Hero," saving the world, righting wrongs, and being adored. But now, as a bitter, disappointed old man, Thomas (Michel Bouquet) has decided that his failure to achieve those dreams was not his fault. His unhappy life was, he believes, the result of having been switched at birth with a baby that grew up in a wealthy and happy neighbor family, a family that—Thomas has decided—was supposed to be *his* family. He finally decides to seek the revenge that he now believes to be simple justice; he's ready to take back the happy life that he's sure was stolen from him. Belgian director Jaco Van Dormael's debut film is skillful and intriguing; he takes the audience on a journey through Thomas's mind and imagination at many different periods of his life, adroitly juggling realistic imagery with childhood fantasy to make us understand Thomas's frustration and eventual paranoia. The art of obsessive excuse-making is a great subject for a movie, though Van Dormael seems less interested exploring it than in his protagonist's redemption. And though the movie just seems to stop suddenly, too conveniently giving us—and Thomas—what its director must have thought to be a generous, happy ending a la *The Last Laugh*, Bouquet's full-bodied, intuitive performance rises above such complaints.

NEXT STOP . . . *The Eighth Day, He Who Must Die, Sansho the Bailiff*

1991 (PG-13) 90m/C *FR* Michel Bouquet, Jo De Backer, Thomas Godet, Mireille Perrier, Sandrine Blancke, Didier Ferney, Hugo Harold Harrisson, Gisela Uhlen, Peter Bohlke; **D:** Jaco Van Dormael; **W:** Jaco Van Dormael; **C:** Walther Vanden Ende; **M:** Pierre Van Dormael. Cesar Awards '91: Best Foreign Film. **VHS, LV, Closed Caption** *PAR, BTV*

TOUS LES MATINS DU MONDE
All the Mornings of the World

One of the most unusual films—at least in subject—to ever become an American art house hit, Alain Corneau's hauntingly beautiful *Tous les Matins du Monde* (*All the Mornings of the World*) is the story of two 17th-century baroque composers. Gérard Depardieu portrays the aged and ailing Marin Marais, who became a successful court musician and composer at Versailles. As a young man, Marais was the protege of Sainte Colombe (Jean-Pierre Marielle), a secretive and spiritual musician whose life was—and still is—largely a mystery. The bulk of the film is formed from flashback sequences in which the young Marais studies with the brilliant and ethereal Sainte Colombe, but provokes his teacher's wrath by having an affair with one of his daughters (Anne Brochet). When he's tossed out of the Sainte Colombe household, Marais acquires what he believes to be "enough" talent by listening to his teacher from a hiding place in the Sainte Colombe barn; deciding one day that his skills are adequate, he departs for a lucrative professional life, having never reached the point at which he even begins to share Sainte Colombe's almost holy connection with his music. Much later in his life, he will regret his haste.

The young Marais is played in the film by Guillaume Depardieu, Gérard's son. It's his film debut, and he proves to be a captivating and gently expressive performer. Everything in the film shows enormous care and thoughtfulness, from its evocative cinematography to the extraordinary musical score, recorded with original instruments of the period. (If CDs wore out the same way LPs used to, my prized soundtrack CD from *Tous les Matins du Monde* would have shredded years ago.) César Awards for Best Picture, Director, Cinematography, and Supporting Actress (Brochet).

NEXT STOP . . . *Un Coeur en Hiver, Amadeus, On the Waterfront*

1992 114m/C *FR* Gerard Depardieu, Guillaume Depardieu, Jean-Pierre Marielle, Anne Brochet, Caroline Sihol, Carole Richert, Violaine Lacroix, Nadege Teron, Miriam Boyer, Michel Bouquet; **D:** Alain Corneau; **W:** Pascal Quignard, Alain Corneau; **C:** Yves Angelo; **M:** Jordi Savall. Cesar Awards '92: Best Cinematography, Best Director (Corneau), Best Film, Best Supporting Actress (Brochet), Best Score. **VHS, LV** *TOU*

TRAFFIC

With the exception of a short, minor television documentary that followed it, the 1971 *Traffic* was to be Jacques Tati's last feature film. Tati's concern here, as always, is the depersonalization of modern society. He settled on a perfect visual metaphor, too—man ensconced in his private automobile, rushing off hither, thither, and yon at the same moment and often in the same direction as millions of other travelers, but all of them are completely isolated from each other. (The actual destination here is Amsterdam—Tati's Monsieur Hulot is a car designer on his way from Paris to a big auto show.) *Traffic* was conceived as a slimmed-down, four-wheel version of Tati's ambitious *Playtime,* in which a modern Paris was divided into glass-and-steel cubicles symbolic of "progress," but which instead simply succeeded in making human contact and meaningful communication impossible. *Traffic* is looser and less painstakingly organized than that earlier superproduction, but the gags (not all of them are on wheels) are less uninspired and

Although a specific incident gives the movie its title—a father risks punishment by cutting down one of the landlord's trees to make new shoes for his son—*The Tree of Wooden Clogs* is for the most part that most difficult kind of story (never mind *epic*) to bring off: a movie made up of small, individual moments without an overwhelmingly linear plot on which to hang them. And yet it works, and works brilliantly. Olmi has captured details of the lives of these people with such a stunning combination of realism and poetry that those accumulated details—and the rhythm of Olmi's editing—*become* the movie's storyline, and a compelling one at that. There is an authentic sense of family and community permeating this movie; Olmi does not try to conjure it with false and gratuitous tearjerking scenes of tragedy. The film is simply a vision of a time and place, populated with richly drawn characters, and it's so skillfully achieved that it becomes a permanent part of our experience. We presented this three-hour movie for one weekend only at the Detroit Institute of Arts exactly twenty years ago. People who saw it still come up to me at the museum and request that it be shown again; they remember moments from it, and they want to take people they know—some born long after that weekend—to see it as well. It's an overwhelming experience. Grand Prize Winner, 1978 Cannes Film Festival.

NEXT STOP . . . *The Sound of Trumpets (Il Posto), La Terra Trema, Bandits of Orgosolo*

1978 185m/C *IT* Luigi Ornaghi, Francesca Moriggi, Omar Brignoll, Antonio Ferrari; *D:* Ermanno Olmi; *W:* Ermanno Olmi; *C:* Ermanno Olmi. Cannes Film Festival '78: Best Film; New York Film Critics Awards '79: Best Foreign Film. **VHS, LV** *FXL*

less urgent. It's a handsome film and Tati/Hulot is such a sympathetic character that you try to like the picture, but it becomes gradually less funny and less vital as it ambles slowly along, as if someone had let the air out of the tires.

NEXT STOP . . . *Playtime, Citizens Band, Weekend*

1971 89m/C *FR* Jacques Tati, Maria Kimberly, Marcel Fraval; *D:* Jacques Tati; *W:* Jacques Lagrange, Jacques Tati; *C:* Eddy van der Enden, Marcel Weiss; *M:* Charles Dumont. **VHS** *HMV*

THE TREE OF WOODEN CLOGS
L'Albero Degli Zoccoli

Director Ermanno Olmi's 1978 epic tells the stories of four sharecropping peasant families in turn-of-the-century Lombardy.

THE TRIAL
Le Proces
Der Prozess
Il Processo

It would appear that Orson Welles felt an affinity with Franz Kafka's story of a man facing the onslaught of an impossible bureaucratic nightmare and who is presumed

guilty no matter what. Anthony Perkins plays Joseph K., the man who finds himself being interrogated without any hint of his alleged crime, and who turns to a mysterious and self-important defense attorney (Welles) for help. As Joseph's situation deteriorates and he sees little chance of exoneration, he begins to believe that it must all be true, that he indeed must be guilty—of *something*. Few Americans saw *The Trial* on its original release, and few have seen it since. Kafka purists don't like it, and even Welles enthusiasts find the picture hard to warm up to. The paradox, of course, is that a successful screen adaptation of *The Trial*, which this is, *can't* be warmed up to; it's designed to be a disorienting, disturbing, joyless glimpse at a world in which the game is over before it's begun. Or, to quote Mark Twain: "When you're born, you're finished." Twenty years after *The Magnificent Ambersons* was taken out of Welles's hands and amputated, with much of the critical and popular world agreeing that he was a genius who "never lived up to his potential," despite the fact that he had continued—against all odds—to do brilliant work, how could this great artist *not* feel like Joseph K., accused, as he always was, of the unforgivable crime of being "Orson Welles?" And the movie reflects those decades of injury (granted, some self-inflicted) with its claustrophobic, uncompromisingly bleak and despairing tone. But underneath this story of a human spirit crushed is Welles the magician, the man who fell so in love with the cinema that he gave everything up for it (and was ridiculed, like *The Blue Angel*'s Professor Emanuel Rath, for his passion). *The Trial*'s imagery is so powerful and its editing so nightmarishly logical that it feels like the product of some new form of stream-of-consciousness directing—but with the discipline and technical skills of a master. Even the disembodied, post-synchronized voices that haunt most of Welles's films (and most European co-productions like this one) work in the movie's favor by suggesting the impersonal, the disembodied, the lifeless functionaries who only follow orders. This is Kafka, all right. It's also every inch a film by Orson Welles. The only Orson Welles. The one

who lived up to his potential. (Franz K. himself might have enjoyed knowing that *The Trial*'s producer, Alexander Salkind, metamorphosed into the force behind three *Superman* movies.) With Romy Schneider, Elsa Martinelli, Jeanne Moreau, and Akim Tamiroff. And if a number of the characters in this movie sound suspiciously like Orson Welles, you're not paranoid, just astute.

NEXT STOP . . . *Touch of Evil, Mr. Arkadin, Franz Kafka's It's a Wonderful Life*

1963 118m/B *FR* Anthony Perkins, Jeanne Moreau, Orson Welles, Romy Schneider, Akim Tamiroff, Elsa Martinelli; *D:* Orson Welles; *C:* Edmond Richard; *M:* Jean Ledrut. **VHS** *CVC, HHT, WFV*

TRISTANA

When adapting the 80-page novel by Benito Pérez Galdós upon which *Tristana* is based, Luis Buñuel remarked that "it allows me to observe some aspects of Spanish life and customs in which I am interested." After seeing *Tristana,* the director's wryly innocuous description may make you burst out laughing. Set in Toledo, Spain, in the late 1920s, during a period of military dictatorship, the film tells the story of Don Lope (Fernando Rey), a vain, aging aristocrat who becomes erotically obsessed with and eventually seduces his young ward, Tristana (Catherine Deneuve). Though Tristana tries to escape Don Lope's insulated and stifling manipulation, she's forced to return when illness forces the amputation of her leg. This might be where any other storyteller would wrap up a moral tale about the consequences of sexual betrayal, but Buñuel simply uses it as a starting point for his savagely witty, utterly clear-eyed portrait of the powerful—and universal—bonds between religion, sexuality, and guilt. *Tristana* is one of those movies that leaves you feeling as if you'd never seen a movie before; the surrealist director's storytelling looks so unforced that the film is almost over before you realize how subversive and even radical it is. The humor in this and other Buñuel masterpieces, such as *The Exterminating Angel* and *The Discreet Charm of the Bour-*

"All I ask is a quiet life together."

—Jiazhen (Gong LI) in *To Live.*

geoisie, begins with the sheerly situational; yet what may at first seem only a bizarre cinematic moment (Don Lope caressing Tristana while trying to comfort her with the sentiment that many men would find her even more exciting since her amputation) attains its full comic stature only when we realize that the forbidden honesty underlying the scene is so liberating as to inspire *relieved* laughter. Brilliantly performed by Rey and Deneuve, *Tristana* is one of the greatest achievements by the cinema's most astute chronicler of desire.

NEXT STOP . . . *Viridiana, Belle de Jour, That Obscure Object of Desire*

1970 (PG) 98m/C *SP IT FR* Catherine Deneuve, Fernando Rey, Franco Nero, Lola Gaos, Antonio Casas, Jesus Fernandez, Vincent Solder; **D:** Luis Bunuel; **W:** Julio Alejandro, Luis Bunuel; **C:** Jose F. Aguayo. Nominations: Academy Awards '70: Best Foreign-Language Film. **VHS** *HTV*

TRIUMPH OF THE WILL
Triumph des Willens

"In all of my films there was … yes; let us say purity," Leni Riefenstahl told *Cahiers du Cinéma* in 1965. "It repulses me so much to be faced with false men that it is a thing to which I have never been able to give artistic form." Considering that she made that remark more than 30 years after creating one of the cinema's most infamous and evil masterworks, you've got to give Riefenstahl some credit. She's like the husband in the old Lenny Bruce routine whose wife walks in while the guy's having energetic sex with his secretary—and he simply denies it. Of course, in the bigger sense, Riefenstahl may not be lying at all; she's simply telling us that she feels no reason to be repulsed at having made this powerfully influential "documentary" record of the 1934 Nazi Party Rally, because there was nothing false or duplicitous about her boss and friend, Adolf Hitler. Riefenstahl is still invited to film festivals where her considerable talents as a filmmaker are celebrated, but it's more than simply an uncomfortable experience to watch this skillfully assembled Nazi recruiting poster, intricately choreographed and filmed by an army of cameramen all under Riefenstahl's command, and then to listen to film students and "scholars" politely applaud her entrance into the theatre as she—and they—proceed to separate the idea of "pure art" from its context, purpose, and consequences. This "purity" without responsibility is one of the cornerstones of Nazi ideology, and is still the basis for Riefenstahl's rationalization and selective memory regarding her pride in the creation of *Triumph of the Will*. Still content to have been "only following orders," Riefenstahl is a living memorial to the denial of truth. Her film, which is filth, survives. She remains its proud creator.

NEXT STOP . . . *Birthplace, Shoah, Night and Fog*

1934 115m/B *GE D:* Leni Riefenstahl; *W:* Leni Riefenstahl; *C:* Sepp Allgeier; *M:* Herbert Windt. **VHS** *NOS, VYY, BAR*

TROIS COULEURS: BLANC
Three Colors: White
White

The centerpiece of Krzysztof Kieslowski's *Trois Couleurs* trilogy acts as a kind of bitter comic relief. It's the story of Karol Karol (Zbigniew Zamachowski), a bewildered, impotent, sad-sack Polish hairdresser who's not only divorced by his sexually frustrated wife Dominique (Julie Delpy), but is cleaned out by her financially as well. Returning to his family in Poland, Karol doggedly washes, curls, and perms his way back to wealth, and he discovers a new economy where people make money by killing other people. It gives him an idea for winning back his ex and for having the last laugh as well. Like her charac-

ter, Dominique's name does not suggest passivity, nor does the name Karol Karol fail to bring to mind Nabokov's enslaved Humbert Humbert. Of course, *Blanc* may be taken as a comic lark and a tart, light diversion between the trilogy's more serious acts, but when one considers that in the French flag the color white stands for equality, it becomes more inviting to look beneath the surface for clues about what the balance of power really means whenever sex, money, men, and women are involved. Agnieszka Holland (*Europa, Europa*) was a co-screenwriter. Best Director Prize, Berlin Film Festival.

NEXT STOP . . . *Trois Couleurs: Bleu, Trois Couleurs: Rouge, A Friend of the Deceased*

1994 (R) 92m/C *FR SI PL* Zbigniew Zamachowski, Julie Delpy, Janusz Gajos, Jerzy Stuhr, Aleksander Bardini, Grzegorz Warchol, Cezary Harasimowicz, Jerzy Nowak, Jerzy Trela, Cezary Pazura, Michel Lisowski, Philippe Morier-Genoud; *Cameos:* Juliette Binoche, Florence Pernel; *D:* Krzysztof Kieslowski; *W:* Krzysztof Kieslowski, Krzysztof Piesiewicz; *C:* Edward Klosinski; *M:* Zbigniew Preisner. Berlin International Film Festival '94: Best Director (Kieslowski). **VHS** *MAX*

TROIS COULEURS: BLEU
Three Colors: Blue
Blue

In 1993, Poland's Krzysztof Kieslowski completed three films which he dubbed the *Trois Couleurs* trilogy, with one film named after each of the colors in the French flag. *Bleu (Blue)*, the first of the films to be released and the most downbeat of the three, is the story of a woman (Juliette Binoche) whose composer husband and child are killed in a traffic accident. In the instant of the crash, she not only lost her family, but also the melodies that her husband would never write. Binoche pulls off something quite extraordinary by keeping us with her during her long, silent stretches of grieving—we always are aware that she's working through the trauma, and that even if she'll never make sense of it (who could?) she's determined to not allow her mourning to become her master. Of the flag's three colors, it is blue that stands for liberty.

The superb scores for all three of the films in this cycle—*Bleu, Blanc (White)*, and *Rouge (Red)*—are by Zbigniew Preisner. Venice Film Festival Awards, Best Picture, Best Actress.

NEXT STOP . . . *Trois Couleurs: Rouge, Trois Couleurs: Blanc, Maborosi*

1993 (R) 98m/C *FR* Juliette Binoche, Benoit Regent, Florence Pernel, Charlotte Very, Helene Vincent, Phillipe Volter, Claude Duneton, Hugues Quester, Florence Vignon, Isabelle Sadoyan, Yann Tregouet, Jacek Ostaszewski; *Cameos:* Emmanuelle Riva; *D:* Krzysztof Kieslowski; *W:* Krzysztof Kieslowski, Krzysztof Piesiewicz, Slawomir Idziak, Agnieszka Holland, Edward Zebrowski; *C:* Slawomir Idziak; *M:* Zbigniew Preisner. Cesar Awards '94: Best Actress (Binoche), Best Film Editing, Best Sound; Los Angeles Film Critics Association Awards '93: Best Score; Venice Film Festival '93: Best Actress (Binoche), Best Film; Nominations: Golden Globe Awards '94: Best Actress—Drama (Binoche), Best Foreign Film, Best Score. **VHS, LV, Letterbox** *TOU*

TROIS COULEURS: ROUGE

Three Colors: Red
Red

Irène Jacob is Valentine, a stunning young fashion model in Geneva whose life unexpectedly intersects with an unhappy, voyeuristic, retired judge (Jean-Louis Trintignant in a warm, dignified, extremely welcome performance) in the third film in Krzysztof Kieslowski's extraordinary and audacious *Trois Couleurs* trilogy. The seeming randomness of their meeting—allowing them both to discover the possibility of new worlds and new ways of looking *at* those worlds—is the real subject of this rather daring and risky film, which works dramatically in ways that depend on what is a genuinely radical conceptual gamble that pays off thrillingly. Kieslowski and his brilliant composer, Zbigniew Preisner, have created in *Rouge*—the color of the French flag that stands for fraternity, but is also associated with violence, eroticism, and life—a portrait of individuals discovering the basic but too-often-neglected joy of *possibility*, and of the innumerable parallel universes that can be entered simply by seizing one of those possibilities—or perhaps more than one. These ideas are never stated directly, but the movie's physical form makes them stand out in stark, exquisite relief. When Kieslowski's camera races along miles of parallel telephone cables, tracking the destination of a single call to one telephone as opposed to any one of millions of others, the mind opens up to the infinite choices we take for granted, and that we tend to put off until another day. Kieslowski proves with *his* choices that the cinema is always capable of more than we imagine, because, as his film reminds us, there are so many *other* imaginations we've yet to encounter. (The major stars of the first two films in the trilogy make unobtrusive and amusing cameo appearances.) Academy Award Nominations for Best Director, Screenplay, and Cinematography.

NEXT STOP . . . *Trois Couleurs: Bleu, Trois Couleurs: Blanc, Fast, Cheap and Out of Control*

1994 (R) 99m/C *FR PL SI* Irene Jacob, Jean-Louis Trintignant, Frederique Feder, Jean-Pierre Lorit, Samuel Lebihan, Marion Stalens, Teco Celio, Bernard Escalon, Jean Schlegel, Elzbieta Jasinska; *Cameos:* Juliette Binoche, Julie Delpy, Benoit Regent, Zbigniew Zamachowski; *D:* Krzysztof Kieslowski; *W:* Krzysztof Kieslowski, Krzysztof Piesiewicz; *C:* Piotr Sobocinski; *M:* Zbigniew Preisner. Cesar Awards '94: Best Score; Independent Spirit Awards '95: Best Foreign Film; Los Angeles Film Critics Association Awards '94: Best Foreign Film; New York Film Critics Awards '94: Best Foreign Film; National Society of Film Critics Awards '94: Best Foreign Film; Nominations: Academy Awards '94: Best Cinematography, Best Director (Kieslowski), Best Original Screenplay; Cesar Awards '94: Best Actor (Trintignant), Best Actress (Jacob), Best Director (Kieslowski), Best Film; Golden Globe Awards '95: Best Foreign Film. **VHS, LV** *MAX*

TWIST & SHOUT

Hab Og Karlighed

Before embarking on the massive project that would become the prize-winning *Pelle the Conqueror*, Danish filmmaker Bille August directed this beguiling coming-of-age story set in the Beatles-saturated Denmark of 1963. Bjorn (Adam Tonsberg) is a drummer whose romance with the lovely Anna (Camilla Søeberg) results in her pregnancy, while Erik (Lars Simonsen), in an effort to deal with a strict father and a seriously depressed mother, struggles to become the stabilizing force in his troubled home. August handles all of this with a refreshing minimum of cliches; while the situations these young people find themselves in are always familiar, the sensitivity with which they're handled makes being a teenager seem like undiscovered country. (The film is a sequel—though self-contained—to August's *Zappa*, which was *not* about Frank.)

NEXT STOP . . . *Zappa, Murmur of the Heart, Time Stands Still*

1984 (R) 107m/C *DK* Lars Simonsen, Adam Tonsberg, Ulrikke Juul Bondo, Camilla Soeberg; *D:* Bille August; *W:* Bille August; *C:* Jan Weincke, Aldo G.R. Aldo Graziatti. **VHS** *NO*

TWO DAUGHTERS
Teen Kanya

This exquisite two-part film by India's Satyajit Ray was adapted from stories by Nobel Prize—winner Rabindranath Tagore. In "The Postmaster," a young man from the city becomes the new postman for a small rural village. A ten-year-old orphan girl befriends him and cares for him when he contracts malaria, but the primitive conditions of the village are too much for him, and he must break the child's heart by telling her he can't stay. In "The Conclusion," a young college graduate resists the girl that the matchmakers have chosen. He selects his own bride instead, but things do not turn out as he imagined. These two tales about the unexpected discovery of love—its different forms, joys, and disappointments—complement each other in an unforced, delicately beguiling way. This is a glowing and complete work of art—not to be considered as simply two short movies stitched together. Gently funny, elegant, and humane, *Two Daughters* warms the spirits like a rare, smooth, generously poured cognac.

NEXT STOP . . . *Mahanagar, Days and Nights in the Forest, Rendezvous in Paris*

1961 114m/B *IN* Chandana Banerjee, Anil Chatterjee, Soumitra Chatterjee; *D:* Satyajit Ray; *W:* Satyajit Ray; *C:* Soumendu Roy; *M:* Satyajit Ray. **VHS** *COL*

✓ TWO ENGLISH GIRLS
Les Deux Anglaises et le Continent
Anne and Muriel

Anne and Muriel (Kika Markham and Stacey Tendeter) are turn-of-the-century English sisters who become acquainted with Claude (Jean-Pierre Léaud) after Anne meets him on a study trip to Paris. Over the next seven years and beyond, the complex relationship between the three—in which love, friendship, pride, and regret play equal parts—will bind them together in unpredictable, heartbreakingly poignant ways. François Truffaut's completely lovely *Two English Girls* is based on the only other novel by Henri-Pierre Roché, the author of *Jules and Jim*. It marked a bold, deeply passionate, profoundly dark departure for the director, and its piercingly pure romanticism is so uncompromising that a first viewing can be dizzying and nearly disorienting. That same form of intense, risky, romantic purity would infuse some of Truffaut's subsequent films, most notably *The Story of Adele H.* and *The Woman Next Door*. But the bittersweet, tender *Two English Girls* is an original, elegant achievement, unique among Truffaut's films. The broodingly beautiful cinematography is by Nestor Almendros, and the musical score is one of Georges Delerue's most haunting and inspired. Originally shortened for its American release, it was fully restored in the 1980s. (Few movies have been known by as many names; the original title of the film—and novel—is *Les Deux Anglaises et le Continent,* but in much of the world, including England, it was called *Anne and Muriel*.)

NEXT STOP . . . *Jules and Jim, The Story of Adele H., The Age of Innocence*

1972 (R) 108m/C *FR* Jean-Pierre Leaud, Kika Markham, Stacey Tendeter, Sylvia Marriott, Marie Mansert, Philippe Leotard; *D:* Francois Truffaut; *W:* François Truffaut; *C:* Nestor Almendros; *M:* Georges Delerue. **VHS, LV** *HMV, FOX*

TWO FRIENDS

Louise (Emma Coles) and Kelly (Kris Bidenko) are two 15-year-old girls whose

friendship has ended. Both girls had had their wishes come true by being accepted for enrollment at the same prestigious school, but Kelly has been forbidden to attend by her hard-line stepfather, who thinks the girl will become a snob. Jane Campion's 1986 *Two Friends* would end here, were it not for the fact that she's placed the end of their story at the beginning of her film. As in Harold Pinter's *Betrayal* (and the *Seinfeld* episode that lampooned it), Campion then works her way back in time through the friendship's deterioration, showing the girls becoming closer and closer over the course of the previous year, and finally believing themselves inseparable, allowing us—if not her characters—a happy ending. The home lives of the girls are lovingly detailed by the director, who's more interested in the moment-to-moment dynamics of adoles-

cent closeness than in its inevitable dissolution, which may be why she dispenses with any pretense of traditional "suspense" right off the bat. Coles and Bidenko are natural and charming performers, but the quality of the sound recording (filmed on 16mm for television) combined with thick and often mumbled Australian accents, may put some viewers off. Stick with it though, to discover the early, already considerable talents of the director who would startle the cinema world with *Sweetie,* and create a worldwide phenomenon with *The Piano.*

NEXT STOP . . . *Sweetie, An Angel at My Table, High Tide (1987)*

1986 76m/C *AU* Kris Bidenko, Emma Coles, Peter Hehir, Kris McQuade; *D:* Jane Campion; *W:* Helen Garner; *C:* Julian Penney; *M:* Martin Armiger. **VHS, Letterbox** *NYF, MIL*

THE TWO OF US

Le Vieil Homme et l'Enfant
Claude
The Old Man and the Boy

Claude Berri's 1967 *The Two of Us* is a film that was both underrated and overrated in its day, for the usual reason that anytime a filmmaker deals with sensitive subject matter, it is expected that the film must be complete, all-encompassing, and definitive, satisfying everyone. Berri's film is his autobiographical memoir of his childhood during World War II, a time when his being Jewish in occupied France could cost him and his family their lives. The eight-year-old Claude (played by Alain Cohen) is sent by his parents to stay with a Catholic family of friends living in the country, but the only problem—and the movie's hook—is that the family's old patriarch, Pépé (Michel Simon), is a Jew-hater who rants to the boy day and night about how Jews look, how they smell, how they have all the money (his antipathy is such that the family keeps him in the dark about the boy's heritage). Claude, needless to say, spends much of the movie's running time trying to keep the old man from seeing him naked. The two develop the predictable friendship, but Berri's determination to generally not stress the most potentially maudlin elements of a scene is admirable. A strength as well is the presence of the great old Michel Simon, who carries with him on screen the extraordinary cinematic legacy of his work in *L'Atalante, Boudu Saved from Drowning,* and so many other classic French films. To his and Berri's credit, they never let the old man become magically transformed into a liberal, progressive thinker; they never even let him discover the truth about his beloved little house guest. Simon's old man will retain his bigotry for the remainder of his life (though there are hints to the contrary), and it's up to us to imagine what he would have become had he assumed any modest position of influence in the Vichy government. But, at least in this movie, he didn't. (Simon's character is actually a composite of a number of people Berri met during the war.) In the end, *The Two of Us* succeeds as personal memoir because it doesn't try to be anything grander than that.

NEXT STOP . . . *Marry Me, Marry Me, Au revoir les Enfants, Forbidden Games*

1968 86m/B *FR* Michel Simon, Alain Cohen, Luce Fabiole, Roger Carel, Paul Preboist, Charles Denner; *D:* Claude Berri; *W:* Claude Berri; *C:* Jean Penzer; *M:* Georges Delerue. **VHS** *NO*

TWO OR THREE THINGS I KNOW ABOUT HER

Deux ou Trois Choses Que Je Sais d'Elle

In the labyrinthine, assaultive, spectacular, and constantly evolving Paris of 1966, a housewife (Marina Vlady) turns to prostitution when day-to-day expenses of life in the big city become overwhelming. The 24 hours that Jean-Luc Godard's film covers is presented like a continuing dream state of motion, space, and images, in which the movie's two stars, Vlady and Paris (each being the "her" of the title), circle around each other and become completely interdependent, like some science fiction, *Demon Seed*—ish notion of a human fused with the glass-and-steel structures around her. At what point have individuals—and cities—irretrievably sold their souls? It's a question Godard poses with the aid of stunning widescreen color images by the legendary cinematographer Raoul Coutard. Experimental, endlessly witty, and still absolutely fresh, this is in its way as impressionistic and poetic a vision of a living metropolis as Dziga Vertov's *The Man with the Movie Camera.*

NEXT STOP . . . *Pierrot le Fou, Alphaville, Playtime*

1966 95m/C *FR* Marina Vlady, Anny Duperey, Roger Montsoret, Jean Narboni, Raoul Levy; *D:* Jean-Luc Godard; *W:* Jean-Luc Godard; *C:* Raoul Coutard. **VHS** *NYF*

UGETSU

Ugetsu Monogatari

In 16th-century Japan, two peasant brothers-in-law, both ambitious in different ways, set out for the city to better themselves. One

unforgettable moments and images such as the morning of ecstasy that follows the first sexual encounter between Genjuro and Lady Wakasa. Simultaneously realistic and otherworldly, this is one of the cinema's great fables about the human toll taken by worldly ambition, and the single greatest ghost story ever filmed. The full title, *Ugetsu Monogatari*, is translated as *Tales of the Pale and Silver Moon After the Rain*. Silver Lion Award, Venice Film Festival.

NEXT STOP . . . *Sansho the Bailiff, Princess Yang Kwei Fei, Kwaidan*

1953 96m/B *JP* Machiko Kyo, Masayuki Mori, Kinuyo Tanaka, Sakae Ozawa; *D:* Kenji Mizoguchi; *W:* Yoshikata Yoda; *C:* Kazuo Miyagawa; *M:* Fumio Hayasaka. Venice Film Festival '53: Silver Prize; Nominations: Academy Awards '55: Best Costume Design (B & W). **VHS, LV, 8mm** *HMV, WFV, DVT*

ULYSSES' GAZE
The Look of Ulysses
To Vlemma Tou Odyssea
The Gaze of Ulysses

A Greek-American filmmaker whose name is only given as A ... (Harvey Keitel) returns to Greece after decades in the U.S. to attend a festival of his work. Obsessed with the history of the Balkans—particularly in light of the current conflict—and obsessed as well with the history of the cinema, A ... is intrigued by rumors of the existence of three reels of film, supposedly photographed by the legendary Manakia brothers, that represent the first film footage ever shot in the Balkans. He is determined to track the film down. Embarking on a Ulysses-like odyssey that will not only take him physically from Greece to Sarajevo but also spiritually from the present to the past, A ... gradually discovers deeply revelatory truths about the borders between countries, the borders between men and women, and the borders between history and cinema. Their common bond, the passage of time, is an important character in this contemplative, three-hour, visionary masterwork by Greek filmmaker Theo Angelopoulos. Though visually stunning, the movie's

Catherine Deneuve looks out the window of her mother's umbrella shop in *The Umbrellas of Cherbourg*.

of the two, Tobei (Sakas Ozawa), who dreams of military glory, encounters catastrophe when he comes across samurai armor and claims another man's victory as his own. The other man, Genjuro (Masayuki Mori), meets and is seduced by the mysterious and overwhelmingly sensuous Lady Wakasa (Machiko Kyo of *Rashomon*). Genjuro's enchantment is so great that he abandons his wife and child for her, before realizing that the Lady Wakasa is actually the ghost of a girl who died before experiencing the joy of womanhood. Kenji Mizoguchi's great, intoxicating *Ugetsu* is drawn from stories by Akinari Ueda, but the haunting images of Mizoguchi's film make it impossible to imagine these tales in any other form. One of the few films to ever convincingly give photographic life to mystical experience, *Ugetsu* is also typical of Mizoguchi's concern with women's frustrations and their oppressed role in Japanese society. *Ugetsu* is filled with

rhythm demands attentiveness and patience, as does the dialogue which at first seems more stilted than stylized. Stay with it. When you come out the other side, you'll feel—correctly—that you've completed an eye-opening spiritual odyssey of your own. Grand Jury Prize, Cannes Film Festival.

NEXT STOP . . . *Landscape in the Mist, The Traveling Players, Before the Rain*

1995 173m/C *GR FR IT* Harvey Keitel, Maia Morgenstern, Erland Josephson, Thanassis Vengos, Yorgos Michalokopoulos, Dora Volonaki; *D:* Theo Angelopoulos; *W:* Theo Angelopoulos, Tonino Guerra, Petros Markaris; *C:* Yorgos Arvanitis; *M:* Eleni Karaindrou. Cannes Film Festival '95: Grand Jury Prize. **VHS** *FXL*

UMBERTO D.

An aged, former civil servant, now trying to live on a completely inadequate government pension, does what he can to maintain a semblance of dignity in spite of his poverty. Umberto is far behind on his rent, and though he's convinced that suicide is the only possible solution to his plight, he's reluctant to leave his beloved dog behind to fight for scraps of food on the mean, post-war Roman streets. Vittorio De Sica's *Umberto D*—one of the world's great movies—is never maudlin or mawkishly sentimental. De Sica's protagonist, played memorably by a non-professional actor and retired professor named Carlo Battisti, remains a gentleman throughout every moment of his horrifying, all-too-familiar plight; he never understands why the rest of the world doesn't behave with kindness and compassion. As we sit there and watch the day-to-day details of Umberto's existence, knowing that there are millions still today in the same hopeless situation, *we* find it hard to understand as well. *Umberto D* cleanses and refreshes the imagination in many ways, and one of the most important is the manner in which it reminds us that great art needn't smash us over the head with its message or jerk unearned tears out of us in order to stir us deeply. The simplicity and unaffected brilliance of *Umberto D* should never be mistaken for casualness; De Sica makes us feel we're seeing a docu-

mentary, yet every detail of script, image, and performance is perfectly designed to achieve an overwhelming emotional impact. (It was De Sica's favorite among his own films.) *Umberto D* has been accurately described as a miracle, and in terms of analysis, it may be best to simply leave it at that. Academy Award Nomination, Best Original Screenplay (Cesare Zavattini).

NEXT STOP . . . *Shoeshine, The Bicycle Thief, Welfare*

1955 89m/B *IT* Carlo Battista, Maria Pia Casilio, Lina Gennari; *D:* Vittorio De Sica; *W:* Cesare Zavattini, Vittorio De Sica; *M:* Alessandro Cicognini. New York Film Critics Awards '55: Best Foreign Film; Nominations: Academy Awards '56: Best Story. **VHS, LV, 8mm, Letterbox** *HMV, HHT, DVT*

THE UMBRELLAS OF CHERBOURG
Les Parapluies de Cherbourg
Die Regenschirme von Cherbourg

In Jacques Demy's brave and bittersweet love story, a 20-year-old Catherine Deneuve plays Genevieve, the teenaged daughter of umbrella shop owner Madame Emery (Anne Vernon). When the war in Algeria means that her adored boyfriend Guy (Nino Castelnuovo) is called to active duty, Genevieve becomes panicked over her discovery that she's pregnant. With the encouragement of her mother, Genevieve decides to marry a wealthy gem dealer who's smitten with her, rather than risk losing Guy during the war and thus having her baby be born fatherless. When Guy inevitably returns, all the parties involved are older and wiser, but their hearts are not convinced. The most immediately noticeable characteristic of *The Umbrellas of Cherbourg* is not just that it's a musical, but that *every* line in the movie is sung. It's disconcerting at first, to the point where you think that a garage mechanic's warbling about an oil change is going to send you right out of the theatre. But Demy cleverly pokes a little fun at his own methods in an early scene: one of the characters sings about how singing at the movies drives him crazy. Suddenly you decide to sit back and let yourself take it in, and you're glad,

because it turns out to be pretty glorious. The music—all 90 minutes of it—is by Michel Legrand, with lyrics by Demy. You'll recognize many of the tunes, two of which later hit pop charts in their English versions as "I Will Wait for You" and "Watch What Happens." The lovely, fairy-tale-like cinematography is by Jean Rabier, and it looks better than ever in the new color restoration of the film that was completed in 1996. A double CD is available of the complete soundtrack as well. Grand Prize, 1964 Cannes Film Festival.

NEXT STOP . . . *Lola, The Young Girls of Rochefort, Jacquot*

1964 90m/C *FR* Catherine Deneuve, Nino Castelnuovo, Anne Vernon, Ellen Farner, Marc Michel, Mireille Perrey, Jean Champion, Alfred Wolff, Dorothee Blanck; **D:** Jacques Demy; **W:** Jacques Demy; **C:** Jean Rabier; **M:** Michel Legrand. Cannes Film Festival '64: Best Film; Nominations: Academy Awards '65: Best Foreign-Language Film, Best Song ("I Will Wait for You"), Best Story & Screenplay, Best Original Score. **VHS** *FXL, ART*

UN COEUR EN HIVER
A Heart in Winter

Stephane (Daniel Auteuil) is a master craftsman who repairs violins with the care, sensitivity, and attention to perfection of a great surgeon. One day, a stunningly beautiful violinist (Emmanuelle Béart) comes into the shop that Stephane and his partner Maxime (André Dussollier) run together. A complicated and potentially messy love story evolves involving the three of them, leading to the quietly sad revelation that as skilled as Stephane may be, he hasn't the temperament—or the willingness to risk failure—that love and art both require. Claude Sautet's delicate and deeply wise portrait of a love that does not triumph could be considered the ultimate music video for grownups. Sautet conjures his characters' feelings through the most subtle directorial nuance; he brings us close and lets each actor's face make the most complicated and contradictory impulses completely palpable. The film's music, almost entirely Ravel, is an integral part of the film's hypnotic rhythm, helping to lead us to that moment—which even Stephane can't fully express verbally—in which he knows that he can go *this* far but no further, and is unwilling to endure the disruptions that would accompany a commitment to passion. He's unable to leave his known, frozen world, a risk-free universe where his heart beats calmly and unexcitedly in its perpetual winter. César Awards for Best Director and Supporting Actor (Dussollier).

NEXT STOP... *Vincent, François, Paul and the Others, Nelly and Monsieur Arnaud, Tous les Matins du Monde*

1993 100m/C *FR* Emmanuelle Beart, Daniel Auteuil, Andre Dussollier, Elisabeth Bourgine, Brigitte Catillon, Maurice Garrel, Miriam Boyer; **D:** Claude Sautet; **W:** Jacques Fieschi, Jerome Tonnerre; **C:** Yves Angelo. Cesar Awards '93: Best Director (Sautet), Best Supporting Actor (Dussollier); Nominations: British Academy Awards '93: Best Foreign Film. **VHS, LV** *REP*

UNDER THE ROOFS OF PARIS
Sous les Toits de Paris

In a teeming, tenement quarter of Paris, a street singer and his best friend both court a charming young girl. Complications ensue, but they don't get in the way of friendship. From this simple wisp of a plot, René Clair created this enchanting and inventive early film musical, which suggested new possibilities for the creative use of sound in filmmaking. Clair had been one of the most vocal enemies of the idea of introducing sound to movies, but when it came, he decided that movies needn't simply be endless dialogue accompanied by static images. Clair stood convention on its head immediately with sequences like an argument that takes place behind a glass door, which, of course, renders the arguers amusingly silent, even in this all-new world of movie sound. Camera movements were accompanied by music and sound effects that complemented and commented on the motion, while overall dialogue was sparse. Songs and music provided most of the commentary, like a comic and satirical Greek chorus. Clair developed many of his innovations with sound still further in his next films, the ingenious *A Nous la Liberté* and his great, incomparably delightful *Le Million*.

NEXT STOP... *The Italian Straw Hat, A Nous la Liberté, L'Atalante*

1929 95m/B *FR* Albert Prejean, Pola Illery, Gaston Modot, Edmond T. Greville; **D:** Rene Clair; **W:** Rene Clair; **C:** Georges Perinal; **M:** Armand Bernard. **VHS** *VYY, NOS, CAB*

UNDERGROUND
Once Upon a Time There Was a Country
Il Etait une Fois un Pays

Marko and Blacky, two wild and crazy Yugoslavian friends, join forces to fight the invading Nazis in 1941, hiding in a cellar to produce much-needed munitions. When the war ends, however, Marko (now dwelling above ground in the "real" world) neglects to inform Blacky, and continues to exploit his patriotic fervor to keep producing the still-in-demand weapons that have so tragically and so profitably become a growth industry. As the nation experiences more wars—and ultimately fractures into non-existence—the two former friends eventually meet again amid the terror and madness of Bosnian battlegrounds. To allude to *Underground* as a comedy is not to be callous—on the contrary, this is one of the darkest visions of the human condition in recent years. But what director Emir Kusturica has given us here is a massive (nearly three-hour), visionary three-ring circus of human folly and tragedy, but one that never fails to entertain and astonish, even while it appalls. As a cry of outrage and despair, *Underground* is remarkably coherent and humane; it is a cynical, powerful, mournful epic that grieves for the loss of a nation and its culture—its final image a perfectly visualized, delicately balanced metaphor that stays in the mind more indelibly that any newsreel footage of inex-

EMIR KUSTURICA
Eastern European Filmmaker

Emil Kusturica's film *Underground* won the Palme d'Or at the Cannes Film Festival in 1995. It has been called a "Balkan blend of weltschmerz and black comedy." It is a bold reconstruction of Yugoslav history from the Nazi invasion of World War II to the present wars. Born November 24, 1955 in Sarajevo, Kusturica has been labeled an apologist for Yugoslavia and a pro-Serb propagandist, but he evades tags. "I really don't have a nationality." When he served on the Cannes jury, he identified himself as a Bosnian.

Kusturica is leery of political fingerpointing. "Heroes don't have nationalities in film," he says. Although his films obviously deal with politics, they also have that Central European surrealistic quality and poetic edge that makes any simple search for a message frustrating.

Kusturica made an English language film, *Arizona Dream*, released in 1992. It starred Johnny Depp, Faye Dunaway, and Jerry Lewis. Vincent Gallo, who also starred in the film, calls Kusturica "a wonderful, compassionate person" but also a "bully, a comedic bully." The director certainly has a temper, although he laughs off a violent incident with his son that had to be broken up by the police. "It was just a stylistic continuation of *Underground*," he says. After the controversy surrounding *Underground*, he vowed to retire from fimmaking, but has done a new film called *Black Cat, White Cat* (1998).

Kusturica lives in a Normandy village with his wife Maya and his son Stribor and daughter Dunya. In his early forties, the director has the remarkable intensity that distinguishes many Eastern European intellectuals. He compares his style to the cinema of Fellini and to the fiction of South Americans—often called "magical realism."

plicable atrocities. The deserving winner of the Palme d'Or at Cannes, *Underground* was turned down by every major American distributor for years, but was finally rescued by Daniel Talbot's indispensable—and often heroic—New Yorker Films.

NEXT STOP . . . *When Father Was Away on Business, Tito and Me, Before the Rain*

1995 192m/C *FR GE HU* Miki Manojlovic, Lazar Ristovski, Mirjana Jokovic, Slavko Stimac, Ernst Stotzner, Srdan Todorovic, Mirjana Karanovic; *Cameos:* Emir Kusturica; *D:* Emir Kusturica; *W:* Emir Kusturica, Dusan Kovacevic; *C:* Vilko Filac; *M:* Goran Bregovic. Cannes Film Festival '95: Best Film; Nominations: Independent Spirit Awards '98: Best Foreign Film. **VHS** *NYR*

UTAMARO AND HIS FIVE WOMEN
Five Women around Utamaro
Utamaro O Meguru Gonin No Onna

Utamaro was a legendary 18th-century Japanese printmaker who gained inspiration from the *demimonde* of Edo, a sordid and disreputable environment of brothels, public drunkenness, and passionate love affairs. The director, Kenji Mizoguchi, was himself an artist concerned with areas of society that are often less than respectable, and the emotional commitment to his subjects that he conveys in his great film tragedies like *Life of Oharu* and *Chikamatsu Monogatari* makes his interest in Utamaro's painting all the more persuasive. Utamaro participated in the sensory excesses of his society only through his art, and Mizoguchi's film lets us experience that strange and sometimes blurred borderline between the artist and his subject. This is a rigorous and fascinating biography, visually beautiful, though not in a league with his greatest masterworks.

NEXT STOP . . . *Ugetsu, Andrei Rublev, Edvard Munch*

1946 89m/B *JP* Minnosuke Bando, Kinuyo Tanaka, Kotaro Bando, Hisato Osawa, Tamezo Mochizuki, Hiroko Kawasaki; *D:* Kenji Mizoguchi; *W:* Yoshikata Yoda; *C:* Shigeto Miki; *M:* Hisato Osawa, Tamezo Mochizuki. **VHS** *NYF, FCT*

VAGABOND
Sans Toit Ni Loi

The brief life of a young woman named Mona (Sandrine Bonnaire), whose frozen body is discovered at the beginning of *Vagabond,* is recounted in a series of flashbacks and interviews with people who encountered her in her aimless travels. Agnes Varda's shattering portrait of a lost soul is a remarkable work of art that never stoops to neatly packaging this woman's despair into an overly neat dramatic framework. Instead, we learn about her past a bit at a time—we learn a little about her parents, her education, her work history. We also witness the responses she provokes in the people she meets, and over time we in the audience momentarily feel some of those same reactions to Mona's appearance, her anger, and her irresponsibility. But it is not that simple. Possibly, just possibly, our discomfort at seeing Mona stems from our understanding her better than we care to admit. Emotional and mental torment are not as easily explained—or soothed—as we would like, or as movies would often have us believe. Varda knows this, and her honest and piercing film reflects it at every turn. We also know that Mona's story is repeated daily, everywhere, and the outcome is often just as tragic. We generally can look away or do our best to relegate such cases to the universe of statistics, but Varda insists that on at least this one occasion, we stare down this terrible mystery to its logical, inevitable end. Bonnaire and the entire cast are extraordinary in what is unquestionably Varda's masterpiece to date.

NEXT STOP . . . *An Angel at My Table, Mouchette, The Fire Within*

1985 105m/C *FR* Sandrine Bonnaire, Macha Meril, Stephane Freiss, Elaine Cortadellas, Marthe Jarnias, Yolanda Moreau; *D:* Agnes Varda; *W:* Agnes Varda; *C:* Patrick Blossier; *M:* Joanne Bruzdowicz. Cesar Awards '86: Best Actress (Bonnaire); Los Angeles Film Critics Association Awards '86: Best Actress (Bonnaire), Best Foreign Film. **VHS, LV** *HMV, TPV*

THE VALLEY OBSCURED BY THE CLOUDS
La Vallee

At the height of its power, the cinema can tap in to the sensibilities of a generation so profoundly that an entire culture can be influenced, whether the film be *Breathless, Easy Rider,* or *2001: A Space Odyssey.* Then again, few sights are sorrier than a talented filmmaker's attempt to tap into the "youth culture" with high-toned, swanky teensploitation pix like Barbet Schroeder's 1972 *The Valley Obscured by the Clouds.* Still, few hippie pictures looked as good as this one, thanks to Nestor Almendros's lush widescreen location cinematography in the jungles of New Guinea. The plot has something to do with an establishment functionary's wife (Bulle Ogier) learning to get down and go natural in the forest while looking for the valley of the gods with some of society's dropouts. The constant Pink Floyd on the soundtrack fills in any of those pesky narrative gaps that tend to crop up when a movie has no plot. Schroeder must have awakened quickly from this experience (quicker than the audience, at least), because his next directorial effort was the bold, alarming documentary *General Idi Amin Dada,* which put Schroeder and Almendros in the middle of a very different jungle, and without Pink Floyd. But it was his next fiction film, the memorable, shocking, surprising *Maîtresse,* that would finally gain Schroeder recognition as a directorial force to be reckoned with.

NEXT STOP . . . *More, In the White City, Apocalypse Now*

1972 106m/C *FR* Bulle Ogier, Michael Gothard, Jean-Pierre Kalfon, Jerome Beauvarlet, Monique Giraudy; **D:** Barbet Schroeder; **W:** Barbet Schroeder; **C:** Nestor Almendros; **M:** Pink Floyd. **VHS** *FCT, WAR, BTV*

VAMPYR

Vampyr, Ou L'Etrange Aventure de David Gray
Vampyr, Der Traum des David Gray
Not Against the Flesh
Castle of Doom
The Strange Adventure of David Gray
The Vampire

Not to be confused with German director F.W. Murnau's 1922 *Nosferatu* (a marvelous film as well, yet different in just about every way), Danish director Carl Dreyer's 1932 *Vampyr* is the agonizingly creepy tale of a female vampire's determined pursuit of her victims. Designed with the familiar but uncomfortable logic of a dream, *Vampyr*—based on J.S. Le Fanu's 1872 story "Carmilla," which also inspired Bram Stoker to create *Dracula*—is less concerned with the particulars of vampirism than with the terrors of the pursued; the process of death is continually imagined by the vampire's potential victims, and they obsess on darkness, defeat, and burial. All of this is achieved through the astounding, hallucinatory cinematography of the great Rudolph Maté (who later, in Hollywood, would photograph a vision from a different kind of dream—Rita Hayworth in *Gilda*) and through the deliberate and inexorable pacing that provides no escape and no sliver of hope in the ghoulish, decaying landscape. (In 1965, Dreyer told *Cahiers du Cinéma* that he and Maté found the key to *Vampyr*'s visual style when a light accidentally hit the lens and fogged one of the takes. After looking at the result, they repeated the "mistake" on each day of the shoot to achieve the same otherworldly effect.)

NEXT STOP . . . *Nosferatu* (1922), *Dracula* (1931), *Nosferatu* (1979)

1931 75m/B *GE FR* Julian West, Sybille Schmitz, Henriette Gerard, Maurice Schutz, Rena Mandel, Jan Hieronimko, Albert Bras; **D:** Carl Theodor Dreyer; **W:** Carl Theodor Dreyer, Christen Jul; **C:** Rudolph Mate; **M:** Wolfgang Zeller. **VHS** *KIV, NOS, SNC*

VAN GOGH

Looking at the greatest works of certain artists, it's sometimes unimaginable to think of being in the same room—or making small talk with—the genius whose hand created the image on the canvas before you. But that is exactly what director Maurice Pialat has done with his gentle and surprisingly moving *Van Gogh*—he has given us a man, not a deity, and has shown us what by all accounts the final 67 days of this man's life consisted of. The film is all small actions and impressions; we see him drinking despite his poor health, putting the moves on a patron's daughter, quietly observing landscapes, ranting over his brother's inability to sell a single work of his art. Nothing is presented urgently; the movie breathes, but never shouts. The scattershot method Pialat uses might not have worked so well or been so engrossing were it not for the central performance of Jacques Dutronc, who seems possessed by the role and radiates intelligence, delicacy, and pain. He's not "acting" up a storm here as some sort of mad genius, nor does he collapse in self-pity as tortured artists are supposed to in the movies. He's just a guy, and that's a radical enough concept to make *Van Gogh* downright avant-garde.

NEXT STOP . . . *The Testament of Orpheus, Lust for Life, Love Is the Devil*

1992 (R) 155m/C *FR* Jacques Dutronc, Alexandra London, Gerard Sety, Bernard Le Coq, Corinne Bourdon; **D:** Maurice Pialat; **W:** Maurice Pialat; **C:** Gilles Henry, Emmanuel Machuel; **M:** Edith Vesperini. Cesar Awards '92: Best Actor (Dutronc). **VHS** *COL, FCT*

THE VANISHING
Spoorloos

A Dutch couple is on holiday when they stop for gas. While in the gas station getting snacks, the wife disappears. For the next three years, the woman's husband doggedly searches for any clue to her whereabouts. Ultimately, in a climactic sequence that can only be called unforgettable, he learns the truth. When critics write about thrillers, they frequently toss around expressions like "it will give you nightmares," when nothing could be further from the truth. In the case of *The Vanishing,* however, nothing could be *closer* to the truth. The film is structured like a long, horribly sadistic practical joke, but it's irresistibly seductive. Much has been written about the power of the movie's ending, but what makes *The Vanishing* especially chilling is the concept and casting of the film's villain, and the methodical way in which he goes about his business. Nothing in the movie seems fantastic, and it's the logical progression of each horrifying step that chills you to the bone and becomes even more upsetting when remembering the film years later. (The director, George Sluizer, did an American remake starring Jeff Bridges and Kiefer Sutherland. It's just awful.)

NEXT STOP . . . *The Lady Vanishes, Psycho, Diabolique*

1988 107m/C *NL FR* Barnard Pierre Donnadieu, Johanna Ter Steege, Gene Bervoets; *D:* George Sluizer; *W:* Tim Krabbe; *C:* Toni Kuhn; *M:* Henny Vrienten. **VHS** *FXL*

VARIETY
Vaudeville
Variete

An acrobat (Emil Jannings) abandons his wife and child to run off with a beautiful young girl (Lya de Putti). When the two of them form a trapeze act with a handsome young acrobat (Warwick Ward), Jannings's well-founded jealousy explodes into deadly violence. E.A. Dupont's silent German classic may not be one of the most subtle melodramas of all time, but it's quite gripping as an example of sheer cinematic bravado. Together with his

great cameraman Karl Freund (*Metropolis, The Last Laugh*), Dupont created a riveting immediacy in *Variety* that made much of the action seem to take place from specific characters' points-of-view. The camera keeps moving and flying through the air, but when it stops, it's often on the come-hither face and voluptuous body of Lya de Putti, who became a sensation as a result of the picture's international success. Jannings is remarkable as the sexually humiliated and dishonored acrobat—it's the kind of part he was always best at, and his performance here ranks with his similarly destroyed Professor Rath in Von Sternberg's *The Blue Angel.*

NEXT STOP . . . *The Last Laugh, Pandora's Box, The Unknown* (1927)

1925 104m/B *GE* Emil Jannings, Lya de Putti, Warwick Ward, Werner Krauss; *D:* E.A. Dupont; *W:* E.A. Dupont; *C:* Karl Freund. **VHS** *VYY, NOS, DVT*

VARIETY LIGHTS
Luci del Varieta
Lights of Variety

The first feature film on which Federico Fellini worked as director (it was co-directed with Alberto Lattuada) is the story of a down-and-out troupe of traveling vaudeville players who cling—naively but necessarily—to the dream that someday they will achieve real fame and stardom. The details of their seedy one-night-stands are presented with swift, gentle, comic poignancy, as are their relationships to each other. But the central love story in *Variety Lights* is that between the performers and their illusions—those they create for their undemanding audiences, and those they must recreate daily for themselves. Those who dismiss the generally delightful *Variety Lights* do so because it's not one the great Fellini films. Granted. But those who say it would never have been noticed were Fellini's name not on it are wrong; the film stands on its own as a transitional moment between neo-realism and the great Italian comedies that followed, but the fun of seeing in it the early seeds of so many of the poetic, Felliniesque elements that would soon fully blossom is

Giulietta Masina
stars as a member
of a vaudeville
troupe in Federico
Fellini's *Variety
Lights*.

Enokizu's case became a sensation in Japan, both because of the brutality of his crimes and because of their seeming senselessness. Beginning with the understanding that there is in fact no such thing as a "senseless" crime, Imamura has structured his film as a series of flashbacks in which we witness the killer's crimes while he awaits conviction and execution for what he has done. We see key incidents from his past, including his unhappy childhood and failed marriage, but to Imamura's credit there's no one moment that appears to be the switch that turned this man into an unrepentant sociopath. As in *Taxi Driver*, we come away with the sensation of knowing this man quite well, yet not having the slightest understanding of what really brought him to this point. It's the welcome opposite of what pictures like this usually try to do, which is to fascistically give us an exact, clean explanation for seemingly random violence (as in Richard Brooks's *In Cold Blood*, when Perry Smith's crummy childhood shows up in near-subliminal flashes at key moments, as if to tell us that *this* is what he was thinking at that very second). It's far more comfortable for someone leaving a film to know precisely what factors will cause the person they're going to drive home with to murder them. Imamura doesn't let us off so easily, and it's the key to his movie's unsettling power.

NEXT STOP... *The Ballad of Narayama, Mishima, Henry: Portrait of a Serial Killer*

1979 129m/C *JP* Ken Ogata, Rentaro Mikuni, Mitsuko Baisho, Chocho Miyako, Mayumi Ogawa, Nijiko Kiyokawa; **D:** Shohei Imamura; **W:** Masuru Baba; **C:** Sinsaku Himeda; **M:** Shinichiro Ikebe. **VHS, LV** *FCT*

irresistible. Irresistible as well is the cast, which includes a remarkably charismatic young woman whom we would soon see more of: Giulietta Masina.

NEXT STOP... *Nights of Cabiria, La Strada, The Iceman Cometh*

1951 93m/B *IT* Giulietta Masina, Peppino de Filippo, Carla Del Poggio, Folco Lulli; **D:** Federico Fellini, Alberto Lattuada; **W:** Federico Fellini, Tullio Pinelli, Ennio Flaiano, Alberto Lattuada; **C:** Otello Martelli; **M:** Felice Lattuada. **VHS** *HMV, CVC*

VENGEANCE IS MINE

Fukusho Suruwa Ware Ni Ari

Shohei Imamura's 1979 film is based on the true history of an infamous murderer and scam artist, called Iwao Enokizu in the film and portrayed mesmerizingly by Ken Ogata.

VERONIKA VOSS

Die Sehns Ucht der Veronika Voss

Based on the true story of a fallen German film star, Rainer Werner Fassbinder's baroque and ghoulish *Veronika Voss* is the closest he ever came to a flat-out horror film. Rosel Zech plays the one-time star who was also a mistress to high-ranking Nazi officials, but by the 1950s is an on-the-nod morphine addict whose supplier—a sadistic female doctor—

is bent on bleeding Veronika of every last possession and shred of self-respect. Determined to make Billy Wilder's *Sunset Boulevard* look like an episode of *Barney*, Fassbinder's heroined heroine literally wallows in decaying, decadent misery and self-pity. As we hear both Veronika and Dean Martin croon "Memories Are Made of This," we see a grim vision of the darker side of the post-war German economic miracle unfolding—a universe of soulless zombies in which progress is merely one more day of waking death, and where recollections of the past are almost as terrifying as glimpses of the future. *Veronika Voss* is both gorgeous and grotesque, and one of the most silken pieces of high melodrama that Fassbinder ever gave us. Grand Prize, 1982 Berlin Film Festival. (There was a spooky soundtrack album, if you can still find it.)

NEXT STOP . . . *The Marriage of Maria Braun , Lola, Sunset Boulevard*

1982 (R) 105m/C *GE* Rosel Zech, Hilmar Thate, Conny Froboess, Anna Marie Duringer, Volker Spengler; **D:** Rainer Werner Fassbinder; **W:** Pea Frolich, Peter Marthesheimer; **C:** Xaver Schwarzenberger; **M:** Peer Raben. **VHS** *FCT*

A VERY CURIOUS GIRL
La Fiancee du Pirate
Dirty Mary
Pirate's Fiancee

This strange little picture created a modest art house buzz in 1969. It is director Nelly Kaplan's merger of a bawdy, farmer's-daughter fable with a hard-line, feminist revenge fantasy. Bernadette Lafont is Marie, the physically desirable but socially outcast form of amusement for the smug and hypocritical men of her small rural village. Her well-plotted revenge finds Marie deciding to charge money for her favors, which puts her in the position of being able to blackmail those who do business with her. It turns out to be an effective way of turning the tables of power, yet the movie is just never inventive enough to be truly engaging, nor vicious enough to really sting. The movie tries to stay whimsical, and the tone just seems all wrong. Its primary attraction—and it's a considerable one—is an electric performance by the wonderful Bernadette Lafont, who energized many key French films of the 1960s and 1970s, including Jean Eustache's landmark epic *The Mother and the Whore*.

NEXT STOP . . . *Such a Gorgeous Kid Like Me, Son of Gascogne, The Mother and the Whore*

1969 (R) 105m/C *FR* Bernadette LaFont, Georges Geret, Michel Constantin, Julien Guiomar, Claire Maurier; **D:** Nelly Kaplan; **W:** Nelly Kaplan, Claude Makovski; **C:** Jean Badal; **M:** Georges Moustaki. **VHS** *NO*

VICTIM

A successful, married English barrister (Dirk Bogarde) with a concealed history of homosexuality finds himself the victim of blackmail after the death of a former lover. When the blackmailers, who are the cause of his young ex-lover's suicide, are caught, Bogarde decides to prosecute them himself, even though it means bringing his hidden past into the light, thereby risking his career and his marriage. Basil Dearden's entertaining and cleverly constructed *Victim* was pretty bold stuff when it was released in 1961, and though time has certainly taken its toll in some respects (homosexuals are referred to as "inverts" in the film), in bigger ways the film still seems revolutionary. Bogarde's character is not treated as insane or as someone who needs to be institutionalized or "cured"; he's the star, and the audience is expected to sympathize with him. Yet it was almost as risky for Bogarde to take this part as it was for his character in the film to take the case. It turned out to be a wise move, for though he'd been acting for decades before *Victim*, it was only after 1961 that the quality of his roles, and the regularity of his accolades, began to grow dramatically.

NEXT STOP . . . *Sapphire, Accident, Death in Venice*

1961 100m/B *GB* Dirk Bogarde, Sylvia Syms, Dennis Price, Peter McEnery, Nigel Stock, Donald Churchill, Anthony Nicholls, Hilton Edwards, Norman Bird, Derren Nesbitt, Alan McNaughton, Noel Howlett, Charles Lloyd Pack, John Barrie, John Bennett; **D:** Basil Dearden; **W:** John McCormick, Janet Green; **C:** Otto Heller; **M:** Philip Green. **VHS** *HMV*

VINCENT, FRANÇOIS, PAUL AND THE OTHERS
Vincent, François, Paul et les Autres

The films of Claude Sautet will always serve as perfect examples of the huge gap that existed—at least a couple of decades ago—between French filmmakers and their Hollywood counterparts. If Hollywood still believes in "high-concept"—plots describable in one sentence—then Sautet represents the true polar opposite. The story of *Vincent, François, Paul and the Others* is less like a simple plot with accompanying subplots than it is like a spinning top; Sautet gives us a fully formed universe of acquaintances, sets them in motion, and lets us revel in the way they remain in a delicate balance. This is a movie about a group of friends and lovers who try to work their problems through with each other, and who do it by talking instead of shooting. Their troubles aren't high-tech, either; there are failing businesses, strained marriages, precarious health—but no approaching asteroids. These people are adults, and act as such, and yet they still love, lust, suffer, and laugh, and they know how to have a good time. What'll they think of next? Starring Yves Montand, Stéphane Audran, Michel Piccoli, Gérard Depardieu, Serge Reggiani, and Marie Dubois.

NEXT STOP . . . *César & Rosalie, Un Coeur en Hiver, Nelly and Monsieur Arnaud*

1976 113m/C *FR* Yves Montand, Gerard Depardieu, Michel Piccoli, Stephane Audran, Serge Reggiani, Marie DuBois; **D:** Claude Sautet; **W:** Claude Sautet, Jean-Loup Dabadie, Claude Neron; **C:** Jean Boffety; **M:** Philippe Sarde. **VHS, LV, Letterbox** *FCT, CVC, TPV*

VIOLETTE
Violette Noziere

Violette is Claude Chabrol's 1978 portrait of the real-life 18-year-old French girl Violette Nozière, who, in 1933, took it upon herself to poison her parents so that she might speed up that irritatingly slow process of waiting for them to die in order to receive her inheritance. Violette (Isabelle Huppert at her most appropriately inscrutable) had other bad habits as well; she was a prostitute and a thief, but compared to the successful murder of her father, the other stuff was small potatoes. Violette's crime caught the public's attention, and when the poisonings were splattered daily over page one, the calm and businesslike teenager became something of a bizarre heroine for surrealists and anarchists, and the target of the sexual fixations of more than a few others. Chabrol's movie has the same dry coolness as his protagonist; there's something vaguely amusing about the director's impersonal, relaxed, but unsentimental view of Violette's far-reaching depravity. It's not a traditional thriller, nor was Violette a traditional killer. With Jean Carmet and Stéphane Audran as dad and mom. Best Actress Award (Huppert), Cannes Film Festival.

NEXT STOP . . . *Le Boucher, The Story of Women, Butterfly Kiss*

1978 (R) 122m/C *FR* Isabelle Huppert, Stephane Audran, Jean Carmet, Jean Francoise, Bernadette LaFont; **D:** Claude Chabrol; **W:** Odile Barski, Frederic Grendel; **C:** Jean Rabier; **M:** Pierre Jansen. Cannes Film Festival '78: Best Actress (Huppert); Cesar Awards '79: Best Supporting Actress (Audran). **VHS** *NYF*

THE VIRGIN SPRING
Jungfrukallan

In Ingmar Bergman's medieval tale, Herr Töre (Max von Sydow) sends his virginal daughter, Karin (Birgitta Pettersson), to carry a load of holy candles to church. As the candles can only be carried by a virgin, Karin's pregnant half-sister Ingeri slips a toad into Karin's bread out of jealousy. Later, on the road, when Karin offers to share her meal with some herdsmen, the toad's sudden appearance angers them. Their resentment escalates, and they rape and murder the girl. Her father discovers what has happened to his beloved daughter when the same herdsmen, unaware that this is the girl's family, try to sell the dead girl's robe to Herr Töre's wife. His revenge is swift, pure, and violent. Afterward, Herr Töre finds his daughter's body, vows to build a church to her memory on the spot, and as he does, a small, flowing spring suddenly appears. *The Virgin Spring* is a straightforward, cleanly told fable about a universe in which God understands the vengeance of the righteous, and forgives it. It's directed with grace and intelligence and beautifully photographed by Sven Nykvist, but it's never been among the most interesting or affecting of Bergman's films. The picture was more popular with audiences than with critics (it won the Oscar for Best Foreign Language Film), and it seemed to open Bergman's cinema to an audience that had previously found his work forbidding, which is not a bad thing. Bergman himself has in recent years said that he's unhappy with the picture, and that in his mind it's "a bad imitation of Kurosawa." Whether he's a better critic than he is a filmmaker—at least in this case—is up to you.

NEXT STOP . . . *Through a Glass Darkly, Winter Light, The Silence*

1959 88m/B *SW* Max von Sydow, Birgitta Valberg, Gunnel Lindblom, Brigitta Pattersson, Axel Duborg; *D:* Ingmar Bergman; *W:* Ulla Isaakson; *C:* Sven Nykvist; *M:* Erik Nordgren. Academy Awards '60: Best Foreign Film; Golden Globe Awards '61: Best Foreign Film; Nominations: Academy Awards '60: Best Costume Design (B & W). **VHS** *HMV*

VIRIDIANA

It was Luis Buñuel's intention that the first film he directed in Spain after his 23-year political exile be both significant and explosive. He succeeded. Viridiana (Silvia Pinal) is an innocent girl who is cajoled into visiting her wealthy and worldly uncle, Don Jaime (Fernando Rey) prior to taking her final vows as a nun. She goes to thank him for helping her with her financial problems through the years, but Don Jaime, it seems, has a few problems of his own. His wife died on their wedding night 30 years earlier, and Viridiana's resemblance to her has been bringing the already obsessed man close to the brink of madness. He drugs Viridiana's tea after beseeching her to try on his dead wife's wedding dress (Don Jaime does that himself from time to time); once she's unconscious on his bed, he gazes at her lasciviously, par-

tially undresses her, but can't finally bring himself to violate her. The next morning, however, he informs Viridiana that she is no longer a virgin, following which he commits suicide. Viridiana and Jorge, Don Jaime's illegitimate son (Francisco Rabal), inherit the Don's estate, and they attempt to create a religious order of their own, inviting beggars, thieves, and derelicts to take shelter there. But these guests take advantage as well as shelter, and it's soon apparent that Buñuel's amazing *Viridiana* is far more than a mere entertainment. Although it isn't exactly the all-out attack on religion it's often described as (though it is filled with traditionally blasphemous imagery, including a contextually startling recreation of Leonardo's *Last Supper*), *Viridiana* is a double-barreled assault on the complacency of simple idealism when unaccompanied by action. Nevertheless, the picture was promptly banned by Franco, and just as promptly won the Grand Prize at the Cannes Film Festival.

NEXT STOP . . . *Nazarin, Simon of the Desert, The Milky Way*

1961 90m/B *SP MX* Silvia Pinal, Francesco Rabal, Fernando Rey, Margarita Lozano, Victoria Zinny; *D:* Luis Bunuel; *W:* Luis Bunuel, Julio Alajandro; *C:* Jose Agayo. Cannes Film Festival '61: Best Film. **VHS** *NOS, HHT, DVT*

VIVA MARIA!

There are two Marias in *Viva Maria!*; they're both dancers in a show traveling through Mexico and, more importantly, they're played by Brigitte Bardot and Jeanne Moreau. They're not pleased with the poverty they encounter in their travels, and they decide to do something about it. Just *what* to do becomes more clear after the Moreau Maria has an affair with a revolutionary leader played by—no kidding—George Hamilton! (Making this picture must be where the tan came from.) When he's killed, the two Marias take their cue, arm themselves, and bomb and blast their way toward liberation for the oppressed. For director Louis Malle, *Viva Maria!* must have been a welcome breather after the grim rigors of *The Fire Within*. And who could ever blame him for grabbing the chance to direct both of these legends in the

LOUIS MALLE

The late Louis Malle's enchanting, deservedly praised *Atlantic City* was one of the surprise critical and box office hits of 1980. A witty, romantic and poetic portrait of a once-graceful world in decay, *Atlantic City* was a very different movie in tone and substance than Malle's previous film, *Pretty Baby*, the controversial portrait of a 12-year-old prostitute that marked Brooke Shields's screen debut.

Such a directorial and thematic about-face was hardly new to Malle; the director himself had already been quoted as saying "I tend to think that I repeat myself, so I try to resist the temptation to return to what I have already explored."

Still, even for Malle—whose career by 1980 had included a celebrated documentary on India, a portrait of the last days of an alcoholic playboy, a futuristic updating of *Alice in Wonderland* and a comedy that culminated in an act of mother/son incest—the project with which he followed *Atlantic City* sounded risky enough to seem downright foolhardy. The program notes of the 1981 New York Film Festival described the plot of *My Dinner with André* as "two men have dinner." The men were Wallace Shawn and André Gregory; they played characters named Wally and André and they were the film's writers as well. As the lights went down at Lincoln Center, I hoped for the best (as I always have at *every* movie) but I secretly braced myself for what I couldn't help but fear would be a textbook example of artistic self-indulgence.

One-hundred and ten minutes later, experiencing a gentle landing after visiting that indescribable, exhilarating peak that is accessible only via the most emotionally resonant and honest works of art, I remembered that there were a thousand other people in the theatre. I knew this because they were on their feet, applauding the man who had understood that this dazzling, structurally brilliant screenplay—the story of two people who are changed forever by "simply" exchanging ideas during the course of a meal—was indeed the stuff of cinema.

Louis Malle knew that all this "simple" dinner conversation required to become a permanent part of our own experience was flawless timing and seemingly effortless direction; that was the only way to draw us in gradually so that we would *listen* to what these two characters were saying to each other. Malle must have understood that, if he brought it off, the movie could provide us with a more emotionally satisfying, intellectually tantalizing exploration of our own lives than many of us undertake in a lifetime. In this one movie, Wally and André's conversation takes the audience on the kind of search Malle must have gone through while preparing each of his films; rethinking preconceived notions, trying on new points-of-view, questioning traditional wisdom. Taking on the direction of *My Dinner with André* was a gamble, not unlike a roll of the dice in Atlantic City.

But what a payoff. As a testament to a brave, unique artist who continually looked at the world in fresh ways, who always learned from what he discovered and who refused to stop evolving either spiritually or artistically, *My Dinner with André*—a film that proves that two hours are all it takes to completely rethink the way we see the universe, each other and ourselves—may be Louis Malle's greatest professional legacy.

same film? BB and JM look great—it's a pairing made in casting heaven—yet there's a noticeable lack of any real sparks when they're on screen together, and a good deal of the comic schtick seems labored and by-the-numbers. Still, *Viva Maria!* is harmless, silly fun, with the emphasis on silly.

NEXT STOP . . . *Zazie dans le Metro, Cat Ballou, Thelma and Louise*

1965 (R) 119m/C *FR IT* Jeanne Moreau, Brigitte Bardot, George Hamilton, Paulette Dubost, Claudio Brook; **D:** Louis Malle; **W:** Louis Malle, Jean-Claude Carriere; **C:** Henri Decae; **M:** Georges Delerue. **VHS** *MGM*

VIVE L'AMOUR
Aiqing Wansui

In crowded modern Taipei, a lonely real-estate agent (Yang Kuei-mei) uses one of her vacant high-rise apartments for an ongoing affair. She's unaware, however, that a young gay man (Lee Kang-sheng) who finds one of her keys has taken to living there himself. Carefully monitoring her comings and goings, their "relationship" becomes a poignant parody of the eternal dilemmas inherent in sharing space with another, as well as a not-so-funny look at the paradox of alienation and loneliness in even the most crowded of cities. Director Tsai Ming-liang's deadpan, ironic comedy of urban angst, sex, and desperation sports as spare and clean a design as the modern apartment building in which much of the film takes place, but its deliberate pace and elliptical structure demand rapt attention. Grand Prize Winner, 1994 Venice Film Festival.

NEXT STOP . . . *Lonesome* (1929), *When the Cat's Away, Two or Three Things I Know About Her*

1994 118m/C *TW* Yang Guimei, Chen Zhaorong, Li Kangsheng; **D:** Tsai Ming-Liang; **W:** Tsai Ming-Liang; **C:** Pen-jung Lioa, Ming-kuo Lin. **VHS** *FXL*

THE WAGES OF FEAR
Le Salaire de la Peur

Four desperate men, stuck hopelessly in a desolate town in Central America, agree to be paid $2,000 each to drive two trucks filled with nitroglycerine over 300 miles of bumpy, decrepit mountain roads so that the nitro can be used to put out a raging oil-well fire. Henri-Georges Clouzot's *The Wages of Fear* is one of the greatest movie thrillers—and one of the most nerve-wracking experiences—of all time. The structure of the movie is genius. First, we learn what we need to about each of the men, who are played by Yves Montand, Folco Lulli, Peter Van Eyck, and Charles Vanel. The tension in their own lives and the despair that brought them to agree to such a situation is made palpable, and friction between them begins to develop as well. Then, they're paired off, put in their trucks, and hit the road. (Having two trucks is insurance. The company paying them thinks they'll be lucky if even one truck makes it without blowing up.) Clouzot has staged some sequences on cliffs, bridges, and washed-out roads (not to mention an encounter with a huge boulder) that are as agonizingly suspenseful as any moments in movie history, and they're stretched out almost beyond our ability to endure them. That's no accident; endurance and courage are exactly what *The Wages of Fear* is about. This is an amazing, shocking, visionary work, thrilling in ways we always hope suspense films will be, yet almost never are. After receiving the Grand Prize at the 1953 Cannes Film Festival, *The Wages of Fear* was cut by more than thirty crucial minutes for its American release, and many of the prints in circulation in the late fifties were shorter still. In the 1980s, a fully restored, 138-minute version was finally released in the U.S., and it's available on video. (Beware of older, shorter, still-circulating public domain versions.) Yes, it was remade by William Friedkin as *Sorcerer* in 1977, and no, it's not nearly as good.

NEXT STOP . . . *Diabolique, Juggernaut, Fires on the Plain*

1955 138m/B *FR* Yves Montand, Charles Vanel, Peter Van Eyck, Vera Clouzot, Folco Lulli, William Tubbs; **D:** Henri-Georges Clouzot; **W:** Henri-Georges Clouzot; **C:** Armand Thirard; **M:** Georges Auric. British Academy Awards '54: Best Film; Cannes Film Festival '53: Best Actor (Vanel), Best Film. **VHS, LV** *HHT, SNC, VYY*

WALKABOUT

Abandoned in the Australian outback after their father commits suicide, a teenaged girl and her little brother must depend on the kindness of a young aborigine in order to survive. Overcoming some inherent racism, the children eventually realize that their notion of what constitutes "civilization" has been stood on its head. Years later, in a coda to the story we've seen, the girl, now grown and married and living in the fast-paced big city, daydreams of the idyllic time that she spent in more natural surroundings. The first film on which former cinematographer Nicolas Roeg received solo directing credit quickly became a cult favorite upon release. It's a physically stunning film that struck a responsive chord with much of the counterculture in 1971, but beneath its photographically impressive, gleaming surface beats an artificial heart. *Walkabout* is an uncomfortably condescend-ing "noble savage" picture in a fancy wrapper—the kind of movie that middle-class American audiences were understandably salivating for during the Vietnam War years. France, after its own "adventure" in Indochina, had already produced *King of Hearts,* in which it was demonstrated that the only sane people in the world were those who'd been declared officially insane. And while *Walkabout* was an Australian production, its simplistic and self-flagellating news flash that "civilization" isn't all that it's cracked up to be was so welcomed by many *cinéastes* that they mistook this stacked deck of pretty picture postcards for philosophically profound art. (They didn't make the same mistake two years later with Ross Hunter's unintentionally hilarious musical remake of *Lost Horizon,* a film that contains the same message as *Walkabout,* but is wrapped in cheesecloth.) Ultimately, it's not the conclusion *Walkabout* reaches that offends (it's probably true), but the simplistic narrative it uses to present its case. To give it its due, the performances are fine, particularly Jenny Agutter as the lost teenager and David Gulpilil as the young man who takes the kids under his wing. And yes, the movie looks great. Still, to paraphrase film historian David Thomson, would any novice find it difficult to make the Australian desert unspectacular?

NEXT STOP . . . *The Last Wave, The Piano, The Man Who Fell to Earth*

1971 (PG) 100m/C *AU* Jenny Agutter, Lucien John, David Gumpilil, John Meillon; *D:* Nicolas Roeg; *W:* Edward Bond; *C:* Nicolas Roeg; *M:* John Barry. **VHS** *HMV*

THE WANNSEE CONFERENCE
Wannseekonferenz

The formalities and basic logistical arrangements for the systematic murder of millions of men, women, and children known as the Final Solution were decided in an 85-minute meeting of 14 Nazi leaders on January 20, 1942. From notes taken by the secretary at the meeting, as well as letters written by Hermann Goering and Adolf Eichmann, screenwriter Paul Mommertz and director Heinz Schirk have recreated—in real screen time—the businesslike but occasionally relaxed gathering that took place that day. *The Wannsee Conference* is one of those cinematic ideas that just seems too simple and too obvious to work—but work it does, and stunningly. Looking at these people joking with each other, drinking their coffee, speaking in only slightly elliptical terms about how to efficiently turn millions of living human beings into piles of dead flesh, and then how to most inexpensively dispose of the mountains of corpses that they intend to create, is to understand—once again—that the most horrifying actions imaginable can grow from the most seemingly ordinary of people when they are above the law. In the film's undramatic, offhanded recreation of what to these Nazis was just one more business meeting, we can grasp a bit of the obscenity of the Nazi denial that their victims were human beings at all. That emotionless mat-

ter-of-factness is more horrifying than any traditional monster movie, all the more so because these monsters were real—as are their spiritual offspring around the world.

NEXT STOP . . . *Shoah, Hotel Terminus: The Life and Times of Klaus Barbie, The Memory of Justice*

1984 87m/C *GE* Dietrich Mattausch, Gerd Brockmann, Friedrich Beckhaus; *D:* Heinz Schirk. **VHS, LV** *HMV, GLV, BTV*

WAR AND PEACE

Thirty years ago, Sergei Bondarchuk's massive, six-hour-plus-change adaptation of Leo Tolstoy's *War and Peace* reputedly cost 100 million dollars, which would be the rough equivalent of 400 million today. That makes *Titanic* and *Batman and Robin* look like low-budget indies by comparison. *War and Peace* may not have been one of the world's great movies, but it is valuable in another way—as a tipoff that the fall of communism was inevitable. The production, hype, and release of the 100 million—dollar *War and Peace* was pure capitalist showmanship, in which the size and scope of the production were the sizzle that was being sold. Though some critics of the day were enthusiastic, they all focused on the cost of the thing rather than its success or failure as literary adaptation. Who can blame them? (We see the same kind of thing today on the front page of the *Wall Street Journal* when, after spending 140 million on *Armageddon,* Jerry Bruckheimer and Disney's Joe Roth say that they wish critics would stop talking about size and flashy style of their movie and simply focus on *Armageddon*'s "substance.") Does anybody actually remember much about *War and Peace,* other than being able to claim you sat through it? I remember that when the picture ended, the audience response was similar to the relieved applause you hear from passengers when a particularly rough flight finally touches down on the runway. I recall some BIG battle scenes and some BIG ballrooms. The color was muddy. Despite the atrocious dubbing, it won the Oscar for Best Foreign Language Film. It *is* available on video in a subtitled version. It's your move, though. I can't spare another six hours. Plus change.

NEXT STOP . . . *War and Peace* (1956), *Napoleon*, *Waterloo*

1968 373m/C *RU* Lyudmila Savelyeva, Sergei Bondarchuk, Vyacheslav Tihonor, Hira Ivanov-Golarko, Irina Gubanova, Antonina Shuranova; *D:* Sergei Bondarchuk; *C:* Jack Cardiff. Academy Awards '68: Best Foreign Film; Golden Globe Awards '69: Best Foreign Film; New York Film Critics Awards '68: Best Foreign Film; Nominations: Academy Awards '68: Best Art Direction/Set Decoration. **VHS, LV** *KUL, TVC, TPV*

THE WAR GAME

Originally commissioned by the BBC as a cautionary tale about the ominous consequences of nuclear catastrophe, Peter Watkins's stunning 47-minute "documentary" was judged too horrifying to be televised, and was immediately shelved by the network. It's likely that even if the film had been shown as scheduled it would have had worldwide attention, but the banning of it—coupled with the subsequent firestorm (pun intended) of public protest—drew enormous attention to the film when it was finally released theatrically in both England and the United States. The premise is simple; a series of worldwide standoffs centering around regional conflicts balloon quickly into an unstoppable, Rube Goldberg-style machine that sets off a nuclear exchange. One small town in England is depicted, and while the town does not suffer a direct hit, the effects on the town of the nearby blast are horrible enough. Watkins stages the whole thing as a documentary, complete with hand-held, grainy, flatly lit camerawork and actors whose delivery is hesitant and unpolished. The resulting illusion of a nightmare caught on the run is of a magnitude that might be compared to the impact of Orson Welles's "War of the Worlds" radio broadcast as heard by those just tuning in in the middle. *The War Game* is one of the most important artifacts of the Cold War, as well as a continuing reminder that the danger—while it may now appear to be diminished—will continue to be very much with us for as long as these weapons exist. Academy Award, Best Documentary Feature.

NEXT STOP . . . *Culloden, The Atomic Cafe, Black Rain* (Imamura)

1965 49m/B Michael Aspel, Peter Graham; *D:* Peter Watkins; *W:* Peter Watkins; *C:* Peter Bartlett. Academy Awards '66: Best Feature Documentary. **VHS** *NOS, SNC, HTV*

WAXWORKS

Paul Leni's 1924 *Waxworks* is a striking and still scary example of German expressionism used to make nightmares come to life. In the film, a poet strolls through a waxworks exhibit at a local carnival, encountering the figures of the tyrannical Haroun al Raschid, Ivan the Terrible, and Jack the Ripper. One at a time, the figures come to life in the mind of the poet, and grotesquely distorted sets and lighting suggest the poet's internalized terrors. Staircases in particular are twisted and forbidding in *Waxworks,* and have been widely interpreted as powerfully suggestive symbols of sexual longing and anxiety. Director Paul Leni—a collaborator of Max Reinhardt's—was quoted in Lotte Eisner's *The Haunted Screen:* "I have tried to create sets so stylized that they evince no idea of reality. It is not extreme reality that the camera perceives, but the reality of the inner event, which is more profoundly effective and moving than what we see through everyday eyes, and I equally believe that the cinema can reproduce this truth, heightened effectively." Leni was referring primarily to the expressionistic techniques that he and directors like F.W. Murnau were experimenting with at the time, but his statement could well be a summary of the basic power of all cinema to create a world based on a heightened, inner reality. Features *The Cabinet of Dr. Caligari*'s Werner Krauss as Jack the Ripper, Emil Jannings as Haroun al Raschid, and Conrad Veidt as Ivan the Terrible, in the sequence that Sergei Eisenstein cited as a major influence on his own interpretation of Ivan 20 years later. The actor who plays the poet is William Dieterle, who in Hollywood in 1939 directed the superb Charles Laughton version of *The Hunchback of Notre Dame.*

NEXT STOP . . . *The Cabinet of Dr. Caligari, The Man Who Laughs, Ivan the Terrible Parts 1 & 2*

1924 63m/B *GE* William Dieterle, Emil Jannings, Conrad Veidt, Werner Krauss, John Gottowt, Olga Belajeff; *D:* Paul Leni; *W:* Henrik Galeen. **VHS** *SNC, NOS, ART*

> "There is an increasing interaction between images and language. One might say that living in society today is almost like living in a vast comic strip."
>
> —Narrator (Jean-Luc Godard) in *Two or Three Things I Know about Her.*

WE ALL LOVED EACH OTHER SO MUCH

Three men (Vittorio Gassman, Nino Manfredi, and Satta Flores) are united over three decades by their friendship and by their love for one extraordinary woman (Stefania Sandrelli). Ettore Scola's enchanting romance begins at the close of World War II, and covers not only the changes in Italy over the years since, but also the evolution of its cinema. Sandrelli's character, an actress, is the movie's link to the movies; Scola's joyous recreation of the evolution of neo-realism into the modern Italian cinema includes appearances by Federico Fellini, Marcello Mastroianni, Anita Ekberg (whose bath in the Trevi fountain in *La Dolce Vita* is lovingly recreated here), and Vittorio De Sica, to whom the film is dedicated. Ettore Scola is one of the most shamefully underrated of Italy's great directors, and the rich, memorable, touching *We All Loved Each Other So Much* is one of his finest achievements.

NEXT STOP . . . *The Easy Life, The Pizza Triangle, La Nuit de Varennes*

1977 124m/C *IT* Vittorio Gassman, Nino Manfredi, Stefano Satta Flores, Stefania Sandrelli, Marcello Mastroianni, Federico Fellini, Anita Ekberg, Vittorio De Sica; **D:** Ettore Scola. **VHS, LV** *COL*

WE THE LIVING

Director Goffredo Alessandrini's sprawling, solemn, three-hour 1942 version of Ayn Rand's first novel was originally designed to be seen as two separate films. *We the Living* is intermittently amusing, usually unintentionally, but is far too grandly self-important to be fully enjoyed as camp. Alida Valli's politically incorrect affair with counter-revolutionary Rossano Brazzi puts her in a precarious position with party officials, and in typical Randian fashion the convoluted plot leads her to a tortured decision over whether or not to abandon her principles while under the thumb of a tyrannical, collectivist system. This picture was made under Mussolini's watch, but it became apparent only after its completion that despite its anti-communist rhetoric, Rand's message was equally vituperative in its disdain for *all* forms of tyranny. It was promptly banned, and went unseen in the U.S. until the late 1980s, when a restored version was re-released theatrically, to modest success. (As lugubrious as this thing is, it's a still hell of a lot more fun than the icily worshipful documentary on Rand, *A Sense of Life,* which was actually nominated for a 1997 Academy Award.)

NEXT STOP . . . *The Fountainhead, Bitter Rice, Seven Beauties*

1942 174m/B *IT* Alida Valli, Rossano Brazzi, Fosco Giachetti; **D:** Goffredo Alessandrini. **VHS, LV** *LUM*

WEDDING IN BLOOD

Middle-aged, adulterous lovers Pierre (Michel Piccoli) and Lucienne (Stéphane Audran) have unleashed a frenzied erotic passion in each other that goes well beyond anything they've ever experienced in their marriages. They can't keep their hands off each other, nor can they resist new forms of sexual expression—like hiding out in a museum after closing time in order to have sex in one of the antique period bedrooms. Their lust is all-encompassing enough to drive them well past any hint of rationality, leading them inevitably to a plan to murder their respective spouses. *Wedding in Blood* is a relatively minor film by Claude Chabrol, but it contains major pleasures—primarily the over-the-top performances of Audran and Piccoli. They're like two kids in a candy store when they're in foreplay mode; the pleasure they feel from being so sexually charged has, ironically, a kind of sweet innocence about it that makes the two would-be killers endearing. Chabrol's script is based on an actual case, but it's really that frantic, stylized groping and groaning that gives the movie a heightened and funny sense of authenticity; it's like a parody of two straitlaced, civilized, middle-class bourgeois who are suddenly shocked but delighted to discover that they're animals, too. The lush cinematography is by Jean Rabier.

CLAUDE CHABROL
French New Wave Director

Director Claude Chabrol's first film, *Le Beau Serge* (1958), is widely regarded as the first lap of France's New Wave in cinema. In 1990 Chabrol was still making waves in France with the eighth movie version of *Madame Bovary*.

Le Beau Serge deals with the return of a young man from the city to his country roots. Chabrol's second film, *Les Cousins,* is about a young provincial who studies law at the Sorbonne and is destroyed by his decadent city cousin. "I was born in Paris, but it was a mistake," Chabrol said, "I'm from the country. My heart belongs to Provence."

His heart and wallet, filled by his early success, also went out to his fellow young filmmakers. Chabrol helped many auteurs make their first films and appeared in small roles in several of them. He was technical adviser to his friend Jean-Luc Godard on the 1959 landmark *Breathless.* Some of his own recent films include *Betty* (1992), *L'enfer* (1994), *La Ceremonie* (1995), and *Rien ne va Plus* (1997).

A fan of mystery writer Georges Simenon, Chabrol is most famous for his detective movies. In his long career, he has spun in and out of critical favor. Asked in 1988 why he made some of his poorly received films, Chabrol replied: "Because at the moment I had nothing better to do, and I think that it is better to work than to loaf."

Chabrol was born June 24, 1930. In 1964, he married actress Stephane Audran, who has starred in many of his major films. They are now divorced. They share a son, and Chabrol has two other sons from a prior marriage.

NEXT STOP . . . *La Femme Infidèle, La Cérémonie, Double Indemnity*

1974 (PG) 98m/C *FR IT* Claude Pieplu, Stephane Audran, Michel Piccoli; **D:** Claude Chabrol; **W:** Claude Chabrol; **C:** Jean Rabier. **VHS** *COL*

WEEKEND

A tense Parisian couple (Mirielle Darc and Jean Yanne) hit the highway to take a weekend motor trip to visit the wife's mother. Along the way they encounter not only a surrealistic traffic jam, but also the stylized and bitterly satirical carnage that comes with it (a woman staggers from the twisted, bloody, flaming wreckage of her car, screaming "My Hermes pocketbook!"). Soon this bourgeois couple will find themselves at the center of a society in the process of self-destruction; on their trip to mom's they will encounter murder, rape, wholesale greed, and cannibalism, all seen as a natural part of a capitalist society eating its own entrails, with no choice left but revolution. Godard's visionary 1967 treatise/position paper/spectacle implies that this is the last chapter in a bourgeois *cinema,* as well. With his radically inventive editing techniques and jarring, ingenious juxtaposition of different styles and story elements, *Weekend* suggests that we must find new ways to tell the same old stories, or we will be condemned to repeat them. Godard shakes up the form of motion pictures as thoroughly as their content, and the result is a funny, brilliant, appalling snapshot of a decade that was about to blow itself apart.

NEXT STOP . . . *Pierrot le Fou, Every Man for Himself, The Cook, the Thief, His Wife & Her Lover*

1967 105m/C *FR IT* Mireille Darc, Jean Yanne, Jean-Pierre Kalfon, Valerie Lagrange, Jean-Pierre Leaud, Yves Beneyton; **D:** Jean-Luc Godard; **W:** Jean-Luc Godard; **M:** Antoine Duhamel. **VHS** *NYF, FCT*

WHEN A WOMAN ASCENDS THE STAIRS
Onna Ga Kaidan O Agaru Toki

Keiko (Hideko Takamine) is a young widow forced to work as a bar hostess in order to support her mother and lazy brother. As she approaches age 30, Keiko comes to realize that her relationships with the men who frequent the bar—some of them married—are leading nowhere. Yet asserting her independence by opening her own bar will prove to be a daunting task. Mikio Naruse was one of the Japanese filmmakers who, like Mizoguchi and Ozu, was interested in—and highly sensitive to—the plight of women in Japanese society. Naruse's films never received significant distribution in the West, however, though a few are available. *When a Woman Ascends the Stairs* isn't considered to be among his finest work, yet it's still a fascinating melodrama with a bitter, memorable aftertaste. Handsomely photographed in a widescreen process, it should be seen in a letterboxed version if at all possible.

NEXT STOP . . . *Sounds from the Mountains, Floating Cloud, Sandokan 8*

1960 110m/B *JP* Hideko Takamine, Tatsuya Nakadai, Masayuki Mori; **D:** Mikio Naruse. **VHS** *WAC*

WHEN FATHER WAS AWAY ON BUSINESS

The title of Emir Kusturica's 1985 film, set in the Sarajevo of the 1950s, refers to the "cover-up" that was invoked in trying to explain a father's whereabouts to the movie's six-year-old protagonist. Dad is in a political prison (he's a bit too vocal with his opinions on Tito), and little Malik is given an early start on the euphemisms and rationalizations that allowed an entire society to delude itself for generations. Kusturica's portrait of survival and human adaptability under such a system is touching, funny, and frightening. Following its Grand Prize at the 1985 Cannes Film Festival, the film became moderately successful in the U.S. (it was shortened by about ten minutes after Cannes for American release), receiving an Academy Award nomination for Best Foreign Language Film. (Still, who could have imagined that just eight years later Kusturica would make *Arizona Dream,* in which Johnny Depp co-starred with Jerry Lewis, who played both a car salesman and an Eskimo? Now *that's* what I call the new world order.) *When Father Was Away on Business* is a good and brave film, but Kusturica would take its themes all the way in his brilliant and visionary *Underground* a decade later.

NEXT STOP . . . *Tito and Me, Man Is Not a Bird, Underground*

1985 (R) 144m/C *YU* Moreno D'E Bartolli, Miki Manojlovic, Mirjana Karanovic; **D:** Emir Kusturica. Cannes Film Festival '85: Best Film; Nominations: Academy Awards '85: Best Foreign-Language Film. **VHS** *FXL*

WHEN THE CAT'S AWAY
Chacun Cherche Son Chat

Fed up with both her job as a modeling agency assistant and her lack of a satisfying love life, the young, vulnerable Chloé (Garance Clavel in a terrifically smart performance) returns to her tiny Parisian apartment from a brief but much-needed vacation only to discover that the one reassuring certainty in her life—her cat Gris-Gris—has disappeared. Chloé had left Gris-Gris in the care of the eccentric Mademoiselle Renée (Renée Le Calm), whose apartment is crammed with cats of every stripe and who seems genuinely heartbroken to inform poor Chloé that Gris-Gris has flown the coop.

W

Renée contacts every one of the aging cat cronies in her grapevine to help locate Gris-Gris (when she puts the word out it's like the dog network's hunt for the kidnapped puppies in *101 Dalmatians*). Chloé's search through the alleys, bars, and back streets of Paris for her missing feline—a search that culminates in at least two happy surprises—turns into an enchantingly funny yet unexpectedly moving journey of the heart. Chloé's Paris is a city changing rapidly; her hope is to find that its romantic spirit is still alive—along with her cat—despite the demolished old buildings and the quickly erected new ones. Cédric Klapisch's charming and refreshingly civilized comedy is a slice of working-class life that may at first seem thin and familiar, but deepens and disarms us as it ambles along, finally depositing us—and Chloé—in a joyous new place that we never saw coming. Klapisch is a director to watch; his economical little storytelling touches—such as Chloé's vacation being represented by a single, brief image of her head sticking out of the water at a beach—are witty and fun, and enrich the meaning of scenes. *When the Cat's Away* is a sneaky, sweet surprise.

NEXT STOP . . . *Boyfriends & Girlfriends, The Daytrippers, Un Air de Famille*

1996 (R) 91m/C *FR* Garance Clavel, Zinedine Soualem, Olivier Py, Renee Le Calm; *D:* Cedric Klapisch; *W:* Cedric Klapisch; *C:* Benoit Delhomme. **VHS** *COL*

THE WHITE BALLOON
Badkonake Sefid

Just before the eagerly anticipated celebration of New Year's Day in Teheran, Razieh (Aïda Mohammadkhani), a seven-year-old girl with an incredibly serious, completely irresistible face, loses the money she was given to buy a special, plump goldfish, a symbol of harmony for the new year. Over the next hour and a half, *The White Balloon* traces, in real time, little Razieh's determined quest to recover the money and return home with her prized fish. *The White Balloon* is a complete delight, though it's not just a simple comedy. The screenplay by Abbas Kiarostami (*Taste of Cherry*) is enormously sensitive to Razieh's plight, and never condescends or dismisses her problem as simple kid's stuff. What charms us is the child's intelligence, ingenuity, and persistence, as well as the elegant, spare direction of first-time filmmaker Jafar Panahi. And if you're looking for a picture with which to introduce children to the "grown-up" world of foreign-language films, *The White Balloon* is an ideal place to jump in. Cannes Film Festival *Camera d'Or* award for Best First Feature.

NEXT STOP . . . *The Bicycle Thief, The Red Balloon, Through the Olive Trees*

1995 85m/C Aida Mohammadkhani, Mohsen Kalifi, Fereshteh Sadr Ofrani, Anna Bourkowska, Mohammad Shahani, Mohammad Bahktiari; *D:* Jafar Panahi; *W:* Abbas Kiarostami; *C:* Farzad Jowdat. New York Film Critics Awards '96: Best Foreign Film. **VHS** *HMK*

THE WHITE SHEIK
Lo Sceicco Bianco

Federico Fellini's first solo directing effort is a poignant and hilarious comic fable about a starry-eyed young woman (Brunella Bova) whose naive infatuation with a pot-bellied Valentino almost destroys her marriage—even though she's still on her honeymoon. The object of her obsession is a white-robed, scimitar-wielding character in the Italian *fumetti*—comic books with tableaux-style photos in place of drawings—who turns out to be posed by someone considerably less dashing in real life than he appears to be on paper. Alberto Sordi contributes a memorable, hilariously pathetic star turn as the White Sheik, and Leopoldo Trieste is immensely sympathetic as the confused husband whose frustration leads him to the acquaintance of a charming prostitute, played by Giulietta Masina. Masina's character was so likable and so charmingly conceived that six years later Fellini would give her a movie of her own which would not only become a classic, but would provide the vehicle for what would be Masina's greatest performance: *Nights of Cabiria*. (Years later, *Cabiria* itself would metamorphose into the stage and film musical *Sweet Charity*).

NEXT STOP . . . *Variety Lights, Nights of Cabiria, The Purple Rose of Cairo*

1952 86m/B *IT* Alberto Sordi, Giulietta Masina, Brunella Bova, Leopoldo Trieste; *D:* Federico Fellini; *W:* Federico Fellini, Tullio Pinelli, Ennio Flaiano; *C:* Arturo Galea; *M:* Nino Rota. **VHS** *HMV, VDM, AUD*

THE WILD CHILD
L'Enfant Sauvage

Though it initially seems like an anomaly among the films of François Truffaut, *The Wild Child* (*L'Enfant Sauvage*) may in fact be the most characteristic film of his career. Set in the 1700s, *The Wild Child* is a dramatization of the facts in a true case as documented in the diary of Dr. Jean Itard, a researcher who took up the task of trying to "civilize" a young boy who was found living alone in the French countryside after having apparently been raised by wolves. Truffaut himself plays Dr. Itard, and an extraordinary young actor named Jean-Pierre Cargol portrays the boy, who was named "Victor" by Itard after he seemed to naturally respond to the sound of the name. *The Wild Child* is in essence another version of Truffaut's semi-autobiographical *The 400 Blows,* but with an ending that suggests that not all of the world's abused kids can overcome their initial damage, no matter how decent or noble the instincts of the child or his potential savior. Itard does his best to remain the detached researcher, but with brilliant restraint and a refreshing lack of sentimentality, Truffaut demonstrates how both doctor and patient—a would-be father and son—are ennobled by their brief relationship. And a sequence in which Itard uncovers in Victor what the researcher calls "the most noble of human attributes"—rebellion against injustice—is powerful enough all be itself to make *The Wild Child* one of Truffaut's finest and most memorable achievements.

NEXT STOP . . . *The 400 Blows, The Mystery of Kaspar Hauser, The Elephant Man*

1970 (G) 85m/B *FR* Jean-Pierre Cargol, Francois Truffaut, Jean Daste, Francoise Seigner, Paul Ville; *D:* Francois Truffaut; *W:* Jean Gruault, Francois Truffaut; *C:* Nestor Almendros; *M:* Antoine Duhamel. National Board of Review Awards '70: Best Director (Truffaut); National Society of Film Critics Awards '70: Best Cinematography. **VHS** *MGM, FCT*

WILD REEDS
Les Roseaux Sauvages

Set in the early 1960s at the end of the French war in Algeria, *Wild Reeds* is a complex, richly textured coming-of-age story about three friends in a French boarding school. François (Gael Morel) is just coming to the realization that he likes boys, and finds himself attracted to the working-class Serge (Stephane Rideau). Serge, however, is developing feelings for Maite (Elodie Bouchez), a young girl who's a friend of François. This would all be troublesome enough, but into the mix steps steps a young, angry, Algerian-born boy (Frederic Gorny) whose rage over the colonialist attitudes of the French permeates everything in his life, including his romantic entanglements. Director André Téchiné pulls off something of a miracle in simply juggling these characters' relationships in a convincing, involving manner, but he goes further. In its surprising, gentle way, *Wild Reeds* becomes a quietly powerful political document as well, demonstrating the far-reaching effects of oppression and repression on the psyches of young people whose emotions are in flux, and whose impressionable personalities are still being formed. Successful on just about every level, this is one of the most remarkable French films of the 1990s.

NEXT STOP . . . *The Disenchanted, Ma Saison Préférée, Hate (La Haine)*

1994 110m/C *FR* Gael Morel, Stephane Rideau, Elodie Bouchez, Frederic Gorny, Michele Moretti; *D:* Andre Techine; *W:* Gilles Taurand, Olivier Massart, Andre Techine; *C:* Jeanne Lapoirie. Cesar Awards '95: Best Director (Techine), Best Film, Best Writing; Los Angeles Film Critics Association Awards '95: Best Foreign Film; National Society of Film Critics Awards '95: Best Foreign Film. **VHS** *FXL*

WILD STRAWBERRIES
Smultron-Stallet

Professor Isak Borg (Victor Sjöström) has awakened from a dream of his own death. It

FRANÇOIS TRUFFAUT

Truffaut was one of the leading members of the New Wave that revitalized French cinema in the late 1950s. He was born in Paris in 1932, and he endured an unhappy home life that was rendered tolerable only through frequent escapes to the cinema. When he was only fourteen he quit school to work in a factory, but he continued to preoccupy himself with moviegoing. By age 20 Truffaut had begun writing for the prominent film journal "Cahiers du Cinema," where he and others such as Jean-Luc Godard, Eric Rohmer, and Claude Chabrol had drawn attention for their advocacy of the auteur theory, which regards the film director as the equivalent of the author.

In addition, Truffaut and other "Cahiers" critics sparked controversy through their harsh disdain for much French filmmaking. Among the many figures offended by Truffaut and his radical cohorts was Truffaut's own father-in-law, a producer of the very films that Truffaut was regularly trashing in his reviews. When Truffaut's father-in-law challenged him to make his own movie, Truffaut responded with *Les Quatres Cents Coups*, a somber, autobiographical account of an alienated boy named Antoine Doinel, who was played with great effectiveness by Jean-Pierre Leaud. *Les Quatres Cents Coups* proved a resounding success, and it immediately established Truffaut as one of the cinema's most promising new filmmakers.

Truffaut followed *Les Quatres Cents Coups* with *Tirez sur le Pianist*, an offbeat drama about a pianist who runs afoul of gangsters. He then scored another significant triumph with *Jules et Jim*, an ingratiating account of an ultimately tragic love triangle. By the mid-1960s, Truffaut and fellow "Cahiers" critics-turned-filmmakers such as Godard reigned as the new leading lights of world cinema. But in succeeding films Truffaut showed less flair and invention. In 1966 he directed an unconvincing version of Ray Bradbury's *Fahrenheit 451*, in English, and in 1969 he resumed the story of Antoine Doinel with *Baisers voles*, an amusing but slight film detailing Doinel's early romances. Two years later, Truffaut continued the Doinel saga with the equally frivolous *Domicile conjugal*, which concerns the protagonist's married life.

In 1972 Truffaut returned to top form with *Les Deux Anglaises et le continent*, an ambitious film of a young French man's relationships with two English women. This film, featuring Leaud as the hero, failed to impress substantially upon its premiere, but it is now regarded as one of Truffaut's greatest achievements.

In 1976 Truffaut launched the film career of actress Isabelle Adjani with *L'Histoire d'Adele H.*, an intense account of a woman's self-destructive obsession with a soldier. Ensuing films, however, were less impressive. *La Chambre verte*, in which he cast himself as a man obsessed with his dead wife, seems lifeless, while a fourth Antoine Doinel film, *L'Amour en Fuite*, seems uninspired. Perhaps most disappointing is *Le Dernier Metro*, a thoroughly conventional drama, set in the French theatre during the German occupation, which recalls the very films that Truffaut decried as a critic. Likewise, the mundane thriller *Vivement Dimanche*, released in 1982, adds little to his reputation. This film, unfortunately, was Truffaut's last. He died of cancer two years later.

is the day on which he is to receive an honorary degree, and he embarks on a motor trip to the university, accompanied by his daughter-in-law, Marianne (Ingrid Thulin). Along the way, the professor's memories are stirred by Marianne's scolding him for his iciness; that emotional coldness seems to run in the Borg family, for it's the same trait that has prompted Marianne to decide to leave her husband. There's a stop along the way for a visit to the house where he grew up, and other passengers are picked up as well, stirring other kinds of remembrances, some long repressed. By the end of the day, the seemingly impenetrable wall the professor has constructed around himself begins to crumble, and the first possibilities of vulnerability and emotional contact with others can be seen. Ingmar Bergman's *Wild Strawberries* isn't exactly beyond criticism, but it's become such an important part of film culture that's it's almost hard to imagine the modern cinema without it. Yes, there are flaws in the picture—some of the pacing seems uneven, and some of the flashback sequences that are supposed to be stylized simply come off as stilted. But these are negligible problems in a wonderful, heartbreakingly beautiful piece of filmmaking. The performances represent some of the finest ensemble work that Bergman has ever produced, but towering above everything is the great and emotionally naked performance of Victor Sjöström. An extraordinary director himself, Sjöström worked in the United States during much of the 1920s, where he created the amazing *He Who Gets Slapped* for Lon Chaney, as well as his directorial masterpiece, the 1928 *The Wind,* starring Lillian Gish. (Boston's Alloy Orchestra has created a superlative new score for *The Wind;* go wherever you have to to hear them accompany it.) Woody Allen, hardly a closet admirer of Bergman's, reproduced the structure of *Wild Strawberries* in his recent *Deconstructing Harry. Wild Strawberries* won the Grand Prize at the Berlin Film Festival, and was an Oscar nominee for Best Original Screenplay.

NEXT STOP . . . *The Seventh Seal, Fanny and Alexander, Citizen Kane*

1957 90m/B *SW* Victor Sjostrom, Bibi Andersson, Max von Sydow, Ingrid Thulin, Gunnar Bjornstrand, Folke Sundquist, Bjorn Bjelvenstam; *D:* Ingmar Bergman; *W:* Ingmar Bergman. Golden Globe Awards '60: Best Foreign Film; Nominations: Academy Awards '59: Best Story & Screenplay. **VHS, LV, 8mm** *VYY, HMV, FOX*

WINGS OF DESIRE
Der Himmel Uber Berlin

Even though movie audiences do tend to have strong and immediate reactions to most everything they see, that old cliche "you'll either love this movie or you'll hate it" is especially true of a couple of dozen pictures I know that keep coming up in conversation. Frank Capra's *It's a Wonderful Life* is one of these (if you're a detractor and are confronted by a fan, it's easiest to simply deny ever having seen it). But for the art house audience, which likes to pride itself on its analytical skills, I know of few movies that provoke the kind of passionate "love it or hate it" reaction as Wim Wenders's 1988 *Wings of Desire.* The story of an angel (Bruno Ganz) who exists in a monochromatic, non-sensual plane of existence until he decides to forsake immortality and heaven for a good cup of coffee and a pretty trapeze artist (Solveig Dommartin), *Wings of Desire* is itself as risky and heartfelt a leap as that which its protagonist takes. Using the divided Berlin that it's set in as a central metaphor, *Wings of Desire* is a conceptually wacky but powerfully eloquent (and daringly elliptical) meditation on the taken-for-granted human capacity for hunger of *every* kind: sex (not just dewy-eyed generic "love") is elevated to the big time here, and sensuality is celebrated in all its forms, rather than reserved as a reward for the deserving. If you squirmed through the flat-footed, literal-minded Nicolas Cage/Meg Ryan remake called *City of Angels,* calm down, take a deep breath, and plunge into *Wings of Desire* anyway. It just might remind you that it *is* a wonderful life. With Otto Sander and Peter Falk.

NEXT STOP . . . *Kings of the Road, Mystery Train, Faraway, So Close!*

1988 (PG-13) 130m/C *GE* Bruno Ganz, Peter Falk, Solveig Dommartin, Otto Sander, Curt Bois; *D:* Wim

W

Wenders; *W:* Wim Wenders, Peter Handke; *C:* Henri Alekan; *M:* Jurgen Knieper. Independent Spirit Awards '89: Best Foreign Film; Los Angeles Film Critics Association Awards '88: Best Cinematography, Best Foreign Film; New York Film Critics Awards '88: Best Cinematography; National Society of Film Critics Awards '88: Best Cinematography. **VHS, LV** *ORI, GLV, MOV*

WINTER LIGHT
Nattvardsgaesterna

The centerpiece of Bergman's "crisis of faith," or "religious" trilogy of films, which began with *Through a Glass Darkly* and ended with *The Silence,* focuses on four central characters: a village priest, Tomas (Gunnar Björnstrand), whose faith is in doubt since the death of his wife; a schoolmistress, Marta (Ingrid Thulin), who is in love with Tomas; and Jonas (Max von Sydow), a fisherman whose obsessive fear of nuclear war is driving his wife, Karin (Gunnel Lindblom), to the edge of her endurance. *Winter Light* is often cited as the least successful of the three films, but this may be simply because of the movie's somewhat elliptical structure and its utter bleakness. Tomas is a man who's just going through the motions of his profession—and unfortunately that profession is based on comforting others with the faith that he no longer has. (One critic likened his dilemma to a man caressing a woman he no longer loves.) There is also the subplot of the fear of nuclear holocaust, which was perhaps a bit too close to home for many in 1962. Nevertheless, though *Winter Light* isn't as structurally or emotionally fully felt as the trilogy's bookends, it remains a haunting elegy for a man who's spent a lifetime consoling others, and is left to wonder who will console him. As always, Bergman has pulled fine performances out of his cast, most notably Björnstrand and Thulin. Stunningly photographed by Sven Nykvist.

NEXT STOP . . . *Through a Glass Darkly, The Silence, The Sacrifice*

1962 80m/B *SW* Gunnar Bjornstrand, Ingrid Thulin, Max von Sydow; *D:* Ingmar Bergman; *W:* Ingmar Bergman; *C:* Sven Nykvist. **VHS, LV** *NLC*

WITCHCRAFT THROUGH THE AGES
Häxan

As much a cult oddity as it is a bona fide classic, Benjamin Christensen's *Witchcraft through the Ages* (*Häxan*) is an inventive and fantastic documentary-like depiction of the history of witchcraft from the Middle Ages to the modern era (1922, at least). Packed with black masses, gothic rituals, and copious nudity, this legendary film has a genuinely erotic pull, which caused it to become a somewhat notorious—and sought after—item over the years. It's quite brilliant visually, and those who have seen the movie tend to remember many of the images for years, even if the specific context of the image has been long forgotten. Christensen, who plays the devil in the film, was a medical school graduate; he chose to go to Hollywood in the mid-1920s where he worked on a few films, but returned to Denmark within a decade. *Witchcraft through the Ages* remained his signature work, and it was banned and suppressed in many countries. It found a new audience in the U.S. as a "head" film in the 1960s, when a new, "underground" version was released, complete with an unnecessary narration spoken by William S. Burroughs. This is a truly unique item—a must.

NEXT STOP . . . *Day of Wrath, The Mysterious Island (1929), Vampyr*

1922 74m/B *SW* Maren Pedersen, Clara Pontoppidan, Oscar Stribolt, Benjamin Christiansen, Tora Teje, Elith Pio, Karen Winther, Emmy Schonfeld, John Andersen; *D:* Benjamin Christiansen; *C:* Johan Ankerstjerne. **VHS** *MPI, GPV, WFV*

WOMAN IN THE DUNES
Suna No Onna
Woman of the Dunes

An entomologist examining beetles in a remote sand dune misses his bus back to the city. Put up for the night by a woman who lives alone at the bottom of a deep sand pit, the entomologist discovers the next morning that he is her prisoner, every bit as trapped as the futilely flailing insects he studies with his magnifying glass. Amid the heat and ever-changing terrain of the shifting sand—which permeates every crevice of the woman's home no matter how often it's shoveled out—the relationship between the two becomes an intense microcosm of sexual co-dependence and a near-Buñuelian examination of the human desire for enslavement. Hiroshi Segawa's cinematography makes the grit and the heat unnervingly palpable, and the haunting score of Toru Takemitsu (recently released on a superb compilation CD) gives *Woman in the Dunes* an otherworldly air. Director Hiroshi Teshigahara received a Special Jury Prize at the Cannes Film Festival for *Woman in the Dunes,* which is such a perfectly realized adaptation of Kobo Abe's novel that it felt as much like a classic on the day of its release in 1964 as it does 34 years later.

NEXT STOP . . . *The Phantom of Liberty, Tristana, Antonio Gaudi*

1964 123m/B *JP* Eiji Okada, Kyoko Kishida, Koji Mitsui, Hiroko Ito, Sen Yano; *D:* Hiroshi Teshigahara; *W:* Kobe Abe; *C:* Hiroshi Segawa; *M:* Toru Takemitsu. Cannes Film Festival '64: Grand Jury Prize; Nominations: Academy Awards '65: Best Director (Teshigahara), Best Foreign-Language Film. **VHS** *CVC, NYF, VDM*

WOMAN IN THE MOON
By Rocket to the Moon
Girl in the Moon

Fritz Lang's visually spectacular but dramatically underwhelming silent science-fiction fantasy was difficult to see for over 20 years following World War II, primarily because the Nazis destroyed so many prints. It's not that they regarded the film as subversive, but rather that they wanted no films circulated around the world which would suggest a German interest in rocketry—at least while von Braun and his cohorts were developing the V-1 and V-2. *Woman in the Moon* stresses the means by which a rocket could—and

did—make such a journey, and Lang's interest in realism led him to use Willy Ley as a technical advisor for the rocket's design and the method by which it would be launched. (Like Lang, Ley also fled to the United States with the coming of the Nazis—he served as an advisor on a number of American science-fiction pictures in the 1950s, and an illustrator for SF magazines.) The original script called for the lunar explorers—four men, a woman, and a child—to discover evidence on the moon that visitors from Atlantis had been there thousands of years earlier. This predated a lot of contemporary *Chariots of the Gods*-type stuff by at least a half century, but eventually, Lang settled for a more pedestrian scenario. (The astronauts end up finding gold and water instead.) *Woman in the Moon* is probably most famous for having introduced the "countdown" to both science fiction and to the world of rocketry. Lang thought it up as a way to generate suspense, figuring that a ship blasting off on a count of "zero" would be cooler than having it launch at the count of "six." The idea stuck, and a tradition was born.

NEXT STOP . . . *A Trip to the Moon, Destination Moon, Metropolis*

1929 115m/B *GE* Klaus Pohl, Willy Fritsch, Gustav von Wagenheim, Gerda Maurus; *D:* Fritz Lang. **VHS** *VYY, IHF, LSV*

A WOMAN IS A WOMAN
Une Femme Est une Femme
La Donna E Donna

Four years before Jacques Demy's *The Umbrellas of Cherbourg,* Jean-Luc Godard tried his hand at a musical of his own. Starting, as Demy did, with music of Michel Legrand, Godard's creation is something of a free-form, improvisational salute to the Hollywood entertainments of Stanley Donen and Vincente Minnelli. There *is* a plot—it has to do with Anna Karina's desire to have a baby by any means necessary, be it Jean-Claude Brialy or Jean-Paul Belmondo—but the substance here is the style, and vice-

THE HOUND SALUTES:
GÉRARD DEPARDIEU
French Actor Most Well-Known in U.S.

For a generation, it has seemed that every French film released in the United States has starred Gérard Depardieu. Indeed, many of them have. About half of the French mega-star's 80-plus films are available in this country, including *Going Places, The Return of Martin Guerre, Get Out Your Handkerchiefs, The Last Metro, Camille Claudel, Cryano de Bergerac, Jean de Florette,* and *Germinal.* His versatility and output are prodigious; Depardieu's played everything from historical figures to beatniks.

"Sixty of my films were boring," he told an interviewer in 1991. "About ten were very good."

Loyal to the French film industry and not fluent in English, Depardieu has failed to conquer America, despite attempts like *Green Card, Bogus, Unhook the Stars, The Man in the Iron Mask,* and even playing Columbus in the epic flop *1492.*

Hollywood wouldn't know how to package him anyway. He is dishevelled and unconventional, not movie-star handsome, a gluttonous bear of a man who is frequently overweight. Yet he is Europe's biggest film star. He was nominated far a Best Actor Oscar for *Cyrano de Bergerac.*

Not by accident are his best roles those of peasants. Depardieu was born in the rural south of Chateauroux, France on December 27, 1948, the third of six children of migrant workers. As a youth, he was a semi-literate car thief, amateur boxer, and Riviera beach bum. He hit Paris at 16 and took speech therapy to become a stage actor.

Depardieu is also a film producer, recording artist, and winemaker. He and his wife Elisabeth have two children, of which his son Guillaume is also an actor.

---

versa. Freeze frames, explanatory titles, sudden, unexpected bursts of song and dance, all on a wide, wide screen densely packed with Raoul Coutard's brightly colored images, lock together to create what Godard described as the first "neo-realist" musical. It's pleasurable and often witty; you can feel the fun Godard must have had in making it, yet it's inoffensively lightweight—a minor work by a major artist.

NEXT STOP . . . *Pierrot le Fou, Contempt, Lola*

1960 88m/C *FR* Jean-Claude Brialy, Jean-Paul Belmondo, Anna Karina, Marie DuBois; **D:** Jean-Luc Godard; **M:** Michel Legrand. **VHS** *INT*

THE WOMAN NEXT DOOR
La Femme d'a Cote

With *The Woman Next Door* in 1981, François Truffaut dared to create a picture that was both deeply felt and unashamedly romantic. Truffaut had just completed *The Last Metro* to wide acclaim and boxoffice success, and while the movie was thoroughly honorable, there was an emotional artificiality about it that felt calculated, dry, and passionless. But *The Woman Next Door,* the story of a suburban husband (Gérard Depardieu) who resumes an affair with a married ex-lover (Fanny Ardant) who moves next door, is nothing but risk. It's a vertiginous, swoony story of uncontrollable, rekindled passion, which audiences either tend to respond to quite deeply or hoot off the screen. Some of the negative response to the film stemmed from the physical screen presence of Ardant (who was Truffaut's lover at the time), one of the few women in movies who looks voracious enough to devour Depardieu for breakfast and still down a couple of Pop-Tarts. But much of the dismissal of this picture came, I think, from some degree of embarrassment on the part of critics at the picture's ruthless emotional force. No "cute" coincidences or wacky situations come out of the woodwork to save these people from their obsessions; they can't see a way out of their dilemma, and they go all the way with their unending sexual need to the point where their feelings are no longer tolerable. *The Woman Next Door* is built on some of the same themes as Truffaut's *The Story of Adele H.,* but that was a love story about one person, and could be viewed more easily as an individual case study in madness. *The Woman Next Door* is cloaked as a far more traditional romance, but it's also a cautionary, "be careful what you wish for" scenario that can have you squirming in your seat with either relief that that isn't you up on the screen, or with envy because you wish it were.

NEXT STOP . . . *The Story of Adele H., The Soft Skin, Vertigo*

1981 (R) 106m/C *FR* Gerard Depardieu, Fanny Ardant, Michele Baumgartner, Veronique Silver, Roger Van Hool; *D:* Francois Truffaut; *W:* Suzanne Schiffman; *M:* Georges Delerue. **VHS, LV** *HMV, FOX*

A WOMAN'S TALE

A Woman's Tale is one of those wonderful movies that it's nearly impossible to convince people to see. They hear that it's about a 78-year-old woman dying of cancer, and believe that it might indeed be very good, but they'll see it later, thanks. The standard device for encouraging people to see a film like this is to point out how "uplifting" it is, but it's not right to play that game with this marvelous piece of work. *A Woman's Tale* stars Australian actress Sheila Florance as the

aforementioned woman, Martha, who's chosen to die at home under the care of a younger nurse. Martha has friends and family who look in on her as well, including a charming gentleman played by Paul Cox regular Norman Kaye (of the same director's marvelous *Man of Flowers*). Bit by bit we learn about her life, her memories, and the things that have shaped her ideas. But she's not simply a spectator. The movie is equally about her continuing impact on those around her. *A Woman's Tale* is eloquent, forthright, and unsentimental; some viewers have been startled by nude scenes featuring a woman of Florance's age, others are put off by the fact that the actress herself was herself dying during the movie's production. Yet this is no exploitative stunt; it's a sensitive, moving, landmark film about coming to terms with age and dying. If you don't have time for that, perhaps you should reconsider just what you're spending your time *on.*

NEXT STOP . . . *Man of Flowers, Wild Strawberries, Near Death*

1992 (PG-13) 94m/C *AU* Sheila Florance, Gosia Dobrowolska, Norman Kaye, Chris Haywood, Myrtle Woods, Ernest Gray, Monica Maughan, Bruce Myles, Alex Menglet; *D:* Paul Cox; *W:* Paul Cox. Australian Film Institute '91: Best Actress (Florance). **VHS, LV, Closed Caption** *ORI, BTV*

WOMEN FROM THE LAKE OF SCENTED SOULS

In a rural Chinese village, a tough-minded businesswoman runs a local sesame-oil factory that attracts the attention of Japanese investors. It seems that the secret ingredient in the oil—the local water, which carries with it much history as well as flavor—can't be reproduced elsewhere. She decides that the money such an investment will bring can be put to good use by buying a bride for her mentally deficient son, and might even make it easier for her to continue the affair she's carrying on behind her clueless, lazy husband's back. *Women from the Lake of Scented Souls* (the original title of which is the slightly less evocative *Sesame Oil Woman*) becomes

Rossy de Palma is
one of the women
caught up in Pedro
Almodovar's farce
*Women on the
Verge of a Nervous
Breakdown.*

more engaging and enjoyably twisted as it
goes along, but be prepared: it might look
more at home on the Lifetime Channel than
on Bravo. Co-winner (with *The Wedding Banquet*) of the Berlin Film Festival's Grand Prize.

NEXT STOP . . . *The Story of Qiu Ju, Ermo, Mildred Pierce*

1994 105m/C *CH* Siqin Gaowa, Wu Yujuan, Lei
Luosheng, Chen Baoguo; *D:* Xie Fei; *W:* Xie Fei; *C:* Bao
Xianran; *M:* Wang Liping. **VHS** *AVI*

WOMEN ON THE
VERGE OF A
NERVOUS
BREAKDOWN
*Mujeres al Borde de un Ataque
de Nervios*

The wonderful Carmen Maura is Pepa, a
woman whose life is coming apart at the

seams, thanks to her elusive, maddening ex-
lover, Ivan (he's just decided to dump her
and she's just discovered she's pregnant), his
new girlfriend, his son (Antonio Banderas),
and his son's girlfriend (the truly weird Rossy
de Palma). With so many people manipulating and controlling her, it's no surprise that
Pepa makes her living dubbing the voices
for movie actors—supplying the emotion
for other people's lives. Oh yes, there are terrorists, too, and suspicious cops, and a pleasantly crazed, flamboyant taxi driver who
keeps picking up Pepa his cab boasts a sign
that reads "Thank You for Smoking"). There is
drugged gazpacho, and a big climactic
scene at the airport, but above all, there is
the joy of comic timing so perfect and satisfying that watching this joyous work by
Pedro Almodóvar is like looking a big, beautiful, perfectly oiled machine, packed with
an impossibly large number of gears, all of
which seem to do just what they're supposed to at exactly the right moment. That's

not to say that *Women on the Verge of a Nervous Breakdown* feels mechanical, either; the thing you marvel at the most is how Almodóvar manages to make such a delicate house of cards seem so alive and spontaneous. A good deal of it has to do with his cast, particularly the great Carmen Maura, who seems to be carrying the whole world on her sturdy shoulders. The design, cinematography, and editing are snappy, ingenious, and always at the service of the genuinely sweet screenplay, which is tough and touching and never misses a step. It works just fine on video, but if you get the chance to see it with a big audience, do.

NEXT STOP . . . *What Have I Done to Deserve This?, The Flower of My Secret, Live Flesh*

1988 (R) 88m/C *SP* Carmen Maura, Fernando Guillen, Julieta Serrano, Maria Barranco, Rossy de Palma, Antonio Banderas; *D:* Pedro Almodovar; *W:* Pedro Almodovar; *C:* Jose Luis Alcaine; *M:* Bernardo Bonazzi. New York Film Critics Awards '88: Best Foreign Film; Nominations: Academy Awards '88: Best Foreign-Language Film. **VHS, LV, Letterbox** *ORI*

THE WONDERFUL CROOK
Pas Si Mechant que Ça

Swiss director Claude Goretta's second theatrical feature received some film festival play, but wasn't released in the U.S. until after the critical raves that greeted *The Lacemaker* two years later. Gérard Depardieu is Pierre, a married man and factory owner whose handmade furniture just isn't selling. He doesn't want to lay off his employees, so he decides that the only decent thing to do is rob a bank. Pierre's new life as a thief comes with a fringe benefit in the form of Nelly (Marlène Jobert), a sympathetic young woman who plays Bonnie to Pierre's Clyde. This is a feather-light, harmless little film that's pleasantly entertaining while you're watching it, but evaporates soon after. Not surprisingly, there's something very *Swiss* about it all; with this material, the dutiful neutrality with which Pierre's dilemma is handled drains a needed sense of foreboding from the film—the picture seems anemic. It's not all sweetness and

light, but a little more messiness might have been just the ticket.

NEXT STOP . . . *The Lacemaker, The Middle of the World, Jonah Who Will Be 25 in the Year 2000*

1975 115m/C *SI FR* Marlene Jobert, Gerard Depardieu, Dominique Labourier, Philippe Leotard, Jacques Debary, Michel Robin, Paul Crauchet; *D:* Claude Goretta; *W:* Claude Goretta; *C:* Renato Berta; *M:* Arie Dzierlatka. *NYR*

THE WORLD OF APU
Apu Sansat
Apur Sansar

In the final film of Satyajit Ray's great *Apu Trilogy*, Apu (played now by Soumitra Chatterjee) is forced to abandon his university studies for lack of funds. Though a strange, unplanned series of circumstances, Apu marries, but the marriage turns out to be a happy one, and Apu believes he has found his place in the world. His wife dies giving childbirth, however, and Apu is so devastated that he will not see his son; instead, he goes on a long journey through the country, alone. Five years later Apu is persuaded to return, and when he sees his son, his love for the boy suddenly transcends all of his deep-seated, festering anger. Now, he truly has found his place in the world. Ray's trilogy is one of the greatest of all film experiences. The flow of narrative, the rhythm of the storytelling, Ravi Shankar's musical score, the visual intimacy, and uninsistent elegance of the acting all reinforce the basic, magnificent story that Ray gives to us. The comic moments in the films seem to flow naturally as well, and are never mere "comic relief." The trilogy has the spaciousness and breadth of a great novel, and it takes us along on Apu's journey through life rather than making us mere spectators. *The Apu Trilogy* can, and does, change you. It opens your eyes once again to the wonder and possibilities of the choices we have, and it reminds us as well of the limitless, untapped potential of the cinema to show us these things.

"I'm sick of being good."

—Pepa (Carmen Maura) in *Women on the Verge of a Nervous Breakdown*.

NEXT STOP . . . *Two Daughters, The Lion King, The Searchers*

1959 103m/B *IN* Soumitra Chatterjee, Sharmila Tagore, Alok Charkravarty, Swapan Makerji; *D:* Satyajit Ray; *W:* Satyajit Ray; *M:* Ravi Shankar. **VHS** *HHT, VYY, DVT*

WOYZECK

Georg Büchner's play, written in 1836, told of an ordinary soldier (Klaus Kinski) who became a victim of the German obsession with militarism. Harassed by his commanders, experimented upon, pushed well beyond reasonable limits of human endurance, Woyzeck finally snapped and turned understandably homicidal. Werner Herzog has made a tense, terse, 82-minute film out of this material, and while there's nothing really wrong with it, the whole project just feels a little superfluous. Additionally, it's hard to imagine Klaus Kinski as a slowly ticking time bomb when he always looks completely demented to begin with. In *Woyzeck,* it's not startling when he finally blows his stack—you just wonder what took him so long. Apparently, Kinski wondered too. In his amusingly titled biography, *All I Need Is Love,* he wrote of filming *Woyzec:* "I don't have to rehearse or listen to Herzog's rubbish. I tell him, I warn him, to keep his trap shut and let me do what I must. He complies." Wouldn't you?

NEXT STOP . . . *Stroszek, Aguirre, the Wrath of God, Full Metal Jacket*

1978 82m/C *GE* Klaus Kinski, Eva Mattes, Wolfgang Reichmann, Josef Bierbichler; *D:* Werner Herzog; *W:* Werner Herzog. **VHS** *NYF*

WUTHERING HEIGHTS
Abismos de Pasion
Cumbres Borrascosas

In his autobiography, Luis Buñuel wrote: "Like all surrealists, I was deeply moved by the novel, and had always wanted to try the movie. I knew I had a first-rate script, but I had to work with actors (the producer) had hired for a musical…including a rumba dancer and a Polish actress. As expected, there were horrendous problems during the shoot, and the results were problematical at best." Of the many versions of Emily Brontë's *Wuthering Heights,* this 1953 Mexican version by Luis Buñuel may be the most eccentric, wildly uneven and least known. This was the period in which Buñuel was in exile from his native Spain, and he made a number of films in Mexico of varying quality and intensity. That variability can be found within *Wuthering Heights,* which consists primarily of barely adequate expository stretches cemented by startling sequences, such as Heathcliff's (Alejandro's) appearance in Cathy's (Catarina's) tomb. It's like looking for a modest prize in a box of stale Crackerjack, though. The rewards are there, but they're best enjoyed by those interested in cataloging the complete works of the great surrealist director. Others will be far more satisfied with the 1939 William Wyler version, which is itself problematical in some ways, but pretty swell nevertheless.

NEXT STOP . . . *Él (This Strange Passion), Viridiana, Wuthering Heights* (1939)

1953 90m/B *MX* Irasema Dilian, Jorge Mistral, Lilia Prado, Ernesto Alonso; *D:* Luis Bunuel. **VHS** *XVC*

XALA
The Curse
Impotence

Senegal's Ousmane Sembène is one of the world's great cinematic satirists, and he's at the height of his powers in this bitter and brilliantly witty tale of a self-satisfied, "Europeanized" black businessman (he washes his Mercedes with Evian) who is suddenly struck down by the dreaded *xala* curse, which causes those afflicted with it to become impotent. As he searches desperately—and in all the wrong places—for a cure, his refusal to recognize the genesis of his condition explodes into both a tragic portrait of cultural enslavement and a razor-sharp satire of man's endless capacity for self-delusion. Censored heavily in Sembène's native Senegal—its Pogo-like "we have met the enemy and he is us" message didn't sit well with authorities—*Xala* is nevertheless one of Sembène's most widely seen and thoroughly entertaining films. Be prepared, however—its last sequence is sobering and unsparing, a reminder that just under the inviting surface of all great satire swims a shark with very sharp teeth.

NEXT STOP . . . *Mandabi, Mephisto, Ran*

1975 123m/C Douta Seck, Makhouredia Gueye, Thierno Leye, Dieynaba Niang, Miriam Niang, Iliamane Sagna, Seune Samb, Abdoulaye Seck, Younouss Seye; *D:* Ousmane Sembene; *W:* Ousmane Sembene; *C:* Georges Caristan, Orlando L. Lopez, Seydina D. Saye, Farba Seck; *M:* Samba Diabara Samb. *NYR*

XICA

A diamond rush in 18th-century Brazil transformed the country's interior into a place of undreamed-of wealth and excess. The legendary black slave Xica da Silva (Zeze Mota) found a way to use another natural formation to achieve riches; her body became the key to capturing the attention of the mining-town's governor, and her status as the unofficial "Empress of Brazil" wasn't far behind. This flamboyant and rollicking fable—part third-world tract and part Vegas act—is filled with music, dancing, and color. It's a lively salute to a true-life heroine, whom director Carlos Diegues (*Bye Bye Brazil*) teasingly refers to as "our Joan of Arc, sort of." (You're guaranteed to go out humming the theme song: "Xica *da,* Xica *da,* Xica *da,* Xica *da* Silva.")

NEXT STOP . . . *Ganga Zumba, Quilombo, Bye Bye Brazil*

1976 109m/C *BR* Zeze Motta, Walmor Chagas, Altair Lima, Jose Wilker, Marcus Vinicius, Elke Maravilha; *D:* Carlos Diegues; *W:* Joao Felicio. **VHS** *NYF, BTV, FCT*

YAABA

This sweetly stirring and eloquent film from Burkina Faso's Idrissa Ouedraogo is the story of a 12-year-old boy who bravely befriends an old woman, even though she's been shunned by her village for being a witch. The boy's affection for her leads to his calling her "yaaba" (grandmother), but soon the social pressures of his daily life and his responsibilities to the others in the community force the boy to make some difficult and very grown-up decisions. Ouedraogo's serene, charming, and piercingly humane fable is told in a straightforward and pleasingly unhurried manner; though it captures the quality of a classic folk tale, it never loses sight of the troubled feelings of its characters, nor does it ever go soft at its center. Suggesting an oft-told legend that might be passed on by a traditional African storyteller—a "griot"—*Yaaba* was described by its director as being "based on tales of my childhood, and on that kind of bedtime storytelling we hear just before falling asleep."

NEXT STOP . . . *Tilaï, Pather Panchali, Forbidden Games, La Promesse*

1989 90m/C Assita Ouedraogo, Rasmane Ouedraogo, Fatimata Sanga, Noufou Ouedraogo, Roukietou Barry, Adama Ouedraogo, Amade Toure, Sibidou Ouedraogo, Adame Sidibe, Kinda Moumouni, Zenabou Ouedraogo, Ousmane Sawadogo; *D:* Idrissa Ouedraogo; *W:* Idrissa Ouedraogo; *C:* Matthias Kalin; *M:* Francis Bebey. *NYR*

YESTERDAY, TODAY AND TOMORROW
Ieri, Oggi e Domani
She Got What She Asked For

Of the many multiple-story films that came out of Italy in the 1960s, Vittorio De Sica's *Yesterday, Today and Tomorrow* was both the best and the most popular. In "Adelina," Sophia Loren makes a shady living on the black market in Naples. When she makes the happy discovery that Italian law prohibits pregnant women from being jailed, she cajoles husband Marcello Mastroianni into keeping her perpetually pregnant (the episode takes place over seven years). In "Anna," Loren is a rich woman who tells her young, starving-artist lover that she cares only for love and passion, and that her money means nothing to her. Clue: she doesn't mean it. The third and most well remembered of the pieces, "Mara," features Loren as

Adelina (Sophia Loren) enjoys life with her husband (Marcello Mastroianni) in *Yesterday, Today and Tomorrow.*

a call-girl who tries to dissuade a young seminary student from giving up the church for her. She does it by taking a week-long vow of chastity, the end of which culminates in the now-legendary strip-tease that Loren does for her favorite client, Mastroianni (the two actors reprised the scene in Robert Altman's *Ready to Wear.*) If you're looking for the De Sica of *The Bicycle Thief* or *Umberto D.,* you'll be disappointed. *Yesterday, Today and Tomorrow* finds the great director in a very different, far more easygoing mode. These pleasant sketches are light, enjoyable, diverting fun, and that's all they're meant to be. De Sica is completely at the service of his actors here, and the undemanding material lets Loren and Mastroianni ham it up so pleasurably that you leave the theatre feeling positively stuffed with *mortadella.*

NEXT STOP . . . *Boccaccio '70, Marriage Italian Style, Woman Times Seven*

1964 119m/C *IT FR* Sophia Loren, Marcello Mastroianni, Tony Pica, Giovanni Ridolfi; *D:* Vittorio De Sica. Academy Awards '64: Best Foreign Film; British Academy Awards '64: Best Actor (Mastroianni). **VHS** *JEF, HHE*

YOJIMBO

Akira Kurosawa's breathtaking, cynical, hilarious *Yojimbo* is the story of a lone samurai (Toshiro Mifune) who wanders into a new town controlled by two warring clans. Equally disdainful of both, the samurai sells his services as a yojimbo (bodyguard) to both sides, profiting handily while scheming to arrange their mutual destruction. *Yojimbo* has a loose, casual feel—as if the events taking place are being worked out as we watch—but it's actually a meticulously designed accomplishment on both a narrative and a technical level. The movie's legendary violence doesn't take up all that much screen time; what there is, however, is high impact. Early in *Yojimbo* is a famous moment in which a dog strolls lazily across a wind-swept street, carrying an object in its mouth. As he approaches the camera, we can see that the object is a severed human hand. Kurosawa doesn't stop there, though; the dog get closer and closer, well after we've identified what he's carrying, until it's right in our faces. Kurosawa's made a comedy, all right, but he's letting us know that we're not getting off the hook too easily—the violence is going to be, in every sense, "in your face." It was a moment that would be expanded upon by American filmmakers during the remainder of the 1960s, culminating in the horrifying juxtaposition of comedy and violence in *Bonnie and Clyde*. *Yojimbo*'s roots, though, are clearly in the American western, and the film ironically became popular in the United States at a time when American westerns were appealing less and less to upscale audiences. (Three years later, *Yojimbo* would be remade, *as* a western, but in Italy, by Sergio Leone. The central role in *A Fistful of Dollars* would be played by Clint Eastwood, and would propel him—and Leone—to a whole new level in their careers. A vastly inferior version by Walter Hill, *Last Man Standing* starring Bruce Willis, would finally bring the story home to America for what would be its worst incarnation. And Bernardo Bertolucci still talks of filming Dashiel Hammet's *Red Harvest,* the book on which Yojimbo itself is reputedly based.) Mifune would play the same character in a charming but much lower-key sequel, *Sanjuro*. Masaru Sato's score for *Yojimbo* is great, as is the widescreen cinematography of Kazuo Miyagawa. Warning: if you don't see *Yojimbo* in a letterboxed version, it will not only not make sense, but you'll completely miss the best visual gags.

NEXT STOP . . . *Sanjuro, Rebellion, A Fistful of Dollars*

1961 110m/B *JP* Toshiro Mifune, Eijiro Tono, Suuzu Yamda, Seizaburo Kawazu, Isuzu Yamada; *D:* Akira Kurosawa; *W:* Hideo Oguni, Shinobu Hashimoto, Akira Kurosawa; *M:* Masaru Sato. Nominations: Academy Awards '61: Best Costume Design (B & W). **VHS, LV, 8mm, Letterbox** *VYY, HHT, NOS*

YOL
The Way

Five Turkish political prisoners are released from their minimum-security prison for one week, to visit their families. Before long, they almost come to wish they had stayed in jail. Disasters of every stripe flood into the lives of these men, and most—like the man who finds that his wife was locked out of their house by his family because she had an affair while he was in jail—are presented as a part of the natural social order of a country so oppressively patriarchal that it has in effect gone quite mad. The writer and credited co-director of the film, Yilmaz Güney, designed the film while himself in prison on political charges; an associate, Serif Gören, did the actual directing of the film based on Güney's instructions. The brutal and ferociously angry *Yol* is nothing if not a testament to artistic dedication and determination. That did not go unnoticed at Cannes, where *Yol* split the 1982 Grand Prize with another overtly political work of fiction, Costa-Gavras's *Missing*.

NEXT STOP . . . *Before the Rain, Commissar, The Silences of the Palace*

1982 (PG) 126m/C *TU* Tarik Akan, Serif Sezer; *D:* Yilmaz Guney, Serif Goren; *W:* Yilmaz Guney; *M:* Sebastian Argol. Cannes Film Festival '82: Best Film. **VHS** *COL, AUD*

THE YOUNG POISONER'S HANDBOOK

In *The Young Poisoner's Handbook,* Hugh O'Conor plays Graham, a young misfit whose chemistry set provides him endless hours of consolation and companionship. After a bit of experimenting, he begins poisoning his stepmum and tracking her progress toward death in a series of charts and journals. Graham is a true sociopath; his worries and anxieties all center around being caught, and he's able to watch his stepmother's increasing agonies (and his family's accompanying worry) in a purely scientific light. He's a little Nazi doctor, pretending at first that he's inter-

ested in some sort of scientific study, but in reality is quite calmly prepared to annihilate anyone who causes him the slightest insult. What's astounding about *The Young Poisoner's Handbook* is that Ross and his extraordinary star Hugh O'Conor (he was Christy Brown in the childhood sequences of *My Left Foot*) have turned this material into very dark comedy, and have brought it off with style and grim wit. The movie is a nightmare (it's based on an actual case), and it never softens Graham's deeds or motives, yet like like other classic movie monsters, Graham is weirdly sympathetic. There's a kind of purity about his drives and ambitions that might be admirable were it not for what his drives and ambitions actually *are*. The movie becomes a kind of Horatio Alger story about succeeding at being monstrous—pulling yourself up by your own bloody bootstraps. You almost root for him until you imagine that it's *your* tea he's bringing you, complete with two sugars

and one cyanide. There are similarities to *A Clockwork Orange* and the director acknowledges this by staging one or two obvious *homage* scenes. He didn't need to, though; *The Young Poisoner's Handbook* is a stronger, smarter, vastly more frightening film.

NEXT STOP . . . *A Clockwork Orange, M, Henry: Portrait of a Serial Killer*

1994 (R) 99m/C *GB* Hugh O'Conor, Anthony Sher, Ruth Sheen, Charlotte Coleman, Roger Lloyd Pack, Paul Stacey, Samantha Edmonds, Charlie Creed-Miles; *D:* Benjamin Ross; *W:* Benjamin Ross, Jeff Rawle; *C:* Hubert Taczanowski; *M:* Robert Lane, Frank Strobel. **VHS, Closed Caption** *CAF*

Z

Costa-Gavras's electrifying thriller is based on the assassination of a Greek anti-war activist and physician (Yves Montand) in the 1960s, and the ensuing, government-toppling investigation. There are a few portions of *Z* that have less impact today than when the film was originally released; most of them are action and chase scenes that have been eclipsed so handily in contemporary movies that they seem a bit quaint. But the meat-and-potatoes of *Z*, which is Jean-Louis Trintignant's relentless investigation into the conspiracy surrounding Montand's murder, can still, as Pauline Kael put it in 1969, "damn near knock you out of your seat." The second half of *Z* is the world's first political music video; the rhythm of the investigation becomes exhilarating, and Françoise Bonnot's staccato editing couples with Mikis Theodorakis's pounding score to produce an irresistible, intoxicating pull. Some complained about what they found to be a bludgeoning, propagandistic tone in Costa-Gavras's style, but when he toned down the punchiness for his extraordinary subsequent film, *The Confession*, almost no one went to see it. One of the most successful foreign-language films of its time, and one of the few to ever be nominated for an Oscar as Best Picture, *Z* was the winner of the Jury Prize at the 1969 Cannes Film Festival.

NEXT STOP . . . *The Confession, Missing, JFK*

1969 128m/C *FR* Yves Montand, Jean-Louis Trintignant, Irene Papas, Charles Denner, Georges Geret, Jacques Perrin, Francois Perier, Marcel Bozzuffi; **D:** Constantin Costa-Gavras; **W:** Constantin Costa-Gavras; **M:** Mikis Theodorakis. Academy Awards '69: Best Film Editing, Best Foreign Film; Cannes Film Festival '69: Special Jury Prize, Best Actor (Trintignant); Golden Globe Awards '70: Best Foreign Film; New York Film Critics Awards '69: Best Director (Costa-Gavras), Best Film; National Society of Film Critics Awards '69: Best Film; Nominations: Academy Awards '69: Best Adapted Screenplay, Best Director (Costa-Gavras), Best Picture; Cannes Film Festival '69: Best Film. **VHS, LV** *FXL*

ZENTROPA

Just after World War II, an American and self-proclaimed pacifist named Leopold finds himself working as a sleeping-car conductor on a huge German railway system called Zentropa. He wants to take part in the post-war rebuilding of Germany, or so he claims, and this is what he comes up with. The railroad—now carrying ordinary passengers but until recently carrying Jews to the ovens—is run by the creepy Max Hartmann, who would like Leo and everyone else to believe that he was *only* following orders. Max's sexy daughter Katharina (Barbara Sukowa) has designs on Leo, but an American agent (Eddie Constantine) has designs on Max; he'd like to arrest him for war crimes. This could be the plot description of any number of mediocre European thrillers, but whatever Lars von Trier's *Zentropa* is, it's not mediocre. I first encountered the picture at a Museum of Modern Art screening—it was part of a superb exhibition the Department of Film mounted in 1991 called *Junction and Journey: Trains and Film*. The experience of watching the film reminded me a bit of the first time I saw Orson Welles's *Touch of Evil;* not because *Zentropa*'s in the same league, exactly (it's not), but because at some point I realized that I had lost track of the plot but was mesmerized anyway. I recall staring at the slow, dark, stylized widescreen images and muttering under my breath: "What the hell *is* this?" I'm still not sure. But if this was von Trier's way of getting noticed, of announcing his arrival on the film scene in a flamboyant way, he succeeded. Von Trier won the Best Director award at Cannes for *Zentropa* (it was originally called *Europa,* but retitled because of the impending release of Agnieszka Holland's *Europa, Europa*. One could only imagine the two films side by side at a multiplex: "One ticket, please." "For *Europa*? Or *Europa, Europa*?"). *Zentropa* sank almost unnoticed beneath the distribution waves in the U.S., but von Trier resurfaced with a far bigger splash in his beguiling *Breaking the Waves.*

NEXT STOP . . . *The Kingdom, Parts I & II, Alphaville, Veronika Voss*

1992 (R) 112m/C *GE* Jean-Marc Barr, Barbara Sukowa, Udo Kier, Eddie Constantine; **D:** Lars von Trier; **W:** Niels Vorsel, Lars von Trier. **VHS, LV, Closed Caption** *TOU*

ZERO FOR CONDUCT
Zero de Conduit

Jean Vigo was 27 when he directed this magnificently poetic, lyrical portrait of youthful

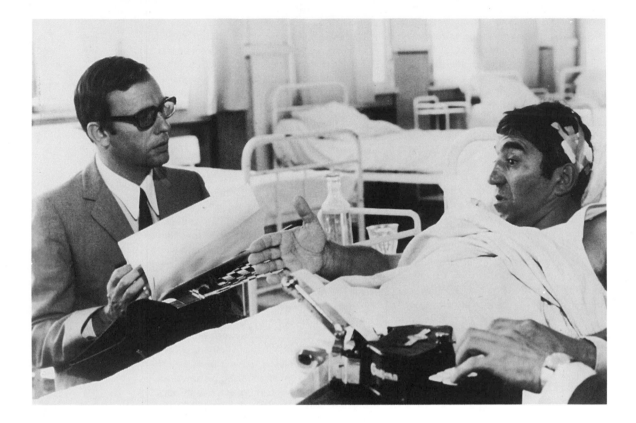

Jean-Louis Trintignant tries to explain what happened in Costa-Gavras's Z.

rebellion at a restrictive French boarding school. The children have just returned to school from a holiday, and are in no mood to take orders from "Sourpuss," the most obnoxious of their instructors. From a spirited, dormitory pillow fight (a hauntingly beautiful slow-motion sequence), a full-scale rebellion erupts—a teacher is tied to his bed, the Jolly Roger is flown on the school roof, and a group of visiting dignitaries are bombarded with junk and forced to retreat from the victorious, triumphant children. *Zero for Conduct* caused an immediate scandal when previewed in 1933, and was, in fact, banned from distribution until 1945, 11 years after the death of its brilliant director. Just 47 minutes long, *Zero for Conduct* is a perfectly shaped work, filled with bold, experimental storytelling techniques and as revolutionary in spirit as its young protagonists. Vigo considered the picture autobiographical, and in light of that, his stylized lampooning of the

adults in the film seems less an expressionistic stunt than emotional cinema-verité. It remains the perfect expression of a child's natural reluctance to surrender to authority, and it's funny, enchanting, and deeply reassuring. There's a nobility in *Zero for Conduct;* not just in the kids but in Vigo's joy at their impulses. As is also true of his heartbreakingly beautiful *L'Atalante,* it's one of the world's great movies.

NEXT STOP . . . *L'Atalante, The 400 Blows, If…*

1933 49m/B *FR* Jean Daste, Robert Le Flon, Louis Lef'evre, Constantin Kelber, Gerard de Bedarieux; **D:** Jean Vigo; **W:** Jean Vigo; **C:** Boris Kaufman. **VHS** *VYY, NOS, HHT*

ZITA

Young, shy Ann (Joanna Shimkus) learns that her adored Aunt Zita (Katina Paxinou) is dying, but she's unable to accept the idea of parting from her great friend and confidant, the woman who has meant everything to her since her childhood. Ann finds it too heartbreaking to remain in the house with the deathly ill Zita, so she runs off into the Parisian night, looking to lose herself in the clubs and cafés, and meeting a young man in the process. When Ann returns home, she's able to face what she encounters there through newly opened eyes. This delicate, quietly contemplative film was directed by Robert Enrico, best-known for his brilliant 30-minute adaptation of Ambrose Bierce's *An Occurrence at Owl Creek Bridge* (the only film Rod Serling ever "outsourced" for his long-running CBS-TV series, *The Twilight Zone*).

Joanna Shimkus turns in a sweet, sympathetic performance as the young woman who understands the need to break from her childhood but is afraid to do so. Jean Boffety's cinematography of the city at night is both otherworldly and intoxicating, and François de Roubaix has contributed a haunting, melancholy musical score. The rarely seen *Zita* is a little knockout, but beware the widely circulated dubbed version at all costs.

NEXT STOP . . . *Forbidden Games, Late Spring, When the Cat's Away*

1968 ?m/C Suzanne Flon, Katina Paxinou, Joanna Shimkus; *D:* Robert Enrico; *C:* Jean Boffety; *M:* François de Roubaix. *NYR*

The "Master Title Index" provides a complete title list of movies reviewed in this book, as well as alternate and/or translated titles, and any movies mentioned within the reviews. The films are listed alphabetically.

The American Friend (1977) *See also* Purple Noon (1960)

American Gigolo *See* Pickpocket (1959)

American Graffiti *See* Hey, Babu Riba (1988); I Vitelloni (1953)

The American Soldier (1970)

Amore in Citta *See* Love in the City (1953)

And God Created Woman (1957)

And Life Goes On… *See* Life and Nothing More … (1992); Taste of Cherry (1996); Through the Olive Trees (1994)

And Now for Something Completely Different *See* The Case of the Mukkinese Battle Horn (1956); Monty Python's The Meaning of Life (1983)

And Now My Love *See* Cat and Mouse (1978)

And the Ship Sails On (1983)

And Woman…Was Created *See* And God Created Woman (1957)

Andrei Rublev (1966) *See also* Gabbeh (1996); The Mirror (1975); The Round-Up (1966); Utamaro and His Five Women (1946)

An Angel at My Table *See* Careful, He Might Hear You (1984); Heavenly Creatures (1994); My Brilliant Career (1979); The Piano (1993); Sweetie (1989); Two Friends (1986); Vagabond (1985)

Angel Heart *See* Insomnia (1997)

Angi Vera (1978) *See also* Time Stands Still (1982)

Angst Essen Selle auf *See* Ali: Fear Eats the Soul (1974)

Anna (1993) *See also* A Slave of Love (1978)

Anna: From Six Till Eighteen *See* Anna (1993)

Anna: Ot Shesti do Vosemnadtsati *See* Anna (1993)

Anne and Muriel *See* Two English Girls (1972)

Another Man, Another Chance *See* A Man and a Woman (1966)

Ansikte mot Ansikte *See* Face to Face (1976)

The Anti-Extortion Woman *See* Minbo—Or the Gentle Art of Japanese Extortion (1992)

Antoine and Colette *See* Confidentially Yours (1983); Love on the Run (1978); Stolen Kisses (1968)

Antonia's Line (1995) *See also* Bhaji on the Beach (1994); Mina Tannenbaum (1993)

Antonio Das Mortes (1968) *See also* Black God, White Devil (1964)

Antonio Gaudi *See* Woman in the Dunes (1964)

Aparajito (1958) *See also* Jalsaghar (1958); Pather Panchali (1954); Phantom India (1969); Salaam Bombay! (1988)

The Apartment *See* L'Avventura (1960)

Apocalypse Now *See* Aguirre, the Wrath of God (1972); The Bird with the Crystal Plumage (1970); The Conformist (1971); Fitzcarraldo (1982); Pixote (1981); The Spider's Stratagem (1970); The Tin Drum (1979); The Valley Obscured by the Clouds (1972)

The Apprenticeship of Duddy Kravitz *See* Outback (1971)

Apu Sansat *See* The World of Apu (1959)

Apu Trilogy *See* Aparajito (1958); The World of Apu (1959)

Apur Sansar *See* The World of Apu (1959)

Arabesque *See* Gertrud (1964)

Arabian Nights (1974) *See also* The Canterbury Tales (1971); The Decameron (1970)

Aranyer Din Ratri *See* Days and Nights in the Forest (1970)

Archangel *See* Careful (1994)

Ariel (1989) *See also* Leningrad Cowboys Go America (1989); The Match Factory Girl (1990)

Arizona Dream *See* When Father Was Away on Business (1985)

Armageddon *See* War and Peace (1968)

Arsenal (1929) *See also* Earth (1930)

Artemisia *See* Camille Claudel (1989)

Ascenseur pour L'Echafaud *See* Frantic (1958)

The Ascent (1976) *See also* Ballad of a Soldier (1960); Commissar (1968)

Ashani Sanket *See* Distant Thunder (1973)

Ashes and Diamonds (1958) *See also* A Generation (1954); Kanal (1956)

Ashik Karib *See* Ashik Kerib (1988)

Ashik Kerib (1988)

The Asphalt Jungle *See* Big Deal on Madonna Street (1958)

At First Sight *See* Entre-Nous (1983)

At War with the Army *See* The Men Who Tread on the Tiger's Tail (1945)

Atame *See* Tie Me Up! Tie Me Down! (1990)

The Atomic Cafe *See* I Live in Fear (1955); The War Game (1965)

Attack of the Crab Monsters *See* Cries and Whispers (1972)

Au Revoir les Enfants (1987) *See also* Forbidden Games (1952); Lacombe, Lucien (1974); The Last Metro (1980); May Fools (1990); The Tin Drum (1979); The Two of Us (1968)

Augustin (1995)

An Autumn Afternoon (1962) *See also* Late Spring (1949); Tokyo Story (1953)

Autumn Sonata (1978) *See also* Face to Face (1976)

The Aviator's Wife *See* Le Beau Mariage (1982); The Marquise of O (1976)

Az en XX. Szazadom *See* My Twentieth Century (1990)

Babette's Feast (1987) *See also* An Autumn Afternoon (1962); A Chef in Love (1996); Like Water for Chocolate (1993); The Magic Flute (1973); Summer Interlude (1950); Tampopo (1986)

Babettes Gaestebud *See* Babette's Feast (1987)

Baby Boom *See* One Sings, the Other Doesn't (1977)

Baby Doll *See* That Obscure Object of Desire (1977)

The Bad Sleep Well (1960) *See also* High & Low (1962)

Badkonake Sefid *See* The White Balloon (1995)

Badlands *See* Butterfly Kiss (1994); La Cérémonie (1995)

Bagdad Cafe *See* Sugarbaby (1985)

The Bailiff *See* Sansho the Bailiff (1954)

Baisers Voles *See* Stolen Kisses (1968)

The Baker's Wife (1933) *See also* Fanny (1932); Harvest (1937)

Ballad of a Soldier (1960)

The Ballad of Narayama (1983) *See also* Black Rain (1988); Himatsuri (1985); Vengeance Is Mine (1979)

Ballada o Soldate *See* Ballad of a Soldier (1960)

Bananas *See* The Battleship Potemkin (1925)

The Band and the Bracelet *See* The Silences of the Palace (1994)

Band of Outsiders (1964) *See also* A Married Woman (1965); Masculine Feminine (1966); My Life to Live (1962)

Bande a Part *See* Band of Outsiders (1964)

Bandit Queen (1994) *See also* Bhaji on the Beach (1994)

Banditi a Orgosolo *See* Bandits of Orgosolo (1961)

Bandits of Orgosolo (1961) *See also* The Gospel According to St. Matthew (1964); The Tree of Wooden Clogs (1978)

Baron Müenchhausen *See* Fabulous Adventures of Baron Munchausen (1961)

Baron of Terror *See* The Brainiac (1961)

Baron Prasil *See* Fabulous Adventures of Baron Munchausen (1961)

Basic Instinct *See* The 4th Man (1979)

Basileus Quartet (1982) *See also* Orchestra Rehearsal (1978)

Basquiat *See* A Bigger Splash (1974)

Batman *See* The Man in the White Suit (1951)

Batman and Robin *See* War and Peace (1968)

Battle Beyond the Stars *See* The Green Slime (1968)

The Battle of Algiers (1966) *See also* The Battleship Potemkin (1925); Burn! (1970); Ten Days That Shook the World (1927)

The Battle of Chile *See* Le Joli Mai (1962); State of Siege (1973)

The Battleship Potemkin (1925) *See also* The Battle of Algiers (1966); I Am Cuba (1964); If… (1969); The Passion of Joan of Arc (1928); Strike (1924); Ten Days That Shook the World (1927)

Bawang Bie Ji *See* Farewell My Concubine (1993)

Baxter (1989)

The Bear *See* Baxter (1989)

Béatrice (1988) *See also* Captain Conan (1996); The Return of Martin Guerre (1983)

Beau Père (1981) *See also* Get Out Your Handkerchiefs (1978)

Beautiful Thing (1995) *See also* The Best Way (1976)

The Beautiful Troublemaker *See* La Belle Noiseuse (1990)

Beauty and the Beast (1946) *See also* The Blood of a Poet (1930); Breaking the Waves (1995); Donkey Skin (1970); Eternal Return (1943); Eyes without a Face (1959); Orpheus (1949); The Testament of Orpheus (1959)

Bed and Board (1970) *See also* The 400 Blows (1959); Love on the Run (1978); Stolen Kisses (1968)

The Bed-Sitting Room *See* Juggernaut (1974)

Bedazzled *See* Bob le Flambeur (1955)

Beethoven *See* Baxter (1989)

Before the Rain (1994) *See also* 1900 (1976); Prisoner of the Mountains (1996); Ulysses' Gaze (1995); Underground (1995); Yol (1982)

Before the Revolution (1965) *See also* The Conformist (1971); Memories of Underdevelopment (1968); A Slave of Love (1978)

Beggars' Opera *See* The Threepenny Opera (1931)

Believe Me *See* Hollow Reed (1995)

Belle de Jour (1967) *See also* The Criminal Life of Archibaldo de la Cruz (1955); La Lectrice (1988); Tristana (1970)

Belle Epoque (1992)

The Belly of an Architect (1991)

Berlin Alexanderplatz (1980) *See also* Heimat 1 (1984); The Kingdom (1995); The Marriage of Maria Braun (1979); The Stationmaster's Wife (1977)

Berlin, Symphony of a Great City *See* The Man with a Movie Camera (1929)

The Best Intentions (1992) *See also* Sunday's Children (1994)

The Best Way (1976) *See also* The Little Thief (1989)

The Best Way to Walk *See* The Best Way (1976)

Betrayal *See* The Go-Between (1971); Two Friends (1986)

A Better Tomorrow (1986) *See also* Hard-Boiled (1992); The Killer (1990)

Betty Blue (1986) *See also* Diva (1982)

Between Us *See* Entre-Nous (1983)

Beware of a Holy Whore (1970)

The Beyond *See* The Bird with the Crystal Plumage (1970)

Beyond and Back *See* Mondo Cane (1963)

Bhaji *See* Bhaji on the Beach (1994)

Bhaji on the Beach (1994) *See also* Bandit Queen (1994)

The Bicycle Thief (1948) *See also* Bandits of Orgosolo (1961); Big Deal on Madonna Street (1958); Bitter Rice (1949); The Gar-

den of the Finzi-Continis (1971); The Icicle Thief (1989); Lamerica (1995); Miracle in Milan (1951); Open City (1945); Pixote (1981); Shoeshine (1947); The Stolen Children (1992); Umberto D. (1955); The White Balloon (1995); Yesterday, Today and Tomorrow (1964)

The Big Chill *See* Jonah Who Will Be 25 in the Year 2000 (1976)

The Big City (1963)

The Big Day *See* Jour de Fete (1948)

Big Deal *See* Big Deal on Madonna Street (1958)

Big Deal on Madonna Street (1958) *See also* Il Bell'Antonio (1960)

The Big Green *See* Shall We Dance? (1997)

The Big Heat *See* M (1931)

Big Night *See* A Chef in Love (1996); Comfort and Joy (1984); Like Water for Chocolate (1993)

A Bigger Splash (1974)

Billy Jack *See* El Topo (1971)

Billy Liar *See* A Kind of Loving (1962)

The Bird with the Crystal Plumage (1970) *See also* Black Sunday (1960)

The Bird with the Glass Feathers *See* The Bird with the Crystal Plumage (1970)

The Birdcage *See* La Cage aux Folles (1978)

Birds of a Feather *See* La Cage aux Folles (1978)

Birthplace (1992) *See also* Night and Fog (1955); The Spider's Stratagem (1970); Triumph of the Will (1934)

Birumano Tategoto *See* The Burmese Harp (1956)

The Bitch *See* La Chienne (1931)

Bitter Harvest *See* Commissar (1968)

Bitter Rice (1949) *See also* We the Living (1942)

The Bitter Tears of Petra von Kant (1972) *See also* The American Soldier (1970); Beware of a Holy Whore (1970); Céleste (1981); In a Year of 13 Moons (1978); The Stationmaster's Wife (1977)

Black Girl (1966) *See also* Borom Sarret (1966); Camp de Thiaroye (1987); Mandabi (1968)

Black God, White Devil (1964) *See also* Antonio Das Mortes (1968)

Black Moon (1975)

Black Narcissus (1947) *See also* I Know Where I'm Going (1945); The Red Shoes (1948)

Black Orpheus (1958)

Black Rain (1988) *See also* Godzilla, King of the Monsters (1956); Rhapsody in August (1991); The War Game (1965)

The Black Sleep *See* The Manster (1959)

The Black Stallion *See* The Red Balloon (1956)

Black Sunday (1960) *See also* The Brainiac (1961)

Blade Runner *See* Alphaville (1965)

Blaise Pascal *See* The Rise of Louis XIV (1966)

Blanc *See* Trois Couleurs: Blanc (1994)

Bleak Moments (1971)

A Blonde in Love *See* Loves of a Blonde (1965)

The Blood of a Poet (1930) *See also* L'Age D'Or (1930); Léolo (1992); Les Enfants Terribles (1950); Orpheus (1949); The Testament of Orpheus (1959)

The Blood of the Beasts *See* Mondo Cane (1963)

Blood Wedding (1981) *See also* Carmen (1983)

The Blow-Out *See* La Grande Bouffe (1973)

Blow-Up (1966) *See also* Comfort and Joy (1984); I Am Curious (Yellow) (1967)

Blue (1993) *See also* Caravaggio (1986); The Double Life of Veronique (1991); Trois Couleurs: Bleu (1993)

The Blue Angel (1930) *See also* Mäedchen in Uniform (1931); The Soft Skin (1964); The Stationmaster's Wife (1977); Torment (1944); Variety (1925)

The Blue Kite (1993) *See also* Farewell My Concubine (1993); To Live (1994)

The Blue Light (1932)

Blue Steel *See* Stray Dog (1949)

Blunt *See* The 4th Man (1979)

The Boat Is Full (1981) *See also* Commissar (1968); Europa, Europa (1991); The Garden of the Finzi-Continis (1971)

Bob le Flambeur (1955) *See also* Borsalino (1970); Le Doulos (1961); Le Samourai (1967); Pépé le Moko (1937)

Bob the Gambler *See* Bob le Flambeur (1955)

Boccaccio '70 (1962) *See also* 8 1/2 (1963); Yesterday, Today and Tomorrow (1964)

Bodas de Sangre *See* Blood Wedding (1981)

The Bodyguards *See* La Scorta (1994)

Bolweiser *See* The Stationmaster's Wife (1977)

Bonaparte and the Revolution *See* Napoleon (1927)

Bonnie and Clyde *See* Breathless (1959); Yojimbo (1961)

Borom Sarret (1966)

Borsalino (1970)

Borsalino and Co. *See* Borsalino (1970)

Boudu Sauve des Eaux *See* Boudu Saved from Drowning (1932)

Boudu Saved from Drowning (1932) *See also* The Crime of Monsieur Lange (1936); The Golden Coach (1952); Smiles of a Summer Night (1955); The Testament of Dr. Cordelier (1959); The Two of Us (1968)

Boy (1969) *See also* In the Realm of the Senses (1976)

A Boy and His Dog *See* Delicatessen (1992)

Boy Meets Girl (1984)

Boyfriends & Girlfriends (1988) *See also* Full Moon in Paris (1984); Le Beau Mariage (1982); Rendezvous in Paris (1995); When the Cat's Away (1996)

The Boys of St. Vincent (1993) *See also* The Devil's Playground (1976)

The Brainiac (1961)

Brazil *See* Delicatessen (1992)

The Break-Up *See* La Rupture (1970)

Breakfast at Tiffany's *See* Liebelei (1932)

Breaking In *See* Comfort and Joy (1984)

Breaking the Waves (1995) *See also* Insomnia (1997); The Kingdom (1995); The Story of Adele H. (1975); Zentropa (1992)

The Breakup *See* La Rupture (1970)

Breathless (1959) *See also* And God Created Woman (1957); Band of Outsiders (1964); Chungking Express (1995); Loulou (1980); Pierrot le Fou (1965); Shoot the Piano Player (1962); The Thief of Paris (1967); The Valley Obscured by the Clouds (1972)

The Bride Wore Black (1968) *See also* Confidentially Yours (1983)

The Bridge *See* Prisoner of the Mountains (1996)

Brief Encounter (1946) *See also* Captain's Paradise (1953); The Lady with the Dog (1959)

A Brief History of Time *See* My Left Foot (1989)

Brigadoon *See* Black Sunday (1960)

Britannia Hospital *See* If... (1969)

Broken English *See* Once Were Warriors (1994)

Bronco Billy *See* The Clowns (1971)

Bronenosets Potemkin *See* The Battleship Potemkin (1925)

The Brood *See* They Came from Within (1975)

Brutti, Sporchi, e Cattivi *See* Down & Dirty (1976)

Bugsy Malone *See* Borsalino (1970)

Bullet in the Head *See* Chungking Express (1995)

Burden of Dreams *See* Aguirre, the Wrath of God (1972); Fitzcarraldo (1982)

The Burmese Harp (1956) *See also* Enjo (1958); Fires on the Plain (1959)

Burn! (1970) *See also* The Battle of Algiers (1966); Sambizanga (1972)

Burnt by the Sun (1994) *See also* Andrei Rublev (1966); Anna (1993); Oblomov (1981); A Slave of Love (1978)

Bushwhacked *See* French Twist (1995)

The Butcher *See* Le Boucher (1969)

The Butcher Boy *See* La Promesse (1996)

Butley *See* The Go-Between (1971); A Month in the Country (1987)

Butterfly Kiss (1994) *See also* Messidor (1977); Violette (1978)

By Rocket to the Moon *See* Woman in the Moon (1929)

Bye Bye Brazil (1979) *See also* Antonio Das Mortes (1968); The Clowns (1971); I Don't Want to Talk about It (1994); Quilombo (1984); Xica (1976)

The Cabinet of Dr. Caligari (1919) *See also* The Golem (1920); The Hour of the Wolf (1968); The Red Desert (1964); Waxworks (1924)

Cabiria *See* Nights of Cabiria (1957); The White Sheik (1952)

Cactus (1986)

Café au Lait (1994) *See also* Hate (1995); A Self-Made Hero (1995)

Cairo Station *See* The Night of Counting the Years (1969)

Calcutta *See* Phantom India (1969)

Calendar *See* The Adjuster (1991); Exotica (1994)

Camila *See* I Don't Want to Talk about It (1994)

Camille Claudel (1989) *See also* French Provincial (1975)

Camouflage *See* Illumination (1973)

The Camp at Thiaroye *See* Camp de Thiaroye (1987)

Camp de Thiaroye (1987) *See also* Sambizanga (1972)

Campanadas a Medianoche *See* Chimes at Midnight (1967)

Canary Murder Case *See* Pandora's Box (1928)

The Canterbury Tales (1971) *See also* Arabian Nights (1974); The Decameron (1970)

Capitaine Conan *See* Captain Conan (1996)

Captain Conan (1996) *See also* L.627 (1992)

Captain's Paradise (1953) *See also* Diary of a Seducer (1995)

Caravaggio (1986)

Cardiogram *See* Freeze-Die-Come to Life (1990)

Career Girls *See* Antonia's Line (1995); Bleak Moments (1971); High Hopes (1988); Orlando (1992); Secrets and Lies (1995)

Careful (1994)

Careful, He Might Hear You (1984)

Carmen (1983) *See also* Blood Wedding (1981); The Hit (1985); The Red Shoes (1948); The Tango Lesson (1997)

Carnival in Flanders (1935) *See also* Children of Paradise (1944)

Carnival of Souls *See* Curse of the Demon (1957); Onibaba (1964)

Caro Diario (1993)

Carousel *See* Faraway, So Close! (1993)

Casablanca *See* King Kong vs. Godzilla (1963)

Casanova *See* City of Women (1981)

Casanova '70 (1965)

The Case of the Mukkinese Battle Horn (1956)

Casino *See* Contempt (1964)

Casque d'Or (1952) *See also* Le Trou (1959)

Castle of Doom *See* Vampyr (1931)

The Castle of the Spider's Web *See* Throne of Blood (1957)

Cat and Mouse (1978) *See also* My New Partner (1984)

Cat Ballou *See* Viva Maria! (1965)

Cat People *See* Curse of the Demon (1957)

Caught *See* La Ronde (1951)

Ceddo (1978) *See also* Black Girl (1966); Borom Sarret (1966); Camp de Thiaroye (1987); Emitai (1971); Guelwaar (1994); Indochine (1992); Tilaï (1990)

Céleste (1981) *See also* Stroszek (1977); Sugarbaby (1985)

Celestial Clockwork (1994)

The Celluloid Closet *See* Okoge (1993)

The Ceremony *See* A Single Girl (1996)

César (1936) *See also* Fanny (1932)

César & Rosalie (1972) *See also* Vincent, François, Paul and the Others (1976)

C'est Arrive Pres de Chez Vous *See* Man Bites Dog (1991)

C'est la Vie *See* Entre-Nous (1983)

Cet Obscur Objet du Desir *See* That Obscure Object of Desire (1977)

Chacun Cherche Son Chat *See* When the Cat's Away (1996)

The Chant of Jimmie Blacksmith (1978) *See also* A Cry in the Dark (1988); The Devil's Playground (1976); La Cérémonie (1995); Outback (1971); Samurai Rebellion (1967)

Chaos *See* Kaos (1985)

Chapayev (1934) *See also* Arsenal (1929)

The Charge of the Light Brigade *See* How I Won the War (1967)

The Charterhouse of Parma *See* Before the Revolution (1965)

Charulata (1964) *See also* The Big City (1963); Devi (1960)

A Chef in Love (1996)

Chelovek s Kinoapparatom *See* The Man with a Movie Camera (1929)

Cheun Gwong Tsa Sit *See* Happy Together (1996)

Chikamatsu Monogatari *See* Gate of Hell (1953); Utamaro and His Five Women (1946)

Children of Paradise (1944) *See also* Carnival in Flanders (1935); French CanCan (1955); La Nuit de Varennes (1982); Le Jour Se Lève (1939);

Les Visiteurs du Soir (1942); The Testament of Dr. Cordelier (1959)

Chimes at Midnight (1967) *See also* Alexander Nevsky (1938); Hamlet (1948); Napoleon (1927); Ran (1985)

Chinatown *See* Le Doulos (1961)

Chloe in the Afternoon (1972) *See also* La Collectionneuse (1967); The Marquise of O (1976)

Chocolat *See* I Can't Sleep (1993); The Scent of Green Papaya (1993)

Chongqing Senlin *See* Chungking Express (1995)

Christ Stopped at Eboli (1979) *See also* La Terra Trema (1948); The Postman (1994); Three Brothers (1980)

Christine *See* Baxter (1989)

Chungking Express (1995) *See also* Happy Together (1996)

Cinderfella *See* Celestial Clockwork (1994)

Cinema Paradiso (1988) *See also* Celestial Clockwork (1994); The Long Day Closes (1992); The Postman (1994)

Citizen Kane *See* La Bete Humaine (1938); Mr. Arkadin (1955); Rashomon (1951); The Red Shoes (1948); Seven Beauties (1976); Wild Strawberries (1957)

Citizens Band *See* Traffic (1971)

City Lights *See* The Killer (1990)

City of Angels *See* Faraway, So Close! (1993); Wings of Desire (1988)

The City of Lost Children (1995) *See also* Delicatessen (1992)

City of Women (1981) *See also* The Man Who Loved Women (1977)

Claire's Knee (1971) *See also* Boyfriends & Girlfriends (1988); Chloe in the Afternoon (1972); Gertrud (1964); La Collectionneuse (1967); Le Beau Mariage (1982); The Marquise of O (1976); My Night at Maud's (1969); Pauline at the Beach (1983); Rendezvous in Paris (1995)

Claude *See* The Two of Us (1968)

Clickety Clack *See* Dodes 'ka-den (1970)

The Cloak *See* The Overcoat (1959)

The Clockmaker *See* The Judge and the Assassin (1975); L.627 (1992)

A Clockwork Orange *See* Going Places (1974); Hate (1995); Mon Oncle d'Amerique (1980); The Young Poisoner's Handbook (1994)

Close to Eden *See* Burnt by the Sun (1994); Dersu Uzala (1975); The Horse

Thief (1987); A Mongolian Tale (1994)

The Clowns (1971) *See also* Cinema Paradiso (1988)

Clueless *See* The Designated Mourner (1997)

Cobweb Castle *See* Throne of Blood (1957)

The Coca-Cola Kid *See* Man Is Not a Bird (1965)

Cocktail Molotov *See* Entre-Nous (1983)

The Cocoanuts *See* Le Million (1931)

Cold Fever *See* Shall We Dance? (1997)

The Collector *See* Tie Me Up! Tie Me Down! (1990)

Colonel Blimp *See* The Life and Death of Colonel Blimp (1943)

Colonel Redl *See* Hanussen (1988); Mephisto (1981)

The Color of Pomegranates *See* Ashik Kerib (1988); Shadows of Forgotten Ancestors (1964)

Combination Platter *See* Egg (1988)

Comfort and Joy (1984) *See also* Local Hero (1983); Love Serenade (1996)

Commissar (1968) *See also* Ballad of a Soldier (1960); Freeze-Die-Come to Life (1990); The Last Metro (1980); Yol (1982)

Como Agua para Chocolate *See* Like Water for Chocolate (1993)

Comradeship *See* Kameradschaft (1931)

A Condemned Man Has Escaped *See* Diary of a Country Priest (1950); Le Trou (1959); A Man Escaped (1957); Pickpocket (1959)

The Confession (1970) *See also* The Ascent (1976); Day of Wrath (1943); Z (1969)

Confidential Report *See* Mr. Arkadin (1955)

Confidentially Yours (1983)

Conflagration *See* Enjo (1958)

The Conformist (1971) *See also* Before the Revolution (1965); The Bird with the Crystal Plumage (1970); A Gentle Woman (1969)

The Conqueror Worm *See* The Brainiac (1961)

Conspirators of Pleasure *See* Jan Svankmejer's Faust (1994)

The Constant Factor *See* Contract (1980); Illumination (1973)

Conte d'Hiver *See* A Tale of Winter (1992)

Contempt (1964) *See also* And God Created Woman (1957); Every Man for Him-

self (1979); A Married Woman (1965); My Life to Live (1962); Pierrot le Fou (1965); A Woman Is a Woman (1960)

Contract (1980) *See also* Illumination (1973)

The Conversation *See* The Day the Sun Turned Cold (1994); Rashomon (1951)

Conversation Piece (1975)

The Cook in Love *See* A Chef in Love (1996)

The Cook, the Thief, His Wife & Her Lover (1990) *See also* Drowning by Numbers (1987); Weekend (1967)

Coup de Foudre *See* Entre-Nous (1983)

Coup de Torchon *See* Life and Nothing But (1989)

Covek Nije Tica *See* Man Is Not a Bird (1965)

Crackers *See* Big Deal on Madonna Street (1958)

The Cranes Are Flying *See* I Am Cuba (1964); The Overcoat (1959)

Crash (1995) *See also* Dead Ringers (1988); They Came from Within (1975)

The Crazy Family *See* The Family Game (1983)

Creepers *See* Suspiria (1977)

Cria (1976) *See also* The Garden of Delights (1970); Léolo (1992); The Nest (1980); Spirit of the Beehive (1973)

Cria Cuervos *See* Cria (1976)

Cries and Whispers (1972) *See also* Face to Face (1976); The Sacrifice (1986)

The Crime of Monsieur Lange (1936) *See also* La Bete Humaine (1938); La Chienne (1931); Le Jour Se Lève (1939)

Crimes and Misdemeanors *See* Le Bonheur (1965); Le Jour Se Lève (1939)

The Criminal Life of Archibaldo de la Cruz (1955) *See also* El (1952); Matador (1986)

Cristo si e fermato a Eboli *See* Christ Stopped at Eboli (1979)

The Crook *See* Cat and Mouse (1978)

The Crowd *See* The Last Laugh (1924)

Crush *See* Okoge (1993)

A Cry in the Dark (1988) *See also* The Chant of Jimmie Blacksmith (1978); Outback (1971)

The Crying Game *See* Blow-Up (1966); The Long Good Friday (1980)

Cuba *See* Juggernaut (1974)

Cul-de-Sac *See* Knife in the Water (1962)

Culloden *See* Edvard Munch (1974); The War Game (1965)

Cumbres Borrascosas *See* Wuthering Heights (1953)

The Curse *See* Xala (1975)

Curse of the Demon (1957)

Curse of the Doll People *See* The Brainiac (1961)

Cybele *See* Sundays & Cybele (1962)

Cyclo *See* The Scent of Green Papaya (1993)

Cyrano de Bergerac *See* The Postman (1994)

Czlowiek z Zelaza *See* Man of Iron (1981)

D2: The Mighty Ducks II *See* Shall We Dance? (1997)

D3: The Mighty Ducks *See* Shall We Dance? (1997)

Da Zdravstvuyet Meksika *See* Que Viva Mexico (1932)

Daikaiju Masura *See* Mothra (1962)

Damage *See* Crash (1995); In the Realm of the Senses (1976); The Lovers (1959); May Fools (1990); The Soft Skin (1964)

The Damned *See* Conversation Piece (1975); The Night Porter (1974)

Dance of the Vampires *See* The Fearless Vampire Killers (1967)

Dandelion *See* Tampopo (1986)

Dans la Ville Blanche *See* In the White City (1983)

Danton *See* La Marseillaise (1937); La Nuit de Varennes (1982); Man of Iron (1981)

Danzón *See* The Tango Lesson (1997)

Daoma Zei *See* The Horse Thief (1987)

Dark Eyes *See* A Slave of Love (1978)

Das Blaue Licht *See* The Blue Light (1932)

Das Boot Ist Voll *See* The Boat Is Full (1981)

Das Cabinet des Dr. Caligari *See* The Cabinet of Dr. Caligari (1919)

Das Tagebuch Einer Verlorenen *See* Diary of a Lost Girl (1929)

David Copperfield *See* Little Dorrit, Film 1: Nobody's Fault (1988)

Dawn of the Dead *See* Suspiria (1977)

Day for Night (1973) *See also* Beware of a Holy Whore (1970); Confidentially Yours (1983); Through the Olive Trees (1994)

Day of Wrath (1943) *See also* Gertrud (1964); Lancelot of the Lake (1974);

Mouchette (1967); The Passion of Joan of Arc (1928); Witchcraft through the Ages (1922)

The Day the Sun Turned Cold (1994)

Daybreak See Le Jour Se Lève (1939)

Days and Nights in the Forest (1970) See also Devi (1960); Distant Thunder (1973); The Middleman (1976); Two Daughters (1961)

Days of Being Wild See Happy Together (1996)

The Daytrippers See When the Cat's Away (1996)

De Eso No Se Habla See I Don't Want to Talk about It (1994)

Dead End See Hate (1995)

Dead of Night (1945) See also Kwaidan (1964); The Tenant (1976)

Dead Ringers (1988) See also Crash (1995); They Came from Within (1975)

The Dead Zone See The Mask (1961); They Came from Within (1975)

The Deadly Invention See The Fabulous World of Jules Verne (1958)

Dear Diary See Caro Diario (1993)

Dearest Love See Murmur of the Heart (1971)

Death and the Green Slime See The Green Slime (1968)

Death and the Maiden See Moonlighting (1982)

Death by Hanging See In the Realm of the Senses (1976)

Death in Venice See Conversation Piece (1975); Victim (1961)

Death of a Bureaucrat (1966) See also Memories of Underdevelopment (1968); Strawberry and Chocolate (1993)

The Decameron (1970) See also Arabian Nights (1974); The Canterbury Tales (1971)

Deconstructing Harry See After the Rehearsal (1984); Wild Strawberries (1957)

Deep End (1970) See also Knife in the Water (1962); Moonlighting (1982)

Delicatessen (1992) See also The City of Lost Children (1995)

Deliverance See Days and Nights in the Forest (1970)

The Demon See Onibaba (1964)

Demon Seed See Two or Three Things I Know About Her (1966)

The Demon's Mask See Black Sunday (1960)

Der Amerikanische Freund See The American Friend (1977)

Der Amerikanische Soldat See The American Soldier (1970)

Der Blaue Engel See The Blue Angel (1930)

Der Dibuk See The Dybbuk (1937)

Der Golem, wie er in die Welt kam See The Golem (1920)

Der Himmel Uber Berlin See Wings of Desire (1988)

Der Letzte Mann See The Last Laugh (1924)

Der Prozess See The Trial (1963)

Dersu Uzala (1975)

The Deserter and the Nomads See The Firemen's Ball (1968)

The Designated Mourner (1997) See also Au Revoir les Enfants (1987); Oblomov (1981)

Destination Moon See Woman in the Moon (1929)

Destroy All Monsters See Mothra (1962)

Deus e o Diabo na Terra do Sol See Black God, White Devil (1964)

Deux ou Trois Choses Que Je Sais d'Elle See Two or Three Things I Know About Her (1966)

Devi (1960)

Devil Doll See Dead of Night (1945)

Devil in the Flesh (1946)

Devil in the Flesh (1987)

The Devil, Probably See Boy Meets Girl (1984)

The Devil Woman See Onibaba (1964)

The Devils (1971) See also The Music Lovers (1971)

The Devil's Envoys See Les Visiteurs du Soir (1942)

The Devil's Eye (1960) See also Les Visiteurs du Soir (1942)

The Devils of Loudun See The Devils (1971)

The Devil's Playground (1976) See also The Chant of Jimmie Blacksmith (1978)

Diabolique (1955) See also The 4th Man (1979); The Vanishing (1988); The Wages of Fear (1955)

Diamond Earrings See The Earrings of Madame de… (1954)

Diary of a Chambermaid (1964)

Diary of a Country Priest (1950) See also A Gentle Woman (1969); Lancelot

of the Lake (1974); Mouchette (1967); Ordet (1955); Thérèse (1986)

Diary of a Lost Girl (1929) See also Pandora's Box (1928); The Threepenny Opera (1931)

Diary of a Seducer (1995) See also La Discrete (1990); La Lectrice (1988)

Diary of a Shijuku Thief See Boy (1969)

Diary of Oharu See Life of Oharu (1952)

Die Angst Tormannes beim Elfmeter See The Goalie's Anxiety at the Penalty Kick (1971)

Die Bitteren Traenen der Petra von Kant See The Bitter Tears of Petra von Kant (1972)

Die Blechtrommel See The Tin Drum (1979)

Die Bleierne Zeit See Marianne and Juliane (1982)

Die Buechse der Pandora See Pandora's Box (1928)

Die Dreigroschenoper See The Threepenny Opera (1931)

Die Ehe der Maria Braun See The Marriage of Maria Braun (1979)

Die Freudlosse Gasse See The Joyless Street (1925)

Die Liebe der Jeanne Ney (1927)

Die Nibelungen (1923) See also M (1931); Metropolis (1926)

Die Nibelungen: Siegfried und Kriemhilds Rache See Die Nibelungen (1923)

Die Regenschirme von Cherbourg See The Umbrellas of Cherbourg (1964)

Die Sehns Ucht der Veronika Voss See Veronika Voss (1982)

Die Verlorene Ehre der Katharina Blum See The Lost Honor of Katharina Blum (1975)

Die Xue Shuang Xiong See The Killer (1990)

Die Zwolfte Stunde See Nosferatu (1922)

Dieu de Tonnerre See Emitai (1971)

Different for Girls See Beautiful Thing (1995); The Best Way (1976)

Diner See I Vitelloni (1953)

Dirty Harry See The Man on the Roof (1976)

Dirty Mary See A Very Curious Girl (1969)

The Discreet See La Discrete (1990)

The Discreet Charm See The Discreet Charm of the Bourgeoisie (1972)

The Discreet Charm of the Bourgeoisie (1972) *See also* The Criminal Life of Archibaldo de la Cruz (1955); The Exterminating Angel (1962); The Hit (1985); The Phantom of Liberty (1974); That Obscure Object of Desire (1977); Tristana (1970)

The Disenchanted *See* La Discrete (1990); Wild Reeds (1994)

Distant Thunder (1973)

Distant Voices, Still Lives (1988) *See also* The Long Day Closes (1992); Once Were Warriors (1994)

Diva (1982) *See also* The Accompanist (1993); Betty Blue (1986); Black Moon (1975); Boy Meets Girl (1984); La Femme Nikita (1991); Moon in the Gutter (1983); Subway (1985)

Divertimento *See* La Belle Noiseuse (1990)

Divorce—Italian Style (1962) *See also* Alfredo, Alfredo (1972); Il Bell'Antonio (1960)

Divorzio All'Italiana *See* Divorce—Italian Style (1962)

Djavulens Oga *See* The Devil's Eye (1960)

Do the Right Thing *See* The Chant of Jimmie Blacksmith (1978)

Docteur Petiot *See* Dr. Petiot (1990)

Dr. Jekyll and Mr. Hyde *See* The Testament of Dr. Cordelier (1959)

Dr. Mabuse: Der Spieler *See* Die Nibelungen (1923)

Dr. Mabuse, Parts 1 & 2 (1922) *See also* The Joyless Street (1925); M (1931); Metropolis (1926); Spies (1928)

Dr. Petiot (1990)

Dr. Strangelove *See* Heavens Above! (1963); I Live in Fear (1955)

Dodes 'ka-den (1970) *See also* Dersu Uzala (1975); The Lower Depths (1936); The Lower Depths (1957); Red Beard (1965); Samurai Rebellion (1967)

A Dog's Life *See* Mondo Cane (1963)

The Dogs of War *See* Burn! (1970)

Doktor Mabuse der Spieler *See* Dr. Mabuse, Parts 1 & 2 (1922)

Domicile Conjugal *See* Bed and Board (1970)

Don Kikhot *See* Don Quixote (1957)

Don Quixote (1957) *See also* Gumshoe (1972)

Dona Flor and Her Two Husbands (1978)

Dona Flor e Seus Dois Maridos *See* Dona Flor and Her Two Husbands (1978)

Donkey Skin (1970) *See also* Beauty and the Beast (1946); Celestial Clockwork (1994); Jacquot (1991)

Don't Look Now *See* Insignificance (1985)

Donzoko *See* The Lower Depths (1957)

Doomed *See* Ikiru (1952)

The Double *See* Kagemusha (1980)

Double Indemnity *See* Bitter Rice (1949); Frantic (1958); Ossessione (1942); Wedding in Blood (1974)

The Double Life of Veronique (1991)

Doulos—The Finger Man *See* Le Doulos (1961)

Down & Dirty (1976)

Down and Out in Beverly Hills *See* Boudu Saved from Drowning (1932)

Down by Law *See* Johnny Stecchino (1992); The Monster (1996)

Dracula *See* Nosferatu (1922); Nosferatu the Vampyre (1979); Vampyr (1931)

Dragon Chow *See* Egg (1988)

The Draughtsman's Contract (1982) *See also* The Belly of an Architect (1991); The Cook, the Thief, His Wife & Her Lover (1990); Drowning by Numbers (1987); The Pillow Book (1995)

Dream of Light *See* La Belle Noiseuse (1990)

A Dream Play *See* After the Rehearsal (1984)

Dreamchild (1985) *See also* Black Moon (1975); Cria (1976); The Long Day Closes (1992)

Dreams (1955) *See also* Akira Kurosawa's Dreams (1990)

Dressed to Kill *See* The Bird with the Crystal Plumage (1970)

Drifting Clouds *See* Ariel (1989); Leningrad Cowboys Go America (1989)

Drowning by Numbers (1987) *See also* The Belly of an Architect (1991); The Draughtsman's Contract (1982); The Pillow Book (1995)

Drunken Angel (1948) *See also* Stray Dog (1949)

Drunken Master (1978)

Drunken Monkey in a Tiger's Eye *See* Drunken Master (1978)

Drunks *See* The Fire Within (1964)

Duck Soup *See* Le Million (1931)

Duel *See* Frantic (1958)

Dune *See* And the Ship Sails On (1983)

The Dybbuk (1937)

Early Spring *See* The Makioka Sisters (1983)

The Earrings of Madame de... (1954) *See also* Generale Della Rovere (1960); La Ronde (1951); La Signora di Tutti (1934); L'Argent (1983); Le Plaisir (1952); Liebelei (1932); Lola Montès (1955)

Earth (1930) *See also* Arsenal (1929); The Man with a Movie Camera (1929)

The Earth Will Tremble *See* La Terra Trema (1948)

The Easy Life *See* We All Loved Each Other So Much (1977)

Easy Rider *See* If... (1969); The Valley Obscured by the Clouds (1972)

Eboli *See* Christ Stopped at Eboli (1979)

The Eclipse (1966) *See also* L'Avventura (1960)

The Edge *See* Once Were Warriors (1994)

Edith & Marcel (1983)

Edvard Munch (1974) *See also* Camille Claudel (1989); La Belle Noiseuse (1990); Utamaro and His Five Women (1946)

Edward II *See* Caravaggio (1986)

Effi Briest (1974)

Efter Repetitionen *See* After the Rehearsal (1984)

Egg (1988)

8 1/2 (1963) *See also* And the Ship Sails On (1983); City of Women (1981); The Clowns (1971); Day for Night (1973); Intervista (1987); Juliet of the Spirits (1965); La Strada (1954); Love in the City (1953); The Tango Lesson (1997)

The Eighth Day *See* Toto le Heros (1991)

Él (1952) *See also* Wuthering Heights (1953)

El Amor Brujo *See* Blood Wedding (1981); Carmen (1983)

El Angel Exterminador *See* The Exterminating Angel (1962)

El Baron del Terror *See* The Brainiac (1961)

El Espiritu de la Colmena *See* Spirit of the Beehive (1973)

El la Nave Va *See* And the Ship Sails On (1983)

El Nido *See* The Nest (1980)

El Topo (1971)

Eléna and Her Men (1956)

Eléna et les Hommes *See* Eléna and Her Men (1956); French Can-Can (1955); The Golden Coach (1952)

The Elephant Man *See* And the Ship Sails On (1983); The Wild Child (1970)

Elevator to the Gallows *See* Frantic (1958)

Elvira Madigan (1967) *See also* The Man on the Roof (1976); Sunday's Children (1994)

The Emigrants (1972) *See also* Jerusalem (1996); The New Land (1973); Pelle the Conqueror (1988)

Emitai (1971) *See also* Borom Sarret (1966); Camp de Thiaroye (1987); Ceddo (1978); Guelwaar (1994); Mandabi (1968); Ramparts of Clay (1971); Shadows of Forgotten Ancestors (1964); Tilaï (1990)

The Empress Yang Kwei Fei *See* Princess Yang Kwei Fei (1955)

The End of St. Petersburg *See* Chapayev (1934)

The English Patient *See* Purple Noon (1960)

The Enigma of Kaspar Hauser *See* Every Man for Himself & God Against All (1975)

Enjo (1958) *See also* The Burmese Harp (1956)

Ensayo de un Crimen *See* The Criminal Life of Archibaldo de la Cruz (1955)

The Entertainer *See* A Kind of Loving (1962); L'Avventura (1960); Look Back in Anger (1958); Saturday Night and Sunday Morning (1960)

Entre-Nous (1983)

The Epic That Never Was *See* Que Viva Mexico (1932)

Episoda Del Mare *See* La Terra Trema (1948)

Eraserhead *See* El Topo (1971); They Came from Within (1975)

Erendira (1983)

Ermo (1994) *See also* The Story of Qiu Ju (1991); Women from the Lake of Scented Souls (1994)

Escape from Alcatraz *See* A Man Escaped (1957)

The Escorts *See* La Scorta (1994)

Et Dieu Crea la Femme *See* And God Created Woman (1957)

E.T.: The Extra-Terrestrial *See* Kaspar Hauser (1993); The Red Balloon (1956)

Etat de Siege *See* State of Siege (1973)

Eternal Return (1943)

Europa *See* Zentropa (1992)

Europa, Europa (1991) *See also* The Accompanist (1993); Fires on the Plain (1959); The Last Metro (1980); Olivier, Olivier (1992); Trois Couleurs: Blanc (1994); Zentropa (1992)

Every Man for Himself (1979) *See also* Last Tango in Paris (1973); Weekend (1967)

Every Man for Himself & God Against All (1975) *See also* Kaspar Hauser (1993)

Everything You Always Wanted to Know About Sex...But Were Afraid to Ask *See* Max, Mon Amour (1986)

Evil Angels *See* A Cry in the Dark (1988)

Exotica (1994) *See also* The Adjuster (1991); The Sweet Hereafter (1996); Ticket to Heaven (1981)

The Exterminating Angel (1962) *See also* Contract (1980); The Criminal Life of Archibaldo de la Cruz (1955); Los Olvidados (1950); The Phantom of Liberty (1974); That Obscure Object of Desire (1977); Tristana (1970)

Eyes of Hell *See* The Mask (1961)

Eyes without a Face (1959) *See also* The Face of Another (1966)

Fabulous Adventures of Baron Munchausen (1961) *See also* The Fabulous World of Jules Verne (1958)

The Fabulous Baker Boys *See* The Stationmaster's Wife (1977)

The Fabulous Baron Munchausen *See* Fabulous Adventures of Baron Munchausen (1961)

The Fabulous World of Jules Verne (1958) *See also* Fabulous Adventures of Baron Munchausen (1961); The Saragossa Manuscript (1965)

The Face *See* The Magician (1958)

The Face of Another (1966) *See also* Odd Obsession (1960); Samurai Rebellion (1967)

Face/Off *See* A Better Tomorrow (1986); Eyes without a Face (1959); The Face of Another (1966); Hard-Boiled (1992); High & Low (1962); The Killer (1990); La Femme Nikita (1991)

Face to Face (1976) *See also* After the Rehearsal (1984); Scenes from a Marriage (1973)

Faces of Death *See* Mondo Cane (1963)

Fag Hag *See* Okoge (1993)

Fahrenheit 451 (1966) *See also* The Bride Wore Black (1968); La Lectrice (1988)

Fallen Angels *See* Happy Together (1996)

The Falls *See* The Draughts-man's Contract (1982); Drowning by Numbers (1987)

The False Note *See* L'Argent (1983)

Falstaff *See* Chimes at Midnight (1967)

The Family Game (1983) *See also* Boy (1969)

Fanny (1932) *See also* César (1936); Marius (1931)

Fanny and Alexander (1983) *See also* Autumn Sonata (1978); Cries and Whispers (1972); The Magic Flute (1973); My Life As a Dog (1985); The Sacrifice (1986); Summer Interlude (1950); Sunday's Children (1994); Wild Strawberries (1957)

Fanny och Alexander *See* Fanny and Alexander (1983)

The Fanny Trilogy *See* The Baker's Wife (1933); French Provincial (1975); Harvest (1937); Jean de Florette (1987); Manon of the Spring (1987)

Fantasia *See* Allegro Non Troppo (1976)

Fantastic Planet (1973) *See also* Nosferatu the Vampyre (1979)

Faraway, So Close! (1993) *See also* Wings of Desire (1988)

Farewell My Concubine (1993) *See also* The Blue Kite (1993); Life on a String (1990); The Piano (1993); Temptress Moon (1996); To Live (1994)

Farinelli (1994)

Farinelli il Castrato *See* Farinelli (1994)

Farinelli the Castrato *See* Farinelli (1994)

Fast, Cheap and Out of Control *See* Project Grizzly (1996); Trois Couleurs: Rouge (1994)

Fata Morgana *See* Heart of Glass (1974)

Fatal Attraction *See* The Soft Skin (1964)

Faust (1926) *See also* Jan Svankmejer's Faust (1994); Mephisto (1981)

Faust-Eine deutsche Volkssage *See* Faust (1926)

Fear Eats the Soul *See* Ali: Fear Eats the Soul (1974)

The Fearless Vampire Killers (1967) *See also* The Green Slime (1968); Nosferatu the Vampyre (1979)

Federico Fellini's 8 1/2 *See* 8 1/2 (1963)

Federico Fellini's Intervista *See* Intervista (1987)

Fellini Satyricon (1969) *See also* Arabian Nights (1974); The Canterbury Tales (1971); La Dolce Vita (1960); Rocco and His Brothers (1960)

Fellini's Casanova *See* Fellini Satyricon (1969)

Fellini's Roma (1972) *See also* Amarcord (1974); Caro Diario (1993); Fellini Satyricon (1969)

Female Perversions *See* Caravaggio (1986); Orlando (1992)

Feng Yue *See* Temptress Moon (1996)

A Few Days in the Life of I.I. Oblomov *See* Oblomov (1981)

The Fifth Element *See* The City of Lost Children (1995); Delicatessen (1992); La Femme Nikita (1991); Le Dernier Combat (1984); Subway (1985)

Film d'Amore et d'Anarchia *See* Love and Anarchy (1973)

Finally, Sunday *See* Confidentially Yours (1983)

Fiorile (1993) *See also* Allonsanfan (1973); Kaos (1985)

Fire *See* Antonia's Line (1995); Bandit Queen (1994); Beautiful Thing (1995); Bhaji on the Beach (1994)

Fire Festival *See* Himatsuri (1985)

The Fire Within (1964) *See also* The Lovers (1959); Taste of Cherry (1996); Vagabond (1985); Viva Maria! (1965)

The Firemen's Ball (1968) *See also* Loves of a Blonde (1965); My Sweet Little Village (1986); My Twentieth Century (1990)

Fires on the Plain (1959) *See also* Black Rain (1988); The Burmese Harp (1956); The Designated Mourner (1997); Harakiri (1962); The Makioka Sisters (1983); Shame (1968); Tokyo Olympiad (1966); The Wages of Fear (1955)

First Name: Carmen *See* Devil in the Flesh (1987); Every Man for Himself (1979)

A Fistful of Dollars (1964) *See also* The Good, the Bad, and the Ugly (1967); Yojimbo (1961)

Fists in the Pocket *See* Devil in the Flesh (1987)

Fitzcarraldo (1982) *See also* Aguirre, the Wrath of God (1972); The Golden Coach (1952)

The 5,000 Fingers of Dr. T *See* The City of Lost Children (1995)

Five Women around Utamaro *See* Utamaro and His Five Women (1946)

The Flame of Torment *See* Enjo (1958)

Flamenco *See* Blood Wedding (1981); Carmen (1983)

Flashdance *See* Black Orpheus (1958)

Flirt *See* Hollow Reed (1995)

Floating Cloud *See* When a Woman Ascends the Stairs (1960)

Floating Weeds *See* Late Spring (1949); Tokyo Story (1953)

Flower *See* The Flower of My Secret (1995)

The Flower of My Secret (1995) *See also* Kika (1994); Women on the Verge of a Nervous Breakdown (1988)

Flower of the Arabian Nights *See* Arabian Nights (1974)

The Flowers of St. Francis (1950) *See also* The Miracle (1948); Monsieur Vincent (1947)

The Fly *See* Dead Ringers (1988); Tetsuo: The Iron Man (1992); They Came from Within (1975)

Fontane Effi Briest *See* Effi Briest (1974)

Fool's Gold *See* Band of Outsiders (1964)

Footloose *See* Shall We Dance? (1997)

For a Few Dollars More *See* The Good, the Bad, and the Ugly (1967)

Forbidden Games (1952) *See also* The Bicycle Thief (1948); Fires on the Plain (1959); Going Places (1974); The Green Room (1978); Is Paris Burning? (1966); Landscape in the Mist (1988); Pather Panchali (1954); Ponette (1995); Purple Noon (1960); Shame (1968); Shoeshine (1947); Small Change (1976); The Tin Drum (1979); The Two of Us (1968); Yaaba (1989); Zita (1968)

Forbidden Planet *See* Throne of Blood (1957)

The Forbidden Quest (1993)

Forgotten Silver *See* Project Grizzly (1996)

The Formula *See* The Man in the White Suit (1951)

47 Ronin, Part 1 (1942) *See also* 47 Ronin, Part 2 (1942)

47 Ronin, Part 2 (1942)

47 Samurai *See* 47 Ronin, Part 1 (1942)

The Fountainhead *See* The Belly of an Architect (1991); We the Living (1942)

Four Flies on Gray Velvet *See* The Bird with the Crystal Plumage (1970); Suspiria (1977)

The 400 Blows (1959) *See also* Bed and Board (1970); The Boys of St. Vincent (1993); Les Mistons (1957); Love on the Run (1978); Monika (1952); My Left Foot (1989); My Life As a Dog (1985); Ponette (1995); Shoot the Piano Player (1962); Small Change (1976); Stolen Kisses (1968); Sugar Cane Alley (1983); The Wild Child (1970); Zero for Conduct (1933)

Four Weddings and a Funeral *See* The Long Day Closes (1992)

The 4th Man (1979)

Fox and His Friends *See* The Bitter Tears of Petra von Kant (1972); In a Year of 13 Moons (1978)

Francesco, Giullare di Dio *See* The Flowers of St. Francis (1950)

Francis, God's Jester *See* The Flowers of St. Francis (1950)

Frankenstein *See* The Golem (1920); Spirit of the Beehive (1973)

Frankenstein Meets the Wolf Man *See* King Kong vs. Godzilla (1963)

Frantic (1958)

A Free Woman *See* The Lost Honor of Katharina Blum (1975); Marianne and Juliane (1982)

Freedom for Us *See* A Nous la Liberté (1931)

Freeze-Die-Come to Life (1990)

French Can-Can (1955) *See also* Eléna and Her Men (1956); The Golden Coach (1952)

French Provincial (1975)

French Twist (1995)

Frenzy *See* Torment (1944)

Fresa y Chocolate *See* Strawberry and Chocolate (1993)

A Friend of the Deceased *See* The Thief (1997); Trois Couleurs: Blanc (1994)

Frissons *See* They Came from Within (1975)

Froken Julie *See* Miss Julie (1950)

The Fugitive *See* A Taxing Woman (1987)

Fukusho Suruwa Ware Ni Ari *See* Vengeance Is Mine (1979)

Full Metal Jacket *See* Gallipoli (1981); Woyzeck (1978)

Full Moon in Paris (1984)

The Funeral (1984) *See also* Tampopo (1986); A Taxing Woman (1987)

Funeral Rites *See* The Funeral (1984)

Fuoco Fatuo *See* The Fire Within (1964)

Gabbeh (1996) *See also* Ashik Kerib (1988); Shadows of Forgotten Ancestors (1964)

The Gallery Murders *See* The Bird with the Crystal Plumage (1970)

Gallipoli (1981)

Gamma Sango Uchu Daisakusen *See* The Green Slime (1968)

Ganga Zumba *See* Black God, White Devil (1964); Quilombo (1984); Xica (1976)

Gangland Boss *See* A Better Tomorrow (1986)

The Gangster's Moll *See* Minbo—Or the Gentle Art of Japanese Extortion (1992)

Garde a Vue *See* The Man on the Roof (1976)

The Garden of Delights (1970) *See also* Half of Heaven (1986)

The Garden of the Finzi-Continis (1971) *See also* Before the Revolution (1965); A Gentle Woman (1969)

The Gate of Heavenly Peace *See* The Blue Kite (1993)

Gate of Hell (1954)

Gates of Heaven *See* Project Grizzly (1996); Stroszek (1977)

The Gaze of Ulysses *See* Ulysses' Gaze (1995)

Gazon Maudit *See* French Twist (1995)

The Gene Krupa Story *See* The Music Lovers (1971)

The General *See* Mon Oncle (1958)

General Idi Amin Dada (1975) *See also* Project Grizzly (1996); The Valley Obscured by the Clouds (1972)

Generale Della Rovere (1960) *See also* Kagemusha (1980); Paisan (1946)

A Generation (1954) *See also* Ashes and Diamonds (1958); Kanal (1956)

A Gentle Creature *See* A Gentle Woman (1969)

A Gentle Woman (1969)

The Gentleman Tramp *See* La Collectionneuse (1967)

Georgy Girl *See* Muriel's Wedding (1994)

The German Sisters *See* Marianne and Juliane (1982)

Germinal (1993) *See also* Margaret's Museum (1995)

Gertrud (1964)

Get Out Your Handkerchiefs (1978) *See also* Beau Père (1981); Going Places (1974); Too Beautiful for You (1988)

Ghost in the Shell *See* Akira (1989)

The Gig *See* Basileus Quartet (1982)

Gilda *See* Vampyr (1931)

Gimme Shelter *See* Sympathy for the Devil (1970)

Ging Chaat Goo Si *See* Police Story (1985)

Ginger & Fred (1986) *See also* And the Ship Sails On (1983); 8 1/2 (1963); Intervista (1987); Juliet of the Spirits (1965)

Girl from Hunan *See* A Mongolian Tale (1994)

Girl in the Moon *See* Woman in the Moon (1929)

Girls in Uniform *See* Mäedchen in Uniform (1931)

Giulietta Degli Spiriti *See* Juliet of the Spirits (1965)

The Glass Eye *See* Dead of Night (1945)

The Go-Between (1971)

The Goalie's Anxiety at the Penalty Kick (1971) *See also* The American Friend (1977)

God of the Sun *See* Emitai (1971)

The Goddess *See* Devi (1960)

The Godfather *See* Burn! (1970); The Emigrants (1972); Heimat 1 (1984); I Am Cuba (1964); Ivan the Terrible, Part 1 (1944); Last Tango in Paris (1973); The New Land (1973); Pépé le Moko (1937); Rocco and His Brothers (1960); Shanghai Triad (1995)

The Godfather Part II *See* The Emigrants (1972); Heimat 1 (1984); The New Land (1973)

The Godfather Parts I & II *See* Berlin Alexanderplatz (1980); Ivan the Terrible, Part 1 (1944)

The Gods and the Dead *See* Erendira (1983)

God's Angry Man *See* General Idi Amin Dada (1975)

The Godson *See* Le Samourai (1967)

Godzilla *See* Godzilla, King of the Monsters (1956); The Green Slime (1968)

Godzilla, King of the Monsters (1956) *See also* The Manster (1959)

Godzilla on Monster Island *See* Mothra (1962)

Godzilla vs. Megalon *See* King Kong vs. Godzilla (1963)

Godzilla vs. Mothra *See* Mothra (1962)

Going Places (1974) *See also* Band of Outsiders (1964); Beau Père (1981); Get Out Your Handkerchiefs (1978)

Gojira *See* Godzilla, King of the Monsters (1956)

The Golden Age *See* L'Age D'Or (1930)

The Golden Coach (1952) *See also* Eléna and Her Men (1956); French Can-Can (1955); Jesus of Montreal (1989)

Golden Marie *See* Casque d'Or (1952)

The Golem (1920)

The Good Fight *See* Land and Freedom (1995)

A Good Marriage *See* Le Beau Mariage (1982)

The Good, the Bad, and the Ugly (1967) *See also* A Fistful of Dollars (1964); The Hidden Fortress (1958); Once Upon a Time in the West (1968); Sanjuro (1962)

Good Will Hunting *See* Insomnia (1997)

Goodbye, Children *See* Au Revoir les Enfants (1987)

Goodfellas *See* The Bitter Tears of Petra von Kant (1972); The Hit (1985); The Stationmaster's Wife (1977)

The Gopher *See* El Topo (1971)

The Gospel According to St. Matthew (1964) *See also* Bandits of Orgosolo (1961); The Decameron (1970); The Flowers of St. Francis (1950); Jesus of Montreal (1989); Mamma Roma (1962); Monsieur Vincent (1947); The Rise of Louis XIV (1966); Thérèse (1986)

The Grail *See* Lancelot of the Lake (1974)

Grand Illusion (1937) *See also* The Ascent (1976); Forbidden Games (1952); The Golden Coach (1952); The Killer (1990); Le Trou (1959); Les Carabiniers (1963); The Life and Death of Colonel Blimp (1943); The Night of the Shooting Stars (1982); Shame (1968)

Grand Prix *See* Crash (1995)

The Grande Bouffe *See* Casanova '70 (1965); 301, 302 (1994)

The Great Day *See* A Special Day (1977)

Great Expectations *See* Little Dorrit, Film 1: Nobody's Fault (1988)

The Great Gabbo *See* Dead of Night (1945)

Greed *See* Toni (1934)

Green Card *See* Kolya (1996)

Green Fields *See* The Dybbuk (1937)

The Green Ray *See* Boyfriends & Girlfriends (1988)

The Green Room (1978) *See also* The Story of Adele H. (1975)

The Green Slime (1968)

The Grifters *See* Gumshoe (1972); The Hit (1985)

Gruppo di Famiglia in un Interno *See* Conversation Piece (1975)

Guantanamera! *See* Death of a Bureaucrat (1966); The Last Supper (1976); Memories of Underdevelopment (1968); Strawberry and Chocolate (1993)

Guelwaar (1994) *See also* Black Girl (1966); Emitai (1971); Mandabi (1968)

Gumshoe (1972) *See also* Confidentially Yours (1983); Saturday Night and Sunday Morning (1960)

Gun Crazy *See* Breathless (1959); Scene of the Crime (1987); Shoot the Piano Player (1962)

Gycklarnas Afton *See* Sawdust and Tinsel (1953)

Hab Og Karlighed *See* Twist & Shout (1984)

Hachigatsu no Kyoshikyoku *See* Rhapsody in August (1991)

The Hairdresser's Husband (1992) *See also* Monsieur Hire (1989); Ridicule (1996)

Half of Heaven (1986)

Halloween *See* The Hour of the Wolf (1968)

Ham Ham *See* Jamón, Jamón (1993)

Hamlet (1948) *See also* Henry V (1989)

Handsome Antonio *See* Il Bell'Antonio (1960)

Hanussen (1988) *See also* Mephisto (1981)

Happiness *See* Le Bonheur (1965)

Happy New Year *See* Edith & Marcel (1983); A Man and a Woman (1966)

Happy Together (1996) *See also* Chungking Express (1995)

Harakiri (1962) *See also* The Human Condition: A Soldier's Prayer (1961); Life of Oharu (1952); Samurai Rebellion (1967); Seven Samurai (1954)

Hard-Boiled (1992) *See also* A Better Tomorrow (1986);

Chungking Express (1995); The Killer (1990)

Harp of Burma *See* The Burmese Harp (1956)

Harvest (1937) *See also* The Baker's Wife (1933); Fanny (1932); French Provincial (1975); Jean de Florette (1987); L'Atalante (1934); Manon of the Spring (1987); Toni (1934)

Hatchet for the Honeymoon *See* Black Sunday (1960)

Hate (1995) *See also* Man Bites Dog (1991); A Self-Made Hero (1995); Wild Reeds (1994)

Hatred *See* Hate (1995)

The Haunted *See* Curse of the Demon (1957)

Häxan *See* Witchcraft through the Ages (1922)

He Who Gets Slapped *See* Wild Strawberries (1957)

He Who Must Die *See* Toto le Heros (1991)

A Heart in Winter *See* Un Coeur en Hiver (1993)

Heart of Glass (1974)

Heartburn *See* Loves of a Blonde (1965)

Heat *See* A Taxing Woman (1987)

Heavenly Creatures (1994) *See also* Léolo (1992); Les Enfants Terribles (1950)

Heavens Above! (1963)

Hei Ma *See* A Mongolian Tale (1994)

Heimat 1 (1984)

Heimat-Eine Deutsche Chronik *See* Heimat 1 (1984)

The Heir to Genghis Khan *See* Storm over Asia (1928)

The Heiress *See* The Makioka Sisters (1983)

Hell in the Pacific *See* Le Dernier Combat (1984)

The Hellstrom Chronicle *See* The Sorrow and the Pity (1971)

Help! *See* Juggernaut (1974)

Henry *See* The Goalie's Anxiety at the Penalty Kick (1971)

Henry V (1945) *See also* Henry V (1989)

Henry V (1989) *See also* Henry V (1945)

Henry: Portrait of a Serial Killer *See* Baxter (1989); Butterfly Kiss (1994); Caro Diario (1993); The Goalie's Anxiety at the Penalty Kick (1971); Vengeance Is Mine (1979); The Young Poisoner's Handbook (1994)

Herz aus Glas *See* Heart of Glass (1974)

The Heterosexuals *See* Les Biches (1968)

Hets *See* Torment (1944)

Hey, Babu Riba (1988) *See also* Tito and Me (1992)

The Hidden Fortress (1958) *See also* The Bad Sleep Well (1960); The Men Who Tread on the Tiger's Tail (1945); Sanjuro (1962); Seven Samurai (1954)

High & Low (1962) *See also* The Man on the Roof (1976); Stray Dog (1949)

High Anxiety *See* The Bride Wore Black (1968)

High Hopes (1988) *See also* Bleak Moments (1971); Life Is Sweet (1990); Secrets and Lies (1995)

High Tide (1987) *See* Two Friends (1986)

Himatsuri (1985)

Hiroshima Mon Amour (1959) *See also* La Jetée (1962); Last Year at Marienbad (1961); L'Avventura (1960); Muriel (1963); Night and Fog (1955); Providence (1977)

The Hit (1985) *See also* Gumshoe (1972)

Hitlerjunge Salomon *See* Europa, Europa (1991)

The Hoary Legends of the Caucasus *See* Ashik Kerib (1988)

The Hole *See* Le Trou (1959)

Holiday *See* Jour de Fete (1948)

Hollow Reed (1995)

The Holy Mountain *See* El Topo (1971)

The Honeymoon Killers *See* Seven Beauties (1976)

Hong Kong Express *See* Chungking Express (1995)

The Hopeless Ones *See* The Round-Up (1966)

Hori, Ma Panenko *See* The Firemen's Ball (1968)

The Horror Chamber of Dr. Faustus *See* Eyes without a Face (1959)

Horse Feathers *See* Le Million (1931)

The Horse Thief (1987) *See also* Life on a String (1990); The Story of Qiu Ju (1991)

The Hospital *See* The Kingdom (1995)

Hostsonaten *See* Autumn Sonata (1978)

The Hot Rock *See* Big Deal on Madonna Street (1958)

Hot Rods to Hell *See* Basileus Quartet (1982)

Hotel Terminus: The Life and Times of Klaus Barbie *See* Birthplace (1992); The Boat Is Full (1981); Dr. Petiot (1990); Salo, or the 120 Days of Sodom (1975); The Sorrow and the Pity (1971); The Wannsee Conference (1984)

The Hour of the Wolf (1968) *See also* The Magic Flute (1973)

House of Fright *See* Black Sunday (1960)

House of Games *See* The 4th Man (1979); General Idi Amin Dada (1975); Mississippi Mermaid (1969); Proof (1991)

House of Pleasure *See* Le Plaisir (1952)

Housekeeping *See* Comfort and Joy (1984); Local Hero (1983)

How I Won the War (1967) *See also* Juggernaut (1974)

How to Marry a Millionaire *See* Moscow Does Not Believe in Tears (1980)

Howards End *See* The Go-Between (1971)

The Human Beast *See* La Bete Humaine (1938)

The Human Condition: A Soldier's Prayer (1961) *See also* The Human Condition: No Greater Love (1958); The Human Condition: Road to Eternity (1959)

The Human Condition: No Greater Love (1958)

The Human Condition: Road to Eternity (1959)

The Hunchback of Notre Dame *See* Waxworks (1924)

Huozhe *See* To Live (1994)

I, a Woman *See* I Am Curious (Yellow) (1967)

I, a Woman Part II *See* I Am Curious (Yellow) (1967)

I Am a Fugitive from a Chain Gang *See* Bandits of Orgosolo (1961)

I Am Cuba (1964) *See also* The Battle of Algiers (1966); Burn! (1970); The Last Supper (1976)

I Am Curious (Blue) *See* I Am Curious (Yellow) (1967)

I Am Curious (Yellow) (1967) *See also* Betty Blue (1986)

I Can't Sleep (1993)

I Don't Want to Talk about It (1994)

I Have a Stranger's Face *See* The Face of Another (1966)

I Hired a Contract Killer *See* The Match Factory Girl (1990)

I Know Where I'm Going (1945) *See also* Local Hero (1983)

I Live in Fear (1955) *See also* Rhapsody in August (1991)

I Remember *See* Amarcord (1974)

I Saw a Dream Like This *See* Akira Kurosawa's Dreams (1990)

I Shot Andy Warhol *See* A

Bigger Splash (1974)

I Soliti Ignoti *See* Big Deal on Madonna Street (1958)

I Vitelloni (1953) *See also* Aparajito (1958); La Dolce Vita (1960); La Strada (1954); Nights of Cabiria (1957); Open City (1945); Rocco and His Brothers (1960)

I Walked with a Zombie *See* Curse of the Demon (1957)

The Iceman Cometh *See* The Lower Depths (1936); The Lower Depths (1957); Variety Lights (1951)

The Icicle Thief (1989) *See also* Allegro Non Troppo (1976)

Ieri, Oggi e Domani *See* Yesterday, Today and Tomorrow (1964)

If... (1969) See also Samurai Rebellion (1967); This Sporting Life (1963); Zero for Conduct (1933)

Ikiru (1952) *See also* Babette's Feast (1987); Blue (1993); Drunken Angel (1948); La Dolce Vita (1960); Rashomon (1951); Red Beard (1965); Rhapsody in August (1991); Taste of Cherry (1996)

Il Bell'Antonio (1960) *See also* Casanova '70 (1965)

Il Buco *See* Le Trou (1959)

Il Conformista *See* The Conformist (1971)

Il Decameron *See* The Decameron (1970)

Il Deserto Rosso *See* The Red Desert (1964)

Il Diario di una Cameriera *See* Diary of a Chambermaid (1964)

Il Diavolo in Corpo *See* Devil in the Flesh (1987)

Il Disprezzo *See* Contempt (1964)

Il Etait une Fois un Pays *See* Underground (1995)

Il Fiore delle Mille e Una Notte *See* Arabian Nights (1974)

Il Generale Della-Rovere *See* Generale Della Rovere (1960)

Il Giardino del Finzi-Contini *See* The Garden of the Finzi-Continis (1971)

Il Ladro di Bambini *See* The Stolen Children (1992)

Il Mostre *See* The Monster (1996)

Il Portiere de Notte *See* The Night Porter (1974)

Il Postino *See* Celestial Clockwork (1994); Christ Stopped at Eboli (1979); The Postman (1994)

Il Posto *See* The Tree of Wooden Clogs (1978)

Il Processo *See* The Trial (1963)

Il Quartetto Basileus *See* Basileus Quartet (1982)

Il Vangelo Secondo Matteo *See* The Gospel According to St. Matthew (1964)

Illicit Interlude *See* Monika (1952); Summer Interlude (1950)

Illuminacja *See* Illumination (1973)

Illumination (1973)

Ilsa: She Wolf of the SS *See* The Night Porter (1974)

I'm All Right, Jack (1959) *See also* A Nous la Liberté (1931); The Case of the Mukkinese Battle Horn (1956); Heavens Above! (1963)

Im Lauf der Zeit *See* Kings of the Road—In the Course of Time (1976)

Imitation of Life *See* Ali: Fear Eats the Soul (1974)

The Immortal Story *See* Mr. Arkadin (1955)

Impotence *See* Xala (1975)

Imprint *See* Fantastic Planet (1973)

Improper Conduct *See* I Am Cuba (1964)

In a Year of 13 Moons (1978) *See also* The American Soldier (1970)

In a Year with 13 Moons *See* In a Year of 13 Moons (1978)

In Celebration *See* This Sporting Life (1963)

In Cold Blood *See* Vengeance Is Mine (1979)

In einem Jahr mit 13 Monden *See* In a Year of 13 Moons (1978)

In for Treatment (1982)

In Love of the Run *See* Love on the Run (1978)

In Search of Noah's Ark *See* Mondo Cane (1963)

In the Course of Time *See* Kings of the Road—In the Course of Time (1976)

In the Name of the Father *See* My Left Foot (1989)

In the Realm of Passion *See* Max, Mon Amour (1986)

In the Realm of the Senses (1976) *See also* The Ballad of Narayama (1983); Boy (1969); Max, Mon Amour (1986); Odd Obsession (1960); The Pillow Book (1995)

In the White City (1983) *See also* The Goalie's Anxiety at the Penalty Kick (1971); The Valley Obscured by the Clouds (1972)

In the Woods *See* Rashomon (1951)

In Weiter Ferne, So Nah! *See* Faraway, So Close! (1993)

The Incredible Journey *See* Baxter (1989)

The Incredible Shrinking Man *See* I Don't Want to Talk about It (1994)

Indochine (1992)

Innocence Unprotected *See* Man Is Not a Bird (1965)

The Innocent (1976) *See also* Senso (1954)

Insignificance (1985)

Insomnia (1997)

Institute Benjamenta *See* Time Stands Still (1982)

Intervista (1987)

Intolerance *See* Napoleon (1927); Strike (1924)

The Intruder *See* The Innocent (1976)

Invaders from Mars *See* The Cabinet of Dr. Caligari (1919)

Invasion of the Neptune Men *See* The Green Slime (1968)

Invention of Destruction *See* The Fabulous World of Jules Verne (1958)

Investigation of a Citizen Above Suspicion *See* La Scorta (1994)

Irma Vep *See* Augustin (1995); Contempt (1964); Police Story (1985)

The Ironman *See* Tetsuo: The Iron Man (1992)

Is Paris Burning? (1966)

Isadora (The Loves of Isadora) *See* Camille Claudel (1989)

Isn't Life a Bitch? *See* La Chienne (1931)

It! The Terror from Beyond Space *See* The Green Slime (1968); Solaris (1972)

The Italian Straw Hat *See* Under the Roofs of Paris (1929)

It's a Wonderful Life *See* Wings of Desire (1988)

It's All True *See* Que Viva Mexico (1932)

It's My Life *See* My Life to Live (1962)

Ivan Grozny 1 *See* Ivan the Terrible, Part 1 (1944)

Ivan Grozny 2 *See* Ivan the Terrible, Part 2 (1946)

Ivan the Terrible *See* Alexander Nevsky (1938); Andrei Rublev (1966); Don Quixote (1957); Ivan the Terrible, Part 1 (1944); Ivan the Terrible, Part 2 (1946); The Lady with the Dog (1959); Waxworks (1924)

Ivan the Terrible, Part 1 (1944)

Ivan the Terrible, Part 2 (1946)

Ivan the Terrible, Part 2: The Boyars' Plot *See* Ivan the Terrible, Part 2 (1946)

Ja Cuba *See* I Am Cuba (1964)

Jackie Chan's Police Force *See* Police Story (1985)

Jackie Chan's Police Story *See* Police Story (1985)

Jacquot (1991) *See also* Le Bonheur (1965); The Umbrellas of Cherbourg (1964)

Jacquot de Nantes *See* Donkey Skin (1970); Jacquot (1991)

Jag Ar Nyfiken—En Film i Gult *See* I Am Curious (Yellow) (1967)

Jag Ar Nyfiken—Gul *See* I Am Curious (Yellow) (1967)

J'Ai Pas Sommeil *See* I Can't Sleep (1993)

Jalsaghar (1958)

Jamón, Jamón (1993) *See also* Belle Epoque (1992)

Jan Svankmejer's Faust (1994)

Jana Aranya *See* The Middleman (1976)

Jaquot *See* Lola (1961)

Jean de Florette (1987) *See also* French Provincial (1975); Germinal (1993); Harvest (1937); Manon of the Spring (1987)

Jean de Florette 2 *See* Manon of the Spring (1987)

Jeanne Dielman *See* The Goalie's Anxiety at the Penalty Kick (1971)

Jeder fur Sich und Gott Gegen Alle *See* Every Man for Himself & God Against All (1975)

Jerusalem (1996) *See also* The Best Intentions (1992); Elvira Madigan (1967); Pelle the Conqueror (1988)

Jesus de Montreal *See* Jesus of Montreal (1989)

Jesus of Montreal (1989)

JFK *See* The Bad Sleep Well (1960); Z (1969)

Jigokumen *See* Gate of Hell (1954)

Joan *See* The Passion of Joan of Arc (1928)

Joe Hill *See* Elvira Madigan (1967)

Johnny Guitar *See* Once Upon a Time in the West (1968)

Johnny Stecchino (1992) *See also* The Monster (1996)

Jonah *See* Jonah Who Will Be 25 in the Year 2000 (1976)

Jonah Who Will Be 25 in the Year 2000 (1976) *See also* La Salamandre (1971); Messidor (1977); The Wonderful Crook (1975)

Jonas—Qui Aura 25 Ans en l'An 2000 *See* Jonah Who Will Be 25 in the Year 2000 (1976)

Jour de Fete (1948) *See also* Playtime (1967)

Journey into Autumn *See* Dreams (1955)

Journey to the Seventh Planet *See* Solaris (1972)

The Joyless Street (1925) *See also* Diary of a Lost Girl (1929); Die Liebe der Jeanne Ney (1927); The Last Laugh (1924); The Threepenny Opera (1931)

Ju Dou (1990) *See also* Red Sorghum (1987); Shanghai Triad (1995)

The Judge and the Assassin (1975) *See also* Béatrice (1988); L.627 (1992); Life and Nothing But (1989)

A Judgment in Stone *See* La Cérémonie (1995)

Juggernaut (1974) *See also* The Wages of Fear (1955)

Jules and Jim (1962) *See also* The Bride Wore Black (1968); Café au Lait (1994); Confidentially Yours (1983); The Soft Skin (1964); Two English Girls (1972)

Jules et Jim *See* Jules and Jim (1962)

Juliet of the Spirits (1965) *See also* City of Women (1981); Fellini Satyricon (1969)

Jungfrukallan *See* The Virgin Spring (1959)

Jurassic Park *See* The Fabulous World of Jules Verne (1958)

Just Before Nightfall *See* La Femme Infidèle (1969); Le Boucher (1969); Les Biches (1968)

Kagemusha (1980) *See also* Dersu Uzala (1975); Dodes 'ka-den (1970); Generale Della Rovere (1960); Storm over Asia (1928)

Kakushi Toride No San Akunin *See* The Hidden Fortress (1958)

Kameradschaft (1931) *See also* Die Liebe der Jeanne Ney (1927); Germinal (1993); Grand Illusion (1937); Margaret's Museum (1995)

Kanal (1956) *See also* Ashes and Diamonds (1958); A Generation (1954); Prisoner of the Mountains (1996)

Kane *See* Mr. Arkadin (1955); Seven Beauties (1976)

Kaos (1985) *See also* Fiorile (1993); The Night of the Shooting Stars (1982); The Saragossa Manuscript (1965)

Kaspar Hauser (1993)

Kavkazsky Plennik *See* Prisoner of the Mountains (1996)

Kazoku Gaimu *See* The Family Game (1983)

Kazoku Game *See* The Family Game (1983)

The Key *See* Odd Obsession (1960)

Kids *See* Hate (1995)

Kika (1994) *See* The Flower of My Secret (1995)

The Killer (1990) *See also* A Better Tomorrow (1986); Chungking Express (1995); Hard-Boiled (1992); Le Samourai (1967)

Killer! *See* This Man Must Die (1970)

The Killing *See* Big Deal on Madonna Street (1958); Bob le Flambeur (1955); Frantic (1958)

Kimono No Kiroku *See* I Live in Fear (1955)

Kind Hearts and Coronets (1949) *See also* Captain's Paradise (1953); The Man in the White Suit (1951)

A Kind of Loving (1962) *See also* This Sporting Life (1963)

King Kong Tai Godzilla *See* King Kong vs. Godzilla (1963)

King Kong vs. Godzilla (1963)

King of Hearts *See* Walkabout (1971)

King of the Hill *See* Mon Oncle Antoine (1971)

The Kingdom (1995) *See also* Berlin Alexanderplatz (1980); Breaking the Waves (1995); Zentropa (1992)

Kings of the Road—In the Course of Time (1976) *See also* The American Friend (1977); Bye Bye Brazil (1979); The Goalie's Anxiety at the Penalty Kick (1971); In the White City (1983); Kings of the Road—In the Course of Time (1976); Wings of Desire (1988)

Kiss Me Goodbye *See* Dona Flor and Her Two Husbands (1978)

Kiss of the Spider Woman *See* Strawberry and Chocolate (1993)

Klute *See* La Lectrice (1988)

Knife in the Water (1962) *See also* Deep End (1970)

Kolya (1996) *See also* My Sweet Little Village (1986)

Komissar *See* Commissar (1968)

Konna Yume Wo Mita *See* Akira Kurosawa's Dreams (1990)

The Koumiko Mystery *See* La Jetée (1962); Le Joli Mai (1962)

Koyaaniqatsi *See* The Man with a Movie Camera (1929); Mondo Cane (1963)

Kriemhild's Revenge *See* Die Nibelungen (1923)

Kumonosujo, Kumonosu-djo *See* Throne of Blood (1957)

Kundun *See* Life on a String (1990)

Kuroi Ame *See* Black Rain (1988)

Kuroneko *See* Onibaba (1964)

Kvinn Odrom *See* Dreams (1955)

Kwaidan (1964) *See also* Akira Kurosawa's Dreams (1990); The Human Condition: A Soldier's Prayer (1961); The Mystery of Rampo (1994); Onibaba (1964); Ugetsu (1953)

L.627 (1992) *See also* The Judge and the Assassin (1975); Les Voleurs (1996); My New Partner (1984)

La Bataille d'Alger *See* The Battle of Algiers (1966)

La Battaglia di Algeri *See* The Battle of Algiers (1966)

La Belle et la Bete *See* Beauty and the Beast (1946)

La Belle Noiseuse (1990) *See also* Edvard Munch (1974); A Month in the Country (1987); The Mother and the Whore (1973); Nelly et Monsieur Arnaud (1995)

La Bete Humaine (1938) *See also* La Chienne (1931)

La Cage aux Folles (1978)

La Cage aux Folles II *See* La Cage aux Folles (1978)

La Cérémonie (1995) *See also* Belle de Jour (1967); Les Bons Debarras (1981); Wedding in Blood (1974)

La Chambre Verte *See* The Green Room (1978)

La Chienne (1931) *See also* Boudu Saved from Drowning (1932); Eléna and Her Men (1956); La Bete Humaine (1938); Mississippi Mermaid (1969)

La Chinoise *See* Before the Revolution (1965); The Crime of Monsieur Lange (1936); Les Carabiniers (1963); Masculine Feminine (1966)

La Cite des Enfants Perdus *See* The City of Lost Children (1995)

La Citte delle Donne *See* City of Women (1981)

La Collectionneuse (1967) *See also* Chloe in the Afternoon (1972)

La Dentielliere *See* The Lacemaker (1977)

La Désenchantée *See* A Single Girl (1996)

La Discrete (1990) *See also* Diary of a Seducer (1995)

La Dolce Vita (1960) *See also* Amarcord (1974); And God Created Woman (1957); 8 1/2 (1963); Fellini's Roma (1972); I Vitelloni (1953); Intervista (1987); L'Avventura (1960); The Lovers (1959); The Miracle (1948); Rocco and His Brothers (1960); We All Loved Each Other So Much (1977)

La Donna E Donna *See* A Woman Is a Woman (1960)

La Double Vie de Veronique *See* The Double Life of Veronique (1991)

La Femme d'a Cote *See* The Woman Next Door (1981)

La Femme du Boulanger *See* The Baker's Wife (1933); Harvest (1937)

La Femme Infidèle (1969) *See also* Wedding in Blood (1974)

La Femme Mariee *See* A Married Woman (1965)

La Femme Nikita (1991) *See also* Le Dernier Combat (1984); Subway (1985)

La Fiancee du Pirate *See* A Very Curious Girl (1969)

La Fille Seule *See* A Single Girl (1996)

La Flor de My Secreto *See* The Flower of My Secret (1995)

La Grande Bouffe (1973) *See also* The Cook, the Thief, His Wife & Her Lover (1990)

La Grande Illusion *See* Grand Illusion (1937)

La Guerre Est Finie *See* Last Year at Marienbad (1961)

La Haine *See* Café au Lait (1994); Hate (1995)

La Jetée (1962) *See also* Le Joli Mai (1962); Stalker (1979)

La Kermesse Heroique *See* Carnival in Flanders (1935)

La Lectrice (1988)

La Lune dans le Caniveau *See* Moon in the Gutter (1983)

La Maman et la Putain *See* The Mother and the Whore (1973)

La Mariee Etait en Noir *See* The Bride Wore Black (1968)

La Marseillaise (1937) *See also* Ridicule (1996)

La Maschera del Demonio *See* Black Sunday (1960)

La Meilleure Façon de Marcher *See* The Best Way (1976)

La Mitad del Cielo *See* Half of Heaven (1986)

La Muerte de un Burocrata *See* Death of a Bureaucrat (1966)

La Noire de... *See* Black Girl (1966)

La Notte (1960) *See also* The Eclipse (1966)

La Notte di San Lorenzo *See* The Night of the Shooting Stars (1982)

La Nuit *See* La Notte (1960)

La Nuit Americaine *See* Day for Night (1973)

La Nuit de Varennes (1982) *See also* Ridicule (1996); We All Loved Each Other So Much (1977)

La Passion Béatrice *See* Béatrice (1988)

La Planete Sauvage *See* Fantastic Planet (1973)

La Prise de Pouvoir par Louis XIV *See* The Rise of Louis XIV (1966)

La Promesse (1996) *See also* Yaaba (1989)

La Ronde (1951) *See also* Belle Epoque (1992); The Earrings of Madame de... (1954); Le Plaisir (1952); Liebelei (1932); Lola (1961); Lola Montès (1955)

La Rupture (1970)

La Salamandre (1971) *See also* Messidor (1977)

La Scorta (1994)

La Signora di Tutti (1934) *See also* Le Plaisir (1952)

La Souffle au Coeur *See* Murmur of the Heart (1971)

La Soufrière *See* General Idi Amin Dada (1975)

La Strada (1954) *See also* Nights of Cabiria (1957); Variety Lights (1951)

La Terra Trema (1948) *See also* Senso (1954); The Tree of Wooden Clogs (1978)

La Tragedie de la Mine *See* Kameradschaft (1931)

La Traversée de Paris *See* Devil in the Flesh (1946)

La Vallee *See* The Valley Obscured by the Clouds (1972)

La Vie de Bohème *See* Ariel (1989); The Match Factory Girl (1990)

La Vie Devant Soi *See* Madame Rosa (1977)

La Vie et Rien d'Autre *See* Life and Nothing But (1989)

L'Accompagnatrice *See* The Accompanist (1993)

The Lacemaker (1977) *See also* A Single Girl (1996); Sundays & Cybele (1962); The Wonderful Crook (1975)

Lacombe, Lucien (1974) *See also* Au Revoir les Enfants (1987); Black Moon (1975); The Conformist (1971); Is Paris Burning? (1966); La Promesse (1996); A Self-Made Hero (1995)

Ladri di Biciclette *See* The Bicycle Thief (1948)

Ladri di Saponette *See* The Icicle Thief (1989)

Lady and the Tramp *See* Baxter (1989)

The Lady from Shanghai *See* Mr. Arkadin (1955)

The Lady Vanishes *See* The Vanishing (1988)

The Lady with the Dog (1959) *See also* The Overcoat (1959)

Ladybird, Ladybird *See* Once Were Warriors (1994)

The Ladykillers *See* The Case of the Mukkinese Battle Horn (1956); I'm All Right, Jack (1959); Kind Hearts and Coronets (1949); The Man in the White Suit (1951)

L'Age d'Or (1930) *See also* The Blood of a Poet (1930); Diary of a Chambermaid (1964); The Phantom of Liberty (1974)

L'Agent de Poche *See* Small Change (1976)

L'Albero Degli Zoccoli *See* The Tree of Wooden Clogs (1978)

The Lament of the Path *See* Pather Panchali (1954)

Lamerica (1995) *See also* La Scorta (1994); Three Brothers (1980)

L'Ami de Mon Ami *See* Boyfriends & Girlfriends (1988)

L'Amour en Fuite *See* Love on the Run (1978)

L'Amour l'Après-Midi *See* Chloe in the Afternoon (1972)

Lan Feng Zheng *See* The Blue Kite (1993)

Lancelot du Lac *See* Lancelot of the Lake (1974)

Lancelot of the Lake (1974) *See also* Béatrice (1988)

Land and Freedom (1995) *See also* Love and Anarchy (1973)

Land of the Pharaohs *See* Subway (1985)

Landscape in the Mist (1988) *See also* L'Avventura (1960); The Night of Counting the Years (1969); Ulysses' Gaze (1995)

L'Anee Derniere a Marienbad *See* Last Year at Marienbad (1961)

Laputa: Castle in the Sky *See* Fantastic Planet (1973)

L'Argent (1983) *See also* A Gentle Woman (1969); Pickpocket (1959)

Lashou Shentan *See* Hard-Boiled (1992)

Lasky Jedne Plavovlasky *See* Loves of a Blonde (1965)

The Last Battle *See* Le Dernier Combat (1984)

The Last Emperor *See* The Bird with the Crystal Plumage (1970)

The Last Laugh (1924) *See also* The Cabinet of Dr. Caligari (1919); Faust (1926); The Joyless Street (1925); Toto le Heros (1991); Variety (1925)

Last Man Standing *See* Yojimbo (1961)

The Last Metro (1980) *See also* The Accompanist (1993); The Woman Next Door (1981)

The Last Movie *See* El Topo (1971)

The Last Seduction *See* The Blue Angel (1930)

The Last Supper (1976)

Last Tango in Paris (1973) *See also* Crash (1995); In the Realm of the Senses (1976); Lovers: A True Story (1990); The Spider's Stratagem (1970); Sugar Cane Alley (1983); That Obscure Object of Desire (1977)

The Last Temptation of Christ *See* The Bitter Tears of Petra von Kant (1972); Day of Wrath (1943); The Flowers of St. Francis (1950); The Gospel According to St. Matthew (1964); Jesus of Montreal (1989)

The Last Wave *See* Picnic at Hanging Rock (1975); Walkabout (1971)

The Last Woman *See* La Grande Bouffe (1973)

Last Year at Marienbad (1961) *See also* La Jetée (1962); Muriel (1963); Night and Fog (1955); Providence (1977)

L'Atalante (1934) *See also* A Propos de Nice (1929); I Know Where I'm Going (1945); Le Jour Se Lève (1939); The Story of Adele H. (1975); The Two of Us (1968); Under the Roofs of Paris (1929); Zero for Conduct (1933)

Late Autumn *See* Late Spring (1949)

Late Spring (1949) *See also* An Autumn Afternoon (1962); Babette's Feast (1987); Tokyo Story (1953); Zita (1968)

The Lavender Hill Mob *See* Big Deal on Madonna Street (1958); Captain's Paradise (1953); Dead of Night (1945); Kind Hearts and Coronets (1949)

L'Aveu *See* The Confession (1970)

L'Avventura (1960) *See also* Blow-Up (1966); The Eclipse (1966); La Notte (1960); Persona (1966); The Red Desert (1964)

The Law *See* Tilaï (1990)

Law of Desire *See* Matador (1986)

Lawrence of Arabia *See* Ivan the Terrible, Part 1 (1944); Saturday Night and Sunday Morning (1960); The Tenant (1976)

Le Beau Mariage (1982)

Le Bonheur (1965) *See* Brief Encounter (1946)

Le Boucher (1969) *See also* La Femme Infidèle (1969); La Rupture (1970); Scene of the Crime (1987); The Story of Women (1988); This Man Must Die (1970); Violette (1978)

Le Carrosse d'Or *See* The Golden Coach (1952)

Le Chaland Qui Passe *See* L'Atalante (1934)

Le Charme Discret de la Bourgeoisie *See* The Discreet Charm of the Bourgeoisie (1972)

Le Chat et la Souris *See* Cat and Mouse (1978)

Le Chèvre *See* Les Compères (1983)

Le Crime de Monsieur Lange *See* The Crime of Monsieur Lange (1936)

Le Dernier Combat (1984) *See also* La Femme Nikita (1991); Subway (1985)

Le Dernier Metro *See* The Last Metro (1980)

Le Diable au Corps *See* Devil in the Flesh (1946)

Le Docteur Petiot *See* Dr. Petiot (1990)

Le Doulos (1961) *See also* Le Samourai (1967)

Le Fantome de la Liberte *See* The Phantom of Liberty (1974)

Le Feu Follet *See* The Fire Within (1964)

Le Genou de Claire *See* Claire's Knee (1971)

Le Graal *See* Lancelot of the Lake (1974)

Le Grand Chemin *See* The Accompanist (1993)

Le Joli Mai (1962)

Le Jour Se Lève (1939) *See also* Children of Paradise (1944); Les Visiteurs du Soir (1942); Pépé le Moko (1937)

Le Journal du Seducteur *See* Diary of a Seducer (1995)

Le Journal d'un Cure de Campagne *See* Diary of a Country Priest (1950)

Le Journal d'une Femme de Chambre *See* Diary of a Chambermaid (1964)

Le Juge et l'Assassin *See* The Judge and the Assassin (1975)

Le Locataire *See* The Tenant (1976)

Le Mandat *See* Mandabi (1968)

Le Mari de la Coiffeuse *See* The Hairdresser's Husband (1992)

Le Mepris *See* Contempt (1964)

Le Million (1931) *See also* A Nous la Liberté (1931); Under the Roofs of Paris (1929)

Le Notti de Cabiria *See* Nights of Cabiria (1957)

Le Peau Douce *See* The Soft Skin (1964)

Le Plaisir (1952) *See also* Lola Montès (1955)

Le Proces *See* The Trial (1963)

Le Retour de Martin Guerre *See* The Return of Martin Guerre (1983)

Le Salaire de la Peur *See* The Wages of Fear (1955)

Le Samourai (1967) *See also* Alphaville (1965); The American Soldier (1970); Bob le Flambeur (1955); Le Doulos (1961)

Le Sang d'un Poete *See* The Blood of a Poet (1930)

Le Sirene du Mississippi *See* Mississippi Mermaid (1969)

Le Testament d'Orphee *See* The Testament of Orpheus (1959)

Le Testament du Docteur Cordelier *See* The Testament of Dr. Cordelier (1959)

Le Trou (1959) *See also* Casque d'Or (1952); A Man Escaped (1957)

Le Vieil Homme et l'Enfant *See* The Two of Us (1968)

Le Voleur *See* The Thief of Paris (1967)

L'Eclisse *See* The Eclipse (1966)

L'Enfant Sauvage *See* The Wild Child (1970)

Leningrad Cowboys Go America (1989) *See also* Ariel (1989)

Léolo (1992) *See also* The Family Game (1983); The Long Day Closes (1992)

The Leopard *See* Conversation Piece (1975); The Innocent (1976); 1900 (1976); Rocco and His Brothers (1960); Senso (1954)

Les Amants du Pont-Neuf *See* Boy Meets Girl (1984)

Les Bas Fonds *See* The Lower Depths (1936)

Les Biches (1968)

Les Bons Debarras (1981)

Les Carabiniers (1963)

Les Compères (1983)

Les Deux Anglaises et le Continent *See* Two English Girls (1972)

Les Diabolique *See* Diabolique (1955)

Les Dimanches de Ville d'Arvay *See* Sundays & Cybele (1962)

Les Enfants du Paradis *See* Children of Paradise (1944)

Les Enfants Terribles (1950) *See also* Eternal Return (1943); The Testament of Orpheus (1959)

Les Jeux Interdits *See* Forbidden Games (1952)

Les Mille et une Recettes du Cuisinier Amoureux *See* A Chef in Love (1996)

Les Mistons (1957)

Les Nuits de la Pleine *See* Full Moon in Paris (1984)

Les Parapluies de Cherbourg *See* The Umbrellas of Cherbourg (1964)

Les Quatre Cents Coups *See* The 400 Blows (1959)

Les Rendez-vous de Paris *See* Rendezvous in Paris (1995)

Les Ripoux *See* My New Partner (1984)

Les Roseaux Sauvages *See* Wild Reeds (1994)

Les Silences du Palais *See* The Silences of the Palace (1994)

Les Somnambules *See* Mon Oncle d'Amerique (1980)

Les Valseuses *See* Going Places (1974)

Les Visiteurs du Soir (1942) *See also* Children of Paradise (1944)

Les Voleurs (1996)

Les Yeux sans Visage *See* Eyes without a Face (1959)

L'Eternel Retour *See* Eternal Return (1943)

Letter from an Unknown Woman *See* The Earrings of Madame de… (1954)

Letter to Jane *See* Every Man for Himself (1979)

Letters from My Windmill *See* Fanny (1932)

L'Evangile Selon Saint-Matthieu *See* The Gospel According to St. Matthew (1964)

L'Histoire d'Adele H. *See* The Story of Adele H. (1975)

L'Homme Qui Aimait les Femmes *See* The Man Who Loved Women (1977)

Liebelei (1932) *See also* La Signora di Tutti (1934); Lola Montès (1955)

The Life and Death of Colonel Blimp (1943) *See also* I Know Where I'm Going (1945)

Life and Nothing But (1989) *See also* Béatrice (1988); Captain Conan (1996); L.627 (1992); A Month in the Country (1987)

Life and Nothing More … (1992)

Life Is Beautiful *See* Johnny Stecchino (1992); The Monster (1996)

Life Is Sweet (1990) *See also* Bleak Moments (1971); High Hopes (1988); Secrets and Lies (1995)

Life of Oharu (1952) *See also* The Lost Honor of Katharina Blum (1975); Princess Yang Kwei Fei (1955); Raise the Red Lantern (1991); Sansho the Bailiff (1954); Utamaro and His Five Women (1946)

Life on a String (1990) *See also* Farewell My Concubine (1993)

The Light Ahead (Fishke der Krumer) *See* The Dybbuk (1937)

Lights of Variety *See* Variety Lights (1951)

Like Water for Chocolate (1993) *See also* Belle Epoque (1992); A Chef in Love (1996); Half of Heaven (1986); Jamón, Jamón (1993)

Lili Marleen *See* The Marriage of Maria Braun (1979)

L'Inde Fantome *See* Phantom India (1969)

L'Innocente *See* The Innocent (1976)

The Lion in Winter *See* I'm All Right, Jack (1959)

The Lion King *See* The World of Apu (1959)

Lisztomania *See* The Devils (1971); The Music Lovers (1971)

Little Big Man *See* Sanjuro (1962)

Little Dorrit *See* Berlin Alexanderplatz (1980)

Little Dorrit, Film 1: Nobody's Fault (1988)

Little Dorrit, Film 2: Little Dorrit's Story (1988)

Little Giants *See* Shall We Dance? (1997)

Little Shop of Horrors *See* Cries and Whispers (1972); L'Avventura (1960)

The Little Theatre of Jean Renoir *See* The Golden Coach (1952)

The Little Thief (1989) *See also* The Best Way (1976)

Little Vera (1988) *See also* Moscow Does Not Believe in Tears (1980)

Little Women *See* My Brilliant Career (1979)

Live Flesh *See* Kika (1994); Matador (1986); Women on the Verge of a Nervous Breakdown (1988)

Living *See* Ikiru (1952)

Living in Oblivion *See* Blow-Up (1966)

Lo Sceicco Bianco *See* The White Sheik (1952)

Local Hero (1983) *See also* Comfort and Joy (1984); Gumshoe (1972); I Know Where I'm Going (1945)

Lola (1961) *See also* Donkey Skin (1970); Jacquot (1991); The Umbrellas of Cherbourg (1964); Veronika Voss (1982); A Woman Is a Woman (1960)

Lola Montès (1955) *See also* The Earrings of Madame de… (1954); La Ronde (1951); La Signora di Tutti (1934); Le Plaisir (1952); Sansho the Bailiff (1954); Eléna and Her Men (1956)

Lolita *See* Heavens Above! (1963); I'm All Right, Jack (1959); The Nest (1980)

The Lonely Wife *See* Charulata (1964)

Lonesome *See* Vive L'Amour (1994)

The Long Day Closes (1992) *See also* Distant Voices, Still Lives (1988)

The Long Good Friday (1980) *See also* The Cook, the Thief, His Wife & Her Lover (1990)

The Long Voyage Home *See* Moon in the Gutter (1983)

The Longest Day *See* Is Paris Burning? (1966)

Look Back in Anger (1958) *See also* Little Vera (1988); This Sporting Life (1963)

The Look of Ulysses *See* Ulysses' Gaze (1995)

L'Opera de Quat'Sous *See* The Threepenny Opera (1931)

Los Olvidados (1950) *See also* The Bicycle Thief (1948); Pixote (1981)

The Lost Honor of Katharina Blum (1975)

The Lost Honor of Kathryn Beck *See* The Lost Honor of Katharina Blum (1975)

Lost Horizon *See* Walkabout (1971)

Lost in America *See* Life Is Sweet (1990)

The Lost Weekend *See* The Hour of the Wolf (1968)

Louisiana Story *See* Bandits of Orgosolo (1961)

Loulou (1980) *See also* A Nos Amours (1984)

Love (1971)

Love Affair, or The Case of the Missing Switchboard Operator *See* Man Is Not a Bird (1965)

Love and Anarchy (1973) *See also* Seven Beauties (1976); Swept Away… (1975)

Love at Twenty *See* Bed and Board (1970); Boccaccio '70 (1962); Confidentially Yours (1983); The 400 Blows (1959); Love on the Run (1978); Stolen Kisses (1968)

Love Eternal *See* Eternal Return (1943)

Love in the City (1953) *See also* Fellini's Roma (1972)

Love Is the Devil *See* Van Gogh (1992)

Love on the Run (1978) *See also* Bed and Board (1970); The 400 Blows (1959); Stolen Kisses (1968)

Love Serenade (1996) *See also* Muriel's Wedding (1994); Proof (1991)

The Loved One *See* The Funeral (1984)

The Lovelorn Minstrel *See* Ashik Kerib (1988)

The Lover *See* Chungking Express (1995)

The Lovers (1959) *See also* Frantic (1958); Loulou (1980)

Lovers: A True Story (1990)

Loves of a Blonde (1965) *See also* The Firemen's Ball (1968); My Sweet Little Village (1986)

The Loves of Jeanne Ney *See* Die Liebe der Jeanne Ney (1927)

Loving Moments *See* Bleak Moments (1971)

The Lower Depths (1936)

The Lower Depths (1957)

The Loyal 47 Ronin *See* 47 Ronin, Part 1 (1942)

L'Ucello dalle Plume di Cristallo *See* The Bird with the Crystal Plumage (1970)

Luci del Varieta *See* Variety Lights (1951)

Luna *See* Before the Revolution (1965); Murmur of the Heart (1971); The Spider's Stratagem (1970)

L'Une Chante, L'Autre Pas *See* One Sings, the Other Doesn't (1977)

Lust for Evil *See* Purple Noon (1960);

Lust for Life *See* A Bigger Splash (1974); Van Gogh (1992)

Lusts of the Flesh *See* Die Liebe der Jeanne Ney (1927)

Lyrical Nitrate *See* The Forbidden Quest (1993)

M (1931) *See also* The Boys of St. Vincent (1993); Die Nibelungen (1923); Dr. Mabuse, Parts 1 & 2 (1922); Le Boucher (1969);

Mäedchen in Uniform (1931); Spies (1928); The Young Poisoner's Handbook (1994)

M. Hire *See* Monsieur Hire (1989)

Ma Nuit Chez Maud *See* My Night at Maud's (1969)

Ma Saison Préférée (1993) *See also* French Provincial (1975); Les Voleurs (1996); Scene of the Crime (1987); Wild Reeds (1994)

Ma Vie en Rose *See* Beautiful Thing (1995); The Best Way (1976)

Maborosi *See* Trois Couleurs: Bleu (1993)

Macbeth *See* Throne of Blood (1957)

Mad Max *See* Akira (1989); Alfredo, Alfredo (1972)

Madam Satan *See* Madame Rosa (1977)

Madame de… *See* The Earrings of Madame de… (1954)

Madame Rosa (1977)

Madame Sousatzka *See* Madame Rosa (1977)

Madame X *See* Madame Rosa (1977)

Mäedchen in Uniform (1931)

The Magic Flute (1973) *See also* The Devil's Eye (1960); The Marquise of O (1976); Smiles of a Summer Night (1955)

The Magician (1958) *See also* After the Rehearsal (1984); Fanny and Alexander (1983); The Hour of the Wolf (1968); La Notte (1960); The Passion of Anna (1970)

The Magnificent Ambersons *See* Ikiru (1952); Sweetie (1989)

The Magnificent Seven *See* Seven Samurai (1954)

Mahanagar *See* The Big City (1963); Charulata (1964); Distant Thunder (1973); The Middleman (1976); The Silences of the Palace (1994); Two Daughters (1961)

Mahler *See* The Music Lovers (1971)

Maîtresse *See* La Salamandre (1971); The Valley Obscured by the Clouds (1972)

Making It *See* Going Places (1974)

The Makioka Sisters (1983) *See also* Tokyo Olympiad (1966)

Malenkaya Vera *See* Little Vera (1988)

Mamma Roma (1962) *See also* The Canterbury Tales (1971); The Decameron (1970); Nights of Cabiria (1957)

A Man and a Woman (1966) *See also* Cat and Mouse (1978); Edith & Marcel (1983)

A Man and a Woman: 20 Years Later *See* A Man and a Woman (1966)

Man Bites Dog (1991)

A Man Escaped (1957)

A Man Escaped, or the Wind Bloweth Where It Listeth *See* A Man Escaped (1957)

The Man in the White Suit (1951)

Man Is Not a Bird (1965) *See also* When Father Was Away on Business (1985)

Man of Aran *See* Bandits of Orgosolo (1961)

Man of Flowers (1984) *See also* Cactus (1986); A Woman's Tale (1992)

Man of Iron (1981) *See also* Man of Marble (1976)

Man of Marble (1976) *See also* Ashes and Diamonds (1958); A Generation (1954); Man of Iron (1981); Moonlighting (1982)

The Man on the Roof (1976) *See also* Elvira Madigan (1967)

The Man Who Fell to Earth *See* Faraway, So Close! (1993); Insignificance (1985); Walkabout (1971)

The Man Who Laughs *See* Waxworks (1924)

The Man Who Loved Women (1977) *See also* The Bride Wore Black (1968); Confidentially Yours (1983); Forbidden Games (1952);

The Man Who Shot Liberty Valance *See* Dersu Uzala (1975)

The Man Who Would Be King *See* Subway (1985)

The Man with a Movie Camera (1929) *See also* A Propos de Nice (1929); Strike (1924); Two or Three Things I Know About Her (1966)

Mandabi (1968) *See also* Black Girl (1966); Borom Sarret (1966); Ceddo (1978); Emitai (1971); Xala (1975)

Manen Pa Taket *See* The Man on the Roof (1976)

Manifesto *See* Man Is Not a Bird (1965)

Manny & Lo *See* Sundays & Cybele (1962)

Manon des Sources *See* Jean de Florette (1987); Manon of the Spring (1987)

Manon of the Spring (1987) *See also* French Provincial (1975); Germinal (1993); Harvest (1937); Jean de Florette (1987)

The Manster (1959)

The Manster—Half Man, Half Monster *See* The Manster (1959)

Marcello Mastroianni: I Remember *See* City of Women (1981); Divorce—Italian Style (1962); Fellini's Roma (1972); Il Bell'Antonio (1960)

Margaret's Museum (1995)

Marianne and Juliane (1982) *See also* One Sings, the Other Doesn't (1977)

Marius (1931) *See also* Fanny (1932)

The Marquise of O (1976)

Marriage Italian Style *See* Yesterday, Today and Tomorrow (1964)

The Marriage of Maria Braun (1979) *See also* The Blue Angel (1930); Effi Briest (1974); French Provincial (1975); Veronika Voss (1982)

A Married Woman (1965)

Marry Me, Marry Me *See* The Two of Us (1968)

Marusa No Onna *See* A Taxing Woman (1987)

Masculin Feminin *See* Masculine Feminine (1966)

Masculine Feminine (1966) *See also* The Mother and the Whore (1973)

M*A*S*H *See* How I Won the War (1967)

The Mask (1961)

Matador (1986) *See also* Kika (1994); Tie Me Up! Tie Me Down! (1990)

The Match Factory Girl (1990) *See also* Leningrad Cowboys Go America (1989)

A Matter of Life and Death *See* Black Narcissus (1947); I Know Where I'm Going (1945); Ikiru (1952); The Life and Death of Colonel Blimp (1943); The Red Shoes (1948)

Max, Mon Amour (1986)

Max, My Love *See* Max, Mon Amour (1986)

May Fools (1990)

McCabe & Mrs. Miller *See* Temptress Moon (1996)

Mean Streets *See* Mamma Roma (1962); Rocco and His Brothers (1960)

Mecaniques Celestes *See* Celestial Clockwork (1994)

Medea *See* Arabian Nights (1974)

Medium Cool *See* Man Bites Dog (1991); Man of Iron (1981)

Megall Az Ido *See* Time Stands Still (1982)

Memorias del Subdesarrollo *See* Memories of Underdevelopment (1968)

Memories of Underdevelopment (1968) *See also* Death of a Bureaucrat (1966); I Am Cuba (1964); The Last Supper (1976); Strawberry and Chocolate (1993)

The Memory of Justice *See* The Sorrow and the Pity (1971); The Wannsee Conference (1984)

The Men Who Tread on the Tiger's Tail (1945)

Menage *See* Okoge (1993)

Mephisto (1981) *See also* The Accompanist (1993); Faust (1926); Hanussen (1988); Xala (1975)

The Merchant of Four Seasons *See* Ali: Fear Eats the Soul (1974); The Bitter Tears of Petra von Kant (1972); Effi Briest (1974); Mother Küsters Goes to Heaven (1976)

Message from Space *See* The Green Slime (1968)

Messidor (1977) *See also* In the White City (1983)

Metisse *See* Café au Lait (1994)

Metropolis (1926) *See also* The Blue Angel (1930); Die Nibelungen (1923); The Golem (1920); Kameradschaft (1931); M (1931); Spies (1928); Variety (1925); Woman in the Moon (1929)

The Middle of the World *See* La Salamandre (1971); The Wonderful Crook (1975)

The Middleman (1976) *See also* The Big City (1963); Days and Nights in the Forest (1970)

A Midwinter's Tale *See* Henry V (1989)

The Mighty Ducks *See* Shall We Dance? (1997)

Mildred Pierce *See* Women from the Lake of Scented Souls (1994)

The Milky Way (1968) *See also* Arabian Nights (1974); Black Moon (1975); El (1952); Erendira (1983); L'Age D'Or (1930); The Phantom of Liberty (1974); Simon of the Desert (1966); Viridiana (1961)

Milou en Mai *See* May Fools (1990)

Milou in May *See* May Fools (1990)

Mina Tannenbaum (1993)

Minbo *See* Minbo—Or the Gentle Art of Japanese Extortion (1992)

Minbo No Onna *See* Minbo—Or the Gentle Art of Japanese Extortion (1992)

Minbo—Or the Gentle Art of Japanese Extortion (1992) *See also* Tampopo (1986); A Taxing Woman (1987)

The Miracle (1948) *See also* Bandits of Orgosolo (1961); The Magician (1958)

Miracle in Milan (1951) *See also* The Garden of the Finzi-Continis (1971); Miss Julie (1950)

Miracolo a Milano *See* Miracle in Milan (1951)

The Mirror (1975) *See also* The Thief (1997)

The Mischief-Makers *See* Les Mistons (1957)

Mishima *See* Enjo (1958); Vengeance Is Mine (1979)

Miss Europe *See* Pandora's Box (1928)

Miss Julie (1950)

Missing *See* The Confession (1970); State of Siege (1973); Yol (1982); Z (1969)

Mississippi Masala *See* Salaam Bombay! (1988)

Mississippi Mermaid (1969) *See also* The Bride Wore Black (1968); Confidentially Yours (1983); Fahrenheit 451 (1966); Scene of the Crime (1987); Shoot the Piano Player (1962); The Soft Skin (1964)

Mr. Arkadin (1955)

Mr. Hulot's Holiday *See* Mon Oncle (1958); Playtime (1967)

Mrs. Dalloway *See* A Month in the Country (1987); Muriel (1963); Sundays & Cybele (1962)

Mitt Liv Som Hund *See* My Life As a Dog (1985)

Modern Times *See* A Nous la Liberté (1931); Jour de Fete (1948); Le Million (1931)

The Mole *See* El Topo (1971)

The Moment of Truth *See* Christ Stopped at Eboli (1979); Three Brothers (1980)

Mommie Dearest *See* The Marriage of Maria Braun (1979)

Mon Homme *See* Beau Père (1981); Going Places (1974); Too Beautiful for You (1988)

Mon Oncle (1958) *See also* Jour de Fete (1948); Playtime (1967)

Mon Oncle Antoine (1971) *See also* Les Bons Debarras (1981)

Mon Oncle d'Amerique (1980) *See also* Hiroshima Mon Amour (1959); Last Year at Marienbad (1961)

Mona Lisa *See* The Long Good Friday (1980)

Mondo Balardo *See* Mondo Cane (1963)

Mondo Cane (1963)

Mondo Pazzo *See* Mondo Cane (1963)

Mondo Trasho *See* Mondo Cane (1963)

Money *See* L'Argent (1983)

The Money Order *See* Mandabi (1968)

A Mongolian Tale (1994)

Monika (1952) *See also* Torment (1944)

Monkey Business *See* Le Million (1931)

Monsieur Hire (1989) *See also* A Nos Amours (1984); Baxter (1989); The Hairdresser's Husband (1992); Man of Flowers (1984); Ridicule (1996)

Monsieur Lange *See* The Crime of Monsieur Lange (1936)

Monsieur Verdoux *See* Captain's Paradise (1953)

Monsieur Vincent (1947)

The Monster (1996) *See also* Johnny Stecchino (1992)

Montenegro *See* Man Is Not a Bird (1965)

A Month in the Country (1987)

Monty Python's Life of Brian *See* Monty Python's The Meaning of Life (1983)

Monty Python's The Meaning of Life (1983)

Moon in the Gutter (1983) *See also* Betty Blue (1986); Diva (1982)

Moonlighting (1982) *See also* Deep End (1970); Knife in the Water (1962)

More *See* The Valley Obscured by the Clouds (1972)

Morocco *See* The Blue Angel (1930)

Moscow Distrusts Tears *See* Moscow Does Not Believe in Tears (1980)

Moscow Does Not Believe in Tears (1980)

Moskwa Sljesam Nje Jerit *See* Moscow Does Not Believe in Tears (1980)

Mosura *See* Mothra (1962)

Mother *See* Storm over Asia (1928)

Mother and Son *See* Andrei Rublev (1966); Ashik Kerib (1988); Cries and Whispers (1972); Solaris (1972)

The Mother and the Whore (1973) *See also* A Very Curious Girl (1969)

Mother Küsters Goes to Heaven (1976) *See also* Ali: Fear Eats the Soul (1974)

Mother Küsters' Trip to Heaven *See* Mother Küsters Goes to Heaven (1976)

Mothra (1962) *See* Godzilla, King of the Monsters (1956)

Mouchette (1967) *See also* Diary of a Country Priest (1950); The Fire Within (1964); Vagabond (1985)

Mui du du Xanh *See* The Scent of Green Papaya (1993)

Mujeres al Borde de un Ataque de Nervios *See* Women on the Verge of a Nervous Breakdown (1988)

Muriel (1963)

Muriel, Or the Time of Return *See* Muriel (1963)

Muriel, Ou le Temps d'un Retour *See* Muriel (1963)

Muriel's Wedding (1994) *See also* The Hit (1985); Love Serenade (1996)

Murmur of the Heart (1971) *See also* Twist & Shout (1984)

The Music Box *See* The Confession (1970)

The Music Lovers (1971) *See also* The Devils (1971)

The Music Room *See* Charulata (1964); Devi (1960); Distant Thunder (1973); Jalsaghar (1958)

The Music Teacher *See* Farinelli (1994)

Mutter Kusters Fahrt Zum Himmel *See* Mother Küsters Goes to Heaven (1976)

My Beautiful Laundrette *See* Gumshoe (1972)

My Brilliant Career (1979) *See also* Careful, He Might Hear You (1984); The Piano (1993)

My Dinner with André *See* The Designated Mourner (1997); May Fools (1990)

My Favorite Season *See* Ma Saison Préférée (1993)

My First Wife *See* Cactus (1986); Man of Flowers (1984)

My Girlfriend's Boyfriend *See* Boyfriends & Girlfriends (1988)

My Left Foot (1989) *See also* The Young Poisoner's Handbook (1994)

My Life As a Dog (1985) *See also* Murmur of the Heart (1971)

My Life to Live (1962) *See also* A Married Woman (1965); Pierrot le Fou (1965)

My Name Is Ivan *See* The Mirror (1975)

My Neighbor Totoro *See* Fantastic Planet (1973)

My New Partner (1984) *See also* Borsalino (1970)

My New Partner II *See* My New Partner (1984)

My Night at Maud's (1969) *See also* Chloe in the Afternoon (1972); Claire's Knee (1971); La Collectionneuse (1967)

My Night with Maud *See* My Night at Maud's (1969)

My Sweet Little Village (1986) *See also* My Twentieth Century (1990)

My Twentieth Century (1990) *See also* Angi Vera (1978)

My Uncle *See* Mon Oncle (1958)

My Uncle, Mr. Hulot *See* Mon Oncle (1958)

The Mysterious Island (1929) *See* Witchcraft through the Ages (1922)

The Mystery of Kaspar Hauser *See* The Boys of St. Vincent (1993); Every Man for Himself & God Against All (1975); Kaspar Hauser (1993); Stroszek (1977); The Wild Child (1970)

The Mystery of Rampo (1994)

Mystery Train *See* Leningrad Cowboys Go America (1989); Wings of Desire (1988)

Na Samyn Dnie *See* Deep End (1970)

Naked *See* Bleak Moments (1971); High Hopes (1988); Life Is Sweet (1990); The Tango Lesson (1997)

Naked Lunch *See* Dead Ringers (1988); They Came from Within (1975)

The Naked Night *See* Sawdust and Tinsel (1953)

Nanook of the North *See* Earth (1930); The Forbidden Quest (1993); Himatsuri (1985)

Napoleon (1927) *See also* La Marseillaise (1937); War and Peace (1968)

Narayama-Bushi-Ko *See* The Ballad of Narayama (1983)

Nashville *See* 32 Short Films about Glenn Gould (1993)

Nattvardsgaesterna *See* Winter Light (1962)

Navigators of the Desert *See* The Night of Counting the Years (1969)

Nazarin *See* Los Olvidados (1950); The Milky Way (1968); Simon of the Desert (1966); Viridiana (1961)

Near Death *See* The Ballad of Narayama (1983); Blue (1993); In for Treatment (1982); A Woman's Tale (1992)

Nelly and Mr. Arnaud *See* Nelly et Monsieur Arnaud (1995)

Nelly et Monsieur Arnaud (1995) *See also* César & Rosalie (1972); Nelly et

Monsieur Arnaud (1995); Un Coeur en Hiver (1993); Vincent, François, Paul and the Others (1976)

Nenette et Boni *See* I Can't Sleep (1993)

The Neon Bible *See* Distant Voices, Still Lives (1988)

Neskolko Dnel iz Zhizni I.I. Oblomov *See* Oblomov (1981)

The Nest (1980) *See also* Cria (1976)

Never Say Never Again *See* Hanussen (1988)

The New Land (1973) *See also* The Emigrants (1972); Jerusalem (1996); Pelle the Conqueror (1988)

The Night *See* La Notte (1960)

Night and Fog (1955) *See also* Birthplace (1992); Hiroshima Mon Amour (1959); Last Year at Marienbad (1961); Salo, or the 120 Days of Sodom (1975); Triumph of the Will (1934)

A Night at the Opera *See* Le Million (1931)

The Night My Number Came Up *See* Dead of Night (1945)

The Night of Counting the Years (1969)

The Night of San Lorenzo *See* The Night of the Shooting Stars (1982)

Night of the Demon *See* Curse of the Demon (1957)

Night of the Hunter *See* Boy (1969); Day of Wrath (1943); Fanny and Alexander (1983); Small Change (1976)

Night of the Living Dead *See* Black Sunday (1960); Outback (1971)

The Night of the Shooting Stars (1982) *See also* Allonsanfan (1973); Fiorile (1993); Kaos (1985)

Night on Earth *See* The Monster (1996)

The Night Porter (1974)

The Night Watch *See* Le Trou (1959)

Nightmare Alley *See* Hanussen (1988)

Nights of Cabiria (1957) *See also* Fellini's Roma (1972); Ginger & Fred (1986); Juliet of the Spirits (1965); La Strada (1954); Loves of a Blonde (1965); Variety Lights (1951); The White Sheik (1952)

Nikita *See* La Femme Nikita (1991)

1900 (1976) *See also* Before the Revolution (1965); The Bird with the Crystal Plumage (1970); Heimat 1 (1984)

1984 *See* The Postman (1994)

99 Women *See* The Green Slime (1968)

Ningen No Joken *See* The Human Condition: Road to Eternity (1959)

Nizza *See* A Propos de Nice (1929)

No Greater Love *See* The Human Condition: A Soldier's Prayer (1961); The Human Condition: Road to Eternity (1959)

No Man's Land *See* Jonah Who Will Be 25 in the Year 2000 (1976)

Nobi *See* Fires on the Plain (1959)

Nobody's Fault *See* Little Dorrit, Film 1: Nobody's Fault (1988)

Nosferatu (1922) *See also* Aguirre, the Wrath of God (1972); Faust (1926); The Golem (1920); Vampyr (1931); Nosferatu the Vampyre (1979)

Nosferatu, A Symphony of Horror *See* Nosferatu (1922)

Nosferatu, A Symphony of Terror *See* Nosferatu (1922)

Nosferatu, Eine Symphonie des Grauens *See* Nosferatu (1922)

Nosferatu the Vampyre (1979) *See also* Nosferatu (1922)

Nostalghia *See* Solaris (1972); Stalker (1979)

Not Against the Flesh *See* Vampyr (1931)

Novecento *See* 1900 (1976)

Noz w Wodzie *See* Knife in the Water (1962)

Nuit et Brouillard *See* Night and Fog (1955)

The Nun's Story *See* Liebelei (1932)

Nuovo Cinema Paradiso *See* Cinema Paradiso (1988)

The Nutty Professor *See* Johnny Stecchino (1992); The Testament of Dr. Cordelier (1959)

Nybyggarna *See* The New Land (1973)

O Dragao da Maldade contra o Santo Guerreiro *See* Antonio Das Mortes (1968)

O Lucky Man! *See* If… (1969)

The Object of My Affection *See* A Special Day (1977)

Oblomov (1981) *See also* Anna (1993); Burnt by the Sun (1994); The Lady with the Dog (1959); A Slave of Love (1978)

Occhi Senza Volto *See* Eyes without a Face (1959)

An Occurrence at Owl Creek Bridge *See* Zita (1968)

October *See* Ten Days That Shook the World (1927)

Odd Obsession (1960) *See also* Enjo (1958); The Mystery of Rampo (1994)

Oedipus Rex *See* Arabian Nights (1974)

Oh! What a Lovely War *See* How I Won the War (1967)

Okoge (1993)

Old Acquaintance *See* Mina Tannenbaum (1993)

The Old Man and the Boy *See* The Two of Us (1968)

Oliver Twist *See* Little Dorrit, Film 1: Nobody's Fault (1988); The Overcoat (1959)

Olivier, Olivier (1992) *See also* Europa, Europa (1991); The Return of Martin Guerre (1983)

Olympia *See* Black Girl (1966); The Blue Light (1932); Tokyo Olympiad (1966)

On the Bridge *See* In for Treatment (1982)

On the Town *See* Lola (1961)

On the Waterfront *See* Tous les Matins du Monde (1992)

Once Upon a Time in America *See* Once Upon a Time in the West (1968)

Once Upon a Time in the West (1968) *See also* The Bird with the Crystal Plumage (1970); The Good, the Bad, and the Ugly (1967); Red Sorghum (1987)

Once Upon a Time There Was a Country *See* Underground (1995)

Once Were Warriors (1994)

One Flew over the Cuckoo's Nest *See* The Firemen's Ball (1968); Loves of a Blonde (1965)

101 Dalmatians *See* When the Cat's Away (1996)

One Plus One *See* Sympathy for the Devil (1970)

One Sings, the Other Doesn't (1977)

Onibaba (1964) *See also* Kwaidan (1964)

Only the French Can! *See* French Can-Can (1955)

Onna Ga Kaidan O Agaru Toki *See* When a Woman Ascends the Stairs (1960)

Open City (1945) *See also* Bitter Rice (1949); Generale Della Rovere (1960); The Gospel According to St. Matthew (1964); Lamerica (1995); Love in the City (1953); The Miracle (1948); Paisan (1946); The Rise of Louis XIV (1966); Shoeshine (1947)

Open Doors *See* Lamerica (1995); The Stolen Children (1992)

Orchestra Rehearsal (1978)

Ordet (1955)

Orfeu Negro *See* Black Orpheus (1958)

The Original Fabulous Adventures of Baron Munchausen *See* Fabulous Adventures of Baron Munchausen (1961)

Orlando (1992) *See also* Caravaggio (1986); The Tango Lesson (1997)

Orphans of the Storm *See* La Marseillaise (1937); Napoleon (1927)

Orphee *See* Orpheus (1949)

Orpheus (1949) *See also* Beauty and the Beast (1946); The Blood of a Poet (1930); Celestial Clockwork (1994); Dead of Night (1945); Eternal Return (1943); Les Enfants Terribles (1950); The Saragossa Manuscript (1965); The Testament of Orpheus (1959)

Ososhiki *See* The Funeral (1984)

Ossessione (1942) *See also* Bitter Rice (1949); La Terra Trema (1948); Lovers: A True Story (1990); Rocco and His Brothers (1960); Senso (1954)

Othello *See* Chimes at Midnight (1967); Hamlet (1948)

Otto e Mezzo *See* 8 1/2 (1963)

Our Daily Bread *See* The Crime of Monsieur Lange (1936)

Our Hospitality *See* Playtime (1967)

Out of the Past *See* Curse of the Demon (1957); Insomnia (1997)

Outback (1971) *See also* Picnic at Hanging Rock (1975)

Outomlionnye Solntsem *See* Burnt by the Sun (1994)

The Outsiders *See* Band of Outsiders (1964)

The Overcoat (1959) *See also* The Lady with the Dog (1959)

The Ox *See* The Emigrants (1972)

The Ox-Bow Incident *See* Tilaï (1990)

Padre Padrone *See* Allonsanfan (1973); Fiorile (1993); Kaos (1985); The Night of the Shooting Stars (1982)

A Page of Madness *See* The Cabinet of Dr. Caligari (1919); Gate of Hell (1954); The Hour of the Wolf (1968)

Pain in the A** *See* La Cage aux Folles (1978); Les Compères (1983)

Paisan (1946) *See also* Ballad of a Soldier (1960); Lamerica (1995); Love in the City (1953); Open City (1945); The Rise of Louis XIV (1966); Shoeshine (1947)

Palombella Rossa *See* Caro Diario (1993)

Pandora's Box (1928) *See also* The Blue Angel (1930); Diary of a Lost Girl (1929); Die Liebe der Jeanne Ney (1927); The Joyless Street (1925); The Threepenny Opera (1931); Variety (1925)

The Parasite Murders *See* They Came from Within (1975)

Pardon Me, Your Teeth Are in My Neck *See* The Fearless Vampire Killers (1967)

Paris Brule-t-il? *See* Is Paris Burning? (1966)

Paris Does Strange Things *See* Eléna and Her Men (1956)

Paris Qui Dort *See* A Nous la Liberté (1931)

Parting Glances *See* Blue (1993)

Pas Si Mechant que Ça *See* The Wonderful Crook (1975)

Pasqualino Settebellezze *See* Seven Beauties (1976)

Pasqualino: Seven Beauties *See* Seven Beauties (1976)

The Passenger *See* Blow-Up (1966); The Red Desert (1964)

Passion *See* Beware of a Holy Whore (1970); Every Man for Himself (1979)

A Passion *See* The Passion of Anna (1970)

The Passion of Anna (1970) *See also* Cries and Whispers (1972); Persona (1966); Scenes from a Marriage (1973); The Silence (1963)

The Passion of Joan of Arc (1928) *See also* Day of Wrath (1943); Gertrud (1964); Ordet (1955); Thérèse (1986)

Passione d'Amoré *See* Down & Dirty (1976); La Nuit de Varennes (1982); A Special Day (1977); Too Beautiful for You (1988)

Pather Panchali (1954) *See also* Aparajito (1958); Jalsaghar (1958); Phantom India (1969); Ponette (1995); Yaaba (1989)

Paths of Glory *See* Captain Conan (1996); Gallipoli (1981); Grand Illusion (1937); Life and Nothing But (1989)

Patty Hearst *See* Devil in the Flesh (1987); Hollow Reed (1995); Marianne and

Jullane (1982); Mother Küsters Goes to Heaven (1976); Pickpocket (1959)

Pauline *See* Pauline at the Beach (1983)

Pauline á la Plage *See* Pauline at the Beach (1983)

Pauline at the Beach (1983) *See also* Celestial Clockwork (1994); Claire's Knee (1971)

Peau d'Ane *See* Donkey Skin (1970)

Pelle *See* Pelle the Conqueror (1988)

Pelle the Conqueror (1988) *See also* The Best Intentions (1992); Jerusalem (1996); Sunday's Children (1994); Twist & Shout (1984)

Pennies from Heaven *See* Dreamchild (1985)

The People vs. Larry Flynt *See* The Firemen's Ball (1968); Loves of a Blonde (1965)

Pépé le Moko (1937)

Peppermint Soda *See* Entre-Nous (1983)

Persona (1966) *See also* After the Rehearsal (1984); Cries and Whispers (1972); The Double Life of Veronique (1991); The Manster (1959); The Return of Martin Guerre (1983); Shame (1968); The Silence (1963)

Persons Unknown *See* Big Deal on Madonna Street (1958)

Peter the First *See* Don Quixote (1957)

Petulia *See* Juggernaut (1974)

Phantom India (1969) *See also* Salaam Bombay! (1988)

The Phantom of Liberty (1974) *See also* Akira Kurosawa's Dreams (1990); The Discreet Charm of the Bourgeoisie (1972); Max, Mon Amour (1986); Woman in the Dunes (1964)

The Phantom of Terror *See* The Bird with the Crystal Plumage (1970)

The Piano (1993) *See also* Belle de Jour (1967); The Hairdresser's Husband (1992); Heavenly Creatures (1994); Two Friends (1986); Walkabout (1971)

Pickpocket (1959) *See also* Diary of a Country Priest (1950); A Gentle Woman (1969); Gertrud (1964); Lancelot of the Lake (1974); L'Argent (1983); A Man Escaped (1957); The Thief of Paris (1967)

Picnic at Hanging Rock (1975) *See also* Gallipoli (1981)

Picnic on the Grass *See* May Fools (1990)

The Pier *See* La Jetée (1962)

Pierrot le Fou (1965) *See also* The American Soldier (1970); Band of Outsiders (1964); Breathless (1959); Contempt (1964); My Life to Live (1962); Two or Three Things I Know About Her (1966); Weekend (1967); A Woman Is a Woman (1960)

The Pillow Book (1995) *See also* The Belly of an Architect (1991); The Cook, the Thief, His Wife & Her Lover (1990); The Draughtsman's Contract (1982)

Pink Flamingos *See* El Topo (1971)

The Pink Panther *See* Big Deal on Madonna Street (1958)

Pinocchio *See* Beauty and the Beast (1946); The City of Lost Children (1995)

Pirate's Fiancee *See* A Very Curious Girl (1969)

Pirds in Peru *See* Betty Blue (1986)

Pixote (1981) *See also* Los Olvidados (1950); Shoeshine (1947)

The Pizza Triangle *See* Alfredo, Alfredo (1972); Down & Dirty (1976); We All Loved Each Other So Much (1977)

A Place in the Sun *See* Que Viva Mexico (1932)

Planet of Incredible Creatures *See* Fantastic Planet (1973)

Play Misty for Me *See* A Fistful of Dollars (1964)

The Player *See* Contempt (1964); Day for Night (1973)

Playtime (1967) *See also* Jour de Fete (1948); Mon Oncle (1958); Traffic (1971); Two or Three Things I Know About Her (1966)

Plein Soleil *See* Purple Noon (1960)

Po Dezju *See* Before the Rain (1994)

Point of No Return *See* La Femme Nikita (1991)

Point of Order *See* Dr. Petiot (1990)

Pokolenie *See* A Generation (1954)

Police *See* Loulou (1980)

Police Force *See* Police Story (1985)

Police Story (1985) *See also* Drunken Master (1978)

Police Story III *See* Drunken Master (1978)

Ponette (1995)

The Poor Outlaws See The Round-Up (1966)

Popeye See Rocco and His Brothers (1960)

Popiol i Diament See Ashes and Diamonds (1958)

Port of Shadows See Pépé le Moko (1937)

Poseidon Adventure See Juggernaut (1974)

The Postman (1994)

The Postman Always Rings Twice See Bitter Rice (1949); The Day the Sun Turned Cold (1994); Frantic (1958); Ju Dou (1990); Lovers: A True Story (1990); Ossessione (1942)

Potemkin See The Battleship Potemkin (1925)

Powaqqatsi See Mondo Cane (1963)

Pred dozhdot See Before the Rain (1994)

Preparez Vous Mouchoirs See Get Out Your Handkerchiefs (1978)

Prima della Rivoluzione See Before the Revolution (1965)

Princess Yang Kwei Fei (1955) See also Sansho the Bailiff (1954); Ugetsu (1953)

Prisoner of the Caucasus See Prisoner of the Mountains (1996)

Prisoner of the Mountains (1996) See also The Ascent (1976); Before the Rain (1994); The Thief (1997)

The Private Life of Henry VIII See The Rise of Louis XIV (1966)

Prix de Beaut... See Pandora's Box (1928)

The Producers See Big Deal on Madonna Street (1958)

Project A See Drunken Master (1978); A Police Story (1985)

Project A, Part II See Police Story (1985)

Project Grizzly (1996)

The Promise See La Promesse (1996)

Proof (1991) See also Les Bons Debarras (1981)

Prospero's Books See The Pillow Book (1995)

Prova d'Orchestra See Orchestra Rehearsal (1978)

Providence (1977) See also Hiroshima Mon Amour (1959); Last Year at Marienbad (1961); Mon Oncle d'Amerique (1980); Muriel (1963); Night and Fog (1955); 32 Short Films about Glenn Gould (1993)

Psycho See Baxter (1989); Dead Ringers (1988); Diabolique (1955); Fahrenheit

451 (1966); La Rupture (1970); L'Avventura (1960); 1900 (1976); Repulsion (1965); The Vanishing (1988)

The Public Enemy See A Better Tomorrow (1986)

Purple Noon (1960) See also The American Friend (1977); Forbidden Games (1952)

The Purple Rose of Cairo See The White Sheik (1952)

Qiu Ju Da Guansi See The Story of Qiu Ju (1991)

Qiu Ju Goes to Court See The Story of Qiu Ju (1991)

Que la Bete Meure See This Man Must Die (1970)

Que Viva Mexico (1932)

Queen Kelly See Que Viva Mexico (1932)

Quemimada! See Burn! (1970)

The Quiet Room See The Tin Drum (1979)

Quilombo (1984) See also Antonio Das Mortes (1968); Black God, White Devil (1964); Black Orpheus (1958); Bye Bye Brazil (1979); Erendira (1983); Xica (1976)

The Raffle See Boccaccio '70 (1962)

Raining Stones See Land and Freedom (1995)

Raise Ravens See Cria (1976)

Raise the Red Lantern (1991) See also Ju Dou (1990); Shanghai Triad (1995); The Story of Qiu Ju (1991)

Ramparts of Clay (1971) See also Indochine (1992); The Scent of Green Papaya (1993); The Silences of the Palace (1994)

Ran (1985) See also Dersu Uzala (1975); Henry V (1945); Kagemusha (1980); Throne of Blood (1957); Xala (1975)

The Rapture See Through a Glass Darkly (1961)

Rashomon (1951) See also The Day the Sun Turned Cold (1994); Drunken Angel (1948); Gate of Hell (1954); I Live in Fear (1955); Ikiru (1952); Princess Yang Kwei Fei (1955); Providence (1977); Stray Dog (1949); Ugetsu (1953)

The Reader See La Lectrice (1988)

Ready to Wear See Yesterday, Today and Tomorrow (1964)

Rear Ravens See Cria (1976)

Rear Window See The Bird with the Crystal Plumage (1970); The Bride Wore Black (1968); Mississippi Mermaid (1969); Monsieur

Hire (1989); Odd Obsession (1960); Proof (1991)

Rebel without a Cause See If... (1969); The Little Thief (1989); Little Vera (1988)

Rebellion See Harakiri (1962); The Human Condition: A Soldier's Prayer (1961); Samurai Rebellion (1967); Yojimbo (1961)

Record of a Living Being See I Live in Fear (1955)

Red See The Double Life of Veronique (1991); Trois Couleurs: Rouge (1994)

The Red and the White See The Round-Up (1966)

The Red Balloon (1956) See also The White Balloon (1995)

Red Beard (1965) See also Dersu Uzala (1975); Dodes 'ka-den (1970); Drunken Angel (1948)

The Red Desert (1964) See also La Notte (1960); L'Avventura (1960)

The Red Shoes (1948) See also Black Narcissus (1947); I Know Where I'm Going (1945); The Life and Death of Colonel Blimp (1943)

Red Sorghum (1987) See also The Horse Thief (1987); Ju Dou (1990); Raise the Red Lantern (1991); The Round-Up (1966); The Story of Qiu Ju (1991)

Reds See The Bird with the Crystal Plumage (1970); Ten Days That Shook the World (1927)

Regain See Harvest (1937)

Rehearsal for a Crime See The Criminal Life of Archibaldo de la Cruz (1955)

Rekopis Znaleziony W Saragossie See The Saragossa Manuscript (1965)

Rembrandt See Carnival in Flanders (1935)

Rendezvous in Paris (1995) See also Diary of a Seducer (1995); Full Moon in Paris (1984); La Discrete (1990); My Night at Maud's (1969); Pauline at the Beach (1983); Two Daughters (1961)

Repentance See Freeze-Die-Come to Life (1990); Moscow Does Not Believe in Tears (1980)

The Replacement Killers See A Better Tomorrow (1986)

Repulsion (1965) See also The Fearless Vampire Killers (1967); Knife in the Water (1962); La Cérémonie (1995); The Tenant (1976); 301, 302 (1994)

Reservoir Dogs *See* Band of Outsiders (1964); The Hit (1985)

The Return of Martin Guerre (1983) *See also* Olivier, Olivier (1992)

Return of the Secaucus Seven *See* Jonah Who Will Be 25 in the Year 2000 (1976)

Revenge of the Vampire *See* Black Sunday (1960)

Rhapsody in August (1991) *See also* Black Rain (1988); The Burmese Harp (1956)

Rich and Famous *See* Mina Tannenbaum (1993)

Richard III *See* Hamlet (1948); Henry V (1945)

Ride the High Country *See* Red Sorghum (1987)

Ridicule (1996) *See also* Monsieur Hire (1989)

Riff Raff *See* Bleak Moments (1971)

Rififi *See* Big Deal on Madonna Street (1958)

Riget *See* The Kingdom (1995)

The Right Stuff *See* Orpheus (1949)

The Rise of Louis XIV (1966) *See also* The Flowers of St. Francis (1950)

Riso Amaro *See* Bitter Rice (1949)

River's Edge *See* Pixote (1981)

The Road *See* La Strada (1954)

The Road to Eternity *See* The Human Condition: A Soldier's Prayer (1961)

The Road Warrior *See* Akira (1989); Le Dernier Combat (1984)

Robert et Robert *See* Cat and Mouse (1978)

RoboCop *See* Ivan the Terrible, Part 1 (1944)

Rocco and His Brothers (1960) *See also* La Terra Trema (1948); L'Avventura (1960); Ossessione (1942); Senso (1954)

Rocco e I Suoi Fratelli *See* Rocco and His Brothers (1960)

Rocco et Ses Freres *See* Rocco and His Brothers (1960)

Rocky *See* In the Realm of the Senses (1976)

The Rocky Horror Picture Show *See* El Topo (1971)

Rodan *See* Godzilla, King of the Monsters (1956)

The Rolling Stones Rock and Roll Circus *See* Sympathy for the Devil (1970)

Roma *See* Fellini's Roma (1972)

Roma, Citta Aperta *See* Open City (1945)

Rome, Open City *See* Open City (1945)

Room at the Top *See* Casque d'Or (1952); Look Back in Anger (1958)

Rope *See* Heavenly Creatures (1994); Purple Noon (1960)

Rosalie Goes Shopping *See* Sugarbaby (1985)

Rosemary's Baby *See* The Fearless Vampire Killers (1967); Knife in the Water (1962); Repulsion (1965); The Tenant (1976)

Rouge *See* Trois Couleurs: Rouge (1994)

'Round Midnight *See* The Judge and the Assassin (1975)

The Round-Up (1966)

Rue Cases Negres *See* Sugar Cane Alley (1983)

Rules of the Game *See* Boudu Saved from Drowning (1932); Boyfriends & Girlfriends (1988); Eléna and Her Men (1956); French Provincial (1975); The Golden Coach (1952); Grand Illusion (1937); The Mother and the Whore (1973); Smiles of a Summer Night (1955); Toni (1934)

The Sacrifice (1986) *See also* The Mirror (1975); Solaris (1972); Winter Light (1962)

The Saga of the Road *See* Pather Panchali (1954)

Saikaku Ichidai Onna *See* Life of Oharu (1952)

Salaam Bombay! (1988)

The Salamander *See* La Salamandre (1971)

Salo, or the 120 Days of Sodom (1975) *See also* Arabian Nights (1974); The Decameron (1970); La Grande Bouffe (1973)

The Saltmen of Tibet *See* The Forbidden Quest (1993)

Sambizanga (1972)

The Samurai *See* Le Samourai (1967)

Samurai Rebellion (1967) *See also* Harakiri (1962); The Human Condition: A Soldier's Prayer (1961)

Sandokan 8 *See* When a Woman Ascends the Stairs (1960)

Sanjuro (1962) *See also* Sanshiro Sugata (1943); Yojimbo (1961)

Sanma No Aji *See* An Autumn Afternoon (1962)

Sans Toit Ni Loi *See* Vagabond (1985)

Sanshiro Sugata (1943)

Sanshiro Sugata Part Two *See* Sanshiro Sugata (1943)

Sansho Dayu *See* Sansho the Bailiff (1954)

Sansho the Bailiff (1954) *See also* 47 Ronin, Part 1 (1942); Life of Oharu (1952); Princess Yang Kwei Fei (1955); Toto le Héros (1991); Ugetsu (1953)

Sapphire *See* Victim (1961)

The Saragossa Manuscript (1965)

Sasom I En Spegel *See* Through a Glass Darkly (1961)

Saturday Night and Sunday Morning (1960) *See also* A Kind of Loving (1962); Look Back in Anger (1958)

Saturday Night Fever *See* Saturday Night and Sunday Morning (1960); Shall We Dance? (1997)

Satyricon *See* Fellini Satyricon (1969)

Sauve Qui Peut *See* Every Man for Himself (1979)

Sauve Qui Peut la Vie *See* Every Man for Himself (1979)

Savage Messiah *See* Camille Claudel (1989); The Devils (1971)

The Savage Planet *See* Fantastic Planet (1973)

Sawdust and Tinsel (1953) *See also* Dreams (1955); Miss Julie (1950); Monika (1952); Torment (1944)

Scanners *See* They Came from Within (1975); Ticket to Heaven (1981)

Scarlet Street *See* La Chienne (1931)

Scene of the Crime (1987) *See also* Ma Saison Préférée (1993)

Scenes from a Marriage (1973) *See also* The Best Intentions (1992); Cries and Whispers (1972); Face to Face (1976); A Gentle Woman (1969)

The Scent of Green Papaya (1993) *See also* Indochine (1992)

Schindler's List *See* The Chant of Jimmie Blacksmith (1978)

The Searchers *See* L'Atalante (1934); A Mongolian Tale (1994); The Story of Adele H. (1975); The World of Apu (1959)

Seconds *See* The Face of Another (1966)

Secrets and Lies (1995) *See also* Bleak Moments (1971); High Hopes (1988); Life Is Sweet (1990)

Seduced and Abandoned *See* Alfredo, Alfredo (1972); Divorce—Italian Style (1962)

The Seducer's Diary *See* Diary of a Seducer (1995)

A Self-Made Hero (1995) *See also* The Accompanist

(1993); Café au Lait (1994);
The Flower of My Secret
(1995)

A Sense of History *See* High
Hopes (1988); Kind Hearts
and Coronets (1949)

A Sense of Life *See* We the
Living (1942)

Senso (1954) *See also* The
Innocent (1976)

Seppuku *See* Harakiri (1962)

Serpico *See* L.627 (1992); La
Scorta (1994)

Sesame Oil Woman *See*
Women from the Lake of
Scented Souls (1994)

Seven Beauties (1976) *See
also* Love and Anarchy
(1973); The Night Porter
(1974); Swept Away…
(1975); We the Living
(1942)

Seven Chances *See* Police
Story (1985)

Seven Samurai (1954) *See
also* 47 Ronin, Part 1
(1942); Once Upon a Time
in the West (1968); Ran
(1985); Red Beard (1965)

The Seventh Seal *See*
Dreams (1955); Fanny and
Alexander (1983); The
Magician (1958); Monty
Python's The Meaning of
Life (1983); Orpheus
(1949); Wild Strawberries
(1957)

Shadow *See* Le Boucher
(1969)

Shadow of a Doubt *See* Le
Boucher (1969); The
Manster (1959); The Story
of Women (1988)

The Shadow Warrior *See*
Kagemusha (1980)

**Shadows of Forgotten
Ancestors** (1964) *See also*
Ashik Kerib (1988);
Gabbeh (1996)

Shadows of Our Ancestors
See Shadows of Forgotten
Ancestors (1964)

**Shadows of Our Forgotten
Ancestors** *See* Shadows
of Forgotten Ancestors
(1964)

Shall We Dance? (1997)

Shall We Dansu? *See* Shall We
Dance? (1997)

Shame (1968) *See also* The
Designated Mourner
(1997); Forbidden Games
(1952); The Passion of
Anna (1970); The Sacrifice
(1986); The Silence (1963)

Shampoo *See* The Hairdresser's Husband (1992)

Shanghai Express *See* The
Blue Angel (1930)

Shanghai Triad (1995) *See
also* Ju Dou (1990);
Temptress Moon (1996)

Shchors *See* Earth (1930)

She Got What She Asked For
See Yesterday, Today and
Tomorrow (1964)

The Sheltering Sky *See* In the
White City (1983)

Sherlock Jr. *See* Cinema Par-
adiso (1988); Drunken
Master (1978); The Icicle
Thief (1989)

Sherman's March *See* Caro
Diario (1993)

She's Gotta Have It *See* Café
au Lait (1994)

Shichinin No Samurai *See*
Seven Samurai (1954)

Shine *See* 32 Short Films
about Glenn Gould (1993)

Shinel *See* The Overcoat
(1959)

Shivers *See* They Came from
Within (1975)

Shoah *See* Birthplace (1992);
The Boat Is Full (1981);
Europa, Europa (1991);
Night and Fog (1955);
Salo, or the 120 Days of
Sodom (1975); Triumph of
the Will (1934); The
Wannsee Conference
(1984)

Shoeshine (1947) *See also*
The Bicycle Thief (1948);
Big Deal on Madonna
Street (1958); Los Olvidados (1950); Miracle in
Milan (1951); Paisan
(1946); The Stolen Chil-
dren (1992); Umberto D.
(1955)

Shonen *See* Boy (1969)

Shoot the Moon *See*
Gumshoe (1972); Scenes
from a Marriage (1973)

Shoot the Pianist *See* Shoot
the Piano Player (1962)

Shoot the Piano Player
(1962) *See also* Jules and
Jim (1962); Moon in the
Gutter (1983)

Short Eyes *See* M (1931)

The Shout *See* The Tin Drum
(1979)

Siegfried *See* Die Nibelungen
(1923)

**Siegfried and Kriemhild's
Revenge** *See* Die Nibelungen (1923)

The Silence (1963) *See also*
The Passion of Anna
(1970); Persona (1966);
Sawdust and Tinsel (1953);
Through a Glass Darkly
(1961); The Virgin Spring
(1959); Winter Light (1962)

The Silence of the Lambs
See The Judge and the
Assassin (1975)

The Silences of the Palace
(1994) *See also* Charulata
(1964); Ramparts of Clay
(1971); Yol (1982)

Silken Skin *See* The Soft Skin
(1964)

Simon del Desierto *See*
Simon of the Desert
(1966)

Simon of the Desert (1966)
See also The Discreet

Charm of the Bourgeoisie
(1972); The Exterminating
Angel (1962); The Garden
of Delights (1970); The
Milky Way (1968); Ordet
(1955); Viridiana (1961)

Singin' in the Rain *See*
French Can-Can (1955)

The Singing Detective *See*
Dreamchild (1985)

A Single Girl (1996) *See also*
Augustin (1995); I Can't
Sleep (1993); La Céré-
monie (1995)

The Sins of Lola Montès *See*
Lola Montès (1955)

**Sisters, or the Balance of
Happiness** *See* Marianne
and Juliane (1982)

Six Degrees of Separation
See A Cry in the Dark
(1988)

A Slave of Love (1978) *See
also* Anna (1993); Burnt by
the Sun (1994); Oblomov
(1981)

The Slingshot *See* My Life As
a Dog (1985)

Slow Motion *See* Every Man
for Himself (1979)

Small Change (1976) *See also*
Day for Night (1973); Les
Mistons (1957); The Little
Thief (1989); Sugar Cane
Alley (1983)

Smiles of a Summer Night
(1955) *See also* Days and
Nights in the Forest
(1970); The Devil's Eye
(1960); The Magic Flute
(1973); Summer Interlude
(1950)

Smultron-Stallet *See* Wild
Strawberries (1957)

The Snapper *See* The Hit
(1985)

The Soft Skin (1964) *See also*
The Bride Wore Black
(1968); Jules and Jim
(1962); Le Bonheur (1965);
The Man Who Loved
Women (1977); Mississippi
Mermaid (1969); The
Woman Next Door (1981)

Solaris (1972) *See also* The
Sacrifice (1986); Stalker
(1979)

Soldier of Orange *See* The
4th Man (1979)

The Soldiers *See* Les Carabiniers (1963)

A Soldier's Prayer *See* The
Human Condition: A Sol-
dier's Prayer (1961)

Sommarlek *See* Summer
Interlude (1950)

Sommarnattens Leende *See*
Smiles of a Summer Night
(1955)

Sommersby *See* Olivier,
Olivier (1992); The Return
of Martin Guerre (1983)

Son of Gascogne *See*
Augustin (1995); A Very
Curious Girl (1969)

The Song of the Road *See* Pather Panchali (1954)

Sorcerer *See* The Wages of Fear (1955)

The Sorrow and the Pity (1971) *See also* The Accompanist (1993); Au Revoir les Enfants (1987); The Boat Is Full (1981); The Designated Mourner (1997); Dr. Petiot (1990); Is Paris Burning? (1966); Lacombe, Lucien (1974); The Last Metro (1980); Night and Fog (1955); A Self-Made Hero (1995); The Story of Women (1988)

Sotto, Sotto *See* Swept Away… (1975)

Soul *See* Earth (1930)

The Sound of Trumpets *See* The Tree of Wooden Clogs (1978)

Sounder *See* Sugar Cane Alley (1983)

Sounds from the Mountains *See* When a Woman Ascends the Stairs (1960)

Sous les Toits de Paris *See* Under the Roofs of Paris (1929)

Souvenirs d'en France *See* French Provincial (1975)

Soy Cuba *See* I Am Cuba (1964)

Spartacus *See* Farewell My Concubine (1993); L'Avventura (1960)

A Special Day (1977) *See also* Allonsanfan (1973)

The Specter of Freedom *See* The Phantom of Liberty (1974)

Speed *See* The 4th Man (1979)

The Spider's Stratagem (1970) *See also* The Bird with the Crystal Plumage (1970); Last Tango in Paris (1973)

Spies (1928) *See also* Dr. Mabuse, Parts 1 & 2 (1922)

Spione *See* Spies (1928)

Spirit of the Beehive (1973) *See also* Cria (1976); Kolya (1996); The Nest (1980)

Spirits of the Dead *See* Boccaccio '70 (1962)

Spivs *See* I Vitelloni (1953)

The Split *See* The Manster (1959)

The Spooky Movie Show *See* The Mask (1961)

Spoorloos *See* The Vanishing (1988)

Stagecoach *See* And the Ship Sails On (1983); The Good, the Bad, and the Ugly (1967); La Nuit de Varennes (1982)

Stairway to Heaven *See* Ikiru (1952)

Stalker (1979) *See also* The Sacrifice (1986); Solaris (1972)

Star 80 *See* City of Women (1981)

Star Wars *See* The Green Slime (1968); The Hidden Fortress (1958); Kind Hearts and Coronets (1949)

Starstruck *See* My Brilliant Career (1979)

State of Siege (1973) *See also* The Confession (1970)

The State of Things *See* Kings of the Road—In the Course of Time (1976)

The Stationmaster's Wife (1977)

Steamboat Bill, Jr. *See* Police Story (1985)

The Stepfather *See* The Adjuster (1991); Béatrice (1988); Beau Père (1981)

The Stolen Children (1992) *See also* La Scorta (1994); Lamerica (1995); Landscape in the Mist (1988)

Stolen Kisses (1968) *See also* Bed and Board (1970); Confidentially Yours (1983); The 400 Blows (1959); Love on the Run (1978)

Storm over Asia (1928)

The Story of Adele H. (1975) *See also* The Bride Wore Black (1968); Camille Claudel (1989); Confidentially Yours (1983); The Green Room (1978); Last Tango in Paris (1973); Le Jour Se Lève (1939); The Man Who Loved Women (1977); Mississippi Mermaid (1969); Small Change (1976); Two English Girls (1972); The Woman Next Door (1981)

The Story of Boys and Girls *See* Jamón, Jamón (1993); Like Water for Chocolate (1993)

The Story of Qiu Ju (1991) *See also* Ermo (1994); Raise the Red Lantern (1991); To Live (1994); Women from the Lake of Scented Souls (1994)

The Story of Women (1988) *See also* Lacombe, Lucien (1974); Violette (1978)

Stowaway in the Sky *See* The Red Balloon (1956)

The Strange Adventure of David Gray *See* Vampyr (1931)

The Strange Ones *See* Les Enfants Terribles (1950)

Stranger than Paradise *See* Ariel (1989); Stroszek (1977)

Stranger's Face *See* The Face of Another (1966)

Strangers on a Train *See* The American Friend (1977); Brief Encounter (1946); Le Beau Mariage (1982); Purple Noon (1960)

Straw Dogs *See* La Femme Infidèle (1969)

Strawberry and Chocolate (1993) *See also* Memories of Underdevelopment (1968)

Stray Dog (1949) *See also* The Bad Sleep Well (1960); Drunken Angel (1948); High & Low (1962); Sanshiro Sugata (1943)

Street of Sorrow *See* The Joyless Street (1925)

Strictly Ballroom *See* Shall We Dance? (1997)

Strike (1924) *See also* Arsenal (1929); The Battleship Potemkin (1925); Chapayev (1934); Storm over Asia (1928); Ten Days That Shook the World (1927)

Stroszek (1977) *See also* Ariel (1989); Céleste (1981); Every Man for Himself & God Against All (1975); Leningrad Cowboys Go America (1989); Woyzeck (1978)

Subway (1985) *See also* Le Dernier Combat (1984)

Such a Gorgeous Kid Like Me *See* A Very Curious Girl (1969)

Sugar Cane Alley (1983) *See also* Mon Oncle Antoine (1971)

Sugarbaby (1985) *See also* Céleste (1981); Egg (1988)

Summer *See* Boyfriends & Girlfriends (1988); Chloe in the Afternoon (1972); Full Moon in Paris (1984); My Night at Maud's (1969); Pauline at the Beach (1983); Rendezvous in Paris (1995); A Tale of Springtime (1992); A Tale of Winter (1992)

Summer Interlude (1950)

Summer with Monika *See* Monika (1952)

Summerplay *See* Summer Interlude (1950)

A Summer's Tale *See* Boyfriends & Girlfriends (1988); A Tale of Springtime (1992); A Tale of Winter (1992)

Suna No Onna *See* Woman in the Dunes (1964)

Sunday *See* A Self-Made Hero (1995)

A Sunday in the Country *See* The Judge and the Assassin (1975)

Sundays & Cybele (1962)

Sunday's Children (1994) *See also* The Best Intentions (1992); The Devil's Eye (1960)

Sunrise *See* Faust (1926); The Last Laugh (1924)

Sunset Boulevard *See* Veronika Voss (1982)

457

Sunset of a Clown See Sawdust and Tinsel (1953)

The Sunshine Boys See Ginger & Fred (1986)

Supercop See Drunken Master (1978)

Suspiria (1977) See also The Bird with the Crystal Plumage (1970); Black Sunday (1960); The Brainiac (1961)

Swann in Love See Céleste (1981)

Sweet Charity See Nights of Cabiria (1957); The White Sheik (1952)

Sweet Dreams See Edith & Marcel (1983)

The Sweet Hereafter (1996) See also The Adjuster (1991); Beau Père (1981); Exotica (1994); This Man Must Die (1970)

Sweetie (1989) See also Love Serenade (1996); The Piano (1993); Two Friends (1986)

Swept Away… (1975) See also Love and Anarchy (1973); Seven Beauties (1976)

Swept Away…By an Unusual Destiny in the Blue Sea of August See Swept Away… (1975)

Switchblade Sisters See Bandit Queen (1994)

Sylvia and the Phantom See Devil in the Flesh (1946)

Sympathy for the Devil (1970)

Szegenylegenyek Nehezeletuck See The Round-Up (1966)

Szerelem See Love (1971)

Taking Off See The Firemen's Ball (1968); Loves of a Blonde (1965)

A Tale of Springtime (1992) See also A Tale of Winter (1992)

A Tale of Winter (1992) See also A Tale of Springtime (1992)

Tales from the Gimli Hospital See Careful (1994)

Tales of Manhattan See L'Argent (1983)

Tales of Ordinary Madness See La Grande Bouffe (1973)

Tales of the Pale and Silver Moon After the Rain See Ugetsu (1953)

The Tall Blond Man with One Black Shoe See A Chef in Love (1996); Les Compères (1983)

Ta'm e Guilass See Taste of Cherry (1996)

Tampopo (1986) See also Babette's Feast (1987); A Chef in Love (1996); The Family Game (1983); The Funeral (1984); Jamón,

Jamón (1993); La Grande Bouffe (1973); The Makioka Sisters (1983); Minbo—Or the Gentle Art of Japanese Extortion (1992); A Taxing Woman (1987)

Tango See Blood Wedding (1981)

Tango & Cash See Andrei Rublev (1966)

The Tango Lesson (1997) See also Orlando (1992)

Tanin No Kao See The Face of Another (1966)

Taste of Cherries See Taste of Cherry (1996)

Taste of Cherry (1996) See also Through the Olive Trees (1994); The White Balloon (1995)

Taxi Blues See Little Vera (1988)

Taxi Driver See Day of Wrath (1943); The Middleman (1976); Pickpocket (1959); Vengeance Is Mine (1979)

A Taxing Woman (1987) See also The Funeral (1984); Minbo—Or the Gentle Art of Japanese Extortion (1992); Tampopo (1986)

A Taxing Woman's Return See Minbo—Or the Gentle Art of Japanese Extortion (1992); Tampopo (1986); A Taxing Woman (1987)

Teen Kanya See Two Daughters (1961)

The Temptation of Dr. Antonio See Boccaccio '70 (1962)

Temptress Moon (1996)

Ten Days That Shook the World (1927) See also The Battleship Potemkin (1925); Chapayev (1934); Strike (1924)

The Tenant (1976) See also Careful (1994); Deep End (1970); The Fearless Vampire Killers (1967); Monsieur Hire (1989); Repulsion (1965)

Tengoku To Jigoku See High & Low (1962)

Terms of Endearment See Autumn Sonata (1978)

Terror of Dracula See Nosferatu (1922)

Testament See Fahrenheit 451 (1966)

Testament in Evil See The Testament of Dr. Cordelier (1959)

The Testament of Dr. Cordelier (1959)

The Testament of Dr. Mabuse See Dr. Mabuse, Parts 1 & 2 (1922)

The Testament of Orpheus (1959) See also Orpheus (1949); Van Gogh (1992)

Tetsuo See Tetsuo: The Iron Man (1992)

Tetsuo: The Iron Man (1992) See also Akira (1989)

Tetsuo II: Body Hammer See Tetsuo: The Iron Man (1992)

Tevye the Milkman See The Dybbuk (1937)

That Obscure Object of Desire (1977) See also The Criminal Life of Archibaldo de la Cruz (1955); Half of Heaven (1986); The Phantom of Liberty (1974); Tristana (1970)

Their First Trip to Tokyo See Tokyo Story (1953)

Thelma and Louise See Viva Maria! (1965)

There's Always Tomorrow See The Bitter Tears of Petra von Kant (1972); Brief Encounter (1946)

Thérèse (1986) See also Monsieur Vincent (1947)

They Came from Within (1975) See also 301, 302 (1994)

They Loved Life See Kanal (1956)

They Who Step on the Tiger's Tail See The Men Who Tread on the Tiger's Tail (1945)

The Thief (1997)

The Thief of Paris (1967) See also Phantom India (1969); Pickpocket (1959)

Thieves See Les Voleurs (1996); Ma Saison Préférée (1993)

The Thin Blue Line See The Confession (1970); A Cry in the Dark (1988)

The Thing with Two Heads See The Manster (1959)

The 39 Steps See Spies (1928)

37.2 Degrees in the Morning See Betty Blue (1986)

37.2 le Matin See Betty Blue (1986)

32 Short Films about Glenn Gould (1993) See also Providence (1977)

This Is Spinal Tap See Leningrad Cowboys Go America (1989); Project Grizzly (1996)

This Man Must Die (1970) See also La Femme Infidèle (1969); La Rupture (1970)

This Sporting Life (1963)

This Strange Passion See Él (1952)

Those Who Tread on the Tiger's Tail See The Men Who Tread on the Tiger's Tail (1945)

A Thousand and One Nights See Arabian Nights (1974)

Three Bad Men in the Hidden Fortress See The Hidden Fortress (1958)

Three Brothers (1980) *See also* Christ Stopped at Eboli (1979)

Three Colors: Blue *See* Trois Couleurs: Bleu (1993)

Three Colors: Red *See* Trois Couleurs: Rouge (1994)

Three Colors: White *See* Trois Couleurs: Blanc (1994)

301, 302 (1994) *See also* The Cook, the Thief, His Wife & Her Lover (1990)

301–302 *See* 301, 302 (1994)

3 Penny Opera *See* The Threepenny Opera (1931)

Three Rascals in the Hidden Fortress *See* The Hidden Fortress (1958)

The Threepenny Opera (1931) *See also* Diary of a Lost Girl (1929)

Throne of Blood (1957) *See also* Chimes at Midnight (1967); Ran (1985)

Through a Glass Darkly (1961) *See also* Monika (1952); The Passion of Anna (1970); Sawdust and Tinsel (1953); Shame (1968); The Silence (1963); The Virgin Spring (1959); Winter Light (1962)

Through the Olive Trees (1994) *See also* Life and Nothing More … (1992); The White Balloon (1995)

THX 1138 *See* Subway (1985)

Tianguo Niezi *See* The Day the Sun Turned Cold (1994)

Ticket to Heaven (1981)

Tie Me Up! Tie Me Down! (1990)

Tight Little Island *See* The Man in the White Suit (1951)

Tightrope *See* The Mask (1961)

Tilaï (1990) *See also* Yaaba (1989)

Time After Time *See* Insignificance (1985)

Time in the Sun *See* Que Viva Mexico (1932)

The Time of Return *See* Muriel (1963)

Time Stands Still (1982) *See also* Hey, Babu Riba (1988); Twist & Shout (1984)

The Tin Drum (1979) *See also* The Lost Honor of Katharina Blum (1975)

Tini Zabutykh Predkiv *See* Shadows of Forgotten Ancestors (1964)

Tirez sur le Pianiste *See* Shoot the Piano Player (1962)

Titanic *See* And the Ship Sails On (1983); French Twist (1995); Heavenly Creatures (1994); War and Peace (1968)

Tito and I *See* Tito and Me (1992)

Tito and Me (1992) *See also* Angi Vera (1978); Kolya (1996); Love (1971); Man of Marble (1976); Time Stands Still (1982); Underground (1995); When Father Was Away on Business (1985)

Tito i Ja *See* Tito and Me (1992)

To Be or Not to Be *See* Generale Della Rovere (1960); Kagemusha (1980); La Cage aux Folles (1978)

To Catch a Thief *See* The Thief of Paris (1967)

To Live (1994) *See also* The Blue Kite (1993); Ermo (1994); Farewell My Concubine (1993); Ikiru (1952)

To Our Loves *See* A Nos Amours (1984)

To Vlemma Tou Odyssea *See* Ulysses' Gaze (1995)

Tokyo Monogatari *See* Tokyo Story (1953)

Tokyo Olympiad (1966)

Tokyo Story (1953) *See also* An Autumn Afternoon (1962); Autumn Sonata (1978); Black Rain (1988); Late Spring (1949); The Makioka Sisters (1983); Red Beard (1965); Seven Beauties (1976)

Tom Jones *See* Saturday Night and Sunday Morning (1960)

Tomorrow Never Dies *See* Drunken Master (1978)

Toni (1934) *See also* Boudu Saved from Drowning (1932)

Too Beautiful for You (1988) *See also* French Twist (1995); Get Out Your Handkerchiefs (1978); Sugarbaby (1985)

Topio Stin Omichli *See* Landscape in the Mist (1988)

Topkapi *See* Big Deal on Madonna Street (1958)

Tora No O Wo Fumu Otokotachi *See* The Men Who Tread on the Tiger's Tail (1945)

Tora! Tora! Tora! *See* Dodes 'ka-den (1970)

Torment (1944) *See also* Miss Julie (1950); Sawdust and Tinsel (1953)

The Total Balalaika Show *See* Leningrad Cowboys Go America (1989)

Toto le Heros (1991)

Toto the Hero *See* Toto le Heros (1991)

Touch of Evil *See* Chimes at Midnight (1967); Going Places (1974); Mr. Arkadin (1955); Zentropa (1992)

A Touch of Zen *See* Sanshiro Sugata (1943)

Touchez Pas au Grisbi *See* Bob le Flambeur (1955); Casque d'Or (1952)

Tous les Matins du Monde (1992) *See also* Carnival in Flanders (1935); Farinelli (1994); 32 Short Films about Glenn Gould (1993); Un Coeur en Hiver (1993)

Tout va Bien *See* Every Man for Himself (1979)

Traffic (1971)

The Traveling Players *See* Bye Bye Brazil (1979); Ulysses' Gaze (1995)

Tre Fratelli *See* Three Brothers (1980)

The Tree of Wooden Clogs (1978) *See also* Lamerica (1995)

The Trial (1963)

The Trial of Joan of Arc *See* The Passion of Joan of Arc (1928)

A Trip to the Moon *See* Woman in the Moon (1929)

Tristana (1970) *See also* Belle de Jour (1967); The Criminal Life of Archibaldo de la Cruz (1955); The Garden of Delights (1970); Half of Heaven (1986); Lovers: A True Story (1990); Swept Away… (1975); Tetsuo: The Iron Man (1992); Woman in the Dunes (1964)

Triumph des Willens *See* Triumph of the Will (1934)

Triumph of the Will (1934) *See also* The Blue Light (1932)

Trois Couleurs *See* Trois Couleurs: Blanc (1994); Trois Couleurs: Bleu; Trois Couleurs: Rouge (1994)

Trois Couleurs: Blanc (1994) *See also* Trois Couleurs: Bleu (1993); Trois Couleurs: Rouge (1994)

Trois Couleurs: Bleu (1993) *See also* Trois Couleurs: Blanc (1994); Trois Couleurs: Rouge (1994)

Trois Couleurs: Rouge (1994) *See also* Trois Couleurs: Blanc (1994); Trois Couleurs: Bleu (1993)

Trop Belle pour Toi *See* Too Beautiful for You (1988)

The Trouble with Harry *See* Death of a Bureaucrat (1966)

The Troubles We've Seen *See* The Sorrow and the Pity (1971)

The Truck *See* Last Year at Marienbad (1961)

The Truman Show *See* Gallipoli (1981); Picnic at Hanging Rock (1975)

Tsubaki Sanjuro *See* Sanjuro (1962)

Tulitkkutehtaan Tytto *See* The Match Factory Girl (1990)

12 Monkeys *See* La Jetée (1962)

28 Up *See* Anna (1993)

20,000 Leagues under the Sea *See* Liebelei (1932)

Twilight of the Cockroaches *See* Fantastic Planet (1973)

Twin Peaks *See* The Kingdom (1995)

Twins *See* Dead Ringers (1988)

Twist & Shout (1984) *See also* Hey, Babu Riba (1988)

Twister *See* The 4th Man (1979)

Twitch of the Death Nerve *See* Black Sunday (1960)

Two Daughters (1961) *See also* The Big City (1963); The World of Apu (1959)

Two English Girls (1972) *See also* Fahrenheit 451 (1966); The Green Room (1978); Jules and Jim (1962)

Two for the Road *See* Saturday Night and Sunday Morning (1960)

Two Friends (1986) *See also* Careful, He Might Hear You (1984); Muriel's Wedding (1994); Sweetie (1989)

Two Mikes Don't Make a Wright *See* High Hopes (1988); Kind Hearts and Coronets (1949)

2001: A Space Odyssey *See* Fellini Satyricon (1969); Himatsuri (1985); Solaris (1972); The Valley Obscured by the Clouds (1972)

The Two of Us (1968) *See also* Kolya (1996)

Two or Three Things I Know About Her (1966) *See also* A Married Woman (1965); Vive L'Amour (1994)

Two Weeks in Another Town *See* Beware of a Holy Whore (1970)

Tystnaden *See* The Silence (1963)

Uccidero Un Uomo *See* This Man Must Die (1970)

Ugetsu (1953) *See also* 47 Ronin, Part 1 (1942); Gate of Hell (1954); Kwaidan (1964); Princess Yang Kwei Fei (1955); Sansho the Bailiff (1954); Utamaro and His Five Women (1946)

Ugetsu Monogatari *See* Ugetsu (1953)

Ugly, Dirty and Bad *See* Down & Dirty (1976)

Ulysses' Gaze (1995) *See also* Landscape in the Mist (1988); The Spider's Stratagem (1970)

Umberto D. (1955) *See also* Miracle in Milan (1951);

Yesterday, Today and Tomorrow (1964)

The Umbrellas of Cherbourg (1964) *See also* Black Orpheus (1958); Donkey Skin (1970); Jacquot (1991); Le Bonheur (1965); Liebelei (1932); Lola (1961); My Life to Live (1962); A Woman Is a Woman (1960)

Un Air de Famille *See* When the Cat's Away (1996)

Un Chien Andalou *See* The Blood of a Poet (1930); L'Age D'Or (1930); That Obscure Object of Desire (1977)

Un Coeur en Hiver (1993) *See also* Basileus Quartet (1982); César & Rosalie (1972); Nelly et Monsieur Arnaud (1995); Orchestra Rehearsal (1978); Tous les Matins du Monde (1992); Vincent, François, Paul and the Others (1976)

Un Condamne a Mort s'Est Echappe, Ou le Vent Souffle ou Il Vent *See* A Man Escaped (1957)

Un Heros Tres Discret *See* A Self-Made Hero (1995)

Un Homme et une Femme *See* A Man and a Woman (1966)

Una Giornata Speciale *See* A Special Day (1977)

Under the Olive Trees *See* Taste of Cherry (1996); Through the Olive Trees (1994)

Under the Roofs of Paris (1929)

Underground (1995) *See also* Before the Rain (1994); Kanal (1956); Love (1971); The Lower Depths (1936); My Twentieth Century (1990); 1900 (1976); Tito and Me (1992); When Father Was Away on Business (1985)

Une Affaire de Femmes *See* The Story of Women (1988)

Une Femme Douce *See* A Gentle Woman (1969); The Lacemaker (1977); Mouchette (1967)

Une Femme Est une Femme *See* A Woman Is a Woman (1960)

Une Noire de… *See* Black Girl (1966)

The Unfaithful Wife *See* La Femme Infidèle (1969)

Unforgiven *See* A Fistful of Dollars (1964)

The Unknown *See* Variety (1925)

The Untouchables *See* The Battleship Potemkin (1925)

The Unvanquished *See* Aparajito (1958)

The Usual Unidentified Thieves *See* Big Deal on Madonna Street (1958)

Utamaro and His Five Women (1946)

Utamaro O Meguru Gonin No Onna *See* Utamaro and His Five Women (1946)

Utvandrarna *See* The Emigrants (1972)

Vagabond (1985) *See also* A Nos Amours (1984); Jacquot (1991); The Little Thief (1989)

The Valley Obscured by the Clouds (1972)

The Vampire *See* Vampyr (1931)

Vampyr (1931) *See also* Day of Wrath (1943); Nosferatu (1922); Witchcraft through the Ages (1922)

Vampyr, Der Traum des David Gray *See* Vampyr (1931)

Vampyr, Ou L'Etrange Aventure de David Gray *See* Vampyr (1931)

Van Gogh (1992) *See also* Edvard Munch (1974)

The Vanishing (1988) *See also* Butterfly Kiss (1994); Insomnia (1997)

Vanya on 42nd Street *See* Basileus Quartet (1982); Days and Nights in the Forest (1970); May Fools (1990)

Vargtimmen *See* The Hour of the Wolf (1968)

Variete *See* Variety (1925)

Variety (1925)

Variety Lights (1951) *See also* Ginger & Fred (1986); Orchestra Rehearsal (1978); The White Sheik (1952)

Vaudeville *See* Variety (1925)

Vengeance Is Mine (1979)

Vernon, Florida *See* Heart of Glass (1974)

Veronika Voss (1982) *See also* Effi Briest (1974); The Marriage of Maria Braun (1979); Zentropa (1992)

Vertigo *See* Black Narcissus (1947); Captain's Paradise (1953); Claire's Knee (1971); Crash (1995); Diabolique (1955); Fahrenheit 451 (1966); The Green Room (1978); The Hairdresser's Husband (1992); The Mystery of Rampo (1994); The Story of Adele H. (1975); The Woman Next Door (1981)

A Very Curious Girl (1969)

A Very Discreet Hero *See* A Self-Made Hero (1995)

Vesnicko Ma Strediskova *See* My Sweet Little Village (1986)

Victim (1961)

Videodrome *See* Tetsuo: The Iron Man (1992); Ticket to Heaven (1981)

Vincent, François, Paul and the Others (1976) *See also* César & Rosalie (1972); Nelly et Monsieur Arnaud (1995); Un Coeur en Hiver (1993)

Vincent, François, Paul et les Autres *See* Vincent, François, Paul and the Others (1976)

Violence et Passion *See* Conversation Piece (1975)

Violette (1978) *See also* The Lacemaker (1977); Les Biches (1968); The Story of Women (1988); This Man Must Die (1970)

Violette Noziere *See* Violette (1978)

The Virgin Spring (1959) *See also* The Devil's Eye (1960)

Viridiana (1961) *See also* The Criminal Life of Archibaldo de la Cruz (1955); Diary of a Chambermaid (1964); The Discreet Charm of the Bourgeoisie (1972); Los Olvidados (1950); The Milky Way (1968); The Nest (1980); Simon of the Desert (1966); Tristana (1970); Wuthering Heights (1953)

Visions of Eight *See* Tokyo Olympiad (1966)

Viskingar Och Rop *See* Cries and Whispers (1972)

Vitelloni *See* I Vitelloni (1953)

Viva Maria! (1965)

Vive L'Amour (1994)

Vivement Dimanche! *See* Confidentially Yours (1983)

Vivre Sa Vie *See* My Life to Live (1962)

Voices of the Moon *See* Intervista (1987)

Volere Volare *See* Allegro Non Troppo (1976); The Icicle Thief (1989)

Vor *See* The Thief (1997)

Voskhozhdeniye *See* The Ascent (1976)

Vredens Dag *See* Day of Wrath (1943)

Vynález Zkázy *See* Fabulous Adventures of Baron Munchausen (1961); The Fabulous World of Jules Verne (1958)

The Wages of Fear (1955) *See also* Diabolique (1955)

Wake in Fright *See* Outback (1971)

Walkabout (1971)

Walkers on the Tiger's Tail *See* The Men Who Tread on the Tiger's Tail (1945)

The Wannsee Conference (1984)

Wannseekonferenz *See* The Wannsee Conference (1984)

The Wanton Contessa *See* Senso (1954)

The Wanton Countess *See* Senso (1954)

War and Peace (1968)

The War Game (1965) *See also* Edvard Munch (1974)

Warnung Vor Einer Helligen Nutte *See* Beware of a Holy Whore (1970)

Waru Yatsu Hodo Yoku Nemuru *See* The Bad Sleep Well (1960)

The Wasp Woman *See* Eyes without a Face (1959)

Waterloo *See* War and Peace (1968)

Waxworks (1924)

The Way *See* Yol (1982)

Ways of Love *See* The Miracle (1948)

We All Loved Each Other So Much (1977) *See also* Down & Dirty (1976); A Special Day (1977)

We the Living (1942)

A Wedding *See* Contract (1980)

The Wedding Banquet *See* Women from the Lake of Scented Souls (1994)

Wedding in Blood (1974) *See also* Les Biches (1968)

Weekend (1967) *See also* Alphaville (1965); Les Carabiniers (1963); Masculine Feminine (1966); Traffic (1971)

Welcome to the Dollhouse *See* The Family Game (1983); Spirit of the Beehive (1973)

Welfare *See* Umberto D. (1955)

The Well-Digger's Daughter *See* The Baker's Wife (1933)

The Well-Made Marriage *See* Le Beau Mariage (1982)

West Side Story *See* The Killer (1990)

What Have I Done to Deserve This? *See* The Flower of My Secret (1995); Kika (1994); Tie Me Up! Tie Me Down! (1990); Women on the Verge of a Nervous Breakdown (1988)

When a Woman Ascends the Stairs (1960) *See also* Life of Oharu (1952)

When Father Was Away on Business (1985) *See also* Angi Vera (1978); Love (1971); Tito and Me (1992); Underground (1995)

When the Cat's Away (1996) *See also* Augustin (1995); Vive L'Amour (1994); Zita (1968)

Where Is My Friend's House? *See* Life and Nothing More … (1992); Through the Olive Trees (1994)

Whiskey Galore *See* The Man in the White Suit (1951)

White *See* The Double Life of Veronique (1991); Trois Couleurs: Blanc (1994)

The White Balloon (1995) *See also* Gabbeh (1996); Life and Nothing More … (1992); Spirit of the Beehive (1973)

White Mischief *See* The Postman (1994)

The White Sheik (1952) *See also* Amarcord (1974); Juliet of the Spirits (1965); Love in the City (1953)

A White White Boy *See* The Mirror (1975)

Whity *See* Beware of a Holy Whore (1970)

Who Framed Roger Rabbit *See* The Icicle Thief (1989)

Who Killed Pasolini? *See* La Scorta (1994)

The Wild Bunch *See* Andrei Rublev (1966); The Good, the Bad, and the Ugly (1967); The Killer (1990); Like Water for Chocolate (1993); Seven Samurai (1954); The Tango Lesson (1997)

The Wild Child (1970) *See also* The Bride Wore Black (1968); Every Man for Himself & God Against All (1975); Kaspar Hauser (1993); Les Mistons (1957); Small Change (1976)

Wild Flower *See* Fiorile (1993)

Wild Horses of Fire *See* Shadows of Forgotten Ancestors (1964)

Wild Reeds (1994) *See also* French Provincial (1975); Les Voleurs (1996); Ma Saison Préférée (1993); Scene of the Crime (1987)

Wild Strawberries (1957) *See also* Dreams (1955); The Magician (1958); A Woman's Tale (1992)

The Wind *See* Wild Strawberries (1957)

Wind from the East *See* Every Man for Himself (1979); Sympathy for the Devil (1970)

Wings of Desire (1988) *See also* Breaking the Waves (1995); Faraway, So Close! (1993); In the White City (1983); Kings of the Road—In the Course of Time (1976); The Tango Lesson (1997)

Winter Light (1962) *See also* The Passion of Anna (1970); The Silence (1963); Through a Glass Darkly

461

(1961); The Virgin Spring (1959)

Witchcraft through the Ages (1922)

Witness *See* Picnic at Hanging Rock (1975)

Wittgenstein *See* Caravaggio (1986)

Woman from the Lake of Scented Souls *See* Ermo (1994)

Woman in the Dunes (1964) *See also* The Exterminating Angel (1962); The Face of Another (1966); Gate of Hell (1954); Samurai Rebellion (1967)

Woman in the Moon (1929) *See also* Metropolis (1926)

The Woman in the Window *See* La Chienne (1931)

A Woman Is a Woman (1960)

The Woman Next Door (1981) *See also* The Bride Wore Black (1968); Confidentially Yours (1983); In the Realm of the Senses (1976); Mississippi Mermaid (1969); Two English Girls (1972)

Woman of the Dunes *See* Woman in the Dunes (1964)

Woman Times Seven *See* Yesterday, Today and Tomorrow (1964)

A Woman's Tale (1992) *See also* Cactus (1986); Man of Flowers (1984)

Women *See* The Flower of My Secret (1995)

The Women *See* Antonia's Line (1995)

Women from the Lake of Scented Souls (1994)

Women on the Verge of a Nervous Breakdown (1988) *See also* The Flower of My Secret (1995); Kika (1994); Matador (1986)

The Wonderful Crook (1975) *See also* The Lacemaker (1977)

The Wonderful, Horrible Life of Leni Riefenstahl *See* The Blue Light (1932) General Idi Amin Dada (1975)

The Wooden Man's Bride *See* The Horse Thief (1987)

The Word *See* Ordet (1955)

The World of Apu (1959) *See also* Aparajito (1958); Jalsaghar (1958); Pather Panchali (1954); Phantom India (1969)

The Worse You Are, the Better You Sleep *See* The Bad Sleep Well (1960)

Woyzeck (1978) *See also* Every Man for Himself & God Against All (1975)

WR: Mysteries of the Organism *See* Man Is Not a Bird (1965)

Wrestling Women vs. the Aztec Mummy *See* King Kong vs. Godzilla (1963)

Written on the Wind *See* Ali: Fear Eats the Soul (1974)

The Wrong Arm of the Law *See* Heavens Above! (1963); I'm All Right, Jack (1959)

Wrong Is Right *See* Man Bites Dog (1991)

Wuthering Heights (1953) *See also* El (1952)

X—The Man with the X-Ray Eyes *See* The Mask (1961)

Xala (1975) *See also* Ceddo (1978); Guelwaar (1994); Sambizanga (1972)

Xica (1976) *See also* Quilombo (1984)

Yaaba (1989) *See also* Tilaï (1990)

Yao a Yao Yao Dao Waipo Qiao *See* Shanghai Triad (1995)

The Year of Living Dangerously *See* Gallipoli (1981); Picnic at Hanging Rock (1975)

Yesterday, Today and Tomorrow (1964) *See also* Boccaccio '70 (1962); Casanova '70 (1965); Love in the City (1953)

Ying Huang Boon Sik *See* A Better Tomorrow (1986)

Yoidore Tenshi *See* Drunken Angel (1948)

Yojimbo (1961) *See also* The Bad Sleep Well (1960); A Fistful of Dollars (1964); Harakiri (1962); The Hidden Fortress (1958); The Men Who Tread on the Tiger's Tail (1945); Samurai Rebellion (1967); Sanjuro (1962); Seven Samurai (1954)

Yokihi *See* Princess Yang Kwei Fei (1955)

Yol (1982)

The Young and the Damned *See* Los Olvidados (1950)

The Young and the Passionate *See* I Vitelloni (1953)

The Young Girls of Rochefort *See* Jacquot (1991); The Umbrellas of Cherbourg (1964)

The Young Poisoner's Handbook (1994) *See also* Mon Oncle d'Amerique (1980); My Left Foot (1989)

Yume *See* Akira Kurosawa's Dreams (1990)

Z (1969) *See also* The Bad Sleep Well (1960); The Confession (1970); La Scorta (1994); Man of Marble (1976); State of Siege (1973)

Zabriskie Point *See* The Eclipse (1966); One Sings, the Other Doesn't (1977)

Zamri Oumi Voskresni *See* Freeze-Die-Come to Life (1990)

Zappa *See* Twist & Shout (1984)

Zazie dans le Metro *See* Murmur of the Heart (1971); Viva Maria! (1965)

A Zed and Two Noughts *See* The Belly of an Architect (1991)

Zelig *See* The Conformist (1971)

Zemlya *See* Earth (1930)

Zendegi Va Digar Hich… *See* Life and Nothing More … (1992)

Zentropa (1992) *See also* The Kingdom (1995)

Zerkalo *See* The Mirror (1975)

Zero de Conduit *See* Zero for Conduct (1933)

Zero for Conduct (1933) *See also* A Propos de Nice (1929); The Devil's Playground (1976); Hate (1995); If… (1969); L'Atalante (1934)

Zire Darakhtan Zeyton *See* Through the Olive Trees (1994)

Zita (1968)

Zuckerbaby *See* Sugarbaby (1985)

Zvenigora *See* Arsenal (1929)

COUNTRY OF ORIGIN INDEX

The "Country of Origin Index" classifies movies by the country of record in which they were produced. Since a film may be financed or produced in more than one country, some videos will appear with more than one country of origin. The codes appear in the review, immediately following the color/black and white designation before the credits. In this index, movies are listed alphabetically by country.

Algerian
The Battle of Algiers

Argentinean
I Don't Want to Talk
About It

Australian
Cactus
Careful, He Might Hear
You
The Chant of Jimmie
Blacksmith
A Cry in the Dark
The Devil's Playground
Gallipoli
Love Serenade
Man of Flowers
Muriel's Wedding
My Brilliant Career
Outback
The Piano
Picnic at Hanging Rock
Proof
Sweetie
Two Friends
Walkabout
A Woman's Tale

Belgian
Farinelli
La Promesse
Man Bites Dog
One Sings, the Other
Doesn't

Brazilian
Antonio Das Mortes
Black God, White Devil
Black Orpheus
Bye Bye Brazil
Dona Flor and Her Two
Husbands
Pixote
Quilombo
Xica

British
Bandit Queen
Beautiful Thing
Before the Rain
The Belly of an Architect
Bhaji on the Beach
A Bigger Splash
Black Narcissus

Bleak Moments
Blow-Up
Blue
Brief Encounter
Butterfly Kiss
Captain's Paradise
Caravaggio
The Case of the
Mukkinese Battle
Horn
Comfort and Joy
The Cook, the Thief, His
Wife & Her Lover
Curse of the Demon
Dead of Night
Deep End
The Designated
Mourner
The Devils
Distant Voices, Still Lives
The Draughtsman's
Contract
Dreamchild
Drowning by Numbers
The Fearless Vampire
Killers
The Go-Between
Gumshoe
Hamlet
Heavens Above
Henry V
High Hopes
The Hit
Hollow Reed
How I Won the War
I Know Where I'm Going
If...
Insignificance
Jan Svankmejer's Faust
Juggernaut
Kind Hearts and
Coronets
A Kind of Loving
Land and Freedom
Les Carabiniers
The Life and Death of
Colonel Blimp
Life Is Sweet
Little Dorrit, Film 1:
Nobody's Fault
Little Dorrit, Film 2: Little
Dorrit's Story
Local Hero
The Long Day Closes

The Long Good Friday
Look Back in Anger
The Man in the White
Suit
Margaret's Museum
Mr. Arkadin
A Month in the Country
Monty Python's The
Meaning of Life
Moonlighting
The Music Lovers
Orlando
The Pillow Book
Providence
The Red Shoes
Repulsion
Salaam Bombay!
Saturday Night and
Sunday Morning
Secrets and Lies
The Tango Lesson
This Sporting Life
Victim
The Young Poisoner's
Handbook

Canadian
The Adjuster
The Boys of St. Vincent
Crash
Dead Ringers
Exotica
Jesus of Montreal
Léolo
Les Bons Debarras
Margaret's Museum
The Mask
Mon Oncle Antoine
My Twentieth Century
The Sweet Hereafter
They Came from Within
32 Short Films about
Glenn Gould
Ticket to Heaven

Chinese
A Better Tomorrow
The Blue Kite
Drunken Master
Ermo
The Horse Thief
Ju Dou
Life on a String
A Mongolian Tale
Raise the Red Lantern

Red Sorghum
Shanghai Triad
The Story of Qiu Ju
To Live
Women from the Lake
of Scented Souls

Cuban
Death of a Bureaucrat
I Am Cuba
The Last Supper
Memories of
Underdevelopment
Strawberry and
Chocolate

Czech
The Fabulous World of
Jules Verne
The Firemen's Ball
Jan Svankmejer's Faust
Kolya
Loves of a Blonde
My Sweet Little Village

Danish
Babette's Feast
Breaking the Waves
Day of Wrath
Gertrud
The Kingdom
Ordet
Pelle the Conqueror
Twist & Shout

Dutch
Antonia's Line
Egg
The Forbidden Quest
The 4th Man
In for Treatment
The Pillow Book
The Vanishing

Finnish
Ariel
Leningrad Cowboys Go
America
The Match Factory Girl

French
A Nos Amours
A Nous la Liberté
The Accompanist
Alphaville

463

The American Friend
And God Created
　Woman
Au Revoir les Enfants
Augustin
Babette's Feast
The Baker's Wife
Band of Outsiders
Basileus Quartet
Baxter
Béatrice
Beau Père
Beauty and the Beast
Before the Rain
Belle de Jour
The Best Way
Betty Blue
Black Moon
Black Orpheus
Bob le Flambeur
Borsalino
Boudu Saved from
　Drowning
Boy Meets Girl
Boyfriends & Girlfriends
Breaking the Waves
Breathless
The Bride Wore Black
Burnt by the Sun
Café au Lait
Camille Claudel
Captain Conan
Carnival in Flanders
Casque d'Or
Cat and Mouse
Celestial Clockwork
César
César & Rosalie
A Chef in Love
Children of Paradise
Chloe in the Afternoon
Christ Stopped at Eboli
The City of Lost
　Children
Claire's Knee
The Confession
Confidentially Yours
The Conformist
Contempt
Conversation Piece
The Crime of Monsieur
　Lange
Day for Night
The Decameron
Delicatessen
Devil in the Flesh
Diabolique
Diary of a
　Chambermaid
Diary of a Country Priest
Diary of a Seducer
The Discreet Charm of
　the Bourgeoisie
Diva
Dr. Petiot
Donkey Skin
The Double Life of
　Veronique
The Earrings of
　Madame De…
Edith & Marcel
Eléna and Her Men
Entre-Nous
Erendira
Eternal Return
Eyes Without a Face
Fahrenheit 451
Fanny

Fantastic Planet
Farinelli
Fellini's Roma
The Fire Within
The Flower of My Secret
Forbidden Games
The 400 Blows
Frantic
French Can-Can
French Provincial
French Twist
Full Moon in Paris
A Gentle Woman
Germinal
Get Out Your
　Handkerchiefs
Going Places
The Golden Coach
Grand Illusion
The Green Room
The Hairdresser's
　Husband
Harvest
Hate
Hiroshima, Mon Amour
I Can't Sleep
In the Realm of the
　Senses
Indochine
Is Paris Burning?
Jacquot
Jean de Florette
Jesus of Montreal
Jour de Fete
The Judge and the
　Assassin
Jules and Jim
L.627
La Belle Noiseuse
La Bete Humaine
La Cage aux Folles
La Cérémonie
La Chienne
La Collectionneuse
La Discrete
La Femme Nikita
La Grande Bouffe
La Jetée
La Lectrice
La Marseillaise
La Nuit de Varennes
La Promesse
La Ronde
La Rupture
The Lacemaker
Lacombe, Lucien
L'Age D'Or
Lancelot of the Lake
Landscape in the Mist
L'Argent
The Last Metro
Last Tango in Paris
Last Year at Marienbad
L'Atalante
Le Beau Mariage
Le Bonheur
Le Boucher
Le Dernier Combat
Le Doulos
Le Joli Mai
Le Jour Se Leve
Le Million
Le Plaisir
Le Samourai
Les Biches
Les Carabiniers
Les Comperes
Les Enfants Terrible

Les Mistons
Les Visiteurs du Soir
Les Voleurs
Life and Nothing But
The Little Thief
Lola
Lola Montès
Loulou
Love on the Run
The Lovers
The Lower Depths
Ma Saison Préférée
Madame Rosa
A Man and a Woman
The Man Who Loved
　Women
Manon of the Spring
Marius
The Marquise of O
A Married Woman
Masculine Feminine
Max, Mon Amour
May Fools
The Milky Way
Mina Tannenbaum
Mississippi Mermaid
Mon Oncle
Mon Oncle D'Amerique
Monsieur Hire
Monsieur Vincent
Moon in the Gutter
Mouchette
Muriel
Murmur of the Heart
My Life to Live
My New Partner
My Night at Maud's
Napoleon
Nelly et Monsieur
　Arnaud
Night and Fog
1900
Nosferatu the Vampyre
Olivier, Olivier
One Sings, the Other
　Doesn't
The Passion of Joan of
　Arc
Pauline at the Beach
Pepe Le Moko
Phantom of Liberty
Pickpocket
Pierrot le Fou
The Pillow Book
Playtime
Ponette
A Propos de Nice
Purple Noon
Ramparts of Clay
Ran
The Red Balloon
Rendezvous in Paris
The Return of Martin
　Guerre
Ridicule
The Rise of Louis XIV
The Sacrifice
Scene of the Crime
A Self-Made Hero
Shanghai Triad
Shoot the Piano Player
The Silences of the
　Palace
A Single Girl
Small Change
The Soft Skin
The Sorrow and the Pity
State of Siege

Stolen Kisses
The Story of Adele H.
The Story of Women
Subway
Sugar Cane Alley
Sundays & Cybele
Sympathy for the Devil
A Tale of Springtime
A Tale of Winter
The Tenant
The Testament of Dr.
　Cordelier
The Testament of
　Orpheus
Thérèse
This Man Must Die
Toni
Too Beautiful for You
Toto le Heros
Tous les Matins du
　Monde
Traffic
The Trial
Tristana
Trois Couleurs: Blanc
Trois Couleurs: Bleu
Trois Couleurs: Rouge
Two English Girls
The Two of Us
Two or Three Things I
　Know About Her
Ulysses' Gaze
Umbrellas of Cherbourg
Un Coeur en Hiver
Under the Roofs of Paris
Underground
Vagabond
The Valley Obscured by
　the Clouds
Vampyr
Van Gogh
The Vanishing
A Very Curious Girl
Vincent, Francois, Paul
　and the Others
Violette
Viva Maria!
Wages of Fear
Wedding in Blood
Weekend
When the Cat's Away
The Wild Child
Wild Reeds
A Woman Is a Woman
The Woman Next Door
The Wonderful Crook
Yesterday, Today and
　Tomorrow
Z
Zero for Conduct

German
Aguirre, the Wrath of
　God
Ali: Fear Eats the Soul
The American Friend
The American Soldier
Berlin Alexanderplatz
Beware of a Holy Whore
The Bitter Tears of Petra
　von Kant
The Blue Angel
The Blue Light
The Cabinet of Dr.
　Caligari
Céleste
The Conformist
The Decameron
Deep End

Diary of a Lost Girl
Die Liebe der Jeanne
    Ney
Die Niebelungen
Dr. Mabuse, Parts 1 & 2
Effi Briest
Erendira
Europa, Europa
Every Man for Himself &
    God Against All
Fabulous Adventures of
    Baron Munchausen
Faraway, So Close!
Faust
Fitzcarraldo
The Goalie's Anxiety at
    the Penalty Kick
The Golem
Hanussen
Heart of Glass
Heimat 1
In a Year of 13 Moons
Joyless Street
Kameradschaft
Kaspar Hauser
Kings of the Road—In
    the Course of Time
The Lacemaker
Land and Freedom
The Last Laugh
Liebelei
The Lost Honor of
    Katharina Blum
M
Mäedchen in Uniform
Marianne and Juliane
The Marquise of O
The Marriage of Maria
    Braun
Metropolis
Mother Küsters Goes to
    Heaven
Nelly et Monsieur
    Arnaud
1900
Nosferatu
Nosferatu the Vampyre
Pandora's Box
Spies
The Stationmaster's
    Wife
Stroszek
Sugarbaby
The Tin Drum
Triumph of the Will
Underground
Vampyr
Variety
Veronika Voss
The Wannsee
    Conference
Waxworks
Wings of Desire
Woman in the Moon
Woyzeck
Zentropa

Greek
Landscape in the Mist
Ulysses' Gaze

Hong Kong
Chungking Express
The Day the Sun Turned
    Cold
Farewell My Concubine
Happy Together
Hard-Boiled
The Killer

A Mongolian Tale
Police Story
Temptress Moon

Hungarian
Angi Vera
Hanussen
Love
Mephisto
My Twentieth Century
The Round Up
Time Stands Still
Underground

Indian
Aparajito
Bandit Queen
The Big City
Charulata
Days and Nights in the
    Forest
Devi
Distant Thunder
Jalsaghar
The Middleman
Pather Panchali
Salaam Bombay!
Two Daughters
The World of Apu

Iranian
Life and Nothing More
    …
The Taste of Cherry
Through the Olive Trees
The White Balloon

Irish
My Left Foot

Israeli
Madame Rosa

Italian
Alfredo, Alfredo
Allegro Non Troppo
Allonsanfan
Amarcord
And the Ship Sails On
Arabian Nights
Bandits of Orgosolo
Basileus Quartet
The Battle of Algiers
Before the Revolution
The Belly of an Architect
The Bicycle Thief
Big Deal on Madonna
    Street
The Bird with the
    Crystal Plumage
Bitter Rice
Black Sunday
Blow-Up
Boccaccio '70
Burn!
The Canterbury Tales
Caro Diario
Casanova '70
Christ Stopped at Eboli
Cinema Paradiso
City of Women
The Clowns
The Conformist
Contempt
Conversation Piece
The Decameron
Devil in the Flesh
Divorce—Italian Style
Down & Dirty

The Eclipse
8 1/2
Farinelli
Fellini Satyricon
Fellini's Roma
Fiorile
A Fistful of Dollars
The Flowers of St.
    Francis
The Garden of the Finzi-
    Continis
Generale Della Rovere
Ginger & Fred
The Good, the Bad and
    the Ugly
The Gospel According
    to St. Matthew
I Vitelloni
The Icicle Thief
Il Bell'Antonio
The Innocent
Intervista
Johnny Stecchino
Juliet of the Spirits
Kaos
La Dolce Vita
La Notte
La Nuit de Varennes
La Scorta
La Signora di Tutti
La Strada
La Terra Trema
Lamerica
Landscape in the Mist
Last Tango in Paris
Last Year at Marienbad
L'Avventura
Les Carabiniers
Love and Anarchy
Love in the City
Mamma Roma
The Miracle
Miracle in Milan
Mississippi Mermaid
Mondo Cane
The Monster
Moon in the Gutter
Muriel
Nelly et Monsieur
    Arnaud
The Night of the
    Shooting Stars
The Night Porter
Nights of Cabiria
1900
Once Upon a Time in
    the West
Open City
Orchestra Rehearsal
Ossessione
Paisan
Pierrot le Fou
The Postman
The Red Desert
Rocco and His Brothers
Salo, or the 120 Days of
    Sodom
Senso
Seven Beauties
Shoeshine
A Special Day
The Spider's Stratagem
The Stolen Children
Suspiria
Swept Away…
Three Brothers
The Tree of Wooden
    Clogs

Tristana
Ulysses' Gaze
Umberto D
Variety Lights
Viva Maria!
We All Loved Each
    Other So Much
We the Living
Wedding in Blood
Weekend
The White Sheik
Yesterday, Today and
    Tomorrow

Japanese
Akira
Akira Kurosawa's
    Dreams
An Autumn Afternoon
The Bad Sleep Well
The Ballad of Narayama
Black Rain
The Burmese Harp
Dersu Uzala
Dodes 'ka-den
Drunken Angel
Enjo
Face of Another
The Family Game
Fires on the Plain
47 Ronin, Part 1
47 Ronin, Part 2
The Funeral
Gate of Hell
Godzilla, King of the
    Monsters
The Green Slime
The Hidden Fortress
High & Low
Himatsuri
Hiroshima, Mon Amour
The Human Condition:
    A Soldier's Prayer
The Human Condition:
    No Greater Love
The Human Condition:
    Road to Eternity
I Live in Fear
Ikiru
In the Realm of the
    Senses
Kagemusha
King Kong vs. Godzilla
Kwaidan
Late Spring
Life of Oharu
The Lower Depths
The Makioka Sisters
The Manster
The Men Who Tread on
    the Tiger's Tail
Minbo—Or the Gentle
    Art of Japanese
    Extortion
Mothra
The Mystery of Rampo
Odd Obsession
Okoge
Onibaba
Princess Yang Kwei Fei
Ran
Rashomon
Red Beard
Rhapsody in August
Samurai Rebellion
Sanjuro
Sanshiro Sugata
Sansho the Bailiff
Seven Samurai

Shall We Dance?
Stray Dog
Tampopo
A Taxing Woman
Tetsuo: The Iron Man
Throne of Blood
Tokyo Olympiad
Tokyo Story
Ugetsu
Utamaro and His Five
    Women
Vengeance Is Mine
When a Woman
    Ascends the Stairs
Woman in the Dunes
Yojimbo

Korean
301, 302

Macedonian
Before the Rain

Mexican
The Brainiac
The Criminal Life of
    Archibaldo de la
    Cruz
Él
El Topo
Erendira
The Exterminating
    Angel
Like Water for
    Chocolate
Los Olvidados
Viridiana
Wuthering Heights

New Zealand
Heavenly Creatures
Once Were Warriors

Norwegian
Edvard Munch

Polish
Ashes and Diamonds
Contract
The Double Life of
    Veronique
The Dybbuk
A Generation
Illumination
Kanal
Knife in the Water
Man of Iron
Man of Marble
Moonlighting
The Saragossa
    Manuscript
Trois Couleurs: Blanc
Trois Couleurs: Rouge

Portuguese
Black Orpheus
In the White City

Russian
Alexander Nevsky
Andrei Rublev
Arsenal

The Ascent
Ashik Kerib
Ballad of a Soldier
The Battleship
    Potemkin
Burnt by the Sun
Chapayev
Commissar
Dersu Uzala
Don Quixote
Earth
Freeze-Die-Come to Life
I Am Cuba
Ivan the Terrible, Part 1
Ivan the Terrible, Part 2
The Lady with the Dog
Little Vera
The Man with a Movie
    Camera
The Mirror
Moscow Does Not
    Believe in Tears
Oblomov
The Overcoat
Prisoner of the
    Mountains
Que Viva Mexico
Shadows of Forgotten
    Ancestors
A Slave of Love
Solaris
Stalker
Storm over Asia
Strike
Ten Days That Shook
    the World
The Thief
War and Peace

Spanish
Belle Epoque
Blood Wedding
Carmen
Chimes at Midnight
Cria
The Criminal Life of
    Archibaldo de la
    Cruz
Don Quixote
The Exterminating
    Angel
The Flower of My Secret
The Garden of Delights
Half of Heaven
Jamon, Jamon
Kika
Land and Freedom
Lovers: A True Story
Matador
The Nest
Spirit of the Beehive
That Obscure Object of
    Desire
Tie Me Up! Tie Me
    Down!
Tristana
Viridiana
Women on the Verge of
    a Nervous
    Breakdown

Swedish
After the Rehearsal
Autumn Sonata
The Best Intentions
Cries and Whispers
The Devil's Eye
Dreams
Elvira Madigan
The Emigrants
Face to Face
Fanny and Alexander
Hour of the Wolf
I Am Curious (Yellow)
Jerusalem
The Magic Flute
The Magician
The Man on the Roof
The Match Factory Girl
Miss Julie
Monika
My Life As a Dog
The New Land
The Passion of Anna
Pelle the Conqueror
Persona
The Sacrifice
Sawdust & Tinsel
Scenes from a Marriage
The Shame
The Silence
Smiles of a Summer
    Night
Summer Interlude
Sunday's Children
Through a Glass Darkly
Torment
The Virgin Spring
Wild Strawberries
The Winter Light
Witchcraft through the
    Ages

Swiss
The Boat Is Full
Chimes at Midnight
In the White City
Jonah Who Will Be 25 in
    the Year 2000
La Salamandre
The Lacemaker
Messidor
Trois Couleurs: Blanc
Trois Couleurs: Rouge
The Wonderful Crook

Taiwanese
Vive L'Amour

Turkish
Yol

Vietnamese
The Scent of Green
    Papaya

Yugoslavian
Hey, Babu Riba
Man Is Not a Bird
Tito and Me
When Father Was Away
    on Business

CAST INDEX

The "Cast Index" provides a complete listing of cast members cited within the reviews. The actors' names are alphabetical by last name, and the films they appeared in are listed chronologically, from most recent to the oldest (please note that only the films reviewed in this book are cited).

Thor Michael Aamodt
Insomnia '97

Tetsuo Abe
Boy '69

Toru Abe
The Human Condition:
No Greater Love '58

Alfred Abel
Metropolis '26
Dr. Mabuse, Parts
1 & 2 '22

Franziskus Abgottspon
Messidor '77

Klaus Abramowsky
Europa, Europa '91

Andrei Abrikosov
Alexander Nevsky '38

Victoria Abril
French Twist '95
Kika '94
Lovers: A True Story '90
Tie Me Up! Tie Me
Down! '90
Max, Mon Amour '86
Moon in the Gutter '83

James Addams
L'Avventura '60

Danny Ades
Aguirre, the Wrath of
God '72

Isabelle Adjani
Camille Claudel '89
Subway '85
Nosferatu the
Vampyre '79
The Tenant '76
The Story of Adele H. '75

Mario Adorf
The Tin Drum '79
The Lost Honor of
Katharina Blum '75
The Bird with the
Crystal Plumage '70

Max Adrian
The Devils '71
The Music Lovers '71

Patricia Adriani
The Nest '80

Ali Affi
One Sings, the Other
Doesn't '77

Jenny Agutter
Walkabout '71

Bjorje Ahistedt
Sunday's Children '94

Lalita Ahmed
Bhaji on the Beach '94

Anouk Aimee
A Man and a Woman '66
8 1/2 '63
Lola '61
La Dolce Vita '60

Tarik Akan
Yol '82

Takejo Aki
The Ballad of
Narayama '83

John Alansu
Love Serenade '96

Hans Albers
The Blue Angel '30

Giorgia Albertazzi
Last Year at
Marienbad '61

Guido Alberti
Casanova '70 '65

Luciano Albertini
Arsenal '29

Andre Aleme
Carnival in Flanders '35

Vera Alentova
Moscow Does Not
Believe in Tears '80

Fabio Alessandrini
The Stolen Children '92

Elizabeth Alexander
The Chant of Jimmie
Blacksmith '78

Grigori Alexandrov
The Battleship
Potemkin '25

Omar Alfonso
Death of a
Bureaucrat '66

Hans Alfredson
The New Land '73
Shame '68

Aina Alfredsson
The Emigrants '72

Alia
Ermo '94

N. Alisova
The Lady with the Dog
'59

Michael Allan
Dead of Night '45

Eric Allen
Bleak Moments '71

Louis Allibert
Le Million '31

Pernilla Allwin
Fanny and
Alexander '83

Roy Alon
The Long Good
Friday '80

Chelo Alonso
The Good, the Bad, and
the Ugly '67

Ernesto Alonso
The Criminal Life of
Archibaldo de la
Cruz '55
Wuthering Heights '53

Domenico Alpi
Before the
Revolution '65

Hector Alterio
Basileus Quartet '82
The Nest '80

Elena Altieri
The Bicycle Thief '48

Francesco Aluigi
Orchestra Rehearsal '78

Enrique Garcia Alvarez
The Exterminating
Angel '62

Mathieu Amalric
Diary of a Seducer '95

Shichisaburo Amatsu
Harakiri '62

Amedee
Forbidden Games '52

Claudio Amendola
La Scorta '94

Clementine Amouroux
Messidor '77

Roland Amstutz
Every Man for
Himself '79

Bertil Anderberg
The Hour of the Wolf '68

Jacqueline Andere
The Exterminating
Angel '62

John Andersen
Witchcraft through the
Ages '22

Bibi Andersson
Babette's Feast '87
Scenes from a
Marriage '73
The Passion of Anna '70

Persona '66
The Devil's Eye '60
The Magician '58
Wild Strawberries '57

Harriet Andersson
Fanny and Alexander '83
Cries and Whispers '72
Through a Glass
    Darkly '61
Dreams '55
Smiles of a Summer
    Night '55
Sawdust and Tinsel '53
Monika '52

Peter Andorai
My Twentieth Century
    '90
Mephisto '81

Marcel Andre
Beauty and the Beast '46

Frederic Andrei
Diva '82

Dana Andrews
Curse of the Demon '57

Andrex Andrisson
La Marseillaise '37

Jorge Angelino
Strawberry and
    Chocolate '93

**Jean-Hugues
    Anglade**
Nelly et Monsieur
    Arnaud '95
La Femme Nikita '91
Betty Blue '86
Subway '85

Annabella
Le Million '31

Francesco Anniballi
Down & Dirty '76

Vito Annicchiarico
Open City '45

**Vladimir Antolek-
    Oresek**
Lancelot of the Lake '74

Laura Antonelli
The Innocent '76

Alexander Antonov
The Battleship
    Potemkin '25

Vittorio Antonucci
The Bicycle Thief '48

Omero Antonutti
Farinelli '94
Kaos '85
Basileus Quartet '82
The Night of the
    Shooting Stars '82

Yoshio Aoki
Harakiri '62

Sugisaku Aoyama
Sanshiro Sugata '43

Steven Appleby
The Mask '61

**Julian (Sonny) Ara-
    hanga**
Once Were Warriors '94

Pilar Aranda
Like Water for
    Chocolate '93

Michiyo Aratama
Kwaidan '64
The Human Condition:
    A Soldier's Prayer
    '61
The Human Condition:
    Road to Eternity '59
The Human Condition:
    No Greater Love '58

Alfonso Arau
El Topo '71

Fanny Ardant
Ridicule '96
Confidentially Yours '83
The Woman Next Door
    '81

David Argue
Gallipoli '81

Imanol Arias
The Flower of My Secret
    '95

Ineko Arima
The Human Condition:
    No Greater Love '58

Ben Aris
If… '69

Yareli Arizmendi
Like Water for
    Chocolate '93

Arletty
Children of Paradise '44
Les Visiteurs du Soir '42
Le Jour Se Lève '39

Gisken Armand
Insomnia '97

John Armstrong
Outback '71

Jurgen Arndt
Céleste '81

Francoise Arnoul
French Can-Can '55

Rosanna Arquette
Crash '95

Antonin Artaud
The Passion of Joan of
    Arc '28
Napoleon '27

**Lorraine Ash-
    bourne**
Distant Voices, Still
    Lives '88

Jane Asher
Dreamchild '85
Deep End '70

Renee Asherson
Henry V '45

Troels Asmussen
Pelle the Conqueror '88

Michael Aspel
The War Game '65

Adrianna Asti
The Phantom of Liberty
    '74
Before the
    Revolution '65

Pacifico Astrologo
Shoeshine '47

Annick Asty
Bed and Board '70

Feodor Atkine
Le Beau Mariage '82

Michel Auclair
French Provincial '75
Beauty and the
    Beast '46

Stephane Audran
Babette's Feast '87
Violette '78
Vincent, François, Paul
    and the Others '76
Wedding in Blood '74
The Discreet Charm of
    the Bourgeoisie '72
La Rupture '70
La Femme Infidèle '69
Le Boucher '69
Les Biches '68

Mischa Auer
Mr. Arkadin '55

Claude Aufaure
The Hairdresser's
    Husband '92

Patrick Auffay
The 400 Blows '59

Pernilla August
Jerusalem '96
The Best Intentions '92

**Jean-Pierre
    Aumont**
Cat and Mouse '78
Day for Night '73

Michel Aumont
Les Compères '83

Daniel Auteuil
Les Voleurs '96
Ma Saison Préférée '93
Un Coeur en Hiver '93
Jean de Florette '87
Manon of the Spring '87

Chikage Awashima
The Human Condition:
    No Greater Love '58

Eddie Axberg
The New Land '73
The Emigrants '72

Felix Aylmer
Hamlet '48
Henry V '45

Sabine Azema
Life and Nothing But '89

Charles Aznavour
Edith & Marcel '83
The Tin Drum '79
Shoot the Piano
    Player '62
The Testament of
    Orpheus '59

Jo Azumi
Harakiri '62

Karin Baal
Berlin Alexanderplatz '80

Balduin Baas
Orchestra Rehearsal '78

Fabienne Babe
Les Voleurs '96

Babita
Distant Thunder '73

Boris Babochkin
Chapayev '34

Alain Bacourt
Mon Oncle '58

Gabriel Bacquier
Manon of the Spring '87

Jean-Pierre Bacri
Entre-Nous '83

Alan Badel
This Sporting Life '63

Laurence Badie
Forbidden Games '52

**Abdolrahma
    Bagheri**
Taste of Cherry '96

**Mohammad Bahk-
    tiari**
The White Balloon '95

Antony Baird
Dead of Night '45

Mitsuko Baisho
Akira Kurosawa's
    Dreams '90
Vengeance Is Mine '79

Manoj Bajpai
Bandit Queen '94

Sijiri Bakaba
Camp de Thiaroye '87

Hylda Baker
Saturday Night and
    Sunday Morning '60

Nebojsa Bakocevic
Hey, Babu Riba '88

Josiane Balasko
French Twist '95
Too Beautiful for You '88

Anna Baldaccini
Boy Meets Girl '84
Every Man for Himself
    '79

Christian Bale
Henry V '89

Michael Balfour
The Canterbury Tales '71

Mireille Balin
Pépé le Moko '37

Mario Balmasada
The Last Supper '76

Antonine Balpetre
Diary of a Country
Priest '50

Humbert Balsan
Lancelot of the Lake '74

David Bamber
High Hopes '88

Janos Ban
My Sweet Little
Village '86

Junzaburo Ban
Dodes'ka-den '70

Antonio Banderas
Tie Me Up! Tie Me
Down! '90
Women on the Verge of
a Nervous
Breakdown '88
Matador '86

Kotaro Bando
Utamaro and His Five
Women '46

Minnosuke Bando
Utamaro and His Five
Women '46

Chandana Banerjee
Two Daughters '61

Kanu Banerjee
Aparajito '58
Pather Panchali '54

Karuna Banerjee
Aparajito '58
Pather Panchali '54

Runki Banerji
Pather Panchali '54

Subir Banerji
Pather Panchali '54

Eun-Jin Bang
301, 302 '94

Donatas Banionis
Solaris '72

Caerthan Banks
The Sweet Hereafter '96

Leslie Banks
Henry V '45

Ildiko Bansagi
Mephisto '81

Li Bao-Tian
Shanghai Triad '95
Ju Dou '90

Chen Baoguo
Women from the Lake
of Scented Souls '94

Jiang Baoying
Shanghai Triad '95

Pierre Barbaud
Hiroshima Mon
Amour '59

Paul Barber
The Long Good
Friday '80

Javier Bardem
Jamón, Jamón '93

Aleksander Bardini
Trois Couleurs: Blanc '94
The Double Life of
Veronique '91

Brigitte Bardot
Viva Maria! '65
Contempt '64
And God Created
Woman '57

Nadia Barentin
A Self-Made Hero '95

Francesco Barilli
Before the
Revolution '65

Lex Barker
La Dolce Vita '60

Raju Barnad
Salaam Bombay! '88

Britta Barnes
Fellini's Roma '72

Biagio Barone
Kaos '85

Pierre Barouh
A Man and a Woman '66

Jean-Marc Barr
Breaking the Waves '95
Zentropa '92

Maria Barranco
Tie Me Up! Tie Me
Down! '90
Women on the Verge of
a Nervous
Breakdown '88

Pierre Barrat
The Rise of Louis XIV '66

Jean-Louis Barrault
La Nuit de Varennes '82
The Testament of Dr.
Cordelier '59
La Ronde '51
Children of Paradise '44

**Marie-Christine
Barrault**
Jesus of Montreal '89
Chloe in the
Afternoon '72
My Night at Maud's '69

Ray Barrett
The Chant of Jimmie
Blacksmith '78

John Barrie
Victim '61

Dorothy Barry
Sweetie '89

Roukietou Barry
Tilaï '90
Yaaba '89

Monique Barscha
Every Man for
Himself '79

Vladimir Barsky
The Battleship
Potemkin '25

Margaret Barton
Brief Encounter '46

Richard Basehart
La Strada '54

Relja Basic
Hey, Babu Riba '88

Antoine Basler
Rendezvous in Paris '95

Alfie Bass
The Fearless Vampire
Killers '67

Albert Basserman
The Red Shoes '48

Othon Bastos
Black God, White
Devil '64

Michal Bat-Adam
Madame Rosa '77

Sylvia Bataille
The Crime of Monsieur
Lange '36

Alexei Batalov
Moscow Does Not
Believe in Tears '80
The Lady with the
Dog '59

Pierre Batcheff
Napoleon '27

Alan Bates
The Go-Between '71
A Kind of Loving '62

Gerald Battiaz
Messidor '77

Carlo Battista
Umberto D. '55

Patrick Bauchau
Entre-Nous '83
La Collectionneuse '67

**Michele
Baumgartner**
The Woman Next
Door '81

Jose Baviera
The Exterminating
Angel '62

Keith Baxter
Chimes at Midnight '67

Nathalie Baye
The Return of Martin
Guerre '83
Beau Père '81
Every Man for Himself
'79
The Green Room '78
The Man Who Loved
Women '77
Day for Night '73

**Gustal
Bayrhammer**
The Stationmaster's
Wife '77

Sean Bean
Caravaggio '86

Emmanuelle Beart
Nelly et Monsieur
Arnaud '95
Un Coeur en Hiver '93
La Belle Noiseuse '90
Manon of the Spring '87

Robert Beauvais
The 400 Blows '59

Jerome Beauvarlet
The Valley Obscured by
the Clouds '72

Xavier Beauvois
Ponette '95

Jacques Becker
Boudu Saved from
Drowning '32

Friedrich Beckhaus
The Wannsee
Conference '84

Reginald Beckwith
Curse of the Demon '57

**Hansjorg
Bedschard**
Messidor '77

Eleanor Beecroft
The Mask '61

Maurice Beerblock
A Man Escaped '57

Olga Belajeff
Waxworks '24

Paulina Belinskaya
Storm over Asia '28

Clara Bellar
Rendezvous in Paris '95

**Jean-Paul
Belmondo**
Borsalino '70
Mississippi Mermaid '69
The Thief of Paris '67
Is Paris Burning? '66
Pierrot le Fou '65
Le Doulos '61
A Woman Is a
Woman '60
Breathless '59

Remy Belvaux
Man Bites Dog '91

Niu Ben
To Live '94

Samy Ben Youb
Madame Rosa '77

Nelly Benedetti
The Soft Skin '64

Augusto Benedico
The Exterminating
Angel '62

Yves Beneyton
The Lacemaker '77
Weekend '67

Feral Benga
The Blood of a Poet '30

Roberto Benigni
The Monster '96
Johnny Stecchino '92

David Bennent
The Tin Drum '79

Heinz Bennent
The Last Metro '80
The Tin Drum '79

Eloise Bennett
A Tale of Springtime '92

Joan Bennett
Suspiria '77

John Bennett
Victim '61

Marcel Berbert
The Green Room '78
Mississippi Mermaid '69

Francoise Berd
A Special Day '77

Eric Berenger
Monsieur Hire '89

Helmut Berger
Conversation Piece '75
The Garden of the Finzi-
Continis '71

Michael Berger
Allonsanfan '73

Nicole Berger
Shoot the Piano
Player '62

Toni Berger
Sugarbaby '85

Thommy Berggren
Sunday's Children '94
Elvira Madigan '67

Hiroko Berghauer
Bed and Board '70

Ingrid Bergman
Autumn Sonata '78
Eléna and Her Men '56

Luis Beristain
The Exterminating
Angel '62
Él '52

Francois Berleand
Captain Conan '96
May Fools '90
Au Revoir les Enfants '87

Charles Berling
Ridicule '96
Nelly et Monsieur
Arnaud '95

Peter Berling
Aguirre, the Wrath of
God '72

Svenolof Bern
The Emigrants '72

Armand Bernard
Napoleon '27

Patrick Bernard
Lancelot of the Lake '74

Roberto Berrardi
Comfort and Joy '84

Glen Berry
Beautiful Thing '95

Jules Berry
Les Visiteurs du Soir '42
Le Jour Se Lève '39
The Crime of Monsieur
Lange '36

Julien Bertheau
That Obscure Object of
Desire '77
The Phantom of
Liberty '74

Pierre Bertin
Eléna and Her Men '56

Roland Bertin
The Hairdresser's
Husband '92
Diva '82

Francesca Bertini
1900 '76

Madeleine Berubet
La Chienne '31

Andre Bervil
Le Trou '59

Gene Bervoets
The Vanishing '88

**Dominique
Besnehard**
A Nos Amours '84

Anne-Marie Besse
Max, Mon Amour '86

Ariel Besse
Beau Père '81

Alyson Best
Man of Flowers '84

Laura Betti
1900 '76
Allonsanfan '73
The Canterbury Tales '71

Didier Bezace
Les Voleurs '96

L.627 '92
The Little Thief '89

Samit Bhanja
Days and Nights in the
Forest '70

Regina Bianchi
Kaos '85

Tino Bianchi
Black Sunday '60

Jean-Luc Bideau
Jonah Who Will Be 25 in
the Year 2000 '76
La Salamandre '71

Kris Bidenko
Two Friends '86

Josef Bierbichler
Woyzeck '78
Heart of Glass '74

Jean-Claude Biette
A Tale of Winter '92

Claudio Bigagli
Fiorile '93
Kaos '85
The Night of the
Shooting Stars '82

Ashley Billard
The Boys of St. Vincent
'93

Raoul Billerey
The Little Thief '89

Teddy Billis
The Testament of Dr.
Cordelier '59

Clara Bindi
Black Sunday '60

Juliette Binoche
Trois Couleurs: Bleu '93

Norman Bird
Victim '61

Jane Birkin
La Belle Noiseuse '90
Blow-Up '66

Serafina Birman
Ivan the Terrible,
Part 2 '46
Ivan the Terrible,
Part 1 '44

Jacqueline Bisset
La Cérémonie '95
Day for Night '73

Erwin Biswanger
Metropolis '26

Chhabi Biswas
Devi '60
Jalsaghar '58

Seema Biswas
Bandit Queen '94

Dragan Bjelogric
Hey, Babu Riba '88

Bjorn Bjelvenstam
Wild Strawberries '57

**Anne Lise Hirsch
Bjerrum**
Pelle the Conqueror '88

Anita Bjork
Miss Julie '50

Halvar Bjork
Autumn Sonata '78
The New Land '73

**Gunnar
Bjornstrand**
Autumn Sonata '78
Face to Face '76
Shame '68
Persona '66
Winter Light '62
Through a Glass
Darkly '61
The Magician '58
Wild Strawberries '57
Dreams '55
Smiles of a Summer
Night '55
Torment '44

Gerard Blain
The American Friend '77

Pierre Blaise
Lacombe, Lucien '74

Julia Blake
Man of Flowers '84

Colin Blakely
This Sporting Life '63

Dominique Blanc
Indochine '92
May Fools '90

Michel Blanc
The Monster '96
Monsieur Hire '89

**Dominique
Blanchar**
L'Avventura '60

Pierre Blanchard
Emitai '71

Roland Blanche
Too Beautiful for You '88

Dorothee Blanck
The Umbrellas of
Cherbourg '64

Sandrine Blancke
Toto le Heros '91

Sylvana Blasi
Bed and Board '70

Martin Blau
Ginger & Fred '86

Charles Blavette
Toni '34

Brian Blessed
Henry V '89

Brenda Blethyn
Secrets and Lies '95

Bernard Blier
Casanova '70 '65

Claire Bloom
Look Back in Anger '58

Roland Blouin
Léolo '92

Rudolf Blumner
M '31

Lothaire Bluteau
Orlando '92
Jesus of Montreal '89

Sergei Bodrov, Jr.
Prisoner of the
Mountains '96

Karl-Heinz Boehm
Mother Küsters Goes to
Heaven '76

Dirk Bogarde
Providence '77
The Night Porter '74
Victim '61

Axel Bogousslavsky
Dr. Petiot '90

Peter Bohlke
Toto le Heros '91

Marquard Bohm
Beware of a Holy
Whore '70

Richard Bohringer
The Accompanist '93
The Cook, the Thief, His
Wife & Her Lover '90
Diva '82

Romane Bohringer
The Accompanist '93
Mina Tannenbaum '93

Curt Bois
Wings of Desire '88
The Boat Is Full '81

James Bolam
A Kind of Loving '62

Iciar Bollain
Land and Freedom '95

Maria Bolme
Sunday's Children '94

Ronaldo Bonacchi
Orchestra Rehearsal '78

Paolo Bonacelli
Johnny Stecchino '92
Christ Stopped at
Eboli '79
Salo, or the 120 Days of
Sodom '75

Gary Bond
Outback '71

**Natalya
Bondarchuk**
Solaris '72

Sergei Bondarchuk
War and Peace '68

Ulrikke Juul Bondo
Twist & Shout '84

Massimo Bonetti
Kaos '85
The Night of the
Shooting Stars '82

**Helena Bonham
Carter**
Margaret's Museum '95

Sandrine Bonnaire
La Cérémonie '95
Monsieur Hire '89
Vagabond '85
A Nos Amours '84

Maria Bonnevie
Insomnia '97
Jerusalem '96

**Berangere
Bonvoisin**
Dr. Petiot '90

Andre Bonzel
Man Bites Dog '91

Katrine Boorman
Camille Claudel '89

Caterina Boratto
Juliet of the Spirits '65
8 1/2 '63

Nelly Borgeaud
The Accompanist '93
The Man Who Loved
Women '77
Mississippi Mermaid '69

Max Born
Fellini Satyricon '69

Jean-Mark Bory
The Lovers '59

Nadege Boscher
Dr. Petiot '90

Maria Bosco
Down & Dirty '76

Dilip Bose
Charulata '64

Elodie Bouchez
Wild Reeds '94

Patrick Bouchitey
The Best Way '76

Jacques Boudet
Farinelli '94

Jean Bouise
La Femme Nikita '91
Le Dernier Combat '84
The Confession '70
I Am Cuba '64

Evelyne Bouix
Edith & Marcel '83

Daniel Boulanger
Bed and Board '70
The Bride Wore Black '68
Breathless '59

Sam Bould
Hollow Reed '95

Carole Bouquet
Too Beautiful for You '88
That Obscure Object of
Desire '77

Michel Bouquet
Tous les Matins du
Monde '92
Toto le Heros '91
Borsalino '70
La Rupture '70
La Femme Infidèle '69
Mississippi Mermaid '69
The Bride Wore Black '68
Monsieur Vincent '47

Corinne Bourdon
Van Gogh '92

Pierre Bourgault
Léolo '92

Elisabeth Bourgine
Un Coeur en Hiver '93

Anna Bourkowska
The White Balloon '95

Jean Bousquet
Scene of the Crime '87

Jean-Pierre Bouvier
Ma Saison Préférée '93

Brunella Bova
The White Sheik '52
Miracle in Milan '51

Guy Boyd
Ticket to Heaven '81

Karin Boyd
Mephisto '81

Charles Boyer
Is Paris Burning? '66
The Earrings of
Madame de... '54

Marie-France Boyer
Le Bonheur '65

Miriam Boyer
Un Coeur en Hiver '93
Tous les Matins du
Monde '92
Jonah Who Will Be 25 in
the Year 2000 '76

Marcel Bozzuffi
Z '69

Mike Bradwell
Bleak Moments '71

Sonia Braga
Dona Flor and Her Two
Husbands '78

Kenneth Branagh
Henry V '89
A Month in the
Country '87

Armando Brancia
Amarcord '74

**Klaus Maria
Brandauer**
Hanussen '88
Mephisto '81

Luisina Brando
I Don't Want to Talk
about It '94

Marlon Brando
Last Tango in Paris '73
Burn! '70

Carlo Brandt
Ridicule '96
Indochine '92

Albert Bras
Vampyr '31
Napoleon '27

Nicoletta Braschi
The Monster '96
Johnny Stecchino '92

Claude Brasseur
Band of Outsiders '64

Pierre Brasseur
Il Bell'Antonio '60
Eyes without a Face '59
Children of Paradise '44

Arthur Brauss
The Goalie's Anxiety at
the Penalty Kick '71

Rossano Brazzi
We the Living '42

Jana Brejchova
Loves of a Blonde '65
Fabulous Adventures
of Baron
Munchausen '61

Marita Breuer
Heimat 1 '84

Jean-Claude Brialy
The Monster '96
La Nuit de Varennes '82
The Judge and the
Assassin '75
The Phantom of Liberty
'74
Claire's Knee '71
The Bride Wore Black '68
A Woman Is a Woman
'60
The 400 Blows '59

**Gennie Nevinson
Brice**
Muriel's Wedding '94

Richard Briers
Henry V '89

Omar Brignoll
The Tree of Wooden
Clogs '78

Michel Briguet
L'Argent '83

Vera Briole
A Single Girl '96

Francoise Brion
Nelly et Monsieur
Arnaud '95

Jim Broadbent
Life Is Sweet '90

Anne Brochet
Tous les Matins du
Monde '92

Gerd Brockmann
The Wannsee
Conference '84

Giulio Brogi
The Spider's
Stratagem '70

Eleanor Bron
Little Dorrit, Film 1:
Nobody's Fault '88
Little Dorrit, Film 2: Little
Dorrit's Story '88

Charles Bronson
Once Upon a Time in
the West '68

Claudio Brook
Simon of the Desert '66
Viva Maria! '65
The Exterminating
Angel '62

Carroll Brooks
Boy Meets Girl '84

Louise Brooks
Diary of a Lost Girl '29
Pandora's Box '28

Pierce Brosnan
The Long Good
Friday '80

Claude Brosset
My New Partner '84

Gudrun Brost
The Hour of the Wolf '68

Amelda Brown
Little Dorrit, Film 1:
Nobody's Fault '88
Little Dorrit, Film 2: Little
Dorrit's Story '88

Bryan Brown
The Chant of Jimmie
Blacksmith '78

Pamela Brown
I Know Where I'm
Going '45

Paul Brown
Butterfly Kiss '94

Coral Browne
Dreamchild '85

Pascale Bruchon
Small Change '76

Werner Bruhns
1900 '76

Genevieve Brunet
The City of Lost
Children '95

Nando Bruno
Open City '45

Peggy Bryan
Dead of Night '45

Bill Bryden
The Mask '61

Yul Brynner
The Testament of
Orpheus '59

Flavio Bucci
Suspiria '77

Horst Buchholz
Faraway, So Close! '93

Gerard Buhr
Bob le Flambeur '55

Genevieve Bujold
Dead Ringers '88
The Thief of Paris '67

Marie Bunel
La Discrete '90

Luis Bunuel
The Discreet Charm of
the Bourgeoisie '72

Anna Buonaiuto
The Postman '94

Alexander Burejev
Prisoner of the
Mountains '96

Simon Burke
The Devil's
Playground '76

Raymond Burr
Godzilla, King of the
Monsters '56

Jackie Burroughs
Careful '94

Ellen Burstyn
Providence '77

David Bursztein
La Belle Noiseuse '90

Richard Burton
Look Back in Anger '58

Sean Bury
If... '69

Ernst Busch
Kameradschaft '31
The Threepenny Opera
'31

Gary Busey
Insignificance '85

Raymond Bussieres
Jonah Who Will Be 25 in
the Year 2000 '76
Casque d'Or '52

Rolan Bykov
Commissar '68
The Overcoat '59

Kathleen Byron
Black Narcissus '47

Sebastian Cabot
Captain's Paradise '53

Garry Cadenat
Sugar Cane Alley '83

Michael Cadman
If... '69

Georges Cahuzac
Napoleon '27

He Caifei
Raise the Red
Lantern '91

Haydee Caillot
A Tale of Winter '92

Clara Calami
Ossessione '42

Sergio Calderon
Erendira '83

Dansogho Camara
Camp de Thiaroye '87

Lina Canelajas
The Garden of
Delights '70

Antonio Cantafora
Intervista '87

Peter Capaldi
Local Hero '83

Lino Capolicchio
Fiorile '93
The Garden of the Finzi-
Continis '71

Patrizia Capparelli
The Decameron '70

Joolia Cappleman
Bleak Moments '71

Capucine
Fellini Satyricon '69

Maria Cardinal
Mouchette '67

Claudia Cardinale
Fitzcarraldo '82
Conversation Piece '75
Once Upon a Time in
the West '68
8 1/2 '63
Il Bell'Antonio '60
Rocco and His Brothers
'60
Big Deal on Madonna
Street '58

Nathalie Cardone
The Little Thief '89

Roger Carel
The Two of Us '68

Lianella Carell
The Bicycle Thief '48

Bruno Carette
May Fools '90

Julien Carette
La Bete Humaine '38
Grand Illusion '37

Joyce Carey
Brief Encounter '46

Jean-Pierre Cargol
The Wild Child '70

Margit Carlquist
Smiles of a Summer
Night '55

Ing-mari Carlsson
My Life As a Dog '85

Jean Carmet
Germinal '93
Violette '78
La Rupture '70
Monsieur Vincent '47

Ian Carmichael
Heavens Above! '63
I'm All Right, Jack '59

George Carney
I Know Where I'm
Going '45

Martine Carol
Lola Montès '55

Jean-Luc Caron
Delicatessen '92

Leslie Caron
Contract '80
The Man Who Loved
Women '77
Is Paris Burning? '66

**Memmo
Carotenuto**
Big Deal on Madonna
Street '58

Renato Carpentieri
Caro Diario '93

Ada Carrasco
Like Water for
Chocolate '93

Peter Carroll
The Chant of Jimmie
Blacksmith '78

Margit Carstensen
Mother Küsters Goes to
Heaven '76
The Bitter Tears of Petra
von Kant '72

Jim Carter
A Month in the
Country '87

Katrin Cartlidge
Breaking the Waves '95
Before the Rain '94

Margherita Caruso
The Gospel According
to St. Matthew '64

Jose Carvalho
In the White City '83

Guy Casabonne
Augustin '95

Alex Casanovas
Kika '94

Maria Casares
La Lectrice '88

The Testament of
Orpheus '59
Orpheus '49
Children of Paradise '44

Antonio Casas
Tristana '70

Salvatore Cascio
Cinema Paradiso '88

Chiara Caselli
Fiorile '93

Maria Pia Casilio
Umberto D. '55

Stefania Casini
Suspiria '77

**Michel
Cassagna**
Every Man for
Himself '79

Jean-Pierre Cassel
La Cérémonie '95
The Discreet Charm of
the Bourgeoisie '72
La Rupture '70
Is Paris Burning? '66

Vincent Cassel
Hate '95
Café au Lait '94

Claudio Cassinelli
Allonsanfan '73

Lou Castel
Beware of a Holy
Whore '70

Nino Castelnuovo
The Umbrellas of
Cherbourg '64

Margit Castensen
Berlin Alexanderplatz '80

Giorgio Cataldi
Salo, or the 120 Days of
Sodom '75

Brigitte Catillon
Un Coeur en Hiver '93
La Lectrice '88

Kim Cattrall
Ticket to Heaven '81

Daniel Cauchy
Bob le Flambeur '55

**Jean-Roger
Caussimon**
French Can-Can '55

Lumi Cavazos
Like Water for
Chocolate '93

Ingrid Caven
In a Year of 13
Moons '78
Mother Küsters Goes to
Heaven '76
The American
Soldier '70
Beware of a Holy
Whore '70

Daniel Ceccaldi
Chloe in the
Afternoon '72
Bed and Board '70
The Soft Skin '64

Carlo Cecchi
La Scorta '94

Clementine Celarie
Betty Blue '86

Adolfo Celi
The Phantom of
Liberty '74

Teco Celio
Trois Couleurs: Rouge '94

Caroline Cellier
Farinelli '94
This Man Must Die '70

Peter Cellier
And the Ship Sails
On '83

Iga Cembrzynska
The Saragossa
Manuscript '65

Athina Cenci
Fiorile '93

Petr Cepek
My Sweet Little
Village '86

Marcel Cerdan, Jr.
Edith & Marcel '83

Alain Chabat
French Twist '95

Walmor Chagas
Xica '76

George Chakiris
Is Paris Burning? '66

**Gobinda
Chakravarty**
Distant Thunder '73

Andrej Chalimon
Kolya '96

**Richard
Chamberlain**
The Music Lovers '71

Jean Champion
The Umbrellas of
Cherbourg '64

Jackie Chan
Police Story '85
Drunken Master '78

Philip Chan
Hard-Boiled '92

Piggy Chan
Chungking Express '95

Judith Chancel
Rendezvous in Paris '95

Norman Chancer
Local Hero '83

Carmen Chaplin
Ma Saison Préférée '93

Geraldine Chaplin
Cria '76

Josephine Chaplin
The Canterbury Tales '71

Graham Chapman
Monty Python's The
Meaning of Life '83

Alok Charkravarty
The World of Apu '59

Charpin
César '36
The Baker's Wife '33
Fanny '32
Marius '31

Geoffrey Chater
If... '69

Anil Chatterjee
The Big City '63
Two Daughters '61

Haren Chatterjee
The Big City '63

**Shubhendu
Chatterjee**
Days and Nights In the
Forest '70

**Soumitra
Chatterjee**
Distant Thunder '73
Days and Nights in the
Forest '70
Charulata '64
Two Daughters '61
Devi '60
The World of Apu '59

Daniel Chatto
Little Dorrit, Film 1:
Nobody's Fault '88
Little Dorrit, Film 2: Little
Dorrit's Story '88

**Emmanuelle
Chaulet**
Boyfriends &
Girlfriends '88

Andre Chaumeau
Dr. Petiot '90

**Jacqueline
Chauveau**
Murmur of the Heart '71

Maury Chaykin
The Sweet Hereafter '96
The Adjuster '91

Andrea Checchi
Black Sunday '60

Micheline Cheirel
Carnival in Flanders '35

Chang Chen
Happy Together '96

Nikolai Cherkassov
Don Quixote '57

Ivan the Terrible,
Part 2 '46
Ivan the Terrible,
Part 1 '44
Alexander Nevsky '38

Patrick Chesnais
La Lectrice '88

Leslie Cheung
Happy Together '96
Temptress Moon '96
Farewell My
Concubine '93
A Better Tomorrow '86

Maggie Cheung
Police Story '85

Maurice Chevit
The Hairdresser's
Husband '92

Minoru Chiaki
The Face of Another '66
The Human Condition:
Road to Eternity '59
The Hidden Fortress '58
Throne of Blood '57
Seven Samurai '54
Rashomon '51

Sofiko Chiaureli
Ashik Kerib '88

Carlos Chionetti
The Red Desert '64

Boris Chirkov
Chapayev '34

Ala Chostakova
The Lady with the
Dog '59

Valerie Chow
Chungking Express '95

A. Christiakov
Storm over Asia '28

**Benjamin
Christiansen**
Witchcraft through the
Ages '22

Julie Christie
The Go-Between '71
Fahrenheit 451 '66

**Francoise
Christophe**
Borsalino '70

Donald Churchill
Victim '61

Bruno Cirino
Allonsanfan '73

Ina Cisse
Tilai '90

Franco Citti
Arabian Nights '74
The Decameron '70
Mamma Roma '62

Aime Clarimond
Monsieur Vincent '47
La Marseillaise '37

Liddy Clark
The Chant of Jimmie
Blacksmith '78

Garance Clavel
When the Cat's Away '96

Samuel Claxton
The Last Supper '76

Yvonne Clech
The Fire Within '64

John Cleese
Monty Python's The
Meaning of Life '83

Aurore Clement
Lacombe, Lucien '74

Pierre Clementi
The Conformist '71
Belle de Jour '67

Carol Cleveland
Monty Python's The
Meaning of Life '83

Philippe Clevenot
The Hairdresser's
Husband '92

Edith Clever
The Marquise of O '76

Vera Clouzot
Diabolique '55
The Wages of Fear '55

Francois Cluzet
Olivier, Olivier '92
The Story of Women '88
Too Beautiful for You '88

Jeremy Clyde
Kaspar Hauser '93

Eva Cobo
Matador '86

Roberto Cobo
Los Olvidados '50

Jean Cocteau
The Testament of
Orpheus '59

Alain Cohen
The Two of Us '68

Charlotte Coleman
The Young Poisoner's
Handbook '94

Emma Coles
Two Friends '86

Gregoire Colin
Before the Rain '94
Olivier, Olivier '92

Luz Maria Collazo
I Am Cuba '64

Toni Collette
Muriel's Wedding '94

Kenneth Colley
The Music Lovers '71

Maxime Collin
Léolo '92

Anne Collings
The Mask '61

Maxime Collion
Dr. Petiot '90

Christoph Colomb
Mandabi '68

Clara Colosimo
Orchestra Rehearsal '78
Alfredo, Alfredo '72

Louisa Colpeyn
Band of Outsiders '64

Karen Colston
Sweetie '89

Robbie Coltrane
Henry V '89

Jean-Paul Comart
L.627 '92

**Laura Duke
Condominas**
Lancelot of the Lake '74

Michel Constantin
A Very Curious Girl '69
Le Trou '59

Eddie Constantine
Zentropa '92
The Long Good Friday
'80
Beware of a Holy
Whore '70
Alphaville '65

Ron Cook
Secrets and Lies '95

Carlos Copello
The Tango Lesson '97

Geoffrey Copleston
The Belly of an
Architect '91

Jean-Paul Coquelin
Le Trou '59

Pancho Cordova
The Exterminating
Angel '62

Annie Cordy
La Rupture '70

Raymond Cordy
A Nous la Liberté '31

Isabel Corey
Bob le Flambeur '55

Caris Corfman
Dreamchild '85

Charles Cork
The Long Good Friday
'80

Aurora Cornu
Claire's Knee '71

Sergio Corrieri
Memories of Under-
development '68
I Am Cuba '64

Silvana Corsini
Mamma Roma '62

Elaine Cortadellas
Vagabond '85

Joaquin Cortes
The Flower of My Secret
'95

Valentina Cortese
Day for Night '73
Juliet of the Spirits '65

Michele Cossu
Bandits of Orgosolo '61

Laurence Cote
Les Voleurs '96

George Coulouris
The Long Good Friday
'80

Nicole Courcel
Sundays & Cybele '62

Richard Courcet
I Can't Sleep '93

Suzanne Courtal
Forbidden Games '52

Robert Cowdra
Saturday Night and
Sunday Morning '60

Victor Cowie
Careful '94

Nicola Cowper
Dreamchild '85

Paul Cox
Careful '94

Peter Coyote
Kika '94

Ruth Cracknell
The Chant of Jimmie
Blacksmith '78

Paul Crauchet
The Wonderful Crook
'75

Michael Crawford
How I Won the War '67

Charlie Creed-Miles
The Young Poisoner's
Handbook '94

Bruno Cremer
Is Paris Burning? '66

Nini Crepon
Dr. Petiot '90

Erno Crisa
Purple Noon '60

Quentin Crisp
Orlando '92

Roger Crouzet
The Thief of Paris '67

Graham Crowden
If… '69

Russell Crowe
Proof '91

Ernesto Cruz
Erendira '83

Penelope Cruz
Jamón, Jamón '93
Belle Epoque '92

Vladimir Cruz
Strawberry and
Chocolate '93

Gyorgy Cserhalmi
Mephisto '81

Peppeddu Cuccu
Bandits of Orgosolo '61

**Maria Grazia
Cucinotta**
The Postman '94

Cao Cuifeng
Raise the Red
Lantern '91

**Wang Xiaoxiao
Cuihua**
Shanghai Triad '95

Roland Culver
Dead of Night '45

Peggy Cummins
Curse of the Demon '57

Alain Cuny
Camille Claudel '89
Basileus Quartet '82
Christ Stopped at Eboli
'79
The Milky Way '68
La Dolce Vita '60
The Lovers '59
Les Visiteurs du Soir '42

Finlay Currie
I Know Where I'm
Going '45

Tony Curtis
Insignificance '85

Cyril Cusack
My Left Foot '89
Little Dorrit, Film 1:
Nobody's Fault '88
Little Dorrit, Film 2: Little
Dorrit's Story '88
Fahrenheit 451 '66

Peter Cushing
Hamlet '48

Mickey Custis
Fires on the Plain '59

Zbigniew Cybulski
The Saragossa
Manuscript '65
Ashes and
Diamonds '58
A Generation '54

Henry Czerny
The Boys of
St. Vincent '93

Ying Da
Farewell My
Concubine '93

**Fernando Ramos
Da Silva**
Pixote '81

Jacques Dacqmine
Germinal '93

Robert Dadies
One Sings, the Other
Doesn't '77

Willem Dafoe
Faraway, So Close! '93

Lil Dagover
Dr. Mabuse, Parts
1 & 2 '22
The Cabinet of Dr.
Caligari '19

Eva Dahlbeck
Dreams '55
Smiles of a Summer
Night '55

Daiba
The Horse Thief '87

Yasuo Daichi
Minbo—Or the Gentle
Art of Japanese
Extortion '92

Jennifer Dale
The Adjuster '91
Ticket to Heaven '81

Marcel Dalio
Grand Illusion '37

Beatrice Dalle
I Can't Sleep '93
Betty Blue '86

John Dalleen
Outback '71

Joe Dallesandro
Black Moon '75

Jiji Dan
The Horse Thief '87

Reiko Dan
Red Beard '65

Dani
Day for Night '73

Ben Daniels
Beautiful Thing '95

Ignat Daniltsev
The Mirror '75

**Ingeborga Dapk-
ounaite**
Burnt by the Sun '94

Mireille Darc
Weekend '67

Florence Darel
The Stolen Children '92
A Tale of Springtime '92

Jon Darling
Sweetie '89

Gerard Darmon
Betty Blue '86
Diva '82

Danielle Darrieux
A Chef in Love '96
Scene of the Crime '87
The Earrings of
Madame de... '54
Le Plaisir '52
La Ronde '51

Jessa Darrieux
The Mother and the
Whore '73

Ivan Darvas
Love '71

Lili Darvas
Love '71

Stella Dassas
Hiroshima Mon
Amour '59

Jean Daste
The Green Room '78
The Wild Child '70
Grand Illusion '37
The Crime of Monsieur
Lange '36
L'Atalante '34
Zero for Conduct '33
Boudu Saved from
Drowning '32

Claude Dauphin
Madame Rosa '77
Is Paris Burning? '66
Casque d'Or '52
Le Plaisir '52

Jean Dautremay
Dr. Petiot '90

Eleanor David
Comfort and Joy '84

Gerd David
The Boat Is Full '81

Stephen Davies
The Long Good
Friday '80

Judy Davis
My Brilliant Career '79

Philip Davis
High Hopes '88

Ninetto Davoli
Arabian Nights '74
The Canterbury Tales '71
The Decameron '70

Marpessa Dawn
Black Orpheus '58

Josette Day
Beauty and the
Beast '46

Matt Day
Muriel's Wedding '94

Daniel Day-Lewis
My Left Foot '89

Jo De Backer
Toto le Heros '91

Moreno D'E Bartolli
When Father Was Away
on Business '85

**Gerard de
Bedarieux**
Zero for Conduct '33

Yvonne de Bray
Eternal Return '43

Grace de Capitani
My New Partner '84

Yvonne De Carlo
Captain's Paradise '53

Renato de Carmine
Allonsanfan '73

Arturo de Cordova
Él '52

Pia de Doses
Fellini's Roma '72

Peppino de Filippo
Boccaccio '70 '62
Variety Lights '51

Marina De Graaf
Antonia's Line '95

Slim De Gray
Outback '71

**Consuelo de
Haviland**
Betty Blue '86

Geert De Jong
The 4th Man '79

David de Keyser
The Designated
Mourner '97

Simon de la Brosse
The Little Thief '89

**Stanislas Carre de
Malberg**
Au Revoir les Enfants '87

**Laurence De
Monaghan**
Claire's Knee '71

**Arthur De Mon-
talembert**
Lancelot of the Lake '74

Robert De Niro
1900 '76

Lourdes De Oliveira
Black Orpheus '58

Rossy de Palma
The Flower of My
Secret '95
Kika '94
Tie Me Up! Tie Me
Down! '90
Women on the Verge of
a Nervous
Breakdown '88

Lya de Putti
Variety '25

**Gaspar de San-
telices**
Death of a
Bureaucrat '66

Vittorio De Sica
We All Loved Each
Other So Much '77
Generale Della
Rovere '60
The Earrings of
Madame de... '54

Christian de Tiliere
Bed and Board '70

**Riccardo De
Torrebruna**
Devil in the Flesh '87

Mauricio De Valle
Black God, White
Devil '64

**Jose-Luis De
Villalonga**
The Lovers '59

**Brigitte de
Villepoix**
Jacquot '91

Marie Dea
Orpheus '49
Les Visiteurs du Soir '42

Jacques Debary
The Wonderful Crook
'75

Michel Debrane
Celestial Clockwork '94

Jean Debucourt
The Earrings of
Madame de... '54
Monsieur Vincent '47

Jan Decleir
Antonia's Line '95

Guy Decomble
The 400 Blows '59
Bob le Flambeur '55
Jour de Fete '48

Marie Dedieu
Bed and Board '70

A. Dedinstev
Storm over Asia '28

Pia Degermark
Elvira Madigan '67

Claude Degliame
Dr. Petiot '90

Cesar del Campo
The Exterminating
Angel '62

Carla Del Poggio
Variety Lights '51

Dulio Del Prete
Alfredo, Alfredo '72

Geraldo Del Rey
Black God, White
Devil '64

Laura Del Sol
The Hit '85
Carmen '83

**Giuditta del
Vecchio**
Léolo '92

Michel Delahaye
Alphaville '65

Suzy Delair
Is Paris Burning? '66

Lisa Delamare
Baxter '89
Monsieur Vincent '47
La Marseillaise '37

Juan deLanda
Ossessione '42

Edouard Delmont
Harvest '37
Toni '34

Alain Delon
Borsalino '70
Le Samourai '67
The Eclipse '66
Is Paris Burning? '66
Purple Noon '60
Rocco and His
Brothers '60

Nathalie Delon
Le Samourai '67

Julie Delpy
Trois Couleurs: Blanc '94
Europa, Europa '91
Béatrice '88

Maly Delshaft
The Last Laugh '24

Claudio Deluca
Small Change '76

Frank Deluca
Small Change '76

Paco DeLucia
Carmen '83

Orane Demazis
French Provincial '75
Harvest '37
César '36
Fanny '32
Marius '31

Kristine Demers
The Boys of St.
Vincent '93

Jacques Demy
The 400 Blows '59

Maggie Dence
Outback '71

Judi Dench
Henry V '89

Catherine Deneuve
Les Voleurs '96
Ma Saison Préférée '93

Indochine '92
Scene of the Crime '87
The Last Metro '80
Donkey Skin '70
Tristana '70
Mississippi Mermaid '69
Belle de Jour '67
Repulsion '65
The Umbrellas of
Cherbourg '64

Maurice Denham
Curse of the Demon '57

Marianne Denicourt
La Belle Noiseuse '90

Jacques Denis
Jonah Who Will Be 25 in
the Year 2000 '76
La Salamandre '71

**Monika
Denisiewicz-
Olbrzychska**
Illumination '73

Brian Dennehy
The Belly of an
Architect '91

Barbara Dennek
Playtime '67

Charles Denner
The Man Who Loved
Women '77
Z '69
The Bride Wore Black '68
The Two of Us '68
The Thief of Paris '67

Manuela Denz
Sugarbaby '85

**Elisabeth
Depardieu**
Jean de Florette '87
Manon of the Spring '87

Gerard Depardieu
Germinal '93
Tous les Matins du
Monde '92
Camille Claudel '89
Too Beautiful for You '88
Jean de Florette '87
Les Compères '83
Moon in the Gutter '83
The Return of Martin
Guerre '83
The Woman Next
Door '81
The Last Metro '80
Loulou '80
Mon Oncle d'
Amerique '80
Get Out Your
Handkerchiefs '78
1900 '76
Vincent, François, Paul
and the Others '76
The Wonderful Crook '75
Going Places '74

**Guillaume
Depardieu**
Tous les Matins du
Monde '92

Edouard Dermithe
The Testament of
Orpheus '59
Les Enfants Terribles '50
Orpheus '49

Jean Desailly
The Soft Skin '64

Jean Desbordes
The Blood of a Poet '30

Alex Descas
I Can't Sleep '93

Hubert Deschamps
The Fire Within '64

**Geory
Desmouceaux**
Small Change '76

Ivan Desny
Les Voleurs '96
Berlin Alexanderplatz
'80
The Marriage of Maria
Braun '79
Lola Montès '55

**Maruschka
Detmers**
Devil in the Flesh '87

Ernst Deutsch
The Golem '20

Chunibala Devi
Pather Panchali '54

Padma Devi
Jalsaghar '58

**Francis
Devlaeminck**
Small Change '76

**Laurent
Devlaeminck**
Small Change '76

Jon DeVries
The 4th Man '79

Patrick Dewaere
Beau Père '81
Get Out Your
Handkerchiefs '78
The Best Way '76
Going Places '74

Bernard Dheran
Ridicule '96

Lea di Lea
The Earrings of
Madame de… '54

**Carmelo
Di Mazzarelli**
Lamerica '95

Matoura Dia
Ceddo '78

Ismaila Diagne
Ceddo '78

Miriam Diaz-Aroca
Belle Epoque '92

Evelyne Didi
Celestial Clockwork '94

Gabino Diego
Belle Epoque '92

Juan Diego
Jamón, Jamón '93

Hans Diehl
The Boat Is Full '81

Gustav Diesl
Pandora's Box '28

William Dieterle
Waxworks '24

Marlene Dietrich
The Blue Angel '30

Albert Dieudonne
Napoleon '27

Anton Diffring
Fahrenheit 451 '66

Arthur Dignam
The Chant of Jimmie
Blacksmith '78
The Devil's
Playground '76

Irasema Dilian
Wuthering Heights '53

Phillip Dinn
The Boys of St.
Vincent '93

Stefano Dionisi
Farinelli '94

**Therese N'Bissine
Diop**
Black Girl '66

Shaghayeh Djodat
Gabbeh '96

Mauricio Do Valle
Antonio Das Mortes '68

Anica Dobra
Tito and Me '92

Gosia Dobrowolska
Careful '94
A Woman's Tale '92

Brian Dodd
The Boys of St.
Vincent '93

Arielle Dombasle
Celestial Clockwork '94
Pauline at the Beach '83
Le Beau Mariage '82

Arturo Dominici
Black Sunday '60

Germana Dominici
Black Sunday '60

Solveig Dommartin
Faraway, So Close! '93
Wings of Desire '88

Peter Donaldson
The Sweet Hereafter '96

Barnard Pierre Donnadieu
Béatrice '88
The Vanishing '88
The Return of Martin Guerre '83

Martin Donovan
Hollow Reed '95

Brian Dooley
The Boys of St. Vincent '93

Edna Dore
High Hopes '88

Francoise Dorleac
The Soft Skin '64

Diana Dors
Deep End '70

Gabrielle Dorziat
Monsieur Vincent '47

Els Dottermans
Antonia's Line '95

Kirk Douglas
Is Paris Burning? '66

Melvyn Douglas
The Tenant '76

Shirley Douglas
Dead Ringers '88

Marie-Laure Dougnac
Delicatessen '92

Freda Dowie
Distant Voices, Still Lives '88

Doris Dowling
Bitter Rice '49

Terry Downes
The Fearless Vampire Killers '67

Jacqueline Doyen
Entre-Nous '83

Drashi
The Horse Thief '87

Milena Dravic
Man Is Not a Bird '65

Ruth Drexel
The Marquise of O '76

Jean Claude Dreyfus
The City of Lost Children '95
Delicatessen '92

Claire Drouot
Le Bonheur '65

Jean-Claude Drouot
La Rupture '70
Le Bonheur '65

Dinara Drukarova
Freeze-Die-Come to Life '90

Jeanie Drynan
Muriel's Wedding '94

Daniel Dublet
Jacquot '91

Marie DuBois
Mon Oncle d'Amerique '80
Vincent, François, Paul and the Others '76
The Thief of Paris '67
Jules and Jim '62
Shoot the Piano Player '62
A Woman Is a Woman '60

Axel Duborg
The Virgin Spring '59

Paulette Dubost
May Fools '90
The Last Metro '80
Viva Maria! '65

Danielle Dubroux
Diary of a Seducer '95

Jean Duceppe
Mon Oncle Antoine '71

Michael Duchaussoy
May Fools '90
This Man Must Die '70
La Femme Infidèle '69

Roger Duchesne
Bob le Flambeur '55

Louis Ducreux
The Double Life of Veronique '91
The Story of Women '88

Gerry Dugan
The Devil's Playground '76

Claire Duhamel
Bed and Board '70

Olympia Dukakis
Jerusalem '96

Paul Dullac
La Marseillaise '37

Sandrine Dumas
The Double Life of Veronique '91

Tamas Dunai
Angi Vera '78

Adrian Dunbar
My Left Foot '89

Claude Duneton
Trois Couleurs: Bleu '93
The Double Life of Veronique '91

Robert Dunham
The Green Slime '68
The Face of Another '66

Anny Duperey
Germinal '93
Les Compères '83

Two or Three Things I Know About Her '66

Vincent Dupont
I Can't Sleep '93

Albert Dupontel
A Self-Made Hero '95

Anna Marie Duringer
Veronika Voss '82
The Lacemaker '77

Andre Dussollier
Un Coeur en Hiver '93
Le Beau Mariage '82

Jacques Dutronc
Van Gogh '92
Every Man for Himself '79

Pierre Dux
La Lectrice '88
Monsieur Vincent '47

Milena Dvorska
My Sweet Little Village '86

Valentine Dyall
Brief Encounter '46

Peter Dyneley
The Manster '59

Clint Eastwood
The Good, the Bad, and the Ugly '67
A Fistful of Dollars '64

Dagmar Ebbesen
Monika '52

Juan Echanove
The Flower of My Secret '95

Dale Edmonds
Paisan '46

Samantha Edmonds
The Young Poisoner's Handbook '94

Nekohachi Edoya
The Funeral '84

Allan Edwall
The Sacrifice '86
Fanny and Alexander '83
The New Land '73
The Emigrants '72

Hilton Edwards
Victim '61

Sergei Eisenstein
The Battleship Potemkin '25

Andre Eisermann
Kaspar Hauser '93

Anita Ekberg
Intervista '87
We All Loved Each Other So Much '77
Boccaccio '70 '62
La Dolce Vita '60

Lars Ekborg
Monika '52

Gosta Ekman
Faust '26

Jack Elam
Once Upon a Time in the West '68

Carmen Elias
The Flower of My Secret '95

Peter Elliott
Curse of the Demon '57

Bob Ellis
Man of Flowers '84

Michael Elphick
Little Dorrit, Film 1: Nobody's Fault '88
Little Dorrit, Film 2: Little Dorrit's Story '88

Paul Eluard
L'Age D'Or '30

Dick Emery
The Case of the Mukkinese Battle Horn '56

Michael Emil
Insignificance '85

Taungaroa Emile
Once Were Warriors '94

Daniel Emilfork
The City of Lost Children '95

Akira Emoto
Shall We Dance? '97

Tameka Empson
Beautiful Thing '95

Lena Endre
Jerusalem '96
Sunday's Children '94
The Best Intentions '92

Tina Engel
The Boat Is Full '81

Constanze Engelbrecht
Fiorile '93

Elisabeth Erikson
The Magic Flute '73

Marie Berthe Ernst
L'Age D'Or '30

Max Ernst
L'Age D'Or '30

Homayon Ershadi
Taste of Cherry '96

Norman Erskine
Outback '71

Jacques Ertand
A Man Escaped '57

Bernard Escalon
Trois Couleurs:
Rouge '94

Manuel Estanillo
Death of a
Bureaucrat '66

Agnes Esterhazy
The Joyless Street '25

Pierre Etaix
Max, Mon Amour '86
Pickpocket '59

Karl Ettlinger
The Joyless Street '25

Wolf Euba
Céleste '81

Jean Eustache
The American Friend '77

Edith Evans
Look Back in Anger '58

Peter Eyre
The Tango Lesson '97
Orlando '92

Jacques Fabbri
Diva '82

Francoise Fabian
My Night at Maud's '69
Belle de Jour '67
The Thief of Paris '67

Luce Fabiole
The Two of Us '68

Pierre Fabre
Bed and Board '70

Aldo Fabrizi
The Flowers of St.
Francis '50
Open City '45

Franco Fabrizi
Ginger & Fred '86
I Vitelloni '53

Gerard Falconetti
Claire's Knee '71

Maria Falconetti
The Passion of Joan of
Arc '28

Peter Falk
Faraway, So Close! '93
Wings of Desire '88

Rossella Falk
8 1/2 '63

Paul Fankeur
Jour de Fete '48

Sergio Fantoni
The Belly of an
Architect '91

Betty Faria
Bye Bye Brazil '79

Mimsy Farmer
Allonsanfan '73

Ellen Farner
The Umbrellas of
Cherbourg '64

David Farrar
Black Narcissus '47

**Rainer Werner Fass-
binder**
The American
Soldier '70
Beware of a Holy
Whore '70

Andrew Faulds
The Devils '71

Rene Faure
The Judge and the
Assassin '75

Claudio G. Fava
The Icicle Thief '89

Kamel Fazaa
The Silences of the
Palace '94

Frederique Feder
Trois Couleurs: Rouge '94

Birgitte Federspiel
Babette's Feast '87

Jorge Fegan
Erendira '83

Friedrich Feher
The Cabinet of Dr.
Caligari '19

Harry Feist
Open City '45

Raphael Fejto
Au Revoir les Enfants '87

**Enrique Alvarez
Felix**
Simon of the Desert '66

Maria Felix
French Can-Can '55

Nicole Felix
Small Change '76

Federico Fellini
Intervista '87
We All Loved Each
Other So Much '77
The Miracle '48

Riccardo Fellini
I Vitelloni '53

Zhang Fengyi
Farewell My
Concubine '93

Colm Feore
32 Short Films about
Glenn Gould '93

Anouk Ferjac
This Man Must Die '70

Fernandel
Harvest '37

Jesus Fernandez
Tristana '70

**Wilhelmenia
Wiggins
Fernandez**
Diva '82

Didier Ferney
Toto le Heros '91

Catherine Ferran
Baxter '89

Antonio Ferrari
The Tree of Wooden
Clogs '78

Andrea Ferreol
The Last Metro '80
Three Brothers '80
The Tin Drum '79
La Grande Bouffe '73

Mel Ferrer
Eléna and Her Men '56

Benoit Ferreux
Murmur of the Heart '71

Babette Ferrier
Chloe in the
Afternoon '72

Martine Ferriere
Mississippi Mermaid '69

Gabriele Ferzetti
Basileus Quartet '82
The Night Porter '74
The Confession '70
L'Avventura '60

Buster Fiddess
Outback '71

Shirley Anne Field
Saturday Night and
Sunday Morning '60

Maurice Fields
A Cry in the Dark '88

**Kristian
Figenschow**
Insomnia '97

Audrey Fildes
Kind Hearts and
Coronets '49

Frank Finlay
Gumshoe '72

Albert Finney
Gumshoe '72
Saturday Night and
Sunday Morning '60

Elena Fiore
Seven Beauties '76

Nada Fiorelli
The Golden Coach '52

Colin Firth
A Month in the
Country '87

Kai Fischer
The Goalie's Anxiety at
the Penalty Kick '71

Vera Fischer
Quilombo '84

Peter Fitz
Au Revoir les Enfants '87

Lewis Fitz-gerald
A Cry in the Dark '88

Neil Fitzpatrick
A Cry in the Dark '88

Georges Flament
The 400 Blows '59
La Chienne '31

Susan Fleetwood
The Sacrifice '86

Jason Flemyng
Hollow Reed '95

Dexter Fletcher
The Long Good
Friday '80

Bjorn Floberg
Insomnia '97

Suzanne Flon
Zita '68

Sheila Florance
A Woman's Tale '92
Cactus '86

Florelle
The Crime of Monsieur
Lange '36

Fiona Florence
Fellini's Roma '72

**Stefano Satta
Flores**
We All Loved Each
Other So Much '77

Henry Fonda
Once Upon a Time in
the West '68

Robert Fontaine
Emitai '71
Black Girl '66

**Genevieve
Fontanel**
The Man Who Loved
Women '77

Tex Foote
Outback '71

Glenn Ford
Is Paris Burning? '66

Delphine Forest
Europa, Europa '91

Veronica Forque
Kika '94

Rudolph Forster
The Threepenny
Opera '31

Pasquale Fortunato
The Conformist '71

Brigitte Fossey
The Man Who Loved
Women '77
Going Places '74
Forbidden Games '52

Meg Foster
Ticket to Heaven '81

Andre Fouche
César '36

Edward Fox
The Go-Between '71

Gro Fraas
Edvard Munch '74

Rolla France
A Nous la Liberté '31

Franco Franchi
Kaos '85

Jean Francoise
Violette '78

Guy Frangin
A Gentle Woman '69

Paul Frankeur
The Phantom of Liberty
'74
The Milky Way '68

Filippa Franzen
The Sacrifice '86

Bill Fraser
Little Dorrit, Film 1:
Nobody's Fault '88
Little Dorrit, Film 2: Little
Dorrit's Story '88

Helen Fraser
Repulsion '65

Hugh Fraser
The Draughtsman's
Contract '82

John Fraser
Repulsion '65

Marcel Fraval
Traffic '71

Charles Frawley
The Devil's
Playground '76

Paul Freeman
The Long Good
Friday '80

Alice Freindlikh
Stalker '79

Stephane Freiss
Vagabond '85

Pierre Fresnay
Monsieur Vincent '47
Grand Illusion '37
César '36
Fanny '32
Marius '31

Bernard Fresson
Germinal '93
The Tenant '76
Hiroshima Mon
Amour '59

Matt Frewer
Monty Python's The
Meaning of Life '83

Sami Frey
César & Rosalie '72
Band of Outsiders '64

Ulf Friberg
Jerusalem '96

Brenda Fricker
My Left Foot '89

Gertrud Fridh
The Hour of the Wolf '68

Rebecca Frith
Love Serenade '96

Willy Fritsch
Woman in the Moon '29
Spies '28

Gert Frobe
Is Paris Burning? '66

Conny Froboess
Veronika Voss '82

Gustav Froehlich
Metropolis '26

Samuel Froler
The Best Intentions '92

Ewa Froling
Fanny and Alexander '83

**Miguel Angel
Fuentes**
Fitzcarraldo '82

Warner Fuetterer
Faust '26

Tatsuya Fuji
In the Realm of the
Senses '76

Susumu Fujita
The Human Condition:
Road to Eternity '59
The Men Who Tread on
the Tiger's Tail '45

Kei Fujiwara
Tetsuo: The Iron Man '92

Samuel Fuller
The American Friend '77
Pierrot le Fou '65

Rikki Fulton
Comfort and Joy '84

Eiji Funakoshi
FIres on the Plain '59

Herve Furic
A Tale of Winter '92

Yvonne Furneaux
Repulsion '65
La Dolce Vita '60

Judith Furse
Black Narcissus '47

Sigge Furst
Shame '68

Jaro Furth
The Joyless Street '25

Susumo Fusuita
Sanshiro Sugata '43

Jean Gabin
French Can-Can '55
Le Plaisir '52
Le Jour Se Lève '39
La Bete Humaine '38
Grand Illusion '37
Pépé le Moko '37
The Lower Depths '36

Christopher Gable
The Music Lovers '71

Gabriel Gabrio
Harvest '37
Pépé le Moko '37

Renee Gadd
Dead of Night '45

Antonio Gades
Carmen '83
Blood Wedding '81

**Charlotte Gains-
bourg**
The Little Thief '89

Janusz Gajos
Trois Couleurs: Blanc '94

Michel Galabru
Belle Epoque '92
La Cage aux Folles '78
The Judge and the
Assassin '75

Eddra Gale
8 1/2 '63

Genevieva Galea
Les Carabiniers '63

Peter Galfy
Time Stands Still '82

Anna Galiena
Jamón, Jamón '93
The Hairdresser's
Husband '92

Frank Gallacher
Proof '91

Peter Gallagher
Dreamchild '85

Jose Gallardo
I Am Cuba '64

Lucy Gallardo
The Exterminating
Angel '62

**Rosa Maria
Gallardo**
The Brainiac '61

Maresa Gallo
Love in the City '53

Michael Gambon
The Cook, the Thief, His
Wife & Her Lover '90

Yvonne Gamy
Manon of the Spring '87

Abel Gance
Napoleon '27

Bruno Ganz
Faraway, So Close! '93
Wings of Desire '88
In the White City '83
Nosferatu the Vampyre
'79
The American Friend '77
The Marquise of O '76

Gaoba
The Horse Thief '87

Lola Gaos
Tristana '70

Siqin Gaowa
Women from the Lake
of Scented Souls '94

Victor Garber
Exotica '94

Greta Garbo
The Joyless Street '25

Delia Garces
Él '52

Mauricio Garces
The Brainiac '61

Lamberto Garcia
The Last Supper '76

Lea Garcia
Black Orpheus '58

Nicole Garcia
Mon Oncle d'
Amerique '80

Raul Garcia
I Am Cuba '64

Cecile Garcia-Fogel
L.627 '92

Luce Garcia-Ville
Last Year at
Marienbad '61

Katya Gardner
Careful '94

Gale Garnett
32 Short Films about
Glenn Gould '93

Ettore Garofolo
Mamma Roma '62

Ivo Garrani
Black Sunday '60

Maurice Garrel
Un Coeur en Hiver '93
La Discrete '90

Micheline Gary
The Testament of Dr.
Cordelier '59

Vittorio Gassman
We All Loved Each
Other So Much '77
Big Deal on Madonna
Street '58
Bitter Rice '49

Faye Gatteau
Olivier, Olivier '92

Francisco Gattorno
Strawberry and
Chocolate '93

Mikkel Gaup
Breaking the Waves '95

Jack Gautier
Playtime '67

Jean-Yves Gautier
A Chef in Love '96

Martine Gautier
May Fools '90

Otto Gebuehr
The Golem '20

Daniel Gelin
Murmur of the Heart '71
Is Paris Burning? '66
The Testament of
Orpheus '59
La Ronde '51

**Francois-Eric
Gendron**
Boyfriends &
Girlfriends '88

Leo Genn
Henry V '45

Lina Gennari
Umberto D. '55

Heinrich George
Metropolis '26

Jan George
The American Soldier
'70

Alika Georgouli
Landscape in the
Mist '88

Henriette Gerard
Vampyr '31

**Brother Nazario
Gerardi**
The Flowers of St.
Francis '50

Richard Gere
Rhapsody in August '91

Georges Geret
A Very Curious Girl '69
Z '69
Diary of a
Chambermaid '64

Nane Germon
Beauty and the
Beast '46

Kurt Gerron
The Blue Angel '30

Valeska Gert
Juliet of the Spirits '65
The Threepenny
Opera '31
The Joyless Street '25

Bankim Ghosh
Charulata '64

Shyamal Ghoshal
Charulata '64

Fosco Giachetti
We the Living '42

Giancarlo Giannini
The Innocent '76
Seven Beauties '76
Swept Away… '75
Love and Anarchy '73

Mel Gibson
Gallipoli '81

Therese Giehse
Black Moon '75
Lacombe, Lucien '74

John Gielgud
Providence '77
Chimes at Midnight '67

Ariadna Gil
Celestial Clockwork '94
Belle Epoque '92

Terry Gilliam
Monty Python's The
Meaning of Life '83

Luigi Gillianni
Boccaccio '70 '62

Ian Gilmour
The Chant of Jimmie
Blacksmith '78

Tom Gilroy
Land and Freedom '95

Teresa Gimpera
Spirit of the Beehive '73

Florence Giorgetti
The Lacemaker '77

Renato Giovannoli
Fellini's Roma '72

Daniele Girard
Bed and Board '70

Remy Girard
Jesus of Montreal '89

Annie Girardot
Rocco and His
Brothers '60

Hippolyte Girardot
Manon of the Spring '87

Bernard Giraudeau
Ridicule '96

Nicolas Giraudi
Scene of the Crime '87

Monique Giraudy
The Valley Obscured by
the Clouds '72

Massimo Girotti
The Monster '96
Senso '54
Ossessione '42

Gudrun Gisladottir
The Sacrifice '86

Anton Glanzelius
My Life As a Dog '85

Sabine Glaser
The Man Who Loved
Women '77

Nicholas Gledhill
Careful, He Might Hear
You '84

Michele Gleizer
Europa, Europa '91

Wienczylaw Glinski
Kanal '56

**Mathias
Gnaedinger**
The Boat Is Full '81

Fritz Gnass
M '31

Thomas Godet
Toto le Heros '91

Judith Godreche
Ridicule '96

Vanda Godsell
This Sporting Life '63

Carl Goetz
Pandora's Box '28

Philippe Goldman
Small Change '76

Richard Golfier
Small Change '76

Francesco Golisano
Miracle in Milan '51

Marina Golovine
Olivier, Olivier '92
The Stolen Children '92

Katerina Golubeva
I Can't Sleep '93

Fernando Gomez
Belle Epoque '92
Spirit of the Beehive '73

Mikhail Gomorov
The Battleship
Potemkin '25

Peter Gonzales
Fellini's Roma '72

Augustin Gonzalez
The Nest '80

Janos Gorbe
The Round-Up '66

Barbara Gordon
Dead Ringers '88

Marius Goring
The Red Shoes '48

Frederic Gorny
Wild Reeds '94

**Vladimir
Gostyukhin**
The Ascent '76

Michael Gothard
The Valley Obscured by
the Clouds '72
The Devils '71

Heinrich Gotho
Metropolis '26

John Gottowt
Waxworks '24
Nosferatu '22

Michael Gough
The Go-Between '71

Olivier Gourmet
La Promesse '96

Siqin Gowa
The Day the Sun Turned
Cold '94

Chantal Goya
Masculine Feminine '66

Peter Graham
The War Game '65

Emma Gramatica
Miracle in Milan '51

Sam Grana
The Boys of St. Vincent
'93

Alexander Granach
Kameradschaft '31
Nosferatu '22

Daisy Granados
Memories of Under-
development '68

Bjorn Granath
Pelle the Conqueror '88

Farley Granger
Senso '54

Charles Granval
Boudu Saved from
Drowning '32

Christiane Graskoff
Mephisto '81

Fernand Gravet
La Ronde '51

Carla Gravina
Alfredo, Alfredo '72

Ernest Gray
A Woman's Tale '92

Nadia Gray
La Dolce Vita '60

Vivean Gray
Picnic at Hanging
Rock '75

Juliette Greco
Eléna and Her Men '56
Orpheus '49

Calvin Green
Exotica '94

Marika Green
Pickpocket '59

Bruce Greenwood
The Sweet Hereafter '96
Exotica '94

Joan Greenwood
Little Dorrit, Film 1:
Nobody's Fault '88
Little Dorrit, Film 2: Little
Dorrit's Story '88
The Man in the White
Suit '51
Kind Hearts and
Coronets '49

Everley Gregg
Brief Encounter '46

Pascal Greggory
Pauline at the
Beach '83
Le Beau Mariage '82

Laurent Grevill
I Can't Sleep '93
Camille Claudel '89

Edmond T. Greville
Under the Roofs of
Paris '29

Denise Grey
Devil in the Flesh '46

Sylvie Grezel
Small Change '76

Lucas Gridoux
Pépé le Moko '37

Hugh Griffith
The Canterbury Tales '71
Kind Hearts and
Coronets '49

Rachel Griffiths
Muriel's Wedding '94

Anouk Grinberg
A Self-Made Hero '95

Nikolai Grinko
Stalker '79
Andrei Rublev '66

Clare P. Grogan
Comfort and Joy '84

Ake Gronberg
Sawdust and Tinsel '53
Monika '52

Frank Groothof
In for Treatment '82

Robert Grubb
Gallipoli '81

Gustav Grundgens
Liebelei '32
M '31

Ilka Gruning
The Joyless Street '25

**Halina
Gryglaszewska**
The Double Life of
Veronique '91

Dominic Guard
Picnic at Hanging
Rock '75
The Go-Between '71

Irina Gubanova
War and Peace '68

Francois Guerin
Eyes without a Face '59

Blanca Guerra
Erendira '83

Ruy Guerra
Aguirre, the Wrath of
God '72

Fausto Guerzoni
Black Orpheus '58
The Bicycle Thief '48

**Makhouredia
Gueye**
Xala '75
Mandabi '68

Giovanni Guidelli
Fiorile '93

Fernando Guillen
Women on the Verge of
a Nervous
Breakdown '88

Yang Guimei
Vive L'Amour '94

Alec Guinness
Little Dorrit, Film 1:
Nobody's Fault '88
Little Dorrit, Film 2: Little
Dorrit's Story '88
Captain's Paradise '53
The Man in the White
Suit '51
Kind Hearts and
Coronets '49

Julien Guiomar
Léolo '92
My New Partner '84
French Provincial '75
A Very Curious Girl '69
The Thief of Paris '67

Lara Guirao
L.627 '92

Henri Guisol
The Crime of Monsieur
Lange '36

Leo Gullotta
La Scorta '94

Eisi Gulp
Sugarbaby '85

David Gumpilil
Walkabout '71

Ted Gunther
The Green Slime '68

Pinaki Sen Gupta
Aparajito '58

Uma Das Gupta
Pather Panchali '54

Stefan Guttler
Heart of Glass '74

Ronald Guttman
The Pillow Book '95

Bertil Guve
Fanny and
Alexander '83

Susanna Haavisto
Ariel '89

Sylvie Habault
Thérèse '86

Nora Habib
Augustin '95

**Eugeniusz
Haczkiewicz**
Moonlighting '82

Michiko Hada
The Mystery of
Rampo '94

Hakan Hagegard
The Magic Flute '73

Brahim Haggiag
The Battle of Algiers '66

Kenichi Hagiwara
Kagemusha '80

Marcelle Hainia
Boudu Saved from
Drowning '32

Zhang Haiyan
Ermo '94

Zouzou El Hakim
The Night of Counting
the Years '69

Georgina Hale
The Devils '71

Brian Hall
The Long Good
Friday '80

May Hallitt
Black Narcissus '47

Dina Halpern
The Dybbuk '37

George Hamilton
Viva Maria! '65

Rosalind Hammond
Muriel's Wedding '94

Paul Hampton
They Came from
Within '75

Ranko Hanai
Sanshiro Sugata '43

Yoshiaki Hanayagi
Sansho the Bailiff '54

Irene Handl
Secrets and Lies '95
Brief Encounter '46

Roger Hanin
Rocco and His
Brothers '60

Holger Juul Hansen
The Kingdom '95

Setsuko Hara
Tokyo Story '53
Late Spring '49

Meiko Harada
Akira Kurosawa's
Dreams '90
Ran '85

**Cezary
Harasimowicz**
Trois Couleurs: Blanc '94

Christine Harbort
Mephisto '81

Jacques Harden
Lola '61

Jonathon Hardy
The Devil's
Playground '76

John Hargreaves
Careful, He Might Hear
You '84

Dennis Harkin
Brief Encounter '46

Jimmi Harkishin
Bhaji on the Beach '94

Jessica Harper
Suspiria '77

Richard Harris
Juggernaut '74
The Red Desert '64
This Sporting Life '63

Cathryn Harrison
Black Moon '75

**Hugo Harold
Harrisson**
Toto le Heros '91

John Harryson
Monika '52

Ian Hart
Hollow Reed '95
Land and Freedom '95

Michel Hart
Dr. Petiot '90

William Hartnell
This Sporting Life '63

Kazuo Hasegawa
Gate of Hell '54

O.E. Hasse
State of Siege '73

Didier Haudepin
The Innocent '76

Cast

481

Sabine Haudepin
The Last Metro '80

Sterling Hayden
1900 '76

Patricia Hayes
Little Dorrit, Film 1:
    Nobody's Fault '88
Little Dorrit, Film 2: Little
    Dorrit's Story '88

Tony Haygarth
A Month in the
    Country '87

Chris Haywood
A Woman's Tale '92
Man of Flowers '84

Ruby Head
The Long Good
    Friday '80

Paul Hebert
Mouchette '67

Amel Hedhili
The Silences of the
    Palace '94

Thomas Heelberg
The Man on the Roof '76

Ahmad Hegazi
The Night of Counting
    the Years '69

Peter Hehir
Two Friends '86

Bernard Helfrich
The Stationmaster's
    Wife '77

Jenny Helia
Toni '34

Erik Hell
The Passion of Anna '70

Brigitte Helm
Die Liebe der Jeanne
    Ney '27
Metropolis '26

Robert Helpmann
The Red Shoes '48

David Hemblen
The Sweet Hereafter '96
Exotica '94
The Adjuster '91

David Hemmings
Juggernaut '74
Blow-Up '66

Ian Hendry
Repulsion '65

Anna Henkel
1900 '76

Uno Henning
Die Liebe der Jeanne
    Ney '27

Anders Henrikson
Miss Julie '50

Judith Henry
Germinal '93
La Discrete '90

Linda Henry
Beautiful Thing '95

Louis Herbert
Forbidden Games '52

Eileen Herlie
Hamlet '48

Irm Hermann
Mother Küsters Goes to
    Heaven '76
Ali: Fear Eats the Soul '74
The Bitter Tears of Petra
    von Kant '72

Marcel Herrand
Children of Paradise '44
Les Visiteurs du Soir '42

Mark Herron
8 1/2 '63

Werner Herzog
Man of Flowers '84

David Hewlett
The Boys of St. Vincent
    '93

Bokuzen Hidari
The Lower Depths '57
Seven Samurai '54

Tonpei Hidari
The Ballad of Narayama
    '83

Jan Hieronimko
Vampyr '31

**Chieko
    Higashiyama**
Tokyo Story '53

Anthony Higgins
Max, Mon Amour '86
The Draughtsman's
    Contract '82

Bernard Hill
Drowning by Numbers
    '87

Max Hiller
The Last Laugh '24

Wendy Hiller
I Know Where I'm Going
    '45

Mikijiro Hira
The Mystery of
    Rampo '94

Thora Hird
A Kind of Loving '62

Ingvar Hirdwall
The Man on the Roof '76

Reiko Hitomi
The Human Condition: A
    Soldier's Prayer '61

Paul Hittscher
Fitzcarraldo '82

Valerie Hobson
Kind Hearts and
    Coronets '49

Dustin Hoffman
Alfredo, Alfredo '72

Thom Hoffman
Orlando '92
The 4th Man '79

**Marco
    Hofschneider**
Europa, Europa '91

Rene Hofschneider
Europa, Europa '91

Vuong Hoa Hoi
The Scent of Green
    Papaya '93

Ticky Holgado
French Twist '95
Delicatessen '92

Stanley Holloway
Hamlet '48
Brief Encounter '46

Ian Holm
The Sweet Hereafter '96
Henry V '89
Dreamchild '85
Juggernaut '74

Max Holsboer
The Blue Light '32

Jany Holt
Café au Lait '94

Miroslav Holub
The Fabulous World of
    Jules Verne '58

Lluis Homar
Celestial Clockwork '94

Inoshiro Honda
King Kong vs.
    Godzilla '63

Yutaka Honda
The Pillow Book '95

Anthony Hopkins
Juggernaut '74

Rolf Hoppe
Mephisto '81

Dennis Hopper
The American Friend '77

Michael Hordern
How I Won the War '67

Camilla Horn
Faust '26

Zbigniew Horoks
Dr. Petiot '90

Jane Horrocks
Life Is Sweet '90

Robert Horton
The Green Slime '68

Laszlo Horvath
Angi Vera '78

Bob Hoskins
The Long Good
    Friday '80

German Houde
Les Bons Debarras '81

Renee Houston
Repulsion '65

Christopher Hovik
Max, Mon Amour '86

Alan Howard
The Cook, the Thief, His
    Wife & Her Lover '90

Trevor Howard
Brief Encounter '46

Sally Ann Howes
Dead of Night '45

Noel Howlett
Victim '61

Christina Hoyos
Carmen '83
Blood Wedding '81

Rudolf Hrusinsky
My Sweet Little
    Village '86

Li Hu
The Day the Sun Turned
    Cold '94

Ji Cun Hua
Red Sorghum '87

Walter Hudd
I Know Where I'm
    Going '45

Charles Hughes
Outback '71

David Hughes
32 Short Films about
    Glenn Gould '93

Wendy Hughes
Careful, He Might Hear
    You '84
My Brilliant Career '79

Yank Huiquin
The Story of Qiu Ju '91

Bill Hunter
Muriel's Wedding '94
The Hit '85

Holly Hunter
Crash '95
The Piano '93

Isabelle Huppert
La Cérémonie '95
The Story of Women '88
Cactus '86
Entre-Nous '83
Loulou '80
Every Man for Himself
    '79
Violette '78
The Lacemaker '77
The Judge and the
    Assassin '75
Going Places '74

John Hurt
The Hit '85

Troy Hurtubise
Project Grizzly '96

Pelle Hvenegaard
Pelle the Conqueror '88

Sin-Hye Hwang
301, 302 '94

Jane Hylton
The Manster '59

Mirta Ibarra
Strawberry and
Chocolate '93

Etsuko Ichihara
Black Rain '88

Raizo Ichikawa
Enjo '58

Eric Idle
Monty Python's The
Meaning of Life '83

Giuseppe Ieraci-tano
The Stolen Children '92

Hisashi Igawa
Rhapsody in August '91
Akira Kurosawa's
Dreams '90
Ran '85
Harakiri '62

Choko Iida
Drunken Angel '48

Pola Illery
Under the Roofs of
Paris '29

Vladimir Ilyine
A Chef in Love '96
Burnt by the Sun '94

Yoshio Inaba
Harakiri '62
Seven Samurai '54

Ciccio Ingrassia
Kaos '85

I. Inkizhinov
Storm over Asia '28

Valeri Inkizhinov
Storm over Asia '28

Franco Interlenghi
I Vitelloni '53
Shoeshine '47

Carolina Iotti
The Tango Lesson '97

Marie Irakane
Bed and Board '70

Enrique Irazoqui
The Gospel According
to St. Matthew '64

Jeremy Irons
Dead Ringers '88
Moonlighting '82

Mitsunori Isaki
Akira Kurosawa's
Dreams '90

Keisuke Ishida
Black Rain '88

Akira Ishihama
Harakiri '62
The Human Condition:
No Greater Love '58

Juzo Itami
The Family Game '83

Emi Ito
Mothra '62

Hiroko Ito
Woman in the Dunes '64

Yumi Ito
Mothra '62

Yunosuke Ito
The Burmese Harp '56
Ikiru '52

Aniko Ivan
Time Stands Still '82

Hira Ivanov-Golarko
War and Peace '68

Vladimir Ivashov
Ballad of a Soldier '60

Daniel Ivernel
Diary of a
Chambermaid '64

Shima Iwashita
An Autumn
Afternoon '62
Harakiri '62

Teresa Izewska
Kanal '56

Glenda Jackson
The Music Lovers '71

Mark "Jacko" Jackson
Outback '71

Philip Jackson
High Hopes '88

Irene Jacob
Trois Couleurs: Rouge '94
The Double Life of
Veronique '91
Au Revoir les Enfants '87

Derek Jacobi
Henry V '89
Little Dorrit, Film 1:
Nobody's Fault '88
Little Dorrit, Film 2: Little
Dorrit's Story '88

Ulla Jacobsson
Smiles of a Summer
Night '55

Maurice Jacquemont
The Return of Martin
Guerre '83

Nicole Jacquet
Every Man for
Himself '79

Claude Jade
Love on the Run '78
Bed and Board '70
Stolen Kisses '68

Richard Jaeckel
The Green Slime '68

Mick Jagger
Sympathy for the
Devil '70

Tadeusz Janczar
Kanal '56

Krystyna Janda
Man of Iron '81
Mephisto '81
Man of Marble '76

Oleg Jankowsky
My Twentieth
Century '90

Emil Jannings
The Blue Angel '30
Faust '26
Variety '25
The Last Laugh '24
Waxworks '24

Jim Jarmusch
Leningrad Cowboys Go
America '89

Marthe Jarnias
Vagabond '85

Ernst Hugo Jarogard
The Kingdom '95

Magda Jaroszowna
Contract '80

John Jarratt
The Chant of Jimmie
Blacksmith '78

Stig Jarrel
The Devil's Eye '60
Torment '44

Belinda Jarrett
Muriel's Wedding '94

Elzbieta Jasinska
Trois Couleurs:
Rouge '94

Giovanni Javarone
Orchestra Rehearsal '78

Jamco Jayang
The Horse Thief '87

Marianne Jean-Baptiste
Secrets and Lies '95

Isabel Jeans
Heavens Above! '63

Ursula Jeans
The Life and Death of
Colonel Blimp '43

Kalina Jedrusik
The Double Life of
Veronique '91

Joanna Jedryka
The Saragossa
Manuscript '65

Barbara Jefford
And the Ship Sails
On '83

Peter Jeffrey
If... '69

Edith Jehanne
Die Liebe der Jeanne
Ney '27

Anne-Marie Jelinek
Black Girl '66

Rudolph Jelinek
Fabulous Adventures
of Baron
Munchausen '61

Roger Jendly
Jonah Who Will Be 25 in
the Year 2000 '76

Cleo Jensen
Elvira Madigan '67

Eugen Jenson
Die Liebe der Jeanne
Ney '27

Zheng Jian
Ju Dou '90

Wang Jianfa
The Story of Qiu Ju '91

Zhou Jie
Temptress Moon '96

Ma Jingwu
The Day the Sun Turned
Cold '94
Raise the Red
Lantern '91

Marlene Jobert
The Wonderful
Crook '75
The Thief of Paris '67
Masculine Feminine '66

Alejandro Jodorowsky
El Topo '71

Brontis Jodorowsky
El Topo '71

Ulf Johansson
The Hour of the Wolf '68

Veronika Johansson
Rendezvous in Paris '95

Georg John
M '31

Gottfried John
Berlin
Alexanderplatz '80
The Marriage of Maria
Braun '79

In a Year of 13
Moons '78
Mother Küsters Goes to
Heaven '76

Lucien John
Walkabout '71

Mervyn Johns
Dead of Night '45

Celia Johnson
Captain's Paradise '53
Brief Encounter '46

Dots Johnson
Paisan '46

Guri Johnson
Insomnia '97

Mirjana Jokovic
Underground '95

Pierre Jolivet
Le Dernier Combat '84

Jonah
Jonah Who Will Be 25 in
the Year 2000 '76

Freddie Jones
And the Ship Sails On '83
Juggernaut '74

Gemma Jones
The Devils '71

Terry Jones
Monty Python's The
Meaning of Life '83

Morten Jorgensen
Pelle the Conqueror '88

Erland Josephson
Ulysses' Gaze '95
Hanussen '88
The Sacrifice '86
After the Rehearsal '84
Fanny and
Alexander '83
Autumn Sonata '78
Face to Face '76
Scenes from a
Marriage '73
Cries and Whispers '72
The Passion of Anna '70
The Hour of the Wolf '68

Jacques Jouanneau
Bed and Board '70

Edouard Joubeaud
Jacquot '91

Alain Jouffroy
La Collectionneuse '67

Raymond Jourdan
The Rise of Louis XIV '66

Louis Jouvet
La Marseillaise '37
The Lower Depths '36
Carnival in Flanders '35

Jovan Jovanovich
The Decameron '70

Joydeb
Charulata '64

Odette Joyeux
La Ronde '51

Jorge Juliao
Pixote '81

Andre Julien
Dr. Petiot '90

Ge Zhi Jun
The Story of Qiu Ju '91

Ye Jun
The Story of Qiu Ju '91

Tito Junco
The Exterminating
Angel '62

Fabio Junior
Bye Bye Brazil '79

Curt Jurgens
And God Created
Woman '57

Fawzia el Kader
The Battle of Algiers '66

Piotr Kadochnikev
Ivan the Terrible,
Part 2 '46
Ivan the Terrible,
Part 1 '44

**Larisa
Kadochnikova**
Shadows of Forgotten
Ancestors '64

Charlotte Kady
L.627 '92

Kyoko Kagawa
The Lower Depths '57
Sansho the Bailiff '54

Teruyuki Kagawa
The Mystery of
Rampo '94

Temur Kahmhadze
A Chef in Love '96

**Alexander
Kaidanovsky**
Stalker '79

Joseph Kairau
Once Were Warriors '94

Jean-Pierre Kalfon
The Valley Obscured by
the Clouds '72
Weekend '67

Mohsen Kalifi
The White Balloon '95

Alexander Kalyagin
A Slave of Love '78

Fritz Kampers
Kameradschaft '31

Nobuo Kaneko
The Human Condition: A
Soldier's Prayer '61
Ikiru '52

Takeshi Kaneshiro
Chungking Express '95

Li Kangsheng
Vive L'Amour '94

Aneeta Kanwar
Salaam Bombay! '88

Mirjana Karanovic
Underground '95
When Father Was Away
on Business '85

Emil Kariewicz
Kanal '56

Anna Karina
Alphaville '65
Pierrot le Fou '65
Band of Outsiders '64
Les Carabiniers '63
My Life to Live '62
A Woman Is a
Woman '60

Tcheky Karyo
La Femme Nikita '91
Full Moon in Paris '84

**Mohamed Ben
Kassen**
The Battle of Algiers '66

Mathieu Kassovitz
A Self-Made Hero '95
Café au Lait '94

Daisuke Kato
Seven Samurai '54
Rashomon '51

Masayuki Kato
The Bad Sleep Well '60

Kokinji Katsura
The Human Condition:
Road to Eternity '59

Gunther Kaufman
In a Year of 13
Moons '78

Hiroko Kawasaki
Utamaro and His Five
Women '46

Seizaburo Kawazu
Yojimbo '61

Yusuke Kawazu
The Human Condition: A
Soldier's Prayer '61
The Human Condition:
Road to Eternity '59

Sylvia Kay
Outback '71

Yuzo Kayama
Red Beard '65

Narumi Kayashima
Rhapsody in August '91

Norman Kaye
A Woman's Tale '92
Cactus '86
Man of Flowers '84

Billy Kearns
Bed and Board '70
Purple Noon '60

Jeremy Keefe
The Boys of St.
Vincent '93

Pat Keen
A Kind of Loving '62

Harvey Keitel
Ulysses' Gaze '95
The Piano '93
La Nuit de Varennes '82

Michael Keith
King Kong vs.
Godzilla '63

Constantin Kelber
Zero for Conduct '33

Hiram Keller
Fellini Satyricon '69

Judy Kelly
Dead of Night '45

Paul Kemp
M '31

Suzy Kendall
The Bird with the
Crystal Plumage '70

Thomas Keneally
The Devil's
Playground '76

Diana Kent
Heavenly Creatures '94

Edith Ker
Delicatessen '92

Evelyne Ker
A Nos Amours '84

Jean Keraudy
Le Trou '59

Michele Kerbash
The Battle of Algiers '66

Samia Kerbash
The Battle of Algiers '66

Jean-Pierre Kerien
Muriel '63

Bill Kerr
Gallipoli '81

Deborah Kerr
Black Narcissus '47
The Life and Death of
Colonel Blimp '43

**Mamaengaroa
Kerr-Bell**
Once Were Warriors '94

Corinne Kersten
Murmur of the Heart '71

**Mohamad Ali
Keshavarz**
Through the Olive
Trees '94

Sarita Khajuria
Bhaji on the Beach '94

Shaheen Khan
Bhaji on the Beach '94

Arsinee Khanjian
The Sweet Hereafter '96
Exotica '94
The Adjuster '91

Farhad Kheradmand
Life and Nothing More
… '92

Udo Kier
Breaking the Waves '95
The Kingdom '95
Zentropa '92
The Stationmaster's
Wife '77
Suspiria '77

Chu-Ryun Kim
301, 302 '94

Sandrine Kimberlain
A Self-Made Hero '95

Maria Kimberly
Traffic '71

Isao Kimura
Stray Dog '49

Ko Kimura
Seven Samurai '54

Dave King
The Long Good
Friday '80

Melinda Kinnaman
My Life As a Dog '85

Roy Kinnear
Juggernaut '74
How I Won the War '67

Tsuyoshi Kinoshita
Boy '69

Klaus Kinski
Fitzcarraldo '82
Nosferatu the
Vampyre '79
Woyzeck '78
Aguirre, the Wrath of
God '72

Nastassia Kinski
Faraway, So Close! '93
Moon in the Gutter '83

Mia Kirshner
Exotica '94

Nino Kirtadze
A Chef in Love '96

Keiko Kishi
The Makioka Sisters '83
Kwaidan '64

Kyoko Kishida
The Face of Another '66
Woman in the
Dunes '64

The Human Condition:
A Soldier's
Prayer '61

Ildiko Kishonti
Mephisto '81

Tanie Kitabayashi
The Burmese Harp '56

Kazuo Kitamura
Black Rain '88

Kinya Kitaoji
Himatsuri '85

Nijiko Kiyokawa
Vengeance Is Mine '79

Koji Kiyomura
The Human Condition:
A Soldier's
Prayer '61

Alf Kjellin
Summer Interlude '50
Torment '44

Bjorn Kjellman
The Best Intentions '92

Ingvar Kjellson
Shame '68

Bodil Kjer
Babette's Feast '87

Nita Klein
Dr. Petiot '90
Muriel '63

Rudolf Klein-Rogge
Spies '28
Metropolis '26
Die Nibelungen '23
Dr. Mabuse, Parts
1 & 2 '22
The Cabinet of Dr.
Caligari '19

Leonid Kmit
Chapayev '34

Esmond Knight
Hamlet '48
The Red Shoes '48
Black Narcissus '47
Henry V '45

Shirley Knight
Juggernaut '74

Akiji Kobayashi
Harakiri '62

Bogumil Kobiela
Ashes and
Diamonds '58

Georg August Koch
Die Nibelungen '23

Marianne Koch
A Fistful of Dollars '64

Momoko Kochi
Godzilla, King of the
Monsters '56

Kokuten Kodo
Sanshiro Sugata '43

Kuninori Kodo
Seven Samurai '54

Max Kohlhase
The Joyless Street '25

Heidi Komarek
The Icicle Thief '89

Maja Komorowska
Contract '80

Chu Kong
The Killer '90

Milos Kopecky
Fabulous Adventures
of Baron
Munchausen '61

Fritz Kortner
Pandora's Box '28

Sylva Koscina
Juliet of the Spirits '65

Josef Kostlinger
The Magic Flute '73

Yoshio Kosugi
The Human Condition:
No Greater Love '58
The Men Who Tread on
the Tiger's Tail '45

Eva Kotamanidou
Landscape in the
Mist '88

Elias Koteas
Crash '95
Exotica '94
The Adjuster '91

Hubert Kounde
Hate '95
Café au Lait '94

Bholanath Koyal
Charulata '64

Akiko Koyama
Boy '69

Andras Kozak
The Round-Up '66

Jeroen Krabbe
Farinelli '94
The 4th Man '79

Michael Kraft
Rendezvous in Paris '95

Werner Krauss
The Joyless Street '25
Variety '25
Waxworks '24
The Cabinet of Dr.
Caligari '19

Lee Kresel
Mothra '62

Elisabeth Kreuzer
Basileus Quartet '82
The American Friend '77
Kings of the Road—
In the Course of
Time '76

Harry Krimer
Napoleon '27

Svetlana Kri-outchkova
Burnt by the Sun '94

Michael Kroecher
Every Man for Himself &
God Against All '75

Max Kronert
The Golem '20

Margareta Krook
Persona '66

Christiane Kruger
Le Dernier Combat '84

Hardy Kruger
Sundays & Cybele '62

Nikolai Kryuchkov
Ballad of a Soldier '60

Eva Krzyzewska
Ashes and Diamonds '58

Akira Kubo
Throne of Blood '57

Jarl Kulle
Babette's Feast '87
Fanny and Alexander '83
The Devil's Eye '60
Smiles of a Summer
Night '55

Magda Kun
Dead of Night '45

Tamiyo Kusakari
Shall We Dance? '97

Machiko Kyo
The Face of Another '66
Odd Obsession '60
Princess Yang Kwei Fei
'55
Gate of Hell '54
Ugetsu '53
Rashomon '51

Barbara Laage
Bed and Board '70

Andre S. Labarthe
My Life to Live '62

Samuel Labarthe
The Accompanist '93

Elisabeth Labi
Orchestra Rehearsal '78

Cateria Sylos Labini
The Icicle Thief '89

Elina Labourdette
Lola '61

Dominique Labourier
Jonah Who Will Be 25 in
the Year 2000 '76
The Wonderful Crook '75

Philippe Labro
Cat and Mouse '78

Marian Labuda
My Sweet Little
Village '86

Ronald Lacey
The Fearless Vampire
Killers '67

Stephen Lack
Dead Ringers '88

Andre Lacombe
Dr. Petiot '90

Ghalia Lacroix
The Silences of the
Palace '94

Violaine Lacroix
Tous les Matins du
Monde '92

Katya Ladan
32 Short Films about
Glenn Gould '93

Taherek Ladania
Through the Olive
Trees '94

Walter Ladengast
Nosferatu the
Vampyre '79

Walter Laderigast
Every Man for Himself &
God Against All '75

Nicole Ladmiral
Diary of a Country
Priest '50

Bernadette LaFont
Violette '78
The Mother and the
Whore '73
A Very Curious Girl '69
The Thief of Paris '67

**Jean-Philippe
LaFont**
Babette's Feast '87

Marie Laforet
Purple Noon '60

Valerie Lagrange
Cat and Mouse '78
Weekend '67
A Man and a Woman '66

Tulsi Lahnin
Jalsaghar '58

Jenny Laird
Black Narcissus '47

Michael Lake
Sweetie '89

Anne Lambert
Picnic at Hanging
Rock '75

**Anne Louise
Lambert**
The Draughtsman's
Contract '82

**Christopher
Lambert**
Subway '85

Duncan Lamont
The Golden Coach '52

Pascal Lamorisse
The Red Balloon '56

Jutta Lampe
Marianne and
Juliane '82

Chus Lampreave
The Flower of My
Secret '95
Matador '86

Gunter Lamprecht
Berlin Alexanderplatz '80

Burt Lancaster
Local Hero '83
1900 '76
Conversation Piece '75

Rodolfo Landa
The Criminal Life of
Archibaldo de la
Cruz '55

Inge Landgut
M '31

Ruth Landshoff
Nosferatu '22

Caroline Lang
L'Argent '83

Fritz Lang
Contempt '64

Amanda Langlet
Pauline at the Beach '83

Victor Lanoux
Scene of the Crime '87

Daniel Lapaine
Muriel's Wedding '94

Ivan Lapikov
Andrei Rublev '66

Sylvie Laporte
La Lectrice '88

Odete Lara
Antonio Das Mortes '68

Leon Larive
Children of Paradise '44

Michele Laroque
Nelly et Monsieur
Arnaud '95

Gerard Lartigau
Indochine '92

Martin LaSalle
Pickpocket '59

Dieter Laser
The Lost Honor of
Katharina Blum '75

Stanislaw Latallo
Illumination '73

**Philippe
Laudenbach**
Confidentially Yours '83

Carole Laure
Get Out Your
Handkerchiefs '78

Christine Laurent
Cat and Mouse '78

Jacqueline Laurent
Le Jour Se Lève '39

Remy Laurent
La Cage aux Folles '78

John Laurie
Hamlet '48

Charlotte Laurier
Les Bons Debarras '81

**Dominque
Lavanant**
The Monster '96

Denis Lavant
Boy Meets Girl '84

Martin Lavut
The Mask '61

Phyllida Law
Before the Rain '94

Denis Lawson
Local Hero '83

Claude Layou
Diary of a Country
Priest '50

Renee Le Calm
When the Cat's Away '96

**Charles Le
Clainche**
A Man Escaped '57

Bernard Le Coq
Captain Conan '96
Van Gogh '92

Robert Le Flon
Zero for Conduct '33

Paul Le Person
The Thief of Paris '67

Robert Le Vigan
The Lower Depths '36

Jean-Pierre Leaud
Diary of a Seducer '95
Love on the Run '78
Day for Night '73
Last Tango in Paris '73
The Mother and the
Whore '73
Two English Girls '72
Bed and Board '70
Stolen Kisses '68
Weekend '67
Masculine Feminine '66
Alphaville '65
Pierrot le Fou '65
The 400 Blows '59
The Testament of
Orpheus '59

Madeleine LeBeau
8 1/2 '63

Samuel Lebihan
Captain Conan '96
Trois Couleurs:
Rouge '94

Francoise Lebrun
The Mother and the
Whore '73

Yvon Lec
Bed and Board '70

Ginette LeClerc
The Baker's Wife '33

Jacqueline Lecomte
Playtime '67

Francis Lederer
Pandora's Box '28

Fernand Ledoux
Les Visiteurs du Soir '42
La Bete Humaine '38

Virginie Ledoyen
A Single Girl '96
La Cérémonie '95

Christopher Lee
Hamlet '48

Danny Lee
The Killer '90

Margaret Lee
Casanova '70 '65

Mark Lee
Gallipoli '81

Sophie Lee
Muriel's Wedding '94

Louis Lef'evre
Zero for Conduct '33

Rene Lefevre
The Crime of Monsieur
Lange '36
Le Million '31

Darling Legitimus
Sugar Cane Alley '83

Margaret Leighton
The Go-Between '71

Arabella Lemaitre
The Flowers of St.
Francis '50

Genevieve Lemon
The Piano '93
Sweetie '89

John Lennon
How I Won the War '67

Lotte Lenya
The Threepenny
Opera '31

Loles Leon
Tie Me Up! Tie Me
Down! '90

Marco Leonardi
Like Water for
Chocolate '93
Cinema Paradiso '88

Philippe Leotard
Cat and Mouse '78
The Wonderful
    Crook '75
Two English Girls '72

Robert Lepage
Jesus of Montreal '89

Paul Leperson
The Phantom of
    Liberty '74

Severine Lerczinska
Boudu Saved from
    Drowning '32

Preben Lerdorff
Day of Wrath '43

Jacques Leroy
Le Samourai '67

Phillippe LeRoy
The Night Porter '74
A Married Woman '65
Le Trou '59

Francois Leterrier
A Man Escaped '57

Rudolf Lettinger
The Cabinet of Dr.
    Caligari '19

Tony Leung
Happy Together '96
Chungking Express '95
Hard-Boiled '92

Sabrina Leurquin
Baxter '89

Francois Levantal
Hate '95

Pavlik Levin
Commissar '68

Raoul Levy
Two or Three Things I
    Know About Her '66

Jose Lewgoy
Fitzcarraldo '82

Fiona Lewis
The Fearless Vampire
    Killers '67

Jonathan Lewis
The Boys of St.
    Vincent '93

Tommy Lewis
The Chant of Jimmie
    Blacksmith '78

Leo Leyden
The Mask '61

Thierno Leye
Xala '75

Jacob Leygraf
Sunday's Children '94

Pierre Leymarie
Pickpocket '59

Johan Leysen
Egg '88

Thierry Lhermitte
Augustin '95
My New Partner '84

Gong Li
Temptress Moon '96
Shanghai Triad '95
To Live '94
Farewell My
    Concubine '93
Raise the Red
    Lantern '91
The Story of Qiu Ju '91
Ju Dou '90
Red Sorghum '87

Anki Liden
My Life As a Dog '85

**Wolfgang
    Liebeneiner**
Liebelei '32

Leon Liebgold
The Dybbuk '37

Albert Lieven
The Life and Death of
    Colonel Blimp '43

Paola Liguori
Intervista '87

Lili Liliana
The Dybbuk '37

Silvia Lillo
Love in the City '53

Altair Lima
Xica '76

Bridget Lin
Chungking Express '95
Police Story '85

Kevin Lin
Temptress Moon '96

Kong Lin
Raise the Red
    Lantern '91

Sven Lindberg
Face to Face '76

Gunnel Lindblom
The Virgin Spring '59

Slawomir Linder
The Saragossa
    Manuscript '65

Peter Lindgren
The New Land '73
I Am Curious (Yellow) '67

Vincent Lindon
Betty Blue '86

**Carl Gustav
    Lindstedt**
The Man on the Roof '76

Pierre Lindstedt
The New Land '73
The Emigrants '72

Gunnel Lindstrom
The Silence '63

Theo Lingen
M '31

Henrik Linnros
Sunday's Children '94

Edilson Lino
Pixote '81

Therese Liotard
One Sings, the Other
    Doesn't '77

Lu Liping
The Blue Kite '93

Eugene Lipinski
Moonlighting '82

Moshe Lipman
The Dybbuk '37

Virna Lisi
Casanova '70 '65

Michel Lisowski
Trois Couleurs: Blanc '94

Boris Livanov
Ten Days That Shook
    the World '27

Roger Livesey
I Know Where I'm
    Going '45
The Life and Death of
    Colonel Blimp '43

Enrico Lo Verso
Lamerica '95
Farinelli '94
La Scorta '94
The Stolen Children '92

Jane Lobre
The Green Room '78
A Gentle Woman '69

Truong Thi Loc
The Scent of Green
    Papaya '93

Philip Locke
And the Ship Sails
    On '83

Phyllis Logan
Secrets and Lies '95

Christopher Logue
The Devils '71

Luisa Loiano
Mamma Roma '62

Tadek Lokcinski
Café au Lait '94

Ulli Lommel
Effi Briest '74
The American
    Soldier '70
Beware of a Holy
    Whore '70

Jacek Lomnicki
Man of Marble '76

Tadeusz Lomnicki
Contract '80
Man of Marble '76
A Generation '54

Alexandra London
Van Gogh '92

Frederic Longbois
Celestial Clockwork '94

**Michael (Michel)
    Lonsdale**
Nelly et Monsieur
    Arnaud '95
Erendira '83
The Phantom of
    Liberty '74
Murmur of the Heart '71
The Bride Wore Black '68
Stolen Kisses '68
Is Paris Burning? '66

Theodore Loos
M '31
Metropolis '26

Ava Loraschi
A Tale of Winter '92

Sophia Loren
A Special Day '77
Yesterday, Today and
    Tomorrow '64
Boccaccio '70 '62

Jean-Pierre Lorit
Trois Couleurs:
    Rouge '94

Peter Lorre
M '31

Nadia Loutfy
The Night of Counting
    the Years '69

Patti Love
The Long Good
    Friday '80

Arthur Lowe
If… '69
This Sporting Life '63
Kind Hearts and
    Coronets '49

Holger Lowenadler
Lacombe, Lucien '74

Klaus Lowitsch
The Marriage of Maria
    Braun '79

Lynn Lowry
They Came from
    Within '75

Benedicte Loyen
Rendezvous in Paris '95

Margarita Lozano
Jean de Florette '87
Manon of the Spring '87
Half of Heaven '86
Kaos '85
The Night of the
    Shooting Stars '82
Viridiana '61

Angela Luce
The Decameron '70

Fabrice Luchini
La Discrete '90
Full Moon in Paris '84

Cast

Joseph Lucien
The City of Lost Children '95

Christian Lude
The Thief of Paris '67

Francoise Lugagne
Diary of a Chambermaid '64

Peter Luhr
The Marquise of O '76

Benny Luke
La Cage aux Folles '78

Folco Lulli
The Wages of Fear '55
Variety Lights '51

Ti Lung
A Better Tomorrow '86

Lei Luosheng
Women from the Lake of Scented Souls '94

Cui Luowen
The Story of Qiu Ju '91

Maria Pia Luzi
La Notte '60

Tom Lycos
Sweetie '89

Melanie Lynskey
Heavenly Creatures '94

Lya Lys
L'Age D'Or '30

Rita Macedo
The Criminal Life of Archibaldo de la Cruz '55

Niall MacGinnis
Curse of the Demon '57

Jack MacGowran
The Fearless Vampire Killers '67

Ignacy Machowski
Contract '80

Fulton Mackay
Local Hero '83

Mary MacLeod
If… '69

Peter MacNeill
Crash '95

Victor Maddern
I'm All Right, Jack '59

Teresa Madruga
In the White City '83

Beverly Maeda
The Face of Another '66

Yona Magalhaes
Black God, White Devil '64

Pupella Maggio
Amarcord '74

Lamberto Maggiorani
The Bicycle Thief '48

Allan Magicovsky
They Came from Within '75

Benoit Magimel
Les Voleurs '96
A Single Girl '96

Anna Magnani
Mamma Roma '62
The Golden Coach '52
The Miracle '48
Open City '45

Barbara Magnolfi
Suspiria '77

Pierre Maguelon
Bed and Board '70

Caludette Maille
Like Water for Chocolate '93

Valerie Mairesse
The Sacrifice '86
One Sings, the Other Doesn't '77

Marne Maitland
Fellini's Roma '72

Swapan Makerji
The World of Apu '59

Patrick Malahide
A Month in the Country '87
Comfort and Joy '84

Zygmunt Malandowicz
Knife in the Water '62

Henrik Malberg
Ordet '55

Pierre Malet
Basileus Quartet '82

Miles Malleson
Captain's Paradise '53
Kind Hearts and Coronets '49
Dead of Night '45

Odile Mallet
The City of Lost Children '95

Mona Malm
The Best Intentions '92

Lennart Malmer
Elvira Madigan '67

Jan Malmsjo
Fanny and Alexander '83
Scenes from a Marriage '73

Birger Malmsten
The Silence '63
Summer Interlude '50

Michael Maloney
Henry V '89

Nick Mancuso
Ticket to Heaven '81

Rena Mandel
Vampyr '31

Gina Manes
Napoleon '27

Gaspard Manesse
Au Revoir les Enfants '87

Nino Manfredi
We All Loved Each Other So Much '77
Down & Dirty '76

Silvana Mangano
Conversation Piece '75
The Decameron '70
Bitter Rice '49

Paulus Manker
My Twentieth Century '90

Claude Mann
French Provincial '75

Ettore Manni
City of Women '81

Miki Manojlovic
Underground '95
When Father Was Away on Business '85

Predrag Manojlovic
Tito and Me '92

Marie Mansert
Two English Girls '72

Leslie Manville
Secrets and Lies '95
High Hopes '88

Jean Marais
Donkey Skin '70
The Testament of Orpheus '59
Eléna and Her Men '56
Orpheus '49
Beauty and the Beast '46
Eternal Return '43

Elke Maravilha
Xica '76

Dominique Marcas
Dr. Petiot '90

Georges Marchal
Belle de Jour '67

Corinne Marchand
Borsalino '70

Guy Marchand
Entre-Nous '83
Loulou '80

Henri Marchand
A Nous la Liberté '31

Elio Marcuzzo
Ossessione '42

Ahmed Marei
The Night of Counting the Years '69

Ivano Marescotti
The Monster '96

Janie Mareze
La Chienne '31

Miriam Margolyes
Little Dorrit, Film 1: Nobody's Fault '88
Little Dorrit, Film 2: Little Dorrit's Story '88

Jean-Pierre Marielle
Tous les Matins du Monde '92

Banduk Marika
Cactus '86

Jacques Marin
Forbidden Games '52

Marisol
Blood Wedding '81

Jane Marken
Children of Paradise '44
Eternal Return '43

Kika Markham
Two English Girls '72

Olivera Markovic
Tito and Me '92

Philippe Maron
Jacquot '91

Christian Marquand
And God Created Woman '57

Evarist Marquez
Burn! '70

Sylvia Marriott
The Story of Adele H. '75
Two English Girls '72

Marjorie Mars
Brief Encounter '46

Claudia Marsani
Conversation Piece '75

Carry Marsh
Dead of Night '45

Bryan Marshall
The Long Good Friday '80

E.G. Marshall
Is Paris Burning? '66

Henri Marteau
Indochine '92
La Femme Infidèle '69

Norma Martel
The Night of the Shooting Stars '82

Jean Martin
The Battle of Algiers '66

Elsa Martinelli
The Trial '63

Marc Martinez
Land and Freedom '95

Mario Ivan Martinez
Like Water for Chocolate '93

Nacho Martinez
Matador '86

Marino Mase
The Belly of an Architect '91
Les Carabiniers '63

Vladimir Mashkov
The Thief '97

Giulietta Masina
Ginger & Fred '86
Juliet of the Spirits '65
Nights of Cabiria '57
La Strada '54
The White Sheik '52
Variety Lights '51

Lea Massari
Christ Stopped at Eboli '79
Allonsanfan '73
Murmur of the Heart '71
L'Avventura '60

Leonide Massine
The Red Shoes '48

Chiara Mastroianni
Diary of a Seducer '95
Ma Saison Préférée '93

Marcello Mastroianni
I Don't Want to Talk about It '94
Intervista '87
Ginger & Fred '86
La Nuit de Varennes '82
City of Women '81
A Special Day '77
We All Loved Each Other So Much '77
Allonsanfan '73
La Grande Bouffe '73
Casanova '70 '65
Yesterday, Today and Tomorrow '64
8 1/2 '63
Divorce—Italian Style '62
Il Bell'Antonio '60
La Dolce Vita '60
La Notte '60
Big Deal on Madonna Street '58

Gabor Mate
My Twentieth Century '90

Maria Mathiesen
Insomnia '97

Jacques Mathou
Ridicule '96
The Hairdresser's Husband '92
Betty Blue '86

Eiko Matsuda
In the Realm of the Senses '76

Yusaku Matsuda
The Family Game '83

Dietrich Mattausch
The Wannsee Conference '84

Eva Mattes
Céleste '81
In a Year of 13 Moons '78
Woyzeck '78
Stroszek '77
The Bitter Tears of Petra von Kant '72

Marinka Matuszewski
The Mother and the Whore '73

Julie Mauduech
Café au Lait '94

Monica Maughan
A Woman's Tale '92
Cactus '86

David Mauhsell
Orchestra Rehearsal '78

Carmen Maura
Women on the Verge of a Nervous Breakdown '88
Matador '86

Nicole Maurey
Diary of a Country Priest '50

Claire Maurier
La Cage aux Folles '78
A Very Curious Girl '69
The 400 Blows '59

Gerda Maurus
Woman in the Moon '29
Spies '28

Antonina Maximova
Ballad of a Soldier '60

Yelena Maximova
Earth '30

Ferdinand "Ferdy" Mayne
The Fearless Vampire Killers '67
Captain's Paradise '53

Ernestine Mazurowna
Jean de Florette '87

Rosy Mazzacurati
La Notte '60

Des McAleer
Butterfly Kiss '94

Ray McAnally
My Left Foot '89

Ruth McCabe
My Left Foot '89

Tom McCamus
The Sweet Hereafter '96

Leigh McCormack
The Long Day Closes '92

Alec McCowen
Henry V '89

Kyle McCulloch
Careful '94

Malcolm McDowell
If... '69

Peter McEnery
Victim '61

Angela Punch McGregor
The Chant of Jimmie Blacksmith '78

Ewan McGregor
The Pillow Book '95

Don McKellar
Exotica '94
The Adjuster '91

Tim McKenzie
Gallipoli '81

Alan McNaughton
Victim '61

Kris McQuade
Two Friends '86

Ray Meagher
The Chant of Jimmie Blacksmith '78

Patricia Medina
Mr. Arkadin '55

Armand Meffre
Jean de Florette '87
Manon of the Spring '87

Mathias Megard
Rendezvous in Paris '95

Armin Meier
Mother Küsters Goes to Heaven '76

John Meillon
Outback '71
Walkabout '71

Maurizio Mein
Intervista '87

Alfonso Mejias
Los Olvidados '50

Susanna Mekhralieva
Prisoner of the Mountains '96

Mariangela Melato
Swept Away... '75
Love and Anarchy '73

Annielo Mele
Shoeshine '47

Breno Mello
Black Orpheus '58

Jean-Pierre Melville
Breathless '59

Murray Melvin
The Devils '71

Ricky Memphis
La Scorta '94

Daniel Mendaille
Kameradschaft '31

Mauro Mendonca
Dona Flor and Her Two Husbands '78

Alex Menglet
A Woman's Tale '92

Oleg Menshikov
Prisoner of the Mountains '96
Burnt by the Sun '94

Yehudi Menuhin
32 Short Films about Glenn Gould '93

Ernest Menzer
Bed and Board '70

Robert Menzies
Cactus '86

Chantal Mercier
Small Change '76

Michele Mercier
Casanova '70 '65
Shoot the Piano Player '62

Jean Mercure
Baxter '89

Macha Meril
Vagabond '85
A Married Woman '65

Franco Merli
Arabian Nights '74

Mary Merrall
Dead of Night '45

Clive Merrison
Heavenly Creatures '94

Franco Mescolini
The Monster '96

Eric Messiter
Kind Hearts and Coronets '49

Otto Messmer
Generale Della Rovere '60

Veronkia Metonidze
Ashik Kerib '88

Raymond Meunier
Le Trou '59

Paul Meurisse
Diabolique '55

Anne-Laure Meury
Boyfriends &
  Girlfriends '88

Myriam Meziere
Jonah Who Will Be 25 in
  the Year 2000 '76

**Vittorio
  Mezzogiorno**
Moon in the Gutter '83
Three Brothers '80

Yiur Mgoyan
Ashik Kerib '88

Ralph Michael
Dead of Night '45

**Yorgos Michalo-
  kopoulos**
Ulysses' Gaze '95

Andre Michaud
A Nous la Liberté '31

Marc Michel
The Umbrellas of
  Cherbourg '64
Lola '61
Le Trou '59

Maria Michi
Paisan '46
Open City '45

Ivan Micholaichuk
Shadows of Forgotten
  Ancestors '64

Alain Midgette
Before the
  Revolution '65

Toshiro Mifune
Samurai Rebellion '67
Red Beard '65
High & Low '62
Sanjuro '62
Yojimbo '61
The Bad Sleep Well '60
The Hidden Fortress '58
The Lower Depths '57
Throne of Blood '57
I Live in Fear '55
Seven Samurai '54
Life of Oharu '52
Rashomon '51
Stray Dog '49
Drunken Angel '48

Toto Mignone
Ginger & Fred '86

Tatsuya Mihashi
High & Low '62
The Burmese Harp '56

Shin-Ichiro Mikami
An Autumn
  Afternoon '62

Anna Mikhalkov
Anna '93

Nadia Mikhalkov
Burnt by the Sun '94
Anna '93

Nikita Mikhalkov
Burnt by the Sun '94
Anna '93

Norihei Miki
Black Rain '88
Himatsuri '85

Rentaro Mikuni
Vengeance Is Mine '79
Kwaidan '64
Harakiri '62
The Burmese Harp '56

Kevin Miles
The Chant of Jimmie
  Blacksmith '78

Sarah Miles
Blow-Up '66

Tomas Milian
Boccaccio '70 '62
Il Bell'Antonio '60

Piro Milkani
Lamerica '95

Peter Millard
32 Short Films about
  Glenn Gould '93

Spike Milligan
The Case of the
  Mukkinese Battle
  Horn '56

Jean-Roger Milo
L.627 '92

Sandra Milo
Juliet of the Spirits '65
8 1/2 '63
Generale Della Rovere
  '60

Michio Minami
The Human Condition:
  Road to Eternity '59

Miou-Miou
Germinal '93
May Fools '90
La Lectrice '88
Entre-Nous '83
Jonah Who Will Be 25 in
  the Year 2000 '76
Going Places '74

Brigitte Mira
Berlin
  Alexanderplatz '80
Mother Küsters Goes to
  Heaven '76
Every Man for Himself &
  God Against All '75
Ali: Fear Eats the
  Soul '74

Isa Miranda
The Night Porter '74
La Ronde '51
La Signora di Tutti '34

Helen Mirren
The Cook, the Thief, His
  Wife & Her Lover '90
The Long Good
  Friday '80

Masao Mishima
Harakiri '62
The Human Condition:
  No Greater Love '58

Jorge Mistral
Wuthering Heights '53

Heather Mitchell
Proof '91

Labina Mitevska
Before the Rain '94

Koji Mitsui
Woman in the Dunes '64

Ken Mitsuishi
The Pillow Book '95

Ichirota Miyagawa
The Family Game '83

Seiji Miyaguchi
The Human Condition:
  No Greater Love '58
Seven Samurai '54

Chocho Miyako
Vengeance Is Mine '79

Nobuko Miyamoto
Minbo—Or the Gentle
  Art of Japanese
  Extortion '92
A Taxing Woman '87
Tampopo '86
The Funeral '84

Eiko Miyoshi
I Live in Fear '55

Genevieve Mnich
The Mother and the
  Whore '73

Teresa Mo
Hard-Boiled '92

Bjorn Moan
Insomnia '97

Tamezo Mochizuki
Utamaro and His Five
  Women '46

Gaston Modot
Casque d'Or '52
Children of Paradise '44
Grand Illusion '37
L'Age D'Or '30
Under the Roofs of
  Paris '29

**Urszula
  Modrzynska**
A Generation '54

**Enrica Maria
  Modugno**
Kaos '85

**Aida Mohammad-
  khani**
The White Balloon '95

Hossein Moharami
Gabbeh '96

Rogheih Moharami
Gabbeh '96

Angela Molina
Half of Heaven '86
That Obscure Object of
  Desire '77

Georgia Moll
Contempt '64

Jordi Molla
Jamón, Jamón '93

Tibor Molnar
The Round-Up '66

Ghislaine Mona
Thérèse '86

Laurent Monnier
Jacquot '91

Roland Monot
A Man Escaped '57

**Bruno
  Monsaingeon**
32 Short Films about
  Glenn Gould '93

Celia Montalvan
Toni '34

Yves Montand
Jean de Florette '87
Manon of the Spring '87
Vincent, François, Paul
  and the Others '76
State of Siege '73
César & Rosalie '72
The Confession '70
Z '69
Is Paris Burning? '66
The Wages of Fear '55

Elsa Montero
Death of a
  Bureaucrat '66

Ofelia Montesco
The Exterminating
  Angel '62

**Martine
  Montgermont**
Dr. Petiot '90

**Yves
  Montmarquette**
Léolo '92

Roger Montsoret
Two or Three Things I
  Know About Her '66

Heinz Moog
Senso '54

Gar Moore
Paisan '46

**Morando
  Morandini**
Before the
  Revolution '65

Marcello Morante
The Gospel According
  to St. Matthew '64

Nonna Mordyukova
Commissar '68

Jeanne Moreau
La Femme Nikita '91
French Provincial '75
Going Places '74
The Bride Wore Black '68
Chimes at Midnight '67
Viva Maria! '65
Diary of a
Chambermaid '64
The Fire Within '64
The Trial '63
Jules and Jim '62
La Notte '60
The 400 Blows '59
The Lovers '59
Frantic '58

Yolanda Moreau
Vagabond '85

Gael Morel
Wild Reeds '94

Rina Morelli
Il Bell'Antonio '60

Linda Moretti
The Postman '94

Michele Moretti
Wild Reeds '94
French Provincial '75

Nanni Moretti
Caro Diario '93

Abraham Morewski
The Dybbuk '37

Michele Morgan
Cat and Mouse '78

Maia Morgenstern
Ulysses' Gaze '95

Masayuki Mori
The Bad Sleep Well '60
When a Woman
Ascends the
Stairs '60
Princess Yang
Kwei Fei '55
Ugetsu '53
Rashomon '51
The Men Who Tread on
the Tiger's Tail '45

P. H. Moriarty
The Long Good
Friday '80

**Philippe Morier-
Genoud**
Trois Couleurs: Blanc '94
Au Revoir les Enfants '87
Confidentially Yours '83

Francesca Moriggi
The Tree of Wooden
Clogs '78

Johnny Morina
The Boys of St.
Vincent '93

Henning Moritzen
Cries and Whispers '72

Gaby Morlay
Le Plaisir '52

Robert Morley
Little Dorrit, Film 1:
Nobody's Fault '88
Little Dorrit, Film 2: Little
Dorrit's Story '88

Emmanuel Morozof
Olivier, Olivier '92

Keijiro Morozumi
The Human Condition:
A Soldier's
Prayer '61

Rachael Morris
Once Were Warriors '94

Temuera Morrison
Once Were Warriors '94

Helen Morse
Picnic at Hanging
Rock '75

Clive Morton
Kind Hearts and
Coronets '49

Gastone Moschin
The Conformist '71

Bertha Moss
The Exterminating
Angel '62

Mireille Mosse
The City of Lost
Children '95

Masahiro Motoki
The Mystery of
Rampo '94

Zeze Motta
Quilombo '84
Xica '76

Catherine Mouchet
Thérèse '86

**John Moulder-
Brown**
Deep End '70

Jean-Paul Moulinot
The Fire Within '64

Charles Moulton
The Baker's Wife '33

Kinda Moumouni
Yaaba '89

Gilberto Moura
Pixote '81

Lisbeth Movin
Day of Wrath '43

Romesh Mukerji
Distant Thunder '73

Majhabi Mukherjee
Charulata '64
The Big City '63

Pradip Mukherjee
The Middleman '76

Shailan Mukherjee
Charulata '64

Suku Mukherjee
Charulata '64

Maxim Munzuk
Dersu Uzala '75

Sachiko Murase
Rhapsody in August '91

Jean Murat
Eternal Return '43
Carnival in Flanders '35

Takehiro Murata
Okoge '93
Minbo—Or the Gentle
Art of Japanese
Extortion '92

Irina Muravyova
Moscow Does Not
Believe in Tears '80

Paule Muret
Every Man for
Himself '79

Hideo Murota
A Taxing Woman '87

Tony Musante
The Bird with the
Crystal Plumage '70

Hans Musaus
Every Man for Himself &
God Against All '75

Alexander Musky
The Joyless Street '25

**Varvara Myas-
nikova**
Chapayev '34

Peter Mygind
The Kingdom '95

Bruce Myles
A Woman's Tale '92
A Cry in the Dark '88

Per Myrberg
Sunday's Children '94

Claire Nadeau
Nelly et Monsieur
Arnaud '95

Mikola Nademsy
Earth '30

Yasushi Nagata
The Human Condition:
No Greater Love '58

Kyozo Nagatsuka
Okoge '93

Taketoshi Naito
The Human Condition:
A Soldier's
Prayer '61

Tatsuya Nakadai
Ran '85
Kagemusha '80
Samurai Rebellion '67
The Face of Another '66
Kwaidan '64
Harakiri '62

High & Low '62
Sanjuro '62
The Human Condition:
A Soldier's
Prayer '61
When a Woman
Ascends the
Stairs '60
The Human Condition:
Road to Eternity '59
Enjo '58
The Human Condition:
No Greater Love '58

Takeo Nakahara
Okoge '93

Aio Nakajima
In the Realm of the
Senses '76

Ryota Nakamoto
Himatsuri '85

Ganjiro Nakamura
Odd Obsession '60
Enjo '58
The Lower Depths '57

Katsuo Nakamura
Kwaidan '64

Satoshi Nakamura
The Manster '59

Tamao Nakamura
The Human Condition:
A Soldier's
Prayer '61

Toshihiko Nakano
Akira Kurosawa's
Dreams '90

Ichiro Nakaya
Harakiri '62

**Rodion
Nakhapetov**
A Slave of Love '78

Shinji Nambara
The Human Condition:
No Greater Love '58

Govind Namdeo
Bandit Queen '94

Agnes Nano
Cinema Paradiso '88

Jessica Napier
Love Serenade '96

Jean Narboni
Two or Three Things I
Know About Her '66

Narenhua
A Mongolian Tale '94

Levan Natroshvili
Ashik Kerib '88

Gustavo Naveira
The Tango Lesson '97

Arnost Navratil
The Fabulous World of
Jules Verne '58

Pavel Nazarov
Freeze-Die-Come to
Life '90

Yuri Nazarov
Little Vera '88

Amedeo Nazzari
Nights of Cabiria '57

Tabata Ndiaye
Ceddo '78

Scott Neal
Beautiful Thing '95

Brent Neale
Careful '94

Claire Nebout
Ponette '95
Scene of the Crime '87

**Raisa
Nedashkovskaya**
Commissar '68

Toshie Negishi
Akira Kurosawa's
Dreams '90

Natalia Negoda
Little Vera '88

Francois Negret
Au Revoir les Enfants '87

Del Negro
Aguirre, the Wrath of
God '72

Carola Neher
The Threepenny
Opera '31

Sigrid Neiiendam
Day of Wrath '43

Sam Neill
The Piano '93
A Cry in the Dark '88
My Brilliant Career '79

Kate Nelligan
Margaret's Museum '95

Margaret Nelson
Picnic at Hanging
Rock '75

Tommaso Neri
The Battle of Algiers '66

Franco Nero
Tristana '70

Derren Nesbitt
Victim '61

Loni Nest
The Joyless Street '25
The Golem '20

Jinpachi Nesu
Ran '85

Sarah Neville
Careful '94

Robyn Nevin
Careful, He Might Hear
You '84

The Chant of Jimmie
Blacksmith '78

Claudette Nevins
The Mask '61

Robert Newton
Henry V '45

Dieynaba Niang
Xala '75

Isseu Niang
Mandabi '68

Miriam Niang
Xala '75

Maurizio Nichetti
The Icicle Thief '89
Allegro Non Troppo '76

Anthony Nicholls
If… '69
Victim '61

Mike Nichols
The Designated
Mourner '97

Nick Nichols
Dead Ringers '88

Alexander Niegreva
Little Vera '88

Asta Nielson
The Joyless Street '25

Leon Niemczyk
Knife in the Water '62

Nikandrov
Ten Days That Shook
the World '27

Esko Nikkari
The Match Factory
Girl '90

**Jose Nilson dos
Santos**
Pixote '81

Maj-Britt Nilsson
Summer Interlude '50

Annibale Ninchi
La Dolce Vita '60

Akira Nishimura
The Bad Sleep Well '60

Aud Egede Nissen
Dr. Mabuse, Parts
1 & 2 '22

Bernard Noel
A Married Woman '65
The Fire Within '64

Magali Noel
Amarcord '74
La Dolce Vita '60
Eléna and Her Men '56

Toshie Nogishi
Okoge '93

Philippe Noiret
The Postman '94
Life and Nothing But '89

Cinema Paradiso '88
My New Partner '84
Three Brothers '80
The Judge and the
Assassin '75
La Grande Bouffe '73

Christine Noonan
If… '69

Ghita Norby
The Kingdom '95
The Best Intentions '92

Nadine Nortier
Mouchette '67

Alex Norton
Comfort and Joy '84

Jerzy Nowak
Trois Couleurs: Blanc '94

Eslinda Nunez
Memories of Under-
development '68

Lena Nyman
Autumn Sonata '78
I Am Curious
(Yellow) '67

Uwe Ochsenknecht
Kaspar Hauser '93

Simon O'Connor
Heavenly Creatures '94

Hugh O'Conor
The Young Poisoner's
Handbook '94
My Left Foot '89

Joseph O'Conor
The Forbidden
Quest '93

Miki Odagari
Ikiru '52

Fritz Odemar
M '31

**Fereshteh Sadr
Ofrani**
The White Balloon '95

Ken Ogata
The Pillow Book '95
The Ballad of
Narayama '83
Vengeance Is Mine '79

Mayumi Ogawa
Vengeance Is Mine '79

Bulle Ogier
The Discreet Charm of
the Bourgeoisie '72
The Valley Obscured by
the Clouds '72
La Salamandre '71

Pascale Ogier
Full Moon in Paris '84

Claudia Ohana
Erendira '83

Yoshi Oida
The Pillow Book '95

Eiji Okada
The Face of Another '66
Woman in the Dunes '64
Hiroshima Mon
Amour '59

Mariko Okada
An Autumn Afternoon
'62

**Nikolai P.
Okholopkov**
Alexander Nevsky '38

Denjiro Okochi
The Men Who Tread on
the Tiger's Tail '45
Sanshiro Sugata '43

Daniel Olbrychski
The Tin Drum '79

Craig Olejnik
Margaret's Museum '95

Lena Olin
After the Rehearsal '84

Enrico Oliveri
Black Sunday '60

Laurence Olivier
Hamlet '48
Henry V '45

Paul Olivier
A Nous la Liberté '31
Le Million '31

Jennifer O'Neill
The Innocent '76

Judy Ongg
The Pillow Book '95

Marian Opania
Man of Iron '81

Liana Orfei
Casanova '70 '65

Pierre Orma
Camp de Thiaroye '87

Luigi Ornaghi
The Tree of Wooden
Clogs '78

Umberto Orsini
César & Rosalie '72

Bruno Ortensi
Shoeshine '47

Hisato Osawa
Utamaro and His Five
Women '46

Per Oscarsson
The New Land '73

Jacek Ostaszewski
Trois Couleurs: Bleu '93

Michael O'Sullivan
Careful '94

Shoji Otake
Tampopo '86
The Funeral '84

Hideji Otaki
Minbo—Or the Gentle
  Art of Japanese
  Extortion '92
Kagemusha '80

Shuji Otaki
A Taxing Woman '87

Nobuko Otowa
Onibaba '64

Nadia Ottaviani
Intervista '87

Miranda Otto
Love Serenade '96

Adama Ouedraogo
Yaaba '89

Assita Ouedraogo
La Promesse '96
Yaaba '89

Noufou Ouedraogo
Yaaba '89

**Rasmane
  Ouedraogo**
La Promesse '96
Tilai '90
Yaaba '89

Sibidou Ouedraogo
Yaaba '89

**Zenabou
  Ouedraogo**
Yaaba '89

Andre Oumansky
Burnt by the Sun '94

**Sverre Anker
  Ousdal**
Insomnia '97

Kati Outinen
The Match Factory
  Girl '90

Najia Overghi
The Silences of the
  Palace '94

Baard Owe
The Kingdom '95

Rena Owen
Once Were Warriors '94

Ayse Owens
The Long Day Closes '92

Eitaro Ozawa
The Human Condition:
  No Greater Love '58

Sakae Ozawa
Princess Yang Kwei
  Fei '55
Ugetsu '53

Shoichi Ozawa
Black Rain '88
The Ballad of
  Narayama '83

Erik Paaske
Pelle the Conqueror '88

Charles Lloyd Pack
If... '69
Victim '61

Roger Lloyd Pack
The Young Poisoner's
  Handbook '94

Genevieve Page
Belle de Jour '67

Marcel Pagliero
Open City '45

Turo Pajala
Ariel '89

Tania Palaiologou
Landscape in the
  Mist '88

Jack Palance
Contempt '64

Michael Palin
Monty Python's The
  Meaning of Life '83

Andrea Palma
The Criminal Life of
  Archibaldo de la
  Cruz '55

Ulf Palme
Dreams '55
Miss Julie '50

Luciana Paluzzi
The Green Slime '68

Nirmal Pandey
Bandit Queen '94

Irene Papas
Erendira '83
Christ Stopped at Eboli
  '79
Z '69

Veronika Papp
Angi Vera '78

Ignazio Pappalardo
Johnny Stecchino '92

Anna Paquin
The Piano '93

Marisa Paredes
The Flower of My Secret
  '95

Mila Parely
Beauty and the
  Beast '46

Anne Parillaud
La Femme Nikita '91

Lorival Pariz
Antonio Das Mortes '68

Cecil Parker
Heavens Above! '63

Dita Parlo
Grand Illusion '37
L'Atalante '34

Patrick Paroux
Delicatessen '92

Christine Pascal
The Best Way '76

Pier Paolo Pasolini
The Canterbury Tales '71
The Decameron '70

Susanna Pasolini
The Gospel According
  to St. Matthew '64

Antonio Passallia
Le Boucher '69

Lars Passgard
Through a Glass
  Darkly '61

Earl Pastko
The Sweet Hereafter '96

Rosana Pastor
Land and Freedom '95

Erszi Pasztor
Angi Vera '78

Patachou
French Can-Can '55

Andre Pataczek
Sweetie '89

Nana Patekar
Salaam Bombay! '88

Daniela Patella
Alfredo, Alfredo '72

Bill Paterson
Comfort and Joy '84

Christian Patey
L'Argent '83

Jean-Marie Patte
The Rise of Louis XIV '66

Brigitta Pattersson
The Virgin Spring '59

Henrik Pauer
Time Stands Still '82

Adam Pawlikowski
Ashes and Diamonds '58

Katina Paxinou
Zita '68
Rocco and His
  Brothers '60

Pooya Payvar
Life and Nothing More
  ... '92

Cezary Pazura
Trois Couleurs: Blanc '94

Maren Pedersen
Witchcraft through the
  Ages '22

Liu Peiqi
Ermo '94

Jean Pelegri
Pickpocket '59

**Jean-Pierre
  Pellegrin**
One Sings, the Other
  Doesn't '77

Ines Pellegrini
Arabian Nights '74

Gilles Pelletier
Jesus of Montreal '89

Matti Pellonpaa
Ariel '89
Leningrad Cowboys Go
  America '89

Lilo Pempeit
Effi Briest '74

Malvina Penne
Chloe in the
  Afternoon '72

John Penrose
Kind Hearts and
  Coronets '49

Marilia Pera
Pixote '81

Esme Percy
Dead of Night '45

Michel Perelon
Cat and Mouse '78

Conchita Perez
Cria '76

Vincent Perez
Indochine '92

Francois Perier
Z '69
Le Samourai '67
The Testament of
  Orpheus '59
Orpheus '49

Anthony Perkins
Is Paris Burning? '66
The Trial '63

Ron Perlman
The City of Lost
  Children '95

Florence Pernel
Trois Couleurs: Bleu '93

Mireille Perrey
The Umbrellas of
  Cherbourg '64

Mireille Perrier
Toto le Heros '91
Boy Meets Girl '84

Jacques Perrin
Cinema Paradiso '88
State of Siege '73
Donkey Skin '70
Z '69

Francoise Perrot
Life and Nothing But '89

Fred Personne
Every Man for Himself
  '79

Jorge Perugorria
Strawberry and
  Chocolate '93

Peter
Ran '85

493

Vladimir Pucholt
Loves of a Blonde '65

Gustav Puttjer
Kameradschaft '31

Olivier Py
When the Cat's Away '96

Zhu Qanging
The Story of Qiu Ju '91

Lu Qi
Farewell My
    Concubine '93

Liu Pei Qu
The Story of Qiu Ju '91

Pu Quanxin
The Blue Kite '93

Sarfuddin Quarassi
Salaam Bombay! '88

Iain Quarrier
The Fearless Vampire
    Killers '67

Anthony Quayle
Hamlet '48

Hugues Quester
Trois Couleurs: Bleu '93
A Tale of Springtime '92

Gerry Quigley
32 Short Films about
    Glenn Gould '93

**Umberto P.
    Quinavalle**
Salo, or the 120 Days of
    Sodom '75

Anthony Quinn
La Strada '54

Frederic Quiring
Olivier, Olivier '92

Kurt Raab
The Stationmaster's
    Wife '77
The American
    Soldier '70
Beware of a Holy
    Whore '70

Birgitte Raabjerg
The Kingdom '95

Francesco Rabal
Tie Me Up! Tie Me
    Down! '90
Belle de Jour '67
The Eclipse '66
Viridiana '61

Francine Racette
Au Revoir les Enfants '87

Goran Radakovic
Hey, Babu Riba '88

Basil Radford
Dead of Night '45

**Jerzy
    Radziwilowicz**
Man of Iron '81
Man of Marble '76

Chips Rafferty
Outback '71

Raimu
César '36
The Baker's Wife '33
Fanny '32
Marius '31

Anne Raitt
Bleak Moments '71

Cecil Ramage
Kind Hearts and
    Coronets '49

Enrique Rambal
The Exterminating
    Angel '62

**Mary Carmen
    Ramirez**
Belle Epoque '92

Charlotte Rampling
Max, Mon Amour '86
The Night Porter '74

Suze Randall
Chloe in the
    Afternoon '72

Salvo Randone
Fellini Satyricon '69

Galatea Ranzi
Fiorile '93

Eva Ras
Man Is Not a Bird '65

Eddy Rasimi
Le Trou '59

Michael Raskine
La Lectrice '88

Frode Rasmussen
Insomnia '97

Fritz Rasp
The Threepenny Opera
    '31
Diary of a Lost Girl '29
Spies '28
Die Liebe der Jeanne
    Ney '27
Metropolis '26

Julien Rassam
The Accompanist '93

Alida Rauffe
César '36
Fanny '32

Aurore Rauscher
Rendezvous in Paris '95

Thyrza Ravesteijn
Antonia's Line '95

Adrian Rawlins
Breaking the Waves '95

Nicholas Ray
The American Friend '77

Cyril Raymond
Brief Encounter '46

Gary Raymond
Look Back in Anger '58

Stephen Rea
Life Is Sweet '90

Sady Rebbot
My Life to Live '62

Michael Redgrave
The Go-Between '71
Mr. Arkadin '55
Dead of Night '45

Vanessa Redgrave
The Devils '71
Blow-Up '66

Liam Redmond
Curse of the Demon '57

**Ekaterina Red-
    nikova**
The Thief '97

Vicky Redwood
The Big City '63

Lou Reed
Faraway, So Close! '93

Oliver Reed
The Devils '71

Saskia Reeves
Butterfly Kiss '94

Benoit Regent
Trois Couleurs: Bleu '93

Serge Reggiani
Cat and Mouse '78
Vincent, François, Paul
    and the Others '76
Le Doulos '61
Casque d'Or '52
La Ronde '51

Regine
My New Partner '84

Hans Leo Reich
Metropolis '26

**Wolfgang Reich-
    mann**
Woyzeck '78

Santa Relli
Jour de Fete '48

Michel Remaudeau
Emitai '71

Albert Remy
Shoot the Piano
    Player '62
The 400 Blows '59
Children of Paradise '44

Renaud
Germinal '93

Madeleine Renaud
Le Plaisir '52

Jeremie Renier
La Promesse '96

Serge Renko
Rendezvous in Paris '95

Ginette Reno
Léolo '92

Jean Reno
La Femme Nikita '91
Subway '85
Le Dernier Combat '84

Pierre Renoir
Children of Paradise '44
La Marseillaise '37

Sophie Renoir
Boyfriends & Girlfriends
    '88
Le Beau Mariage '82

Eva Renzi
The Bird with the
    Crystal Plumage '70

Alejandro Repulles
Aguirre, the Wrath of
    God '72

Catherine Retore
Messidor '77

Jean-Luc Revol
A Tale of Winter '92

Fernando Rey
The Hit '85
That Obscure Object of
    Desire '77
Seven Beauties '76
The Discreet Charm of
    the Bourgeoisie '72
Tristana '70
Chimes at Midnight '67
Viridiana '61

Silvano Rey
The Last Supper '76

Hossein Rezai
Through the Olive
    Trees '94

Catherine Rich
Captain Conan '96

Claude Rich
Captain Conan '96
The Bride Wore Black '68
Is Paris Burning? '66

Jean Richard
Eléna and Her Men '56

Jean-Louis Richard
The Last Metro '80

Pierre Richard
A Chef in Love '96
Les Compères '83

Joely Richardson
Hollow Reed '95
Drowning by
    Numbers '87

John Richardson
Black Sunday '60

**Miranda
    Richardson**
The Designated
    Mourner '97

Natasha Richardson
A Month in the Country '87

Carole Richert
Tous les Matins du Monde '92

Paul Richter
Die Nibelungen '23
Dr. Mabuse, Parts 1 & 2 '22

Stephane Rideau
Wild Reeds '94

Giovanni Ridolfi
Yesterday, Today and Tomorrow '64

Leni Riefenstahl
The Blue Light '32

Peter Riegert
Local Hero '83

Mariana Rigillo
The Postman '94

Alexandre Rignault
Eternal Return '43

Caterina Rigoglioso
Love in the City '53

Shane Rimmer
Dreamchild '85

Vince Rimmer
Careful '94

Dante Rino
The Golden Coach '52

Jacques Rispal
Bed and Board '70

Lazar Ristovski
Underground '95
Tito and Me '92

June Ritchie
A Kind of Loving '62

Emmanuelle Riva
Hiroshima Mon Amour '59

Cecilia Rivera
Aguirre, the Wrath of God '72

Enrique Rivero
The Blood of a Poet '30

Jean Riveyre
Diary of a Country Priest '50

Julien Riviere
Les Voleurs '96

Marie Riviere
A Tale of Winter '92

Jason Robards, Jr.
Once Upon a Time in the West '68

Jessie Robbins
The Fearless Vampire Killers '67

Yves Robert
The Judge and the Assassin '75

Alice Roberts
Pandora's Box '28

Ewan Roberts
Curse of the Demon '57

Nancy Roberts
Black Narcissus '47

Rachel Roberts
Picnic at Hanging Rock '75
This Sporting Life '63
Saturday Night and Sunday Morning '60

George Robey
Henry V '45

Liliane Robin
Breathless '59

Michel Robin
The Wonderful Crook '75

Sophie Robin
A Tale of Springtime '92

Bruce Robinson
The Story of Adele H. '75

Madeleine Robinson
Camille Claudel '89

Jacques Robiolles
Bed and Board '70

German Robles
The Brainiac '61

Flora Robson
Black Narcissus '47

Daniela Rocca
Divorce—Italian Style '62

Luigina Rocchi
Arabian Nights '74

Jean Rochefort
Ridicule '96
The Hairdresser's Husband '92

Ebbe Rode
Babette's Feast '87
Gertrud '64

Nina Pens Rode
Gertrud '64

Celia Rodriguez
I Am Cuba '64

Jose Antonio Rodriguez
The Last Supper '76

Norman Rodway
Chimes at Midnight '67

Roger-Pierre
Mon Oncle d' Amerique '80

Helena Rojo
Aguirre, the Wrath of God '72

Ruben Rojo
The Brainiac '61

Kirsten Rolffes
The Kingdom '95

Beatrice Romand
Le Beau Mariage '82
Claire's Knee '71

Pierre Romans
Dr. Petiot '90

Luis Romay
Death of a Bureaucrat '66

Maurice Ronet
Beau Père '81
La Femme Infidèle '69
The Fire Within '64
Purple Noon '60
Frantic '58

Thorkild Roose
Day of Wrath '43

Rosanna Rory
Big Deal on Madonna Street '58

Francoise Rosay
Carnival in Flanders '35

Gabrielle Rose
The Sweet Hereafter '96
The Adjuster '91

Guy Rose
If... '69

Rosette
A Tale of Winter '92
Pauline at the Beach '83

Cathy Rosier
Le Samourai '67

Lee Ross
Secrets and Lies '95

Salvatore Rossi
Kaos '85

Norman Rossington
Saturday Night and Sunday Morning '60

Carlo Rota
32 Short Films about Glenn Gould '93

Tim Roth
The Cook, the Thief, His Wife & Her Lover '90
The Hit '85

Bendt Rothe
Gertrud '64

Brigitte Rouan
Olivier, Olivier '92

Jean-Paul Roussillon
Baxter '89

Catherine Rouvel
Borsalino '70
La Rupture '70

Josef Rovensky
Diary of a Lost Girl '29

Gitali Roy
Charulata '64

Lise Roy
The Boys of St. Vincent '93

Sandhya Roy
Distant Thunder '73

Regis Royer
La Lectrice '88

Saul Rubinek
Ticket to Heaven '81

Sergio Rubini
Intervista '87

Christian Ruche
La Lectrice '88

Franz Rudnick
Marianne and Juliane '82

Rufus
Erendira '83
Jonah Who Will Be 25 in the Year 2000 '76

Heinz Ruhmann
Faraway, So Close! '93

Carlos Ruiz de la Tejera
Death of a Bureaucrat '66

Janice Rule
Gumshoe '72

Jenny Runacre
The Canterbury Tales '71

Kicki Rundgren
My Life As a Dog '85

Claire Rushbrook
Secrets and Lies '95

Clive Russell
Margaret's Museum '95

Theresa Russell
Insignificance '85

Margaret Rutherford
Chimes at Midnight '67

Sif Ruud
Face to Face '76

Raisa Ryazanova
Moscow Does Not Believe in Tears '80

Georg Rydeberg
The Hour of the Wolf '68

Eli Ryg
Edvard Munch '74

Chishu Ryu
Akira Kurosawa's
Dreams '90
An Autumn
Afternoon '62
The Human Condition:
A Soldier's
Prayer '61
Tokyo Story '53
Late Spring '49

Daisuke Ryu
Ran '85

Bruno S
Stroszek '77
Every Man for Himself &
God Against All '75

Yacef Saadi
The Battle of Algiers '66

Hend Sabri
The Silences of the
Palace '94

Sabu
Black Narcissus '47

Keiji Sada
An Autumn
Afternoon '62
The Human Condition:
Road to Eternity '59
The Human Condition:
No Greater Love '58

Isabelle Sadoyan
Trois Couleurs: Bleu '93

**Marianne
Saegebrecht**
Sugarbaby '85

Elena Safonova
The Accompanist '93

Libuse Safrankova
Kolya '96

Iliamane Sagna
Xala '75

He Saifei
Temptress Moon '96

**Hubert Saint
Macary**
Diary of a Seducer '95

Louis Sainteve
Forbidden Games '52

Frankie Sakai
Mothra '62

Sumiko Sakamota
The Ballad of
Narayama '83

Yoshiko Sakuma
The Makioka Sisters '83

Kinzo Sakura
Tampopo '86

Fabian Salas
The Tango Lesson '97

Abel Salazar
The Brainiac '61

El Hedi Ben Salem
Ali: Fear Eats the
Soul '74

**Enrico Maria
Salerno**
The Bird with the
Crystal Plumage '70

John Salew
Kind Hearts and
Coronets '49

Lyda Salmonava
The Golem '20

Elina Salo
The Match Factory
Girl '90

Gino Saltamerenda
The Bicycle Thief '48

Renato Salvatori
State of Siege '73
Burn! '70
Rocco and His
Brothers '60
Big Deal on Madonna
Street '58

Seune Samb
Xala '75

Isaac Samberg
The Dybbuk '37

Udo Samel
Kaspar Hauser '93

Will Sampson
Insignificance '85

Lu Man San
The Scent of Green
Papaya '93

Maite Sanchez
Cria '76

Dominique Sanda
1900 '76
The Conformist '71
The Garden of the Finzi-
Continis '71
A Gentle Woman '69

Otto Sander
Faraway, So Close! '93
Wings of Desire '88
The Marquise of O '76

Dirk Sanders
Pierrot le Fou '65

**Christopher
Sandord**
Deep End '70

Stefania Sandrelli
Jamón, Jamón '93
We All Loved Each
Other So Much '77
1900 '76
Alfredo, Alfredo '72
The Conformist '71
Divorce—Italian
Style '62

Ibrahim Sane
Camp de Thiaroye '87

Fatimata Sanga
Yaaba '89

Walter Santesso
La Dolce Vita '60

Jorge Sanz
Belle Epoque '92
Lovers: A True Story '90

Martine Sarcey
The Thief of Paris '67

Kali Sarkar
Jalsaghar '58

Jacqueline Sassard
Les Biches '68

Kei Sato
Onibaba '64

Kei Sato
Harakiri '62

Lyudmila Savelyeva
War and Peace '68

Iya Savvina
The Lady with the
Dog '59

**Ousmane
Sawadogo**
Yaaba '89

Abbas Sayah
Gabbeh '96

Carmela Sazio
Paisan '46

Dolly Scal
Pickpocket '59

Franco Scaldati
Kaos '85

Valentina Scalici
The Stolen Children '92

Renato Scarpa
The Postman '94
The Icicle Thief '89

Doris Schade
Marianne and
Juliane '82

Clemens Scheitz
Stroszek '77

Clemens Scheitz
Heart of Glass '74

Wolfgang Schenck
Effi Briest '74

Karl Scheydt
The American
Soldier '70

Jean Schlegel
Trois Couleurs:
Rouge '94

**Guylaine
Schlumberger**
My Life to Live '62

Daniel Schmid
The American Friend '77

Walter Schmidinger
Hanussen '88

Nathalie Schmidt
Europa, Europa '91

Sybille Schmitz
Vampyr '31
Diary of a Lost Girl '29

Magda Schneider
Liebelei '32

Maria Schneider
Last Tango in Paris '73

Romy Schneider
César & Rosalie '72
The Trial '63
Boccaccio '70 '62

G.H. Schnell
Nosferatu '22

Margareta Schoen
Die Nibelungen '23

Emmy Schonfeld
Witchcraft through the
Ages '22

Max Schreck
Nosferatu '22

Greta Schroder
Nosferatu '22
The Golem '20

Werner Schroeter
Beware of a Holy
Whore '70

Rudolf Schuendler
Suspiria '77

Maurice Schultz
The Passion of Joan of
Arc '28

Reinhold Schunzel
The Threepenny
Opera '31

Maurice Schutz
Vampyr '31

Ellen Schwannecke
Mädchen in
Uniform '31

Hanna Schygulla
La Nuit de Varennes '82
Berlin
Alexanderplatz '80
The Marriage of Maria
Braun '79
Effi Briest '74
The Bitter Tears of Petra
von Kant '72
Beware of a Holy
Whore '70

Edith Scob
The Milky Way '68
Eyes without a Face '59

Paul Scofield
Henry V '89

Martin Scorsese
Akira Kurosawa's
Dreams '90

Jenny Seagrove
Local Hero '83

Josef Sebanek
Loves of a Blonde '65

Jean Seberg
Breathless '59

Abdoulaye Seck
Xala '75

Douta Seck
Sugar Cane Alley '83
Xala '75

Zohra Segal
Bhaji on the Beach '94

Dortha Segda
My Twentieth
Century '90

Mil Seghers
Antonia's Line '95

Francoise Seigner
The Wild Child '70

Louis Seigner
The Eclipse '66

Edda Seipel
The Marquise of O '76

Kyoko Seki
Ikiru '52

Peter Sellers
Heavens Above! '63
I'm All Right, Jack '59
The Case of the
Mukkinese Battle
Horn '56

Willy Semmelrogge
Every Man for Himself &
God Against All '75

Pinaki Sen Gupta
Jalsaghar '58

Ramani Sen Gupta
Aparajito '58

Koreya Senda
The Face of Another '66
Gate of Hell '54

Momar Nar Sene
Black Girl '66

Subrata Sensharma
Charulata '64

Rade Serbedzija
Before the Rain '94

Nikolai Sergueiev
Andrei Rublev '66

Meika Seri
In the Realm of the
Senses '76

Assumpta Serna
Matador '86

Jacques Sernas
La Dolce Vita '60

Julieta Serrano
Tie Me Up! Tie Me
Down! '90
Women on the Verge of
a Nervous
Breakdown '88
Matador '86

Adrienne Serrantie
Mon Oncle '58

Michel Serrault
Nelly et Monsieur
Arnaud '95
Dr. Petiot '90
La Cage aux Folles '78
Diabolique '55

Henri Serre
The Fire Within '64
Jules and Jim '62

Mo Sesay
Bhaji on the Beach '94

Roshan Seth
Little Dorrit, Film 1:
Nobody's Fault '88
Little Dorrit, Film 2: Little
Dorrit's Story '88

Gerard Sety
Van Gogh '92

Younouss Seye
Xala '75

Athene Seyler
Curse of the Demon '57

Carolyn Seymour
Gumshoe '72

Delphine Seyrig
The Discreet Charm of
the Bourgeoisie '72
Donkey Skin '70
The Milky Way '68
Stolen Kisses '68
Muriel '63
Last Year at
Marienbad '61

Serif Sezer
Yol '82

**Mohammad Sha-
hani**
The White Balloon '95

Amelia Shankley
Dreamchild '85

Omar Sharif
Juggernaut '74

Chanda Sharma
Salaam Bombay! '88

Fiona Shaw
My Left Foot '89

Moira Shearer
The Red Shoes '48

Ruth Sheen
The Young Poisoner's
Handbook '94
High Hopes '88

Jacques Shelly
A Nous la Liberté '31

Lei Lao Sheng
The Story of Qiu Ju '91

Anthony Sher
The Young Poisoner's
Handbook '94

George Shevtsov
Love Serenade '96

Vladek Sheybal
Kanal '56

Misa Shimizu
Okoge '93

Joanna Shimkus
Zita '68

Takashi Shimura
Kwaidan '64
The Bad Sleep Well '60
Throne of Blood '57
Godzilla, King of the
Monsters '56
I Live in Fear '55
Seven Samurai '54
Ikiru '52
Rashomon '51
Stray Dog '49
Drunken Angel '48
The Men Who Tread on
the Tiger's Tail '45
Sanshiro Sugata '43

Eitaro Shindo
Sansho the Bailiff '54

Masayuki Shionoya
Okoge '93

Zarifeh Shivah
Through the Olive
Trees '94

Stephan Shkurat
Earth '30

Vasily Shukshin
Commissar '68

**Antonina
Shuranova**
War and Peace '68

**Shun Chun
Shusheng**
Shanghai Triad '95

Jin Shuyuan
Raise the Red
Lantern '91

**Jean-Chretien
Sibertin-Blanc**
Augustin '95

Nadia Sibirskaia
The Crime of Monsieur
Lange '36

Adame Sidibe
Yaaba '89

Simone Signoret
Madame Rosa '77
The Confession '70
Is Paris Burning? '66

Diabolique '55
Casque d'Or '52
La Ronde '51

Caroline Sihol
Tous les Matins du
Monde '92
Confidentially Yours '83

**Djemal
Sikharulidze**
Prisoner of the
Mountains '96

Lidio Silva
Black God, White
Devil '64

Silvagni
The Rise of Louis XIV '66

Aldo Silvani
La Strada '54

Joe Silver
They Came from
Within '75

Veronique Silver
The Woman Next
Door '81

Jean Simmons
Hamlet '48
Black Narcissus '47

Francois Simon
Christ Stopped at
Eboli '79

Jean-Daniel Simon
Camp de Thiaroye '87

Luc Simon
Lancelot of the Lake '74

Michel Simon
The Two of Us '68
L'Atalante '34
Boudu Saved from
Drowning '32
La Chienne '31

Simone Simon
Le Plaisir '52
La Ronde '51
La Bete Humaine '38

Lars Simonsen
Twist & Shout '84

Victor Sjostrom
Wild Strawberries '57

Stellan Skarsgard
Insomnia '97
Breaking the Waves '95

Georg Skarstedt
Monika '52

Lena Skerla
The Fire Within '64

Sonia Skiba
Heart of Glass '74

Claire Skinner
Life Is Sweet '90

Stephane Slima
Mina Tannenbaum '93

Pete Smith
Once Were Warriors '94

Rinaldo Smordoni
Shoeshine '47

Jofre Soares
Antonio Das Mortes '68

Mario Socrate
The Gospel According
   to St. Matthew '64

Camilla Soeberg
Twist & Shout '84

Vladimir Sokoloff
The Lower Depths '36
Die Liebe der Jeanne
   Ney '27

Andrei Sokolov
Little Vera '88

Marilyn Solaya
Strawberry and
   Chocolate '93

Vincent Solder
Tristana '70

Laly Soldevilla
Spirit of the Beehive '73

Paul Soles
Ticket to Heaven '81

Madeleine Sologne
Eternal Return '43

Yuri Solomin
Dersu Uzala '75

Anatoli Solonitzin
Stalker '79
Andrei Rublev '66

Elena Solovei
Oblomov '81
A Slave of Love '78

Jimmy Somerville
Orlando '92

Noriko Songoku
Okoge '93

Elga Sorbas
The American
   Soldier '70

Alberto Sordi
I Vitelloni '53
The White Sheik '52

Jean Sorel
Belle de Jour '67

Charo Soriano
The Garden of Delights
   '70

Sander Soth
Time Stands Still '82

Luchy Soto
The Garden of
   Delights '70

Zinedine Soualem
When the Cat's Away '96

Renee Soutendijk
The 4th Man '79

Catherine Spaak
Le Trou '59

Odoardo Spadaro
The Golden Coach '52

James Spader
Crash '95

Pasquale Spadola
Kaos '85

Timothy Spall
Secrets and Lies '95
Life Is Sweet '90

Sebastian Spence
The Boys of St.
   Vincent '93

Will Spendler
Sugarbaby '85

Volker Spengler
Veronika Voss '82
In a Year of 13
   Moons '78
The Stationmaster's
   Wife '77

Jeremy Spenser
Kind Hearts and
   Coronets '49

Tony Sperandeo
La Scorta '94

Laurent Spielvogel
The Monster '96

Jacques Spiesser
Baxter '89

Paul Stacey
The Young Poisoner's
   Handbook '94

Robert Stack
Is Paris Burning? '66

**Ernest Stahl-
   Nachbaur**
M '31

Enzo Staiola
The Bicycle Thief '48

Marion Stalens
Trois Couleurs:
   Rouge '94

Terence Stamp
The Hit '85

Wadeck Stanczak
Scene of the Crime '87

Lionel Stander
Once Upon a Time in
   the West '68

Jiri Stanislay
Moonlighting '82

Alison Steadman
Life Is Sweet '90

Barbara Steele
They Came from Within
   '75
8 1/2 '63
Black Sunday '60
La Dolce Vita '60

Jan Steen
Antonia's Line '95

Bernice Stegers
City of Women '81

Renate Steiger
The Boat Is Full '81

Franz Stein
M '31

Albert Steinruck
The Golem '20

Aram Stephane
French Provincial '75

Nicole Stephane
Les Enfants Terribles '50

Robert Stephens
Henry V '89

Miroslava Stern
The Criminal Life of
   Archibaldo de la
   Cruz '55

**Jean-Francois
   Stevenin**
Olivier, Olivier '92
Small Change '76

Paul Stevens
The Mask '61

Juliet Stevenson
Drowning by
   Numbers '87

Alexandra Stewart
Black Moon '75
Day for Night '73
The Fire Within '64

Slavko Stimac
Underground '95

Nigel Stock
Victim '61

Vaclav Stockel
The Firemen's Ball '68

Shirley Stoler
Seven Beauties '76

Paolo Stoppa
Miracle in Milan '51

Olaf Storm
Metropolis '26

Ernst Stotzner
Underground '95

Meryl Streep
A Cry in the Dark '88

Oscar Stribolt
Witchcraft through the
   Ages '22

Elaine Stritch
Providence '77

Axel Strobye
Pelle the Conqueror '88

Woody Strode
Once Upon a Time in
   the West '68

Jerzy Stuhr
Trois Couleurs: Blanc '94

Hans Sturm
The Golem '20

Ricardo Suarez
Death of a
   Bureaucrat '66

Fujio Suga
The Human Condition:
   A Soldier's
   Prayer '61

Ichiro Sugai
Sansho the Bailiff '54

Kin Sugai
The Funeral '84

Haruko Sugimura
Tokyo Story '53
Late Spring '49

Barbara Sukowa
Zentropa '92
Marianne and
   Juliane '82
Berlin
   Alexanderplatz '80

Peter Sumner
The Chant of Jimmie
   Blacksmith '78

Folke Sundquist
Wild Strawberries '57

Asao Suno
Fires on the Plain '59

Donald Sutherland
1900 '76

Dudley Sutton
Orlando '92
The Devils '71

Janet Suzman
And the Ship Sails On
   '83
The Draughtsman's
   Contract '82

Semyon Svashenko
Earth '30
Arsenal '29

Zdenek Sverak
Kolya '96

Josef Svet
The Firemen's Ball '68

Anna Svierker
Day of Wrath '43

Robert Swann
If... '69

Cast

Tilda Swinton
Orlando '92
Caravaggio '86

Basil Sydney
Hamlet '48

Shafiq Syed
Salaam Bombay! '88

Eric Sykes
Heavens Above! '63

Eugena Sylvaw
The Passion of Joan of
   Arc '28

Kary Sylway
Face to Face '76
Cries and Whispers '72

Sylvia Syms
Victim '61

Eva Szabo
Angi Vera '78

Laszlo Szabo
Alphaville '65

Oleg Tabakov
Oblomov '81

Said Taghmaoui
Hate '95

Sharmila Tagore
Days and Nights in the
   Forest '70
Devi '60
The World of Apu '59

Hiromasa Taguchi
Shall We Dance? '97

Tomoroh Taguchi
Tetsuo: The Iron Man '92

Kwako Taichi
Himatsuri '85

Hideko Takamine
When a Woman
   Ascends the
   Stairs '60

Akira Takarada
Minbo—Or the Gentle
   Art of Japanese
   Extortion '92

Tadao Takashima
King Kong vs.
   Godzilla '63

Naoto Takenaka
Shall We Dance? '97
The Mystery of
   Rampo '94

Ryo Takeuchi
Harakiri '62

Osamu Takizawa
Fires on the Plain '59

Tetsuro Tamba
Harakiri '62

Akim Tamiroff
Alphaville '65

The Trial '63
Mr. Arkadin '55

Kinuyo Tanaka
Sansho the Bailiff '54
Ugetsu '53
Life of Oharu '52
Utamaro and His Five
   Women '46

Yoshiko Tanaka
Black Rain '88

Kiyoko Tange
Dodes 'ka-den '70

Cecile Tanner
Every Man for
   Himself '79

Guo Tao
To Live '94

Jun Tatara
The Human Condition:
   Road to Eternity '59

Nick Tate
A Cry in the Dark '88
The Devil's
   Playground '76

Sharon Tate
The Fearless Vampire
   Killers '67

Jacques Tati
Traffic '71
Playtime '67
Mon Oncle '58
Jour de Fete '48

Sven-Bertil Taube
Jerusalem '96

**Aino Taube-
   Henrikson**
Face to Face '76

Nils Tavernier
Mina Tannenbaum '93
L.627 '92
Béatrice '88
The Story of Women '88

Grigor Taylor
La Notte '60

Valerie Taylor
Repulsion '65

Ludmila Tcherina
The Red Shoes '48

Tora Teje
Witchcraft through the
   Ages '22

Izabella Telezynska
The Music Lovers '71

Isabel Telleria
Spirit of the Beehive '73

Stacey Tendeter
Two English Girls '72

Tengger
A Mongolian Tale '94

Johanna Ter Steege
The Vanishing '88

Akira Terao
Akira Kurosawa's
   Dreams '90
Ran '85

**Margarita
   Terekhova**
The Mirror '75

Nadege Teron
Tous les Matins du
   Monde '92

Nigel Terry
Caravaggio '86

Terry-Thomas
I'm All Right, Jack '59

Laurent Terzieff
Germinal '93
The Milky Way '68

Nicky Tesco
Leningrad Cowboys Go
   America '89

Fabio Testi
The Garden of the Finzi-
   Continis '71

Anne Teyssedre
A Tale of Springtime '92

Katharina Thalbach
Kaspar Hauser '93
The Tin Drum '79

Hilmar Thate
Veronika Voss '82

Ernest Thesiger
Henry V '45

David Thewlis
Life Is Sweet '90

Olivette Thibault
Mon Oncle Antoine '71

Hertha Thiele
Mädchen in
   Uniform '31

**Jean-Baptiste
   Thierree**
Muriel '63

Victorie Thivisol
Ponette '95

Al Thomas
Outback '71

Hugh Thomas
If… '69

Florence Thomassin
Mina Tannenbaum '93

Greg Thomey
The Boys of St.
   Vincent '93

Derek Thompson
The Long Good
   Friday '80

Emma Thompson
Henry V '89

Jack Thompson
The Chant of Jimmie
   Blacksmith '78
Outback '71

R.H. Thomson
Ticket to Heaven '81

Luc Thuillier
Monsieur Hire '89

Ingrid Thulin
After the Rehearsal '84
Cries and Whispers '72
The Hour of the Wolf '68
The Silence '63
Winter Light '62
The Magician '58
Wild Strawberries '57

Xie Tian
Temptress Moon '96

Marie Tifo
Les Bons Debarras '81

Vyacheslav Tihonor
War and Peace '68

**Viatcheslav
   Tikhonov**
Burnt by the Sun '94

Charles Tingwell
A Cry in the Dark '88

Heather Tobias
High Hopes '88

Yuri Tobubeyev
Don Quixote '57

Yukiko Todoroki
Sanshiro Sugata '43

Marko Todorovic
Hey, Babu Riba '88

Srdan Todorovic
Underground '95

Ugo Tognazzi
La Cage aux Folles '78
La Grande Bouffe '73
Love in the City '53

Haruko Togo
I Live in Fear '55

Yu Tokui
Shall We Dance? '97

Lubor Tolos
The Fabulous World of
   Jules Verne '58

Yuri Tolubeyev
The Overcoat '59

Ricky Tomlinson
Butterfly Kiss '94

Kenneth Tong
Police Story '85

Eijiro Tono
Yojimbo '61
The Human Condition:
   No Greater Love '58

Adam Tonsberg
Twist & Shout '84

David Toole
The Tango Lesson '97

Jean Topart
The Testament of Dr.
    Cordelier '59

Roland Topor
Nosferatu the
    Vampyre '79

Silva Torf
The Joyless Street '25

Toni Tornado
Quilombo '84

Regina Torne
Like Water for
    Chocolate '93

Kristina Tornqvist
Pelle the Conqueror '88

Mari Torocsik
Love '71

Ana Torrent
The Nest '80
Cria '76
Spirit of the Beehive '73

Philippe Torreton
Captain Conan '96
L.627 '92

Toto
Big Deal on Madonna
    Street '58

**Francois
    Toumarkine**
La Discrete '90

Amade Toure
Yaaba '89

Roland Toutain
Eternal Return '43

Yann Tregouet
Trois Couleurs: Bleu '93

Jerzy Trela
Trois Couleurs: Blanc '94

**Johanne-Marie
    Tremblay**
Jesus of Montreal '89

Leopoldo Trieste
Cinema Paradiso '88
Divorce—Italian
    Style '62
I Vitelloni '53
The White Sheik '52

**Jean-Louis
    Trintignant**
A Self-Made Hero '95
Trois Couleurs:
    Rouge '94
Confidentially Yours '83
La Nuit de Varennes '82
The Conformist '71
My Night at Maud's '69
Z '69
Les Biches '68

Is Paris Burning? '66
A Man and a Woman '66
And God Created
    Woman '57

Marie Trintignant
Ponette '95
The Story of Women '88

**Elisabeth
    Trissenaar**
Berlin
    Alexanderplatz '80
In a Year of 13
    Moons '78
The Stationmaster's
    Wife '77

Massimo Troisi
The Postman '94

Francois Truffaut
The Green Room '78
Day for Night '73
The Wild Child '70
The 400 Blows '59

Raoul Trujillo
The Adjuster '91

Ralph Truman
Henry V '45

Kenneth Tsang
The Killer '90

**Ludmila
    Tselikovskaya**
Ivan the Terrible,
    Part 2 '46
Ivan the Terrible,
    Part 1 '44

Rigzin Tseshang
The Horse Thief '87

Yoshio Tsuchiya
Red Beard '65

Junichi Tsujita
The Family Game '83

Shinya Tsukamoto
Tetsuo: The Iron Man '92

**Ryonosuke
    Tsukigata**
Sanshiro Sugata '43

William Tubbs
The Wages of Fear '55
Paisan '46

Bill Tung
Police Story '85

Mustapha Ture
Mandabi '68

V. Tzoppi
Storm over Asia '28

Stratos Tzortzoglou
Landscape in the
    Mist '88

Ryohei Uchida
The Human Condition:
    Road to Eternity '59

Kichijiro Ueda
Rashomon '51

Kenjiro Uemura
The Human Condition:
    Road to Eternity '59

Gisela Uhlen
Toto le Heros '91
The Marriage of Maria
    Braun '79

Liv Ullmann
Autumn Sonata '78
Face to Face '76
The New Land '73
Scenes from a
    Marriage '73
Cries and Whispers '72
The Emigrants '72
The Passion of Anna '70
The Hour of the Wolf '68
Shame '68
Persona '66

**Marianne O.
    Ulrichsen**
Insomnia '97

Jolanta Umecka
Knife in the Water '62

**Deborah Kara
    Unger**
Crash '95

Vanna Urbino
Jules and Jim '62

Mary Ure
Look Back in Anger '58

Janez Urhovec
Man Is Not a Bird '65

Irma Urrila
The Magic Flute '73

Jun Usami
Late Spring '49

Peter Ustinov
Lola Montès '55

Kari Vaananen
Leningrad Cowboys Go
    America '89

Pierre Val
Captain Conan '96

Dominique Valadie
A Single Girl '96

**Charlotte
    Valandrey**
Orlando '92

Birgitta Valberg
Shame '68
The Virgin Spring '59

Anne Valery
Kind Hearts and
    Coronets '49

Rosa Valetti
M '31
The Blue Angel '30

Frederick Valk
Dead of Night '45

Alida Valli
Suspiria '77
1900 '76
The Spider's
    Stratagem '70
Eyes without a Face '59
Senso '54
We the Living '42

Romolo Valli
The Garden of the
    Finzi-Continis '71

Raf Vallone
Bitter Rice '49

**Willeke Van
    Ammelrooy**
Antonia's Line '95

**Tomas Van
    Bromssen**
My Life As a Dog '85

Lee Van Cleef
The Good, the Bad, and
    the Ugly '67

**Sylvie van den
    Elsen**
L'Argent '83

**Frederic Van Dren
    Driessche**
A Tale of Winter '92

Peter Van Eyck
The Wages of Fear '55

Jo Van Fleet
The Tenant '76

Roger Van Hool
The Woman Next
    Door '81

Robert Van Loon
Paisan '46

Henry van Lyck
Every Man for Himself &
    God Against All '75

**Veerle Van
    Overloop**
Antonia's Line '95

Pierre Vaneck
Erendira '83
Is Paris Burning? '66

Charles Vanel
Three Brothers '80
Diabolique '55
The Wages of Fear '55

Manuela Vargas
The Flower of My
    Secret '95

Cast

501

Michael Vartan
Fiorile '93

Jose Luis Lopez Vasquez
The Garden of
Delights '70

Robert Vattier
The Baker's Wife '33

Natalie Vavilova
Moscow Does Not
Believe in Tears '80

Claude Vega
Bed and Board '70

Misa Vehara
The Hidden Fortress '58

Conrad Veidt
Waxworks '24
The Cabinet of Dr.
Caligari '19

Hans Man Int Veld
In for Treatment '82

Marijke Vengelers
Egg '88

Thanassis Vengos
Ulysses' Gaze '95

Maribel Verdu
Belle Epoque '92
Lovers: A True Story '90

Bernard Verley
The Phantom of
Liberty '74
Chloe in the
Afternoon '72
The Milky Way '68

Francoise Verley
Chloe in the
Afternoon '72

Anne Vernon
The Umbrellas of
Cherbourg '64

Howard Vernon
Alphaville '65
Bob le Flambeur '55

John Vernon
A Special Day '77

Pablo Veron
The Tango Lesson '97

Veruschka
Blow-Up '66

Charlotte Very
Trois Couleurs: Bleu '93
A Tale of Winter '92

Christophe Vesque
Bed and Board '70

Karin Viard
Delicatessen '92

Gala Videnovic
Hey, Babu Riba '88

Laszlo Vidovszky
My Twentieth Century
'90

Eric Viellard
Boyfriends &
Girlfriends '88

Vesa Vierikko
The Match Factory
Girl '90

Florence Vignon
Trois Couleurs: Bleu '93

Nelson Villagra
The Last Supper '76

Marthe Villalonga
Ma Saison Préférée '93

Astrid Villaume
Pelle the Conqueror '88

Paul Ville
The Wild Child '70

Ferdinando Villella
Orchestra Rehearsal '78

Carmen Villena
Blood Wedding '81

Jacques Villeret
Edith & Marcel '83

James Villiers
Repulsion '65

Dominique Vincent
The Rise of Louis XIV '66

Helene Vincent
Trois Couleurs: Bleu '93

Marcus Vinicius
Xica '76

Enzo Vitale
Seven Beauties '76

Antoine Vitez
The Green Room '78
My Night at Maud's '69

Hansa Vithal
Salaam Bombay! '88

Kim Vithana
Bhaji on the Beach '94

Michel Vitold
Basileus Quartet '82
The Confession '70
The Testament of Dr.
Cordelier '59

Judith Vittet
The City of Lost
Children '95

Monica Vitti
The Phantom of Liberty
'74
The Eclipse '66
The Red Desert '64
La Notte '60
L'Avventura '60

Rajesh Vivek
Bandit Queen '94

Marina Vlady
Chimes at Midnight '67
Two or Three Things I
Know About Her '66

Sandra Voe
Breaking the Waves '95

Karl Michael Vogler
Deep End '70

Ruediger Vogler
Faraway, So Close! '93
Marianne and
Juliane '82
Kings of the Road—
In the Course of
Time '76

Dimitrie Vojnov
Tito and Me '92

Michel Voletti
A Tale of Winter '92

Ludmilla Volinskaya
Commissar '68

Dora Volonaki
Ulysses' Gaze '95

Gian Marie Volonte
Christ Stopped at
Eboli '79
A Fistful of Dollars '64

Franco Volpi
Johnny Stecchino '92

Phillipe Volter
Trois Couleurs: Bleu '93
The Double Life of
Veronique '91

Frederick Von Ledenberg
Ginger & Fred '86

Heidi von Palleske
Dead Ringers '88

Erich von Stroheim
Grand Illusion '37

Max von Sydow
Jerusalem '96
The Best Intentions '92
Pelle the Conqueror '88
The New Land '73
The Emigrants '72
The Passion of Anna '70
The Hour of the Wolf '68
Shame '68
Winter Light '62
Through a Glass
Darkly '61
The Virgin Spring '59
The Magician '58
Wild Strawberries '57
Miss Julie '50

Margarethe von Trotta
Beware of a Holy
Whore '70

Hans von Twardowski
The Cabinet of Dr.
Caligari '19

Gustav von Wagenheim
Woman in the Moon '29
Nosferatu '22

Hertha von Walther
M '31

Julia Vonderlinn
In the White City '83

Milena Vukotic
The Phantom of
Liberty '74
The Discreet Charm of
the Bourgeoisie '72

Michael Wade
The Boys of St.
Vincent '93

Elsie Wagstaff
Saturday Night and
Sunday Morning '60

Anton Walbrook
Lola Montès '55
La Ronde '51
The Red Shoes '48
The Life and Death of
Colonel Blimp '43

Gunn Walgren
Fanny and
Alexander '83

Aurora Walker
Él '52

Bill Walker
The Mask '61

Jeffrey Walker
Proof '91

Kerry Walker
The Piano '93

Sarah Walker
Man of Flowers '84

Anita Wall
Scenes from a
Marriage '73

Max Wall
Little Dorrit, Film 1:
Nobody's Fault '88
Little Dorrit, Film 2: Little
Dorrit's Story '88

Eli Wallach
The Good, the Bad, and
the Ugly '67

Angela Walsh
Distant Voices, Still
Lives '88

Harriet Walter
May Fools '90

Martin Walz
The Boat Is Full '81

Faye Wang
Chungking Express '95

Grzegorz Warchol
Trois Couleurs: Blanc '94

Roy Ward
The Forbidden Quest '93

Sophie Ward
Little Dorrit, Film 1:
Nobody's Fault '88
Little Dorrit, Film 2: Little
Dorrit's Story '88

Warwick Ward
Variety '25

David Warner
Providence '77

Norbert Wartha
Céleste '81

Richard Warwick
If... '69

Mona Washbourne
If... '69

Andre Wasley
Forbidden Games '52

Eriko Watanabe
Shall We Dance? '97

Fumio Watanabe
Boy '69

Ken Watanabe
Tampopo '86

Alberta Watson
The Sweet Hereafter '96

Anthony Watson
The Long Day Closes '92

Emily Watson
Breaking the Waves '95

Naunton Wayne
Dead of Night '45

Jacki Weaver
Picnic at Hanging
Rock '75

Hugo Weaving
Proof '91

Chloe Webb
The Belly of an
Architect '91

Timothy Webber
The Boys of St.
Vincent '93

Rupert Webster
If... '69

Paul Wegener
The Golem '20

Li Wei
Ju Dou '90

Ding Weimin
Raise the Red
Lantern '91

**Isabelle
Weingarten**
The Mother and the
Whore '73

Elizabeth Welch
Dead of Night '45

Gertrude Welcker
Dr. Mabuse, Parts
1 & 2 '22

Orson Welles
Chimes at Midnight '67
Is Paris Burning? '66
The Trial '63
Mr. Arkadin '55

Kenneth Welsh
Margaret's Museum '95

Ariadne Welter
The Brainiac '61
The Criminal Life of
Archibaldo de la
Cruz '55

Jiang Wen
Red Sorghum '87

Lara Wendell
Intervista '87

Wim Wenders
The American Friend '77

Elizabeth Wenst
Kameradschaft '31

Zhang Wenyao
The Blue Kite '93

Fritz Wepper
Le Dernier Combat '84

Jan Werich
Fabulous Adventures
of Baron
Munchausen '61

Oskar Werner
Fahrenheit 451 '66
Jules and Jim '62
Lola Montès '55

Otto Wernicke
M '31

Julian West
Vampyr '31

Geir Westby
Edvard Munch '74

Alison Whelan
My Left Foot '89

Harriet White
Paisan '46

Billie Whitelaw
Gumshoe '72

Bernhard Wicki
La Notte '60

Nina Widerberg
Elvira Madigan '67

Ellen Widmann
M '31

Bud Widom
The Green Slime '68

Dorothea Wieck
Mäedchen in
Uniform '31

Matthias Wieman
The Blue Light '32

Nalma Wifstrand
The Hour of the Wolf '68
The Magician '58

James Wilby
Dreamchild '85

Brian Wilde
Curse of the Demon '57

**Catherine
Wilkening**
Jesus of Montreal '89

Jose Wilker
Bye Bye Brazil '79
Dona Flor and Her Two
Husbands '78
Xica '76

Dean Williams
Distant Voices, Still
Lives '88

Heathcote Williams
The Tango Lesson '97
Orlando '92

Andre Wilms
Monsieur Hire '89

Lambert Wilson
The Belly of an
Architect '91

Marc Wincourt
Murmur of the Heart '71

Angela Winkler
The Tin Drum '79
The Lost Honor of
Katharina Blum '75

Olof Winnerstrand
Torment '44

Kate Winslet
Heavenly Creatures '94

Shelley Winters
The Tenant '76

Karen Winther
Witchcraft through the
Ages '22

Googie Withers
Dead of Night '45

John Wittig
Pelle the Conqueror '88

Alfred Wolff
The Umbrellas of
Cherbourg '64

Sven Wollter
The Sacrifice '86
The Man on the Roof '76

Anthony Wong
Hard-Boiled '92

David Wood
If... '69

John Wood
Orlando '92

Salvador Wood
Death of a
Bureaucrat '66

Myrtle Woods
A Woman's Tale '92

**Helmut
Woudenberg**
In for Treatment '82

Jiang Wu
To Live '94

Vivian Wu
The Pillow Book '95

Patrick Wymark
Repulsion '65

Robert Wyndham
Dead of Night '45

Keenan Wynn
Once Upon a Time in
the West '68

Yang Liu Xia
The Story of Qiu Ju '91

Li Xuejian
Shanghai Triad '95

Raghubir Yadav
Bandit Queen '94
Salaam Bombay! '88

Moustapha Yade
Ceddo '78

Koji Yakusho
Shall We Dance? '97
Tampopo '86

Isuzu Yamada
Yojimbo '61
The Lower Depths '57
Throne of Blood '57

Isao Yamagata
Gate of Hell '54

So Yamamura
The Human Condition:
No Greater Love '58
Princess Yang Kwei
Fei '55
Tokyo Story '53

Tsutomu Yamazaki
A Taxing Woman '87
Tampopo '86
The Funeral '84
Kagemusha '80

Suuzu Yamda
Yojimbo '61

Kan Yanagidani
The Human Condition:
Road to Eternity '59

Oleg Yankovsky
The Mirror '75

Philip Yankovsky
The Mirror '75

Jean Yanne
Indochine '92

Cast

This Man Must Die '70
Le Boucher '69
Weekend '67

Sen Yano
Woman in the Dunes '64

Shoji Yasui
The Burmese Harp '56

Rikiya Yasuoka
Tampopo '86

Marjorie Yates
The Long Day Closes '92

Sally Yeh
The Killer '90

Tran Nu Yen-Khe
The Scent of Green
    Papaya '93

Michelle Yeoh
Drunken Master '78

Zhang Yi
Ju Dou '90

Hideko Yoshida
The Pillow Book '95

Yitsuko Yoshimura
Onibaba '64

Sayuri Yoshinaga
The Makioka Sisters '83

Ge You
To Live '94
Farewell My
    Concubine '93

Cho Yuen
Police Story '85

Siu Tien Yuen
Drunken Master '78

Wu Yujuan
Women from the Lake
    of Scented Souls '94

Saori Yuki
The Family Game '83

Chow Yun-Fat
Hard-Boiled '92
The Killer '90
A Better Tomorrow '86

**Krystyna
    Zachwatowicz**
Man of Marble '76

Ludmila Zaisova
Little Vera '88

Ichiro Zaitsu
The Funeral '84

**Zbigniew
    Zamachowski**
Trois Couleurs:
    Blanc '94

Zaira Zambello
Bye Bye Brazil '79

Billy Zane
Orlando '92

Bruno Zanin
Amarcord '74

Dominique Zardi
La Femme Infidèle '69
Le Trou '59

**Waclaw
    Zastrzezynski**
Ashes and Diamonds '58

Zatloukalova
The Fabulous World of
    Jules Verne '58

Edward Zebrowski
Illumination '73

Rosel Zech
Veronika Voss '82

Michalis Zeke
Landscape in the
    Mist '88

Mai Zetterling
Torment '44

Monica Zetterlund
The New Land '73
The Emigrants '72

Stephanie Zhang
Augustin '95

Chen Zhaorong
Vive L'Amour '94

Wai Zhi
The Day the Sun Turned
    Cold '94

Ge Zhijun
Ermo '94

Tuo Zhong Hua
The Day the Sun Turned
    Cold '94

Lin Zi
The Story of Qiu Ju '91

Terri Zimmern
The Manster '59

Victoria Zinny
Viridiana '61

Hanns Zischler
Kings of the Road—
    In the Course of
    Time '76

Istvan Znamenak
Time Stands Still '82

Jean-Pierre Zola
Mon Oncle '58

Zouzou
Chloe in the
    Afternoon '72

Ladislav Zupanic
My Sweet Little
    Village '86

Yoshitaka Zushi
Akira Kurosawa's
    Dreams '90
Dodes'ka-den '70

Milos Zutic
Hey, Babu Riba '88

Elsa Zylberstein
Farinelli '94
Mina Tannenbaum '93

DIRECTOR INDEX

The "Director Index" lists all directors credited in the main review section, alphabetically by last names. Make sure you also check back to the "Cast Index" to see if your favorite director may have also done an acting cameo in a film.

Dodo Abashidze
Ashik Kerib '88

Jovan Acin
Hey, Babu Riba '88

Percy Adlon
Sugarbaby '85
Céleste '81

Goffredo Alessan-drini
We the Living '42

Grigori Alexandrov
Ten Days That Shook the World '27

Marc Allegret
Fanny '32

Pedro Almodovar
The Flower of My Secret '95
Kika '94
Tie Me Up! Tie Me Down! '90
Women on the Verge of a Nervous Breakdown '88
Matador '86

Gianni Amelio
Lamerica '95
The Stolen Children '92

Lindsay Anderson
If… '69
This Sporting Life '63

Theo Angelopoulos
Ulysses' Gaze '95
Landscape in the Mist '88

Michelangelo Antonioni
Blow-Up '66
The Eclipse '66
The Red Desert '64
La Notte '60
L'Avventura '60
Love in the City '53

Manuel Gutierrez Aragon
Half of Heaven '86

Vicente Aranda
Lovers: A True Story '90

Alfonso Arau
Like Water for Chocolate '93

Denys Arcand
Jesus of Montreal '89

Dario Argento
Suspiria '77
The Bird with the Crystal Plumage '70

Gillian Armstrong
My Brilliant Career '79

Alexander Askoldov
Commissar '68

Jacques Audiard
A Self-Made Hero '95

Bille August
Jerusalem '96
The Best Intentions '92
Pelle the Conqueror '88
Twist & Shout '84

Claude Autant-Lara
Devil in the Flesh '46

Gabriel Axel
Babette's Feast '87

Hector Babenco
Pixote '81

Josiane Balasko
French Twist '95

Bruno Barreto
Dona Flor and Her Two Husbands '78

Shirley Barrett
Love Serenade '96

Alexei Batalov
The Overcoat '59

Mario Bava
Black Sunday '60

Jacques Becker
Le Trou '59
Casque d'Or '52

Jean-Jacques Beineix
Betty Blue '86
Moon in the Gutter '83
Diva '82

Marco Bellocchio
Devil in the Flesh '87

Remy Belvaux
Man Bites Dog '91

Maria-Luisa Bemberg
I Don't Want to Talk about It '94

Roberto Benigni
The Monster '96
Johnny Stecchino '92

Daniel Bergman
Sunday's Children '94

Ingmar Bergman
After the Rehearsal '84
Fanny and Alexander '83
Autumn Sonata '78
Face to Face '76
The Magic Flute '73
Scenes from a Marriage '73
Cries and Whispers '72
The Passion of Anna '70
The Hour of the Wolf '68
Shame '68
Persona '66
The Silence '63
Winter Light '62
Through a Glass Darkly '61
The Devil's Eye '60
The Virgin Spring '59
The Magician '58
Wild Strawberries '57
Dreams '55
Smiles of a Summer Night '55

Sawdust and Tinsel '53
Monika '52
Summer Interlude '50

Claude Berri
Germinal '93
Jean de Florette '87
Manon of the Spring '87
The Two of Us '68

Bernardo Bertolucci
1900 '76
Last Tango in Paris '73
The Conformist '71
The Spider's Stratagem '70
Before the Revolution '65

Jean-Louis Bertucelli
Ramparts of Clay '71

Luc Besson
La Femme Nikita '91
Subway '85
Le Dernier Combat '84

Bertrand Blier
Too Beautiful for You '88
Beau Père '81
Get Out Your Handkerchiefs '78
Going Places '74

Sergei Bodrov
Prisoner of the Mountains '96

Carl Boese
The Golem '20

Jerome Boivin
Baxter '89

Mauro Bolognini
Il Bell'Antonio '60

Sergei Bondarchuk
War and Peace '68

Andre Bonzel
Man Bites Dog '91

505

VideoHound's
WORLD CINEMA

John Boulting
Heavens Above! '63
I'm All Right, Jack '59

Roy Boulting
Heavens Above! '63

Serge Bourguignon
Sundays & Cybele '62

Bruno Bozzetto
Allegro Non Troppo '76

Kenneth Branagh
Henry V '89

George Breakston
The Manster '59

Robert Bresson
L'Argent '83
Lancelot of the Lake '74
A Gentle Woman '69
Mouchette '67
Pickpocket '59
A Man Escaped '57
Diary of a Country
   Priest '50

Luis Bunuel
That Obscure Object of
   Desire '77
The Phantom of
   Liberty '74
The Discreet Charm of
   the Bourgeoisie '72
Tristana '70
The Milky Way '68
Belle de Jour '67
Simon of the Desert '66
Diary of a
   Chambermaid '64
The Exterminating
   Angel '62
Viridiana '61
The Criminal Life of
   Archibaldo de la
   Cruz '55
Wuthering Heights '53
Él '52
Los Olvidados '50
L'Age D'Or '30

Jane Campion
The Piano '93
Sweetie '89
Two Friends '86

Marcel Camus
Black Orpheus '58

Leos Carax
Boy Meets Girl '84

Marcel Carne
Children of Paradise '44
Les Visiteurs du Soir '42
Le Jour Se Lève '39

Marc Caro
The City of Lost
   Children '95
Delicatessen '92

Fabio Carpi
Basileus Quartet '82

Alberto Cavalcanti
Dead of Night '45

Alain Cavalier
Thérèse '86

Liliana Cavani
The Night Porter '74

Claude Chabrol
La Cérémonie '95
The Story of Women '88
Violette '78
Wedding in Blood '74
La Rupture '70
This Man Must Die '70
La Femme Infidèle '69
Le Boucher '69
Les Biches '68

Gurinder Chadha
Bhaji on the Beach '94

Jackie Chan
Police Story '85

**Benjamin
Christiansen**
Witchcraft through the
   Ages '22

Pavel Chukhrai
The Thief '97

Grigori Chukrai
Ballad of a Soldier '60

Rene Clair
A Nous la Liberté '31
Le Million '31
Under the Roofs of
   Paris '29

Rene Clement
Is Paris Burning? '66
Purple Noon '60
Forbidden Games '52

Maurice Cloche
Monsieur Vincent '47

**Henri-Georges
Clouzot**
Diabolique '55
The Wages of Fear '55

Jean Cocteau
The Testament of
   Orpheus '59
Orpheus '49
Beauty and the
   Beast '46
The Blood of a Poet '30

Gerard Corbiau
Farinelli '94

Alain Corneau
Tous les Matins du
   Monde '92

**Constantin Costa-
Gavras**
State of Siege '73
The Confession '70
Z '69

Paul Cox
A Woman's Tale '92
Cactus '86
Man of Flowers '84

Kenneth Crane
The Manster '59

Charles Crichton
Dead of Night '45

David Cronenberg
Crash '95
Dead Ringers '88
They Came from
   Within '75

Danniel Danniel
Egg '88

**Jean-Pierre
Dardenne**
La Promesse '96

Luc Dardenne
La Promesse '96

Terence Davies
The Long Day Closes '92
Distant Voices, Still
   Lives '88

Jaime de Arminan
The Nest '80

**Christian de
Chalonge**
Dr. Petiot '90

Guiseppe de Santis
Bitter Rice '49

Vittorio de Seta
Bandits of Orgosolo '61

Vittorio De Sica
The Garden of the Finzi-
   Continis '71
Yesterday, Today and
   Tomorrow '64
Boccaccio '70 '62
Umberto D. '55
Miracle in Milan '51
The Bicycle Thief '48
Shoeshine '47

Basil Dearden
Victim '61
Dead of Night '45

Jean Delannoy
Eternal Return '43

Peter Delpeut
The Forbidden
   Quest '93

Jacques Demy
Donkey Skin '70
The Umbrellas of
   Cherbourg '64
Lola '61

Claire Denis
I Can't Sleep '93

Jacques Deray
Borsalino '70

Michel DeVille
La Lectrice '88

Carlos Diegues
Quilombo '84
Bye Bye Brazil '79
Xica '76

Jacques Doillon
Ponette '95

**Alexander
Dovzhenko**
Earth '30
Arsenal '29

**Carl Theodor
Dreyer**
Gertrud '64
Ordet '55
Day of Wrath '43
Vampyr '31
The Passion of Joan of
   Arc '28

Danielle Dubroux
Diary of a Seducer '95

Martine Dugowson
Mina Tannenbaum '93

E.A. Dupont
Variety '25

Julien Duvivier
Pépé le Moko '37

Nana Dzhordzadze
A Chef in Love '96

Christine Edzard
Little Dorrit, Film 1:
   Nobody's Fault '88
Little Dorrit, Film 2: Little
   Dorrit's Story '88

Atom Egoyan
The Sweet Hereafter '96
Exotica '94
The Adjuster '91

Sergei Eisenstein
Ivan the Terrible,
   Part 2 '46
Ivan the Terrible,
   Part 1 '44
Alexander Nevsky '38
Que Viva Mexico '32
Ten Days That Shook
   the World '27
The Battleship
   Potemkin '25
Strike '24

Robert Enrico
Zita '68

Ildiko Enyedi
My Twentieth
   Century '90

Victor Erice
Spirit of the Beehive '73

Jean Eustache
The Mother and the
   Whore '73

**Rainer Werner Fass-
binder**
Veronika Voss '82
Berlin
   Alexanderplatz '80
The Marriage of Maria
   Braun '79
In a Year of 13 Moons '78
The Stationmaster's
   Wife '77

Mother Küsters Goes to
  Heaven '76
Ali: Fear Eats the Soul '74
Effi Briest '74
The Bitter Tears of Petra
  von Kant '72
The American
  Soldier '70
Beware of a Holy
  Whore '70

Xie Fei
A Mongolian Tale '94
Women from the Lake
  of Scented Souls '94

Federico Fellini
Intervista '87
Ginger & Fred '86
And the Ship Sails
  On '83
City of Women '81
Orchestra Rehearsal '78
Amarcord '74
Fellini's Roma '72
The Clowns '71
Fellini Satyricon '69
Juliet of the Spirits '65
8 1/2 '63
Boccaccio '70 '62
La Dolce Vita '60
Nights of Cabiria '57
La Strada '54
I Vitelloni '53
Love in the City '53
The White Sheik '52
Variety Lights '51

Marco Ferreri
La Grande Bouffe '73

Jacques Feyder
Carnival in Flanders '35

Anne Fontaine
Augustin '95

Milos Forman
The Firemen's Ball '68
Loves of a Blonde '65

Bill Forsyth
Comfort and Joy '84
Local Hero '83

Georges Franju
Eyes without a Face '59

Stephen Frears
The Hit '85
Gumshoe '72

Kinji Fukasaku
The Green Slime '68

Pal Gabor
Angi Vera '78

Abel Gance
Napoleon '27

Pietro Germi
Alfredo, Alfredo '72
Divorce—Italian
  Style '62

Francois Girard
32 Short Films about
  Glenn Gould '93

Jean-Luc Godard
Every Man for
  Himself '79
Sympathy for the
  Devil '70
Weekend '67
Masculine Feminine '66
Two or Three Things I
  Know About Her '66
Alphaville '65
A Married Woman '65
Pierrot le Fou '65
Band of Outsiders '64
Contempt '64
Les Carabiniers '63
My Life to Live '62
A Woman Is a
  Woman '60
Breathless '59

Serif Goren
Yol '82

Claude Goretta
The Lacemaker '77
The Wonderful
  Crook '75

Marleen Gorris
Antonia's Line '95

Ernst Gossner
Jan Svankmejer's
  Faust '94

Peter Gothar
Time Stands Still '82

Peter Greenaway
The Pillow Book '95
The Belly of an
  Architect '91
The Cook, the Thief, His
  Wife & Her Lover '90
Drowning by
  Numbers '87
The Draughtsman's
  Contract '82

Ruy Guerra
Erendira '83

**Tomas Gutierrez
  Alea**
Strawberry and
  Chocolate '93
The Last Supper '76
Memories of Under-
  development '68
Death of a
  Bureaucrat '66

Lasse Hallstrom
My Life As a Dog '85

Robert Hamer
Kind Hearts and
  Coronets '49
Dead of Night '45

David Hare
The Designated
  Mourner '97

Wojciech Has
The Saragossa
  Manuscript '65

Jack Hazan
A Bigger Splash '74

Yosif Heifitz
The Lady with the
  Dog '59

Werner Herzog
Fitzcarraldo '82
Nosferatu the
  Vampyre '79
Woyzeck '78
Stroszek '77
Every Man for Himself &
  God Against All '75
Heart of Glass '74
Aguirre, the Wrath of
  God '72

Yim Ho
The Day the Sun Turned
  Cold '94

P.J. Hogan
Muriel's Wedding '94

Agnieszka Holland
Olivier, Olivier '92
Europa, Europa '91

Inoshiro Honda
Mothra '62
Godzilla, King of the
  Monsters '56

Tran Anh Hung
The Scent of Green
  Papaya '93

Kon Ichikawa
The Makioka Sisters '83
Tokyo Olympiad '66
Odd Obsession '60
Fires on the Plain '59
Enjo '58
The Burmese Harp '56

Shohei Imamura
Black Rain '88
The Ballad of
  Narayama '83
Vengeance Is Mine '79

Markus Imhoof
The Boat Is Full '81

Juzo Itami
Minbo—Or the Gentle
  Art of Japanese
  Extortion '92
A Taxing Woman '87
Tampopo '86
The Funeral '84

Peter Jackson
Heavenly Creatures '94

Gualtiero Jacopetti
Mondo Cane '63

Benoit Jacquot
A Single Girl '96

Miklos Jancso
The Round-Up '66

Derek Jarman
Blue '93
Caravaggio '86

Jean-Pierre Jeunet
The City of Lost
  Children '95
Delicatessen '92

**Alejandro
  Jodorowsky**
El Topo '71

Terry Jones
Monty Python's The
  Meaning of Life '83

Claude Jutra
Mon Oncle Antoine '71

Chen Kaige
Temptress Moon '96
Farewell My
  Concubine '93
Life on a String '90

Mikhail Kalatozov
I Am Cuba '64

Vitaly Kanevski
Freeze-Die-Come to
  Life '90

Nelly Kaplan
A Very Curious Girl '69

Shekhar Kapur
Bandit Queen '94

Wong Kar-Wai
Happy Together '96
Chungking Express '95

Mathieu Kassovitz
Hate '95
Café au Lait '94

Aki Kaurismaki
The Match Factory
  Girl '90
Ariel '89
Leningrad Cowboys Go
  America '89

Abbas Kiarostami
Taste of Cherry '96
Through the Olive
  Trees '94
Life and Nothing More
  … '92

**Krzysztof
  Kieslowski**
Trois Couleurs: Blanc '94
Trois Couleurs: Rouge '94
Trois Couleurs: Bleu '93
The Double Life of
  Veronique '91

Anthony Kimmins
Captain's Paradise '53

**Teinosuke
  Kinugasa**
Gate of Hell '54

Cedric Klapisch
When the Cat's Away '96

Masaki Kobayashi
Samurai Rebellion '67
Kwaidan '64
Harakiri '62
The Human Condition: A
  Soldier's Prayer '61
The Human Condition:
  Road to Eternity '59
The Human Condition:
  No Greater Love '58

Director

Marja Kok
In for Treatment '82

Alexander Korda
Marius '31

Ted Kotcheff
Outback '71

Grigori Kozintsev
Don Quixote '57

Akira Kurosawa
Rhapsody in August '91
Akira Kurosawa's
    Dreams '90
Ran '85
Kagemusha '80
Dersu Uzala '75
Dodes'ka-den '70
Red Beard '65
High & Low '62
Sanjuro '62
Yojimbo '61
The Bad Sleep Well '60
The Hidden Fortress '58
The Lower Depths '57
Throne of Blood '57
I Live in Fear '55
Seven Samurai '54
Ikiru '52
Rashomon '51
Stray Dog '49
Drunken Angel '48
The Men Who Tread on
    the Tiger's Tail '45
Sanshiro Sugata '43

Diane Kurys
Entre-Nous '83

Emir Kusturica
Underground '95
When Father Was Away
    on Business '85

Rene Laloux
Fantastic Planet '73

Albert Lamorisse
The Red Balloon '56

Fritz Lang
M '31
Woman in the Moon '29
Spies '28
Metropolis '26
Die Nibelungen '23
Dr. Mabuse, Parts
    1 & 2 '22

Alberto Lattuada
Love in the City '53
Variety Lights '51

**Jean-Claude
    Lauzon**
Léolo '92

David Lean
Brief Encounter '46

Patrice Leconte
Ridicule '96
The Hairdresser's
    Husband '92
Monsieur Hire '89

Mike Leigh
Secrets and Lies '95

Life Is Sweet '90
High Hopes '88
Bleak Moments '71

Claude Lelouch
Edith & Marcel '83
Cat and Mouse '78
A Man and a Woman '66

Paul Leni
Waxworks '24

Sergio Leone
Once Upon a Time in
    the West '68
The Good, the Bad, and
    the Ugly '67
A Fistful of Dollars '64

Richard Lester
Juggernaut '74
How I Won the War '67

Carlo Lizzani
Love in the City '53

Ken Loach
Land and Freedom '95

Joseph Losey
The Go-Between '71

Pavel Lozinski
Birthplace '92

Bigas Luna
Jamón, Jamón '93

Peter Lynch
Project Grizzly '96

Hettie Macdonald
Beautiful Thing '95

**Alexander
    MacKendrick**
The Man in the White
    Suit '51

John MacKenzie
The Long Good
    Friday '80

Guy Maddin
Careful '94

Dusan Makavejev
Man Is Not a Bird '65

**Mohsen
    Makhmalbaf**
Gabbeh '96

Karoly Makk
Love '71

Sarah Maldoror
Sambizanga '72

Louis Malle ✓
May Fools '90
Au Revoir les Enfants '87
Black Moon '75
Lacombe, Lucien '74
Murmur of the Heart '71
Phantom India '69
The Thief of Paris '67
Viva Maria! '65
The Fire Within '64
The Lovers '59
Frantic '58

Milcho Manchevski
Before the Rain '94

Francis Mankiewicz
Les Bons Debarras '81

Chris Marker
La Jetée '62
Le Joli Mai '62

Goran Markovic
Tito and Me '92

Francesco Maselli
Love in the City '53

Jean-Pierre Melville
Le Samourai '67
Le Doulos '61
Bob le Flambeur '55
Les Enfants Terribles '50

Vladimir Menshov
Moscow Does Not
    Believe in Tears '80

Jiri Menzel
My Sweet Little
    Village '86

Nikita Mikhalkov
Burnt by the Sun '94
Anna '93
Oblomov '81
A Slave of Love '78

Gavin Millar
Dreamchild '85

Claude Miller
The Accompanist '93
The Little Thief '89
The Best Way '76

Tsai Ming-Liang
Vive L'Amour '94

Kenji Mizoguchi
Princess Yang Kwei
    Fei '55
Sansho the Bailiff '54
Ugetsu '53
Life of Oharu '52
Utamaro and His Five
    Women '46
47 Ronin, Part 1 '42
47 Ronin, Part 2 '42

Moshe Mizrahi
Madame Rosa '77

Edouard Molinaro
La Cage aux Folles '78

Mario Monicelli
Casanova '70 '65
Big Deal on Madonna
    Street '58

**Thomas
    Montgomery**
King Kong vs.
    Godzilla '63

Jocelyn Moorhouse
Proof '91

Nanni Moretti
Caro Diario '93

Yoshimitsu Morita
The Family Game '83

Terry Morse
Godzilla, King of the
    Monsters '56

F.W. Murnau
Faust '26
The Last Laugh '24
Nosferatu '22

Mira Nair
Salaam Bombay! '88

Takehiro Nakajima
Okoge '93

Mikio Naruse
When a Woman
    Ascends the
    Stairs '60

Maurizio Nichetti
The Icicle Thief '89

Bruno Nuytten
Camille Claudel '89

Pat O'Connor
A Month in the
    Country '87

**Kazuyoshi
    Okuyama**
The Mystery of
    Rampo '94

Laurence Olivier
Hamlet '48
Henry V '45

Ermanno Olmi
The Tree of Wooden
    Clogs '78

Marcel Ophuls
The Sorrow and the
    Pity '71

Max Ophuls
Lola Montès '55
The Earrings of
    Madame de... '54
Le Plaisir '52
La Ronde '51
La Signora di Tutti '34
Liebelei '32

Nagisa Oshima
Max, Mon Amour '86
In the Realm of the
    Senses '76
Boy '69

Katsuhiro Otomo
Akira '89

Idrissa Ouedraogo
Tilaï '90
Yaaba '89

Yasujiro Ozu
An Autumn
    Afternoon '62
Tokyo Story '53
Late Spring '49

G.W. Pabst
Kameradschaft '31
The Threepenny
    Opera '31
Diary of a Lost Girl '29
Pandora's Box '28

Die Liebe der Jeanne
   Ney '27
The Joyless Street '25

Marcel Pagnol
Harvest '37
César '36
The Baker's Wife '33

Euzhan Palcy
Sugar Cane Alley '83

Jafar Panahi
The White Balloon '95

Sergei Paradjanov
Ashik Kerib '88
Shadows of Forgotten
   Ancestors '64

Chul-Soo Park
301, 302 '94

Pier Paolo Pasolini
Salo, or the 120 Days of
   Sodom '75
Arabian Nights '74
The Canterbury Tales '71
The Decameron '70
The Gospel According
   to St. Matthew '64
Mamma Roma '62

Maurice Pialat
Van Gogh '92
A Nos Amours '84
Loulou '80

Vassili Pitchul
Little Vera '88

Benoit Poelvoorde
Man Bites Dog '91

Roman Polanski
The Tenant '76
The Fearless Vampire
   Killers '67
Repulsion '65
Knife in the Water '62

Gillo Pontecorvo
Burn! '70
The Battle of Algiers '66

Angela Pope
Hollow Reed '95

Sally Potter
The Tango Lesson '97
Orlando '92

Michael Powell
The Red Shoes '48
Black Narcissus '47
I Know Where I'm
   Going '45
The Life and Death of
   Colonel Blimp '43

Emeric Pressburger
The Red Shoes '48
Black Narcissus '47
I Know Where I'm
   Going '45
The Life and Death of
   Colonel Blimp '43

Vsevolod Pudovkin
Storm over Asia '28

Michael Radford
The Postman '94

Mort Ransen
Margaret's Museum '95

Satyajit Ray
The Middleman '76
Distant Thunder '73
Days and Nights in the
   Forest '70
Charulata '64
The Big City '63
Two Daughters '61
Devi '60
The World of Apu '59
Aparajito '58
Jalsaghar '58
Pather Panchali '54

Karel Reisz
Saturday Night and
   Sunday Morning '60

Edgar Reitz
Heimat 1 '84

Sheldon Renan
Akira '89

Jean Renoir
The Testament of Dr.
   Cordelier '59
Eléna and Her Men '56
French Can-Can '55
The Golden Coach '52
La Bete Humaine '38
Grand Illusion '37
La Marseillaise '37
The Crime of Monsieur
   Lange '36
The Lower Depths '36
Toni '34
Boudu Saved from
   Drowning '32
La Chienne '31

Alain Resnais
Mon Oncle
   d'Amerique '80
Providence '77
Muriel '63
Last Year at
   Marienbad '61
Hiroshima Mon
   Amour '59
Night and Fog '55

Tony Richardson
Look Back in Anger '58

Leni Riefenstahl
Triumph of the Will '34
The Blue Light '32

Dino Risi
Love in the City '53

Jacques Rivette
La Belle Noiseuse '90

Glauce Rocha
Antonio Das Mortes '68
Black God, White
   Devil '64

Nicolas Roeg
Insignificance '85
Walkabout '71

Julian Roffman
The Mask '61

Eric Rohmer
Rendezvous in Paris '95
A Tale of Springtime '92
A Tale of Winter '92
Boyfriends &
   Girlfriends '88
Full Moon in Paris '84
Pauline at the Beach '83
Le Beau Mariage '82
The Marquise of O '76
Chloe in the
   Afternoon '72
Claire's Knee '71
My Night at Maud's '69
La Collectionneuse '67

Francesco Rosi
Three Brothers '80
Christ Stopped at
   Eboli '79

Benjamin Ross
The Young Poisoner's
   Handbook '94

Roberto Rossellini
The Rise of Louis XIV '66
Generale Della
   Rovere '60
The Flowers of St.
   Francis '50
The Miracle '48
Paisan '46
Open City '45

Ken Russell
The Devils '71
The Music Lovers '71

Leontine Sagan
Mäedchen in
   Uniform '31

Chadi Abdel Salam
The Night of Counting
   the Years '69

Carlos Saura
Carmen '83
Blood Wedding '81
Cria '76
The Garden of
   Delights '70

Claude Sautet
Nelly et Monsieur
   Arnaud '95
Un Coeur en Hiver '93
Vincent, François, Paul
   and the Others '76
César & Rosalie '72

Fred Schepisi
A Cry in the Dark '88
The Chant of Jimmie
   Blacksmith '78
The Devil's
   Playground '76

Heinz Schirk
The Wannsee
   Conference '84

John Schlesinger
A Kind of Loving '62

Volker Schlondorff

The Tin Drum '79
The Lost Honor of
   Katharina Blum '75

Barbet Schroeder
General Idi Amin
   Dada '75
The Valley Obscured by
   the Clouds '72

Carl Schultz
Careful, He Might Hear
   You '84

Ettore Scola
La Nuit de Varennes '82
A Special Day '77
We All Loved Each
   Other So Much '77
Down & Dirty '76

Peter Sehr
Kaspar Hauser '93

Ousmane Sembene
Camp de Thiaroye '87
Ceddo '78
Xala '75
Emitai '71
Mandabi '68
Black Girl '66
Borom Sarret '66

Larisa Shepitko
The Ascent '76

Jim Sheridan
My Left Foot '89

Kaneto Shindo
Onibaba '64

Alf Sjoberg
Miss Julie '50
Torment '44

Vilgot Sjoman
I Am Curious
   (Yellow) '67

Erik Skjoldbjaerg
Insomnia '97

Jerzy Skolimowski
Moonlighting '82
Deep End '70

George Sluizer
The Vanishing '88

John N. Smith
The Boys of St.
   Vincent '93

Thierno Faty Sow
Camp de Thiaroye '87

Masayuki Suo
Shall We Dance? '97

Jan Svankmajer
Jan Svankmejer's
   Faust '94

Jan Sverak
Kolya '96

Istvan Szabo
Hanussen '88
Mephisto '81

Juan Carlos Tabio
Strawberry and
    Chocolate '93

Lee Tamahori
Once Were Warriors '94

Alain Tanner
In the White City '83
Messidor '77
Jonah Who Will Be 25 in
    the Year 2000 '76
La Salamandre '71

Andrei Tarkovsky
The Sacrifice '86
Stalker '79
The Mirror '75
Solaris '72
Andrei Rublev '66

Jacques Tati
Traffic '71
Playtime '67
Mon Oncle '58
Jour de Fete '48

Bertrand Tavernier
Captain Conan '96
L.627 '92
Life and Nothing But '89
Béatrice '88
The Judge and the
    Assassin '75

Paolo Taviani
Fiorile '93
Kaos '85
The Night of the
    Shooting Stars '82
Allonsanfan '73

Vittorio Taviani
Fiorile '93
Kaos '85
The Night of the
    Shooting Stars '82
Allonsanfan '73

Andre Techine
Les Voleurs '96
Wild Reeds '94
Ma Saison Préférée '93
Scene of the Crime '87
French Provincial '75

**Hiroshi
    Teshigahara**
The Face of Another '66
Woman in the
    Dunes '64

Ralph L. Thomas
Ticket to Heaven '81

Moufida Tlatli
The Silences of the
    Palace '94

Ricardo Tognazzi
La Scorta '94

Roland Topor
Fantastic Planet '73

Giuseppe Tornatore
Cinema Paradiso '88

Fina Torres
Celestial Clockwork '94

Jacques Tourneur
Curse of the Demon '57

Jan Troell
The New Land '73
The Emigrants '72

Fernando Trueba
Belle Epoque '92

Francois Truffaut ✓
Confidentially Yours '83
The Woman Next
    Door '81
The Last Metro '80
The Green Room '78
Love on the Run '78
The Man Who Loved
    Women '77
Small Change '76
The Story of Adele H. '75
Day for Night '73
Two English Girls '72
Bed and Board '70
The Wild Child '70
Mississippi Mermaid '69
The Bride Wore Black '68
Stolen Kisses '68
Fahrenheit 451 '66
The Soft Skin '64
Jules and Jim '62
Shoot the Piano
    Player '62
The 400 Blows '59
Les Mistons '57

Shinya Tsukamoto
Tetsuo: The Iron Man '92

Chano Urueto
The Brainiac '61

Roger Vadim
And God Created
    Woman '57

Jaco Van Dormael
Toto le Heros '91

Eric Van Zuylen
In for Treatment '82

Agnes Varda
Jacquot '91
Vagabond '85
One Sings, the Other
    Doesn't '77
Le Bonheur '65

Georgy Vassiliev
Chapayev '34

Sergei Vassiliev
Chapayev '34

Francis Veber
Les Compères '83

Paul Verhoeven
The 4th Man '79

Dziga Vertov
The Man with a Movie
    Camera '29

Daniel Vigne
The Return of Martin
    Guerre '83

Jean Vigo
L'Atalante '34
Zero for Conduct '33
A Propos de Nice '29

Christian Vincent
La Discrete '90

Luchino Visconti
The Innocent '76
Conversation Piece '75
Boccaccio '70 '62
Rocco and His
    Brothers '60
Senso '54
La Terra Trema '48
Ossessione '42

**Josef von
    Sternberg**
The Blue Angel '30

Lars von Trier
Breaking the Waves '95
The Kingdom '95
Zentropa '92

**Margarethe von
    Trotta**
Marianne and
    Juliane '82
The Lost Honor of
    Katharina Blum '75

Andrzej Wajda
Man of Iron '81
Man of Marble '76
Ashes and
    Diamonds '58
Kanal '56
A Generation '54

Regis Wargnier
Indochine '92

Michal Waszynski
The Dybbuk '37

Peter Watkins
Edvard Munch '74
The War Game '65

Paul Wegener
The Golem '20

Peter Weir
Gallipoli '81
Picnic at Hanging
    Rock '75

Orson Welles
Chimes at Midnight '67

The Trial '63
Mr. Arkadin '55

Wim Wenders
Faraway, So Close! '93
Wings of Desire '88
The American Friend '77
Kings of the Road—In
    the Course of
    Time '76
The Goalie's Anxiety at
    the Penalty Kick '71

Lina Wertmuller
Seven Beauties '76
Swept Away… '75
Love and Anarchy '73

Bo Widerberg
The Man on the Roof '76
Elvira Madigan '67

Robert Wiene
The Cabinet of Dr.
    Caligari '19

**Michael
    Winterbottom**
Butterfly Kiss '94

John Woo
Hard-Boiled '92
The Killer '90
A Better Tomorrow '86

Zhou Xiaowen
Ermo '94

**Mitsuo
    Yanagimachi**
Himatsuri '85

Zhang Yimou
Shanghai Triad '95
To Live '94
Raise the Red
    Lantern '91
The Story of Qiu Ju '91
Ju Dou '90
Red Sorghum '87

**Krzysztof
    Zanussi**
Contract '80
Illumination '73

Cesare Zavattini
Love in the City '53

Karel Zeman
Fabulous Adventures
    of Baron
    Munchausen '61
The Fabulous World of
    Jules Verne '58

**Tian
    Zhuangzhuang**
The Blue Kite '93
The Horse Thief '87

Claude Zidi
My New Partner '84

WRITER INDEX

The "Writer Index" provides a complete listing of writers cited within the reviews. The listings are alphabetical by last name, and the films are listed chronologically, from most recent to the oldest. Some actors and directors will show up here as they tend to do a lot of writing themselves.

Kobe Abe
The Face of Another '66
Woman in the
    Dunes '64

**Herbert
    Achternbusch**
Heart of Glass '74

Jovan Acin
Hey, Babu Riba '88

Percy Adlon
Sugarbaby '85
Céleste '81

Gilles Adrien
The City of Lost
    Children '95
Delicatessen '92

Julio Alajandro
Viridiana '61

Luis Alcoriza
The Exterminating
    Angel '62
Él '52

Julio Alejandro
Tristana '70

Michel Alexandre
L.627 '92

Grigori Alexandrov
Que Viva Mexico '32

Arif Aliev
Prisoner of the
    Mountains '96

Jim Allen
Land and Freedom '95

Pedro Almodovar
The Flower of My
    Secret '95
Kika '94
Tie Me Up! Tie Me
    Down! '90
Women on the Verge of
    a Nervous
    Breakdown '88
Matador '86

Gianni Amelio
Lamerica '95
The Stolen Children '92

Sergio Amidei
Shoeshine '47
Open City '45

Theo Angelopoulos
Ulysses' Gaze '95
Landscape in the
    Mist '88

**Gianfranco
    Angelucci**
Intervista '87

Jean Anouilh
Monsieur Vincent '47

**Michelangelo
    Antonioni**
Blow-Up '66
The Eclipse '66
The Red Desert '64
La Notte '60
L'Avventura '60

Vicente Aranda
Lovers: A True Story '90

Denys Arcand
Jesus of Montreal '89

Marcel Archand
The Earrings of
    Madame de... '54

Marek Arenstein
The Dybbuk '37

Dario Argento
Suspiria '77
The Bird with the
    Crystal Plumage '70
Once Upon a Time in
    the West '68

**Alexander
    Askoldov**
Commissar '68

Olivier Assayas
Scene of the Crime '87

Jacques Audiard
A Self-Made Hero '95
Baxter '89

Bille August
Jerusalem '96
Pelle the Conqueror '88
Twist & Shout '84

Jean Aurel
Confidentially Yours '83
Le Trou '59

Jean Aurenche
The Judge and the
    Assassin '75
Forbidden Games '52
Devil in the Flesh '46

Gabriel Axel
Babette's Feast '87

Rafael Azcona
Belle Epoque '92
La Grande Bouffe '73

Masuru Baba
Vengeance Is Mine '79

Hector Babenco
Pixote '81

Giya Badridze
Ashik Kerib '88

John Baines
Dead of Night '45

Josiane Balasko
French Twist '95

Bela Balazs
The Threepenny
    Opera '31

**Enrique Pineda
    Barnet**
I Am Cuba '64

Bruno Barreto
Dona Flor and Her Two
    Husbands '78

Shirley Barrett
Love Serenade '96

Odile Barski
Violette '78

Elio Bartolini
The Eclipse '66

Mario Bava
Black Sunday '60

Jerome Beaujour
A Single Girl '96

Marcel Beaulieu
Farinelli '94

Jacques Becker
Le Trou '59
Casque d'Or '52

**Jean-Jacques
    Beineix**
Betty Blue '86
Moon in the Gutter '83
Diva '82

Bela Belazs
The Blue Light '32

Marco Bellocchio
Devil in the Flesh '87

Remy Belvaux
Man Bites Dog '91

**Maria-Luisa
    Bemberg**
I Don't Want to Talk
    about It '94

Roberto Benigni
The Monster '96
Johnny Stecchino '92

Charles Bennett
Curse of the Demon '57

Leo Benvenuti
Alfredo, Alfredo '72

Luc Beraud
The Accompanist '93
The Best Way '76

John Berger
La Salamandre '71

Ingmar Bergman
Sunday's Children '94
The Best Intentions '92
After the Rehearsal '84
Fanny and
    Alexander '83
Autumn Sonata '78
Face to Face '76
Scenes from a
    Marriage '73
Cries and Whispers '72
The Passion of Anna '70
The Hour of the Wolf '68
Shame '68
Persona '66
The Silence '63
Winter Light '62
Through a Glass
    Darkly '61
The Devil's Eye '60
The Magician '58
Wild Strawberries '57
Dreams '55
Smiles of a Summer
    Night '55
Sawdust and Tinsel '53
Monika '52
Summer Interlude '50
Torment '44

Claude Berri
Germinal '93
Jean de Florette '87
Manon of the Spring '87
The Two of Us '68

**Bernardo
    Bertolucci**
1900 '76
Last Tango in Paris '73
The Conformist '71
The Spider's
    Stratagem '70
Once Upon a Time in
    the West '68
Before the
    Revolution '65

**Giuseppe
    Bertolucci**
1900 '76

Luc Besson
La Femme Nikita '91
Subway '85
Le Dernier Combat '84

Bertrand Blier
Too Beautiful for You '88
Beau Père '81
Get Out Your
    Handkerchiefs '78
Going Places '74

Sergei Bodrov
Prisoner of the
    Mountains '96

Jerome Boivin
Baxter '89

Edward Bond
Walkabout '71

Pascal Bonitzer
La Belle Noiseuse '90

Andre Bonzel
Man Bites Dog '91

Telsche Boorman
French Twist '95

Pierre Bost
The Judge and the
    Assassin '75
Forbidden Games '52
Devil in the Flesh '46

Nouri Bouzid
The Silences of the
    Palace '94

**Frank Cottrell
    Boyce**
Butterfly Kiss '94

Francois Boyer
Forbidden Games '52

Bruno Bozzetto
Allegro Non Troppo '76

Gerard Brach
Jean de Florette '87
Manon of the Spring '87
The Tenant '76
The Fearless Vampire
    Killers '67
Repulsion '65

Ray Bradbury
Fahrenheit 451 '66

Melvin Bragg
The Music Lovers '71

Kenneth Branagh
Henry V '89

Robert Bresson
L'Argent '83
Lancelot of the Lake '74
A Gentle Woman '69
Pickpocket '59
A Man Escaped '57
Diary of a Country
    Priest '50

Riwia Brown
Once Were Warriors '94

Joyce Bunuel
Black Moon '75

Luis Bunuel
That Obscure Object of
    Desire '77
The Phantom of Liberty
    '74
The Discreet Charm of
    the Bourgeoisie '72
Tristana '70
Belle de Jour '67
Simon of the Desert '66
Diary of a
    Chambermaid '64
The Exterminating
    Angel '62
Viridiana '61
The Criminal Life of
    Archibaldo de la
    Cruz '55
Él '52
L'Age D'Or '30

Aldo Buzzi
Love in the City '53

Anne Cameron
Ticket to Heaven '81

Jane Campion
The Piano '93
Sweetie '89

Cuca Canals
Jamón, Jamón '93

Leos Carax
Boy Meets Girl '84

Marc Caro
The City of Lost
    Children '95
Delicatessen '92

Fabio Carpi
Basileus Quartet '82

**Jean-Claude Car-
    riere**
May Fools '90
Max, Mon Amour '86
The Return of Martin
    Guerre '83
Every Man for
    Himself '79
The Tin Drum '79
That Obscure Object of
    Desire '77
The Phantom of
    Liberty '74
The Discreet Charm of
    the Bourgeoisie '72
Borsalino '70
The Milky Way '68
Belle de Jour '67
The Thief of Paris '67
Viva Maria! '65
Diary of a
    Chambermaid '64

Robert Caswell
A Cry in the Dark '88

Jean Cau
Borsalino '70

Alain Cavalier
Thérèse '86

Liliana Cavani
The Night Porter '74

Jean Cayrol
Muriel '63
Night and Fog '55

Vincenzo Cerami
The Monster '96
Johnny Stecchino '92

Claude Chabrol
La Cérémonie '95
The Story of Women '88
Wedding in Blood '74
La Rupture '70
La Femme Infidèle '69
Le Boucher '69
Les Biches '68

Gurinder Chadha
Bhaji on the Beach '94

Graham Chapman
Monty Python's The
    Meaning of Life '83

Zhang Chengzhi
A Mongolian Tale '94

Valentin Chernykh
Moscow Does Not
    Believe in Tears '80

Hal E. Chester
Curse of the Demon '57

Luigi Chiarini
Love in the City '53

Pavel Chukhrai
The Thief '97

Grigori Chukrai
Ballad of a Soldier '60

Rene Clair
A Nous la Liberté '31
Under the Roofs of
    Paris '29

T.E.B. Clarke
Dead of Night '45

John Cleese
Monty Python's The
    Meaning of Life '83

Rene Clement
Purple Noon '60
Forbidden Games '52

**Henri-Georges
    Clouzot**
The Wages of Fear '55

Jean Cocteau
The Testament of
    Orpheus '59
Les Enfants Terribles '50
Orpheus '49
Beauty and the Beast '46
Eternal Return '43
The Blood of a Poet '30

Catherine Cohen
Indochine '92

**Jacques
    Companeez**
Casque d'Or '52

**Shane Con-
    naughton**
My Left Foot '89

Alec Coppel
Captain's Paradise '53

**Francis Ford
    Coppola**
Is Paris Burning? '66

Andree Corbiau
Farinelli '94

Gerard Corbiau
Farinelli '94

Alain Corneau
Tous les Matins du
    Monde '92

Jean Cosmos
Captain Conan '96

**Constantin Costa-
    Gavras**
Z '69

Maurizio Costanzo
A Special Day '77

Noel Coward
Brief Encounter '46

Paul Cox
A Woman's Tale '92
Cactus '86
Man of Flowers '84

David Cronenberg
Crash '95
Dead Ringers '88
They Came from
  Within '75

Frederick Curiel
The Brainiac '61

Bohdan Czeszko
A Generation '54

Jean-Loup Dabadie
Vincent, François, Paul
  and the Others '76
César & Rosalie '72

Salvador Dali
L'Age D'Or '30

**Suso Cecchi
  D'Amico**
The Innocent '76
Conversation Piece '75
Big Deal on Madonna
  Street '58

Danniel Danniel
Egg '88

**Jean-Pierre
  Dardenne**
La Promesse '96

Luc Dardenne
La Promesse '96

Georges Darien
The Thief of Paris '67

Terence Davies
The Long Day Closes '92
Distant Voices, Still
  Lives '88

Jaime de Arminan
The Nest '80

**Christian de
  Chalonge**
Dr. Petiot '90

Ennio de Concini
Devil in the Flesh '87
Divorce—Italian
  Style '62
Black Sunday '60

Claude de Givray
Bed and Board '70
Stolen Kisses '68

Vinitius De Moraes
Black Orpheus '58

Giuliani G. De Negri
The Night of the
  Shooting Stars '82

Guiseppe de Santis
Bitter Rice '49

Vittorio de Seta
Bandits of Orgosolo '61

Vittorio De Sica
Umberto D. '55
The Bicycle Thief '48

Richard DeKoker
Juggernaut '74

Alvaro del Amo
Lovers: A True Story '90

Franklin Delessert
The Mask '61

Peter Delpeut
The Forbidden
  Quest '93

Jacques Demy
The Umbrellas of
  Cherbourg '64

Claire Denis
I Can't Sleep '93

Alan Dent
Hamlet '48
Henry V '45

Jacques Deray
Borsalino '70

Edmundo Desnoes
Memories of Unde-
  rdevelopment '68

Michel DeVille
La Lectrice '88

Rosalinde DeVille
La Lectrice '88

Graziano Diana
La Scorta '94

Carlos Diegues
Quilombo '84
Bye Bye Brazil '79

John Dighton
Kind Hearts and
  Coronets '49

Peter Dobai
Hanussen '88

Jacques Doillon
Ponette '95

**Alexander
  Dovzhenko**
Earth '30
Arsenal '29

Ginette Doynel
The Golden Coach '52

**Carl Theodor
  Dreyer**
Gertrud '64
Day of Wrath '43
Vampyr '31

Danielle Dubroux
Diary of a Seducer '95

Martine Dugowson
Mina Tannenbaum '93

E.A. Dupont
Variety '25

Marguerite Duras
Hiroshima Mon
  Amour '59

Julien Duvivier
Pépé le Moko '37

Christine Edzard
Little Dorrit, Film 1:
  Nobody's Fault '88
Little Dorrit, Film 2: Little
  Dorrit's Story '88

Atom Egoyan
The Sweet Hereafter '96
Exotica '94
The Adjuster '91

Ilya Ehrenburg
Die Liebe der Jeanne
  Ney '27

Sergei Eisenstein
Ivan the Terrible,
  Part 2 '46
Ivan the Terrible,
  Part 1 '44
Alexander Nevsky '38
Que Viva Mexico '32
The Battleship
  Potemkin '25

Caroline Eliacheff
La Cérémonie '95

Bob Ellis
Cactus '86
Man of Flowers '84

Yuhei Enoki
The Mystery of
  Rampo '94

Ildiko Enyedi
My Twentieth
  Century '90

Victor Erice
Spirit of the Beehive '73

Laura Esquivel
Like Water for
  Chocolate '93

Jean Eustache
The Mother and the
  Whore '73

Diego Fabbri
Generale Della
  Rovere '60

Jean-Pol Fargeau
I Can't Sleep '93

**Rainer Werner Fass-
  binder**
Berlin Alexanderplatz '80
The Marriage of Maria
  Braun '79
In a Year of 13 Moons '78
The Stationmaster's
  Wife '77
Mother Küsters Goes to
  Heaven '76
Ali: Fear Eats the Soul '74
Effi Briest '74
The Bitter Tears of Petra
  von Kant '72
The American Soldier '70
Beware of a Holy
  Whore '70

Xie Fei
Women from the Lake
  of Scented Souls '94

Bi Feiyu
Shanghai Triad '95

Joao Felicio
Xica '76

Federico Fellini
Intervista '87

Ginger & Fred '86
And the Ship Sails
  On '83
City of Women '81
Orchestra Rehearsal '78
Amarcord '74
Fellini's Roma '72
The Clowns '71
Fellini Satyricon '69
Juliet of the Spirits '65
8 1/2 '63
Boccaccio '70 '62
La Dolce Vita '60
Nights of Cabiria '57
La Strada '54
I Vitelloni '53
The White Sheik '52
Variety Lights '51
The Flowers of St.
  Francis '50
The Miracle '48
Paisan '46
Open City '45

Michel Fermaud
The Man Who Loved
  Women '77

Jesus Ferrere
Matador '86

Marco Ferreri
La Grande Bouffe '73

Michel Fessler
Ridicule '96

Jacques Fieschi
Nelly et Monsieur
  Arnaud '95
Un Coeur en Hiver '93

Bill Finger
The Green Slime '68

Ennio Flaiano
Juliet of the Spirits '65
8 1/2 '63
Boccaccio '70 '62
La Dolce Vita '60
La Notte '60
Nights of Cabiria '57
La Strada '54
I Vitelloni '53
The White Sheik '52
Variety Lights '51

Anne Fontaine
Augustin '95

Milos Forman
The Firemen's Ball '68

Bengt Forslund
The New Land '73
The Emigrants '72

Bill Forsyth
Comfort and Joy '84
Local Hero '83

Adolfo Franci
Shoeshine '47

Nikolaj Frobenius
Insomnia '97

Pea Frolich
Veronika Voss '82
The Marriage of Maria
  Braun '79

Pal Gabor
Angi Vera '78

Antonio Gades
Carmen '83
Blood Wedding '81

Henrik Galeen
Waxworks '24
Nosferatu '22
The Golem '20

Louis Gardel
Indochine '92

Helen Garner
Two Friends '86

Dominique Garnier
Dr. Petiot '90

Paul Gegauff
This Man Must Die '70
Purple Noon '60

Pietro Germi
Alfredo, Alfredo '72
Divorce—Italian
    Style '62

Jerome Geronimi
Diabolique '55

Vera Gherarducci
Bandits of Orgosolo '61

Alfredo Giannetti
Divorce—Italian
    Style '62

Boris Giller
Prisoner of the
    Mountains '96

Terry Gilliam
Monty Python's The
    Meaning of Life '83

Jose Giovanni
Le Trou '59

Andre Girard
La Chienne '31

Francois Girard
32 Short Films about
    Glenn Gould '93

Tomas Gislason
The Kingdom '95

Jean-Luc Godard
Every Man for
    Himself '79
Weekend '67
Two or Three Things I
    Know About Her '66
Alphaville '65
A Married Woman '65
Band of Outsiders '64
Contempt '64
My Life to Live '62
Breathless '59

Jakub Goldberg
Knife in the Water '62

Jorge Goldenberg
I Don't Want to Talk
    about It '94

Marilyn Goldin
Camille Claudel '89
French Provincial '75

Claude Goretta
The Wonderful
    Crook '75

Marleen Gorris
Antonia's Line '95

Peter Gothar
Time Stands Still '82

Sam Grana
The Boys of St.
    Vincent '93

Simon Gray
A Month in the
    Country '87

Janet Green
Victim '61

Peter Greenaway
The Pillow Book '95
The Belly of an
    Architect '91
The Cook, the Thief, His
    Wife & Her Lover '90
Drowning by
    Numbers '87
The Draughtsman's
    Contract '82

Frederic Grendel
Violette '78
Diabolique '55

Jean Gruault
Mon Oncle
    d'Amerique '80
The Green Room '78
The Story of Adele H. '75
The Wild Child '70
Jules and Jim '62

Jerry Gruza
Deep End '70

Tonino Guerra
Ulysses' Gaze '95
Landscape in the
    Mist '88
Ginger & Fred '86
And the Ship Sails
    On '83
The Night of the
    Shooting Stars '82
Amarcord '74
Blow-Up '66
The Eclipse '66
Casanova '70 '65
The Red Desert '64
La Notte '60
L'Avventura '60

Jean Guinee
L'Atalante '34

Yilmaz Guney
Yol '82

**Tomas Gutierrez
Alea**
Strawberry and
    Chocolate '93
Memories of Under-
    development '68
Death of a
    Bureaucrat '66

Willi Haas
The Joyless Street '25

Willis Hall
A Kind of Loving '62

Robert Hamer
Kind Hearts and
    Coronets '49

Peter Handke
Wings of Desire '88
The Goalie's Anxiety at
    the Penalty Kick '71

Jonathan Harvey
Beautiful Thing '95

Keiji Hasebe
Enjo '58

Izo Hashimoto
Akira '89

**Shinobu
    Hashimoto**
Dodes 'ka-den '70
Samurai Rebellion '67
Harakiri '62
Yojimbo '61
The Bad Sleep Well '60
The Hidden Fortress '58
Throne of Blood '57
I Live in Fear '55
Seven Samurai '54
Ikiru '52
Rashomon '51

**Anthony Havelock-
    Allan**
Brief Encounter '46

Sandy Haver
The Mask '61

Steve Hayes
Fantastic Planet '73

Jack Hazan
A Bigger Splash '74

Liu Heng
The Story of Qiu Ju '91
Ju Dou '90

Alain Henry
Entre-Nous '83

Gyula Hernadi
The Round-Up '66

Werner Herzog
Fitzcarraldo '82
Nosferatu the
    Vampyre '79
Woyzeck '78
Stroszek '77
Every Man for Himself &
    God Against All '75
Heart of Glass '74
Aguirre, the Wrath of
    God '72

Yim Ho
The Day the Sun Turned
    Cold '94

Carl Hoffmann
Faust '26

P.J. Hogan
Muriel's Wedding '94

Agnieszka Holland
Trois Couleurs: Bleu '93
Olivier, Olivier '92
Europa, Europa '91

Frantisek Hrubin
The Fabulous World of
    Jules Verne '58

Yu Hua
To Live '94

Tran Anh Hung
The Scent of Green
    Papaya '93

Evan Hunter
High & Low '62

**Rustam Ibragim-
    bekov**
Burnt by the Sun '94

Kon Ichikawa
Tokyo Olympiad '66

Masato Ide
Ran '85
Kagemusha '80

Eric Idle
Monty Python's The
    Meaning of Life '83

Slawomir Idziak
Trois Couleurs: Bleu '93

Shohei Imamura
Black Rain '88
The Ballad of
    Narayama '83

Markus Imhoof
The Boat Is Full '81

Ulla Isaakson
The Virgin Spring '59

Toshiro Ishido
Black Rain '88

Juzo Itami
Minbo—Or the Gentle
    Art of Japanese
    Extortion '92
A Taxing Woman '87
Tampopo '86
The Funeral '84

Simona Izzo
La Scorta '94

Peter Jackson
Heavenly Creatures '94

Gualtiero Jacopetti
Mondo Cane '63

Benoit Jacquot
A Single Girl '96

Hans Janowitz
The Cabinet of Dr.
    Caligari '19

Derek Jarman
Blue '93
Caravaggio '86

Henri Jeanson
Pépé le Moko '37

Michael Jenkins
Careful, He Might Hear
You '84

Jean-Pierre Jeunet
The City of Lost
Children '95
Delicatessen '92

**Alejandro
Jodorowsky**
El Topo '71

Terry Johnson
Insignificance '85

Evan Jones
Outback '71

Terry Jones
Monty Python's The
Meaning of Life '83

Christen Jul
Vampyr '31

S.A. Kacyzna
The Dybbuk '37

Vitaly Kanevski
Freeze-Die-Come to
Life '90

Nelly Kaplan
A Very Curious Girl '69

Wong Kar-Wai
Happy Together '96
Chungking Express '95

Mathieu Kassovitz
Hate '95
Café au Lait '94

Aki Kaurismaki
The Match Factory
Girl '90
Ariel '89
Leningrad Cowboys Go
America '89

Norman Kaye
Cactus '86

Barrie Keefe
The Long Good
Friday '80

Shu Kei
Temptress Moon '96

Abbas Kiarostami
Taste of Cherry '96
The White Balloon '95
Through the Olive
Trees '94
Life and Nothing
More … '92

**Krzysztof
Kieslowski**
Trois Couleurs: Blanc '94
Trois Couleurs:
Rouge '94
Trois Couleurs: Bleu '93
The Double Life of
Veronique '91

Riyuzo Kikushima
High & Low '62
The Bad Sleep Well '60

The Hidden Fortress '58
Throne of Blood '57

**Teinosuke
Kinugasa**
Gate of Hell '54

Jack Kirkland
The Golden Coach '52

Cedric Klapisch
When the Cat's Away '96

Yuri Klepikov
The Ascent '76

Claude Klotz
The Hairdresser's
Husband '92

**Andrei Kon-
chalovsky**
Andrei Rublev '66

Dusan Kovacevic
Underground '95

Tim Krabbe
The Vanishing '88

Akira Kurosawa
Rhapsody in August '91
Akira Kurosawa's
Dreams '90
Ran '85
Kagemusha '80
Dersu Uzala '75
Dodes 'ka-den '70
High & Low '62
Yojimbo '61
The Bad Sleep Well '60
The Hidden Fortress '58
The Lower Depths '57
Throne of Blood '57
I Live in Fear '55
Seven Samurai '54
Ikiru '52
Rashomon '51
The Men Who Tread on
the Tiger's Tail '45

Diane Kurys
Entre-Nous '83

Emir Kusturica
Underground '95

Irakli Kvirikadze
A Chef in Love '96

**Tadeusz
Kwiatkowski**
The Saragossa
Manuscript '65

Hans Kyser
Faust '26

Jacques Lagrange
Traffic '71

Rene Laloux
Fantastic Planet '73

**Peter Martin
Lampel**
Kameradschaft '31

Fritz Lang
M '31

Metropolis '26
Dr. Mabuse, Parts
1 & 2 '22

Arlette Langmann
Germinal '93
A Nos Amours '84

Leo Lania
The Threepenny
Opera '31

Pierre Laroche
Les Visiteurs du Soir '42

Alberto Lattuada
Variety Lights '51

Christine Laurent
La Belle Noiseuse '90

**Jean-Claude
Lauzon**
Léolo '92

Auguste Le Breton
Bob le Flambeur '55

Alain Le Henry
A Self-Made Hero '95

David Lean
Brief Encounter '46

Patrice Leconte
The Hairdresser's
Husband '92
Monsieur Hire '89

Gerard Lee
Sweetie '89

Lilian Lee
Farewell My
Concubine '93

Suh-Goon Lee
301, 302 '94

Mike Leigh
Secrets and Lies '95
Life Is Sweet '90
High Hopes '88
Bleak Moments '71

Claude Lelouch
Cat and Mouse '78
A Man and a Woman '66

Sergio Leone
Once Upon a Time in
the West '68
The Good, the Bad, and
the Ugly '67

Rudolf Leonhard
Diary of a Lost Girl '29
Die Liebe der Jeanne
Ney '27

Raoul Levy
And God Created
Woman '57

Robert Liebmann
The Blue Angel '30

**Father Antonio
Lisandrini**
The Flowers of St.
Francis '50

Carlo Lizzani
Bitter Rice '49

Jean-Bernard Luc
Monsieur Vincent '47

Bigas Luna
Jamón, Jamón '93

Ruggero Maccari
A Special Day '77
Down & Dirty '76

Giulio Macchi
The Golden Coach '52

Angus MacPhail
Dead of Night '45

Guy Maddin
Careful '94

Dusan Makavejev
Man Is Not a Bird '65

**Mohsen
Makhmalbaf**
Gabbeh '96

Claude Makovski
A Very Curious Girl '69

Luigi Malerba
Love in the City '53

Louis Malle
May Fools '90
Au Revoir les Enfants '87
Black Moon '75
Lacombe, Lucien '74
Murmur of the Heart '71
The Thief of Paris '67
Viva Maria! '65
The Fire Within '64
The Lovers '59

Milcho Manchevski
Before the Rain '94

Guido Manuli
Allegro Non Troppo '76

Xiao Mao
The Blue Kite '93

Petros Markaris
Ulysses' Gaze '95

Chris Marker
La Jetée '62

Goran Markovic
Tito and Me '92

**Christopher
Marlowe**
Faust '26

Henri Marquet
Jour de Fete '48

**Gabriel Garcia
Marquez**
Erendira '83

**Peter
Marthesheimer**
Veronika Voss '82
The Marriage of Maria
Braun '79

Olivier Massart
Wild Reeds '94

Rene Masson
Diabolique '55

Zenzo Matsuyama
The Human Condition:
    Road to Eternity '59

Toshiro Mayazumi
Enjo '58

Carl Mayer
The Cabinet of Dr.
    Caligari '19

John McCormick
Victim '61

Don McKellar
32 Short Films about
    Glenn Gould '93

Enrico Medioli
Conversation Piece '75

Jean-Pierre Melville
Le Samourai '67
Bob le Flambeur '55
Les Enfants Terribles '50

David Mercer
Providence '77

**Anne-Marie
    Mieville**
Every Man for
    Himself '79

Nikita Mikhalkov
Burnt by the Sun '94
Anna '93

Annie Miller
The Little Thief '89

Claude Miller
The Accompanist '93
The Little Thief '89
The Best Way '76

Paula Milne
Hollow Reed '95

Tsai Ming-Liang
Vive L'Amour '94

David Mingay
A Bigger Splash '74

Moshe Mizrahi
Madame Rosa '77

Yoko Mizuki
Kwaidan '64

Patrick Modiano
Lacombe, Lucien '74

Edouard Molinaro
La Cage aux Folles '78

Mario Monicelli
Big Deal on Madonna
    Street '58

Indro Montanelli
Generale Della
    Rovere '60

Jocelyn Moorhouse
Proof '91

Nanni Moretti
Caro Diario '93

Father Felix Morion
The Flowers of St.
    Francis '50

Yoshimitsu Morita
The Family Game '83

Marcel Moussey
Shoot the Piano
    Player '62
The 400 Blows '59

Takeo Murata
Godzilla, King of the
    Monsters '56

Yuri Nagibin
Dersu Uzala '75

Kenji Nakagami
Himatsuri '85

Takehiro Nakajima
Okoge '93

Mario Nascimbene
The Night of Counting
    the Years '69

Ronald Neame
Brief Encounter '46

Claude Neron
Vincent, François, Paul
    and the Others '76
César & Rosalie '72

Maurizio Nichetti
The Icicle Thief '89

Daria Nicolodi
Suspiria '77

Bruno Nuytten
Camille Claudel '89

Hideo Oguni
Ran '85
Dodes 'ka-den '70
High & Low '62
Yojimbo '61
The Bad Sleep Well '60
The Hidden Fortress '58
The Lower Depths '57
Throne of Blood '57
I Live in Fear '55
Seven Samurai '54
Ikiru '52

**Colo Tavernier
    O'Hagan**
Béatrice '88
The Story of Women '88

**Kazuyoshi
    Okuyama**
The Mystery of
    Rampo '94

Laurence Olivier
Henry V '45

Ermanno Olmi
The Tree of Wooden
    Clogs '78

Max Ophuls
Lola Montès '55
The Earrings of
    Madame de… '54

Erik Orsenna
Indochine '92

John Osborne
Look Back in Anger '58

Nagisa Oshima
Max, Mon Amour '86
In the Realm of the
    Senses '76
Boy '69

Katsuhiro Otomo
Akira '89

Karl Otten
Kameradschaft '31

Ottiero Ottieri
The Eclipse '66

Idrissa Ouedraogo
Tilaï '90
Yaaba '89

Yasujiro Ozu
An Autumn
    Afternoon '62
Tokyo Story '53

G.W. Pabst
Pandora's Box '28

Marcel Pagnol
Harvest '37
César '36
The Baker's Wife '33
Fanny '32
Marius '31

Enrico Palandri
Devil in the Flesh '87

Euzhan Palcy
Sugar Cane Alley '83

Michael Palin
Monty Python's The
    Meaning of Life '83

Jaroslav Papousek
The Firemen's Ball '68

Pier Paolo Pasolini
Arabian Nights '74
The Gospel According
    to St. Matthew '64
Mamma Roma '62
Il Bell'Antonio '60

Ivan Passer
The Firemen's Ball '68

Anna Pavignano
The Postman '94

Pyotr Pavlenko
Alexander Nevsky '38

Senel Paz
Strawberry and
    Chocolate '93

Patricia Petit
The Scent of Green
    Papaya '93

Sandro Petraglia
Fiorile '93
The Stolen Children '92

Nicholas Phipps
Captain's Paradise '53

Maurice Pialat
Van Gogh '92
A Nos Amours '84

**Krzysztof
    Piesiewicz**
Trois Couleurs: Blanc '94
Trois Couleurs:
    Rouge '94
Trois Couleurs: Bleu '93
The Double Life of
    Veronique '91

Tullio Pinelli
Ginger & Fred '86
Juliet of the Spirits '65
8 1/2 '63
Boccaccio '70 '62
La Dolce Vita '60
Nights of Cabiria '57
La Strada '54
Love in the City '53
The White Sheik '52
Variety Lights '51

Harold Pinter
The Go-Between '71

Benoit Poelvoorde
Man Bites Dog '91

Jean Poiret
La Cage aux Folles '78

Roman Polanski
The Tenant '76
The Fearless Vampire
    Killers '67
Repulsion '65
Knife in the Water '62

Gillo Pontecorvo
The Battle of Algiers '66

Andrea Porporati
Lamerica '95

**Alfredo Torres
    Portillo**
The Brainiac '61

Dennis Potter
Dreamchild '85

Sally Potter
The Tango Lesson '97
Orlando '92

Michael Powell
The Red Shoes '48
Black Narcissus '47
I Know Where I'm
    Going '45

Emeric Pressburger
The Red Shoes '48
Black Narcissus '47
I Know Where I'm
    Going '45

Jacques Prevert
Children of Paradise '44
Les Visiteurs du Soir '42
The Crime of Monsieur
    Lange '36

Peter Prince
The Hit '85

Giani Puccini
Bitter Rice '49

Pascal Quignard
Tous les Matins du
Monde '92

Michael Radford
The Postman '94

Mort Ransen
Margaret's Museum '95

Jeff Rawle
The Young Poisoner's
Handbook '94

Satyajit Ray
The Middleman '76
Distant Thunder '73
Days and Nights in the
Forest '70
Charulata '64
The Big City '63
Two Daughters '61
Devi '60
The World of Apu '59
Aparajito '58
Jalsaghar '58
Pather Panchali '54

Jean Redon
Eyes without a Face '59

Ivan Reiner
The Green Slime '68

Richard Reitinger
Faraway, So Close! '93

Edgar Reitz
Heimat 1 '84

Jean Renoir
The Testament of Dr.
Cordelier '59
The Golden Coach '52
La Bete Humaine '38
Grand Illusion '37
La Marseillaise '37
The Crime of Monsieur
Lange '36
The Lower Depths '36
Toni '34
Boudu Saved from
Drowning '32
La Chienne '31

Bernard Revon
Bed and Board '70

Claude Rich
The Accompanist '93

Jean-Louis Richard
Day for Night '73
The Bride Wore Black '68
Fahrenheit 451 '66
The Soft Skin '64

Leni Riefenstahl
Triumph of the Will '34
The Blue Light '32

Albert Riera
L'Atalante '34

Jacques Rivette
La Belle Noiseuse '90

Glauce Rocha
Antonio Das Mortes '68
Black God, White
Devil '64

Eric Rohmer
Rendezvous in Paris '95
A Tale of Springtime '92
A Tale of Winter '92
Boyfriends &
Girlfriends '88
Full Moon in Paris '84
Pauline at the Beach '83
Le Beau Mariage '82
The Marquise of O '76
Chloe in the
Afternoon '72
Claire's Knee '71
My Night at Maud's '69
La Collectionneuse '67

Brunello Rondi
Orchestra Rehearsal '78
Juliet of the Spirits '65
8 1/2 '63
La Dolce Vita '60
La Strada '54

Jean-Pierre Ronssin
La Discrete '90

Francesco Rosi
Three Brothers '80
Christ Stopped at
Eboli '79

Benjamin Ross
The Young Poisoner's
Handbook '94

Roberto Rossellini
Generale Della
Rovere '60
The Flowers of St.
Francis '50
Paisan '46

Stefano Rulli
The Stolen Children '92

Ken Russell
The Devils '71

Chadi Abdel Salam
The Night of Counting
the Years '69

Vaclav Sasek
The Firemen's Ball '68

Carlos Saura
Carmen '83
Blood Wedding '81
Cria '76

Claude Sautet
Nelly et Monsieur
Arnaud '95
Vincent, François, Paul
and the Others '76
César & Rosalie '72
Borsalino '70

**Johan Lindstroem
Saxon**
Elvira Madigan '67

Furio Scarpelli
The Postman '94
Big Deal on Madonna
Street '58

Giacomo Scarpelli
The Postman '94

Fred Schepisi
A Cry in the Dark '88

The Chant of Jimmie
Blacksmith '78
The Devil's
Playground '76

Suzanne Schiffman
Confidentially Yours '83
The Woman Next
Door '81
The Last Metro '80
The Man Who Loved
Women '77
Small Change '76
The Story of Adele H. '75
Day for Night '73

Volker Schlondorff
The Tin Drum '79

Barbet Schroeder
General Idi Amin
Dada '75
The Valley Obscured by
the Clouds '72

Yevgeni Schwarz
Don Quixote '57

**Aleksander
Scibor-Rylski**
Man of Iron '81
Man of Marble '76

Ettore Scola
La Nuit de Varennes '82
A Special Day '77
Down & Dirty '76

Peter Sehr
Kaspar Hauser '93

Shinichi Sekizawa
Mothra '62

Ousmane Sembene
Camp de Thiaroye '87
Ceddo '78
Xala '75
Emitai '71
Black Girl '66

Jorge Semprun
The Confession '70

Mala Sen
Bandit Queen '94

Mario Serandrei
Black Sunday '60

**Alessandro
Sermoneta**
Lamerica '95

Wallace Shawn
The Designated
Mourner '97

Larisa Shepitko
The Ascent '76

Jim Sheridan
My Left Foot '89

David Sherwin
If... '69

Alan Sillitoe
Saturday Night and
Sunday Morning '60

Charles Sinclair
The Green Slime '68

Alf Sjoberg
Miss Julie '50

Jerzy Skolimowski
Deep End '70
Knife in the Water '62

John N. Smith
The Boys of St.
Vincent '93

Norman Snider
Dead Ringers '88

Franco Solinas
The Battle of Algiers '66

L. Solovyov
The Overcoat '59

Thierno Faty Sow
Camp de Thiaroye '87

Charles Spaak
Grand Illusion '37
The Lower Depths '36

**Jerzy Stefan
Stawinski**
Kanal '56

Peter F. Steinbach
Heimat 1 '84

David Stone
Repulsion '65

David Storey
This Sporting Life '63

Ramon Suarez
Death of a
Bureaucrat '66

Bloeslav Sulik
Deep End '70

Masayuki Suo
Shall We Dance? '97

Jan Svankmajer
Jan Svankmejer's
Faust '94

Zdenek Sverak
Kolya '96
My Sweet Little
Village '86

Meera Syal
Bhaji on the Beach '94

Istvan Szabo
Hanussen '88

Yasuhiko Takiguchi
Harakiri '62

Alain Tanner
In the White City '83
Messidor '77
Jonah Who Will Be 25 in
the Year 2000 '76
La Salamandre '71

Sooni Taraporevala
Salaam Bombay! '88

Andrei Tarkovsky
The Mirror '75
Andrei Rublev '66

Jacques Tati
Traffic '71
Jour de Fete '48

Frank Taubes
The Mask '61

Gilles Taurand
Les Voleurs '96
Wild Reeds '94

Bertrand Tavernier
Captain Conan '96
L.627 '92
Life and Nothing But '89
The Judge and the
	Assassin '75

Paolo Taviani
Fiorile '93
Kaos '85
The Night of the
	Shooting Stars '82
Allonsanfan '73

Vittorio Taviani
Fiorile '93
Kaos '85
The Night of the
	Shooting Stars '82
Allonsanfan '73

Vincent Tavier
Man Bites Dog '91

Andre Techine
Les Voleurs '96
Wild Reeds '94
Ma Saison Préférée '93
French Provincial '75

Moufida Tlatli
The Silences of the
	Palace '94

George Toles
Careful '94

Jerome Tonnerre
Un Coeur en Hiver '93

Roland Topor
Fantastic Planet '73

Giuseppe Tornatore
Cinema Paradiso '88

Fina Torres
Celestial Clockwork '94

Jan Troell
The New Land '73
The Emigrants '72

Massimo Troisi
The Postman '94

Francois Truffaut
Confidentially Yours '83
The Man Who Loved
	Women '77
Small Change '76
Day for Night '73
Two English Girls '72
Bed and Board '70
The Wild Child '70
Mississippi Mermaid '69
The Bride Wore Black '68
Stolen Kisses '68
Fahrenheit 451 '66
The Soft Skin '64
Jules and Jim '62
Shoot the Piano
	Player '62
The 400 Blows '59

Shinya Tsukamoto
Tetsuo: The Iron Man '92

Keinosuke Uegusa
Drunken Angel '48

Ghislain Uhry
Black Moon '75

Pierre Uytterhoeven
A Man and a Woman '66

Roger Vadim
And God Created
	Woman '57

Ladislao Vajda
The Threepenny
	Opera '31
Die Liebe der Jeanne
	Ney '27

Thanassis Valtinos
Landscape in the
	Mist '88

Jaco Van Dormael
Toto le Heros '91

Agnes Varda
Jacquot '93
Vagabond '85
One Sings, the Other
	Doesn't '77
Le Bonheur '65

Georgy Vassiliev
Chapayev '34

Sergei Vassiliev
Chapayev '34

Francis Veber
Les Compères '83
La Cage aux Folles '78

Dziga Vertov
The Man with a Movie
	Camera '29

Vittorio Vettreni
Love in the City '53

Eric Vicaut
Ridicule '96

Gore Vidal
Is Paris Burning? '66

Daniel Vigne
The Return of Martin
	Guerre '83

Jean Vigo
L'Atalante '34
Zero for Conduct '33
A Propos de Nice '29

Christian Vincent
La Discrete '90

C.G. Viola
Shoeshine '47

Jacques Viot
Black Orpheus '58

Luchino Visconti
The Innocent '76
Conversation Piece '75
Boccaccio '70 '62

Gino Vissentini
Il Bell'Antonio '60

Karl Vollmoller
The Blue Angel '30

Thea von Harbou
M '31
Metropolis '26
Dr. Mabuse, Parts
	1 & 2 '22

Lars von Trier
Breaking the Waves '95
The Kingdom '95
Zentropa '92

**Margarethe von
	Trotta**
Marianne and
	Juliane '82

Slavko Vorkapich
The Mask '61

Niels Vorsel
Zentropa '92

Natto Wada
Fires on the Plain '59
Enjo '58
The Burmese Harp '56

Annette Wademant
The Earrings of Madame
	de… '54

Andrzej Wajda
Ashes and
	Diamonds '58

Laszlo Wajda
Kameradschaft '31

Des Walsh
The Boys of St.
	Vincent '93

Frances Walsh
Heavenly Creatures '94

Regis Wargnier
Indochine '92

Keith Waterhouse
A Kind of Loving '62

Remi Waterhouse
Ridicule '96

Peter Watkins
Edvard Munch '74
The War Game '65

Paul Wegener
The Golem '20

Lu Wei
To Live '94
Farewell My
	Concubine '93

Peter Weir
Gallipoli '81

Orson Welles
Chimes at Midnight '67

Wim Wenders
Faraway, So Close! '93
Wings of Desire '88
The American Friend '77
Kings of the Road—
	In the Course of
	Time '76
The Goalie's Anxiety at
	the Penalty Kick '71

Lina Wertmuller
Seven Beauties '76
Swept Away… '75
Love and Anarchy '73

Gerald Wexler
Margaret's Museum '95

Bo Widerberg
The Man on the Roof '76
Elvira Madigan '67

David Williamson
Gallipoli '81

Barry Wong
Hard-Boiled '92

Kar-Wei Wong
Happy Together '96

John Woo
Hard-Boiled '92
The Killer '90
A Better Tomorrow '86

Charles Wood
How I Won the War '67

**Yevgeny
	Yevtushenko**
I Am Cuba '64

Valentin Yezhov
Ballad of a Soldier '60

Yoshikata Yoda
Sansho the Bailiff '54
Ugetsu '53
Utamaro and His Five
	Women '46

Lang Yun
Ermo '94

Krzysztof Zanussi
Contract '80
Illumination '73

Barnardino Zapponi
The Clowns '71

Cesare Zavattini
The Garden of the Finzi-
	Continis '71
Boccaccio '70 '62
Umberto D. '55
Miracle in Milan '51
The Bicycle Thief '48
Shoeshine '47

Edward Zebrowski
Trois Couleurs: Bleu '93

Karel Zeman
Fabulous Adventures
	of Baron
	Munchausen '61
The Fabulous World of
	Jules Verne '58

Rui Zhang
The Horse Thief '87

Claude Zidi
My New Partner '84

Ulrich Zieger
Faraway, So Close! '93

Carl Zuckmayer
The Blue Angel '30

CINEMATOGRAPHER INDEX

The "Cinematographer Index" provides a complete listing of cinematographers, or directors of photography, as they are also known, cited within the reviews. The listings are alphabetical by last name, and the films are listed chronologically, from most recent to the oldest.

Arne Abrahamsen
Gertrud '64

Barry Ackroyd
Land and Freedom '95

Remi Adefarasin
Hollow Reed '95

Jose F. Aguayo
Tristana '70
Viridiana '61

Pierre Aim
Hate '95
Café au Lait '94

Yuzuru Aizawa
The Bad Sleep Well '60

Jose Luis Alcaine
Jamón, Jamón '93
Belle Epoque '92
Lovers: A True Story '90
Tie Me Up! Tie Me
Down! '90
Women on the Verge of
a Nervous
Breakdown '88

Henri Alekan
Wings of Desire '88
Beauty and the
Beast '46

Sepp Allgeier
Triumph of the Will '34
Diary of a Lost Girl '29

Nestor Almendros
Confidentially Yours '83
Pauline at the Beach '83
The Last Metro '80
The Green Room '78
Love on the Run '78
Madame Rosa '77
The Man Who Loved
Women '77
The Marquise of O '76
General Idi Amin
Dada '75
The Story of Adele H. '75
Chloe in the
Afternoon '72
Two English Girls '72

The Valley Obscured by
the Clouds '72
Claire's Knee '71
Bed and Board '70
The Wild Child '70
My Night at Maud's '69
La Collectionneuse '67

John A. Alonzo
The Hit '85

Herbert S. Alpert
The Mask '61

Karl Andersson
Day of Wrath '43

Yves Angelo
The Accompanist '93
Germinal '93
Un Coeur en Hiver '93
Tous les Matins du
Monde '92
Baxter '89

Johan Ankerstjerne
Witchcraft through the
Ages '22

Thierry Arbogast
Ridicule '96
Ma Saison Préférée '93
La Femme Nikita '91

Ricardo Aronovich
Celestial Clockwork '94
Providence '77
Murmur of the Heart '71

Yorgos Arvanitis
Ulysses' Gaze '95
Landscape in the
Mist '88

Yushun Atsuta
An Autumn
Afternoon '62
Tokyo Story '53

Jean Bachelet
The Crime of Monsieur
Lange '36
The Lower Depths '36

Jean Badal
A Very Curious Girl '69

Ian Baker
A Cry in the Dark '88
The Chant of Jimmie
Blacksmith '78
The Devil's
Playground '76

Michael Ballhaus
The Marriage of Maria
Braun '79
The Stationmaster's
Wife '77
Mother Küsters Goes to
Heaven '76
The Bitter Tears of Petra
von Kant '72
Beware of a Holy
Whore '70

Diane Baratier
Rendezvous in Paris '95

Robert Barberske
Kameradschaft '31

Leonida Barboni
Divorce—Italian
Style '62

Boris Baromykin
Fantastic Planet '73

Peter Bartlett
The War Game '65

Julio Battiferri
Swept Away… '75

Mario Battistoni
The Icicle Thief '89

Mario Bava
Black Sunday '60

Alfonso Beato
The Flower of My
Secret '95
Antonio Das Mortes '68

Claude Beausoleil
Le Bonheur '65

Etienne Becker
Phantom India '69

**Youssef Ben
Youssef**
The Silences of the
Palace '94

Henning Bendtsen
Gertrud '64

Georges Benoit
The Baker's Wife '33

Louis Berger
L'Atalante '34

Georgi Beridze
A Chef in Love '96

Gabriel Beristain
Caravaggio '86

Steven Bernstein
Like Water for
Chocolate '93

Renato Berta
May Fools '90
Au Revoir les Enfants '87
Full Moon in Paris '84
Every Man for
Himself '79
Messidor '77
Jonah Who Will Be 25 in
the Year 2000 '76
The Wonderful Crook '75

Luca Bigazzi
Lamerica '95

Hilding Bladh
Dreams '55

Patrick Blossier
Jacquot '91
Dr. Petiot '90
Vagabond '85

Martin Bodin
Torment '44

Jean Boffety
Vincent, François, Paul
and the Others '76
César & Rosalie '72
Zita '68

Alun Bollinger
Heavenly Creatures '94

Andre Bonzel
Man Bites Dog '91

Jean Bourgoin
Black Orpheus '58
Mon Oncle '58
Mr. Arkadin '55
La Marseillaise '37

Russell Boyd
Gallipoli '81
Picnic at Hanging
    Rock '75

Vladimir Brylyakov
Freeze-Die-Come to
    Life '90

L.H. Burel
Pickpocket '59
A Man Escaped '57
Diary of a Country
    Priest '50

Jack Cardiff
War and Peace '68
The Red Shoes '48
Black Narcissus '47

Georges Caristan
Ceddo '78
Xala '75

Carlo Carlini
Generale Della
    Rovere '60
I Vitelloni '53

Francois Catonne
Indochine '92

**Caroline
    Champetier**
A Single Girl '96

Gu Changwei
Farewell My
    Concubine '93
Ju Dou '90
Life on a String '90
Red Sorghum '87

Dominique Chapuis
Mina Tannenbaum '93
The Little Thief '89
Sugar Cane Alley '83

**Pierre-Laurent
    Chenieux**
Tilaï '90

Yiu-tsou Cheung
Police Story '85

Alain Choquart
Captain Conan '96
L.627 '92

Vladimir Chukhnov
The Ascent '76

Denys Clerval
Erendira '83
Mississippi Mermaid '69
Stolen Kisses '68

Antonio Climatl
Mondo Cane '63

Ghislan Cloquet
Donkey Skin '70
A Gentle Woman '69
Mouchette '67
The Fire Within '64
Le Trou '59
Night and Fog '55

Alfio Contino
The Night Porter '74

Denys Coop
This Sporting Life '63
A Kind of Loving '62

Rafael Corkidi
El Topo '71

Michael Coulter
The Long Day Closes '92

Curt Courant
La Bete Humaine '38

Raoul Coutard
Max, Mon Amour '86
The Confession '70
The Bride Wore Black '68
Two or Three Things I
    Know About Her '66
Alphaville '65
A Married Woman '65
Band of Outsiders '64
Contempt '64
The Soft Skin '64
Jules and Jim '62
Breathless '59

Luis Cuadrado
Spirit of the Beehive '73

**Massimo Dalla-
    mano**
A Fistful of Dollars '64

Acacio De Almeida
In the White City '83

Gerard de Battista
French Twist '95

Jan De Bont
The 4th Man '79

Bruno de Keyzer
Life and Nothing But '89
Béatrice '88
Little Dorrit, Film 1:
    Nobody's Fault '88
Little Dorrit, Film 2: Little
    Dorrit's Story '88

Pasquale De Santis
L'Argent '83
Three Brothers '80
Christ Stopped at
    Eboli '79
A Special Day '77
The Innocent '76
Conversation Piece '75
Lancelot of the Lake '74

Vittorio de Seta
Bandits of Orgosolo '61

Henri Decae
Le Samourai '67
The Thief of Paris '67
Viva Maria! '65
Purple Noon '60
The 400 Blows '59

Frantic '58
Bob le Flambeur '55

Isabelle Dedieu
Thérèse '86

Benoit Delhomme
When the Cat's Away '96
The Scent of Green
    Papaya '93

Tonino Delli Colli
Intervista '87
Ginger & Fred '86
Seven Beauties '76
Salo, or the 120 Days of
    Sodom '75
Lacombe, Lucien '74
The Decameron '70
Once Upon a Time in
    the West '68
The Good, the Bad, and
    the Ugly '67
The Gospel According
    to St. Matthew '64
Mamma Roma '62

Daniil Demutsky
Earth '30
Arsenal '29

Franco Di Giacomo
The Postman '94
The Night of the
    Shooting Stars '82

Carlo Di Palma
The Monster '96
Blow-Up '66
The Red Desert '64

Dario Di Palma
Down & Dirty '76
The Clowns '71

Gianni Di Venanzo
The Eclipse '66
Juliet of the Spirits '65
8 1/2 '63
La Notte '60
Big Deal on Madonna
    Street '58
Love in the City '53

Georges Diane
Hate '95

**Desmond
    Dickinson**
Hamlet '48

**Fyodor
    Dobronravov**
Dersu Uzala '75

Alan Dostie
32 Short Films about
    Glenn Gould '93

Christopher Doyle
Happy Together '96
Temptress Moon '96
Chungking Express '95

Jean-Marie Dreujou
Augustin '95

Stuart Dryburgh
Once Were Warriors '94
The Piano '93

Appolinari Dudko
Don Quixote '57

Guy Dufaux
Jesus of Montreal '89

Patrick Duval
Distant Voices, Still
    Lives '88

Albert Duverger
L'Age D'Or '30

Teodoro Escamilla
Carmen '83
Blood Wedding '81
The Nest '80
Cria '76

Jean-Yves Escoffier
Boy Meets Girl '84

Jean-Marc Fabre
A Self-Made Hero '95

Abdel Aziz Fahmy
The Night of Counting
    the Years '69

**Rainer Werner Fass-
    binder**
In a Year of 13 Moons '78

Roger Fellous
Diary of a
    Chambermaid '64

Gabriel Figueroa
Simon of the Desert '66
The Exterminating
    Angel '62
Él '52

Vilko Filac
Underground '95

Gunnar Fischer
The Devil's Eye '60

Gerry Fisher
Juggernaut '74
The Go-Between '71

Freddie Francis
Saturday Night and
    Sunday Morning '60

Benito Frattari
Mondo Cane '63

Karl Freund
Metropolis '26
Variety '25
The Golem '20

Jing Sheng Fu
A Mongolian Tale '94

**Yasumichi
    Fukuzawa**
Dodes'ka-den '70

Arturo Galea
The White Sheik '52

Yuri Gantman
Dersu Uzala '75

Marcello Gatti
Burn! '70
The Battle of Algiers '66

Lu Gengxin
Ermo '94

Valery Ginsberg
Commissar '68

Basco Giurato
Cinema Paradiso '88

Pierre William Glenn
Small Change '76
The Judge and the Assassin '75
Day for Night '73

Agnes Godard
I Can't Sleep '93

Aldo G.R. Aldo Graziatti
Twist & Shout '84

Marcel Grignon
Is Paris Burning? '66

Ennio Guarnieri
The Garden of the Finzi-Continis '71

Yoshimasa Hakata
Okoge '93

Willy Hameister
The Cabinet of Dr. Caligari '19

Ismail Lakhdar Hamina
Camp de Thiaroye '87

Peter Hannan
Insignificance '85

Kazutami Hara
Akira Kurosawa's Dreams '90

Nicolas Hayer
Orpheus '49

Otto Heller
Victim '61

Gilles Henry
Van Gogh '92

Ronald Hill
The Golden Coach '52

Erwin Hillier
I Know Where I'm Going '45

Sinsaku Himeda
Vengeance Is Mine '79

Carl Hoffmann
Die Nibelungen '23
Dr. Mabuse, Parts 1 & 2 '22

Antonin Horak
The Fabulous World of Jules Verne '58

Yong Hou
The Blue Kite '93

Roger Hubert
Children of Paradise '44
Eternal Return '43

Slawomir Idziak
Trois Couleurs: Bleu '93
The Double Life of Veronique '91
Contract '80

Hideo Ito
In the Realm of the Senses '76

Takeo Ito
Drunken Angel '48
The Men Who Tread on the Tiger's Tail '45

Hossein Jafarian
Through the Olive Trees '94

Augustin Jimenez
The Criminal Life of Archibaldo de la Cruz '55

Farzad Jowdat
The White Balloon '95

Mario Garcia Joya
Strawberry and Chocolate '93

Robert Juillard
Forbidden Games '52

Jurgen Jurges
Faraway, So Close! '93
Ali: Fear Eats the Soul '74
Effi Briest '74

Mahmoud Kalari
Gabbeh '96

Matthias Kalin
Yaaba '89

Per Kallberg
The Man on the Roof '76

Vilen Kalyuta
Burnt by the Sun '94

Boris Kaufman
L'Atalante '34
Zero for Conduct '33
A Propos de Nice '29

Mikhail Kaufman
The Man with a Movie Camera '29

Takashi Kawamata
Black Rain '88

Naoke Kayano
Shall We Dance? '97

Michel Kelber
Devil in the Flesh '46

John Kenway
Bhaji on the Beach '94

Darius Khondji
The City of Lost Children '95
Delicatessen '92

Edward Klosinski
Trois Couleurs: Blanc '94
Man of Iron '81
Illumination '73

Setsuo Kobayashi
Fires on the Plain '59

Hajime Koizumi
Mothra '62

Lajos Koltai
Hanussen '88
Time Stands Still '82
Mephisto '81
Angi Vera '78

Robert Krasker
Senso '54
Brief Encounter '46
Henry V '45

Eric Kress
The Kingdom '95

Henning Kristiansen
Babette's Feast '87

Jules Kruger
Pépé le Moko '37

Toni Kuhn
The Vanishing '88

Walter Robert Lach
Die Liebe der Jeanne Ney '27
The Joyless Street '25

Christian Lacoste
Black Girl '66

Giuseppe Lanci
Caro Diario '93
Fiorile '93
Johnny Stecchino '92
Devil in the Flesh '87
Kaos '85

Jeanne Lapoirie
Les Voleurs '96
Wild Reeds '94

Federico G. Larraya
A Fistful of Dollars '64

Robert Le Febvre
Casque d'Or '52

Pavel Lebeshev
Prisoner of the Mountains '96
Anna '93
The Ascent '76

Georges Leclerc
The Testament of Dr. Cordelier '59

Richard Leiterman
Ticket to Heaven '81

Claude Lelouch
A Man and a Woman '66

Pierre Letarte
The Boys of St. Vincent '93

Pierre Lhomme
Camille Claudel '89
The Mother and the Whore '73

Hans Liechti
The Boat Is Full '81

Waldemar Lima
Black God, White Devil '64

Ming-kuo Lin
Vive L'Amour '94

Pen-jung Lioa
Vive L'Amour '94

Jerzy Lipman
Knife in the Water '62
Kanal '56

Dietrich Lohmann
Effi Briest '74
The American Soldier '70

Jacques Loiseleux
A Nos Amours '84

Orlando L. Lopez
Xala '75

William Lubtchansky
La Belle Noiseuse '90
Every Man for Himself '79

Marcel Lucien
Boudu Saved from Drowning '32

Yang Lun
Ju Dou '90

Igor Luther
The Tin Drum '79

Bernard Lutic
Boyfriends & Girlfriends '88
Entre-Nous '83
Le Beau Mariage '82

Emmanuel Machuel
Van Gogh '92

Laurent Machuel
Diary of a Seducer '95

Kenneth Macmillan
Henry V '89
A Month in the Country '87

Guy Maddin
Careful '94

Yonezo Maeda
Minbo—Or the Gentle Art of Japanese Extortion '92
A Taxing Woman '87
The Funeral '84
The Family Game '83

Svatopluk Maly
Jan Svankmejer's Faust '94

Bahram Manocheri
Bleak Moments '71

Heinrich Marandzhjan
The Overcoat '59

Alain Marcoen
La Promesse '96

Chris Marker
La Jetée '62

Otello Martelli
Boccaccio '70 '62
I Vitelloni '53

Variety Lights '51
The Flowers of St.
    Francis '50
Bitter Rice '49

Jurgen Martin
Céleste '81

Mario Masini
Allegro Non Troppo '76

Rudolph Mate
Vampyr '31

Christian Matras
The Earrings of
    Madame de... '54
Grand Illusion '37

Thomas Mauch
Fitzcarraldo '82
Stroszek '77
Aguirre, the Wrath of
    God '72

Alfredo Mayo
Kika '94

Seamus McGarvey
Butterfly Kiss '94

Martin McGrath
Muriel's Wedding '94

Phil Meheux
The Long Good
    Friday '80

Ashok Mehta
Bandit Queen '94

Chris Menges
Comfort and Joy '84
Local Hero '83
Gumshoe '72

Barnard Menoud
Every Man for
    Himself '79

Jacques Mercanton
Jour de Fete '48

Shigeto Miki
Utamaro and His Five
    Women '46

Katsuji Misawa
Akira '89

Subrata Mitra
Charulata '64
The Big City '63
Devi '60
Aparajito '58
Jalsaghar '58

Kazuo Miyagawa
Kagemusha '80
Tokyo Olympiad '66
Enjo '58
Ugetsu '53
Rashomon '51

Yoshio Miyajima
Kwaidan '64
Harakiri '62
The Human Condition:
    Road to Eternity '59

Jean Monsigny
Tilaï '90

Carlo Montuori
The Bicycle Thief '48

Oswald Morris
Look Back in Anger '58

Andrei Moskvin
Don Quixote '57
Ivan the Terrible,
    Part 2 '46

Sergei Mukhin
Ballad of a Soldier '60

Robby Muller
The Tango Lesson '97
Breaking the Waves '95
The American Friend '77
Kings of the Road—
    In the Course of
    Time '76
The Goalie's Anxiety at
    the Penalty Kick '71

Asakazu Nakai
Dersu Uzala '75
High & Low '62
Throne of Blood '57
I Live in Fear '55
Seven Samurai '54
Ikiru '52

Armando Nannuzzi
La Cage aux Folles '78
Il Bell'Antonio '60

Bruno Nuytten
Jean de Florette '87
Manon of the Spring '87
The Best Way '76
French Provincial '75
Going Places '74

Sven Nykvist
The Sacrifice '86
After the Rehearsal '84
Fanny and Alexander '83
Autumn Sonata '78
Face to Face '76
The Tenant '76
Black Moon '75
Scenes from a
    Marriage '73
Cries and Whispers '72
The Passion of Anna '70
The Hour of the Wolf '68
Shame '68
Persona '66
The Silence '63
Winter Light '62
Through a Glass
    Darkly '61
The Virgin Spring '59

Curt Oertel
The Joyless Street '25

Ermanno Olmi
The Tree of Wooden
    Clogs '78

Miroslav Ondricek
If... '69

Luc Pages
A Tale of Winter '92

Aiace Parolini
Alfredo, Alfredo '72

Peter Pau
The Killer '90

Stanley Pavey
Dead of Night '45

Homayun Payvar
Taste of Cherry '96
Life and Nothing
    More ... '92

Julian Penney
Two Friends '86

Jean Penzer
Get Out Your
    Handkerchiefs '78
The Two of Us '68

Georges Perinal
The Life and Death of
    Colonel Blimp '43
A Nous la Liberté '31
The Blood of a Poet '30
Under the Roofs of
    Paris '29

Andre Perlstein
Cat and Mouse '78

Jorgen Persson
Jerusalem '96
The Best Intentions '92
Elvira Madigan '67

**Aleksandar
Petkovic**
Man Is Not a Bird '65

Jacek Petrycki
Europa, Europa '91

**Tony Pierce-
Roberts**
Moonlighting '82

Bronislau Pikhart
The Fabulous World of
    Jules Verne '58

Roland Pointoizeau
The Testament of
    Orpheus '59

Dick Pope
Secrets and Lies '95

Roger Pratt
High Hopes '88

Jean Rabier
The Story of Women '88
Violette '78
Wedding in Blood '74
This Man Must Die '70
La Femme Infidèle '69
Le Bonheur '65
The Umbrellas of
    Cherbourg '64

Jose Ortiz Ramos
The Brainiac '61

Franz Rath
Marianne and Juliane '82

Gustav Rathje
M '31

Lubomir Rejthar
Fantastic Planet '73

Michel Remaudeau
Emitai '71

Claude Renoir
Eléna and Her Men '56
The Golden Coach '52
Monsieur Vincent '47
Toni '34

Georgy Rerberg
The Mirror '75

Edmond Richard
That Obscure Object of
    Desire '77
The Phantom of Liberty
    '74
The Discreet Charm of
    the Bourgeoisie '72
Chimes at Midnight '67
The Trial '63

Gunther Rittau
The Blue Angel '30
Metropolis '26
Die Nibelungen '23

**Jean-Francois
Robin**
Nelly et Monsieur
    Arnaud '95
Betty Blue '86

Alexei Rodionov
Orlando '92

Nicolas Roeg
Walkabout '71
Fahrenheit 451 '66

Gernot Roll
Kaspar Hauser '93
Heimat 1 '84

Giuseppe Rotunno
And the Ship Sails On
    '83
City of Women '81
Orchestra Rehearsal '78
Amarcord '74
Fellini's Roma '72
Fellini Satyricon '69
Boccaccio '70 '62

Philippe Rousselot
Too Beautiful for You '88
Moon in the Gutter '83
Diva '82

Soumendu Roy
The Middleman '76
Distant Thunder '73
Days and Nights in the
    Forest '70
Two Daughters '61

Giuseppe Ruzzolini
Arabian Nights '74
Allonsanfan '73

Robert Saad
They Came from
    Within '75

Farhad Saba
Through the Olive
    Trees '94

Odd Geir Saether
The Man on the Roof '76
Edvard Munch '74

Takao Saito
Rhapsody in August '91
Akira Kurosawa's
  Dreams '90
Dodes 'ka-den '70
High & Low '62

Timo Salminen
Ariel '89

Vic Sarin
Margaret's Museum '95

Paul Sarossy
The Sweet Hereafter '96
Exotica '94
The Adjuster '91

Yasushi Sasakibara
The Mystery of
  Rampo '94

Seydina D. Saye
Xala '75

Edward Scaife
Curse of the Demon '57
Captain's Paradise '53

Aldo Scavarda
Before the
  Revolution '65
L'Avventura '60

Martin Schafer
Kings of the Road—
  In the Course of
  Time '76

**Jorge Schmidt-
  Reitwein**
Nosferatu the
  Vampyre '79
Every Man for Himself &
  God Against All '75
Heart of Glass '74

Hans Schneeberger
The Blue Light '32

Eugene Schufftan
Metropolis '26

**Xaver Schwarzen-
  berger**
Veronika Voss '82
Berlin Alexanderplatz
  '80

Chris Seager
Beautiful Thing '95

John Seale
Careful, He Might Hear
  You '84

Farba Seck
Xala '75

Guido Seeber
The Joyless Street '25

Hiroshi Segawa
The Face of Another '66
Woman in the
  Dunes '64

Seizo Sengen
Boy '69

Eduardo Serra
The Hairdresser's
  Husband '92

**Eugene (Eugen
  Shufftan)
  Shuftan**
Eyes without a Face '59

Aleksander Sigayev
Chapayev '34

Sandi Sissel
Salaam Bombay! '88

Igor Slabnevich
Moscow Does Not
  Believe in Tears '80

Douglas Slocombe
The Music Lovers '71
The Fearless Vampire
  Killers '67
Kind Hearts and
  Coronets '49
Dead of Night '45

Vladimir Smutny
Kolya '96

Piotr Sobocinski
Trois Couleurs:
  Rouge '94

Jaromir Sofr
My Sweet Little
  Village '86

Yuri Sokol
Cactus '86
Man of Flowers '84

Dante Spinotti
Basileus Quartet '82

Oliver Stapleton
The Designated
  Mourner '97

Willy Stassen
Antonia's Line '95

Charly Steinberger
Deep End '70

Vittorio Storaro
1900 '76
Last Tango in Paris '73
The Conformist '71
The Bird with the
  Crystal Plumage '70

Harry Stradling
Carnival in Flanders '35

Goran Strindberg
Miss Julie '50

Ramon Suarez
Memories of Under-
  development '68
Death of a
  Bureaucrat '66

Kohei Sugiyama
Gate of Hell '54

Peter Suschitzky
Crash '95
Dead Ringers '88

**Hubert
  Taczanowski**
The Young Poisoner's
  Handbook '94

Masao Tamai
Godzilla, King of the
  Monsters '56

Masaki Tamura
Tampopo '86
Himatsuri '85

Jiri Tarantik
Fabulous Adventures
  of Baron
  Munchausen '61
The Fabulous World of
  Jules Verne '58

**Jean-Jacques
  Tarbes**
My New Partner '84
Borsalino '70

Gilbert Taylor
Repulsion '65

Manuel Teran
Before the Rain '94

Ubaldo Terzano
Black Sunday '60

Armand Thirard
And God Created
  Woman '57
Diabolique '55
The Wages of Fear '55

**Erling Thurmann-
  Andersen**
Insomnia '97

Eduard Tisse
Ivan the Terrible,
  Part 2 '46
Ivan the Terrible,
  Part 1 '44
Alexander Nevsky '38
Que Viva Mexico '32
The Battleship
  Potemkin '25

Maseo Tochizawa
The Ballad of
  Narayama '83

Luciano Tovoli
Suspiria '77
Bandits of Orgosolo '61

Jan Troell
The New Land '73
The Emigrants '72

Shinya Tsukamoto
Tetsuo: The Iron Man '92

Masaharu Ueda
Rhapsody in August '91
Akira Kurosawa's
  Dreams '90
Kagemusha '80

Sergei Urusevsky
I Am Cuba '64

Charlie Van Damme
One Sings, the Other
  Doesn't '77

Eddy van der Enden
Traffic '71

**Walther Vanden
  Ende**
Farinelli '94
Toto le Heros '91

Sacha Vierny
The Pillow Book '95
The Belly of an
  Architect '91
The Cook, the Thief, His
  Wife & Her Lover '90
Drowning by
  Numbers '87
The Draughtsman's
  Contract '82
Beau Père '81
Mon Oncle d'
  Amerique '80
Belle de Jour '67
Muriel '63
Last Year at
  Marienbad '61
Hiroshima
  Mon Amour '59
Night and Fog '55

Radoslav Vladic
Tito and Me '92

Mario Vulpiani
La Grande Bouffe '73

Fritz Arno Wagner
Kameradschaft '31
M '31
The Threepenny
  Opera '31
Diary of a Lost Girl '29
Die Liebe der Jeanne
  Ney '27
Nosferatu '22

Lau Wai-Keung
Chungking Express '95

Mandy Walker
Love Serenade '96

Wing-Heng Wang
Hard-Boiled '92

Tony Wannamker
Project Grizzly '96

David Watkin
The Devils '71
How I Won the War '67

Jan Weincke
Twist & Shout '84

Marcel Weiss
Traffic '71

Brian West
Outback '71

Billy Williams
Dreamchild '85

Willy
Harvest '37

Jerzy Wojcik
Ashes and Diamonds '58

Cinematographer

Wing-hang Wong
The Killer '90
A Better Tomorrow '86

Albert Wywerka
The Dybbuk '37

Yu Xaioqun
The Story of Qiu Ju '91

Alexander Xenofontov
Chapayev '34

Bao Xianran
Women from the Lake of Scented Souls '94

Chi Xiaonin
The Story of Qiu Ju '91

Yoshikazu Yamasawa
The Green Slime '68

Kazuo Yamazaki
The Hidden Fortress '58
The Lower Depths '57

Minoru Yokoyama
The Burmese Harp '56

Hou Yong
The Day the Sun Turned Cold '94
The Horse Thief '87

Yasuhiro Yoshioka
Boy '69

Lu Yue
Shanghai Triad '95
To Live '94

Vadim Yusov
Anna '93
Andrei Rublev '66

Jacek Zaleski
Europa, Europa '91

Fei Zhao
The Horse Thief '87

Bernard Zitzermann
La Cérémonie '95

COMPOSER INDEX

The "Composer Index" provides a complete listing of composers, arrangers, lyricists, or bands that have provided an original music score for a film. The names are alphabetical by last name, and the films are listed chronologically, from most recent to the oldest.

Andre Claveau
Lacombe, Lucien '74

Rene Cloerec
Devil in the Flesh '46

Jean Constantin
The 400 Blows '59

Bill Conti
The Garden of the Finzi-Continis '71

Ray Cook
Careful, He Might Hear You '84

Carmine Coppola
Napoleon '27

Joseph Cosma
La Bete Humaine '38

Vladimir Cosma
Les Compères '83
Diva '82

Carlo Crivelli
Devil in the Flesh '87

Carlos D'Alessi
Delicatessen '92

Oswald D'Andrea
Captain Conan '96

John Dankworth
Saturday Night and Sunday Morning '60

Mychael Danna
The Sweet Hereafter '96
Exotica '94
The Adjuster '91

David Darling
Faraway, So Close! '93

Peter Dasent
Heavenly Creatures '94

Jean-Louis Daulne
Café au Lait '94

Marie Daulne
Café au Lait '94

Peter Maxwell Davies
The Devils '71

Elsa Davis
Cactus '86

Miles Davis
Frantic '58

Emillo De Diego
Blood Wedding '81

Luis De Pablo
Spirit of the Beehive '73

Francois de Roubaix
Zita '68
Le Samourai '67

Manuel De Sica
The Icicle Thief '89
The Garden of the Finzi-Continis '71

Claude Debussy
Basileus Quartet '82
L'Age D'Or '30

Georges Delerue
Confidentially Yours '83
The Woman Next Door '81
The Last Metro '80
Get Out Your Handkerchiefs '78
Love on the Run '78
Day for Night '73
Two English Girls '72
The Conformist '71
The Two of Us '68
Viva Maria! '65
Contempt '64
The Soft Skin '64
Muriel '63
Jules and Jim '62
Shoot the Piano Player '62
Hiroshima Mon Amour '59

Simon des Innocents
Le Beau Mariage '82

Alexandre Desplat
A Self-Made Hero '95

Leonid Desyatnikov
Prisoner of the Mountains '96

Orlando Di Lasso
Every Man for Himself & God Against All '75

Manu Dibango
Ceddo '78

Andrew Dickson
Secrets and Lies '95

Loek Dikker
The 4th Man '79

Andrew Dixon
High Hopes '88

Francois Dompierre
Jesus of Montreal '89

Gaetano Donizetti
Man of Flowers '84

Patrick Doyle
Indochine '92
Henry V '89

John Du Prez
Monty Python's The Meaning of Life '83

Anne Dudley
Hollow Reed '95

Laurence Dufrene
Man Bites Dog '91

Antoine Duhamel
Ridicule '96
Belle Epoque '92
Bed and Board '70
The Wild Child '70
Mississippi Mermaid '69
Stolen Kisses '68

Weekend '67
Pierrot le Fou '65

Charles Dumont
Traffic '71

Trevor Duncan
La Jetée '62

Arie Dzierlatka
Messidor '77
The Wonderful Crook '75
Chloe in the Afternoon '72

Brian Easdale
Black Narcissus '47

Nicolas Economou
Marianne and Juliane '82

Hanns Eisler
Night and Fog '55

Micky Erbe
Ticket to Heaven '81

Sebastien Erms
Rendezvous in Paris '95
A Tale of Winter '92

Bengt Ernryd
The New Land '73

Carlos Farinas
I Am Cuba '64

Francois Farrugia
Celestial Clockwork '94

George Fenton
Land and Freedom '95

Simon Fisher
Caravaggio '86

Charles Fox
The Green Slime '68

Cesar Franck
Céleste '81

Fred Frith
The Tango Lesson '97

Giovanni Fusco
The Eclipse '66
The Red Desert '64
L'Avventura '60
Hiroshima Mon Amour '59

Roel A. Garcia
Chungking Express '95

Girogio Gaslini
La Notte '60

Roberto Gerhard
This Sporting Life '63

Michael Gibbs
Hard-Boiled '92

Ronan Girre
Le Beau Mariage '82

Alain Goraguer
Fantastic Planet '73

Stuart Gorling
Dreams '55

Jay Gottlieb
La Discrete '90

Patrick Gowers
A Bigger Splash '74

Ron Grainer
A Kind of Loving '62

Enrique Granados
Kika '94

Stephane Grappelli
May Fools '90
Going Places '74

Allan Gray
I Know Where I'm Going '45

Philip Green
Victim '61

Edvard Grieg
M '31

Murray Grindlay
Once Were Warriors '94

Francis Gromon
Marius '31

Jean Jacques Grunenwald
Diary of a Country Priest '50
Monsieur Vincent '47

Zhang Guangtain
Shanghai Triad '95

Herbie Hancock
Blow-Up '66

John Harle
Butterfly Kiss '94

Max Harris
Dreamchild '85

Richard Hartley
The Designated Mourner '97

Tadashi Hattori
The Men Who Tread on the Tiger's Tail '45

Fumio Hayasaka
I Live in Fear '55
Sansho the Bailiff '54
Seven Samurai '54
Ugetsu '53
Ikiru '52
Rashomon '51
Drunken Angel '48

Hikaru Hayashi
Boy '69

Pierre Henry
The Man with a Movie Camera '29

Bernard Herrmann
The Bride Wore Black '68
Fahrenheit 451 '66

Werner R. Heymann
Faust '26

Marc Hillman
Baxter '89

Joachim Holbek
Breaking the Waves '95
The Kingdom '95

Friedrich Hollander
The Blue Angel '30

Toshiyuki Honda
Minbo—Or the Gentle
    Art of Japanese
    Extortion '92
A Taxing Woman '87

Arthur Honegger
Harvest '37

Gottfried Huppertz
Metropolis '26
Die Nibelungen '23

Abdullah Ibrahim
Tilaï '90

Akira Ifukube
The Burmese Harp '56
Godzilla, King of the
    Monsters '56

Alberto Iglesias
The Flower of My
    Secret '95

Shinichiro Ikebe
Rhapsody in August '91
Akira Kurosawa's
    Dreams '90
The Ballad of
    Narayama '83
Kagemusha '80
Vengeance Is Mine '79

Ernest Irving
Kind Hearts and
    Coronets '49

Chu Ishikawa
Tetsuo: The Iron Man '92

Pierre Jansen
Violette '78
La Rupture '70
La Femme Infidèle '69

Maurice Jarre
The Tin Drum '79
Is Paris Burning? '66
Sundays & Cybele '62
Eyes without a Face '59

Maurice Jaubert
The Green Room '78
The Man Who Loved
    Women '77
Small Change '76
The Story of Adele H. '75
L'Atalante '34

Geir Jenssen
Insomnia '97

Jorgen Jersild
Gertrud '64

Zhao Jiping
Temptress Moon '96
To Live '94

Farewell My
    Concubine '93
The Story of Qiu Ju '91

**Antonio Carlos
    Jobim**
Black Orpheus '58

**Alejandro Jodor-
    owsky**
El Topo '71

Alain Jomy
The Accompanist '93
The Little Thief '89
The Best Way '76

Eleni Karaindrou
Ulysses' Gaze '95
Landscape in the
    Mist '88

Kara Karayev
Don Quixote '57

Ali Akbar Khan
Devi '60

**Nusrat Fateh Ali
    Khan**
Bandit Queen '94

Wojciech Kilar
Contract '80
Illumination '73

Chuji Kinoshita
The Human Condition:
    Road to Eternity '59

Jurgen Knieper
Wings of Desire '88
The American Friend '77
The Goalie's Anxiety at
    the Penalty Kick '71

Mark Knopfler
Comfort and Joy '84
Local Hero '83

Krzysztof Komeda
Knife in the Water '62
The Dybbuk '37

Ka-Fai Koo
A Better Tomorrow '86

Andrezej Korzynski
Man of Iron '81
Man of Marble '76

Yuji Koseki
Mothra '62

Joseph Kosma
The Testament of Dr.
    Cordelier '59
Children of Paradise '44
Grand Illusion '37
The Crime of Monsieur
    Lange '36

Jan Krenz
Ashes and Diamonds '58
Kanal '56

Djavashir Kuliev
Ashik Kerib '88

Milan Kymlicka
Margaret's Museum '95

Yves Laferriere
Jesus of Montreal '89

Francis Lai
My New Partner '84
Cat and Mouse '78
A Man and a Woman '66

Hans Landberger
The Golem '20

Robert Lane
The Young Poisoner's
    Handbook '94

Bob Last
Orlando '92

Felice Lattuada
Variety Lights '51

**Angelo Francesco
    Lavagnino**
Chimes at Midnight '67

Raul Lavista
Simon of the Desert '66
The Exterminating
    Angel '62

Maurice Lecouer
Erendira '83

Jean Ledrut
The Trial '63

Michel Legrand
The Go-Between '71
Donkey Skin '70
Band of Outsiders '64
The Umbrellas of
    Cherbourg '64
My Life to Live '62
A Woman Is a
    Woman '60

Roger Legrand
Manon of the Spring '87

Axel Linstadt
Kings of the Road—
    In the Course of
    Time '76

Wang Liping
Women from the Lake
    of Scented Souls '94

Zdenek Liska
Fabulous Adventures
    of Baron
    Munchausen '61
The Fabulous World of
    Jules Verne '58

Ismaila Lo
Camp de Thiaroye '87

Lowell Lo
The Killer '90

Evan Lurie
The Monster '96
Johnny Stecchino '92

Baaba Maal
Guelwaar '94

Manuel Malou
French Twist '95

Nikos Mamangakis
Kaspar Hauser '93
Heimat 1 '84

Franco Mannino
Conversation Piece '75

Karel Mares
The Firemen's Ball '68

**Yannis
    Markopolous**
Cactus '86

Andrzej Markowski
A Generation '54

Diego Masson
Black Moon '75

Brian May
Gallipoli '81

John McCulloch
Careful '94

Murray McNabb
Once Were Warriors '94

Nacho Mendez
El Topo '71

Wim Mertens
The Belly of an
    Architect '91

Minoru Miki
In the Realm of the
    Senses '76

Paul Misraki
Alphaville '65
And God Created
    Woman '57

Tamezo Mochizuki
Utamaro and His Five
    Women '46

Federico Mompoll
Cria '76

Francis Monkman
The Long Good
    Friday '80

Patrick Moraz
La Salamandre '71

Ennio Morricone
La Scorta '94
Tie Me Up! Tie Me
    Down! '90
Cinema Paradiso '88
La Cage aux Folles '78
Salo, or the 120 Days of
    Sodom '75
Arabian Nights '74
Allonsanfan '73
The Bird with the
    Crystal Plumage '70
Burn! '70
The Decameron '70
Once Upon a Time in
    the West '68
The Good, the Bad, and
    the Ugly '67
The Battle of Algiers '66
Before the
    Revolution '65
A Fistful of Dollars '64

Composer

Georges Moustaki
A Very Curious Girl '69

Kunihiko Murai
Tampopo '86

Jean Murat
I Can't Sleep '93

Michel Musseau
Celestial Clockwork '94

Stanley Myers
Dreamchild '85

Ken Myhr
Project Grizzly '96

Mario Nascimbene
Love in the City '53

John Neschling
Pixote '81

Jose Nieto
Lovers: A True Story '90

Sergei Nikitin
Moscow Does Not
    Believe in Tears '80

Stefan Nilsson
Jerusalem '96
The Best Intentions '92

Erik Nordgren
The Emigrants '72
The Devil's Eye '60
The Virgin Spring '59

Per Norgard
Babette's Feast '87

Filip Nowak
Ashes and Diamonds '58

Michael Nyman
The Piano '93
The Hairdresser's
    Husband '92
The Cook, the Thief, His
    Wife & Her Lover '90
Drowning by
    Numbers '87
The Draughtsman's
    Contract '82

George Oddner
The New Land '73

Nino Oliviero
Mondo Cane '63

Riz Ortolani
Mondo Cane '63

Hisato Osawa
Utamaro and His Five
    Women '46

Yoshihide Otomo
The Day the Sun Turned
    Cold '94
The Blue Kite '93

**Vyacheslav
    Ovchinnikov**
Andrei Rublev '66

Albinoni Pachelbel
Every Man for Himself &
    God Against All '75

Gino Paoli
Before the
    Revolution '65

Daniele Paris
The Night Porter '74

Charlie Parker
Murmur of the Heart '71

Tom Paxton
Stroszek '77

**Krzysztof
    Penderecki**
The Saragossa
    Manuscript '65

Jorge Perez
The Criminal Life of
    Archibaldo de la
    Cruz '55

Giovanni Pergolese
Cactus '86

Jean-Claude Petit
Jean de Florette '87
Manon of the Spring '87

Laurent Petitgrand
Faraway, So Close! '93

Goffredo Petrassi
Bitter Rice '49

Piero Piccioni
Three Brothers '80
Swept Away… '75
Il Bell'Antonio '60

Franco Piersanti
Lamerica '95
The Stolen Children '92

Jacques Pinault
Boy Meets Girl '84

Pink Floyd
The Valley Obscured by
    the Clouds '72

Nicola Piovani
Caro Diario '93
Fiorile '93
Jamón, Jamón '93
Intervista '87
Ginger & Fred '86
Kaos '85
The Night of the
    Shooting Stars '82

Gianfranco Plenizio
And the Ship Sails
    On '83

Gillo Pontecorvo
The Battle of Algiers '66

Gavriil Popov
Chapayev '34

Michel Portal
Dr. Petiot '90
Max, Mon Amour '86

Rachel Portman
High Hopes '88

Sally Potter
The Tango Lesson '97

**Kvarteto Mesta
    Prahi**
A Single Girl '96

Zbigniew Preisner
Trois Couleurs: Blanc '94
Trois Couleurs: Rouge
    '94
Trois Couleurs: Bleu '93
The Double Life of
    Veronique '91
Europa, Europa '91

Craig Preuss
Bhaji on the Beach '94

Andre Previn
The Music Lovers '71

Sergei Prokofiev
Ivan the Terrible,
    Part 2 '46
Ivan the Terrible,
    Part 1 '44
Alexander Nevsky '38

Henry Purcell
A Nos Amours '84

Xiao-Song Qu
The Horse Thief '87

Peer Raben
Veronika Voss '82
Berlin Alexanderplatz
    '80
The Marriage of Maria
    Braun '79
In a Year of 13 Moons '78
The Stationmaster's
    Wife '77
The American
    Soldier '70
Beware of a Holy
    Whore '70

Satyajit Ray
Distant Thunder '73
Days and Nights in the
    Forest '70
Charulata '64
The Big City '63
Two Daughters '61
Jalsaghar '58

Django Reinhardt
Lacombe, Lucien '74

Patrick Roffe
Baxter '89

Jean-Louis Roques
Germinal '93

Hilding Rosenberg
Torment '44

Renzo Rossellini
Generale Della Rovere
    '60
The Flowers of St.
    Francis '50

Nino Rota
Orchestra Rehearsal '78
Amarcord '74
Love and Anarchy '73
Fellini's Roma '72
The Clowns '71
Fellini Satyricon '69

Juliet of the Spirits '65
8 1/2 '63
Boccaccio '70 '62
La Dolce Vita '60
Purple Noon '60
Rocco and His
    Brothers '60
Nights of Cabiria '57
La Strada '54
I Vitelloni '53
The White Sheik '52

**Christopher
    Rousset**
Farinelli '94

Miklos Rozsa
Providence '77

Xia Ru-jin
Ju Dou '90

Carlo Rustichelli
Alfredo, Alfredo '72
Divorce—Italian
    Style '62

Camille Saint-Saens
Au Revoir les Enfants '87
Effi Briest '74

Kojun Saito
An Autumn
    Afternoon '62
Tokyo Story '53

**Samba Diabara
    Samb**
Xala '75

Philippe Sarde
Les Voleurs '96
Nelly et Monsieur
    Arnaud '95
Ma Saison Préférée '93
L.627 '92
Beau Père '81
Madame Rosa '77
Vincent, François, Paul
    and the Others '76
French Provincial '75
The Judge and the
    Assassin '75
Lancelot of the Lake '74
La Grande Bouffe '73
César & Rosalie '72

Erik Satie
The Fire Within '64

Masaru Sato
High & Low '62
Yojimbo '61
The Bad Sleep Well '60
The Hidden Fortress '58
The Lower Depths '57
Throne of Blood '57

Jordi Savall
Tous les Matins du
    Monde '92

Domenico Scarletti
The Exterminating
    Angel '62
The Devil's Eye '60

Poul Schierbeck
Day of Wrath '43

Alfred Schnittke
The Ascent '76
Commissar '68

Franz Schubert
Au Revoir les
Enfants '87

John Scott
Outback '71

Vincent Scotto
Pépé le Moko '37
César '36
The Baker's Wife '33
Fanny '32

Ilona Seckaz
Antonia's Line '95

Gyorgy Selmeczi
Time Stands Still '82
Angi Vera '78

Jean-Marie Senia
Diary of a Seducer '95
Jonah Who Will Be 25 in
the Year 2000 '76

Akira Senju
The Mystery of
Rampo '94

Eric Serra
La Femme Nikita '91

Ravi Shankar
The World of Apu '59
Aparajito '58
Pather Panchali '54

Howard Shore
Crash '95
Dead Ringers '88

**Dimitri
Shostakovich**
Ariel '89
Ten Days That Shook
the World '27

Isaak Shvartz
Dersu Uzala '75

N. Sidelnikov
The Overcoat '59

Zoran Simjanovic
Tito and Me '92

Bruce Smeaton
A Cry in the Dark '88
The Chant of Jimmie
Blacksmith '78
The Devil's
Playground '76

Picnic at Hanging
Rock '75

Neil Smolar
The Boys of St.
Vincent '93

Martial Solal
Breathless '59

Ondrej Soukup
Kolya '96

Cat Stevens
Deep End '70

Oscar Straus
The Earrings of
Madame de... '54

Igor Stravinsky
La Belle Noiseuse '90

Frank Strobel
The Young Poisoner's
Handbook '94

L. Subramaniam
Salaam Bombay! '88

Yoshikazu Suo
Shall We Dance? '97

Jiri Sust
My Sweet Little
Village '86

**Rabindranath
Tagore**
Charulata '64

Toru Takemitsu
Black Rain '88
Himatsuri '85
Ran '85
Dodes'ka-den '70
The Face of Another '66
Kwaidan '64
Woman in the Dunes '64
Harakiri '62

Tengger
A Mongolian Tale '94

Mikis Theodorakis
Z '69

Maurice Thiriet
Children of Paradise '44

Ken Thorne
Juggernaut '74
How I Won the War '67

Ton That Tiet
The Scent of Green
Papaya '93

Armando Trovaioli
A Special Day '77
Down & Dirty '76
Boccaccio '70 '62

Toshiaki Tsushima
The Green Slime '68

**Simon Fisher
Turner**
Blue '93

Pierro Umiliani
Big Deal on Madonna
Street '58

Jean-Louis Valero
Boyfriends &
Girlfriends '88

Pierre Van Dormael
Toto le Heros '91

Georges Van Parys
Diabolique '55
The Earrings of
Madame de... '54
Casque d'Or '52

Giuseppe Verdi
Little Dorrit, Film 1:
Nobody's Fault '88
Little Dorrit, Film 2: Little
Dorrit's Story '88

Edith Vesperini
Van Gogh '92

Jose Maria Vitier
Strawberry and
Chocolate '93

Antonio Vivaldi
The Golden Coach '52

Henny Vrienten
The Vanishing '88

Popul Vuh
Fitzcarraldo '82
Heart of Glass '74
Aguirre, the Wrath of
God '72

Gyorgy Vukan
Hanussen '88

William Walton
Hamlet '48
Henry V '45

**Andrew Lloyd
Webber**
Gumshoe '72

Kurt Weill
The Threepenny
Opera '31

Lars Johan Werle
The Hour of the Wolf '68

**Francois
Wertheimer**
One Sings, the Other
Doesn't '77

Roger White
Bandit Queen '94

Jean Wiener
A Gentle Woman '69
The Crime of Monsieur
Lange '36
The Lower Depths '36

Marc Wilkinson
If... '69

Herbert Windt
Triumph of the Will '34

Dag Wiren
Miss Julie '50

Zhou Xiaowen
Ermo '94

Shoji Yamashiro
Akira '89

Gabriel Yared
Camille Claudel '89
Betty Blue '86
Moon in the Gutter '83
Every Man for
Himself '79

Jean Yatove
Jour de Fete '48

Narciso Yepes
Forbidden Games '52

Joji Yuasa
The Funeral '84

Wolfgang Zeller
Vampyr '31

Jiping Zhao
Ju Dou '90

Hans Zimmer
Insignificance '85
Moonlighting '82

Mikhail Ziv
Ballad of a Soldier '60

Composer

CATAGOREY INDEX

The "Category Index" includes subject terms ranging from straight genre descriptions, like "Drama" or "Comedy", to more specific themes, like "Hit Men" or "Paris". These terms can help you identify unifying themes, settings, and events. Category terms are listed alphabetically. So enjoy the hunt!

Action Adventure
See also Adventure
    Drama; Macho Men;
    Martial Arts
A Better Tomorrow
Dersu Uzala
Fabulous Adventures of
    Baron Munchausen
Hard-Boiled
The Hidden Fortress
Kagemusha
King Kong vs. Godzilla
My New Partner
Police Story
Samurai Rebellion
Sanjuro
Subway
Yojimbo

Adapted from a Book
The Accompanist
The American Friend
Ashes and Diamonds
Bandit Queen
Belle de Jour
Berlin Alexanderplatz
Betty Blue
The Bicycle Thief
Black Narcissus
Borsalino
The Bride Wore Black
The Canterbury Tales
Captain Conan
Chapayev
Charulata
Christ Stopped at Eboli
The Confession
Confidentially Yours
Contempt
Crash
A Cry in the Dark
Dead Ringers
Devil in the Flesh
The Devils
Diary of a Lost Girl
Don Quixote
Dona Flor and Her Two
    Husbands
The Dybbuk
Effi Briest
The Emigrants
Enjo
Erendira

Fahrenheit 451
Fanny
Farewell My Concubine
Faust
Fellini Satyricon
The Fire Within
Fitzcarraldo
The Garden of the Finzi-
    Continis
A Generation
Germinal
The Goalie's Anxiety at
    the Penalty Kick
The Green Room
Harvest
High & Low
Hiroshima, Mon Amour
Is Paris Burning?
Jan Svankmejer's Faust
Jean de Florette
Jerusalem
Jules and Jim
Kind Hearts and
    Coronets
Kwaidan
La Belle Noiseuse
La Bete Humaine
La Cérémonie
La Chienne
La Rupture
The Lacemaker
Life of Oharu
Like Water for
    Chocolate
Lola Montès
The Lost Honor of
    Katharina Blum
The Man on the Roof
Manon of the Spring
Mephisto
Mississippi Mermaid
A Month in the Country
Moon in the Gutter
My Brilliant Career
My Left Foot
The New Land
Nosferatu
Nosferatu the Vampyre
Oblomov
Once Were Warriors
Orlando
The Overcoat
Pelle the Conqueror
Picnic at Hanging Rock

The Postman
Prisoner of the
    Mountains
Purple Noon
Rhapsody in August
Salo, or the 120 Days of
    Sodom
The Saragossa
    Manuscript
Saturday Night and
    Sunday Morning
A Self-Made Hero
Shoot the Piano Player
Solaris
The Story of Qiu Ju
The Sweet Hereafter
Ten Days That Shook
    the World
The Tenant
That Obscure Object of
    Desire
The Tin Drum
The Trial
Tristana
Two English Girls
Ugetsu
Wages of Fear
Walkabout
War and Peace
We the Living
The World of Apu
Wuthering Heights

Adapted from a Fairy Tale
Beauty and the Beast
The Blue Light
Donkey Skin
Les Visiteurs du Soir

Adapted from a Play or Musical
Beautiful Thing
Black Orpheus
Blood Wedding
Chimes at Midnight
Day of Wrath
The Designated
    Mourner
The Devils
The Golden Coach
Hamlet
Henry V
La Cage aux Folles

La Ronde
Les Enfants Terrible
Look Back in Anger
The Lower Depths
Marius
Miss Julie
Ordet
Ran
The Threepenny Opera
Throne of Blood
Woyzeck

Adapted from a Story
Ashik Kerib
Babette's Feast
Brief Encounter
Curse of the Demon
The Decameron
A Gentle Woman
The Go-Between
I Don't Want to Talk
    About It
Kaos
The Lady with the Dog
Le Plaisir
Life on a String
Margaret's Museum
The Red Shoes
Strawberry and
    Chocolate
Three Brothers
Two Daughters
Vampyr

Adapted from an Article
Olivier, Olivier
Two or Three Things I
    Know About Her

Adapted from an Opera
Carmen
Farewell My Concubine
Fitzcarraldo
The Magic Flute

Adapted from Memoirs or Diaries
Bandit Queen
Caro Diario
Céleste

Edvard Munch
Jacquot
The Pillow Book

Adapted from the Radio
The Devil's Eye
Mr. Arkadin

Adolescence
See Coming of Age; Hell High School; Teen Angst

Adoption & Orphans
See also Hard Knock Life; Only the Lonely
Pixote
Secrets and Lies
Sugar Cane Alley
Sundays & Cybele

Adventure Drama
See also Action Adventure; Drama
Alexander Nevsky
Himatsuri
Juggernaut
The Killer
Ran

Africa
Borom Sarret
Emitai
General Idi Amin Dada
Guelwaar
Pepe Le Moko
Tilaï
Yaaba

Alcoholism
See On the Rocks

Amnesia
See also Identity
Sundays & Cybele

Angels
Faraway, So Close!
Miracle in Milan
Wings of Desire

Animation & Cartoons
Allegro Non Troppo
Fantastic Planet

Anthology
See also Comedy Anthologies
The Decameron
Kaos
Kwaidan
Le Plaisir
Love in the City
Paisan
Rendezvous in Paris

Anti-War War Movies
See also Satire & Parody
The Burmese Harp
Fires on the Plain
Forbidden Games
Gallipoli
Grand Illusion
Henry V

Les Carabiniers
Prisoner of the Mountains
The Tin Drum
The War Game

Archaeology
See Big Digs

Art & Artists
Andrei Rublev
The Belly of an Architect
A Bigger Splash
The Blue Light
Camille Claudel
Caravaggio
The Designated Mourner
Edvard Munch
Entre-Nous
Hour of the Wolf
La Belle Noiseuse
My Left Foot
Rendezvous in Paris
The Testament of Orpheus
Utamaro and His Five Women
Van Gogh

Asia
See also China; Japan
Indochine
The Scent of Green Papaya

Assassinations
See also Hit Men; Spies & Espionage
The American Friend
The American Soldier
Antonio Das Mortes
Ashes and Diamonds
La Femme Nikita
La Scorta
Love and Anarchy
State of Siege
Yojimbo
Z

At the Movies
See also Behind the Scenes
Cinema Paradiso
The Long Day Closes
Tampopo

Australia
See Down Under

Automobiles
See Motor Vehicle Dept.

Avant-Garde
Band of Outsiders
The Blood of a Poet
Boy Meets Girl
Breathless
Careful
Hiroshima, Mon Amour
La Jetée
Les Carabiniers
Lola
Phantom of Liberty
Repulsion
The Testament of Dr. Cordelier
The Testament of Orpheus
Veronika Voss

B/W & Color Combos
Andrei Rublev
If…
A Man and a Woman
Stalker
Wings of Desire

Ballet
See also Dance Fever
Carmen
The Red Shoes
Summer Interlude
Suspiria

Bathroom Scenes
The Cook, the Thief, His Wife & Her Lover
Diabolique
They Came from Within
Tie Me Up! Tie Me Down!

Behind Bars
See Great Escapes; Men in Prison

Behind the Scenes
See also At the Movies
Augustin
Beware of a Holy Whore
Contempt
La Dolce Vita
Through the Olive Trees
Ulysses' Gaze

Berlin
See also Germany
Berlin Alexanderplatz
Faraway, So Close!
Wings of Desire

Big Battles
See also World War I; World War II
Alexander Nevsky
The Battleship Potemkin
Gallipoli
Henry V
Ran
Ten Days That Shook the World
War and Peace

Big Digs
The Mask
The Night of Counting the Years

Big Ideas
See also Ethics & Morals
Blue
The Designated Mourner
Diary of a Seducer
Faraway, So Close!
1900

Biography
See This is Your Life

Black Comedy
See also Comedy; Comedy Drama; Satire & Parody
Ariel
Careful
The Cook, the Thief, His Wife & Her Lover

The Criminal Life of Archibaldo de la Cruz
Delicatessen
Él
The Exterminating Angel
The Firemen's Ball
The 4th Man
The Funeral
The Garden of Delights
Kind Hearts and Coronets
Léolo
Life Is Sweet
Man Bites Dog
Matador
Max, Mon Amour
Muriel's Wedding
Seven Beauties
That Obscure Object of Desire
Tie Me Up! Tie Me Down!
Toto le Heros
Trois Couleurs: Blanc
Underground
Women on the Verge of a Nervous Breakdown

Black Gold
Breaking the Waves
Local Hero

Blindness
See also Physical Problems
Cactus
The Killer
Life on a String
Proof

Bloody Mayhem
See also Horror
The Brainiac
Hard-Boiled
The Killer
Ran

Boating
See Sail Away

Books
Fahrenheit 451
La Lectrice
Providence

Bounty Hunters
A Fistful of Dollars
The Good, the Bad and the Ugly

Bringing Up Baby
See also Parenthood; Pregnant Pauses
Monika
A Woman Is a Woman

Buddies
A Better Tomorrow
Captain Conan
Entre-Nous
Freeze-Die-Come to Life
Gallipoli
Grand Illusion
Hate
Heavenly Creatures
Jules and Jim

Kings of the Road—In
     the Course of Time
Le Doulos
Les Comperes
Mina Tannenbaum
One Sings, the Other
     Doesn't
The Red Balloon
Strawberry and
     Chocolate
Ugetsu
Vincent, Francois, Paul
     and the Others

Canada
The Adjuster
The Boys of St. Vincent
Dead Ringers
Margaret's Museum
The Sweet Hereafter

Cannibalism
See also Edibles; Horror
The Cook, the Thief, His
     Wife & Her Lover
Delicatessen

Carnivals &
     Circuses
Black Orpheus
The Cabinet of Dr.
     Caligari
The Clowns
Elvira Madigan
La Strada
Lola Montès
Sawdust & Tinsel
Variety
Variety Lights

Chases
See also Road Trip
Breathless
Stray Dog
This Man Must Die

Child Abuse
The Boys of St. Vincent
Hollow Reed
The Stolen Children

Childhood Visions
Au Revoir les Enfants
Careful, He Might Hear
     You
Cinema Paradiso
Cria
Diva
Fanny and Alexander
Forbidden Games
Jacquot
Kolya
Léolo
The Mirror
My Life As a Dog
The Night of the
     Shooting Stars
Pelle the Conqueror
The Pillow Book
Pixote
Ponette
The Red Balloon
Salaam Bombay!
The Silences of
     the Palace
Small Change
Spirit of the Beehive
Sunday's Children
The Tin Drum

Tito and Me
Toto le Heros
Walkabout
When Father Was Away
     on Business
Zero for Conduct

Children
See Animation &
     Cartoons;
     Childhood Visions

China
See also Asia
The Blue Kite
The Day the Sun
     Turned Cold
Ermo
Farewell My Concubine
The Horse Thief
Ju Dou
The Killer
Princess Yang Kwei Fei
Raise the Red Lantern
Red Sorghum
Shanghai Triad
The Story of Qiu Ju
Temptress Moon
To Live
Women from the Lake
     of Scented Souls

Christmas
See also Holidays
Ma Saison Préférée
A Tale of Winter

CIA
See Spies & Espionage

Circuses
See Carnivals & Circuses

Classic Horror
See also Horror
Black Sunday
The Cabinet of Dr.
     Caligari
Nosferatu
Pandora's Box
Vampyr
Witchcraft through the
     Ages

Cold War
See Red Scare

Comedy
See also Black Comedy;
     Comedy Drama;
     Comic Adventure;
     Horror Comedy;
     Musical Comedy;
     Romantic Comedy;
     Satire & Parody;
     Slapstick Comedy
Augustin
Big Deal on Madonna
     Street
Boudu Saved from
     Drowning
Comfort and Joy
Divorce—Italian Style
How I Won the War
Intervista
Johnny Stecchino
Jonah Who Will Be 25 in
     the Year 2000
Kika
La Cage aux Folles

La Grande Bouffe
Leningrad Cowboys
     Go America
Les Comperes
Love Serenade
Mon Oncle
Mon Oncle D'Amerique
My Sweet Little Village
Pauline at the Beach
Shall We Dance?
Small Change
Tampopo
Traffic
When the Cat's Away

Comedy
     Anthologies
See also Comedy
Boccaccio '70
Monty Python's The
     Meaning of Life

Comedy Drama
See also Black Comedy;
     Comedy
Amarcord
Antonia's Line
Arabian Nights
Babette's Feast
The Baker's Wife
Band of Outsiders
Baxter
Beautiful Thing
Bed and Board
The Best Way
Bhaji on the Beach
Bleak Moments
Borsalino
Carnival in Flanders
Caro Diario
Celestial Clockwork
César
César & Rosalie
A Chef in Love
Chimes at Midnight
Chloe in the Afternoon
Chungking Express
City of Women
Claire's Knee
The Decameron
The Devil's Eye
Don Quixote
Ermo
Ginger & Fred
Hey, Babu Riba
I Vitelloni
Insignificance
Jamon, Jamon
Kolya
La Discrete
La Dolce Vita
La Ronde
Like Water for
     Chocolate
The Little Thief
Local Hero
Love in the City
Loves of a Blonde
Marius
The Marriage of Maria
     Braun
May Fools
Murmur of the Heart
My Life As a Dog
My Twentieth Century
Oblomov
A Self-Made Hero
Stroszek
Sugarbaby

Sweetie
Swept Away…
A Tale of Springtime
A Taxing Woman
The Thief of Paris
Tito and Me
Ugetsu
Yesterday, Today and
     Tomorrow

Coming of Age
See also Teen Angst
A Nos Amours
Amarcord
Aparajito
Au Revoir les Enfants
Beautiful Thing
The Blue Kite
Cria
The Devil's Playground
Fellini Satyricon
The 400 Blows
A Generation
I Don't Want to Talk
     About It
I Vitelloni
Les Mistons
The Long Day Closes
Monika
Murmur of the Heart
My Brilliant Career
My Life As a Dog
Pather Panchali
Pauline at the Beach
Ramparts of Clay
The Scent of Green
     Papaya
The Silences of the
     Palace
Summer Interlude
Time Stands Still
Twist & Shout
Two Daughters
The Wild Child
Wild Reeds

Contemporary Noir
See also Film Noir
The American Friend
Betty Blue
Le Samourai
Purple Noon

Cooking
See Edibles

Cops
See also Detectives
Chungking Express
The Designated
     Mourner
Diva
Hard-Boiled
Hate
High & Low
L.627
La Scorta
Le Samourai
Les Voleurs
The Man on the Roof
My New Partner
Police Story

Corporate
     Shenanigans
The Bad Sleep Well
The Crime of Monsieur
     Lange
Local Hero

The Man in the White
Suit
A Taxing Woman

Courtroom Drama
See also Order in the Court

Crime & Criminals
See also Crime Sprees;
Fugitives;
Organized Crime;
Serial Killers
Bandit Queen
Borsalino
Breathless
Casque d'Or
Confidentially Yours
Diva
Dr. Mabuse, Parts 1 & 2
Down & Dirty
Frantic
High & Low
La Salamandre
La Scorta
Le Jour Se Leve
Le Samourai
Les Voleurs
Moon in the Gutter
Ossessione
Pepe Le Moko
Pickpocket
Pierrot le Fou
Pixote
Rashomon
Shanghai Triad
Vengeance Is Mine
Victim
Violette
Wedding in Blood

Crime Drama
See also Drama
High & Low
Le Samourai
The Long Good Friday
M
Purple Noon

Crime Sprees
See also Fugitives
Butterfly Kiss
Messidor

Crop Dusters
Earth
Harvest
Jean de Florette
Pelle the Conqueror
The Tree of Wooden
Clogs

Cult Items
The American Friend
Blow-Up
Breathless
The Cabinet of Dr.
Caligari
Careful
Contempt
Crash
The Devils
El Topo
Eyes Without a Face
The Fearless Vampire
Killers
La Cage aux Folles
Last Tango in Paris
Leningrad Cowboys Go
America
The Manster

Culture Clash
Leningrad Cowboys Go
America
Moonlighting

Dance Fever
See also Ballet
Black Orpheus
Blood Wedding
Carmen
French Can-Can
Ginger & Fred
Shall We Dance?
The Tango Lesson

Death & the
Afterlife
See also Angels; Ghosts,
Ghouls, & Goblins;
Occult; Suicide
Devi
Dona Flor and Her Two
Husbands
Donkey Skin
The Funeral
Gallipoli
The Green Room
Monty Python's The
Meaning of Life
Ponette
A Woman's Tale

Detectives
See also Cops
Alphaville
Cat and Mouse
Gumshoe
La Rupture
Mr. Arkadin
My New Partner
Stolen Kisses
Stray Dog

Devils
The Devils
Faust
Jan Svankmejer's Faust
Les Visiteurs du Soir

Director/Star
Teams:
Kurosawa &
Mifune
The Bad Sleep Well
Drunken Angel
The Hidden Fortress
High & Low
Rashomon
Red Beard
Sanjuro
Seven Samurai
Stray Dog
Throne of Blood
Yojimbo

Director/Star
Teams: Woo &
Fat
A Better Tomorrow
Hard-Boiled
The Killer

Divorce
See also Marriage
Divorce—Italian Style
Hollow Reed
Scenes from a Marriage

Doctors & Nurses
See also Evil Doctors;
Hospitals &
Medicine; Sanity
Check; Shrinks
Dead Ringers
Dr. Mabuse, Parts 1 & 2
Dr. Petiot
Drunken Angel
Eyes Without a Face
Monty Python's The
Meaning of Life
Persona
Red Beard

Docudrama
See also Documentary
The Battle of Algiers
A Cry in the Dark
Pickpocket
The Rise of Louis XIV
Ten Days That Shook
the World
32 Short Films about
Glenn Gould

Documentary
See also Docudrama
Anna
A Bigger Splash
Birthplace
Caravaggio
The Clowns
General Idi Amin Dada
Le Joli Mai
The Man with a
Movie Camera
Mondo Cane
Night and Fog
Phantom India
Project Grizzly
The Sorrow and the Pity
Tokyo Olympiad
Triumph of the Will
The War Game
Witchcraft through
the Ages

Dogs
See King of Beasts
(Dogs)

Down Under
The Chant of Jimmie
Blacksmith
A Cry in the Dark
Gallipoli
Heavenly Creatures
Love Serenade
Muriel's Wedding
My Brilliant Career
Once Were Warriors
Outback
Walkabout

Drama
See also Adventure
Drama; Comedy
Drama; Historical
Drama; Musical
Drama; Romantic
Drama; Tearjerkers;
Tragedy
A Nos Amours
The Adjuster
After the Rehearsal
Aguirre, the Wrath
of God
Akira Kurosawa's
Dreams

Allonsanfan
The American Soldier
And God Created
Woman
And the Ship Sails On
Angi Vera
Antonio Das Mortes
Aparajito
The Ascent
Ashes and Diamonds
Ashik Kerib
Au Revoir les Enfants
An Autumn Afternoon
Autumn Sonata
The Bad Sleep Well
Ballad of a Soldier
Bandit Queen
Bandits of Orgosolo
Basileus Quartet
Béatrice
Before the Revolution
Belle de Jour
The Belly of an Architect
Berlin Alexanderplatz
Beware of a Holy Whore
The Bicycle Thief
The Big City
Bitter Rice
Black Girl
Black God, White Devil
Black Narcissus
Black Orpheus
Black Rain
Blood Wedding
The Blue Angel
The Blue Kite
The Boat Is Full
Bob le Flambeur
Borom Sarret
Boy
Boy Meets Girl
The Boys of St. Vincent
Breaking the Waves
The Burmese Harp
Burn!
Burnt by the Sun
Butterfly Kiss
Bye Bye Brazil
Camp de Thiaroye
Careful, He Might Hear
You
Casque d'Or
Ceddo
Céleste
The Chant of Jimmie
Blacksmith
Chapayev
Christ Stopped at Eboli
Cinema Paradiso
Commissar
The Confession
The Conformist
Contempt
Conversation Piece
Crash
Cria
Cries and Whispers
The Crime of Monsieur
Lange
A Cry in the Dark
Day for Night
Deep End
Devi
The Devil's Playground
Diary of a Country Priest
Diary of a Lost Girl
Die Liebe der
Jeanne Ney

Category

535

The Two of Us
Two or Three Things I
  Know About Her
Ulysses' Gaze
Umberto D
Utamaro and His Five
  Women
Vagabond
The Valley Obscured by
  the Clouds
Van Gogh
Variety Lights
Veronika Voss
Victim
Vincent, Francois, Paul
  and the Others
Viridiana
Wages of Fear
Walkabout
Weekend
When a Woman
  Ascends the Stairs
When Father Was Away
  on Business
The White Balloon
The Wild Child
Wild Reeds
Wild Strawberries
The Winter Light
Woman in the Dunes
A Woman's Tale
Women from the Lake
  of Scented Souls
The World of Apu
Woyzeck
Xala
Xica
Yaaba
Yol
Zita

Dream Girls
City of Women
Exotica
La Collectionneuse
Les Mistons

Drugs
See Pill Poppin'

Eating
See Cannibalism;
  Edibles

Edibles
See also Cannibalism
Babette's Feast
A Chef in Love
The Cook, the Thief, His
  Wife & Her Lover
La Grande Bouffe
Life Is Sweet
Like Water for
  Chocolate
Monty Python's The
  Meaning of Life
Tampopo
301, 302

Ethics & Morals
See also Big Ideas
Chloe in the Afternoon
The Funeral
The Judge and the
  Assassin
La Ronde
L'Avventura
Muriel
Ran

The Sacrifice
The Story of Women
Viridiana

Evil Doctors
See also Doctors &
  Nurses; Mad
  Scientists
Dead Ringers
Dr. Mabuse, Parts 1 & 2

Existentialism
See The Meaning of Life

Experimental
See Avant-Garde

Explorers
The Forbidden Quest
The Valley Obscured by
  the Clouds

Family Ties
See also Parenthood
Antonia's Line
Autumn Sonata
Beau Père
Beautiful Thing
Belle Epoque
The Blue Kite
Burnt by the Sun
Careful, He Might Hear
  You
A Chef in Love
Cries and Whispers
The Day the Sun Turned
  Cold
Dead Ringers
Devi
Diary of a Seducer
Die Liebe der Jeanne
  Ney
Distant Voices, Still Lives
Donkey Skin
Down & Dirty
The Emigrants
Erendira
Ermo
Eternal Return
Eyes Without a Face
Face to Face
Fanny and Alexander
Farinelli
Fiorile
The Flower of My Secret
The Funeral
The Garden of Delights
The Garden of the Finzi-
  Continis
Heimat 1
High & Low
Hollow Reed
I Don't Want to Talk
  About It
I Live in Fear
Indochine
Jalsaghar
Jamon, Jamon
Kind Hearts and
  Coronets
La Cérémonie
La Promesse
La Rupture
La Terra Trema
Landscape in the Mist
Late Spring
Léolo
Les Bons Debarras
Les Comperes

Les Enfants Terrible
Les Voleurs
Life and Nothing More
  …
Life Is Sweet
Like Water for
  Chocolate
Little Dorrit, Film 1:
  Nobody's Fault
Little Dorrit, Film 2: Little
  Dorrit's Story
The Long Day Closes
Love
Ma Saison Préférée
The Makioka Sisters
Mamma Roma
Margaret's Museum
Marianne and Juliane
May Fools
Mon Oncle
Mon Oncle Antoine
A Mongolian Tale
Mouchette
Murmur of the Heart
My Twentieth Century
The New Land
1900
Olivier, Olivier
Once Were Warriors
Onibaba
Ordet
The Pillow Book
Ponette
Ran
Rhapsody in August
Rocco and His Brothers
Secrets and Lies
Seven Beauties
The Silence
The Silences of the
  Palace
The Stolen Children
Sugar Cane Alley
Sunday's Children
The Sweet Hereafter
Sweetie
A Tale of Winter
Temptress Moon
The Thief
Three Brothers
Through a Glass Darkly
Ticket to Heaven
Time Stands Still
Tito and Me
To Live
Tokyo Story
The Tree of Wooden
  Clogs
Trois Couleurs: Blanc
Trois Couleurs: Bleu
Violette
Viridiana
Walkabout
The White Balloon
Women on the Verge of
  a Nervous
  Breakdown
The World of Apu

Fantasy
See also Animation &
  Cartoons
A Nous la Liberté
Ashik Kerib
The Blood of a Poet
The City of Lost
  Children
Donkey Skin
Dreamchild

Eternal Return
The Fabulous World of
  Jules Verne
Faraway, So Close!
The Golem
Jan Svankmejer's Faust
Les Visiteurs du Soir
The Magician
Miracle in Milan
Orpheus
The Red Balloon
The Saragossa
  Manuscript
Stalker
The Testament of Dr.
  Cordelier
The Testament of
  Orpheus
Waxworks
The White Sheik
Wings of Desire
Zero for Conduct

Farming
See Crop Dusters

Female Bonding
See also Women
Antonia's Line
Two Friends

Femme Fatale
The Blue Angel
Casque d'Or
Drowning by Numbers
La Femme Nikita
Pepe Le Moko
Ran

Fifties
See Nifty '50s

Film Noir
See also Contemporary
  Noir
Bob le Flambeur
Frantic
High & Low
Le Doulos

Filmmaking
See also At the Movies;
  Behind the Scenes
The Adjuster
Contempt
Day for Night
Intervista
Jacquot
A Slave of Love
The Tango Lesson
Ulysses' Gaze

Firemen
Fahrenheit 451
The Firemen's Ball

Flashback
Antonia's Line
Exotica
The Forbidden Quest
Les Voleurs
The Silences of the
  Palace
301, 302
Two Friends
Walkabout

Folklore &
  Mythology
Antonio Das Mortes

Black Orpheus
Die Niebelungen
Donkey Skin
Faust
Life on a String

Food
See Edibles

France
See also Paris
The Accompanist
Black Girl
Borsalino
Breathless
Carnival in Flanders
César
Dr. Petiot
Harvest
Hate
Is Paris Burning?
La Cérémonie
La Collectionneuse
La Marseillaise
The Lacemaker
The Last Metro
Last Tango in Paris
Le Joli Mai
Le Million
Le Trou
Marius
May Fools
Napoleon
Ridicule
A Tale of Winter

Friendship
See Buddies

Front Page
See also Mass Media;
    Shutterbugs
The Forbidden Quest
La Dolce Vita
Man of Iron

Fugitives
Bandits of Orgosolo
Le Doulos
Stray Dog

Gambling
Bob le Flambeur
Dona Flor and Her Two
    Husbands
Le Million

Gangs
See also Crime &
    Criminals;
    Organized Crime
A Better Tomorrow
Borsalino
Diva
Pierrot le Fou
Shoot the Piano Player

Gays
See also Gender
    Bending; Lesbians
Arabian Nights
Beautiful Thing
The Best Way
Blue
The Conformist
Happy Together
Hollow Reed
I Can't Sleep
La Cage aux Folles
The Music Lovers

Okoge
The Pillow Book
Strawberry and
    Chocolate
Victim
Vive L'Amour
Wild Reeds

Gender Bending
See also Gays; Lesbians;
    Role Reversal
In a Year of 13 Moons
La Cage aux Folles

Germany
See also Berlin
Ali: Fear Eats the Soul
Berlin Alexanderplatz
The Blue Angel
Dr. Mabuse, Parts 1 & 2
Faraway, So Close!
Kaspar Hauser
Marianne and Juliane
The Marriage of Maria
    Braun
Mephisto
The Stationmaster's
    Wife
Triumph of the Will
Wings of Desire
Woyzeck

**Ghosts, Ghouls, &
    Goblins**
See also Death & the
    Afterlife; Occult
Dona Flor and Her Two
    Husbands
The Kingdom
Kwaidan
Ugetsu

Go Fish
La Terra Trema
Love Serenade

Governesses
See The Help: Female

Grand Hotel
The Night Porter
A Single Girl

Great Britain
See also London;
    Scotland
Bhaji on the Beach
Distant Voices, Still Lives
High Hopes
The Long Day Closes
The Long Good Friday
The War Game

Great Escapes
See also Men in Prison;
    POW/MIA; War,
    General
La Nuit de Varennes
Le Trou
A Man Escaped

Growing Older
See also Death & the
    Afterlife; Late
    Bloomin' Love
After the Rehearsal
The Ballad of Narayama
Chimes at Midnight
The Firemen's Ball
Ginger & Fred

I Can't Sleep
Lamerica
The Last Laugh
Ma Saison Préférée
Pelle the Conqueror
Ran
Rhapsody in August
Tokyo Story
Toto le Heros
Umberto D
When a Woman
    Ascends the Stairs
Wild Strawberries
A Woman's Tale

Hard Knock Life
See also Homeless
Eléna and Her Men
Lamerica
The Match Factory Girl
Salaam Bombay!

Heists
See also Scams, Stings &
    Cons
The Bicycle Thief
Big Deal on Madonna
    Street
Bob le Flambeur

Hell High School
See also School Daze;
    Teen Angst
If…
Zero for Conduct

The Help: Female
Diary of a
    Chambermaid
I Can't Sleep
In the White City
La Cérémonie
The Silences of the
    Palace
That Obscure Object of
    Desire

Historical Drama
See also Medieval
    Romps; Period Piece
Andrei Rublev
The Ballad of Narayama
The Battle of Algiers
The Battleship
    Potemkin
Children of Paradise
The Devils
Fellini Satyricon
47 Ronin, Part 1
47 Ronin, Part 2
Gallipoli
Gate of Hell
Henry V
Ivan the Terrible, Part 1
Ivan the Terrible, Part 2
Kaspar Hauser
La Marseillaise
La Nuit de Varennes
The Marquise of O
Napoleon
The Passion of Joan of
    Arc
The Rise of Louis XIV
Senso
Ten Days That Shook
    the World
Thérèse
The Wannsee
    Conference

Hit Men
See also Assassinations
Hard-Boiled
The Killer
La Femme Nikita
Le Samourai

The Holocaust
See also Germany;
    Judaism; Nazis &
    Other Paramilitary
    Slugs; World War II
Au Revoir les Enfants
Birthplace
Europa, Europa
The Garden of the Finzi-
    Continis
Kanal
The Last Metro
Night and Fog
The Wannsee
    Conference

Homeless
See also Hard Knock Life
Distant Thunder
Dodes 'ka-den
Kanal
Los Olvidados
The Lower Depths
Salaam Bombay!

Homosexuality
See Gays; Lesbians

Horror
See also Bloody
    Mayhem;
    Cannibalism; Classic
    Horror; Horror
    Comedy; Killer
    Bugs; Mad
    Scientists; Monsters,
    General; Occult;
    Satanism;
    Supernatural
    Horror; Vampires
Dead of Night
Dead Ringers
Eyes Without a Face
The Kingdom
The Mask
Nosferatu the Vampyre
Suspiria
They Came from Within
301, 302

Horror Comedy
See also Horror
The Fearless Vampire
    Killers
The Kingdom

**Hospitals &
    Medicine**
See also Doctors &
    Nurses; Sanity
    Check; Shrinks
Dead Ringers
Hard-Boiled
In for Treatment
The Kingdom

Housekeepers
See The Help: Female

Identity
See also Role Reversal
My Brilliant Career

Category

Orlando
Secrets and Lies
Sundays & Cybele
Vincent, Francois, Paul
   and the Others

Immigration
The Emigrants
I Can't Sleep
La Promesse
The New Land
Pelle the Conqueror

India
Aparajito
Bandit Queen
The Big City
Black Narcissus
Charulata
Days and Nights in the
   Forest
Distant Thunder
Jalsaghar
The Middleman
Pather Panchali
Two Daughters
The World of Apu

Island Fare
The Passion of Anna
The Postman
Swept Away…

Italy
Amarcord
The Bicycle Thief
Christ Stopped at Eboli
Cinema Paradiso
The Conformist
Divorce—Italian Style
Fellini Satyricon
Fellini's Roma
The Garden of the
   Finzi-Continis
Kaos
La Dolce Vita
La Scorta
La Terra Trema
Love and Anarchy
Love in the City
Mamma Roma
1900
Open City
Orchestra Rehearsal
Ossessione
Paisan
The Postman
Shoeshine
The Tree of Wooden
   Clogs

Japan
See also Asia; Tokyo
Akira
The Ballad of Narayama
Black Rain
Boy
Dodes 'ka-den
Enjo
47 Ronin, Part 1
47 Ronin, Part 2
Hiroshima, Mon Amour
Life of Oharu
The Makioka Sisters
The Men Who Tread on
   the Tiger's Tail
Minbo—Or the Gentle
   Art of Japanese
   Extortion

Okoge
The Pillow Book
Ran
Rashomon
Red Beard
Samurai Rebellion
Sansho the Bailiff
Seven Samurai
Shall We Dance?
Ugetsu
Utamaro and His Five
   Women

Journalism
See Front Page

Judaism
See also The Holocaust
Au Revoir les Enfants
Commissar
The Dybbuk
The Garden of the Finzi-
   Continis
The Golem
The Last Metro
The Sorrow and the Pity
The Two of Us

Jungle Stories
Aguirre, the Wrath of
   God
Fitzcarraldo
Wages of Fear

Justice Prevails…?
See also Order in the
   Court
A Cry in the Dark
The Day the Sun Turned
   Cold
Hollow Reed
The Story of Qiu Ju

Kidnapped!
See also Missing Persons
The City of Lost
   Children
Tie Me Up! Tie Me
   Down!

Killer Bugs
Mothra
They Came from Within

**King of Beasts
(Dogs)**
Baxter
A Cry in the Dark
Umberto D

Kings
See Royalty

Labor & Unions
See also Miners &
   Mining
I'm All Right Jack
Man of Iron
Man of Marble
Moonlighting
Strike

Late Bloomin' Love
See also Growing Older
Ali: Fear Eats the Soul
Brief Encounter
Devil in the Flesh
Devil in the Flesh
A Man and a Woman
Stroszek

Law & Lawyers
See also Order in the
   Court
Minbo—Or the Gentle
   Art of Japanese
   Extortion
The Sweet Hereafter
Trois Couleurs: Rouge
Victim

Lesbians
See also Gays; Gender
   Bending
The Bitter Tears of Petra
   von Kant
Butterfly Kiss
Entre-Nous
French Twist
Les Voleurs
Mäedchen in Uniform
The Silence

**Live Action/Anima-
tion Combos**
Fabulous Adventures of
   Baron Munchausen
Jan Svankmejer's Faust

London
See also Great Britain;
   Royalty
Beautiful Thing
Full Moon in Paris
The Long Good Friday
Moonlighting
Secrets and Lies
The Young Poisoner's
   Handbook

Loneliness
See Only the Lonely

Lottery Winners
Babette's Feast
Le Million

Macho Men
See also Action
   Adventure
A Fistful of Dollars
The Good, the Bad, and
   the Ugly
Police Story

Mad Scientists
See also Science &
   Scientists
The City of Lost
   Children
The Manster

Made for Television
See TV Movies

Mafia
See Organized Crime

Marriage
See also Divorce; War
   Between the Sexes;
   Wedding Hell
The Adjuster
Alfredo, Alfredo
The Best Intentions
Blood Wedding
Breaking the Waves
Captain's Paradise
Charulata
Chloe in the Afternoon
Claire's Knee

Crash
Divorce—Italian Style
Dona Flor and Her Two
   Husbands
Donkey Skin
Drowning by Numbers
Effi Briest
Él
Entre-Nous
The Flower of My Secret
French Twist
A Gentle Woman
Gertrud
Get Out Your
   Handkerchiefs
The Hairdresser's
   Husband
Il Bell'Antonio
The Innocent
Ju Dou
Juliet of the Spirits
A Kind of Loving
La Bete Humaine
La Chienne
La Notte
L'Atalante
Late Spring
Le Beau Mariage
Le Bonheur
Life of Oharu
Loulou
The Lovers
Ma Saison Préférée
The Makioka Sisters
The Marriage of Maria
   Braun
A Married Woman
Max, Mon Amour
Muriel's Wedding
The Music Lovers
Odd Obsession
The Piano
Raise the Red Lantern
Saturday Night and
   Sunday Morning
Scenes from a Marriage
The Shame
The Soft Skin
The Stationmaster's
   Wife
Too Beautiful for You
Wedding in Blood
The Woman Next Door
Women from the Lake
   of Scented Souls

Martial Arts
Drunken Master
Sanshiro Sugata

Mass Media
See also Front Page;
   Radio
A Cry in the Dark
The Lost Honor of
   Katharina Blum

**May-December
Romance**
See also Coming of Age;
   Growing Older;
   Romantic Comedy;
   Romantic Drama
Nelly et Monsieur
   Arnaud
That Obscure Object of
   Desire

The Meaning of Life
The Designated
    Mourner
Land and Freedom
Monty Python's The
    Meaning of Life
Wings of Desire

Medieval Romps
See also Historical
    Drama; Period Piece
Béatrice
The Decameron
Donkey Skin
Lancelot of the Lake
Onibaba
Ran
Rashomon
The Return of Martin
    Guerre
Seven Samurai

Meltdown
Black Rain
I Live in Fear
Rhapsody in August
The Sacrifice
The War Game

Men
See also Macho Men;
    Repressed Men; War
    Between the Sexes
La Grande Bouffe
The Young Poisoner's
    Handbook

Men in Prison
See also Fugitives; Great
    Escapes; POW/MIA
Le Trou
A Man Escaped
Shoeshine
Yol

Mexico
Like Water for
    Chocolate
Los Olvidados
Que Viva Mexico

Middle East
See also Terrorism
Guelwaar
Life and Nothing More
    ...
The Silences of the
    Palace
The Taste of Cherry
Through the Olive Trees
The White Balloon

Military: Foreign
The Ascent
Gallipoli
Prisoner of the
    Mountains

Miners & Mining
Germinal
Kameradschaft
Margaret's Museum
Xica

Minnesota
The Emigrants
The New Land

Missing Persons
See also Kidnapped!

Picnic at Hanging Rock
The Vanishing

Mistaken Identity
See also Gender
    Bending; Role
    Reversal
Generale Della Rovere
High & Low
Johnny Stecchino
Mississippi Mermaid
The Monster
My Twentieth Century
Purple Noon
The Return of Martin
    Guerre
A Self-Made Hero
Toto le Heros

**Modern
    Shakespeare**
Chimes at Midnight
Ran
Throne of Blood

Monsters, General
See also Ghosts, Ghouls,
    & Goblins; Killer
    Bugs; Mad
    Scientists; Vampires
The Brainiac
Godzilla, King of the
    Monsters
The Manster
Mothra

Montreal
See also Canada
Jesus of Montreal
Léolo

Motor Vehicle Dept.
Crash
This Man Must Die
Traffic
Wages of Fear

Music
See also Rock Stars on
    Film
The Accompanist
Allegro Non Troppo
Basileus Quartet
Carmen
Diva
Leningrad Cowboys Go
    America
The Music Lovers
Orchestra Rehearsal
The Piano
Shoot the Piano Player
32 Short Films about
    Glenn Gould
Tous les Matins du
    Monde
Un Coeur en Hiver

Musicals
Le Million
The Music Lovers
The Red Shoes
The Threepenny Opera
Umbrellas of Cherbourg
A Woman Is a Woman

Mystery & Suspense
See also Psycho-Thriller
Alphaville
The American Friend

The Bird with the
    Crystal Plumage
The Bride Wore Black
Cat and Mouse
Confidentially Yours
Diva
The Draughtsman's
    Contract
Frantic
Juggernaut
La Cérémonie
The Man on the Roof
Monsieur Hire
The Mystery of Rampo
Picnic at Hanging Rock
Repulsion
Scene of the Crime
The Spider's Stratagem
Stray Dog
This Man Must Die
The Vanishing
Violette
Z
Zentropa

Mythology
See Folklore &
    Mythology

**Nazis & Other Para-
    military Slugs**
See also Germany; The
    Holocaust; Judaism;
    World War II
The Conformist
Europa, Europa
Hanussen
Kanal
The Last Metro
Madame Rosa
A Man Escaped
Mephisto
The Night Porter
Open City
The Sorrow and the Pity
Triumph of the Will
Zentropa

Negative Utopia
See also Post
    Apocalypse;
    Technology-
    Rampant
Alphaville
Metropolis

Newspapers
See Front Page

Nifty '50s
The Long Day Closes
Moscow Does Not
    Believe in Tears
The Thief
When Father Was Away
    on Business

Nightclubs
The Blue Angel
French Can-Can
La Cage aux Folles
Le Samourai
Shanghai Triad
A Woman Is a Woman

**Not-So-True
    Identity**
Europa, Europa
Olivier, Olivier
The Thief

Nuclear Disaster
See Meltdown

Nuns & Priests
See also Religion
Black Narcissus
The Boys of St. Vincent
The Devils
The Devil's Playground
Diary of a Country Priest
Jesus of Montreal
Thérèse

Obsessive Love
Betty Blue
Brief Encounter
Chungking Express
Él
Temptress Moon
Wuthering Heights

Occult
See also Satanism;
    Witchcraft
The Brainiac
Curse of the Demon
The Devils
The Devil's Eye
Dona Flor and Her Two
    Husbands
The Dybbuk
Half of Heaven
Hanussen
The Kingdom
The Magician
Ticket to Heaven
Witchcraft through the
    Ages

Oceans
See Go Fish

Oedipal Allegories
See also Family Ties
Hamlet
Murmur of the Heart

Oil
See Black Gold

Oldest Profession
Belle de Jour
Caravaggio
Diary of a Lost Girl
Diva
Erendira
Jamon, Jamon
La Chienne
Life of Oharu
Lola Montès
Madame Rosa
Mamma Roma
Man of Flowers
My Life to Live
Nights of Cabiria
Pandora's Box
Sansho the Bailiff
Two or Three Things I
    Know About Her
Utamaro and His Five
    Women

On the Rocks
See also Pill Poppin'
Dona Flor and Her Two
    Husbands
Drunken Angel
The Fire Within
Once Were Warriors

Category

539

Chapayev
Que Viva Mexico
Strike
Ten Days That Shook
   the World

Prostitutes
See Oldest Profession

Psychiatry
See Shrinks

Psycho-Thriller
See also Mystery &
   Suspense
Blow-Up
Day of Wrath
The Day the Sun
   Turned Cold
Diabolique
Knife in the Water
La Rupture
Le Boucher
The Passion of Anna
Repulsion
The Tenant
Through a Glass Darkly
The Vanishing
Vengeance Is Mine
The Young Poisoner's
   Handbook

Psychotics/
   Sociopaths
Repulsion
The Tenant
Tetsuo: The Iron Man
The Young Poisoner's
   Handbook

Queens
See Royalty

Radio
See also Mass Media
Comfort and Joy
Love Serenade

Rags to Riches
See also Price of Fame;
   Wrong Side of the
   Tracks
The Last Laugh
Trois Couleurs: Blanc

Rape
See also Sexual Abuse
Bandit Queen
Diary of a Lost Girl
Kika
Landscape in the Mist
Olivier, Olivier
Rashomon

Rebel With a Cause
See also Rebel Without a
   Cause
The Burmese Harp
La Marseillaise
Man of Marble
Memories of
   Underdevelopment
Sansho the Bailiff
Sympathy for the Devil

Rebel Without
   a Cause
See also Rebel With a
   Cause
Breathless

Going Places
If…

Red Scare
See also Russia/USSR
Anna
Arsenal
Chapayev
Commissar
Death of a Bureaucrat
Earth
Indochine
Man of Iron
Man of Marble
Mother Küsters Goes to
   Heaven
Strike
Tito and Me
When Father Was Away
   on Business

Religion
See also Judaism; Nuns
   & Priests; Saints
Before the Rain
Breaking the Waves
Devi
Enjo
The Flowers of St.
   Francis
The Gospel According
   to St. Matthew
Guelwaar
Heavens Above
Jerusalem
The Milky Way
The Miracle
Monsieur Vincent
Ordet
The Passion of Joan
   of Arc
Through a Glass Darkly
The Winter Light

Repressed Men
See also Men
Bleak Moments
Él

Rescue Missions
The City of Lost
   Children
Seven Samurai

Revenge
Black Sunday
Fiorile
Hamlet
Harakiri
Manon of the Spring
The Match Factory Girl
This Man Must Die
Trois Couleurs: Blanc
The Virgin Spring
The White Sheik

Road Trip
See also Chases; Motor
   Vehicle Dept.
Ariel
Ashik Kerib
Butterfly Kiss
Bye Bye Brazil
Kings of the Road—In
   the Course of Time
La Strada
Lamerica
Landscape in the Mist

Leningrad Cowboys Go
   America
Pierrot le Fou
The Saragossa
   Manuscript
Sawdust & Tinsel
Weekend

Rock Stars on Film
Blow-Up
How I Won the War

Role Reversal
See also Gender
   Bending; Identity
Kagemusha
La Femme Nikita
La Ronde
Persona
The Tango Lesson

Romance
See Late Bloomin' Love;
   Romantic Comedy;
   Romantic Drama;
   Romantic Triangles

Romantic Comedy
Alfredo, Alfredo
Belle Epoque
Boyfriends & Girlfriends
Café au Lait
Captain's Paradise
Casanova '70
Diary of a Seducer
Dona Flor and Her Two
   Husbands
French Twist
Get Out Your
   Handkerchiefs
I Know Where I'm Going
Il Bell'Antonio
La Collectionneuse
La Lectrice
Le Beau Mariage
The Man Who Loved
   Women
My Night at Maud's
Okoge
Smiles of a Summer
   Night
Stolen Kisses
Too Beautiful for You
We All Loved Each
   Other So Much

Romantic Drama
The Accompanist
Ali: Fear Eats the Soul
Beauty and the Beast
Before the Rain
The Best Intentions
Betty Blue
The Bitter Tears of Petra
   von Kant
The Blue Light
Breathless
Brief Encounter
Cactus
Camille Claudel
Carmen
Charulata
Days and Nights in the
   Forest
Devil in the Flesh
Devil in the Flesh
Effi Briest
Eléna and Her Men
Fanny

Full Moon in Paris
A Gentle Woman
The Go-Between
The Hairdresser's
   Husband
Indochine
Jules and Jim
La Notte
La Strada
The Lady with the Dog
Le Bonheur
Liebelei
Life and Nothing But
Little Dorrit, Film 2: Little
   Dorrit's Story
Lola
Loulou
Love on the Run
The Lovers
Lovers: A True Story
A Man and a Woman
Man Is Not a Bird
Margaret's Museum
Mississippi Mermaid
Nelly et Monsieur
   Arnaud
The Nest
Pepe Le Moko
The Piano
Princess Yang Kwei Fei
Red Sorghum
Rendezvous in Paris
The Return of Martin
   Guerre
Shoot the Piano Player
A Slave of Love
The Soft Skin
A Special Day
A Tale of Winter
Through the Olive Trees
Tilaï
Tristana
Twist & Shout
Two Daughters
Two English Girls
Un Coeur en Hiver
Vive L'Amour
War and Peace
We the Living
Wedding in Blood
Wings of Desire
The Woman Next Door
Wuthering Heights

Romantic Triangles
Café au Lait
The Cook, the Thief, His
   Wife & Her Lover
Dead Ringers
French Twist
Jules and Jim
Les Voleurs
Liebelei
Love Serenade
The Lovers
Saturday Night and
   Sunday Morning
A Tale of Winter
Tilaï
Vive L'Amour

Rome
See also Italy
The Belly of an Architect
Fellini Satyricon
Fellini's Roma
Ginger & Fred
La Dolce Vita
A Special Day
The White Sheik

Category

541

VideoHound's
WORLD CINEMA

Royalty
See also Historical
    Drama; Medieval
    Romps; Period Piece
Alexander Nevsky
Chimes at Midnight
Donkey Skin
Eléna and Her Men
Farinelli
Henry V
Ivan the Terrible, Part 1
Ivan the Terrible, Part 2
Kaspar Hauser
Kind Hearts and
    Coronets
La Nuit de Varennes
Lancelot of the Lake
Orlando
Princess Yang Kwei Fei
Ridicule
The Rise of Louis XIV
The Saragossa
    Manuscript
The Silences of the
    Palace
Storm over Asia
Throne of Blood

Russia/USSR
See also Red Scare
Anna
The Ascent
The Battleship
    Potemkin
Burnt by the Sun
Commissar
Dersu Uzala
Freeze-Die-Come to Life
Ivan the Terrible, Part 1
Ivan the Terrible, Part 2
Little Vera
The Man with a Movie
    Camera
The Mirror
Moscow Does Not
    Believe in Tears
The Music Lovers
Prisoner of the
    Mountains
A Slave of Love
The Thief
War and Peace
We the Living

Sail Away
See also Go Fish
And the Ship Sails On
The Battleship
    Potemkin
Captain's Paradise
Juggernaut
Knife in the Water
Swept Away…

Saints
See also Religion
The Flowers of St.
    Francis
The Passion of Joan
    of Arc
Thérèse

Sanity Check
See also Doctors &
    Nurses; Hospitals &
    Medicine; Shrinks
Aguirre, the Wrath of
    God
Camille Claudel

Dead of Night
Devi
Devil in the Flesh
Dr. Mabuse, Parts 1 & 2
Eyes Without a Face
The 4th Man
The Goalie's Anxiety at
    the Penalty Kick
The Hairdresser's
    Husband
Heavenly Creatures
Mother Küsters Goes to
    Heaven
The Red Desert
Solaris
The Story of Adele H.
The Tenant
The Testament of Dr.
    Cordelier
Vengeance Is Mine

Satanism
See also Devils; Occult
Black Sunday
The Devils
The Devil's Eye

Satire & Parody
See also Black Comedy;
    Comedy
Beau Père
Big Deal on Madonna
    Street
Contract
Death of a Bureaucrat
Diary of a
    Chambermaid
The Discreet Charm of
    the Bourgeoisie
Down & Dirty
The Family Game
Going Places
Gumshoe
Heavens Above
High Hopes
The Icicle Thief
I'm All Right Jack
Jamon, Jamon
L'Age D'Or
Man Bites Dog
The Man in the White
    Suit
The Milky Way
Minbo—Or the Gentle
    Art of Japanese
    Extortion
Monty Python's The
    Meaning of Life
Orchestra Rehearsal
Phantom of Liberty
A Propos de Nice
Simon of the Desert
Sympathy for the Devil
A Very Curious Girl
The White Sheik
Xala

Scams, Stings &
Cons
See also Heists
Kind Hearts and
    Coronets
Lamerica
Lovers: A True Story
The Monster
Ossessione

School Daze
See also Hell High
    School

Au Revoir les Enfants
Black Narcissus
The Devil's Playground
Europa, Europa
Heavenly Creatures
Mädchen in Uniform
Wild Reeds

Sci Fi
See also Fantasy
Akira
Alphaville
The Fabulous World of
    Jules Verne
Fahrenheit 451
Fantastic Planet
Godzilla, King of the
    Monsters
The Green Slime
King Kong vs. Godzilla
La Jetée
The Manster
Metropolis
Mothra
Solaris
Stalker
Tetsuo: The Iron Man
Woman in the Moon

Science & Scientists
See also Mad Scientists
Illumination
The Man in the White
    Suit
Woman in the Dunes

Scotland
See also Great Britain
Breaking the Waves
Comfort and Joy
I Know Where I'm Going
Local Hero

Serial Killers
See also Crime &
    Criminals; Crime
    Sprees
Butterfly Kiss
I Can't Sleep
M
Man Bites Dog
The Monster

Sex & Sexuality
See also Torrid Love
    Scenes
The Adjuster
And God Created
    Woman
Belle de Jour
Belle Epoque
Betty Blue
Bitter Rice
The Blue Angel
Boccaccio '70
Breaking the Waves
The Canterbury Tales
Carnival in Flanders
Casanova '70
César & Rosalie
Claire's Knee
The Cook, the Thief, His
    Wife & Her Lover
Crash
The Decameron
Devil in the Flesh
Devil in the Flesh
The Devils
The Devil's Eye
The Devil's Playground

Diary of a
    Chambermaid
Divorce—Italian Style
Dreams
The Eclipse
Él
Every Man for Himself
Exotica
Fellini Satyricon
The 4th Man
Get Out Your
    Handkerchiefs
I Am Curious (Yellow)
In the Realm of the
    Senses
Indochine
Jamon, Jamon
Kika
La Collectionneuse
La Ronde
Last Tango in Paris
Le Boucher
Like Water for
    Chocolate
Loulou
Lovers: A True Story
The Man Who Loved
    Women
A Married Woman
Miss Julie
Monsieur Hire
Monty Python's The
    Meaning of Life
The Mother and the
    Whore
My Life to Live
Pauline at the Beach
The Pillow Book
Repulsion
Scene of the Crime
The Stationmaster's
    Wife
Sugarbaby
Temptress Moon
That Obscure Object of
    Desire
Tie Me Up! Tie Me
    Down!
The Valley Obscured by
    the Clouds
A Very Curious Girl
Wedding in Blood
The Woman Next Door
Women on the Verge of
    a Nervous
    Breakdown
Xica
Yesterday, Today and
    Tomorrow

Sexual Abuse
See also Rape
The Boys of St. Vincent
The Devils
The Night Porter

Ships
See Sail Away

Showbiz Dramas
Day for Night
La Dolce Vita
The Last Metro

Shrinks
See also Doctors &
    Nurses
Face to Face
The Young Poisoner's
    Handbook

Shutterbugs
See also Front Page
Blow-Up
Proof

Silent Films
Arsenal
The Battleship
  Potemkin
The Cabinet of Dr.
  Caligari
Diary of a Lost Girl
Die Liebe der Jeanne
  Ney
Die Niebelungen
Dr. Mabuse, Parts 1 & 2
Earth
Faust
The Golem
Joyless Street
The Last Laugh
The Man with a Movie
  Camera
Metropolis
Napoleon
Nosferatu
Pandora's Box
The Passion of Joan of
  Arc
A Propos de Nice
Spies
Storm over Asia
Strike
Ten Days That Shook
  the World
Variety
Waxworks
Witchcraft through the
  Ages
Woman in the Moon

Slapstick Comedy
See also Comedy
The Case of the
  Mukkinese Battle
  Horn
Drunken Master
Jour de Fete
The Monster
Playtime

Slavery
Burn!
The Last Supper
Quilombo
Sansho the Bailiff
Xica

Slice of Life
See also True Stories
Amarcord
The Bicycle Thief
The Big City
Black God, White Devil
Bleak Moments
César
Delicatessen
Dodes 'ka-den
Egg
Every Man for Himself &
  God Against All
The Family Game
Fanny and Alexander
The Funeral
Happy Together
High Hopes
Jalsaghar
Joyless Street
La Terra Trema

Late Spring
The Little Thief
Local Hero
Look Back in Anger
Love on the Run
Ma Saison Préférée
Mamma Roma
Marius
The Middleman
A Mongolian Tale
My Sweet Little Village
Once Were Warriors
Saturday Night and
  Sunday Morning
A Single Girl
Stroszek
Sugarbaby
Toni
The Tree of Wooden
  Clogs
Twist & Shout
The White Balloon
Women from the Lake
  of Scented Souls

South America
Aguirre, the Wrath of
  God
Black Orpheus
Bye Bye Brazil
Fitzcarraldo
Happy Together
I Don't Want to Talk
  About It
Quilombo
Xica

Space Operas
The Green Slime
Heavens Above
Solaris
Stalker
Woman in the Moon

Spaghetti Western
A Fistful of Dollars
The Good, the Bad and
  the Ugly
Once Upon a Time in
  the West

Spain
Belle Epoque
Land and Freedom

Spies & Espionage
See also Terrorism
A Generation
Spies

Sports
The Goalie's Anxiety at
  the Penalty Kick
Monty Python's The
  Meaning of Life
This Sporting Life
Tokyo Olympiad

Suicide
See also Death & the
  Afterlife
Delicatessen
The Fire Within
A Gentle Woman
Last Tango in Paris
Mäedchen in Uniform
Mother Küsters Goes to
  Heaven
Mouchette

The Taste of Cherry
The Tenant

Supernatural
Horror
See also Classic Horror;
  Horror
The Brainiac
Curse of the Demon
Kwaidan

Survival
See also Negative
  Utopia; Post
  Apocalypse
Black Rain
Erendira
The Forbidden Quest
Kameradschaft
Le Dernier Combat
The Life and Death of
  Colonel Blimp
Little Dorrit, Film 1:
  Nobody's Fault
Little Dorrit, Film 2: Little
  Dorrit's Story
Walkabout

Suspense
See Mystery & Suspense

Tearjerkers
La Bete Humaine
La Chienne
Le Jour Se Leve
Miss Julie
The Nest
Under the Roofs of Paris

Technology-
Rampant
A Nous la Liberté
Metropolis
Mon Oncle

Teen Angst
See also Coming of Age;
  Hell High School
Beautiful Thing
Fellini's Roma
Heavenly Creatures
If…
La Promesse
Les Enfants Terrible
Les Mistons
The Little Thief
Mon Oncle Antoine
Monika
Mouchette
Time Stands Still
Twist & Shout
Two Friends
The Young Poisoner's
  Handbook

Television
See Mass Media; TV
  Movies

Terrorism
See also Crime &
  Criminals; Spies &
  Espionage
Juggernaut
Marianne and Juliane
Women on the Verge of
  a Nervous
  Breakdown

This is Your Life
Amarcord
Au Revoir les Enfants
Bandit Queen
The Best Intentions
A Bigger Splash
Camille Claudel
Caravaggio
Caro Diario
Céleste
Chapayev
A Chef in Love
Dreamchild
Edith & Marcel
Edvard Munch
Europa, Europa
Fanny and Alexander
Farinelli
La Salamandre
La Signora di Tutti
Monsieur Vincent
The Music Lovers
My Left Foot
Napoleon
The Rise of Louis XIV
The Story of Adele H.
Sunday's Children
The Testament of
  Orpheus
Thérèse
32 Short Films about
  Glenn Gould
Van Gogh
Veronika Voss

Thrillers
See also Mystery &
  Suspense; Psycho-
  Thriller
Insomnia
La Femme Infidele

Tokyo
See also Japan
Akira
An Autumn Afternoon
Dodes 'ka-den
Godzilla, King of the
  Monsters
Hiroshima, Mon Amour
Mothra
Okoge
Tokyo Story

Torrid Love Scenes
See also Sex & Sexuality
Betty Blue
The Cook, the Thief, His
  Wife & Her Lover
Dona Flor and Her Two
  Husbands
In the Realm of the
  Senses
Last Tango in Paris
The Lovers
Moon in the Gutter
1900
Swept Away…
The Woman Next Door

Tragedy
See also Drama;
  Tearjerkers
Deep End
Effi Briest
Gate of Hell
Hamlet
Jalsaghar
Jules and Jim

Category

543

Margaret's Museum
The Nest
Princess Yang Kwei Fei
Ran
Shadows of Forgotten
  Ancestors
The Sweet Hereafter
Throne of Blood
Tilaï
Trois Couleurs: Bleu
Variety
The Virgin Spring
The Woman Next Door

Trains
La Bete Humaine
My Twentieth Century
Once Upon a Time in
  the West
Subway
A Tale of Winter
Zentropa

True Crime
See also Crime &
  Criminals; This is
  Your Life; True
  Stories
Dr. Petiot
I Can't Sleep

True Stories
See also This is Your Life;
  True Crime
Au Revoir les Enfants
The Boys of St. Vincent
A Cry in the Dark
Dead Ringers
Elvira Madigan
Enjo
Europa, Europa
Every Man for Himself &
  God Against All
Farinelli
Fitzcarraldo
Heavenly Creatures
Jerusalem
Kaspar Hauser
The Last Supper
A Man Escaped
Marianne and Juliane
My Left Foot
Olivier, Olivier
The Passion of Joan
  of Arc
Quilombo
The Return of Martin
  Guerre
Vengeance Is Mine
Violette
The Wannsee
  Conference
Wedding in Blood
The Wild Child
The Young Poisoner's
  Handbook

TV Movies
After the Rehearsal
Berlin Alexanderplatz
The Boys of St. Vincent
The Clowns
Face to Face

The Magic Flute
The Rise of Louis XIV
The Testament of Dr.
  Cordelier
Two Friends

Twins
See also Family Ties
Dead Ringers
The Double Life of
  Veronique

UFOs
See Space Operas

Vacations
Claire's Knee
La Collectionneuse
Pauline at the Beach
A Tale of Winter

Vampires
The Fearless Vampire
  Killers
Nosferatu
Nosferatu the Vampyre
Vampyr

**War Between the
Sexes**
See also Divorce;
  Marriage
The Best Intentions
Carmen
Divorce—Italian Style
Juliet of the Spirits
La Discrete
The Marriage of Maria
  Braun
My Brilliant Career
Pauline at the Beach
A Taxing Woman
Women on the Verge of
  a Nervous
  Breakdown
Yesterday, Today and
  Tomorrow

War, General
See also Anti-War War
  Movies; Big Battles;
  Postwar; POW/MIA;
  Terrorism; World
  War I; World War II
Alexander Nevsky
Ballad of a Soldier
The Battle of Algiers
Before the Rain
Camp de Thiaroye
Chapayev
Henry V
The Hidden Fortress
How I Won the War
La Marseillaise
La Nuit de Varennes
Land and Freedom
The Life and Death of
  Colonel Blimp
Napoleon
Prisoner of the
  Mountains
Senso
The Shame

Storm over Asia
Ulysses' Gaze
War and Peace

Wedding Hell
See also Marriage;
  Wedding Bells
The Bride Wore Black
Contract
Wedding in Blood

Wild Kingdom
See also Killer Bugs; King
  of Beasts (Dogs)
A Cry in the Dark
Max, Mon Amour

Witchcraft
See also Occult
Black Sunday
Day of Wrath
The Devils

Women
See also Dream Girls;
  Femme Fatale
Antonia's Line
Bandit Queen
Bhaji on the Beach
The Big City
Black Girl
Commissar
Dreams
The Flower of My Secret
Jamon, Jamon
Juliet of the Spirits
Lola Montès
Mäedchen in Uniform
Marianne and Juliane
Messidor
Mina Tannenbaum
Moscow Does Not
  Believe in Tears
My Brilliant Career
My Twentieth Century
One Sings, the Other
  Doesn't
The Pillow Book
The Scent of Green
  Papaya
The Silences of the
  Palace
A Single Girl
The Story of Qiu Ju
The Story of Women
The Tango Lesson
301, 302
Utamaro and His Five
  Women
Viva Maria!
When a Woman
  Ascends the Stairs
Women from the Lake
  of Scented Souls
Women on the Verge of
  a Nervous
  Breakdown

World War I
Arsenal
Captain Conan
Devil in the Flesh
Dr. Mabuse, Parts 1 & 2

Gallipoli
Grand Illusion
The Life and Death of
  Colonel Blimp
Life and Nothing But

World War II
See also The Holocaust;
  Postwar; POW/MIA
The Accompanist
The Ascent
Ashes and Diamonds
Au Revoir les Enfants
Black Rain
The Boat Is Full
Brief Encounter
The Burmese Harp
Christ Stopped at Eboli
Distant Thunder
Distant Voices, Still Lives
Dr. Petiot
Europa, Europa
Fires on the Plain
Forbidden Games
The Garden of the Finzi-
  Continis
Generale Della Rovere
A Generation
The Human Condition:
  A Soldier's Prayer
The Human Condition:
  No Greater Love
The Human Condition:
  Road to Eternity
Is Paris Burning?
Kanal
The Last Metro
The Life and Death of
  Colonel Blimp
The Little Thief
A Man Escaped
Mephisto
The Mirror
Night and Fog
The Night of the
  Shooting Stars
Open City
Paisan
Salo, or the 120 Days of
  Sodom
Seven Beauties
The Sorrow and the Pity
The Tin Drum
Triumph of the Will
The Two of Us
Underground
The Wannsee
  Conference

Writers
See also This is Your Life
The Flower of My Secret
My Brilliant Career
The Pillow Book
301, 302

**Wrong Side of the
Tracks**
See also Rags to Riches
Careful, He Might Hear
  You
The Lacemaker
This Sporting Life

DISTRIBUTOR LIST

The "Distributor List" below explains the three-letter distributor codes found at the end of each review. If the movie is available on video, look up the code here and then refer to the "Distributor Guide" for the address, phone, fax and other pertinent information for the distributor. Please note, however, that studio distributors do not sell to the general public; they act as wholesalers selling only to retail outlets. You will find that many video stores provide an ordering service for hard-to-find videos. See the "Video Sources" list at the front of the book for a list of establishments that may be able to help you find what you're looking for.

AOV—Admit One Video
ART—Artisan Entertainment
AUD—Audio-Forum
AVI—Arrow Video, Inc./Arrow Entertainment
BAR—Barr Films
BFA—Phoenix/Coronet/ BFA Films and Video (R)
BMG—BMG
BST—ETD
BTV—Baker & Taylor Video
CAB—Cable Films & Video
CAF—Cabin Fever Entertainment
CCB—Critics' Choice Video, Inc.
CCN—Cinevista
COL—Columbia Tristar Home Video (W)
CRC—Criterion Collection
CTH—Corinth Video
CTL—Capitol Entertainment and Home Video (W)
CVC—Connoisseur Meridian Films
DVT—Discount Video Tapes, Inc./Hollywood's Attic (W)
ERG—Ergo Media Inc. (R)

EVE—Evergreen Entertainment
FCT—Facets Multimedia, Inc.
FOX—CBS/Fox Video
FRF—First Run Features
FST—Festival Films (R)
FUS—Fusion Video
FXL—Fox/Lorber Home Video
FXV—Twentieth Century Fox Home Entertainment
GKK—Goodtimes Entertainment
GLV—German Language Video Center
GPV—Grapevine Video
GVV—Glenn Video Vistas, Ltd. (R)
HBO—HBO Home Video (W)
HEG—Horizon Entertainment
HHE—Hollywood Home Entertainment
HHT—Hollywood Home Theatre
HMK—Hallmark Home Entertainment
HMV—Home Vision Cinema
HTV—Hen's Tooth Video (W)

IFC—International Film Circuit, Inc.
IGP—Ignatius Press
IHF—International Historic Films, Inc.
IME—Image Entertainment
INC—Increase/SilverMine Video (W)
ING—Ingram Entertainment Inc. (W)
INT—Interama, Inc. (R)
JEF—JEF Films, Inc.
KEP—Keep the Faith Inc.
KIV—Kino on Video (W)
KUI—Knowledge Unlimited, Inc.
KUL—Kultur Video (W)
LSV—LSVideo, Inc.
LUM—Lumivision Corp.
MAX—Miramax Pictures Home Video
MET—Metromedia Entertainment
MGM—MGM Home Entertainment
MIL—Milestone Film & Video
MLB—Mike #LeBell's Video (R)
MLT—Music for Little People
MOV—Movies Unlimited (R)
MPI—MPI Home Video

545

MRV—Moore Video

MVD—Music Video Distributors

NCJ—National Center for Jewish Film

NLC—New Line Home Video

NOS—Nostalgia Family Video

NYF—New Yorker Video

NYR—Not Yet Released

ORI—Orion Home Video

PAR—Paramount Home Video

PBS—PBS Home Video

PGV—Polygram Video (PV)

PMS—Professional Media Service Corp.

REP—Republic Pictures Home Video

RHI—Rhino Home Video

RXM—Rex #Miller

SIG—Signals

SMW—Something Weird Video

SNC—Sinister Cinema

STP—Streamline Pictures

SWC—Simon Wiesenthal Center

TAI—Tai Seng Video Marketing

THV—Trimark Home Video

TIM—Timeless Video Inc.

TLF—Time-Life Video and Television

TOU—Buena Vista Home Video

TPV—Tapeworm Video Distributors

TRI—Triboro Entertainment Group

TVC—The Video Catalog

USH—Universal Studios Home Video

VCD—Video City Productions/ Distributing

VCI—VCI Home Video

VCN—Video Connection

VDA—Video Action (W)

VDC—Vidcrest

VDM—Video Dimensions (W)

VEC—Valencia Entertainment Corp.

VES—Vestron Video

VHE—VCII Home Entertainment, Inc.

VTR—Anchor Bay

VYY—Video Yesteryear

WAC—World Artists Home Video

WAR—Warner Home Video, Inc.

WAX—Waxworks/Videoworks, Inc.

WBF—Water Bearer Films

WFV—Western Media Systems

WST—White Star

XVC—Xenon

DISTRIBUTOR GUIDE

The "Distributor Guide" provides contact information, including address, phone, fax and toll-free numbers, for the distributors indicated within the reviews. Each movie in the main section has at least one distributor code located at the end of the entry. The key to these codes, preceding this guide, will lead you to the appropriate distributor. Those reviews with the code **OM** are on moratorium, meaning that they were distributed at one time, but aren't currently. Since it was once available, an On Moratorium title may show up at your local video store. If the distributor for a movie is not known, the code **NO** will follow the review. New theatrical releases (and some older titles) that haven't made it to video at press time have the designation **NYR** (not yet released). Three warnings: 1) Not all movies are available on video; 2) From year to year, a small minority of distributors move without telling anyone, or just plain go out of business; and 3) Studio distributors do not sell to the general public—they generally act as wholesalers, selling only to retail outlets. Many video stores provide an ordering service. Try checking the "Video Sources" section in the front of the book for a few suggested outlets to help you find the title you're looking for.

ADMIT ONE VIDEO (AOV)
PO Box 66, Sta. O
Toronto, ON, Canada M4A
 2M8
416-463-5714
Fax: 416-463-5714

ANCHOR BAY (VTR)
500 Kirts Blvd.
Troy, MI 48084
248-362-4400
800-786-8777
Fax: 248-362-4454

**ARROW VIDEO, INC.
 /ARROW
 ENTERTAINMENT (AVI)**
135 W. 50th St., Ste. 1925
New York, NY 10020
212-258-2200
Fax: 212-245-1252

**ARTISAN ENTERTAINMENT
 (ART)**
15400 Sherman Way
PO Box 10124
Van Nuys, CA 91410-0124
818-988-5060
800-677-0789
Fax: 818-778-3259

AUDIO-FORUM (AUD)
96 Broad St.
Guilford, CT 06437
203-453-9794
800-243-1234

Fax: 203-453-9774
e-mail: 74537.550@
 compuserve.com

**BAKER & TAYLOR VIDEO
 (BTV)**
700 N. Austin
Niles, IL 60714
800-775-2800

BARR FILMS (BAR)
12801 Schabarum
Irwindale, CA 91706

BMG (BMG)
1540 Broadway, 2yth Fl.
New York, NY 10036
216-543-6466

**BUENA VISTA HOME VIDEO
 (TOU)**
PO Box 908
Lakewood, CA 90714-0908
310-233-3120

**CABIN FEVER
 ENTERTAINMENT (CAF)**
100 W. Putnam Ave.
Greenwich, CT 06830
203-863-5200
Fax: 203-863-5258

CABLE FILMS & VIDEO (CAB)
PO Box 7171, Country Club Sta.
Kansas City, MO 64113
913-362-2804
800-514-2804

Fax: 913-341-7365
e-mail: catchwave@
 sprintmail.com

**CAPITOL ENTERTAINMENT
 AND HOME VIDEO (CTL)**
6205 Adelaide Dr.
Bethesda, MD 20817
301-564-9700
Fax: 301-564-0797
e-mail:
 capent@capitolent.com
web: http://
 www.capitolent.com

CBS/FOX VIDEO (FOX)
PO Box 900
Beverly Hills, CA 90213
562-373-4800
(888)223-4FOX
Fax: 562-373-4803

CINEVISTA (CCN)
560 W. 43rd, No. 8J
New York, NY 10036
212-947-4373
800-341-CINE
Fax: 212-947-0644

**COLUMBIA TRISTAR HOME
 VIDEO (COL)**
Sony Pictures Plz.
10202 W. Washington Blvd.
Culver City, CA 90232
310-280-5418
Fax: 310-280-2485
web:http://www.spe.sony.com

CONNOISSEUR MERIDIAN FILMS (CVC)
1575 Westwood Blvd., Ste. 205
Los Angeles, CA 90024
310-231-1350
800-529-2300
Fax: 310-231-1359
web: http://www.
    meridianvideo.com

CORINTH VIDEO (CTH)
34 Gansevoort St.
New York, NY 10014
212-463-0305
800-221-4720
Fax: 212-929-0010

CRITERION COLLECTION (CRC)
c/o The Voyager Co.
578 Broadway
New York, NY 10012
212-431-5199
800-446-2001
web: http:// www.
    criterionco.com

CRITICS' CHOICE VIDEO, INC. (CCB)
PO Box 749
Itasca, IL 60143
630-775-3300
800-367-7765
Fax: 630-775-3340

DISCOUNT VIDEO TAPES, INC./HOLLYWOOD'S ATTIC (DVT)
PO Box 7122
Burbank, CA 91510
818-843-3366
Fax: 818-843-3821
web: http://www.
    discountvideotapes.com

ERGO MEDIA INC. (ERG)
668 American Legion Dr.
PO Box 2037
Teaneck, NJ 07666
201-692-0404
800-695-3746
Fax: 201-692-0663
e-mail: ergo@intec.com
web: http://www.
    jewishvideo.com

ETD (BST)
13950 Senlac Dr., Ste. 300
Farmers Branch, TX 75234
972-406-0866
800-541-1008

EVERGREEN ENTERTAINMENT (EVE)
6100 Wilshire Blvd., Ste. 1400
Los Angeles, CA 90048

FACETS MULTIMEDIA, INC. (FCT)
1517 W. Fullerton Ave.
Chicago, IL 60614
773-281-9075

800-331-6197
Fax: 773-929-5437

FESTIVAL FILMS (FST)
6115 Chestnut Ter.
Excelsior, MN 55331-8107
612-470-2172
800-798-6083
Fax: 612-470-2172
e-mail: fesfilms@aol.com
web: http://members.aol.com/
    festfilms/

FIRST RUN FEATURES (FRF)
153 Waverly Pl.
New York, NY 10014
212-243-0600
800-229-8575
Fax: 212-989-7649

FOX/LORBER HOME VIDEO (FXL)
419 Park Ave. S., 20th Fl.
New York, NY 10016
212-686-6777
Fax: 212-685-2625

FUSION VIDEO (FUS)
100 Fusion Way
Country Club Hills, IL 60478
708-799-2073
Fax: 708-799-8375
web: http://www.
    fusion-intl.com

GERMAN LANGUAGE VIDEO CENTER (GLV)
7625 Pendleton Pike
Indianapolis, IN 46226-5298
317-547-1257
800-252-1957
Fax: 317-547-1263
web: http://www.
    germanvideo.com

GLENN VIDEO VISTAS, LTD. (GVV)
6924 Canby Ave., Ste. 103
Reseda, CA 91335
818-881-8110
Fax: 818-981-5506
e-mail:
    mglass@worldnet.att.net

GOODTIMES ENTERTAINMENT (GKK)
16 E. 40th St., 8th Fl.
New York, NY 10016-0113
212-951-3000
Fax: 212-213-9319
e-mail: order@gtent.com
web: http:// www.
    goodtimes.com

GRAPEVINE VIDEO (GPV)
PO Box 46161
Phoenix, AZ 85063
602-973-3661
Fax: 602-973-2973
web: http://www.
    grapevinevideo.com

HALLMARK HOME ENTERTAINMENT (HMK)
6100 Wilshire Blvd., Ste. 1400
Los Angeles, CA 90048
213-634-3000
Fax: 213-549-3760

HBO HOME VIDEO (HBO)
1100 6th Ave.
New York, NY 10036
212-512-7400
Fax: 212-512-7498
web: http://www.
    hbohomevideo.com

HEN'S TOOTH VIDEO (HTV)
2805 E. State Blvd.
Fort Wayne, IN 46805
219-471-4332
Fax: 219-471-4449

HOLLYWOOD HOME ENTERTAINMENT (HHE)
6165 Crooked Creek Rd., Ste. B
Norcross, GA 30092-3105

HOLLYWOOD HOME THEATRE (HHT)
9830 Charlieville Blvd.
Beverly Hills, CA 90212
310-203-9868

HOME VISION CINEMA (HMV)
5547 N. Ravenswood Ave.
Chicago, IL 60640-1199
773-878-2600
800-826-3456
Fax: 773-878-8406
web: http://www.
    homevision.com

HORIZON ENTERTAINMENT (HEG)
45030 Trevor Ave.
Lancaster, CA 93534
805-940-1040
800-323-2061
Fax: 805-940-8511

IGNATIUS PRESS (IGP)
33 Oakland Ave.
Harrison, NY 10528-9974
914-835-4216
Fax: 914-835-8406

IMAGE ENTERTAINMENT (IME)
9333 Oso Ave.
Chatsworth, CA 91311
818-407-9100
800-473-3475
Fax: 818-407-9111

INCREASE/SILVERMINE VIDEO (INC)
6860 Canby Ave., Ste. 118
Reseda, CA 91335
818-342-2880
800-233-2880
Fax: 818-342-4029
e-mail: quksil@aol.com

INGRAM ENTERTAINMENT INC. (ING)
2 Ingram Blvd.
La Vergne, TN 37086-7006
615-287-4000
800-621-1333
web: http://www.
ingramentertainment.com

INTERAMA, INC. (INT)
301 W. 53rd St., Ste. 19E
New York, NY 10019
212-977-4830
Fax: 212-581-6582
e-mail: InteramaNY@aol.com

INTERNATIONAL FILM CIRCUIT, INC. (IFC)
PO Box 1151
Old Chelsea Station, NY 10011
212-779-0660
Fax: 212-779-9129
e-mail: ifcplanet@aol.com

INTERNATIONAL HISTORIC FILMS, INC. (IHF)
PO Box 29035
Chicago, IL 60629
773-927-2900
Fax: 773-927-9211
web: http://www.IHFfilm.com

JEF FILMS, INC. (JEF)
Film House
143 Hickory Hill Cir.
Osterville, MA 02655-1322
508-428-7198
(888)JEF-FILM
Fax: 508-428-7198
e-mail: finchleyrd@aol.com

KEEP THE FAITH INC. (KEP)
PO Box 10544
10 Audrey Pl.
Fairfield, NJ 07004
201-244-1990
Fax: 201-244-1990

KINO ON VIDEO (KIV)
333 W. 39th St., Ste. 503
New York, NY 10018
212-629-6880
800-562-3330
Fax: 212-714-0871
e-mail: kinoint@infunnse.com
web: http://www.kino.com

KNOWLEDGE UNLIMITED, INC. (KUI)
Box 52
Madison, WI 53701-0052
608-836-6660
800-356-2303
Fax: 608-831-1570
e-mail: ku-mail@ku.com
web: http://www.ku.com

KULTUR VIDEO (KUL)
195 Hwy. No. 36
West Long Branch, NJ 07764
908-229-2343
800-458-5887
Fax: 908-229-0066

e-mail:
kultur@monmouth.com
web: http://www.
monmouth.com/~kultur

MIKE LEBELL'S VIDEO (MLB)
75 Freemont Pl.
Los Angeles, CA 90005
213-938-3333
Fax: 213-938-3334
e-mail: mlvideo@aol.com

LSVIDEO, INC. (LSV)
PO Box 415
Carmel, IN 46032

LUMIVISION CORP. (LUM)
877 Federal Blvd.
Denver, CO 80204-3212
303-446-0400
800-776-LUMI
Fax: 303-446-0101

METROMEDIA ENTERTAINMENT (MET)
1888 Century Park E., Ste. 700
Los Angeles, CA 90067
310-282-0550
Fax: 310-201-0798

MGM HOME ENTERTAINMENT (MGM)
2500 Broadway
Santa Monica, CA 90404-6061
310-449-3000
Fax: 310-449-3100

MILESTONE FILM & VIDEO (MIL)
275 W. 96th St., Ste 28C
New York, NY 10025
212-865-7449
Fax: 212-222-8952
e-mail: milesfilm@aol.com

REX MILLER (RXM)
Rte. 1, Box 457-D
East Prairie, MO 63845
314-649-5048

MIRAMAX PICTURES HOME VIDEO (MAX)
500 S. Buena Vista St.
Burbank, CA 91521
800-413-5566

MOORE VIDEO (MRV)
PO Box 5703
Richmond, VA 23220-0703
804-745-9785
Fax: 804-745-9785

MOVIES UNLIMITED (MOV)
3015 Darnell Rd.
Philadelphia, PA 19154
215-637-4444
800-466-8437
Fax: 215-637-2350
e-mail: movies@
moviesunlimited.com
web: http://www.
moviesunlimited.com

MPI HOME VIDEO (MPI)
16101 S. 108th Ave.
Orland Park, IL 60462
708-460-0555
Fax: 708-873-3177

MUSIC FOR LITTLE PEOPLE (MLT)
Box 1460
Redway, CA 95560
707-923-3991
800-346-4445
Fax: 707-923-3241

MUSIC VIDEO DISTRIBUTORS (MVD)
O'Neill Industrial Center
1210 Standbridge St.
Norristown, PA 19401
610-272-7771
800-888-0486
Fax: 610-272-6074

NATIONAL CENTER FOR JEWISH FILM (NCJ)
Brandeis University
Lown Bldg. 102
Waltham, MA 02254-9110
617-899-7044
Fax: 617-736-2070
e-mail: ncjf@
logos.cc.branders.eu

NEW LINE HOME VIDEO (NLC)
116 N. Robertson Blvd.
Los Angeles, CA 90048
310-967-6670
Fax: 310-854-0602

NEW YORKER VIDEO (NYF)
16 W. 61st St., 11th Fl.
New York, NY 10023
212-247-6110
800-447-0196
Fax: 212-307-7855

NOSTALGIA FAMILY VIDEO (NOS)
PO Box 606
Baker City, OR 97814
503-523-9034
800-784-8362
Fax: 503-523-7115

NOT YET RELEASED (NYR)
United States

ORION HOME VIDEO (ORI)
MGM
2500 Broadway
Santa Monica, CA 90404-6061
310-449-3000
Fax: 310-449-3100

PARAMOUNT HOME VIDEO (PAR)
Bluhdorn Bldg.
5555 Melrose Ave.
Los Angeles, CA 90038
213-956-3952

PBS HOME VIDEO *(PBS)*
Catalog Fulfillment Center
PO Box 4030
Santa Monica, CA 90411
800-531-4727
800-645-4PBS

**PHOENIX/CORONET/BFA
FILMS AND VIDEO** *(BFA)*
2349 Chaffee Dr.
St. Louis, MO 63146
314-569-0211
800-777-8100
Fax: 314-569-2834
e-mail:
   BFAEduc@worldnet.att.net
   Phoenix films@
   worldnet. att.net

POLYGRAM VIDEO (PV)
(PGV)
825 8th Ave.
New York, NY 10019
212-333-8000
800-825-7781
Fax: 212-603-7960

**PROFESSIONAL MEDIA
SERVICE CORP.** *(PMS)*
19122 S. Vermont Ave.
Gardena, CA 90248
310-532-9024
800-223-7672
Fax: 800-253-8853
e-mail: promedia@class.org

**REPUBLIC PICTURES HOME
VIDEO** *(REP)*
5700 Wilshire Blvd.,
   Ste. 525 North
Los Angeles, CA 90036-3659
213-965-6900
Fax: 213-965-6963

RHINO HOME VIDEO *(RHI)*
10635 Santa Monica Blvd.,
   2nd Fl.
Los Angeles, CA 90025-4900
310-828-1980
800-843-3670
Fax: 310-453-5529

SIGNALS *(SIG)*
7000 Westgate Dr.
St. Paul, MN 55114
612-659-3700
800-669-5225
Fax: 612-659-0083
e-mail: kyle@rivertrade.com

**SIMON WIESENTHAL
CENTER** *(SWC)*
9760 W. Pico Blvd.
Los Angeles, CA 90035-4792
310-553-9036
Fax: 310-553-8007

SINISTER CINEMA *(SNC)*
PO Box 4369
Medford, OR 97501-0168
541-773-6860
Fax: 541-779-8650

SOMETHING WEIRD VIDEO
(SMW)
PO Box 33664
Seattle, WA 98133
206-361-3759
Fax: 206-364-7526

STREAMLINE PICTURES
(STP)
2908 Nebraska Avenue
Santa Monica, CA 90404-4109
310-998-0070
800-846-1453
Fax: 310-998-1145
web: http://www.
   insv.com/streamline

**TAI SENG VIDEO
MARKETING** *(TAI)*
170 S. Spruce Ave., Ste. 200
San Francisco, CA 94080
415-871-8118
800-888-3836
Fax: 415-871-2392
e-mail: webstaff@taiseng.com
web: http://www.taiseng.com

**TAPEWORM VIDEO
DISTRIBUTORS** *(TPV)*
27833 Hopkins Ave., Unit 6
Valencia, CA 91355
805-257-4904
Fax: 805-257-4820
e-mail: tapewo01@
   interserv.com
web: http://www.
   tapeworm.com

**TIME-LIFE VIDEO AND
TELEVISION** *(TLF)*
1450 E. Parham Rd.
Richmond, VA 23280
804-266-6330
800-621-7026

TIMELESS VIDEO INC. *(TIM)*
9943 Canoga Ave., Ste. B2
Chatsworth, CA 91311
818-773-0284
800-478-6734
Fax: 818-773-0176

**TRIBORO ENTERTAINMENT
GROUP** *(TRI)*
12 W. 27th St., 15th Fl.
New York, NY 10001
212-686-6116
Fax: 212-686-6178

TRIMARK HOME VIDEO
(THV)
2644 30th St.
Santa Monica, CA 90405-3009
310-314-2000
Fax: 310-392-0252

**TWENTIETH CENTURY FOX
HOME ENTERTAINMENT**
(FXV)
PO Box 900
Beverly Hills, CA 90213
310-369-3900
(888)223-4FOX
Fax: 310-369-5811

**UNIVERSAL STUDIOS HOME
VIDEO** *(USH)*
100 Universal City Plz.
Universal City, CA 91608-9955
818-777-1000
Fax: 818-866-1483

**VALENCIA ENTERTAINMENT
CORP.** *(VEC)*
45030 Trevor Ave.
Lancaster, CA 93534-2648
805-940-1040
800-323-2061
Fax: 805-940-8511

VCI HOME VIDEO *(VCI)*
11333 E. 60th Pl.
Tulsa, OK 74146
918-254-6337
800-331-4077
Fax: 918-254-6117
e-mail: vcihomevideo@
   mail.webter.com

**VCII HOME
ENTERTAINMENT, INC.**
(VHE)
13418 Wyandotte St.
North Hollywood, CA 91605
818-764-1777
800-350-1931
Fax: 818-764-0231

VESTRON VIDEO *(VES)*
c/o Live Home Video
15400 Sherman Way
PO Box 10124
Van Nuys, CA 91410-0124
818-988-0303
800-367-7765
Fax: 818-778-3194
e-mail: cust_serv@
   live-entertainment.com

VIDCREST *(VDC)*
PO Box 69642
Los Angeles, CA 90069
213-650-7310
Fax: 213-654-4810

VIDEO ACTION *(VDA)*
708 W. 1st St.
Los Angeles, CA 90012
213-687-8262
800-422-2241
Fax: 213-687-8425

THE VIDEO CATALOG *(TVC)*
7000 Westgate Dr.
St. Paul, MN 55114
612-659-3700
800-733-6656
Fax: 612-659-0083
e-mail: kyle@rivertrade.com

**VIDEO CITY PRODUCTIONS/
DISTRIBUTING** *(VCD)*
4266 Broadway
Oakland, CA 94611
510-428-0202
Fax: 510-654-7802

VIDEO CONNECTION *(VCN)*
3123 W. Sylvania Ave.
Toledo, OH 43613
419-472-7727
800-365-0449
Fax: 419-472-2655

VIDEO DIMENSIONS
(VDM)
322 8th Ave., No. 1701
New York, NY 10001
212-929-6135
Fax: 212-929-6135
e-mail: video@cultvideo.com
web: http://www.
cultvideo.com/video.html

VIDEO YESTERYEAR *(VYY)*
Box C
Sandy Hook, CT 06482
800-243-0987
Fax: 203-797-0819
e-mail: video@yesteryear.com

WARNER HOME VIDEO, INC.
(WAR)
4000 Warner Blvd.
Burbank, CA 91522
818-954-6000

WATER BEARER FILMS
(WBF)
48 W. 21st St., No. 301
New York, NY 10010
212-242-8686
800-551-8304
Fax: 212-242-4560
e-mail: WBFVideo@aol.com
web: http://www.wbf.com

WAXWORKS/VIDEOWORKS,
INC. *(WAX)*
325 E. 3rd St.
Owensboro, KY 42303
502-926-0008
800-825-8558
Fax: 502-685-0563

WESTERN MEDIA SYSTEMS
(WFV)
30941 W. Agoura Rd., Ste. 302
Westlake Village, CA 91361
818-889-7350
Fax: 818-889-7350

WHITE STAR *(WST)*
195 Hwy. 36
West Long Branch, NJ 07764
908-229-2343

800-458-5887
Fax: 908-229-0066

WORLD ARTISTS HOME
VIDEO *(WAC)*
5150 Wilshire Blvd., Ste. 506
Los Angeles, CA 90036
213-933-7057
800-821-1205
Fax: 213-933-2356
e-mail:
world@worldarfists.com
web:http://www.
worldartist.com/world

XENON *(XVC)*
211 Arizona Ave.
Santa Monica, CA 90401